CHILD PSYCHOLOGY

The Modern Science

SECOND EDITION

ROSS VASTA
State University of New York at Brockport

MARSHALL M. HAITH
University of Denver

SCOTT A. MILLER
University of Florida

JOHN WILEY & SONS, INC.
New York • Chichester • Brisbane • Toronto • Singapore

ACQUISITIONS EDITOR   Karen Dubno
DEVELOPMENTAL EDITORS   Barbara Heaney; Beverly Peavler, Naples Editing Services
MARKETING MANAGER   Catherine Faduska
PRODUCTION EDITOR   Jennifer Knapp
PRODUCTION COORDINATOR   Erica Smythe, HRS Electronic Text Management
TEXT DESIGNER   Karin Kincheloe and Nancy Field
MANUFACTURING MANAGER   Susan Stetzer
PHOTO EDITOR   Lisa Passmore
ILLUSTRATION COORDINATOR   Edward Starr
COVER DESIGNER   Levavi/Levavi
COVER PHOTO   Russell D. Curtis/Photo Researchers

This book was set in 10/12 New Baskerville by ATLIS Graphics and printed and
bound by Von Hoffmann Press. The cover was printed by Lehigh Press.

Recognizing the importance of preserving what has been written, it is a
policy of John Wiley & Sons, Inc. to have books of enduring value published
in the United States printed on acid-free paper, and we exert our best
efforts to that end.

The paper in this book was manufactured by a mill whose forest management programs include
sustained yield harvesting of its timberlands. Sustained yield harvesting principles ensure that
the number of trees cut each year does not exceed the amount of new growth.

Library of Congress Cataloging-in-Publication Data
Vasta, Ross.
    Child psychology : the modern science / Ross Vasta, Marshall M.
Haith, Scott A. Miller.—2nd ed.
        p.   cm.
    Includes bibliographical references and index.
    ISBN 0-471-59890-9
    1. Child psychology.   I. Haith, Marshall M., 1937–   .
II. Miller, Scott A., 1944–   .   III. Title.
BF721.V345   1995   94-27437
155.4—dc20   CIP

Printed in the United States of America

10 9 8 7 6 5 4 3 2 1

PREFACE

*I*n preparing the second edition of *Child Psychology: The Modern Science,* our primary goals remained the same as for the first edition: to serve instructors' needs, to maximize student learning, and to reflect accurately and comprehensively the discipline of developmental psychology as it exists today. Once again, we believe we have achieved these goals in ways that set this textbook apart from the others.

A CONTEXTUALIST APPROACH

The most important and distinctive feature of *Child Psychology* is its emphasis on the contextualist view of human development. Inspired by Urie Bronfenbrenner's seminal work, and fueled by the rediscovery of Lev Vygotsky's writings, modern developmental psychology has increasingly adopted a contextualist perspective. The child is not viewed as a passive recipient of environmental influences, but as an active producer of those influences. From the very beginning, the infant engages in a transactional "dance" with the caregiver, each regulating the behavior of the other. As the child grows, development interacts in critical ways with the social contexts in which it occurs, the two most important being the family system and the school environment. Cognitive development also is believed to reflect this contextual interplay, as evidenced by the rise in popularity of Vygotsky's sociocultural view of intelligence.

Unfortunately, developmental texts have not kept pace with this trend. Too often, contextual material has been included simply in the form of separate chapters on family and school influences, appended to the end of the book. As such, the discussion of these influences comes too late to be of maximal pedagogical value. Determinants residing in these contextual settings should instead be interwoven in the story of development and considered at the point where the relevant aspect of development is being discussed. If we wish to discuss, for example, how family size or class size affects intelligence, the place to present that material is in the chapter on intelligence, not in chapters on the family and the school near the end of the course. One solution to this problem—undoubtedly employed by many instructors—is to extract pieces of material from the later chapters and insert them where they belong. This approach, however, is awkward and unsatisfying.

In the first edition of *Child Psychology,* we offered a better solution. Material on the family, school, and other contextual influences was integrated into the main body of the text. This allows the course to move from one area of development to another in a topical manner, while including the broad tapestry of variables that affect each area. In the second edition, we have retained this integrated organization, while adding even more contextualist material.

We begin by introducing the ecological perspective in Chapter 2, where we also discuss the major theories that dominate the field today. Thereafter, each chapter includes one or two Development in Context sections that describe specific examples of how context affects our thinking about the issue at hand. For example, in Chapter 3 (Research Methods) we describe Glen Elder's research on the life course. In Chapter 9 (Information Processing) we present

Ceci and Bronfenbrenner's now-classic cupcakes-in-the-oven research. In Chapter 14 (Moral Development) we describe Belsky's evolutionary theory of reproductive strategies. And in Chapter 16 (Peer Relations) we examine children's social networks as assessed by Brenda Bryant's neighborhood walk technique. Some of the boxed sections also consider contextual influences, such as the nature of bilingual language acquisition (Box 11-2), whether the typical high school environment favors males over females (Box 15-4), and Bronfenbrenner's comparative research on children in the Soviet Union and United States (Box 16-1). Most importantly, we weave contextual material throughout the entire text, examining specific influences (e.g., social class, race, culture) in virtually every chapter.

Cultural Diversity

The growing recognition that culture represents an extremely important context of development has been reflected in a dramatic increase in cross-cultural and multicultural research within the discipline. We have incorporated this trend by including a good deal more culturally diverse material in this second edition. In addition to the examples given in the previous section, we also describe the use of marijuana by pregnant mothers in Jamaica (Chapter 5), the development of mathematical skills among Brazilian street vendors (Chapter 10), comparisons of infant–caregiver attachment patterns in Germany, Japan, Israel, and the United States (Chapter 12), and Margaret Mead's classic cross-cultural research on gender differences (Chapter 15).

Scientific Orientation

In this text we treat child psychology as a natural science and present it in a way that reflects its scientific underpinnings. In addition to providing a full chapter on research methods (Chapter 3), we discuss specific methodological issues frequently throughout the book, such as using microgenetic methods to study emerging cognitive abilities in Chapter 3, comparing research designs for determining genetic influences on development in Chapter 4, and examining techniques for studying infants' response to novelty in Chapter 10.

State-of-the-Art Coverage

Information is being generated in developmental psychology at a staggering rate. To prepare a text-

book of manageable proportions, authors must make some tough decisions. We have chosen to present a state-of-the-art treatment of child psychology that focuses principally on the very latest issues and findings—like gene therapy, psychoteratology, the role of action in perception, manual exploration in blind children, the social bases of early memory, maternal separation anxiety, the gender script model, and family contributions to peer relations. To keep the second edition at the cutting edge of the field, we added many new studies and over 1000 new references, while keeping the book's length relatively brief.

Although our focus is on current work, we recognize that some truly classic studies should be known by every student of human development. In such cases, we present the material in boxed sections labeled "Classics of Research."

Balanced Theoretical Presentation

Rather than emphasizing any single theoretical orientation, our book examines child psychology from the perspectives of the three principal traditions that characterize the discipline today—the cognitive-developmental approach, the environmental/learning approach, and the ethological approach. The fundamental tenets of these three orientations are first presented in Chapter 2. Then, most of the chapters within Parts III and IV begin by examining what the three traditions have to say about that topic area and go on to consider relevant research findings and applications. As a consequence, the student can approach the substantive material in these chapters with a conceptual structure that facilitates interpretation, comparison, and critical analysis. For example, Chapter 14, on moral development, begins by outlining Piaget's and Kohlberg's stage theories of moral reasoning and then examines recent studies designed to test the validity and scope of these models.

Organization

The 16 chapters of this text are organized topically and grouped into four parts. Part I provides the general foundation of the discipline, covering history, theory, and research methods. In keeping with the research-oriented approach of the text, these topics are presented in some detail. Part II focuses on biological and physical development, including genetics, prenatal development, birth, growth, and motor development. Part III investigates sensory and perceptual development, cognitive processes, and language acquisition. Part IV describes social and personality development, including emotional development, attachment, the self-system, moral reasoning, prosocial and antisocial behavior, gender role development, and peer relations.

The internal organization of the chapters within Parts III and IV is developmental. The topic area—be it language, gender roles, or another topic—begins with the newborn and describes development through adolescence. This approach helps students to appreciate the continuity of growth within each area and to understand the ongoing interactions between biological processes and contextual influences.

Pedagogical Features

In our effort to be complete and up-to-date, we have not forgotten that this is a textbook whose audience includes college sophomores. We have designed into the book a number of features to maximize the likelihood that students will learn the material.

Readability and Simplicity   We have worked hard to make our text, above all, interesting and accessible to the student reader. We believe that the text's comfortable writing style and the clarity with which concepts are introduced, discussed, and interrelated will enable students to read and understand a rigorous treatment of the issues.

In addition, rather than presenting long and tedious discussions of research findings that are likely to overwhelm students, we first decided what concepts and principles we wished students to come away with and then carefully selected research findings and real-world examples to illustrate and support this material. As a consequence, we believe that we have produced a text that communicates the essence and excitement of developmental psychology simply and efficiently.

Boxed Features   Boxes are used selectively in this text and are of four thematic types. The "Classics of Research" boxes, mentioned earlier, present studies of enduring historical value, even if no longer of major relevance to contemporary thinking in the area (e.g., Hartshorne and May's research on moral character or Terman's studies of genius). The "Research Focus" boxes discuss provocative and cutting-edge findings or interesting research methods, such as emergenesis (Chapter 4), neonatal imitation (Chapter 8), and language learning in apes (Chapter 11). The "Applications" boxes describe techniques developed for use by parents, educators, and therapists in the natural environment, such as

attempts to boost children's IQ (Chapter 10) or to change children's gender stereotypes (Chapter 15). Finally, the "Social Applications" boxes present recent work aimed at preventing or ameliorating social problems relevant to children, such as curbing media violence (Chapter 14) and controlling aggression by youth gangs (Chapter 16).

Running Glossary   Boldfaced glossary items in the text highlight terms of continuing importance to the reader. These items are defined in the margin on the page on which they first appear, as well as at the end of the book, providing students with a convenient guide for reviewing the material.

"To Recap" Sections   In addition to a Conclusion at the end of each chapter, there is a summary at the end of each major section in a chapter. This organization encourages students to pause and reflect on what they have just read and helps set the stage for the section that follows. Feedback from the first edition indicated that students found these sections very helpful.

"For Thought and Discuss on Questions"   A feature new to the second edition is a set of questions at the end of each chapter that are designed to foster critical thinking. Each question notes a finding or principle from the chapter and asks the student to apply it to an issue of real-world or personal relevance.

Illustration Program   We reworked many of the figures and drawings from the first edition to create new, effective illustrations in a full-color format. We also carefully selected many color photos that depict situations and events described in the text, along with some that illustrate laboratory techniques and other research methods.

Supplementary Materials

Accompanying the text, once again, is a full package of materials to support student learning and classroom teaching. The package includes the following:

• The *Student Study Guide* contains chapter outlines, learning objectives, key terms, application exercises, self-test questions, and practice exams. The study guide was prepared by Alastair Younger of the University of Ottawa, who coauthored the study guide for the first edition.

• The *Instructor's Resource Guide* contains guidelines for the first-time instructor, chapter outlines, learning objectives, key terms, lecture topics, discussion questions, in-class and out-of-class activities, supplemental readings, videoguide, and media materials. It was prepared by Susan Siaw and Meg Clark of the California State Polytechnic University, Pomona.

• The *Test Bank* provides approximately 100 questions for each chapter, keyed to the text in a multiple-choice, true/false, and essay format. Each question notes the text page on which the correct answer can be found, and whether the question is factual or conceptual.

• The *Computerized Test Bank* is available for the IBM or the Macintosh.

• *Overhead Transparencies* present approximately 100 figures and tables from the text.

• *Videotapes* include both *Early Images* and three tapes from the Annenberg series *Discovering Psychology*. *Early Images* is a 30-minute videotape created by Marshall Haith, including 27 image sequences accompanied by music and other sounds based on three decades of perceptual work on human infants. The video illustrates four major domains that have been studied and that are important for infants: visual stimulation, visual tracking, sound-picture correlations, and the formulation of visual and auditory expectations. The tapes from *Discovering Psychology* include "The Developing Child," "Language Development," and "Sex & Gender."

ACKNOWLEDGMENTS

Many people assisted us in preparing this second edition. At Wiley, the revision was handled skillfully and with great perspicacity by our developmental editor, Barbara Heaney. Among the many production people involved in the project, we would like to single out Lisa Passmore, for her beautiful work with the photographs, and Jenni Knapp, for cheerfully dealing with the many details and problems associated with turning the manuscript into a bound book. As with the first edition, we received invaluable advice and assistance from our freelance consultant, Beverly Peavler. At our home campuses, we are grateful for the work and technical help provided by a number of individuals: at Brockport, Carol Miles and Deirdre Rosenberg; at Denver, Nancy Pleiman, Joan Bihun, Tara Wass, and Diane Fox; and at Florida, Pat Miller, Cecile Chapman, and Michelle Boyer. We also would like to thank Joe Fagan for permitting us to use several photographs from his lab, Micki Chi for providing the original photograph for Figure 9-4, and Heather Holmes for her help in the preparation of several chapters.

Finally, we have no doubt that the book would not even exist without the continuing support, encouragement, and patience of our wives and children. They deserve our most special thanks.

We would like to acknowledge the contributions of the following reviewers, whose many comments and suggestions were extremely helpful in preparing this revision of the text.

Karen Bauer, University of Delaware
Ed Cornell, University of Alberta
James Dannemiller, University of Wisconsin, Madison
Vernon Hall, Syracuse University
Kenneth Kallio, State University of New York, Geneseo
Wallace Kennedy, Florida State University
Gary Levy, University of Wyoming
Kevin MacDonald, California State University, Long Beach
Lisa Oakes, University of Iowa
Cynthia O'Dell, Indiana University
Bina Raval, Towson State University
Karl Rosengren, University of Illinois at Urbana-Champaign
Ellin Scholnick, University of Maryland
Kathleen Sexton-Radek, Elmhurst College
Susan Siaw, California Polytechnic State University, Pomona
Gregory Simpson, University of Kansas
Nanci Stewart Woods, Austin Peay State University
Leonard Volenski, Seton Hall University

We would like to thank Gail S. Goodman, of the University of California, Davis, and Jeffrey T. Coldren, of the University of Toledo, for sharing with us their students' evaluation of the first edition of *Child Psychology*. Their comments were very useful in planning the second edition. We would also like to thank the following for their responses to our questionnaire for the second edition:

Gordon F. Brown, Pasadena City College
Roger V. Burton, SUNY Buffalo
Melissa Faber, The University of Toledo
Beverly I. Fagot, University of Oregon
Mary Ann Fischer, Indiana University, Northwest
Gail S. Goodman, University of California, Davis
Vernon Haynes, Youngstown State University
Christine Kenitzer, Texas Tech University
Elizabeth Lemerise, Western Kentucky University
Gary Levy, University of Wyoming
Angeline Lillard, University of San Francisco
Kevin MacDonald, California State University, Long Beach
Margie McMahan, Cameron University
Derek Montgomery, Bradley University
Vicky Phares, University of South Florida
Marite Rodriguez-Haynes, Clarion University
Gayle Scroggs, Cayuga Community College
Susan Siaw, California Polytechnic State University, Pomona
Nicholas R. Santilli, John Carroll University
Frank J. Sinkavich, York College of Pennsylvania
Rita Smith, Millersville University of Pennsylvania

Ross Vasta   Marshall M. Haith   Scott A. Miller

ABOUT THE AUTHORS

Age 5

ROSS VASTA is Professor of psychology at the State University of New York at Brockport. He received his undergraduate degree from Dartmouth College in 1969 and his Ph.D. in clinical and developmental psychology from State University of New York at Stony Brook in 1974. He has spent sabbatical years at the University of California, Davis and at the University of North Carolina at Chapel Hill. In 1987 he was awarded the SUNY Chancellor's Award for Excellence in Teaching. His previous books include *Studying Children: An Introduction to Research Methods, Strategies and Techniques of Child Study,* and *Six Theories of Child Development.* He is currently editor of the annual series *Annals of Child Development.* His research interests include physical child abuse and gender differences in spatial abilities.

Age 5

MARSHALL M. HAITH is The John Evans Professor of psychology at the University of Denver and National Institute of Mental Health Research Scientist. He earned his Ph.D. from UCLA in 1964. After completing postdoctoral work at Yale University, he held positions at Harvard University,

University of Geneva, and Rene Descartes University in Paris. He has been a Guggenheim Fellow and a Fellow at the Center for Advanced Study in the Behavioral Sciences. He has previously authored *Day Care and Intervention Programs for Infants under Two Years of Age* and *Rules That Babies Look By: The Organization of Newborn Visual Activity* and is a coauthor of *The Development of Future-Oriented Processes,* with J. B. Benson, R. Roberts, Jr., and B. Pennington. Along with J. J. Campos, he edited Volume 2 of *Mussen's Handbook of Child Psychology.* His research interests include infant perception, the formation of expectations in early infancy, and the development of information-processing skills.

Age 8

SCOTT A. MILLER is Professor of psychology at the University of Florida. After completing his undergraduate work at Stanford University in 1966, he entered the Institute of Child Development at the University of Minnesota, where he earned his Ph.D. in 1971. His initial appointment was at the University of Michigan. He is a Fellow of Division 7 (Developmental) of the American Psychological Association. He has previously authored *Developmental Research Methods* and coauthored, with John Flavell and Patricia Miller, *Cognitive Development,* 3rd edition. His research has been in cognition, focusing on Piaget's work, children's understanding of logical necessity, and parents' beliefs about children.

BRIEF CONTENTS

CONTENTS

Part One

FOUNDATIONS OF A SCIENCE

Chapter 1

INTRODUCTION AND PERSPECTIVE

*T*his book describes the modern science of child psychology. In it, we trace the growing child's behavior and development from the embryo's beginnings in the mother's womb to the child's introduction to the adult world in adolescence. We also describe the many factors that affect children's development and we examine how researchers go about the business of scientifically studying them.

Attempts to explain children's development go as far back as history can trace. But child psychology as a science is only about 100 years old. How does an interesting topic suddenly become defined as a science? Or, more specifically, how has the study of children in the past century differed from that in the previous 3,000 years?

The answer lies simply in the method of study. For investigation to be scientific, it must follow certain rules known as the *scientific method*. These rules specify, for example, how research evidence should be gathered, how it may be analyzed, and what sorts of conclusions researchers may draw from their findings. Scientists have used this method to study an endless number of phenomena, from stars to starfish. In this book, we examine how they use it to study children.

At first glance, understanding child development may not appear to be very difficult. Certainly the typical behaviors of infants and young children—including their speech, their interactions with others, and even the ways they think—are simpler than those same behaviors in adults. But it is a mistake to conclude that the *processes* involved are simple. Psychologists have learned that human development is a complex and intricate puzzle, and unraveling its mysteries has proved to be a major challenge. Since the methods of science were first applied to the study of children 100 years ago, we have learned a great deal. Yet the more we learn, the more apparent it becomes that we have only scratched the surface.

DEVELOPMENTAL PSYCHOLOGY

To begin, it is important to understand exactly what psychology is and what psychologists study. Psychology is the scientific study of behavior. The behavior that most psychologists study is human behavior. But any species—from mice to mynah birds to monkeys—can be examined legitimately from a psychological (and developmental) perspective.

Developmental psychology
The branch of psychology devoted to the study of changes in behavior and abilities over the course of development.

Developmental psychology, one of the largest of psychology's many subfields, is concerned with *the changes in behavior and abilities that occur as development proceeds.* Developmental researchers examine both what the changes are and why they occur. To put it another way, developmental research has two basic goals. One is to describe children's behavior at each point in their development. This involves such questions as, When do babies begin to walk? What are the typical mathematical abilities of a 5-year-old? How do sixth graders usually resolve conflicts with their peers? The second goal is to identify the causes and processes that produce changes in behavior from one time to the next. This involves determining the effects of such factors as the child's genetic inheritance, the biological and structural characteristics of the human brain, the physical and social environment in which the child lives, and the types of experiences that the child encounters.

Developmental psychologists study behavior changes at all phases of the life cycle. Most, though, have focused on the period that ends with adolescence. For this reason, *developmental psychology* and *child psychology* have traditionally referred to the same body of scientific knowledge. That situation is changing, however. In recent years, a good deal of developmental research has been directed toward issues related to adulthood and old age, which has led to the emergence of **life-span de-velopmental psychology.** This book, however, focuses on the traditional early period (and so we have chosen the title *Child Psychology*).

Why Study Children?

If developmental psychologists can study any species of animal and any period in the life cycle, why has so much of their research traditionally concentrated on humans during the childhood years? There are at least five answers to this question.

Period of Rapid Development

Because developmental researchers are interested in studying change, it makes sense for them to focus on a period when much change occurs. And during the first part of the life of most species, more developmental changes take place than during any other period. In humans, physical growth, for example, is greater in the first year than in any other year. (In fact, by age 2 most children have already attained one half of their adult height.) Similarly, changes involving social interactions, the acquisition and use of language, memory and reasoning abilities, and virtually all other areas of human functioning are greatest during childhood.

Long-Term Influences

An equally important reason for studying children is that the events and experiences of the early years strongly affect the individual's later development. As the poet Wordsworth once noted (and many psychologists have since reiterated), "The child is father to the man." In fact, almost all psychological theories suggest that who we are today depends very much on our development and experiences as children, although we will see that the various theories make the connection in different ways.

Insight into Complex Adult Processes

Not all psychologists are primarily concerned with early development. But even researchers who are attempting to understand complex adult behaviors often find it useful to examine what those behaviors are like during periods when they are not so complex. For example, most people can produce long and detailed sentences. In turn, most other people can easily understand these sentences. Humans are capable of complex communication because our languages follow systems of rules. But determining what these rules are and how they are used has proved very difficult. One approach to this problem is to study language as it is being acquired. Infants initially produce phrases of only one or two words. Yet even these first word combinations appear to follow rules (which we discuss in Chapter 11). By examining early speech, language researchers are gaining insight into the mechanisms of our more complex adult speech. Thus in language acquisition, as well as in many other areas, the growing child is a "showcase" of developing skills and abilities, and researchers interested in different aspects of human development have taken advantage of this fact to help them understand adult behavior.

Social Policy Applications

Most developmental psychologists conduct their research in laboratory settings, where they investigate theoretical questions regarding basic psychological processes. Nevertheless, the products of this research can sometimes benefit children in the real world.

Life-span developmental psychology
The study of developmental issues across the life cycle.

Social policy
The principles used by a society to decide which social problems to address and how to deal with them.

Our world is plagued by social problems, such as poverty, illiteracy, drugs, and crime. **Social policy** refers to the way a society approaches these problems (Garbarino, Gaboury, & Plantz, 1992). Legislators and other policymakers, for example, often turn to psychologists to provide them with "usable knowledge" regarding the effects of these problems on children and possible ways to treat them (Thompson, 1993; Zigler & Finn-Stevenson, 1992). In some cases, in fact, developmental research is designed to address specific social issues. For example, we will see in Chapter 12 that the growing need for mothers to work outside the home has led to a dramatic increase in the number of young children in day care. As a result, many studies in recent years have examined the relation between day care experiences and various aspects of children's behavior and development. And not all applications of developmental research involve social problems. Laboratory findings are being extended to classroom teaching methods and parental disciplinary techniques, for example. Simply put, one reason we study children is to make their lives better.

Interesting Subject Matter

A final and very important reason why so many developmental psychologists have directed their efforts toward understanding children is that the human child is a fascinating and wondrous creature. When we consider that children have attracted attention from artists, poets, and scholars in many other fields of study, it is perhaps not surprising that psychologists, too, have found this subject matter appealing. The ease with which a naive 2-year-old acquires her native language (while the adult often struggles in foreign language classes) and the creativity of a youngster playing with invisible friends are just two examples of the inherently intriguing characteristics that all growing children display. Yet much of a child's development remains a mystery, and at this point science has more questions than answers.

• Children's fascinating behavior and inherent appeal undoubtedly contribute to their being of great interest to developmental researchers.

✔ *To Recap...*

Developmental psychologists use the scientific method to study changes in behavior. The two basic goals of their research are to describe behaviors and abilities at each phase of development and to explain why the behaviors change. Any species at any age level is legitimate subject matter for developmental psychology. But most developmental research over the years has involved children, for five reasons: childhood is a period of rapid development, early experiences have long-term effects, complex processes are easier to understand as they are forming, the knowledge of basic processes can help to solve some of the problems of childhood, and children are inherently interesting to study.

HISTORICAL VIEWS OF CHILDHOOD

It is clear that modern psychologists consider childhood an immensely important period. Perhaps for similar reasons, our Western culture views children as warranting a great deal of attention, care, and shelter from harm. Many laws have been designed expressly to protect children from dangerous toys, dangerous substances, and even dangerous parents. Our belief that all children deserve a free public education and that they should not be exploited in factories, for example, similarly reflects the view that childhood is a special and important time. But these attitudes toward children have not always existed. In fact, they reflect a relatively recent conception of early development (Greenleaf, 1978; Hart, 1991). To understand our modern view of the child, it is helpful to examine briefly views of childhood from earlier points in history. Because child psychology is a science whose roots are in Western culture, this survey will be restricted to that tradition. In the remainder of the text, however, we consider contemporary aspects of child development in cultures throughout the world.

Ancient Greece and Rome

The eras of the Greek and Roman civilizations, which extend from about 600 B.C. to about 400 A.D., are regarded by modern historians as periods of great enlightenment. Especially in the realm of learning, these societies recognized the major impact of the childhood years on later development. Early educational training, at least for the children of the upper classes, was highly valued (Borstelmann, 1983).

• In contrast to earlier historical periods, children today are viewed as physically and psychologically vulnerable, and are accorded a special place in Western society.

Yet the status of children during these times was hardly enviable. Although such great thinkers as Plato and Aristotle wrote of the importance of education, they also defended practices that today would seem unthinkable. *Infanticide,* the killing of newborns, was routine and viewed as an appropriate way to deal with babies who were illegitimate, unhealthy, or simply unwanted. Female infants were most in jeopardy. They were generally seen as necessary only for their eventual reproductive value, so many Greek and Roman families "kept" only one daughter (Breiner, 1990; Langer, 1974).

Severe punishment and the sexual exploitation of children were neither uncommon nor considered wrong or cruel. The Romans, for example, bought and sold children for various purposes, including domestic work and service in brothels for the sexual pleasure of adults (Mounteer, 1987). And in neighboring Carthage, children were killed and buried in the foundations of public buildings or burned in mass graves as sacrifices to the gods (Weld, 1968). So although the ancient world recognized the importance of the childhood years, it clearly did not display the caring and protective attitudes toward children that exist today.

The Medieval and Renaissance Periods

Prior to the fall of the Roman Empire (in approximately 400 A.D.), the position of children had slowly begun to improve, partly as a result of the spread of Christianity and the Church's attempts to promote a new image of children. Following Rome's collapse, this practice continued as the Church took a strong stand against infanticide and offered parents of unwanted children the alternative of shipping them away to convents and monasteries—an arrangement that benefited both parties. (The Church, however, remained generally powerless in preventing the killing of twins, who were considered to be the obvious products of adultery.) Although educational training during this period reached one of its lowest levels in recorded history, the Church was somewhat successful in providing simple reading and writing instruction to children involved in religious studies (Sommerville, 1982).

As the medieval period progressed, the view of childhood continued to improve as religious writings began to glorify the innocence and purity of children. In the 12th century, for example, December 6 was set aside to honor the patron saint of all children, St. Nicholas. That holiday was later moved to coincide with the celebration of the birth of Christ and became our modern Christmas.

Unfortunately, the abuse and exploitation of children remained commonplace throughout the medieval period, and the folklore of the age reveals that childhood remained a perilous time. In fact, it has even been suggested that childhood as we know it did not exist during the Middle Ages. Once children were old enough to participate in household and community labor (at about the age of 7), they became a part of the larger society and were, according to some historians, simply treated as less experienced adults (Aries, 1962; Hoyles, 1979; McCoy, 1988). Although some scholars do not agree entirely with this theory, there is little doubt that children of the medieval period had a very difficult life (Demaitre, 1977; Kroll, 1977; Pollock, 1983).

The Renaissance began to emerge early in the 14th century and extended into the 17th. It was marked by a revival of interest in Greco-Roman art, literature, and thought that in turn prompted a general rebirth of Western civilization. This era also saw an increased concern for the welfare of children. In Florence, Italy—generally considered the birthplace of the Renaissance—charitable institutions known as *foundling homes* were set up to take in sick, lost, and unwanted children. These homes were typically supported by donations from wealthy individuals.

Unfortunately, many homeless children did not survive even in these institutions, and many others never came under this sort of care. But the foundling homes, which eventually spread throughout Western Europe, were significant in that they represented a new and growing belief that society is at least in part responsible for the care and protection of its youngsters (Trexler, 1973).

The Renaissance also was marked by the reemergence of scientific investigation in such fields as astronomy, medicine, and physics. The science of psychology did not yet exist, so the study of human development was primarily the concern of philosophers and religious scholars. Some early scientific thinkers, such as Galileo, believed that physical and biological mechanisms were the basis for understanding human behavior. But the Church disagreed with any nonspiritual explanations of behavior and, being a powerful social force at the time, was effective in discouraging their study.

The Reformation

Throughout the medieval period and much of the Renaissance, "the Church" referred to the Roman Catholic Church. But early in the 16th century, a variety of Protestant sects arose. One of the most important of these sects from the perspective of child psychology was the Puritans, led by John Calvin (1509–1564).

The Puritans were perhaps the first to offer a comprehensive model of child development. In many ways, their view was a rejection of the earlier belief in the child's purity. Instead of seeing them as innocents, Calvin argued that children are born with original sin and are naturally inclined toward evil unless given the proper guidance and instruction (Pollock, 1987). Yet he also believed that children have a great capacity for learning at an early age and that parents therefore have the opportunity (and the obligation) to train them properly.

The Puritans took child rearing very seriously. They were, in fact, the first group to write manuals to aid parents in this task. The Calvinist approach was to encourage the child to become independent and self-reliant and, most of all, to develop self-control. Because sin and evil were seen as ever-present problems, it was crucial that the child learn to resist temptations early and effectively. The Puritans eventually made their way to colonial America, and are among the best known of the early New England settlers. Stories have depicted the harsh disciplinary practices urged on parents by the "fire-and-brimstone" preachers of the day, such as Jonathan Edwards. In reality, however, the Calvinists preached that firm guidance would prevent children from misbehaving and would thus eliminate the need for more severe forms of punishment (Sommerville, 1978).

The Puritans put great emphasis on education, particularly reading (Moran & Vinovskis, 1985). Because of this they were the first to write books specifically for children. Although most of the books had religious or moral themes, a few were made somewhat entertaining in an attempt to make the task of learning a bit more pleasant.

Descartes's Dualistic Model

In order to understand the views of child development that emerged in the 17th century and beyond, we must take a short side trip to discuss the contribution of René Descartes (1596–1650). Descartes, a French mathematician and philosopher, was not specifically interested in child development. But his model of human behavior laid the groundwork for what would eventually become the science of psychology.

The essence of Descartes's philosophy was that the mind and the body are separate from one another. The human mind, he argued, does not have a material form and does not follow the physical laws of science. Its function is to reason and make decisions and then carry out these decisions by commanding the body to perform whatever is required. He also believed that the human mind contains certain "innate ideas," including the concepts of "perfection" and "infinity," as well as a number of mathematical principles. These two beliefs—that the mind exists and that it contains certain inborn ideas—led Descartes to conclude that only God could have created it.

Descartes's description of the human mind as nonphysical, God-given, and dominant over people's earthly bodies was consistent with the Church's views, and so his ideas met with little religious opposition. This tacit acceptance by the Church was important for science in general—and eventually for psychology—because it allowed Descartes to develop a theoretical model of the human body that was based solely on mechanical and physical principles. Here he focused on involuntary behaviors, such as the inner workings of the body's organ systems, simple reflexes, and even some cognitive processes (e.g., memory and certain forms of learning). These behaviors, he argued, were controlled by a relatively simple stimulus-and-response system and were similar to the mechanical functioning of a machine.

Cartesian dualism
René Descartes's idea that the mind and body are separate, which helped clear the way for the scientific study of human development.

In essence, then, Descartes divided the investigation of human behavior into two separate realms—one concerned with the psychological functioning of the mind and the other with the physical workings of the body. The concept that the mind exists independently of the body, which is referred to as **Cartesian dualism,** remains a matter of debate in psychology even today. But the historical importance of Descartes's mind–body division was that it removed the scientific investigation of the body from the scrutiny of the Church, thus permitting researchers to pursue whatever questions or issues they saw fit to study. This new view of human behavior, in turn, ushered in the modern study of psychology.

✔ To Recap...

The concept of childhood has changed dramatically over time. The ancient Greeks and Romans viewed children largely as property that was both exchangeable and expendable. During the medieval period, the Church helped to elevate society's image of children by stressing their purity and innocence. At the same time the Church hindered scientific study, which reemerged as an area of interest during the Renaissance, by permitting only religious explanations of human behavior. The Puritan sect, arising out of the Reformation, constructed the first comprehensive model of child development. It was based on the idea of the child's inherent evil and inclination toward sin. René Descartes cleared the way for the scientific study of human behavior by proposing a dualistic system in which the nonphysical mind governed the mechanical functioning of the physical body.

EARLY THEORISTS

With the introduction of Descartes's mind–body distinction, scholarly debate over the nature of human development intensified, and several very different points of view emerged. Three early scholars—John Locke, Jean-Jacques Rousseau, and Charles Darwin—offered theories of human behavior that are the direct ancestors of the three major theoretical traditions that characterize the science of child psychology today. These three modern traditions include one model that focuses on the influence of the child's environment, a second that emphasizes the role of the child's cognitive development, and a third that is most concerned with the evolutionary origins of behavior.

John Locke (1632–1704)

In 17th-century England, Descartes's theory was extended by a group of philosophers known as the British Empiricists. The most famous of these was John Locke, a physician whose liberal political views may have contributed to his belief that all children are created equal.

Locke accepted Descartes's distinction between the mind and the body, but he rejected the concept of innate ideas. To Locke, the mind of a newborn infant was like a piece of white paper—a **tabula rasa** ("blank slate"). Locke believed that knowledge came to the child only through experience and learning. Children were therefore neither innately good nor innately evil. They were simply the products of their environment and upbringing—an idea that is today referred to as **environmentalism.** In some ways, Locke's descriptions of how children learn were several hundred years ahead of their time (Borstelmann, 1983). For example, he believed that children acquire knowledge through the principles of reward, punishment, and imitation and that if children repeatedly experience two things occurring together, they will then form an association between them (Locke, 1690/1824). These proposed mechanisms, we will see in the next chapter, remain important elements of our modern view of human learning.

Locke's writings were not all academic. He also offered advice to parents on the best methods for raising their children. Although he stressed the use of rewards and punishments, Locke did not favor material rewards (e.g., candy and toys) or physical punishment. Discipline, he believed, should involve praise for appropriate behaviors and scolding for inappropriate behaviors. Locke also discussed the importance of stimulating children to begin learning at a very early age. And in one major departure from his environmentalist philosophy, he suggested that children have an inborn curiosity that parents should encourage and carefully guide (Locke, 1693/1964).

Locke's ideas gained wide acceptance among British and European scholars, as well as the general public. But in less than 100 years, this strong environmentalist model was to be replaced by a very different conception of the child.

Jean-Jacques Rousseau (1712–1778)

Jean-Jacques Rousseau was born in Switzerland but spent most of his life in France, where he became the leading philosopher of his day. He is considered the father of French romanticism, a movement in which artists and writers emphasized themes of sentimentality, naturalness, and innocence. These ideas found their way into Rousseau's conception of the child.

Rousseau's views on development are presented in his novel Émile (1762). In this famous work, Rousseau describes the care and tutoring of a male child from infancy to young adulthood. Using this literary vehicle, Rousseau described his theoretical views of child development and offered suggestions on the most appropriate methods of child rearing and education (Mitzenheim, 1985).

Fundamental to Rousseau's theory was his return to Descartes's view that children are born with knowledge and ideas, which unfold naturally with age.

• John Locke, a 17th-century British philosopher, foreshadowed later environmentalists by proposing that a newborn's mind was like a blank sheet of paper on which environment and experiences wrote the script of the child's life.

Tabula rasa
Latin phrase, meaning "blank slate," used to describe the newborn's mind as entirely empty of inborn abilities, interests, or ideas.

Environmentalism
The theory that human development is best explained by examination of the individual's experiences and environmental influences.

• Jean Jacques Rousseau, an 18th-century French philosopher, described his nativistic views of human development in *Émile*, a novel about the growth and upbringing of a young French boy.

Development, in this view, proceeds through a predictable series of stages that are guided by an inborn timetable. The child's innate knowledge includes such things as the principles of justice and fairness and, above all, a sense of conscience. In effect, Rousseau had returned to the theme of the inborn goodness and purity of the child. Rousseau also believed that whatever knowledge the child does not possess innately is acquired gradually from interactions with the environment, guided by the child's own interests and level of development. Thus the wisest approach to child rearing is not to formally instruct children but rather to have them learn through a process of exploration and discovery. By clearly emphasizing innate processes as the driving forces in human development, Rousseau's theory contrasted with the environmentalistic ideas of Locke and would today be referred to as **nativism.**

Nativism
The theory that human development results principally from inborn processes that guide the emergence of behaviors in a predictable manner.

Rousseau further believed that the development of the child repeats the cultural history of the human race. Émile, he said, was a *noble savage,* much as the primitive cave dwellers had been. They were "noble" because they possessed an innate goodness that characterizes all humans; they were "savage" because their ideas were simple and unsophisticated.

Rousseau's suggestions for educating Émile contain at least three ideas that today are espoused by some educational theorists. First, children should be exposed to a particular body of knowledge only after they display a cognitive "readiness" to learn it. Second, children learn best when they are exposed to information or ideas and then allowed to acquire an understanding of them through their own discovery process. Finally, both education and child rearing should foster a permissive rather than a highly disciplined style of interaction (Thomas, 1979).

Rousseau's theory met with opposition in 18th-century America, because the Calvinists' doctrine of inborn sin and their belief in strict discipline were not compatible with this more romanticized view of the child. In Europe, however, Rousseau's ideas had a major impact, and his nativistic view of development was hailed by both scientific and political writers. His ideas, like Locke's, were both revolutionary and ahead of their time. And as we will see, they would reappear 200 years later in the work of another Swiss theorist, Jean Piaget.

• Charles Darwin's theory of evolution, developed in the mid-19th century, was quickly adopted by the early developmental psychologists and laid the foundation for the modern fields of ethology and sociobiology.

Charles Darwin (1809–1882)

The third major ancestor of modern developmental thought was the British biologist Charles Darwin. Although he is best known for his theory of evolution, presented in *The Origin of Species* (1859), Darwin was also a keen observer of child development. Indeed, his detailed record of the growth and behavior of his infant son, "Doddy," is one of the first developmental studies (Darwin, 1877).

Darwin's evolutionary theory begins with the assumption that individual members of the same species vary in many characteristics, so that some are faster, some are stronger, some are lighter, and so on. A second assumption is that most species produce more offspring than their environment can support, which means that the individual members must compete for survival. Depending on the environment, some variations may increase the chances for survival, such as providing better ways of avoiding danger or acquiring food. If so, individuals possessing these traits are more likely to survive and so pass them along to future generations. Through this process, which Darwin called **natural selection,** the species continually evolves to ever more adaptive forms. At the same time, less useful variations gradually disappear.

Natural selection
An evolutionary process proposed by Charles Darwin in which characteristics of an individual that increase its chances of survival are more likely to be passed along to future generations.

If accurate, this model means that some of the present-day behaviors of humans (or any other animal) had their origins countless years ago, when they were important for the survival of an earlier form of our species. This theoretical attempt to explain current behavior by appealing to its original evolutionary value is today the focus of *ethology* (discussed in the next chapter).

Darwin's theory of evolution did not directly address the issue of child development. But his views led other biologists of the time, such as Ernst Haeckel, to propose the principle of **recapitulation** (Haeckel, 1906/1977). According to this theoretical notion, the development of the individual—that is, *ontogeny*—proceeds through stages that parallel the development of the entire species—that is, *phylogeny*. This principle is often stated more briefly as "ontogeny recapitulates phylogeny." As applied to our species, it means that human development—beginning with its earliest embryonic and prenatal forms and continuing with the physical, motor, and social development of the growing child—follows a progression of behaviors similar to those that evolved through the various prehuman species (Wertheimer, 1985).

Recapitulation theory
An early biological notion, later adopted by psychologist G. Stanley Hall, that the development of the individual repeats the development of the species.

Although it is no longer scientifically supported, the idea that the child's development repeats that of the species had great appeal for some early developmentalists. And by providing a theory that both explained the developing behaviors observed by Rousseau and others and served as a framework for future research on human development, Darwin's writings helped launch the scientific study of the child (Charlesworth, 1992; Dixon & Lerner, 1992).

✔ *To Recap...*

Even before psychology emerged as a separate discipline, three early scholars presented important models of human development. John Locke based his approach on the strict environmentalist position that all knowledge is acquired through experience and learning. Jean-Jacques Rousseau proposed a nativistic model in which child behavior unfolds according to inborn processes. Charles Darwin's theory of evolution offered the possibility that many human behaviors had their origins in the past, when they were valuable for our ancestors' survival.

PIONEERS OF CHILD PSYCHOLOGY

The belief that the development of the child is related to the evolution of the species gave birth to the science of developmental psychology. But the evolutionary perspective was joined by other theoretical models as child development quickly became the focus of increasing amounts of scientific debate and research. Only a few of the individuals who contributed to the rise of this movement are discussed here. Our purpose is not to provide a detailed history of child study but rather to point out the origins of some important ideas and controversies that remain a part of modern developmental science.

G. Stanley Hall (1846–1924)

The psychologist credited with founding the field of developmental psychology is G. Stanley Hall. Hall conducted and published the first systematic studies of children in the United States and has been referred to as the "father of child psychology" (Appley, 1986).

Hall received his Ph.D. from Harvard in 1878 under the famous psychologist William James. He spent the next 2 years working in Germany, where he became familiar with a child study project being conducted in Berlin. On his return to the United States, Hall decided to replicate this study. In the fall of 1882, he administered questionnaires to all the first-grade children in the Boston school district to determine for the first time precisely what sorts of everyday knowledge American children usually possessed when they began school. The questions included such items as, What season is it? Where are your elbows? and Where does butter come from? Hall published the results of this research in 1883 under the title "The Contents of Children's Minds." Although interesting, the findings contained nothing particularly new or surprising. Nevertheless, Hall became convinced that more of this sort of descriptive information was necessary for understanding the normal development of children.

In 1891, he thus began a larger project designed to gather data on children of all ages and from all regions of the country. Once again Hall used questionnaires, but this time he sent them to parents, teachers, and other adults who had frequent contact with children. In addition to asking many specific questions, he invited the respondents to include anecdotal descriptions of incidents or situations that might shed light on children's development. Unfortunately, Hall's research was not well designed and he was not prepared to deal his results. The information that poured in from these questionnaires took many forms, with the respondents approaching the questions in a wide variety of ways. In the end, Hall was left with a vast accumulation of data that were difficult to interpret and impossible to summarize (White, 1992).

Genetic psychology
G. Stanley Hall's original term for developmental psychology that stressed the evolutionary basis of development.

Hall's attempts to make a theoretical contribution to psychology were also less than successful. Excited by Darwin's writings, he adopted the view that children's behavior and development recapitulate the evolution of the species. This view led him to label the study of child development **genetic psychology,** meaning the study of development from its genesis, or earliest beginnings (Grinder, 1967). Hall also felt that education and child rearing should encourage the "natural" tendencies of the child that reflect the behavior and development of earlier forms of the species.

• Some of the pioneers of psychology invited by G. Stanley Hall to Clark University in 1909. Hall is seated front center, and Sigmund Freud is seated front left.

He was especially interested in the period of adolescence, which he believed marked the end of biological recapitulation and the first opportunity for the child to develop individual talents and abilities (Hall, 1904).

By the turn of the century, however, advances in biological research had made it clear that no simple recapitulation process exists in human development (Coleman, 1971). Furthermore, many American psychologists were beginning to favor a more environmentalist view, which held that children acquire knowledge and skills through experience and that their behavior can be best explained by learning processes. Even before Hall's death in 1924, genetic psychology had become more commonly known as developmental psychology, and environmentally oriented researchers, using rigorous experimental methods, had taken an entirely new direction in child study (Cairns, 1983).

Although neither his research nor his theoretical ideas ultimately had much impact, Hall did make some lasting contributions to the field (Hilgard, 1987; Ross, 1972). As an educator at Clark University in Worcester, Massachusetts, Hall trained the first generation of child researchers. He also established several scientific journals for reporting the findings of child development research, and he founded and became the first president of the American Psychological Association. Finally, a more indirect contribution was his invitation to Sigmund Freud to present a series of lectures in the United States—an event that, as we will see, led to the introduction of psychoanalytic theory into American psychology.

John B. Watson (1878–1958)

The philosophical or theoretical view that is generally shared by the scientists of a given period is referred to as its **Zeitgeist**—a German term meaning "the spirit of the times." When a science is very young, the Zeitgeist can change dramatically from one time to the next. Major shifts in thinking regarding one of the most basic issues of human development—what causes changes in behavior in growing children—had already occurred several times in the centuries before the science of developmental psychology emerged in the mid-1800s. We saw that the Zeitgeist of the 17th century was Locke's environmentalist view of human development. This model was replaced first by Rousseau's nativistic explanation and then by the evolutionary theories of Darwin and Hall. As the 20th century dawned, the pendulum began to swing away from biological interpretations of development and back toward the environmentalist position.

Zeitgeist
"The spirit of the times," or the ideas shared by most scientists during a given period.

John B. Watson was the first major psychologist to adopt Locke's belief that human behavior can be understood principally in terms of experiences and learning. But his new approach, which he called **behaviorism,** differed radically from the existing psychological attitudes regarding what psychologists should study and which methods of investigation they should use (Horowitz, 1992).

Behaviorism
A theory of psychology, first advanced by John B. Watson, that human development results primarily from conditioning and learning processes.

Watson received his Ph.D. in 1903 from the University of Chicago. His early career was devoted to the study of physiological processes and animal psychology. Descartes's dualism was very evident among psychologists at this time. Some, like Watson, studied the physiological workings of the body. But many were exclusively concerned with the psychological functioning of the human mind, especially consciousness and issues revolving around how the outside world is experienced internally and how individual perceptions are combined to form ideas and thoughts. Their most common research method was **introspection,** which involved engaging subjects in a task or problem and then having them try to look inward and report on the processes occurring in their minds.

Introspection
A research method for investigating the workings of the mind by asking subjects to describe their mental processes.

Watson found this approach unsatisfactory for a number of reasons. In large part, he was dissatisfied with the method of introspection itself and the fact that little agreement was ever found across subjects' descriptions of their internal experiences. As a result, scientific progress on these issues seemed to be at a standstill. In addition, Watson held that any evidence that could not be measured and verified by others lacked scientific validity. Finally, his interest in animal psychology led him to reject any method that could not also be used to study other species.

Watson was equally dissatisfied with what was being studied. He felt strongly that psychology should follow the example of the other natural sciences and deal only with objective, observable subject matter—in this case, observable behavior. He further believed that the goal of psychology should be to predict and control behavior, not to achieve a subjective understanding of the mind's inner workings.

These ideas were radical for the time, but Watson's persuasive writing style, combined with a bit of luck, soon propelled behaviorism into the forefront of psychological theory (Cohen, 1979). Watson joined the psychology faculty at Johns Hopkins University in 1908. Within several years he became chairman of the prestigious psychology department, president of the American Psychological Association, and editor of *Psychological Review,* the most important journal in the field. Watson used these positions as platforms from which to present his views and to market behaviorism to the scientific community.

The basic tenet of behaviorism was that changes in behavior result primarily from conditioning processes, rather than from inborn biological mechanisms. Watson argued that learning occurred through the process of association, as described in the work of the Russian physiologist Ivan Pavlov (1849–1936). Pavlov had shown that any simple reflex is composed of a stimulus and a response that are biologically related to one another. For example, he demonstrated that meat powder is a stimulus that naturally elicits the response of salivation in dogs. A biologically unrelated stimulus—such as the sound of a bell—can, however, acquire the power to cause this same response, if it is repeatedly associated with the natural stimulus. Pavlov established such an association simply by ringing a bell just before presenting meat powder to his dogs. After a number of these pairings, the bell alone could cause the dogs to salivate. At this point, both stimuli could produce the salivation response, but one did so naturally (i.e., biologically), whereas the other did so as a result of conditioning.

Conditioned reflex method
John B. Watson's name for the Pavlovian conditioning process in which reflexive responses can be conditioned to stimuli in the environment.

Watson believed that this simple conditioning process, which he called the **conditioned reflex method,** explained how human behavior changes over time. All human behavior, he argued, begins as simple reflexes. Then, through an association process like the one Pavlov described, various combinations of simple behaviors become conditioned to many stimuli in the environment. The longer the conditioning process continues, the more complex the stimulus–response relations become. Language ("verbal behavior," to Watson), for example, begins as simple infant sounds that grow in complexity as they continue to be conditioned to the objects and events in the surrounding environment. Furthermore, as speech grows more and more sophisticated, it gradually develops a subvocal (silent) form, which we know as thinking, reasoning, and problem solving. Watson therefore believed that it was crucial for psychologists to study infants and young children—not to observe early physical changes but to study the first steps in the conditioning process that produces complex human behavior.

The Pavlovian conditioning process that formed the core of Watson's behavioristic theory was relatively straightforward and easy to understand. And it was this simplicity, along with Watson's close adherence to the methods of the other natural sciences, that led American psychologists of the time to embrace behaviorism as a major advance in scientific thinking. A new Zeitgeist had emerged.

In 1920, however, Watson was forced to resign from Johns Hopkins when the revelation of an affair with a graduate student, followed by a divorce from his wife, created a scandal. He left academic life and turned to a career in business, where his interest in psychology moved away from scholarly issues. Watson began writing magazine articles and books about his behavioristic approach for the general public. *Psychological Care of the Infant and Child,* published in 1928, presented his views on child rearing, and it proved to be a very successful and influential book. Watson's suggestions to parents were based on a virtually pure environmentalism— that is, no abilities or personality characteristics were inborn, so children were entirely the products of their upbringing and environment. This view had great appeal for many parents, who delighted in believing that any child had the potential to become a great athlete, surgeon, or Supreme Court justice, if only given the proper training.

Watson's career was brief, but his contributions to psychology were significant. His criticism of introspective research and his call for objective methods of study brought early experimental psychology in line with the other natural sciences. Today, virtually all experimental psychology is based on the methods that Watson espoused, including the precise specification of experimental procedures, the emphasis on observable and measurable behaviors, and the use of objective and verifiable measures rather than subjective experiences (Brewer, 1991). However, Watson's strict environmentalist views and the major role he assigned to conditioned reflexes are no longer taken very seriously.

Sigmund Freud (1856–1939)

In 1909, as Watson was introducing behaviorism to the scientific world, another important event took place. G. Stanley Hall invited some of the most eminent psychologists of the day, including several European scholars, to come to Clark University to celebrate the institution's 20th anniversary (Hall and Freud are seen seated together on page 14). It was on this occasion that Sigmund Freud, in a series of five lectures, first outlined his grand theory of psychological development. American psychologists were not immediately receptive to Freud's model, and it proved to be no obstacle to Watson's emerging behavioral and experimental movement. But the seeds of psychoanalytic thought had been planted in American soil, and in time Freud's views would attract a good deal of attention both inside and outside the psychological community.

Freud spent most of his early life in Vienna, Austria, where he trained as a medical student. In 1885, bored with medical practice, he traveled to Paris to learn the technique of hypnosis from the French physician Charcot. It was during this time that Freud began to develop many of his ideas regarding the powerful role of the unconscious. On his return to Vienna, Freud established a private practice and began refining both his theory and the methods of psychoanalysis.

Freud made two major contributions to psychology. His greatest impact was in the area of clinical psychology, where his model of personality and his techniques of psychoanalysis underlie what is still a major school of thought in psychotherapy. His contribution to developmental psychology was his stage theory of psychosexual

Libido
Sigmund Freud's term for the sexual energy that he believed is possessed by all children from birth and then moves to different locations on the body over the course of development.

Erogenous zones
According to Freud's theory of psychosexual development, the areas of the body where the libido resides during successive stages of development. The child seeks physical pleasure in the erogenous zone at which the libido is located.

• Freud proposed that, during the anal stage, successful toilet training is important to the child's psychosexual development.

Repression
Freud's term for the process through which desires or motivations are driven into the unconscious, as typically occurs during the phallic stage.

Identification
The Freudian process through which the child adopts the characteristics of the same-sex parent during the phallic stage.

Fixation
The condition in which some of the libido inappropriately remains in one of the erogenous zones, causing the adult to continually seek physical pleasure in that area.

development. Although he actually spent very little time observing children's growth and development directly, he used his patients' and his own recollections of childhood experiences to construct a comprehensive model of child development.

The central theme of Freudian developmental theory is that each child is born with a certain amount of sexual energy, called **libido,** that is biologically guided to certain locations on the body, called the **erogenous zones,** as the child grows. Sexual energy, in this model, refers simply to the ability to experience physical pleasure. The arrival of the libido at each location marks a new stage in the child's psychosexual development. And during that stage, the child receives the greatest physical pleasure in that erogenous zone.

Freud's model was not purely biological, however, and he firmly believed that children's experiences during each stage strongly affect their later development. Successful movement from stage to stage requires that children receive the proper amount of physical pleasure from each erogenous zone. Freud therefore cautioned parents not to frustrate children by being overly strict, but he warned that being too indulgent or permissive could cause problems, as well. In other words, children should experience enough pleasure, but not too much. Unfortunately, both Freud's advice and his theoretical predictions were always rather vague as to how much pleasure was enough.

According to the psychosexual model, human development unfolds in five stages. During the *oral stage,* from birth to about 18 months, the libido is located at the mouth. The infant's principal source of physical pleasure is sucking, and all objects tend to find their way into the child's mouth. When and how much infants are breast-fed and how they are eventually weaned are the events in this stage that Freud felt have the strongest long-term influence. The period from 18 months to 3 years marks the *anal stage,* in which the child attains physical pleasure first from having bowel movements and later from withholding them. Not surprisingly, positive toilet-training experiences are the major concern during this stage.

The most complex of Freud's stages is the *phallic stage,* which lasts roughly from ages 3 to 5. The erogenous zone is the genital area, and the child's physical pleasure is derived from the direct stimulation of the genital organs. Sometimes this stimulation is produced by the child through touching, or masturbation, and sometimes it is accidentally produced by the parent, as during bathing or hugging. During this stage, according to Freud, children become sexually attracted to the parent of the opposite sex. But they soon begin to experience feelings of conflict as they realize that the same-sex parent is a powerful rival. Children presumably resolve this conflict in two ways. First, they force their desires into the unconscious, a process called **repression,** which also wipes out their memory of these feelings. Then, they compensate for this loss by making a determined effort to adopt the characteristics of the same-sex parent, a process called **identification.**

The *latency stage* occurs in the middle and later childhood years, from ages 6 to 12. During this stage, the libido remains repressed and inactive. It reemerges at puberty in the *genital stage,* when once again the child develops an attraction toward the opposite sex. Now, however, it is more appropriately directed toward peers, rather than parents.

Freud's theory of child development is actually a theory of personality formation. It assumes that many aspects of the adult personality result from events during the childhood psychosexual stages. If the child's experiences during a stage are not what they should be, some portion of the libido will remain **fixated** in that erogenous zone, rather than moving onto the next one. For example, if a child is not given the appropriate amount of oral gratification during the first stage, the libido will remain partially fixated at the mouth. Later in life, this fixation will be manifested in the adult's continually seeking physical pleasure in this erogenous zone—perhaps by smoking, chewing on pencils, or having an unusual interest in kissing. Many everyday behaviors of this sort, in fact, were explained by Freud as being symptoms of early developmental difficulties.

Although Freud's theory had some influence on American developmentalists, they never fully accepted it, for a number of reasons. First, it is vague and makes few clear predictions. As a result, its key elements cannot be scientifically verified or disproved. Research studies that have attempted to test Freud's ideas—by examining the relation between breast-feeding or toilet-training practices and later personality characteristics, for example—fail to support his model (Caldwell, 1964; Ferguson, 1970). Furthermore, Freud's heavy reliance on unobservable mechanisms, such as unconscious motives, is not consistent with American psychology's belief that science should be based on measurable and verifiable observations.

In spite of its failings, Freud's theory of child development includes two fundamental concepts that are still generally accepted today. The first is his rejection of either a purely nativistic or a strictly environmentalist explanation of human behavior. Freud was the first major developmentalist to argue for an **interactionist perspective,** which sees both inborn processes *and* environmental factors as making strong contributions to the child's development. Today, almost all child psychologists subscribe to an interactionist position. The second is Freud's suggestion that early experiences can have important effects on behavior in later life. Again, most contemporary developmentalists agree with this idea, although few would explain these effects in terms of unresolved childhood conflicts hidden in the adult's unconscious (Beier, 1991; Emde, 1992).

Interactionist perspective
The theory that human development results from the combination of nature and nurture factors.

Arnold Gesell (1880–1961)

In science, we have seen, the pendulum of philosophical thought continually swings back and forth. Just as scientists begin to accept a particular way of looking at things, someone seems to come along with an important criticism of that view or with new evidence that supports some earlier position. So when the Zeitgeist swings back toward a prior point of view, it is usually because of new research findings and a more complete theoretical explanation of the facts. Accordingly, when developmentalists began returning to the biological model of child development in the 1930s, it was not because they once again accepted recapitulation theory. Rather, they were persuaded to reconsider the nativistic viewpoint by the research and ideas of one of G. Stanley Hall's most successful students, Arnold Gesell.

Gesell completed his doctoral work at Clark University in 1906 and went on to obtain a medical degree at Yale University. In 1911, he established the Yale Clinic of Child Development, where he spent almost 50 years studying and describing development in the typical child.

Although he did not agree with Hall's view that human development mirrors the evolution of the species, Gesell did believe that development is guided primarily by genetic processes. He therefore felt that growth and the emergence of motor skills (crawling and sitting, for example.) should follow very predictable patterns. In this scheme, the environment plays only a minor role—perhaps affecting the age at which certain skills appear but never affecting the sequence or pattern of development. The complex of biological mechanisms that guide development Gesell described simply as **maturation.** The resulting patterns of growth and development were as yet unknown, and Gesell set about to identify them.

Maturation
The biological processes assumed by some theorists to be primarily responsible for human development.

• Among Arnold Gessell's most important contributions to developmental psychology were his innovative research techniques, including an observation dome that permitted photographing the child unobtrusively from any angle.

Norms
A timetable of age ranges indicating when normal growth and developmental milestones are typically reached.

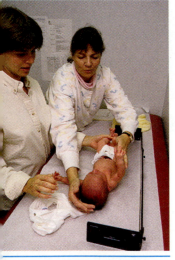

• Gesell's method of comparing children's development to norms representing the average range of development continues to be used today.

Using observational methods and hundreds of children of many different ages as subjects, Gesell conducted the first large-scale study to examine children's behavior in great detail. This research revealed a high degree of uniformity in children's development. They did not all develop at the same rate—some walked earlier and others later—but the pattern of development was very consistent. For example, almost all children walked before they ran, ran before they skipped, and skipped before they hopped. From his work, Gesell established statistical **norms**—a sort of developmental timetable that describes the usual order in which children display various early behaviors and the age range within which each behavior normally appears (Gesell & Thompson, 1938). These norms proved very valuable to physicians and parents as general guidelines for evaluating developmental progress—so much so that they continue to be revised and used today.

To acquire this sort of descriptive information, Gesell did not rely on the outdated research methods of the past. In fact, the sophisticated research techniques he developed for observing and recording children's behavior are among his most important contributions to psychology (Thelen & Adolph, 1992). Gesell pioneered in the use of film cameras to record children's behavior. He also developed the first one-way viewing screens, and he constructed a photographic dome that allowed observations from all angles without disturbing the child under study.

Gesell wrote books for parents containing advice that could have been given by Rousseau 200 years earlier. He suggested, for instance, that babies be fed only when they display signs of hunger and that they be allowed to sleep, play, or explore according to their own natural schedules. Parents should be patient and enjoy their children's current abilities and behaviors rather than try to hurry them along toward more mature skills. Furthermore, education should be flexible and geared to each child's interests and personal style of learning. Gesell's advice was not quite as permissive as Rousseau's, and he did believe that parents need to include some limits and structure in the child's life. But he felt strongly that, if largely left alone, children will develop naturally and properly, according to their inborn biological plans (Gesell & Ilg, 1943).

Gesell's contributions in some areas were substantial and important. His methodological innovations helped to advance the field of developmental research, and his establishment of norms greatly expanded our knowledge of children's everyday skills and behavior. But Gesell's strongly biological philosophy, like most extreme viewpoints, was an oversimplification, because it largely neglected the crucial role of environmental factors. As a result, his theoretical model failed to have a long-term impact on developmental thought (Hilgard, 1987). However, Gesell's emphasis on patterns of unfolding behavior and his focus on similarities in children's development may have helped prepare American psychologists to accept the more influential views of another of Rousseau's theoretical descendants, Jean Piaget.

Jean Piaget (1896–1980)

If we had to select the one psychologist whose work has had the greatest influence on the study of child development, we would have to consider Jean Piaget a very strong candidate. His ideas have inspired more research than those of any other theorist, and his conception of human development revolutionized thinking about children and their behavior. Piaget differs from the other pioneers discussed here in that his theoretical views are still widely accepted in some form by many of today's developmental psychologists. For this reason, we discuss Piaget in several places in this text. This chapter briefly describes his background and overall approach to psychology. Later chapters cover his theoretical views and the research that addresses them.

• Jean Piaget is one pioneer of child psychology whose early ideas remain largely accepted today by many researchers.

Piaget was born and raised in Switzerland. From boyhood, he was interested in science, particularly biology and animal behavior, and his Ph.D., which he received in 1918, was based on research with mollusks. Although he left this area of study, his background in biology is reflected in his theory of child development.

Piaget had always been drawn to the study of psychology, and after earning his doctorate, he briefly studied the techniques of psychoanalysis. He soon moved from Switzerland to Paris, where he became involved in the development of intelligence tests for children.

Intelligence testing was a new field at this time, and two of its founders, Alfred Binet and Theodore Simon, were attempting to develop questionnaires that could predict children's success in school. Binet and Simon first devised questions that represented the knowledge typical of children at a given age. Then they developed norms so that any child's test performance—that is, the number of correct answers—could be compared with the average performance of other children of the same age. These tests improved on Hall's early questionnaires by including precise testing and scoring procedures that did not allow for subjective interpretations.

Piaget was hired by Simon to administer the tests, which gave him his first real experience with developmental work. But unlike his employers, Piaget became less interested in the number of test items children answered correctly than in the reasons for their incorrect responses. Children of different ages, he observed, not only knew different amounts of information but also looked at the world in very different ways. Their answers revealed *qualitative* (style-related) differences in thinking beyond the *quantitative* (amount-related) differences in factual information.

After 2 years in Paris, Piaget returned to Switzerland and began his own research on the development of children's knowledge. Some of his research questions were quite philosophical. What does it mean to know something? Do all people perceive and store knowledge in the same way? Is what you learn affected by what you already know? The branch of philosophy that deals with these kinds of issues is called *epistemology.* Piaget called his own area of interest **genetic epistemology,** by which he meant the study of the nature of knowledge in young children and how it changes as they grow older (*genetic* meaning "developmental").

Genetic epistemology
Jean Piaget's term for the study of children's knowledge and how it changes with development.

Piaget's theory is described in detail in the next chapter and in Chapter 8. Briefly, it is concerned with identifying the commonalities in children's development rather than with determining how children differ from one another. Unlike Hall, Piaget was interested not in the precise knowledge children possess but rather in how they go about acquiring and using that knowledge. He did not care, for example, *what children know* when they enter school, as much as *how children think.*

In 1925, the first of Piaget's three children was born. Piaget spent a great deal of time studying development in his own children. Often he would invent simple experiments or situations to examine how they approached problems of different sorts. He later used many of these experiments in his research with other children.

To find support for his theory, Piaget developed his own research technique. Whereas Gesell's methods involved observing children without interfering with them, Piaget challenged children with simple tasks and verbal problems that required solutions and explanations. His technique, known as the **clinical method,** involved a loosely structured interview in which he asked whatever questions or pursued whatever issues he felt would reveal the child's way of reasoning. Piaget might have begun by asking each of a number of children the same question, such as, Is a rose prettier than a flower? His follow-up questions, however, would depend on the nature of the child's responses.

Clinical method
Piaget's principal research method, which involved a semistructured interview with questions designed to probe children's understanding of various concepts.

Piaget's research initially attracted some attention in the United States during the 1920s and 1930s. But his writings were difficult for American psychologists to understand because they contained many terms and concepts that were different from the scientific language they were using. And his somewhat informal methods of investigation were viewed as a problem by more rigorous experimental researchers. During the 1940s and 1950s, as American child psychology once again turned toward environmental and conditioning models, interest in Piaget's theory disappeared.

Beginning in the late 1950s, however, American psychologists began to rediscover Piaget's work. His theoretical writings were translated into more familiar concepts, and his studies were replicated under controlled experimental conditions (Flavell, 1963). Among the first to endorse Piaget's theories were educators, who began to develop school curricula based on his ideas. Research psychologists soon also grew interested in Piaget's theoretical views. Their own experiments supported his predictions and confirmed the existence of qualitative differences in the behavior of children of different ages. In addition, his theory generated many new questions that psychologists felt could and should be investigated, questions about children's understanding of time, logic, causality, and other kinds of fundamental knowledge, for example.

Piaget died in 1980. As late as 1975, he was continuing to revise his model in response to new data and findings generated by his research team in Geneva (Beilin, 1989). Piaget's many books on child psychology remain the greatest contribution to the field by a single scholar (Beilin, 1992).

Lev Vygotsky (1896–1934)

Another pioneer of child psychology whose ideas continue to find considerable acceptance is Lev Vygotsky. As with Piaget, we present Vygotsky's background and general theoretical approach here and in later chapters we discuss his ideas in more detail.

Vygotsky was born in Russia in the same year as Piaget, and their early work occupied the same period. Yet their backgrounds were very different. These differences are reflected in the contrasting models of human development they constructed (Glassman, 1994; Kozulin, 1990).

Vygotsky was not trained in science but instead received a law degree from Moscow University. He went on to study literature and linguistics and eventually received a Ph.D. for a book he wrote on the psychology of art. Whereas Piaget wrote a dissertation on the biology of mollusks, one of Vygotsky's major works as a student was an essay on Shakespeare's *Hamlet*.

• Lev Vygotsky's sociocultural theory of cognitive development, originally published more than fifty years ago, has generated great interest in modern developmentalists.

An interesting similarity between the two scholars, however, is that both received little attention from Western scientists until the 1960s, when their work was translated into English, and their theories began to be tested experimentally. Piaget, of course, was still active at this time and continued to contribute to the scientific advances brought about by his theory. Vygotsky, however, had died at 37 and never lived to see his ideas pursued by other researchers. In fact, his writings were initially misunderstood and so were banned in the former Soviet Union for over 20 years. Thus, his work remained unknown even to many of his contemporary Soviet psychologists.

To understand Vygotsky's theory, it is important to appreciate the political environment of the time. Vygotsky began working in psychology shortly after the Russian Revolution, in which Marxism replaced the rule of the czar. The new Marxist philosophy stressed socialism and collectivism. Individuals were expected to sacrifice their personal goals and achievements for the betterment of the larger society. Sharing and cooperation were encouraged, and the success of any individual was seen as reflecting the success of the culture. Marxists also placed a heavy emphasis on history, believing that any culture could be understood only through examination of the ideas and events that had shaped it.

Vygotsky's model of human development incorporated these elements and so has been termed a *sociocultural* (or *sociohistorical*) approach. For him, the individual's development is a product of his or her culture. Development, in Vygotsky's theory, referred largely to mental development, such as thought, language, and reasoning processes. These abilities were assumed to develop through social interactions with others (especially parents) and thus represented the shared knowledge of the culture. Mental abilities and processes similarly were viewed in terms of the historical sequence of events that produced them. Whereas Piaget believed that all children's cognitive development follows a very similar pattern of stages, Vygotsky saw intellectual abilities as being much more specific to the culture in which the child was reared (Miller, 1993).

Today, the sociocultural approach has become one of the most influential movements in developmental psychology. We discuss the specific psychological mechanisms proposed by Vygotsky and others of this tradition in later chapters.

✔ *To Recap...*

The scientific study of children began with the questionnaire research of G. Stanley Hall, who also proposed a theory of development based on the principle of evolutionary recapitulation. John B. Watson helped to make child psychology a natural science by introducing objective research methods based on observable and measurable behaviors. His behavioristic theory of development held that the conditioned reflex was the fundamental unit of development and that environmental and experiential factors were primarily responsible for changes in behavior. Sigmund Freud proposed a stage theory of child development that grew out of his clinical work in psychoanalysis. Modern developmentalists have little interest in Freud's theory, but his interactionist viewpoint and his emphasis on childhood experiences remain important concepts. Arnold Gesell's research with children renewed interest in the biological perspective by offering evidence that inborn maturational processes account for developmental changes. His observational studies produced age-related norms of behavior that have been valuable to both professionals and parents. Jean Piaget is perhaps the most influential developmental theorist to date. His genetic epistemology was concerned with understanding the form of children's knowledge and the qualitative changes it undergoes as they develop. Lev Vygotsky proposed a sociocultural model of human, and especially mental, development that reflected Marxist beliefs in the social and cultural basis of individual development and the importance of viewing development in historical perspective.

ISSUES IN DEVELOPMENTAL PSYCHOLOGY

In our brief look at the views espoused by the early theorists and pioneers of developmental psychology, we have come across a number of recurring questions. Three issues, in particular, have run through scientific thinking about development almost from the very beginning, and they continue to be a source of debate today. These issues revolve around the questions of nature versus nurture, continuity versus discontinuity, and normative versus idiographic development.

Nature versus Nurture

The most basic and long-standing issue in child psychology (and perhaps in all of psychology) involves the degree to which behavior and development result from inborn, biological, **nature** factors or environmental, experiential, **nurture** factors. This debate has existed at least since Locke and Rousseau first proposed their rather pure environmental and nativistic models of child development. The nurture view was later taken up by Watson and other learning theorists, while the nature position formed the basis of the theories of Hall and Gesell. The modern debate, however, is far more complex than in these early days of psychology (Plomin & McClearn, 1993).

As we indicated earlier, virtually all child researchers today subscribe to some form of interactionist position, in which both nature and nurture are assumed to contribute to human development. Several theoretical models describing how our

Nature versus nurture debate
The scientific controversy regarding whether the primary source of developmental change rests in biological (nature) factors or environmental and experiential (nurture) factors.

• The role of nature and nurture factors in human development has been at the heart of many theoretical debates in developmental psychology.

genes and environment may work together to guide our behavior are discussed in Chapters 2 and 4. Nevertheless, the nature–nurture debate has not ended. Some theorists, despite their overall interactionist philosophy, contend that specific aspects of behavior have primarily a biological basis. Others believe that the same behavior is the result of environmental factors. For example, when a kindergartner hits a classmate who has just taken his toy, some psychologists are more likely to believe that the child's aggressive response is principally a biological reaction to frustration. Others will contend that it probably represents a behavior the child learned by watching and interacting with others. And even when a behavior is assumed to result from a combination of nature and nurture factors, many questions usually remain regarding the precise role that each plays in the process.

The nature–nurture issue can often be seen, for example, in the area of gender-role development. Once a sex difference in behavior has been identified—such as the finding that males are generally more adept than females at spatial tasks that involve mentally rotating a figure to a different orientation (Halpern, 1992)—explanations for the difference can take at least three different forms. The difference can be attributed to nature, as in the contention that the brains of males and females are structured differently. It can be attributed to environmental factors, as in the argument that boys receive more encouragement from parents and teachers to engage in activities that promote spatial skills. Or it can involve an interactionist explanation, such as the possibility that boys innately prefer activities involving spatial relations and, as a result, spend more time improving these skills.

Nature versus nurture questions, such as the one just described, arise in almost every topic we consider in this text. At times, however, they appear under different labels, such as heredity versus environment, maturation versus learning, or emergent abilities versus acquired skills. All of these debates, nevertheless, tend to involve the same fundamental question.

Continuity versus Discontinuity

Continuity versus discontinuity debate
The scientific controversy regarding whether development is constant and connected (continuous) or uneven and disconnected (discontinuous).

A second long-standing issue in child psychology is whether development displays **continuity** or **discontinuity.** This debate actually has two components (Emde & Harmon, 1984). One involves the pattern of development. Continuity theorists believe that development is smooth and stable, with new abilities, skills, and knowledge gradually added at a relatively uniform pace. Discontinuity theorists hold that development occurs at different rates, alternating between periods of little change and periods of abrupt, rapid change. The second component involves the connectedness of development. Continuity theorists contend that early behaviors build on one another to form later behaviors or, at least, that development early in life is somehow clearly tied to development later on. Discontinuity theorists suggest that some aspects of development emerge relatively independently of what has come before and cannot be predicted from the child's previous behavior (Clarke & Clarke, 1976).

The continuity model is often associated with the belief that human behavior consists of many individual skills that are added one at a time, usually through learning and experience. As children acquire more and more of these skills, they combine and recombine them to produce increasingly complex abilities. This approach emphasizes quantitative change—the simpler elements being essentially added together to produce the more advanced capabilities—and often characterizes environmentalist models of development. In contrast, psychologists who favor the discontinuity model usually hold that development is guided primarily by internal biological factors. Stage theorists, for example, argue that the unevenness of children's development reflects the discontinuous nature of the changes taking place in the underlying structures of the body and brain. Thus, development often involves qualitative changes that are more than just simple combinations of previous abilities or behaviors. In their models, development remains relatively stable while the child is in a given stage, but movement to the next stage brings an abrupt shift in the child's abilities.

Like the nature versus nurture issue, the question of continuity versus discontinuity is not cut-and-dried. Psychologists on both sides of the debate agree that some developmental processes are more accurately described by one model, others by the competing model (Rutter, 1987).

Normative versus Idiographic Development

Normative versus idiographic development
The question of whether research should focus on identifying commonalities in human development (normative development) or on the causes of individual differences (idiographic development).

Universals of development
Aspects of development or behavior that are common to children everywhere.

A third issue that commonly arises in child psychology is actually less a matter of debate than of a researcher's focus when studying development. Some psychologists are concerned with **normative** development, meaning the commonalities that exist in the development of all children. Others focus on **idiographic** development, meaning the individual differences that exist among children.

Normative research often is based on a biological view of development. Gesell and, to a lesser degree, Piaget, are examples. These theorists typically conceive of development as unfolding predictably, guided by internal biological processes and largely unaffected by environmental factors. This perspective thus principally focuses on the "average" child, with the primary goal of identifying and describing how normal development proceeds from step to step. A related issue involves the search for **universals of development**—those behaviors or patterns of development that characterize all children, everywhere (as Piaget sought to identify).

Idiographic research centers on the individual child and the factors that produce human diversity. Genes are certainly responsible for some of the individual

• Normative research attempts to identify commonalities among children, whereas idiographic research is concerned with why one child is different from the next.

differences among people. But the idiographic perspective also considers the environmental and experiential processes that serve to mold and shape children into unique individuals. Researchers use this approach to study aspects of development that display **cultural relativism**—the way in which such aspects differ from one culture to another.

Contemporary research on language development illustrates these two perspectives. Some theorists believe that language abilities emerge similarly for all children because they are controlled in large part by specific mechanisms in the brain. Correspondingly, their studies search for common patterns of linguistic development among children of a given language, as well as for characteristics that are universal across the many thousands of languages throughout the world. Theorists more concerned with individual differences in speech development typically study environmental influences on language acquisition—such as the type of speech adults use when talking with children—in order to determine which factors cause language to develop differently in different children.

Cultural relativism
The idea that certain behaviors or patterns of development vary from one culture to another.

✔ *To Recap...*

Three issues arise frequently in child psychology research. The nature versus nurture issue focuses on whether the primary source of developmental change is inborn and biological or environmental and experiential. The continuity versus discontinuity issue concerns whether the pattern of development is constant or uneven and whether development shows connectedness—that is, whether early characteristics predict later ones. The normative versus idiographic issue involves the researcher's preference for focusing either on the commonalities of children's development and the search for universals or on the factors that produce individual differences among children, such as cultural influences.

CONCLUSION

Our brief look backward in this chapter should have made one point clear—the more scholars have observed children and learned about early development, the more they have come to appreciate the importance of the childhood years for understanding all of human behavior. As this fact became increasingly obvious, two things happened. First, we realized that because children are not fully developed organisms they are more vulnerable than adults, so we began to treat them better. Second, we began to study children much more closely, using all of the available tools of science. Today, children are accorded a very special status in our society, and developmental psychology has taken its place among the other natural sciences.

Although child study is still young compared with other physical and biological sciences, our understanding of developmental processes is progressing so rapidly that it is difficult to keep up with the information that is being generated by researchers. The remainder of the text, therefore, focuses on the current state of the field rather than on historical issues and research. And yet, as we proceed from topic to topic, some of the recurring controversies may sound familiar and reminiscent of the fundamental differences that arose between Locke and Rousseau, Watson and Gesell, or Binet and Piaget.

FOR THOUGHT AND DISCUSSION

1.   We suggest five reasons why developmental psychologists have traditionally focused their work on children. *Can you think of any others? What are some behaviors that can only be studied in children? What behaviors or aspects of children's development are you particularly interested in learning about in this course?*

2.   Descartes believed that the mind is nonphysical and separate from the body. *What do you think? How could you prove it?*

3.   We state that childhood today is seen as a special time. *What are some specific examples (beyond those in the text) of how our society treats children differently from adults?*

4.   One theme that has preoccupied philosophers and psychologists involves whether children are born with a tendency to be good, evil, or neither. *What do you think? Do you think this is a question that scientists should study?*

5.   Some aspects of development are believed to be continuous from early childhood, whereas others are thought to be discontinuous. *Which aspects of your own personality have remained the same since you were a young child? Which have changed? Relate this stability and change to nature and nurture factors.*

Chapter 2

THEORIES OF CHILD DEVELOPMENT

*D*evelopmental psychologists usually describe themselves in terms of their areas of research interest. One psychologist, for example, might concentrate on infants, studying how perceptual abilities develop during the first months of life. Another might be concerned with identifying the ways in which children's social skills affect their success in the classroom. But in addition to their research interests, most psychologists also characterize themselves in terms of a particular theoretical orientation—that is, their view of how development occurs and which factors they believe are most responsible for changes in children's behavior.

Today, the large majority of child psychologists identify themselves with one of three general theoretical views—the cognitive-developmental approach, the environmental/learning approach, or the ethological approach. This chapter outlines the principal ideas and underlying assumptions of these three theories. Then, as we discuss various topics throughout the rest of the book, we will compare and contrast the approaches taken by each of the theories, including the types of questions they ask and the research methods they prefer.

Of course, more than three models of human development exist. We have chosen to describe only these three for two reasons. First, they are presently the most popular, and so they guide most of the research being conducted today. Second, each of the theories is comprehensive and attempts to explain many areas of child development. Some theories that focus on more limited aspects of development are discussed in later chapters.

COGNITIVE-DEVELOPMENTAL MODELS

The cognitive-developmental approach encompasses a number of related theories and kinds of research. For years, this approach was most closely associated with the work of Piaget. However, in the past 2 decades, information-processing models and sociocultural analyses have also become very popular among cognitive developmentalists.

As we saw in Chapter 1, the roots of the cognitive- developmental tradition lie in the 18th-century writings of Jean-Jacques Rousseau. This early nativistic view suggested that human development unfolds predictably with little or no environmental influence. Modern cognitive-developmental theorists assign a much greater role to environmental influences than did Rousseau, reflecting the interactionist perspective of all contemporary theories. Nevertheless, one characteristic of most cognitive models is an emphasis on "nature" factors.

A more important characteristic of this approach, however, is implied by the name *cognitive-developmental. Cognition* refers to knowing, and the central idea underlying these theories is that children's behavior reflects the structure, or organization, of their knowledge or intelligence. How we think and what we know are assumed to guide how we behave. Some basic goals for psychologists of this tradition, therefore, are to specify what children know, how this knowledge is organized, and how it changes or develops.

As an example, consider a topic touched on at the end of the last chapter, the development of gender roles. Cognitive-developmentalists believe that the first step children take in acquiring gender roles is to develop an understanding of the categories "male" and "female." This understanding includes their learning whether they are male or female and which behaviors are considered appropriate for each gender. This knowledge then presumably leads them to behave in ways typical of little boys or little girls. Note that, according to this approach, the environment does not act directly on children's behavior; it acts indirectly by changing children's cognition. (We discuss the cognitive-developmental explanation of sex typing more fully in Chapter 15.)

Our discussion of the major cognitive-developmental models begins with Jean Piaget (1896–1980). Not only is his theory the oldest in this tradition, but it has provided psychology with its richest and most elaborate account of developmental changes in cognitive abilities (Miller, 1993).

Piaget's Theory

As a student of biology and zoology, Piaget learned that survival requires adaptation. Any individual organism, as well as any entire species, must adapt to constant changes in the environment. Piaget therefore viewed the development of human cognition, or intelligence, as the continual struggle of a very complex organism trying to adapt to a very complex environment (Piaget & Inhelder, 1968).

According to Piaget's theory, human development can be described in terms of **functions** and **cognitive structures.** The functions are inborn biological processes that are the same for everyone and remain unchanged throughout our lives. The purpose of these functions is to construct internal cognitive structures. The structures, in contrast, change repeatedly as the child grows.

Cognitive Structures

The most fundamental aspect of Piaget's theory, and often the most difficult to comprehend, is his belief that intelligence is a process—not something that a child *has* but something that a child *does.* Piaget's child understands the world by acting or operating on it.

Consider how Piaget would describe an infant's knowledge of a ball. This knowledge consists of various actions that the infant can perform with the ball— pushing it, throwing it, mouthing it, and so on. These actions are examples of **schemes**—the cognitive structures of infancy—and they involve two elements: an object in the environment (such as a ball) and the child's reaction to the object. A scheme is not a physical structure, however, in the way that the hypothalamus is a structure in the brain. Rather, a scheme is a psychological structure that reflects the child's underlying knowledge and guides his or her interactions with the world. It is the nature and organization of these schemes (or other cognitive structures during later development) that define the child's intelligence at any given moment.

Several further points about Piaget's cognitive structures are important to note. One is that they are flexible. A scheme, for example, is not a rigid relationship between object and action—that is, an infant does not display exactly the same behavior with every ball encountered. Similarly, an action can be adapted to different objects. The way a ball is grasped is somewhat different from the way a rattle is grasped. And the way either of these objects is sucked is somewhat different from the way a nipple is sucked.

Cognitive structures are flexible in still another sense—they change over time. A particular scheme, such as grasping, shows more and more skill as the infant applies it to more and more objects. In this way, a baby's repertoire of schemes eventually becomes more individualized, or *differentiated,* so that a ball becomes primarily an object to be thrown, a rattle primarily an object to be shaken, and a nipple primarily an object to be sucked.

Functions
Piaget's term for the biologically based tendencies to organize knowledge into cognitive structures and to adapt to challenges from the environment.

Cognitive structures
Piaget's term for the interrelated systems of knowledge that underlie and guide intelligent behavior.

Schemes
Piaget's term for the cognitive structures of infancy. A scheme consists of a set of skilled, flexible action patterns through which the child understands the world.

• According to Piaget, babies' early schemes involve interactions with simple objects.

Beyond these simple schemes of infancy, new and higher-level cognitive structures gradually emerge. An 8-year-old confronted with a ball, for example, still has all of the earlier schemes available (although sucking is not a very likely response!). But the older child can also comprehend a ball by using mental operations, such as assigning it certain properties (color, size) or actions (bouncing, hitting) or capabilities (being a member of the class "round things").

For Piaget, *development* refers to this continual reorganization of knowledge into new and more complex structures. Much of our discussion in Chapter 8 concerns what these structures are and how they change with development.

Functions

The functions that guide human development are also central to Piaget's theory. Piaget stressed two general functions, both of which he adapted from his training in biology. One is **organization.** Organization refers to the fact that all cognitive structures are interrelated and that any new knowledge must be fitted into the existing system. According to Piaget, it is this need for organization—for integrating new information, rather than simply adding it on—that forces our cognitive structures to become ever more elaborate.

The second general function is **adaptation.** Adaptation refers to the tendency of the organism to fit with its environment in ways that promote survival. It is composed of two subprocesses. **Assimilation** is the tendency to understand new experiences in terms of existing knowledge. Whenever we encounter something new, we try to make sense of it in terms of our existing cognitive structures. The infant who brings everything to his mouth to suck is demonstrating assimilation, as is the toddler who calls all men "Daddy." Note that there may be some distortion of the environmental reality in such efforts (not all men, of course, are Daddy). But trying to fit new things into what we already know is a necessary part of adapting to the world.

When new information is too different or too complex to be integrated into existing structures, **accommodation** occurs—that is, cognitive structures change in response to new experiences. The infant eventually learns that not all objects are to be sucked (and that different objects need to be sucked in different ways), just as the toddler learns that different labels or names need to be applied to different men. For Piaget, such changes reflect accommodation to the demands of the environment. Thus it is primarily through accommodation that the number and complexity of children's cognitive structures increase.

Assimilation and accommodation are assumed to operate closely together. The growing child is continually making slight distortions of information to assimilate it into existing structures, while also making slight modifications in these structures to accommodate new objects or events. The interplay of these two functions illustrates another important aspect of Piaget's theory, the concept of **constructivism.** Children's knowledge of events in their environment is not an exact reproduction of those events—it is not like a perfect photograph of what they have seen or a precise recording of what they have heard. Children take information from the environment and bend, shape, or distort it until it fits comfortably into their existing cognitive organization. As we said earlier, they *operate* on it. Even when they accommodate structures to allow for new experiences, the accommodation is seldom complete, and some distortion of the information remains. Thus, when a 6-, an 8-, and a 10-year-old watch a movie or hear a lecture, they come away with somewhat different messages, even though they may have seen or heard precisely the same stimulus input. Each child acts on the information somewhat differently, fitting it

Organization
The tendency to integrate knowledge into interrelated cognitive structures. One of the two biologically based functions stressed in Piaget's theory.

Adaptation
The tendency to fit with the environment in ways that promote survival. One of the two biologically based functions stressed in Piaget's theory.

Assimilation
Interpreting new experiences in terms of existing cognitive structures. One of the two components of adaptation in Piaget's theory.

Accommodation
Changing existing cognitive structures to fit with new experiences. One of the two components of adaptation in Piaget's theory.

Constructivism
Piaget's belief that children actively create knowledge rather than passively receive it from the environment.

into a somewhat different set of structures. This is what Piaget meant by his claim that the child *constructs* knowledge about the world, rather than simply receiving and registering it.

The processes of assimilation, accommodation, and construction of new knowledge begin at birth and extend throughout life. Each new construction makes the cognitive system a bit more powerful and adaptive. In addition to these small-scale changes, however, Piaget maintained that at some points during development major, far-reaching modifications are required. At these points, the cognitive system, because of both biological maturation and past experiences, has completely mastered one level of functioning and is ready for new, qualitatively different challenges—challenges that go beyond what the current set of schemes can handle. It is at these points that the child moves to a new stage of development.

Stages of Development

Piaget was a stage theorist. In his view, all children move through the same stages of cognitive development in the same order. Each stage is a qualitatively distinct form of functioning, and the structures that characterize each stage determine the child's performance in a wide range of situations.

There are four such general stages, or **periods,** in Piaget's theory. Chapter 8 discusses the four periods and also evaluates the general claim that development is divided into stages. Here we settle for a brief overview.

The **sensorimotor** period represents the first 2 years of life. The infant's initial schemes are simple reflexes. Gradually, these reflexes are combined into larger, more flexible units of action. Knowledge of the world is limited to physical interactions with people and objects. Most of the examples of schemes given earlier—grasping, sucking, and so on—occur during infancy.

During the **preoperational** period, from roughly 2 to 6 years, the child begins to use symbols to represent the world cognitively. Words and numbers take the place of objects and events, and actions that formerly had to be carried out physically can now be performed mentally, through the use of internal symbols. The preoperational child is not yet skilled at symbolic problem solving, however, and various gaps and confusions are evident in the child's attempts to understand the world.

Many of these limitations are overcome when the child reaches the period of **concrete operations,** which lasts approximately from ages 6 to 11. Concrete operational children are able to perform mental operations on the bits of knowledge that they possess. They can add them, subtract them, put them in order, reverse them, and so on. These mental operations permit a kind of logical problem solving that was not possible during the preoperational period.

The final stage is the period of **formal operations,** which extends from about age 11 through adulthood. This period includes all of the higher level abstract operations that do not require concrete objects or materials. The clearest example of such operations is the ability to deal with events or relations that are only possible, as opposed to those that actually exist. Mentally considering all of the ways certain objects could be combined, or attempting to solve a problem by cognitively examining all of the ways it could be approached, are two operations that typically cannot be performed until this final stage.

The accuracy of Piaget's theory has been studied extensively over the years. In Chapter 8 we consider the evidence psychologists have gathered that both supports and questions various aspects of this theory.

Periods
Piaget's term for the four general stages into which his theory divides development. Each period is a qualitatively distinct form of functioning that characterizes a wide range of cognitive activities.

Sensorimotor
Form of intelligence in which knowledge is based on physical interactions with people and objects. The first of Piaget's periods, extending from birth to about 2 years.

Preoperational
Form of intelligence in which symbols and mental actions begin to replace objects and overt behaviors. The second of Piaget's periods, extending from about 2 to 6 years.

Concrete operations
Form of intelligence in which mental operations make logical problem solving with concrete objects possible. The third of Piaget's periods, extending from about 6 to 11 years.

Formal operations
Form of intelligence in which higher level mental operations make possible logical reasoning with respect to abstract and hypothetical events and not merely concrete objects. The fourth of Piaget's periods, beginning at about 11 years.

Information-Processing Models

A second form of cognitive theory is the information- processing approach, which we describe in detail in Chapter 9. Information-processing theorists conceptualize human cognition as a system composed of three parts. First, there is information in the world that provides the input to the system. Stimulation enters our sensory receptors in the form of sights, sounds, tastes, and so on. Second, there are processes in the brain that act on and transform the information in a variety of ways (hence the name of this approach). These include encoding it into symbolic forms, comparing it with previously acquired information, storing it in memory, retrieving it when necessary, and similar processes. Most of the psychologists working in the information-processing tradition have concentrated on this middle part of the system, designing their experiments to reveal the nature of these internal processes and how they interact with one another. The third part of the system is the output, which is our behavior—speech, social interactions, writing, and so on.

As you have probably noticed, there is an inescapable connection between the information-processing approach to cognition and the operation of a computer. Some theorists make this connection very strongly. Their goal is to construct computer programs that simulate human behavior, so that ultimately we will be able to specify our cognitive processes in precise mathematical and logical terms. More often, however, researchers use the computer analogy simply as a way of thinking about information flowing through a system, where it is processed and reemerges in a different form. This approach has been very useful in guiding psychological research on children's problem solving, memory, reading, and other cognitive processes (Kail & Bisanz, 1992; Klahr, 1989, 1992).

In recent years, the information-processing view has probably become the leading approach to the study of human cognition (Miller, 1993). Its popularity in part reflects the growing interest in *cognitive science,* an interdisciplinary field in which researchers in biology, mathematics, philosophy, and neuroscience, among others, are attempting to understand the workings of the human mind (e.g., Posner, 1989; Osherson, 1990).

Not all information-processing research has been concerned with children, and much of it has not been directed to developmental issues. Nevertheless, the approach has infused many areas of child psychology, and it will turn up throughout the text in topics as diverse as perception, language, gender roles, and aggression.

• Information-processing models of development compare the functions of the human mind to those of a computer.

Social Models of Cognition

The cognitive-developmental tradition has always been principally concerned with children's cognitive abilities. But in recent years, it also has become increasingly involved with children's social development, as the boundaries between these two areas of human development have steadily blurred. The increased interest in social processes among psychologists of this tradition has occurred for two different reasons. On the one hand, cognitive processes have been shown to influence social experiences. On the other, social interactions are thought to influence cognitive development.

Social Cognition

Many modern developmentalists believe that social development is affected by the nature and level of the child's cognitive skills. How children interact with others depends, for example, on how clearly they conceptualize interpersonal relationships, how accurately they interpret other children's behavior, how well they can apply information gained in previous situations to their current circumstances, and so forth. We will see in later chapters that such skills reflect fundamental aspects of children's emerging cognitive abilities. Children's social interactions, therefore, are at least somewhat affected by the sophistication of their cognitive development.

This is not to say, however, that the cognitive processes involved in social experiences are identical to those involved in nonsocial experiences. Although Piaget seemed to assume that the cognitive factors involved in understanding people and social relationships are the same as those that underlie mastery of the physical world (Piaget, 1963, 1964), most developmentalists today feel that the two are in some ways quite different. As a result, a new area of study has evolved known as **social cognition** (Pryor & Day, 1985; Shantz, 1983).

How might understanding the social world differ from understanding the physical world? One major difference is that people possess certain characteristics not found in nonliving things. For example, people have motives and intentions that may lead them to choose one behavior or another, sometimes in ways that are difficult to predict. Also, people have feelings and emotions that influence their behaviors and that may be important components of those behaviors. And perhaps most importantly, people interact—that is, when acted on, people act back. An inanimate thing, such as a leaf or a cup, may respond when we act on it. But when we act on a cup, we need not be concerned about what mood it is in, or what it hopes will happen, or what it will say in response. Nor, of course, do we need to be concerned about how *it* may act on *us*.

Modern theorists do not deny that there are important similarities between physical cognition and social cognition (Flavell, Miller, & Miller, 1993; Marini & Case, 1989, 1994). But their primary interest is in differences of the sort just described, and much research—within both the Piagetian and the information-processing frameworks—is underway to investigate children's understanding of social phenomena (Dodge, 1986a; Miller & Aloise, 1989). You will encounter such studies at several points in the book—with respect to children's concept of the self, for example (Chapter 13), the ways in which they reason about moral issues (Chapter 14), and their understanding of what it means to be a friend (Chapter 16).

Social cognition Knowledge of the social world and interpersonal relationships.

Sociocultural Models

The kinds of research just described focus on how children's cognitive level enables them to understand their social world. But researchers have also been interested in the reverse process—that is, in how social experiences affect children's cognitive development.

The most influential contemporary theory of how social experience affects cognitive development is that of the Soviet psychologist Lev Vygotsky, discussed briefly in Chapter 1. The theory itself is not new. As we saw, all of Vygotsky's work was conducted in the 1920s and 1930s. But only in recent years have developmental psychologists in the West begun to apply Vygotsky's ideas to children's cognitive and social development.

Vygotsky's theory emphasizes a number of related elements (Kozulin, 1990; Wertsch & Tulviste, 1992). Perhaps most generally, it emphasizes culture as a determinant of individual development. Humans are the only species that has created cultures, and every human child develops in the context of a culture. Culture makes two sorts of contributions to the child's intellectual development. First, children acquire much of the content of their thinking—that is, their knowledge—from it.

• Vygotsky believed that children acquire cognition through shared experiences with others in their culture who are more knowledgeable.

Tools of intellectual adaptation
Vygotsky's term for the techniques of thinking and problem solving that children internalize from their culture.

Dialectical process
The process in Vygotsky's theory whereby children learn through problem-solving experiences shared with others.

Internalization
Vygotsky's term for the child's incorporation, primarily through language, of bodies of knowledge and tools of thought from the culture.

Second, children acquire the processes or means of their thinking—what Vygotskians call the **tools of intellectual adaptation**—from the surrounding culture. In short, culture teaches children both what to think and how to think.

How does culture exert its influences? Vygotsky believed that cognitive development results from a **dialectical process** whereby the child learns through shared problem-solving experiences with someone else—usually a parent or teacher, sometimes a sibling or peer (Belmont, 1989; Tudge & Rogoff, 1989). Initially, the person interacting with the child assumes most of the responsibility for guiding the problem solving, but gradually this responsibility transfers to the child. Although these interactions can take many forms, Vygotsky stressed language interchanges. It is primarily through their speech that adults are assumed to transmit to children the rich body of knowledge that exists in the culture. As learning progresses, the child's own language comes to serve as his or her primary tool of intellectual adaptation. Eventually, for example, children can use internal speech to direct their own behavior in much the same way that the parents' speech once directed it. This transition reflects the final Vygotskian theme, development as a process of **internalization.** Bodies of knowledge and tools of thought at first exist outside the child, in the surrounding culture. Development consists of gradual internalization—primarily through language—of these forms of cultural adaptation (Rogoff, 1990, 1991).

Undoubtedly part of the reason for the current popularity of Vygotsky's theory lies in its fit with contemporary ideas about the importance of social factors and contexts in explaining children's behavior. We have much to say about such matters throughout this book. And we return specifically to Vygotsky in Chapter 10 when we discuss theories of intelligence and again in Chapter 14 when we examine the development of self-control.

✔ *To Recap...*

The cognitive-developmental approach to human development is based on the belief that cognitive abilities are fundamental and that they guide children's behavior. The key to understanding children's behavior, then, lies in understanding how their knowledge is structured at any given time and how it changes as they grow.

Piaget described human development in terms of inborn functions and changing cognitive structures. With development, the structures become progressively more complex and differentiated. Changes in structures are guided by two functions, organization and adaptation. Adaptation, in turn, consists of assimilation and accommodation. These processes reflect Piaget's constructivist view of development—the belief that children construct their understanding of the world rather than passively receive it from the environment. As children do this, they pass through four stages, or periods, of development: the sensorimotor period, the preoperational period, the period of concrete operations, and the period of formal operations.

Information-processing models conceptualize cognition as a computer-like system with three parts. Stimulation from the outside world makes up input, the first part; mental processes act on that information and represent the second part; and behavior of various sorts makes up the output of the system, the third part.

Social cognition refers to children's knowledge about people and social processes. Cognitive researchers have increasingly come to believe that understanding the social world differs in important ways from understanding the physical world. For example, people—unlike inanimate objects—have feelings and motives and interact with each other. Psychologists favoring a sociocultural approach contend that social processes are crucial in the development of children's cognitive abilities. Vygotsky's theory stresses the child's gradual internalization of culturally provided forms of knowledge and tools of adaptation, primarily through interchanges with parents.

ENVIRONMENTAL/LEARNING APPROACHES

Just as Rousseau was the ancestor of the cognitive-developmental approach, so John Locke was the great-grandfather of the learning tradition. Locke's belief that environment and experiences are the keys to understanding human behavior—a view that John B. Watson translated into behaviorism early in this century—continues to be the guiding principle for many child psychologists today.

The essence of the environmental/learning view is that a great deal of human behavior, especially social behavior, is acquired rather than inborn. Of course, modern behavioral psychologists, like cognitive-developmental psychologists, are interactionists. They accept as obvious the fact that biological and cognitive factors make important contributions to human development. But they do not share the belief that our biology and evolutionary history largely dictate our development (a view discussed in the next part of this chapter). Nor do they accept the idea that cognition is the fundamental process in psychological development and that changes in behavior always reflect advances in cognitive abilities. Children's behavior, they feel, can be independent of their cognitions.

Consider the earlier example concerning the relation between children's understanding of gender and their gender-role behavior. Cognitive-developmentalists contend that children first develop an understanding that they are male or female and then attempt to behave consistently with their gender, as when a girl comes to prefer playing with dolls to playing with trucks. Environmental/learning theorists, in contrast, hold that children's toy preferences (as well as other gender-related behaviors) do not necessarily grow out of what they know about their gender but often result from what happened when they played with certain toys. A girl, for example, may have received approval from people in her social environment (e.g., her parents or friends) for playing with dolls and disapproval for playing with trucks. These responses, not her understanding of her gender, may be primarily responsible for her later choices and may also contribute to her understanding of the gender concept.

Defining Learning

Learning
A relatively permanent change in behavior that results from practice or experience.

A greater emphasis on environmental factors has led behavioral researchers to focus on the processes by which the environment exerts its influence—namely, the principles of conditioning and learning. When psychologists use the term **learning,** they are not referring simply to what goes on in a classroom (although, hopefully, a good deal of it takes place there, too). Instead, psychologists view learning in a much more general sense, defining it as *a relatively permanent change in behavior that results from practice or experience.* This definition has three important elements.

The first part of the definition ("relatively permanent") distinguishes learned changes in behavior from changes that are only temporary and that often reflect physiological processes—such as when behavior changes as a result of sleep, illness, or fatigue. The second part ("change in behavior") means that, even though learning may ultimately result from chemical and neurological changes in the brain, psychologists are interested in how learning affects observable behavior. If a psychologist were interested in determining whether a child had learned a list of words, for example, the psychologist would need to demonstrate that learning had occurred by examining some aspect of the child's behavior—for example, whether the child can write, recite, or recognize the words after looking at them. The final part of the definition ("results from practice or experience") is meant to separate learned changes in behavior from changes caused by more general biological processes, such as growth, pregnancy, or even death.

• B. F. Skinner's revision of Watson's early behavioristic views down-played the role of Pavlovian processes in human development and introduced principles of operant conditioning.

Reflex
A biological relation in which a specific stimulus reliably elicits a specific response.

Respondent behavior
Responses based on reflexes, which are controlled by specific eliciting stimuli. The smaller category of human behaviors.

B. F. Skinner and Behavior Analysis

In Chapter 1 we saw that John B. Watson's attempt to build a comprehensive theory of child development based on learning principles failed, in part, because Pavlovian conditioning could not explain the bulk of human behavior. Watson's model was based on the conditioning of reflexes. But except in very young infants, reflexes comprise only a small part of human behavior. How, then, can a learning theory attempt to account for the whole range of typical child behaviors? One answer emerged in the work of another pioneer of behaviorism, B. F. Skinner (Gewirtz & Pelaez-Nogueras, 1992).

Skinner accepted the role of Pavlovian conditioning of reflexes, but he added to learning theory a second type of behavior and, correspondingly, a second type of learning. According to his model, all behavior falls into one of two categories. The first involves reflexes. As we have seen, a **reflex** is composed of a stimulus that reliably elicits a response. This relation is biological and inborn. The responses involved in the simple reflexes that all organisms display Skinner called **respondent behaviors.** The salivation response that meat powder elicited in Pavlov's dogs is an example. The most important characteristic of a respondent behavior is that it is completely controlled by the stimulus that elicits it—quite simply, the response occurs when the stimulus is present and does not occur when the stimulus is absent. In humans, respondent behaviors are particularly obvious during infancy and include such reflexive behaviors as sucking in response to a nipple placed in the mouth and grasping in response to an object touching the palm of the hand.

Children and adults also display a few respondent behaviors, usually in the form of simple physiological responses (blinking and sneezing) and emotional responses (some aspects of fear, anger, and sexual arousal).

Operant behaviors are very different. We can think of them, roughly, as voluntary responses, and they comprise the vast majority of all human behaviors. Operant behaviors are controlled by their effects—that is, by the consequences they produce. In general, pleasant consequences make the behaviors more likely to occur again, whereas unpleasant consequences have the opposite result (Skinner, 1953).

Skinner's model of learning has been applied to children's development by Sidney Bijou and Donald Baer (Bijou, 1989; Bijou & Baer, 1961, 1965, 1978), who pioneered the environmental/learning approach to developmental psychology known as **behavior analysis.** The goal of behavior analytic theory is to explain how children's innate capabilities interact with their experiences and environment to produce changes in their behavior and development—which is, of course, remarkably similar to the goal of cognitive-developmental theory and most other interactional theories of child development. What distinguishes behavior analysis is that (1) it relies heavily on learning processes as explanations for developmental change and (2) it avoids explanations based on unobservable cognitive processes, such as Piaget's mental operations and the computer-like mental mechanisms of the information-processing approach.

Behavior analysis also views human development as passing through three stages, termed the *foundational stage* (infancy), the *basic stage* (childhood and adolescence), and the *societal stage* (adulthood and old age). These stages, however, mainly describe observable changes in the way the individual interacts with the environment rather than underlying cognitive abilities (Bijou, 1989).

Types of Learning

To understand environmental/learning accounts of child development, we must consider the various types of conditioning and learning that operate on the child. In this section, we examine four forms of learning; habituation, respondent conditioning, operant conditioning, and discrimination learning.

Habituation

The simplest form of learning involves respondent behaviors and is called **habituation.** Habituation occurs when a reflex response temporarily disappears as a result of being elicited repeatedly by the same stimulus. For example, if we clap our hands loudly near an infant, the infant will display a full-body startle reflex. If we continue to clap our hands at frequent intervals (say, every 15 seconds), the size of the startle response will decrease steadily until it may be difficult to detect at all. This simple change in behavior illustrates learning through the habituation process.

How do we know, though, that habituation really represents some form of learning? Maybe the infant's muscles have simply become too fatigued to produce the response any longer—a change in behavior that, according to our earlier definition, we could not consider to be learned. To demonstrate that fatigue is not the reason for the decreased response, we need only change the stimulus. Assume, for instance, that the repeated hand clapping has reduced the startle to a very low level. Now, after waiting 15 seconds, we sound a loud buzzer instead of clapping our hands. With great reliability, the startle response will reappear at the same high level it showed when we first clapped our hands. The recovery of a habitu-

Operant behavior
Voluntary behavior controlled by its consequences. The larger category of human behaviors.

Behavior analysis
B. F. Skinner's environmental/learning theory, which emphasizes the role of operant learning in changing observable behaviors.

Habituation
The decline or disappearance of a reflex response as a result of repeated elicitation. The simplest type of learning.

• Habituation is a simple learning process that explains why babies can sleep in noisy surroundings.

Dishabituation
The recovery of a habituated response that results from a change in the eliciting stimulus.

Respondent (classical) conditioning
A form of learning, involving reflexes, in which a neutral stimulus acquires the power to elicit a reflexive response (UCR) as a result of being associated (paired) with the naturally eliciting stimulus (UCS). The neutral stimulus then becomes a conditioned stimulus (CS).

Unconditioned stimulus (UCS)
The stimulus portion of a reflex, which reliably elicits a respondent behavior (UCR).

Unconditioned response (UCR)
The response portion of a reflex, which is reliably elicited by a stimulus (UCS).

Conditioned stimulus (CS)
A neutral stimulus that comes to elicit a response (UCR) through a conditioning process in which it is consistently paired with another stimulus (UCS) that naturally evokes the response.

ated response that occurs as a result of a change in the eliciting stimulus is known as **dishabituation.**

Habituation plays only a small role in children's development. One relatively common example is the way infants learn to sleep through routine household noises. If given enough exposure, babies habituate very quickly to slamming doors, ringing telephones, and other such sounds that might otherwise continually wake them. Unfortunately, many parents are unaware of the habituation process and so try to keep everyone very quiet during nap times. The absence of typical household stimuli, however, may prevent the habituation process from occurring and, ironically, make the infant more likely to awaken at the first bark of the family dog. Just as anyone who lives next to railroad tracks learns to sleep through the midnight trains, babies learn to sleep through household noises if given the opportunity.

Although habituation does not account for a great deal of children's development, psychologists have discovered that it can be a very useful technique for studying infants' sensory and memory abilities. We examine how this works in later chapters.

Respondent Conditioning

The basic elements of Pavlov's **classical conditioning**—now called **respondent conditioning**—were introduced in the Chapter 1. This form of learning begins with any reflex, which is described as an **unconditioned stimulus (UCS)** that reliably elicits an **unconditioned response (UCR).** Learning occurs when a neutral stimulus is paired with the UCS and, as a result, acquires the ability to elicit the UCR. (Technically, the response it produces may not always be precisely identical to the UCR, but it is very close.) Because the neutral stimulus acquires its effectiveness through this conditioning process, it is now called a **conditioned stimulus (CS).**

We can illustrate this process with an example involving children's emotional responses, the aspect of human development where respondent conditioning plays its largest role. Fear responses, for instance, can be naturally elicited by a number of stimuli, a very common one being pain. Suppose a child visits the dentist for the first time. The stimuli in that environment—the dentist, the office, the instruments, and so forth—are neutral to the child and so have no particular emotional effect on his behavior. During the visit, however, suppose that the child experiences pain (UCS) that elicits fear (UCR). The various neutral stimuli become associated with the UCS (because they are paired with it) and thus become conditioned stimuli (CS) for the fear response. The child has now acquired a fear of the dentist. In the same way, many common fears of childhood can be learned responses to places or objects that previously were not frightening. (See Box 2-1 for a classic demonstration of the conditioning of fear.)

Note that in habituation, learning results in a change in the response, which gradually gets weaker. By contrast, in respondent conditioning the response remains the same and learning involves a change in the stimulus, which begins as neutral but becomes effective in producing the response.

A related process in respondent conditioning is **stimulus generalization.** Here, not only a neutral stimulus but other stimuli that are similar become conditioned. In our example, the child may come to fear not only his own dentist but all dentists, or perhaps even anyone wearing a white medical coat. When this sort of generalized fear becomes a serious problem, it is termed a **phobia.** A common example is a child who is bitten by a dog and becomes frightened of all dogs. Similarly, therapists frequently encounter children who have had a bad emotional experience at school (e.g., being injured or embarrassed) and then display a generalized fear of going to school called *school phobia.*

This brings us to one final aspect of respondent conditioning. The relation between a CS and a UCR is a conditioned, or learned, relation that also can be unlearned. A CS acquires its power to elicit the response by being paired with a UCS, and to maintain this power, such pairing must continue to take place, at least occasionally. If a CS is repeatedly presented alone, it will gradually lose its effectiveness in eliciting the response and return to being a neutral stimulus. This process is called **respondent extinction.** Suppose the child in our example returns to the dentist often without experiencing pain. The dentist and other conditioned stimuli in the situation will gradually cease to elicit fear. Likewise, if phobic children have repeated encounters with friendly dogs, or many days at school without distress, these fears, too, will gradually undergo extinction. Of course, not all fears result from respondent conditioning, and other factors can contribute to this aspect of children's emotional development as well.

Operant Conditioning

A third type of learning is called **operant conditioning.** Unlike habituation and respondent conditioning, operant conditioning is assumed by learning theorists to be very important for understanding the typical behavior of children.

Operant behaviors, we have seen, are influenced by their effects, and many of the everyday behaviors of children occur simply because they resulted in desirable consequences in the past. Any consequence that makes a response more likely to occur again is called a **reinforcer.** Consider the following examples. The same child may (1) share her toys with a friend because doing so often produces similar sharing by the other child, (2) throw a temper tantrum in the supermarket because this usually results in her mother buying her candy, (3) twist and shake the knob of the playroom door because this behavior is effective in getting it open, (4) work hard at her skating lessons because her coach praises her when she performs well, and

Stimulus generalization
A process related to respondent conditioning in which stimuli that are similar to the conditioned stimulus (CS) also acquire the power to elicit the response.

Phobia
A fear that has become serious and may have been generalized to an entire class of objects or situations.

Respondent extinction
A process related to respondent conditioning in which the conditioned stimulus (CS) gradually loses its power to elicit the response as a result of no longer being paired with the unconditioned stimulus (UCS).

Operant conditioning
A form of learning in which the probability of occurrence of an operant behavior changes as a result of its reinforcing or punishing consequences.

Reinforcer
A consequence that increases the likelihood of a behavior that it follows.

• Some activities, like putting together a puzzle, are reinforced simply by the consequence of achieving the solution.

LITTLE ALBERT AND LITTLE PETER: CONDITIONING AND COUNTERCONDITIONING FEAR

Perhaps the most famous research conducted by John B. Watson involved the conditioning of a fear response in an 11-month-old child named Albert B. (Watson & Rayner, 1920). The study was designed to show that fear is an unconditioned response that can be easily conditioned to a variety of common stimuli.

Watson believed that children fear dogs, dentists, and the like because they associate these objects or persons with an unconditioned stimulus for fear, such as pain or a sudden loud noise. To illustrate this process, Watson first exposed Albert to a tame white laboratory rat, which produced only mild interest. On several later occasions, Watson presented the rat to Albert and then made a loud noise (UCS) behind Albert. The noise elicited a pronounced fear response (UCR) in the form of crying and trembling. Very soon, the sight of the rat alone was enough to make Albert cry in fear—it had become a conditioned stimulus (CS) for that response. Watson went on to show that objects similar to the rat, such as cotton or a white fur coat, now also elicited the fear response.

A few years later, Watson and an associate named Mary Cover Jones applied the fear-conditioning process in reverse (Jones, 1924). A 3-year-old named Peter was brought to them with an intense fear of rabbits and other furry creatures. The researchers rea-soned that if this fear had been learned (conditioned), it could be unlearned. Their method for eliminating the fear response to the rabbit they called *countercondi-tioning*. This involved presenting the conditioned stim-ulus in such a way that it would not elicit the fear re-sponse but would instead elicit a competing emotional response—in this case, the pleasure derived from eat-ing. On the first day of treatment, Peter was placed in a high chair and fed his lunch. At the same time, a caged rabbit was displayed on the other side of the room, far enough away so that the fear response did not occur. Each day, while Peter ate, the rabbit was moved slightly closer. In the end, Peter was not at all disturbed at having the rabbit sit next to him while he ate his lunch. The rabbit was no longer a conditioned stimulus for fear and had instead become associated with pleasure.

An experiment of the sort conducted with Little Albert would not be permitted today, because psychol-ogists now have strict ethical guidelines for research that would prohibit a child from being exposed to this type of fear experience (see Chapter 3). The experi-ment with Little Peter, however, is very similar to the type of fear-reduction therapy used today by clinical psychologists and would be considered a form of be-havior modification.

Positive reinforcer
A reinforcing consequence that involves the presenta-tion of something pleasant following a behavior.

Negative reinforcer
A reinforcing consequence that involves the removal of something unpleasant fol-lowing a behavior.

Punisher
A consequence that de-creases the likelihood of a behavior that it follows.

(5) put her pillow over her head when her baby brother is crying because this be-havior helps reduce the unpleasant sound.

It should be obvious from this list that reinforcers can take many forms. Nevertheless, all of them fall into one of two categories. Those that involve getting something good are called **positive reinforcers,** and those that involve getting rid of something bad are called **negative reinforcers.** Some common classes of rein-forcement are presented in Table 2-1.

It should also be apparent from our list of examples that the reinforcement process does not work only on desirable or beneficial responses. Reinforcement in-creases the likelihood of any behavior that leads to a pleasant consequence, whether we would typically view that behavior as appropriate (sharing toys), inap-propriate (throwing a tantrum in a supermarket), or just neutral (opening a door).

Not all consequences are reinforcing, however. Behavior sometimes produces effects that are unpleasant, and these *reduce* the likelihood that the behavior will occur again. Such consequences are called **punishers.** We usually think of punish-ment as something that is delivered by parents or teachers for misbehavior. But the

TABLE 2-1 ● Common Classes of Reinforcers

Type	Description
Consumable reinforcers	Candy, ice cream, soda pop, and other edibles (especially when the child is hungry) reliably reinforce behaviors in almost all children.
Social approval and attention	Praise and attention are extremely powerful reinforcers for many youngsters. Unfortunately, some children are given attention only for undesirable behaviors and, as a result, these are the behaviors that are reinforced.
Stimulation and activity reinforcers	Reinforcers can take the form of many simple activities. Listening to music, playing sports, solving puzzles, and (for an infant) watching a mobile turn above the crib all provide stimulation that is reinforcing to most children.
Negative reinforcement	The removal or avoidance of an unpleasant situation can be very reinforcing. In the classroom, children often display appropriate behaviors to avoid discipline from the teacher.
Acquired (conditioned) reinforcers	Consequences that are not inherently reinforcing can acquire this capacity by being associated with effective reinforcers. Money and academic grades, for example, are of little interest to infants, but they can acquire strong reinforcement value for older children as they become associated with other desirable consequences.

principle of punishment, like its reinforcement counterpart, is simply part of nature's learning process that "teaches" organisms which responses are wise to repeat and which are better to avoid. Punishment, too, can involve **positive punishers** (i.e., getting something bad, like a spanking, a failing grade, or a scraped knee) or **negative punishers** (i.e., losing something good, like a new baseball, a chance to sit by a friend at lunch, or television privileges for a week). Either way, behaviors that lead to these consequences become less likely to occur again.

What constitutes a punishing consequence can vary from child to child. This point is important, because it is common for adults to assume they are administering punishment to a child when, in fact, the consequence can be having the opposite result. In the classroom, for example, the teacher may view scolding a child who is clowning around as punishment. But because "attention" can be such a powerful reinforcer for many children, this response from the teacher (and perhaps the reactions of the rest of the class) may actually make the clowning behavior more, rather than less, likely to recur. As a disciplinary technique, punishment can also have other important drawbacks, as described in Box 2-2.

Discrimination Learning

A fourth type of learning, called **discrimination learning,** is very closely related to operant conditioning. Sometimes the same behavior by the same child produces different consequences, depending on the circumstances. For example, being aggressive may lead to praise on the football field but punishment in the classroom.

Positive punisher
A punishing consequence that involves the presentation of something unpleasant following a behavior.

Negative punisher
A punishing consequence that involves the removal of something pleasant following a behavior.

Discrimination learning
A type of learning in which children come to adjust their behavior according to stimuli that signal the opportunity for reinforcement or the possibility of punishment.

EFFECTS AND SIDE EFFECTS OF PUNISHMENT BY PARENTS OR TEACHERS

Punishment is a consequence that decreases the likelihood of the behavior that it follows. We typically think of punishment as the discipline dispensed by parents, such as spanking, taking away television or other privileges, or confining the child to his or her room. Most parents use these techniques in the hope that the punished behavior will not occur again. Indeed, moderate to strong punishment, if delivered clearly and consistently, is effective in reducing undesirable behaviors. (Mild punishment, in contrast, can actually increase the behavior, if the attention that comes with it is the only attention the child normally receives.)

At the same time, punishment can produce a number of side effects that parents may not anticipate. First of all, strong punishers can elicit aggression and other emotional behaviors in children, including crying, tantrums, and head banging. Second, the individual who delivers the punishment sometimes becomes so closely associated with punishment in general that the child may begin to avoid interaction with that person. Third, punishment can reduce an entire class of responses—sometimes including behaviors that are not a problem. For example, the child who is punished by the teacher for speaking out of turn may react by decreasing the rate of all verbal participation in class. Fourth, parents who use punishment may be serving as models for behavior that they do not want to see their children imitate. The fact that many delinquent children were exposed to physical punishment in childhood (Bandura & Walters, 1959) and that abused children frequently grow up to be abusing parents (Parke & Collmer, 1975) may reflect, in part, the children's imitation of aggression by the parents. Fifth, punishment is not a good teaching device because it only tells children what they did wrong, not what they should be doing instead. Finally, punishment has an addictive quality. Because it often is successful in temporarily

• Punishment should be used sparingly as a disciplinary tool because it can produce side effects.

ending the child's aversive behavior, it negatively reinforces parents who use it and makes them more likely to use it again in similar situations.

Punishment should always be used in combination with reinforcement for the appropriate behaviors we wish the child to display. Even then, it should be used sparingly, and preferably as a negative consequence, such as removing something desirable, rather than as a positive consequence, such as slapping or spanking.

Discriminative stimuli
Stimuli that provide information as to the possibility for reinforcement or punishment.

Or acting cute may be effective in getting favors from Grandma but have no effect at all on Mommy. In both cases, the potential consequence of the behavior is signaled to the child by certain stimuli in the environment. In the first case, the stimulus is the physical setting—the football field versus the classroom—and in the second, it is the person with whom the child is interacting. Stimuli that provide information regarding the potential consequences of behavior are called **discriminative stimuli.**

Discrimination learning is the process by which children learn to "read" such stimuli so they can adjust their behavior accordingly. The precise details of this process are fairly complex. In general, children learn to discriminate whether their behavior will produce reinforcement or punishment in two ways: (1) through some sort of trial-and-error process, in which they have repeated experiences with the stimuli, the behaviors, and the consequences or (2) through observing someone else's behavior produce the consequences in a particular situation—a process we consider shortly.

Social-Learning Theory

Over the years, the environmental/learning tradition has grown more like the other two major traditions (in fact, all three approaches continue to move closer together) (Miller, 1993). In this section, we consider a second approach within the behavioral tradition, **social-learning theory,** that has become increasingly concerned with how cognitive factors influence development (Grusec, 1992; Zimmerman, 1983).

Social-learning theory
A form of environmental/ learning theory that adds observational learning to respondent and operant learning as a process through which children's behavior changes.

The leading spokesperson for the social-learning viewpoint, which he refers to as *social cognitive theory,* has been Albert Bandura (1986, 1989). Like other behavioral psychologists, Bandura believes that cognitive development alone does not explain childhood changes in behavior and that learning processes are responsible for much of children's development. But some learning processes, he feels, are affected by the child's cognitive abilities. This is especially true for the more complex types of learning that Bandura believes are involved in children's development beyond the infant years. We turn to one of these types next.

Observational Learning

Skinner's addition of operant conditioning to Watson's Pavlovian conditioning greatly expanded learning theory's ability to explain children's behavior. Nevertheless, some problems remained. One was that children sometimes acquire new behaviors simply by seeing someone else perform them. A second was that children sometimes become more or less likely to perform a behavior after seeing another person experience reinforcing or punishing consequences for that behavior. Neither of these facts is easily explained by a type of learning in which changes in behavior occur only when children experience direct consequences for their actions.

Bandura solved this problem by proposing that as children grow their development is increasingly based on a fifth type of learning—**observational learning.** Learning by observation occurs when the behavior of an *observer* is affected by witnessing the behavior (and often its consequences) of a *model.* In developmental psychology, the observers are children, and the models include parents, teachers, siblings, classmates, storybook heroes, sports celebrities, television personalities, and even cartoon characters—in short, just about anyone.

Observational learning
A form of learning in which an observer's behavior changes as a result of observing a model.

Bandura and other researchers have pursued three important issues regarding the modeling process: (1) Which models are most likely to influence a child's behavior? (2) Under what circumstances is this influence most likely to occur? (3) How does the child's behavior change as a result of observational learning? All of these issues have been studied extensively in recent years (Bandura, 1989).

Our answer to the first question, for the moment, must be simply that a model who possesses a characteristic that children find attractive or desirable—such as talent, intelligence, power, good looks, or popularity—is most likely to be imitated.

More detailed discussion of this issue is postponed until later chapters, because a number of other factors, such as the child's level of development and the types of behaviors being modeled, must also be considered.

Identifying the circumstances under which modeling is most effective also can be complex. But one of the most important factors is whether the model receives reinforcing or punishing consequences for the behavior. One of Bandura's most important contributions to social-learning theory was his demonstration that consequences of a model's behavior can affect the behavior of an observer. When a child sees a model receive reinforcement for a response, the child receives **vicarious reinforcement** and, like the model, becomes more likely to produce that same response. The opposite is true when the child receives **vicarious punishment** as a result of witnessing a model being punished. In some sense, then, observational learning is the same as operant learning, except that the child experiences the consequences vicariously rather than directly.

The most obvious and perhaps the most important result of modeling is **imitation,** which occurs when children copy what they have seen. Imitation can take such varied forms as eating the breakfast cereal a professional athlete claims to eat, climbing on a chair to steal a cookie from the shelf after seeing an older brother do it, or copying the problems a teacher is writing on the blackboard. Imitations need not always be precise replications of what was observed. **Selective imitation** occurs when children, as a result of observing a model, acquire general skills or behaviors that follow some "rule." For example, some psychologists believe that young children learn to imitate the structure of adults' speech (prepositional phrases, interrogatives, and so on) even though they may not imitate its exact content (Snow, 1983; Whitehurst & deBaryshe, 1989). As we have seen, imitation is especially likely to occur when the model has received reinforcement for the behavior.

A second result of modeling occurs when the observer becomes less likely to perform a behavior that has just been modeled. This effect, known as **response in-**

Vicarious reinforcement
Reinforcing consequences experienced when viewing a model that affect an observer similarly.

Vicarious punishment
Punishing consequences experienced when viewing a model that affect an observer similarly.

Imitation
Behavior of an observer that results from and is similar to the behavior of a model.

Selective imitation
Behavior of an observer that follows the general form or style of the behavior of a model but is not a precise copy.

Response inhibition (counterimitation)
Behavior of an observer that is directly opposite that of a model; often the result of vicarious punishment.

• Imitation is an important process by which children acquire new skills and behaviors.

hibition (or sometimes **counterimitation**), is a frequent result of vicarious punishment. The teacher who publicly disciplines an unruly child in order to "set an example" for the rest of the class is counting on observational learning to inhibit similar behaviors in the other children (a strategy that, of course, may backfire if the attention to the misbehaver proves to be reinforcing).

Children do not always immediately display behavior learned from models. A striking illustration of this point occurred in one of Bandura's early studies, in which one group of youngsters observed a model rewarded for displaying new aggressive behaviors toward an inflated toy clown, while a second group saw those same behaviors punished. When given an opportunity to play with the doll themselves, the children who witnessed the reinforcement imitated many of the model's aggressive acts toward the doll, whereas the group who observed punishment did not. But when later offered rewards for reproducing the aggressive behaviors, both groups were able to perform them quite accurately (Bandura, 1965). Obviously, all of the children had acquired (learned) the new behaviors, even though the vicariously experienced punishment had inhibited some children from performing them. This distinction between acquisition and performance has been of particular interest to researchers studying the potential effects of viewing violence on television. Defenders of this form of programming point out that children usually do not appear to display the violence themselves after watching such programs. But critics suggest that the children may nevertheless be learning violent or aggressive behaviors, which they may later display in situations where there is an incentive to do so—such as when interacting with peers who encourage aggressive or delinquent behaviors. These critics further charge that because such acts of aggression typically occur later on and in unrelated situations, we often do not realize that they were inspired by the television programs the children watched (Liebert & Sprafkin, 1988).

The acquisition-performance distinction is very evident in Bandura's theoretical formulation of observational learning, depicted in Figure 2-1. Bandura believes that learning by observation involves four separate processes. The first two account

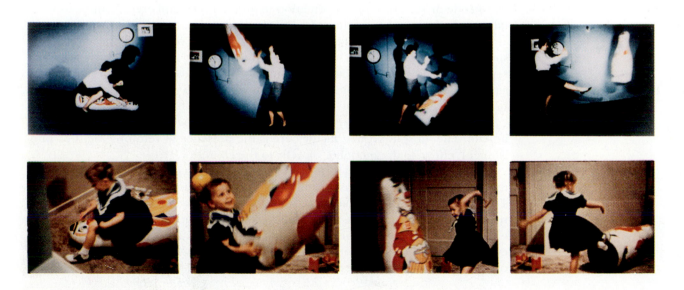

• Albert Bandura's early research showed that children exposed to filmed violence were capable of very accurately imitating of the model's aggressive acts when given the opportunity to reproduce them.

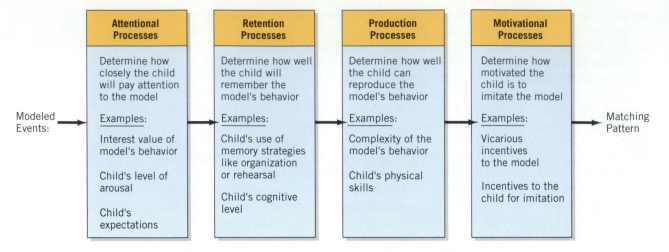

Modeled Events: →

Attentional Processes	Retention Processes	Production Processes	Motivational Processes
Determine how closely the child will pay attention to the model	Determine how well the child will remember the model's behavior	Determine how well the child can reproduce the model's behavior	Determine how motivated the child is to imitate the model
Examples:	Examples:	Examples:	Examples:
Interest value of model's behavior	Child's use of memory strategies like organization or rehearsal	Complexity of the model's behavior	Vicarious incentives to the model
Child's level of arousal	Child's cognitive level	Child's physical skills	Incentives to the child for imitation
Child's expectations			

→ Matching Pattern

Figure 2-1   Bandura's model of observational learning. Adapted from Albert Bandura, *Social Learning Theory,* © 1977, p. 23. Reprinted by permission of Prentice-Hall, Inc., Englewood Cliffs, New Jersey.

for the acquisition, or learning, of a model's behavior, and the other two control the performance, or production, of these behaviors (Bandura, 1977b).

Attentional processes determine how closely the child pays attention to what the model is doing. This component is influenced, in part, by characteristics of the model, such as how much the child likes or identifies with the model, as well as by characteristics of the child observer, such as the child's expectations or level of emotional arousal.

Retention processes refer to how well the child can store the modeled information in memory for later use. These processes depend, for example, on the child's ability to code or structure the information in an easily remembered form or to mentally or physically rehearse the model's actions.

Production processes control how well the child can reproduce the model's responses. In many cases, the child possesses the necessary responses. But sometimes, reproducing the model's actions may involve brand-new skills. It is one thing to carefully watch a circus juggler, but it is quite another to go home and repeat those behaviors accurately.

Motivational processes determine which models and behaviors a child chooses to imitate. The most important factor here is the presence of reinforcement or punishment, either to the model or directly to the child.

One way to think of this formulation is to imagine a child viewing a model and then to consider the reasons why the child might *not* imitate the model's actions. The child might not have paid attention to what the model was doing, might not recall the model's responses, might not possess the physical skills to repeat the model's behaviors, or might feel little motivation to do what the model has done. In everyday life, children do not, of course, imitate everything they see. Bandura's theory suggests four important reasons why this is the case.

Reciprocal Determinism

Bandura's social-cognitive analysis is truly interactional in nature. It is based on his view that human development reflects the interaction of the person (P), the per-

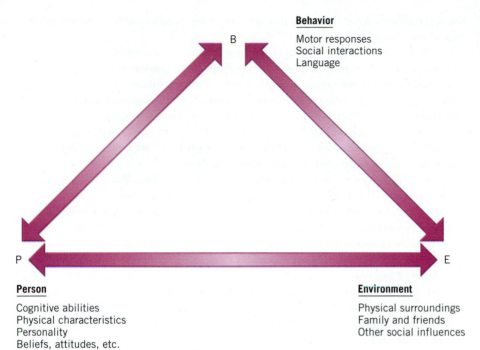

Behavior
Motor responses
Social interactions
Language

B

P

E

Person
Cognitive abilities
Physical characteristics
Personality
Beliefs, attitudes, etc.

Environment
Physical surroundings
Family and friends
Other social influences

Figure 2-2 Bandura's model of reciprocal determinism. Adapted from "The Self System in Reciprocal Determinism" by Albert Bandura, 1978, *American Psychologist, 33,* p. 335. Copyright 1978 by the American Psychological Association. Adapted by permission.

son's behavior (B), and the environment (E). Bandura describes this process of interaction as **reciprocal determinism** (Bandura, 1978).

As illustrated in Figure 2-2, the reciprocal determinism model forms a triangle of interactions. The person includes the child's cognitive abilities, physical characteristics, personality, beliefs, attitudes, and so on. These, of course, influence both the child's behavior and the child's environment—children choose not only what they want to do (P → B) but also where and with whom to do it (P → E). These influences are reciprocal, however. Children's behavior (and the reactions it engenders) can affect their feelings about themselves and their attitudes and beliefs about other things (B → P). Likewise, much of children's knowledge about the world and other people results from information they receive from television, parents, textbooks, and other environmental sources (E → P). Environment, of course, also affects behavior. As learning theorists contend, the consequences of children's behavior and the models they observe can powerfully influence what they do (E → B). But children's behavior also contributes to creating their environment. A child who shares and cooperates with his classmates is likely to attract many friends, whereas the opposite may be the case for a child who behaves selfishly or aggressively (B → E).

Bandura's addition of observational learning to the environmental/learning tradition, along with his willingness to incorporate cognitive aspects of development, has greatly increased the explanatory power of social-learning theory and has made it the most important learning-based approach. We consider the role of this model in many aspects of children's development throughout the text.

Reciprocal determinism
Albert Bandura's proposed process describing the interaction of a person's characteristics and abilities (P), behavior (B), and environment (E).

✔ *To Recap...*

Environmental/learning theories begin with the assumption that much of children's typical behavior is acquired through conditioning and learning principles. Here, learned behaviors are distinguished from behaviors that are temporary, unobservable, or based solely on biological processes.

Behavior analysis is one form of learning theory. It is based on B. F. Skinner's distinction between respondent behaviors and operant behaviors. In this view, four types of conditioning and learning are assumed to operate on children: habituation (and dishabituation), respondent conditioning, operant conditioning, and discrimination learning. Habituation and respondent conditioning are controlled by eliciting stimuli. In contrast, operant conditioning and discrimination learning are controlled by their consequences. Consequences that make behavior more probable are called reinforcers; those that make behavior less probable are called punishers.

Social-learning theory, based largely on the ideas of Albert Bandura, proposes a greater role for cognitive factors than does behavior analysis. An important assumption of this theory is that observational learning occurs when an observer's behavior changes as a result of viewing the behavior of a model. Consequences experienced when viewing a model, called vicarious reinforcement and vicarious punishment, can affect the behavior of an observer. The most important result of modeling is imitation, which may exactly copy the observed behavior or may abstract it to a general form. Response inhibition, a second possible result of modeling, occurs when imitation of an observed behavior becomes less likely—usually because the model has received punishment for it. Bandura distinguishes between the acquisition of a modeled response and its performance. Acquisition is determined by the observer's attentional and retentional processes, whereas performance is controlled by the observer's production and motivational processes.

Bandura refers to his theoretical model of human development as reciprocal determinism. It holds that human development results from the complex interaction of characteristics of the person, the person's behavior, and the environment.

ETHOLOGY

Ethology
The study of development from an evolutionary perspective.

Sociobiology
A branch of biology that attempts to discover the evolutionary origins of social behavior.

The third major theoretical approach in modern child psychology is **ethology,** the study of development from an evolutionary perspective. The historical roots of this tradition can be traced to the work of Charles Darwin (1809–1882). More recently, a similar approach has sprung up in the field of biology and is called **sociobiology** (Wilson, E. O., 1975), a term referring to the biological or evolutionary origins of social behavior. Although among the three theoretical models we are discussing the ethological tradition has the fewest followers, it is growing rapidly, and its ideas and findings are being applied to more and more areas of child development (Hinde, 1983, 1989; MacDonald, 1988a; Schleidt, 1991).

Behavior and Evolution

According to ethologists, behavior has two kinds of determinants, or causes—immediate and evolutionary. The immediate determinants are the more obvious. They include the environment in which the behavior occurs, the animal's recent experiences, and the state or condition of the animal—whether it is hungry, tired, or angry, for example. These determinants relate to how the behavior is useful to the individual. A behavior's evolutionary determinants are less clear. Presumably they were important in the natural selection process and contributed to the species' survival and reproduction. Evolutionary determinants help explain how a behavior may be valuable, not just to the individual, but to the entire species. To explain behaviors like hunting for prey or constructing a dam, we must consider both the immediate circumstances, like the availability of prey or of appropriate building materials, and factors in the animal's evolutionary past, like the climate and terrain in which the behaviors evolved.

Ethologists are, of course, most interested in studying the evolutionary causes of behavior. Although they have some interest in the role of conditioning and learning principles in behavior (Chiszar, 1981), most of their efforts are concentrated on understanding how inborn processes affect development. These processes might include the genetic mechanisms that transmit physical and behavioral characteristics from one generation to the next and the biological mechanisms that control the occurrence of instinctual patterns of behavior.

In trying to understand the ethological approach, it is important to keep in mind that, from an evolutionary perspective, our species is the product of millions of years of change. What we are today represents only a small part of an enormous process. For this reason, ethology views human beings as only one of the 5 million or so species that presently inhabit the earth, and it considers human development within the context of the entire animal kingdom. It should not be surprising, then, that much of the research conducted within this tradition involves nonhuman species.

Classical Ethology

Ethology first gained scientific recognition in the 1930s with the work of two pioneers in animal study, Konrad Lorenz and Niko Tinbergen. Lorenz was born in Austria in 1903 and died in 1989. He is famous for his naturalistic studies of the imprinting process, discussed shortly. Tinbergen was born in the Netherlands in 1907 and also died in 1989. His approach to research was more experimental than Lorenz's, but he too conducted many detailed studies of animal behavior (Tinbergen, 1951, 1973). Both of these men were zoologists by training, and their early investigations focused exclusively on nonhuman animals. Nevertheless, their research laid the groundwork for the growing trend toward the application of ethological principles to child development, and in 1973 they were jointly awarded a Nobel Prize for their pioneering research.

Innate Mechanisms

During the past 50 years or so, ethologists have discovered a number of important links between evolutionary processes and behavior—most of these links based on work with other species. In this section we consider some of these findings.

Ethologists have identified four qualities that characterize virtually all innate, or inborn, behaviors. First, they are *universal* to all members of the species. Second, since they are usually biologically programmed responses to very specific stimuli, they *require no learning or experience.* Third, they are normally *stereotyped,* meaning that they occur in precisely the same way every time they are displayed. Finally, they are only *minimally affected by environmental influences* (in the short run, that is; natural selection pressures affect them across generations) (Eibl-Eibesfeldt, 1975, 1989). Countless examples of these behaviors have been identified in virtually every known species, ranging from the nest-building behaviors of ants, to the pecking responses of chickens, to the herding behaviors of antelopes.

In humans, such innate behaviors are most evident during infancy. An inborn response like sucking, for example, is found in all babies, does not need to be learned, occurs in a stereotyped pattern, and is very little influenced by the environment (at least during the first weeks of life).

The idea of a stimulus that biologically elicits a simple reflexive response, like sucking, is neither new nor of interest only to ethologists (as the work of Pavlov and Watson clearly demonstrates). But ethologists have typically been interested in more complex *sequences* of innate behaviors, which they originally termed *fixed action patterns.* These are the chains of responses that, for example, spiders produce in spinning a web, beavers in constructing a dam, or bears in caring for newborn cubs. Today, researchers realize that such sequences are not quite as rigid, or fixed, as was once thought, and so they are now referred to as **modal action patterns** (Dewsbury, 1978). A modal action pattern is triggered by a specific stimulus in the animal's environment, known as a sign stimulus, or what Lorenz called an **innate releasing mechanism** (Lorenz, 1981). A classic example of such a mechanism was demonstrated by Tinbergen (1973) in his work with the stickleback.

The stickleback is a freshwater fish with three sharp spines. In winter, the males stay in schools and are rather inactive. But as the water temperature rises in spring, it sets off a distinctive pattern of mating behaviors. First, each stickleback leaves the school and builds a tunnel-like nest in the sand, which he defends as his own territory against other males. When a female approaches the area above the nest, the male begins his courtship by stabbing her with one of his spines. He then swims down to the nest in an unusual zigzag pattern. The stabbing and swimming motion apparently excites the female, who follows him to his nest. When she enters it, the male places his face against her tail and begins to quiver. This stimulates the female to release her eggs, which the male fertilizes by releasing his sperm. He then chases her away and waits for another female to approach. This ritual continues until five or so females have released eggs in the nest. The male subsequently cares for the

Modal action pattern
A sequence of behaviors elicited by a specific stimulus.

Innate releasing mechanism
A stimulus that triggers an innate sequence or pattern of behaviors. Also called a sign stimulus.

• Konrad Lorenz found that newly hatched goslings, when permitted to follow him around for a short time, would imprint to him and thereafter treat him as their mother.

developing eggs, driving away intruders and fanning the water with his tail to provide them with sufficient oxygen.

In addition to observing this mating process in the wild, Tinbergen studied sticklebacks in the laboratory. There he exposed the fish to wooden models of other sticklebacks of various colors and shapes to determine experimentally which stimuli are necessary to trigger and maintain the chain of behaviors. The details of these experiments are not crucial for our purposes, but the work does raise several important issues.

One involves the relevance of these sorts of modal action patterns for human development. Is there any relation, for example, between the seduction ritual of male sticklebacks and the behavior of male college students? Probably not. But ethologists believe certain response patterns in humans are, in fact, triggered by very specific stimuli.

A related issue concerns the nature versus nurture question. The stickleback does not need to learn the complex courtship responses; they are elicited biologically by stimuli in the environment. This does not mean, however, that other aspects of the stickleback's behavior do not change in response to experiences or consequences. Conversely, even though some aspects of human behavior clearly result from learning processes, ethologists contend that this does not rule out the possibility that other aspects of human behavior—perhaps even complex behavior patterns—are controlled by innate evolutionary processes.

Tinbergen's research strategy also illustrates how ethologists combine naturalistic and laboratory methods. The great majority of their investigations involve the observation of behaviors in the natural settings where they evolved. In this way, the researcher can examine how an animal's responses typically occur. The behaviors are also studied in more structured settings, however, where the researcher can control the conditions under which events take place and can subject an animal's rituals and routines to various experimental tests. This approach is useful for identifying the critical variables that actually control the behavior.

Sensitive Periods

We indicated earlier that ethologists also have an interest in the effects of learning and experience. In this area, though, they are principally concerned with how an animal's genetic or biological makeup can influence the learning process (Bolles & Beecher, 1988). For example, ethologists argue that animals are biologically programmed so that they learn certain things most easily during certain periods of development. One of the most dramatic examples of this relationship is illustrated by Lorenz's research on **imprinting,** the process by which newborns of some species form an emotional bond with their mothers.

Lorenz was the first ethologist to study imprinting extensively, and from his naturalistic observations he provided a fascinating account of this early attachment process (Lorenz, 1937). In many bird species, where the young can walk almost immediately after hatching, baby birds soon begin to follow the mother as she moves about. Lorenz theorized that this simple act of following is responsible for the strong social bond that develops between the newborn and the parent. To confirm his suspicion, Lorenz removed just-hatched goslings from their mother and had them follow another animal, or various nonliving objects that he pulled along, or even himself. As he predicted, the young birds quickly imprinted to whatever they followed and thereafter treated it as their mother.

Lorenz further discovered that one of the most important influences on imprinting was the age of the chicks. If the act of following occurred during a period

Imprinting
A biological process in which the young of some species acquire an emotional attachment to the mother.

Sensitive (critical) period
A period of development during which certain behaviors are more easily learned.

• Ethologists believe that evolutionary processes play some role in the behavior of all species.

that began several hours after birth and lasted until sometime the next day, the attachment bond reliably developed. When the following occurred only before or after this period, however, little or no imprinting resulted. Lorenz assumed that the boundaries of the period were fixed absolutely, so he called it the **critical period.** A great deal of research has since been conducted on this attachment mechanism in birds and other species. We now know that imprinting can occur outside of this period, although with great difficulty (Hess, 1973; Hoffman, H.S., 1987), and so the term **sensitive period** has become generally preferred (Bateson, 1979; Immelmann & Suomi, 1981).

Sensitive periods are not restricted to imprinting or even to the area of mother–infant attachment. Researchers in a number of disciplines—including biology, psychology, and psychiatry—have applied the concept to many different aspects of development (Bornstein, 1987). In children, the idea of a sensitive period for learning has been investigated in areas as diverse as language acquisition (Newport, 1991) and gender-role development (Money & Annecillo, 1987), as we will see in subsequent chapters.

Applications to Human Development

Our main interest in ethological theory is its application to child development, and modern researchers are finding many areas of development where evolutionary determinants may be important (DeKay & Buss, 1992; Scarr, 1992). Most of these specific applications are discussed later in the text. Here we introduce several of the more general principles and themes.

Sociobiology

We said earlier that some biologists have attempted to apply evolutionary principles to human social behavior. This new area of research began rather dramatically in 1975 with the publication of a book by a Harvard biologist, E. O. Wilson, entitled *Sociobiology: The New Synthesis.* According to Wilson's radical and somewhat controversial theory, genes are very selfish structures whose only interest is to ensure their own survival from generation to generation.

We have already seen that genes are responsible for specific physical characteristics (color of fur, size of ears, and so on). When a characteristic is valuable for survival or reproduction, the genes that produced it are more likely to be passed along to the next generation. Sociobiologists believe that genes produce not only physical traits but social behaviors, although these theorists admit that the process by which a gene can produce a behavior is not yet completely understood. Social behaviors that are more adaptive for survival thus are assumed to undergo the same natural selection process as physical traits.

The sociobiological view can be illustrated by a frequently cited example. Consider a mother who risks her life to save her child from danger. According to the traditional ethological model, this response by the mother should not have an evolutionary basis, because natural selection would not favor behaviors that reduce an individual's chances of survival. Sociobiologists, however, contend that the mother's genes have in some way programmed her to do whatever she can to ensure that her genes are passed onto future generations. Because her child carries many of those same genes, and because he would have many reproductive years ahead of him, evolutionary mechanisms drive the mother to sacrifice her life to save his (Dawkins, 1976; Porter & Laney, 1980).

Wilson suggests that genetic effects on social behavior, however, are better understood at the level of the culture or society, rather than the individual. He claims, for example, that many of our cultural practices, such as taboos against incest and laws against murder or assault, reflect an evolutionary process that favors individuals whose social behaviors are in line with what is best for the survival of the species. The behaviors of these individuals are thus more likely to be passed along to future generations, whereas undesirable behaviors are not. This new theory has been both praised and criticized (Green, 1989; Lerner & von Eye, 1992). But it has sparked a great deal of debate and has drawn increasing attention to the evolutionary perspective.

Human Ethology

Ethological principles have increasingly been applied to our own species (Archer, 1992; Eibl-Eibesfeldt, 1989). Ironically, the reasoning that makes this theory so believable with respect to nonhuman species has made it difficult to apply to people. Many lower animals exhibit complex and sophisticated behaviors that appear to be well beyond the intelligence of their species. Ants and other colonizing insects, for example, have highly developed societies, efficient divisions of labor, and extremely effective techniques for survival. Yet the brains of these animals are very primitive, and their capacity for learning is correspondingly limited. The most reasonable explanation for their masterful behavior, therefore, is that it evolved over millions of years and is now simply genetically programmed to occur. We humans, on the other hand, are most obviously distinguished from other species by our advanced cognitive abilities. Most of us like to think that the intellectual abilities that characterize our species—reasoning, decision making, problem solving, and so on—are the source of our complex patterns of behavior. Attributing important aspects of human behavior to genetic programming, therefore, is often seen as unnecessary and even degrading (Gould, 1982).

The reluctance to view human behavior as anything but conscious and deliberate is one reason why psychologists did not begin to consider human ethology seriously until the 1960s. Even then, initial attempts to apply ethological principles to the humans were for the most part limited to books written for the general public, such as *The Naked Ape* by Desmond Morris (1967) and *The Territorial Imperative* by Robert Ardrey (1966). This situation has been changing rapidly, however.

Bowlby's Influence

As early as the 1940s, Lorenz suggested that physical characteristics of babies, such as the shape of their head and the sound of their cry, might serve as stimuli to trigger caregiving by mothers (Lorenz, 1950). Developmental psychologists likewise had little difficulty interpreting infants' early reflexive behaviors in terms of their evolutionary value to the species. Nevertheless, the scientific application of the ethological model to child development is usually considered to have begun in 1969, when John Bowlby published the first of his three volumes on the subject (Bowlby, 1969, 1973, 1980).

Bowlby, a British physician and psychoanalyst, was the first to attract child psychologists to an evolutionary interpretation of human development (Bretherton, 1992). As a clinician, Bowlby had witnessed the emotional problems of children who had been raised in institutions. Such children often have difficulty forming and maintaining close relationships. Bowlby attributed this problem to the children's lack of a strong attachment to their mothers during infancy. His interest in this area eventually led him to an ethological explanation of how and why the mother–infant bond is established.

Bowlby's theory is an interesting mix of ethology and Freud (Sroufe, 1986). Like Freud, Bowlby believes that the quality of early social relationships is critical to later development and that these first experiences are carried forward by processes in the unconscious. Of particular importance is the development of expectations by the infant that the mother will be available and responsive. Bowlby's theory reiterates the fundamental principle of classical ethology that a close mother–infant bond is crucial in humans (and in most higher level species) for the survival of the young. Infants who remain near the mother can be fed, protected, trained, and transported more effectively than infants who stray from her side. The behaviors used by the mother and infant to keep the pair in close contact must therefore be innate and controlled by a variety of releasing stimuli (we discuss these behaviors in Chapter 12). Bowlby further maintains that the attachment bond develops easily during a sensitive period, but after this time it may become impossible for the child ever to achieve a truly intimate emotional relationship (Bowlby, 1988).

Other Areas

Bowlby's work has encouraged a great deal of additional research on attachment and bonding processes in humans (e.g., Ainsworth, 1973). But more importantly for this tradition, it began a general movement toward examining other aspects of child development within an evolutionary context (Blurton-Jones, 1972). Psychologists of this persuasion have since investigated children's aggression, peer interactions, cognitive development, and many other topics.

Ethologists have also influenced developmental research methods. Observational methods have always been used by child researchers, but there has been a renewed interest in studying children in their natural environments (Bronfenbrenner, 1979; McCall, 1977). Observational techniques that do not influence or intrude on children's normal social interactions, for example, are being increasingly added to more experimental approaches to studying these behaviors. We can reasonably conclude, then, that the ethological tradition has established itself as an important perspective in contemporary developmental psychology.

✔ *To Recap...*

Ethology is based on the principles of evolution as first proposed by Charles Darwin. Ethologists believe that behaviors have both immediate and evolutionary determinants. These scientists are primarily concerned with innate behaviors, and they attempt to explain complex response patterns in terms of their survival value for the species.

Lorenz and Tinbergen, two founders of the ethological movement, identified four characteristics of innate behavior: it is universal, it is stereotyped, it requires no learning, and it is minimally affected by the environment. Ethologists have described how complex sequences of inherited responses (modal action patterns) are triggered by stimuli in the environment and how innate mechanisms, such as imprinting, influence the learning process.

Sociobiology is a recent attempt to explain social behavior in terms of an evolutionary model in which the survival of the genes supersedes any other goal. This mechanism is believed to be principally expressed in cultural and social structures.

Human ethology did not emerge until recently because evolutionary processes did not appear necessary to explain complex human behaviors. As a result of Bowlby's research on the attachment process, many aspects of child development now are being studied from an ethological perspective.

DEVELOPMENT IN CONTEXT: The Ecological Approach

Whereas the three approaches we have just described guide most of the research conducted by child psychologists, a fourth perspective has emerged in recent years and is proving very influential. This perspective is not a new theoretical model, because it cuts across the other three traditions. Instead, it represents a different way of thinking about human development and a different approach to studying the factors that influence it (Garbarino & Abramowitz, 1992).

Scientific research on children's development traditionally has taken place in laboratory settings. There are good reasons for this. The most important is that scientific investigation demands careful experimental control, so that the scientist can isolate the factors of interest and eliminate those that are extraneous. Until recently, the laboratory has afforded the only setting in which such control could be achieved.

Some researchers, however, have questioned the wisdom of this practice, pointing to an obvious fact—children's development does not generally take place in laboratories. It takes place at home, with the family; at school, with classmates and teachers; in the park, with neighbors and peers; and, more generally, within a larger social and cultural environment. In short, development always occurs in a context. And, more importantly, the context often influences the course of that development. This realization has produced a growing interest in studying children in the settings where their development typically occurs and in examining how the context influences, and is influenced by, the child's behavior.

The idea of studying development in context—called the **ecological approach**—is not a new one. Darwin argued that to understand the evolutionary value of any behavior, we must consider the ecological niche in which it evolved. For some time now, child researchers have been aware of the usefulness of an ecological perspective. The first important example of ecological psychology took place in the 1940s and 1950s, when Barker and Wright (1951, 1955) conducted a series of studies in which teams of observers recorded children's interactions in homes and schools, noting both their behaviors and the physical environments in which they occurred. This method of study, however, did not arouse much interest among developmental researchers of the time.

The recent resurgence of interest in the ecological perspective can be traced to two sources. One is the development of more sophisticated methods for studying behavior in the natural environment (Vasta, 1982a). The other is the publication of an influential book by Urie Bronfenbrenner, a psychologist at Cornell University. In *The Ecology of Human Development* (1979), Bronfenbrenner revitalized this approach by providing researchers with a conceptual framework in which ecological issues could be studied. His model, known as **ecological systems theory,** has since been revised (Bronfenbrenner, 1986, 1989, 1993) and has generated a number of related efforts by other researchers (Belsky, 1980; Lerner & Lerner, 1987, 1989; Leyendecker & Scholmerich, 1991).

Ecological systems theory is based on the notion that to completely understand development we must consider how the unique characteristics of a child interact with that child's surroundings. The child possesses a variety of personal characteristics, the most important of which are those that Bronfenbrenner describes as *developmentally instigative*—that is, capable of influencing other people in ways that are important to the child. Examples include a child's physical appearance, social skills, intellectual abilities, and personality. The environment is viewed as a series of interrelated layers, with those closest to the child having the most direct impact and those farther away influencing the child more indirectly.

Ecological approach
An approach to studying development that focuses on individuals within their environmental contexts.

Ecological systems theory
Urie Bronfenbrenner's theory that emphasizes the interrelations of the individual with layers of environmental context.

• Ecological systems theory holds that development varies depending on the context in which it occurs, including the people and the physical resources.

Transactional influence
A bidirectional, or recipro-cal, relationship in which in-dividuals influence one an-other's behaviors.

Microsystem
The environmental system closest to the child, such as the family or school. The first of Bronfenbrenner's lay-ers of context.

Mesosystem
The interrelationships among the child's microsystems. The second of Bronfenbrenner's layers of context.

• Urie Bronfenbrenner's work has revitalized inter-est in the ecological ap-proach to studying human development.

Bronfenbrenner contends that the child and the environment continually in-fluence one another in a bidirectional, or **transactional,** manner (Bell, 1979; Sameroff, 1975). For example, suppose a child has the developmentally instigative characteristics of being bright and articulate. These may affect her environment by causing her parents to send her to a better school, which in turn may influence her by improving her academic skills, which again affects her environment by attracting friends who have high career aspirations, and so forth in an ongoing cycle of in-teraction and development. These sorts of interactions, Bronfenbrenner argues, are very difficult to study if the child is removed from the natural environment in which they occur.

The processes through which such interactions occur are not unique to the ecological model. The biological, cognitive, and learning mechanisms we have al-ready discussed are all assumed to operate within these interactions. For this rea-son, researchers from all three of the theoretical traditions have begun to pursue their interests within an ecological framework.

Figure 2-3 shows Bronfenbrenner's ecological model of development. At the center is the child. Nearest the child is the **microsystem,** which for most children includes the family, the school, the church, the playground, and so forth, along with the relationships that the child forms within these settings. The microsystem possesses physical characteristics, such as the size of the child's house, the amount of nearby playground equipment, and the number of books in the child's day-care center. It also consists of people, including the child's immediate family, the other children on the block, the child's teacher, and so on. These people, in turn, possess characteristics that may be relevant to the child's development, such as the socio-economic status of the peer group, the educational background of the parents, and the political attitudes of the teacher. The microsystem is not constant but changes as the child grows.

The **mesosystem** refers to the system of relationships among the child's mi-crosystems. This might include the parents' relationship with the child's teacher and the relationship between the child's siblings and neighborhood friends. In gen-eral, the more interconnected these systems are the more the child's development is likely to be supported in a clear and consistent way.

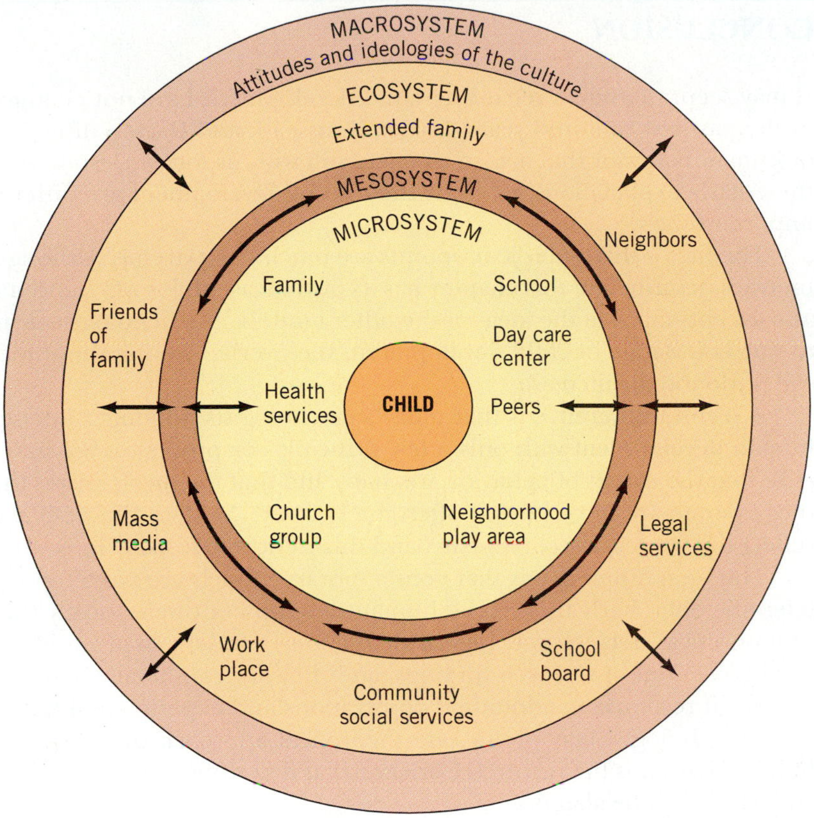

Figure 2-3 Bronfenbrenner's ecological model of the environment. U. Bronfenbrenner, from C. Kopp/Krakow, *The Child,* © 1982 by Addison-Wesley Publishing Co., Inc., Reading, Massachusetts. Figure 12.1 on page 648. Reprinted with permission of the publisher.

The **exosystem** refers to social settings that can affect the child but in which the child does not participate directly: the local government, which decides how strictly air pollution standards will be enforced or which families will be eligible for welfare payments; the school board, which sets teachers' salaries and recommends the budget for new textbooks and equipment; and the parents' place of employment, which establishes policies regarding paid paternity leaves and on-site day-care facilities.

Finally, there is the **macrosystem,** which involves the culture and subculture in which the child lives (Cole, 1992). The macrosystem affects the child through its beliefs, attitudes, and traditions. Children living in the United States may be influenced, for example, by beliefs regarding democracy and equality and perhaps the virtues of capitalism and free enterprise. In certain parts of the country, children may also be affected by regional attitudes regarding the importance of rugged individualism or the desirability of a slower pace of life. And if a child lives in an ethnic or racially concentrated neighborhood, the values and cultural traditions of that group may add yet another source of influence. The macrosystem is generally more stable than the others. But it, too, can change as a society evolves—for example, from a liberal political era to a conservative one, or from economic prosperity to depression, or from peace to war (Elder & Caspi, 1988).

Context can affect any and all aspects of children's behavior and development. For that reason, we have spread our discussion of various contextual influences over the many topics covered in this text. Each of the chapters that follows includes a section such as the one you have just read, labeled "Development in Context," that illustrates contextual influences related to the topic.

Exosystem
Social systems that can affect children but in which they do not participate directly. Bronfenbrenner's third layer of context.

Macrosystem
The culture or subculture in which the child lives. Bronfenbrenner's fourth layer of context.

CONCLUSION

It may seem that ideas regarding child development have not changed very much in the past few hundred years. Locke, Rousseau, and Darwin offered explanations of human behavior that are, in essence, still with us today. Despite similarities with these early explanations, modern theories of development are different in several important ways.

The first is that today's viewpoints are much less extreme. Although each of the theories described in this chapter has its own ideas, philosophy, and methods, each also accepts many of the ideas of the other models. As psychologists continue to add to our knowledge of child development, the overlap among the three approaches will undoubtedly increase.

A second difference is that today's psychologists no longer attempt to explain human development with only a few principles or processes. We have come to realize that the causes of behavior are many and that the mechanisms through which they operate are intricate and often interrelated. Modern theoretical explanations reflect this increasing complexity, and this trend too is likely to continue.

The final difference is that contemporary models are based on a great deal of scientific data. Early theories of human development were mostly the products of philosophical debates and logical deductions. Modern explanations, in contrast, have grown out of research findings, and they are continually being modified and revised in response to additional observations and experimental data. A particular child psychologist may prefer one theoretical approach over another, but in the final analysis, it is the research evidence that determines which theories will survive and which will be abandoned.

FOR THOUGHT AND DISCUSSION

1. This chapter described the three major traditions of modern child psychology. *Which approach to explaining human development—cognitive, environmental, or ethological—fits best with your own thinking regarding how we develop?*

2. Information-processing theorists conceptualize the mind in terms of computer operations. *What do you think are some advantages to this approach? Do you feel that viewing the mind as a machine makes it impossible for these theorists to investigate the more emotional aspects of human behavior?*

3. In Box 2-2 we discuss some problems with using punishment as a disciplinary technique. *Should parents be free to spank or slap their children? What about teachers or child-care workers? Explain your answer.*

4. One aspect of both Bandura's concept of reciprocal determinism and Bronfenbrenner's ecological model is that people, to some degree, produce their own environments. *Can you think of some ways in which you have produced some of the desirable aspects of your environment? Have you produced any negative aspects? What could you do to change them?*

5. Ethologists contend that while many of our behaviors evolved millions of years ago when they were useful for survival, some of these behaviors now no longer serve this function. *Try to think of some everyday behaviors—your own or those of others—that may have an evolutionary basis but that probably are no longer useful or adaptive.*

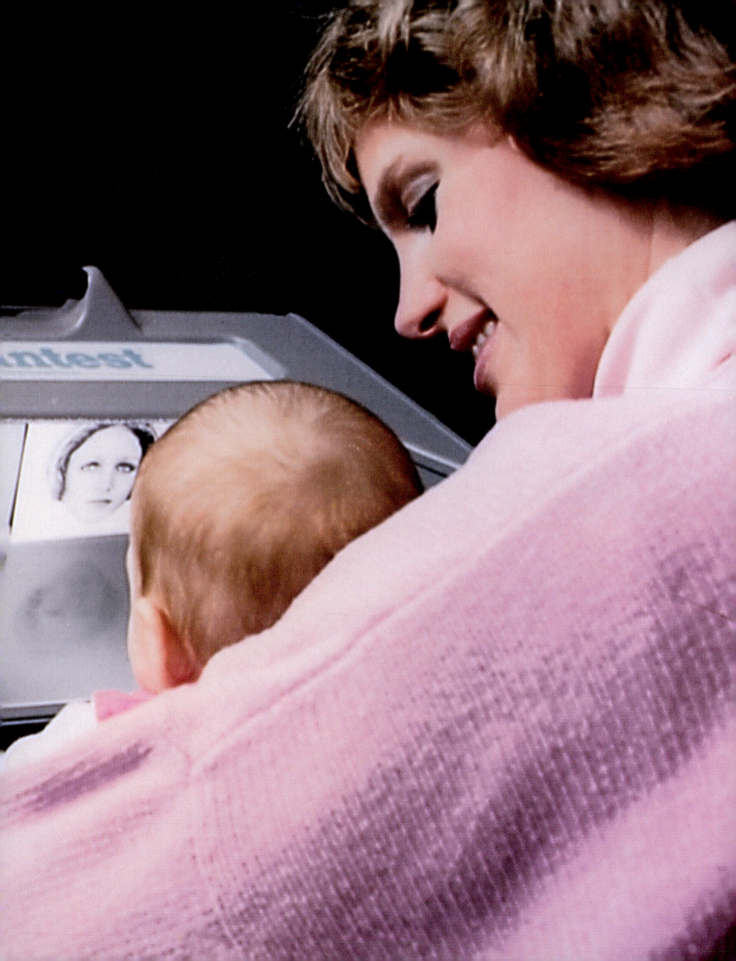

Chapter 3

RESEARCH METHODS

*T*he developing child may seem quite different from atoms fusing to produce nuclear energy or leaf cells making food from light and carbon dioxide through photosynthesis. Yet the research methods used by developmental psychologists are fundamentally the same as those used by physicists, biologists, and researchers in the other natural sciences.

The study of the child became scientific in the 19th century, when G. Stanley Hall began using questionnaires to study children's everyday knowledge. Since then, the research methods used by child psychologists have advanced impressively in quantity, quality, and sophistication. These advances, in turn, have been largely responsible for the enormous growth in the understanding of developmental processes that has occurred in this century (Appelbaum & McCall, 1983; Vasta, 1982b).

We begin this chapter by outlining some of the fundamental ideas and concepts that are basic to all scientific research. We then consider the principal research methods used in developmental psychology. Last, we discuss the sometimes thorny issue of research ethics.

SCIENTIFIC RESEARCH

Scientific method
The system of rules used by scientists to conduct and evaluate their research.

The approach scientists use to study any problem or issue is known as the **scientific method.** The method is essentially a system of rules for investigation that scientists use to design and conduct their research, to evaluate their results, and to communicate their findings to other scientists. These rules have evolved over hundreds of years, and they can be applied to the study of virtually anything.

The Role of Theory

Theory
A broad set of statements describing the relation between a phenomenon and the factors assumed to affect it.

Law (principle)
A predicted relation between a phenomenon and a factor assumed to affect it that is supported by a good deal of scientific evidence.

Hypothesis
A predicted relation between a phenomenon and a factor assumed to affect it that is not yet supported by a great deal of evidence. Hypotheses are tested in experimental investigations.

In Chapter 2, we discussed several important theories, but we did not actually define the term. In psychology, a **theory** is a set of statements describing the relation between behavior and the factors assumed to influence it. A specific statement that has a good deal of research evidence to support it is called a **law** or **principle**—the principle of reinforcement is a good example. A statement that simply postulates a relation is called a **hypothesis.**

Theories have two important roles in scientific research. The first is to organize research findings. As investigators acquire knowledge, they use theories to fit the information together into a coherent explanation of the behaviors and processes being studied. Once the knowledge is organized, it is sometimes obvious that certain questions remain to be answered or that specific relations probably exist even though they do not yet have substantial supporting evidence. A second role of theories, then, is to guide new research by indicating to investigators which hypotheses should be tested next.

Developmental psychologists do not investigate children's functioning by randomly studying any question that pops into their heads. Their research is typically guided by an underlying theory and their theoretical orientation. Thus, cognitive-developmentalists tend to investigate characteristics of children's knowledge; environmental/learning theorists study ways in which a behavior is acquired through experience; and ethologists examine various innate patterns of responses. Beyond producing such general interests, developmental theories also serve to generate very specific hypotheses regarding the causes of behavior. As a result, the great majority of research studies are part of systematic programs that involve testing one hypothesis after another.

Objectivity

Scholars in fields other than the sciences—literature, music, and art, for example—often rely on individual tastes, personal opinions, and other subjective judgments. In contrast, scientists emphasize **objectivity**—that is, they attempt to define and deal with the matters they investigate in ways that can, at least in principle, be agreed on by everyone.

One result of the emphasis on objectivity in child psychology is the focus on *observable* behaviors. Recall that in child psychology, our two primary goals—to describe children's behavior at each point in their development and to identify the causes and processes that produce changes in behavior from one point to the next—center on behavior. Furthermore, although developmental psychologists of all traditions acknowledge the importance of internal cognitive processes, they can investigate these mechanisms only by observing their effects on some aspect of behavior. We study assimilation and accommodation, for example, by observing a child's reactions to new experiences; we study intelligence by calculating a child's performance on an IQ test; and we study self-esteem by observing how a child interacts in social situations. In each case, the cognitive process or operation can be revealed and investigated only through its effect on behavior.

A related characteristic of scientific objectivity is that the events or behaviors studied must be *measurable*. Simply put, this means that in psychological research, the aspect of development being studied must always be defined and described in terms of specific behaviors that we can somehow count. Say, for example, we are interested in studying children's altruism—their willingness to aid someone else. We might decide to define altruism in terms of sharing behaviors and then develop a procedure wherein we count the number of pennies that each child donates to a

Objectivity
A characteristic of scientific research; it requires that the procedures and subject matter of investigations should be formulated so that they could, in principle, be agreed on by everyone.

• An important characteristic of psychological research is the focus on objective definitions and measurable behaviors.

charity under very specific conditions. Or say we want to investigate an infant's attachment to her mother. We could define attachment in terms of the child's crying, smiling, and searching behaviors and then measure the amount of time that elapses before the infant displays each of these behaviors after the mother has left the room. In these examples, we have defined the abstract concepts of "altruism" and "attachment" in terms of behaviors we can describe and measure very precisely.

Factors that we suspect may influence children's behaviors must also be *quantifiable*. Physical determinants—the number of children in a classroom and the amount of alcohol that a pregnant mother has consumed, for example—are relatively easy to describe in this way. Determinants that have to do with the behaviors of others—social approval and modeling, for instance—are more difficult to deal with, but they too must be carefully defined and described so that they are measurable.

The precise measurement of behaviors and their causes is of utmost importance because scientific research identifies cause-and-effect relations by focusing on change. The typical way psychologists determine whether a hypothesis is accurate—that is, whether a particular factor causes a particular behavior—is to conduct an experiment that examines whether changes in the suspected factor produce changes in the behavior of interest. Unless these factors and behaviors have been measured very accurately, it may be difficult to determine whether any changes have, in fact, taken place. Developmental psychologists have an additional concern for accurate measurement. Even when they are merely describing, rather than explaining, behaviors, the differences between the responses of, for example, a 2-month-old and those of a 4-month-old may only be detectable if those responses have been measured with great exactness.

Objectivity therefore reduces the chances of *bias* entering into the scientific process. By using methods that are observable, measurable, and quantifiable, researchers hope to eliminate the possibility of their findings being influenced by such factors as their prior expectancies, beliefs, or preferences.

Throughout this text, we describe many research studies. These studies vary greatly from one another in the issues under study, the methods used to collect data, and the types of subjects involved. All of them, however, share the characteristics we have just described. They focus on changes in observable responses, and they deal with behaviors and events that have been measured and quantified with as much precision as possible.

✔ To Recap...

The scientific method consists of the rules that researchers use to conduct and describe their investigations. Scientific theories play two important roles in the research process. First, they help to organize the information gathered from scientific studies. Second, they guide researchers to the important questions that need to be examined next. Scientific research also requires objectivity, which in psychology leads to a focus on observable behaviors and to a requirement that behaviors and their determinants be described in ways that are measurable and quantifiable.

TYPES OF RESEARCH

Research in psychology generally falls into one of three categories: descriptive, correlational, or experimental. Here we briefly discuss each of these approaches as they apply to the study of children.

Descriptive Research

The oldest form of psychological research is the purely descriptive approach. When applied to children, **descriptive research** consists of simply observing children and recording what is seen. No formal attempt is made to identify relations among the children's behaviors and any other factors. Early *baby biographies,* such as those in which Darwin and others kept daily records of the behaviors of their infants, provided the first systematic descriptive data on human development. G. Stanley Hall's questionnaire findings and, later, Arnold Gesell's norms—both of which described the typical skills and abilities of children of various ages—also used the descriptive method.

Today, descriptive research of this sort is not very common. Normally it is conducted only when very little is known about a topic. Even then, it is often only a first step in a research plan that will go on to use more sophisticated methods of investigation.

Descriptive research Research based solely on observations, with no attempt to determine systematic relations among the variables.

Correlational Research

The next step beyond observing and describing events is identifying systematic relations that exist in the observations. More specifically, researchers attempt to identify correlations among variables. A **variable** is any factor that can take on different values along some dimension. Common examples include human physical characteristics—height, weight, age, and so on—and physical aspects of the environment—temperature, room size, amount of food eaten, and number of people in a family, for instance. Human behaviors, if properly defined, can also be variables and can vary along a number of different dimensions. Examples of behavioral variables might include how many times a child asks the teacher for help (*frequency*), how loudly a baby cries (*intensity*), or how long a child practices the piano (*duration*).

Variable Any factor that can take on different values along a dimension.

A **correlation** is a statement that describes how two variables are related. For example, we might wonder whether children's ages are correlated with—that is, systematically related to—their heights. To answer this question, we might observe and record the heights of 100 children, who vary in age from 2 to 12, and examine whether changes in the one variable correspond to changes in the other. In this case, we would discover a clear correlation between the variables of age and height—that is, as children increase in age, they generally increase in height as well. This type of relation, in which two variables change in the same direction, is described as a **positive correlation.**

Correlation The relation between two variables, described in terms of its direction and strength.

What about the relation between a child's age and the number of hours each day that the child spends at home? Here we would also discover a systematic relation, but the variables involved would move in opposite directions—as a child's age increases, the amount of time the child spends at home generally decreases. This sort of relation is called a **negative correlation.** Finally, we might investigate the relation between a child's height and the number of children in the child's classroom. In this case, we would likely find that the two variables are not related to one another at all and so have no correlation.

Positive correlation A correlation in which two variables change in the same direction.

Negative correlation A correlation in which two variables change in opposite directions.

Correlations can be described not only in terms of their direction (positive or negative) but also in terms of their strength. A strong correlation means that two variables are closely related. In such cases, knowing the value of one variable gives us a good indication of the value of the second variable. As a correlation grows weaker, the amount of predictability between the variables decreases. When the variables become completely unrelated, knowledge of the value of one gives us no clue as to the value of the other.

Correlation coefficient (r)
A number between +1.00 and −1.00 that indicates the direction and strength of a correlation between two variables.

Scatter diagram
A graphic illustration of a correlation between two variables.

The direction of a correlation is indicated by a plus or minus sign, and its strength is indicated by a numerical value that can be calculated from a simple statistical formula. The result is called the **correlation coefficient (r),** which can range between +1.00 and −1.00. A correlation coefficient of +.86 indicates a strong positive correlation, and +.17 indicates a weak positive correlation. Similarly, −.93, −.41, and −.08 denote, respectively, a strong, a moderate, and a weak negative correlation. A coefficient of 0.00 indicates that there is no correlation between two variables. Correlations can also be depicted graphically with a **scatter diagram,** some examples of which are shown in Figure 3-1.

To illustrate both the usefulness and the limitations of correlational research, let us consider a hypothetical example. Suppose some researchers are interested in determining whether there is a relation between children's reading ability and the amount of time that they watch the educational television program "Sesame Street." To begin, the researchers randomly select a number of children and determine a value for each child's reading ability, perhaps by giving the children a reading test on which they can score between 0 and 100. Then the researchers determine the value of the viewing variable, perhaps by having parents record the number of hours each week that the child watches "Sesame Street." Finally, the researchers calculate the correlation between the two sets of scores and discover that the variables have a correlation coefficient of +.78, as shown in Figure 3-2. What can they conclude from these findings?

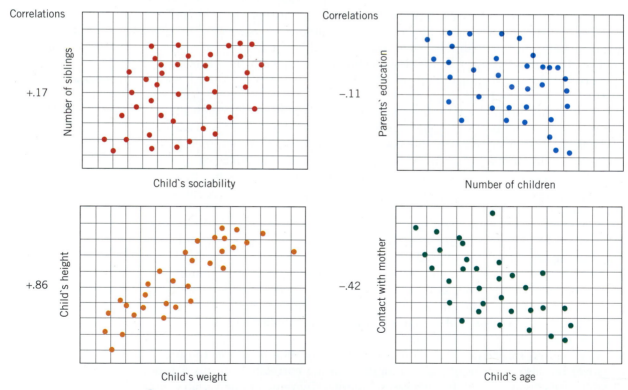

Figure 3-1   Scatter diagrams illustrating correlations between two variables. Each dot represents one child and shows the child's values for the two variables. One value is plotted from the vertical axis and the other from the horizontal axis. The left two graphs show positive correlations, and the right two graphs show negative correlations.

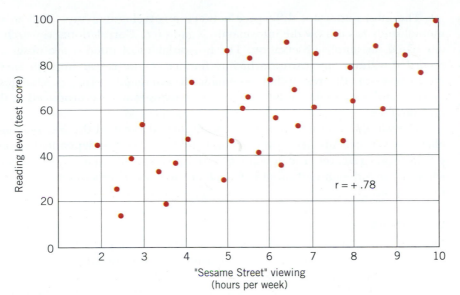

Figure 3-2 A scatter diagram of a hypothetical correlation between children's viewing of "Sesame Street" and their reading level. The correlation coefficient (r) shows a strong positive relation between the two variables.

Since the two variables display a strong positive correlation, we might be tempted to believe that the study shows that viewing "Sesame Street" leads to better reading skills—or in more general terms, that one of the variables has an effect on the other. But herein lies a major limitation of correlational research—*a correlation cannot be used to show causality between the variables*. The correlation in the example may accurately reveal the pattern and strength of the viewing–reading relation, but it cannot reveal cause and effect between the variables. Why not?

If we think carefully about the example, we will realize that some other conclusions cannot be ruled out. For example, rather than the TV viewing having an effect on the reading, the reverse is equally plausible. That is, children who are better readers may enjoy "Sesame Street" more than children who are poorer readers and may therefore watch it more often. Another possibility is that the two variables are both influenced by some third variable that we have not measured. For instance, both might be affected by the educational background of the child's parents. Indeed, there is a good chance that the better educated a child's parents are, the more likely they are to encourage both reading and the viewing of educational television. Thus, while correlational research is a valuable tool for identifying and measuring systematic relations, it cannot be used to explain them. Explanation requires a more powerful research method—the experimental approach.

Correlational research, nevertheless, can play an important role in the scientific research process. Like descriptive research, correlational studies are often sources of interesting and provocative questions. These questions may be formed into specific research hypotheses that investigators can go on to examine using more rigorous methods of research.

Experimental Research

The most popular and important type of research in developmental psychology is the experiment. Like a simple correlational study, a simple experiment often involves investigating the relation between just two variables. Unlike correlational research, however, experimentation permits us to infer cause-and-effect relations between the variables involved.

The most important difference between a correlational study and an experimental study lies in how the information is gathered. Correlational research is usually based on simple observation. The two variables of interest are observed and recorded without any intrusion or interference by the researchers. In an experiment, however, the researcher systematically *manipulates*—that is, changes—one variable and then looks for any effects the changes may have produced in the second variable.

The variable that is systematically manipulated is called the **independent variable.** The variable affected by the manipulation is called the **dependent variable.** In psychological research, the dependent variable is typically some aspect of behavior, whereas the independent variable is a factor the researcher suspects may influence that behavior.

Independent variable
The variable in an experiment that is systematically manipulated.

Dependent variable
The variable that is predicted to be affected by an experimental manipulation. In psychology, usually some aspect of behavior.

Group Studies

Most of the experimental research conducted by developmental psychologists involves a method that compares the behavior of groups of subjects exposed to different manipulations of a variable.

Let us consider how researchers might use the experimental method to address the question of whether watching "Sesame Street" affects reading level. First, the researchers need a hypothesis that clearly identifies the independent and dependent variables. If the hypothesis is that viewing "Sesame Street" improves reading ability, then the independent variable is the amount of viewing, and the dependent variable is the child's reading level. The next step involves systematically manipulating the independent variable. As in the correlational approach, the researchers select a number of children, but here they randomly divide them into, say, four groups. The first group is required to watch 2 hours of "Sesame Street" each week; the second group, 4 hours; the third group, 8 hours; and the fourth group, 10 hours. After perhaps 6 months, the researchers readminister the reading test to all the children and examine how the different groups perform. Possible results are shown in Figure 3-3. If the differences in performance are sufficiently large (as determined by the appropriate statistical tests), not only can the researchers conclude that the two variables are systematically related, but they can also make the causal statement

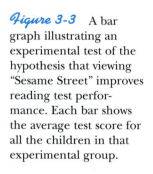

Figure 3-3   A bar graph illustrating an experimental test of the hypothesis that viewing "Sesame Street" improves reading test performance. Each bar shows the average test score for all the children in that experimental group.

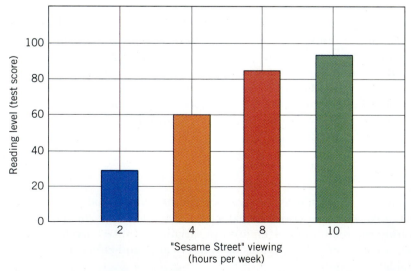

that viewing "Sesame Street" improves children's reading ability. The psychologists' hypothesis now has been supported by experimental data.

Reversal-Replication Studies

Although experimental research most often involves exposing groups of subjects to different values of an independent variable, there is an alternative called the **reversal-replication design** (or sometimes the **ABAB design**). In this method, the independent variable is systematically presented and removed, and effects on the dependent variable are noted. The main advantage of this design is that fewer subjects are needed. In fact, it can be used in an experiment involving a single child. Consider, for example, how we might use this method to test the hypothesis that the presence of the mother causes infants to smile more often. In this experiment, the independent variable would be the presence or absence of the mother, and the dependent variable would be the amount the infant smiles. As Figure 3-4 indicates, the basic procedure of the experiment involves counting the number of times the infant smiles per minute during a 20-minute daily session in which the mother is either present or absent.

In conducting the experiment, the researcher must first determine the *baseline,* or initial level of the behavior being observed. In this example, the baseline is the amount that the infant smiles "naturally," meaning when the mother is not present. Then in the second, or *treatment,* phase the independent variable is introduced. As shown in Figure 3-4, there is a clear increase in smiling when the mother is present. The change in the infant's behavior is consistent with the researcher's hypothesis, but there are not yet sufficient data to establish a causal relation between the presence of the mother and the increased smiling. Why not? The change in the infant's behavior might have resulted from other factors—a better overall "mood," perhaps—that only coincidently occurred when the mother was present.

Reversal-replication (ABAB) design
An experimental design in which the independent variable is systematically presented and removed several times. It can be used in studies involving very few subjects.

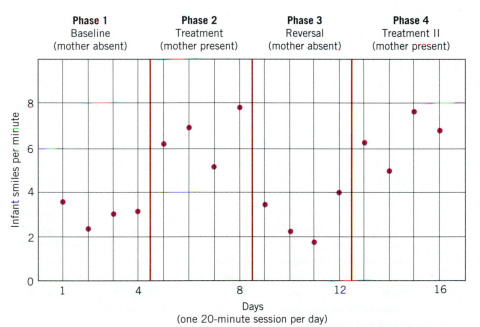

Figure 3-4   A reversal–replication design showing a causal relation between the presence of the mother (the independent variable) and the amount an infant smiles (the dependent variable). The third and fourth phases replicate the procedures and results of the first two phases.

To determine whether the change in behavior was only accidently related to the change in the independent variable, the researcher attempts to *replicate* the procedure and results. In the next step, then, the independent variable is again removed. This is called the *reversal*, or withdrawal, phase. In our example, we can see that the infant's behavior returns to its baseline level. Finally, the independent variable is presented once more in a second treatment phase. If the subsequent change in behavior is the same as during the first treatment phase, then the researcher has enough evidence to infer a causal relation between the independent and dependent variables. Since the amount the infant smiles does indeed increase once again, the researcher can reasonably conclude that the baby's smiling is affected by the mother's presence.

Additional Considerations

Experimental research is a powerful scientific tool, not only because it can reveal cause-and-effect relations but also because it can be applied to a wide variety of problems and settings. Much of the experimentation conducted by child psychologists takes place in laboratories, especially when conditions must be carefully controlled and monitored. But experimental research can also be conducted in field settings—playgrounds, classrooms, or children's homes, for example—where the child's behavior is studied under more natural or typical conditions.

The experimental approach is of paramount importance in the study of child development, and examples of experiments appear frequently in the pages that follow. Here, we have outlined only the most basic concepts involved in this method. But many detailed procedures not discussed here must be followed before we can be confident that an experiment is scientifically sound. These involve such matters as how the subjects of the study are selected and assigned to groups, under what conditions the data are gathered, which statistical tests are conducted, and so forth. Furthermore, experimental studies—as well as correlational studies—are typically much more complex than we have indicated. For one thing, a single study often involves a number of variables rather than just two, and sometimes several hypotheses are tested at once. Finally, no single experiment should ever be taken as definitive. Before science can feel confident about a finding, the results generally must be replicated several times and by different experimenters. Discussions of all these issues can be readily found in texts devoted to methodology in developmental psychology (e.g., Miller, 1987; Vasta, 1979).

✔ To Recap...

The three major research methods used by child psychologists are descriptive research, correlational research, and experimentation. The descriptive approach involves simple observation and is used today primarily as a first step in exploring areas about which little is known. Correlational studies are used to identify relations between variables and to describe them in terms of their direction and strength. This method cannot produce conclusions regarding cause and effect. The experimental approach involves testing hypotheses by systematically manipulating the independent variable and examining the effects thereby produced on the dependent variable. As a result, it allows researchers to draw conclusions regarding cause and effect. Experimental studies may involve groups of subjects exposed to different values of an independent variable. They may also involve only a few subjects, who are exposed to the repeated presentation and removal of an independent variable in a reversal-replication design.

STUDYING DEVELOPMENT

Development, as we have seen, involves changes in behavior over time. Consequently, many of the issues of interest to developmental researchers focus on how children's behavior at one age differs from their behavior at another age. Sometimes these issues are mainly descriptive, such as how a child's speech progresses from the one-word utterances of the toddler, to the ill-formed sentences of the preschooler, to the reasonably accurate sentences of the preadolescent. At other times they focus on the determinants of behavior, such as the possible effects of day-care programs on a child's later social adjustment to school. For either type of question, however, the psychologist needs a research method that will allow the comparison of behaviors at different ages. Four methods are available for this purpose—the longitudinal study, the cross-sectional study, a method that combines the two, and the microgenetic technique.

Longitudinal Research

One approach to studying children's behavior at different ages is the **longitudinal design.** The logic of this approach is quite simple—the behaviors of interest are first measured when the child is very young and then measured again at various intervals. The main advantage of this method is that it allows the researcher to study directly how each behavior changes as the child grows older (Menard, 1991; Mussen, 1987).

Longitudinal design
A research method in which the same subjects are studied repeatedly over time.

The number of years required for a longitudinal study can vary considerably. Some questions can be explored within a relatively brief time frame. For example, determining whether different techniques of caring for premature infants have different effects on the age at which the babies begin to walk and talk should take only about 18 months to 2 years of observation. Other questions, such as whether a child's early disciplinary experiences influence his or her own use of punishment as a parent, may need to extend over decades.

Longitudinal studies can be either correlational or experimental. If we measure behaviors at one age and then again at a later age, we can determine the consistency of the behaviors by calculating the correlation between the two sets of measurements. Experimental longitudinal studies usually involve introducing a ma-

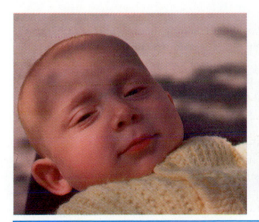

• In longitudinal research, the same individuals are studied over a period of time, sometimes many years.

TERMAN'S STUDIES OF GENIUS

There have been many famous longitudinal studies in developmental psychology, but the first major one was Lewis Terman's investigation of intellectually gifted children. This classic research remains especially noteworthy in that it followed a very large group of subjects for almost their entire lives and generated some fascinating findings (Cravens, 1992).

Terman was a psychologist at Stanford University and is best known for having developed one of the first IQ tests, the Stanford-Binet, which we will describe when we discuss intelligence testing in Chapter 10. In the course of administering his new test, Terman became interested in the children who scored at the very highest levels. In 1921 he selected approximately 1,400 extremely intelligent 11-year-olds in California to participate in a longitudinal project he titled *Genetic Studies of Genius* (Terman, 1925).

Terman was not interested in only the IQ scores of his subjects. He also collected a great deal of information on their families, schools, physical characteristics, mental and medical health, personality traits, and more. Thereafter, at intervals of about 10 years, Terman readministered many of the same tests and measures to find out whether gifted children develop differently from their peers of normal intelligence.

The subjects of his study, who became known as "Termites," proved to be quite different than the conventional wisdom of the time would have predicted. Rather than supporting the stereotype that genius chil-

dren are sickly, meek, and social misfits, Terman's subjects in fact proved to be quite the opposite. As they grew they were found to be healthier, wealthier, more professionally successful, and even happier than most others in society.

Two findings that Terman reported when he initially tested his subjects proved to be somewhat controversial. One was that the gifted children came from wealthier, better educated families. The other was that many more males than females were identified as having high IQ scores. Both of these findings today are regarded skeptically by psychologists and may have resulted from flaws or biases in the way in which Terman selected his subjects (Shurkin, 1992).

Terman died in 1957, but his research was continued by others, including Robert Sears, a Termite who had become a developmental psychologist. In 1972, when the subjects had reached their 60s, they were asked to describe what aspects of their lives they had found most satisfying or rewarding. Interestingly, the majority of them pointed to their families—not their wealth, social status, or professional success—as having been their greatest source of happiness (Sears, 1977).

Most of the Termites have now died. Nevertheless, the vast amount of information collected by Terman's research team is still being studied by scientists who continue to generate new questions and better ways to look at the data.

nipulation at one point in development and then examining its effects on the dependent variables of interest at some later point, or points, in development.

Two types of research questions are particularly well suited to the longitudinal approach (Magnusson et al., 1991). The first concerns the persistence, or stability, of behaviors. If, for instance, we wish to determine the extent to which a child's temperament (an aspect of personality) remains constant throughout life, the best approach is to measure this characteristic in the same children periodically and examine the correlations among the sets of scores. Aspects of behavior that display continuity of development, as described in Chapter 1, are especially suited for longitudinal study. The second type of question that works well with the longitudinal method involves the effects of early experiences on later behavior. If we wish to determine whether certain events or conditions that occur during a child's early years—divorce, an infant stimulation program, or the quality of diet, for instance—produce long-term effects, the clearest answers will be obtained with an experimental longitudinal approach. For example, we might identify a group of children who have participated in an early stimulation program and a group who have not and then follow both groups for a number of years to see if differences emerge in their school success. (An early longitudinal study is presented in Box 3-1).

Despite the obvious value of the longitudinal approach, the method does have certain disadvantages. One of the most common problems is *subject attrition,* the loss of individuals under study, which can occur for a variety of reasons. Families may move away, children may become ill or develop other problems that interfere with participation in the study, or the parents may simply lose interest and withdraw from the project. Other problems may develop because subjects are tested repeatedly. For example, a study concerned with the stability of a child's intelligence requires that IQ tests be administered at regular intervals. However, repeated experience with tests, in and of itself, may make a child "test wise" to the types of answers or responses that are expected. This can, in turn, improve the child's performance. A third disadvantage directly relates to the fact that longitudinal studies are often designed to last for many years. There is a very real possibility that the issues involved or the instruments used at the beginning of the study may become outdated. For example, the experimental questions posed at the outset of the project may become less important as the years pass and other research findings are published. Similarly, the tests and instruments used may become obsolete. Finally, there is a major practical disadvantage. Since it often requires a large research staff and many hours of observation or testing, longitudinal research can be very expensive.

DEVELOPMENT IN CONTEXT: Studying the Life Course

One interesting variation on longitudinal research is the study of the life course. Such investigations focus on how major personal and environmental events affect an individual. The dependent measures of interest here, however, are not the short-term impacts of such events which psychologists usually study. Rather, the emphasis is on how these events can alter the course of the individual's entire life (Elder, 1985).

Generally, such research is archival rather than experimental. This means that the investigators use existing longitudinal studies that have gone on for many years as their source of data. By examining the records of these studies—often tracing one individual's life at a time—the life-course researcher can study new questions of current interest that may not have been a specific focus of the original project. And because the research uses data that have already been gathered, longitudinal issues can be studied in a fraction of the time normally required (Elder & Caspi, 1988).

Studies of the life course have taken several forms. Some have examined the impact of major historical events or conditions on the lives of the people in a particular generation. Examples include the effects of the Great Depression of the 1930s and the effects of World War II on children and young adults (Elder, 1974). Other studies have looked at the role of life transitions—for example, the age at which a woman decides to marry, to have her first child, or to enter the work force (Elder, Caspi, & Downey, 1986).

A newer interest of life-course researchers is the long-range effects of early personality characteristics (Caspi & Elder, 1988). A guiding assumption of research in this area is that an individual's relationship to his or her environment is transactional. Recall from Chapter 2 that this means a person to some degree produces a

• Research on the life course has investigated the effects of major historical events, such as the Great Depression of the 1930s, on the lives of individuals involved.

certain type of environment, to which he or she then continues to be exposed. For example, studies have examined the lives of some shy children (Caspi, Elder, & Bem, 1988) and explosive children (Caspi, Elder, & Bem, 1987). Although few long-term effects of shyness in girls were identified, boys who were shy and unassertive later showed delays in marrying, fathering children, and establishing stable careers. Explosive, ill-tempered boys were more likely to drop out of school and ultimately to have poorer jobs, less job satisfaction, and more marital problems. Ill-tempered girls, too, tended to have less stable marriages as adults and to be married to men of lower socioeconomic status. The researchers believe these children, because of their shyness or explosiveness, engendered certain reactions in people and so gradually gravitated toward (or away from) certain social experiences and groups. These patterns, in turn, influenced the lives of these individuals for many years.

Cross-Sectional Research

Cross-sectional design
A research method in which subjects of different ages are studied simultaneously to examine the effects of age on some aspect of behavior.

An alternative to longitudinal research is the **cross-sectional design.** Here, researchers examine developmental differences in behavior by studying children of different ages. When an experiment is set up in this way, the age of the subjects simply becomes an independent variable in the research design.

The major advantage of this approach, of course, is that it is much less time-consuming than the longitudinal method. Rather than waiting 5 years to determine, say, how memory processes in 3-year-olds differ from memory processes in 8-year-olds, we can simply study a group of 3-year-olds and a group of 8-year-olds at the same time. The shortness of the time required also means that such experiments are rarely plagued by the problems of subject attrition, repeated testing, outdated issues and instruments, and high cost.

Two important disadvantages, nevertheless, are presented by this approach. The first is that questions of early experience and behavior stability cannot be investigated with this method. It is impossible to determine the impact of an early event or the persistence of an early trait by examining those behaviors in *different* older children.

Cohort effect
A problem sometimes found in cross-sectional research, in which subjects of a given age are affected by factors unique to their generation.

A second problem is known as the **cohort effect.** This phenomenon stems from the fact that certain aspects of people's behavior are influenced by the unique events and conditions experienced by their particular age group or generation. For example, suppose we were investigating the cognitive skills of individuals at ages 25, 35, and 60 and found that the 35-year-olds performed better on our various reasoning and problem-solving tests than the younger or older groups. Would these results allow us to conclude that cognitive development peaks after early adulthood and then declines? Such an interpretation is certainly consistent with our data. But another explanation arises when we consider the educational backgrounds of our three groups of subjects. The 65-year-olds were raised during the Depression, when many youngsters were forced to leave school early and find jobs. The 25-year-olds were raised during the late 1960s, when much greater emphasis was being placed on children's social and emotional development. But the 35-year-olds began attending school shortly after the launching of the Soviet satellite *Sputnik*, which stimulated a major U.S. effort to improve scientific and mathematical training. The point here is that our subjects are members of three cohorts, or peer groups, that had different educational experiences. The performance differences we observe therefore may not reflect the differences in their ages so much as their different life experiences.

Combining Longitudinal and Cross-Sectional Research

To obtain the best features of the longitudinal and cross-sectional designs, researchers sometimes combine the two methods into a **cross-sequential design.** The combined approach begins with a simple cross-sectional investigation, during which groups of children of different ages are studied simultaneously. The same groups are then studied again at one or more later times to provide a longitudinal perspective on the question.

For instance, an investigator might begin by measuring the amount of competitiveness displayed by 4-year-olds, 7-year-olds, and 10-year-olds playing a game. Three years later, the investigator retests the children, whose ages are now 7, 10, and 13. This procedure makes two types of data comparisons possible. Cross-sectional comparisons among the children can be made at both the initial testing and the later testing to see whether children at the different ages show different levels of competitiveness. In addition, the stability of each child's competitiveness can be examined by a comparison of the child's scores at the two ages.

The combined design also permits the investigator to check directly for two of the common problems associated with the individual designs. If the data for the groups at ages 7 and 10 during the first testing differ from the data for these groups during the second testing, then these differences are very likely the result of either a cohort effect (a cross-sectional design problem) or a repeated-testing effect (a longitudinal design problem). In either case, the investigator will need to exercise caution in drawing conclusions regarding both age-related differences in competitiveness and the stability of the behavior over time. But if the data from these corresponding groups are very similar, the researcher can have considerable confidence in the results of the study.

Cross-sequential design
A research method combining longitudinal and cross-sectional designs.

Microgenetic Studies

A somewhat newer approach to examining developmental change involves the intensive study of a small number of children over a brief period of time. The purpose of this **microgenetic method** is to investigate changes in important developmental processes *as they are occurring* (Siegler & Crowley, 1991, 1992).

Recall from Chapter 1 that some aspects of human development are thought to be discontinuous—they are relatively stable for a period of time but then move abruptly to a higher level. Investigators attempting to understand the nature of such changes have used the microgenetic approach in the hope of examining the particular developmental process as it goes from one level to the next. Much of the research using this approach has been concerned with children's cognitive abilities, probably because the concept of discontinuous change is consistent with the view of development held by most cognitive-developmental psychologists.

A microgenetic study begins with several children of around the age at which a developmental change is expected to occur. The behavior of interest is observed and measured repeatedly in these children. For example, if the experiment is concerned with the children's use of a particular cognitive strategy for solving a certain type of problem (a common focus of such research), the children may be asked to complete many such problems over a period of weeks. In such an experiment, the researcher not only assesses the correctness of the children's solutions, but also examines precisely how they approach each problem, perhaps by asking them to describe what they are doing. In this way, the investigator attempts to identify when a child moves from the use of a simpler cognitive strategy to a more sophisticated

Microgenetic method
A research method in which a small number of subjects are observed repeatedly in order to study an expected change in a developmental process.

one. By examining this process very carefully, the researcher may acquire a better understanding of exactly how it works. In Chapter 9 we describe an experiment that investigated how children develop a particular strategy for adding numbers.

While the microgenetic method can yield a great deal of new information about a developmental process, it too has drawbacks. One practical problem is that the many observations required over a compressed period of time can make this approach expensive. The other is that great care must be taken to ensure that the repeated assessment of the child's abilities does not itself cause changes in the behavior of interest (Pressley, 1992).

✔ To Recap...

Many developmental issues require comparisons of children's behavior at different ages. The longitudinal method assesses the behavior of the same children over a period of time. It is particularly useful for addressing questions concerning the effects of early experience on later behavior and the stability of behavior. The longitudinal method commonly suffers from problems with subject attrition, the effects of repeated testing, and the fact that issues and instruments may become outdated. It is also expensive. Cross-sectional research is less time-consuming than longitudinal research because it involves simultaneously studying children of different ages. However, it is sometimes plagued by the cohort effect. The longitudinal and cross-sectional approaches can be combined into the cross-sequential design, which offers some of the advantages of both methods. The microgenetic method is used to study emerging developmental changes by intensively assessing the behavior of a small number of children over a brief period of time.

OTHER RESEARCH TACTICS

Many additional research methods are commonly used by developmental investigators. Here, we describe cross-cultural research and comparative research, two popular approaches encountered throughout the text.

Cross-Cultural Research

An important theme of modern child psychology is that development must be studied in context. We saw in Bronfenbrenner's model (Chapter 2) that a very important context in which children develop is the culture of their people. How can we determine the influence of culture on a particular aspect of behavior or development?

Cross-cultural studies
Research designed to determine the influence of culture on some aspect of development and in which culture typically serves as an independent variable.

One approach is to study the same behavior in different cultures. **Cross-cultural studies** accomplish this by using the child's culture as an independent variable in the experiment and examining its effects on the dependent variable(s) of interest. Such studies have been conducted in areas as diverse as gender roles, moral reasoning, and perceptual abilities (Harkness & Super, 1987; Wagner & Stevenson, 1982).

An important use of this experimental method is to investigate nature–nurture questions, such as occur frequently in research on language development. English-speaking children generally follow a relatively predictable pattern of language acquisition. Certain grammatical structures are displayed before others (such as active sentences before passive sentences), and certain types of errors and omissions are very common among all children of a given age. Do these similarities mean that

• Cross-cultural studies can sometimes help determine whether patterns of behavior among members of one culture are universal to humans or result from common environmental influences.

language development is guided by inborn biological mechanisms and is therefore essentially the same for all humans? Or do they simply reflect the fact that most children in a given culture are exposed to very similar language models by parents, teachers, and others?

One fruitful approach to answering this question is to examine patterns of language acquisition in several cultures. If children in very different language environments display similar progressions in their development of grammatical structures and speech distortions, we have good evidence to support the belief that language development is genetically guided. If we find differences between cultural groups, however, we can conclude that environmental factors contribute to the language acquisition process (an issue we pursue further in Chapter 11).

Comparative Research

Psychologists also study behaviors across species. Although **comparative research** of this sort has served many different purposes, traditionally developmentalists have performed animal experiments for two reasons. First, researchers of the ethological tradition study animal behavior for clues to the evolutionary origins of similar human behaviors. For instance, determining how the imprinting process causes newborn birds to develop social attachments to their mothers may help child researchers to understand the mechanisms involved in the development of attachment between human infants and their mothers. Similarly, studying the play-fighting that commonly occurs among pups of many species may provide insights into the rough-and-tumble social interactions of young children.

More frequently, however, comparative research permits developmental psychologists to conduct studies that would be prohibited with human subjects for ethical reasons. What happens, for instance, to an infant who is reared for 6 months

Comparative research
Research conducted with nonhuman species in order to provide information relevant to human development.

• Comparative research investigates similar behaviors across different species.

without a mother? Does the visual system develop normally in an infant raised in total darkness? Do injections of sex hormones during the mother's pregnancy affect the later social behavior of the offspring? These, as well as many other questions, would be impossible to address experimentally with humans. Using other species, researchers have studied each of these issues in the laboratory.

✔ *To Recap...*

Cross-cultural research is useful for studying the influence of culture on development and for addressing some nature–nurture issues. Comparative research is conducted by ethologists to identify similarities in behavior processes between humans and nonhuman species. It also provides a way of experimentally addressing questions that would be unethical to investigate with human subjects.

ETHICAL ISSUES

No one would question the fact that psychological research often produces findings that benefit children, adults, and society as a whole. Nevertheless, almost any research involving human subjects can pose a variety of risks. Investigators therefore have an obligation to determine exactly what potentially negative effects may result from their experiments and to consider whether these risks outweigh the potential value of the research findings (Fisher & Tryon, 1988, 1990; Rheingold, 1982a; Sieber, 1992).

Concern over ethical issues has not always been as great as it is today. Early investigators had few restrictions on their research, as is evidenced by such questionable experiments as John B. Watson's conditioning of 11-month-old Little Albert. Today, however, attention is becoming increasingly focused on safeguarding children's rights and well-being.

Potential Risks

An obvious concern in any experiment is the possibility of physical injury to the child, although this problem is relatively rare in developmental research. A more common, and often more subtle, issue involves potential psychological harm to the child. Some experimental hypotheses may require, for example, observing how children respond when they cannot solve a problem, are prohibited from playing with an attractive toy, or are exposed to violent behavior. These procedures may produce various negative emotions, such as feelings of failure, frustration, or stress. The concern here is that the children may continue to experience these emotions for some time after leaving the experimental situation.

A somewhat less obvious category of problems involves violations of privacy. If a researcher secretly gains access to a child's school records, or if observations are conducted without a child's knowledge, or if data regarding a child or a family become public knowledge, the legal and ethical rights of these subjects may be violated.

Safeguards

The concern for ethical research practices has led to the development of safeguards designed to avoid or eliminate potential risks. These safeguards have, by and large, become a routine part of modern research procedures. In addition, professional scientific organizations have developed codes of ethical standards to guide their members. *Ethical Principles in the Conduct of Research with Human Participants* (1982), published by the American Psychological Association, and "SRCD Ethical Standards for Research with Children" (1990), published by the Society for Research in Child Development and reproduced in part in Table 3-1, are two important examples.

Perhaps the most important measure used to ensure that research is conducted ethically is *peer review*. Before beginning a research study, investigators are encouraged, and in many situations required, to submit the research plan to other scientists for their comments and approval. This practice permits an objective examination of the procedures by knowledgeable individuals who are not personally involved in the research. Peer review committees weigh the possible value of the research findings against potential risks. Sometimes, they offer suggestions as to how likely negative effects might be prevented or minimized. Almost all of the research carried out at colleges and universities or funded by government organizations follows this practice.

Another basic safeguard for protecting children's rights is the requirement for researchers to obtain the *informed consent* of the participants in the study. Any research conducted with children requires the written permission of both the parents and the institution (school, day-care center, and so on) where the research will take place. In addition, each child must be made aware of the general procedures of the study. Most important, the child has the right to refuse to participate or to withdraw from the study at any time, regardless of the fact that the parents have given their permission.

In situations where the research procedures may produce negative feelings in the child, the investigator must provide some means of reducing those feelings before the child leaves. For example, if a child is participating in an experiment in which he or she experiences failure, the investigator might end the research session by having the child perform a relatively easy task that will ensure success. Also, to whatever extent seems reasonable, the investigator should at some point explain to the child the purpose of the study and the child's role in it, a procedure called *debriefing*.

Maintaining *subject confidentiality* is also a crucial aspect of ethical research. Whenever possible, the identities of the participants and information about their individual performance should be concealed from anyone not directly connected

• Researchers who study children are required to ensure that neither physical nor psychological harm to the child is likely to result from their procedures.

TABLE 3-1 ● Ethical Standards for Research with Children, Society for Research in Child Development

Children as research participants present ethical problems for the investigator that are different from those presented by adult participants. Children are more vulnerable to stress than adults and, having less experience and knowledge than adults, are less able to evaluate the social value of the research and less able to comprehend the meaning of the research procedures themselves. In all cases, therefore, the child's consent or assent to participate in the research, as well as the consent of the child's parents or guardians, must be obtained.

In general, no matter how young children are, they have rights that supersede the rights of the investigator. The investigator is therefore obligated to evaluate each proposed research operation in terms of these rights, and before proceeding with the investigation, should obtain the approval of an appropriate Institutional Review Board.

The principles listed below are to be subscribed to by all members of the Society for Research in Child Development. These principles are not intended to infringe on the right and obligation of researchers to conduct scientific research.

Principle 1. Non-harmful Procedures:

The investigator should use no research operation that may harm the child either physically or psychologically. The investigator is also obligated at all times to use the least stressful research operation whenever possible. Psychological harm in particular instances may be difficult to define; nevertheless its definition and means for reducing or eliminating it remain the responsibility of the investigator. When the investigator is in doubt about the possible harmful effects of the research operations, consultation should be sought from others. When harm seems inevitable, the investigator is obligated to find other means of obtaining the information or to abandon the research.

Principle 2. Informed Consent:

Before seeking consent or assent from the child, the investigator should inform the child of all features of the research that may affect his or her willingness to participate

and should answer the child's questions in terms appropriate to the child's comprehension. The investigator should respect the child's freedom to choose to participate in the research or not by giving the child the opportunity to give or not give assent to participation as well as to choose to discontinue participation at any time. Assent means that the child shows some form of agreement to participate without necessarily comprehending the full significance of the research necessary to give informed consent. Investigators working with infants should take special effort to explain the research procedures to the parents and be especially sensitive to any indicators of discomfort in the infant.

In spite of the paramount importance of obtaining consent, instances can arise in which consent or any kind of contact with the participant would make the research impossible to carry out. Nonintrusive field research is a common example. Conceivably, such research can be carried out ethically if it is conducted in public places, participants' anonymity is totally protected, and there are no foreseeable negative consequences to the participant.

Principle 3. Parental Consent:

The informed consent of parents, legal guardians or those who act in loco parentis (e.g., teachers, superintendents of institutions) similarly should be obtained, preferably in writing. Informed consent requires that parents or other responsible adults be informed of all the features of the research that may affect their willingness to allow the child to participate. Not only should the right of the responsible adults to refuse consent be respected, but they should be informed that they may refuse to participate without incurring any penalty to them or to the child.

Principle 4. Additional Consent:

The informed consent of any persons, such as school teachers for example, whose interaction with the child is the subject of the study, should also be obtained. As with the child and parents or guardians informed consent requires that the persons interacting with the child during

with the research. Anonymity often is achieved through the practice of assigning numbers to the subjects and then using these numbers instead of names during the analysis of the data.

Finally, all research psychologists have some ethical responsibilities that go beyond the protection of their subjects. For example, scientists who report data that may be controversial or that may affect social policy decisions have an obligation to describe the limitations and degree of confidence they have in their findings. In addition, investigators should normally provide their research subjects with some gen-

TABLE 3-1 ● (*Continued*)

the study be informed of all features of the research which may affect their willingness to participate.

Principle 5. Incentives:

Incentives to participate in a research project must be fair and must not unduly exceed the range of incentives that the child normally experiences. Whatever incentives are used, the investigator should always keep in mind that the greater the possible effects of the investigation on the child, the greater is the obligation to protect the child's welfare and freedom.

Principle 6. Deception:

Although full disclosure of information during the procedure of obtaining consent is the ethical ideal, a particular study may necessitate withholding certain information or deception. Whenever withholding information or deception is judged to be essential to the conduct of the study, the investigator should satisfy research colleagues that such judgment is correct. If withholding information or deception is practiced, and there is reason to believe that the research participants will be negatively affected by it, adequate measures should be taken after the study to ensure the participant's understanding of the reasons for the deception.

Principle 7. Anonymity:

To gain access to institutional records, the investigator should obtain permission from responsible authorities in charge of records. Anonymity of the information should be preserved and no information used other than that for which permission was obtained.

Principle 8. Mutual Responsibilities:

From the beginning of each research investigation, there should be clear agreement between the investigator and the parents, guardians or those who act in loco parentis, and the child, when appropriate, that defines the responsibilities of each. The investigator has the obligation to honor all promises and commitments of the agreement.

Principle 9. Jeopardy:

When, in the course of research, information comes to the

investigator's attention that may jeopardize the child's well-being, the investigator has a responsibility to discuss the information with the parents or guardians and with those expert in the field in order that they may arrange the necessary assistance for the child.

Principle 10. Unforeseen Consequences:

When research procedures result in undesirable consequences for the participant that were previously unforeseen, the investigator should immediately employ appropriate measures to correct these consequences, and should redesign the procedures if they are to be included in subsequent studies.

Principle 11. Confidentiality:

The investigator should keep in confidence all information obtained about research participants. The participants' identities should be concealed in written and verbal reports of the results, as well as in informal discussion with students and colleagues.

Principle 12. Informing Participants:

Immediately after the data are collected, the investigator should clarify for the research participant any misconceptions that may have arisen. The investigator also recognizes a duty to report general findings to participants in terms appropriate to their understanding.

Principle 13. Reporting results:

Because the investigator's works may carry unintended weight with parents and children, caution should be exercised in reporting results, making evaluative statements, or giving advice.

Principle 14. Implications of Findings:

Investigators should be mindful of the social, political and human implications of their research and should be especially careful in the presentation of findings from the research. This principle, however, in no way denies investigators the right to pursue any area of research or the right to observe proper standards of scientific reporting.

Source: Excerpted from "SRCD Ethical Standards for Research with Children," 1990, *SRCD Newsletter, Winter,* pp. 5–6.

eral information about the final results of the research, as an acknowledgment of the importance of the subjects' contribution to the overall research process.

✔ *To Recap...*

Research with human subjects always involves a balance between the potential value of the findings and any risks that may be involved. The most common categories of risk include physical and psychological harm to the child and violations of privacy. Certain safeguards are now routinely used. They include prior review of research plans by other scientists; obtaining the informed consent of parents, teachers, and children involved in a research study; elimination of any experimentally produced negative feelings through extra procedures; debriefing as to the purpose of the research; and strict maintenance of confidentiality. Additional ethical requirements include taking some responsibility for the social ramifications of research findings and providing feedback to participants about the outcome of the research project.

CONCLUSION

Our primary reason for devoting a chapter to issues of methodology is to emphasize the fact that effective research methods are crucial for advancing scientific knowledge. Uncovering new scientific truths involves a number of essential components. It begins, of course, with the perceptive insights of an astute researcher. But even the most astute researcher cannot answer important theoretical questions without adequate research techniques. For example, the existence of atoms and genes was first proposed many years ago. But only with the aid of such technological advances as the particle accelerator and the electron microscope have scientists actually been able to confirm these predictions. Similarly, psychologists have long debated the physical and cognitive capabilities of the newborn. Only in the past 2 decades, however, have research techniques been developed that permit many of these questions to be studied scientifically.

Another important reason for introducing methodological issues at this point is that later chapters present a good deal of research evidence to support descriptions of developmental progress and processes. This evidence, for the most part, has been gathered through the methods described here, so it is helpful to approach it with an understanding of the differences between the correlational and experimental designs, longitudinal and cross-sectional experiments, and so on. Moreover, these basics prepare the way for the more specific techniques and procedures used in certain areas of study, which we describe as they come into play.

FOR THOUGHT AND DISCUSSION

1.   Psychologists study children using methods that are objective and quantifiable. *Can you think of ways children are studied by other kinds of scholars that do not display these characteristics? What do you think are some advantages of each approach?*

2.   We gave an example of a study that showed that children's reading level and their viewing of "Sesame Street" were correlated, but that could not indicate whether one variable influenced the other. *Suggest some aspects of children's behavior that might correlate with their viewing of violence on TV. What are some possible explanations for these correlations?*

3.   Studies of the life course indicate that major historical or political events can affect the development of an entire generation. *Can you think of any major events of this sort that have affected the life course of people your age? How might your life have been different had they not occurred?*

4.   Comparative developmental research involves the use of nonhuman species. One ethical requirement of research with humans is that subjects' participation is voluntary. *Does research with animals violate the spirit of this requirement? Do you think 3-year-olds can give informed consent for research participation?*

Part Two

BIOLOGICAL AND PHYSICAL DEVELOPMENT

Chapter 4

GENETICS: THE BIOLOGICAL CONTEXT OF DEVELOPMENT

*N*ow that we have laid the historical, theoretical, and methodological groundwork for the science of child psychology, we can begin to examine the development of the individual child. But where do we begin? People often think of birth as the beginning of development. However, we will see in the next chapter that crucial aspects of development take place while the fetus is developing inside the mother. Perhaps conception, then, is the appropriate starting point. But conception, too, is a continuation rather than the initiation of the developmental process. Even before the sperm from the father fertilizes the egg of the mother, important genetic processes have been at work in both parents that will have major impact on the child. To understand the development of the child, then, we must begin with the child's parents and how they pass their heredity onto the next generation.

Furthermore, hereditary transmission is only one part of the genetics story. Our genes guide, regulate, and affect our development throughout our lives. Precisely how genes affect development and exactly how much of our behavior genes control are major issues facing researchers. Indeed, the role that genes play in human development is one of the most exciting and controversial issues in modern child psychology. Unlike most of the other topics that we will discuss, genetics crosses into the fields of biology and biochemistry. Thus, in order to explain what psychologists mean when they say that genes "cause" behavior, in this chapter we focus on some key concepts from those fields. But we emphasize the psychological perspective, because psychologists are interested primarily in how genetic processes affect behavior. First, we discuss the basic concepts behind gene functioning. Then we consider genetic disorders and why they occur. Third, we address the relation between genes and behavior. Finally, we discuss new ideas about how genes turn on and off to affect behavioral development and how genes and environment interact to produce the behavior that we see.

MECHANISMS OF INHERITANCE

How does a single fertilized cell "know" to develop into a person rather than a chimpanzee? How does a baby inherit the characteristics of his or her parents—black or white skin, red or brown hair, tall or short stature? How does a single cell give rise to trillions of other cells that become different parts of the body—the fingers, the heart, the brain, the skin, and so on?

Such questions lie at the heart of the puzzle of inheritance, a puzzle that has engaged thoughtful people since the beginning of time. At last, the fascinating workings of human genetic processes are becoming understood, and this understanding is yielding answers. The field of genetics has experienced tremendous growth over the past few decades, and our knowledge of genetic mechanisms has grown accordingly. Not surprisingly, this knowledge involves an account of life itself.

Cell Division

Perhaps the most fundamental, and certainly the most common, genetic activity is the reproduction of cells. Indeed, in the time that it takes you to read this sentence, more than 100 million cells in your body will reproduce themselves (about 25 million cell divisions occur per second) (Curtis, 1983).

All cells have three major subdivisions, shown in Figure 4-1: the nucleus; the cytoplasm, which surrounds the nucleus; and the cell membrane, which encases the cell. The genetic material, DNA, lies in the nucleus and is organized into chemical strands called **chromosomes**.

There are many specialized types of cells, but here we concern ourselves with two broad types—body cells and germ cells. Body cells, by far the larger category, contain 23 pairs of chromosomes, 46 in all, in their nuclei. Germ cells (sperm and ova) contain 23 single chromosomes. This difference is the key to how each type of cell reproduces.

Body cells reproduce by a process called **mitosis**. Through this process, diagramed on the left-hand side of Figure 4-2, each parent cell produces two identical "child" cells. The body cell prepares for mitosis by doubling in size, and each of its 46 chromosomal strands duplicates itself, producing two identical strands connected near their centers, like an X (4-2a). During mitosis, these joined strands line up at the cell's midline (4-2b), and each X breaks apart into two identical chromosomal strands. One set moves toward one side of the cell; the other set, toward the other side. A nucleus forms around each set of chromosomes, and finally the cell itself divides in two (4-2c). With mitosis complete, each new cell contains 46 chromosomes and is genetically identical to the parent cell.

Almost all cells reproduce by mitosis. The only exception is germ cells. Because germ cells—a sperm and an ovum—combine at conception, each can have only 23 chromosomes, so that the cell they combine to form will have 46. To maintain the required number of chromosomes, germ cells reproduce through a process called **meiosis**, diagramed on the right-hand side of Figure 4-2.

Meiosis begins with a specialized sex cell that has 46 chromosomes, or 23 pairs. As in mitosis, the 46 chromosomes duplicate themselves into two strands that remain attached, like an X (Figure 4-2a). But then a different and significant event occurs. Each of the 46 X-shaped bodies pairs up with its partner (Figure 4-2d—remember, the 46 chromosomes comprise 23 pairs) and, by a process called **crossing over**, exchanges genetic material with it. The process of crossing over is crucial to each person's uniqueness. Because of this exchange of material, the two strands that form each X are no longer identical, and neither are the pairs of Xs. Crossing over virtually assures that no two people (unless they develop from the same fertilized egg, as identical twins do) will ever be exactly the same. Figure 4-3 is a greatly simplified representation of such an exchange.

As in mitosis, the Xs then line up at the midline of the cell, but they do not yet break apart. Instead, one X from each pair migrates toward one pole of the cell,

Chromosome
One of the bodies in the cell nucleus along which the genes are located. The nucleus of each human cell has 46 chromosomes, with the exception of the germ cells, which have 23.

Mitosis
Replication of the chromosomal material of the cell nucleus followed by cell division, resulting in two identical cells.

Meiosis
Replication in sex cells, which consists of two cell divisions, resulting in four germ cells that are all genetically different.

Crossing over
The exchange of genetic material between chromosomes during meiosis.

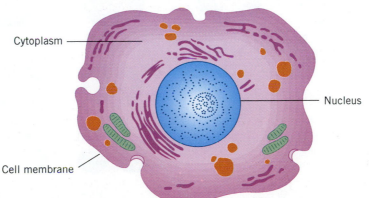

Figure 4-1 Major subdivisions of the cell.

Cytoplasm

Nucleus

Cell membrane

and its partner migrates toward the other. Nuclei form, and the cell divides in two (Figure 4-2*e*). When this first stage of meiosis is complete, the two resulting cells are genetically different from each other.

In the next stage of meiosis, the chromosomes in each body cell again line up at the cells' midline (Figure 4-2*f*). Now the Xs break apart, and again new cells are formed. Each of the four cells that results from meiosis has only 23 chromosomes. Because crossing over occurred, each leg of each X is unique, which makes each of these germ cells different from one another, as well as from the parent cell (Figure 4-2*g*). When one of these germ cells combines with a germ cell from a mate, the new cell is the mold for all the trillions of other body cells that will develop.

Think about the fact that every one of the 23 chromosomes in a germ cell probably represents a one-of-a-kind combination of genetic material and that these 23

Figure 4-2   Mitosis and meiosis. Mitosis results in two cells identical with the parent cell and with each other (left). Meiosis results in four cells different from the parent cell and from each other (right). Adapted from *Biology: Exploring Life* (p. 152) by G. D. Brum & L. K. McKane, 1989, New York: John Wiley & Sons. Copyright © 1989 by John Wiley & Sons, Inc. Adapted by permission of John Wiley & Sons, Inc.

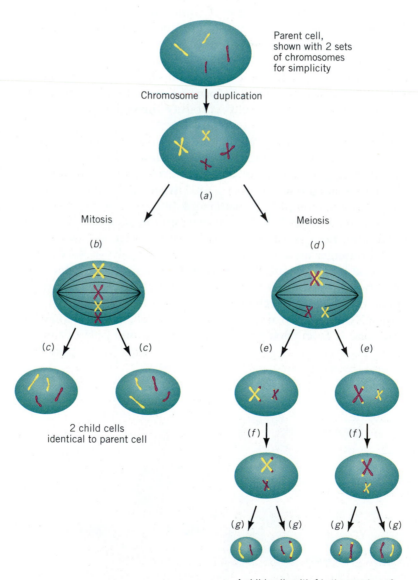

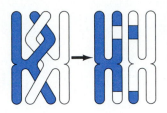

Figure 4-3 Crossing over results in the exchange of genetic material. After the crossover, all four strands are different. Adapted from *Biology: Exploring Life* (p. 44) by G. D. Brum & L. K. McKane, 1989, New York: John Wiley & Sons. Copyright © 1989 by John Wiley & Sons, Inc. Adapted by permission of John Wiley & Sons, Inc.

chromosomes must combine with another set of original chromosomes from the other germ cell to form the template for a new individual. This should help to make it clear why people come in so many sizes, colors, and shapes. To get a better idea of what chromosomes do, we "zoom in" on one next.

Inside the Chromosome

Although it was generally accepted, by the early 1940s, that the "stuff of inheritance" is carried on the chromosomes in units called **genes**, no one had ever seen a gene. Indeed, no one even had a very good idea of what one was or what it did. Research on viruses had suggested that a long and complicated molecule called **deoxyribonucleic acid (DNA)** was the carrier of genetic information. By the early 1950s, researchers had discovered that a remarkable constant holds across all cells of a given species: With the exception of the germ cells, each cell contains exactly the same amount of DNA as every other cell; germ cells carry exactly half the DNA of other cells. The big breakthrough in genetics came in 1953 when James Watson and Francis Crick reported that they had uncovered the structure of the DNA molecule (Watson & Crick, 1953). The tale of their discovery is one of the most exciting detective stories in modern science (Watson, 1968), and the discovery itself earned them the Nobel Prize in 1962. Most importantly, their findings opened the door for an understanding of the structure of the gene and how life reproduces.

Watson and Crick found that the DNA molecule has the structure of a double helix, much like the sides of a spiral staircase joined by rungs, as shown at the top of Figure 4-4. These rungs are composed of four bases: adenine (A), thymine (T), guanine (G), and cytosine (C). Each rung is called a *nucleotide* and consists of a linked pair of these bases. Only two types of pairings occur—adenine pairs with thymine and cytosine pairs with guanine—so the only rungs that occur are A–T and G–C. The rungs may appear in any sequence, and it is the sequence that comprises the coded information carried by the gene (Capecchi, 1994).

Since each nucleotide base can link to only one other base, each half-rung of the DNA molecule can serve as a blueprint for the other half. It is this feature that permits the chromosome to replicate itself during cell division. The chromosome "unzips" down the length of the staircase, breaking the links that connect the bases at the middle of each rung. The half-rungs then pair, base by base, with new material to form two new identical copies of the original DNA sequence, as shown at the bottom of Figure 4-4.

Just how are DNA, genes, and chromosomes organized? Earlier, we said that DNA is organized into chemical strands called chromosomes. In other words, each chromosome is made of DNA. The DNA is in turn made up of nucleotides; each nucleotide is a rung in a chemical staircase, as just shown. A gene is a particular section of DNA—a portion of a chromosome—made up of a number of nucleotides.

Some numbers will clarify these relations. Each body cell contains 23 pairs of chromosomes. All of these chromosomes together contain about 100,000 genes.

Gene
The unit of inheritance; a segment of DNA on the chromosome that can guide the production of a protein or an RNA molecule.

Deoxyribonucleic acid (DNA)
The chemical material that carries genetic information on chromosomes. Capable of self-replication, the DNA molecule is made up of complementary nucleotides wound in a stair-like, double-helix structure.

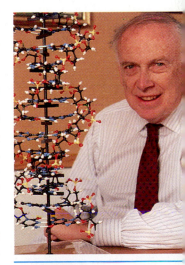

• James Watson received the Nobel Prize with Francis Crick for discovering the structure of the DNA molecule.

Figure 4-4   Structure and replication of DNA.

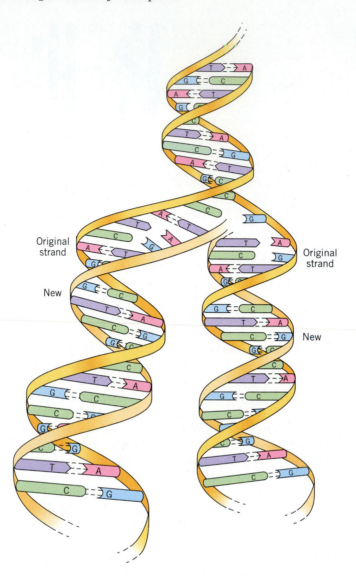

On average, a gene contains about 1,000 nucleotides, but some contain as many as 2 million. In all, each cell contains about 3 billion nucleotides. These numbers underscore our point about why each individual is unique. The crossing-over process of meiosis combined with the special mix of genes from the two parents makes the possibilities for unique combinations virtually limitless (Landegren et al., 1988).

Another interesting point involves the enormous amount of information stored by DNA. It is estimated that the DNA in each cell carries as much information as all the editions of the *Encyclopedia Britannica* published since 1768. Yet, according to estimates, a strand of DNA stretching from the earth to the sun (about 93 million miles) would weigh only half a gram.

The precise sequence of the nucleotides in a gene is extremely important. For example, 450 base pairs make up a gene that controls a characteristic of red blood cells. Only one base pair out of the 450 differentiates a person who has normal blood from one who suffers from the devastating blood disease, sickle-cell anemia. In some genes, the sequence of nucleotides is so rigidly specified by heredity that it is essentially a "familial fingerprint." So-called DNA fingerprinting has been used to convict murderers and rapists and to identify paternity of children (Jeffreys, Brookfield, & Semeonoff, 1992). But DNA fingerprinting has also served to free the innocent. In 1993, a man was freed after serving 9 years in prison for raping and killing a 9-year-old girl because DNA analysis of semen stains on the girl's clothes showed that he had not committed the crime (*Denver Post*, 1993). The number and precise sequence of nucleotides in the genes also supply the answer to the question posed earlier about how the cell "knows" to develop into a human rather than a chimpanzee. The sequence is especially critical because approximately 98% of human DNA is also found in the DNA of the chimpanzee (*Science*, 1988).

There are two kinds of genes—structural genes and regulator genes. The job of the *structural genes* is to guide the production of proteins, which serve many different functions in the body. The actual production task—a complex one that we will not consider in detail here—is actually carried out by various types of ribonucleic acid (RNA).

The job of *regulator genes* is to control the activities of other genes. Recall that in each individual, each body cell contains exactly the same chromosomal material, and hence the same genes, as every other cell. Normally, protein production by the overwhelming majority of genes in any particular cell is suppressed, so that the cells in a particular organ, like the heart, liver, or brain, only produce proteins that are appropriate for that organ. Regulator genes play a crucial role in this suppression (Beardlsey, 1991).

How do the regulator genes "know" what the specialized task of a cell is? How do they know that the products of a heart cell rather than a liver cell are required? Does the very first cell, the fertilized ovum, somehow contain the instructions for what each descendant cell should produce and repress? Or might cells, like people, "behave" in different ways depending on what is going on around them?

Fairly recently, scientists in the United States were able, for the first time, to split the 6-day-old embryo of a horse into two equal cell clusters. They reimplanted the two embryos into two separate adult females. If all of the instructions for these cells were determined in the fertilized ovum, the baby horses at birth should have been monsters—either a front half alone or a rear half (or a left or right side). However, both females gave birth to complete and normal colts.

Clearly, cells have the potential at early stages to develop in quite different ways. Like a complete person, a cell is influenced by its environment—other cells. Regulator genes turn the functioning of structural genes on and off depending on what is going on around them. The full story of gene regulation is not yet known, but how cells control protein production and how these controls change with development are among the most interesting questions that microbiologists study (Marx, 1992).

We have seen that genes produce proteins, but how do genes affect the physical structures and behaviors we actually observe? The earliest answers to this question came from an unusual source. Although modern technology has fostered breathtaking discoveries, our understanding of how genes function leans heavily on the discoveries of a man who had little more at his disposal than a garden and some pea plants.

Mendel's Experiments

The researcher who provided the first glimpse at the mechanism of inheritance drew his conclusions from careful observation of only the *results* of the processes we have outlined. He was Gregor Mendel (1822–1884), an Austrian monk who is recognized as the father of modern genetics. Based on his extensive work with pea plants, Mendel proposed a theory of inheritance in 1865.

Mendel wondered how pea plants pass on such characteristics as flower color to the next generation. To study this process, he mated purple-flowered and white-flowered plants. The historical view at the time held that the offspring is a mix of the parents' traits. Thus, Mendel should have expected that the resulting plants would be lavender-flowered. Surprisingly, however, all of the first-generation offspring had purple flowers. Had the white trait disappeared in these offspring? Mendel decided to mate the new purple-flowered offspring with each other. Now, one might expect that all of the second-generation plants would have purple flowers like the parent plants. Surprise again, because about one fourth of the second-generation offspring bore white flowers, whereas the remaining plants bore purple ones.

Through many similar experiments involving color and other characteristics, Mendel developed a theory to account for his observations. He hypothesized that each observable characteristic, or trait—such as color—is associated with the presence of two elements, now called genes, one inherited from each parent. Today, we call the observable trait the **phenotype** and the inherited elements the **genotype**. Because the observed trait was not a simple mix of influences from the two genes—purple-flowered and white-flowered pea plants do not produce lavender-flowered offspring—Mendel concluded that the gene from one parent must dominate the gene from the other parent.

Phenotype
The observable expression of a genotype.

Genotype
The genetic constitution that an individual inherits; may refer to the inherited basis of a single trait, a set of traits, or all of a person's traits.

Principles of Gene Transmission

To illustrate Mendel's theory, we will assume that each original white- or purple-flowered plant—we will call these the parent plants—had either two purple genes or two white genes, as diagrammed in Figure 4-5. Each "child" of a purple and a white mating must then possess one purple-flowered and one white-flowered gene. The "purple gene" from one parent must suppress the "white gene" from the other, however, because all of these child plants are purple.

Now things get interesting. The fact that each child plant carries both a *dominant* purple gene and a *recessive* white gene (a gene not expressed in the presence of a dominant gene) creates the opportunity for important variety in their offspring, the "grandchildren plants." Since each of the child plants can pass along only one of its two genes, four combinations can occur in the grandchild plants: purple from both parents; purple from parent 1 and white from parent 2; white from parent 1 and purple from parent 2; and white from both parents. If each of these four combinations has an equal chance to occur, and if the purple gene dominates whenever it is present, three fourths of the grandchildren plants will be purple, and one fourth will be white. This is exactly what Mendel observed.

It is perhaps as intriguing to think about the *process* of Mendel's discovery as the discovery itself. He simply observed some differences among pea plants, wondered what caused them, and then proceeded with a few straightforward experiments to make one of the great scientific discoveries of all time. Many such discoveries are based on everyday curiosity, hard thinking, and logic. As one of our students noted, "Mendel was just good at looking at things, wasn't he?"

Mendel's insights are captured in two principles. The *principle of segregation* states that each inheritable trait is passed on to the offspring as a separate unit. The *principle of independent assortment* asserts that these units are passed on independently of one another. Mendel confirmed this second concept in experiments in

• The pioneering work of Gregor Mendel with pea plants paved the way for the modern science of genetics.

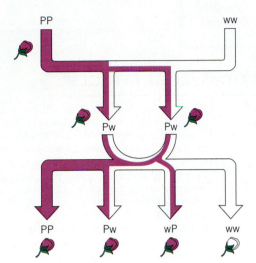

PP — ww

"Parent" plants have only purple or only white genes

Pw — Pw

"Child" plants received one gene from each parent; but since purple is dominant, all are purple

PP — Pw — wP — ww

Four combinations, or genotypes, are possible in "grandchildren" plants

Figure 4-5 The four combinations of genes that can result after two generations when the original mating occurred between a plant with two dominant genes for color and a plant with two recessive genes for color.

which he demonstrated that one trait, such as flower color, is inherited independently of another trait, such as stem length. A plant might be purple-flowered and long-stemmed, for example, or purple-flowered and short-stemmed.

Mendel's principles capture much of the truth about inheritance throughout the huge variety of life forms. For example, his discovery of dominant and recessive traits applies to many human characteristics, as well as to pea plants, as shown in Table 4-1. One commonly cited example is eye color; the gene for brown eye color is dominant, while that for blue eye color is recessive. Thus, a mother and father who both possess brown–blue gene combinations for eye color have brown eyes themselves and are 3 times as likely to produce a brown-eyed child as a blue-eyed child.

Revisions of Mendel's Principles

While decades of research have supported Mendel's basic ideas, new findings have qualified these ideas in several important ways. First, single traits can be affected by more than one gene. Intelligence and height are examples of phenotypes affected by many genes. The effect of these genes may differ in strength, however, with some genes exerting much stronger effects than others (Goldsmith, 1993; McLearn et al., 1991). Second, genes can display **incomplete dominance**, being neither entirely dominant nor entirely recessive. For example, sickle-cell anemia is passed on through a recessive gene. However, the blood of people who have a re-

Incomplete dominance
The case in which a dominant gene does not completely suppress the effect of a recessive gene on the phenotype.

TABLE 4-1 ● Some Common Dominant and Recessive Traits

Dominant	*Recessive*
Brown eyes	Blue, gray, or green eyes
Normal hair	Baldness (in men)
Dark hair	Blond hair
Normal skin coloring	Albinism
Normal color vision	Color blindness

EMERGENESIS: GENETIC "SPECIAL EFFECTS"

Having just read Mendel's theory, you might expect that individual genes simply combine, one by one, to make up the final sum of a person's traits. According to this thinking, the degree of phenotypic similarity between two individuals should depend simply on the number of genes they have in common.

However, look at Figure 4-6*a*. It shows an artist's sketch of the faces of two actors most people judge to be attractive. Now look at Figure 4-6*b*. It shows how children of this couple might look if facial features of the parents are passed on independently as Mendel showed. We can see that the faces of the offspring differ more than a little in attractiveness from the faces of the "parents." Clearly, there is something special about the *combination* of features in the actors' faces that makes us judge them to be attractive. Attractiveness, then, seems to emerge from special combinations of features, a phenomenon that is called *emergenesis*.

Genius, too, appears to reflect a special—and rare—combination of genes. If genius depended on the possession of a certain number of "intelligence" genes, we would expect genius and near-genius to run in families. But often this is not the case. Consider Carl Friedrich Gauss, generally regarded as one of the greatest mathematicians of all time. Born of uneducated parents, he had taught himself to read and to do arithmetic by the time he was 3 years old.

When Gauss was 10, the village schoolmaster thought to keep his large class occupied by writing down the integers from 1 to 100 and then finding their sum. Moments later he was startled to see little Carl at his desk with just a single number on his slate. "There 'tis" said the boy and then sat with his hands folded while the rest of the class toiled on. . . . The boy had at once perceived that the problem reduced to $(1 + 100) + (2 + 99) + \cdots + (50 + 51) = 50(101) = 5,050$. (Lykken et al., 1992, p. 1573).

Gauss appeared to have come from another planet with respect to his parents and even his 6 children, none of whom had a distinguished career. Other geniuses who stood out as unusual from their families include Jean-Jacques Rousseau (discussed in Chapter 1), Michael Faraday, William Shakespeare, and Benjamin Franklin.

Researchers today are studying emergenesis to identify what behavioral traits might be emergenic. One group of scientists has identified such traits as well-being, interest in arts and crafts, and self-adjustment as possible candidates (Lykken et al., 1992).

You've probably noticed that Michael Jordan and Nancy Kerrigan do not simply lie on a continuum of athletic ability. They stand out noticeably from their talented peers. Emergenesis helps us to think about why. Some casts of the genetic dice produce truly unique outcomes.

cessive gene for sickle-cell anemia and a dominant normal gene has some of the characteristics of the disease. Third, the environment can play a crucial role in the expression of genes. For example, the fur color of the Arctic fox changes with temperature from white in winter to brown in summer, so the fox is camouflaged in both the winter snow and the brown underbrush of summer. It is not known whether any human traits display such clear evidence of *environment–gene interaction*—that is, environmental influence on gene expression. Finally, Mendel assumed that each characteristic was passed on independently. In fact, some characteristics cluster together. For example, although color blindness and hemophilia are controlled by different genes, these two traits occur together more frequently

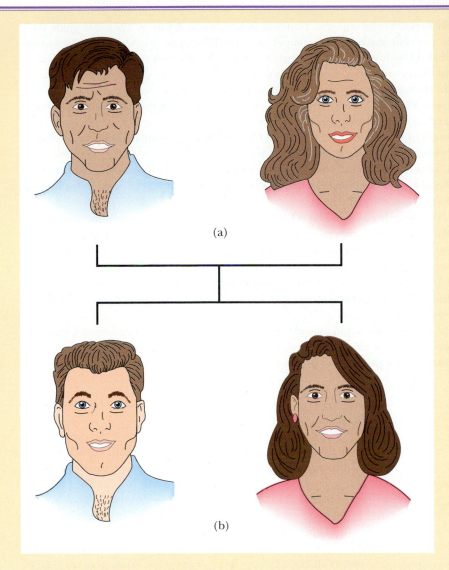

Figure 4-6 Artist's rendition of (a) two actors' faces and (b) how the faces of their offspring might appear if features of the parents were randomly recombined. From "Emergenesis" by D. T. Lykken, M. McGue, A. Tellegen, & T. J. Bouchard, Jr., 1992, *American Psychologist, 47,* 1569. Copyright by the APA.

than we would expect by chance. This clustering occurs because each chromosome carries many genes, and genes that lie close together on the same chromosome often "travel together" during the crossing-over process of meiosis. Genes that lie on different chromosomes *do* assort independently, however, and genes that lie on the same chromosome are increasingly likely to sort independently the farther apart they are.

While it is important to understand the relations between individual genes and the traits they produce, the whole plant or human being is made up of many, even thousands, of traits that often interact. Box 4-1 discusses why traits must be considered in patterns rather than individually.

✔ To Recap...

Genes carry hereditary information from one generation to the next. They also guide the reproduction of cells and the production of proteins throughout life. Cell reproduction occurs by mitosis in body cells and by meiosis in germ cells. Mitosis results in two identical cells with 46 chromosomes apiece, whereas meiosis produces four different germ cells, each with 23 chromosomes. When germ cells from the two sexes combine, they form a cell with the typical 46 chromosomes. This cell serves as the mold for the manufacture of trillions of identical cells through mitosis.

The "stuff of inheritance" is DNA, a double-helix-shaped molecule in the cell nucleus that contains billions of nucleotides. The nucleotides on a chromosome are subdivided into genes, some structural and some regulatory. Structural genes direct the production of proteins. Regulatory genes direct the rate and timing of structural gene activity, facilitating or supressing gene activity as required.

Mendel's research with pea plants led to the first scientific theory of inheritance, based on the concept of dominant and recessive genes. His principles of segregation and independent assortment are generally accepted today, although they have been qualified by several important exceptions: single traits may be affected by more than one gene; genes may be neither completely dominant nor completely recessive; the environment may influence phenotypic characteristics; and genes on the same chromosome may not assort independently.

While it is important to understand the particular relation between genes and traits, individuals are made up of many traits that interact; thus, we must also pay attention to special combinations of traits that can produce unexpected effects.

GENETIC DISORDERS

Although in the great majority of cases, a person's genetic makeup results in normal development, a small proportion of individuals have genetic disorders. Some human disorders are entirely hereditary and are passed along to offspring according to the same principles of inheritance that determine eye color and nose shape. Other disorders are not inherited but may result from errors during division of the germ cell in meiosis. Chromosomal abnormalities may also be produced by radiation, drugs, viruses, chemicals, and perhaps by the aging process. We limit our discussion here to genetic errors in the 22 pairs of chromosomes that play no role in determining sex, the **autosomes**. Our discussion of sex chromosome disorders appears in Chapter 15.

Autosomes
One of the 22 pairs of chromosomes other than the sex chromosomes.

Hereditary Disorders

Abnormal genes are passed along to offspring according to the Mendelian probabilities that hold for any trait. Whether these defective genes express themselves in the phenotype depends on whether they are dominant or recessive. If the defective gene inherited from one parent is recessive, the gene from the other parent usually assures normal functioning.

Dominant Traits

Dominant autosomal genes that cause severe problems typically disappear from the species, because the affected people usually do not live to reproduce. In a few cases, however, severely disabling dominant genes are passed on, because they do not become active until relatively late in the affected individuals' lives. These people may reproduce before they know that they have inherited the disease.

An example is **Huntington's chorea**. The age of onset of this disease varies, but it typically strikes people between about 30 and 40 years of age. Quite suddenly, the nervous system begins to deteriorate, resulting in uncontrollable muscular movements and disordered brain function. In the 17th century, three brothers came to the United States from England, all carrying the abnormal gene for Huntington's chorea. By 1965, more than a 1,000 affected individuals could be traced directly to this family. The disease became well known to many Americans when the folksinger Woody Guthrie died from it. Until recently, the children of a person stricken with Huntington's chorea had no way of knowing whether they, too, carried the gene and could pass it on to their offspring. Late in 1983, scientists discovered that the gene for Huntington's chorea is carried on chromosome 4. (Chromosomes are identified by numbers from 1 to 23.) Ten years later, in 1993, researchers located the exact gene responsible for the disease. Furthermore, a technique has been perfected for determining whether a person has inherited the gene (The Huntington's Disease Collaborative Research Group, 1993; Morell, 1993). Table 4-2 shows several hereditary diseases that are caused by single genes and the location of these genes on particular chromosomes.

Huntington's chorea
An inherited disease in which the nervous system suddenly deteriorates, resulting in uncontrollable muscular movements and disordered brain function. The disease typically strikes people between about 30 and 40 years of age and ultimately causes death.

Recessive Traits

Like Mendel's purple flowers, which showed no effect of the white color gene that they carried, parents can pass along problem recessive genes that have no effect on them. If both parents carry a recessive gene responsible for a disease, these genes can combine in the offspring to produce the disease, just as two brown-eyed parents can produce a blue-eyed child. It has been estimated that, on average, each of us carries four potentially lethal genes as recessive traits (Scarr & Kidd, 1983). But because most of these lethal genes are rare, it is very unlikely that we will mate with someone who has a matching recessive gene. Even then, the likelihood of a child's receiving both recessive genes is 1 in 4.

One class of diseases carried by recessive genes produces inborn errors of metabolism, which cause the body to mismanage sugars, fats, proteins, or carbohydrates (Schweitzer & Desnick, 1983). An example is **Tay-Sachs disease**, in which the nervous system disintegrates because of the lack of an enzyme that breaks down fats in brain cells. The fatty deposits swell, and the brain cells die. Tay-Sachs disease is rare in the general population, occurring in only 1 in 300,000 births. However, among Ashkenazic Jews, who account for more than 90% of the Jewish population of the United States, it occurs in 1 out of every 3,600 births. Infants afflicted with the disease appear normal at birth and through their first half-year. Then at about 8 months of age, they usually become extremely listless, and often by the end of their 1st year, they are blind. Most stricken children die by the age of 6. At present, there is no treatment for the disorder.

Tay-Sachs disease
An inherited disease in which the lack of an enzyme that breaks down fats in brain cells causes progressive brain deterioration. Affected children usually die by the age of 6.

A more encouraging story can be told about **phenylketonuria (PKU)**, a problem involving the body's management of protein. This disease occurs when the body fails to produce an enzyme that breaks down phenylalanine, an amino acid. As a result, abnormal amounts of the substance accumulate in the blood and harm the developing brain cells. Infants with PKU are typically healthy at birth but, if untreated, begin to deteriorate after a few months of life as the blood's phenylalanine level mounts. Periodic convulsions and seizures may occur, and the victims usually

Phenylketonuria (PKU)
An inherited metabolic disease caused by a recessive gene. It can produce severe mental retardation if dietary intake of phenylalanine is not controlled for the first several years of life.

TABLE 4-2 ● Some Hereditary Diseases and the Locations of the Genes on Chromosomes That Control Them

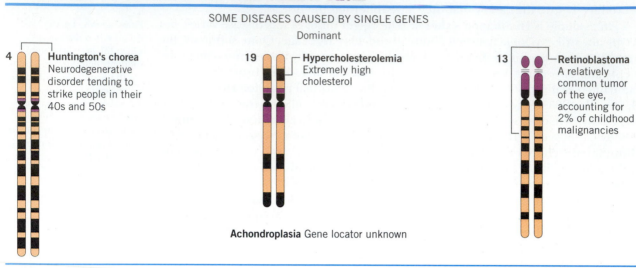

SOME DISEASES CAUSED BY SINGLE GENES

Dominant

4 Huntington's chorea
Neurodegenerative disorder tending to strike people in their 40s and 50s

19 Hypercholesterolemia
Extremely high cholesterol

13 Retinoblastoma
A relatively common tumor of the eye, accounting for 2% of childhood malignancies

Achondroplasia Gene locator unknown

Recessive

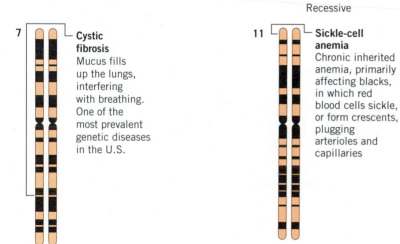

7 Cystic fibrosis
Mucus fills up the lungs, interfering with breathing. One of the most prevalent genetic diseases in the U.S.

11 Sickle-cell anemia
Chronic inherited anemia, primarily affecting blacks, in which red blood cells sickle, or form crescents, plugging arterioles and capillaries

12 Phenylketonuria
An inborn error of metabolism that frequently results in mental retardation

Congenital deafness
gene locator unknown

15 Tay-Sachs disease
Fatal hereditary disorder involving lipid metabolism often occuring in Ashkenazi Jews and French Canadians

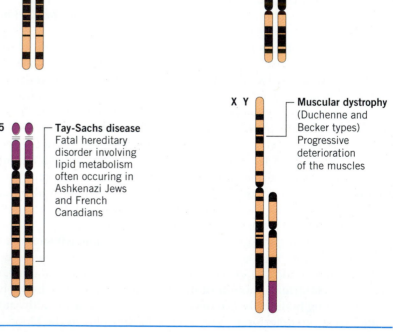

X Y Muscular dystrophy
(Duchenne and Becker types) Progressive deterioration of the muscles

become severely retarded, sometimes requiring institutionalization for the remainder of their lives.

Our understanding of how PKU disrupts normal metabolism has led to one of the rare victories of science over genetic abnormalities. Once the mechanism of the disease was discovered, special diets were developed that are low in phenylalanine and thus prevent its accumulation in the bloodstream. These special diets, begun shortly after birth, permit the affected child to develop normally. Because of the dramatic results of timely intervention in this disease, newborn babies are now routinely tested for PKU at birth through a simple urine-screening procedure.

It was thought that after the critical early-childhood period had passed, phenylketonurics could return to an unrestricted diet. However, recent evidence suggests that whereas a high phenylalanine level no longer produces obvious retardation in older children, there may be subtle effects on cognitive performance later in life (Diamond, 1993; Weglage et al., 1993; Welsh et al., 1990).

The lesson in the PKU story is that genes do not determine the fate of an individual with finality. How or whether a gene's influence is played out can depend on interactions with the environment.

A recessive genetic anomaly that does not involve disturbances in metabolism is **sickle-cell anemia (SCA)**. People who have inherited a gene for this recessive trait from both parents have red blood cells that do not contain normal hemoglobin, a protein that carries oxygen throughout the body. Instead, they contain an abnormal hemoglobin that causes red blood cells to become "sickled," as shown in Figure 4-7. These sickled cells tend to clog small blood vessels instead of easily passing through them as they normally would, thus preventing blood from reaching parts of the body. An unusual oxygen demand, perhaps brought on by physical exertion, may cause the sufferer to experience severe pain, tissue damage, and even death because of the inadequate supply of oxygen. Even people who have only one gene for SCA show some of the characteristics of this condition. (As we saw, this is one of the exceptions to Mendel's principles.) However, because most of their cells are normal, these individuals rarely suffer ill effects.

Sickle-cell anemia (SCA)
An inherited blood disease caused by a recessive gene. The red blood cells assume a sickled shape and do not distribute oxygen efficiently to the cells of the body.

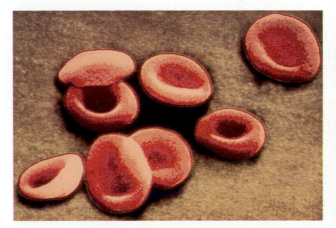 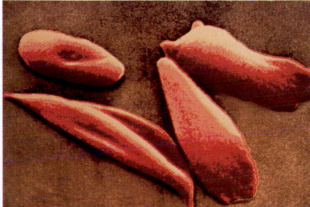

Figure 4-7 Scanning electron micrographs of red blood cells from normal individuals (left) and individuals with sickle-cell anemia (right).

About 9% of African Americans carry the recessive gene for SCA. Among the Bamba, a tribe in Africa, the incidence has been reported to be as high as 39%. Such a high rate of occurrence seems surprising from a Darwinian perspective, by which nonadaptive traits are weeded out through natural selection, because individuals who have two genes for SCA frequently die young and produce few children. How, then, could such a characteristic be preserved through evolution? The answer reveals a rare instance in which a gene is maladaptive for one purpose but adaptive for another. Scientists noted that the Bamba live in areas where the incidence of malaria is high, but Bamba children who carry the SCA gene are about half as likely to have malarial parasites as those who do not (Allison, 1954). Although it is unclear how this gene offers resistance to malaria, its presence appears to permit more carriers to grow up and have children, even though 1 in 4 will have SCA. Apparently, the negative effects of malarial parasites on reproduction are greater than the effects of carrying the SCA gene.

It is likely that many new findings are on the horizon of genetic research. Within the last few years, investigators have discovered that a type of Alzheimer's disease that runs in families is caused by an alteration in chromosome 14. In 1989, investigators announced success in their search for the gene for cystic fibrosis on chromosome 7. This is the most common genetic disorder among Caucasians. In 1993, a gene defect located on chromosome 21 was found to be responsible for amytrophic lateral sclerosis. This devastating nerve degenerative disease is known as Lou Gehrig's disease, after the well-known baseball player. It is also the disease that afflicts Stephen Hawking, the brilliant British physicist (Hooper, 1992; Loehlin, Willerman, & Horn, 1988; Marx, 1993). The genetic locus of many other diseases may be discovered in the near future as part of the Human Genome Project, discussed in Box 4-2. On average, a new gene is discovered every day, and by 1994, over 4,000 had been identified. (Gottesman, 1993; Nowak, 1994).

The discoveries of precise locations of genes that cause physical disorders has raised hope that we might also be able to find genes that account for behavioral disorders. Perhaps we will. There have been several reports in recent years of discoveries of chromosomal locations for alcoholism, aggressiveness, manic-depressive disease, schizophrenia, hyperactivity, and other behavioral disorders (Ackerman, 1992; Aldhous, 1993; Brunner et al., 1993; Hauser et al., 1993). Most recently, scientists have even reported evidence for localization of a homosexuality gene on the X (sex) chromosome (Hamer et al., 1993). But we must be cautious in interpreting these claims. Indeed, we regularly read about such reports in daily newspapers and magazines, because they are highly controversial (Horgan, 1993; Powledge, 1993). Scientific knowledge depends heavily on demonstrating that results are replicable, and additional studies have often not obtained the same findings (Mann, 1994). Some investigators believe that no single gene will ever be found that alone accounts for a complex behavior. Time will tell.

• African children who carry a recessive gene for sickle-cell anemia have a reduced likelihood of contracting malaria.

Structural Defects in the Chromosome

The genetic abnormalities we have been discussing are all passed along according to the regular principles of inheritance. However, genetically based abnormalities may also result from physical alterations in chromosomes. These "errors" often occur during meiosis in one of the parents, and they can involve any of the 22 autosomes or the sex chromosome. As mentioned, environmental hazards can also damage chromosomes.

THE HUMAN GENOME PROJECT

If scientists knew where each of the 100,000 genes were in the 46 human chromosomes, they would be in a better position to learn what each of these genes does. The potential benefits would be enormous. Health scientists, for example, would possess the tools to identify defective genes that produce thousands of inherited diseases. In many cases, these defects could be detected even before people showed their effects, and preventive treatment might be possible. Locating the genes on the chromosomes is referred to as *mapping the genome.*

But such mapping is only one step toward understanding. If scientists knew the exact sequence of nucleotides in each gene, they would be able to specify how the gene is defective. This knowledge would open up the possibility of correcting the defective sequence. Establishing the sequence of the 3 billion nucleotides in the DNA molecule is referred to as *sequencing the genome.*

The year 1989 was a banner year for these goals. That was the year in which the United States launched the Human Genome Project, headed by James Watson, one of the researchers who discovered the structure of the DNA molecule. This project has been likened to the Manhattan Project, which produced the atomic bomb, and the Apollo program, which placed the first man on the moon (Cantor, 1990; Watson, 1990). One official exclaimed: "It's going to tell us everything. Evolution, disease, everything will be based on what's in that magnificent tape called DNA" (Jaroff, 1989, p. 63).

The task is not only exciting but overwhelming. By mid-1993, about 1 million of the 3 billion nucleotides had been sequenced, and the capacity for sequencing had reached about 1 million per year. At this rate, it will take 3,000 years to sequence the whole genome (Collins & Galas, 1993; Jaroff, 1989; National Institute of Health, 1993; Roberts L., 1988).

But the hope is that new technology will make it possible to complete the job of mapping and sequencing the genome within 15 years at a cost to the U.S.

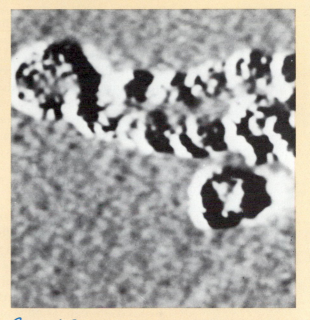

Figure 4-8 The first published high-resolution photograph of a strand of DNA, taken with a scanning tunneling microscope. From "Direct Observation of Native DNA Structures with the Scanning Tunneling Microscope" by T. P. Beebe, 1989, *Science, 243,* p. 371. Copyright 1989 by the AAAS. Reprinted by permission.

government of $3 billion. Automatic sequencers are being developed that can sequence between 100,000 and 1 million nucleotides per day. Furthermore, scientists in the San Francisco area reported in 1989 that they had taken the first clear photograph of DNA— seen in Figure 4-8—through a revolutionary technique. It may be possible in the future for scientists to read the "code of life" from photographs of this type (Beebe et al., 1989).

Down syndrome
A chromosomal disorder typically associated with an extra chromosome 21. Its effects include mental retardation and a characteristic physical appearance.

• Children with Down syndrome have physical features that include flattened faces and folds on the eyelids.

One of the most frequently observed effects of structural abnormality is **Down syndrome**, named after John Langdon H. Down, the physician who first described it. Infants afflicted with this disorder are moderately to severely retarded and share a distinctive appearance that includes a flattened face and folded eyelids. They also tend to have poor muscle tone, delayed responsiveness, and reduced emotional expression. Down syndrome was identified in 1957, marking the first time that a human disease had been directly linked to a chromosomal disorder. Babies with Down syndrome have an extra chromosome, usually an extra chromosome 21, as illustrated in Figure 4-9.

The likelihood that a couple will produce a child with Down syndrome increases dramatically with the age of the mother. Fewer than 1 in 1,000 babies of mothers under 30 have Down syndrome, whereas the incidence is 74 times greater for women between the ages of 45 and 49. (Still, only a small proportion of births to these older mothers involve Down syndrome.) The age of the father is not as important, but the father does contribute the extra chromosome in 20 to 30% of cases (Behrman & Vaughan, 1987).

Serious problems can also be caused by the deletion of material from a chromosome. For example, the deletion of a small amount of genetic material from chromosome 15 produces *cri du chat*, or "cry of the cat," syndrome. Affected infants, who have a catlike cry, suffer mental retardation and neuromuscular problems. Another example is Wilm's tumor, which occurs when genetic material is missing from one of the two copies of chromosome 11. Children who have this disorder have no iris, the colored part of the eye, and are more likely to have cancer of the kidney during infancy or early childhood. Some other factor or factors must also be involved, though, as 60% of the affected children do not develop cancer. There have even been cases in which one identical twin contracted cancer and the other did not (Yunis, 1983).

Given the billions of sperm cells generated by the male and the 2 million or so ova generated by the female, we should not be surprised at the occurrence of genetic

Figure 4-9   Chromosomes for a child with Down syndrome. Note the extra chromosome 21.

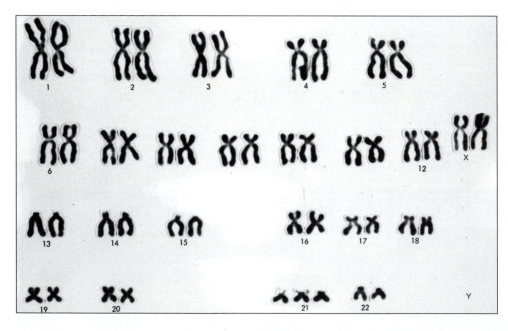

imperfections. Indeed, such variations, or *mutations*, are the driving force behind evolution. When the "errors" have, by chance, been adaptive, they have resulted in improvements in the species or even the inauguration of a new species. Still, the overwhelming majority of these "experiments of nature" are maladaptive. Fortunately, through a natural screening process, about 90% of all genetic abnormalities result in miscarriage rather than live birth. So although more than 5,000 single-gene abnormalities have been identified in humans (Capecchi, 1994; McKusick, 1992), only about 1% of all babies have detectable chromosomal abnormalities.

One important application of the rapid accumulation of knowledge about genetic disorders involves genetic counseling of prospective marital partners and parents. We discuss this topic in Chapter 5.

✔ *To Recap...*

Certain disorders are transmitted genetically on the autosomes according to Mendelian principles. Huntington's chorea is caused by a dominant gene that is expressed in all carriers, whereas Tay-Sachs disease, phenylketonuria, and sickle-cell anemia are caused by recessive genes expressed only when the individual inherits the defective gene from both parents. Other genetic diseases, such as Down syndrome, are caused by structural defects in chromosomes, which may occur during meiosis in one of the parents.

GENES AND BEHAVIOR

We have seen something of how genes operate inside the cell and how they affect external characteristics, such as eye and hair color. Occasionally, genes can even produce physical abnormalities and intellectual deficits, as in Down syndrome. But what do genes have to do with our understanding of normal psychology and the development of behavior? Some scientists would say "a great deal," whereas others would say "very little." As we have seen, virtually all psychologists believe that both genes and environment determine behavior, but they differ in which one they emphasize. The debate as to whether nature (genes) or nurture (experience and environment) is the main factor in producing individual differences in psychological development has been heated and prolonged.

It is helpful to make two distinctions when thinking about the nature versus nurture controversy. The first concerns the behavior in question. When we consider physical attributes, such as athletic ability and mechanical dexterity, it seems likely that genetic endowment exerts a strong influence. However, if we focus on more culturally defined behaviors, such as moral behavior and social skills, logic dictates that we recognize the influence of experience. Since genetic factors undoubtedly influence some behaviors more strongly than others, it is important to be precise about which behaviors we are discussing.

The second distinction is whether the focus is on similarities between people or their differences. No one would deny that genetic influences explain why people are different from frogs or chimpanzees in body structure, thinking and speaking ability, and so on. Can we therefore conclude that humans' intelligence and ability to communicate are genetically determined? It depends. While genetic differences help to explain psychological differences between species, they may or may not contribute to differences among members of the same species. It is these differences among people, individual differences, that are the focus of debate over whether heredity or environment is most influential.

Science is just beginning to develop adequate techniques to explore how much and in what way genes and environment interact to produce behavioral and developmental differences. Here we examine the methods modern researchers are using to study these questions and consider some of the preliminary answers that are emerging.

Methods of Study

How do researchers study the influence of genes on observable human traits, including behavior? As we will see, this is an exceedingly complex problem. People are not pea plants; scientists are not free to mate humans of their choice to see how the offspring will turn out. Thus, they have had to depend on observation, experiments of nature, and careful analyses of their data. The methods that researchers use include family studies, adoption studies, twin studies, and combinations of these approaches. These methods belong to the field of **behavior genetics**, the study of the role that genes play in individual differences in behavior.

Family Studies

Because children inherit 50% of their genetic constitution from each parent, similarities among family members are not surprising. The family-study approach looks for continuities of characteristics over generations of the same family. One famous example is Henry Goddard's study of the Kallikak family, published in 1912.

During the Revolutionary War, a soldier whom Goddard called Martin Kallikak (a pseudonym) had an illegitimate son by a retarded tavern maid. Later, Kallikak married a woman of normal intelligence from a respected family. Goddard traced five generations of Kallikak's offspring from these two lines. Of the 480 or so descendants of the tavern maid, he identified many as criminal, alcoholic, or "immoral" and 25% as retarded. In contrast, the 496 descendants from Kallikak's marriage were all intellectually normal, according to Goddard, and most occupied respected positions in their communities. Goddard attributed the differences between the two family lines to the different genetic endowments of Kallikak's two mates. Unfortunately, he ignored the vastly different environments, rearing practices, and experiences of the two lines of descendants. Indeed, difficulty in distinguishing between hereditary and environmental influences is inherent in this research method. As one investigator put it, lots of things run in families—cake recipes, for example. In other words, family resemblances do not necessarily result only from genetic influence.

Family studies can, however, suggest characteristics that might involve genetic factors and thereby encourage more definitive research. For example, researchers investigated several cases of specific dyslexia—certain reading and spelling difficulties in people who are otherwise normal or above normal in intelligence—that appeared among several generations of males in the same family. Chromosomal analyses revealed that a segment of DNA on one particular chromosome was more similar among the affected males than could be expected by chance alone. This similarity did not occur in unaffected family members, nor was a similarity found for any other chromosome among the affected males (Pennington & Smith, 1983).

We cannot assume as a result of these studies that all instances of dyslexia—or any other complex behavioral disorder—are affected by the malfunction of a single gene. Indeed, a location on another chromosome has been discovered that is also associated with the occurrence of dyslexia. Furthermore, not all people who have dyslexia have other family members who are affected. And among those affected in

Behavior genetics
A field of study that explores the role of genes in producing individual differences in behavior.

the same family, not all have identical genes in the suspected regions of the chromosomes that have been identified. It is likely, then, that several factors typically produce such problems (Barinaga, 1994; DeFries & Gillis, 1993; Smith, Kimberling, & Pennington, 1991). Still, family studies can help researchers focus on the genetic underpinnings of such behavior.

Adoption Studies

If Goddard could have arranged for some of Martin Kallikak's descendants on the illegitimate side to be raised in the homes of the married-family descendants, and vice versa, he could have better separated the influences of genes and environment. Essentially, this is the logic of studying the development of adopted children. The question is, will a child turn out to be more like the biological parent, with whom he or she shares a considerable genetic constitution, or more like the adoptive parent, with whom he or she shares an environment?

Twin Studies

Approximately 1 of every 85 births yields twins, providing investigators with an interesting opportunity to study the role of genetic similarity. Twins come in two varieties. **Identical twins** develop from the same fertilized egg and are called **monozygotic twins** (*mono*, "one"; *zygote*, "fertilized egg"). They have exactly the same genetic composition. **Fraternal twins** develop from two different eggs and are called **dizygotic twins** (*di*, "two"). Their genetic makeup is no more similar than that of any two children who have the same parents; on average, 50% of the genes of dizygotic twins are the same. Assuming that identical twins share environments that are no more similar than those shared by fraternal twins, any greater similarity between identical twins may be attributed to their greater genetic similarity.

Identical (monozygotic) twins
Twins who develop from a single fertilized ovum and thus inherit identical genetic material.

Fraternal (dizygotic) twins
Twins who develop from separately fertilized ova and who thus are no more genetically similar than other siblings.

Combined Twin-Study and Adoption-Study Approaches

There is one major problem with the twin-study approach: How can we be certain that a family treats a set of fraternal twins as similarly as a set of identical twins? Because identical twins look more alike, parents and others may expect them to act more alike. Such expectations may influence how people behave toward the children and, as a result, may affect how the children themselves behave. A method

• Identical twins, whose genetic makeup is precisely the same, are commonly employed in research designs examining the effects of genes on human development.

that avoids these problems involves twins who are separated early in life and raised in different adoptive homes. If genes play no role in creating individual differences in behavior, then identical twins raised apart should be no more alike than fraternal twins raised apart. Although this combined approach is the most desirable, it also is the most difficult to pursue, because so few twins are raised apart.

Influences of Genes on Psychological Characteristics

Scientists have applied these research methods to a number of human behavioral characteristics. In three areas, in particular, genes appear to play an important role: psychiatric disorders, intellectual performance, and personality.

Psychiatric Disorders

Schizophrenia—a disorder that produces confused thought and language, hallucinations, and unpredictable actions—has been of special interest, because it is the most frequently occurring severe psychiatric disorder. In fact, about 50% of all psychiatric patients in resident state and county hospitals are diagnosed as having schizophrenia (Gottesman & Shields, 1982).

Family studies have shown that children of mothers who have schizophrenia are about 10 times as likely as children of normal mothers to develop schizophrenia (Hanson, Gottesman, & Meehl, 1977). And people who have schizophrenia are 8 times more likely to have a close relative with the disorder than are those who do not have schizophrenia (Gottesman & Shields, 1982). Do these statistics reflect a genetic source of the disorder? Or does the greater incidence of schizophrenia in close relatives reflect a similarity in their environments?

Adoption studies have been particularly important in providing an answer to this question, because they compare genetically similar children raised in different environments. Children of schizophrenic mothers who are placed in adoptive homes are around 10 times as likely to develop schizophrenia as either the natural children of the adoptive parents or adopted children of normal mothers (Plomin, 1986). Thus, heredity seems to play a role in the development of the disease.

A large twin study also points toward genetic influences in schizophrenia. Investigators studied 164 pairs of identical male twins and 268 pairs of fraternal male twins who were veterans of World War II. The researchers developed *concordance rates* for schizophrenia in these twins—that is, rates at which schizophrenia developed in both members of a pair of twins. The concordance rates were 30.9% for identical twins and 6.5% for fraternal twins (Kendler & Robinette, 1983).

Whatever the effect of genes on the development of schizophrenia, however, heredity cannot be the whole story. If it were, identical twins would be 100% concordant for schizophrenia, and fraternal twins would be 50% concordant; we have seen that this is not the case. Furthermore, schizophrenic mothers produce schizophrenic children only about 1 time in 10. It is clear, then, that environmental factors also play a role (Holzman & Matthysse, 1990).

Less extreme psychiatric disorders, such as depression and the cyclic swings between moods that occur in bipolar disorder (manic depression) have also been linked to genetic influences. Relatives of patients affected with these disorders (called *affective disorders*) are about 9 times as likely to have similar problems as other people (Plomin, 1986). Moreover, there is a strikingly higher concordance for these affective disorders among identical twins than fraternal twins—around

65% concordance for identical twins and 21% for fraternal twins (Plomin, Owen & McGuffin, 1994).

Intellectual Performance

Whereas some mental disorders may not show up until adolescence or early adulthood, intellectual performance can be assessed in infancy. For this reason, and because standardized measures of intellectual functioning are so readily available, more studies have been carried out on the genetic basis of individual differences in intelligence than on any other psychological characteristic.

Family, adoption, and twin studies have all been used to investigate this issue. The evidence from all these studies paints a fairly clear picture—there are similarities in the intelligence of genetic relatives that cannot be entirely accounted for by similarities in their environments. In fact, based on all the available data, it is estimated that approximately 50% of the differences among people on IQ tests may be attributable to genetic factors (McGue et al., 1993; Plomin et al., 1994). (This is *not* the same as saying that 50% of a particular person's intelligence is determined at birth. We discuss this issue in more detail in Chapter 10.)

Table 4-3 summarizes more than 200 studies of identical and fraternal twins raised in their own homes and provides an example of the findings that have been reported. For every measure of intelligence or achievement, identical twins were more similar than fraternal twins. Additional evidence that genetics plays a significant role in intellectual development comes from studies using the combined twin-adoption method. We describe these studies in Chapter 10.

It is important to emphasize that the evidence for genetic influences on intellectual performance, as well as on other attributes, concerns the average *relation* between performances of individuals and not the absolute *level* of those performances.

TABLE 4-3 ● Average Correlations from Several Twin Studies of Various Abilities

		Average Correlation	
Trait	Number of Studies	Identical Twins	Fraternal Twins
Ability			
General intelligence	30	.82	.59
Verbal comprehension	27	.78	.59
Number and mathematics	27	.78	.59
Spatial visualization	31	.65	.41
Memory	16	.52	.36
Reasoning	16	.74	.50
Clerical speed and accuracy	15	.70	.47
Verbal fluency	12	.67	.52
Divergent thinking	10	.61	.50
Language achievement	28	.81	.58
Social studies achievement	7	.85	.61
Natural science achievement	14	.79	.64
All abilities	211	.74	.54

Source: Adapted from "Heredity and Environment: Major Findings from Twin Studies of Ability, Personality and Interests" by R. C. Nichols, 1978, *Homo, 29*, Table 1, p. 163. Adapted by permission.

Studies have shown repeatedly that environment affects the level of intellectual performance as well, with more intellectually stimulating home conditions generally producing higher IQ scores (e.g., Scarr & Weinberg, 1983). Thus, we can say that the IQ scores of identical twins are typically more similar than the IQ scores of nontwins but that the scores of all these people will be higher if they are raised in intellectually stimulating environments.

Personality

Personality refers to consistency in an individual's behavior in different situations with regard to such characteristics as dominance, fearfulness, social openness, and sensation seeking. Identical twins are more similar in personality than fraternal twins, their correlations being about .25 higher than those for fraternal twins (Floderus-Myrhed, Pederson, & Rasmuson, 1980; Loehlin & Rowe, 1992; Nichols, 1978). Such findings suggest that genetics plays an important role in personality development.

This conclusion should not be surprising when we consider how evolution, and therefore heredity, might play a role in, say, fears. Certain fears may be important for survival. Fear of snakes, for example, is so common in the general population it is unlikely to have been always acquired through direct experience with snakes. And evidence indicates that at least some fears are more likely to be shared by identical twin adolescents and adults than by their fraternal twin counterparts. More than 400 twins were asked about a variety of fears, including fear of rats and snakes, dangerous places, harm to a loved one, and looking foolish in front of others. The fears reported by identical twins were more similar than those of fraternal twins, the correlation being about .25 higher (Rose & Ditto, 1983).

Anecdotes about the similarity of identical twins reared apart are almost eerie. Researchers related the following stories about two sets of identical twins who were reared apart and met for the first time as adults.

> . . . at their first adult reunion, [the identical twins] discovered that they both used Vademecum toothpaste, Canoe shaving lotion, Vitalis hair tonic, and Lucky Strike cigarettes. After that meeting, they exchanged birthday presents that crossed in the mail and proved to be identical choices, made independently in separate cities. (Lykken et al., 1992, p. 1565)
>
> Only 2 of the more than 200 individual twins reared apart were afraid to enter the acoustically shielded chamber used in our psychophysiology laboratory, but both separately agreed to continue if the door was wired open—they were a pair of [identical] twins. When at the beach, both women had always insisted on entering the water backwards and then only up to their knees. (Lykken et al., 1992, p. 1565)

Of course, coincidences do occur by chance, and we are more likely to find them when we look hard for them, as we might in twins. Furthermore, no one ever reports on all the behaviors that twins do *not* share. Still, the researchers quoted here did not find similar coincidences among the nonidentical twins reared apart, which suggests that, in fact, there is something to the observations they report.

Other behaviors that reflect personality, such as attitudes, beliefs, and the use of leisure time, also appear to be affected by genetic makeup. Investigators found that identical twins who were reared apart were more similar in their religious interests, attitudes, and values than fraternal twins raised apart. Genetic factors accounted for around 50% of the similarities between the twins (Waller et al., 1990). Even the relative likelihood of divorcing one's marriage partner seems subject to genetic influence. If one identical twin experiences divorce, the chance that the other twin will experience divorce is 6 times that for the general population. The likelihood falls to 2 times the population average for a fraternal twin. Of course, there is no such thing as a "divorce gene"; the increase in risk for divorce is probably related to personality characteristics affected by genetic inheritance (McGue & Lykken, 1992).

Geneticists estimate that about 50% of the differences in personality among people can be attributed to genetic differences (Bouchard, 1994). You may recall that this is about the same percentage as for differences in intelligence. These estimates reflect the much higher correlation between identical than fraternal twins for measures of IQ and personality. We saw in Table 4-3, for example, that the average correlation for "all abilities," a measure of intelligence, was .20 higher for identical twins than for fraternal twins. We also saw that, with regard to personality, the correlation for identical twins was about .25 higher than for fraternal twins.

Instead of looking at the difference in correlations, consider their absolute size. The correlation for "all abilities" is .74 for identical twins and .54 for fraternal twins. But it is lower for personality attributes: .52 for identical twins and .25 for fraternal twins (Nichols, 1978). These findings are typical. Whether we look at identical or fraternal twins, the correlation is consistently stronger for intelligence than for personality. How can we explain this?

Where intelligence is concerned, something *in addition to* heredity must be contributing to the similarities within sets of twins. That something must be environment. The twins' shared experience from the environment must affect their intelligence more than it affects their personalities (Holden, 1987; Scarr & Kidd, 1983).

Just how much does common experience within the environment affect personality then? A relevant finding involves children with different biological parents who are adopted into the same home. These children show only a small correlation in personality during early childhood. Later, rather than increasing as a result of the shared household, the correlation actually diminishes to near zero in adolescence (Scarr et al., 1981; Scarr, 1992). Does this mean that environment has very little effect on personality? Not at all.

> Growing up together in the same family does not make siblings similar in personality. This does not imply that family influences are unimportant. The point is that environmental influences that affect personality do not operate on a family-by-family basis but rather on an individual-by-individual basis ... even an event that affects every individual in the family [such as the death of the family dog] will not be experienced in the same manner by each individual. Thus, the shared event is really a nonshared experience. (Braungart et al., 1992, p. 46)

While it is commonly acknowledged that children from the same family may differ strikingly from one another, psychologists have only recently considered the issue of *nonshared environments*—the unique experiences that children have from objectively similar events (Emde et al., 1992; Goldsmith, 1993; Hoffman, 1991; Plomin & Daniels, 1987). Infants and children are not mere observers of what goes on around them. They select what interests them, interpret what is going on around them, and create their own internal reality (Scarr, 1993).

Even very young babies display personality differences, which may be forerunners of their later tendencies to experience events differently. Some are irritable and cry frequently, whereas others are placid and smile a lot. Some naturally cuddle, whereas others tense up, arch their backs, and give a sense of noncuddliness or even rejection. Some can quietly watch a mobile for many minutes, whereas others

TABLE 4-4 ● Mean Behavioral Scores for Motor Activity, Crying, Fretting, Vocalizing, and Smiling for Caucasian-American, Irish, and Chinese 4-Month-Old Infants

Behavior	American	Irish	Chinese
Motor activity	48.6	36.7	11.2
Crying (in seconds)	7.0	2.9	1.1
Fretting (% trials)	10.0	6.0	1.9
Vocalizing (% trials)	31.4	31.1	8.1
Smiling (% trials)	4.1	2.6	3.6

Source: From "The Idea of Temperament: Where Do We Go from Here" by J. Kagan, D. Arcus, and N. Snidman, 1993, in R. Plomin & G. E. McClearn (Eds.), *Nature, Nurture, and Psychology,* Washington D.C.: APA Publications.

need constant action to stay happy. These aspects of personality, which relate to emotional expressiveness and responsiveness, are referred to as *temperament*. Some aspects of temperament persist well into the early school years and may eventually form the basis for adult personality. (We take up this subject again in Chapter 12.)

Does genetic constitution influence temperament? Apparently it does, at least to some extent. As early as 3 months of age, and throughout the early years of life, identical twins are more similar in their attention, activity, and involvement in testing than fraternal twins (Braungart et al., 1992; Emde et al., 1992; Matheny, 1980).

An intriguing finding by Jerome Kagan and his colleagues suggests that genetic factors may influence differences in personality and practices between people of different nations. They studied how three groups of 4-month-old infants reacted to auditory, olfactory, and visual stimuli. As shown in Table 4-4, Chinese children were much less likely to cry and fret and produced much less motor activity than Caucasian-American or Irish babies (Kagan, Arcus, & Snidman, 1993). These findings support those from an earlier study of Asian-American and Caucasian-American newborn babies that showed the Caucasian infants to be more easily arousable (Freedman & Freedman, 1969). Kagan and his colleagues speculate that these differences in genetic predisposition may play a role in the tendency of Eastern cultures to adopt life philosophies more serene than those of the West. Regardless, the general idea that genetic differences might influence how people design their environments—and that these environmental designs in turn affect behavior in children—has been echoed by several authors. Once again, we see the complexity of the interplay between genetic and environmental influences on behavior (McGuffin & Katz, 1993; Plomin, Loehlin, & DeFries, 1985; Rowe, 1993).

✔ *To Recap...*

Psychologists have used four research strategies to study the influence of heredity on behavior—family studies, adoption studies, twin studies, and a combination of the twin study and the adoption study. In three areas in particular—certain psychiatric disorders, intellectual performance, and personality—evidence confirms that genes do play a significant role. Most convincingly, identical twins raised in different environments are more alike than fraternal twins who are raised together.

At the same time, studies have shown that the environment also influences these behaviors. Even identical twins, who have exactly the same genetic endowment, may differ in whether they develop a mental disorder, in their intellectual performance, and in their personalities. Behavior genetics studies have demonstrated that differences in how twins (and others) experience the same environment affect some of these traits more than others.

GENE TIMING AND GENE-ENVIRONMENT INTERACTIONS

Until recently, scientists believed that genes exert a fairly constant influence on development and that a person's genetic structure remains stable. These beliefs have come under intense scrutiny in the past several years, as researchers have increasingly turned their attention to how gene expression changes with development. One reason gene influences change is that genes themselves produce different amounts of proteins at different ages. A second reason is that environmental opportunities change as the child grows, which permits genetic influences to act in different ways at different ages. Recent research suggests still another reason to question traditional beliefs: Some genes may move around on the chromosome, altering even the basic genetic structure!

Changing Gene Actions and Developmental Pacing

An example of how gene influences change with development is the period of puberty, a time when hormonal changes initiate menstruation in females and the appearance of pubic hair and genital maturation in both sexes. Certain genes that had previously been "turned off" are "turned on" (by regulator genes) in adolescence. Another example involves physical aspects of human development, such as growth and height, that are characterized by spurts and plateaus. The rhythm of these life events is referred to as **developmental pacing**, a concept that raises important questions.

Developmental pacing
The rate at which spurts and plateaus occur in an individual's physical and mental development.

First of all, is pacing entirely regulated by genes, or does the environment play a role? Studies with identical twins have demonstrated striking coincidences in the timing of such events as the thinning and graying of hair, the hardening of nails, and the occurrence and even the position of dental cavities (Farber, 1981; Kallman, 1953). Yet in spite of the fact that these universal physical events follow a reasonably predictable schedule and tend to occur synchronously in identical twins, they are not free from environmental influence. For example, both nutrition and stress appear to affect the age of onset of menstruation in females (Katchadourian, 1977; Moffitt et al., 1992).

A second question, and one more interesting to psychologists, is whether spurts and plateaus similar to those for physical growth also occur in behavior—for example, in intellectual and temperamental development. Infants are only moderately consistent from one age to the next in how they perform on sensory and motor tasks or assessments of temperament, and the relative rankings of babies in a group often change. Psychologists have wondered whether these variations arise from inadequacies in the measurements themselves or differences in how quickly babies change. If real differences in the rates of change do occur, they may be due, in part, to genetically controlled differences in developmental pacing. And if this is the case, we should expect a greater similarity (more concordance) in the developmental spurts and plateaus of identical twins than in those of fraternal twins.

This interesting possibility has some support. Matheny (1983) studied the concordance of *change* in temperament for 300 identical and fraternal twins from 6 to 24 months of age. In general, profiles of change were more similar for identical

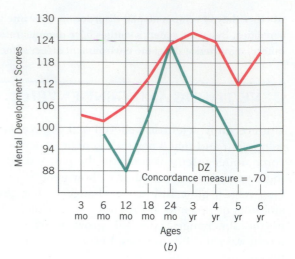

Figure 4-10 Concordance in IQ changes in (*a*) identical, or monozygotic (MZ), twins and (*b*) fraternal, or dizygotic (DZ), twins from 3 months to 6 years of age. The scales are different to accommodate different ranges of scores. The important point is that changes in performance are more similar for monozygotic twins. Adapted from "The Louisville Twin Study: Developmental Synchronies in Behavior" by R. S. Wilson, 1983, *Child Development, 54,* p. 301. Copyright 1983 by The Society for Research in Child Development, Inc. Adapted by permission.

than for fraternal twins. Matheny concluded that the changes were at least partially regulated by genetic factors. Wilson (1983, 1986a) reported on the intellectual development of almost 500 pairs of identical and fraternal twins who were monitored from the ages of 3 months to 15 years. Wilson developed a measure of concordance to describe the degree of similarity in these changes, which varied from 0 (no concordance) to 1 (perfect concordance). Figure 4-10 shows examples of how the developmental scores changed over this period; the concordance measure reflects the degree to which one twin's increases and decreases corresponded to like changes in the other twin. The identical twins were more concordant in their shifts in performance than the fraternal twins. The greater concordances for identical twins support the view that human development is subject to continuing genetic influence and that different genes are effective at different times (Cardon & Fulker, 1994; Fulker & Cardon, 1993; Plomin et al., 1993).

Demonstrating that genes influence behavior is one thing. Explaining how this happens is quite another. Indeed, identifying the "process" of genetic influence is one of the most important challenges facing modern science. At this time, no convincing theory explains how gene products—proteins—are related to behavior (Rowe, 1993). But psychologists have developed interesting ideas about how genes and the environment interact.

Genes and the Environment: Models of Interaction

It is important to remember that in spite of their impressive similarities, identical twins, with their identical genes, are not 100% concordant on any known behavioral trait. Clearly, to understand behavior, we must take a look at how genes and the environment cooperate. Here we examine models that attempt to explain how heredity and environment interact to affect behavior.

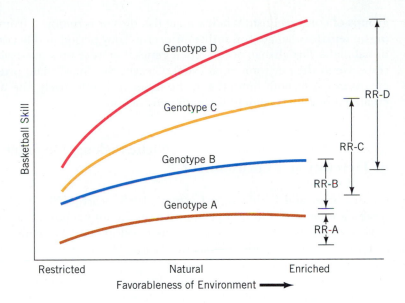

Figure 4-11 The reaction range concept, showing the simultaneous influences of genes and environment. Adapted from "Developmental Genetics and Ontogenetic Psychology: Overdue Détente and Propositions from a Matchmaker" by I. I. Gottesman, 1974. In A. D. Pick (Ed.), *Minnesota Symposia on Child Psychology*, Vol. 8, p. 60. Copyright 1974 by the University of Minnesota Press. Adapted by permission.

One model, proposed by Gottesman (1974), is essentially a limit-setting model. According to it, genes do not determine development precisely. Instead, they establish a **reaction range** within which development will occur. Environmental factors then determine where in this range we end up.

Figure 4-11 illustrates this model by showing the ranges of possible basketball skill that might exist for four genotypes. In each case, the reaction range (**RR**) is determined by genotype. The individual's position within the reaction range is determined by the environmental factors of experience and coaching, identified on the figure as restricted, natural (average), or enriched. Genotype A might represent a rare type of dwarfism. The flatness of the curve reflects the very limited variation in basketball prowess that can be produced in individuals of this type by even very dramatic differences in experience and coaching. Genotypes B and C might represent females and males, respectively, who are of average height and coordination for their genders. Their potential performance varies more than for Genotype A and depends more on how much opportunity they have had to play and how skilled their coaches have been. Finally, Genotype D might represent well-coordinated males who are taller than 6 ft 6 in. Their potential for outstanding performance is greater than that of any of the other groups, as is their range of potential.

There are two important points to note in Figure 4-11. First, the reaction ranges vary in size. Second, they overlap. Similar examples could be constructed for mathematics performance or musical ability or any of a number of other traits or skills. The reaction ranges might be larger or smaller for different behavioral traits, reflecting the varying roles of heredity and environment.

Gottlieb (1991, 1992) takes issue with the reaction range model in his *epigenetic* view of development. He argues that genes and the environment interact much more dynamically than the limit-setting model portrays. By referring to the "coaction of genes and the environment," he suggests that genetic influences are not set—the actions of the genes themselves can be influenced by the environment. Furthermore, genes and environment change and cooperate at every stage of development to determine behavior. One stunning example is found in small social

Reaction range
The amount by which a trait can vary as a result of experience within the limits set by genetic inheritance.

groups of coral reef fish. When a male fish dies or is removed from the group, one of the females changes sex and color over a 2-day period and becomes a fully functional male. The change occurs when genes that were previously silent "turn on" in response to the environmental event. Clearly, the "new" male presents a changed environment to both himself and the other fish. Effectively, the environment has created a new environment through gene action.

DEVELOPMENT IN CONTEXT: Niche-Picking: Ongoing Interactions of Heredity and Environment

Sandra Scarr and Kathleen McCartney (1983; Scarr, 1988, 1992, 1993) have suggested a somewhat different perspective on the interaction between genes and the environment, one that also changes as development proceeds. Their model describes three basic relations—passive, evocative, and active—through which genotype and the environment work together to support behavior.

A *passive* relation exists when the child's environment is created mainly by the parents. Because the parents and the child usually have very similar genotypes, the environment created by the parents is usually consistent with and supportive of the child's genotype. For example, musically inclined parents are likely to have musically inclined children, and they are likely to provide a "musical" home for their children.

An *evocative* relation exists when the child evokes certain responses from others (recall Bronfenbrenner's notion of developmentally instigative behaviors, discussed in Chapter 2). These responses form a part of the child's environmental context, which is generally consistent with the child's genotype, as he or she plays an active part in creating it. For example, a happy and gregarious baby is likely to elicit smiling, laughing, and similar signs of friendliness from others.

Finally, an *active* relation exists when a child engages in niche-picking. According to this theory children drift toward "niches" in the environment—the library, the athletic field, the rock concert—that reflect their own interests and talents and are therefore in accord with their genotypes.

This model does not downplay the importance of the environment. Rather, it views the environment as enhancing the child's genetic predispositions through

• According to Scarr and McCartney's model, niche-picking occurs when children choose environments that reflect and support their genetic predispositions.

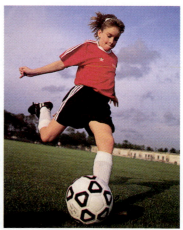

each of the three relations. The model helps explain two interesting findings: 1) nonbiological siblings who are raised in the same home are more similar to one another in the early years than in adolescence, and 2) the psychological characteristics of an adopted child become increasingly similar to those of the biological mother and less similar to those of the adoptive mother. These findings may result from the fact that the rearing parents have substantial control over the children's environment in the early years, thereby producing some uniformity in the experience of siblings. As the children grow older, however, they become increasingly able to choose their own environments and experiences. If their choices are affected partly by the gene pool they share with their biological parents, these environments will support their genotypes and make them behave less like one another and more like their genetic parents (Greenfield & Childs, 1991; Plomin & DeFries, 1985; Scarr & Weinberg, 1983).

The models just described emphasize a point already made: The central question about heredity and environment is not which is more important but how both interact as a child develops. A little thought reveals that the interaction can become quite complex. As we saw earlier, even a cell's function depends on its "environment." Suppose increases in stress around final exam time affect the hormones circulating in your bloodstream, changing the environment of certain brain cells. The cells' functioning is affected, along with any influences they have on behavior. At this level of complexity, it becomes very difficult to say what is cause and what is effect.

Recent discoveries may complicate the picture even more. One of the things scientists thought they could depend on was that genes would stay in the same place on the DNA molecule. After all, their position on the molecule affects how they are turned on and off and how they affect other genes. However, even this assumption has been abandoned. Although her findings were ignored for 3 decades, Barbara McClintock received the Nobel Prize in 1983 for her discovery that genes can change their location and function on the DNA molecule. To our knowledge, no one has incorporated this information about "jumping genes" into theories of behavior. However, it would not be surprising if links between behavioral and environmental phenomena and changes in gene location were found in the not-so-distant future.

✔ *To Recap...*

Human physical development, and perhaps other aspects of development, is characterized by spurts and plateaus that result from the activation of certain genes only at certain times. The pattern by which this activation occurs—known as developmental pacing—is more synchronous in identical twins and so shows genetic influence. Nevertheless, environment also plays a role.

Various models address how genes and the environment interact to affect behavior. Gottesman proposed a limit-setting model by which genes set a reaction range, and environmental factors determine the final outcome. Gottlieb suggests an interactive model whereby genes and environment affect one another to cooperatively affect behavior. Scarr and McCartney suggested a third model by which children's behavior is influenced by three relations between genotype and environment: the passive relation, the evocative relation,

and the active relation. Gene–environment interactions are complex and may be complicated further by findings indicating that the organization of genes on the DNA molecule may change over time.

CONCLUSION

Research into the effect of genes on behavior is very new, and so our conclusions here must be somewhat more tentative than they will be for other topics. Still, two general conclusions appear to be relatively sound.

The first is that increasing our understanding of genetic processes is both crucial and difficult. As the research reported in this chapter clearly indicates, genetic mechanisms play an important role both in the transmission of our ancestors' heritage and in the everyday regulation of our development and functioning. Yet it seems highly unlikely that complex human traits such as intelligence and personality will ultimately be attributable to the functioning of a single gene or even a few genes. Although the malfunction of a single gene (e.g., the gene responsible for PKU) can do enormous damage in a sphere such as intelligence, normal intellectual activity may well depend on the adequate functioning of hundreds of genes. (A car, after all, requires thousands of parts to function normally, but it takes only a malfunctioning carburetor to radically impair automotive functioning.) Thus genes affect behavior but not in a simple way (Plomin, 1993).

The second conclusion is that genetics will not give the whole answer. The same research that reveals genetic processes in many aspects of development also indicates limits to the influence of these inborn factors. Both the environment and experience are major determinants of human behavior in every area and at every point in development.

Perhaps the best way to think about the nature versus nurture issue, then, is to keep in mind the fact that any genetic process occurs within an environmental context. We will not completely understand such processes by studying them in isolation. Similarly, we will not fully understand environmental factors without taking into account the genetic and hereditary bases of behavior. Thus the only reasonable course of action would seem to be to grant the important contributions of both heredity and the environment and then move ahead with the task of learning how they interrelate to influence human behavior and human development.

FOR THOUGHT AND DISCUSSION

1.   We mentioned that genes may play a larger role in some behaviors than in others and that this issue has sometimes been a source of scientific controversy. *Which do you think plays the larger role in the following behaviors, genes or environment? 1) musical ability, 2) athletic skill, and 3) interpersonal skills. What leads you to these conclusions? How could you explore this issue?*

2.   As a result of *crossing over*, every sperm and ovum is genetically unique. *If this process did not occur, would children look more or less similar to their siblings and parents? Why?*

3.   The concept of emergenesis suggests that special combinations of genes can produce traits that are unique. *In addition to the examples given in the text (beauty, genius, athletic prowess), can you think of some other rare physical or behavioral characteristics that might reflect this process? What about in other species?*

4. Research is continuing to identify the genes responsible for various disorders. This knowledge often permits physicians to determine who is likely to display a disorder, although they cannot necessarily prevent or treat it. *What are some of the potential positive effects of such knowledge? Can you think of any ramifications of this technology that are not positive?*

5. The concept of *nonshared environment* relates to the fact that children in the same family do not necessarily share the same experiences. *Think about your own childhood. Can you identify ways in which you and your siblings experienced different environments? Can you speculate on how these different experiences may have led you down different life paths?*

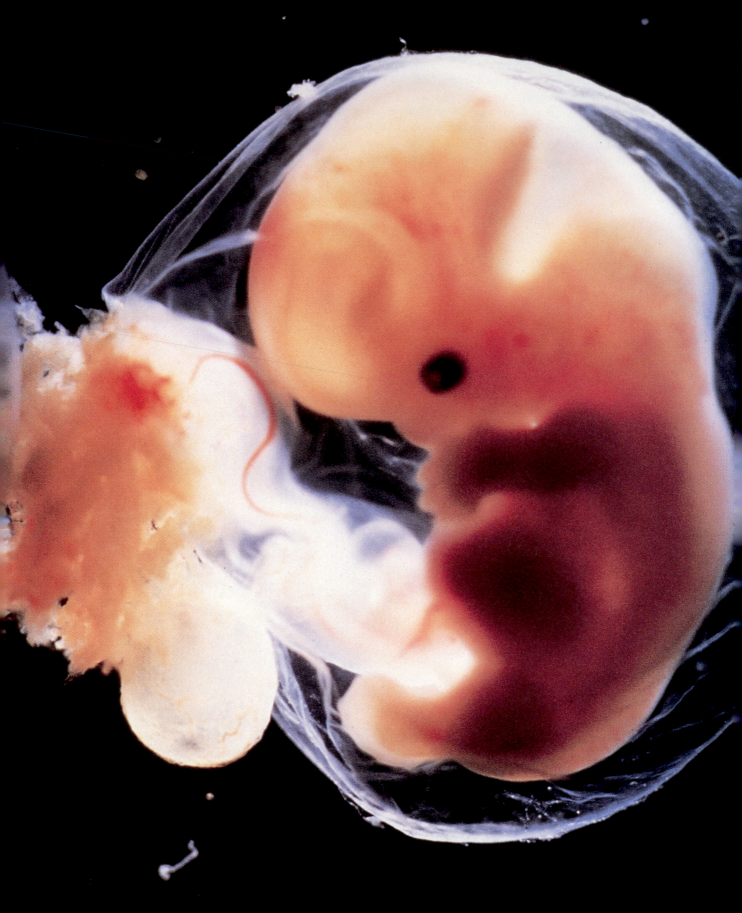

Chapter 5

PRENATAL DEVELOPMENT

*T*hroughout the cycle of human development, no period is marked by such dramatic changes as the 9 months between conception and birth. Yet the events that occur during prenatal development are often unappreciated, perhaps because they are hidden from view. Within only a few weeks after fertilization a single cell "explodes" into billions of cells, each with a highly specialized task. These cells will make up a fully differentiated human, consisting of eyes, ears, arms, legs, brain, and internal body organs.

You can probably imagine how creative the people from ancient cultures must have been as they tried to explain how a fully formed creature could emerge at birth. As late as the 18th century, some theories on the subject held that individuals were fully formed even before conception. One theory, animaliculism, proposed that each sperm cell contained a tiny individual like the one shown in Figure 5-1. The individual would grow when deposited in a woman's womb. Another theory held that the fully formed organism resided instead in the ovum (Needham, 1959).

Just a bit more than 100 years ago, a Swiss zoologist, peering through a microscope, became the first person to see a sperm enter an egg, fertilize it, and produce the cell for a new embryo. Such discoveries in the late 18th century led to our current understanding of fertilization and prenatal development (Touchette, 1990; Wasserman, 1988). This understanding has also led to knowledge about factors that impair development, including genetic defects, infections, drugs, and environmental poisons. Increasingly, physicians are able to detect and even treat health problems in the growing fetus. These are the topics of this chapter.

STAGES OF PRENATAL DEVELOPMENT

Even though it is the largest cell in the body, the ovum is no larger than the period at the end of this sentence, and the sperm cell that fertilizes it weighs less than

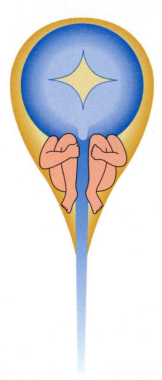

Figure 5-1   Copy of a 17th-century drawing of a sperm. The miniature human was thought to enlarge after entering the ovum.

1/30,000 as much (Scheinfeld, 1972). Yet this tiny genetic package will grow into a baby billions of times larger in only 9 months. Every stage of development along the journey from conception to birth represents a mix of the influences of nature and nurture. Even the genetic material that the mother and father contribute to the offspring can be affected by environmental factors, such as radiation. And other environmental factors, such as nutrition, infections, and drugs, can also influence development. In this section, we follow the baby's prenatal development through three stages, or periods—the period of the zygote, the period of the embryo, and the period of the fetus. But first we consider the starting point of development—conception.

Conception

Prenatal development begins at **conception**, or fertilization, when a sperm unites with an ovum to form a single cell, called a **zygote**. As we saw in Chapter 4, this event creates the template for a genetically unique human being. The zygote receives 23 chromosomes from the mother and 23 from the father, and these 46 chromosomes will replicate over and over through mitosis.

Once every 28 or so days, about halfway through a menstrual cycle, ovulation occurs, and an ovum begins to travel through the fallopian tube toward the uterus. If the female has sexual intercourse with a fertile male a few days before, during, or after ovulation, one of several million sperm produced by a single ejaculation may reach the ovum and penetrate it. How does it happen that this one particular sperm finds the ovum? One view is that with so many sperm available, at least one is likely to happen, by chance, onto the traveling ovum. However, recent evidence suggests that rather than blind luck operating, the ovum emits a chemical "signal" that helps to select the relatively few sperm that are in suitable condition to fertilize the ovum (Roberts, 1991). Within about an hour of penetration, the genetic material from the sperm and the ovum merge to form a zygote, and development of a new individual begins. Scientists have learned to create new human life through a procedure that artificially copies the result of this fertilization process. (Researchers recently cloned a fertilized human egg, a procedure described in Box 5-1.)

Conception
The entry of the genetic material from a male germ cell (sperm) into a female germ cell (ovum); fertilization.

Zygote
A fertilized ovum.

• Millions of sperm from the father enter the vagina of the mother, but only several hundred reach the ovum and only one actually fertilizes it.

The Period of the Zygote (Conception to 2nd Week)

The zygote multiplies rapidly as it moves through the fallopian tube. By the time it reaches the uterus, about 4 days after fertilization, the cell mass looks something like a mulberry. This assembly of cells carries the foundation for the future fetus, the structure in which the fetus will live, and the lifeline that will connect it to the mother's uterus.

Approximately 6 days after fertilization, the cells of the zygote become sticky and attach to the wall of the uterus, where implantation begins. Now the cells begin to specialize, some forming an inner cell mass, which will become the embryo, and some forming a surrounding cell mass, which will become support structures for the embryo. Figure 5-2 diagrams the events of the 1st week of human development. The zygote is still only about 0.01 in. long (Rugh & Shettles, 1971).

Implantation takes about a week. During this time, the zygote actually digests pathways into the lining of the uterus, giving it access to nourishment from the mother's blood. Finally, the zygote is totally buried in the uterine wall, and the period of the zygote ends. About 2 weeks have passed since fertilization, which corresponds to the first missed menstrual period. By the time a woman suspects she may be pregnant, then, prenatal development is well under way.

CLONING HUMAN BEINGS

Over 60 years ago, Aldous Huxley fantasized about the future consequences of technology and social planning in *Brave New World*. He drew the chilling image of human hatcheries that would breed "test-tube babies" who had the appropriate genetic mix to meet society's needs (Huxley, 1932). One class of mass-produced humans would carry out the menial tasks of society while another class would become the doctors and intellectuals. Fact crept toward fantasy in 1978, when doctors succeeded in combining a human sperm and egg in a glass petri dish and then reimplanted the egg in the mother's uterus. The mother gave birth to Louise Joy Brown, the first human born through in vitro fertilization.

The event fueled a major dispute. While some saw this procedure as contrary to nature and the first step toward fulfillment of Huxley's nightmare, others saw it as a godsend for parents who wanted children but suffered from fertility problems.

The fire flamed anew in 1993, when a team at George Washington University, led by Jerry Hall, announced that a human zygote had been cloned for the first time. After chemically dissolving the membrane surrounding a fertilized egg, the researchers separated the two cells of a zygote and surrounded each with an artificial membrane to replace the original. The separated zygotes now contained identical DNA, and each began to multiply as it would under normal circumstances. A similar phenomenon occurs naturally when a zygote splits to give rise to identical twins. This technique has been available for use with livestock, but this was the first time it had been employed with humans (Kohlberg, 1993).

The cloned zygotes were not reimplanted into the mother's uterus, because they were known to be damaged, so no artificially cloned humans were born as a result of this research. But the new possibility gave rise to a chorus of ethical questions surrounding the capability to create identical creatures outside the womb. Could we freeze one zygote to see how its twin turned out before deciding whether to implant—or, alternatively, kill—the second? Would it be possible to create teams of Einsteins to do society's intellectual work or to mass-produce Huxley's drones to do the menial labor? Perhaps a woman could give birth to her own twin, letting her fulfill, vicariously, the life dreams she was unable to accomplish. All these scenarios are imaginable but highly unlikely. The cloning procedure was developed to aid infertile couples who might be unable to produce large quantities of fertilized eggs on their own.

To date, fertilization techniques currently in use have been successful in producing healthy and contributing citizens who are not noticeably different from those produced naturally. Between 1988 and 1993, for example, around 5,300 babies were born in Great Britain through in vitro fertilization (Winston & Handyside, 1993). These children are physically, emotionally, socially, and intellectually equivalent to their peers (Golombok et al., 1993; Morin et al., 1989).

Discussions about the ethical implications of advances in fertilization science will take place, as they should. Technology should serve society's needs while adhering to its ethical values. Hopefully, with this principle in mind, scientists will make sure Huxley's nightmare remains pure fantasy.

The Period of the Embryo (3rd to 8th Week)

Embryo
The developing organism from the 3rd week, when implantation is complete, through the 8th week after conception.

The period of the **embryo** begins when implantation is complete and lasts for around 6 weeks. All major internal and external structures form during this period. In the 3rd week, the inner cell mass differentiates into three germ layers from which all body structures will emerge. Initially, two layers form—the *endodermal* layer and the *ectodermal* layer. The endodermal cells will develop into internal organs and glands. The ectodermal cells form the basis for parts of the body that maintain contact with the outside world—the nervous system; the sensory parts of the eye, nose, and ear; tooth enamel; skin; and hair. The third cell layer then appears between the endodermal and ectodermal layers. This is the *mesodermal* layer, which will give rise to muscles, cartilage, bone, the heart, sex organs, and some

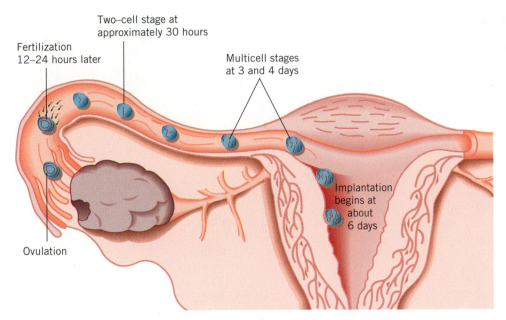

Fertilization
12–24 hours later

Ovulation

Two–cell stage at
approximately 30 hours

Multicell stages
at 3 and 4 days

Implantation
begins at
about
6 days

Figure 5-2 Schematic representation of the events of the first week of human development.

glands. A primitive heart begins to form and, by the end of the 3rd week, connects to the vessels and begins to beat to form a primitive cardiovascular system, the first organ system to become functional (Moore, 1983).

Around the beginning of the 4th week, the embryo looks something like a tube about 0.1 in. long. The shape of the embryo gradually changes, however, because cell multiplication is more rapid in some locations than others. Now the environment begins to affect how cells develop. Cells do not simply follow a predetermined biological plan as the embryo's development unfolds but are affected by their neighbors. (For example, a normal eye lens is most likely to develop if the forming lens tissue has an opportunity to grow first near other endodermal tissue, then near mesodermal tissue, and finally near ectodermal tissue [Jacobson, 1966].) Thus, even at this very early stage, with biological events that seem genetically programmed, parts of the organism develop normally or abnormally depending on what is going on around them. By the end of the 4th week, the embryo assumes a curved form, as shown in Figure 5-3. We can distinguish a bump below the head, which is the primitive heart, and the upper and lower limbs, which have just begun to form as tiny buds.

The embryo's body changes less in the 5th week, but the head and brain develop rapidly. The upper limbs now form, and the lower limbs appear and look like small paddles. In the 6th week, the head continues to grow rapidly, and differentiation of the limbs occurs as elbows, fingers, and wrists become recognizable. It is now possible to discern the ears and eyes. The limbs develop rapidly in the 7th week, and stumps appear that will form fingers and toes.

By the end of the 8th week, the embryo has distinctly human features. Almost half of the embryo consists of the head. The eyes, ears, toes, and fingers are easily distinguishable. All internal and external structures have formed. Thus, in 8 weeks, a single, tiny, undifferentiated cell has proliferated into a remarkably complex organism consisting of millions of cells differentiated into heart, kidneys, eyes, ears, nervous system, brain, and other structures. Its mass has increased a staggering 2 million percent. Figure 5-4 gives some indication of the magnitude of this change.

Seeing this wonderfully well-ordered unfolding, we can hardly help but wonder what makes it happen. Although we do not know all the answers, some of

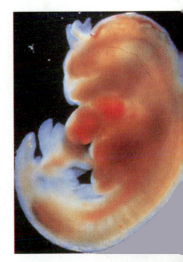

Figure 5-3 An embryo at 4 weeks.

Figure 5-4 Human
ova and embryos showing
growth and body form
from 3 to 8 weeks.
Adapted from *Textbook of
Embryology,* 5th ed. (p. 87)
by H. E. Jordan and J. E.
Kindred, 1948, New York:
Appleton-Century-Crofts.
Copyright 1948 by
Appleton-Century-Crofts.
Adapted by permission.

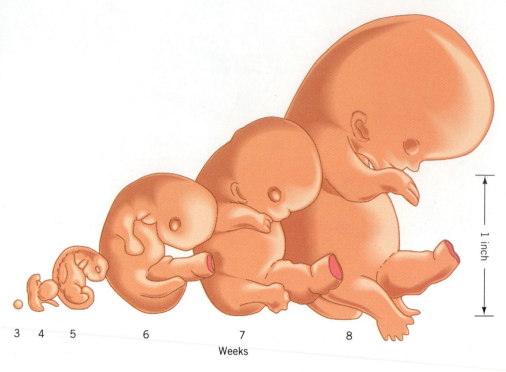

the processes have become clearer in the last few years. As mentioned, part of the development of cells depends on other cells around them, and the dynamic interaction of cells is well established (Melton, 1991; Stern, 1992). However, the sequence and timing with which cells differentiate and multiply to form body parts is largely under genetic control. The regulator genes that specify sequence and timing are called *homeotic genes.* One writer has referred to them as "smart genes" (Beardlsey, 1991). Amazingly, the basic form of these genes has been conserved from beetles to humans over a billion years of evolution. The genes make proteins that tell the body segments what kind of part to make—head, arms, legs, and so on. Interestingly, the homeotic genes are ordered on the chromosome in the same sequence as the segments of the body that they control—head, neck, arms, and so on. The genes overlap so that one controls the next in line, making each gene "turn on" at the right time. If one set of homeotic genes is disrupted, the whole system breaks down. Fortunately, the way that these genes "talk" to one another usually is predictable and orderly (Beardsley, 1991; Marx, 1992).

The Prenatal Environment

Just as the embryo's inner cell mass changes rapidly in the early weeks of development, so does the surrounding cell mass. Structures that arise from these cells during the period of the zygote develop by the end of the embryonic stage into three major support systems: the amniotic sac, the placenta, and the umbilical cord, illustrated in Figure 5-5.

The **amniotic sac** is a watertight membrane filled with fluid. As the embryo grows, the amniotic sac comes to surround it, cushioning and supporting it within the uterus and providing an environment with a constant temperature.

Amniotic sac
A fluid-containing enclosure, secured by a watertight membrane, that surrounds and protects the embryo and fetus.

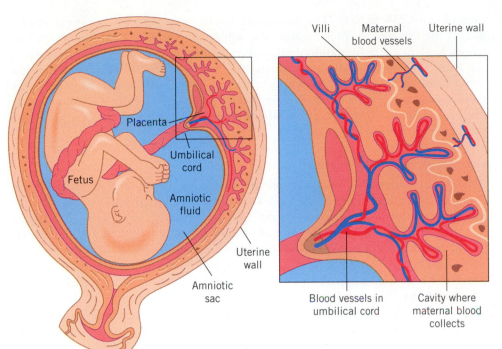

Villi   Maternal blood vessels   Uterine wall

Placenta

Umbilical cord

Fetus

Amniotic fluid

Uterine wall

Amniotic sac

Blood vessels in umbilical cord

Cavity where maternal blood collects

Figure 5-5   Maternal structures that support the embryo and fetus include the placental villi, amniotic sac, placenta, and umbilical cord.

The **placenta**, formed from both the mother's tissue and the embryo's tissue, is the organ the mother and the embryo (later the fetus) use to exchange materials. Linking the embryo to the placenta is the **umbilical cord**, which houses the blood vessels that carry these materials.

The exchange of materials takes place in the placental villi. These ornate-looking structures (shown in Figure 5-5) are small blood vessels immersed in the mother's blood but separated from it by a very thin membrane. The membrane is semipermeable—that is, only molecules of a certain size can pass through it, including some viruses and chemicals. Blood itself does not pass between the mother and the fetus. However, oxygen and nutrients do pass from the mother's blood to the villi, and waste products of the fetus pass into the mother's blood to be carried away and excreted. The intricate and winding networks of the placental villi comprise an area half the size of a tennis court (Beaconsfield, Birdwood, & Beaconsfield, 1980).

Placenta
An organ formed by both embryonic and uterine tissue where the embryo attaches to the uterus. This organ exchanges nutrients, oxygen, and wastes between the embryo or fetus and the mother through a very thin membrane that does not allow the passage of blood.

Umbilical cord
A soft cable of tissue and blood vessels that connects the fetus to the placenta.

The Period of the Fetus (9th to 38th Week)

At the end of the 8th week, the period of the **fetus** begins. The principal tasks for the fetus are to further develop the already formed organ structures and to increase in size and weight. Beginning its 3rd month weighing only 0.2 oz. and measuring 2 in. in length, the average fetus will be born 266 days after conception weighing about 7 to 8 lb and measuring about 20 in. in length. Fetal growth begins to slow around the 8th month, which is good for both the mother and the fetus. If the growth rate did not slow, the fetus would weigh 200 pounds at birth.

Fetus
The developing organism from the 9th week to the 38th week after conception.

External Changes

During this period, the fetus's appearance changes drastically. The head grows less than other parts of the body, changing its ratio from 50% of the body mass at 12

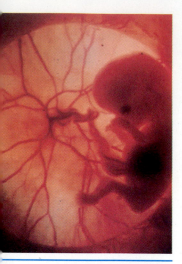

• Until birth, the fetus remains immersed in fluid within the amniotic sac, receiving oxygen and nourishment through the umbilical cord. The fetus in the photo is 12 weeks into gestation.

weeks toward 25% at birth. The skin, which has been transparent, begins to thicken during the 3rd month. Facial features, which appeared almost extraterrestrial at 6 weeks, become more human-looking as the eyes move from the sides of the head to the front. The eyelids seal shut near the beginning of the 3rd month and remain shut for the next 3 months. Nails appear on fingers and toes by the 4th month, and pads appear at the ends of the fingers that will uniquely identify the individual for life. Head hair also begins to grow. A bone structure begins to support a more erect posture by 6 months.

Growth of Internal Organs

Changes in external appearance are accompanied by equally striking internal changes. By 3 months, the brain has assumed the basic organization that will mark its later functional subdivisions—seeing, hearing, thinking, and so on. The 100 billion cells of the adult brain are already present in the fetus by the 5th month, but the 14 trillion connections they will make between themselves and incoming and outgoing nerve cells will not be completed until well after birth. The most complex telephone system in the world is no match for this intricately wired human communication device. Nerve cell growth and establishment of connections, begun at 19 days, continue throughout fetal development. A major mystery facing scientists is how the single undifferentiated zygote cell can give rise to billions of fibers that properly connect eyes, ears, touch sensors, muscles, and the parts of the brain. Although an inborn plan of some sort must guide how this wiring proceeds, it is clear that environmental factors and interactions between nerve cells also play a role, as no two brains are wired identically, not even those of identical twins, who have exactly the same genetic material (Barnes, 1986; Edelman, 1987; Rakic et al., 1986).

Other internal organs continue to develop. Sexual development becomes apparent in males by the end of the 3rd month with the appearance of external sexual organs. In females, the precursors of ova, or *oocytes*, form on the outer covering of the ovaries; all the oocytes the female will ever possess will be present at birth. The fallopian tubes, uterus, and vagina develop, and the external labia become discernible.

Early Signs of Behavior

Fetal activity begins in the 3rd month, when the fetus is capable of forming a fist, wiggling the toes, and swallowing; the mother, however, feels none of this. The fetus also appears to become sensitive to environmental stimulation, for it moves its whole body in response to a touch stimulus. By the 4th month, the eyes are sensitive to light through the lids, and by the 5th month a loud noise may activate the fetus. During this same month, the fetus swims effortlessly, a luxury gradually lost later as quarters become increasingly cramped. The fetus is now capable of kicking and turning and may begin to display rhythms of sleep and activity. By the 7th month, brain connections are sufficient for the fetus to exhibit a sucking reflex when the lips are touched.

Toward Independence

The later stages of prenatal development ready the fetus to live outside the mother's body. The fetus, although separate from the mother in many ways during development, is nevertheless completely dependent on her for survival during most of the prenatal period. Recall that the support system in the uterus provides oxygen, nutrients, waste disposal, and a constant temperature for the fetus. Although physicians have made marked progress in saving premature babies, they have been unable to lower the "age of viability" under around 23 to 24 weeks of fetal age. The major obstacle to independent life for a fetus born prematurely is the immaturity of the air sacs of the lungs, which will have to exchange carbon dioxide for oxygen (Kolata, 1989). The fetus's inability to digest food or control body temperature is also a problem, and fat has not yet formed under the skin to assist in temperature regulation.

By 6 to 7 months of age, the fetus has a chance of survival outside the mother's body. The brain is sufficiently developed to provide at least partial regulation of breathing, swallowing, and body temperature. However, the baby born after only 7 months of development will need to be provided with extra oxygen, will have to take food in very small amounts, and will have to live for several weeks in an incubator for temperature control. In the 8th month, fat appears under the skin, and although the digestive system is still too immature to adequately extract nutrients from food, the fetus begins to store maternal nutrients in its body. But even a baby born at 8 months is susceptible to infection. Beginning in the 8th month, the mother's body contributes disease-fighting antibodies to the fetus that she has developed through her own exposure to foreign bodies. This process is not complete until 9 months of fetal age and is important, because these antibodies help to protect babies from infection until around 6 months of age, when they can produce their own in substantial amounts.

✔ *To Recap...*

Prenatal development begins with conception and proceeds through the period of the zygote, the period of the embryo, and the period of the fetus. At conception, a sperm cell penetrates an egg cell, thereby joining the 23 chromosomes from the father with 23 chromosomes from the mother to form a zygote. The zygote multiplies rapidly as it migrates toward the uterus. There, it becomes fully implanted by the end of the 2nd week after conception.

Now an embryo, the cell mass rapidly differentiates into organs and structures. In the 6 weeks that make up the period of the embryo, a mulberry-like cluster of cells is transformed into a complex and differentiated organism with a heart, kidneys, eyes, ears, a nervous system, and a brain. The support structures needed for protection and growth—the amniotic sac, the placenta, and the umbilical cord—are also completed.

At the end of the 8th week, the fetal period begins. The primary task for the fetus is growth and further development of organ systems. Behavior begins in the 3rd month. The fetus grows toward increasing independence but is unable to survive before about 23 to 24 weeks of fetal age, mainly because the air sacs of the lungs are unable to transfer oxygen to the blood. As the fetus matures, the lungs become increasingly able to perform this function, the digestive system becomes able to extract nutrients from food, and fat appears to provide insulation for temperature control. In the last months, the fetus takes antibodies from the mother to protect against infection in the early months following birth. By 9 months following conception, the normal fetus is ready to face the external world.

TERATOLOGY: HISTORY, PRINCIPLES, AND NATURAL EVENTS

It is natural to think that prenatal development depends only on genes and that the environment begins to affect the baby only after birth. But, although the uterus may not seem like an environment in the usual sense, it is the only home the embryo and fetus know. We will see that a number of factors affect the quality of this "home" and determine whether development is normal or abnormal—indeed, whether development can occur at all.

Approximately 3 to 5% of all live-born babies are identified as malformed at birth. Some malformations are difficult to detect at first but become apparent with age. Thus, by the early school years, approximately 6 to 7% of children are identified as having congenital malformations—that is, malformations that existed at birth. Many more babies would be born with malformations, were it not for a natural prenatal process that results in miscarriage, or spontaneous abortion. It is estimated that 90% of some kinds of malformations end in spontaneous abortions and that without this natural screening process, the observed incidence of congenital malformation would be 12% or more (Shepard, 1986; Warkany, 1981).

We have already seen that genetic defects cause some abnormalities. Malformations may also be caused by infectious diseases, poor nutrition, age, and perhaps even the mother's emotional state, as well as by drugs and other environmental hazards. Nongenetic agents that can cause malformation in the embryo and fetus are referred to as **teratogens** (*tera* is a Latin base meaning "monster"). The term *teratology* refers to the study of the effect of teratogens on prenatal development.

Teratogen
An agent that can cause abnormal development in the fetus.

Much of our discussion of teratogens will focus on their physical effects. Indeed, teratogens are defined in terms of their creation of physical malformations. However, psychologists have noted increasingly that teratogens can have psychological and behavioral effects as well. This realization has given rise to a new field, called **psychoteratology**. Researchers in this field use behavior rather than physical outcomes to study the potentially damaging effects of teratogens and have found that behavioral effects may show up in the absence of physical effects. Thus, in many cases, behavioral measures may be more sensitive than physical measures (Fein et al., 1983; Voorhees & Butcher, 1982; Voorhees & Mollnow, 1987; Weiss, 1983).

Psychoteratology
The discovery and study of the harmful effects of teratogens through the use of behavioral measures, such as learning ability.

Historical Ideas

The field of teratology achieved scientific status only recently, but it has an interesting history. The birth of malformed babies probably gave rise to at least some of the creatures of Greek mythology, such as the one-eyed cyclops and the various creatures that are part human and part beast (Warkany, 1977). Whereas monsters were sometimes idolized in antiquity, people in the medieval period believed that the birth of malformed babies portended catastrophe, and malformed infants and children were often put to death. Some believed that these babies were produced through the mating of humans with animals, and it was not unusual for mothers and midwives who delivered malformed babies to be put on trial for witchcraft. Such practices gradually gave way to the more benign belief that maternal fright, thoughts, and impressions could create a monster birth (Warkany, 1981). Running parallel to these theories were ancient beliefs that the food and drink a pregnant woman ingested could affect the fetus. In the Bible, an angel admonishes a woman named Manoah that when she conceives a son, she should "drink no wine nor strong drink, and eat not any unclean thing" (Judges 13:4).

Despite the apparent fact that people of biblical times believed that maternal nourishment could affect the development of the fetus, an enormous time lapsed before people fully realized the potential effects of the external world on the fetus. People generally believed that the embryo and fetus lived in a privileged environment, protected against harm by the placenta and its amniotic world.

By 1930, however, there was general recognition that X-rays could produce intrauterine growth retardation, microcephaly (an abnormally small head and brain), and small eyes. And by the mid-1940s, it had become obvious that a pregnant mother who contracted rubella (German measles) during the early months of pregnancy had a relatively high chance of producing a baby with congenital abnormalities of the eye, ear, heart, and brain. Still, these events were seen as exceptional. A major disaster finally shook people's faith in the "privileged environment" belief, but only as recently as the early 1960s.

A mild and seemingly harmless sedative, Thalidomide, appeared on the market in the late 1950s, and many pregnant women—some who did not even know they were pregnant—took it. Physicians soon noticed a sharp increase in the number of babies born with defective limbs. Careful questioning of mothers, analysis of doctors' prescriptions, and epidemiological research implicated Thalidomide as the culprit. The field of teratology experienced a dramatic surge as a result of this event and has been expanding rapidly ever since. Table 5-1 provides a partial list of the maternal conditions and teratogens that may harm the fetus. We will discuss most of these after we consider some general principles that govern the action of teratogens.

General Principles

Around 1,600 agents have been examined for teratogenic effects, and about 30 of them are known to cause defects in humans (Shepard, 1986). Evaluating an agent for teratogenic effects, however, is fraught with problems. For obvious reasons, animals must be the "guinea pigs" for substance testing, but the potential teratogen may not have the same effect on animal and human fetuses. Furthermore, people often take more than one drug. Complicating investigations further, a particular drug may only do damage when combined with another drug, or a disease, or stress.

Six principles capture important features of how teratogens act (Hogge, 1990; Wilson, 1977b).

    1. *A teratogen's effect depends on the genetic makeup of the organism exposed to it.* A prime example is Thalidomide. The human fetus is extremely sensitive to this substance, but rabbits and rats are not. That is one reason Thalidomide was not at first suspected to be a teratogen. Testing performed on these animals revealed no ill effects. The principle of genetic differences in sensitivity also applies to individuals within a species. Some babies are malformed because their mothers drank alcohol during pregnancy, but others are apparently not affected by this practice.

    2. *The effect of a teratogen on development depends partly on timing.* Even before conception, teratogens can affect the formation of the parents' sex cells. Formation of female sex cells begins during fetal life, and formation of sperm can occur up to 64 days before the sperm are expelled. Thus, a fetus can be affected by drugs that the pregnant grandmother took decades earlier or by X-ray exposure that the father experienced many weeks before conception (Tuchmann-Duplessis, 1975). For 2 to 3 weeks after conception, the zygote's fluids do not mix with those of the mother, so the zygote is relatively impervious to some teratogens. After the zygote has attached to the uterus, however, substances in the mother's bloodstream can mix with the blood of the embryo,

TABLE 5-1 ● Some Teratogens and Conditions That May Harm the Fetus

Teratogen	Potential Effect
Therapeutic Drugs	
Aspirin	In large quantities, miscarriage, bleeding, newborn respiratory problems
Barbiturates	Newborn respiratory problems
Diethylstilbestrol (DES) (a drug to prevent miscarriage)	Genital abnormalities in both sexes, vaginal and cervical cancer in adolescent females
Isoretinoin (a vitamin A derivative for treating acne)	Malformations of the head and ears, heart and central nervous system defects, behavior problems
Phenytoin (an anticonvulsant drug)	Threefold increase in likelihood of heart defects and growth retardation
Streptomycin	Hearing loss
Tetracycline	Most commonly, staining of teeth; can also affect bone growth
Thalidomide	Deformed limbs, sensory deficits, defects in internal organs, death
Street Drugs	
Cocaine and crack	Growth retardation, premature birth, irritableness in the newborn, withdrawal symptoms
Heroin and methadone	Growth retardation, premature birth, irritableness in the newborn, withdrawal symptoms, sudden infant death syndrome
LSD and marijuana	Probable cause of premature birth and growth retardation when used heavily; originally implicated in chromosomal breakage, but this effect is uncertain
Maternal Condition	
Age	For teenage women and women over 35, lighter-weight babies than women in the optimal childbearing years; likelihood of Down syndrome birth increases with advancing age
Alcohol use	Brain and heart damage, growth retardation, mental retardation, fetal alcohol syndrome
Diabetes	A threefold increase in all types of birth defects, including babies born without a brain, with spina bifida, and with heart defects
Malnutrition	Increased likelihood of growth retardation, prematurity, inattention; poor social interactive ability, especially when mother also has a history of malnutrition before pregnancy
Phenylketonuria (PKU)	Growth retardation of brain and head, mental retardation, heart defects
Smoking	Growth retardation, prematurity
Infections	
AIDS (acquired immunodeficiency syndrome)	Congenital malformations; leaves infant vulnerable to infections of all types
Cytomegalovirus	Deafness, blindness, abnormal head and brain growth, mental retardation
Herpes	Mental retardation, eye damage, death
Rubella	Mental retardation, eye damage, deafness, heart defects
Syphilis	Mental retardation, miscarriage, blindness, deafness, death
Toxoplasmosis	Abnormalities in brain and head growth, mental retardation
Environmental Hazards	
Lead	Miscarriage, anemia, mental retardation
Mercury	Abnormal head and brain growth, motor incoordination, mental retardation
PCBs	Growth retardation
Radiation	Leukemia, abnormal brain and body growth, cancer, genetic alterations, miscarriage, stillbirth

and the embryo enters a particularly sensitive period. Teratogens can produce organ malformation from 2 to 8 weeks, because this is a time when organs are forming. After the organs have formed, teratogens primarily produce growth retardation or tissue damage (Goldman, 1980). Which organ is affected by a teratogen depends in part on which organ is forming. (See Figure 5-6 for critical periods for organ development.) Rubella is an example of how crucial timing can be. Rubella affects only 2 to 3% of the offspring of mothers infected within 2 weeks after their last period, whereas it affects 50% of offspring when infection occurs during the 1st month following conception, 22% when it occurs during the 2nd month, and 6 to 8% when it occurs during the 3rd month. The incidence falls to very low levels thereafter. Whether ear, eye, heart, or brain damage results depends on the stage of the formation of each organ when the mother is infected (Kurent & Sever, 1977; Murata et al., 1992; Whitley & Goldenberg, 1990).

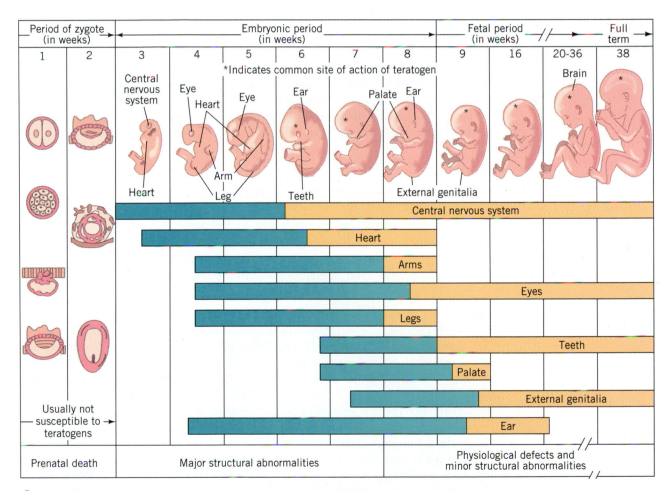

Figure 5-6 A schematic illustration of the sensitive or critical periods in prenatal development. Sensitivity to teratogens is greatest from 3 to 9 weeks after conception, the period when organ formation occurs. The most critical age period of vulnerability for each organ is shown in green and continuing periods where the likelihood of damage declines is shown as orange. Adapted from *Before We Are Born*, 3rd ed. (p. 118) by K. L. Moore, 1989, Philadelphia: Saunders. Copyright 1989 by W. B. Saunders Company. Adapted by permission.

3. *The effect of a teratogen may be unique.* For example, Thalidomide produces gross limb defects, whereas rubella primarily affects sensory and internal organs.

4. *The abnormal development caused by teratogens may result in malformation, growth retardation, functional and behavioral disorders, or death.*

5. *Teratogens differ in how they gain access to the fetus.* Radiation passes to the fetus directly through the mother's body, for example, whereas chemicals usually travel to the fetus through the blood and across the placental membrane. Physical blows are partially cushioned by the mother's body and the amniotic fluid. The mother's blood may be able to filter some potentially harmful chemicals to protect the fetus. The placenta, too, serves as a filter, but not a complete barrier—materials may be slowed by this filter, but will not necessarily be stopped. Some teratogens move past this filter faster than others.

6. *The likelihood and degree of abnormal development increase with the fetus's dosage of the harmful agent, from no effect to a lethal one.*

Natural Challenges

Much current media attention focuses on potential teratogens that mothers voluntarily consume or that the modern industrial environment exposes them to. However, the mother and fetus have always faced natural challenges from the environment. Infectious diseases can harm the fetus, and the quality of the mother's nutrition affects how the fetus develops. Parental age and even maternal experiences and stress may also have an effect.

Infectious Diseases

Several viral and bacterial infections in the mother can damage the fetus. We discuss some of the more common ones here.

Rubella   Rubella virus can damage the central nervous system of the fetus, resulting in blindness, deafness, and mental retardation. The heart, liver, and bone structure may also be damaged, depending on the timing of infection.

Herpes   Two viruses in the herpes group can produce central nervous system damage. One is cytomegalovirus (CMV), the most common intrauterine viral infection. CMV may cause abnormal brain and head growth, encephalitis, blindness, and mental retardation. It is estimated that 33,000 infants are born with CMV each year, but only 10% of them are seriously affected. Because pregnant mothers are often unaware that they have been infected by CMV, doctors have made little progress in discovering the specific effects of fetal exposure at particular ages. CMV can be transmitted by sexual contact, blood transfusions, or mixing of body fluids (Behrman & Vaughan, 1987).

Another herpes virus, herpes virus type 2, infects the genitals of adults. This virus had reached epidemic levels in the United States by the early 1980s. In the infant, herpes 2 can cause encephalitis, central nervous system damage, and blood-clotting problems. Most herpes 2 infections of infants occur following direct contamination by the mother's infected birth canal. Intrauterine infection, though rare, has effects similar to those of CMV (Murata et al., 1992; Whitley & Goldenberg, 1990).

AIDS Another virus reached epidemic levels in the 1980s—the human immuno-deficiency virus (HIV), which causes acquired immunodeficiency syndrome, or AIDS. The virus cannot live in air; it is transmitted from one person to another exclusively through body fluids. There are three major avenues for transmission. The first is through sexual intercourse by way of male semen or female vaginal fluids. The second is through blood exchange. Many people have been infected with the virus through transfusions of blood donated by infected individuals, but improved blood screening has reduced this threat dramatically. Currently, HIV-infected blood is exchanged most commonly through intravenous drug injection by addicts who use the same needle (Palca, 1990). The third means of transmission is from mother to infant (for an example, see European Collaborative Study, 1991). Box 5-2 discusses pediatric AIDS around the world. In addition to causing AIDS, the human immunodeficiency virus can act as a teratogen. Some infected babies are born with facial deformities—larger-than-normal eye separation, boxlike foreheads, flattened nose bridges, and misshapen eye openings.

Influenza and Mumps A number of other viruses, including influenza A and mumps, have harmful effects on embryological development in animals. Their effect on the human fetus is unclear, but mumps in early pregnancy does increase the chance of miscarriage (Behrman & Vaughan, 1987; Kurent & Sever, 1977).

Toxoplasma Gondii Nonviral infections can also produce embryological defects. Toxoplasma gondii is a protozoan that infects adults, probably through ingestion of undercooked contaminated meat products and possibly also through infection from animals, principally cats. A mother infected by this organism may show no effect or may have symptoms similar to those caused by mononucleosis. The fetus may experience a range of effects from none at all to severe central nervous system damage, including abnormal brain and head growth and mental retardation (Whitley & Goldenberg, 1990).

Syphilis and Gonorrhea Syphilis and gonorrhea are sexually transmitted diseases. After declining for several years, the incidence of syphilis began to increase in the late 1980s. This disease is caused by a spirochete, a type of bacteria which can infect the fetus and cause central nervous system damage, deformities of the teeth and skeleton, and even death. The fetus is relatively resistant to infection from the syphilis spirochete until the 4th or 5th month (Bergsma, 1979).

Gonorrhea is also caused by a bacterial agent. Its incidence has been reported to be as high as 30% in some populations. Premature birth, premature rupture of membranes, and spontaneous abortion are associated with gonorrhea. The fetus is affected in about 30% of cases; the most common problem is eye infection, which can lead to blindness if untreated. Fortunately, almost all newborns are treated with silver nitrate eye drops at birth to prevent this problem (Murata et al., 1992; Whitley & Goldenberg, 1990).

Nutrition

As mentioned earlier, trillions of cells are manufactured from the original fertilized egg to form the fully developed fetus. During prenatal development, cells increase not only in number but also in size. As Table 5-2 illustrates, the baby and its accompanying support system will weigh 25 to 30 lb by the 9th month of pregnancy, billions of times the weight of the fertilized egg.

PEDIATRIC AIDS: THE CONSEQUENCES OF A PANDEMIC

AIDS was first described in 1981 (Slutsker et al., 1992). In the 10 years following that report, 200,000 cases were identified in the United States alone. The growth in cases of HIV infection occurred mainly among ho-

mosexual males in the United States in the early 1980s, but by the late 1980s new infections in men and women were approximately equal—now the occurrence of new infection is higher among females

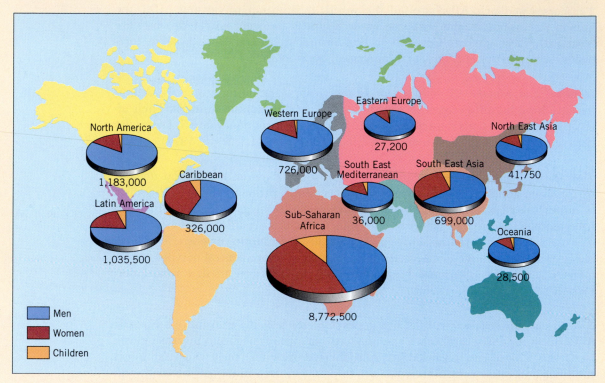

Figure 5-7 Estimated numbers of HIV-infected men, women, and children in major areas of the world. Based on data from AIDS in the World, 1992, p. 30.

Where does all of this mass come from? The answer is obvious—from the mother. Thinking about the issue this way brings home the importance of maternal nutrition. The quality of the fetus's cells can be no better than that of the nutrients the mother supplies through the placental circulation system. Oddly, this simple fact is often not fully appreciated. Earlier, we said that, at least in the early stages of development, the functioning of cells depends on the "environment" they are in. The quality of the mother's nutrition is probably the most important environmental influence on the fetus and newborn baby (Morgane et al., 1993).

The prospective mother, then, must supply nutrients for the fetus and its support system. In part, her ability to do this depends on her nutrition during pregnancy. But

• Intervention programs in Africa have been success-ful in reducing the incidence of HIV infection.

(Mann, Tarantola, & Netter, 1992a, 1992b). AIDS is currently the number-two killer (following unintentional injuries) among males in the United States and the number-six killer among females (Selik, Chu, & Buehler, 1993).

AIDS, of course, is not simply a U.S. problem. As Figure 5-7 shows, HIV infection is a worldwide pandemic, affecting almost 12 million persons on every continent. And many of its victims are children.

Around 30% of the pregnant women who are infected with HIV pass the virus on to their offspring, either to the fetus or to the baby during birth or shortly thereafter through breastfeeding. By 1992, 1.1 million children had been infected by HIV around the world. In both infants and mothers, the AIDS virus destroys the body's natural defenses to infection, leaving the infected individuals vulnerable to diseases they otherwise would be able to fight successfully. But babies typically develop AIDS following an HIV infection much more quickly than adults do. About half of the infants infected near the time of birth die within 2 years, and an additional 30% die within 5 years (Bailey, 1992; Lallemont et al., 1992; Weiss, 1993).

AIDS continues to spread rampantly. As many as 120 million people may be infected by the year 2000, and it is expected that as many as 10 million of these will be children. It is estimated that 90% of the new cases of HIV infection between 1993 and 2000 will be in developing countries (Merson, 1993). The disease compounds with the many others that people in these countries confront in trying to help their young survive. Infected mothers in developing countries face an awful decision regarding breastfeeding. Whereas they risk transmitting HIV to their infants through breast milk, if they do not breast-feed, their babies are 3 times as likely to die from other infections (Heymann, 1992).

There is no immediate hope for a cure for those who have been infected by HIV or for a vaccine to protect uninfected people from future infection (Cohen, 1992, 1993). What can be done? Our best hope today is education. For example, in Kinshasa, Zaire, an intervention program reduced the incidence of HIV infection from 18% to 2% a year through education, counseling, peer support, treatment for sexually transmitted diseases, and condoms (Mann, Tarantola, & Netter, 1992a).

The United Nations has recognized the disaster that potentially awaits the world. Hopefully, its efforts to educate citizens everywhere, coupled with an unprecedented research effort, will slow and eventually halt this pandemic.

it also depends to a great extent on her nutritional status before pregnancy. Both the mothers and their fetuses fare more poorly when the mother suffers long-term malnutrition than when the mother has good prepregnancy nutrituion (Rosso, 1990). Additionally, how well the placenta passes nutrients to the fetus, maternal disease, and genetic factors can affect fetal nutrition.

Maternal malnutrition can have devastating effects on the fetus. Autopsies of severely malnourished stillborn infants from third-world countries reveal that their brains weighed up to one third less than expected. Deficits in the size of major internal organs of between 6 and 25% have been found in the United States in infants born to urban poor families (Naeye, Diener, & Dellinger, 1969; Parekh et al., 1970).

TABLE 5-2 • Weight Gain during Pregnancy

Development	Weight Gain (lb)
Infant at birth	$7\frac{1}{2}$
Placenta	1
Increase in mother's blood volume to supply placenta	4
Increase in size of mother's uterus and muscles to support it	$2\frac{1}{2}$
Increase in size of mother's breasts	3
Fluid to surround infant in amniotic sac	2
Mother's fat stores	5–10
Total	25–30

Source: Reprinted by permission from page 495 of *Understanding Nutrition*, Fourth Edition by E. N. Whitney and E. M. N. Hamilton; Copyright © 1987 by West Publishing Company. All rights reserved.

Malnutrition is associated with increased rates of spontaneous abortion, infant death, and congenital defects. Pregnant women who have inadequate diets are also more likely to have small and premature babies (Bauerfeld & Lachenmeyer, 1992). (Problems associated with low birth weight are discussed in Chapter 6.)

As is sometimes the case with teratogens, however, it can be difficult to isolate the effects of malnourishment from other factors. Malnutrition is often accompanied by inadequate housing and health care and inferior education and sanitation, as well as the daily stress of poverty. Unfortunately, catastrophes sometimes provide a means for separating out the influences of at least some of these factors. During World War II, for example, the entire populations of many countries had severely limited food supplies not associated with the other factors. Food supplies in the Netherlands were especially scarce, and, in addition to a decline in conceptions, there was a substantial increase in miscarriages, stillbirths, and congenital malformations.

Food quantity is not the only issue in maternal nutrition. The pregnant woman and her fetus have special dietary needs. Proteins, vitamins, and minerals are especially important. Animal studies reveal that protein deficits produce damage to the kidneys, intestines, and skeletal growth in the fetus. Low intake of certain vitamins can affect the eyes and internal organs and increase the number of malformations (Rosso, 1990; Shepard, 1977). Trace elements in the diet are also important. An absence of iron in the mother's blood can produce anemia in her baby. Diets lacking iodine are associated with an increased likelihood of cretinism, a severe thyroid deficiency that causes physical stunting and mental deficiency. (Pharoah et al., 1981). Deficits of copper, manganese, and zinc produce central nervous system damage and other negative effects in rats, and zinc deficiency has been implicated in the occurrence of anencephaly (absence of the cortex of the brain) in people in Turkey and other Eastern countries. Vegetarians should be aware that they are vulnerable to deficiencies of vitamins, especially B12, iron, and zinc, as well as to inadequate caloric intake (Cavdar et al., 1980; Rosso, 1990).

Convincing evidence of the importance of one B vitamin, folic acid, has recently become available. Deficits of folic acid in pregnant mothers had been associated with neural tube defects—anencephaly and nonclosure of the spinal cord (spina bifida)—in babies. A well-designed study carried out in several countries investigated this association. Pregnant women were randomly assigned to 1 of 4 groups: (a) supplementation with folic acid, (b) supplementation with a mixture of seven other vitamins, (c) supplementation with both folic acid and vitamins, and (d) neither folic acid nor vitamin supplementation. The frequency of neural tube defects was 3.5 times higher for groups b and d, which did not receive folic-acid supplementation, than for groups a and c, which did (MRC Vitamin Study Research Group, 1991).

What is the intellectual fate of babies who are malnourished during fetal life? The outcome depends, to a large extent, on their childhood environments. Children who were malnourished as fetuses because of World War II but had adequate diet and stimulation as infants and children showed no long-term intellectual deficit. Many Korean children suffered malnutrition during the Korean War but were later adopted by Americans who provided them with good nutrition and education. These children later performed as well on intellectual and achievement tests as children who had not suffered early malnutrition. The general conclusion is that an enriched home environment may compensate for many of the effects of early malnutrition, but the outcome also depends on when during pregnancy the malnutrition occurred and how severe it was (Morgane et al., 1993; Stein & Susser, 1976; Vietze & Vaughan, 1988; Winick, Knarig, & Harris, 1975; Zeskind & Ramey, 1981). On the other hand, babies who are malnourished both as fetuses and after birth are more likely to show delayed motor and social development. They become relatively inattentive, unresponsive, and apathetic (Barrett, Radke-Yarrow, & Klein, 1982; Bauerfeld & Lachenmeyer, 1992). Fortunately, health organizations worldwide have recognized the lasting consequences of early nutritional deficits and have initiated attempts to supplement the diets of both pregnant women and their infants. Supplemented babies are more advanced in motor development and more socially interactive and energetic, an encouraging sign that the consequences of bad nutrition may be avoided (Barrett, et al., 1982; Joos et al., 1983).

Excesses of nutrients can also be damaging. For example, you may recall from Chapter 4 that people with the disease phenylketonuria (PKU) are unable to break down the amino acid phenylalanine. Mothers who have phenylketonuria, even though they have protected themselves through early dietary restrictions, still have excesses of phenylalanine circulating in their blood. The fetus, though genetically normal, may suffer brain damage from intrauterine exposure to this excess product. Mothers, however, can protect the fetus by maintaining a restricted diet during pregnancy (Koch & Cruz, 1991). Excesses of the sugar galactose in diabetic mothers may cause cataracts and other physical problems, even death, in the fetuses; the babies at birth are more likely to have passive muscle tone and to be less attentive (Langer, 1990). Just as deficits in iodine can cause problems, excess iodine can detrimentally affect thyroid function in the fetus (Pharoah et al., 1981). Excess vitamin supplementation has been implicated in birth defects in both humans and animals (Rosso, 1990).

Maternal Experiences and Stress

Of all the factors that might influence the fetus, none has generated more speculation than that of the mother's own experiences. The belief that the mother's mental impressions could affect the fetus is quite old. We may chuckle when we hear the old wives' tale about how a pregnant woman's child will favor classical music if the mother listens to Beethoven. But surveys in modern times in the United States and Europe have revealed that many people still believe that birthmarks are caused by maternal frights or unsatisfied food cravings. For example, an unsatisfied craving for strawberries might produce a strawberry-colored birthmark (Ferriera, 1969).

Modern investigators have dismissed beliefs in magical influences on the fetus and have focused on psychological factors that have fairly well documented influences on the body. For example, psychological stress increases the activity of the adrenal glands. The secretions from these glands enter the mother's blood and can be transmitted to the fetus through the placenta. Additionally, hormones released during stress can reduce the blood flow and oxygen available to the fetus (Thompson, 1990). Thus, identifiable physical pathways exist by which maternal emotional states could affect the fetus.

Here is another area in which investigators have used behavior rather than physical malformations to study teratogens. Animal studies have demonstrated that maternal stress can increase emotionality in offspring (Thompson & Grusec, 1970). Although it is, of course, less easy to conduct such experiments with humans, some evidence suggests similar effects. For example, Sontag found sharply increased activity of fetuses in mothers who had just experienced an emotional shock (e.g., death in the family or divorce), and he reported that, after birth, these babies had feeding and digestive difficulties (Sontag, 1944, 1966).

Investigators have used various methods to assess the effects of stress in pregnant women and have examined the relation between the stress and, among other things, abnormalities in the newborn. High levels of reported anxiety were related to such problems as increases in fetal activity, congenital malformations, irritability, and feeding and digestive difficulties in the baby (Davids, DeVault, & Talmadge, 1961; Ferriera, 1969; Ottinger & Simmons, 1964; Sontag, 1944, 1966; Stott, 1969).

Again, there are problems in interpreting these relations because of limitations in researchers' ability to control all of the factors that might be related to anxiety. Often, mothers' reports of anxiety were obtained after their babies were born. Perhaps these reports of anxiety were influenced by the babies' malformation or irritability rather than the other way around—the cause-and-effect problem mentioned in Chapter 3. Further, there is often no way to separate prenatal and postnatal influences on the infant. A mother who has reported a great deal of prenatal anxiety may handle her infant differently, for example, and it may be this handling that makes her baby irritable. One study showed that women who reported marital difficulties and ambivalence about their pregnancies later reported more problems, including depression, when their babies were 5 months of age (Field et al., 1985). Depressed mothers have less optimal interactions with their babies, and it appears that the mothers' negative judgments about their babies reflected the mothers' own states and their impact on their infants rather than their anxiety during pregnancy (Cohn et al., 1990; Field et al., 1985; Vaughn et al., 1987). Finally, the genetic relation between the mother and her baby may be the operative factor rather than the prenatal experience. A mother who is genetically predisposed to anxiety, which might reflect abnormal hormonal activity, could pass this genetic predisposition on to her fetus (Copans, 1974; Joffe, 1969).

A recent study avoided some of the problems of prior studies by using low birth weight and early delivery as measures of the effects of stress on babies. These measures do not depend on the babies' postnatal interactions with their mothers or on the mothers' judgments of the babies. A group of women completed anxiety questionnaires during their pregnancy. Independent of other medical risk factors, there was a relation between a woman's reported anxiety and the likelihood that she would give birth early or have a low-birth weight baby. The physical pathways already described could have been responsible for these outcomes. It is also possible that women under stress do not look after their health—failing, for example, to get adequate rest or nutrition—which, in turn, might be responsible for the outcomes (Lobel, Dunkel-Schetter, & Scrimshaw, 1992).

Clearly, the question of whether maternal experiences affect the fetus is a difficult one to answer. There seems little doubt that a relation exists between maternal stress and the likelihood of problems in the offspring. But we do not know why the relation exists or how strong it is (Istvan, 1986).

Parental Age

The typical age at which a woman gives birth to her first child has risen dramatically over the past 2 decades in the United States. Between 1970 and 1986, the rate of first births to mothers between the ages of 30 and 39 rose 136%. Although the optimal maternal childbearing years generally have been thought to be between 25 and 29 years of age, age has become less important in mothers who have chosen to delay their first birth past these years. Today, such mothers are better educated than was the case decades ago and are more likely to seek early prenatal care and be in good health. Babies born to mothers between 30 and 34 years of age are now almost as heavy as those born to mothers in the optimal range (Ventura, 1989). (Birth weight is a widely used indicator of newborn status.)

As we saw in Chapter 4, increased maternal age is associated with an increased likelihood of giving birth to a baby with Down syndrome. A mother's chances of giving birth to a Down syndrome infant are almost 74 times greater at age 49 than at age 30 (Hook & Lindsjo, 1978).

The father's age also carries a risk for the fetus, because the relative frequency of mutation in the father's sperm increases with age. Down syndrome is attributable to the father rather than the mother in 20 to 30% of the cases (Behrman & Vaughan, 1987). Another genetic disorder related to the father's age is achondroplasia, a mutation that becomes dominant in the child who inherits it and causes bone deformities. The most obvious characteristics are dwarfism and a large head with a prominent forehead and a depressed bridge of the nose. As shown in Figure 5-8, the relative likelihood that a child will inherit achondroplasia increases with the father's age much as the relative likelihood of Down syndrome increases with the mother's age (Friedman, 1981).

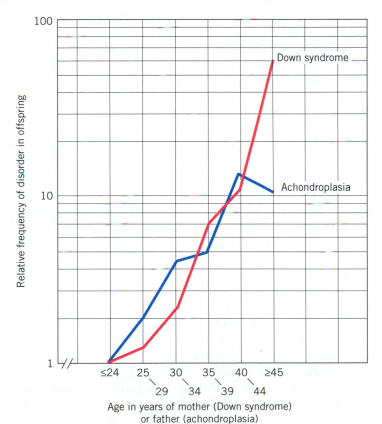

Figure 5-8 Relative frequency of Down syndrome and achondroplasia in the offspring of mothers (Down syndrome) and fathers (achondroplasia) of various ages. From "Paternal Age Effect" by J. M. Friedman. Reprinted with permission from The American College of Obstetricians and Gynecologists (*Obstetrics and Gynecology*, Vol. 57, 1981, p. 746).

• Teenage pregnancy has skyrocketed in recent years. Babies of teenage mothers generally do less well than average. It is unclear what roles biological, social, and economic factors play in this outcome.

In general, babies who are born to mothers in their teens are also at greater risk. Around 500,000 babies a year are born to teenage mothers in the United States, so this is a major concern (Newberger, Melnicoe, & Newberger, 1986). There is some disagreement about whether the negative effect of early motherhood is due mostly to poorer prenatal care for teenage mothers or to their biological immaturity. One study showed that even when teenage mothers received the same prenatal care as older mothers, they were more likely to give birth to babies who were premature or underweight (Leppert, Namerow, & Barker, 1986). Other evidence, however, suggests that the less advantaged socioeconomic status of teenage mothers is responsible for the negative effect on their babies (Murata et al., 1992).

✔ To Recap...

Teratology is the study of agents that thwart normal prenatal development. The emerging field of psychoteratology focuses on the behavioral effects of teratogens. These effects may not always be obvious at birth, but behavioral assessments may detect effects even when no physical evidence exists.

Six principles describe how teratogens act: (1) the effect depends on the genetic makeup of the organism exposed, (2) the effect depends on timing, (3) the effect may be unique to the teratogen, (4) the effects may include death or serious disorders, (5) teratogens gain access to the fetus in different ways, and (6) the effect increases with the level of exposure.

There are a number of natural challenges to the health of the embryo and the fetus. Infectious diseases, such as rubella and AIDS, can cause severe damage. Nutritional factors are important for normal fetal growth, so poor nutrition is also harmful. The ultimate effect of fetal malnutrition depends in part on postnatal nutrition and on the level of stimulation in the environment. Although there is strong suspicion that maternal stress and experiences during pregnancy can affect the fetus, the evidence is still somewhat circumstantial. Parental age demonstrably affects the risk for the fetus, however. As the age of the parents increases, there is increased risk of Down syndrome and achondroplasia. On average, teenage women are more likely to have premature or underweight babies than women in the optimal childbearing age range, but the reasons might have more to do with socioeconomic factors than with the mother's age.

TERATOLOGY: DRUGS AND ENVIRONMENTAL CHEMICALS

To this point we have considered natural challenges to the health of the fetus. There are also hazards that people create in the form of chemicals. Such chemicals include those that people ingest—both on purpose and by accident—and substances released into the environment. These chemicals constitute a clear avenue by which the environment can affect the baby before birth.

Drugs

"The desire to take medicine is, perhaps, the greatest feature which distinguishes us from animals." So said Sir William Osler, a medical historian (Finnegan & Fehr, 1980). People in our culture today consume chemicals not only as medicines to treat specific conditions but as means to induce various mental states. Many such substances—alcohol, caffeine, and nicotine—have become so much a part of daily life that we often do not think of them as drugs. A *drug*, however, can be defined as any substance other than food intended to affect the body. The average pregnant woman takes 4 to 10 drugs of some sort during pregnancy, and up to 80% of the drugs are not prescribed by a doctor.

We mentioned earlier that the effects of Thalidomide dramatically increased awareness of the potential damage that chemicals can do to the fetus. The tragic consequences of the sedative became apparent in the early 1960s, soon after the drug appeared on the market. Depending on when a mother took the drug, her baby was born with malformations of the eyes and ears, deformation of the internal organs, or fusing of the fingers and toes. Some babies were born with a rare defect called *phocomelia*—a condition in which the limbs are drastically shortened and the hands and feet are connected to the torso like flippers.

The teratogenic effects of Thalidomide were especially surprising because doctors considered it to be a mild drug. The women who took it experienced no apparent side effects, and the drug produced no harmful effects on the offspring of pregnant animals on which it was tested. Clearly, we had a lot to learn about how chemicals affect the fetus, and we still do. This incomplete knowledge makes it all the more ill advised for pregnant women to ingest drugs that they could avoid.

"Street Drugs"

The increasing availability of powerful mood- and mind-altering illegal drugs since the 1960s, has been a major health concern in the United States. Unfortunately, the increase has provided substantial evidence about the dangers of drug intake by pregnant women, both to themselves and to their fetuses. Addictive drugs have come under special scrutiny.

For example, heroin addicts are more likely to suffer medical complications in pregnancy and labor, and their newborn babies more likely to undergo drug withdrawal symptoms. Frequently, addiction to heroin is compounded by poor nutrition and inadequate health care; almost 75% of addicts do not see a physician during pregnancy. Forty to 50% of heroin-dependent women who are observed during the prenatal period have medical complications, including anemia, cardiac disease, hepatitis, tuberculosis, hypertension, and urinary infections. They are more likely to miscarry or to give birth prematurely. Their babies are usually lighter than normal and are more likely to suffer brain bleeding, low blood sugar, and jaundice. Heroin-dependent expectant mothers may use methadone, a synthetic drug designed to help break the heroin habit, but methadone is also addictive and is associated with sudden infant death syndrome (in which the baby unexpectedly stops breathing and dies). Furthermore, infants withdrawing from methadone may show withdrawal symptoms more severe than those associated with withdrawal from heroin (Chasnoff et al., 1984; Finnegan & Fehr, 1980; Householder et al., 1982). Offspring of heroin-addicted mothers are less well coordinated at 4 months of age and are less attentive at 1 year (Voorhees & Mollnow, 1987). Some of the effects of heroin addiction have also been observed in babies born to mothers who use cocaine or crack, as described in Box 5-3.

Pregnant women who use heroin and cocaine are more likely than nonusers to be single, economically disadvantaged, and uneducated. They are less likely to practice good nutrition and more likely to use other drugs, including alcohol, and to smoke. For these reasons, it is very difficult to separate the effect of these drugs from an overall configuration of risks to the fetus and mother.

The use of the hallucinogens marijuana and LSD accelerated rapidly in the 1960s and 1970s and created concern about their teratogenic potential. Early research suggested that chromosome breakage was more frequent in users of these drugs and that the users were more likely to experience miscarriages or have babies

BEGINNING LIFE WITH TWO STRIKES: COCAINE-EXPOSED BABIES

On December 15, 1988, Seminole County officials in Florida arrested Toni Suzette Hudson, age 29, making her the first mother to be charged with dealing drugs to an unborn fetus. Her son, Michael, born on November 15, was a cocaine addict at birth.

Unfortunately, Michael's situation is not especially unusual. A conservative estimate is that at least 100,000 fetuses a year are exposed to cocaine (Hawley & Disney, 1992). The ready availability of cocaine, especially in the much cheaper form of hard crack, has increased use of the drug to epidemic proportions. As of 1985, 22 million Americans had admitted using cocaine at least once. It seems likely that the increasing availability of crack renders that figure a pale estimate of today's usage.

Cocaine affects the fetus indirectly through reduced maternal blood flow to the uterus, limiting the fetus's supply of nutrients and oxygen. Additionally, cocaine passes through the placenta and enters the fetus's bloodstream, where it gains direct access to the brain in as little as 3 minutes. In the brain, cocaine affects chemical nerve transmitters in addition to increasing heart rate and blood pressure.

Cocaine-exposed babies are more likely to be miscarried or born dead. If they are born alive, they are more likely to be premature or to suffer retarded growth. They also are more likely to be difficult to arouse and irritable, and they may show frequent jitteriness and shaking. They may have difficulty in regulating their level of alertness and sleep patterns, and be hard to handle (Committee on Substance Abuse, 1990; Hawley & Disney, 1992).

Despite all of these difficulties, studies have turned up conflicting findings regarding how cocaine babies turn out. Some studies have reported that exposed babies later are more impulsive than nonexposed babies and less able to function in unstructured settings. But other studies report few or no long-term effects that can be attributed to cocaine exposure alone. This is largely because cocaine research shares the same difficulties as research on many other teratogens. Mothers who use cocaine are more likely to use other drugs and to smoke and drink. In addition, they are more likely to live in poverty and chaos, to be undernourished and in poor health, and to be depressed. Given this complex of factors, which often exist both before and after a child is born, it is difficult to pinpoint the role of prenatal cocaine exposure on the child's development (Barone, 1993; Gingras et al., 1992; Hawley & Disney, 1992; Hawley et al., 1993).

Indeed, investigators are becoming more sensitive to the effects of the postnatal environment of the cocaine-exposed child. Given an irritable baby who has difficulty falling into regular sleep patterns and a mother who is depressed, has few resources, and continues her drug habit, there is little likelihood that a healthy mother–infant interaction will develop. Many investigators believe that the quality of this relationship and the postnatal environment are the major determinants of the child's outcome (Mayes, 1992).

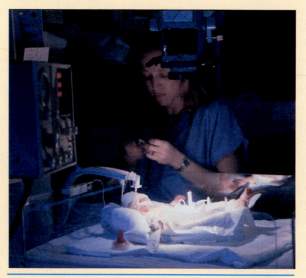

• Newborn babies who have been exposed to cocaine as fetuses are more likely to be premature, jittery, and irritable and to have disrupted sleep patterns.

Some legal authorities believe that pregnant mothers who use drugs should be actively prosecuted as Toni Hudson was. They believe that such mothers are unfit to care for their children. Others argue that it would be counterproductive to worsen a child's future prospects by removing her or him from the mother. They make the case that resources should be committed to helping these mothers kick the drug habit and providing them with education and support to enable them to provide a stable home for their children.

with limb malformations. As with heroin and cocaine, however, the effects of the drugs are difficult to separate from other environmental and health-care practices.

Recent research suggests that the heavy use of marijuana may cause newborns to be jittery and to habituate poorly to visual stimuli (Jones & Lopez, 1990). However, two other recent studies suggest that the moderate use of marijuana has much less extreme effects if the users otherwise engage in good health practices. A study in Ottawa, Canada, in which mothers had good prenatal care, found no effect on the offspring of maternal marijuana users at 2, 3, 5, or 6 years of age, although the exposed children did have lower verbal and memory scores when they were 4 years old (Fried, O'Connell & Watkinson, 1992).

DEVELOPMENT IN CONTEXT: Ganja Use in Jamaica

A study in Jamaica underlines the importance of considering cultural context in health-care practices. As we have noted, one of the most difficult tasks that scientists face in evaluating the effects on the fetus is separating these effects from other factors. In North America, marijuana consumption may be associated with alcohol consumption, smoking, poor nutrition and health care, antisocial behavior, and economic level. It is hard to separate these factors from the influence of marijuana alone.

In Jamaica, marijuana is referred to as ganja. Ganja use is very common among pregnant women in Jamaica and is not associated with the use of other drugs, smoking, or alcohol consumption. Furthermore, social disapproval is not a factor in ganja use in Jamaica. In fact, the smoking of ganja is seen to be a sign of independence from men, economically and socially. Often, women of lower economic status who smoke ganja earn money by selling it and use the money to provide food and housing that is less available to nonsmokers.

An extensive study of offspring of ganja-using mothers found that they performed as well on assessments at 1 month and 5 years of age as children of nonusers; in fact, on a few measures, the 1-month-olds and the 5-year-olds did better (although the differences were small and may have reflected the better access to resources of the ganja-using mothers). Although further research must be done on this issue, we can see how studying varying cultures can help us to better evaluate the effects of drug use (Dreher, 1989; Dreher & Hayes, 1993; Dreher, Nugent, & Hudgins, 1994; Stephens, 1991; Hayes et al., 1991).

Therapeutic Drugs

Many pregnant women take prescribed drugs as part of a continuing regimen of health care—for example, to treat diabetes or blood-clotting tendencies—or as treatments for health problems brought on by the pregnancy. Some of these drugs may increase the risk of fetal problems, creating the need to weigh the risk to the fetus from taking the drug against the risk to the mother of not taking it (Warkany, 1981). Anticoagulants, anticonvulsants (for epileptics), antibiotics, and even heavy use of aspirin have been implicated in increased likelihood of fetal growth retardation, fetal malformations, and fetal and newborn death, especially when taken during the first 3 months of pregnancy. The action of these drugs is often not straightforward. For example, aspirin, which is harmless at a particular dosage in rats, can be teratogenic if administered with benzoic acid, a widely used food preservative. However, it should be kept in mind that the danger from these drugs is fairly low and that by far the majority of mothers taking them have healthy infants. Indeed, there is still considerable controversy over whether some of these drugs are teratogenic at all (Hopkins, 1987; Jones et al., 1988; Majewski & Steger, 1984; Wilson, 1977a).

The effects of sex hormones are more clear. These hormones are sometimes used to treat breast cancer in women and to reduce the likelihood of miscarriage. The use of sex hormones in early pregnancy has been associated with central nervous system malformations in offspring and, more frequently, with masculinization of the external genitalia of females. Some pregnant women took a particularly damaging synthetic hormone, diethylstilbestrol (DES), in the 1950s and early 1960s to reduce the likelihood of miscarriage. Much later, physicians discovered that a high percentage of the female children of these women developed vaginal and cervical problems when they reached adolescence, and some of these offspring developed cancer of the cervix (Harper, 1981; Shepard, 1977; Wilson, 1977a). Recently, evidence has accumulated that the male offspring of mothers who took DES are more likely to develop testicular cancer and to have a lowered sperm count (Sharpe & Skakkebaek, 1993). The studies of sex hormones illustrate yet another problem in detecting teratogenic agents—the possible delay by many years of any observable effect.

Some drugs offer unique benefits but are also powerful teratogens and create considerable controversy. Accutane, a medication for the treatment of disfiguring acne, came on the market in the early 1980s. Within a year, reports of birth defects associated with its use began to appear. By 1988, at least 62 deformed babies had been born to Accutane-using mothers, and the figure may now be as high as 600. Many people argue that the drug should be taken off the market, especially because young women who use it may become pregnant unknowingly or be unaware of its effects. Others argue that it is unfair to deprive people who are not at risk (e.g., males) of the unique therapeutic benefits of Accutane. The manufacturer of the drug has compromised by adding strong warning statements to the label and urging dermatologists to have women screened for pregnancy before they write a prescription for its use (Sun, 1988).

The effects of one prescription sedative, Thalidomide, have already been described. Research on barbiturates and tranquilizers—both depressants—has turned up mixed results. Although some investigators have found associations between congenital defects and sedatives, others have not. Phenobarbital, however, has been associated with congenital defects and blood coagulation problems in the newborn (Jones, Johnson, & Chambers, 1992). Tranquilizers such as diazepam (Valium) and chlordiazepoxide (Librium) can produce cleft palate in mice, and cleft palates have been reported in humans to be 4 times as frequent when these tranquilizers were taken in the first 3 months of pregnancy. Millions of people take these drugs each year (Goldman, 1980; Voorhees & Mollnow, 1987).

Caffeine

Caffeine, a drug present in coffee, tea, chocolate, and some soft drinks, is the drug most commonly consumed in pregnancy. Strangely, the possible effect of caffeine on the fetus has received relatively little attention. As is often the case, one of the problems in determining the effect of caffeine is separating out its effects from the effects of other drugs, such as nicotine and alcohol. Some studies have associated caffeine use with an increased likelihood of miscarriage, premature birth, lower birth weight, and poorer muscular development and reflexes in the newborn (Heller, 1987; Jacobson et al., 1984). However, a later study failed to support these findings, identifying only a small effect on the baby's sleep regularity and a relation between the amount of caffeine consumed and difficulty in consoling the infant (Hronsky & Emory, 1987). The need for more research in this area is evident.

Nicotine

Between one fourth and one third of the women of childbearing age in North America smoke. The effects of nicotine and cigarette smoke on the fetus have been well investigated. Smoking is known to impair the functioning of the placenta, especially oxygen exchange. The following are some risks to women who smoke while they are pregnant:

- On average, their babies are smaller.
- The likelihood of premature delivery and complications increases with the number of cigarettes they smoke per day.
- Their babies are 25 to 56% more likely to die at birth or soon thereafter (Murata et al., 1992).
- Their babies are as much as 50% more likely to develop cancer (Stjernfeldt et al., 1986).
- According to longitudinal studies, detrimental effects on their children's height and reading ability may last into early adolescence (Fogelman, 1980). Other studies found that a poorer performance on language and cognitive tasks was associated with how much the mothers smoked while pregnant (Fried, O'Connell, & Watkinson, 1992).
- Impulsivity and attentional deficits may also be lasting problems; a recent study found these problems in 6-year-olds whose mothers smoked while pregnant (Fried, Watkinson, & Gray, 1992).

Even passive exposure of pregnant nonsmoking women to others' smoke apparently affects the growth of the fetus (Martin & Bracken, 1986).

Alcohol

In the United States, alcohol is the most widely used drug that is known to harm the fetus. It poses a major preventable health problem. Among the causes of birth defects in the United States, alcohol ranks 3rd, just behind Down syndrome and spina bifida. It is the leading cause of congenital mental retardation in the Western world (Murata et al., 1992; Warren & Bast, 1988). Withdrawal effects in newborns of mothers who drink heavily can mimic those of drug addiction (Abel, 1980, 1981).

Although the effects of alcohol on the fetus were suspected in the 18th century, a clear picture of the consequences of chronic maternal alcoholism on the fetus did not emerge until 1973, when investigators described **fetal alcohol syndrome**, a unique set of features in the fetus caused by the mother's alcohol consumption (Jones et al., 1973). A photo of a child with this syndrome appears in Figure 5-9. Limb and facial malformations, congenital heart disease, failure to thrive, anomalies of the external genitalia, growth retardation, mental retardation, and learning disabilities are associated with fetal alcohol syndrome (Rosett, 1980; Wilson, 1977a). Behavior problems compound these difficulties, as infants with fetal alcohol syndrome are irritable, sleep less well, are difficult to feed, and frequently regurgitate (Rosett, 1980). By school age, these children are more likely to have difficulty in sustaining effort and attention and to have language problems and motor-performance deficits (Larsson, Bohlin, & Tunell, 1985; Streissguth et al., 1985).

Research indicates that chronic alcohol use by the mother increases the risk to the fetus by almost 50%. Some of the effects just described, however, have been ob-

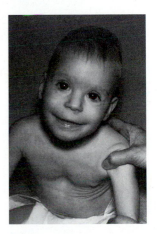

Figure 5-9 Infant born with fetal alcohol syndrome.

Fetal alcohol syndrome
A set of features in the infant caused by the mother's ingestion of alcohol during pregnancy; typically includes facial malformations and other physical and mental disabilities.

served in infants whose mothers were not chronic alcohol users but who drank sporadically and heavily. Furthermore, the effects of alcohol can be increased by smoking and other drugs. What level of alcohol use during pregnancy is safe? One expert has cautioned against chronic use exceeding 45 drinks per month or 6 drinks at any one time; these levels double or triple the risk of congenital malformations, growth retardation, and functional abnormalities in the fetus (Rosett, 1980). The effects of relatively low levels of alcohol consumption are less clear. In one study, even alcohol consumption within the limits of what could be defined as social drinking reduced alertness in newborns and their ability to habituate to a repeated stimulus, and the effects may be observable years later (Streissguth, Sampson, & Barr, 1989). However, in two studies, children of low-risk women with good prenatal care who consumed less than one drink per day performed as well as the offspring of nondrinkers on tests of cognition and language and measures of attention and impulsivity (Fried, O'Connell, & Watkinson, 1992; Fried, Watkinson, & Gray, 1992).

Environmental Chemicals

The number and amount of chemicals in our environment have increased explosively since the beginning of the Industrial Revolution. Insecticides, herbicides, fungicides, solvents, detergents, food additives, and miscellaneous other chemicals have become part and parcel of our daily existence. Each year, thousands of new compounds are synthesized by industry or created as a result of reactions in the environment. One expert recently estimated that humans are exposed to significant amounts of approximately 5 million of these environmental chemicals. Only a small fraction of them are tested as potential teratogens in pregnant laboratory animals (Ames, 1979).

Researchers often find that chemicals are potentially teratogenic in animals, but the doses that they use are typically quite large. People generally experience comparable doses only in rare instances, such as industrial accidents or concentrated dumping (for example, in Love Canal, a former chemical dumping ground near Niagara Falls). The rates of defective births and spontaneous abortions are monitored routinely in many hospitals in the United States, providing a measure of protection against long-term chronic exposure of undiscovered teratogens. However, as we have seen, complex interactions among chemicals and delayed effects can often make detection difficult.

A clear example of the effects of environmental chemicals comes from Cubatão, a small town in an industrial valley in Brazil. Cubatão was slowly choking through pollution of its streams, air, and countryside. Thousands of tons of particulate matter were being discharged into the air from smokestacks, and huge amounts of organic matter and heavy metals were being dumped into the streams. Through an ambitious cleanup program the town reduced discharges of particulate matter by 72%, organic waste into rivers by 93%, and heavy metals by 97%. With the cleanup, the infant mortality rate in Cubatão dropped to one half the 1984 rate (Brooke, 1991).

Of the various chemicals present in the environment, metals have come under special scrutiny. Mercury and lead have been suspected teratogens for many years. A disaster comparable to that caused by Thalidomide occurred in Japan between 1954 and 1960, when people ate fish from a bay that had been contaminated with mercury from industrial dumping. Many mothers who ate the fish gave birth to infants with severe neurological symptoms resembling cerebral palsy. Prenatal exposure to lead from automobile exhausts and lead-base paints has been implicated in increased miscarriages, neuromuscular problems, and mental retardation (Bellinger et al., 1986; Wilson, 1977c). Follow-ups of children who experienced high lead exposure as babies reveal negative effects even after 11 years on vocabulary, motor coordination, reading ability, and higher level thinking (Needleman et al., 1990).

Another group of environmental chemicals that can harm fetuses are polychlorinated biphenyls (PCBs), widely used as lubricants, insulators, and ingredients in paints, varnishes, and waxes. Cooking oil used in Japan in 1968 and in Taiwan in 1979 was accidentally contaminated by PCBs, and pregnant women who used the oil were more likely to have stillborn infants and infants with darkly pigmented skin. In the United States, PCB levels are relatively high in fish taken from Lake Michigan. Offspring of mothers who ate these fish were smaller at birth, had somewhat smaller heads, and were more likely to startle and be irritable. Babies who had detectable PCB levels in their blood at birth performed more poorly on various visual measures at both 7 months and 4 years of age (Jacobson et al., 1985; Jacobson et al., 1992; Jacobson & Jacobson, 1988;). PCBs are widely distributed and appear to be well established in the food chain, though not at levels that are typically detrimental to fetuses (Rogan, 1982).

✔ *To Recap...*

Not only natural challenges but also exposure to drugs and chemicals may pose risks to the developing embryo and fetus. "Street drugs," though illegal, have become increasingly available over the past 3 decades and can have highly negative effects on the fetus. Babies of drug-addicted mothers may be born addicted, and they are likely to have many developmental problems. Therapeutic drugs may also be harmful, as was the case with Thalidomide.

Some substances are so common in our daily lives that we may fail to think of them as drugs. Caffeine, nicotine, and alcohol are examples. No firm conclusions have been drawn regarding the effects of caffeine consumption during pregnancy. Nicotine and alcohol are another matter. Smoking has consistently been shown to affect growth and to increase the risk of premature delivery and birth complications. Alcohol consumption can produce a range of physical malformations and intellectual consequences, including fetal alcohol syndrome.

Exposure to harmful chemicals can also occur through taking in the chemical by-products of industry in the food we eat and the air we breathe. Mercury and lead have been documented as particularly teratogenic, and PCBs also appear harmful.

PREVENTING, DETECTING, AND TREATING BIRTH DEFECTS

We noted earlier that through a natural process of screening, spontaneous abortion ends fetal development in most cases in which the fetus has genetic abnormalities or a problem exists in the uterine environment. Although there are thousands of genetic abnormalities and scores of challenges to the fetus, it is important to view these risks in perspective. More than 90% of infants are born healthy and normal, and the large majority of the remaining infants have minor problems that can be corrected or that will be outgrown.

Still, small percentages can translate to large numbers of people, and statistics provide little comfort to those affected. It has been estimated that in a single year as many as 200,000 babies may be born with birth defects in the United States and that 15 million Americans have some kind of handicap caused by a birth defect

(Sorenson, Swazey, & Scotch, 1981). Can anything be done to prevent birth defects? How can a mother be sure the baby she is carrying is healthy? And how can birth defects be treated?

Prevention

At present, not all birth defects can be prevented. The causes of some are not controllable; the causes of others are not even known. There are, however, certain steps that significantly lower the risk from teratogens. A woman planning to become pregnant can, for example, avoid drinking alcohol, smoking, and taking unnecessary drugs, and she can eat prudently. Prenatal care is very important both for assessing risk and for monitoring the woman's progress and the fetus's development. In fact, some experts advise women to see a physician even before they conceive (Murata et al., 1992).

Rapid progress in the area of genetics has made it possible for people to exert some control over the incidence of genetic problems. **Genetic counseling** consists of a range of activities focused on determining the likelihood that a couple will conceive a child with a genetic disorder. Couples who are contemplating pregnancy often want to know the chances that their baby will be normal. DNA analysis of their blood may be done to determine if they are carriers of a defective dominant or recessive gene, as in the case of Tay-Sachs disease or cystic fibrosis (see Box 5-4). If one parent is a carrier of a defective dominant gene that is autosomal, the chances are 1 in 2 that their baby will be normal. If both parents are carriers of the same defective recessive gene, the chances are 3 in 4 that their baby will be healthy. Defective genes on the sex chromosome affect the chances differently, depending on whether the fetus is a male or female and whether the mother or father is the carrier. When couples are at risk and the woman has become pregnant, parents often consider procedures for assessing whether the fetus is normal.

Screening for Abnormalities

There has been significant progress in detecting problems in newborn infants, which opens up the possibility for early treatment. Phenylketonuria (PKU) can again serve as an example. Although scientists understood at the beginning of the 1960s what caused PKU and how to treat it through diet, they had no method for determining which newborn infants had PKU. By the time they discovered the defect in a child, irreversible damage had occurred. Then, in 1961, a blood test was developed that could detect excess phenylalanine in the blood. Infants with PKU were put on a special diet until they were around 7 years of age to prevent the severe retardation, seizures, and skin lesions characteristic of the untreated PKU patient. By the late 1960s, approximately 90% of all babies in the United States were being screened at birth. Today, PKU is no longer a major health problem (Rowley, 1984).

Even more dramatic advances permit parents to learn about the status of the fetus as early as 9 to 11 weeks into a pregnancy and, as we shall see, sometimes in the first days following conception.

Ultrasound Imaging

Ultrasound imaging uses soundlike waves to provide a continuous picture of the fetus and its environment. The level of detail in this image permits identification of the sex of the fetus by 16 to 20 weeks and reveals abnormal head growth; defects of the heart, bladder, and kidneys; some chromosomal anomalies; and neural tube defects (Anderson & Allison, 1990; Golbus, 1983; Nakahara et al., 1993; Stoll et al.,

• As research has furthered our knowledge of factors that can harm the fetus, agencies have become increasingly effective in alerting the expectant mother.

Genetic counseling
The advising of prospective parents about genetic diseases and the likelihood that they might pass on defective genetic traits to their offspring.

Ultrasound imaging
A noninvasive procedure for detecting physical defects in the fetus. A device that produces soundlike waves of energy is moved over the pregnant woman's abdomen, and reflections of these waves form an image of the fetus.

A POPULATION APPROACH TO GENETIC SCREENING

A highly successful program of genetic population screening has demonstrated the value of a well-publicized effort to inform parents of reproductive risks. The program, the first of its kind, was initiated in 1970 to identify carriers of Tay-Sachs disease. This disorder is carried as a recessive gene in about 1 of 29 American Jews. If two carriers mate, 1 of 4 of their children, on average, will have Tay-Sachs disease. The effort to identify carriers, begun through a community education and neighborhood-based screening campaign in the Baltimore, Maryland–Washington, D.C. area, had tested more than 354,000 Jewish adults by 1981. Virtually all of the couples identified as carriers elected to have amniocentesis during their pregnancies, which numbered 912 by 1981, and 202 fetuses were diagnosed as having Tay-Sachs. All but 13 of these pregnancies were voluntarily terminated by the parents; the babies born to the remaining 13 were afflicted with Tay-Sachs, as predicted. The incidence of this fatal disease was thus reduced by 65 to 75% over the prior decade (Kaback, 1982).

In 1990, a similar program on a much larger scale was contemplated to screen parents for cystic fibrosis. The Tay-Sachs program had targeted 1 to 2 million people, but geneticists were now considering screening the entire U.S. population of reproductive age—perhaps 100 to 200 million people. One in 25 Caucasians is a carrier of cystic fibrosis, which puts the level of risk in the general population near the level of risk for Tay-Sachs in American Jews. Current tests can identify about 70% of cystic fibrosis carriers, and efforts are underway to develop techniques for identifying the remaining 30% (Roberts, 1990).

A multitude of ethical issues arise from our increasing skill in fetal screening. Should damaged fetuses be aborted? If so, how disabling must the genetic defect be? If a child was diagnosed as genetically damaged as a fetus, should insurance companies be able to deny the child insurance, given that the companies know that health expenses will be exorbitant, compared to those of other children?

1993). Ultrasound imaging is also helpful for diagnostic procedures that require collection of amniotic fluid or tissue, such as amniocentesis and chorionic villus sampling. Finally, ultrasound can determine whether there is more than one fetus.

As with many technological advances, concerns have arisen about how ultrasound imaging is used. Because China has developed a one-child policy and its citizens favor males, ultrasound imaging is being used there to determine the sex of the fetus in order to identify female fetuses for abortion. The practice is spreading in Asia, upsetting the ratios of male to female births. The ratio has reached 118.5 male per 100.0 female births in China (Kristof, 1993).

Amniocentesis

An especially important tool for assessment is **amniocentesis**, because it provides samples of both the amniotic fluid and fetal cells in the fluid that have been sloughed off. A needle is passed through the mother's abdomen and into the amniotic cavity to collect the fluid. Analysis of the fluid can reveal abnormalities. For example, alpha-feto protein (FEP), a substance the fetus produces, circulates in the amniotic fluid. Abnormally high levels of FEP occur when the fetus has certain types of damage to the brain, the central nervous system, or the liver and kidneys.

Chromosomal analysis of the fetal cells can also indicate problems. Women over the age of 35 frequently opt to have amniocentesis because of their heightened risk of having babies with Down syndrome, a defect that shows up in a chromosomal cell analysis. Interestingly, awareness of the risk associated with maternal age, coupled with the availability of amniocentesis and the option of terminating pregnancy, has completely changed the maternal age distribution of Down syndrome

Amniocentesis
A procedure for collecting cells that lie in the amniotic fluid surrounding the fetus. A needle is passed through the mother's abdominal wall into the amniotic sac to gather discarded fetal cells. These cells can be examined for chromosomal and genetic defects.

• Ultrasound imaging permits identification of abnormalities in the developing fetus, as well as other characteristics like gender, size, and position.

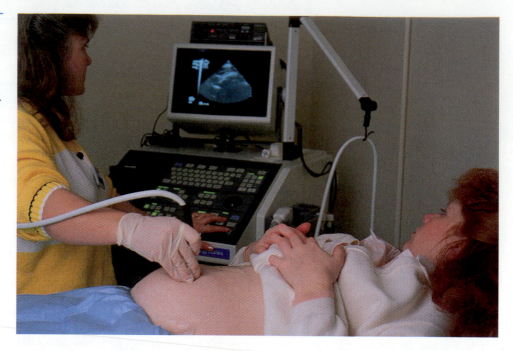

births. Now, 80% of afflicted babies are delivered to mothers under age 35, because amniocentesis is not a routine procedure for these women (Behrman & Vaughan, 1987). Fetal cells can also be tested for genetic defects such as sickle-cell anemia, cystic fibrosis, and Duchenne muscular dystrophy (Winston & Handyside, 1993). The list of detectable diseases increases almost daily with increasing knowledge of which genes produce particular diseases.

The amniocentesis procedure does increase the risk of miscarriage, but only by around 0.5 percent (Cunningham, MacDonald, & Gant, 1989). Another problem with amniocentesis is that it is most effective after the period during which abortion is safest for the mother. Chorionic villus sampling, a relatively new procedure, can make information about the fetus available much earlier.

Chorionic Villus Sampling

Chorionic villus sampling (CVS)

A procedure for gathering fetal cells earlier in pregnancy than is possible through amniocentesis. A tube is passed through the vagina and cervix so that fetal cells can be gathered at the site of the developing placenta.

In a procedure called **chorionic villus sampling (CVS)** cells are collected from the chorion, a part of the placenta. A small tube is inserted through the cervix and into the fetal placenta to collect a sample of fetal cells. These cells reveal large-scale defects of the chromosomes or more minute defects in the DNA. CVS is possible as early as 9 to 11 weeks but carries a slightly higher risk of miscarriage than amniocentesis, around 2% (Cunningham et al., 1989).

Test-Tube Screening

Scientists have succeeded in screening embryos in the test tube before they are implanted in the mother's uterus. Egg cells are collected from the mother and then fertilized in a petri dish through in vitro fertilization as described earlier. One cell is removed from each embryo when it reaches the eight-cell stage. From this one cell, the sex of the embryo can be determined, and, within a few hours, the DNA of the cell can be checked for suspected anomalies. Chloe O'Brien, born in England on April, 1992, was the first baby to be born by in vitro fertilization following DNA analysis before implantation. The parents were carriers of the cystic fibrosis gene. If they had conceived in the normal fashion and had discovered that their fetus had cystic fibrosis by the other techniques described, they would have faced a decision on abortion. By this technique, they were assured that the embryo that was implanted was free of this disease, and Chloe is doing fine (Fogle, 1992; Handyside et al., 1992).

It is possible to detect almost 200 disorders through various screening techniques. However, only around 10% of women who have at-risk pregnancies participate in prenatal screening (Fletcher, 1983). The risk of problem pregnancy is higher for a woman who (1) has had miscarriages or has had offspring with congenital disorders, (2) is outside the optimal childbearing age range, (3) has relatives (or the father has relatives) with genetic abnormalities, (4) is poor and has inadequate medical supervision and nutrition, or (5) takes drugs during pregnancy.

Treatment

The growing sophistication of diagnostic procedures has made early detection of developmental abnormalities more and more possible. But what happens when a fetus is found to be developing abnormally? Of course, the parents may decide to terminate the pregnancy. But sometimes there are treatment alternatives. Developments in the medical treatment of fetuses parallel the rapid advances in early diagnosis. The current and projected approaches to prenatal treatment fall into three categories—medical therapy, surgery, and genetic manipulation.

Medical Therapy

Medical therapy is currently the most widely available of the three methods. An example is the provision of extra vitamins to the mother when enzyme deficiencies are discovered in the blood of the fetus (Golbus, 1983).

An exciting first in medical therapy was reported in mid-1989. Parents in Lyons, France, whose first child had died in infancy of a hereditary disorder, learned that the fetus the mother was carrying had the same disorder. The disease consists of an immune deficiency that leaves the infant open to almost any infection. Doctors decided to try to treat the fetus while he was still in the womb. They injected immune cells from the thymus and liver of two aborted fetuses into the umbilical cord, the first time this had been done. After the baby was born, the injected cells multiplied (Elmer-DeWitt, 1994).

Researchers recently discovered that women who have AIDS are less likely to pass the disease on to their fetuses if they have certain antibodies in their blood. It may be possible to immunize AIDS-carrying pregnant mothers to increase the number of these antibodies (Stephens, 1990).

Surgery

The use of fetal surgery is illustrated by the experience of a pregnant woman who had earlier given birth to an infant with hydrocephaly, an abnormal accumulation of fluid inside the skull that results in brain damage. An ultrasound diagnosis indicated that the fetus was accumulating fluid on the brain and would likely suffer brain damage if treatment was delayed until birth. Surgeons at the University of Colorado Medical School, working through a long hollow tube inserted through the mother's abdomen and the amniotic sac, inserted a small valve in the back of the fetus's head to permit the excess fluid to drain, thereby relieving pressure on the brain. The fetus survived the surgery and, at 16 months of age, appeared to be normal (Clewell et al., 1982; Fadiman, 1983).

Physicians are now able to carry out surgery on fetuses to avoid the damage caused by blockage of the urinary tract and a small number of other problems

Figure 5-10 Brain surgery on a monkey fetus. The fetus was taken halfway out of the uterus for the procedure and then replaced to continue development inside the mother.

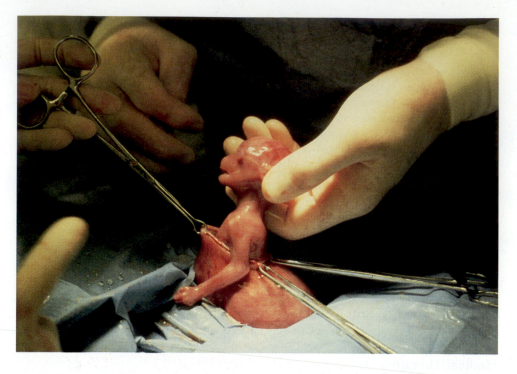

(Ohlendorf-Moffat, 1992). In the near future, fetuses who have a neural tube defect may also be treatable. Neural tube defects often result in infants being born with an opening in the back of the head through which part of the brain protrudes. The current treatment involves removing the external brain tissue and closing the skull after birth, which often leaves the infant blind and mentally retarded. Working with monkeys, researchers at the National Institute of Child Health and Human Development have operated on fetuses by removing them from the uterus and conducting a similar operation, as shown in Figure 5-10. Apparently, the brain tissue at least partially regenerates, because the monkey fetuses, carried to term, are able to see. This treatment may someday be available for human fetuses who would otherwise face a bleak future (Fadiman, 1983; Kolata, 1983).

Genetic Engineering

Probably the greatest promise for prenatal treatment lies in the field of genetic engineering. Suppose we could detect, say, the lack of an enzyme in a fetus's blood and could identify the specific gene that caused the defect. Working in the laboratory with a blood sample from the fetus, we would "clip out" the defective gene and insert a synthetic gene. After producing many copies of the blood cells containing the repaired chromosome, we would inject them into the fetus, where they would survive and replicate and provide sufficient amounts of the enzyme for normal development.

In September 1990, scientists undertook the first federally approved attempt at human gene therapy of this kind. It involved a 4-year-old girl who suffered from ADA deficiency, a severe and incurable disease of the immune system. Cells were extracted from the little girl, and harmless viruses were used to carry the needed

ADA gene into the cells. The cells—a billion or so—were then reinjected into the child's bloodstream. The cells are producing the needed ADA, but the child will need repeated treatments. Currently, scientists are working on techniques to make repeated treatments unnecessary by carrying out similar procedures during the fetal stage. They will try to replace the cells in the fetus that give rise to all of the ADA-producing cells; thus these cells will not die during the lifetime of the patient (Capecchi, 1994; Karson, Polvino, & Anderson, 1992).

Ethical Considerations

The ability to diagnose abnormal development raises innumerable ethical questions—questions that people may find difficult to answer. Today's fetal screening techniques can detect the presence of sickle-cell anemia, Huntington's chorea, Down syndrome, cystic fibrosis, and numerous other maladies. What are the consequences of this knowledge? If no treatment is possible, the options—bringing a child with a serious disorder into the world or deciding to terminate the pregnancy—may seem equally undesirable (Kolata, 1986).

Increasingly, special interest groups and the federal government have sought to become involved in this decision process. Movements are now underway to prevent the use of federal or state funds for abortions and even to make any abortion illegal. Proponents of these movements argue from a moral and ethical "pro-life" perspective. Opponents emphasize the individual mother's right to make a personal, moral, and ethical choice. They also point out that prohibitions would discriminate against poorer citizens, who may not have personal funds to pay for abortion.

In a related area, two successive United States presidents have made different decisions regarding research on the use of aborted fetal tissue to treat various illnesses. President George Bush banned research with fetal tissue, and President Bill Clinton lifted this ban soon after he took office. Those who oppose such research argue that women might seek more abortions in order to sell their fetuses for research. Others claim that this is extremely unlikely and that the research could lead to humanitarian treatments for those who suffer from certain diseases, such as Parkinson's, for whom fetal tissue provides the only hope.

Another related issue, the treatment of severely damaged newborn infants, emerges when no abortion is performed. This issue, too, is controversial, as in the case of Baby Jane Doe. On October 11, 1983, Baby Jane Doe was born on Long Island with hydrocephalus, spina bifida, and microcephaly. Her parents had two options: They could approve two operations, after which it was likely that she would live past age 20 but be paralyzed, severely retarded, and in pain. Or they could refuse to permit surgery, in which case she would likely die before the age of 3. They chose not to allow surgery. But others felt it was not their choice to make alone. Most significantly, the U.S. Justice Department, for the first time, sued on behalf of the medical rights of a handicapped infant. Ultimately, the U.S. Supreme Court ruled against the government, putting the matter to rest in June, 1986 (Holden, 1986).

Decisions regarding the health and life of a fetus or infant are intensely emotional and deeply embedded in social, ethical, and moral convictions. They are also very personal. As new technologies are developed, the fine line that separates these personal beliefs and feelings on the one side, and the government's role in protecting the rights of fetuses and infants on the other, may become increasingly tenuous.

✔ *To Recap...*

We have progressed dramatically in our understanding of prenatal diseases and in our ability to diagnose and treat them. In some cases, the most useful approach is prevention, perhaps through genetic counseling.

During pregnancy, diagnostic procedures provide a window on prenatal development that was unknown only a few decades ago. Ultrasound imaging can detect growth anomalies, such as abnormal head growth. Amniocentesis and chorionic villus sampling provide fetal cells that can be analyzed for chromosomal defects and several genetic problems, as well as some other disorders. Screening has even been carried out on embryos in test tubes.

When problems are detected, treatment can sometimes proceed even while the fetus is still in the uterus. Medical therapy is one possibility, as when there are chemical imbalances. Surgery is a second possibility. On the horizon is the possibility of gene therapy.

As we become more skilled at understanding genetics, screening for and diagnosing problems, and developing treatment alternatives, however, individuals and society at large face a new array of ethical dilemmas.

CONCLUSION

We live at a time when knowledge and technology in many fields are expanding at a dizzying pace. Nowhere are the effects of progress more dramatic than in biology and health-related fields. The field of prenatal development has benefited enormously from these advances.

Only relatively recently have we developed an understanding of the processes of conception and embryological development. It has been especially important for us to learn that differentiation of body parts and limbs occurs in the first 8 weeks or so after conception. With this knowledge, we have been better able to understand why infections and certain drugs have more devastating effects on the organism during the early prenatal period than later.

Our awareness that the placenta does not always filter out chemicals and toxins from the mother's blood, and that these substances thus enter the bloodstream of the fetus, has had profound effects. Scientists actively look for causes of abnormal development that were previously ignored. Environmental pollutants, drugs, and other chemicals are suspect, and it is now routine to test new chemicals for toxic effects on the fetus. The new field of psychoteratology may provide even more sensitive indicators of harmful substances. Although we may not always know how or why these substances affect the fetus, at least we are learning when they do. Partly because of this knowledge, the ratio of birth deaths to live births in the United States has reached an all-time low.

An important message from this information is that the baby is in an environment from the moment of conception. By the time of birth, interactions between genes and the environment have been at play during the full 9 months of development.

One might come away from this chapter fearful about all the things that threaten a baby's prenatal development. Keep in mind that, in fact, the very large majority of babies are born healthy and intact. Fortunately, as we have learned about the dangers that the fetus faces, we have been increasingly able to take precautions that will increase the likelihood that the newborn will get a healthy start. In the next chapter, we discuss the tools the baby brings into the external world and several principles of growth and development.

FOR THOUGHT AND DISCUSSION

1. The embryo stage is the most vulnerable time for the developing baby. But since this period occurs between 3 and 8 weeks after conception, many women do not realize that they are pregnant until after this point. *What ramifications might knowledge of this vulnerability have for college students and other young people who are sexually active? How would you suggest a young woman behave if she suspected she was pregnant?*

2. As we saw, many physical and behavioral problems of development result from inadequate prenatal care, such as failure to maintain an appropriate diet or exposure to teratogens of various kinds. *How might this knowledge affect one's beliefs regarding problems of development in impoverished areas or among disadvantaged people? What sorts of alternative explanations for these problems would it challenge?*

3. It is now clearly documented that exposing the developing fetus to large quantities of alcohol or drugs can cause serious developmental problems. *Under the circumstances, should pregnant mothers who knowingly ingest these teratogens be prosecuted for child abuse? Could this policy have any important drawbacks?*

4. Prenatal testing permits us to learn many things about the fetus before birth, including the baby's sex. *What are some potential advantages of learning whether the baby is male or female many months before birth? What are some possible problems with knowing? Would you want to know?*

5. We mentioned two diseases for which population screening has been undertaken or is being contemplated. Such screening is very expensive. *If you had to make the decision to approve such a project, what factors would you consider? What might be some potential dangers in implementing a policy to genetically screen people in a population?*

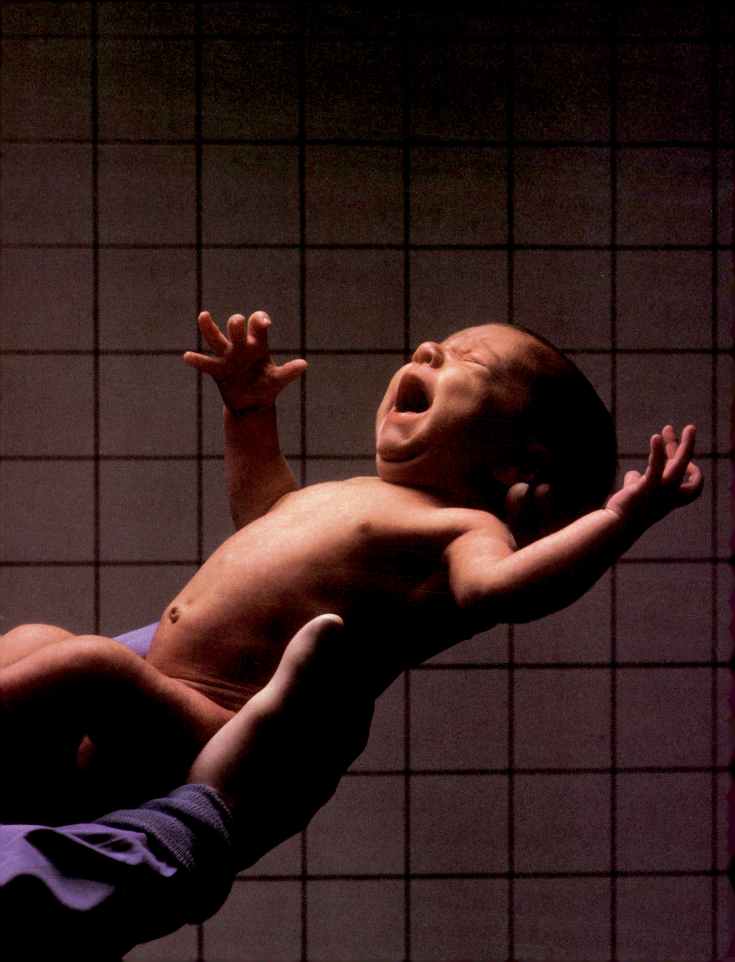

Chapter 6

BIRTH, PHYSICAL GROWTH, AND THE DEVELOPMENT OF SKILL

*p*hysical growth is a hallmark of development. In Chapter 5, we witnessed the explosive growth and specialization of the human organism during the 9 months before birth. In this chapter, we watch the baby enter the world and develop physically from birth through adolescence. Increases in physical size will not be our only concern. We will also consider how the baby acquires skills that permit the manipulation of objects and exploration of the environment, skills that have enormous psychological impact. Psychological and physical growth depend crucially on the maturation of the brain, so we devote part of our discussion to how the brain develops and operates. In addition, we follow physical changes that prepare the adolescent for reproductive capability, changes that affect the person's self-image and identity. Our story starts with birth and surrounding events—the *perinatal period*.

BIRTH AND THE PERINATAL PERIOD

Birth is truly momentous. No other event in life involves such dramatic changes and requires so much adaptation in such a brief period. Normally, the events surrounding birth proceed smoothly. In this technological age, we sometimes forget that humans and their predecessors accomplished the feat over millions of years without advanced equipment and trained professionals. Occasionally, however, modern technology is crucial to the preservation of life. After briefly describing the physical process of birth, we consider deviations from the normal state of affairs, especially those involving the infant at risk.

Labor and Delivery

Typically around 38 weeks after fertilization, the birth process begins, probably triggered by a signal from a small area of the brain of the fetus that monitors the status of developing organs (Palca, 1991). The aging placenta, increasingly less able to provide the needed nourishment for the fetus, may also play a role. Labor begins when the muscles of the mother's uterus begin to contract rhythmically, initially every 15 to 20 minutes and then at shorter and shorter intervals. The complete birth process typically requires 8 to 16 hours for the first baby and half that for later babies (Guttmacher, 1973). Labor consists of three stages, shown in Figure 6-1. The first stage begins with a narrowing of the uterus and ends with the full dilation (widening) of the neck of the uterus. The second stage ends when the fetus leaves the vagina, after which the placenta and remaining membranes are delivered, completing the final stage.

Although the stages of birth are, of course, the same in all cultures, there are many variations in how cultures think about and deal with birth. Practices have changed fairly rapidly in the United States. As recently as 1972, only 27% of American hospitals permitted fathers into the delivery room. By 1980, 80% of these hospitals had an open policy. Research suggests that the father's presence can have a positive influence on both the mother and the infant (Parke & Beitel, 1986). Cultural variations in labor and delivery are discussed in Box 6-1.

Culture also affects the likelihood that the mother will survive pregnancy and childbirth. In the United States, because of improved health care, maternal deaths per 100,000 women of childbearing age fell from approximately 660 in 1931 to 7.4 in 1986. But around the world, even today, 500,000 women each year lose their lives from complications of pregnancy and labor. In Nigeria, for example, the death rate is still 800 per 100,000. And in one rural region of Ghana there are 1,700 maternal

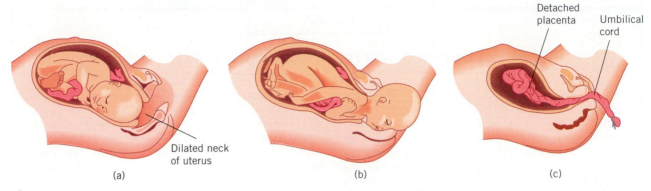

Detached placenta

Umbilical cord

Dilated neck of uterus

(a)   (b)   (c)

𝒯igure 6-1   The three stages of labor: (*a*) The neck of the uterus dilates, (*b*) the baby is delivered, and (*c*) the placenta is expelled.

deaths per 100,000. Often, pregnant women simply do not have health-care facilities available to them, or transportation to health facilities is poor. But, sometimes, a cultural clash is the problem. An area in Accra, Ghana, has a large population of Muslim refugees from Mali whose custom is to wear long black dresses. For native Ghanans, the color black symbolizes evil and death, so hospitals do not accept women who come to them in black and try to get the women to change their dress. The Muslim women resist this attempt and simply refuse to go to the hospitals. Thus, they do not receive necessary care (*Carnegie Quarterly*, 1993).

Babies face challenges during the birth process also, although no one really knows how much stress the baby experiences during birth. However, being pressed by the muscular contractions of the uterus, squeezed through the birth canal, and thrust into a completely new world of air, light, cold, and sound is, to say the least, unfamiliar. For the mother, birth can be both exhausting and exhilarating. And for an older sibling, the arrival of a new brother or sister often caps many months of discussion and anticipation, and the beginning of a new role in the family (Mendelson, 1990).

As we have noted, the great majority of births proceed normally. However, for every normal process there are deviations. Babies are usually born by vaginal deliv-

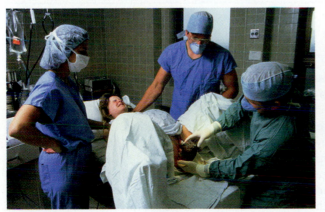 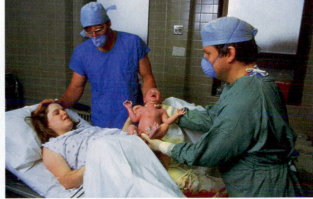

• In Western society, birth typically takes place in a hospital with the mother lying on her back. Medication for pain, once administered routinely, has given way to more natural methods of dealing with the physical discomfort.

CULTURAL ATTITUDES TOWARD BIRTH

Some people believe that in most Western countries, pregnancy, labor, and delivery are treated as if they were the symptoms of an illness. Pregnant women are encouraged to visit the doctor regularly. Most give birth in a hospital, lying down (some say for the convenience of the doctor), and have been given drugs to block pain. Often, after the baby is born, doctors and nurses, not the baby's mother, take over the baby's care, at least for a while.

Does something unique to Western civilization encourage us to look at pregnancy as a sort of disability and birth as a process requiring medical intervention? Apparently not. Among the Cuna Indians of Panama, for example, a pregnant woman must visit the medicine man daily for herbal medicines and is given medication throughout labor. Intervention in labor is practiced in many cultures: The pregnant woman's abdomen may be massaged, perhaps with masticated roots or melted butter, or even constricted to help push the baby out. It is said that for difficult cases, midwives of Burma tread on the woman's abdomen with their feet.

Nevertheless, the attitude of the West is often contrasted with that of cultures in which birth is seen as an everyday occurrence. Among the Jarara of South America, for example, labor and birth are so much a part of daily life that a woman may give birth in a passageway or shelter in view of everyone. In many cultures, women give birth alone. And non-Western women commonly deliver in an upright position—kneeling, sitting, squatting, and even standing—rather than lying down (Mead & Newton, 1967).

There has been a trend in the West toward making birth more "natural." A British obstetrician, Grantly Dick-Read, wrote a book called *Natural Childbirth* in 1933 and a second, called *Childbirth Without Fear,* in 1944 to put forth the view that Western societies had created an association between childbirth and pain. Fear of pain, he said, actually created tension and muscle cramping that produced pain unnecessarily. These ideas were reinforced by Dr. F. Lamaze (1970) in *Painless Childbirth.* Lamaze's popular method of preparation for childbirth is based on conditioning through breathing and muscle exercises and on educating the mother about pregnancy and labor.

A parallel movement has emphasized the baby's experience of childbirth. In *Birth Without Violence* (1975), Dr. F. Leboyer argued that the infant's transition into the outside world—already stressful because of the birth process itself—should not be made more difficult by bright lights, noise, and insensitive handling. Leboyer introduced a more gentle approach to limit the assault on the baby's senses—a darkened and quiet room, gentle massage, and a warm bath.

Is the "naturalist" trend right? Is the "illness" orientation wrong? The fact is, research in this field is inadequate to allow us to draw any firm conclusions about what might be "best" for the mother or the baby. What seems remarkable is the ability of mothers and newborns, in general, to thrive despite the varying rituals with which their cultures surround them.

---

ery but may be born by cesarean section. Babies usually are born after approximately 9 months of gestation but may be born prematurely or postmaturely. Babies are usually born without mechanical assistance but the physician may need to assist the birth with special devices. Although important deviations are relatively rare, they can be worrisome or even devastating for those affected. Scientists have devoted great effort to developing technologies for optimizing the outcomes of abnormal birth as well as for understanding its consequences. Their efforts have resulted in a substantial decline in the United States of deaths in the newborn period, both for whites, for whom the mortality rate has been comparatively low, and for African Americans, for whom the rate has been much higher (see Table 6-1). Still, in 1993, the United States ranked behind most other industrialized nations in newborn mortality rate statistics (Anderson, 1993).

TABLE 6-1 ● U.S. Infant Mortality Rates 1915–1990 (Deaths in the first year per 1,000 live births)

Year	African Americans	Whites	All Races
1915	150.4	92.8	95.7
1920	117.4	73.3	76.7
1925	105.3	65.0	69.0
1930	90.5	55.2	60.4
1935	80.1	49.2	53.2
1940	72.9	43.2	47.0
1945	56.2	35.6	38.3
1950	43.9	26.8	29.2
1955	43.1	23.6	26.4
1960	44.3	22.9	26.0
1965	41.7	21.5	24.7
1970	32.6	17.8	20.0
1975	26.2	14.2	16.1
1980	21.4	11.0	12.6
1985	18.2	9.3	10.6
1987	17.9	8.6	10.1
1988	17.6	8.5	10.0
1989	17.7	8.2	9.7
1990	17.0	7.7	9.1
1991			8.9
1992			8.5

Source: Based on information from U.S. Department of Health and Human Services, National Center for Health Statistics, Vital Statistics of the United States, 1987, and Monthly Vital Statistics Reports from 1993.

Technological advances permit the monitoring of the fetus's state during birth. Physicians can visualize the fetus, the umbilical cord, and the placenta by ultrasound to determine, for example, if there is danger that the umbilical cord will wrap around the fetus's neck (which can cause strangulation), and they can record the heart rate of the fetus and its activity electronically through the mother's abdomen. The physician may intervene when the fetus is in a breech position (that is, positioned with the feet rather than the head toward the vagina), when labor is not progressing normally, when the birth canal seems too narrow, or when there are signs of **fetal distress** as indicated by a heart rate that is abnormally high or low (Anderson & Allison, 1990). The physician may assist through the use of forceps or a vacuum or may deliver the fetus by cesarean section, through an incision in the mother's abdomen.

Technological progress hardly ever escapes controversy, and birth events are no exception. Some argue that the increased sensitivity of monitoring techniques prompts too many doctors to choose cesarean delivery. The rate of cesarean deliveries skyrocketed from 5% in 1969 to 25% in 1990 and estimates from current trends suggest that the rate will rise to as high as 40% by the year 2000 (Guillemin, 1993). Others point to the increases in survival rates of newborns and a decline in birth defects such as cerebral palsy, which are thought to be related to difficult

Fetal distress
A condition of abnormal stress in the fetus; may be reflected during the birth process in an abnormal fetal heart rate.

births. As is often the case, we need more information and research in order to judge the merits of this procedure for mother and infant.

The Concept of Risk

Parents worry about whether their baby will be normal. In more than 9 out of 10 cases, the baby is born on time, and they are able to breathe a sigh of relief when the doctor tells them the baby is fine. But some parents and their babies are not so fortunate. Approximately 3% of all babies born in the United States each year, 120,000 or so infants, are born with major malformations. In addition, some babies are considered to be **at risk** for developmental delays and cognitive and social problems. Psychologists believe that the earlier they can identify these babies, the earlier they can intervene to help. Thus, they have carried out hundreds of studies over the past 2 decades to try to discover what factors put infants in the highest category of risk. Three indicators have received significant attention—maternal and family characteristics, the physical compromise of the newborn, and the performance of the newborn on behavioral assessments.

At risk
A term describing babies who have a higher likelihood of experiencing developmental problems than other babies.

Maternal and Family Characteristics

Around 85% of the risk of severe developmental problems can be attributed to what happens in the prenatal period. As mentioned in the preceding chapter, several maternal factors increase risk for the fetus, including the mother's use of drugs or alcohol, exposure to viral infections during pregnancy, smoking, and poor nutrition. A major factor in the United States is the failure of the mother to seek prenatal care from a physician. Of mothers who saw a doctor at any time during pregnancy, only 6% had low-birthweight babies, whereas the figure was 3.5 times greater for mothers who did not see a doctor (Bronfenbrenner, 1989). Low birthweight is an important indicator of risk. We have already seen that infant mortality is higher among African Americans than among whites. So, too, is low birthweight. This may reflect the fact that whereas only about 20% of pregnant white women fail to see a doctor in the first 3 months of pregnancy, the comparable figure for African-American women is 38% (Kopp & Kaler, 1989).

Failure to see a doctor partly reflects the financial resources available to the mother. Indeed, financial problems increase the likelihood of low birthweight by sixfold (Binsacca et al., 1987). Babies born to families who have strained financial resources, poor social support, and little education are more at risk than are those born to more advantaged families. One set of experts recently made the following projection of the percent of newborn babies that will face various risk factors by the year 2000:

- Not wanted (12%)
- Born at low birthweight and/or premature (7%)
- Mothers are substance abusers (11%)
- Parents are alcoholics (10%)
- Mothers are teenagers (10%)
- Mothers are not married (30%)
- Mothers have not completed high school (20%)
- Family income is below the federal poverty line (23%) (Barnard, Morisset, & Spieker, 1993, p. 386)

Physical Compromise of the Newborn

A second general indicator of risk is evidence of physical problems in the newborn—most frequently, low birthweight. Around 6 to 7% of the babies born annually in the United States (around 250,000) have a low birthweight, below 2,500 grams (about 5.5 pounds). Of all infant deaths that are not due to major malformations, 70% are associated with low birthweight; stated in other terms, low-birthweight babies are about 40 times more likely to die in the first month of life than are babies born at normal weight (Erickson & Bjerkedal, 1982; Freda et al., 1990; *March of Dimes Report,* 1989). Furthermore, about 7% of the larger babies and 15% of the smaller ones in the low-birthweight group will suffer serious developmental difficulties (Kopp & Kaler, 1989). Why do these babies have problems?

The newborn must make a number of adaptations to the outside world. Temperature control and nutrition are no longer provided by the mother's body, but these needs are rather easily met by the parents or other providers. However, the baby must assume three critical functions on his own—elimination of wastes, independent blood circulation, and breathing. Of these adaptations, breathing is the most likely to cause problems. Remember that the fetus, who has lived in a water world for almost 9 months, must draw his first breath within seconds after birth. Because oxygen remains in the blood for a while after the umbilical cord has been cut, a breathing delay of even 5 minutes may not be harmful. However, some babies have difficulty initiating or maintaining breathing. Babies who are born light in weight are much more likely to have breathing problems than normal-weight babies.

Failure to breathe prevents the delivery of oxygen to cells in the body. Certain problems before birth can also have this effect. A deficit of oxygen in the cells, called **anoxia,** can cause the cells to die. The brain cells are especially sensitive to oxygen deficits. Severe anoxia may damage the brain area that controls movement of the limbs, for example, resulting in a spastic-type movement referred to as cerebral palsy (Apgar & Beck, 1974).

Anoxia
A deficit of oxygen supply to the cells that can produce brain or other tissue damage.

Low-birthweight babies may be placed in two categories. One group comprises babies whose birthweights are low because they were born **preterm,** before the end of the normal gestation period—that is, the normal 38 weeks of pregnancy. We will consider the preterm infant in a moment.

Preterm
A term describing babies born before the end of the normal gestation period.

Babies may also be born with a low birthweight because their fetal growth was retarded. Such babies are considered to be **small for gestational age (SGA).** Babies in this category have weights among the bottom 10% of babies born at a particular gestational age. They may be born at the expected gestational age of 9 months, or they may be born earlier (and so be both SGA *and* preterm). In either case, they are unusually light for their stage of development. Several factors appear to increase the likelihood that babies will be born so light, including chromosomal abnormalities, congenital infections, poor maternal nutrition, and maternal substance abuse. Often, the cause is unknown (Allen, 1984; Lubchenko, 1981).

Small for gestational age (SGA)
A term describing babies born at a weight in the bottom 10% of babies of a particular gestational age.

SGA babies tend to have poor muscle tone and to appear limp when held. They do not arouse easily, and they orient relatively poorly to visual stimulation (Als et al., 1976). Recent investigations suggest that these babies are disadvantaged beyond the newborn period. At 7 months of age, SGA babies have poorer recognition memory than babies born at normal weight (Gotlieb, Baisini, & Bray, 1988). SGA babies who are also preterm perform more poorly on verbal tests of IQ in the preschool period than do preterm babies whose weights were appropriate for their ages (Dowling & Bendell, 1988). However, their eventual developmental course depends heavily on the quality of their postbirth environment (Gorman & Pollitt, 1992).

Whether SGA babies eventually catch up with their peers seems also to depend on their growth patterns as fetuses. In one study, fetuses who had normal rates of head growth up to 34 weeks of gestational age attained normal body size and mental performance by 4 years of age. Fetuses whose head growth had faltered prior to 34 weeks were much smaller than their peers at 4 years, and their mental ability was impaired (Tanner, 1990).

What about babies who are light because they are preterm? Steady improvement in technology has produced a dramatic decline in deaths due to preterm birth. While a birthweight below 2,500 grams (5.5 pounds) is classified as low, babies weighing only one fifth that much (a little more than a pound) have at least a 25% chance of living, and the odds rise to more than 90% for babies who weigh at least 1,000 grams (about 2.2 pounds) (Minde, 1993). One consequence of this progress is that very tiny babies who would once have died at birth are now kept alive, and these babies face strong challenges to life and well being. The lighter the baby, the higher the risk.

Preterm babies often face the breathing problems described earlier, and many are prone to the bursting of tiny blood vessels in the brain, which produces bleeding and contributes to the infant's risk. Even disregarding these physical challenges, the preterm baby may, at least for a time, lag behind a normal-term baby. Because the preterm infant is comparable to a fetus still in the womb, we might expect her to be less advanced than the normal-term baby. However, even when the normal-term and preterm infant are matched for the number of days following fertilization, the preterm infant usually has poorer muscle tone and less mature brain patterns and is more disorganized and more difficult to soothe (Als, Duffy, & McAnulty, 1988; Duffy, Als, & McAnulty, 1990; Kopp, 1983; Parmelee & Sigman, 1983).

Studies indicate that preterm infants may be less attentive and have poorer memory than normal-term infants during the first year of life but differences tend to disappear over time (Parmelee & Sigman, 1983). Typically, by the elementary school years, no obvious differences remain between preterm and normal-term children. Although there is some evidence of a higher frequency of educational and behavioral problems, especially in boys, it is hard to disentangle these effects from those of the context in which the child is raised (Kopp & Parmelee, 1979). Preterm infants are more likely to be born to less advantaged families, and a family's economic status has a strong impact on developmental outcome (Kopp, 1983; Kopp & Parmelee, 1979; Minde, 1993; Parmelee & Sigman, 1983; Sameroff & Chandler, 1975).

Physical and Behavioral Assessment

Still a third indicator of risk is poor performance on standard assessments. Perhaps as a sign of things to come, almost all babies born in the United States begin life with a test. Such assessments help the tester to organize observations of the newborn and to record them for reference by others. Tests are used to screen babies for disorders, to determine whether a baby's nervous system is intact, and to characterize how a newborn responds to social and physical stimuli. Even though newborns are new to the external world, they possess a surprising range of behaviors and functions. Tests assess many—more than 85% of—such behaviors and functions (Francis, Self, & Horowitz, 1987; Self & Horowitz, 1979). Here, we consider the main categories of newborn assessments and the most often-used tests: the Apgar exam, the Prechtl test, and the Brazelton Neonatal Behavioral Assessment Scale.

In 1953, Dr. Virginia Apgar introduced a test that permits obstetricians to record objectively the status of the newborn, and it has become the standard for the baby's first assessment. The *Apgar exam* focuses on five of the newborn's vital functions, which are measured by heart rate, respiration, muscle tone, response to a mildly painful stimulus, and skin color. The newborn receives a score from 0 to 2 on each of these items with 2 the optimal score. For example, the baby earns a 2 for the heart rate category if the heart beats 100–140 times per minute; a 1 if the rate is less than 100; and a 0 if no beat is detectable. Babies are typically assessed on the five categories almost immediately after birth. The highest possible score is, of course, 10. In a study of almost a thousand babies, 77% received a score of 8–10, 17% a score of 3–7, and 6% a score of 0–2 (Apgar, 1953).

Investigators use the Apgar to discover babies who may need special monitoring and attention through early infancy. Several factors tend to lower the Apgar score, including maternal depression, anxiety, smoking, drinking, and labor medication. Infants who later succumb to sudden infant death syndrome and other causes of early mortality have frequently earned lower Apgar scores at birth. Psychologists have also examined the relation between a newborn's Apgar score and intellectual functioning later in infancy and early childhood. The results have been mixed, with some investigators reporting a positive relation but others reporting no relation when socioeconomic status, race, and gender are taken into consideration (Francis et al., 1987).

The Apgar exam assesses vital life processes and can be quickly administered, but the results provide only limited information. An extensive assessment of neurological functioning, which we will refer to as the *Prechtl test,* is much more informative (Prechtl, 1977; Prechtl & Beintema, 1964). This examination includes items similar to those in the Apgar but also assesses alertness, spontaneous movements and tremors, facial expressions, muscle tone, reactions to placement in a variety of postures, and around 15 reflexes. Babies who show fetal distress during birth or who need assistance with instruments to pass through the birth canal earn lower scores on the Prechtl test (Leijon, 1980; Prechtl, 1968). Labor medication and premature birth also tend to depress scores on this test (Belsey et al., 1981; Forslund & Bjerre, 1983).

The questions addressed by the Apgar and Prechtl tests, such as how well the newborn is managing such functions as breathing, independent blood circulation, and certain reflexes, are obviously important. But such measurements may tempt us to think of the newborn as something of a machine whose vital functions operate at a certain level of efficiency and who responds in a certain way to stimuli. The newborn is a much more complex creature, with a wealth of behavioral tools. Moreover, newborn babies differ substantially in how they behave, and these differences may affect how parents and others treat them. For these reasons, investigators have focused increasingly on tests of how well the newborn's behavior is organized (Brazelton, 1984; Rosenblith, 1961).

The *Brazelton Neonatal Behavioral Assessment Scale* is the most comprehensive of these tests. A fundamental concept underlying this scale is that the seemingly fragile and helpless newborn possesses organized behaviors for dealing with both attractive stimuli, such as pleasant sights, sounds, and tastes, and offensive stimuli, such as loud noises and pin pricks (Brazelton, Nugent, & Lester, 1987). Assessors observe babies in a number of states, or levels of alertness, to obtain a sense of the baby's style and temperament. A unique feature of the exam is that it evaluates the newborn's ability to habituate. Habituation, as you may recall from Chapter 2, is a simple form of learning in which a reflex response to a stimulus declines or disappears when the stimulus repeatedly occurs. The exam includes items in four general categories: attention and social responsiveness, muscle tone and physical movement, control of

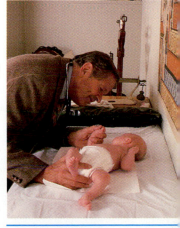

• T. Berry Brazelton developed a widely used scale for assessing the newborn.

alertness (habituation, irritability, and excitability), and physiological response to stress. The baby's performance on these measures provides indicators of well-being and risk. For example, a baby who is unable to habituate to a repeated stimulus or to remain alert may fall into a higher risk category. Infants who have difficulty maintaining alertness as newborns are more likely to have medical problems and developmental delays at 1 year of age (Francis et al., 1987; Tynan, 1986).

All the newborn assessments discussed here do a fairly good job of characterizing how a baby is doing in the early period. However, they are poor predictors of ultimate intelligence and personality, and none of the risk factors we have discussed is very dependable when considered in isolation. This fact may seem surprising to anyone who has seen a very light baby in the newborn intensive-care nursery. A 2-pound baby—who is little more than tubes, only able to breathe with a mechanical respirator, and perhaps suffering internal brain bleeding—may seem to be on the verge of death. Amazingly, such a baby is more than likely to turn out fine (Sostek et al., 1987). The best predictor of developmental difficulties is the number of risk factors to which an infant is subjected. The greater the number, the more likely that the infant will have problems (Sameroff et al., 1993).

 ## DEVELOPMENT IN CONTEXT: Infants at Risk: Environment Holds the Key

Some babies who are born at risk have suffered brain or central nervous system damage that affects their functioning throughout life. However, for many babies born at risk, whether they achieve normal development appears to depend largely on the context in which they are reared. Most of the research illustrating this fact has been carried out with preterm infants, so we will focus on that work. But many of these factors are at play in determining the outcome of any baby at risk.

One factor is the quality of the relationship that forms between the parents and the baby. At-risk babies often pose special challenges to this relationship. For example, the preterm baby may spend weeks in a plastic enclosure, in a special-care hospital nursery where parents have little opportunity to hold and cuddle her. When the baby comes home, she is likely to have an irritating cry, be difficult to soothe, and have irregular patterns of sleep and wakefulness (Frodi et al., 1988; Parmelee & Garbanati, 1987).

These real problems are aggravated by people's reactions to preterm babies. In one study, several sets of parents were shown a film of a 5-month-old baby after they had been told that the baby was either "normal," "difficult," or "premature" (a term the researchers used for both SGA and preterm babies). Parents who were told that the baby was premature judged crying segments of the film to be more negative than did other parents, and physiological measures indicated that they experienced the baby's cries as more stressful (Frodi et al., 1978). Other investigators have observed that parents treat their premature children differently even after apparent differences between them and their full-term counterparts have disappeared (Barnard, Bee, & Hammond, 1984a; Beckwith & Parmelee, 1986). The tendency to expect negative behavior from premature infants has been referred to as "prematurity stereotyping" (Stern & Karraker, 1992). Such stereotypes increase the possibility that a negative cycle between parent and infant will be set in motion. Of course, the degree to which this is true depends in part on the tolerance and flexibility of the caregivers. We consider this issue again in Chapter 12.

A contributor to disruption of the parent–infant relationship in the past was the policy of hospitals not to permit the parents to hold or touch their infant in the special-care nursery because of the fear of infection. We can easily imagine how a mother's confidence in caring for her baby might be jeopardized after being limited for 6 to 8 weeks after birth to watching the baby through a transparent incubator shield with all sorts of plastic tubes running to and fro. As investigators increasingly appreciated the importance of the very earliest social interactions between mother and infant, things began to change. A group at Stanford University took the daring step of permitting parents to handle their infants in the special-care nursery and demonstrated that no increased danger of infection resulted (Barnett et al., 1970). Subsequent work demonstrated that handling enhanced mothers' self-confidence in responding to their babies (Leiderman & Seashore, 1975; Seashore et al., 1973).

A related factor is the lack of stimulation that infants often experience when they must spend time in the hospital. The temperature-controlled, patternless plastic chambers in which they are placed deprive them not only of human physical contact but of sensory input as well. Several studies have demonstrated the positive effects of providing stimulation for preterm infants. For example, in one study preterm babies were placed on a gently oscillating waterbed that mimics the stimulation the baby receives in the womb. The waterbed babies had fewer episodes in which breathing stopped than babies treated conventionally (Korner, 1985). Other investigators introduced special massage programs and extra visual, auditory, and movement stimulation for preterm infants, both in the nursery and following hospital discharge. The effects were improved weight gain and intellectual development over the first year of life compared with preterm infants who did not receive special enrichment (Anisfeld et al., 1993; Powell, 1974; Scafadi et al., 1986; Scarr-Salapatek & Williams, 1973). However, there is increasing concern that, for some premature babies, added stimulation becomes overstimulation and has a negative rather than positive effect. Increasingly, investigators are suggesting that each baby

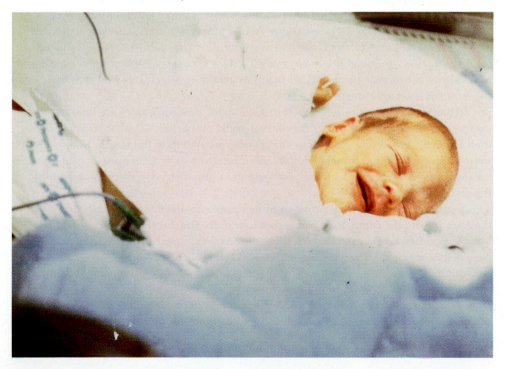

• Premature babies benefit from opportunities to control their exposure to a mild stimulus that changes, such as the "breathing bear" discussed in the text.

must be considered individually. One creative idea is to provide stimulation that the babies themselves can decide to experience or avoid. For example, one investigator placed a "breathing" teddy bear in the baby's bed, which the baby could either contact or avoid. Premature babies who had the breathing bear tended to stay near it more than those who had a nonbreathing bear, and they spent a longer amount of time in quiet sleep (Thoman, 1993; Thoman, Ingersoll, & Acebo, 1991).

Another factor that may affect the development of the preterm infant, as mentioned, is the family's socioeconomic status. By 2 to 3 years of age, children born preterm into families that have strong financial resources seem indistinguishable from children born at term. These more positive outcomes for infants of more advantaged parents might be related to the reduction of other stresses in the parents' lives—fewer financial problems and lower incidence of sickness, for example—and to their better access to and use of health and psychological professionals. Family stresses tend to reduce the emotional availability of parents for their infants, their tolerance for negative behavior, and their ability to organize family tasks (Hoy, Bill, & Sykes, 1988). Enrichment programs have been shown to be effective for families with low-birthweight infants both for increasing the child's cognitive capabilities and for reducing behavior problems at 2 and 3 years of age (Brooks-Gunn et al., 1993). Of course, the contextual factors we have considered here affect the development of all babies. What recent research has told us is that these factors are especially important for babies born at risk (Rauh et al., 1988).

✔ *To Recap...*

Labor begins with regular contractions of the uterus and passes through three stages. Most births proceed normally, and technological advances have helped to improve the outcomes of those that do not.

Psychologists have been particularly interested in identifying babies born at risk for developmental problems. One indicator of risk is maternal and family characteristics. Whether the mother receives prenatal care from a physician seems especially important.

A second indicator of risk is physical compromise of the newborn, most frequently identified by low birthweight. Low-birthweight babies have more difficulties in adjusting physically to life outside the womb. Difficulty in breathing, which may lead to anoxia, is the most common adjustment problem.

Babies' birthweights may be low for two reasons. Preterm babies are light because they were born before the end of the normal gestation period. SGA babies are small even for their gestational age because of growth retardation in the womb. Both types show differences from normal-weight infants, and these differences may persist for several years. However, at least for preterm babies, the differences may disappear by the early school years.

A third indicator of risk is provided by newborn assessments. These tests include the Apgar exam, the commonest and easiest to use; the Prechtl test, which adds more neurological functions to the characteristics tested by the Apgar exam; and the Brazelton Neonatal Behavioral Assessment Scale, the most comprehensive test.

Ultimately, no single risk indicator predicts intelligence or personality especially well. The number of risk factors seems to be the best predictor of developmental problems. In addition, the outcome of a baby born at risk depends on the quality of the relationship with the parents, the availability of early stimulation, and the family's socioeconomic status.

THE ORGANIZED NEWBORN

Look at a newborn baby, and you will see that his face, if he is awake, changes expression rapidly for no apparent reason, and his legs and arms often flail around with no seeming purpose or pattern. A sleeping baby is less active, but her sleep is punctuated by twists, turns, startles, and grunts—a fairly unorganized picture. Seeing these behaviors, you can understand why, during most of the history of child psychology, people considered the newborn a passive and helpless creature whose activity was essentially random. Any organized behavior depended on external stimulation. Is it true that the newborn comes into the world with no organized patterns of behavior for sleeping, eating, getting the caregiver's attention, or even moving? Must caregivers teach the baby all these things?

Research on newborn behavior since the 1960s has drastically changed our views. Certainly the newborn is not as coordinated or predictable as the 2-year-old, but his behavior is neither random nor disorganized. The newborn possesses natural rhythms of activity that generate patterns of sleeping and wakefulness, eating, and motion. Moreover, the newborn is equipped with many reflexive responses to external stimulation. These rhythms and reflexes help babies to manage their energy resources as well as their responses to external stimulation. The newborn also possesses some organized behavioral patterns for investigating and controlling the environment through looking, sucking, and crying. We now look more carefully at this organized newborn.

States of Alertness

Often, when grandparents and friends come to the hospital to see the new baby, the first question they ask the nurse is, "Is she asleep or awake?" Actually, there are other possibilities as well. Thirty years ago, Peter Wolff, at the Harvard Medical School, carefully watched several newborn babies for many hours and was struck by how much their levels of alertness varied yet how similar these levels were from one baby to another (Wolff, 1959, 1966). He captured these observations by defining six states of infant alertness: (1) quiet, or deep, sleep; (2) active, or light, sleep; (3) drowsiness; (4) alert inactivity; (5) alert activity; and (6) crying. These states are described in Table 6-2.

Several aspects of these states and how they change with age make them very useful for understanding early development, for assessing the effects of various factors—such as teratogens—on development, and for comparing one infant with another. The states become more distinct with age, and investigators believe that this change provides information about how the baby's brain matures. In addition, the amount of time babies spend in each state and the ease with which babies move from one state to the next change with age. Therefore, physicians can examine how various factors, such as preterm birth, teratogens, birth medication, and mother–infant interaction affect early development by studying their effect on how soon the various states become organized and differentiated.

Recordings of brain activity, made by means of an **electroencephalograph** (EEG), reveal that states become increasingly distinct with age. Recordings from a fetus of 29 weeks gestational age reveal the same brain-wave pattern across all states, whereas the patterns for full-term 3-month-olds are well differentiated (Parmelee & Sigman, 1983; Sadeh & Anders, 1993). The sample recording in Figure 6-2 shows

Electroencephalograph (EEG)
An instrument that measures brain activity by sensing minute electrical changes at the top of the skull.

TABLE 6-2 ● States of the Infant

State	Characteristics
Deep sleep	Regular breathing; eyes closed with no eye movements; no activity except for occasional jerky movements
Light sleep	Eyes closed but rapid eye movements can be observed; activity level low; movements are smoother than in deep sleep; breathing may be irregular
Drowsiness	Eyes may open and close but look dull when open; responses to stimulation are delayed, but stimulation may cause state to change; activity level varies
Alert inactivity	Eyes open and bright; attention focused on stimuli; activity level relatively low
Alert activity	Eyes open; activity level high; may show brief fussiness; reacts to stimulation with increases in startles and motor activity
Crying	Intense crying that is difficult to stop; high level of motor activity

that the brain-wave patterns of babies in quiet sleep and active sleep become increasingly different with age.

The time distribution of sleep states also changes rapidly with age, as shown in Figure 6-3. Whereas the fetus of 25 weeks gestational age engages almost exclusively in active sleep, the newborn spends about half the time in active sleep and half in quiet sleep. By 3 months, quiet sleep occurs twice as much as active sleep (Berg & Berg, 1987; Gardner, Karmel & Magnano, 1992; Korner et al., 1988; Parmelee & Sigman, 1983). In active sleep, babies periodically move and breathe irregularly, but the most notable feature is that they frequently move their eyes back and forth with their eyelids closed (as do adults), so this sleep state is often called **rapid eye movement,** or **REM, sleep.**

The shift from dominantly active, or REM, sleep to dominantly quiet sleep has aroused considerable speculation about the function of REM sleep. In the adult, REM sleep constitutes only about 20% of total sleep time and is associated with

Rapid eye movement (REM) sleep
A stage of irregular sleep in which the individual's eyes move rapidly while the eyelids are closed.

Figure 6-2 With age, the brain waves associated with the various states become increasingly distinct. Adapted from "Perinatal Brain Development and Behavior" by A. H. Parmelee and M. D. Sigman, 1983. In P. H. Mussen (Ed.), *Handbook of Child Psychology: Vol. 2, Infancy and Developmental Psychobiology,* 4th ed. (p. 116), New York: John Wiley & Sons. Copyright 1983 by John Wiley & Sons, Inc. Adapted by permission of John Wiley & Sons, Inc.

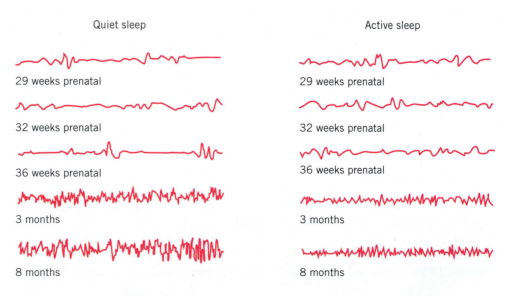

Quiet sleep

29 weeks prenatal

32 weeks prenatal

36 weeks prenatal

3 months

8 months

Active sleep

29 weeks prenatal

32 weeks prenatal

36 weeks prenatal

3 months

8 months

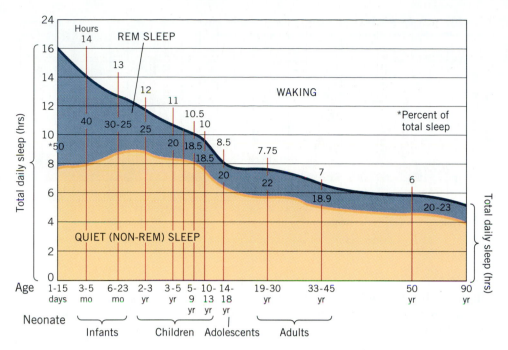

Figure 6-3 Although the total amount of sleep time declines with age, the drop is most noticeable for REM sleep during the first 2 to 3 years of life. The amount of quiet sleep is about the same for newborns and 3-year-olds, but the percent of sleep time spent in the REM state declines from around 50% to around 25% over this time span. From "Ontogenic Development of the Human Sleep–Dream Cycle" by H. P. Roffwarg, J. N. Muzio, and W. C. Dement, 1966, *Science, 152,* p. 608. Copyright 1966 by the AAAS. Reprinted by permission. The figure reproduced here contains revisions made by Roffwarg et al. since the original publication in 1966.

dreaming (Aserinsky & Kleitman, 1955). Roffwarg and his associates (1966) speculated that the high frequency of REM activity in early development reflects a kind of internal "motor" that keeps nerve pathways active until the baby receives enough external stimulation to maintain their integrity, an idea that was subsequently confirmed (Kandel & O'Dell, 1992). Consistent with this idea is the finding that babies who have longer awake periods, which presumably provide needed stimulation, have shorter REM periods during sleep (Boismer, 1977; Denenberg & Thoman, 1981).

A striking change in the organization of states occurs around 3 months of age. Whereas the adult usually enters the quiet sleep state from a state of wakefulness, the newborn typically enters REM sleep from the waking state. The adult pattern emerges at around 3 months (Parmelee & Sigman, 1983). Investigators believe the change reflects an important stage of brain maturation.

Since the organization of sleep states—how well they are differentiated, their time distribution, and the order in which they appear—reflects brain maturation, we might expect babies at risk to be less organized than other infants. Indeed, state organization is affected in babies of alcoholic and drug-addicted mothers. And babies who are unstable in how they distribute their time in various states between 2 and 5 weeks of life are more likely than relatively stable babies to have later medical and behavioral problems (Parmelee & Sigman, 1983; Thoman et al., 1981). There is also a relation between infrequent eye movements during active sleep and mental retardation (Garcia-Coll et al., 1988; Tynan, 1986).

To this point, we have talked about infant states in terms of the internal processes they reflect. But states also play an important role in infants' interactions with the environment. Babies are more receptive to stimuli and learn more readily when they are in states of alertness than when they are crying, asleep, or drowsy (Berg & Berg, 1987; Parmelee & Sigman, 1983; Thoman, 1990). Thus, states affect the impact of external events. Conversely, external events can affect an infant's state. For example, a monotonous sound may cause a baby who is in an active sleep state to shift to a state of quiet sleep (Brackbill, 1975; Wolff, 1966). A crying baby

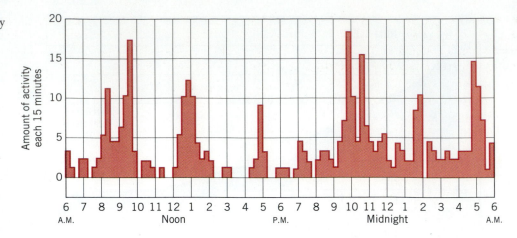

Figure 6-4 The activity of a 6-day-old baby rises and falls over a 24-hour period in a repeating rhythm that averages 4 hours in duration. Adapted from L. W. Sander, G. Stechler, P. Burns, and H. L. Julia, "Early Mother–Infant Interaction and 24-Hour Patterns of Activity and Sleep," *Journal of the American Academy of Child Psychiatry, 9,* p. 110, 1970, Copyright by The American Academy of Child and Adolescent Psychiatry. Adapted by permission.

will often shift to a quiet, alert state if an adult picks her up, puts her to his shoulder, and gently rocks her up and down (Korner & Thoman, 1970; Pederson & Ter Vrugt, 1973).

Rhythms

Most children and adults have regular patterns of daily activity. For the most part, they sleep at night, are awake during the day, and eat at fairly predictable times. We can say that their daily patterns obey a repeating rhythm. On the other hand, one need only look at the reddened, tired eyes of a new parent to know that the newborn baby's habits are not so regular. Can we conclude, then, that the baby enters the world with no rhythms at all and must be taught by the parents when to eat, when to sleep, and when to wake? Not at all. Newborn babies are very rhythmic creatures. The newborn's biological clock just seems to tick at a different rate than ours, and it gradually shifts into synchrony with ours as the baby ages.

The newborn's states, like the adult's, occur as rhythms that cycle within other rhythms. The newborn baby engages in a cycle of active and quiet sleep that repeats each 50 to 60 minutes. (A similar cycle exists in the adult with a duration of 90 to 100 minutes.) This cycle is coordinated with a cycle of wakefulness that occurs once every 3 to 4 hours (Aserinsky & Kleitman, 1955; Parmelee & Sigman, 1983; Sander et al., 1970). What produces this behavior? We might suspect that the sleep–wake cycle reflects a cycle of hunger or of external disruption by caregivers. However, the cycle seems to be internally governed. Even before the first feeding and with external distractions held to a minimum, newborns still display roughly these same sleep–wake cycles (Emde, Swedberg, & Suzuki, 1975). The pattern of activity over the 24-hour day for a 6-day-old baby in Figure 6-4 reflects this sleep–wake cyclicity.

Much to the relief of their parents, infants gradually adapt to the 24-hour light–dark cycle. Sleep periods become longer at night as awake periods lengthen during the day, with longer sleep at night emerging around 5 to 6 weeks of age. By 12 to 16 weeks, the pattern of sleeping at night and being awake during the day is fairly clearly established, although the baby sleeps about the same amount as the newborn (Berg & Berg, 1987).

Even though the rhythms of the newborn seem to be biologically programmed, they are not free from environmental influences. For example, newborn babies who stay in their mothers' rooms in the hospital begin to display day–night differences in their sleep cycles earlier than babies who stay in the hospital nursery (Sander et al., 1970). These rooming-in babies also spend more time in quiet sleep and less time crying than babies in nursery groups (Keefe, 1987). Apparently, prenatal experience can also affect rhythmic activity. Newborns who have alcoholic or drug-dependent mothers have more difficulty in synchronizing their various sleep–wake rhythms and in adapting to the night–day cycle (Parmelee & Sigman, 1983; Sander et al., 1977).

Organized Behavior of the Newborn

We have seen that the newborn baby has identifiable states of alertness and that these states fit into overall rhythms. Newborns are also equipped with several specific behavior patterns that occur in response to specific stimuli, such as the startle reaction to a loud sound. These highly stereotyped behavior patterns, which occur as brief responses to specific stimuli, are called **reflexes.** The newborn also initiates activities and is capable of sustaining them over considerable periods of time. Looking behavior, sucking, and crying are examples of such activities, which we will refer to as *congenitally organized behaviors*.

Reflex
An automatic and stereotyped response to a specific stimulus.

Reflexes

The newborn's reflexes, even those we seldom see, are interesting and important, because they provide information about the state of the brain and the nervous system. The presence or absence of reflexes and their developmental course provides information about a particular baby's neural apparatus (Kessen, Haith, & Salapatek, 1970). For example, an infant should reflexively bend to the left side when the doctor runs her thumb along the left side of the baby's spinal column. If this reflex occurs on the left side, but not the right side, it is possible that the nerves are damaged on that side.

Some reflexes last throughout life. But the reflexes that have been of most interest are those that disappear in the first year of life, because their disappearance indicates the development of more advanced brain functions. Table 6-3 lists some of the more common reflexes as well as the stimuli that produce them and their developmental course. We discuss only a few of these reflexes here.

The **rooting reflex** is the first to appear. If one strokes a newborn's cheek next to the side of his mouth, the baby will turn his head to that side and search with his mouth. This reflex is adaptive, because it helps the baby find the nipple of the mother's breast for feeding. This reflex appears as early as 2 to 3 months gestational age and represents the first indication that the fetus can respond to touch (Hooker, 1958; Minkowski, 1928). Rooting generally disappears in infants around 3 to 4 months of age (Peiper, 1963).

The **palmar reflex** enables the newborn to hang unsupported when the reflex is elicited by pressure against the palm of her hand, as shown in Figure 6-5*a*. After this reflex disappears, at 3 to 4 months of age, the child will not again be able to support her own weight in this way until around 4 or 5 years of age (McGraw, 1940). The **moro reflex** consists of a series of reactions to sudden sound or the loss of head support. First the infant thrusts her arms outward, opens her hands, arches her back, and stretches her legs outward. Then she brings her arms inward in an embracing motion with fingers formed into fists. The absence of a moro reflex is a sign of brain damage, and its failure to disappear after 6 or 7 months of age is also cause for concern. Moro, who first described the reflex (Moro, 1918), argued that it was

Rooting reflex
The turning of the infant's head toward the cheek at which touch stimulation is applied, followed by opening of the mouth.

Palmar reflex
The infant's finger grasp of an object that stimulates the palm of the hand.

Moro reflex
The infant's response to loss of head support or to a loud sound, consisting of thrusting of the arms and fingers outward, followed by clenching of the fists and a grasping motion of the arms across the chest.

TABLE 6-3 ● Newborn Reflexes

Name	Testing Method	Response	Developmental Course	Significance
Blink	Flash a light in infant's eyes	Closes both eyes	Permanent	Protects eyes from strong stimuli
Biceps reflex	Tap on the tendon of the biceps muscle	Contracts the biceps muscle	Brisker in the first few days than later	Absent in depressed infants or those with congenital muscular disease
Knee jerk or patellar tendon reflex	Tap on the tendon below the patella or kneecap	Quickly extends or kicks the knee	More pronounced in the first 2 days than later	Absent or difficult to obtain in depressed infants or infants with muscular disease; exaggerated in hyper-excitable infants
Babinski	Gently stroke the side of the infant's foot from heel to toes	Flexes the big toe dorsally; fans out the other toes; twists foot inward	Usually disappears near the end of the 1st year; replaced by plantar flexion of big toe in the normal adult	Absent in infants with defects of the lower spine; retention important in diagnosing poor myelination of motor tracts of the brainstem in older children and adults
Withdrawal reflex	Prick the sole of the infant's foot with a pin	Flexes leg	Constantly present during the first 10 days; present but less intense later	Absent with sciatic nerve damage
Plantar or toe grasp	Press finger against the ball of the infant's foot	Curls all toes under	Disappears between 8 and 12 months	Absent in infants with defects of the lower spinal cord
Tonic neck reflex	Lay baby down on back	Turns head to one side; baby assumes fencing position, extending arm and leg on this side, bending opposite limbs, and arching body away from direction faced	Found as early as 28th prenatal week; frequently present in first weeks, disappears by 3 or 4 months	Paves way for eye–hand coordination

Tonic neck reflex
The infant's postural change when the head is turned to the side, consisting of extension of the arm on that side and clenching of the other arm in what looks like a fencer's position.

Stepping reflex
The infant's response to being held in a slightly forward, upright position with feet touching a horizontal surface, consisting of stepping movements.

a relic of an adaptive reaction by primates to grab for support while falling, but others have disputed this argument (e.g., Peiper, 1963). Indeed, as with many newborn reflexes, the biological function of the moro reflex is obscure.

Several reflexes of the newborn occur in the absence of specific external stimulation. The **tonic neck reflex,** or fencer's position, is a common example. When the newborn's head turns to one side, he tends to extend the arm on that side while flexing the arm on the opposite side, as shown in Figure 6-5*b*.

Many components of reflexes are integrated into later locomotor activity (Capute et al., 1978; Thelen, 1981; Zelazo, 1976). An example is the **stepping reflex,** shown in Figure 6-5*c*. Although this reflex usually disappears by around 3 months of age, it becomes increasingly strong if it is practiced (Zelazo, Zelazo, & Kolb, 1972; Zelazo et al., 1993).

TABLE 6-3 ● Newborn Reflexes (*Continued*)

Name	Testing Method	Response	Developmental Course	Significance
Palmar or hand grasp	Press rod or finger against the infant's palm	Grasps the object with fingers; can suspend own weight for brief period of time	Increases during the 1st month and then gradually declines and is gone by 3 or 4 months	Weak or absent in depressed babies
Moro reflex (embracing reflex)	Make a sudden loud sound; let the baby's head drop back a few inches; or suspend baby horizontally, then lower hands rapidly about six inches and stop abruptly	Extends arms and legs and then brings arms toward each other in a convulsive manner; fans hands out at first, clenches them tightly	Begins to decline in 3rd month, generally gone by 5th month	Absent or constantly weak moro indicates serious disturbance of the central nervous system; may have originated with primate clinging
Stepping or automatic walking reflex	Suport baby in upright position with bare feet on flat surface; move the infant forward and tilt him slightly from side to side	Makes rhythmic stepping movements	Disappears in 2 to 3 months	Absent in depressed infants
Swimming reflex	Hold baby horizontally on stomach in water	Alternates arm and leg movements, exhaling through the mouth	Disappears at 6 months	Demonstrates coordination of arms and legs
Rooting reflex	Stroke cheek of infant lightly with finger or nipple	Turns head toward finger, opens mouth, and tries to suck finger	Disappears at approximately 3 to 4 months	Absent in depressed infants; appears in adults with severe cerebral palsy
Babkin or palmarmental reflex	Apply pressure on both of baby's palms when lying on back	Opens mouth, closes eyes, and turns head to midline	Disappears in 3 to 4 months	Inhibited by general depression of central nervous system

Source: Excerpted from *Child Psychology: A Contemporary Viewpoint,* 2nd ed. (Table 4-1) by E. M. Hetherington and R. D. Parke, 1979; New York; McGraw–Hill. Copyright 1979 by McGraw–Hill, Inc. Excerpted by permission.

Although there is an automatic quality to reflexes, environmental factors do affect their appearance (Brazelton, 1973; Peiper, 1963; Touwen, 1976). For example, a satiated baby may not show a rooting response, and most reflexes are sensitive to state. Still, reflexes do seem tied to specific stimuli and are rarely seen in their absence. This is not the case for the behaviors we refer to as congenitally organized behaviors.

Congenitally Organized Behaviors

The newborn enters the world with several well-organized behaviors. Looking, sucking, and crying are three behaviors that, unlike reflexes, are often not elicited by a discrete, identifiable stimulus. These behaviors provide infants with means to get nourishment and to control and explore their environments.

The newborn's looking behavior is often unexpected (Crouchman, 1985). New parents may be amazed by the fact that their baby, even in the first moments of life,

Figure 6-5   Some new-
born reflexes: (*a*) palmar,
(*b*) stepping, and (*c*)
tonic neck.

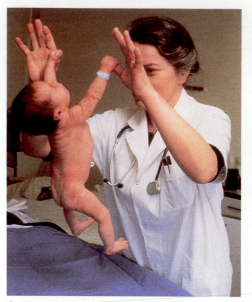

a   *b*

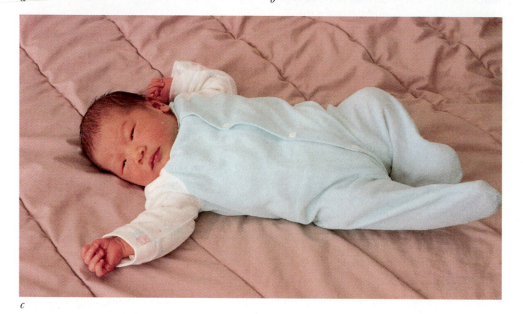

c

will lie with eyes wide open, seemingly examining them and other objects in the room. In a room that is dimly lit, the light coming through the window may be an especially attractive target. And babies do not simply respond reflexively to light when they look. As early as 8 hours after birth, and in complete darkness, babies open their eyes wide and engage in frequent eye movements, as though they were searching for something to explore (Haith, 1991). We will have more to say about early perception in the next chapter. Our point now is that looking behavior shows that newborns possess tools for acting on their world as well as for reacting to it.

In some respects, sucking seems to fit the definition of a reflex, since it is easily elicited by oral stimulation, at least when the newborn is hungry. However, in other respects it is not reflexlike. Babies may suck spontaneously, even during sleep. The sucking act adapts to a variety of conditions, varies depending on whether or not nutriment is provided and how long the feeding session has been going on, lasts over extended periods of time, and may vary with what the baby is sucking and how much fluid he gets with each suck (Crook, 1979; Kaye, 1967; Kessen et al., 1970). The adaptability of sucking sets it apart from the reflexes we discussed in the preceding section.

Sucking is a marvelously coordinated act. Babies suck one to two times each second, and each suck requires an orchestration of actions. Milk is extracted from the nipple both by suction (as with a straw) and by a squeezing action, and these actions must be coordinated with both breathing and swallowing. Some babies show sucking coordination from birth, while others may require a week or so of practice (Halverson, 1946; Peiper, 1963).

No other behavior seems to serve quite as many purposes as sucking for newborns. Of course, it is a way for them to get nourishment. But, it is a primary means by which they begin to explore the world. Even at birth, many babies suck their fingers and thumbs, and it appears that some newborns have even practiced this as fetuses. Later they will continue to explore with their mouths as they become increasingly better able to grasp and find new objects (Rochat, 1989). Indeed, Piaget (1954) remarked that the first changes in sucking are "the beginning of psychology." Sucking also is the first complex action babies adapt to the variations the world presents to them. For example, newborn babies suck differently on a nipple than on a tube and suck soft tubes differently than rigid ones (Dubignon & Campbell, 1968; Lipsitt & Kaye, 1965). A baby who has fed on the breast may have difficulty feeding from a bottle nipple. And sucking behavior is sensitive to sensory events. Babies who are sucking tend to stop when they see something start to move or when they hear a voice (Bronshtein et al., 1958; Haith, 1966). Additionally, sucking plays a social role in the process of attachment between mother and infant (Bowlby, 1969; Crook, 1979). Finally, sucking seems to buffer the infant against pain and overstimulation. Agitated babies quiet when they suck on a pacifier (Kessen & Leutzendorff, 1963). One study found that crying during circumcision was reduced by about 40% when babies were permitted to suck on a pacifier (Gunnar, Fisch, & Malone, 1984). This finding confirms experimentally what civilizations have known for some time; for thousands of years, Jewish babies have been encouraged to suck on wine-soaked cotton during circumcision.

A third organized behavior of the newborn is crying. Like sucking, crying orchestrates various components of behavior, such as respiration, vocalizing, and muscular tensing, in a rhythmic pattern. Psychologists have been interested in crying both as a tool for diagnosing nervous system integrity and for its social role.

Wolff (1969) distinguished three types of cries in the very young infant—a hungry, or basic, cry; a mad, or angry, cry; and a pain cry. The first two are similar in pitch but different in that the mad cry forces more air through the vocal cords, producing more variation. The pain cry has a more sudden onset with a much longer initial burst and a longer period of breath-holding between cries. Other researchers have identified the types slightly differently, as expressing hunger, fear, or pain (Wasz-Hockert, Michelsson, & Lind, 1985). Adults have little difficulty in distinguishing various cries based on their timing and patterning (Zeskind, Klein, & Marshall, 1992).

The crying of healthy newborn infants is fairly characteristic in both pitch and rhythm. An atypical cry can signal problems. Babies who are immature or brain damaged produce higher-frequency cries with abnormal timing patterns (Lester, 1976, 1984). Babies who show evidence of malnutrition at birth or who are preterm often also have higher-pitched cries with abnormal timing patterns

(Zeskind, 1983; Zeskind & Lester, 1978). Infants who have genetic anomalies, such as the *cri du chat* syndrome (in which the infant's cry sounds like that of a cat) and Down syndrome, also have atypical cries, indicating that the cry reflects central nervous system functioning.

Some investigators have speculated that babies influence early social relationships with their caregivers by the nature of their cries (Lester, 1984). Cries of babies at risk are perceived as more grating, piercing, and aversive than the cries of other babies, and "difficult" babies seem to have more aversive cries than "easy" babies (Lounsbury & Bates, 1982; Zeskind & Lester, 1978). Cries experienced as aversive, as noted, may set in motion a negative cycle between baby and caregiver.

More broadly, crying is a major factor in early social interaction because it is one of the infant's basic tools for bringing caregivers closer. In one study, mothers and fathers displayed heightened stress when shown a film of a baby crying (Frodi et al., 1978). Clearly, adults dislike hearing babies cry, so they typically do something to quiet the crying baby. When a baby fusses for no apparent reason, parents may try various techniques for soothing him (Emde, Gaensbauer, & Harmon, 1976). Picking up a baby is an effective quieter. Swaddling, or wrapping a baby snugly in a blanket, and pacifiers are also sometimes effective, as is continuous or rhythmic sound (Brackbill et al., 1966; Campos, 1989). Even in the first month of life, we can see crying controlled by events other than food or pain relief; infants often stop crying if they have interesting things to watch or sounds to listen to (Wolff, 1969). The baby learns very early to use crying to control her social environment, sometimes producing what Wolff has called the "fake cry" to get the caregiver's attention as early as 3 weeks of age.

The three congenitally organized behaviors of looking, sucking, and crying are gradually perfected by the infant to explore and control the physical and social world. As Robert Emde noted in his presidential address to the Society for Research in Child Development, babies are not only organized but organizing (Emde, 1994), and these are the first tools the baby has for organizing the world. Of course, other skills, such as reaching, grasping, and walking, also play a role, and elaborate emotional behavior such as smiling and laughing will enrich the social repertoire of the developing infant. We consider the physical accomplishments of the infant in the next section, leaving the more social components of development for Chapter 12.

✔ *To Recap...*

The activity of newborns is not random but is organized into states, rhythms, reflexes, and congenitally organized behaviors. The newborn's level of alertness is typically categorized according to six states varying from quiet sleep to crying. Several aspects of these states change with age, providing information about early development. Although state organization is primarily controlled by internal factors, state can be affected by external stimulation. Conversely, the baby's response to stimulation is affected by the state he or she is in.

The newborn's states occur in rhythmic cycles. A basic rest–activity cycle is coordinated with a longer sleep–wake cycle. With age, the baby gradually adapts to the 24-hour light–dark cycle.

Other evidence for behavioral organization is found in reflexes. Although some reflexes last through life, others, such as the rooting, palmar, moro, and tonic-neck reflexes, disappear during the first year. These reflexes and their developmental courses provide important information about the integrity of the central nervous system.

Congenitally organized behaviors such as looking, crying, and sucking are available at birth but, unlike reflexes, are not easily attributable to a particular stimulus. These are examples of prepared behaviors that the infant possesses for exploring and controlling the physical and social aspects of the world.

MOTOR DEVELOPMENT

Looking, crying, and sucking have obvious limitations as tools to control the environment. Imagine for a moment that you cannot move around or grasp objects and manipulate them at will. In effect, you must depend on others to provide interesting objects for you to inspect. This brief exercise may give you a sense of the newborn's limited options for acting on the physical world. But before long, the limited newborn is a go-for-everything, grab-anything 9-month-old. This rapid transformation is a key feature of development in human infancy, in effect giving the baby "power tools" for acquiring knowledge and for gaining a sense of competence through increasing self-control.

Motor Development in Infancy

Motor development can be divided into two general categories. The first includes **locomotion** and **postural development,** which concern control of the trunk of the body and coordination of the arms and legs for moving around. The second category is **prehension,** the ability to use the hands as tools for such things as eating, building, and exploring. The acquisition of these motor skills gives babies infinitely more options for acting on their worlds (Kopp & Parmelee, 1979).

Table 6-4 presents some of the milestones of motor development at selected ages. Motor skills depend on one another to a substantial extent. For example, the infant's ability to control the upper-body posture for sitting frees the hands for grabbing objects. We should note that the ages given in the table are approximate markers. Babies—just as adults, who vary widely in athletic prowess—differ in when they master particular skills.

Principles and Sequence in Motor Development

Skills are not developed in a happenstance sequence. Rather, the progression of skill obeys two general principles. The first principle of development is that it tends to proceed in a **proximodistal** direction—that is, body parts closest to the center of the body are brought under control before parts farther out. The acquisition of skill in using the arms, hands, and fingers provides a good example. The newborn can position himself toward an object but cannot reach it. Although most of his arm movements seem random, he does direct some of them toward the general vicinity of the object. In the second month of life, he sweeps his hand more deliberately near the object and gradually contacts it more consistently (White & Held, 1966). By 4 months of age, he can often grab at objects in a way that looks convincingly deliberate, but he uses the whole hand, with little individual finger control. Gradually, he coordinates his fingers (Rochat, 1989). At 6 months of age, he will reach with one hand for a cube with all fingers extended. Once he has it in hand, he may transfer it from hand to hand and rotate his wrist so he can see it from various perspectives. By 9 months, the baby can grasp a pellet neatly between forefinger and thumb, and the 1-year-old can hold a crayon to make marks on paper (White, Castle, & Held, 1964).

Locomotion
The movement of an individual through space. Psychologists have been most interested in movements that individuals control themselves, such as walking and crawling.

Postural development
The increasing ability of babies to control parts of their body, especially the head and the trunk.

Prehension
The ability to grasp and manipulate objects with the hands.

Proximodistal
Literally, near-to-far. This principle of development refers to the tendency of body parts to develop in a trunk-to-extremities direction.

TABLE 6-4 • Motor Milestones

Age in Months	Locomotion and Postural Development	Prehension and Manipulative Skills
0	Turns head to side when lying on stomach; poor head control when lifted; alternating movements of legs when on stomach as if to crawl	Reflex grasp—retains hold on ring
3	Head erect and steady when held vertically; when on stomach, elevates head and shoulders by arms or hands or elbows; sits with support; anticipates adjustment of lifting	Grasps rattle; reaches for object with two hands
6	Sits alone momentarily; pulls self to sitting position with adult's hand as puller; rolls from back to stomach	Grasps cube with simultaneous flexion of fingers; reaches with one hand and rotates the wrist; transfers cube between hands
9	Sits alone; pulls self to sitting position in crib; makes forward progress in prone position toward toy; walks holding on to furniture	Opposes thumb and finger in seizing cube; picks up pellet with forefinger and thumb
12	Stands alone; lowers self to sitting from a standing position; walks with help; creeping perfected; into everything	Holds crayon adaptively to make a mark
18	Walks well (since about 15 months) and falls rarely; climbs stairs or chair	Throws balls into box; scribbles vigorously; builds tower of 3 or more blocks
24	Walks up and down stairs; walks backward; runs	Places square in form board; imitates folding of paper; piles tower of 6 blocks; puts blocks in a row to form a train

Source: Based on information from *Manual for the Bayley Scales of Infant Development,* by N. Bayley, 1969, New York: Psychological Corporation; and "The Denver Developmental Screening Test" by W. K. Frankenburg and J. Dodds, 1967, *Journal of Pediatrics, 71,* pp. 181–191.

Cephalocaudal
Literally, head-to-tail. This principle of development refers to the tendency of body parts to mature in a head-to-foot progression.

The second principle is that control over the body develops in a **cephalocaudal,** or head-to-foot, direction. The newborn who is placed on her stomach can move her head from side to side, although her head must be supported when she is lifted to someone's shoulder. The 3-month-old infant holds her head erect and steady in the vertical position before she can push off the mattress with her hands to lift her head and shoulders and look. At 6 months, she can pull herself to a sitting position and may even be able to drag herself around a bit, but only at around 9 months can she use her legs with her hands to move herself forward by creeping or crawling. By the time the infant is 12 months old, the mother is likely to walk into the baby's bedroom and find her standing in the crib, rattling the side bars and perhaps distressed because she cannot figure out how to sit down again! Within 6 months after the baby's first birthday, her legs are usually under sufficient control to permit walking without support. Then the real fireworks begin, as she is into everything.

The top portion of Figure 6-6 presents a picture of the typical baby's stages of progression toward self-produced locomotion. Essentially, this sequence involves a transfer of responsibility for transportation from the hands to the legs. But babies reach milestones of locomotion at different ages. And as the lower parts of Figure

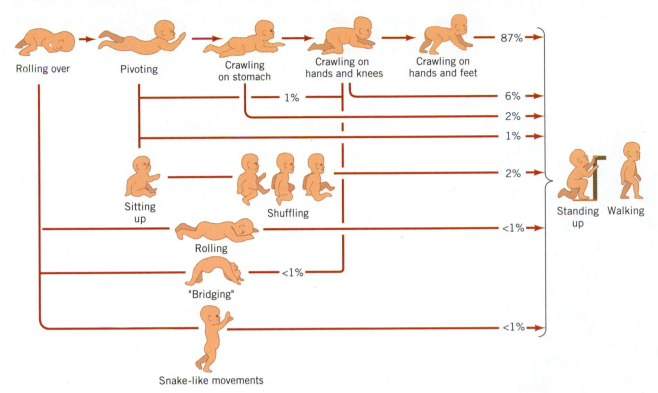

Rolling over   Pivoting   Crawling on stomach   Crawling on hands and knees   Crawling on hands and feet   87%

1%   6%   2%   1%

Sitting up   Shuffling   2%   Standing up   Walking

Rolling   <1%

"Bridging"   <1%

Snake-like movements   <1%

Figure 6-6   Most babies follow a fairly regular sequence in learning to walk, gradually transferring responsibility for movement from the arms to the feet. But some skip certain stages of crawling, and others never crawl at all. Adapted from "Early Development of Locomotion: Significance of Prematurity, Cerebral Palsy and Sex" by R. H. Largo, L. Molinari, M. Weber, L. C. Pinto, and G. Duc, 1985, *Developmental Medicine and Child Neurology, 27,* pp. 183–191, Figure 2. Copyright 1985 by MacKeith Press. Adapted by permission.

6-6 illustrate, they can reach them in different ways. Note that 87% follow a progression that starts with rolling over and progresses through various styles of crawling to standing and then walking. But some babies go from a belly crawl to standing without passing through intermediate stages, and others never crawl at all (Largo et al., 1985). Figure 6-6 illustrates both how different—and how resourceful—babies can be.

The progression of locomotor skills in infancy reflects increasing timing, balance, and coordination. These components have only recently yielded to careful analysis, as scientists have adapted techniques used in sports science. Researchers at the University of Denver, for example, use videotape to record the motions of body parts as the baby acquires skill in crawling toward objects (Benson, 1990). As shown in Figure 6-7, the baby wears a black body suit that has small reflective markers (the kind that bicyclists and runners wear at night) at the shoulder, elbow, wrist, hip, knee, and ankle. From the videotape playback, a computer can record the location of these bright spots 60 times each second to determine the path, velocity, and timing of the movement of each joint. Weekly observations of infants from 6 months to the age of competent crawling (10 to 12 months of age) reveal that babies often go through a sequence in coordinating their limbs. First, the baby coordinates one side of the body—for example, the right side—dragging the other side along. Then she gradually coordinates the left side, while giving up some coordination of the

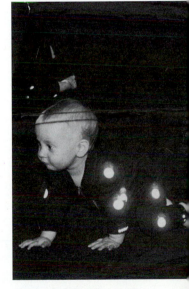

Figure 6-7   Scientists use computerized techniques to track light reflections on babies' joints to study how babies acquire skill in crawling. (Photo by permission of Dr. Janette Benson, University of Denver)

right side. Finally, she coordinates both sides to become an efficient crawler. During these advances, the baby gains control of the timing of motion of each limb—learning, for example, to begin the advance of the left knee as the right arm is completing its backward thrust (Benson, 1990; Freedland, 1993).

Maturation and Experience in the Emergence of Motor Skills

Because motor skills emerge in a fairly predictable sequence and at fairly predictable times, we might suppose that these skills are genetically programmed. But a glance back at Figure 6-6 reminds us that there is no rigidly fixed genetic program for the unfolding of at least some motor events. And once again, the environment can play a role, by encouraging the infant to display a skill at a particular time.

Differences in when American infants and African infants accomplish important milestones are illustrative. African infants generally sit, stand, and walk from one to several months earlier than American infants (Geber & Dean, 1957; Konner, 1976; Super, 1981). However, practice, not heredity, seems to account for at least some of the difference. One investigator found that the Kipsigis in western Kenya believe that their infants will not sit, stand, or walk without practice. Thus, they energetically practice their infants in these skills—for example, building a special hole in the ground with sand to reinforce their infants' sitting skills quite early in infancy. For skills that are not practiced, like crawling and rolling over, the Kenyan babies are not precocious (Super, 1981). These observations have been replicated in the laboratory. Babies who practice stepping step more than babies who practice other activities (Zelazo et al., 1993).

Still, while practice is important in motor development, babies in all known cultures reach the major milestones within an age range that encompasses only a few months. It is important not to overlook the universality of these milestones (Kopp, 1979). Every normal infant walks, and all normal infants eventually pick up objects in approximately the same fashion. How we move around and how we manipulate objects reflects in part how our bodies are made—it would simply make no sense for us to move around by crawling upside down on hands and feet or to try to pick up objects with the backs of our hands. Our genetic endowment, then, sets the stage and prepares us for various accomplishments. These accomplishments are played out through interaction with a real world of events and objects (von Hofsten, 1989). Box 6-2 describes an early investigation of this issue.

The Psychological Implications of Motor Development

Motor development is not something that simply happens to the baby. To a great extent, it is something the baby causes through a desire to act on the world. Robert White (1959) referred to this desire as **effectance motivation** and to the infant's growing competence as *effectance,* a competence that creates a sense of mastery. Through motor development the baby gains control of his body, which, in turn, he uses as a tool. Once able only to grasp objects that people put in his hand, the baby becomes sufficiently coordinated to lunge for his grandma's eyeglasses or an interesting saltshaker and now is at least partial master of his own experience. The feat of mastery sometimes seems like an end unto itself. The nonwalking baby who has spent months watching people move to and fro on their feet smiles with glee after she takes those first two or three steps, as though to say, "I can do it, too!"

Learning to move around is not only a motor accomplishment for babies; it also helps them to organize their world (Bushnell & Boudreau, 1993). Benson and

• Kipsigis (in Kenya, Africa), believe that their infants need practice to learn certain postural skills, such as sitting. Photo used by permission of Dr. Charles Super, Pennsylvania State University.

Effectance motivation
The desire of the infant or child to become effective in acting on the environment and in coping with the objects and people in it.

DOES MOTOR DEVELOPMENT DEPEND ON PRACTICE OR ON MATURATION?

During the 1920s and 1930s, the Zeitgeist in developmental psychology leaned heavily toward biological explanations of children's development. We saw in Chapter 1 that G. Stanley Hall's early evolutionary views were revised and resurrected during this period by his student Arnold Gesell at Yale University.

One major theoretical issue of the time concerned children's motor development. Learning-oriented psychologists, like John B. Watson, had argued that the crawling, climbing, and walking displayed by all normal infants represent reflexes that are conditioned through experience and practice. But Gesell and other biologically oriented theorists believed that these behaviors simply emerge according to a genetic timetable. Simple biological maturation, not conditioning and learning principles, guide their appearance.

To compare these two alternatives, Gesell developed a research method called the co-twin control. A pair of identical twins was used, so that biological factors would be the same for the two infants. Gesell then selected one infant, whom he termed twin T, to receive training and extra practice each day at climbing stairs and related motor skills. The control infant, twin C, received no extra practice. After 6 weeks of training, twin T had become a very accomplished climber—but so had twin C. Gesell interpreted these findings to mean that the climbing skill must have been a result of the children's biological development and not their practice or experience (Gesell & Thompson, 1929). Studies of the same sort by other researchers appeared to confirm this conclusion (McGraw, 1935).

Later research, however, demonstrated that Gesell's conclusions had been a bit simplistic. Whereas extra training may not accelerate children's motor development, some amount of experience appears necessary for development to occur normally. Infants deprived of physical stimulation or the opportunity to move about were found to have delayed motor development (Dennis, 1960; Dennis & Najarian, 1957). When such infants were then given extra stimulation, their motor skills improved rapidly (Sayegh & Dennis, 1965).

The method of the co-twin control was a useful technique for comparing the effects of maturation and learning (which is, of course, a specific case of nature versus nurture). But as psychologists now agree, both of these processes are essential for normal motor development.

Uzgiris (1985) demonstrated how babies' control over their own transportation contributes to their spatial understanding. An investigator on one side of a low table hid an attractive toy in a depression to the left or right and then covered the two depressions with identical cloths while a baby on the other side of the table watched. Then the baby either cruised around the table or was picked up by an adult and placed on the opposite side, reversing the left or right location of the toy (from the baby's perspective). Babies were much more accurate in keeping track of the spatial location of the toy when they moved themselves than when an adult moved them. Thus, babies seem to understand spatial relations better when they control their own movements. If you think about it, this finding won't surprise you. You may have experienced the same phenomenon if you have ever tried to get back to an unfamiliar place when you were the passenger rather than the driver of the car that took you there the first time.

A baby's control over body movement also fosters an appreciation of the meaning of distance and heights. Infants first become wary of heights at just about the time they are capable of self-produced locomotion (Bertenthal & Campos, 1990). Later, when babies can control how close they are to their caregivers, they use their motor skills for exploration when they feel safe and for comfort when they feel insecure, as we will see again in Chapter 12 (Ainsworth, 1983).

• An infant's first steps are a major milestone of development, not only increasing his or her mobility in the environment, but also creating a sense of competence and mastery.

Motor Development Beyond Infancy

How infants acquire motor skills has attracted a great deal of attention. Less is known about the development of motor skill between infancy and the age at which children become relatively skilled athletes. A recent summary of what is known about this area provides the basis for the following discussion (Gallahue, 1989).

By the second birthday, most children have overcome their battle with gravity and balance and are able to move about and handle objects fairly efficiently. Their early abilities form the basis for skills that appear between 2 and 7 years of age. Three sets of fundamental movement skills emerge: locomotor movements, manipulative movements, and stability movements. Locomotor movements include walking, running, jumping, hopping, skipping, and climbing. Manipulative movements include throwing, catching, kicking, striking, and dribbling. Stability movements involve body control relative to gravity. They include bending, stretching, turning, swinging, rolling, dodging, head standing, and beam walking. These fundamental skills typically appear in all children and are further refined by those adolescents who develop exceptional athletic skills. Skilled skaters, dancers, and gymnasts, for example, creatively combine highly refined locomotor and stability movements.

Fundamental movement skills develop through three stages. In the first stage, the child tries to execute the movement pattern, but preparatory and follow-through components are missing. An elementary or transitional stage follows. Here, the child enjoys more control over the required movements, but they do not all fit together into an integrated pattern. By the third, mature, stage all components are well integrated into a coordinated and purposeful act. Figure 6-8 is a schematic diagram of these stages for one type of manipulative movement, throwing.

The refinement of motor skills depends a great deal on the development of the muscles and the nerve pathways that control them, but other factors are important as well. Motor skills also depend on sensory and perceptual skills, for example. And children acquire many of their motor skills in play, which involves social and physical interaction. One important aspect of motor skills is reaction time—the time required for the external stimulus to trigger the ingoing nerve pathways, for the individual to make a decision, and for the brain to activate the muscles through the outgoing nerve pathways. Reaction time improves substantially through the preschool and elementary school years, even for simple motor movements. Although reaction time improves in the early years, there is a correlation between

Initial

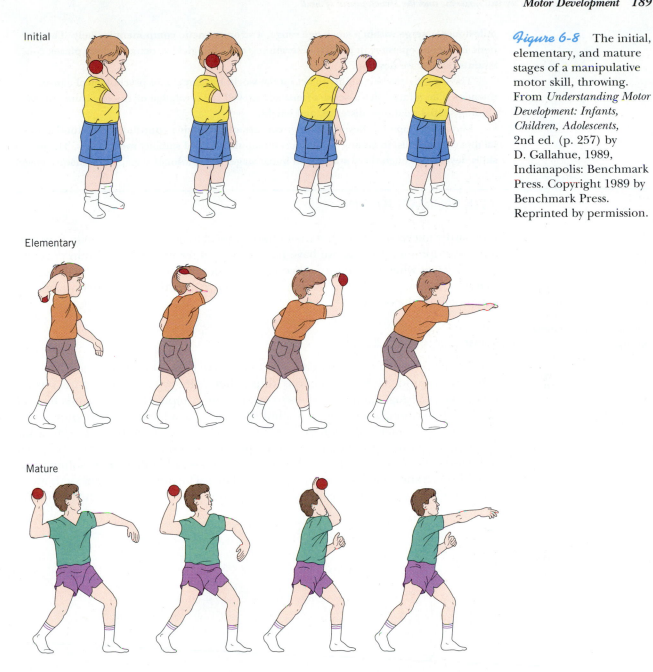

Elementary

Mature

Figure 6-8 The initial, elementary, and mature stages of a manipulative motor skill, throwing. From *Understanding Motor Development: Infants, Children, Adolescents,* 2nd ed. (p. 257) by D. Gallahue, 1989, Indianapolis: Benchmark Press. Copyright 1989 by Benchmark Press. Reprinted by permission.

a child's reaction time in early infancy and the preschool years (Bard, Hay, & Fleury, 1990; Cratty, 1986; Dougherty & Haith, 1993). We look more closely at the development of the brain and nervous system in the following section.

✔ To Recap...

Motor development can be categorized as (1) locomotion and postural development or (2) prehension. In both these areas, control over the body develops in a cephalocaudal and a proximodistal direction. Individual differences in the unfolding of some motor events, as well as the effects of practice, offer evidence that motor development is not rigidly genetically programmed. However, because motor development is universal and developmental milestones emerge within a small age range, a strong genetic component is likely. The genetic influence operates in part by determining our biological structure, which places constraints on how we develop.

The infant's growing ability to act on the world has important psychological consequences. The infant gains a sense of mastery as well as knowledge of the environment, including spatial relations, distance, and height.

Motor development beyond infancy consists of increasing coordination of fundamental movement skills, including locomotor, manipulative, and stability movements. These skills develop through three stages—an initial stage, a transitional stage, and a mature stage.

THE HUMAN BRAIN

It is hardly necessary to say that the brain is central to every sort of human function and development. Already, we have had cause to refer indirectly to brain development, such as when we mentioned connections between behavior and neurological maturity in newborns. In this section, we look more directly at the structure and development of the brain.

Structure of the Brain

The brain contains approximately 100 billion nerve cells, or **neurons;** each of these cells has around 3,000 connections with other cells, which adds up to several quadrillion message paths. Needless to say, no one completely understands how all of these communication paths work, but there is quite a lot that we do know.

Like every other cell, each neuron has a nucleus and a cell body. But neurons are unique among cells in that they develop extensions on opposite sides, as shown in Figure 6-9. On the incoming side, the extensions—called **dendrites**—often form a tangle of strands that look like the roots of plants. The outgoing extension is more like a single tap root and is called an **axon.** Axons usually extend farther from the

Neuron
A nerve cell, consisting of a cell body, axon, and dendrites. Neurons transmit activity from one part of the nervous system to another.

Dendrite
One of a net of short fibers extending out from the cell body in a neuron; receives activity from nearby cells and conducts that activity to the cell body.

Axon
A long fiber extending from the cell body in a neuron; conducts activity from the cell body to another cell.

Figure 6-9   A nerve cell, or neuron.

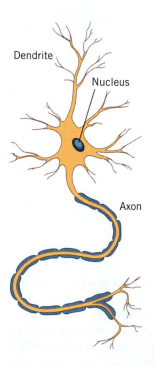

Dendrite

Nucleus

Axon

cell than dendrites and may be quite long. They are often covered by a sheath of a fatty substance, **myelin,** that insulates them and speeds message transmission. The extensions of adjoining cells do not quite touch. They are separated by minute fluid-filled gaps called **synapses.** Information is passed along a neuron as an electrical signal. The transmission of activity from an axon to a dendrite across the synapse is accomplished by the flow of chemicals called **neurotransmitters.**

The brain has three major parts. The **brainstem** includes the cerebellum, which controls balance and coordination. The **midbrain** serves as a relay station and controls breathing and swallowing. The **cerebrum** is the highest brain center and includes the left and right hemispheres and the bundle of nerves that connect them. Of most interest to psychologists is the relatively thin shell of "gray matter" that covers the brain, called the **cerebral cortex.** This structure appears to be the most recently evolved part of the brain and is crucial for the functioning of the senses, language, memory, thought, and decision making, and the control of voluntary actions. Particular areas of the cerebral cortex have particular responsibilities, although some areas are more specialized than others. The cortex has over 40 different functional areas (Shatz, 1992). Some specialized tasks are identified in Figure 6-10. The areas for visual, auditory, and touch sensation have been mapped particularly well, as has the area for motor action. Spreading out from the primary sensory areas (for example, sight, learning, and touch) are association areas that involve complex interconnections among brain cells for higher level perception and memory functions. The front areas of the brain seem to serve even higher level functions of sensory integration and goal organization.

Development of the Brain

Scientists only partially understand how the brain, in its amazing complexity, develops. It begins as a hollow tube; the neurons are generated along the outer walls of this tube and then travel to their proper locations (Kolb, 1989). Scientists have identified three stages in this process. The first is cell production. Most neurons are produced between 10 and 26 weeks following conception, which means that the fetal brain generates these cells at a rate of 250,000 per minute. After around 28 weeks, few neurons are produced, and no more will be produced for the rest of the person's life. Indeed, the brain overproduces neurons and then trims them back by as much as 50% (Baringa, 1993; Cowan, 1979; Huttenlocher, 1990; Kolb, 1989; Raff et al., 1993).

Once the cells have been produced near the center of the brain, they must migrate outward to their proper locations. This cell migration is the second stage of early brain development. How do the neurons "know" where to go? That question has not been answered. It seems likely that there is a chemical attraction between the target location and the migrating neuron. Migration is complete by 7 months gestational age (Huttenlocher, 1990; Rakic, 1988).

When the neuron has found its home, the third stage, cell elaboration, begins. In this process, axons and dendrites form synapses with other cells. Cell elaboration continues for years after birth and produces as many as 100% more synapses than will eventually exist in the adult. Thus, as they are being formed, synapses are also being cut back. The paring of synapses occurs earlier in the primary sensory areas than elsewhere. For example, the visual cortex is trimmed to the adult level by 11 years of age, but the frontal areas, which play a role in complex thought processes, are not reduced to the adult level until 16 years of age (Huttenlocher, 1990). Experience plays an important role in the eventual sculpting of the connections of the brain through this process. Neurons and their connections compete for sur-

Myelin
A sheath of fatty material that surrounds and insulates the axon, resulting in speedier transmission of neural activity.

Synapse
The small space between neurons where neural activity is communicated from one cell to another.

Neurotransmitter
A chemical that transmits electrical activity from one neuron across the synaptic junction to another neuron.

Brainstem
The lower part of the brain, closest to the spinal cord; includes the cerebellum, which is important for maintaining balance and coordination.

Midbrain
A part of the brain that lies above the brainstem; serves as a relay station and as a control area for breathing and swallowing and houses part of the auditory and visual systems.

Cerebrum
The highest brain center; includes both hemispheres of the brain and the interconnections between them.

Cerebral Cortex
The thin sheet of gray matter, consisting of six layers of neurons, that covers the brain.

Figure 6-10 Some areas of the cerebral cortex are specialized for particular functions; this diagram shows only a few.

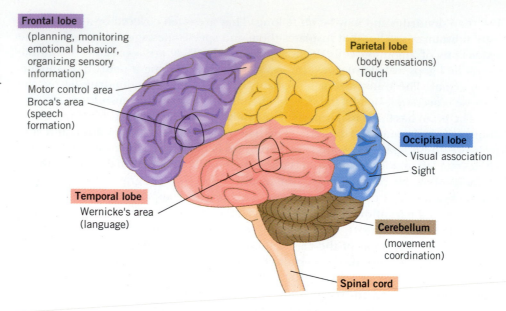

Frontal lobe
(planning, monitoring emotional behavior, organizing sensory information)
Motor control area
Broca's area (speech formation)

Parietal lobe
(body sensations) Touch

Occipital lobe
Visual association
Sight

Temporal lobe
Wernicke's area (language)

Cerebellum
(movement coordination)

Spinal cord

vival, and the ones that are used through experience appear to survive, while those that are not used disappear (Barnes, 1990; Diamond, 1991; Kandel & O'Dell, 1992; Siegler, 1989b).

The fetus's brain grows faster than any other organ (except, perhaps, the eye), and this pace continues in infancy. At birth, the baby's body weight is only 5% of adult weight, whereas the brain weighs 25% of its adult value. By three years of age, the brain has attained 80% of its ultimate weight, compared with 20% for body weight (Morgan & Gibson, 1991; Tanner, 1990). However, the brain does not mature uniformly.

The first area to mature is the primary motor area. It may not be surprising to learn that within this area, the locations that control activity near the head mature first and maturation proceeds downward. This is the direction in which motor control proceeds, the cephalocaudal progression. Similarly, the areas that correspond to the arms mature earlier than those that control the fingers, which corresponds to the proximodistal principle of motor development.

Not far behind the motor area in maturity are the primary sensory areas—touch, vision, and hearing, in that order. Maturation seems to spread out from these sensory areas into the association areas. Myelin formation, or *myelination,* is one index of maturation. The tracts that control fine motor movement continue to myelinate until about age 4, and the areas concerned with attention and consciousness continue to myelinate up to puberty (Tanner, 1990).

Hemispheric Specialization

The two hemispheres of the brain are not perfectly symmetrical. In at least some respects, the left brain and the right brain are specialized. The left side of the brain is usually more specialized for language performance and the right side for spatial and mathematical tasks. Another way to think about this distinction is that the left side is more oriented to language and concepts, and the right side is more oriented to images. Pictures of the brain produced by a technique called positron emission tomography (PET) have confirmed that the left side of the brain is typically more active during language tasks and the right side more active during mathematical tasks. At the same time, however, these pictures show that most tasks, like reading and listening, involve many areas of the brain (Corina, Vaid, & Bellugi, 1992; Posner et al., 1988). We might also note that in some people, the right, rather than the left, side of the brain appears to be dominant for language, or there is mixed dominance. Left-handers more frequently fall into these categories than right-handers. Problems with reading performance are sometimes associated with mixed or right-side dominance for language. Children who have dyslexia, but who have otherwise normal or superior intelligence, are more likely to lack strong left-brain dominance than normal readers, for example.

The basis for hemispheric specialization appears quite early. For example, electrical brain recordings in newborn infants reveal more activity in response to speech sounds on the left than on the right side (Molfese & Molfese, 1979). An interesting question is whether left–right functions are fixed. Some studies have supported the position that either hemisphere can pick up the function of the other if the intact hemisphere is still in a formative stage. For example, one researcher, after reviewing several studies of infants who had lost the use of the left hemisphere, concluded that such children could acquire language normally if their brain damage occurred before 2 years of age (Lenneberg, 1967). More recent research has made it clear that the matter may not be so simple, however. How brain damage affects a person's performance depends on a number of factors, including what function is involved and what environment the person experiences afterwards (Kolb, 1989). In Chapter 15, we will see that hemispheric specialization may also play a role in certain gender differences in development.

✔ *To Recap...*

The brain operates through networks of communication that involve billions of neurons and several quadrillion neuron pathways. Messages travel along neurons as electrical signals, which are picked up by the incoming dendrites and passed along by the outgoing axons. Neurotransmitters allow messages to travel across the synapses.

The brain has three major parts—the brainstem, the midbrain, and the cerebrum. Of most interest to psychologists is the cerebral cortex, which controls higher level brain functions. Some areas of the cortex are specialized for various functions, including visual, auditory, and touch sensation.

Development of the fetal brain includes three stages: cell production, cell migration, and cell elaboration. No neurons are produced after around 28 weeks of fetal age, but cell elaboration continues for years. Both neurons and synapses are overproduced and then cut back, and the cutting-back process continues into adolescence. Experience plays a role, partly through affecting which neurons and synapses will die.

The left and right hemispheres of the brain are, to some extent, specialized. Evidence suggests that even at birth, the left side of the brain is prepared to control language functioning and the right side to control spatial and mathematical functioning. However, under certain circumstances, one hemisphere may be able to pick up the functions of the other.

HUMAN GROWTH

Physical growth, as we have said, is a hallmark of development. Growth continues through childhood, but not uniformly. As Arnold Gesell put it, growth does not proceed as a balloon inflates, with each part expanding equally fast (Gesell, 1954).

Rather, the overall rate of growth slows and speeds during the growth years, and different body parts grow at different rates. In this section, we discuss the unfolding of whole-body growth, adolescent sex differentiation, and factors that affect physical growth and development.

Growth in Size

We saw in Chapter 5 that the fetus's growth rate is dramatically high, necessarily slowing as birth approaches. This general slowing trend characterizes growth up to adolescence.

Figure 6-11 shows an average growth curve for males and females. As you can see, boys and girls are approximately the same height until around 10 years of age. A growth spurt typically occurs between 10 and 12 years of age for girls and 12 and 14 years of age for boys. This age difference accounts for the common observation that girls, on average, are taller than boys in grades 7 and 8, a relation that permanently reverses a few years later. In North America and northern and western Europe, where good records have been kept, we know that height increases are just about completed by 15.5 years of age in girls and 17.5 years in boys; less than 2% of growth is added afterwards (Malina, 1990; Tanner, 1990).

Charts like the one in Figure 6-11 may give the impression that there is, or should be, a "normal" growth rate. But few children exactly fit the averages such charts depict. It is obvious that individuals reach quite different ultimate heights and weights, but it may be less apparent that their *rates* of growth may also differ. To illustrate, Figure 6-12 shows a growth curve for three girls. Girl B reached menarche, the onset of menstruation, before girls A and C. She was taller than both

• Physical growth does not proceed at a steady rate, but slows and speeds up throughout childhood.

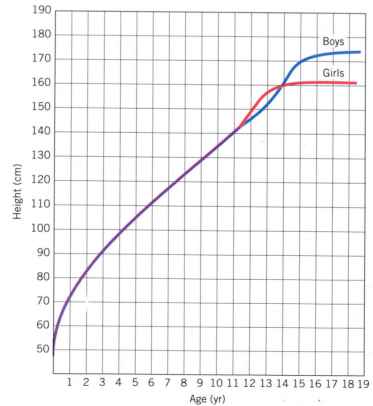

Figure 6-11 Typical male and female growth curves. Birth length doubles by around the 4th year, but growth slows, and length doubles again only around the 13th year. Adult height can be estimated by doubling the height of males at 24 months and of females at 18 months (Lowrey, 1978; Tanner, 1990). From "Standards for Growth and Growth Velocities" by J. M. Tanner, R. H. Whitehouse, and M. Takaishi, 1966, *Archives of Disease in Childhood, 41,* p. 467. Copyright 1966 by *Archives of Disease in Childhood.* Reprinted by permission.

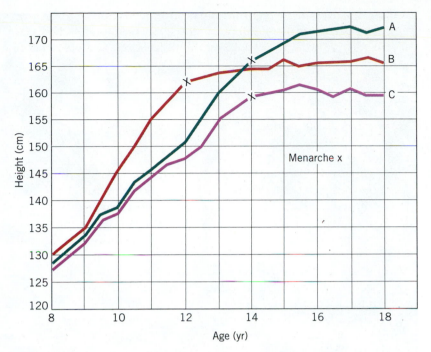

Figure 6-12 Curves showing the heights of three girls over time. Age of menarche is indicated by an *x*. Adapted from "Individual Patterns of Development" by N. Bayley, 1956, *Child Development, 27,* p. 52. Copyright 1956 by The Society for Research in Child Development, Inc. Adapted by permission.

at age 12 but was ultimately shorter than girl A. Such differences in age of onset of the growth spurt are likely to accompany differences in age of puberty. Differences in the rate of maturation may have lasting implications for personality development, a topic to which we return later.

Factors that may produce individual differences in growth rate include malnutrition and disease. Researchers, for example, recorded the growth rate of one child who suffered from two episodes of inadequate nutrition (Prader, Tanner, & von Harnack, 1963). The child's growth was severely affected; but after the episodes were over, the child did not simply return to his normal rate of growth. Rather, there was remarkable acceleration in growth, which returned him to his expected growth path. This "catch-up" growth is relatively common as an aftermath of disease or limited malnutrition (Tanner, 1963).

How might we distinguish a child whose rate of maturation is slow from a child who is genetically targeted for a small adult stature? A technique for making this distinction establishes the skeletal maturity, or **bone age,** of the child, which may differ from his or her chronological age. Children's bones develop from cartilage, which breaks down near the center as bone forms. This process extends outward toward the bone ends, called the *epiphyses.* As growth reaches completion, the epiphyses close; at this point, no further growth is possible. One can determine from an X-ray how a child's bone development compares with that of his or her peers and approximately how much more growth is likely to occur (Tanner, 1990).

Bone age

The degree of maturation of an individual as indicated by the extent of hardening of the bones.

Changes in Body Proportion and Composition

Another sort of variability in growth rate concerns the rates at which different parts of the body develop. Figure 6-13 shows a graph of proportional growth of the body. Most noticeably, the size of the head changes, from 50% of total body length at 2 months of fetal age, to 25% by birth, and to only about 10% by adulthood. This sequence reflects the cephalocaudal, or top-down, sequence of development described earlier.

• The pace of growth during childhood and adolescence is influenced by both nature and nurture factors.

We have seen that a spurt in height accompanies adolescence. More of this height comes from trunk growth than leg growth, but in one of the few violations of the cephalocaudal and proximodistal principle, leg growth precedes trunk growth by 6 to 9 months. Parents often wonder whether children at this stage will always be all hands and feet (Tanner, 1990).

Internal organs also follow individual paths of growth, as you might expect from our discussion of the brain. Up to around 6 to 8 years of age, the brain grows much faster than the body in general. In contrast, the reproductive organs grow much slower. Then the rate of brain growth slows to a gradual halt, whereas the reproductive system reaches a plateau between 5 and 12 years of age and surges at around 14 years of age.

The proportion of fat to muscle also changes with age, and it differs for boys and girls. The fetus begins to accumulate fat in the weeks before birth, and this process continues until around 9 months after birth. After that, fat gradually declines until around 6 to 8 years of age. Girls have a bit more fat than boys at birth. This difference increases gradually through childhood until about 8 years of age and then increases more rapidly. During the adolescent growth spurt, girls continue to gain fat faster than males, although there is a sharp decline in the rate of fat accumulation when they are growing fastest. Muscle growth also occurs during adolescence, more strikingly for boys than for girls (Malina, 1990). However, because girls reach their growth spurt before males, there is a 2-year period in which girls, on average, have more muscle than boys. Changes in body proportions that occur in adolescence result in greater shoulder width and muscular development in males and broader hips and more fat in females.

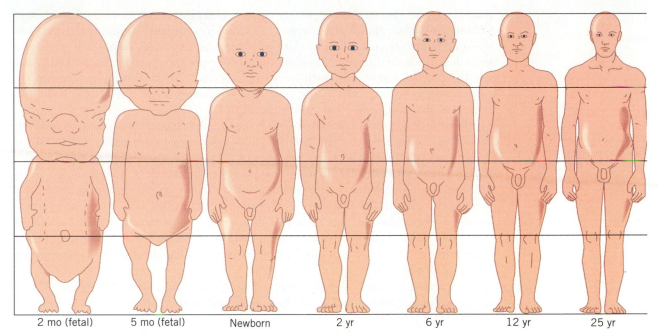

| 2 mo (fetal) | 5 mo (fetal) | Newborn | 2 yr | 6 yr | 12 yr | 25 yr |

Figure 6-13 Body proportions at several ages. From *Growth* (p. 118) by W. J. Robbins, S. Brady, A. G. Hogan, C. M. Jackson, and C. W. Greene, 1928, New Haven: Yale University Press.

Sex Differentiation and Puberty

We have already seen that gender affects body size and composition. Now we look more closely at the physical aspects of gender in the growth years and especially in adolescence. Other aspects of sex differentiation are discussed in Chapter 15.

Early Sex Differentiation

The father's sperm determines the sex of the fetus by contributing either an X (female) or a Y (male) chromosome to the 23rd pair. In the fetus, the gonads (ovaries in females and testes in males) look the same for males and females when they first appear. However, they develop somewhat faster in the male. It is interesting to note that the fetus will become female unless direction is provided. If no male hormones are secreted in the early weeks, the fetus develops female sex organs. Male hormones also appear to affect the hypothalamus, which will later play a role in the cyclic menstruation of the female. The secretion of the hormone testosterone seems to affect brain wiring so that the male becomes noncyclic in hormone production in adulthood. Apparently, if this wiring pattern is not established between 10 and 14 weeks after fertilization, the fetus is female.

Sex differentiation continues from birth until puberty, with girls developing somewhat faster than boys, as mentioned. Still, boys and girls share relatively similar heights, body proportions, and body composition in the years between birth and puberty, at least relative to the differences that occur during puberty.

Adolescence and Puberty

Accompanying the dramatic changes in growth at the beginning of adolescence is the most substantial surge of differentiation between the two sexes since the fetal period. These changes occur when certain chemicals—hormones—provided by various endocrine glands are released into the bloodstream. Ultimately, these glandular activities are controlled by the hypothalamus. Especially important glands for growth and sexual differentiation in adolescence are the gonads, the adrenals, and the thyroid. In addition, growth hormone, secreted by the pituitary, activates the production of a hormone in the liver that stimulates bone growth (Kulin, 1991; Paikoff & Brooks-Gunn, 1990; Stanhope, 1989).

Puberty
The period in which chemical and physical changes in the body occur to enable sexual reproduction.

Besides the growth spurt already discussed, adolescence is marked by **puberty,** the series of changes that culminate in sexual maturity and the ability to reproduce. Puberty usually begins between the ages of 10 and 14, somewhat earlier for girls than for boys. In males, the first sign of puberty, which occurs at around age 11 on average, is an enlargement of the testes and a change in the texture and color of the scrotum. Later, the penis enlarges, pubic hair appears, and sperm production begins, followed by the appearance of hair under the arms and on the face. Near the end of puberty, the larynx lengthens, causing the male voice to become deeper. Male adolescents sometimes announce this lengthening through an embarrassing breaking of the voice.

For females, the first sign of puberty is breast budding, which may occur as early as 8 years of age and as late as 13 years, followed by the appearance of pubic hair.

Figure 6-14 Several physical changes that occur during puberty in males and females. Average age at which each change begins and ends is shown, as well as the range of ages for individuals. For example, breast development in females begins, on average, at 10.5 years and is complete by 15 years. But a particular female may begin development as early as 8 years of age and another may complete development as late as 18 years of age. (Adapted from Marshall and Tanner, 1970.)

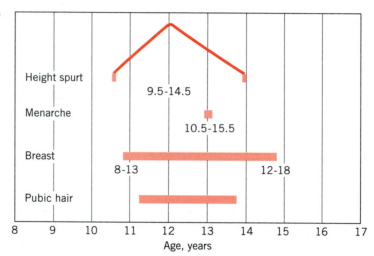

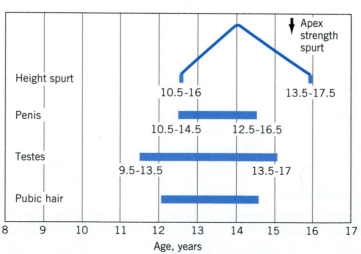

Menarche occurs relatively late in puberty—on average, at around 13 years in northern and central Europe and North America. Variation is high, but 95% of girls begin menarche between 11 and 15 years of age. Usually, ovulation follows the onset of menarche by 1 or 2 years. Figure 6-14 illustrates the average age of onset and offset of several physical changes in puberty as well as the strikingly large range of ages at which these changes occur.

How fast adolescents move through puberty varies as widely as when they start. For example, it may take a girl as few as 1.5 years or as many as 5 years to complete puberty. Suppose we were studying a single class of boys and girls in elementary school. If we recorded when the first student began puberty and followed the group until the last student finished puberty, chances are we would have to follow the group for a full 10 years (Petersen, 1987). Within the middle years, you can imagine how much variation in maturation there would be and how these differences might play out in social relations, self-image, and confidence.

Attitudes Toward Puberty

Psychologists studying adolescence tended in the past to focus on physical changes. As investigators have learned more about the dynamics of adolescent change, however, they have increasingly emphasized the roles that social and cultural factors play. More and more, investigators talk about "biosocial" or "psychobiological" factors in adolescence rather than only biological factors (Collins, 1988; Lerner, Lerner, & Tubman, 1989; Smith, 1989).

For example, consider how girls react to the onset of menarche. This event usually heightens a girl's self-esteem and her prestige among peers. However, girls who are psychologically unprepared for menarche, because they lack information about it, have more negative feelings about its onset. Later in life, these girls are more negative about menstruation, report more severe symptoms, and are more self-conscious than other girls (Brooks-Gunn, 1987, 1991).

Social factors also influence how adolescents feel about changes in their bodies and how early or late maturation affects their self-images. At least in the United States, the socially approved female is thin. But as we have seen, females add fat in puberty, and their hips broaden. In contrast, males add muscle and shoulder width, characteristics that fit "ideal" cultural images for the male. Not surprisingly, early-maturing females tend to be more dissatisfied with their bodies during puberty than late-maturing females, whereas the opposite is true for males. The dissatisfaction of early-maturing females and the satisfaction of early-maturing males relate to their satisfaction with their weight and proportions (Crockett & Petersen, 1987; Dornbusch et al., 1987; Lerner, 1987). A study in Helsinki, Finland, in which children were studied at 11, 13, 15, and 18 years of age, revealed that males were more satisfied with their bodies than females at all ages. Both sexes were more satisfied with their bodies at 18 years of age than they had been before, however, reflecting an acceptance of body changes (von Wright, 1989).

Only limited research exists on how early and late maturers succeed later in life. When studied as young adults, adolescent boys who had been early maturers had more stable vocations than late maturers. They scored higher on tests of sociability, dominance, self-control, and responsibility. Late maturers scored higher on nurturance but had more negative self-concepts and more feelings of rejection by others and were more likely to have suffered maladjustment in late adolescence. On the positive side, late-maturing boys seemed more able than earlier maturers to face their emotions and feelings (Brooks-Gunn & Reiter, 1990; Jones, 1957; Mussen & Jones, 1957). Of course, individuals vary substantially, and the climate of the family in which a child grows strongly moderates the effects of maturation rate.

Factors That Affect Growth and Maturation

Genetic heritage plays a major part in the growth and maturation of a child. Thus, children tend to resemble their biological parents—tall parents, for example, usually have taller children than do short parents. But as you probably suspect by now, growth and maturation are also influenced by the context of development. Following a discussion of the role of heredity, we will discuss some contextual factors—nutrition, exercise, social class, disease, abuse, and psychological trauma—that affect growth rate.

Heredity

You may remember from Chapter 4 that investigators sometimes compare similarities in identical twins with similarities in fraternal twins to determine how much genetic factors influence particular behaviors. A similar strategy yields information about the role of heredity in the onset and pace of puberty and body structure. One study of twins has been underway in Louisville, Kentucky, for over 30 years, and more than 500 twins have been studied. Identical twins became increasingly similar in height up to around 4 years of age and stabilized at a very high correlation of around .94. Fraternal twins of the same sex did the opposite. At birth, their correlation in height was .77, but it then diverged to .59 at 2 years and .49 at 9 years, where it stabilized. A similar pattern for similarities in weight was observed (Wilson, 1986b). Identical twins are also more similar than fraternal twins in their spurts and lags in growth (Mueller, 1986).

Several other measures support the role of heredity in the rate of maturation. Identical twins display much higher similarity in the age of eruption of their teeth than do fraternal twins, and they are more similar in the pace of bone development, as well as in breast development in girls and testicular development in boys. The age of onset of menarche differs by less than 4 months in identical twins. One study revealed that even when identical twins were raised apart, the onset of menarche differed by an average of only 2.8 months. Fraternal twins raised together typically differ by 6 to 12 months in the age of onset. These two studies imply that genes play a substantial role in maturation, a conclusion supported by relations between age of onset of menarche between mother and daughter (Bailey & Garn, 1986). Presumably, the role is played out through systems that regulate hormone production.

If genetic factors influence maturation and eventual stature, we might expect to find maturational differences among genetic groups. In fact, these do occur. Asians reach puberty faster than Europeans and move through it more quickly but achieve a smaller stature. Africans proceed through adolescence at about the same pace as do Europeans and Americans; but when they have equivalent quality of life, they reach a taller stature (Evelyth, 1986).

Nutrition

It should come as no surprise that relations have been found between the adequacy of nutrition and growth. Nutrition affects the brain as well, and symptoms of undernutrition have often been accompanied by evidence of intellectual impairment. General undernutrition contributes to slow growth and later onset of puberty (Tanner, 1987).

Undernutrition is thought to be especially damaging during gestation and the early years of life, because brain growth is so rapid during this period. Growth occurs in two ways; by increases in the number of cells and by increases in cell size. Increases in cell number usually characterize early growth, while increases in cell size are responsible for some early growth and for all growth after about 18 months.

• Zinc deficiency can produce abnormal metabolism and growth failure (child on left).

Thus, the impact of malnutrition is qualitatively different at different ages, and it is thought to be especially damaging during the early period. Brains of children in Chile who died from malnutrition in their first or second year showed lower brain weight, less brain protein, fewer brain cells, and less myelin than expected. Research with rats reveals an especially damaging effect of combined prenatal and postnatal malnutrition. Whereas malnutrition during either period alone reduced the number of brain cells by 15%, malnutrition during the two periods combined resulted in a 60% loss, and there is evidence that a similar relation holds for humans (Bálazs et al., 1986; Winick, 1971).

Recent studies indicate that the effects of early malnutrition are not as irreversible as was once thought. Dietary correction and stimulating environments can have remarkable recuperative effects. However, some negative effects may not be reversible, and prevention is clearly better than treatment (Lozoff, 1989). Recent studies in Brazil and Colombia document the effects of preventive measures. When food supplementation was provided from mid-pregnancy to the time the child was 3 years of age, benefits for both growth and weight could be observed even 3 years after the intervention ceased (Paine et al., 1992; Super, Herrera, & Mora, 1990).

Undernutrition can affect intellectual development even apart from physical changes in the brain, because of its effect on energy level. Undernourishment in babies makes them more apathetic, which reduces their energy for social interaction and the development of social bonds. Moreover, it affects the time that they have for learning about their environment. Their apathy may be especially damaging during critical periods of development (Cravioto & Arrieta, 1986).

In addition to simply getting enough food, children need balance in their diets. For example, a zinc deficiency can be particularly disruptive for normal metabolism and can cause growth failure, atrophy of the testes, and decreased size of the accessory sex glands. Marijuana abusers tend to be especially vulnerable to zinc deficiencies (Farrow, Rees, & Worthington-Roberts, 1987).

Eating disorders represent an area of nutrition that has received increasing attention in recent years. **Anorexia nervosa** is one such disorder. The anorexic, most often a young female, voluntarily engages in severe dietary restriction—she starves herself. The effects include muscle wasting; dry skin; thin, dry, and brittle hair; constipation, dehydration; and sleep disturbance. Sometimes growth and development are impeded, menstruation may cease, and breast development may be permanently affected. Adolescent anorexics often have a distorted concept of nourishment and body image.

Another eating disorder is **bulimia,** which involves food binging and sometimes self-induced vomiting or an excessive consumption of laxatives. These practices often damage the teeth, irritate the gums, and produce cracked and damaged lips, and they may alter body fluid balance. Bulimics, like anorexics, have a distorted concept of nourishment, and they often suffer guilt and depression (Hsu, 1990; Leon, 1991; Rees & Trahms, 1989).

Obesity, or excess fat storage, is one of the most common disorders in the United States today. Obesity is usually defined as weight 20% or more over a standard weight for height. Obesity appears to be a particular problem among Hispanic Americans (Olvera-Ezzell, Power, & Cousins, 1990). It may result from genetic predisposition, overeating, or a combination of both; it frequently has an early onset, by 4 or 5 years of age (Eichorn, 1970, 1979). Obesity has several effects on development. Obese females tend to begin puberty earlier than nonobese females, for example, and obese males hit their growth spurt earlier. Obesity also has psychological consequences. Many obese children feel insecure and are overprotected by their parents. They may frequently experience school difficulties, neu-

• Eating disorders during adolescence often result from a preoccupation with weight and from distorted concepts of body image.

Anorexia nervosa
A severe eating disorder, usually involving excessive weight loss through self-starvation, typically found in teenage girls.

Bulimia
A disorder of food binging and sometimes purging by self-induced vomiting or excessive use of laxatives, typically observed in teenage girls.

Obesity
A condition of excess fat storage; often defined as weight more than 20% over a standardized 'ideal' weight.

roses, and social problems. A vicious cycle may become established in which social and psychological problems induce eating, and weight gain further contributes to the problems.

Exercise

Physical activity generally has beneficial effects on development, but there is some evidence of negative effects if exercise is taken to extremes. Very strenuous exercise in highly intensive training programs (for example, training for wrestling) may reduce growth rate (Gallahue, 1989). Ballet dancers exercise strenuously and strive to keep their bodies slim, factors that seem to be related to their tendency to reach menarche at a later age than nondancers (Brooks-Gunn, 1987). The regularity of the menstrual cycle is affected by exercise once menarche has begun. Female athletes who train intensively often experience irregular menstrual periods during their training regime (Firsch, 1984).

 DEVELOPMENT IN CONTEXT: **Social Class, Culture, and Poverty**

The quality of life, measured in terms of physical resources, is clearly better in developed than developing countries. The death rates of children are 10 times higher in developing than developed countries; one estimate indicates that 11 million fewer children would die each year if the poor countries of the world had the same death rates as the wealthy countries (Altman, 1993). However, citizens of even the wealthiest countries do not have uniform access to resources.

In virtually every country in the world, there are differences in social classes, and these differences determine access to nutrition and health care. Differences in physical development between social classes are consistently found. As you can see in Figure 6-15, for example, there is much less difference in height among young boys of the higher socioeconomic class across several countries than between higher and lower socioeconomic classes within a country. Of course, social class itself is not the cause of such physical variations; rather, they represent many differences in nutrition, health care, disease, environmental enrichment, and opportunity.

The United States is not immune to these problems. Some 14.3 million children under 18 years of age live in poverty, about one in every five U.S. children. And the likelihood of being poor is not evenly distributed among racial groups. Whereas approximately 40% of African-American families and 35% of Hispanic-American families with children are poor, only 13% of white families live in poverty (SRCD Newsletter, 1993). Furthermore, poverty is a growing problem. By 1990, the poverty rate was one third higher than in the 2 preceding decades (Duncan, Brooks-Gunn, & Klebanov, 1994; Halpern, 1993). The discrepancy between rich and poor has grown as well. Throughout the 1980s, the income of the top 20% of U.S. families increased by $7,172 per year, whereas that of the bottom 20% decreased by $347 (SRCD Newsletter, 1993).

Behind these grim statistics are children and parents who have inadequate access to health care, housing, and nutrition. The gravest consequence of these conditions is death. In a recent study in Washington, D.C., death rates among children was 7 times higher in the poorest counties than in the richest counties (Halpern, 1993).

A child's well-being may be affected even before conception. Poor women are more likely to have inferior health before pregnancy and inadequate health care during pregnancy. They are also more likely to experience high levels of stress during pregnancy and to engage in harmful health behavior. Consequently, the fetus

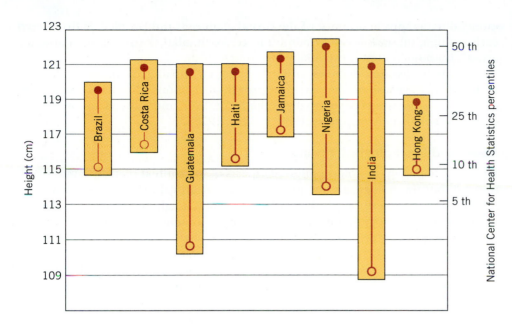

Figure 6-15 Average heights of 7-year-old boys in several countries. The solid circles at the top indicate the heights of boys from the higher socioeconomic classes, and the open circles at the bottom indicate the heights of boys from the lower socioeconomic classes. Adapted from 'Genetics, Environment, and Growth: Issues in the Assessment of Nutritional Status' by R. Martorell, 1984. In A. Velasquez & H. Bourges (Eds.), *Genetic Factors in Nutrition* (p. 382), Orlando, FL: Academic Press. Copyright 1984 by Academic Press. Adapted by permission.

is more likely to experience intrauterine stress, a contributor to premature labor and delivery and to low birthweight. "In other words, under conditions of poverty, an infant is significantly more likely to be born constitutionally vulnerable and to be a difficult-to-care-for baby" (Halpern, 1993, p.74).

The daily grind of poverty and typically overcrowded living conditions following birth can compound a baby's constitutional vulnerability. Poverty can drain parents' energy and undermine their self-confidence and feeling of control over their lives. Exhaustion, irritability, anger, and a feeling of futility are often the result, with consequences for the parent–child relationship. Parents may not have the psychological resources to share their infant's joy and pleasure, which would provide the parent positive feedback for meeting the infant's needs (Halpern, 1993).

Not all poor families are the same, of course. Some children grow up poor in extended families where neighborhood and social support is ample and where the social network pulls together to help children rise to the challenge of limited resources and excel. Still, there can be little doubt that these children and families face formidable odds.

The Clinton presidential administration has made several proposals to address some of the problems of the poor, including one that would make health care more accessible. But some people argue that caring for the poor is not the government's responsibility. Clearly, the problems of poverty and adequate health care for all will be with us for years to come.

Physical Abnormality

Growth depends crucially on normal functioning of the pituitary and thyroid glands. In adolescence, sex-gland secretions play an important role in the growth spurt. Abnormalities in the functioning of any of these glands can produce dwarfism or giantism. If diagnosed in time, glandular abnormalities can be corrected. For example, some children fail to grow because of a deficit in growth hormone, due perhaps to a tumor of the hypothalamus. If this problem is discovered early enough, substances can be administered to stimulate the pituitary to produce growth hormone, often substantially speeding growth.

Metabolic diseases, diabetes, and infections can impair growth, and certain genetic diseases are also accompanied by growth aberrations. Problems can also be produced by diseases of such organs as the heart, liver, and kidneys and by various bone diseases (Kreipe & Strauss, 1989; Lowrey, 1978).

Abuse and Psychological Trauma

We have focused up to now on physical aspects of the context of growth and development, but psychological trauma can also impair growth. A failure-to-thrive syndrome has been described in infants who fail to gain weight for no obvious reasons other than psychological disturbances or maltreatment and abuse by parents. Frequently, these babies gain weight quite readily when their care is transferred to hospital personnel (Benoit, 1993; Drotar, 1988; Drotar et al., 1990).

An interesting report on 13 children between the ages of 3 and 11 years provides an example of how psychological trauma can affect growth. These children lived in homes that were unusually stressful as a result of marital strife or alcohol abuse, and there were several cases of child abuse. The children appeared to have abnormally low pituitary gland activity, and their growth rates were substantially impaired. Shortly after they were removed from parental care, the circulation of growth hormone from the pituitary increased, and the growth of most of the children accelerated (Powell, Brasel, & Blizzard, 1967). Clearly, there is at least some environmental control over a characteristic that was once thought to be controlled almost exclusively by genetics.

This is of special concern in the United States, where child abuse is reaching alarming levels. The National Center on Child Abuse and Neglect reported 160,932 cases of confirmed abuse of children under age 3 in the United States in 1990. A majority of the 1,200 children who died from abuse that year were under 3 years of

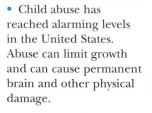

• Child abuse has reached alarming levels in the United States. Abuse can limit growth and can cause permanent brain and other physical damage.

age (Mrazek, 1993). Because most cases are not reported, it is difficult to know how much abuse occurs, but it is estimated that 2.2 million children a year are abused, 25% of them under 2 years of age. Several intervention programs have shown that the likelihood of abuse can be reduced in families at risk, and child-care advocates have proposed many ideas for dealing with this problem. To date, however, no wide-ranging programs have been undertaken by the U.S. government (Zigler, Hopper, & Hall, 1993).

Secular Trends

There is evidence that growth rates have changed over recent history in some parts of the world. In Europe and North America, after about 1900, the average height of 5- to 7-year-olds increased 1 to 2 centimeters per decade, and the average height of 10- to 14-year-olds increased 2 to 3 centimeters per decade. Adult height, however, increased only 0.6 centimeters per decade between 1880 and 1960. Thus, the increase in children's heights apparently reflected a trend toward faster maturation more than a trend toward greater ultimate stature. Indeed, it was fairly typical for people to grow until age 25 or so before this century, whereas growth usually continues today only until about age 18 or 19. The trend toward faster maturation has also been noticeable in the age of menarche, which has decreased over the last century (Meredith, 1963; Tanner, 1987). Earlier maturation can be explained by better living conditions—better nourishment, better health care, and lowered incidence of disease. The trend began to level off about 2 decades ago.

✔ *To Recap...*

Growth is continuous through childhood but does not proceed uniformly. The rate of growth gradually slows, then spurts at adolescence and stops soon afterward. Of course, growth rates vary widely among children, as do the heights ultimately reached. Bone age is one way to distinguish a child who will be a short adult from one who is maturing slowly. Different parts of the body develop at different rates, following a cephalocaudal progression. Body organs also vary in rates of maturation; the brain, for example, develops very early.

Boys and girls grow fairly similarly until adolescence. Girls typically experience the adolescent growth spurt and puberty earlier than boys. Boys add more height once their growth spurt has begun, as well as more muscle mass and shoulder width. Girls add relatively more fat and hip width. The adolescent's attitude toward these changes may reflect social and cultural factors, such as the amount of information he or she has about the changes and the body image that society holds up as ideal.

Many factors influence growth and maturation. Genetic heritage is clearly important, but such environmental factors as nutrition, exercise, social class, disease, abuse, and psychological trauma also come into play. Some of these environmental variables, such as better nutrition, accelerated growth rates in many developed countries during the 20th century.

CONCLUSION

This chapter concludes a set of three chapters that concern the more physical aspects of human psychological development. In Chapters 4 and 5, we focused on genetics and prenatal development. In Chapter 6, we discussed the behaviors and physical equipment the baby brings to the world and how this basic equipment develops through infancy, childhood, and adolescence.

Until recently, psychologists have not been very open to considering the physical and biological bases of behavior. Rather, a tension existed between the more physically based and the more psychologically based disciplines, with psychologists more focused on demonstrating that social and nonbiological factors influence behavior. However, the mood seems to be changing. As we have seen, biological influences that we might at first imagine would act on their own are found, on closer examination, to cooperate with environmental factors to produce their ultimate effect. We have seen many examples of this interdependence—for instance, in the effects of health care on birth mortality, of the family setting on the outcome of infants at risk, of prenatal exposure to cocaine on the newborn's state organization and rhythms, of practice on motor development, and of psychological trauma on growth. The discovery that experience affects virtually every domain of behavior and virtually every physical process has relieved psychologists of their earlier preoccupation. Tensions that once existed between psychologists and biologists have largely disappeared, yielding more integrated efforts to understand how biological factors and experience collaborate to influence human development.

No better evidence of this collaboration exists than in the successful efforts of psychologists, biologists, and neuroscientists to have the decade of the 1990s declared the "decade of the brain." President George Bush signed a resolution to this effect in October 1989, committing the United States to the expenditure of significant research dollars and efforts aimed at understanding both the psychological and biological mysteries of this most important organ. Perhaps, by the turn of the 21st century, exciting advances in our understanding of human development will reflect the wisdom of this national commitment to better understanding.

FOR THOUGHT AND DISCUSSION

1.   We have seen that birth is not the beginning of development. But during the prenatal period, nature factors exert much more influence that nurture factors. *What, then, do you view as the major developmental significance of birth? Try to imagine what early postnatal development would be like if humans gestated for a longer period, say, two years (like elephants).*

2.   Birthing practices in Western countries have changed in interesting ways. Until the mid-20th century, births generally took place at home with family members. Then there was a dramatic shift to delivering in hospitals, with impersonal medical procedures replacing traditional ones. Now the pendulum has swung back toward more natural methods in which the family once again is included. *What might be some advantages of this recent trend? What about disadvantages? Can you think of any other aspects of child-rearing that have displayed this same return to more traditional methods? Can you predict some that might do so?*

3.   It is clear that the newborn is much more sophisticated and complex than was once believed. *Why do you think even trained professionals so grossly underestimated babies' abilities? Assume we continue to do so today. What other remarkable abilities might we someday discover that babies possess?*

4.   Physical development follows cephalocaudal and proximodistal progressions. *Think about these trends from an evolutionary perspective. Can you think of reasons why it would be adaptive for development to occur in these ways?*

5.   We said that the development of the synapses in the brain goes on for a number of years after birth. *Why do you think humans have evolved this way, rather than with all of the connections already established? How would development be different if they were?*

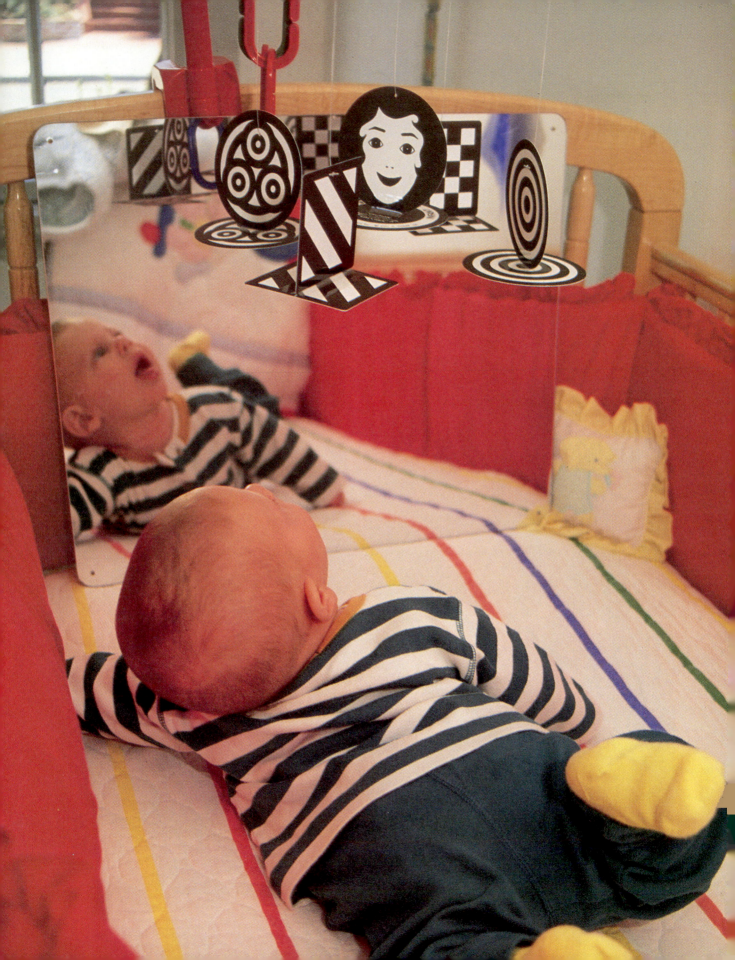

Chapter 7

SENSORY AND PERCEPTUAL DEVELOPMENT

*A*ll that we know about ourselves and the world has come to us through our senses. As obvious as this claim may seem, philosophers have argued its merits. Are people born with innate, organized categories for perceiving the world, or must everything be experienced to be known? A philosopher named Molyneux posed the question as follows. A man is born blind but is suddenly able to see as an adult. The man had learned to distinguish a sphere and a cube by touch when he was blind. Will he be able to recognize which is which by sight alone? John Locke (1694/1959) said no, arguing that experience is necessary to understand the relation between vision and touch (the empiricist position). Others predicted that the previously blind man would be able to identify the two objects by vision alone, because knowledge of the relations among properties of objects is inborn (the nativist position).

Such questions have motivated studies of perceptual development, especially development in infancy. What do the infant and child know about their world at various ages? How do they acquire new knowledge? And how does their genetic endowment affect what they learn?

We must distinguish among three processes in order to talk about perceptual development—sensation, perception, and attention. **Sensation** refers to the detection and discrimination of sensory information—for example, hearing and distinguishing high and low tones. **Perception** refers to the interpretation of sensations and involves *recognition* ("I've heard that song before") and *identification* ("That was thunder"). **Attention** refers to the selectivity of perception, as when a child fails to hear his mother calling because he is attending to the television.

In this chapter, we examine the capacities that babies have for learning about the objects and people in their world and how these capacities develop. After we consider the sensory and perceptual modes separately, we see how children coordinate information from these modes. We then discuss how the child integrates perception and attention with action in the smooth flow of behavior. We begin by taking a look at what the three major theories say about perceptual development.

THEORIES OF SENSORY AND PERCEPTUAL DEVELOPMENT

The three theories of development that we have described—environmental/learning, ethological, and cognitive-developmental—have somewhat different ideas about perceptual development. As you might expect, however, they agree on several fundamental issues. All of these theories acknowledge that experience affects perceptual development, for example, and all of them acknowledge that our biological machinery plays an important role in how we experience the things that go on around us.

Environmental/Learning Approaches

Learning theorists emphasize the role of experience in perceptual development. According to this view, a child builds perceptual impressions through associations. For example, when a baby sees a face for the first time, she sees no relation among the eyes, eyebrows, nose, mouth, ears, and hairline. After seeing many faces, the baby comes to see all of these elements as belonging together. Only then can she recognize a familiar face or distinguish one face from another (Hebb, 1949).

Sensation
The experience resulting from the stimulation of a sense organ.

Perception
The interpretation of sensory stimulation based on experience.

Attention
The selection of particular sensory input for perceptual and cognitive processing and the exclusion of competing input.

Through experience babies also learn to connect sights with sounds, touch with vision, and so on. The sound of a human voice seems, at first, no more likely to accompany the sight of a face than does the sound of a horn. Only experience makes the combination of face and voice more natural than face and horn. So, along with John Locke, learning theorists would answer Molyneux's question with a resounding no. The blind man must see and feel the sphere and the cube at the same time to understand the relations between the visual and tactile sensations.

Learning theory helps to make sense of such phenomena as our inability to distinguish easily among faces of people who belong to races that are unfamiliar. An Asian, for example, may have difficulty distinguishing among Caucasian males of similar height and hair color, because she is relatively unfamiliar with the particular features of Caucasian faces.

Research on the central nervous system illustrates how experience affects the functioning of even single sensory cells. Normally, each cell (neuron) in the visual area of the brain is stimulated by one type of visual element, such as vertical edges, but not by other elements, such as horizontal edges. Other brain cells respond to horizontal edges but are insensitive to vertical edges. Still other cells "like" angles, or diagonal lines, or other visual elements. Most theorists believe that when a stimulus repeatedly activates combinations of such cells—as when a baby looks at a square—the connections among these cells grow stronger. Eventually, the cells fire in synchrony, and a person sees a whole square rather than a combination of lines and intersections (Hebb, 1949). The important point here is that these cells are sensitive to experience at an early age (Antonini & Stryker, 1993).

This sensitivity to experience appears to reflect a kind of Darwinian "survival of the fittest" battle among brain cells (Edelman, 1987; 1993). As we noted in Chapter 6, many of the neurons we are born with die early in life. Researchers believe that visual experience activates some cells, which survive, but that other cells or their interconnections are not activated, and these die or their synapses are trimmed back. Thus, experience is important to the survival of cells and their connections (Burkhalter, 1991; Greenough & Black, 1992; Rakic, 1991).

Ethological Theory

The ethological theorists emphasize the natural equipment that animals and humans have evolved for gathering information from their world. They pay special attention to how our sensory receptors are built to pick up physical energy and to inform us about aspects of the physical world.

James and Eleanor Gibson have developed an ethological theory of perceptual development that contrasts strikingly with the learning approach (Gibson, 1966; Adolph, Eppler, & Gibson, 1993). The Gibsons do not believe that perception involves combining pieces of input through experience. Instead, they argue that objects in the world give off physical energy that is already organized and can be perceived in its entirety. Perceptual development, they suggest, consists of a child's increasing sensitivity to the organization of this energy and also to which properties of objects and people remain stable and which properties change. In general, ethological theorists would be more likely to answer Molyneux's question with a yes, because they would assume that natural relations exist between vision and touch.

The Gibsonian analysis suggests that even infants should be sensitive to the synchrony of visual and auditory events, and this appears to be the case. When young babies watch people speak, they can detect when speakers' lip movements are not synchronized with the sounds that they hear (Kuhl & Meltzoff, 1988). This ability is difficult to account for by traditional learning theories, which emphasize the need for certain sound–vision experiences. Such experiences are fairly limited for very young infants. Notice that theorists generally assume that the earlier in development a perceptual skill occurs, the less likely that it has been acquired by experience.

Cognitive-Developmental Theories

Cognitive theories of perception emphasize the role of knowledge in how we interpret the world. In a classic study that illustrated the role of cognition in perception, Jerome Bruner had middle-class and poor children look at a quarter and then select a circle that they thought matched the size of the quarter. Poorer children selected larger circles than middle-class children, suggesting that the quarter looked larger to them, presumably because it was of greater value (Bruner & Goodman, 1947).

Bruner suggested, in fact, that cognitive processes precede perception rather than the other way around—that a person may not perceive an object until he or she has categorized it (Bruner, Goodnow, & Austin, 1956). Although this idea may seem unlikely, it is not difficult to demonstrate cognitive effects on perception. For example, look at the picture in Figure 7-1. What is it? Now, look at the upside-down word in the caption of the figure. Once you know what the picture is, you perceive it differently, and it is no longer possible to perceive it the way you did before. Clearly, cognitive categorization can affect perception.

Piaget also emphasized the role of cognition in perception. He believed that a child's stage of cognitive development controls how the child perceives the world. Through infancy, babies increasingly integrate perceptual modes like touch and vision, which helps them understand that, for example, a felt object and a seen object are the same. (Piaget, then, would answer Molyneux's question with a no; experience is necessary to properly identify previously felt objects by vision alone.) The influence of cognition on perception continues well past infancy. For example, children in the early school years (the preoperational period) have difficulty attending to more than one perceptual dimension, which interferes with their ability

Figure 7-1 A Dalmatian.

to solve certain problems (Piaget & Inhelder, 1969). We pursue this research in more detail in the next chapter.

The information-processing model represents another cognitive approach to perception. Researchers who take this approach suggest that, like a computer, the brain processes information through a series of steps: perceptual input, internal modifications, memory, and output. The relevant questions about perceptual development, then, involve how these processes change with age and how these changes are related to the amount of information a child can process. For example, a child's growing improvement in reading may involve a number of cognitive and percep-tual abilities, such as improvements in vision, recognition that clusters of lines and intersections form independent letters, skill in seeing several letters at the same time, and so on.

✔ *To Recap...*

The **environmental/learning approach** to perceptual development emphasizes the role of experience. In this view, development occurs as babies learn through experience to construct increasingly detailed and complex perceptions from the separate input of the senses. It appears that experience affects single sensory cells and connections between these cells.

Ethologists place less emphasis on experience and believe that even babies perceive sensory information comprehensively, not as separate pieces of input from different senses. Development consists of increasing sensitivity to the structure of incoming information, as well as to which properties change and which remain constant.

Finally, the cognitive approach emphasizes how knowledge can affect perception. Piaget believed the child's stage of development controls how she perceives the world, and the information-processing approach focuses on how sensory information is transformed as it is processed by the brain.

TOUCH AND PAIN, SMELL AND TASTE, MOTION AND BALANCE

Now we turn to an examination of what young babies actually perceive. We have much less information about the sensory modes of touch, smell, taste, and body balance and motion than about hearing or vision. Nevertheless, these sensory capacities are vitally important to the survival of young organisms. In most animals, these capacities develop earlier than hearing and vision, so we will consider them first (Rachell & Gottlieb, 1992).

Touch and Pain

Anyone who wonders whether the newborn baby senses touch or experiences pain should watch the baby's reaction to a heel prick for a blood sample or to circumcision (Reisman, 1987). Newborn babies also show touch reflexes such as those described in Chapter 6. In fact, the fetus displays its first sign of sensitivity to external stimulation through reactions to touch. As early as the second month following conception, the fetus responds to stroking at the side of the mouth (tested in naturally aborted fetuses). Touch sensitivity increases over the first several days of life (Haith, 1986; Lipsitt & Levy, 1959).

Touching is important for relations between children and adults. A hand placed on the newborn's chest can soothe a crying episode, and gentle stroking can quiet even premature babies (MacFarlane, 1977; Oehler & Eckerman, 1988). For older infants, touching produces more positive affect and visual attention during interactions between infant and caregiver (Stack & Muir, 1992). You probably know about the attachment of the Peanuts character Linus to his blanket. In fact, many babies become best friends with their blankets and draw comfort from the facial stroking that they afford. We discuss this matter further in Chapter 12.

Haptic perception
The perceptual experience that results from active exploration of objects by touch.

Psychologists refer to the active, exploratory use of touch as **haptic perception.** By the end of the first year of life, infants can recognize a familiar object by exploration with the hand alone (Rose, Gottfried, & Bridger, 1981a). This perception improves with age. Young preschoolers tend to explore forms with their fingers haphazardly. Nevertheless, even blind 3-year-olds can haptically explore a novel object in one orientation and then recognize that object in a new orientation, a skill that requires forming a mental image of the felt object and then transforming it mentally to the new orientation (Landau, 1991). As children become more skilled in finger tracing of object contours with age, their recognition performance improves even further (Pick & Pick, 1970).

Smell and Taste

When can babies smell odors? How would we be able to tell, as we can't ask? Researchers have examined this question by observing whether babies, when presented with a smell, will make a face, turn their heads, or do nothing at all. Even newborns turn their heads away from a cotton swab that smells bad (Rieser, Yonas, & Wikner, 1976). Babies produce positive facial expressions in response to banana, strawberry, and vanilla smells and negative expressions in response to smells of rotten eggs and fish (Crook, 1987; Steiner, 1977, 1979). Thus, the newborn's sense of smell is keen, and it improves over the first few days of life (Lipsitt, Engen, & Kaye, 1963).

• Touching and stroking can calm babies and also increase their visual attention to the caregiver.

Infants use this ability as early as the first week of life to distinguish their mothers' smells. One researcher placed a breast pad from the mother next to one cheek of the baby and a breast pad from another woman next to the other cheek. By the sixth day of life, the baby turned more frequently toward the mother's breast pad, a discrimination that could only have been made by smell (MacFarlane, 1975). Babies can also distinguish a female stranger's breast pad from a pad worn under the stranger's arm, but only if the stranger is lactating (Porter et al., 1992).

Babies are also sensitive to taste at birth. As the fluid that a baby sucks is sweetened, the baby sucks harder, consumes more, and tends to quiet faster from crying episodes (Blass & Smith, 1992; Nowlis & Kessen, 1976; Smith et al., 1992). Interestingly, babies sometimes slow down their sucking rate with increasing sweetness, perhaps because they prefer to take a little time to savor the taste between sucks (Crook, 1987; Lipsitt, 1977). As seen in Figure 7-2, newborn babies can also distinguish between different tastes. Even at 2 hours of age, babies make different facial expressions when they taste sweet and nonsweet solutions, and they also differentiate sour, bitter, and salty tastes (Rosenstein & Oster, 1988). At around 4 months of age, they begin to prefer salty tastes, which they found aversive as newborns (Harris, Thomas, & Booth, 1990).

The fact that newborns reject certain fluids and that they grimace in response to negative odors and tastes indicates that they come into the world with likes and dislikes. Within months, the older infant will challenge you to find his mouth with a spoon that contains something he decides he dislikes just by looking at it.

Vestibular Sensitivity

Vestibular sensitivity refers to our ability to detect gravity and the motion of our bodies, which helps us to maintain body posture. In adults, disturbance

Vestibular sensitivity
The perceptual experience that results from motion of the body and from the pull of gravity.

Figure 7-2   A newborn tasting (*a*) a sweet solution, (*b*) a bitter solution, and (*c*) a sour solution. From "Differential Facial Responses to Four Basic Tastes in Newborns" by D. Rosenstein and H. Oster, 1988, *Child Development, 59,* pp. 1561–1563. Copyright 1988 by The Society for Research in Child Development, Inc. Reprinted by permission.

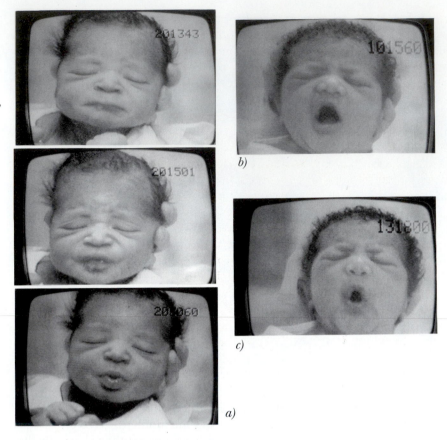

of the vestibular sense causes dizziness and an inability to remain standing in the dark.

Newborns are sensitive to vestibular stimulation along all three axes of motion—front-to-back, up-and-down, and side-to-side (Reisman, 1987; Werner & Lipsitt, 1981). The soothing properties of rocking and jiggling for crying babies clearly demonstrate this sensitivity. The effectiveness of these maneuvers depends on both how much and how fast they occur (Pederson & Ter Vrught, 1973). Postural adjustments also affect responsiveness, so that babies are often more alert in a vertical than in a horizontal posture (Korner & Thoman, 1970).

A novel study examined the relation between vestibular and visual perception in providing the infant with a sense of self-motion. Usually, visual cues and vestibular cues are consistent in telling us whether we are moving or stationary. However, sometimes conflict between these cues produces confusing effects. For example, if you are seated in a nonmoving train, next to another nonmoving train, your train may seem to move backward when the other train begins to move forward. Your vision tells you one thing, while your vestibular sense tells you another. Vision wins out for a moment, but your stomach may take a turn when you realize what has happened. Pilots are taught to trust their instruments rather than their impressions, as both their sight and their vestibular sense may mislead them. Lee and Aronson (1974) asked whether infants depend primarily on vision rather than vestibular input to maintain posture. They placed toddling infants (13 to 16 months old) in a "fake" room with walls that could move as the floor remained stationary. When the front and side walls moved, visual cues told the infant that she was moving forward, while vestibular cues said she was not moving at all. Apparently, the visual cues won out, as babies often fell backward in this situation. A similar phenomenon occurs in babies who are only old enough to sit up (Bertenthal, 1993). As children get older, however, they become increasingly accurate in using body cues (Wapner, 1969; Wapner & Werner, 1965).

✔ *To Recap...*

Touch and pain, smell and taste, and body balance and motion (vestibular sensitivity) are well developed at birth. Even the fetus is sensitive to touch, and touch sensitivity increases over the first days of life. Touch is a vital component of several adaptive reflexes. It also has important social effects, and babies use touch to explore the environment. Newborns are sensitive to both smell and taste. They prefer pleasant odors to unpleasant ones and can distinguish their mother's body smells from those of other women. Similarly, babies suck harder to get sweeter fluid and consume more of it. As early as 2 hours after birth, babies can distinguish not only sweet but also sour, bitter, and salty tastes.

Newborns are also sensitive to vestibular stimulation, responding to both position and movement, but even older babies tend to rely on vision when vestibular and vision cues contradict each other.

HEARING

Hearing is one of our most important senses, because a great deal of information about the world comes to us from sound alone. Cars approaching from behind, a ringing telephone, music from a stereo, and, most importantly, human speech—all are perceived through the sense of hearing.

How do we know that a newborn baby can hear? By using naturally occurring responses to sounds such as the moro reflex (discussed in Chapter 6) or the tendency of babies to tighten the eyelids, turn the head and eyes toward the source of a sound, or become quiet. Changes in the baby's heart rate and breathing also occur in response to sounds (Aslin, Pisoni, & Jusczyk, 1983).

Even the fetus can hear. Electrical recordings of brain responses demonstrate sound reception in fetuses as early as the 25th week after conception, about 3.5 months before full-term birth (Parmelee & Sigman, 1983). These findings indicate that fetuses receive sound impulses, but how do they respond to sound?

Two investigators used ultrasound imaging to answer this question. Ultrasound techniques, as mentioned in Chapter 5, create a picture of the fetus. The images showed that, although fetuses did not respond to auditory stimuli before 24 weeks after conception, after 28 weeks virtually all fetuses clamped their eyelids in response to sound. All of the fetuses who did not respond (1 to 2%) were born with hearing deficits or serious impairments (Birnholz & Benacerraf, 1983).

But, we might ask, how good is the sound quality available to the fetus? One curious mother decided to answer this question by swallowing a microphone (she "drank the microphone," as she described it) and recording the sound of her own voice and other sounds. The stomach recording was quite muffled, but one could clearly discern the mother's intonations (Fukahara, Shimura, & Yamanouchi, 1988). Box 7-1 discusses other evidence that the fetus can do more than merely detect sound (Cooper & Aslin, 1989).

IS THE FETUS LISTENING TO THE MOTHER?

In 1980, DeCasper and Fifer reported a surprising finding: Babies less than 4 days old could discriminate their mothers' voices from strangers' voices. The most reasonable interpretation was that the babies became familiar with their mothers' voices in the womb. The finding was based on a clever exploitation of the natural pacifier-sucking rhythm of infants, which consists of bursts of sucks separated by brief rests. For one half of the babies, recordings of their mothers' voices were played when they paused longer than average between bursts, and recordings of strangers' voices were played when they paused less than average. This relation was reversed for the remaining babies. Babies adjusted their pauses to increase their exposure to their mothers' voices in preference to the strangers' voices.

Of course, it is conceivable that the babies had become familiar with their mothers' voices in the few days after birth; if so, they should also have preferred to listen to their fathers' voices over strange male voices. They did not, even though they had often been exposed to their fathers' voices (DeCasper & Prescott, 1984). In fact, babies preferred a recording of a heart sound to their fathers' voices (Panneton, Kelman, & DeCasper, 1984).

The case for familiarity having come from fetal exposure would be strengthened if the infant could recognize a particular event that was only experienced before birth. DeCasper and Spence (1986) asked pregnant women to read aloud one of two stories each day in the last 6 weeks of pregnancy. Their newborn babies were then given the opportunity to hear a recording of the familiar story or of a new story. Babies adjusted their sucking to hear a voice reading a familiar story more than a new story, whether it was the mother's voice reading the story or a stranger's voice (DeCasper & Spence, 1991).

These findings indicate that fetuses can become familiar both with their mothers' voices and with specific sound patterns the mothers produce. Recent evidence suggests that fetuses may also be picking up something more general about their own native languages. Newborn french babies discriminated a woman speaking French from the same woman speaking Russian. Babies of non-French-speaking mothers could not make this discrimination (Mehler et al., 1988).

Because these findings seem so astonishing, investigators have been especially careful to carry out their studies in a controlled manner. Cautious and skeptical reviewers have found no apparent flaw in them (Cooper & Aslin, 1989). However, because investigators in the past have encountered so much difficulty even in demonstrating fetal responses to sound or in finding newborn learning, prudence suggests that we withhold final judgment until these findings are replicated reliably in other laboratories. Nevertheless, current evidence suggests that the fetus may, indeed, be listening.

Sensitivity to Sound

Newborn babies appear to be less sensitive to sound than are adults (Aslin, Pisoni, & Jusczyk, 1983). A newborn can hear only sounds somewhat louder than a quiet whisper at a distance of about 4.5 feet, whereas an adult can easily hear a whisper at this distance. Fluid in the middle ear may be part of the problem.

Sensitivity to sound varies with the pitch of the sound in both infant and adult. Adult sensitivity is poorer for high and low sounds than for intermediate ones. While newborn babies hear relatively better at low than high frequencies, by 6 months of age auditory sensitivity has improved more for higher than for lower sounds and is as good as adult sensitivity (Schneider & Trehub, 1985a, 1985b; Schneider, Trehub, & Bull, 1980; Werner & Bargones, 1992). Sensitivity to sound increases only until around 10 years of age. Sensitivity to higher frequencies peaks even earlier and does not improve beyond about 4 or 5 years (Trehub et al., 1988).

Sensitivity measurements determine how loud a sound must be for the infant to detect it. However, we are normally exposed to sounds that are much louder than this threshold level. For a full understanding of the infant's hearing capacity, we must also know how well the infant can discriminate sounds that differ in various characteristics, such as in intensity, frequency, and duration.

Discriminating Sounds

Infants are able to distinguish differences in intensity, or loudness, at an early age. For example, after a 6-month-old becomes familiar with a sound approximately as loud as an ordinary conversation at a distance of about 3 feet, a small increase in intensity produces a noticeable change in heart rate (Moffitt, 1973). Twelve-month-olds can detect even very slight shifts in intensity (Trehub & Schneider, 1983).

How well do infants distinguish among sound frequencies? By 5 months of age, infants are almost as good as adults at distinguishing among high-frequency tones that vary only slightly (Werner & Bargones, 1992). By 9 months of age, they can pick out melodies, even when the key changes (Trehub, Thorpe, & Morrongiello, 1987). That means they can perceive the relations among the frequencies, even when the frequencies themselves change because of the key change.

Some sounds are more effective than others in recruiting infants' attention. Low tones are more effective in quieting babies, whereas higher tones tend to distress them (Eisenberg, 1970, 1976). Babies are better at discriminating complex sounds than we might suspect. Recently, investigators discovered that babies between 4 and 7 months of age could tell the difference between a lullaby and an adult-directed song even when the song and lullaby came from a foreign culture (Unyk & Schellenberg, 1991).

Babies are especially sensitive to the characteristics of sound that will be important for language perception. Even newborns can distinguish differences in the duration of sounds (Clifton, Graham, & Hatton, 1968). And they can distinguish between sounds that have the same frequency and intensity but differ in how fast they reach maximum intensity (Kearsley, 1973), an especially important feature for distinguishing speech sounds. Young infants prefer to listen to sounds that fall within the frequency range of the human voice, and they will listen to a human voice in preference to a bell (Eisenberg, 1970, 1976). Babies use their discriminative sensitivities to distinguish speech sounds as early as 1 month of age (Aslin, Pisoni, & Jusczyk, 1983; Burnham, Earnshaw, & Quinn, 1987).

DEVELOPMENT IN CONTEXT: Music to Our Ears: Cultural Influences on Perception of Tunes

Perception seems so immediate and direct that it is natural to assume that what one person sees and hears is the same as what another person sees and hears. Yet this is not always the case. For example, native speakers of English easily perceive a stream of spoken English sounds as a string of distinctive words, but a similar stream spoken in German, Chinese, or Russian may sound to them like a bewildering flow of noise, with one word running into the next and little clue even for when one sentence ends and the next one begins. Clearly, language perception depends on the context in which it develops.

But might language be perceived in a special way because it is a social stimulus? Is it possible that our perceptions of other sound stimuli might be universal across cultures and not as sensitive to context? A recent experiment on music perception examined this possibility (Lynch et al., 1990).

The research was carried out with 6-month-olds and adults. The investigators used seven-tone melodies based either on Western major and minor scales or on a Javanese scale of a different structure. To Western listeners, Javanese melodies sound odd.

Listeners heard a repeating melody from one of these scales, occasionally interrupted by a seven-note sequence that was mistuned, in that the fifth note had a small frequency change. Babies had been trained to turn their heads to produce an animated toy sequence when they heard the mistuned sequence, and adults had been trained to raise their hands. The question was, could babies and adults pick up the same amount of mistuning for the Western and the Javanese scales?

The adults, who were not musicians, detected the mistuning much more easily in the Western melody than in the Javanese melody. The babies also detected the mistuned melodies, but they were no better at doing so for the Western than the Javanese melody. These results suggest that humans are born with the ability to perceive musicality across a wide range of sound structures. But this ability gradually changes, becoming more sensitive for types of music often heard than for those seldom or never heard. Music perception, then, is apparently sensitive to cultural influences, as is the case for language perception (Kuhl, 1993; Werker, 1991).

Sound Localization

An important property of sounds is the direction they come from. Even newborns distinguish very general sound location. They turn their eyes and heads toward a sound source to the left or right if the sound is relatively continuous. Rattles and human voices are most effective in eliciting this response (Braddick & Atkinson, 1988; Mendelson & Haith, 1976). Recent work indicates that this response disappears around the second month of life and reappears in the third or fourth month in a more vigorous form. When the response reemerges, it is faster, suggesting that a different brain center has taken control of this ability (Field, J., 1987; Muir & Clifton, 1985).

Over the first year and a half of life, babies make increasingly fine distinctions of auditory space (Ashmead, et al., 1991; Morrongiello, 1988a, 1988b, 1988c). To accomplish this feat, they must solve an interesting and very general problem of growing organisms, one of appropriate recalibration, or readjustment. The problem is that accurate sound localization depends in large part on the detection of the time difference between when sound arrives at the two ears. For example, a sound on the right produces energy that reaches the right ear before it reaches the left ear. With age, the head grows larger, so that the distance between the two ears increases. Therefore, a sound that comes from the same off-center location produces a larger time difference in an older child than in a younger child. Since even the newborn displays some accuracy in locating sounds, the baby must perform a recalibration to accommodate growth at an older age, continually adjusting the relation between sound cues and what these cues mean for where the sound-producing object is (Clifton et al., 1988; Fenwick, Hillier, & Morrongiello, 1991). This is a general problem for the baby in many action systems—eye movements, head movements, reaching, and walking, to name a few. And no one knows how it happens.

The location of sounds varies not only with direction but also with distance. Even 6-month-olds are sensitive to the distance of a sound but distinguish approaching sounds better than receding sounds (Morrongiello, Hewitt, & Gotowiec, 1991).

✔ *To Recap...*

The fetus can hear at least as early as several months prior to birth. But newborns appear to be less sensitive to sound than adults. Within the first year, however, the infant's hearing at high frequencies is as good as the adult's. Infants can discriminate sounds on the basis of intensity, frequency, and duration. Especially important are sound discriminations that are central to the perception of speech. Even newborns distinguish differences in duration and the rate of change of sound intensity, and infants are most attentive to sounds that fall within the voice range. The baby's ability to localize sounds is present at birth and then fades somewhat, to reappear at 4 months in a more efficient form. This ability becomes more precise over the first 18 months of life.

VISION

Take a moment to look around and appreciate the richness and complexity of your visual environment. You can see variations in brightness and color, as well as texture, and you can tell which surfaces are hard and which are soft. Looking around, you can see dozens of objects and many items of function—light switches that can be flicked, containers that hold objects, shelves that support books, chairs that you can sit in. Vision provides an immense amount of information about the world, and you know how to interpret this information easily.

Now, consider what this world must look like to a newborn baby. First, can the newborn see? If so, how well? When the baby can see well enough to make out objects, how does he know that one object is in front of another, that an object can serve as a container, or even that the container—say, a cup—is separate from the table on which it rests? How does a baby know that a tree she sees through a window is outside the room rather than part of the glass? From this small sample of questions, you can see how much the baby has to learn. In the past 2 decades, we have discovered a great deal about how this learning progresses. Here, we first consider two basic questions: How good is the newborn baby's vision, and how quickly does it improve?

Sensory Capabilities

We have known for some time that newborn babies can see something. New parents notice that their baby often turns her head toward a source of light, such as a window. In the first days of life, awake babies can also distinguish light intensity. They open their eyes widely in darkness and close them in bright light; typically, they choose to look at moderate light levels (Haith, 1980; Hershenson, 1964). Babies find visual movement especially attractive even at birth, and they become increasingly sensitive to movement over the first several months of life (Aslin & Shea, 1990; Burnham, 1987; Nelson & Horowitz, 1987).

Visual Acuity

The newborn baby will look more at patterned than at unpatterned displays. For example, if we show an awake baby a picture of a black-and-white bull's-eye and a gray card that are equally bright, the baby will look more at the pattern than at the card (Fantz, 1961). We can use this pattern-looking tendency to measure the baby's visual acuity, or how sharply he can see things. (Box 7-2 describes how the technique for doing such research was developed.)

WHAT DO BABIES SEE? THE WORK OF ROBERT FANTZ

A key problem in understanding perceptual development is that we cannot easily communicate with infants. People have wondered since the beginning of time what the newborn baby can see and when the baby can tell one color or face or shape from another. Through much of the modern era of psychology, researchers have approached these questions somewhat indirectly. For example, an investigator might measure the heart rate or respiration of a baby looking at a picture of a face and then see whether changes occur when the baby looks at a picture of the facial features (mouth, eyes, nose) scrambled up in a different pattern; if so, the investigator might conclude that there is something special about faces for the infant. Other indirect approaches use learning procedures. If a baby can learn to turn her head right when a red stimulus appears and left for a blue stimulus, presumably the baby can discriminate red and blue.

Robert Fantz made a discovery that profoundly affected research on infant vision (Fantz, 1961). Fantz observed that babies look at different things for different periods of time. Perhaps one could simply measure how much more babies look at one display than another to study what the baby can see and discriminate in the displays. This direct approach would eliminate the need for cumbersome electrodes to measure physiological changes or the tedium of training and learning procedures.

The solution to measuring where babies look was quite straightforward. The researcher shows the baby two displays, side by side. With properly adjusted lighting, the researcher can see the reflection of these displays on the surface of the baby's eye, much as you can see the reflection of a window in daylight in the eyes of a partner you are talking to. When the baby looks at one of the displays, that display is reflected from the surface of the eye over the black pupil opening. The researcher, using two stopwatches, can record how long the baby looks at each display.

Researchers have used this powerful technique to study a host of issues concerning infant vision, including visual acuity, color perception, form perception, face recognition, and picture perception. Because an infant's interest in a particular visual display declines over time and recovers for novel stimuli, investigators have also been able to use this technique to study how an infant's memory develops and how various types of developmental problems (such as Down syndrome and prematurity) affect perceptual processing and mem-ory (Bornstein & Sigman, 1986; Fagan et al., 1986).

A remarkable fact about the Fantz discovery is how obvious it seems, after the fact. Many great contributors to science have been able to see the obvious among the complex and to find significance in what others have overlooked.

Visual accommodation
The automatic adjustment of the lens of the eye to produce a focused image of an object on the light-sensitive tissue at the back of the eye.

To measure visual acuity, we can show babies a gray picture next to a second picture that contains vertical black and white stripes. Ordinarily, the baby looks longer at the striped picture. Over repeated presentations, we make the stripes more narrow and compressed, which also makes them more difficult to distinguish from the gray picture. Eventually, the baby no longer looks more at the striped pattern, presumably because he can no longer tell the difference between the two pictures. Using this approach, researchers have estimated that the newborn's acuity is about 20/400 to 20/800 (meaning that a normal-vision adult sees at 400 to 800 feet what the newborn sees at 20 feet), compared with normal adult acuity of 20/20. By 3 months of age, acuity improves to around 20/100; by 12 months, it approximates that of the adult (Banks & Salapatek, 1983; Dobson & Teller, 1978). Figure 7-3 shows how a picture of a face might look to infants at 1, 2, and 3 months of age from a distance of about 6 inches.

Why do younger infants have poorer vision? Early studies of infants younger than 1 month of age suggested that the lens of the eye did not vary its focus with distance, a process called **visual accommodation** (Haynes, White, & Held, 1965).

 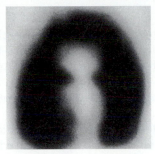  

Figure 7-3 Visual acuity improves dramatically during the first months of life, as illustrated in computer estimations of what a picture of a face looks like to 1-, 2-, and 3-month-olds at a distance of about 6 inches. All estimations were taken from the original, which illustrates adult acuity (seen on the far right). From "The Recognition of Facial Expressions in the First Two Years of Life: Mechanisms of Development" by Charles A. Nelson, *Child Development, 58,* Figure 1, p. 892. Copyright 1987 by the Society for Research in Child Development, Inc. Reprinted by permission. These photos were made available by Martin Banks and Arthur Ginsburg.

Rather, the lens seemed to be fixed for optimal focus at a distance of about 7 to 8 inches. Because this is the typical distance of the mother's face from the baby's eyes during feeding, ethologists constructed a nice story about why evolution might use such a trick to assure that the baby would be attracted to the mother's face.

Evolutionary explanations are often very seductive, but they can also be wrong, as this one was. In fact, the baby's lens is not fixed, but it does not vary with distance as the adult's does. At birth, the brain circuits that are responsible for accommodation are simply not sufficiently mature to pick up minor differences in the precision of focus. Thus, variations for focal distance in the early weeks of life are relatively useless. It appears to be only happenstance that the lens has a relatively fixed focus at around 7 to 8 inches. Accommodation improves between 1 and 3 months of age and is almost adultlike by 6 months of age (Aslin & Smith, 1988; Banks & Salapatek, 1983; Hainline & Abramov, 1992).

Peripheral Vision

The part of the eye that provides acute vision covers a very small portion of the visual field—a circular area about the size of a quarter at arm's length. Yet our visual world seems continuous and complete; we do not see it as if we were looking through a long quarter-size tube. This is because our **peripheral vision,** which is less detailed, covers much more of the visual field. The peripheral vision of the 1-month-old is much smaller than that of the adult, but significant improvement occurs by 3 months of age (Braddick & Atkinson, 1988).

Peripheral vision
The perception of visual input outside the area on which the individual is fixating.

Color Vision

When can babies see color? Babies tend to look at colored objects, and that tendency has helped psychologists to answer this question. Babies can differentiate red from green even at birth (Adams, 1989). However, there is some question about how similar their color perception is to the adult's. The adult possesses three color receptors—one each for blue, red, and green. Only two receptors are required for color sensitivity, so the baby could respond to color even if she had only two functioning types. It is clear, however, that by 2 months of age, all color receptors are functioning (Teller & Bornstein, 1987). By 3 months, babies prefer yellow and red over blue and green (Adams, 1987).

Binocular Vision

Binocular vision
The ability of the two eyes to see the same aspects of an object simultaneously.

Because our eyes are in different locations, they see slightly different pictures of the world. The coordination of these two pictures is called **binocular vision**. The closer the object, the larger the difference between the pictures. Therefore, binocular vision provides the brain with information about distance. Furthermore, when the brain fuses the two pictures into a single image, the perceiver experiences stereoscopic, or three-dimensional, depth.

To investigate the development of binocular vision, researchers had babies wear goggles with a green filter over one eye and a red filter over the other. (This technique was used on television during halftime for a Super Bowl game to create stereoscopic depth on the television screen.) Stimuli were presented so that a baby who did not fuse the images from the two eyes saw unrelated red and green splotches. However, if the baby's brain fused the images, a geometric form appeared on the screen and moved from side to side. The investigators watched to see whether the babies tracked the "phantom" object as it moved across the screen. Using this ingenious technique, they found such tracking as early as 3.5 months of age. There is general agreement now that stereoscopic vision is not present at birth and that its onset occurs between 3 and 5 months of age (Aslin & Smith, 1988; Atkinson & Braddick, 1988; Fox et al., 1980).

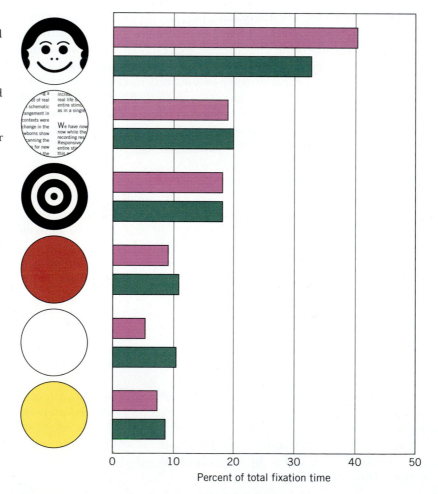

Figure 7-4   Stimuli that Robert Fantz showed to infants. The length of the purple bars indicates the average time that 2- to 3-month-olds looked at the stimulus, and the length of the green bars indicates looking time for 3- to 6-month-olds. From R. Fantz, 1961, "The origin of form perception." *Scientific American, 204,* p. 72. Copyright 1961 by *Scientific American.* Reprinted by permission.

Percent of total fixation time

Visual Pattern and Contrast

For many years, many people believed that newborn babies were blind or, at best, simply capable of reflexively looking at a source of light. As suggested in the discussion of visual acuity, Robert Fantz proved them wrong. Even newborn babies looked longer at a patterned display than at a nonpatterned display, as shown in Figure 7-4.

Investigators later developed the techniques shown in Figure 7-5 to measure what parts of displays newborns look at. They discovered that newborns look primarily at high-contrast edges—for example, where black and white meet—and move their eyes back and forth over those contrast edges (Haith, 1980, 1991).

As babies get older, they prefer patterns that are more densely packed. Whereas 3-week-olds look longer at a 6-by-6 checkerboard than a 12-by-12 or a 24-by-24 checkerboard, 6-week-olds are more likely to look longest at the intermediately complex display and 3-month-olds at the most complex display (Karmel & Maisel, 1975). An early theory held that babies prefer increasing complexity (that is, more checks) as they get older and become more complex themselves. However, several investigators pointed out that, as the number of checks increases, so does the amount of black-white edge in the display. Most investigators now believe that babies are attracted to the displays that offer the most edge contrasts that they can see at a particular age (Banks & Salapatek, 1983; Karmel & Maisel, 1975). Why? Perhaps these findings suggest what babies are trying to accomplish with their visual behavior.

When babies move their eyes over edges, they activate cells of the visual areas of the brain. The strongest brain activity occurs when the baby adjusts the eye so that images of the edges fall near the center of the eye—that is, when the baby looks straight at the edges. Also, the more detail the baby can see, the stronger the activation. Haith (1980) has suggested that the baby's visual activity in early infancy reflects a biological "agenda" for the baby to keep brain-cell firing at a high level. This agenda makes sense because, as we have seen, cells in the brain compete to establish connections to other cells. Activity tends to stabilize the required connections, while inactive pathways deteriorate (Greenough, Black, & Wallace, 1987).

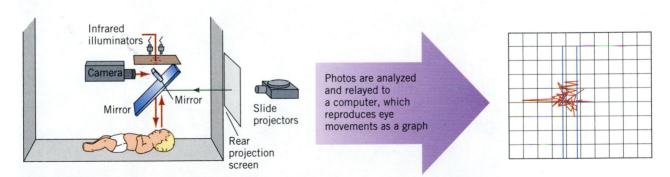

Figure 7-5 Studying how babies look at stimuli. A camera records the baby's eye movements as he or she looks at a reflected image. Pictures of the eye are then analyzed. Measurements of the positions of the center of the pupil and the reflected infrared light spots identify where the baby's eye fixated when the picture was taken. All this information is relayed to a computer that reconstructs the baby's eye movements in graphic form. Shown is a reconstruction of a newborn's fixations on a vertical bar.

Fortunately, this agenda brings the baby to areas of the visual display that are also psychologically meaningful. Edges provide information about the boundaries of objects, their relation in depth, and where they can be grasped.

Thus, the baby appears to be "programmed" to engage in visual activity that is very adaptive. This activity produces the sensory input needed to maintain and tune the neural apparatus and also focuses the baby's attention on the most informative parts of the visual world. Once again, we can see that the young infant is anything but passive. Babies do not need prompting to find interesting things to look at. Even the newborn possesses tools to get necessary experience for normal development.

Visual Relations

The agenda that biology sets for the newborn makes sense initially, but growing babies move beyond simply exciting their own brains and begin to appreciate the organization among parts of the visual world. Mother's face soon is seen as a whole rather than as eyebrows, eyes, ears, a nose, and so on. As one famous child psychiatrist put it, the infant is a "meaning maker" (Emde, 1994).

Several lines of evidence suggest that, while newborns are sensitive to very simple relations among stimuli, babies really begin to "put things together" between 1 and 3 months of age (Haith, 1986; Kleiner & Banks, 1987; Slater et al., 1991). Interestingly, this is a period that marks several transitions in the infant's life—a time when several reflexes disappear, brain-wave patterns change, smiling occurs, and the baby begins to sleep through the night (Emde, Gaensbauer, & Harmon, 1976). Apparently, important brain changes occur during this period.

Researchers tested this idea by showing babies a pattern of bars that formed a circular or square pattern, as shown in Figure 7-6. In some patterns, one bar was misaligned. An adult sees the one misaligned bar as strange, because she sees all the other bars as going together. The misalignment had no effect on the visual fixations of 1-month-olds, but 3-month-olds looked longer around the displaced bar than

• Psychologists exploit babies' natural inclination to look at patterned displays to learn what babies can see and discriminate.

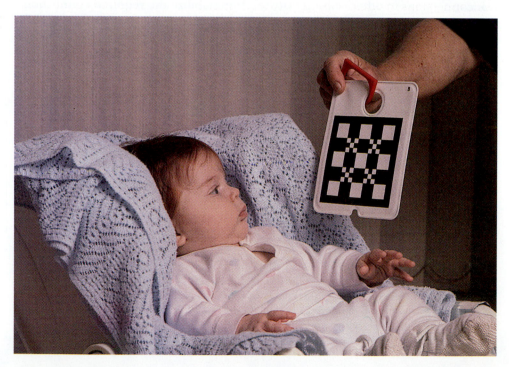

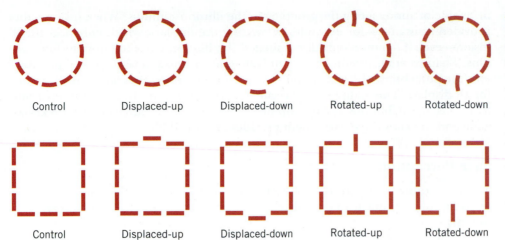

Figure 7-6 Stimuli used in the study by Van Giffen and Haith. Babies were shown the control stimulus three times, in alternation with one of the experimental figures. From "Infant Visual Response to Gestalt Geometric Forms" by K. Van Giffen and M. M. Haith, 1984, *Infant Behavior and Development, 7,* Figure 1, p. 338. Copyright 1984 by Ablex Publishing Corp. Reprinted by permission.

around the properly aligned ones (Van Giffen & Haith, 1984). Thus, between 1 and 3 months of age, babies begin to see the organization in visual displays rather than only the details.

Of course, babies do not appreciate all possible visual relations by 3 months of age. As you can demonstrate to yourself by walking into a modern art gallery, the perception of organization takes time and effort and, as we have seen, knowledge. Some 5- and 7-month-olds were shown the display in Figure 7-7*a* (Bertenthal, Campos, & Haith, 1980). Adults report perceiving a square that overlays full circles at each of the corners in this display. They also report faint edges that connect the corners of the square, even though no such edges exist. Of course, adults have considerable knowledge about such things as squares and how a square might block the view of circles behind it. Babies looked at the arrangement in 7-7*b* (the same elements, with some rotated to destroy the illusion) until their looking habituated. Then some babies were shown the illusion stimulus in 7-7*a*, and others saw the second nonillusion stimulus in 7-7*c*, both of which involved a change in two corner elements. Five-month-olds did not consistently detect either of these changes. However, 7-month-olds detected the change when it involved the illusion in 7-7*a*, indicating that they were perceptually grouping its elements. Are younger infants

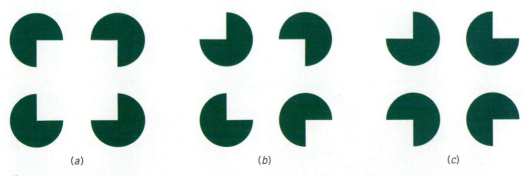

(a) (b) (c)

Figure 7-7 Stimuli used in studies by Bertenthal (all three stimuli) and Shapiro (*a* and *b* only). From "Development of Visual Organization: The Perception of Subjective Contours" by B. I. Bertenthal, J. J. Campos, and M. M. Haith, 1980, *Child Development, 51,* Figure 1, p. 1073. Copyright 1980 by The Society for Research in Child Development, Inc. Reprinted by permission.

incapable of appreciating the grouping in the illusion stimulus? When investigators provided assistance—for example, by rotating the displays, which enhances the illusion—even 4.5-month-olds discriminated the illusion from the nonillusion stimulus (Shapiro et al., 1983). The point is that, as for most developmental phenomena, the perception of visual organization is not something that happens all at once for all displays. The ability to appreciate visual organization begins between 1 and 3 months of age, but this ability continues to improve and is affected by both knowledge and the cues the environment provides (Haith, 1993).

Face Perception

The face contains the arrangement of visual elements that babies are most interested in. Infants appear to recognize the organization of face features as early as 2 months of age, when they look more at a schematic picture of a face than at the same features in a scrambled array. Facial features in these pictures change in importance with age, with first the eyes, then the eyes and nose, and then the eyes, nose, and mouth assuming importance in attracting attention and in eliciting smiling (Johnson et al., 1992; Maurer, 1985).

A problem with this research is that most investigators have used pictures of faces or two-dimensional displays of black-and-white elements. Perhaps babies at earlier ages perceive real faces in a holistic fashion but cannot appreciate "faceness" in schematic two-dimensional displays. That, in fact, seems to be the case. Investigators used equipment similar to that described earlier to record exactly where infants look on real, live faces (Figure 7-8). Babies at 5 weeks of age tend to look near the high-contrast borders of the face—the edges where skin and hair or chin and garment meet. Thus, they behave like newborns, who fixate near the black-and-white edges of figures, presumably to activate visual brain areas. However, babies only 2 weeks older spend most of their time looking at the internal features of the face, especially the eyes. Fixation on these internal features may reflect a new perceptual organization of the face into a whole rather than a collection of elements (Hainline, 1978; Haith, Bergman, & Moore, 1977; Maurer & Salapatek, 1976). Curiously, when the adult in this experiment talked, the older babies looked even more at the adult's eyes rather than at the mouth. Since adults enjoy eye contact, and babies like to be talked to, this tendency may enhance an ongoing positive interaction between parent and infant.

Figure 7-8 Apparatus very similar to that shown in Figure 7-5 is used to record a baby's fixations on a face. Computer reconstructs the baby's fixations on a face (a) when the adult was quiet (left) and (b) when the adult talked. A rotating arrow shows the sequence of fixations and where the baby began and ended looking (b).

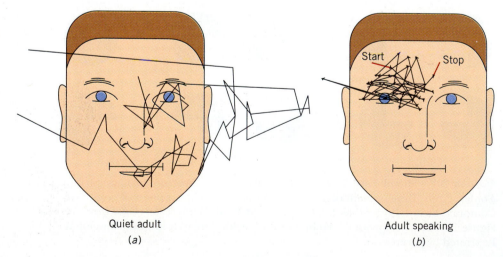

Quiet adult
(a)

Adult speaking
(b)

The sensitivity of babies to emotional expressions in the face grows slowly over the first 2 years of life (Nelson, 1987). However, even 3-month-olds look longer at faces as the intensity of the smile increases, and this tendency appears to depend on experience (see Figure 7-9). Babies whose mothers call attention to themselves and smile when their babies look at them are the babies who show the strongest preferences for smiley faces (Kuchuk, Vibbert, & Bornstein, 1986). We will see in Chapter 12 that by the end of the first year, babies can differentiate a number of other expressions of emotion.

Objects and Their Properties

The ability of babies to appreciate the relations among visual elements—for example, lines, angles, and edges—is important for their perception of the objects that populate the world. But a problem arises in accounting for how we "know" objects from vision alone. The images that objects produce in our eyes change with distance and with other variations such as lighting. How do we come to know that varying images represent the same object? To answer this question, we need to distinguish between proximal and distal characteristics in perception. **Proximal stimulation** refers to the physical energies that reach the eye (or other sensory receptors). **Distal properties** refer to the properties of the object itself—its color, size, and so on. Whereas the distal properties of an object remain constant, the proximal stimulation a person receives changes with distance, lighting, and the object's orientation. How do infants learn that different proximal impressions belong to the same distal object? How do they solve the problem of maintaining perceptual constancy in spite of sensory change (Aslin, 1987a)?

Proximal stimulation
Physical energies that reach sensory receptors.

Distal properties
The actual properties of an object—color, size, and so on—as opposed to proximal stimulation.

The Constancies

As an object moves farther away from us, its image on the eye shrinks. Yet the object continues to appear the same size, at least up to a point. For example, a child standing in front of you seems shorter than an adult standing across the street even though the child casts a larger image on your eyes than the adult. This phenomenon is called **size constancy**. Size constancy is not present before 3 months of age. Some size constancy is present in most infants by 5 to 7 months; whether 4-month-

Size constancy
The experience that the physical size of an object remains the same even though the size of its projected image on the eye varies.

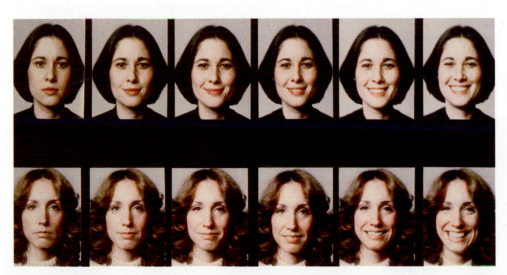

Figure 7-9 Stimuli used in Kuchuk study to examine infants' sensitivity to the intensity of a smile. From "The Perception of Smiling and Its Experiential Correlates in Three-Month-Old Infants" by A. Kuchuk, M. Vibbert, and M. H. Bornstein, 1986, *Child Development, 57*, p. 1056. Copyright 1986 by The Society for Research in Child Development, Inc. Reprinted by permission.

olds have it or not depends on the maturity of their binocular vision (Aslin, 1987b). It is important to note, though, that "some size constancy" is not *complete* size constancy. The ability to judge the size of objects with changing distance improves up to at least 10 or 11 years of age (Day, 1987).

Objects also change apparent shape as they rotate or as we move around them. **Shape constancy** refers to the stability of our perception in the face of changes in the shape of the image on the eye. Some shape constancy exists for infants as young as 3 months of age (Bower, 1966; Caron, Caron, & Carlson, 1979; Day & McKenzie, 1973). However, shape constancy may not exist this early for irregular shapes (Cook & Birch, 1984). As with many developmental accomplishments, then, shape constancy may not be an all-or-nothing affair. It appears to exist at 3 or 4 months of age under some conditions but not others (Dodwell, Humphrey, & Muir, 1987).

Objects in the world also continually change in brightness. Still, a dark dress continues to look dark whether it is dimly lit in a storeroom or brightly illuminated by direct sunlight. **Brightness constancy** may exist as early as 7 weeks of age for objects that are not too small (Dannemiller, 1985). Finally, **color constancy** refers to the perception of a color as the same despite changes in the hue of light (for example, the fluorescent light of a department store versus sunlight). Color constancy is only partially available by 4 months of age (Dannemiller & Hanko, 1987).

Visual constancies are important because they address the fundamental question of how stable the world is for the infant in the first half-year of life. After all, if such constancies were absent, each time a baby saw an object at a different distance, or in a different orientation, or in a different light, it would appear to be a different object. Instead of one mother, the infant would experience a different mother every time he saw her from a different angle.

Invariances

Perceptual constancies result from the fact that many features of objects and the environment remain stable. Think about the images that you receive as you move around a stationary object or as the object itself moves, and you will notice that even with change, there is stability. J. J. Gibson pointed out this stability and called it **invariance** (Gibson, 1966). Of course, there are obvious things that remain constant or nearly constant, such as the color and brightness of the object. But there is also a less obvious stability that Gibson refers to as higher order invariance. For example, imagine that you are looking at a checkerboard that rotates around its vertical axis as a top would spin. As the checkerboard rotates, the checks approaching you get larger, and those receding get smaller. Yet the relation in size between the near and far checks is constant from the top of the checkerboard to the bottom. In fact, all the size relations change in an orderly fashion. Moreover, the shape of the image, with its consistently straight edges, could only be generated by certain objects; for example, it could not be generated by a checkered ball. In brief, although changing perspectives of objects produce changing images, the changes are predictable. The stable *relations* among the elements of an object provide the viewer with sufficient cues to develop a concept of the object, no matter what the perspective.

Are babies sensitive to those cues? The answer is yes, at least under some circumstances. For example, some infants were shown a lollipop-shaped object like the one in the top row of Figure 7-10 until they habituated. When they were shown the same object in an upside-down orientation, they behaved as though they had never seen it. Other babies saw the same object in several orientations—but not upside-down—until they tired of it (bottom row of Figure 7-10). When they saw the

---

Shape constancy
The experience that the physical shape of an object remains the same even though the shape of its projected image on the eye varies.

Brightness constancy
The experience that the brightness of an object remains the same even though the amount of light it reflects back to the eye changes (because of shadows or changes in the illuminating light).

Color constancy
The experience that the color of an object remains the same even though the wavelengths it reflects back to the eye change (because of changes in the color of the illuminating light).

Invariance
The stability in the relations among some properties of an object as other properties change.

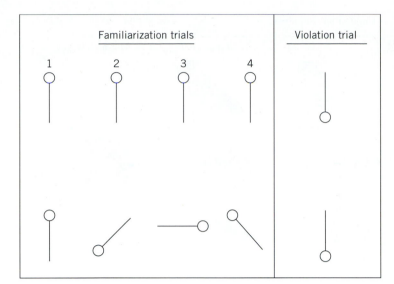

Figure 7-10 Lollipop stimulus used in the McGurk study to examine infants' sensitivity to orientation. From "Infant Discrimination of Orientation" by H. McGurk, 1972, *Journal of Experimental Child Psychology, 14,* Figure 1, p. 154. Copyright 1972 by Academic Press. Reprinted by permission.

upside-down orientation for the first time, they behaved as though they were seeing the same old lollipop. The babies who had seen multiple perspectives, then, were able to appreciate the lollipop as the same object in a new orientation, because their experience led them to note its invariance (McGurk, 1970).

A similar principle seems to operate in the recognition of faces. Infants at 4, 6, and 7 months of age saw a picture of a side view of a face repeatedly until they habituated. When saw a front view of the same face, they behaved as though it were the face of a new person. Other infants first saw the face in a variety of side views—left, right, and angled up or down. When they tired of these poses, they were shown the face looking straight ahead. Here, infants of different ages acted differently. The 7-month-olds behaved as though the face was familiar, but the 4- and 6-month-olds did not. The younger babies reacted to the frontal view as a new face even after they had seen a variety of poses (Cohen & Strauss, 1979). A related finding holds for emotional expressions. By 10 months of age, infants recognize a happy face even when it is displayed by an unfamiliar person, whereas 7-month-olds do not (Ludemann, 1991). These studies suggest that babies are capable of forming psychological categories—for example, a "happy face" category.

Another study demonstrated that 9-month-olds may form concepts even when each item they see is different. After having seen pictures of several different birds, shown in Figure 7-11, babies looked much longer at a picture of a horse than at a new bird. Apparently, they had formed a mental category, "bird," with which they had become bored. They became interested again when they saw a picture from a different category (Roberts, K., 1988). Increasingly, then, we are learning that babies are capable of forming categories of perception to organize the world.

What Objects Do

Our knowledge about objects in the visual world is more extensive than we may realize. For example, we know that some objects can move, whereas others cannot. Some objects (such as a sponge) can be deformed, whereas others remain rigid. We assume that objects are whole and continuous even when they are partly blocked from view. Furthermore, we can often judge the softness and hardness of surfaces

Figure 7-11   Category stimuli used in Roberts's study. From "Retrieval of Basic-Level Category in Prelinguistic Infants" by K. Roberts, 1988, *Developmental Psychology, 24*, Figure 1, p. 23. Copyright 1988 by the American Psychological Association. Reprinted by permission.

by their texture and how they reflect light. The question is, what properties of objects do infants know about? Recent research provides valuable insights into this question.

Object Rigidity and Motion

What we can do with objects tells us something about their properties. For example, we can alter rigid objects, like sticks, in certain ways and deformable objects, like sponges, in other ways. Do babies know anything about how objects can be transformed? One researcher showed infants an object that moved in three different ways that are possible for rigid objects—rotation along two different axes and zooming. Then, the object either underwent a fourth type of rigid motion or was squeezed. Infants at 5 months of age looked longer at the squeezing, suggesting that they were surprised (Gibson, Owsley, & Johnston, 1978). Thus, at least by 5 months of age, babies can tell the difference—by sight alone—between objects that are rigid and those that are pliable.

A Swedish psychologist illustrated how motion provides information by outfitting a person with small lights placed at the body joints and filming the person in darkness. When the films showed the person standing still, the viewer perceived a random array of light points. However, when the film showed the person walking, the viewer perceived what is termed "biological motion" (Johansson, 1973). Babies appear to understand this point-light biological motion by 3 to 5 months of age (Bertenthal, 1993; Bertenthal & Pinto, in press). We can conclude that babies are able to use motion to understand the properties of objects and to organize their perception of forms.

Object Continuity

Because we know about objects, we see them as continuous and whole even when our view is partially blocked. For example, when a person stands in front of a table, blocking the midsection of the table from our view, we naturally infer that the two ends of the table are connected. In a sense, we perceive a whole table. Do young infants also perceive objects as continuous and whole when they are partially blocked by other objects?

In one set of experiments, 4-month-old babies looked at a partly blocked object until their interest declined—for example, a long rod partly hidden by a block, as shown in the top of Figure 7-12*a*. Then the researchers showed them a continuous rod paired with two rod pieces, identical to what they were able to see with the block in place. Presumably, if the babies had thought earlier that the rod was continuous, they should have looked longer at the two separated rods than at the more "typical" continuous rod. They did not, which suggests that they had not perceived a single whole rod behind the block (Spelke, 1985). In a variation of this procedure, babies actually saw a bar move out from in front of a sphere that it had partially blocked, as illustrated in the top of Figure 7-12*b*. The movement of the bar revealed either a whole sphere or two separated sphere parts (bottom 7-12*b*). Again, the babies paid no special attention to the separated parts. The researchers tried several displays—including a face, as shown in Figure 7-12*c*—but had no success in demonstrating that infants could infer more about the objects than what they could see (Kellman & Spelke, 1983; Schmidt & Spelke, 1984).

These findings seem amazing. Is it possible that, for example, babies see people as cut into pieces when they stand behind a table? Probably not. In all of these studies, the partially hidden object was stationary, and so was the baby. In the real world, when we see one object partially blocked by another, our own movement produces more displacement of the closer object than of the "pieces" of the farther object. This is a clue that the blocked object is continuous. Furthermore, the blocked object itself may move, providing another clue. In fact, when infants can see, for example, a sphere move behind a blocking rod (that is, the two sphere parts move simultaneously), these infants later look at the separated sphere parts as

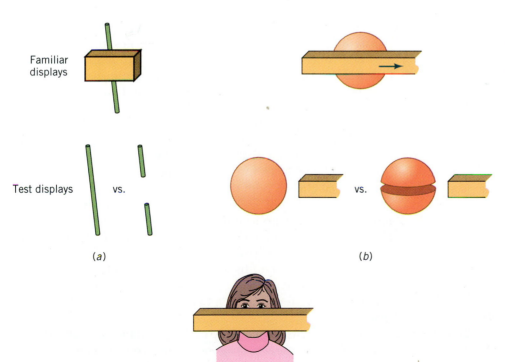

Familiar displays

Test displays   vs.

(a)   (b)

(c)

Figure 7-12 Some pictures used to study object perception in infants. From "Perception of Unity, Persistence, and Identity: Thoughts on Infants' Conceptions of Objects" by E. S. Spelke, 1985. In J. Mehler & R. Fox (Eds.), *Neonate Cognition: Beyond the Blooming Buzzing Confusion* (Figures 6.1, 6.2, and 6.3, pp. 91–93), Hillsdale, NJ: Erlbaum. Copyright 1985 by Lawrence Erlbaum Associates. Reprinted by permission.

though they had not seen them before. Under these conditions, infants apparently perceive the moving sphere as whole (Kellman, Spelke, & Short, 1986; Spelke, 1988, Van de Walle & Spelke, 1993). However, experience may be necessary for this accomplishment, because newborns do not seem to be able to infer that a moving object is whole even when it moves behind another object that partially blocks it (Slater et al., 1990).

Based on several experiments of the kind just described, Spelke has argued that infants in the early months of life understand object continuity, along with some other properties of objects. However, they do not understand some other properties (such as the effects of gravity) until the second year of life (Spelke, 1991; Spelke et al., 1992). These ideas are controversial (in that others believe young babies have only a minimal understanding of continuity and other such properties) and await further investigation.

The Spatial Layout

To this point, we have considered infants' fundamental perceptual capacities and their perception of patterns and objects. The visual world, however, consists of multiple objects—a landscape of objects and events that lie in particular spatial relations to one another (Gibson, 1988). To understand more about how the baby perceives this richer world, we now consider the issues of depth and space perception.

Depth and Distance

As babies acquire the ability to move around, they also develop an ability to get into trouble. One potential danger is that they might fall over edges, if they cannot perceive that a surface that supports them drops off. Eleanor Gibson and Richard Walk (1960) first tested infants' perception of depth by using a unique device called a visual cliff, shown in Figure 7-13. The visual cliff consists of a transparent sheet of plexiglass on which the infant can crawl. A patterned cloth lies just beneath the clear surface on one side. Under the other side is the same cloth pattern, but it lies several feet below the clear surface. Infants able to crawl were placed on a small platform just at the edge of the boundary between "safe" and "deep." Although their mothers called to them from across the deep side, the infants were unwilling to cross, apparently because they perceived the depth and danger.

When does the ability to perceive the depth of the deep side develop? An ingenious approach to this question, one that can be used with infants too young to crawl, involves measuring infants' heart rates as the experimenter lowers them to the clear surface of the visual cliff on both the deep and the safe sides. The heart rate of infants as young as 2 months of age slowed when they were lowered to the deep side, which indicated that they noticed the difference and were interested in it. However, the heart rate of 9-month-olds increased, suggesting that they were afraid, and they were also unwilling to cross over to the deep side. The shift from interest to fear occurs after about 7 months of age, when babies begin to take responsibility for their own movement, such as by crawling or by pushing themselves around in walkers (Campos & Bertenthal, 1989; Campos, Bertenthal, & Kermoian, 1992; Scarr & Salapatek, 1970).

How are babies able to perceive depth? One of the possibilities involves binocular vision. However, a baby who has only one good eye behaves the same on the visual cliff as babies with two good eyes (Walk & Dodge, 1962), indicating that binocular vision is not essential for perceiving depth. The more likely possibility seems to be **motion parallax**. As mentioned earlier, when we move, nearer objects appear to

Figure 7-13 Around the time that babies develop skill in crawling, they become fearful of heights in the absence of support, as they display in their reluctance to cross a visual cliff.

Motion parallax
An observer's experience that a closer object moves across the field of view faster than a more distant object when both objects are moving at the same speed or when the objects are stationary and the observer moves.

change position faster than farther objects (Kellman & von Hofsten, 1992). Slight head movements seem to cue infants about the relative distance of the deep side.

You can see by looking at photographs or pictures that several other cues to distance are available to infants. These cues, like motion parallax, can be appreciated with one eye alone, so we refer to them as **monocular cues**. For example, railroad tracks appear to converge at a distant point. Objects that are nearer may hide objects that are farther along the same line of sight (a dime, held in the right position, can block an object as large as the moon). Finally, the relative size of objects provides a cue about their distance. If we see a picture in which a dog is larger than a car, we assume the car is farther away, and we can even judge their relative distance from one another, because we know how big cars and dogs are (remember size constancy).

Several experiments have evaluated when infants use these types of cues. For example, Granrud and Yonas (1984) used the array shown in Figure 7-14 to test infants' sensitivity to depth produced by one object blocking another. Whereas 7-month-olds reached more frequently for the part of the two-dimensional display that seemed closest, 5-month-olds did not. Similar types of experiments indicate that infants become sensitive to monocular cues for depth between 5 and 7 months of age (Arterberry, Bensen, & Yonas, 1991; Aslin & Smith, 1988).

Aside from monocular cues for depth, there are also **kinetic cues**, which are produced by movement of the observer or of the objects. We have already discussed one kinetic cue, motion parallax. Objects provide additional cues when they are on a collision course with the observer. Here, as the size of the object in the eye increases, it blocks more and more of the background, and all of the parts of the object get larger. Babies blink more when objects approach them than when they move away even at 1 month of age. The likelihood of a blink to an approaching object increases from 16% at 6 weeks of age to 75% at 10 weeks (Petterson, Yonas, & Fisch, 1980).

Monocular cue
A visual cue that is available to one eye only or that does not depend on the combined information available to the two eyes.

Kinetic cue
A visual cue that informs the observer about the relative distance of an object either through movement of the object or movement of the observer.

• At around 6–7 months of age, infants become sensitive to monocular cues for points with distance.

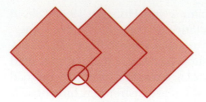

Figure 7-14   A stimulus used by Yonas and his colleagues to test infants' depth perception. From "Development of Visual Space Perception" by A. Yonas and C. Owsley, 1987. In P. Salapatek & Cohen (Eds.), *Handbook of Infant Perception, Vol. 2: From Perception to Cognition* (Figure 1, p. 99), Orlando, FL: Academic Press. Copyright 1987 by Academic Press. Reprinted by permission.

When do infants perceive depth? As with most questions of development, there is no absolute answer. Sensitivity to different depth cues occurs at different ages. Babies use kinetic depth cues between 1 and 3 months of age, binocular cues around 4 to 5 months, and monocular static cues around 6 to 7 months (Yonas, Arterberry, & Granrud, 1987; Yonas & Granrud, 1985; Yonas & Owsley, 1987).

Keeping Track of Locations in Space

We will see in Chapter 13 that the young infant only gradually learns the distinction between self and the external world of objects. Early in development, the baby understands the world egocentrically—that is, the understanding of space and objects is tied to the baby's own actions and body. Thus, if a baby finds an object to her right, she expects to find that object on her right again, even if she rotates her body. Gradually, babies learn to use stable landmarks in the environment to find objects, because these provide reliable cues that do not change as the baby moves around (Piaget, 1952).

A clever study by Linda Acredolo (1978) examined this issue for infants at 6, 11, and 16 months of age. In the wall to each side of the infant was a window. Infants learned to turn and look at one window—say, the one on the left—to make an interesting visual display appear. For half the infants, there was a colored star around the window where the display would appear, to serve as a landmark. The remaining infants had no landmark. After infants learned the left-turn response, their chair was rotated 180 degrees. Now the correct response was a right turn. If a baby was responding with reference only to his own body, he would continue to look to the left. If he could use the landmark, or if he could compensate for the rotation of his body, he would look to the right. Whether or not the landmark was present, 6-month-olds turned to the left side—that is, they used their bodies as the frame of reference rather than the landmark. The 11-month-olds also tended to turn left when no landmark was present but were able to use the landmark to respond when it was present. Finally, the oldest group responded correctly whether the landmark was present or not. Although the tendency for 9-month-old infants to use landmarks can be increased by making the landmarks extremely attention getting, 6-month-olds remain relatively imperturbable (Acredolo, 1978; Acredolo & Evans, 1980; Rieser, 1979).

One factor that seems to affect how infants organize space is their opportunity to move themselves around. Like a passenger in a car, the passively moved baby may not understand how she got from one place to another or the spatial consequences of the move. A study by Benson and Uzgiris (1985) examined the role that self-produced motion plays in spatial understanding for 9- to 12-month-old infants. As a baby watched from one side of a platform, an experimenter on the other side hid an object in a left or right compartment. The compartments were then covered with identical cloths. To retrieve the hidden object, the baby had to move around the platform to the opposite side. As a consequence, when the object was originally hidden on the infant's left side, the infant could find it on the right side.

Critical to their success was whether infants could navigate around the platform on their own. Babies were more successful when they transported themselves. When they were carried, they more often responded with reference to their own bodies, not taking account of their spatial reorientation. If a baby's ability to move around affects his understanding of space, one might expect motor-handicapped infants to be delayed on spatial-performance tasks, even if they are equivalent to normal babies on cognitive tasks. Indeed, this is the case (Telzrow et al., 1988). Babies' control over their own movement through space apparently plays an important role in how well they understand the spatial world.

✔ *To Recap...*

Newborns can see, although visual acuity does not approach adult levels until about 12 months of age. Peripheral vision, color vision, and stereoscopic vision all are present in the early months of life. From birth, babies show interest in the visual contrasts presented by light–dark edges. One interpretation of this interest is that babies have an inborn agenda to engage in activity that stimulates their visual brain centers. At around 2 to 3 months of age, babies become increasingly interested in organized displays and faces rather than simple visual detail and contrast. The internal features of the face, especially the eyes, are particularly attractive after this age transition.

During the first half year of life, babies become quite sensitive to the properties of objects. They are able to appreciate that a single object offers many visual perspectives, as we can see in their ability to maintain size, shape, brightness, and color constancy. Perceptual constancies result from the fact that many features of objects remain stable even as our perspective changes. A bit later, babies appear to understand something about a subtle stability called higher order invariance. Some evidence suggests that these older babies construct visual categories in which similar objects can be placed.

Babies in the first half year are also learning what objects do. They seem to know something about what transformations are possible for rigid as opposed to pliable objects, as well as being able to interpret point-light biological motion. Babies do not, however, appear to infer that an object that is partially hidden from their view is continuous and whole unless they can see the object move.

Studies of how infants appreciate the spatial layout illustrate several important principles. Infants become sensitive to several kinds of cues for determining the distance of objects, with kinetic cues becoming effective first, then binocular cues, and finally monocular static cues. Although babies detect depth on a visual cliff at around 2 to 3 months of age, their fear of depth develops only around the time they learn to crawl. During the first half year, babies organize space and the objects in it with reference to their own bodies. Later, they can use landmarks in the visual field. This accomplishment permits them to appreciate that objects occupy a stable location independent of their own activity.

INTERMODAL PERCEPTION

Up to this point, we have discussed the various perceptual modes separately. But, of course, we actually perceive most objects, people, and events in our world through more than one mode. A dog, for example, provides a great deal of visual information. It also supplies auditory information through barking, panting, and moving around. Touch may provide another cue as the dog sidles up against your leg. Unfortunately, the dog may stimulate yet another perceptual mode, smell, from a distance of several feet. Although these perceptual cues may sometimes be available simultaneously, you probably can tell that the dog is nearby with only a few of them, maybe even one alone.

How the child comes to realize that cues from different senses "go together" has puzzled psychologists and philosophers for some time (Bushnell, 1994; Walker-Andrews & Dickson, 1993). One issue focuses on how our senses are related and how this relation changes with development. As we have seen, Piaget (1952) argued that the sensory modes are separate at birth and that the baby integrates them only through experience. For example, the baby can relate touch and vision only when he learns to look at objects as his hand grasps them. In contrast, others have argued that the baby is unaware of which sensory mode is stimulated by, say, a light or a sound (Bower, 1974). In this view, the senses are completely intermingled at birth, and the baby learns to separate them through experience.

A second issue concerns the mental image or representation that results from perception. As we saw in our example, stimulation of different perceptual modes can produce the same mental representation—say, of a dog—but how do they come to do so? This is the issue that opened the chapter: whether a previously blind person could recognize by vision alone an object that he had known only by touch. And it is the issue at the heart of how we can know a dog by vision, by sound, by feel, and even by smell. One possibility is that the baby learns to associate all the cues that the dog provides through repeatedly experiencing them together. Eventually, one cue triggers associations to the other cues, resulting in a mental representation, "dog." Before this, the child may have different representations for each mode—in a sense, a visual dog, a sounding dog, a feeling dog, and a smelling dog. The other possibility is that the child perceives a unitary dog from the beginning (Gibson, 1988b; Spelke, 1987) because the child detects visual, auditory, touch, and smell cues as invariant properties of dogs. The detection of any one property indicates the presence of the whole animal.

Researchers generally have approached infants' use of intermodal relations in one of two ways (Rose & Ruff, 1987). Many studies focus on how exploring in one mode triggers exploration in a different mode. Other studies focus on how input from different senses comes to indicate a single mental representation.

Exploratory Intermodal Relations

We appreciate the spatial location of objects through many sensory modes—vision, audition, touch, and sometimes even smell. Investigators have asked whether infants are born with a knowledge of space used by all the different sensory modes. If so, this shared knowledge could provide a basis for the intercoordination of the senses. For example, you know where to look when a person calls your name from behind or to the side. Does a newborn baby, who has had no opportunity to associate sound location and visual location, do the same?

As we mentioned earlier, the answer is yes. Newborns turn their eyes and head toward the sound of a voice or a rattle if the sound continues for several seconds (Clifton et al., 1981; Mendelson & Haith, 1976). And the interrelation among sense modes is not limited to sound and vision. You will remember that one of the infant's earliest reflexes involves turning the head toward the cheek being stroked, an exploratory action that helps the newborn to find the nipple. Similar relations exist between smell and vision; we noted that a 6-day-old baby will turn toward a breast pad that exudes the odor of the mother's milk (MacFarlane, 1975).

An important example of exploratory relations between perceptual modes is the relation between vision and reaching. The infant's reach for a rattle that she sees illustrates how vision can trigger tactile exploration. Babies do not reach and grasp objects accurately before 4 or 5 months of age, but much earlier they move their arms in the right direction, perhaps as early as birth (McDonnell, 1979; Spelke, 1987; von Hofsten, 1988; White, Castle, & Held, 1964).

These are examples of relations among the sensory modes that are present at birth, presumably because they have evolutionary value. But they are not fixed relations; they must be confirmed and sharpened by experience. For example, the newborn can localize a sound and look at the object that makes it with only crude accuracy (Bechtold, Bushnell, & Salapatek, 1979). Better performance seems to depend on repeated experience and correction of errors. Still, inborn relations between sensory modes do seem to exist. We call these *prepared relations*—relations for which the baby is predisposed but that are modifiable by experience. A certain amount of modifiability is useful, so that the interrelated systems can be "tuned," or recalibrated. If tuning were not possible, children would have no means by which they could adapt to such physical changes as the distance between their eyes and ears or the changing length of their arms and legs.

The examples of exploratory activity just described support the idea that relations among the sensory modes exist quite early. Next, though, we must ask whether babies realize they are exploring the same object in the two modes. This question raises the issue of mental representation (Rose & Ruff, 1987).

• Babies explore novel objects with multiple modalities, including vision and touch (not necessarily a comforting tendency for household pets!).

Intermodal Representation

Researchers have used two approaches to ask how early babies can use different perceptual modes to form a mental representation of an object. The first examines whether babies can transfer the benefit of experience from one mode to another. The second examines whether babies know that the same object is stimulating two modes. Psychologists have used these approaches to examine relations between haptic and visual perception and between vision and audition.

Haptic–Visual Relations

Babies' use of the relations between haptic and visual information provides the earliest evidence that stimulation in different sensory modes can activate the same mental representation. As noted earlier, haptic perception refers to active exploration by means of touch, as when a baby handles a rattle. To test for intermodal transfer between haptic and visual perception, investigators provided 1-month-old infants an opportunity to suck on either a nubby (bumpy) nipple or a smooth nipple. They then presented the infants pictures of the nubby and smooth nipples, side by side. Infants looked longer at the nipple they had sucked (Meltzoff & Borton, 1979). Although this finding suggests that cross-modal cues can specify the same object for infants at an amazingly early age, we should be careful in reaching conclusions. First, several experimenters have been unable to replicate the results even with older infants (Brown & Gottfried, 1986; Rose, Gottfried, & Bridger, 1981b). Second, even if transfer did occur, babies might have matched the cues from different modes on a very general basis. For example, they might have matched the two nubby nipples on the general basis of roughness without necessarily thinking that they were the same object (Rose & Ruff, 1987).

Investigators have tested somewhat older infants for the ability to recognize objects visually that they have previously explored only by hand. Whether this ability is present in the first half year of life is in doubt (Ruff & Kohler, 1978; Streri &

Pecheux, 1986), but babies between 6 and 12 months of age more clearly demonstrate that they can make the match (Rose & Orlian, 1991; Rose & Ruff, 1987). Babies are also able to learn about an object visually and then recognize that object by touch, but only if they are already somewhat familiar with the object (Bushnell, 1994).

An ingenious study examined whether babies can detect differences between what they feel and what they see. The baby was given the impression that he was reaching for an object reflected in a mirror, but in actuality, he was reaching for an object hidden behind the mirror. On trick trials, the baby felt a furry object while seeing a smooth object, or vice versa. On nontrick trials, the objects matched. Whereas 8-month-olds did not show different facial expressions for trick and nontrick trials, 9.5- and 11-month-olds showed more surprise during the trick trials, indicating that they perceived the mismatch (Bushnell, 1982).

Auditory–Visual Relations

Can babies detect a lack of correspondence between a sound and a visual event? Interestingly, babies naturally look at visual events that correspond to the sounds they hear. For example, Spelke (1976) showed infants two films, side by side. One film showed a person playing peekaboo, and the other showed a hand hitting a wooden block and a tambourine. A sound track was played that was appropriate to one of the films. Babies looked more at the film that matched the sound track, suggesting that they recognized the visual–sound correspondence.

Babies can also match auditory and visual events when the matching involves tempo and rhythm and when it involves sounds that accompany a moving object's changes in direction (Bahrick, Walker, & Neisser, 1981; Lewkowicz, 1992a; Mendelson & Ferland, 1982). And by 4 months of age, babies have some idea about the types of sounds new objects will make when they bang together, a feat that requires knowledge of several properties of objects—for example, their hardness and whether there is one item or several items involved in the collision (Bahrick, 1983, 1988, 1992). But not until 9 months of age do infants show clear evidence that they understand that approaching objects make increasingly louder sounds (Moore, 1993; Morrongiello & Fenwick, 1991).

Babies also appreciate sound–visual relations when they involve people. A baby looks longer at his mother's face when he hears his mother's voice than when he hears a stranger's voice (Cohen, 1974). Furthermore, as early as 3.5 months of age, a baby looks more at her mother when she hears her mother's voice and at her father when she hears his voice (Spelke & Owsley, 1979). By 4 months of age, babies look more at a male face when they hear a male voice and more at a female face when they hear a female voice, even when both faces and voices are unfamiliar (Walker-Andrews & Raglioni, 1988). Some sensitivities seem even more subtle. Infants between 2.5 and 4 months of age are sensitive to the lack of synchrony between the movement of lips and the sounds they hear, and they also respond to the match of mood in the voice and the face when sadness or happiness is expressed (Walker, 1982).

Infants then, are surprisingly good at picking up the commonality in cues from different senses. The baby's awareness that different cues from the same objects are coordinated greatly simplifies the task of organizing the overwhelming number of stimuli in the world into more manageable chunks. It is important to remember, though, that intermodal capabilities emerge at different times. At first, for example, infants simply appreciate that synchrony exists between visual and auditory events. More subtle forms of intermodal perception appear in steps as the baby matures (Lewkowicz, 1992b).

The beginning of this section described two basic approaches toward the development of intermodal perception. From the research on intermodal exploration, it is obvious that babies come into the world with a number of inborn relations between sensory modes. Nevertheless, it also seems that forming mental representations of objects from the inputs of many perceptual modes requires some experience. As always, nature and nurture work together to guide development.

✔ *To Recap...*

Most of our perceptual experience reflects the involvement of several sensory modes rather than a single one. Psychologists have wondered how children come to know that these perceptual cues "go together." In investigating this issue, they have focused on exploratory relations and mental representations.

Exploratory intermodal relations exist at birth, but they are tuned by experience. In the first half year of life, babies seem to have difficulty forming the same mental representation from different sensory modes. However, there is reasonable evidence that babies in the second half year do develop mental representations that bridge haptic and visual modes as well as the auditory and visual modes.

It appears that prepared relations between perceptual modes exist at birth but that experience plays a significant role in tuning and elaborating these relations.

THE DEVELOPMENT OF ATTENTION

Because perceptual and sensory processes are triggered by external stimuli, it may seem that these processes are passive and simply activated by events in the world. However, the perceptual modes are the mind's tools for gathering information about the environment, and the mind uses these tools actively.

We have all experienced lapses of attention—driving a car with our mind in "neutral" or reading several pages in a book while thinking of something else. Clearly, attention plays a central role in what information the mind takes in. In children, too, attention and alertness, along with intentions, goals, and inclinations, affect how they perceive the world.

Attention in Infancy

Even newborn infants attend to mild sounds and sights. Their bodies become quieter, they stop what they were doing (such as sucking), they widen their eyes, and their heart rates slow. These changes in behavior appear designed to optimize the babies' readiness to receive stimuli. They were first described by Sokolov (1960) as the **orienting reflex** and can be observed, for example, when newborns attend to moving lights, to sounds that change gradually, or to sounds of low frequency (Eisenberg, 1970; Haith, 1966; Kearsley, 1973). However, if the physical stimuli are too intense or the changes too abrupt, infants close their eyes and become agitated, and their heart rates increase. This is a protective reaction called the **defensive reflex** (Finlay & Ivinskis, 1987; Graham & Clifton, 1966; Kearsley, 1973). The orienting and defensive reflexes appear to be the baby's earliest forms of positive and negative attention.

We have already discussed other indicators of newborns' attention, such as their tendency to look toward the location of a sound and to turn their heads toward cheek stimulation or an attractive odor. However, investigators typically are

Orienting reflex
A natural reaction to novel stimuli that enhances stimulus processing and includes orientation of the eyes and ears to optimize stimulus reception, inhibition of ongoing activity, and a variety of physiological changes.

Defensive reflex
A natural reaction to novel stimuli that tends to protect the organism from further stimulation and that may include orientation of the stimulus receptors away from the stimulus source and a variety of physiological changes.

Selective attention
A concentration on a stimulus or event with attendant disregard for other stimuli or events.

more interested in the development of **selective attention**, the ability of the infant to focus on one stimulus rather than another. Even newborns have the capacity for at least a simple form of selective attention, choosing to look at displays of intermediate levels of brightness and pattern variability over extreme levels (Hershenson, 1964; Hershenson, Munsinger, & Kessen, 1965) and at patterned over nonpatterned displays (Fantz, 1963). Newborns also adjust their sucking activity to hear their mothers' voices rather than the voices of strange women (Cooper & Aslin, 1989; DeCasper & Fifer, 1980). This capacity for selective attention provides a powerful tool for investigating infant perception, as we have already seen.

What controls the infant's attention? This question has not yet been settled, but Jerome Kagan has provided the most complete set of ideas. He suggests that from birth to around 3 months of age, infants attend to patterns that contain contour and movement. From approximately 3 months to 12 months of age, they attend to things that seem surprising or discrepant from what they know. For example, when shown clay models of regular and distorted faces, babies looked more at the distorted faces. From 12 months on, babies attend to events that provoke them to form hypotheses, or guesses, about what is going on in their world. For example, a child might see his mother with a bandage on her face and try to figure out what happened (Kagan, 1970).

It is interesting to note that even young babies differ from one another in their attentional activity, which may be stable over time. A recent experiment, for example, found that babies who sustain more visual attention on stimuli at 5 months of age also tend to sustain attention in free play at 3.5 years of age (Ruddy, 1993b).

Selective Attention in Older Children

Although infants are capable of selective attention, there is a general shift, with age, from control of attention by external stimuli to stronger self-regulation based on the individuals' own goals and intentions. Flavell (1985) identified four important aspects of attention that develop with age.

1.   *Control* of attention improves with age as attention span increases and distractibility decreases. For example, children under 2.5 years of age are easily distracted from watching television programs by toys in the room and other events in the house. Soon enough, however, it may become quite difficult to pull them away from the set (Anderson et al., 1986).

2.   *Adaptability* of attention to the task also changes. When an experimenter tells children to pay attention to a particular task, older children do so and disregard things that are not central to it. Younger children, however, focus on many more of the irrelevant aspects and so do not perform as well on the main task (Hagen & Hale, 1973; Hale, 1979).

3.   Still another feature of attentional change is *planfulness*. When an experimenter asks children to judge whether two complex pictures are the same, younger children often use a haphazard comparison strategy, not examining all of the details before making a judgment. Older children are more systematic, comparing each detail across pictures, one by one (Vurpillot, 1968).

4.   Finally, children become better at adjusting their attentional *strategies* as they gather information from a task. For example, experienced readers change their reading speed as the difficulty of the text changes, while younger

readers tend to maintain a fairly regular reading speed regardless of difficulty (Day, 1975).

How do we select among things to attend to? Obviously, we can move our eyes to focus on one object rather than another. But selecting among things that we hear depends more on internal processes. A clear example of auditory selectivity is the "cocktail party" phenomenon, which refers to our ability to track one conversation through the noise of many others.

Children's ability to listen selectively appears to be related to Flavell's adaptability component of attention. In one study, researchers asked children to put on earphones that simultaneously played a male and a female voice. The children were instructed to listen to only one of the voices. When asked for information about what the voices said, younger children were much more likely to report information from both of the voices, whereas older children were more likely to report from only the target voice (Maccoby, 1967, 1969). Thus, the ability to focus attention increases with age for auditory input. This also seems to be true for switching auditory attention. In a listening task, children were asked to switch their attention back and forth between different signals to the two ears. Consistent with a developmental improvement in adapatability, 11-year-olds performed better at the task than 8-year-olds (Pearson, 1991).

✔ *To Recap...*

Even at birth, some sensory stimuli arouse interest, or an orienting reflex, in the newborn, whereas others produce rejection, or a defensive reflex. We are not yet certain what governs babies' attention. One model proposes that infants first attend to patterns and contours, then to discrepant stimuli, and then to events that require cognitive effort to be understood.

Older children display better selective attention. There is a general shift, with age, from stimulus control to self-control of attention. Four important aspects of attention that develop with age are control, adaptability, planfulness, and strategies.

PERCEPTION AND ACTION

As we have seen, we play a large role in determining what we will perceive. Much of our perceptual effort is expended for a good reason—so that we can operate on the world effectively: "We perceive in order to act and we act to perceive" (Pick, 1992). As we act—as we move and as objects in the world move around us—we deal with a continuous flow of changing energy. Only a moment's thought about the perceptual flow of events for an ice skater or a tennis player makes the point obvious. Perception occurs on a plane of action, then, and action, in turn, modifies perception in a seamless and continuing experience. Psychologists have only recently begun to explore the ramifications of this insight (Bertenthal, 1993; Schmuckler, 1993).

Action Systems in Infancy

Even for the newborn, perception is affected by action. For example, we saw that newborns turn their heads toward a stimulus that rubs against their cheeks and turn their eyes and heads toward a sound source. These actions are responses to sensory stimuli, yet these actions, in turn, affect how and which additional stimuli the newborn will perceive.

The looking activity of young infants is a good example of the role of action in perception. When alert and active, young infants make new visual fixations two or three times each second. Newborn infants even search actively with their eyes in darkness, indicating that their perceptual system is active even when there is no stimulus to produce a reaction. They continue to search when a light is turned on until they find light–dark edges. When they do, they cross back and forth over those edges, adjusting their visual scanning as necessary. They seem to come into the world with a set of rules for acting:

1.   If awake and the light is not too bright, open eyes.

2.   If in darkness, search around.

3.   If find light, search for contrasting edges.

4.   If find edges, stay near them and cross back and forth over them.

5.   As the clustering of edges increases, scan the edges more and more narrowly.

This inborn set of rules serves the biological function of activating visual cells in the brain and assuring that cells form proper hookups with each other (Haith, 1980, 1991). Such rules also illustrate that, from the earliest moments of a newborn's external life, action affects perception as well as perception affects action.

Action can also anticipate perception. Very recent research demonstrates that young infants can anticipate perceptual events before they occur, through the formation of expectations. Babies 3.5 months of age saw attractive pictures alternating in left-hand and right-hand positions on a computer screen. Each picture appeared for 0.7 second, followed by a delay of 1 second. After about 15 seconds of experience with this series, most infants moved their eyes, during the 1-second delay, to the place where the next picture would appear. Even when they did not move their eyes during the delay, it was clear that they expected a picture to appear, because they responded to it within about 0.4 second on average—substantially faster than when the appearance of the pictures was unpredictable (Haith, 1994; Haith, Hazan, & Goodman, 1988). One interpretation of this finding is that infants form expectations in order to free themselves from simply reacting to each event as it occurs (Haith, Wentworth, & Canfield, 1993).

Babies also use other action tools to investigate objects—for example, their mouths and tongues. Although this type of exploration has not been studied extensively, we have already seen that infants can visually recognize an object when they have only been given the opportunity to mouth it (Rochat, 1993).

As infants grow, their actions interplay with perception over an increasingly broad scope. At first, the eyes, mouth, and hands are the action systems, and the hands and mouth can only explore objects that are brought to the infant. Efficient reaching for objects usually begins around 5 months of age and broadens the infant's horizons substantially. Now babies can use actions more effectively to express what they want to do and can acquire attractive objects somewhat independently (sometimes to the mortification of parents as a saltshaker goes flying in an upscale restaurant).

When infants begin to move around by themselves, the fun really begins! As we have seen, this accomplishment produces new experiences and sometimes new un-

derstandings—such as the onset of fear of heights (Campos et al., 1978). Moving around independently also requires new perceptual learning. This is so because, for babies in the first year of life, their perception of space is not separate from the actions they perform. For example, babies who were able to reach around a barrier for a hidden object had to relearn the task when they were required to crawl around the barrier to get it (Lockman, 1984). Reaching around a barrier and moving the body around the same barrier to retrieve an object may seem like similar tasks to an adult, but to a baby they are quite different and affect her perception of space and barriers.

Action Systems in Older Children

Action systems continue to develop through childhood. Increasingly, cognitive strategies play a role in how these systems are deployed. Here, we look at development in the areas of visual scanning and action skills.

Visual Scanning

One of the hallmarks of development is the child's ability to develop and use strategies to reach a goal. Studies of eye fixations illustrate what strategies children use to examine visual displays and how new information changes these strategies.

In one experiment, children were shown pairs of houses like those in Figure 7-15 and were asked to judge whether the houses in each pair were identical or different. The experimenter recorded the children's eye fixations and movements as they looked at the two houses. Each house had several windows of varying shapes with varying decorations. A thorough examination of the houses required that each window be compared between houses, one by one.

Striking differences between children 4 and 9 years of age emerged. The younger children appeared to have little or no plan for the task. Rather than comparing the corresponding windows in a pair of houses, the younger children often

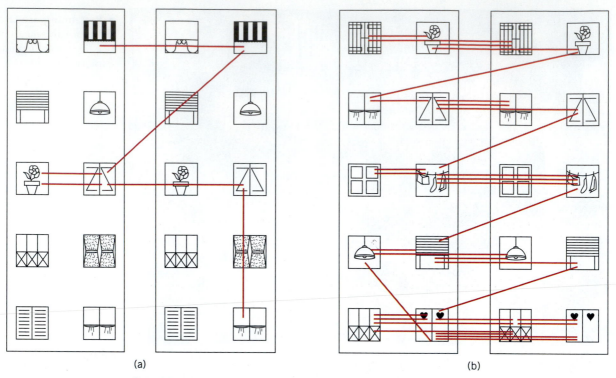

(a)   (b)

Figure 7-15   Reconstruction of a fixation sequence by (*a*) an inefficient child and (*b*) an efficient child. Their task was to judge whether the windows in two houses were identical or different. From E. Vurpillot, R. Castelo, and C. Renard, 1975, *Année Psychologique, 75,* Figure 2, pp. 362–363. Reprinted by permission of Presses Universitaires de France.

looked at windows in different locations, in a haphazard order, and did not check all windows before deciding the houses were the same. Older children, in contrast, scanned comparable windows, systematically checking each pair of windows before making a "same" decision. They were also more efficient, ending their inspection as soon as a difference between windows permitted them to say "different" (Vurpillot, 1968; Vurpillot & Ball, 1979).

In general, studies of scanning and reading reveal increased carefulness in patterning information, more flexibility in search, and lowered distractibility as children move from preschool to middle-elementary school years (Day, 1975).

Action Skills

Action skills—behaviors that require physical coordination, such as reaching, walking, and catching—involve a complex interplay between perception and various parts of the motor system. The development of these skills is made more complicated by the fact that the growing body and limbs change in size, weight, and proportion. Perception plays a key role in the continuing adjustment required for skill development, providing feedback about the relative accuracy of performance. Feedback here indicates the difference between reaching a goal (such as catching a ball) and not reaching it (missed it by 6 inches!).

One study examined how children of different ages adjust action to perception in the development of skill (Hay, 1984). Glass wedges placed in front of the eyes of children between 5 and 11 years of age created a shift in the apparent location of visual objects (much like the apparent shift of underwater objects as seen from above). If the child did not watch his arm as it moved toward the object, but simply reached directly for the object where it appeared to be, he would reach too far to one side and miss. The 5-year-olds tended to make more direct reaches, correcting hand position only after the hand had reached the apparent position of the object. The 7-year-olds made slower or more hesitant reaches, with starts and stops followed by small corrections near the end. Children 9 and 11 years of age were more likely to begin with a direct movement, gradually slowing their reach as they approached the object, and making corrective movements near the end. Apparently, the 5-year-olds paid little attention to feedback, whereas the 7-year-olds overemphasized it, much as an unpracticed driver oversteers a sliding car. By 9 years of age, children used feedback more effectively.

Does the coordination between perception and action decline from early childhood to adulthood? A visit to the local video game parlor will convince any doubter that children are capable of highly sophisticated perceptual–action skills. In fact, it is commonly assumed that children are much more competent in such skills than adults. However, we should not forget that children have more practice and are more motivated to engage in such activities.

Ralph Roberts developed a technology for exploring this issue, as illustrated in Figure 7-16 (Roberts et al., 1991). He asked adults and 4-, 7- and 12-year-olds to play the video game Asteroids over several sessions in the laboratory, so he could watch them as they evolved from novices to intermediates. None had ever played video games before. The tasks in the game are to maneuver a spaceship so that it is not hit by flying rocks and to try to shoot down the rocks. The fast movement of the

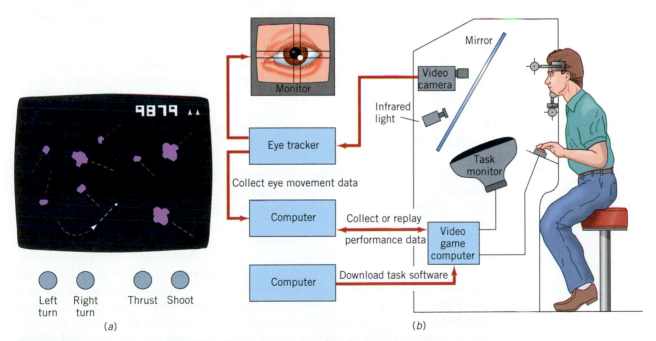

(a)   (b)

Figure 7-16 (a) In the Asteroids video game, a player controls a spaceship with buttons that can rotate the nose of the ship counterclockwise (left-turn button), rotate the nose clockwise (right-turn button), move the ship forward (thrust button), and fire missiles from the ship's nose. The object of the game is to destroy the moving asteroids with a missile and not to allow the asteroids to hit the ship. (b) As a person plays the game, a camera records the player's eye fixations. A computer records the screen presented to the player, the player's eye fixations, and the player's button presses 60 times each second. Researchers can analyze these data to find out precisely how looking and action are orchestrated.

game makes it perceptually demanding, and there are several buttons that the player can push to control turning and flying the spaceship and shooting its gun. A computer recorded all of the game displays and all of the players' actions, including eye movements, for later analysis. People in all age groups initially simplified the task by using as few controls as possible—for example, pressing only the spaceship's right-turn and fire buttons. The younger groups maintained this strategy throughout and therefore never got much better. The older groups, however, tried new strategies with time, learning to move or fly the spaceship around the screen. The shift to new strategies had a short-term cost, because new flyers tend to run into things, thereby destroying their spaceship. Ultimately, however, the ability to fly produced better performance. We can see similarities to the earlier discussion of attention and eye-movement strategies. Here too, development consists of increasing flexibility in the use of skills and increasing use of strategies (Roberts, 1989). There is hope beyond grade school, after all!

✔ To Recap...

Perception and action are interwoven even in infancy. Reflexes in newborns affect visual perception. The tools for seeking visual input are available at birth, and infants apparently use these tools to stimulate themselves through the inspection of high-contrast edges. Babies also develop expectations for regular events, which permit them to assume some control over their actions.

As babies become more adept, they use other action systems to modify their perceptual experience. Visually guided reach and self-produced locomotion dramatically change the opportunities that infants have to affect their own experience. Their control of their own movement through space contributes to their understanding of spatial stability but may require new learning.

Action tools continue to develop through the school years and often reveal cognitive and perceptual strategies that children use at particular ages. Increasingly, children make use of feedback to adapt to changing perception–action circumstances.

CONCLUSION

We began this chapter by noting that virtually all of the knowledge we possess has come to us through our perceptual apparatus. Small wonder, then, that perceptual development has been a central interest for scientists trying to understand the development of the human mind.

The last 2 decades or so of research have taught us that many earlier ideas about infants were wrong. Many experts thought babies were blind and deaf at birth, an idea that lent support to the empiricist view that perceptual capacities were based solely on experience and learning. We now know that all of the perceptual systems function even before the fetus has reached the age of normal-term birth. We live in the age of the "competent infant," in which many new capabilities have been discovered and infancy seems much less a period of perceptual disability than once believed.

At the same time, we must be careful not to attribute too much skill to the infant. A recent "superbaby" craze (reinforced by articles in such widely read publications as *Time* and *Newsweek* magazines) has led many people to think that babies can do almost anything. However, even in terms of very basic sensory processes—in detecting and discriminating the physical energies that stimulate the receptors—it is clear that the newborn baby has a great deal left to accomplish. And as we have seen, perceptual tools must be increasingly refined.

One of the most crucial problems in developmental psychology is that we have few concepts for talking about partial accomplishments. We ask if the baby has color vision or melody perception or intermodal perception and so on. When we find evidence that the baby does, often that is the end of our questioning. But no one really believes that, for example, the melody perception of the infant is as good as the melody perception of the adult. The problem is that although we can understand how a baby can see more or less clearly, because we can experience out-of-focus images for ourselves, we do not have concrete examples of imperfect color vision, melody perception, or intermodal perception. Until we can find a way to talk about imperfect accomplishments clearly, we will fail to have a complete understanding of perceptual development.

It is useful to think of the baby as coming into the world with the essential *tools* for taking in and seeking out perceptual information. This is most obviously the case with eye movements. Other tools will soon mature, such as grasping, reaching, crawling, and walking. These tools are present at birth or mature during infancy in babies of every culture. However, the *content* of perception, the actual information gathered, is highly dependent on experience. Whether a baby becomes familiar with faces that are brown, yellow, or white or learns to understand French, Chinese, or English depends on the culture in which he or she is raised.

As in most cases, then, the diametrically opposed nature and nurture views are both correct. Evolution has provided a creature with all of the tools necessary to collect information about the world. Experience determines exactly what that information will be.

FOR THOUGHT AND DISCUSSION

1. Molyneux's question concerned the relation between touch and vision. But it could have concerned other senses. *Think of some other combinations of senses for which we could ask the same question. Would the answers to these questions have the same implications for the nature–nurture issue as did Molyneux's original question?*

2. Investigators have demonstrated that some aspects of newborns' perceptual abilities appear to be innate whereas others are acquired through experience. *Why is it important for research psychologists to be able to make these distinctions? Do you think they have any potential practical importance?*

3. The development of the visual system appears to be influenced, in part, by experience. *If you were trying to optimize, or even accelerate, this development, how would you design a nursery for infants aged 1 month to 6 months?*

4. We described the three major approaches to perceptual development—environmental/learning, ethological, and cognitive-developmental. *Identify the research finding in the chapter that you feel poses the greatest difficulty for each of the three theories. Given what we know, which theory do you feel best accounts for perceptual development?*

5. In discussing the interrelation of action and perception, we dealt mostly with laboratory findings. *Apply the concepts we described—intermodal perception, attentional strategies, and the relation between action and perception—to analyze an example of "real life" athletic performance.*

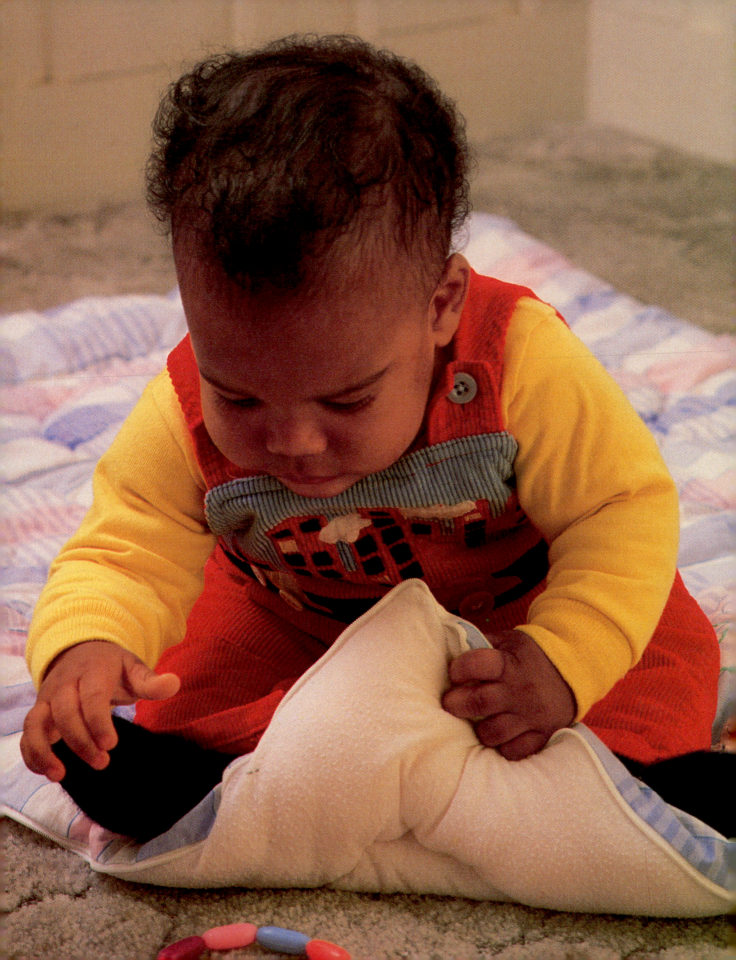

Chapter 8

COGNITIVE DEVELOPMENT: THE PIAGETIAN APPROACH

We closed the last chapter with a message of both competence and limitations. We saw that the infant's perceptual abilities are considerably more impressive than psychologists once believed. But we saw as well that even the modern "superbaby" is not equivalent to an adult and that major improvements in perceptual ability occur within the short span of infancy. Determining the ways in which the perceptual world of the infant both resembles and differs from that of the adult is one of the most fascinating challenges in modern child psychology. So too is tracing the interplay of biological and environmental factors that transform the "competent newborn" into the fully competent adult.

The same points apply, perhaps even more forcefully, to the subject of our next three chapters—children's cognitive development. By **cognition** we refer to all of the higher order mental processes by which humans attempt to understand and adapt to their world—processes that go by such labels as *thinking, reasoning, learning,* and *problem solving.* Here, too, the research of recent years has taught us that infants and young children are often far more competent than we used to believe. Yet the child's thinking may also differ from that of the adult in many ways, and these differences continue to intrigue and to baffle researchers and parents alike. Discovering the mixture of competence and limitations that characterizes thought at different points in childhood is one of the two great challenges that the researcher of cognitive development faces. The second is to discover how the limitations are overcome and how new forms of competence emerge. These challenges reflect the two general goals of developmental psychology identified in Chapter 1: to describe development and to explain it.

Across the next three chapters, we consider three general approaches to these questions. First we focus on the cognitive-developmental approach, as represented by the work of Jean Piaget. We examine both Piaget's original theory and research and more recent studies that in some way test, modify, or extend the Piagetian position. In Chapter 9 our attention shifts to another major representative of the cognitive-developmental approach—the information-processing perspective. Finally, in Chapter 10 we consider the intelligence test approach. We will see that these perspectives are in many respects complementary rather than contradictory and that a full model of cognitive development requires insights gained from all three approaches.

Cognition
Higher order mental processes, such as reasoning and problem solving, through which humans attempt to understand the world.

PIAGET'S THEORY

We begin with an elaboration of some of the points made about Piaget's approach in Chapters 1 and 2. We then go on to give a fuller account of the Piagetian picture of development.

Piaget's training included heavy doses of both biology and philosophy. From philosophy came much of the content of his work. Piaget's goal throughout his career was to use the study of children to answer basic philosophical questions about the nature and origins of knowledge. His research thus shows a consistent focus on what have long been central topics in philosophy: the child's understanding of space, time, and causality, of number and quantity, of classes and relations, of invariance and change. Undoubtedly one reason Piaget's studies have attracted so much attention is that they identify such basic and important forms of knowledge. Another reason is Piaget's surprising, and controversial, claim that these basic forms of knowledge often take a long time to develop.

From biology Piaget took ideas about both the structure and the function of intelligence. A basic principle in biology is that of *organization*. An organism is never simply a random collection of cells, tissues, and organs; rather, organisms are always highly organized systems. One job of the biologist is to discover what the underlying organization is. Piaget maintains that the same principle applies to human intelligence. For Piaget, the essence of intelligence does not lie in individually learned responses or isolated memories; the essence lies in the underlying organization. This organization takes the form of the various *cognitive structures* that the developing child constructs. The job of the psychologist is to discover what these structures are.

Biology also contributed to the functional side of Piaget's theory. Another basic biological principle is that of *adaptation*. All organisms adapt to the environments in which they must survive, often by means of very complex mechanisms. The biologist tries to discover what these mechanisms of adaptation are. Human intelligence, according to Piaget, is an adaptive phenomenon—indeed, it may be the primary means by which humans adapt to the environmental challenges they face. Adaptation occurs through the complementary processes of *assimilation* and *accommodation*. Whenever we interact with the environment, we assimilate the environment to our current cognitive structures—that is, we fit it in or interpret it in terms of what we already understand. Yet at the same time we are continually accommodating our structures to fit with the environment—that is, altering our understanding to take account of new things. It is through innumerable instances of assimilation and accommodation that cognitive development occurs.

The term *development* reflects one final influence from biology. Organisms are not static. Rather, they change, both across the lifetime of the individual and across the history of the species. Still one more task for the biologist, therefore, is to describe and explain the changes that occur. Intelligence, too, changes as the child develops, and the child psychologist must describe and explain these changes. For Piaget, there is not a single organization or set of cognitive structures that defines childhood intelligence. As children develop they construct qualitatively different structures, structures that allow a progressively better understanding of the world. It is these qualitatively different structures that define the Piagetian *stages of development*. Thus Piaget, like many cognitive-developmentalists, was a stage theorist.

Piaget divided development into four general stages, or periods. These periods were introduced in Chapter 2 and are summarized in Table 8-1. Much of the rest of this chapter consists of a description of the Piagetian periods of development. Although we focus on Piaget, we also consider related research by others. We will be able to see, therefore, how contemporary research is building on and extending the important work begun by Piaget.

✔ *To Recap...*

Piaget's approach to studying cognitive development was influenced by his training in both philosophy and biology. His training in philosophy led to an emphasis on basic forms of knowledge, such as concepts of space and causality. His training in biology led to the belief that intelligence reflects both organization, as knowledge is integrated into cognitive structures, and adaptation, as the child adjusts to challenges from the environment. Adaptation occurs through the complementary processes of assimilation and accommodation. As these processes lead to developmental change, children move through four qualitatively distinct stages, or periods, of cognitive functioning.

TABLE 8-1 ● Piaget's Four Periods of Development

Period	Ages (yrs)	Description
Sensorimotor	0–2	Infants understand the world through the overt actions performed on it. These actions reflect the sensorimotor schemes. Across infancy, the schemes become progressively more complex and interrelated. Decentering occurs, and the infant comes to understand object permanence.
Preoperational	2–6	The child can now use representations rather than overt actions to solve problems. Thinking is consequently faster, more efficient, more mobile, and more socially sharable. The child's initial attempts at representational functioning also show limitations, including egocentrism and centration.
Concrete operational	6–12	The advent of operations allows the child to overcome the limitations of preoperational thought. Operations are a system of internal mental actions that underlie logical problem solving. The child comes to understand various forms of conservation, as well as classification and relational reasoning.
Formal operational	12–adult	The further development of operations leads to a capacity for hypothetical-deductive reasoning. Thought begins with possibility and works systematically and logically back to reality. The prototype for such logical reasoning is scientific problem solving.

COGNITION DURING INFANCY: THE SENSORIMOTOR PERIOD

The first of Piaget's periods is the sensorimotor period. It is the period of infancy, extending from birth until about age 2.

You can gain some idea of the magnitude of cognitive advance during this period by imagining (or remembering, if you are a parent) the following two scenes: bringing a newborn home from the hospital and planning a 2-year-old's birthday party. Only 2 years separate the two events. Yet how different are the sorts of things that one can do with, say to, and expect of the two children! As Flavell, Miller, and Miller (1993) put it, "these two organisms scarcely seem to belong to the same species, so great are the cognitive as well as the physical differences between them" (p. 23). It is Piaget's work that provides us with our most complete picture of exactly what these differences are.

Studying Infant Intelligence

Piaget's conclusions about infant development are based on the study of his own three children from birth through the end of infancy (Piaget, 1951, 1952, 1954). We can add immediately that this restriction does *not* apply to his conclusions concerning later development, which are based on the study of thousands of children. For infancy, however, Piaget's research is limited to a sample of three.

• Piaget remains the field's most influential theorist of cognitive development. Many of his most important insights derived from his skill as an observer of children's behavior.

Piaget's method of studying his infants combined naturalistic observation with experimental manipulation. Both Piaget and his wife Valentine (herself a trained psychologist) spent many hours simply watching the everyday behavior of their babies in their everyday settings. But these naturalistic observations were supplemented by frequent small-scale experiments. If, for example, Piaget was interested in his daughter's ability to cope with obstacles, he would not necessarily wait until an obstacle happened along. Instead, he might interpose a barrier between daughter and favorite toy and then record her response to this challenge.

There are both strengths and weaknesses in Piaget's methodology. On the positive side, the method combines two attributes that are relatively rare in developmental research: the observation of behavior in the natural setting and the longitudinal study of the same children as they develop. It seems clear that this approach (helped along, of course, by Piaget's genius) permitted insight into forms and sequences of development that could not have been gained solely from controlled laboratory study.

Perhaps the most obvious limitation of Piaget's method concerns the sample. A sample of three is a shaky basis for drawing conclusions about universals of human development—especially when all three are from the same family and are being observed by their own parents! It was clearly important that Piaget's observations be replicated with both larger and more representative samples and more objective techniques of data collection. A number of such replication studies now exist, and they are positive enough in general outline to tell us that Piaget's picture of infancy was reasonably accurate (Harris, 1983). The replications are by no means completely supportive, however. We will note corrections and extensions as we go.

The Six Substages

Piaget divided the sensorimotor period into six substages. In the descriptions that follow, the ages should be taken simply as rough averages. What is important in a stage theory is not the age but the *sequence*—the order in which the stages come. This is assumed to be the same for all children.

Stage 1: Exercising Reflexes (Birth to 1 Month)

Piaget's label for the first stage reflects his predominantly negative conception of the newborn's abilities. In his view, the newborn's adaptive repertoire is limited to simple, biologically provided reflexes. Thus the newborn sucks when a nipple rubs against the lips, grasps when an object grazes the palm, and orients when an appropriate visual stimulus appears. These behaviors are seen as automatic responses to particular environmental stimuli, and they show only slight change during the first month of life.

It should be clear from Chapter 6 that Piaget underestimated the newborn's behavioral competence. Indeed, most of what he labeled "reflexes" we would today refer to as "congenitally organized behaviors," a term that reflects the complexity and the coordination that behaviors such as sucking and looking may show. Even in Piaget's view, however, these initial behaviors are important. They are important because they are the building blocks from which all future development proceeds. Development occurs as the behaviors are applied to more and more objects and events—in Piaget's terms, as babies assimilate more and more things—and as their behaviors begin to change in response to these new experiences—in Piaget's terms, as they begin to accommodate. As the initially inflexible behaviors begin to be modified by experience, the infant is entering the second of the sensorimotor substages.

Stage 2: Developing Schemes (1 to 4 Months)

As the infant changes, so does Piaget's terminology, from *reflexes* to *sensorimotor schemes*. We stressed earlier that Piaget sought to identify the cognitive structures that characterize a particular period of development. **Sensorimotor schemes** are the cognitive structures of infancy. The term refers to the skilled and generalizable action patterns by which the infant acts on and makes sense of the world. We can speak, for example, of a "sucking scheme," in the sense that the infant has an organized pattern of sucking that can be applied to innumerable different stimuli. Nipples, of course, are sucked; but so are rattles, stuffed toys, and fingers. Similarly, there is a "grasping scheme," a skilled behavior of grasping that can be applied to virtually any object that the infant encounters.

The notion of scheme captures an emphasis central to Piaget's theory—the role of action in intelligence. For Piaget, intelligence at every period of development involves some form of action on the world. During infancy, the actions are literal and overt. The infant knows the world through behaviors such as sucking, grasping, looking, and manipulating.

Schemes undergo two sorts of development during the second substage. First, individual schemes become progressively refined. The grasping of the 1-month-old is a rather primitive affair; the hard, thin rattle and the soft, fat stuffed toy may both be grasped in essentially the same way. The grasping of the 4-month-old is considerably more skilled and attuned to environmental variation. Such development does not stop at 4 months, of course. Particular schemes may continue to evolve throughout infancy.

The second change is that initially independent schemes begin to be coordinated. Rather than being performed in isolation, therefore, the schemes are now combined into larger units. Of particular importance is the fact that schemes involving the different sensory modes—sight, hearing, touch, taste, smell—begin to be brought together. Thus, the infant hears a sound and turns toward the source of the sound, a coordination of hearing and vision. Or the infant looks at an object and then reaches out to grasp and manipulate it, a coordination of vision and

Sensorimotor schemes Skilled and generalizable action patterns by which infants act on and understand the world. In Piaget's theory, the cognitive structures of infancy.

touch. Piaget believed that this ability to coordinate what one sees and what one touches is especially important for the infant's exploration of the world.

Recent studies indicate that Piaget underestimated the degree of early coordination between the senses. As we saw in Chapter 7, even newborns show a tendency to turn toward the source of a sound (Clifton et al., 1981; Morrongiello, 1988a). Other studies have suggested that the rudiments of visually directed reaching may be present quite early (Bower, Broughton, & Moore, 1970; von Hofsten, 1982). By 3 or 4 months, infants can use information from one sensory mode to form expectations about what they will experience in another. They have some knowledge, for example, of what sounds can or cannot go with what sights (Spelke, 1979, 1987), and they can use tactile information to guide their visual exploration of objects (Gibson & Walker, 1984). These findings do not negate Piaget's claim that intermodal coordination improves across the early months. But they do suggest that the beginnings of such coordination are present earlier than he believed.

Stage 3: Discovering Procedures (4 to 8 Months)

Although infants act on the environment from birth, their behavior in the first few months has an inner-directed quality. When a young baby manipulates a stuffed toy, for example, the baby's interest seems to lie more in the various finger movements being performed than in the toy itself. In Piaget's terms, the stage 2 infant uses schemes for the pure pleasure of using them—grasping for the sake of grasping, sucking for the sake of sucking, and so on. One characteristic of stage 3 is that the infant begins to show a clearer interest in the outer world. The schemes begin to be directed away from the baby's own body and toward exploration of the environment. Thus, the stage 3 infant who manipulates a toy does so because of a real interest in exploring that object.

One manifestation of this greater awareness of the environment is that the infant discovers procedures for reproducing interesting events. The stage 3 infant might accidentally kick a doll suspended above the crib, making the doll jump, and then spend the next 10 minutes happily kicking and laughing. Or the infant might happen to create an interesting sound by rubbing a toy against the bassinet hood, thus initiating an activity that may continue indefinitely. The infant is beginning to develop a very important kind of knowledge—what it is that he or she can do to produce desirable outcomes. That this knowledge is still far from perfectly developed is implied by the term *accidentally*. What the stage 3 infant shows is a kind of after-the-fact grasp of causality. Once the infant has accidentally hit upon some interesting outcome, he or she may be able to reproduce it. What the infant cannot yet do is figure out in advance how to produce interesting effects.

There is another limitation of stage 3 behavior. The procedures that the baby has developed may sometimes be applied inappropriately, almost as though the baby believes that a particular procedure can produce *any* interesting outcome that he or she might desire. The following observation from Piaget illustrates this sort of **magical causality**. The numbers at the start indicate the baby's age—7 months and 7 days.

> At 0;7 (7) he looks at a tin box placed on a cushion in front of him, too remote to be grasped. I drum on it for a moment in a rhythm which makes him laugh and then present my hand (at a distance of 2 cm. from his, in front of him). He looks at it, but only for a moment, then turns toward the box; then he shakes his arm while staring at the box (then he draws himself up, strikes his coverlets, shakes his head, etc.; that is to say, he uses all the "procedures" at his disposition). He obviously waits for the phenomenon to recur. (Piaget, 1952, p. 201)

Observations such as this reveal just how limited the stage 3 grasp of causality is.

Magical causality
The belief that a generally effective causal action can produce any outcome of interest, even in the absence of physical contact between cause and effect. A characteristic of stage 3 of the sensorimotor period.

Stage 4: Intentional Behavior (8 to 12 Months)

The stage 3 infant can reproduce interesting outcomes only after happening upon them by chance. During stage 4, this restriction disappears. The stage 4 infant *first* perceives some desirable goal and *then* figures out how to achieve it. In so doing, the infant demonstrates the first genuinely **intentional behavior**.

In Piaget's analysis, intentional behavior involves an ability to separate *means* and *end*. The infant must be able to use one scheme as a means to lead to some other scheme, which then becomes the goal, or end. The typical situation for studying intentional behavior concerns response to obstacles. Suppose the baby is about to reach for a toy and we drop a pillow between hand and toy. How does the baby respond? Simple though this problem may seem, the infant before stage 4 cannot solve it. The younger infant may storm ineffectually at the pillow or may immediately activate the goal scheme—that is, do to the pillow what he would have done to the toy. What the stage 3 infant does *not* do—and the stage 4 infant does—is first push the pillow aside and then reach for the toy. This sort of adaptive problem solving requires a separation of means and end. The infant must use the push-aside scheme as a means to get to the reach-and-play scheme, the desired end.

Piaget regarded the development of intentional behavior as a hallmark of infant intelligence. Indeed, he referred to this stage 4 acquisition as "the first actually intelligent behavior patterns" (Piaget, 1952, p. 210).

Stage 5: Novelty and Exploration (12 to 18 Months)

Piaget's name for stage 5 is "the discovery of new means through active exploration." The word *new* conveys a major difference between stage 4 and stage 5. The behavior of the stage 4 infant, although certainly intelligent, is essentially conservative. The infant at stage 4 tends to use mostly familiar schemes to produce a small range of mostly familiar effects. The stage 5 infant, in contrast, begins deliberately and systematically to *vary* his or her behaviors, thus creating both new schemes and new effects.

The advances of stage 5 are evident when the infant has some problem to solve. The stage 5 infant is not limited to reproducing previously successful solutions or slight variants of them. Instead, the infant can discover completely new solutions through a very active process of trial and error. Piaget documented, for example, how infants at this stage come to discover that a faraway goal can be retrieved by means of a string and that a stick can be used to push, pull, or otherwise act on some distant object. Note that these behaviors can be considered the first instances of a very important human achievement—the ability to use tools (Flavell et al., 1993).

The stage 5 infant also experiments for the pure pleasure of experimentation. An example familiar to many parents is the "high-chair behavior" of the 1-year-old. The baby leans over the edge of her high chair and drops her spoon to the floor, carefully noting how it bounces. The parent retrieves and returns the spoon, whereupon the baby leans over the other side of the chair and drops the spoon again, perhaps with a bit more force this time. The parent again returns the spoon, and this time the baby flings it across the room—whereupon the exasperated parent gives up and removes either baby or spoon from the situation. For most of us, not being Piaget, it may be difficult to appreciate that cognitive development is occurring in this situation. Yet it is through such active experimentation that infants learn about the world.

Intentional behavior
In Piaget's theory, behavior in which the goal exists prior to the action selected to achieve it; made possible by the ability to separate means and end.

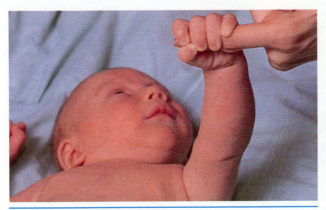

• In Piaget's theory, babies act upon the world from birth. During stage 1 of the sensorimotor period these actions are limited to the exercise of inborn reflexes.

• A hallmark of sensorimotor stage 5 is the ability to experiment in new ways to produce novel outcomes.

• As infants progress through the sensorimotor substages, they become increasingly interested in the outer environment and increasingly skilled at acting upon it to produce interesting outcomes.

Stage 6: Mental Representation (18 to 24 Months)

The first five sensorimotor substages are a time of remarkable cognitive progress. Yet there is still one more great advance to be made.

During the first five substages all of the infant's adaptation to the world occurs through overt behavior. Even the stage 5 infant's problem solving is based on trying out one behavior after another until a solution is reached. The advance that occurs at stage 6 is that the infant becomes capable for the first time of **representation**—of thinking about and acting on the world *internally* and not merely externally. It is this advance that will bring the sensorimotor period to an end.

Let us consider two examples. One concerns Piaget's daughter Jacqueline, who is carrying some blades of grass through the house.

> Jacqueline, at 1;8 (9) arrives at a closed door—with a blade of grass in each hand. She stretches out her right hand toward the knob but sees that she cannot turn it without letting go of the grass. She puts the grass on the floor, opens the door, picks up the grass again and enters. But when she wants to leave the room things become complicated. She puts the grass on the floor and grasps the doorknob. But then she

Representation
The use of symbols to picture and act on the world internally.

perceives that in pulling the door toward her she will simultaneously chase away the grass which she placed between the door and the threshold. She therefore picks it up in order to put it outside the door's zone of movement. (Piaget, 1952, p. 339)

When Jacqueline pauses with her hand on the doorknob the second time she is apparently doing two things. She is imagining the problem—the door sweeping over the grass. And she is imagining the solution—moving the grass beyond the sweep of the door. She is thus doing a kind of mental problem solving, based on an internal use of representations or symbols, that is not possible earlier in infancy.

The second example comes from Piaget's other daughter, Lucienne. Lucienne (who is 16 months old) and her father are playing a game in which he hides a watch chain in a matchbox and she attempts to retrieve it. After several easy versions of the game Piaget makes it harder: He reduces the opening of the matchbox to only 3 millimeters, too narrow for Lucienne to perform her usual solution of inserting a finger to hook part of the chain. How does the child respond?

She looks at the slit with great attention; then, several times in succession, she opens and shuts her mouth, at first slightly, then wider and wider! Apparently Lucienne understands the existence of a cavity subjacent to the slit and wishes to enlarge that cavity. . . . Soon after this phase of plastic reflection, Lucienne unhesitatingly puts her finger in the slit and, instead of trying as before to reach the chain, she pulls so as to enlarge the opening. She succeeds and grasps the chain. (Piaget, 1952, pp. 337-338)

In Piaget's analysis, the opening of the mouth is a symbol for the opening of the matchbox, and it is this symbol that allows Lucienne to solve the problem. Note that Piaget apparently caught Lucienne during a transitional period. Had he tried the game a month or so earlier, the mouth opening would have been unlikely. Instead, Lucienne would probably have approached the problem in typical stage 5 fashion, experimenting through overt trial and error. Had he tried the game a month or so later, the mouth opening would again have been unlikely. An older Lucienne could generate and use a purely internal symbol. Because Lucienne is transitional, on the brink of using representations but not yet very good at it, she still has to externalize her symbol.

For Piaget, it is the onset of representation that defines the movement from the sensorimotor period to the next period of development, the preoperational. We will have more to say about representational ability when we discuss the preoperational period.

Table 8-2 summarizes the six sensorimotor substages.

The Notion of Object Permanence

Any brief summary of Piaget's sensorimotor studies necessarily omits many interesting aspects of infant development. But one aspect must receive some attention, both because of its importance in Piaget's theory and because it has been the target of dozens of follow-up studies. This is the phenomenon of object permanence.

The term **object permanence** refers to our knowledge that objects have a permanent existence that is independent of our perception of them. It is the knowledge, for example, that a toy does not cease to exist just because one can no longer feel it, or a rattle just because one can no longer hear it, or Mommy just because one can no longer see her. It is hard to imagine a more basic piece of knowledge than this. Yet Piaget's research suggests that infants do not at first understand ob-

Object permanence
The knowledge that objects have a permanent existence that is independent of our perceptual contact with them. In Piaget's theory, a major achievement of the sensorimotor period.

TABLE 8-2 ● **The Six Sensorimotor Substages**

Stage	Ages (mos.)	Description
1. Exercising reflexes	0–1	The infant is limited to exercising inborn reflexes—for example, sucking and grasping.
2. Developing schemes	1–4	The reflexes evolve into adaptive schemes. The schemes begin to be refined and coordinated.
3. Discovering procedures	4–8	Behavior becomes more outwardly oriented. The infant develops procedures for reproducing interesting events.
4. Intentional behavior	8–12	The first truly intentional behavior emerges. The infant can separate means and end in pursuit of a goal.
5. Novelty and exploration	12–18	The infant begins to vary the schemes systematically to produce new effects. Problems are solved through an active process of trial and error.
6. Mental representation	18–24	The capacity for representational or symbolic functioning emerges. Mental problem solving begins to replace overt trial and error.

ject permanence and that this understanding develops only gradually across the whole span of infancy.

Piaget described the development of object permanence in terms of the same six-stage progression that he used for the sensorimotor period as a whole. During the first two stages—that is, the first 3 or 4 months—babies show essentially no evidence that they realize objects exist apart from their own actions on them. Should a toy drop out of sight, for example, the 2-month-old acts for all the world as though it no longer exists. The young infant will not search for a vanished object and is likely instead to turn fairly quickly to some other activity. At most, the baby at this stage may follow an object with his eyes or stare for awhile at the place where an object has just disappeared.

It is only during the third stage, at about 4 to 8 months, that babies begin to search for vanished objects. At first, however, the search shows a number of curious limitations. The infant may search, for example, if the object is partially hidden but not if it is totally hidden. The search may even depend on how much of the object is hidden. If only a corner of a sought-after toy is visible, the baby may sit perplexed. As soon as a bit more is revealed, however, the baby may happily reach out and retrieve the toy. Search may also depend on whether the infant's own action or something else makes the object disappear. The baby who pushes a toy over the edge of the high chair may look down at the floor to find it; should Papa Piaget do the pushing, however, search is less likely. For Piaget, this observation is evidence that the infant's knowledge of the object still depends on his or her action on it.

Another interesting stage 3 behavior was revealed not in Piaget's original studies but in more recent work. We place a toy in front of a 6-month-old. The infant reaches for the toy and closes his fingers around it, at which point we drop a cloth over both hand and toy. Despite the fact that they are now holding the toy, many babies at this stage are unable to retrieve it! Some simply sit there in confusion; others bring out their empty hands. Apparently the tactile cues from the toy are not sufficient in the absence of any visual evidence of its existence (Gratch, 1972; Gratch & Landers, 1971).

Stage 4 marks an important step forward with regard to object permanence. The infant at this stage (at about 8 to 12 months) can now search systematically and intelligently for hidden objects. The stage 4 infant searches even when the object is completely gone and even when it was not her own actions that made it disappear. Yet there are still limitations in the understanding of permanence, and they are revealed when the infant must cope with more than one hiding place. The following passage describes Piaget's initial observation of this phenomenon.

> Let us cite an observation made not on our children but on an older cousin who suggested to us all the foregoing studies. Gerard, at 13 months, knows how to walk, and is playing ball in a large room. He throws the ball, or rather lets it drop in front of him and, either on his feet or on all fours, hurries to pick it up. At a given moment the ball rolls under an armchair. Gerard sees it and, not without some difficulty, takes it out in order to resume the game. Then the ball rolls under the fringe of the sofa; he bends down to recover it. But as the sofa is deeper than the armchair and the fringe does prevent a clear view, Gerard gives up after a moment; he gets up, crosses the room, goes right under the armchair and carefully explores the place where the ball was before. (Piaget, 1954, p. 65)

Piaget went on to study this strange-looking behavior more systematically. He might hide a toy under a pillow to his daughter's left two or three times, each time allowing her to retrieve it successfully. Then, while the daughter watched, he would hide the same toy under a blanket to her right. The baby would watch the toy disappear under the blanket and then turn and search under the pillow! What seemed to define the object was not its objective location but her previous success at finding it—it became "the thing that I found under the pillow." For Piaget, this behavior (which has come to be labeled the **A$\overline{\text{B}}$ error**—that is, A-not-B) is evidence that, even at this stage, the baby's knowledge of objects is not freed from her own actions on them.

The infant does, of course, eventually overcome this limitation. The stage 5 infant (about 12 to 18 months) can handle the sort of multiple-hiding-place problems that baffle the younger baby. But there is still one more limitation. The infant at this stage can handle such problems only if the movements of the object are visible—that is, if he can see the object as it is moved from one hiding place to another. Suppose, however, that the movements are not visible—that the task involves what Piaget labeled *invisible displacements*. Piaget might hide a toy in his fist, for example, and then move the fist in succession through hiding places A, B, and C before bringing it out empty. To infer the movements of a hidden object, the infant must be able to represent the object when it is not visible. Thus, solution of this problem is found only at stage 6, when the capacity for symbolic functioning emerges.

The work on object permanence illustrates two very general themes in Piaget's approach to development. One is the notion of development as a process of **progressive decentering**. According to Piaget, the infant begins life in a state of profound **egocentrism**; that is, he or she literally cannot distinguish between self and outer world. The newborn and the young infant simply do not know what is specific to the self (one's own perceptions, actions, wishes, and so on) and what exists apart from the self. This egocentrism is reflected most obviously in the absence of object permanence. For the young baby, objects exist only to the extent that she is acting on them. Only gradually, across infancy, does the baby decenter and grow more aware of both self and world.

The second theme is the importance of **invariants** in development. We live in a world of constant flux, a world in which all sorts of things (for example, what we

A$\overline{\text{B}}$ error
Infants' tendency to search in the original location where an object was found rather than in the most recent hiding place. A characteristic of stage 4 of object permanence.

Progressive decentering
Piaget's term for the gradual decline in egocentrism that occurs across development.

Egocentrism
In infancy, an inability to distinguish the self (e.g., one's actions or perceptions) from the outer world. In later childhood, an inability to distinguish one's own perspective (e.g., visual experience, thoughts, feelings) from that of others.

Invariants
Aspects of the world that remain the same even though other aspects have changed. In Piaget's theory, different forms of invariants are understood at different stages of development.

can or cannot see, how things look) change from one moment to the next. Piaget maintained that one important kind of knowledge that the child must acquire is a knowledge of what it is that stays the same—remains invariant—in the face of constant change. The first and most basic cognitive invariant is object permanence—the realization that the existence of objects is invariant despite changes in our perceptual experience of them. We will encounter other, more advanced invariants when we discuss the later Piagetian stages.

More Recent Work on Object Permanence

Object permanence has received more research attention than any other aspect of sensorimotor development. It provides a good context, therefore, for talking about how later researchers have attempted to test and to extend Piaget's work.

Did Piaget Underestimate the Infant's Ability?

No researcher has questioned Piaget's assertion that the infant's understanding of objects is at first limited. Replication studies have amply confirmed Piaget's claims about the kinds of errors infants make when they must search for hidden objects (Harris, 1983, 1989b; Uzgiris & Hunt, 1975). Nevertheless, many researchers have wondered whether the infant's understanding is really as limited as Piaget believed. A particular concern has been Piaget's emphasis on motor search behaviors in assessing object permanence—that is, behaviors such as lifting a cloth or pushing aside a screen. It seems logically possible that an infant knows perfectly well that an object still exists but simply fails to show the kinds of active search behaviors that Piaget required.

How else might we assess what infants know about objects? The most informative approach has made use of the habituation phenomenon described in Chapter 2. *Habituation*, you may recall, refers to a decline in response to a repeated stimulus; conversely, *dishabituation* refers to the recovery of response when the stimulus changes. Researchers have probed infants' understanding of objects by seeing what sorts of changes in objects they are likely to notice and dishabituate to. Of particular interest has been response to impossible changes—that is, events that seem to violate the laws of object permanence.

A study by Baillargeon (1987a) provides an example. In this study, babies were first shown a screen that rotated, like a drawbridge, though a 180-degree arc (see Figure 8-1*a*). Although this event was initially quite interesting, after a number of repetitions the babies' attention dropped off, showing that they had habituated to the rotation. At this point a wooden box was placed directly in the path of the screen (see Figure 8-1*b*). Note that the baby could see the box at the start of a trial but that the box disappeared from view once the screen had reached its full height. In one experimental condition, labeled the "Possible event" in the figure, the screen rotated to the point at which it reached the box and then stopped—as indeed it should, given the fact that a solid object was in its path. In the other condition, labeled the "Impossible event," the screen rotated to the point of contact with the box and then kept right on going through its full 180-degree arc! (This outcome was made possible by a hidden platform that dropped the box out of the way.)

Any adult confronted with the event just described would probably be quite surprised, because he or she would know that the box still existed behind the screen, even though it could no longer be seen. Infants as young as 4.5 months apparently possess the same knowledge. Their attention did not increase when they viewed the possible event; looking times shot up, however, when the screen appeared to pass

Figure 8-1 The Baillargeon test of object permanence. Infants were first habituated to the event shown in part (*a*). Response was then measured to either the possible event in part (*c*), in which the screen rotates to point of contact with the box and stops, or the impossible event in part (*b*), in which the screen continues to move through the area occupied by the box. Adapted from "Object Permanence in $3\frac{1}{2}$- and $4\frac{1}{2}$-Month-Old Infants" by R. Baillargeon, 1987, *Developmental Psychology, 23*, p. 656. Copyright 1987 by the American Psychological Association. Adapted by permission.

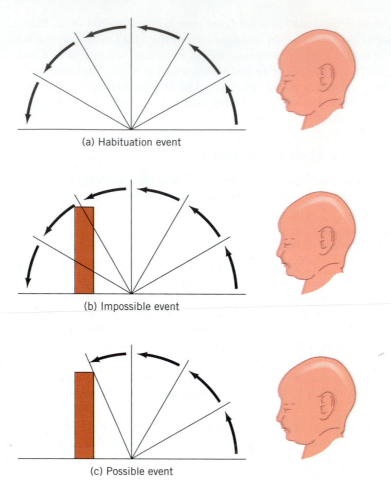

(a) Habituation event

(b) Impossible event

(c) Possible event

magically through a solid object. The most plausible explanation for such recovery of interest is that the infants knew that the box must still exist and therefore expected the screen to stop.

Young infants know something about not only the existence but also the properties of hidden objects. In a further experiment, Baillargeon (1987b) replaced the hard and rigid box with a soft and compressible ball of gauze. Infants were not surprised by the continued rotation of the screen in the soft-object case, indicating that they retained information about not only the presence but also the compressibility of the hidden object. Infants can also retain and use information about the location of hidden objects. Baillargeon (1986) showed babies a toy car that moved along a track, disappeared behind a screen, and reemerged at the other end. Following habituation, the infants saw a box placed behind the screen, in one case next to the track (possible event) and in the other case directly on the track (impossible event); they then watched the car again make its journey from one side of the screen to the other. Infants looked longer at the impossible event, thus indicating that they remembered not only that the box still existed but *where* it was—and that they drew different implications from the two locations.

The experiments just described are but a few examples of the ingenious ways in which modern researchers have attempted to discover what young babies know about objects (Baillargeon, 1993; Spelke et al., 1992). Such experiments are difficult to do and to interpret, and not all psychologists agree on their meaning (Fischer & Bidell, 1991; Rutkowska, 1991). Many, however, believe that studies such as Baillargeon's indicate that babies have some knowledge of object permanence several months earlier than Piaget reported. Yet researchers also agree that babies do not show active search behaviors for hidden objects until about 8 or 9 months, just as Piaget observed. Why babies' ability to organize intelligent behaviors lags so far behind their initial knowledge is one of the most intriguing questions in modern infancy research.

The A$\overline{\text{B}}$ Error

Perhaps because it is so counterintuitive, the A$\overline{\text{B}}$ error of the stage 4 child has been the most often studied aspect of object permanence. Recall that A$\overline{\text{B}}$ refers to the infant's tendency to search in an initial hiding place, rather than in the place into which an object has just disappeared. Recent research verifies that the error does occur, but it also indicates that a host of factors can affect the probability of occurrence. The error may depend on the memory demands of the task, for example. Infants may err if forced to wait for a few seconds before searching but respond perfectly if allowed to search immediately (Diamond, 1985; Fox, Kagan, & Weiskopf, 1979). The error may also depend on the number of possible locations. The infant may be less likely to search at location A if other possible hiding places exist than if A and B are the only response options (Bjork & Cummings, 1984; Sophian & Sage, 1983). Both of these findings suggest the operation of factors not considered by Piaget. On the other hand, factors that *were* stressed by Piaget do not always prove to be important. For example, search at A is not always affected by how often the infant has previously found the object at A, nor is it necessarily affected by whether it is the infant or the experimenter who has done the finding at A (Evans, 1973; Sophian & Wellman, 1983). Neither of these outcomes fits very easily with Piaget's "egocentric" interpretation of why the error occurs.

The message that emerges from these studies is that the A$\overline{\text{B}}$ phenomenon, while genuine, is more complicated than Piaget's theory indicates. Investigators are still trying to determine exactly when and why it occurs (Baillargeon, DeVos, & Graber, 1989; Diamond, Cruttenden, & Neiderman, 1994; McClelland et al., 1993; Wellman, Cross, & Bartsch, 1986). One interesting suggestion from recent research is that brain maturation may play a role (Bell & Fox, 1992; Diamond, 1991a, 1991b). We know that areas of the cerebral cortex are central to the operation of memory, and memory is clearly one component of successful A$\overline{\text{B}}$ performance. The cerebral cortex also underlies the ability to inhibit behavior, and inhibition too is necessary for success at the task: To retrieve the object at B, the infant must be able to resist the tendency to reach toward the previously correct site at A. Maturational advances in the brain areas that mediate memory and inhibition coincide with advances in performance on the A$\overline{\text{B}}$ task. Furthermore, damage to these areas is associated with problems with tasks of object permanence. Indeed, even *adults* with brain damage and consequent memory problems will make the A$\overline{\text{B}}$ error (Schacter et al., 1986).

An Overall Evaluation

Piaget's work remains our most influential and informative account of infant cognitive development. Nevertheless, the more recent studies of object permanence suggest several corrections to the initial Piagetian picture—corrections that probably can be extended to Piaget's sensorimotor work as a whole.

CAN NEWBORNS IMITATE?

A father leans over the crib and makes a funny face at his 3-day-old daughter—sticking out his tongue, wrinkling his nose, and in general acting the way adults often act around young babies. The daughter stares at this strange display and then appears, at least to the father's eyes, to wrinkle *her* nose, and stick out *her* tongue. The delighted father concludes that babies—or at least *his* baby—can imitate from early in life.

Until recently, psychologists would have dismissed this account as the wishful exaggeration of a proud parent. The newborn, after all, is in many respects not a highly competent organism. And imitation of facial expressions is a rather complex cognitive achievement. To imitate a behavior like tongue protrusion, the infant must somehow translate a purely visual stimulus into the tactile-motor commands necessary to produce the behavior. Such imitation thus requires the kind of intermodal coordination that has generally been denied the very young infant. To these theoretical arguments can be added some empirical data. Piaget (1951) included an examination of imitation among his sensorimotor studies, and he reported that imitation of the sort just described is not found until at least 7 or 8 months. In his view, young infants imitate only those behaviors

that they already produce spontaneously and those that they can see or hear themselves perform. Thus, the infant might imitate a particular finger movement, for which there is perceptible feedback, but not a behavior like opening the mouth or sticking out the tongue.

Some recent evidence has provided a strong challenge to this traditional view. Across a series of studies, Meltzoff and Moore (1977, 1983a, 1983b, 1985, 1989, 1992) have examined infants' responses when an adult stands over them and behaves like our hypothetical father—for example, opening his mouth or sticking out his tongue. Their procedure involves videotaping the infant's face as the model performs the target behaviors. The tapes are then scored by a rater who is unaware of the behavior being modeled (see Figure 8-2). Meltzoff and Moore report that even newborns can imitate both mouth opening and tongue protrusion, producing these behaviors reliably more often in response to the model than in the model's absence.

As might be expected, the claim of such remarkable precocity has not gone unchallenged (Abravanel & Sigafoos, 1984; Bjorklund, 1987b; Jones & Ridge, 1991; Kaitz et al., 1988; Poulson et al.,

First, Piaget often underestimated the infant's ability. How great the underestimation is has been a matter of dispute. But when studies have suggested revisions in Piaget's age norms, the revisions have almost always been in a downward direction. This conclusion applies not just to object permanence but to such topics as causality (Leslie, 1988; Leslie & Keeble, 1987), problem solving (Willatts, 1990), and imitation (Meltzoff, 1990b; Poulson, Nunes, & Warren, 1989). Box 8-1 provides a dramatic example with respect to very early forms of imitation.

Second, at least some of the underestimation in Piaget's work stems from his emphasis on motor behavior in assessing the infant's knowledge—that is, the focus on behaviors such as reaching, manipulating, bringing objects together, and in general acting on the world. With modern research techniques, such as the habituation procedure, we depend less on such overt behaviors, and our picture of infant competence has correspondingly grown more positive.

Third, Piaget may have overemphasized motor behavior not only methodologically but theoretically. In his theory, infants learn about and understand the world primarily by literally acting on it—by reaching for and grasping objects, manipulating them in various ways, and so on. Such behaviors are undoubtedly an important part of infant intelligence. But Piaget probably underestimated the role that

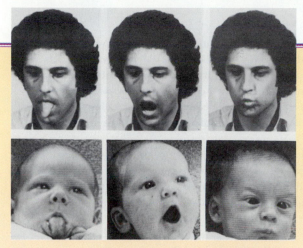

Figure 8-2 Adult model and infant response in Meltzoff and Moore's study of neonatal imitation. Even very young infants appear to imitate the adult's facial expressions. From "Imitation of Social and Manual Gestures by Human Neonates" by A. N. Meltzoff and M. K. Moore, 1977, *Science, 298*, p. 75. Copyright 1977 by the American Association for the Advancement of Science. Reprinted by permission.

1989). Not all researchers have been able to replicate Meltzoff and Moore's findings. In a recent review of 26 studies, Anisfeld (1991) concluded that tongue protrusion was the only gesture for which there was consistent, across-study evidence of adult–child matching; findings with respect to other gestures were too limited or too contradictory to permit conclusions. Furthermore, not all researchers interpret positive results as evidence of genuine imitation. An alternative possibility, favored by ethologically oriented workers, is that mouth opening and tongue protrusion are biologically wired-in responses to specific eliciting stimuli. In this view, the adult's movement automatically elicits a similar movement from the infant, much as other congenitally organized actions are elicited by their own appropriate stimuli. Neonatal "imitation" is thus not true imitation but rather a simpler response not dependent on intermodal matching. And this response eventually simply disappears, rather than developing into the more complex imitation of later infancy.

At present, the status of neonatal imitation is one of the most controversial topics in infant research (Anisfeld, 1991; Bornstein & Lamb, 1992). Research efforts continue, both to verify the phenomenon and to distinguish among the various explanations for its occurrence. If valid, however, Meltzoff and Moore's findings would constitute perhaps the most dramatic illustration of competence that exists earlier than Piaget claimed.

purely perceptual learning plays in infant development (Bebko et al., 1992; Bremner, 1993; Mandler, 1992).

✔ To Recap...

The first of Piaget's stages of development is the sensorimotor period, which extends from birth until about age 2. Infant intelligence is characterized in terms of sensorimotor schemes, and development occurs through the processes of assimilation and accommodation—incorporating new elements into the schemes and modifying the schemes in response to new experiences. This conception of infant intelligence reflects Piaget's emphasis on the child's own actions as a source of knowledge.

The sensorimotor period is divided into six substages. The starting point consists of various inborn reflexes. The reflexes evolve into adaptive schemes, and the schemes become more refined, externally oriented, and intercoordinated as the infant develops. A particularly noteworthy kind of coordination of schemes is found at stage 4 with the coordination of means and end into the first truly intentional behavior. The culmination of the sensorimotor period is the onset of mental representation at stage 6.

An especially important sensorimotor achievement is object permanence. Piaget's research suggests that infants only gradually come to understand object permanence through a series of stages in which the existence of the object is freed from the infant's actions on it. For Piaget, this phenomenon illustrates the gradual decentering process through which the egocentrism of the newborn gives way to a more objective understanding of the world. Object permanence is also an example of Piaget's emphasis on the child's mastery of invariants.

Later studies have largely confirmed the descriptive picture provided by Piaget. In some cases, however (e.g., the AB̄ error of stage 4), more recent research has indicated the importance of factors not considered in Piaget's theory. And a general conclusion from later research is that Piaget often underestimated infants' knowledge.

THOUGHT IN THE PRESCHOOLER: THE PREOPERATIONAL PERIOD

The preoperational period extends from about age 2 to about age 6. The "about" is again important. Piagetian age norms are always rough guidelines, and particular children may develop more quickly or more slowly than the average.

We noted at the beginning of the chapter that childhood cognition is a mixture of competence and limitations. At no time during development is this mixture—surprisingly adultlike abilities on the one hand and glaring, hard-to-believe errors on the other—quite so striking or so challenging to explain as during the preoperational period. Some of the most fascinating contemporary research in child psychology is directed to exploring the mysteries of the preoperational mind.

More About Representation

Symbolic function
The ability to use one thing (such as a mental image or word) as a symbol to represent something else.

As we saw, the defining characteristic of the movement from sensorimotor to preoperational is the onset of representational ability, or what Piaget called the **symbolic function.** Piaget defined the symbolic function as the ability to use one thing to represent something else—to use one thing as a *symbol* to stand for some other thing, which then becomes the *symbolized*. Symbols can take a variety of forms. They can be motor movements, as when the opening of Lucienne's mouth symbolized the opening of the matchbox. They can be mental images, as may have been the case when Jacqueline thought through the blades-of-grass problem. They can be physical objects, as when a 3-year-old grabs a broom and rides it as if it were a horse. And, of course, they can be words.

What is the evidence that a general capacity for representational functioning emerges near the end of infancy? Piaget cited five kinds of behavior that become evident at this time, all of which seem to require representational ability and none of which he had observed earlier in infancy (Mandler, 1983; Piaget, 1951). We have discussed two of these behaviors: the internal problem solving of stage 6 and the ability to handle the invisible displacements version of the object permanence problem. Another, discussed in Chapter 11, is the first appearance of words. What Piaget stressed here is the ability not simply to label present objects but to talk about objects or events *in their absence*. The latter is clearly a symbolic achievement.

Deferred imitation
Imitation of a model observed some time in the past.

A fourth piece of evidence is the appearance of **deferred imitation**. Although babies imitate from early in life, they can at first imitate only models that are directly in front of them. It is only near the end of infancy, according to Piaget, that the baby begins to imitate models from the past—for example, some behavior that an older brother performed the week before. The ability to imitate behavior from the past clearly implies the capacity to store that behavior in some representational form.

The final index of the symbolic function is familiar to any parent. It is the emergence of **symbolic play**. Now is the time that the child's play begins to be enriched by the ability to use one thing in deliberate pretense to stand for something else. Now is the time that sticks turn into boats, sand piles into cakes, and brooms into horses.

Was Piaget correct about the emergence of representational ability? We have seen that a consistent theme from modern research is that babies are often more capable than Piaget indicated. Such is probably the case as well with respect to the onset of representation. Although the importance of the transition described by Piaget is not in dispute, later research suggests that simple forms of symbolic functioning probably emerge earlier in infancy than he believed (Mandler, 1988; Meltzoff, 1990b).

Strengths of Preoperational Thought

In Piaget's theory, the cognitive structures of later stages are always more powerful and more adaptive than those of earlier stages. Consequently, the onset of representational intelligence marks a major advance in the child's cognitive abilities.

Representational, in-the-head problem solving is superior to sensorimotor problem solving in a number of ways. Representational intelligence is considerably faster and more efficient. Rather than trying out all possible solutions overtly, a necessarily slow and error-prone process, the representational child can try them out internally, using representations rather than literal actions. When the representational child *does* act, the solution can be immediate and adaptive. Representational intelligence is also considerably more mobile. Sensorimotor intelligence is limited to the here and now—what is actually in front of the child to be acted on. With representational intelligence, however, the child can think about the past and imagine the future. The scope of cognitive activity is thus enormously expanded.

Representational intelligence is also socially sharable in a way that sensorimotor intelligence is not. With the acquisition of language, the child can communicate ideas to others and receive information from them in ways that are not possible without language. Piaget's theory does not place as much stress on either language or cultural transmission as do many other theories (for example, the Vygotskian position discussed in Chapter 2). Nevertheless, Piaget did consistently cite social experience as one of the factors that account for development (Piaget, 1964). And both the extent and the nature of social experience change greatly once the child has entered the preoperational period.

The preoperational period is also a time of specific cognitive acquisitions. It is the time during which the child develops a form of knowledge that Piaget labeled **qualitative identity** (Piaget, 1968). Qualitative identity refers to the realization that the qualitative, or generic, nature of something is not changed by a change in its appearance. It is the realization, for example, that a wire remains the same wire even after it has been bent into a different shape or that water remains the same water even though it may look different after being poured from a glass to a pie pan. (Note, though, that the child does not yet realize that the length of the wire or the quantity of water remains the same—this is a more advanced form of knowledge.) It should be clear that qualitative identity, like object permanence, reflects a central Piagetian theme—the importance of mastering invariants in the environment.

Symbolic play
Form of play in which the child uses one thing in deliberate pretense to stand for something else.

• One of the clearest signs of the preoperational child's representational skills is the emergence of symbolic play. With her newfound symbolic skills, the 2-year-old readily transforms a pot into a hat.

Qualitative identity
The knowledge that the qualitative nature of something is not changed by a change in its appearance. In Piaget's theory, a preoperational achievement.

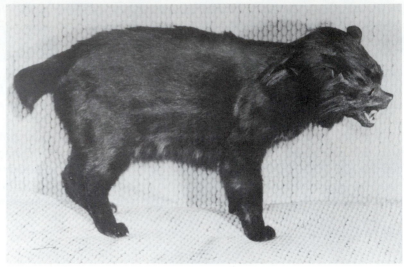

Figure 8-3   Cat transformed into dog, used by De Vries in the study of qualitative identity. Young preoperational children seem to believe that the cat has really become a dog; older preoperational children realize that the identity is unchanged. From "Constancy of Generic Identity in the Years Three to Six" by R. De Vries, 1969, *Monographs of the Society for Research in Child Development, 34* (3, Serial No. 127), p. 8. Copyright 1969 by the Society for Research in Child Development. Reprinted by permission.

A striking illustration of the phenomenon of qualitative identity comes in a study by De Vries (1969). De Vries first exposed her preschool subjects to a docile black cat. The cat was then transformed, by means of a very realistic mask, into a fierce-looking dog (see Figure 8-3). Following the transformation, De Vries questioned the children about what kind of animal they now saw. What kind of sound would it make, for example, and what kind of food would it like to eat? Most of the 3-year-olds seemed quite convinced that the cat had become a dog. In contrast, most of the 5- and 6-year-olds were able to overcome the perceptual cues and affirm qualitative identity. They realized that the cat was still a cat and would always remain a cat.

Appearance–reality distinction

Distinction between how objects appear and what they really are. Understanding the distinction implies an ability to judge both appearance and reality correctly when the two diverge.

A related, but more general, phenomenon that has received considerable research attention in recent years is labeled the **appearance–reality distinction.** As the name suggests, the appearance–reality distinction concerns children's ability to distinguish between the way things appear and the way they really are. Suppose, for example, that we show a child a red car, cover the car with a filter that makes it look black, and then ask what color the car "really and truly is." A 3-year-old is likely to reply "black"; a 6-year-old will almost certainly (and perhaps scornfully) say "red." Suppose next that we present a stone disguised as an egg and ask what this strange object "looks like." The 3-year-old, knowing the "really and truly" in this case (the apparent egg really is a stone), answers "stone"; the 6-year-old, again showing a capacity to distinguish appearance from reality, replies "egg." Problems in distinguishing appearance and reality are not limited to the visual realm; children also come to realize that sounds or smells or touches may sometimes mislead, giving a false impression of their underlying source (Flavell, Flavell, & Green, 1983; Flavell, Green, & Flavell, 1989). And children must come to understand that people, as well as objects, can present misleading appearances—they may look nice, for example, when they are actually mean (Flavell et al., 1992). Interestingly, the developmental progression from lack of understanding to eventual mastery in this area is not specific to our culture; children from the People's Republic of China, for example, respond in the same way to such tasks as do American children (Flavell, Zhang, Zou, Dong, & Qi, 1983). In no culture do children completely master the distinction between appearance and reality by age 6; all of us remain susceptible to being fooled by misleading appearances. But the preoperational child makes major strides in mastering this important kind of knowledge (Flavell, 1986, 1992b).

The preoperational child also makes major strides with respect to a variety of forms of interrelated knowledge that fall under the heading of theory of mind. Psychologists use the term **theory of mind** to refer to children's understanding of the mental world—what they think about such phenomena as thoughts, beliefs, desires, and intentions. Do children realize, for example, that there is a distinction between the mental and the nonmental—that thoughts are in our minds and not part of the physical world? Do they realize, despite this distinction, that the mental and the nonmental are connected—that our experiences lead us to have certain thoughts and beliefs, and that these thoughts and beliefs in turn direct our behavior? Do they appreciate the distinctions among different mental states—the fact that to think something is not necessarily the same as to know something, or that the intention to achieve a goal is no guarantee that the goal will actually be reached? Piaget (1929) was one of the first to explore questions of this sort in some of his earliest studies. Contemporary researchers, however, have gone well beyond these Piagetian beginnings. Indeed, theory of mind has emerged in just the last half dozen or so years as one of the most active arenas for research in cognitive development (Astington, 1993; Montgomery, 1992; Perner & Astington, 1992; Russell, 1992; Wellman, 1990).

A topic of particular interest to theory-of-mind researchers has been the child's understanding of **false belief:** the realization that it is possible for people to hold beliefs that are not true. This topic is interesting because it provides evidence with respect to one of the issues identified in the preceding paragraph—the child's ability to separate the mental from the nonmental. Consider the scenario depicted in Figure 8-4. To any adult, the answer to the question of where Sally will search for her marble is obvious—in the basket, where she last saw it. She has no way, after all, of knowing that the marble has been moved during her absence. Note, however, that to arrive at this answer we must set aside our own knowledge of the true state of affairs to realize that Sally could believe something that differs from this true state—that she could hold a false belief. We can do this only if we realize that beliefs are mental representations that need not correspond to reality.

Three-year-old children typically have great difficulty in understanding false beliefs. Most 3-year-olds will fail tasks such as the one in Figure 8-4. Most 3-year-olds also have difficulty in recapturing their own false beliefs. In another common false belief task, children are shown a container that turns out to have unexpected contents—for example, a crayon box that actually holds candles. When asked what they initially believed was in the box, most 3-year-olds reply "candles," answering in terms of their current knowledge rather than their original, false belief. Four-year-olds are much more likely to understand that they can hold a belief that is false and that a representation can change even when the reality does not. They are also more likely to realize that others could hold false beliefs in tasks of either the crayon-box or hidden-marble sort. More generally, as children develop across the preschool years, they gradually come to understand more and more about the mental world, both in their own minds and in those of others. As with the appearance–

Theory of mind
Thoughts and beliefs concerning the mental world.

False belief
The realization that people can hold beliefs that are not true. Such understanding, which is typically acquired during the preoperational period, provides evidence of the ability to distinguish the mental from the nonmental.

Figure 8-4 Example of a false belief task. To answer correctly, the child must realize that beliefs are mental representations that may differ from reality. From *Autism: Explaining the Enigma* (p.160) by U. Frith, 1989, Oxford: Basil Blackwell. Copyright 1989 by Basil Blackwell. Reprinted by permission.

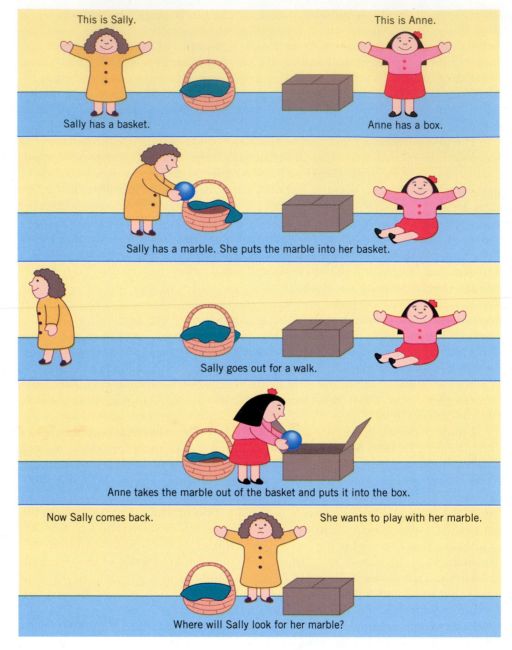

reality distinction, such understanding is not complete by age 6. But the preschool years are a time of significant progress.

The examples that we have described hardly exhaust the list of preoperational accomplishments. Indeed, one of the efforts of the last part of Piaget's career was to identify preoperational achievements that had been missed in his earlier studies (Beilin, 1989, 1992a, 1992b; Piaget, 1979, 1980). And when we turn to language development in Chapter 11, we will see that the years from 2 to 6 constitute a time of truly remarkable progress with respect to this critical and uniquely human ability.

Limitations of Preoperational Thought

Despite the positive features just noted, most of what Piaget had to say about preoperational thought concerns weaknesses rather than strengths. The weaknesses all stem from the fact that the child is attempting to operate on a new plane of cognitive functioning, that of representational intelligence. The 3-year-old who is quite skilled at the sensorimotor level turns out to be not at all skilled at purely mental reasoning and problem solving. Hence the term *preoperational*—to refer to the fact that the child lacks the "operations" that allow effective problem solving at the representational level.

Egocentrism

We saw that infancy begins in a state of profound egocentrism and that a major achievement of infancy is the gradual decentering through which the infant learns what is specific to the self and what exists apart from the self. The preoperational period also begins in a state of egocentrism, but this time at a representational rather than a sensorimotor level. In Piaget's view, the young preoperational child has only a very limited ability to represent the psychological experiences of others—to break away from his own perspective to take the point of view of someone whose perspective is different from his own. Instead, the 3- or 4-year-old often acts as though everyone shares his particular point of view—sees what he sees, feels what he feels, knows what he knows, and so on. Note that egocentrism does not mean egotism or selfishness, but simply a difficulty in taking the point of view of another.

Preoperational egocentrism is evident in a variety of contexts. Perhaps the most readily evident example is children's speech. Piaget's first book, *The Language and Thought of the Child* (Piaget, 1926), examined both naturally occurring conversations between children and experimentally elicited speech of various sorts. Piaget found that the children's speech was often hopelessly jumbled and hard to decipher, even when they clearly were trying their best to communicate. Table 8-3 presents some examples from an experiment in which children attempted to retell a story (the phrases in brackets are Piaget's comments on their efforts). Piaget attributed such *egocentric speech* to the young child's basic cognitive egocentrism. Young children often fail to assume the perspective of their listener, acting instead as though the listener already knows everything that they know. Certainly anyone who has listened to a 3-year-old relate the events of his or her day has some appreciation for this claim.

Piaget also studied the child's ability to assume the visual perspective of another (Piaget & Inhelder, 1956). The best known task for studying such visual perspective taking is the three-mountains problem pictured in Figure 8-5. After having a child walk around the display, the researchers seated the child on one side and moved a doll to various locations around the board. The child's task was to indicate what the doll would see from the different locations. For many young children, the answer was clear: The doll would see exactly what they saw. Again, the young child acts as though his or her own perspective is the only one possible.

Centration

The concept of **centration** refers to the young child's tendency to focus on only one aspect of a problem at a time. As an example, let us consider what is perhaps the most famous Piagetian task—the **conservation** problem. Specifically, we examine a conservation of number problem (Piaget & Szeminska, 1952). To construct such a

Centration
Piaget's term for the young child's tendency to focus on only one aspect of a problem at a time, a perceptually biased form of responding that often results in incorrect judgments.

Conservation
The knowledge that the quantitative properties of an object or collection of objects are not changed by a change in appearance. In Piaget's theory, a concrete operational achievement.

TABLE 8-3 ● Children Retell a Story: Some Piagetian Examples of Egocentric Speech

Story Presented to the Children

Once upon a time, there was a lady who was called Niobe, and who had 12 sons and daughters. She met a fairy who had only one son and no daughter. Then the lady laughed at the fairy because the fairy only had one boy. Then the fairy was very angry and fastened the lady to a rock. The lady cried for 10 years. In the end she turned to a rock, and her tears made a stream which still runs today.

Examples of Children's Reproductions

Met (6;4), talking of Niobe: "The lady laughed at this fairy because she [who?] only had one boy. The lady had 12 sons and 12 daughters. One day she [who?] laughed at her [at whom?]. She [who?] was angry and she [who?] fastened her beside a stream. She [?] cried for 50 months, and it made a great big stream." Impossible to tell who fastened, and who was fastened.

Gio (8 years old) "Once upon a time there was a lady who had 12 boys and 12 girls, and then a fairy a boy and a girl. And then Niobe wanted to have some more sons [than the fairy. Gio means by this that Niobe competed with the fairy, as was told in the text. But it will be seen how elliptical is his way in expressing it]. Then she [who?] was angry. She [who?] fastened her [whom?] to a stone. He [who?] turned into a rock, and then his tears [whose?] made a stream which is still running to-day."

Source: Adapted from *The Language and Thought of the Child* (pp. 99, 116, 121) by J. Piaget, 1926, New York: Harcourt Brace. Adapted by permission.

problem, we might begin by laying out two rows of five chips, as shown in the first column of Figure 8-6. As long as the chips are arranged in one-to-one correspondence, even a 3- or 4-year-old can tell us that the two rows have the same number. But suppose that, while the child watches, we spread one of the rows so that it is longer than the other and then ask the child again about the number. What virtually every 3- and 4-year-old will say is that the longer row now has more. If we ask the child why, the child finds the answer obvious: because it is longer. In Piaget's terms, the child *centrates* on the length of the row and hence fails to conserve the number.

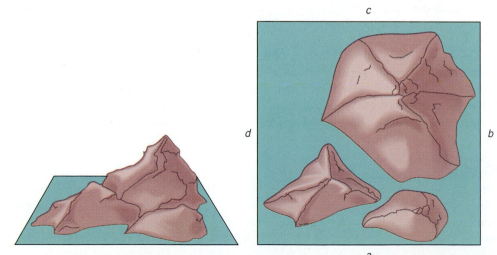

Figure 8-5 Piaget's three-mountains problem for assessing visual perspective taking. The child's task is to judge how the display looks to someone viewing it from a different perspective. From *The Child's Conception of Space* (p. 211) by J. Piaget and B. Inhelder, 1956, London: Routledge and Kegan Paul. Copyright 1956 by Routledge and Kegan Paul. Reprinted by permission.

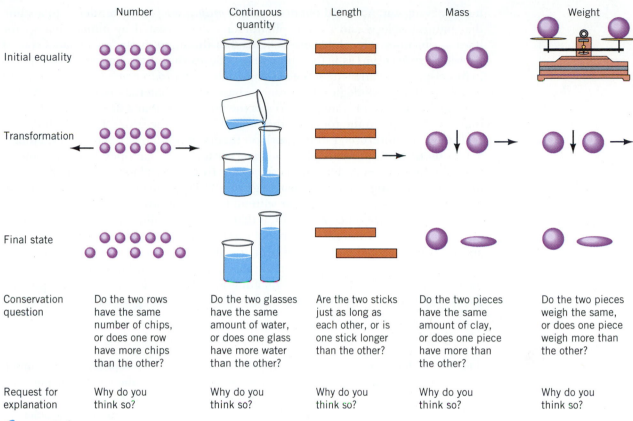

	Number	Continuous quantity	Length	Mass	Weight
Initial equality					
Transformation					
Final state					
Conservation question	Do the two rows have the same number of chips, or does one row have more chips than the other?	Do the two glasses have the same amount of water, or does one glass have more water than the other?	Are the two sticks just as long as each other, or is one stick longer than the other?	Do the two pieces have the same amount of clay, or does one piece have more than the other?	Do the two pieces weigh the same, or does one piece weigh more than the other?
Request for explanation	Why do you think so?	Why do you think so?	Why do you think so?	Why do you think so?	Why do you think so?

Figure 8-6 Examples of Piagetian conservation problems.

Centration, then, is a perceptually biased form of responding that is characteristic of young children. For the young child, what seems to be critical is how things look at the moment. The child's attention is captured by the most salient, or noticeable, element of the perceptual display, which in the number task is the length of the rows. Once her attention has been captured, the child finds it difficult to shift attention and take account of other information—for example, the fact that the rows differ not only in length but also in density. The result is that the child is easily fooled by appearance and often, as in the conservation task, arrives at the wrong answer.

It is no accident that the words *egocentrism* and *centration* are similar. In a general sense, both refer to the same idea—that young children tend to adopt a single perspective, to judge in terms of what is immediately obvious, to take account of only certain information, and so on. Indeed, in his later writings Piaget dropped the often misunderstood label *egocentric* and used the term *centered* to refer to both of the phenomena discussed here (Vuyk, 1981).

Other Preoperational Limitations

Piaget's studies identified several further confusions that preoperational thought may show (Piaget, 1929, 1951). Young children's thinking is often imbued with *animism*, or the tendency to endow inanimate objects with the qualities of life. The young child who indicates that the sun shines "because it wants to" is engaging in animistic thinking, as is the child who is concerned that a piece of paper will be

• One of the most basic forms of conservation is the conservation of quantity. To conserve quantity, the child must avoid centering on the misleading perceptual appearance.

hurt by being cut. A related phenomenon is *artificialism,* or the tendency to assume that natural objects and natural phenomena were created by human beings for human purposes. The child who believes that the night exists "so we can sleep" is showing artificialism, as is the child who believes that the moon was invented to light people's way after the sun goes down. The term *realism* refers to the tendency to believe that psychological phenomena have a real, material existence. A familiar example to parents of young children is the conviction that a dream is a real thing that is right there in the room (at the window? under the bed?). Piaget's studies of realism were a forerunner of the work on theory of mind described earlier. Finally, Piaget used the term *transductive reasoning* for a form of preoperational reasoning that qualifies neither as deduction (reasoning from general to particular) nor as induction (reasoning from particular to general). Transductive thought, in contrast, moves from particular to particular with no consideration of the general principles that link particular events. The result is that the young child often shows confusions about how and why two events relate. Piaget's daughter Lucienne provides an example: "I haven't had my nap so it isn't afternoon."

Is the young child's thinking really as egocentric, centrated, and confused as Piaget claimed? A brief answer is "sometimes but by no means always." We provide a fuller answer after considering the next of the Piagetian periods.

✔ To Recap...

The second developmental period in Piaget's progression is the preoperational. The onset of representational intelligence marks a major advance over sensorimotor functioning. The child's intellectual adaptations are now faster, more efficient, more mobile, and more socially sharable. The preoperational period is also a time of specific cognitive acquisitions, including qualitative identity, the appearance–reality distinction, and the understanding of false belief.

The movement from sensorimotor to representational brings problems as well as advances, a fact that is signaled by the term preoperational. The young child's thinking is often egocentric, showing an inability to break away from his or her own perspective to adopt the perspective of others. The young child's thinking also shows centration, a tendency to be captured and misled by what is perceptually obvious. The child's failure to conserve is one manifestation of centration.

MIDDLE CHILDHOOD INTELLIGENCE: THE CONCRETE OPERATIONAL PERIOD

The concrete operational period is the period of middle childhood. It extends from about age 6 to about age 11 or 12.

Discussions of the cognitive differences between preschoolers and grade-schoolers typically present a long list of contrasts (Flavell et al., 1993; Ginsburg & Opper, 1988). If forced to sum up the differences in a single phrase, however, most child psychologists would probably say something like "the older child is just more *logical.*" This is not to say that preschoolers are totally illogical; such would be far from the truth. But the preschooler's attempts at logical reasoning are often scattered and incomplete, working impressively in some contexts but going badly astray in others. The young child seems to lack an overall logical system that can be applied with confidence to a wide range of problems, particularly the kinds of scientific and logical problems that Piaget (with his training in philosophy) stressed. The older child, in contrast, does possess such a system.

To examine the differences between the preoperational and the concrete operational, we first present a sampling of the relevant Piagetian tasks. We then move on to Piaget's theory of the differences between the preoperational and concrete operational periods.

A Sampling of Tasks

For the most part, Piaget used the same tasks to study the preoperational and concrete operational periods. The difference between periods lies in the pattern of response. The preoperational child fails all of the tasks, whereas the concrete operational child begins to succeed at them. The older child's success is not instantaneous, however. The concrete operational concepts differ in difficulty, and their mastery is spread across the whole period of middle childhood.

Conservation

The conservation of number problem described earlier is just one example of a conservation task. Conservation can be examined in any quantitative domain. And indeed, Piaget and his coworkers studied just about every form of conservation that can be imagined. There are studies of conservation of mass, weight, and volume; of length, area, and distance; of time, speed, and movement (Piaget, 1969, 1970; Piaget & Inhelder, 1974; Piaget, Inhelder, & Szeminska, 1960). Some examples are shown in Figure 8-6. As can be seen, the typical starting point is a demonstration that two stimuli are equal on some quantitative dimension. While the child watches, one of the stimuli is transformed so that they no longer look equal. To conserve the quantity, the child must be able to overcome the misleading perceptual appearance. And this is precisely what the preoperational child cannot do.

Different forms of conservation are mastered at different times. Conservation of number is typically one of the first to be acquired, appearing by about age 5 or 6 in most U.S. samples. Conservation of mass and conservation of continuous quantity are also relatively early achievements. Conservation of length and conservation of weight are more difficult, typically coming 2 or 3 years after the first conservations. Other forms of conservation emerge still later.

Conservation represents another form of invariant. During the sensorimotor period, the infant masters the invariant of object permanence—the knowledge that the existence of objects is invariant. During the preoperational period, the child comes to understand qualitative identity—the knowledge that the qualitative nature of objects is invariant. And during the concrete operational period, the child masters the various forms of conservation—the knowledge that *quantitative* properties of objects are invariant.

Classes

Piaget's major work on classes appears in a book entitled *The Early Growth of Logic in the Child* (Inhelder & Piaget, 1964). The word *logic* is important. A number of investigators, both before and since Piaget, have studied how children form groups or classes when asked to sort an array of objects. Do they sort on the basis of color or shape, for example, and can they consistently follow whatever criteria they select? Piaget also studied such "free sorting" behavior. His finding again points out limitations. Young children's sorting is often inconsistent and illogical, based more on pictorial, or *figural*, properties than on objective similarity. A young child, for example, might begin by sorting on the basis of shape, then switch to color, then switch to items that make a picture. Piaget's real interest, however, was not simply

Class inclusion
The knowledge that a subclass cannot be larger than the superordinate class that includes it. In Piaget's theory, a concrete operational achievement.

• The ability to reason about classes is an important achievement of the concrete operational period.

Seriation
The ability to order stimuli along some quantitative dimension, such as length. In Piaget's theory, a concrete operational achievement.

Transitivity
The ability to combine relations logically to deduce necessary conclusions—for example, if A > B and B > C then A > C. In Piaget's theory, a concrete operational achievement.

in the child's ability to group objects sensibly; it was in the child's understanding of the structure or logic of any classification system formed.

The best known task for probing the child's understanding of classes is the **class inclusion** problem. Suppose that we present the child with 20 wooden beads, 17 of them red and 3 of them white. The child agrees that some of the beads are red, some are white, and all are wooden. We then ask the child whether there are more red beads or more wooden beads. Or we might ask which would make a longer necklace, all the red beads or all the wooden beads. However we word the question, the preoperational response is the same: There are more red beads than wooden beads. The child is apparently unable to think about a bead as belonging simultaneously to both a subclass (all the red ones) and a superordinate class (all the wooden ones). Instead, once the child has focused on the perceptually salient subclass—all the many red beads—the only comparison left is with the other subclass—the very few white beads. Note again the role of centration in the preoperational child's thinking—the tendency to focus on what is perceptually obvious and to ignore other information. The result is that the child makes a fundamental logical error and judges that a subclass is larger than its superordinate class.

The concrete operational response is again quite different. The concrete operational child can solve this and other versions of the class inclusion problem. Furthermore, the concrete operational child, according to Piaget, appreciates the *logical necessity* of the class inclusion answer. The child knows not simply that there are not more roses than flowers or more dogs than animals. The child who truly understands the structure of classes knows that there can *never* be more roses or more dogs—that it is logically impossible for a subclass to be larger than the superordinate class (S. A. Miller, 1986).

Relations

In addition to classes, the child must come to understand the relations between classes. Thus, another large set of Piagetian tasks has to do with various aspects of relational reasoning.

A deceptively simple-looking problem in relational reasoning is the **seriation** task (Piaget & Szeminska, 1952). To study seriation of length, we might present 10 sticks of different lengths haphazardly arranged on a table. The child's task is to order the sticks in terms of length. We might expect that any child who is persistent enough will eventually arrive at the correct solution through trial and error. Yet most young children fail the task. They may end up with just two or three groups of "big" and "little" sticks rather than a completely ordered array. Or they may line up the tops of the sticks but completely ignore the bottoms. Even if the child succeeds through trial and error, he or she is unlikely to be able to solve further variants of the problem—for example, to insert new sticks into a completed array. What seriation requires, according to Piaget, is a systematic and logical approach in which the child is able to think of each stick as being simultaneously longer than the one that precedes it and shorter than the one that comes after it. It is this sort of two-dimensional, noncentrated approach to problem solving that the preoperational child lacks.

The preoperational child also fails to appreciate the **transitivity** of quantitative relations (Piaget et al., 1960). Suppose we work with three sticks—A, B, and C—that differ only slightly in length. We show the child that A is longer than B and that B is longer than C. We then ask about the relative lengths of A and C but do not allow the child to compare them perceptually. Solving this task requires the ability to add together the two premises (A > B and B > C) to deduce the correct answer (A > C).

The concrete operational child has this ability (though not immediately—transitivity emerges at about 7 or 8). The preoperational child does not and so is likely to fall back on guessing or some other irrelevant strategy.

Note the similarity between transitivity and class inclusion. In both cases, the correct answer follows as a logically necessary implication from the information available. Thus, it is not simply a fact that A happens to be longer than C; if A is longer than B and B longer than C, then A *has to be* longer than C. We can see again Piaget's emphasis on the development of very basic forms of logical reasoning.

The Concept of Operations

Interesting though the empirical studies may be, Piaget's primary purpose was never simply to document what children do or do not know. His goal was always to use children's overt performance as a guide to their underlying cognitive structures. During middle childhood, these structures are labeled *concrete operations.*

We will not attempt a full presentation of Piaget's theory of concrete operations, because the theory is very complicated. Nevertheless, it is important to convey some idea of what Piaget meant by **operations**. Operations are in many respects similar to the sensorimotor schemes. One similarity is implied by the very name *operation.* An operation, like a sensorimotor scheme, always involves some form of action—"operating" on the world in order to understand it. A further similarity is that operations, like schemes, do not exist in isolation but are organized into a larger system of interrelated cognitive structures.

Operations
Piaget's term for the various forms of mental action through which older children solve problems and reason logically.

There are also differences between sensorimotor schemes and concrete operations. A major difference concerns how actions are expressed. Sensorimotor schemes are always expressed in overt action—reaching, grasping, manipulating, or the like. Operations, in contrast, are a system of *internal* actions. They are, in fact, the logical, in-the-head form of problem solving that the child has been slowly moving toward ever since the onset of representational intelligence.

Let us apply the notion of intelligence-as-internal-action to one of the concepts discussed earlier—working with classes, for example. Piaget argued that what a child knows about classes is a function of various mental actions that the child can perform. Simply to think about an object as belonging to a certain class is a form of action. Classes are not environmental givens; rather, they are cognitive constructions. To add together two subclasses (for example, red beads and white beads) to get the superordinate class (wooden beads) is a form of action. To compare the sizes of two subclasses, or of subclass and superordinate, is a form of action. In general, classification is a matter of mental activity—of creating and disbanding classes, comparing different classes, and logically adding, subtracting, or multiplying classes.

What about conservation? Piaget identified various mental actions through which the child might arrive at a correct conservation judgment. In the conservation of number task, the child might reason that the change in one dimension—say, the length of the row—is compensated by, or canceled out by, the change in the other dimension—the spacing between objects. Such reasoning by means of *compensation* involves a kind of logical multiplication of the two dimensions (increase in length times decrease in density implies no change in number). Or the child might reason that the spreading transformation can be undone and the starting point of equality reestablished, a form of reasoning that Piaget labeled *inversion* or *negation.* Both compensation and inversion are examples of a more general Piagetian notion, the concept of **reversibility**. Reversibility is a property of opera-

Reversibility
Piaget's term for the power of operations to correct for potential disturbances and thus arrive at correct solutions to problems.

tional structures that allows the cognitive system to correct, or "reverse," potential disturbances and thus to arrive at an adaptive, nondistorted understanding of the world. It is this power that concrete operational thought has and that preoperational thought lacks.

The Concept of Stage

Thus far in our review of the Piagetian stages we have not really discussed what it means to claim that there are stages of development. The concrete operational period provides a good context for discussion of this issue, because it is with regard to this period that the concept of stage has been most extensively debated.

Most theorists agree that a stage theory must meet at least three criteria to be valid. One is that there be *qualitative* as well as quantitative changes with development—changes in how the child thinks and not just in how much the child knows or how quickly the child can do things. Piagetians maintain that development does in fact show qualitative change from one period to the next. They would argue, for example, that there is a qualitative, in-kind difference between a sensorimotor child, who must act out all of his or her adaptation to the world, and a preoperational child, who can solve problems mentally through the use of symbols. Similarly, there is a qualitative difference between the preoperational response to a conservation task and the concrete operational response. Younger children treat conservation as a problem in perceptual estimation, judging always in terms of how things look. Older children do not even need to look at the stimuli; for them, conservation is a matter of logical reasoning, not perceptual judgment.

A second criterion is that the stages come in an invariant sequence. In a stage theory like Piaget's, each stage builds on the one before. No stage can be attained until the preceding one has been mastered. It is impossible, for example, for the child to become preoperational without the sensorimotor developments that make representational thought possible. Similarly, concrete operations are built on the achievements of the preoperational period. This claim of sequence applies not only to the four general periods but also to the substages within a period—for example, the six sensorimotor substages.

The final criterion is the one that has created the most problems. Piaget's theory maintains that each stage can be characterized by a set of interrelated cognitive structures—for example, the concrete operations of middle childhood. Once developed, these structures determine performance on a wide range of cognitive tasks. This position implies that there should be important *concurrences* in development. That is, if two or more abilities are determined by the same underlying structures, then they should emerge at the same time. Children's cognitive endeavors should therefore show a good deal of consistency.

The problem for Piaget's theory is that children's performance is often far from consistent. They may, for example, succeed on some presumably concrete operational tasks yet fail totally on others. Piaget did not claim perfect consistency; he was the first, in fact, to demonstrate that various concrete operational concepts may be mastered at different times. Most commentators, however, believe that Piaget never satisfactorily explained the inconsistencies that his research uncovered. And research since his has revealed even more inconsistency in development, including instances in which abilities that Piaget explicitly claimed as concurrences are mastered at different times (de Ribaupierre, Rieben, & Lautrey, 1991; Jamison, 1977; Kreitler & Kreitler, 1989; Toussaint, 1974). The studies we describe in the next section raise even more questions about whether it makes sense to talk about a child being "in" the preoperational or concrete operational stage.

What, then, is the status of the concept of stage? The issue continues to be much debated, with no clear resolution in sight (Fireman & Beilin, 1990; Flavell, 1982a, 1982b; Flavell et al., 1993; Miller, 1993). Some researchers continue to believe that Piaget's stage model is basically accurate, even though specific details may need correcting. Others (including researchers whose work we discuss in the next chapter) believe that cognitive development does in fact occur in stages but that the stages are different from those posited by Piaget. And still others believe that the concept of stage serves no useful purpose and should be abandoned.

More on the Preoperational–Concrete Operational Contrast

Is young children's thinking really as riddled with deficiencies as Piaget claims? Are the differences between early childhood and later childhood really so great? A number of research programs in recent years have suggested that the answer to both questions is no. We discuss this research under three headings: perspective taking, number, and classes.

Perspective Taking

We begin with the concept of visual perspective taking that Piaget's three-mountains task is meant to tap. As an examination of Figure 8-5 makes clear, the three-mountains task requires more than simply avoiding an egocentric response. To come up with the correct answer, the child must engage in a fairly complicated process of spatial calculation. Perhaps the young child's problems with this task tell us more about such spatial computation skills than about egocentrism.

When the task is simplified, young children often look considerably less egocentric. Children as young as 3 can predict the other's viewpoint when familiar toys rather than Piagetian mountains serve as landmarks (Borke, 1975). Even 2-year-olds can demonstrate some awareness of the other's viewpoint in very simple situations (Klemchuk, Bond, & Howell, 1990). When asked to show another person a picture, for example, the 2-year-old holds the picture vertically so that its face is toward the viewer rather than toward the self (Lempers, Flavell, & Flavell, 1977). Similarly, 2-year-olds realize (popular myth notwithstanding) that the fact that *their eyes* are closed does not mean that other people also cannot see (Flavell, Shipstead, & Croft, 1980). Even 18-month-olds will point to objects that they want an adult to notice, a behavior that suggests some realization that the adult does not necessarily share their perspective (Rheingold, Hay, & West, 1976). All of these behaviors, it is true, represent only very simple forms of perspective taking. Nevertheless, they do imply some ability to separate another's point of view from one's own.

Children's ability to tailor their speech to the needs of others also turns out to be more advanced than one would expect from Piaget's accounts of egocentric speech. Four-year-olds use simpler speech when talking to 2-year-olds than when talking either to other 4-year-olds or to adults (Shatz & Gelman, 1973). Thus, they adjust the level of their communication to the cognitive resources of the listener. Indeed, even 2-year-olds talk somewhat differently to infant siblings than to adults (Dunn & Kendrick, 1982). Children can also adjust to temporary variations in what the listener knows, as opposed to the general differences that exist between babies and adults. They describe an event differently, for example, depending on whether the adult to whom they are talking was present when the event occurred (Menig-Peterson, 1975), and they make different inferences about what listeners know as a function of differences in listeners' past experiences (Mossler, Marvin, & Greenberg, 1976).

Evidence for early perspective taking skills is not limited to the studies reviewed here. The finding is quite general across a variety of different forms of perspective taking (Flavell, 1992b; Forrester, 1992; Newcombe, 1989; Newcombe & Huttenlocher, 1992; Shantz, 1983). In no case is the 3- or 4-year-old's performance fully equivalent to that of the older child. But it is often more advanced than we once believed.

Number

As we saw, the aspect of numerical understanding that most interested Piaget is the child's ability to conserve number in the face of a perceptual change. Later studies have not disproved Piaget's contention that a full understanding of conservation of number—or, for that matter, any form of conservation—is a concrete operational achievement. Recent work does suggest, however, that there may be earlier, partial forms of understanding that were missed in Piaget's studies.

As with perspective taking, investigators have simplified the conservation task in various ways. They have reduced the usual verbal demands, for example, by allowing the child to pick candies to eat or juice to drink rather than answer questions about "same" or "more." Or they have made the context for the question more natural and familiar by embedding the task within an ongoing game. Although such changes do not remove the nonconservation error completely, they often do result in improved performance by supposedly preoperational 4- and 5-year-olds (Donaldson, 1982; Gold, 1987; Miller, 1976, 1982).

If the task is sufficiently simplified, even 3-year-olds can show some knowledge of the invariance of number. Rochel Gelman devised a game using two plates with toy mice glued to them—one with two mice and the other with three. The plates were hidden and the child was allowed to uncover one of them. During the first part of the game, the child learned that the three-mice plate was the "winner" and the two-mice plate the "loser." Then, in a critical test trial, the three-mice plate was surreptitiously transformed while hidden. In some cases, the length of the row was shortened; in other cases, one of the mice was removed. The children were unfazed by the change in length, continuing to treat the plate as a winner. They thus showed some ability to separate number from perceptual appearance. An actual change in number, however, was responded to quite differently, eliciting surprise, search behaviors, and various attempts at an explanation (e.g., "Jesus took it"). The children thus showed a recognition that number, at least in this situation, should remain invariant (Gelman, 1972).

Gelman has also studied other aspects of young children's understanding of number (Gelman, 1982, 1991; Gelman & Gallistel, 1978; Greeno, Riley, & Gelman, 1984). She has demonstrated, for example, that children's early counting is considerably less rote and confused than Piagetians used to believe. Gelman and Gallistel identified five principles that a counting system must honor (see Table 8-4). Their research indicates that children as young as 3 or 4 have some understanding of these principles. Young children do not always follow the principles perfectly, and their specific ways of applying them may differ from those of the adult (e.g., the 3-year-old who demonstrates the stable-order principle by always counting, "1, 2, 6"). Nevertheless, both Gelman's work and that of other researchers (Becker, 1993; Wynn, 1992b) indicates that counting is a frequent, systematic, rule-governed behavior from early in life. Gelman argues that children's early numerical abilities show a number of similarities to their early linguistic abilities. We will see in Chapter 11 that nativistic explanations have been common in the attempt to account for young children's remarkable language skills. Gelman suggests that

TABLE 8-4 ● **What Young Children Know About Number: The Gelman and Gallistel Counting Principles**

Principle	Description
One–one principle	Assign one and only one distinctive number name to each item to be counted.
Stable-order principle	Always recite the number names in the same order.
Cardinal principle	The final number name at the end of a counting sequence represents the number of items in the set.
Abstraction principle	The preceding counting principles can be applied to any set of entities, no matter how heterogeneous.
Order-irrelevance principle	The items in a set can be counted in any order.

Source: Based on information from *The Child's Understanding of Number* by R. Gelman and C. R. Gallistel, 1978. Cambridge, MA: Harvard University Press.

there may be an important biological underpinning to human numerical competence as well.

The suggestion that biological factors contribute to numerical development finds dramatic support in recent research with infants. Investigators have used habituation to determine whether infants are sensitive to the numerical value of a set (Cooper, 1984; Starkey & Cooper, 1980; Strauss & Curtis, 1984; Trehub, Thorpe, & Cohen, 1991; Trieber & Wilcox, 1984; van Loosbroek & Smitsman, 1990). In these studies, the infant is first repeatedly shown collections of a particular size until attention drops off. A new set size is then presented. Do infants notice the change? As long as the set sizes are small, infants as young as 3 months apparently do. There is even evidence (still controversial) that infants may be capable of simple forms of addition and subtraction (Wynn, 1992a, 1993)! Of course, such early numerical competence does not negate a role for later experience; children still have much to learn about number, and parents and teachers play important parts in this learning process (Durkin, 1993; Saxe, Guberman, & Gearhart, 1987). But the infancy studies suggest that such learning may build upon a very early sensitivity to number.

Classes

The class inclusion concept has been the subject of dozens of follow-up studies. Probably the clearest conclusion from these studies is that different forms of the class inclusion problem vary greatly in difficulty (Winer, 1980). In some cases, mastery comes even later than Piaget reported (Trabasso et al., 1978; Winer, 1978). In other cases, however, alterations in task format have suggested that young children do have some understanding of the inclusion relation (Markman, 1981, 1989; Smith, 1979). As with the other developments considered in this section, use of familiar stimuli and simplified wording seems to be important in drawing out whatever fragile knowledge the young child may possess.

Early understanding has been demonstrated for other aspects of classification in addition to class inclusion. The child's ability to form coherent classes depends on what stimuli are used. Eleanor Rosch has drawn some important distinctions concerning the ways in which the world can be cut into classes (Rosch, 1973; Rosch et al., 1976). She argues that certain categories, which she calls *basic-level* categories, lend themselves most naturally to classification and therefore should be developmentally earliest to emerge. "Chair" and "table" are basic-level categories, for example; "furniture" is not. Rosch also argues that some things are more typical members of a category than others. Thus "robin" and "sparrow" are typical members of the category "bird"; "ostrich" and "penguin" are not. Research confirms that children's classification performance does depend in part on what classes and members are presented. Use of basic-level categories results in a marked improvement in children's ability to sort consistently (Mervis & Crisafi, 1982). With the proper choice of classes and members, even 2- and 3-year-olds show some classification ability (Sugarman, 1983).

Children's ability to reason about the members of a class also depends on the stimuli that are used. As we have seen, young children's reasoning tends to be perceptually oriented, concentrating on surface features rather than underlying essences. Often, however, this conclusion has emerged from tasks using arbitrary and unfamiliar stimuli, such as geometric forms in the study of class inclusion. Even 4-year-olds are capable of penetrating beneath the surface when the classes involved are more natural and familiar ones, such as plants or animals. If taught, for example, that a tropical fish breathes under water and a dolphin breathes above water, 4-year-olds conclude that a shark will breathe under water, basing their inference on category membership (both the tropical fish and the shark are fish) rather than perceptual similarity (the shark looks much more like the dolphin than like the tropical fish) (Gelman & Markman, 1986, 1987). In general, recent research suggests that preschool children are developing a rich set of beliefs concerning biological categories, beliefs that often (as in the shark example) go beyond perceptual appearance in adaptive ways (Gelman & Wellman, 1991; Hatano et al., 1993; Keil, 1992; Rosengren et al., 1991; Springer & Keil, 1991). These beliefs, to be sure, are not yet equivalent to mature, adult-level knowledge. But they are a good starting point.

An Overall Evaluation

The consistent message that emerges from these studies is that the preschool child is more competent than Piaget's research and theory would lead us to believe. The studies reviewed here are just a small fraction of the evidence for this statement (Flavell, 1992a; Gelman & Baillargeon, 1983; Halford, 1989; Karmiloff-Smith, 1992; Siegal, 1991; Sugarman, 1987; Wellman & Gelman, 1992). Box 8-2 presents some further examples, along with a discussion of the practical implications of certain forms of early understanding.

This is not to say that Piaget's description of preoperational thinking is totally inaccurate. It is not. Young children *are* often egocentric, centrated, and illogical. They fail in a wide range of tasks that older children succeed on, and they often need simplified situations or special help to show whatever competence they possess. Piaget was correct in asserting that there are important limitations in early childhood thinking and important developmental changes between early childhood and middle childhood. But he may have somewhat misjudged the nature of both the limitations and the change.

DEVELOPMENT IN CONTEXT: Cross-Cultural Research and Piaget

One of the general issues identified in Chapter 1 concerns normative versus idiographic approaches to the study of development. It should be clear that Piaget's work falls squarely under the normative heading. The emphasis in Piagetian research is always on similarities rather than differences among children. All children are assumed to pass through the same stages of development. And all children are assumed to master concepts such as object permanence and conservation.

The study of development in other cultures provides a natural testing ground for the Piagetian claim of universality. We have long known that children growing up in the United States show the same basic patterns of development that Piaget first identified in children in Geneva some 40 or 50 years ago. But suppose we find a culture in which children's experiences are markedly different from those that are typical in Western societies. Will development still follow the Piagetian mold?

The answer turns out to be yes and no. A study by Dasen (1975) provides a good example. Dasen examined three groups of children: Canadian Inuits, Australian aborigines, and Ivory Coast Africans. Both the Inuits and the Australian aborigines depend on hunting for their subsistence, and members of both groups lead a nomadic existence, moving from place to place as need dictates. Dasen hypothesized, therefore, that such cultures might promote the development of spatial skills—abilities such as navigating through a strange environment, remembering and utilizing landmarks, and reversing one's route to get back to the starting point. In contrast, the Ivory Coast economy depends on agriculture rather than hunting, and the Ivory Coast way of life is correspondingly a good deal more sedentary, the emphasis being on accumulating and exchanging agricultural goods. Because of the emphasis on agricultural exchange, the hypothesis in this case was that the culture would promote concepts of quantity and volume.

To test these predictions, Dasen administered a battery of Piagetian tasks to children from each of the three cultures. The children were between 6 and 14 years old, and the tasks were directed to forms of knowledge that Piaget had found to emerge during this period. The particular tasks were selected, however, to reflect the cultural emphases just discussed. Thus, some of the tasks measured spatial skills—for example, the sorts of visual perspective taking tapped by Piaget's three-mountains problem. It was these measures on which the Inuit and aborigine children were expected to do well. Other tasks were directed to quantitative skills—for example, conservation of weight and conservation of volume. These were the tasks on which the Ivory Coast children were expected to excel. The results did indeed confirm these expectations.

Dasen's study is by no means the only demonstration that specific experiences can affect the development of Piagetian concepts. Cross-cultural research indicates that development can be sped up or slowed down depending on the availability of certain experiences and that even the order in which certain abilities emerge may vary from one culture to another (Dasen & Heron, 1981; Laboratory of Comparative Human Cognition, 1983; Mwamwenda, 1992).

At the same time, cross-cultural research also provides support for the Piagetian claim of universality. No one has found a culture in which children do not eventually acquire such basic forms of knowledge as object permanence and conservation, or in which children master conservation without going through an initial phase of nonconservation, or in which the order of the four general periods of development is reversed.

Cross-cultural studies, then, reveal both variation and consistency, depending on which aspects of development we consider. And context undoubtedly contributes to both sorts of outcome. The particular context in which children grow up can nurture the development of particular skills, as studies like Dasen's make clear. But similarities in the contexts that children encounter also help to create similarities in how children develop. There is no environment, after all, in which objects cease to exist when out of sight or in which quantities are not conserved in the face

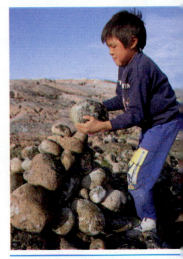

• Inuit children, and children of other nomadic cultures, have well-developed spatial abilities.

THE COCKROACH IN THE MILK: CHILDREN'S BELIEFS ABOUT THE CAUSES OF ILLNESS

Would you drink a glass of milk that had a cockroach floating in it? Would you drink a glass of milk from which a cockroach had been removed? Most adults answer no to both questions. And so, it turns out, do most 3- and 4-year-olds (Siegal, 1988; Siegal & Share, 1990).

The cockroach study is part of a growing research literature directed to children's understanding of the causes of illness (Gochman, 1988; Harbeck & Peterson, 1992; Harbeck-Weber & Peterson, 1993; Sigelman et al., 1993; Springer & Belk, 1993; Springer & Ruckel, 1992). Such research addresses interesting scientific questions about children's ability to engage in cause and effect reasoning—for example, to understand the role of invisible contaminants in the second cockroach scenario. Such research is also of clear applicational interest. Despite the medical advances of recent decades, children and adolescents remain at risk for a number of serious health problems, including AIDS (see Box 5-2) (Tinsley, 1992; Williams & Miller, 1991). Efforts to help children develop health-maintaining behaviors—and to cope with illness when it does occur—

must build upon knowledge of what children themselves think about the causes of illness.

Although Piaget himself never studied beliefs about illness, his general stage model yields a number of predictions. Probably the clearest is that the understanding of young, preoperational children will be confused and incomplete. Preoperational children would be expected to focus on tangible and observable causes of illness, with little ability to conceptualize unseen contributors, such as germs. They would also be expected to reason inaccurately about cause and effect, perhaps generalizing particular causes too broadly or inferring causation from the mere proximity of some event to the onset of illness. And they would be expected to show a form of reasoning that Piaget (1932) labeled immanent justice. As we discuss more fully in Chapter 14, *immanent justice* refers to the belief that punishment automatically follows the occurrence of a misdeed. Young children who become ill may believe that they are being punished for being bad.

Research provides some support for all of these predictions (Bibace & Walsh, 1981; Kister & Patterson, 1980; Simeonsson, Buckley, & Monson, 1979). Studies have

of a perceptual change. And there is no environment in which children cannot perform the kinds of actions on the world that Piaget considered critical to the development of intelligence. Thus, one explanation for similarities in human cognition lies in the similar contexts in which that cognition develops.

✔ To Recap...

The third developmental period in Piaget's theory is the period of concrete operations. During this period, the child gradually masters the different forms of conservation. The concrete operational child also comes to understand various aspects of classification (including class inclusion) and relational reasoning (including transitivity). Piaget attributed these and other achievements of middle childhood to the formation of concrete operations, an organized system of internal mental actions. One criticism of this theory is that development is not as consistent as the notion of underlying structure implies.

Recent research suggests that Piaget overstated the differences between early childhood and middle childhood. When tested in simplified situations, preschool children often show more competence than on standard Piagetian tasks. Young children are not as consistently egocentric as Piaget suggested, and they demonstrate the rudiments of skills that will develop more fully during middle childhood.

shown, for example, that preschool children may offer vague or magical explanations for illness (e.g., colds come from the sun), and that they have only an incomplete grasp of more appropriate causal mechanisms (not only colds but scraped knees can be caught from someone else). As Piaget's work would predict, young children often espouse a belief in immanent justice, claiming that getting sick is a punishment for misbehavior. And as we would also expect from Piaget, there are clear changes with age: As children develop, their reasoning about illness gradually sheds its earlier confusions and becomes more differentiated, more internally oriented, more sensitive to unseen causes, and more accurate in its identification of cause-and-effect relations.

What, then, of the finding that even 3-year-olds can appreciate the danger of an invisible contaminant? We have seen that children's apparent competence often varies with method of questioning, and such has proved to be the case with understanding of illness. The emphasis in recent research has been on simplified techniques that attempt to draw out whatever knowledge the child may have. For example, researchers may use closed-choice rather than open-ended questions, or word the situations in the third person (e.g., "another little boy...") rather than with respect to the child himself. Such techniques do not remove all developmental differences—4-year-olds still understand less than adolescents. But young children do demonstrate more knowledge than earlier studies suggested. They often show a preference for physical causes, such as germs, over psychological ones, such as immanent justice. They realize, as in the cockroach test, that a cause need not be visible but also that there must be some physical contact between cause and effect (a cockroach next to the milk is not sufficient). And they show some awareness that different ailments may have different causal bases.

What are the implications of these findings for health practices with regard to children? The earlier generation of studies identified confusions and gaps in knowledge that both practitioners and parents need to recognize. Young children should be helped, for example, to understand how particular causal agents work, and they should be reassured that they are not to blame if they become ill. Most generally, information about both specific illnesses and general health practices should be tailored to the child's level of understanding. What the recent research indicates, however, is that this understanding is more advanced than the traditional Piagetian picture suggests. Even preschool children may be capable of learning useful information about germs and contamination and contagion. Thus even young children can play an important role in both maintaining and restoring health.

ADOLESCENT AND ADULT: THE FORMAL OPERATIONAL PERIOD

Formal operations is the final period in Piaget's stage hierarchy. It can be given a beginning but not an end point, because once acquired, formal operations are assumed to last throughout the lifetime. The onset of the period is usually dated at about 12 or 13, around the beginning of adolescence. But formal operations may emerge later than this or not at all. As we will see, the evidence suggests that not everyone reaches the formal operational period.

Characteristics of Formal Operational Thought

We have already discussed the meaning of the term *operations*. But what about the term *concrete*? The *concrete* part of the label refers to the basic limitation of concrete operational thought. As we saw, the concrete operational child, in contrast to the sensorimotor child, does operate cognitively by means of representations rather than overt actions. Nevertheless, concrete operational children are still limited to dealing largely with what is directly in front of them—with what is concrete, tangible, real. What the child at this stage cannot yet do at all well is deal with the hypo-thetical—with the whole world of possibility rather than immediate reality.

Formal operational thinkers show no such limitation. The distinguishing characteristic of the formal operational period is the capacity for **hypothetical–deductive reasoning**. The formal operational thinker moves easily and surely through the world of what-ifs, might-bes, and if-thens. The adolescent, in fact, often seems more at home with the hypothetical—with imagined worlds, counterfactual propositions, life dreams and schemes—than in the world of mundane reality. The *deductive* part of *hypothetical–deductive* is also important. To qualify as formal operational, thought must do more than simply imagine possibilities. The formal operational thinker possesses a rigorous logical system for evaluating hypotheses and deducing necessary outcomes. As the term *operations* implies, this system again involves various forms of mental action.

Piaget's favorite way of characterizing the difference between concrete operations and formal operations was to talk about a reversal in the relation between reality and possibility. For the concrete operational child, the starting point is always immediate reality. From this point, the child can make very limited extensions into the hypothetical. In a conservation of number task, for example, the child who imagines pushing the chips back together *is* going beyond what is immediately given, but in a very limited way. For the formal operational thinker, in contrast, the starting point is the world of possibility—whatever it is that *might* be true. From this starting point in the possible, the thinker works back to what happens to be true in the situation under study.

A Research Example: Reasoning About Pendulums

Inhelder and Piaget's (1958) tasks for studying formal operations consist mostly of problems in scientific reasoning. In one task, for example, the subject must determine what factors (length, thickness, shape, and so on) influence the bending of a rod. In another, the subject must experiment with various chemical solutions to determine which combinations produce a specified outcome. Among the other content areas examined are projection of shadows, determinants of floating, conservation of motion, and laws of centrifugal force.

The example that we will describe is drawn from the domain of physics. In this task, the subject is shown a simple pendulum consisting of a weight hanging on a string. Various other weights and strings are also available for experimentation. The subject's job is to figure out what determines the frequency of oscillation of the pendulum—that is, how fast the pendulum swings back and forth. Is it the heaviness of the weight? The length of the string? The height from which the weight is dropped? The force with which it is pushed? Or perhaps some combination of two or more of these factors?

It turns out that the only factor that really has an effect is the length of the string. But the point is not that the formal operational subject knows this in advance, because he or she probably does not. The point is that the formal operational subject possesses a set of cognitive structures that will allow systematic solution of the problem. The solution requires first identifying each of the potentially important variables—weight, length, and so on—and then systematically testing them out, varying one factor at a time while holding other factors constant. The subject must be able to generate all of the possible variables (and sometimes combinations of variables), keep track of what has been done and what still needs to be done, and draw logical conclusions from the overall pattern of results. In the case

Hypothetical-deductive reasoning
A form of problem solving characterized by the ability to generate and test hypotheses and to draw logical conclusions from the results of the tests. In Piaget's theory, a formal operational achievement.

of the pendulum problem, the performance of all relevant tests will lead to the conclusion that if the string is short the pendulum swings fast, and *only* if the string is short does the pendulum swing fast. Thus, the length is both a necessary and a sufficient determinant of oscillation.

As with all Piagetian stages, the achievements of formal operations are clearest when contrasted with the preceding period. The concrete operational child is unlikely to solve the pendulum problem. The 9- or 10-year-old faced with such a task will do some intelligent things, including an accurate testing of some of the possible variables. But the younger child is not able to generate and examine the full range of possibilities on which a logical conclusion depends. Instead, the child may find that a heavy weight on a short string swings fast and conclude that both the weight and length are important, a conclusion that is not valid in the absence of further tests.

Note that the formal operational approach to the problem embodies the kind of reversal between reality and possibility that Piaget stressed. The formal operational subject begins by considering all of the various possibilities—maybe the weight is important, maybe the length is important, and so on. At first, these are merely hypotheses. None of them is anything that the subject has yet observed, and most of them will turn out to be false. Yet it is only by systematically considering all the possibilities that the subject can determine what happens to be true. Thus, the movement of thought is from the possible to the real.

More Recent Work on Formal Operations

Research on formal operations has addressed the same general issues that we discussed with respect to earlier Piagetian stages. A basic question is whether Piaget accurately diagnosed what his subjects knew. Later studies using the Inhelder and Piaget tasks have typically found lower levels of performance than Inhelder and Piaget reported (Shayer, Kucheman, & Wylam, 1976; Shayer & Wylam, 1978). Indeed some studies have found substantial proportions of adult subjects who fail the usual formal operational tasks (Commons, Miller, & Kuhn, 1982).

The suggestion that Piaget may have *overestimated* ability runs counter to what we identified earlier as a common conclusion about Piagetian procedures—namely, that they typically lead to some underestimation of children's competence. Some researchers have suggested that underestimation may also occur at the formal operational level. The Inhelder and Piaget tasks are unfamiliar to most subjects, and the usual method of administering them may not elicit the subject's optimal performance. Studies have shown that the addition of a simple hint or prompt concerning the appropriate procedure can lead to a marked improvement on later trials (Danner & Day, 1977; Stone & Day, 1978). More extended training procedures, as well as other sorts of procedural simplifications, have elicited at least some elements of formal operational performance in children as young as 9 or 10 (Fabricius & Steffe, 1989; Kuhn, Ho, & Adams, 1979; Siegler & Liebert, 1975).

Another possible approach is to vary the content of the tasks. Perhaps people tend to be formal operational when reasoning about content that they are interested in and familiar with. For some subjects, the natural science problems used by Inhelder and Piaget may provide such content; other subjects, however, may require tasks in literary analysis, or auto mechanics, or cooking. Piaget himself, in fact, suggested this possibility in one of his later articles about formal operations (Piaget, 1972). Although research to date is limited, there is some support for the idea. For example, De Lisi and Staudt (1980) demonstrated that college students'

• Formal-operational reasoning is not limited to the science laboratory. The navigational achievements of Micronesian sailors depend on a complex system of computations and logical deductions.

ability to reason at a formal operational level depended on the fit between academic training and specific task: Physics majors did best on the Inhelder and Piaget pendulum task, English majors excelled on a task involving analysis of literary style, and political science majors earned their highest scores on a problem in political reasoning. Findings from cross-cultural research are also compatible. Although subjects from non-Western cultures seldom perform well on the Inhelder and Piaget problems, they may show impressive levels of performance when operating in more familiar and culturally important domains. For example, prior to the availability of magnetic compasses, Micronesian navigators sailed their canoes for hundreds of miles from one island to another without the aid of navigational instruments, an achievement no Western sailor would attempt to duplicate. The navigators' ability to maintain course depended on a complex—and culturally transmitted—computational system in which star positions, rate of movement, and fixed reference points were systematically combined in ways that seem fully equivalent to the highest levels of performance shown by Inhelder and Piaget's (1958) subjects (Hutchins, 1983).

The importance of specific interests and training is also found in studies of logical reasoning (Overton, 1990) and in work on scientific problem solving (Stanovich, 1993a). Research in both areas shows the same variability in performance as does research on formal operations: surprisingly good performance by young children in some studies, surprisingly poor performance by older children and adults in others. The latter finding is perhaps the more striking. Adolescents and adults faced with reasoning tasks of the if-then sort often fail to draw logically valid conclusions from the available information. Similarly, even adults' scientific problem-solving efforts often go astray, a particular problem being a failure to separate theory from evidence and hence to obtain evidence that could serve to test the theory (Kuhn, 1991, 1992b). Such demonstrations of less-than-optimal performance fit with Piaget's suggestion that not everyone reaches the highest stage of cognitive functioning. At the least, they confirm De Lisi and Staudt's (1980) conclusion that we only sometimes operate at our best.

We can note finally that Piaget's theory of formal operations has been subject to some of the same criticisms as his claims concerning concrete operations. The degree of within-stage consistency is again an issue. Although some studies report fairly strong correlations among formal operational tasks (Eckstein & Shemesh, 1992), low to moderate relations are probably a more common finding (Martorano, 1977). Furthermore, the specific logical structures that Piaget believed underlie formal operational performance have been severely criticized by logicians (Braine & Rumaine, 1983; Ennis, 1976; Parsons, 1960). As with earlier Piagetian stages, few dispute that Piaget identified interesting forms of thought or that his theory may partially explain what is happening. But the theory does not seem to be completely satisfactory, and debates about the best way to characterize this level of thinking therefore continue (Byrnes, 1988a, 1988b; Gray, 1990; Keating, 1988).

✔ To Recap...

The final period described by Piaget's theory is the period of formal operations, which typically begins around adolescence. The distinguishing characteristic of formal operations is the capacity for hypothetical-deductive reasoning. The formal operational thinker begins with possibility—all the hypotheses that might apply to the task under study—and ends with reality—the particular solution that a systematic and logical testing of hypotheses shows to be true. Such thinking is revealed most clearly in tasks of scientific reasoning, such as the pendulum problem.

Although later research has confirmed Piaget's general account of adolescent thought, questions have arisen concerning the adequacy of his assessment methods, with some researchers reporting poorer performance than that obtained by Piaget and some reporting better performance. Questions have also arisen concerning the accuracy of Piaget's specific model of formal operations.

COGNITIVE CHANGE

Our discussion thus far has been directed to one of the two basic questions in developmental psychology: What are the most important changes that occur in the course of development? We turn now to the second general question: How can we explain these changes? A developmental theory must specify not only the interesting milestones of development but also the processes by which these milestones emerge.

Piaget's Theory

Piaget's position on the nature–nurture issue is definitely an interactionist one. In his theory, biology and experience act together to produce changes in the child's cognitive abilities.

More specifically, Piaget (1964, 1983) identified four general factors that contribute to cognitive change. Three of the factors are found to some extent in every theory of development. First, biological maturation plays a role. Learning and development occur always within constraints set by the child's maturational level, and some kinds of development may be impossible until maturation has progressed sufficiently. In any stage theory, biological factors contribute to both the nature and the timing of the changes. Some commentators, in fact, believe that Piaget's theory implies an even greater biological contribution than he himself typically stated (Beilin, 1971; Fodor, 1980).

Equilibration
Piaget's term for the biological process of self-regulation that propels the cognitive system to higher and higher forms of equilibrium.

Equilibrium
A characteristic of a cognitive system in which assimilation and accommodation are in balance, thus permitting adaptive, nondistorted responses to the world.

Experience is also important. Piaget divided experience into two categories: physical experience and social experience. The former category includes the child's interactions with inanimate objects; the latter, the child's interactions with people. In both cases, Piaget stressed the importance of assimilation and action. Children must fit experiences, physical or social, into what they already understand. And they must actively construct new knowledge, as opposed to having knowledge imposed ready-made upon them.

Every theory talks in some way about maturation, physical experience, and social experience. The fourth factor is more uniquely Piagetian. It is **equilibration**, another legacy of Piaget's biological training. Piaget used the term to refer to the general biological process of self-regulation. It was for him the most important of the four factors, the one that in a sense explained the other three.

What did Piaget mean by self-regulation? The notion is easiest to understand in conjunction with a closely related Piagetian construct, **equilibrium**. Equilibrium refers to balance within the cognitive system. It exists when the child's cognitive structures can respond to any environmental challenge without distortion or misunderstanding. For Piaget, such an adaptive response implies a balance between assimilation and accommodation. The child neither distorts reality to make it fit existing structures (which would be an excess of assimilation) nor distorts current knowledge in an attempt to make sense of something new (which would be an excess of accommodation). It is the self-regulating process of equilibration that guards against such distortions and acts to maintain equilibrium.

Piaget cited equilibration as the ultimate explanation for several aspects of development. Equilibration accounts for the organization in development. As we saw, inputs from maturation and from various kinds of experience are not simply lumped together; rather, they are coordinated into cognitive structures. According to Piaget, there must be some more general factor that accounts for such coordination. This general factor is the self-regulating process of equilibration. Thus, it is equilibration that directs the integration of sensorimotor schemes during infancy and the coordination of knowledge about classes and knowledge about relations during middle childhood.

Equilibration also serves to explain motivation. In Piaget's view, the cognitive system seeks always to reach and to maintain states of equilibrium, because equilibrium characterizes adaptive behavior. Suppose, however, that the child encounters some new event that cannot immediately be understood. This new event will evoke disequilibrium, or cognitive conflict—some sort of disturbing imbalance within the cognitive system. The child will feel a need to get rid of the conflict and will continue to think and to act until the event is understood and equilibrium restored.

Equilibration accounts finally for the directionality in development—for the fact that development moves always in an upward, progressive direction. When disequilibrium exists, only certain kinds of resolution are satisfactory. Conceivably, the child could remove the disequilibrium by distorting the input or regressing to some lower level of understanding. But this does not happen. When equilibrium is restored, it exists at a higher, better level of understanding. It is in this way that misunderstanding evolves into understanding and lower stages into higher ones.

It should be clear that equilibration, at least as we have discussed it so far, is a *very* general notion. Even if the general construct makes sense, it does not tell us how specific cognitive changes come about. Piaget did attempt at various points to specify the equilibration process more exactly (Piaget, 1957, 1977). Most critics, however, have concluded that none of the versions is very satisfactory, and the theory remains vague and hard to test (Bryant, 1990; Chapman, 1992; Rotman, 1977;

Zimmerman & Blom, 1983). A reasonable conclusion is that Piaget provided a general framework within which a theory of change could be constructed, but that he himself never succeeded in filling in the framework.

Despite the limitations in Piaget's theory of cognitive change, many educators have turned to his writings for ideas about how children learn and about how experiences in school can be made more rewarding. Box 8-3 discusses applications of Piaget's theory to the school setting.

Experimental Training Studies

We turn now from theory to evidence. How might we study the process of cognitive change? There are a number of possible approaches, some of which are discussed in the coming chapters. Here, we concentrate on the approach that has been most common in the Piagetian literature—the training study.

In a training study, we begin with a sample of children who have not yet mastered some Piagetian concept—say, some form of conservation. We begin also with some theory of what particular subskills or kinds of knowledge underlie conservation. We then provide the children, usually in some controlled laboratory setting, with experiences that we think might help them to master these prerequisites and hence to understand conservation. Following the training we administer a posttest to determine whether understanding has improved. If understanding *has* improved, then it may be that our laboratory manipulation tells us something about the real-life routes to conservation.

Several hundred training studies have been carried out in the last 30 years or so. It seems fair to say that this massive effort has not led to the gains in knowledge that researchers initially hoped for (Flavell et al., 1993; Kuhn, 1992a). Nevertheless, three general conclusions can be drawn (Beilin, 1978; D. Field, 1987; Kuhn, 1974).

1. *Training is difficult but by no means impossible.* Instilling a concept like conservation is not a matter of simply pointing out the correct answer. A number of sensible-looking procedures have had no success at all. Such negative outcomes are compatible with Piaget's theory, for they attest to the reality of preoperational thinking and to the slow, gradual nature of cognitive change. Nevertheless, the majority of training studies have reported positive outcomes. By now, there is no longer any doubt that conservation and other Piagetian concepts *can* be experimentally taught.

2. *The success of training depends on the developmental level of the child.* Perhaps the clearest prediction that Piaget's theory makes about training is that the child's readiness should determine its success. Training is beneficial only if the child is already close to mastering the concept, because it is only then that the child will be able to assimilate the new information and make the necessary accommodations to it. Training studies provide general support for this prediction. Training usually works best with older, more mature samples, and very young children are unlikely to be successfully trained. Piaget's theory, however, does not spell out the components of "readiness" very exactly. Hence, specific tests of readiness have been difficult to make, and the notion that learning must wait upon development remains controversial. In some studies, children as young as 4 have been successfully trained in concepts like conservation. This finding fits with an idea discussed earlier—namely, that preoperational children often possess more competence than Piaget believed.

PIAGET AND THE SCHOOL

As we have seen, Piaget's research was inspired by issues in philosophy and was very theoretically oriented. It thus falls in the "basic" rather than "applied" science category. Yet Piaget wrote two books about education (Piaget, 1971, 1976). And others have written extensively about the educational implications of his work (Cowan, 1978; Duckworth, 1987; Ginsburg & Opper, 1988; Kamii & DeVries, 1993; Wadsworth, 1978).

What do Piaget's theory and research have to say about education? Four principles are most often cited. One is the importance of readiness. This principle follows from Piaget's emphasis on assimilation. Experience—educational or otherwise—does not simply happen to the child; rather, it must always be assimilated to current cognitive structures. A new experience will be beneficial only if the child can make some sense of it. Teaching that is too far beyond the child's level is unlikely to have any positive impact.

A second, related principle concerns the motivation for cognitive activity. Educational content that is too advanced is unlikely to be interesting, but the same applies to content that is too simple. What is needed is content that is slightly beyond the child's current level, so that it provides experiences familiar enough to be assimilated yet challenging enough to provoke disequilibrium.

We can hardly work at the child's level unless we know what that level is. A third contribution from Piaget is a wealth of information about what a child does or does not know at different points in development. The message, to be sure, is in part negative—constraints on what can be taught before certain points, cautions about how much development can be accelerated. More positively, Piaget's studies often identify steps and sequences through which particular content domains are mastered. We can thus determine not only where the child is but also the natural next steps for development.

A final principle is more functional. It concerns Piaget's emphasis on intelligence as action. Piaget distrusted educational methods that are too passive, or too rote, or too verbal. In his view, education should build on the child's natural curiosity and natural tendency to act on the world in order to understand it. Knowledge is most meaningful when children construct it themselves rather than have it imposed on them. This principle is expressed in the title of one of Piaget's books about education—*To Understand Is to Invent*.

---

3.   *A wide variety of different training methods have had success.* Some successful training studies have used procedures derived from Piaget's theory—training in reversibility, for example (Wallach, Wall, & Anderson, 1967), or induction of cognitive conflict (Murray, 1982). But other successful studies have used procedures that seem quite distant from what Piaget stressed; examples in this category include operant conditioning (Bucher & Schneider, 1973) and television modeling (Waghorn & Sullivan, 1970). It is difficult to see how Piaget's or any theory can encompass all of the training methods that have proved, in laboratory settings, to be successful. How relevant these laboratory demonstrations are for real-life development remains debatable, because the laboratory situation is always somewhat different from the child's natural environment. To the extent that training studies *are* relevant, however, they suggest that there may be multiple routes to the mastery of concepts like conservation. Some children may acquire conservation through one set of experiences and processes, other children through a different set, and other children through yet a different set.

✔ *To Recap...*

In addition to specifying important changes, a developmental theory must explain how the changes occur. Piaget identified four general factors that contribute to development: matu-

• The Piagetian approach to education stresses the child's own exploration and self-discovery.

Given these guiding principles, what might we expect a Piagetian classroom to look like? Kamii (1985, 1989) provides some examples, centered on the teaching of first- and second-grade arithmetic. The classrooms she describes are less structured looking than those with which most of us are familiar. Rather than using workbooks and preset assignments, teachers attempt to capitalize on the child's spontaneous interests and on the natural activities of everyday life. Thus, a lesson might be built around counting the day's lunch money, or dividing supplies among members of the class, or carrying out a cooking project. Games that nurture mathematical thinking are also prominent— for example, a version of dominoes in which points are gained from even-numbered combinations or a version of tic-tac-toe in which numbers replace the Xs and Os. Peer interaction is encouraged, both during the games and more generally, since the clash of different viewpoints can be an important spur to creative thinking.

Despite the flexibility of the approach, the classrooms described by Kamii are by no means without plans or structures. The guidance and suggestions provided by the teacher are rooted in Piagetian research concerning the natural course of mathematical development. This means, for example, that subtraction is built on a prior understanding of addition and that work with abstract numerical symbols follows the chance to experiment with concrete objects. It means also a continual emphasis on self-discovery— children being free to invent their own approaches to mathematical problem solving rather than having a single approach imposed on them. Kamii's (1985) title thus mirrors Piaget's—*Young Children Reinvent Arithmetic.*

ration, physical experience, social experience, and equilibration. Equilibration is the biological process of self-regulation—the tendency to move toward higher and higher levels of equilibrium. In Piaget's theory it accounts for the organization, motivation, and directionality of development.

The main methodology through which change has been examined is the training study. In a training study, we attempt to teach new knowledge (such as some form of conservation) to children who do not yet possess it. Such studies have demonstrated that training is possible, but they have not yet solved the problem of how real-life change comes about.

CONCLUSION

It is difficult in a single chapter to convey the impact of Piaget's work on the field of child psychology. American child psychologists began to discover Piaget in the late 1950s and the early 1960s, in part because translations of his books began to appear at this time and in part because of the publication of an excellent summary of the work by John Flavell (1963). Since that time, Piaget's writings have inspired literally thousands of studies of children's thinking. The tasks and findings described in this chapter are just a small sampling from this huge research yield (Chapman, 1988; Ginsburg & Opper, 1988; Miller, 1993; Modgil & Modgil, 1976; Voyat, 1982).

Piaget's influence has also extended to the study of topics that he himself had little to say about. We consider a Piagetian-based approach to language development in Chapter 11. And we show in the concluding chapters of the book how Piaget's thinking has influenced the study of children's social development.

At the same time, the research effort of the last 20 years, perhaps inevitably, has revealed a number of problems in Piaget's research and theory. The major criticisms should by now be apparent. Piaget often underestimated children's ability, perhaps especially during the infant and preschool years. Development is not as orderly and consistent as Piaget's stage model seems to imply. Even if the concept of stages is valid, the logical models that Piaget used to characterize the stages are questionable. And Piaget never offered a completely satisfactory explanation of cognitive change. The information-processing perspective, to which we turn in the next chapter, is a major contemporary alternative to Piaget. Psychologists in this tradition do not necessarily deny the insights of Piaget's work; indeed, one subset of information-processing theorists label themselves "neo-Piagetians," to indicate that they are building on a foundation laid by Piaget. The information-processing approach does, however, offer a number of contrasts to Piaget that modern researchers have found attractive.

FOR THOUGHT AND DISCUSSION

1.   Although Piaget's discussions of assimilation focus on infants and children, the process of assimilation is assumed to apply throughout the life span. *Can you think of recent examples from your own life in which your response to some new experience showed the operation of assimilation?*

2.   Modern researchers of infant cognitive development have attempted to devise assessment procedures that are less motorically demanding than the methods used by Piaget. The Baillargeon studies of object permanence are one example. *Imagine that you wished to study infants' understanding of cause-and-effect relations, using procedures similar to those of Baillargeon. What kinds of experiments might you devise?*

3.   Piaget suggested that children are often egocentric—that is, they are unable to break away from their own perspective to take the point of view of someone else. *Are adults also sometimes egocentric? Try to think of experiences you have had in which an adult (possibly yourself) demonstrated egocentrism in his or her interactions with others.*

4.   As we have seen, recent research, using simplified techniques, suggests that young children are more competent than Piaget believed across a number of content areas (e.g., perspective taking, classification, conservation). *Consider the topic of false belief. Is it possible that young children are more competent here as well—that is, that they understand more about false belief than is indicated by the kind of experiments described in the text? How would you modify these experiments to probe for early knowledge?*

5.   When tested with tasks of the sort described by Piaget, children younger than 5 or 6 typically fail to conserve quantities in the face of a misleading perceptual change. Such demonstrations, however, involve experimentally contrived situations in which children are explicitly asked about quantity. *Can you think of naturally occurring situations in which children might fail to conserve? More generally, can you think of real-life settings in which both the achievements and the limitations identified by Piaget might be demonstrated?*

6.   The training-study methodology provides one way to test theories of how cognitive change come about. *Imagine that you wished to devise a conservation training study (or series of studies) based on Piaget's theory. How would your research proceed, and*

what would you predict? Imagine that you wished to take a social-learning approach. In this case, what would be your procedures and predictions?

7. Stage theories such as Piaget's imply that there should be a good deal of consistency in level of cognitive functioning, both within an individual and among individuals of the same age. *Think about the validity of this claim with respect to children you know. Are you more impressed by the similarities or differences among children of the same age? Are you more impressed by the consistency or inconsistency of any one child's level of thinking? Think about the claim with respect to yourself and your peers. Are you all in the same stage of cognitive development?*

Chapter 9

COGNITIVE DEVELOPMENT: THE INFORMATION-PROCESSING APPROACH

A 6-year-old is about to set out for his second day of school. He pauses at the door to collect his pile of books, carefully placed there the night before as a reminder to himself not to forget them. On the way to school, he notes the various landmarks that define his route—the sign at the corner that means turn left, the big tree that tells him that school is just around the bend. Once in the classroom, he struggles again with the task—a fairly new one for him and most first graders—of sitting quietly and paying attention despite all the distracting events around him. There are, in fact, new and important things to pay attention to—letters that must be distinguished from each other, numbers that add together to make other numbers. Not everything is work, however. At recess there is a chance—if only he can remember the rules!—to play the interesting new game learned the day before.

Although much of the content of the first grader's experiences may be new, the psychological processes that underlie his behavior are longstanding ones. From early in life, the child has attended to some aspects of the surrounding environment and ignored others. From early in life, the child has stored information in memory and used this stored knowledge to guide future behavior. From the time that the child could first get around independently, he has needed to note and to remember the spatial environment. And from early in life, the child has taken in information, learned rules, and solved problems—all with regard to both the physical and the social world.

The kinds of psychological processes just sketched are the concern of the information-processing approach to children's intelligence, an approach we examine in this chapter. First, we summarize some of the most important characteristics of information-processing theory and research. We then move on to aspects of child development that have especially intrigued information-processing researchers. We consider several important areas of development, including memory, representa-

• Children's environments present information and cognitive challenges of many sorts. How children come to understand and to respond adaptively to these challenges are the concerns of the information-processing approach.

tion and problem solving, and academic skills. The chapter concludes, as did Chapter 8, with the challenging issue of cognitive change.

THE NATURE OF THE APPROACH

Information processing is a general label for all of the psychological activities touched on in the example above. All involve information of some sort (a spatial landmark, a numerical symbol, an instruction from the teacher), and all involve some kind of processing of this information (attention to critical features, comparison with past memory input, selection of a response). The goal of the information-processing approach is to specify these underlying psychological processes—and the developmental changes they undergo—as exactly as possible. As noted in the preceding chapter, information processing has emerged as a major contemporary approach to the study of children's thinking (Kail & Bisanz, 1992; Klahr, 1989, 1992; Miller, 1993; Siegler, 1983, 1991).

Two images are instructive in characterizing the information-processing approach. One is the flowchart. The other is the computer.

The Flowchart Metaphor

Shown in Figure 9-1 is the symbolic representation of a typical information-processing theory. The particular theory, which deals with memory, contains a number of details that need not concern us here. But its general features are characteristic of the information-processing approach. The starting point is some environmental input, and the end point is some response output. Between stimulus and response a number of psychological processes intervene. In the case of

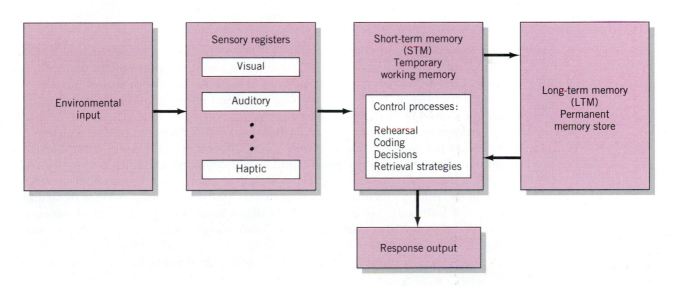

Figure 9-1 An example of an information-processing model of memory. This example illustrates the kind of flowchart representation with which information-processing theorists attempt to describe the sequence of information processing. From "The Control of Short-Term Memory" by R. C. Atkinson and R. M. Shiffrin, 1971, *Scientific American, 225*, p. 82. Copyright 1971 by Scientific American, Inc. Reprinted by permission.

memory, the initial input is assumed to be acted on and transformed in various ways. Imagine, for example, that our first grader has just heard a word for the first time. This word first enters the sensory register—in this case, the auditory register—where a literal image of a stimulus can be held for perhaps a second at most. The word then moves to short-term memory, which is the center for active and conscious processing. Although information typically stays for only a few seconds in short-term memory, various strategies (some of which we consider shortly) may prolong its lifetime considerably. Finally, the word may be transferred to long-term memory, where (as the name suggests) it can exist indefinitely. Getting the word to long-term memory is, of course, the teacher's goal when she presents a new term to be learned. And all of us in fact do have thousands of words stored in permanent memory.

As the figure indicates, more general psychological processes also play a role. Control processes of various sorts affect the maintenance of information and the movement from one store to another. Mechanisms to generate responses are necessary to explain the eventual overt response—for example, the child's ability to say a word that he has recently learned.

The origin of the term *flowchart* should be evident from this example. Information-processing theorists attempt to capture the orderly flow of information through the cognitive system. The origin of the term *information processing* should also be evident. Information is acted on, or processed, in various ways as it moves through the system. The external stimulus and external response—the concerns of traditional learning theory—are only the end points. The real goal of the psychologist—or so maintains the information-processing theorist—is to specify as completely and precisely as possible what comes between stimulus and response. And as our example suggests, even in a seemingly simple case, such as hearing a new word, there may be quite a bit going on.

The Computer Metaphor

The preceding section described a cognitive system that can transform a variety of inputs into a variety of outputs in a systematic and intelligent way. In doing so, it uses stored information and stored rules of various sorts. What sort of intelligent system operates in this way? To anyone immersed in modern Western society, the answer should be obvious—a computer.

Information-processing theorists find the computer a useful tool on a variety of levels. At the most general level, the computer serves as a helpful metaphor for thinking about human cognition. Human and computer are alike in a number of ways. Both store representations or symbols and manipulate these symbols to solve problems. Both perform a variety of such manipulations in an incredibly rapid and powerful fashion. Despite this power, both are limited in the amount of information that they can store and manipulate. Both, however, can learn from experience and modify their rule systems in a progressively adaptive direction. Understanding the operations of computer intelligence may thus lead to insights about human intelligence as well.

Information-processing theorists have drawn from modern computer technology in more specific ways as well. Any theorist of intelligence must decide on a language with which to formulate his or her theory. Piaget, for example, used the language of symbolic logic in constructing his models of cognitive structures. Information-processing theorists have often adopted preexisting computer languages for their theories. The kind of flowchart language depicted in Figure 9-1, for example, was developed by workers in computer science. Such languages have the virtues of precision and (at least to the information-processing theorist) familiarity; they therefore are good vehicles for testing and communicating theories.

At the most specific level, the computer makes possible one of the prime methodologies of the information-processing approach—the **computer simulation**. In a computer simulation, the researcher attempts to program a computer to produce some segment of intelligent behavior in the same way that humans produce the behavior. The idea is to build into the computer program whatever knowledge and rules are thought to be important for the human problem solver. Suppose, for example, that we have a theory of how first graders solve simple addition problems. We might program our computer with the same rules that the children are thought to use and then see how *it* responds to the same tasks. How successfully the program generates the target behavior—in this case, the pattern of first-grade responses—then becomes a test of the investigator's theory of how children arrive at their answers.

> **Computer simulation**
> Programming a computer to perform a cognitive task in the same way that humans are thought to perform it. An information-processing method for testing theories of underlying process.

Comparisons with Piaget

Because our fullest discussion of intelligence to this point has involved the Piagetian approach, comparing the information-processing approach with this view should be instructive. There are both similarities and differences between the two systems.

Information-processing approaches to child development are similar to Piaget's approach in several respects. First, much of the content studied is similar. Information-processing researchers have recognized the importance of the concepts first identified by Piaget, and much of their own research involves attempts to apply information-processing techniques to Piagetian tasks and abilities. Second, similarity exists at a general theoretical level. Information-processing theories, like Piagetian theory, fall within the cognitive-developmental approach to child development. Information-processing theorists agree with Piaget that a complex system of mental rules underlies cognitive performance and that one job of the theorist is to discover what these rules are. Finally, some information-processing theorists follow Piaget in dividing development into distinct stages. Although the stages are not identical to Piaget's, they typically show some important similarities. Because of their grounding in Piaget, this group of information-processing theorists is often referred to as neo-Piagetian (Case, 1992a; Demetriou, Shayer, & Efklides, 1993; Fischer, 1980; Halford, 1993).

The issue of stages, however, also provides an instance of differences between the information-processing and Piagetian approaches. Not all information-processing theorists subscribe to a stage model of development. And even those who may find stages useful differ in important ways from Piaget. The stages proposed by Piaget are the broadest, most general stages that the field of child psychology has seen. To say that a child is in the stage of concrete operations is to make a strong (and, as we saw, debatable) claim about how the child will perform on a wide range of cognitive tasks. Information-processing stage theories tend to be more limited in scope, focusing on particular skills and particular aspects of the child's development. A model might, for example, concentrate on the acquisition of spatial skills, without making any claims about the child's level of performance on other tasks. One way to summarize this difference is to say that the information-processing theorist's stages are more *domain-specific*—that is, more concerned with distinct aspects, or domains, of development.

Other differences between the information-processing and Piagetian approaches can be inferred from the flowchart and computer metaphors. Piaget's theoretical emphasis was always on the logical rules that he thought underlie problem solving, such as the concrete operations of middle childhood and the formal operations of adolescence. He had little to say about many more process-oriented questions that are central to the information-processing researcher. How exactly does the child attend to new information? How is this information taken in and represented in memory? How is it retrieved in the service of problem solving? It would be difficult to construct a full flowchart model of problem solving, let alone a computer simulation, from Piaget's theoretical accounts. Information-processing theorists attempt to develop models that are both more specific and more complete than those offered by Piaget.

These goals of the information-processing approach have both methodological and theoretical implications. Methodologically, the emphasis on precision and testability has led to a number of distinctive methods for studying children's thinking. We have already mentioned one such method—the computer simulation technique—and we describe others later. Theoretically, the emphasis on completeness has meant a concern with a variety of aspects of children's development in addition to the kinds of logical reasoning stressed by Piaget. Much of the work on attention discussed in Chapter 7 was carried out within an information-processing perspective. The same is true for much of the work on memory that we consider next.

✔ To Recap...

The information-processing perspective is a major contemporary approach to the study of cognitive development. Information-processing researchers attempt to describe the underlying cognitive activities, or forms of information processing, that occur between stimulus input and response output. In this attempt, they draw from modern computer science, both for general ideas about human intelligence and for specific languages and methods with which to formulate and test their theories

Like Piaget's theory, information-processing theories fall within the cognitive-developmental approach to development. In addition to sharing Piaget's emphasis on underlying rules or structures, information-processing researchers study many of the same concepts studied by Piaget, and some such researchers (sometimes called neo-Piagetians) propose stage theories that have ties to Piaget's stages. Most information-processing theorists do not subscribe to the kinds of broad, general stages offered by Piaget, however. Their own models are more domain-specific, and they attempt to construct models that are more precise, more complete, and more testable than those proposed by Piaget.

MEMORY IN INFANCY

Children can be affected by their experiences only if they can somehow retain information from these experiences over time. Questions of memory—of how information is taken in, stored, and retrieved—are therefore central to information-processing accounts of development. Because development starts in infancy, the examination of memory must also start with the infant (Olson & Sherman, 1983).

We begin our discussion with a very basic question: Can babies remember? We have already encountered a number of findings that tell us the answer is yes. Many of the phenomena from Piaget's sensorimotor studies demonstrate the presence of memory—for example, the infant's ability to activate a familiar scheme when confronting a familiar object or to search for a plaything that has disappeared. Many of the findings from the study of infant perception discussed in Chapter 7 also imply the use of memory—for example, the effects of experience on the perception of musical melodies. Much of the behavior that we as adults produce would be impossible if we did not remember and were not guided by past experience. The same is true of infants.

How well do babies remember? This question is harder to answer. Even a young infant's memory is in some respects surprisingly good. In other respects, however, infant memory is limited, and many important developmental advances have yet to come.

Psychologists distinguish between two basic forms of memory. **Recognition memory** refers to the realization that some perceptually present stimulus or event has been encountered before. You would be demonstrating recognition memory, for example, if you realized that you had already seen the flowchart memory model (Figure 9-1) when you encountered the same figure in some other book. **Recall memory** refers to the retrieval of some past stimulus or event when the stimulus or event is *not* perceptually present. You would be demonstrating recall memory if you were able to draw the flowchart model (or at least parts of it!) in the absence of any stimulus input. We begin with recognition, then move on to recall.

Recognition memory
The realization that some perceptually present stimulus or event has been encountered before.

Recall memory
The retrieval of some past stimulus or event that is not perceptually present.

Recognition Memory

Methods of Study

How might we determine whether babies can recognize stimuli that they have encountered before? The most common method of study has been the habituation–dishabituation procedure. Habituation is possible only if the infant can recognize a repeated stimulus as something that has been experienced previously; similarly, dishabituation can occur only if the infant can compare the new stimulus to some memory of the original. Classical (or respondent) conditioning and operant conditioning have also been used to explore infant memory. As noted in Chapter 2, learning refers to the lasting effects of experience on behavior, and thus any demonstration of learning necessarily tells us something about memory as well.

One way in which operant conditioning has been employed to study infant memory is pictured in Figure 9-2. As the figure shows, the ribbon linking ankle and mobile confers a potential power on the infant: Kicking the ankle will make the mobile jump. Infants as young as 2 months can learn this relation; the rate of kicking increases when the kicking pays off in the reinforcement of a dancing mobile (Rovee-Collier, 1987). Once this response has been established, various modifications can be introduced to probe the infant's memory. We can test for recognition of the training mobile, for example, by comparing response to a novel mobile with response to the familiar one. Or we can test the duration of the memory by seeing how the infant responds a day or a week or a month after the original conditioning.

Memory in Newborns

A number of questions about infant memory have been explored with these procedures. A natural first question is how early in life babies can remember. The answer seems clear—from birth (or possibly even earlier—recall the suggestion in Chapter 7 that babies may remember some events that they experienced prenatally). Habituation studies are one basis for this conclusion. Habituation is not easy to demonstrate in newborns, and for years infant researchers disagreed about whether

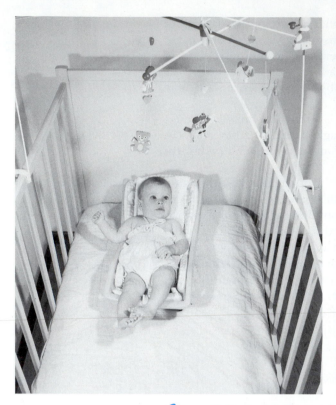 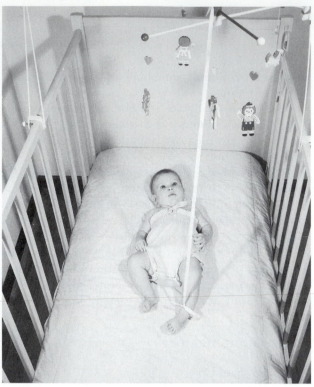

Figure 9-2   An experimental arrangement for studying infants' ability to learn and remember. When the ribbon is attached to the baby's ankle (as in the right-hand photo), kicking the leg makes the mobile above the crib move. Learning is shown by increased kicking whenever the ribbon is attached and the mobile is present. These photos were made available by Dr. C. K. Rovee-Collier.

such early habituation was possible (Slater & Morison, 1991). It now seems clear, however, that a newborn infant—given optimal circumstances—can show habituation across a range of modalities: visual (Slater, Morison, & Rose, 1984), auditory (Zelazo, Weiss, & Tarquino, 1991), and tactile (Kisilevsky & Muir, 1984). Thus newborns do possess some degree of recognition memory. Even infants born 4 weeks prematurely demonstrate some recognition memory soon after birth (Werner & Siqueland, 1978).

Conditioning studies are a further source of evidence for neonatal memory. As with habituation, conditioning can be difficult to produce in very young infants, and the question of whether newborns can be conditioned was for many years a topic of debate. Today, however, most researchers agree that both classical and operant conditioning are possible from birth (Lipsitt, 1990). We have, in fact, already seen some examples of the latter. Recall the finding (Box 7-1) that newborns prefer a stimulus that they have been exposed to prenatally (DeCasper & Fifer, 1980). The newborns showed this preference by adjusting their sucking to produce the desired stimulus—for example, their own mothers' voices. Adjusting behavior to obtain reinforcement is a form of operant conditioning. As with habituation, even premature infants are capable of operant conditioning soon after birth (Thoman & Ingersoll, 1993). An example of classical conditioning in newborns comes from a study in which 1- and 2-day-old infants received a sucrose solution delivered to the lips (Blass, Ganchrow, & Steiner, 1984). The solution functioned as an uncondi-

• One of the most rewarding signs of infant memory is the baby's pleasure at recognizing his parents.

tioned stimulus that elicited the unconditioned response of sucking. The conditioned stimulus consisted of the experimenter's stroking the baby's forehead immediately before delivery of the sucrose. After a few pairings of the stroking with the solution, the babies began to suck in response to the stroking alone—a clear indication that conditioning had occurred.

Developmental Changes

Although memory may be operative from birth, newborns' and young infants' memories are not as powerful as those of older infants. Developmental improvements of various sorts occur during the first year or so of life. One important change is in how long material can be retained. Most demonstrations of memory in newborns involve only a few seconds between presentation of a stimulus and the test for recognition of that stimulus. What such studies show, then, is very short-term memory. As infants develop, the length of time across which they can remember their experiences steadily increases, soon reaching quite impressive levels. By 5 months of age, babies can recognize a stimulus, after a delay of 2 weeks, that they saw for only 2 minutes (Fagan, 1973)! We should add, however, that even the newborn is not limited to very brief memories. One recent study (Swain, Zelazo, & Clifton, 1993) provides evidence that newborns can remember speech sounds across a period of 24 hours. And the studies of memory for speech sounds experienced prenatally (DeCasper & Spence, 1991—see Box 7-1) have typically involved even longer intervals between the last prenatal exposure and the first postnatal test.

The mobile procedure shown in Figure 9-2 provides another approach to assessing the durability of infant memory. The question is how long babies can remember the association between kicking and the movement of the mobile. This procedure, too, reveals both impressive early capacity and developmental improvements in long-term memory with age (Howe & Courage, 1993; Rovee-Collier & Bhatt, 1993). Two-month-olds, for example, can remember the association for 3 days; by 3 months of age the span has stretched to 8 days, and by 6 months some retention is still evident 21 days after conditioning (Rovee-Collier, 1987; Rovee-Collier & Shyi, 1992). Memory is even better if the infant is given a brief reminder during the delay period. In a study by Sullivan (1982), the experimenter jiggled the mobile on the 13th day of the delay period while the infant simply watched. Infants given this reminder showed much more kicking on day 14 than a control group that received no such help. Such priming of memory through a brief reencounter with the original experience is referred to as **reactivation**. Naturally occurring instances of reactivation may be a major way in which forgetting is prevented and memories are kept alive (Rovee-Collier & Hayne, 1987).

Reactivation
The preservation of the memory for an event through reencounter with at least some portion of the event in the interval between initial experience and memory test.

In addition to the duration of memory, another basic question concerns what information the infant retains. Babies' habituation to a stimulus tells us that they recognize *some* aspect of the stimulus, but it does not tell us exactly what they are remembering. This dimension of memory also shows developmental improvements across infancy. Older infants can remember both more information and more complex information than younger infants (Olson & Sherman, 1983; Rose, 1981). Older infants can also abstract and remember general categories of information and not just specific stimuli (Bornstein & Lamb, 1992; Younger, 1993). In one study, for example, 12- to 24-month-old infants were shown a series of pictures of various kinds of food (bread, hot dogs, salami, and so on). The infants were then given a choice of looking at either of two stimuli: a previously unseen item from the food category (an apple) or an item from a new category (a chair). Infants looked longer at the chair than the apple, thus demonstrating that they recognized not just specific foods but the general category of food and that they found a new category more interesting than a familiar one (Ross, 1980). Other studies with similar procedures have demonstrated even earlier categorization skills, most notably for face stimuli. Infants of about 7 to 8 months have been shown to categorize faces on the basis of gender (Fagan, 1976), orientation (Cohen & Strauss, 1979), and expression (Ludemann & Nelson, 1988).

Categorization skills can also be demonstrated in operant conditioning studies with the dancing-mobile procedure. Suppose that instead of presenting a single mobile to be learned, we complicate the baby's task by offering a series of different mobiles, only some of which pay off in reinforcement. We might reinforce response to a series of blue mobiles, for example, but not to mobiles of other colors. Or we might vary the pictures on the mobile, or the complexity of the overall design, or the pattern in which different mobiles are presented across days. In so doing, we can determine whether the baby can recognize and respond appropriately to a general class of stimuli, and not just a single specific exemplar. By 3 months of age babies are in fact capable of this kind of learning and memory. They can learn to respond to a general category of stimuli, such as all the mobiles of a particular shape or a particular color (Hayne, Greco-Vigorito, & Rovee-Collier, 1993; Hayne, Rovee-Collier, & Perris, 1987). They can also learn a more abstract rule for response—for example, to respond if the mobile is new but not if it is one that they have seen before (Fagen et al., 1984). The ability to move beyond specific experiences to form more general categories is an essential component in our attempts to make sense of the world. The habituation and conditioning studies suggest that this ability emerges very early.

Recall Memory

The studies just reviewed indicate clearly that recognition memory is present from birth. But what about recall? Can infants not only recognize familiar stimuli or events but also actively call such stimuli or events to mind?

Recall memory is considerably more difficult to study in infancy than is recognition memory, because infants cannot produce the responses that are used to study recall in older subjects (such as verbal reports or drawing). There is, in fact, no clear agreement on exactly what a young infant might do that would demonstrate recall and thus no agreement on exactly when recall emerges. It does seem clear that recall is present by the end of infancy, as many of the behaviors from Piaget's sensorimotor stage 6 imply. An infant could not show deferred imitation, for example, without the ability to recall a model from the past, nor could she produce words appropriately without some capacity for recall.

Recently, some researchers have suggested that simple forms of recall may emerge considerably earlier in infancy (Mandler, 1988, 1990). The infant's search for vanished objects is one possible index. By the end of the first year most infants can find objects that are hidden in a single location (Piaget's stage 4 of object permanence). Most have also learned the permanent locations for familiar and valued objects, such as the cupboard in which a favorite cereal is kept (Ashmead & Perlmutter, 1980). The ability to find an object that one has not seen for days would certainly seem to imply some capacity for recall.

Recent studies of deferred imitation provide further evidence for recall memory in infancy. These studies indicate that the capacity to reproduce a model from the past emerges earlier than Piaget believed. By 9 months of age infants can imitate a novel action that they viewed a full 24 hours earlier (Meltzoff, 1988b), and by 14 months the retention span has stretched to 1 week (Meltzoff, 1988a). Infants can remember and imitate not just isolated behaviors but simple sequences of action. Thirteen-month-olds, for example, can reproduce three-action sequences for such events as giving Teddy Bear a bath (first place in tub, then wash with sponge, then dry with towel) or constructing a simple rattle (place ball

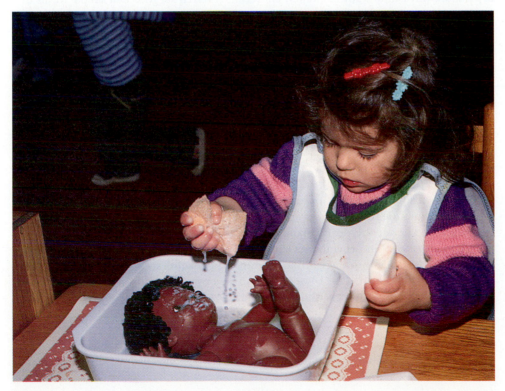

• Memory for the order of events emerges early in life. Even 1-year-olds can remember simple sequences, such as the order to follow in giving a doll a bath.

in large cup, invert small cup into large, shake) (Bauer & Mandler, 1992). Memory for the order in which events occur is an important form of knowledge to which we will return shortly. These studies indicate that such memory has its origins in infancy.

We saw that infants' ability to recognize familiar stimuli may eventually extend across a considerable period of time. Less is known about the durability of early recall, but there is some evidence for long-term retention here as well. In a study by Cutts and Ceci (1988), infants between 8 and 18 months of age learned to remove a puppet's glove to obtain a treat hidden inside. Four months after the learning sessions the puppet and glove were reintroduced. Many (although not all) of the infants immediately pulled the glove off, thus demonstrating some memory for the earlier situation. Even more impressive long-term memory is suggested in a study by McDonough and Mandler (1989). McDonough and Mandler first taught their 11-month-old subjects to imitate simple sequences of actions, as in the Teddy Bear and rattle tasks described above. When the infants were retested as 23-month-olds they showed some ability to reproduce the actions that they had seen modeled a full year earlier! The question of the persistence of infant memories is another topic to which we will return shortly.

✔ *To Recap...*

Infants can remember from birth. Habituation, classical conditioning, and operant conditioning all imply memory, and all have been demonstrated in newborn babies. With development, the span of time across which the infant can retain material increases, as does the amount and the complexity of the material that can be retained.

Habituation and conditioning studies demonstrate recognition memory. Recall memory is more difficult to study in infancy, but recent research suggests that simple forms of recall may emerge by the end of the first year. Infants' ability to search for vanished objects provides one kind of evidence for this conclusion. Imitation of models from the past provides another.

MEMORY IN OLDER CHILDREN

Beyond infancy, most studies of how children remember have concentrated on various forms of recall. The most general change in this type of memory is an obvious one: Older children remember better than younger children. This fact was undoubtedly apparent to parents and teachers long before there was research to verify it. It has also long been apparent to test makers. All of the IQ tests described in Chapter 10 include memory as one of their components. On the average, the older the child, the better the performance on such memory measures.

Developmental improvements in memory are of considerable practical importance, because they influence what parents and teachers expect of children and how they treat children. The 10-year-old can be entrusted with a string of verbal instructions that would overtax the memory of a 4-year-old. Such improvements are also of theoretical interest. How can we explain the fact that older children remember better than younger ones? Several kinds of explanation have been offered, and each seems to capture part of the basis for developmental change. Here we consider three possible contributors to the developmental improvement in memory: greater use of mnemonic strategies, greater knowledge about memory, and more powerful cognitive structures.

The Role of Strategies

Imagine that you are confronted with the following task. A list of words (such as that in Table 9-1) is presented at the rate of one every 5 seconds. There is a 30-second delay following the last word, and you must then recall as many of the words as possible. How might you proceed? Adults faced with such a task are likely to do any of a variety of things to help themselves remember. They may say the words over and over again as the list is presented and during the delay period. They may seek to make the list more memorable by grouping the words into categories—noting, for example, that several of the items name foods and several others name animals. Or they may attempt to create associations among the words by imagining a scenario in which several of the words are linked—for example, a mental image of a cow eating a banana while riding a bicycle.

The approaches just sketched are examples of **mnemonic strategies**. A mnemonic strategy is any technique that people use in an attempt to help themselves remember something. The examples just given correspond, in fact, to three of the most often studied strategies in research on memory: *rehearsal* of the items to be recalled (the saying-over-and-over technique), *organization* of the items into conceptual categories (grouping into foods, animals, and so on), and *elaboration* of the items by linkage in some more general image or story (the picture of the cow on the bicycle).

An increase in the tendency to use strategies is one important source of the improvements in memory that come with age. Dozens of studies have demonstrated that older children are more likely than younger children to generate and employ mnemonic strategies (Bjorklund, 1990; Hasselhorn, 1990; Ornstein, Baker-Ward, & Naus, 1988; Schneider & Pressley, 1989). This finding holds for the three strategies just mentioned: rehearsal (Flavell, Beach, & Chinsky, 1966), organization (Moely, 1977), and elaboration (Kee & Guttentag, 1994). It also holds for other mnemonic strategies that develop across childhood—for example, the ability to direct one's attention and effort in optimal ways, such as by attending to central rather than irrelevant information (Miller, 1990) or by concentrating on difficult rather than easy items (Dufresne & Kobasigawa, 1989).

Do strategies work? The answer in general is yes: Children who use strategies show better recall than children who do not. Children do not always benefit from their initial attempts to employ a strategy, perhaps because executing a new strategy places too much demand on their limited information-processing resources. This failure of a recently developed strategy to facilitate recall is labeled a **utilization deficiency** (Miller & Seier, in press). Usually, however, even young children derive some benefit from the use of strategies; their main problem is simply that they do not generate strategies in the first place. Before about age 5 or 6, it apparently simply does not occur to children that it makes sense to *do* something to help themselves remember. This failure to generate strategies spontaneously, even though the child is capable of executing and benefiting from a strategy, is referred to as a **production deficiency** (Flavell, 1970).

Strategies increase not only in frequency but also in complexity as children get older. Rehearsal is a relatively simple strategy and is, in fact, one of the first to emerge, typically appearing at about age 6 or 7. Organization appears somewhat

TABLE 9-1 ● **Items to be Recalled on a Short-Term Memory Test**

Cow	Truck
Tree	Hat
Banana	Bear
Bicycle	Apple
Dog	Flag
Orange	Horse

Mnemonic strategies
Techniques (such as rehearsal or organization) that people use in an attempt to remember something.

Utilization deficiency
The failure of a recently developed mnemonic strategy to facilitate recall.

Production deficiency
The failure to generate a mnemonic strategy spontaneously.

later, and elaboration later still. There are also developmental changes in complexity within a particular strategy. Younger children's rehearsal efforts, for example, tend to be limited to naming each item as it appears. Older children are more likely to repeat larger chunks of the list each time ("cow," "cow-tree," "cow-tree-banana," and so on—Ornstein, Naus, & Liberty, 1975). Similarly, younger children tend to rehearse only when the items are perceptually present, whereas older children also recognize the value of rehearsing the items in their absence (Locke & Fehr, 1970). In general, older children can generate more complex strategies than younger children, they are better able to match particular strategy to particular task, and they are more skilled at executing their strategies—all of which contributes to their superior memory performance.

We noted that on many memory tasks, children younger than 5 or 6 do not display strategies. Does this mean that the young child is totally incapable of generating a mnemonic strategy? Not at all. If the task is sufficiently simplified, even quite young children may show rudimentary strategies. In one study, for example, 3-year-olds played a game in which they had to keep track of a toy dog that had been hidden under one of several cups. During the delay between hiding and retrieval, many of the children sat with their eyes glued to the critical cup and a finger planted firmly on it (Wellman, Ritter, & Flavell, 1975). These are simple strategies, to be sure, but they *are* strategies, and they are available to even young children. Furthermore, they work. Children who produced such strategies showed better recall than children who did not. Other studies using a similar hide-and-seek procedure have demonstrated that children as young as 18 to 24 months can produce and benefit from simple strategies (DeLoache, Cassidy, & Brown, 1985; Wellman, 1988). The general conclusion to be drawn from such research should sound familiar from the discussion of preschoolers' strengths in Chapter 8. Young children are by no means as competent as older children—in memory or in logical reasoning. When tested in simple and familiar contexts, however, they can sometimes show surprising abilities.

Just as strategies may begin to develop earlier than experts once thought, so they may continue to develop beyond the grade-school years that have been the focus of most memory research. Recent studies have shown that complex mnemonic strategies continue to be refined well into adolescence and even adulthood (Pressley, Levin, & Bryant, 1983). Of particular interest to researchers have been the various study strategies that students develop to cope with school material. Study strategies include specific techniques such as note taking and outlining. They also include more general methods, such as allocation of study time to important or not-yet-mastered material and self-testing to determine what has been learned and what needs to be studied further. With development, children come to use such strategies more and more frequently, and the complexity of the strategies that they are capable of generating also increases. Furthermore, children (and also adolescents and adults) benefit from their strategies. Research reveals a clear relation between the use of appropriate study strategies and the quality of the child's learning (Brown et al., 1983; Paris & Oka, 1986; Pressley, Forrest-Pressley, & Elliot-Faust, 1988). Thus, once again, strategies work (a reassuring message to any student who takes pages of notes!).

The research on study strategies is of interest not only because it extends the developmental picture to older ages but also because of its focus on important content drawn from the child's everyday experience. One limitation of much of the research on strategies is that it has examined memory for arbitrary and meaningless material (such as the list of words in Table 9-1). The work on study strategies veri-

• Mnemonic strategies are not limited to laboratory settings. Study strategies can help to ensure that important material is remembered.

fies that strategies are indeed important in the child's real-life attempts to commit important information to memory. Furthermore, this work has a clear applicational message: If we can help children learn ways to study, then we can improve their chances of success in school. In recent years a number of intervention programs have verified the value of explicitly teaching children to use mnemonic strategies (Brown & Campione, 1990; Brown, Palincsar, & Armbruster, 1984; Pressley et al., 1988). These experimental studies are complemented by naturalistic research that demonstrates that many teachers do in fact promote the development of adaptive study strategies through various classroom practices (Moely et al., 1992).

Research on strategies illustrates one important theme of the information-processing approach (Siegler, 1991). The child's—and, for that matter, the adult's—information-processing capacities are always limited. Only a limited amount of information can fit in short-term memory, for example, and this information typically can be held only briefly. If new information can be rehearsed, however, its lifetime can be extended considerably. If the child can think in terms of categories and not just individual items, then much more can be retained. Much of development consists of the creation of techniques to overcome information-processing limitations and thereby increase the power of the cognitive system. Mnemonic strategies are a prime example of such techniques.

DEVELOPMENT IN CONTEXT: Don't Forget to Take the Cupcakes out of the Oven: Memory at Home and in the Lab

Consider the following set of tasks (Ceci & Bronfenbrenner, 1985): remembering to take one's daily vitamins, remembering to catch the morning bus, remembering to send an anniversary card, and remembering to turn off the bath water before the bathroom floods. All of these activities fall clearly under the heading of what we normally mean by "memory." Yet they differ in two ways from most of the memory tasks that we have considered to this point. First, most memory studies have concentrated on memory of past events—a set of pictures presented the day before, a list of words recently read. As the examples illustrate, however, often the direction of memory is not backward but forward: remembering to carry out some activity in the future. Memory that is directed to future activities is referred to as **prospective memory**.

The second difference concerns the context for the memory. Most memory studies have examined performance in laboratory settings, often for arbitrary sets of material. But there is clearly nothing arbitrary or laboratory-bound about taking pills or catching the bus. The same point applies, of course, to most of the memory activities that each of us engages in every day.

These two emphases—prospective memory and memory in context—have been brought together in an intriguing series of studies by Ceci and Bronfenbrenner (1985; Ceci, Bronfenbrenner, & Baker, 1988). Ceci and Bronfenbrenner's subjects (10- and 14-year-olds) were given one of two tasks to carry out: baking cupcakes or charging a motorcycle battery. In both cases, the critical element of task performance was the timing: remove the cupcakes from the oven (or the cables from the battery) after 30 minutes. A wall clock was available so that the children could monitor the time. Also available for the child's use during the 30-minute wait was a Pac Man game, placed at some distance from both the oven (or battery) and the clock. This arrangement ensured that the children would have to make some effort to check the clock, and that their clock checking could be easily recorded by an observer. A final aspect of the study concerned context. Half of the children were

Prospective memory
Memory directed to the performance of future activities.

tested in a university setting, and half were tested in their own homes. In the case of the home testing, the observers were the children's own older siblings.

What is the optimal pattern of clock checking for a task like baking cupcakes? Ceci and Bronfenbrenner hypothesized that the most efficient performers would show a U-shaped pattern. During the first minutes, clock checking should be high, as subjects attempt to synchronize their psychological clocks with the actual clock. Once this synchronization is accomplished, clock checking should drop off for a while, only to rise again as the end of the 30-minute interval nears. Children who show this pattern (labeled by Ceci and Bronfenbrenner as *strategic monitoring*) should be able to perform their assigned task successfully and still have plenty of time left over for Pac Man. Such children can be contrasted with two other groups—those who accomplish the task, but only at the expense of continually watching the clock, and those whose monitoring of time is so sporadic that they let the cupcakes burn.

Ceci and Bronfenbrenner found that different children did in fact show different patterns of clock checking. But more interesting were the effects of context. The total amount of time spent watching the clock was greater in the laboratory than in the home. This finding related to a second finding: Strategic monitoring was greater in the home than in the lab. Thus, children were more likely to discover the optimal strategy when tested in the familiar setting of their own home. The lab–home contrast also affected the operation of other variables in the study. Older children were more strategic than younger children, for example, but only when tested in the laboratory setting. Similarly, the gender-typed nature of the tasks (baking versus batteries) produced some differential effects for boys and girls—again, however, only in the laboratory context.

The most general point that the Ceci and Bronfenbrenner research makes concerns the importance of taking context into account when assessing children's cognitive abilities. The children in their study showed one level of strategic performance when assessed in the laboratory (the usual setting for psychology research) but a different, higher level of performance when tested at home. Similarly, the laboratory test led to one set of conclusions about age and gender differences, yet the pattern proved different when the children were observed at home. Ceci and Bronfenbrenner stress that their intent is not to question the value of laboratory study but rather to call for research that explores the complete range of contexts in which children's abilities develop and are demonstrated. And as we saw in Chapter 2, it is Bronfenbrenner himself who has provided the fullest analysis of the various settings and systems within which children develop.

The Role of Metamemory

Although strategies are an important source of developmental improvements in memory, they are not the only contributor. What children know about memory also changes with age, and these changes in knowledge contribute to changes in memory.

Metamemory refers to knowledge about memory. It includes knowledge about memory in general—for example, the fact that recognition tasks are easier than recall tasks or that a short list of items is easier to memorize than a long list. It also includes knowledge about one's own memory—for example, the ability to judge whether one has studied an assignment long enough to do well on an exam.

Psychologists have been interested in metamemory for two general reasons. First, it is an important outcome of the child's cognitive development. Traditionally,

Metamemory
Knowledge about memory.

research on cognitive development has concentrated on the child's understanding of external stimuli and events—in some cases physical stimuli (as in Piaget's conservation tasks) and in some cases social ones (as in studies of social cognition). Children's thinking is not limited to external stimuli, however; it also encompasses the internal, mental world. Flavell (1971) was among the first child psychologists to focus explicitly on "thinking about thinking," and he coined the term *metacognition* to refer to thoughts that have mental or psychological phenomena as their target. With metamemory, the focus is on thoughts about memory.

Children's thinking about memory changes in a variety of ways as they develop. Here we note just a few of the questions that have been examined. A basic question is whether the child realizes that there is such a thing as memory. Even young children do show some such knowledge. They may behave differently, for example, when told to remember something than when told simply to look, thus demonstrating some awareness that remembering may require special cognitive activities (Baker-Ward, Ornstein, & Holden, 1984). They also have some understanding of the relative difficulty of different memory tasks. By age 5 or 6, most children realize that familiar items are easier to remember than unfamiliar ones (Kreutzer, Leonard, & Flavell, 1975), that short lists are easier to learn than long ones (Wellman, 1977), that recognition is easier than recall (Speer & Flavell, 1979), and that forgetting becomes more likely over time (Lyon & Flavell, 1993). In other respects, however, young children's metamemory is limited. They do not always show differential behavior when faced with an explicit request to remember (Appel et al., 1972). They do not yet understand many phenomena of memory, such as the fact that related items are easier to recall than unrelated ones (Kreutzer et al., 1975) or that remembering the gist of a story is easier than remembering the exact words (Kreutzer et al., 1975; Kurtz & Borkowski, 1987; Myers & Paris, 1978). And their assessment of their own mnemonic abilities is far too optimistic. In one study, for example, over half of the preschool and kindergarten subjects predicted that they would be able to recall all 10 items from a list of 10, a performance that no child in fact came close to achieving (Flavell, Friedrichs, & Hoyt, 1970). Furthermore, young children do not adjust their expectations readily in response to feedback; even after recalling only 2 or 3 items on one trial, they may blithely assert that they will get all 10 on the next attempt (Yussen & Levy, 1975). Older children are both more modest and more realistic in assessing their own memories (Schneider & Pressley, 1989).

The second general reason for interest in metamemory concerns its possible contribution to developmental changes in memory performance. We stated the argument at the beginning of this section. Older children know more about memory than younger children; older children also remember better than younger children. It is easy to see how these two facts might be related. Knowledge of the demands of different sorts of memory tasks should help the child to select the best strategy for remembering. Knowledge of one's own memory should be important in deciding such things as how to allocate attention and what material to study further.

Obvious though the knowledge–behavior relationship seems, demonstrating it empirically has proved surprisingly difficult. Many studies that have assessed both metamemory and memory performance (focusing usually on the child's use of strategies) have reported only modest correlations, at best, between the two (Cavanaugh & Perlmutter, 1982). Thus, the knowledge that children can demonstrate about memory does not always relate clearly to how they perform on memory tasks. The following quotation, taken from one of the first metamemory studies, suggests a possible reason for this discrepancy. In it, a little girl describes a wonderfully complex procedure for memorizing phone numbers (her metaknowledge) but then suggests at the end that her actual behavior might be quite different.

> Say the number is 633-8854. Then what I'd do is—say that my number is 633, so I won't have to remember that, really. And then I would think now I've got to remember 88. Now I'm 8 years old, so I can remember, say my age two times. Then I say how old my brother is, and how old he was last year. And that's how I'd usually remember that phone number. [Is that how you would most often remember a phone number?] Well, usually I write it down. (Kreutzer, Leonard, & Flavell, 1975, p. 11)

Despite the difficulty in establishing knowledge–behavior links, most researchers remain convinced that the growth of metamemory is one source of developmental improvement in memory. It is simply hard to believe that what children know does not exert an important influence on how they behave. And indeed, the most recent studies of the issue have been more successful than the earlier work at identifying relations between knowledge and behavior (Borkowski, Milstead, & Hale, 1988; Fabricius & Cavalier, 1989; Hasselhorn, 1992; Melot & Corroyer, 1992; Schneider & Pressley, 1989). One promising approach has been to train children in various forms of metamemory and then look for possible effects on subsequent memory performance (Ghatala et al., 1985; Pressley, Borkowski, & O'Sullivan, 1985). Such training does in fact improve memory. Like the work on mnemonic strategies, research such as this is potentially valuable for its applied usefulness as well as its theoretical implications. For example, it may prove possible to help children with memory problems by teaching them about memory itself. Indeed, some of the most successful of the strategy training programs discussed earlier included instruction in metamemory. Apparently, children are most likely to benefit from memory training if they learn not only what to do but *why* to do it. (Although accurate metamemory is generally desirable, young children's limited metamemory may sometimes be beneficial. Box 9-1 discusses this issue.)

The studies of metamemory illustrate a second general theme of the information-processing approach. We have stressed the information-processing theorist's emphasis on the many different processes that go into intelligent behavior. These processes do not occur in isolation, however, nor do they occur without direction. The child must somehow select and coordinate specific cognitive activities, and a full model of intelligence must explain how this selection and coordination occur. The case of mnemonic strategies provides a good illustration. A strategy like rehearsal does not simply happen. Rather, other cognitive processes must decide that rehearsal is an appropriate strategy, monitor its execution, and evaluate its success. In short, some sort of "executive" must control the more specific forms of information processing. Work on metamemory is directed to one sort of executive control—the child's knowledge of memory as a determinant of the ways in which he or she goes about remembering.

The Role of Knowledge

Our final explanation for developmental improvements in memory is perhaps the most straightforward. It concerns the effects of knowledge on memory. Memory and knowledge are in fact closely related. What we know about a topic is an important determinant of how well we remember information about that topic. Older children generally know more about all sorts of things than do younger children, and thus older children generally remember better than do younger children.

Studies that have attempted to specify the ways in which knowledge affects memory have taken a variety of directions. We discuss such research under three (overlapping) headings: constructive memory, expertise, and scripts.

Constructive Memory

The notion of constructive memory is easiest to introduce through example. Table 9-2 presents an example used in research with grade-school children. Children were first read the story and then asked the eight questions listed beneath it.

Any reader is likely to spot a difference between the first four questions and the last four. The first four tap verbatim memory for information that was directly given in the story. The last four, however, concern information that was never explicitly provided. We are never told, for example, that Linda likes to take care of animals. Yet any adult reader of the story knows that she does. And so, it turns out, do most young children.

The ability to answer questions 5 through 8 is a function of constructive memory. **Constructive memory** refers to the ways in which people's general knowledge system structures and reworks the information they take in and thus affects what they remember. The basic idea is that we do not simply record memories as a tape recorder would. Memory always involves acting on and integrating new experiences in light of what we already know—it always involves an attempt to understand, not merely to record. In our attempt to understand, we continually draw inferences and go beyond the information given. The eventual memory is therefore truly a construction and not merely a direct duplication of experience. And this is why we, and the 6-year-old, can come away from the story in Table 9-2 knowing that Linda likes to take care of animals.

Let us consider another example. Eleven-year-olds were read sentences such as "His mother baked a cake" and "Her friend swept the kitchen floor" (Paris & Lindauer, 1976). Later they were asked to recall the sentences. Half of the children were given retrieval cues—hints that might help them remember. The retrieval cues were the names of the instruments implied by the sentences—*oven* for the sen-

Constructive memory Effects of the general knowledge system on how information is interpreted and thus remembered.

TABLE 9-2 ● Story Used in Study of Constructive Memory With Children

Linda was playing with her new doll in front of her big red house. Suddenly she heard a strange sound coming from under the porch. It was the flapping of wings. Linda wanted to help so much, but she did not know what to do. She ran inside the house and grabbed a shoe box from the closet. Then Linda looked inside her desk until she found eight sheets of yellow paper. She cut the paper into little pieces and put them in the bottom of the box. Linda gently picked up the helpless creature and took it with her. Her teacher knew what to do.

1. Was Linda's doll new?
2. Did Linda grab a match box?
3. Was the strange sound coming from under the porch?
4. Was Linda playing behind her house?
5. Did Linda like to take care of animals?
6. Did Linda take what she found to the police station?
7. Did Linda find a frog?
8. Did Linda use a pair of scissors?

Source: From "Integration and Inference in Children's Comprehension and Memory" by S. G. Paris, 1975. In F. Restle, R. Shiffrin, J. Castellan, H. Lindman, and D. Pisoni (Eds.), *Cognitive Theory*, Vol. 1 (p. 233), Hillsdale, NJ: Erlbaum. Copyright 1975 by Lawrence Erlbaum Associates. Reprinted by permission.

THE BENEFITS OF BEING WRONG

Young children are often inaccurate in judging their own memories, predicting that they will remember more than they actually do. Such overoptimism extends to other cognitive domains as well. It is found in preschool children's beliefs about their ability to imitate a model's behaviors. In one study, for example (Bjorklund, Gaultney, & Green, 1993), many 3-year-olds predicted that they would be able to imitate a model who juggled three balls at a time, even though none could actually reproduce such a challenging behavior. Overoptimism is also common in young grade-school children's self-assessments of academic ability (Stipek, 1984; Stipek & Mac Iver, 1989). Children who are just beginning school tend to offer quite high, and also quite unrealistic, assessments of how well they will do at math or reading, and they show only a limited ability to adjust their beliefs when actual performance falls short of expectation.

Holding inaccurate beliefs is generally regarded as undesirable, and indeed much of cognitive development consists of replacing erroneous beliefs with more accurate ones. In a recent article, however,

Bjorklund and Green (1992) propose that the kinds of metacognitive errors just described may actually be adaptive for young children. Their argument is a motivational one. Suppose—to take the imitation task as an example—that 3-year-olds realized just how unlikely they are to succeed at juggling three balls at a time and just how far they are from ever achieving such mastery. If children in fact perceived their own abilities this accurately, then they would have little motivation to persist at the task: Why try something that you are certain to fail? It is precisely because young children do not clearly realize their own limitations that they are motivated to keep trying—not just at imitating complex behaviors but at dozens of other childhood tasks as well. And it is through such persistence that the limitations are gradually overcome and mastery attained.

Bjorklund and Green's argument can be applied to research on memory strategies. Recall that one finding from the study of strategies is that children's first attempts to apply a strategy often yield little or no benefit, a phenomenon labeled *utilization deficiency*. Why

tence about baking, *broom* for the sentence about sweeping, and so on. Children given the cues recalled more than children who received no such help. But why should such cues be helpful? The sentences, after all, did not contain the words *oven* and *broom*. The cues were helpful because the children had gone beyond the information given in the sentences to fill in the missing elements. Having already inferred what the instrument must be, they were easily able to use *oven* or *broom* as a cue to what they had actually heard. Indeed, these implicit cues were just as effective as explicit cues drawn directly from the sentences (*cake, floor*, and so on).

It seems clear that memory is constructive from early in life. At every age, children filter new experiences through their existing knowledge systems, and what they ultimately remember depends on how they interpret experiences. Constructive memory does change across childhood, however, and the changes are of two general sorts. First, with increased age, memory becomes even more constructive, as children become increasingly active in processing information and increasingly likely to draw inferences that allow them to go beyond the literal input. In the retrieval-cues study just described, for example, 7- and 9-year-olds showed little benefit from the implicit cues that were so helpful for 11-year-olds (Paris & Lindauer, 1976). Although certainly capable of inferring "oven" from "baked a cake," the younger children apparently did not spontaneously make such inferences. Second, with increased age, the complexity of the inferences that children

should children persist at using a strategy that is not working for them? One possible explanation is that they do not realize the strategy is not working—they have enough metamemory competence to know that the strategy can be helpful but not enough to monitor and evaluate their own use of it. Another possibility is that they realize that the strategy is not working yet but that they remain optimistic about the future: *Next* time it will pay off. In either case, young children's metacognitive optimism keeps them from giving up after a few failures. And because they do not give up, they become more skilled at executing the strategy, and eventually they begin to profit from it.

Bjorklund and Green's analysis extends beyond metacognition to other limitations of preschool cognition. They suggest ways, for example, in which preschoolers' egocentrism may actually aid their cognitive and social development, as well as advantages that may result from young children's slowness at processing information. The general point is that the long period of immaturity that characterizes human development is not necessarily negative. Young children's immaturity may help them learn what they need to learn.

• Young children often believe that they can accomplish tasks that are beyond their abilities. Such overoptimism may be beneficial, because it helps children to persevere even if they initially fail.

can draw increases as their cognitive abilities increase. In the injured-bird story, for example, even most 5-year-olds could answer questions 7 and 8. Questions 5 and 6, however, require a somewhat higher-order inference and hence were solved at a slightly later age.

Another example of constructive memory will help to make one final point. The example comes from Piaget's only research on memory. Piaget and Inhelder (1973) presented 3- to 8-year-old children with the stimulus shown in the top half of Figure 9-3. The sticks in the figure constitute a *seriated array*—that is, an array in which the stimuli are perfectly ordered along some quantitative dimension, in this case, length. As we saw in Chapter 8, Piaget's previous research had established that an understanding of seriation is a concrete operational achievement, typically coming at age 6 or 7. One week after they had seen the sticks, the children in Piaget's study were asked to draw what they had seen. The bottom half of the figure shows the kinds of drawings that the youngest children produced. It can be seen that the children's memories were not only wrong but systematically wrong. Their drawings, in fact, corresponded exactly to the various errors that preoperational children make in attempting to solve the seriation task. Piaget's interpretation was that the children assimilated the input to their preoperational understanding of seriation. In so doing, they reworked and distorted the experience. The eventual memory thus reflected their understanding and not simply the literal stimulus.

Figure 9-3 Stimulus and typical responses in Piaget and Inhelder's study of constructive memory: (*a*) the seriated array presented to the children and (*b*) what 4- and 5-year-olds remembered a week later. The memory distortions result from the young child's preoperational assimilation of the stimulus.

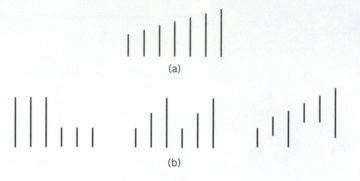

The point that the Piagetian research makes is that constructive memory can operate in a negative as well as a positive direction. When some new experience is too advanced for the child, the child's memory of the experience is likely to be simplified and perhaps even distorted. Other factors besides cognitive level can sometimes result in such "constructive" distortions. It has been shown, for example, that children's beliefs about gender differences may influence how they process information about males and females. Children who viewed pictures in which gender-stereotypic activities were reversed (e.g., a girl sawing and a boy playing with dolls) showed a tendency on a later memory test to "correct" these images, reporting, for example, that it was the boy who did the sawing (Martin & Halverson, 1983a). Similarly, children's beliefs about different ethnic groups have been shown to influence what they remember about members of those groups (Bigler & Liben, 1993).

The constructive nature of memory, then, is a mixed blessing. In general, constructive memory is a positive force, helping us to understand experience more adaptively. But in particular instances, constructive memory can distort and mislead. In Box 9-2 we discuss one situation in which it may be essential to know how accurate children's memories are.

Expertise

Like constructive memory, expertise is easiest to introduce through example. The subject for a study by Chi and Koeske (1983) was a 4-year-old boy who, thanks to a large collection of dinosaur books and very patient parents, knew much more about dinosaurs than do most 4-year-olds. Figure 9-4 shows the experimenters' representation of a subset of the knowledge that the boy was able to demonstrate with respect to the dinosaurs that he knew best. As the figure indicates, in addition simply to knowing the names of many dinosaurs (only about half of which are shown in the figure), the boy knew a number of their characteristic features, such as their diet and method of locomotion, as well as which dinosaurs shared these properties with which others. The question explored in the research was whether all this knowledge would affect what the boy was able to remember about dinosaurs. The answer was clearly positive. The memory tests involved a comparison between two lists of dinosaurs: those that the boy knew best (which are the ones shown in Figure 9-4) and those for which he had less knowledge. When presented with 20 dinosaur names to recall, the boy averaged 9 right for names from the first list and 4 right for names from the second. When retested a year later, he was able to provide the names for 11 of 20 pictures of dinosaurs from the first list but only 2 of 20 for those from the second list.

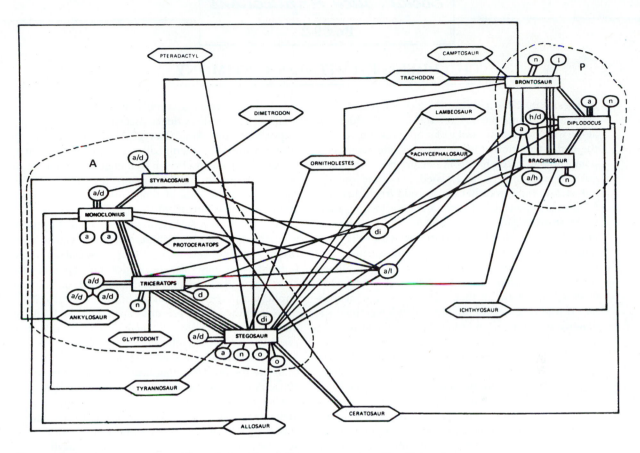

Figure 9-4 Representation of knowledge about dinosaurs possessed by Chi and Koeske's 4-year-old subject. The number of lines between dinosaurs indicates their degree of connection in the child's representation. A = armored; P = giant plant eater. Small letters indicate traits known by the child: a = appearance; d = defense mechanism; di = diet; h = habitat; l = locomotion; n = nickname; o = other. From "Network Representation of a Child's Dinosaur Knowledge" by M. T. H. Chi and R. D. Koeske, 1983, *Developmental Psychology, 19*, p. 33. Copyright 1983 by the American Psychological Association. Reprinted by permission.

The Chi and Koeske (1983) study demonstrates the effects of expertise on memory. The term **expertise** (also sometimes labeled *content knowledge* or the *knowledge base*) refers to organized factual knowledge about some content domain—that is, what we know about some subject. In contrast to the knowledge embodied in Piagetian stages, expertise is content-specific; someone's expertise may be high with regard to dinosaurs, birds, and chess but low when the topic turns to baseball, cooking, or physics. When expertise *is* high, then memory also tends to be high. Variations in expertise contribute to variations in memory within individuals. Chi and Koeske's 4-year-old, for example, remembered well known dinosaurs better than less well known ones, and his memory was undoubtedly better for dinosaurs than it would have been for many other topics. Variations in expertise also contribute to differences in memory between individuals. Most 4-year-olds, for example, would undoubtedly have recalled fewer dinosaurs than did Chi and Koeske's 4-year-old expert. And variations in expertise contribute to differences in memory between older and younger

Expertise
Organized factual knowledge with respect to some content domain.

CHILDREN'S EYEWITNESS TESTIMONY

In Hawaii in 1984 a 3-year-old girl complained one evening of being burned on the leg, refused to be alone with her father, and woke up screaming during the night. Questioned by her parents, she described a man who had taken her from her preschool the previous day and hugged and kissed her while she was naked. She indicated that a 4-year-old friend had also been present, and this friend, after overhearing some of the story, began to make similar statements herself. Over the next several months the two girls were questioned more than 30 times by parents, doctors, and lawyers. Although their claim of having been abused remained consistent, specific details of their stories changed, and some of their statements were inconsistent or clearly false. Eventually, the judge granted the defense attorneys' motion to disqualify the girls as witnesses, ruling that the repeated questioning had so distorted their memories that they could no longer separate reality from fantasy (Cole & Loftus, 1987).

Often, the uncertain memories of young children are simply an interesting and perhaps even charming phenomenon. As this example illustrates, however, there are times when it is critically important to know how accurately children can recount their experiences. In cases of suspected abuse, the apparent child victim is often the only witness. Can the testimony of a young child be trusted? Should such testimony be admissible in court?

In recent years, a number of researchers have attempted to provide evidence that speaks directly to this important question (Doris, 1991; Goodman & Bottoms, 1993; Ornstein, Larus, & Clubb, 1991). Such researchers face an obvious challenge. Experiences of abuse are typically highly traumatic, they may continue for extended periods of time, and they involve the child as a participant and not merely a bystander (Goodman, Aman, & Hirschman, 1987). Furthermore, what children say about abuse may involve more than simply what they remember. Complex social and emotional factors may also be important, such as the child's guilt about being a participant or reluctance to implicate a parent or friend. All of these characteristics make memory for abuse different from the kinds of memory that psychologists usually study—or that they *can* easily study in an ethically acceptable way.

Researchers have tried in various ways to discover or devise memory tests that bear some similarity to the abuse situation. Perhaps the most promising approach has been to study memory for naturally occurring traumatic experiences—for example, going to the dentist (Peters, 1991) or receiving an injection (Goodman et al., 1991). Although such experiences can hardly equal the trauma of abuse, they do capture some of its characteristics. In some studies, researchers have also attempted to simulate the types of questioning that suspected victims of abuse must undergo. A child may be

individuals. Older children possess more expertise for most topics than do younger children, and this greater expertise is one reason that they remember more.

How does expertise affect memory? One way is through the form in which the knowledge is represented. If, for example, the representation includes the sort of rich network of similarities and associations pictured in Figure 9-4, then recalling one item (such as brontosaur) may trigger the recall of related items (brachiosaur, diplodocus, and so on). Another way is through effects on other contributors to memory, such as memory strategies and metamemory. Research has shown that children use strategies most effectively in content areas where their expertise is high (Bjorklund, Muir-Broaddus, & Schneider, 1990; Gaultney, Bjorklund, & Schneider, 1992). Similarly, metacognitive assessments of one's own memory are more accurate among experts for the material in question than among novices (Schneider, Korkel, & Weinert, 1989).

A study by Chi (1978) offers an interesting extension of the work just discussed. Her study examined memory for the positions of chess pieces on a chessboard.

questioned several times across a period of weeks, for example, or the interviewer may include some deliberately leading questions in an attempt to determine how suggestible the child is. Children may be told to "keep a secret" about what happened to them during the experimental session (Bottoms et al., 1990), or a police officer rather than research assistant may do the questioning (Tobey & Goodman, 1992).

Such studies suggest several conclusions about children as witnesses (Ceci & Bruck, 1993a, 1993b; Davies, 1993; Goodman & Bottoms, 1993; Goodman & Schwartz-Kenney, 1992). First, research verifies that recall memory improves with age and that older children typically report more of their experiences than younger children. The memories of 3-year-olds (the youngest age group tested in such research) are especially shaky. Second, in at least some cases, young children are more suggestible than older children or adults—that is, more likely to be influenced by leading questions from an adult authority figure. These findings indicate the need for caution in accepting the reports of young children who have undergone repeated and leading questioning, as was true in the Hawaii case. On the other hand, in many studies, memory differences between children and adults are not very great. The memory problems that children do show are mainly errors of omission rather than commission—that is, they may fail to report certain details, but they do not typically introduce false information. A similar point applies to suggestibility. Children may agree with the implication of a leading question, but they seldom incorporate the suggestion into their later free reports. These findings tell us that any clearly spontaneous mentions of abuse by children must be taken very seriously.

Having offered these conclusions, we should add that there remains much controversy about exactly what the research shows and what the implications are for children's legal testimony. The issue of suggestibility is especially controversial (Ceci & Bruck, 1993b; Doris, 1991). It is clear that young children *are* sometimes suggestible, and of course even one false report may be devastating for the individual involved. On the other hand, there is also evidence that specific questioning may be necessary to elicit certain kinds of information from children—in particular, information about genital touch (Saywitz et al., 1991). Striking the right balance between helpful elicitation and misleading directiveness is clearly a very difficult task. Fortunately, one point on which all researchers agree is that more study is necessary, and the topic of eyewitness memory is currently the focus of an extraordinarily active research effort. Among the topics being explored in this research is the issue of how best to question children in court—for example, the possibility of obtaining testimony via videotape or closed-circuit television. Testifying in court can add to the trauma of an already traumatic situation (Goodman et al., 1992), and it is therefore important to devise procedures that can both maximize accuracy and minimize further stress.

Subjects were 10-year-old children and adults. In striking contrast to the usual developmental trend, Chi found that the 10-year-olds' recall was far superior to that of the adults. This seemingly inexplicable finding is made explicable when we add a further detail of the study: The 10-year-olds were all expert chess players, whereas the adults were all novices. Thus again greater expertise led to greater memory. This study makes the point, however, that it is expertise, not simply age, that is critical. Other researchers have also found that young subjects can equal or even outperform older ones when the content is something they know well—such as cartoon figures (Lindberg, 1980), names of classmates (Bjorklund & Zeman, 1982), or rules of soccer (Schneider, Korkel, & Weinert, 1987).

The work on expertise brings us to another general theme of the information-processing approach. The role of factual knowledge has come to be stressed very heavily in contemporary information-processing accounts of not only memory but also reasoning and problem solving (Bjorklund, 1987a; Chi & Ceci, 1987; Chi, Glaser, & Farr, 1988). The argument is straightforward. The more children already know, the more they will understand of any new experience. The more they understand, the more they will remember. And the more they understand and remember, the more likely they are to reason and to solve problems in effective and adaptive ways.

Scripts

The main points of our discussion of knowledge and memory have been that knowledge affects memory and that as knowledge changes so does memory. There are, of course, many ways in which knowledge changes as children develop, including the build-up of expertise in numerous content areas. One such change, however, is worth singling out for special attention, both because of its general importance and because it has been the focus of much recent research on memory in early childhood. This is the development of scripts.

Script
A representation of the typical sequence of actions and events in some familiar context.

We can define a **script** formally as a representation of the typical sequence of actions and events in some familiar context. Less formally, a script refers to knowledge of the way things typically go. Each of us, for example, possesses a restaurant script, which represents the typical sequence of events in dining at a restaurant: entering the restaurant, sitting down, ordering the meal, eating, paying, and leaving. Our restaurant script, like scripts in general, is not tied to any specific example. Rather it is a *general* representation that can apply to any number of specific restaurants.

Children also form scripts. Indeed, the emergence of scripts for a wide range of familiar experiences may be one of the most important achievements of early childhood cognitive development. Among the scripts that have been studied are going to a restaurant, attending preschool, going to a birthday party, visiting a museum, eating dinner, making cookies, taking a bath, and going to bed at night (Farrar & Goodman, 1990; Nelson, 1986; Nelson & Gruendel, 1981). Table 9-3 presents some examples of children's birthday party scripts, elicited in response to the question "What happens when you have a birthday party?" The numbers in parentheses indicate the age of the child. As can be seen from the examples, scripts increase in both completeness and complexity as children develop.

Much of the interest in children's scripts has concerned their effects on memory. Scripts are in fact both product and process of the constructive nature of the memory system. They are product in the sense that they reflect the child's abstraction, from numerous specific experiences, of the essential general features of some familiar event. Scripts, as we have been stressing, are not reproductions of any specific episode; rather, they are constructions of what typically occurs. Once formed, however, scripts influence how future experiences are processed and remembered (Hudson, 1990a; Nelson & Hudson, 1988). Children asked to remember stories based on familiar scripts show best recall for central events and poorer recall for details that are peripheral to the script (McCartney & Nelson, 1981). Stories that preserve the structure of familiar scripts are typically remembered better than stories that violate a script (Mandler, 1983), although sometimes a deviation from an expected script (e.g., a cat eating pickles) may be so striking that it proves especially memorable (Davidson & Hoe, 1993). Children may even rearrange details in their recall to make a story fit a script. In one study, for example, children heard a story in which the statement "children brought presents" came at the end of a description of a birthday party. In later retelling the story, some children moved the present-bringing earlier in the story, and others replaced it with "children took presents [party favors] home"—certainly a more natural conclusion to a birthday party (Hudson & Nelson, 1983). In general, children seem to be especially sensitive to the

• Scripts are representations of the typical structure of familiar events. Even preschoolers may have learned a simple making-cookies script.

TABLE 9-3 • Examples of Children's Birthday Party Scripts

You cook a cake and eat it. (3 yr, 1 mo)

Well, you get a cake and some ice cream and then some birthday (?) and then you get some clowns and then you get some paper hats, the animal hats and then and then you sing "Happy Birthday to you," and then then then they give you some presents and then you play with them and then that's the end and then they go home and they do what they wanta. (4 yr, 9 mo)

First, uhm . . . you're getting ready for the kids to come, like puttin' balloons up and and putting out party plates and making cake. And then all the people come you've asked. Give you presents and then you have lunch or whatever you have. Then . . . uhm . . . then you open your presents. Or you can open your presents anytime. Uhm . . . you could . . . after you open the presents, then it's probably time to go home. If you're like at Foote Park or something, then it's time to go home and you have to drive all the people home. Then you go home too. (6 yr, 7 mo)

Well, first you open your mail box, and you get some mail. And then you see that there's an invitation for you. Read the invitation. Then you ask your parents if you can go. Then you . . . uhm . . . go to the birthday party and you get a ride there, and after you get there you usually wait for everyone else to come. Then usually they always want to open one of the presents. Sometimes then they have three games, then they have the birthday cake, then sometimes they open up the other presents or they could open them up all at once. After that they like to play some more games and then maybe your parents come to pick you up. And then you go home. (8 yr, 10 mo)

Source: From "Generalized Event Representations: Basic Building Blocks of Cognitive Development" by K. Nelson and J. Gruendel, 1981. In M. E. Lamb and A. L. Brown (Eds.), *Advances in Developmental Psychology*, Vol. 1 (p. 135), Hillsdale, NJ: Erlbaum. Copyright 1981 by Lawrence Erlbaum Associates. Reprinted by permission.

order in which events occur, and they learn new scripts most readily when the events in the script follow a natural logical or causal sequence (Bauer, 1992; Boyer, Barron, & Farrar, in press; Fivush, Kuebli, & Clubb, 1992). Recall from our earlier discussion that even infants can learn the order of events for simple sequences of action.

As with constructive memory in general, the effects of scripts on memory are mixed. A script can sometimes lead to memory distortions, as when some unexpected event is reworked to fit an established script. In addition, young children who are just forming scripts may have difficulty separating the typical and the novel, and they may remember new events less well because they merge such events with the typical events of the script (Farrar & Goodman, 1990, 1992). For the most part, however, scripts—like knowledge in general—aid the memory process. Scripts free us from having to attend to the mundane and predictable, and they provide frameworks within which new experiences can be understood and thus remembered.

DEVELOPMENT IN CONTEXT: How Parents Teach Their Children to Remember

Memory is clearly a basic cognitive capacity. Memory is present from birth, it operates in much the same way in all infants and children, and it undergoes predictable changes as children develop. Furthermore, memory—as well as developmental changes in memory—is closely linked to the cognitive system as a whole, as the work that we have just considered reveals.

To say that memory is basic, however, is not to say that it is unaffected by experience. We have seen that there are seldom all-or-nothing answers to the nature–nurture question, and this principle applies to the development of memory as well. Children's experiences affect their memories from early in life. In recent years there has been considerable interest in the effects of one particular type of experience—the way that parents talk about past events with their young children (Fivush, 1991, 1993; Hudson, 1990b; McCabe & Peterson, 1991; Reese & Fivush, 1993).

Parents do in fact talk about the past with their children. Conversations about such matters as doctor visits, shopping excursions, and family trips are common occurrences in many households. Furthermore, different parents talk about the past in somewhat different ways. Table 9-4 presents examples of two styles of parental conversation that have been identified by researchers. These styles, we should note, are really points along a continuum. As the examples suggest, parents in the elaborative category provide a richer narrative structure than do parents in the repetitive category. Not only do they furnish more information in their own speech, but they make more extended and supportive efforts to elicit information from their children. They also talk more often about the past than do repetitive parents. The child of an elaborative parent is therefore given more chance to be an active participant in conversations about the past, as well as more chance to be successful in his or her recall efforts. Such a child is also provided with more general and more frequent models of how to remember and talk about past experience.

As we might expect, then, children of elaborative parents are generally more successful at recalling past events than are children of repetitive parents, not only in conversations with their own parents but also when tested by an independent adult (Fivush, 1991; Hudson & Sidoti, 1988; Nelson, 1993a). Differences are evident not only in the amount of recall but also in the *style* of recall, with children of elaborative parents more likely to approximate an adultlike narrative style marked by

• Parents often talk about past experiences with their children. Such conversations may be an important contributor to children's earliest memories.

TABLE 9-4 ● Examples of Elaborative and Repetitive Styles in Conversations Between Parent (P) and Child (C)

Elaborative

P: Did we see any big fishes? What kind of fishes?

C: Big, big, big.

P: And what's their names?

C: I don't know.

P: You remember the names of the fishes. What we called them. Michael's favorite kind of fish. Big mean ugly fish.

C: Yeah.

P: What kind is it?

C: um, ba.,

P: A ssshark?

C: Yeah.

P: Remember the sharks?

C: Yeah.

P: Do you? What else did we see in the big tank at the aquarium?

C: I don't know.

P: Remember when we first came in, remember when we first came in the aquarium? And we looked down and there were a whole bunch of birdies in the water? Remember the names of the birdies?

C: Ducks!

P: Nooo! They weren't ducks. They had on little suits. Penguins. Remember, what did the penguins do?

C: I don't know.

P: You don't remember?

C: No.

P: Remember them jumping off the rocks and swimming in the water?

C: Yeah.

P: Real fast. You were watching them jump in the water, hm.

C: Yeah.

Repetitive

P: How did we get to Florida, do you remember?

C: Yes.

P: How did we get there? What did we do? You remember?

C: Yeah.

P: You want to sit up here in my lap?

C: No.

P: Oh, okay. Remember when we went to Florida, how did we get there? We went in the _____ ?

C: The ocean.

P: Well, be _____ , when we got to Florida we went to the ocean, that's right, but how did we get down to Florida? Did we drive our car?

C: Yes.

P: No, think again, I don't think we drove to Florida. How did we get down there, remember, we took a great big _____ ? Do you remember?

Source: From "Parental Styles of Talking About the Past" by E. Reese and R. Fivush, 1993, *Developmental Psychology, 29,* p. 606. Copyright 1993 by the American Psychological Association. Reprinted by permission.

clear temporal and causal relations and helpful orienting and contextual information (e.g., "Remember when we. . .?"). In general, children who engage in such conversations with their parents seem to be learning not only what to remember but *how* to remember—that is, how to organize and to communicate their memories of the past. They are also learning something about the value of such memories and about the value of sharing one's memories with others.

Of course, not all parent–child conversations involve past events. Parents' discussions of ongoing activities have been shown to facilitate their children's subsequent recall of these activities (Tessler, 1991). And parents' structuring of *future* events (e.g., "When you start school next week. . . .") can help their children to understand and be ready for new experiences (Nelson, 1993a).

The theoretical basis for much of the work on parents' contributions to memory has been Vygotsky's (1978) theory. The effects of parents on both what and how their children remember are clearly compatible with Vygotsky's emphasis on the social bases for individual development. Also compatible with Vygotskian theory are the developmental changes in parent–child interactions that this research reveals. When children are very young, it is the parent who carries most of the burden, directing the conversation and drawing information from the child. As children develop, they gradually assume a more active and more equal role in discussions about the past.

Conversations with parents can nurture memories of a variety of sorts, including the kinds of script memory discussed in the previous section. Such conversations may be especially important, however, with respect to the form of memory that is labeled autobiographical. The term **autobiographical memory** refers to memories that are specific, personal, and long-lasting—to memories that are part of one's life history, that have to do with the *self*. A child who can recount the typical activities in a kindergarten day is demonstrating script memory. A child who can remember the time that she spilled the paints, or the day that she won the big race, is demonstrating autobiographical memory. What a number of theorists have suggested is that autobiographical memory may emerge in the context of conversations with parents (Bauer, 1993a; Fivush & Reese, 1992; Hudson, 1990b; Nelson, 1993a, 1993b). Such contexts provide a narrative framework within which personal memories can be elicited and rehearsed, as well as a motivation—sharing with others—for talking about and remembering one's past.

This proposal is relevant to the problem of **infantile amnesia**: the common inability to remember experiences from the first 2 or 3 years of life. The puzzle of why we cannot remember very early experiences has long intrigued theorists, dating back to Freud's proposal that such forgetting results from repression of forbidden sexual desires. A number of other explanations have been offered since Freud, and the topic remains the focus of a good deal of theoretical debate (Howe & Courage, 1993). The work on autobiographical memory provides another possible solution to the puzzle. One way to describe infantile amnesia is to say that there is no autobiographical memory for the events of infancy. If the emergence of autobiographical memory depends on the social sharing of memories, then its absence in the infant, who cannot use language, becomes understandable.

Autobiographical memory
Specific, personal, and long-lasting memory regarding the self.

Infantile amnesia
The inability to remember experiences from the first 2 or 3 years of life.

✔ To Recap. . .

Most examinations of memory beyond infancy have focused on recall memory, which improves with age across the childhood years. Three general kinds of explanation have been offered for this improvement. One important source of improvement is the development of mnemonic strategies, such as rehearsal and organization. In general, the tendency to use strategies, the complexity of the strategies, and the skill with which the strategies are executed all increase with age. The emphasis on strategies reflects one important theme of the information-processing approach—the existence of limits on information-processing resources and the need to develop techniques (such as mnemonic strategies) to overcome the limits.

A second approach to explaining developmental improvements in memory stresses the child's metamemory, which includes knowledge about memory in general and one's own memory in particular. Both sorts of knowledge increase with age. Although attempts to link metamemory to memory performance have sometimes been unsuccessful, recent evidence suggests that increases in knowledge do lead to improvements in performance. The work on metamemory reflects another theme of the information-processing approach—the need for executive control to select and coordinate cognitive activities.

A third approach stresses the effects of the general knowledge system on memory. Studies of constructive memory demonstrate that memory often involves inferences and constructions that go beyond the literal input. Older children are more likely to engage in such constructive processing than younger children. Older children also possess greater content-specific expertise than do younger children, and this factor is another contributor to developmental improvements in memory. Finally, an aspect of cognitive development that appears to be especially closely related to memory is the emergence of scripts, or knowledge of the typical structure of familiar events. Studies of parent–child interaction indicate that conversations with parents contribute to the development of various forms of memory, including scripts and autobiographical memory.

REPRESENTATION AND PROBLEM SOLVING

As noted, the general conclusion that older children remember better than younger ones is hardly surprising. The really interesting questions about children's memory have to do with exactly how and exactly why memory improves with age. It is these questions on which we have been focusing—and these questions for which the information-processing approach has proved so informative.

No one has to read a textbook to learn that children's ability to represent information and to solve problems also improves dramatically across childhood. The tasks that the school system sets for its students, the ways in which parents attempt to reason with and control their children, the opportunities and the expectations that society in general holds—all are quite different for 15-year-olds than for 5-year-olds. Again, the challenge for the researcher is to describe exactly how children's abilities change—and then to explain why these changes come about.

In this section we consider three contributors to developmental improvements. We begin with two general sorts of development that information-processing researchers believe may account for much of children's knowledge: the formation of schemas and the construction of rules. We then consider a central theme in current information-processing theorizing, the contribution of memory to children's problem solving.

The Development of Schemas

We have already considered the development of scripts and their role in children's memory. The concept of schema is closely related to the concept of script. A **schema** is defined as a general representation of the typical structure of a familiar

Schema
A general representation of the typical structure of familiar experiences.

experience. Comparing this definition with that for script, we can see that schema is the more general of the two notions. Scripts are a kind of schema—namely, schemas for familiar events (having a birthday party, taking a bath, and so on). But events are not the only familiar experiences for which we form schemas. In this section we add some further examples as part of a more general consideration of the role of schemas in children's cognitive development.

Imagine hearing the phrases "once upon a time" and "happily every after." You could probably make several assumptions with some confidence: that the phrases are taken from a story, that the first phrase opens the story and the second one closes it, that the story is of a certain, fairy-tale-like sort, and that various events (introduction of characters, presentation of a goal, presentation of obstacles to the goal, overcoming of the obstacles, and so on) occur in a particular sequence between the opening and the close. You could make these assumptions because of your knowledge of how stories typically go—in other words, because you possess a schema for the typical structure of stories. Your story schema, like schemas in general, involves knowledge of both the typical elements for some familiar aspect of the environment (such as the parts of a story) and the relations among the elements (such as the introduction of goals before the description of actions to achieve the goals). Furthermore, your story schema, like schemas in general, is a *general* representation of familiar experience. A schema for stories is not tied to any specific example; rather, it is a general framework that can encompass any number of different stories (Mandler, 1984). Table 9-5 presents an example of one kind of story schema, along with a (not very cheerful) story that fits the schema. It should be clear that an indefinite number of stories could be generated within this general framework.

Besides event schemas (or scripts) and story schemas, people also form *scene schemas*—that is, general representations of how places look (Mandler, 1983, 1984). We know, for example, what objects are likely to be found in what places (stoves in kitchens, buildings on streets), as well as the likely spatial relations among the ob-

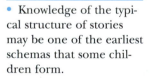

• Knowledge of the typical structure of stories may be one of the earliest schemas that some children form.

TABLE 9-5 ● Example of a Story Schema

1. Setting	Introduction of the protagonist; contains information about the social, physical, or temporal context in which the story events occur.
2. Initiating Event	An action, an internal event, or a physical event that serves to initiate the story line or cause the protagonist to respond emotionally and to formulate a goal.
3. Internal Response	An emotional reaction and goal, often incorporating the thought of the protagonist that causes him or her to initiate action.
4. Attempt	An overt action or series of actions, carried out in the service of attaining a goal.
5. Consequence	An event, action, or end state, marking the attainment or nonattainment of the protagonist's goal.
6. Reaction	An internal response expressing the protagonist's feelings about the outcome of his or her actions or the occurrence of broader, general consequences resulting from the goal attainment or nonattainment of the protagonist.

Example of a Well-Formed Story

Setting	1. Once there was a big grey fish named Albert.
	2. He lived in a big icy pond near the edge of a forest.
Initiating event	3. One day, Albert was swimming around the pond.
	4. Then he spotted a big juicy worm on the top of the water.
Internal response	5. Albert knew how delicious worms tasted.
	6. He wanted to eat that one for his dinner.
Attempt	7. So he swam very close to the worm.
	8. Then he bit into him.
Consequence	9. Suddenly, Albert was pulled through the water into a boat.
	10. He had been caught by a fisherman.
Reaction	11. Albert felt sad.
	12. He wished he had been more careful.

Source: From "Children's Concept of Time: The Development of a Story Schema" by N. L. Stein and C. G. Glenn, 1982. In W. J. Friedman (Ed.), *The Developmental Psychology of Time* (p. 258), New York: Academic Press. Copyright 1982 by Academic Press. Reprinted by permission.

jects. The latter knowledge includes both specific information (chairs go next to tables) and more general, invariant information (objects do not float in space). Scene schemas come in more forms than do story schemas. They are also likely to be activated more often in our daily interactions with the environment.

What is the psychological significance of schemas? Most generally, schemas represent important kinds of knowledge about the world. Often, when we think of knowledge we think of esoteric kinds of information—the rules of calculus, for example, or the names of foreign capitals. Knowledge takes many forms, however, and one very fundamental sort concerns the typical structure of everyday experience. It is this kind of knowledge that is captured in schemas.

The further significance of schemas lies in their effects on cognitive processing. Schemas affect how we take in information and how we direct our own behavior. The effects of scripts on memory are one illustration of this point. The same conclusion applies to other kinds of schemas, such as story and scene schemas. The knowledge that readers possess about stories has been shown to affect their response to stories in a variety of ways: how they divide stories into components, how much reading time they devote to different parts of the story, and how they finish incomplete stories or construct stories themselves (Mandler, 1984; Mandler & Goodman, 1982). Similarly, scene schemas have been shown to influence the ways in which scenes are perceived and also the memory for scenes over time (Fabricius, Hodge, & Quinan, 1993; Saarnio, 1993a).

We saw that simple scripts emerge early in life. Other kinds of schemas can also be found in young children. Even 2-year-olds have simple scene schemas for familiar places such as a room within a house (Ratner & Myers, 1981). For example, given an array of items to choose from, they can identify which items are likely to be found in the kitchen and which in the bathroom (although an occasional sandbox in the kitchen is not unheard of at this age). Young children also possess simple story schemas. Children as young as 3 know some of the conventions for stories (such as the "Once upon a time" beginning), and they have some ability to produce stories that fit story schemas (Mandler, 1983). Of course, both the range of schemas that children possess and the accuracy and complexity of individual schemas increase with development. Older children do not place sandboxes in kitchens. By middle childhood scene schemas are considerably more sophisticated than they were at age 2 or 3 (Saarnio, 1993b). And children's ability to use story schemas, both to understand stories and to generate their own stories, is much more advanced by age 8 or 10 than it was at age 4 (Stein & Glenn, 1982; Trabasso, Stein, & Johnson, 1981).

The range of childhood schemas is hardly exhausted by the examples that we have cited. Children also form schemas for social experiences and social relations. One especially important kind of social schema concerns beliefs about gender and about differences between the sexes. We discuss such *gender schemas* in Chapter 15.

The Development of Rules

We suggested earlier that comparing the information-processing and Piagetian approaches could be helpful in understanding each. This section and the next give us a further chance to make such a comparison. In both cases we consider programs of research that have been influenced by Piaget, both in the ideas behind them and in the particular tasks that they examine. As we will see, however, the conclusions that they reach about children's reasoning and problem solving are somewhat different from Piaget's.

Rules
Procedures for acting on the environment and solving problems.

Robert Siegler (1976, 1978, 1981) has proposed that much of children's cognitive development can be characterized in terms of the construction of **rules**. Rules are procedures for acting on the environment and solving problems. They take the form of "if . . . then" statements. If *A* is the case, do *X*; if *B* is the case, do *Y*; and so forth. A simple and familiar example concerns the rules for behavior at traffic lights: If the light is green, proceed; if the light is red, stop (unfortunately, rules for yellow lights seem to be more variable!).

Many situations, of course, require more thought than does approaching a traffic light, and it is these more complex situations to which Siegler's research has been directed. Figure 9-5 presents one example—a balance-scale problem originally devised by Inhelder and Piaget (1958) to study formal operational reasoning. The child is shown a simple balance scale on which varying numbers of weights can be placed at varying distances from the fulcrum. The task is to predict whether the scale will balance or whether one side or the other will go down. Successfully performing the task requires that the child realize that both weight and distance are important and that she know how to combine the two factors in cases of conflict. The original Piagetian research revealed that children of different ages gave quite

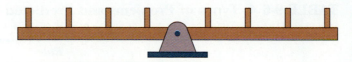

Figure 9-5 Balance scale used in Siegler's research. Metal disks can be placed on any of the eight pegs.

different responses to the task, responses that Piaget analyzed in terms of the logical structures of concrete and formal operations.

Siegler (1976, 1978) used the same task but a different methodology and form of analysis. He began by carefully considering all of the various ways in which children might go about attempting to solve the balance scale problem. Such task analysis is a characteristic information-processing methodology (Kail & Bisanz, 1982). Based on this task analysis, Siegler identified four rules that children might use in solving balance problems. At the simplest level, rule 1, the child judges that the side with more weights will go down or that, if the number of weights on each side is equal, the scale will balance. The child using rule 2 also judges solely in terms of number of weights when the weights on each side are different; if the weights are equal, however, the rule 2 child can also take distance into account. The rule 3 child, in contrast, always considers both weight and distance and is correct whenever one or both are equal. If the two factors are in conflict, however (i.e., more weight on one side, greater distance on the other), the child becomes confused, does not know how to resolve the conflict, and (in Siegler's words) "muddles through." Finally, the rule 4 child has mastered the weight-times-distance rule: Downward force equals amount of weight multiplied by distance from the fulcrum. The rule 4 child can therefore solve any version of the task.

A task analysis identifies possible ways of responding, but it does not tell us whether children actually use these bases. Siegler's next step, therefore, was to test the psychological reality of the proposed rules. He devised six types of balance scale problems, carefully constructed to yield different patterns of response across the different rules. Both the problem types and the predicted responses are shown in Table 9-6. Siegler presented five versions of each problem type (hence 30 problems in all) to children ranging in age from 5 to 17. Children were considered to be using a particular rule if at least 26 of their 30 responses matched the response predicted by the rule. The responses did indeed match. Fully 90% of the children followed one of the four rules consistently. As expected, the complexity of the preferred rule increased with age; most 5-year-olds used rule 1, whereas by age 17, rules 3 and 4 were most common. Finally, a particularly interesting finding was that accurate performance on the problems involving conflict actually declined with age. Although declines with age are normally unexpected, this finding fit nicely with the predictions of the rule analysis. As can be seen in Table 9-6, the developmentally primitive rules 1 and 2 yield perfect performance on these problems, whereas the more advanced rule 3 results only in chance performance.

Siegler and others have applied his rule-assessment methodology to a wide range of tasks and related abilities (Klahr & Robinson, 1981; Ravn & Gelman, 1984; Siegler, 1981). Siegler's (1981) own research has demonstrated the value of rules in explaining performance on a variety of Piagetian problems in addition to the balance scale—for example, conservation of number and conservation of continuous quantity. The explanation is, to be sure, in some respects similar to Piaget's. In the case of conservation, for example, Siegler and Piaget agree that children solve the problem through mental action that logically combines information from both of the relevant dimensions (e.g., height and width in the case of quantity).

TABLE 9-6 ● **Types of Problems and Predicted Responses on the Siegler Balance Scale Task**

Problem Type	Rule			
	I	*II*	*III*	*IV*
Balance	100	100	100	100
Weight	100	100	100	100
Distance	0 (Should say "Balance")	100	100	100
Conflict-Weight	100	100	33 (Chance responding)	100
Conflict-Distance	0 (Should say "Right down")	0 (Should say "Right down")	33 (Chance responding)	100
Conflict-Balance	0 (Should say "Right down")	0 (Should say "Right down")	33 (Chance responding)	100

Source: From "The Origins of Scientific Reasoning" by R. S. Siegler, 1978. In R. S. Siegler (Ed.), *Children's Thinking: What Develops?* (p 115), Hillsdale, NJ: Erlbaum. Copyright 1978 by Lawrence Erlbaum Associates. Reprinted by permission.

There are, however, two differences between Siegler's and Piaget's accounts, differences that in general divide the information-processing and Piagetian approaches. One concerns specificity and testability. Rules are more precisely defined than are Piagetian operations, and the rule-assessment methodology provides a more rigorous test of a proposed explanation than is typically the case in Piagetian research. The second difference is theoretical. Operations are general structures that are assumed to determine performance on a wide range of tasks, and the expectation therefore is that children will be quite consistent in their level of performance. Rules, however, may be more domain-specific, and there is no assumption that performance will necessarily be consistent from one task to another. And Siegler in fact finds that the same child may use rules of different levels on different tasks.

Although both this section and the next use Piagetian examples, we should stress that the approaches being considered have by no means been limited to Piagetian tasks. Siegler, for example, has recently extended his research to the study of academic skills such as addition, subtraction, and reading. We consider some of this work later.

The Contribution of Memory to Problem Solving

We have noted that some information-processing theorists are labeled neo-Piagetian because their ideas are especially closely tied to those of Piaget. In this section we examine one such theory, that of Robbie Case (1985, 1986, 1992a, 1992b).

Like Piaget, Case divides development into distinct stages—stages in many respects similar to Piaget's. A major difference between the two approaches is the emphasis that Case places on memory. In his theory, the total problem-solving resources available to the child are divided into two components—operating space and short-term storage space. The term **operating space** refers to the resources necessary to carry out whatever cognitive operations are being employed for the problem at hand. In the case of the Siegler balance scale task, for example, a child who used rule 2 would first count the number of weights on each side of the fulcrum. Assuming that the weights were equal, the child would then count the number of pegs from the fulcrum. Finally, the child would use the information about weight or distance to predict which side would go down. Each of these operations would require a certain amount of operating space. Note that the term *space* is used somewhat metaphorically, for there is no reference to some actual physical area in the brain. The reference, rather, is to how much of the available mental energy must be used for the activity in question.

Performing operations is one part of problem solving; remembering the results of those operations is another part. The phrase **short-term storage space** refers to the resources the child needs to store results from previous operations while carrying out new ones. The rule 2 child, for example, would need to remember both the overall goal of the task and the results of each preceding operation in order to execute the sequence just described. Without such memory, there could be little hope of a successful solution.

Let us consider another example. Figure 9-6 shows a task in proportional reasoning. The dark beakers contain orange juice, and the clear beakers contain water. The child is asked to imagine that the beakers in each set are poured into a pitcher and to judge which mixture will taste more strongly of juice—that from set A or that from set B. One way to solve the most difficult versions of the task (such as problem *d*) is as follows: count the number of juice beakers in each set and note the size of the difference, count the number of water beakers in each set and note the size of the difference, and compare the results of these two operations. If the juice difference is larger, decide that the set with more juice is juicier; if the water difference is larger (as is the case in the example), decide that the set with more water is less juicy. Thus, to solve the task, the child must perform a number of distinct operations. And the child must remember the results of the operations.

The balance scale and orange juice tasks are just two of many problems whose solution depends on combining results from several cognitive operations. Such

Operating space
In Case's theory, the resources necessary to carry out cognitive operations.

Short-term storage space
In Case's theory, the resources necessary to store results from previous cognitive operations while carrying out new ones.

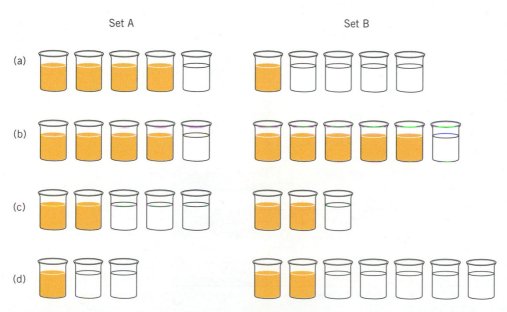

Figure 9-6 Example of a task in proportional reasoning. The dark beakers contain orange juice, and the clear beakers contain water. The child's task on each trial is to determine whether set A or set B would produce a juicier tasting drink. From *Intellectual Development* (p. 184) by R. Case, 1985, New York: Academic Press. Copyright 1985 by Academic Press. Adapted by permission.

combining is possible only if short-term storage space is sufficient to hold all of the relevant results. In Case's theory, limitations in short-term storage space are a major determinant of young children's difficulties in problem solving. Because they can keep track of only a few things at a time, young children can do only a few things at a time. Correspondingly, advances in problem solving occur as short-term storage space expands, and the child can begin to combine operations that previously could only be performed separately. In the case of the juice problem, for example, it is not until age 9 or 10 that the child has sufficient storage space to combine all of the operations described in the preceding paragraph. More generally, the stage progressions in Case's theory are defined largely in terms of the new combinations made possible by increases in short-term storage capacity.

Why does short-term storage capacity increase? There are two possible explanations. One possibility, shown in Figure 9-7*a*, is that the total problem-solving resources expand with age. As the total resources grow, so does the space available for short-term storage. In this view, older children simply have more resources available to them. Thus, it is not surprising that they can remember more and do more.

Plausible though this model may seem, Case's research leads him to prefer a second possibility. This possibility, shown in Figure 9-7*b*, is that the growth in storage capacity results from a decrease in the space used to perform operations. Cognitive resources must always be divided between the two components of operations and storage; if fewer resources are needed for one component, then more are available for the other. In this second view, developmental changes in storage result from increases in operational efficiency. As children develop, they become more skilled at performing cognitive operations. Hence, they have more space left over for storage, and hence they can do more and more.

Accepting this second explanation leads naturally to another question: Why does operational efficiency increase? Case proposes two contributors. One is practice. With practice, cognitive activities of many sorts become more skilled and efficient. Thus, what once took effort and attention may eventually become automatic and routine. (We return to this notion, called *automatization*, in our discussion of

Figure 9-7 Two models for explaining developmental increases in short-term storage space. (*a*) In model 1, the total processing resources increase with age. (*b*) In model 2, processing resources remain constant, but operating space decreases.

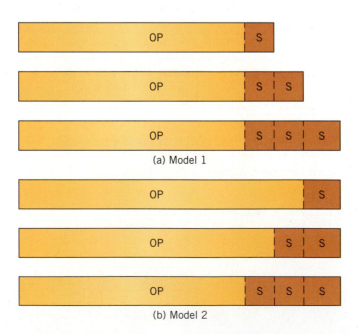

(a) Model 1

(b) Model 2

cognitive change.) The second factor is biological maturation. Children develop at about the same pace, and this similarity suggests a biological contribution to development. Furthermore, Case notes that major changes in brain development occur at about the same time as the stage-to-stage transitions identified in his theory. Finally, recent research indicates that speed of information processing increases at a regular rate from early childhood to adulthood (Hale, 1990; Kail, 1991, 1992; Kail & Park, 1992, 1994). This increase in speed is so consistent across tasks and across samples that it appears to be maturational in origin.

Case's theory is one of the most ambitious information-processing efforts to date, and not all aspects of it have won acceptance (Flavell, 1984; Siegler, 1986). Its most general claim, however, is widely held: Memory improves as children develop, and improvements in memory contribute to improvements in reasoning and problem solving (Howe & Rabinowitz, 1990).

✔ *To Recap...*

Like memory, children's representation and problem solving improve dramatically over the childhood years. One important development is the formation of schemas, or representations of the typical structure of familiar experiences. In addition to event schemas (scripts), story schemas and scene schemas are among the childhood schemas that have been studied. Schemas emerge early in life and increase in complexity as children develop. Once formed, they affect how children process information and respond to the environment.

The development of rules is another contributor to developmental change. Children's understanding of a variety of concepts can be formulated in terms of the mental rules that guide responding. Solution of balance scale problems, for example, consistently follows one of four general rules, and the complexity and the appropriateness of the rules increase with age.

Short-term storage space is a third contributor to problem solving. Solutions to many problems require the ability to combine results from a number of cognitive operations. This is possible only if the child has sufficient storage space to remember past results while performing new operations. Older children have greater storage capacity than younger children, and so they are capable of more complex forms of reasoning and problem solving. Current evidence suggests that the increase in storage capacity results from an increase in operational efficiency, which in turn results from both biological maturation and practice at executing operations.

ACADEMIC ABILITIES

Thus far our examples of information-processing research have been drawn largely from two content domains: the development of memory and the understanding of Piagetian concepts. One of the strengths of the information-processing approach, however, is its applicability to a wide range of topics. In this section we discuss some information-processing research that has clear applicational as well as theoretical interest—studies directed to the development of skills stressed in school. We begin with arithmetic, then move on to reading.

Arithmetic

Suppose that you were asked how you come up with the answer to simple addition problems such as 4 + 2 and 3 + 5. Your response would probably be that you simply know—that you have memorized the answer to such often-encountered problems. And you would probably be right—all of us *have* memorized a number of basic arithmetical facts. But what about young children who are just beginning to learn about mathematics? How do they come up with *their* answers?

A number of recent research programs have examined the strategies that children use in solving arithmetic problems (Ashcraft, 1990; Baroody, 1992; Bisanz & LeFevre, 1990; Widaman et al., 1992). Here we concentrate on some research by Robert Siegler and associates (Kerkman & Siegler, 1991; Siegler & Jenkins, 1989; Siegler & Shipley, in press; Siegler & Shrager, 1984). Shown in Table 9-7 are strategies that young children might use to solve the 3 + 5 problem. The retrieval strategy corresponds to the expected strategy for adults—retrieving from memory a previously memorized answer. Other possible strategies clearly vary in both sophistication and likelihood of success.

How can we determine which strategy a child is using? Siegler and colleagues use a variety of techniques. One possibility is simply to watch children as they work on the problems. Some strategies (putting up fingers, counting out loud) are overt and thus directly observable. Another possibility is to ask children how they arrive at their answers. Although verbal reports are not infallible guides to mental processes (in children or anyone), they can provide useful information. Table 9-8 presents some examples of children's self-reports on their use of the min strategy, or the strategy of counting up from the larger of two addends. A third approach makes use of a central information-processing methodology: the measurement of response time as a guide to processes of solution. A child using the count-from-first-addend strategy, for example, should take longer to solve 3 + 7 than to solve 3 + 5; a child using the min strategy, however, should be equally quick on the two problems. Examination of response times across a range of problems can help to specify the strategies being used. Finally, Siegler has tested his full model of children's knowledge of addition (only part of which is captured in Table 9-7) with another basic information-processing method, computer simulation. His success at programming a computer to generate the kinds of response patterns shown by children suggests that his theory really has identified the processes that guide behavior.

One of the most interesting findings from the Siegler program of research concerns the diversity of strategies that children use. We might have expected that a child at any point in development would have a single method of solving addition problems. In fact, children typically employ a number of different strategies, sometimes going with one approach, sometimes trying something different. Children's selection among strategies is not random but rather often adaptively geared to the problem at hand. They may, for example, use the retrieval strategy for simple and familiar problems but fall back on one of the more certain counting strategies when faced with a more complex task. In general, they seem to strive for a balance of speed and accuracy, selecting the fastest strategy that is likely to yield a correct response. With development, there is a predictable progression from less efficient to more efficient strategies, culminating in the ability to retrieve answers from memory rather than continually having to calculate them anew. With development, speed and accuracy increase as well. These increases come in part from the emergence of more efficient strategies and in part from increased skill in executing any particular strategy.

These conclusions about strategy use are not limited to addition. They apply as well to other forms of arithmetic. As we discuss shortly, they also apply to reading.

In addition to developmental differences in strategy use, there also are clear individual differences. Children of a given age vary greatly in the strategies that they prefer and the skill with which they execute those strategies. Siegler (1988) identi-

● Counting on the fingers is one of the first arithmetical strategies that children develop.

TABLE 9-7 ● Children's Strategies for Solving Simple Addition Problems

Strategy	Typical Use of Strategy to Solve 3 + 5
Sum	Put up 3 fingers, put up 5 fingers, count fingers by saying "1, 2, 3, 4, 5, 6, 7, 8."
Finger recognition	Put up 3 fingers, put up 5 fingers, say "8" without counting.
Short-cut sum	Say "1, 2, 3, 4, 5, 6, 7, 8," perhaps simultaneously putting up one finger on each count.
Count-from-first-addend	Say "3, 4, 5, 6, 7, 8" or "4, 5, 6, 7, 8," perhaps simultaneously putting up one finger on each count.
Min (count-from-larger-addend)	Say "5, 6, 7, 8," or "6, 7, 8," perhaps simultaneously putting up one finger on each count beyond 5.
Retrieval	Say an answer and explain it by saying "I just knew it."
Guessing	Say an answer and explain it by saying "I guessed."
Decomposition	Say "3 + 5 is like 4 + 4, so it's 8."

Source: Adapted from *How Children Discover New Strategies* (p. 59) by R. S. Siegler and E. Jenkins, 1989, Hillsdale, NJ: Erlbaum. Copyright 1989 by Lawrence Erlbaum Associates. Adapted by permission.

fied three general patterns of arithmetical performance among first graders: "good students," "not-so-good students," and "perfectionists." Good students and not-so-good students differed in ways that would be expected. Good students were faster and more accurate in executing strategies than were not-so-good students, and they also used retrieval more often and less mature strategies less often than the not-so-good group. Perfectionists, in contrast, were just as skilled at executing strategies and just as accurate as the good students, but they were least likely of all to use retrieval to arrive at their answers. Apparently, perfectionists set a high premium on avoiding mistakes, and they therefore often opted for slow but certain methods of solution.

Research such as Siegler's has implications for the teaching of arithmetic. Perhaps the most general implication is that teachers should be sensitive to the beliefs and strategies that children bring to the classroom setting. We saw in Chapter 8 that learning about numbers begins very early in life, and thus it is not surprising that even first graders have their own strategies for solving arithmetic problems. Teachers should realize, furthermore, that not all first graders will have the same strategies, and that instruction, as far as possible, should be adjusted to the individual child's level of development. As Siegler (1988) notes, lower level strategies such as counting on one's fingers should not necessarily be discouraged; children may need experience with the simpler strategies to arrive at answers that they can eventually retrieve from memory. Recall that this same principle emerged in our discussion of the implications of Piaget's work for education (Box 8-3): Be sensitive to the natural sequence of development and to the need for advanced knowledge to build upon lower level understanding. In Box 9-3 we consider further some implications of information-processing research for the teaching of arithmetic, including an application to teacher training.

Reading

Reading is a source of great joy for many people and a source of great sorrow for many others. Despite thousands of hours of school instruction, many children

TABLE 9-8 ● **Protocols Illustrating Children's Use of the Min Strategy to Solve Addition Problems**

Experimenter (E):	How much is 6 + 3?
Lauren (L):	(Long pause) Nine.
E:	OK, how did you know that?
L:	I think I said . . . I think I said . . . oops, um . . . I think he said . . . 8 was 1 and . . . um . . . I mean 7 was 1, 8 was 2, 9 was 3.
E:	OK.
L:	Six and three are nine.
E:	How did you know to do that? Why didn't you count "1, 2, 3, 4, 5, 6, 7, 8, 9"? How come you did "6, 7, 8, 9"?
L:	Cause then you have to count all those numbers.
E:	OK, well how did you know you didn't have to count all of those numbers?
L:	Why didn't . . . well I don't have to if I don't want to.
Experimenter (E):	OK, Brittany, how much is 2 + 5?
Brittany (B):	2 + 5—(whispers)—6, 7—it's 7.
E:	How did you know that?
B:	(excitedly) Never counted.
E:	You didn't count?
B:	Just said it—I just said after six something—seven—six, seven.
E:	You did? Why did you say 6, 7?
B:	'Cause I wanted to see what it really was.
E:	OK, well—so, did you—what—you didn't have to count at one, you didn't count 1, 2, 3, you just said 6, 7?
B:	Yeah—smart answer.
Experimenter (E):	OK, Christian, How much is 1 + 24?
Christian (C):	1 + 24!?
E:	Yep.
C:	Umm . . . . 25.
E:	How did you know that?
C:	I . . . counted in my head.
E:	How did you count it in your head?
C:	What was it again?
E:	1 + 24.
C:	I went . . . 1, 2, 3, 4, 5, si . . . I went, 24 + 1, I, well, ... I'll try to get you to understand, ok?
E:	OK.
C:	I went 24 + 1 . . . (whispers) 24 . . . (whispers) 25 . . . that's what I did.
E:	OK, that's good, well why didn't you count 1, 2, 3, 4, 5, 6, 7, 8, 9, 10, all the way to 24?
C:	Aww, that would take too long . . . silly.

Source: From *How Children Discover New Strategies* (pp. 66, 80, 91) by R. S. Siegler and E. Jenkins, 1989, Hillsdale, NJ: Erlbaum. Copyright 1989 by Lawrence Erlbaum Associates. Reprinted by permission.

RULES AND ARITHMETIC: GETTING RID OF BUGS

Imagine that you are a fourth-grade teacher and one of your pupils turns in the answer sheet shown in the accompanying table. What could you conclude about this child's knowledge of subtraction?

At first glance, it is tempting to conclude simply that the child still has a lot to learn about how to subtract. Most of the answers are incorrect, and there is no readily apparent pattern to the errors. On closer inspection, however, it becomes clear that the student's behavior is far from random. In fact, the errors result from two specific confusions about the rules of subtraction. One confusion concerns the rules for borrowing. Whenever this student needs to borrow from a column, he continues to borrow from every remaining column, whether borrowing is necessary or not. It is this confusion that accounts for the errors on problems 1, 4, and 7. The second confusion concerns the rules for subtracting from 0. Whenever the top digit in a column is 0, the student writes the bottom digit as the answer. It is this confusion that leads to the mistakes on problems 2, 5, and 8.

The confusions illustrated in the table are examples of "bugs" in the student's rules for subtraction (Brown & Burton, 1978; Brown & Van Lehn, 1982). In computer science, the term *bug* refers to an error in a computer program. Brown and colleagues use the term in much the same way in referring to children's knowledge of arithmetic. A bug, therefore, is a systematic error in an otherwise correct system of rules. A bug does not result in random responding—the responses shown in the table are quite systematic and predictable. Nor does the existence of bugs imply a complete absence of understanding—the answers in the table reflect a fair degree of knowledge about subtraction. Bugs do mean, however, that knowledge is incomplete and errors will occur.

Once they are pointed out, the bugs in the table are easy enough to see. Identifying bugs, however, can be a major challenge. The approach taken by Brown and colleagues is a version of Siegler's (1976) rule-assessment methodology. They begin with a long list of bugs that might arise in a child's understanding of arithmetic—a list based both on task analysis and on samples of children's arithmetic performance. A set of problems is then constructed to test for the existence of the hypothesized bugs. As with Siegler's rules, spe-

cific predictions can be made about the patterns of answers that would result from different methods of solution. For example, a child whose only confusion was the subtracting-from-0 bug would miss all problems in which 0 occurred in the top row and be correct on all other problems. Note that the predictions are quite specific—not just success or failure, but the exact error that the bug would produce.

The studies carried out by Brown and associates verify that bugs of various sorts exist and that the rule-assessment approach is a useful technique for revealing them. The main goal of their work, however, has been to train teachers to recognize and correct bugs. To this end, two computerized games (BUGGY and DEBUGGY) were developed. The games involve interaction between teacher and computer. The computer produces an example of a particular bug, the teacher forms a hypothesis about the bug and generates some further problems to test the hypothesis, the computer responds to the problems, the teacher revises the hypothesis and tests again, and so forth. Teachers who work with these programs have been shown to benefit in two general ways. First, they become more skillful at detecting particular bugs. They learn, for example, not to zero in too quickly on a single hypothesis and not to present problems that serve only to confirm rather than to test their ideas. The second benefit is more general and perhaps even more important. BUGGY and DEBUGGY help teachers to realize that children's errors are not necessarily the result of carelessness or lack of motivation or inability to follow rules. Rather, a child may be quite systematic and logical in applying a rule system, but the rules with which he is working may be incorrect in certain respects. Knowing exactly what a child's problems are is a first step in correcting those problems.

Examples of Subtraction Bugs

1.	662	2.	140	3.	389	4.	631	5.	905
	−357		−21		−344		−402		−624
	205		121		45		129		321

6.	477	7.	456	8.	700
	−56		−38		−395
	21		318		495

never develop satisfactory reading skills. Can research help to identify the problems and suggest solutions?

Reading as a cognitive activity is in fact closely bound to many of the cognitive processes discussed throughout this chapter. Strategies are again important, for example. Siegler's (1988) research has shown that children develop strategies for identifying words that are analogous to their strategies for adding numbers. They use retrieval from memory, for example, for high-certainty targets and fall back on slower sounding-out strategies when faced with less well known words. There are again individual differences, with good readers more likely to use retrieval than poor readers. Strategies are also important when children move beyond individual words and attempt to comprehend text. Comprehension monitoring is central to effective reading—that is, continual self-checking to be sure that what has been read is understood, coupled with rereading and other correction procedures when comprehension fails. Older children are generally better at comprehension monitoring than younger children, and good readers are better than poor readers (Garner, 1990). Monitoring their reading efforts may be the most important metacognitive skill that many people exercise.

The developments discussed in regard to representation and problem solving also play a role in reading. The formation of story schemas can help children to understand text that fits an established schema (Garner, 1993). More generally, knowledge of a variety of sorts can be brought to the task of comprehension, and again there are both developmental and individual differences in the ability to use existing knowledge to make sense of new information (Siegler, 1991). Memory is important as well. The kind of short-term storage space stressed in Case's (1985) theory is critical for reading—to understand even a single sentence, readers must be able to hold in memory the first words read as they progress to later words in the sentence. Difficulties with short-term memory are one contributor to problems in reading (Siegel, 1993a).

Thus far our focus has been on the ultimate goal in reading—namely, comprehension of text. But a number of more basic processing steps must be executed before comprehension becomes an issue: perception of letters, translation of letters into sounds, combination of individual sounds into words. Here, too, research has provided a wealth of information about how reading occurs and about differences between good and poor readers (Adams, 1990; Rack, Hulme, & Snowling, 1993; Rayner, 1993). One finding, in particular, emerges as important with respect to both developmental and individual differences, and that concerns the role of phonological awareness. The term **phonological awareness** refers to both the general realization that letters correspond to sounds and the ability to perform specific letter-to-sound translations. It refers, in short, to children's ability to "crack the code"—to figure out how squiggles on paper can yield the sounds and words of the language. So defined, phonological awareness would appear to be central to reading, and research suggests that this is the case (Siegel, 1993b; Stanovich, 1988). Deficits in phonological decoding skills are a major contributor to severe reading difficulties. And the early emergence of phonological awareness is a good predictor of eventual reading ability. Indeed, measures of phonological awareness in preschool are a better predictor of subsequent reading than are measures of IQ (Goswami & Bryant, 1990).

The studies of phonological awareness are relevant to the long-standing debate between two approaches to the teaching of reading: the phonics and whole-word approaches. A **phonics** approach to reading instruction stresses letter-sound correspondences and the build-up of words from individual units; a **whole-word** approach

• Reading is one of the most important cognitive skills that children develop. Information-processing researchers attempt to identify the many specific components that make successful reading possible.

Phonological awareness
The realization that letters correspond to sounds and the ability to perform specific letter-to-sound translations.

Phonics
An approach to reading instruction that stresses letter–sound correspondences and the build-up of words from individual units.

Whole-word
An approach to reading instruction that stresses learning and visual retrieval of entire words.

stresses learning and visual retrieval of entire words without working through individual sounds. As Siegler (1991) notes, one reason that the debate has continued is that there is no simple right answer to the question of how best to teach reading. Both methods work well for some children and fail to work for others, and a full program of reading instruction must undoubtedly incorporate aspects of both approaches. Nevertheless, many researchers and practitioners believe that the findings from reading research indicate a need for a greater emphasis on phonics than is the case in many school systems today (Chall, 1983; Perfetti, 1991; Vellutino, 1991).

✔ *To Recap...*

Studies of arithmetic indicate that children develop a variety of strategies to solve arithmetical problems and that they typically use several strategies rather than just one. With increased age, there is a gradual ascendance of more efficient strategies (such as retrieval), and within any age good students are more advanced in strategy selection and more skilled in strategy execution than are weaker students.

Studies of reading indicate that basic cognitive processes stressed in information-processing theory are important for reading. Strategies (such as comprehension monitoring), general knowledge (such as story schemas), and short-term memory all contribute to reading comprehension. Also important is phonological awareness, the realization that letters correspond to sounds and the ability to perform specific letter-to-sound translations.

COGNITIVE CHANGE

In Chapter 8 we concluded that Piaget never succeeded in providing a fully detailed and satisfactory theory of cognitive change. Much the same criticism has often been leveled against information-processing theorists (Miller, 1993). Most information-processing accounts have been more successful at specifying the various levels or states of understanding through which the cognitive system moves than at explaining the transition from one state to another.

In this section we consider the explanations for cognitive change that have been offered in information-processing theories to date (Klahr, 1989, 1992; Miller, 1993; Siegler, 1989; Siegler & Jenkins, 1989; Siegler & Munakata, 1993). We begin with some general points about the information-processing approach to explaining cognitive change. We then discuss several specific mechanisms of change that have been proposed by theorists in this tradition.

General Points

A number of guiding principles characterize information-processing attempts to explain cognitive development. A first principle is that we cannot explain the transition from one state to another until we have a good understanding of exactly what the states are and therefore exactly what is changing. In the words of Klahr and Wallace (1976), "A theory of transition can be no better than the associated theory of what it is that is undergoing that transition" (p. 14). Thus, the information-processing theorist's precise accounts of the different forms of knowledge that develop across childhood are not simply of interest in themselves. They are a necessary basis for formulating a theory of change.

A second principle is related. The kinds of change that a child can show in response to new experience depend on the child's current level of knowledge. New strategies, rules, and the like must always be built on an existing base. In a broad sense, therefore, information-processing theorists agree with Piaget about the importance of *readiness* for cognitive change. Their approach to the concept, however, differs from Piaget's in two ways. First, as noted in the discussion of conservation training studies, Piaget's theory is often vague with respect to exactly what the important components of readiness are. Information-processing accounts attempt to provide a more precise and testable description of the prerequisites for cognitive change. Second, Piaget's notion of readiness, like the stages on which it is based, is a very broad notion that extends to numerous aspects of the child's development. Thus, the preoperational child may be said to be unprepared to learn a wide range of logical concepts. Information-processing theorists are more domain-specific in their approach to readiness. A child's readiness to master some new set of skills may depend largely on his or her prior experience with related skills. And the child's readiness for one kind of learning may not be the same as his or her readiness for another kind of learning.

A third principle is that many different mechanisms may contribute to development. Some theories have attempted to explain development primarily in terms of one general, all-inclusive principle. Piaget's concept of equilibration is one well-known example. Some early versions of learning theory, with their almost exclusive emphasis on reinforcement as a source of change, are another example. Information-processing theorists have been more eclectic in their approach, proposing a number of different mechanisms that may contribute to change. We discuss some of these mechanisms shortly.

A final distinctive emphasis in the information-processing approach to change is methodological—an emphasis on experimental procedures through which processes of change can be studied directly. Information-processing researchers have utilized a variety of techniques to study the process of change. Case's (1985) research, for example, makes use of both the training-study strategy discussed earlier and naturalistic observations of children's problem-solving efforts. As we discuss shortly, Siegler (1976) has also applied the training study approach to performance on the balance scale task. Some information-processing researchers have attempted to develop *self-modifying computer simulations*—that is, computer programs that can use available input to transform themselves from lower to higher levels of cognitive performance (Klahr, 1992). Theories of the steps and processes through which children make cognitive progress can be tested by seeing whether such steps and processes can be successfully simulated on the computer. Finally, an especially informative approach in recent research has been the *microgenetic method* discussed in Chapter 3. In a microgenetic study, the researcher presents tasks for children to solve (such as problems in elementary arithmetic) and then observes their behavior as they work repeatedly and intensively on such problems—perhaps dozens of hours of observation spread across several weeks. The attempt is to capsulize the time frame for cognitive change and to observe within a relatively short period processes that ordinarily would be spread across a much longer time (Siegler & Crowley, 1991, 1992; Siegler & Jenkins, 1989). The microgenetic method was the source for many of Siegler's conclusions about elementary arithmetic discussed in the previous section.

Mechanisms of Change

As noted, information-processing theorists have proposed a number of different change mechanisms. Here we consider three: encoding, automatization, and strategy construction.

Siegler (1991) defines **encoding** as "identifying the most important features of objects and events and using the features to form internal representations" (p. 10). Encoding is thus related to what we normally mean by attention, but it carries some further implications as well. One is the idea that information processing is always active rather than passive, because the child attends to only some features of the environment and uses only some features to arrive at judgments. The other is the emphasis on how the child interprets or represents the encoded information. Encoding involves not simply attending but also forming some sort of representation of what has been attended to, and it is this representation that guides subsequent problem solving.

Let us consider how the concept of encoding can be applied to Siegler's balance-scale task. Recall that children who use rule 1 base their judgments solely on the number of weights. Siegler (1976) tested such children's encoding of the relevant information. First, he allowed the children to observe an arrangement of the scale for 10 seconds. Then he covered the scale, brought another scale forward, and asked the children to reproduce the arrangement that they had just seen. Both 5-year-old and 8-year-old rule 1 users were tested. Siegler found that the 5-year-olds could reproduce only the weights and not the distances, evidence that they had encoded only weight. The 5-year-olds also failed to benefit from training trials on which they were shown the results of various configurations of weight and distance. As Siegler notes, the children's failure to learn from training is not surprising, given that they never encoded the critical information. The 8-year-olds, in contrast, were able to encode both weight and distance, even though they did not yet use distance information in making their judgments. Because of their sensitivity to both variables, the 8-year-olds were able to benefit from the same training that had been ineffective with the 5-year-olds.

Siegler's work suggests a three-phase sequence in the relation between developmental level and encoding. Initially, children's reasoning and encoding are at the same level; they encode only some features and they use only these features in their reasoning. The 5-year-old rule 1 users exemplify this phase. Eventually, children begin to encode new features of the world, even though at first they may not realize the significance of these features. The 8-year-old rule 1 users are at this phase. Finally, with relevant experience, children can integrate their various encodings, and their reasoning advances to a new level.

A second mechanism is **automatization**. As noted in the context of Case's (1985) theory of the role of memory in problem solving, there is a characteristic progression in the development of any cognitive skill. At first, the skill—precisely because it is new—requires considerable attention and effort, and few resources may be left for any other sort of cognitive processing. With practice, however, execution of the skill becomes more and more automatic, cognitive resources are freed, and more advanced forms of problem solving become possible. Automatization is a primary mechanism by which the cognitive system overcomes inherent limitations on the amount of information that can be processed.

The same can be said for a third mechanism, **strategy construction**. Like automatization, strategies serve to overcome processing limitations by increasing the efficiency with which information is handled. The child who realizes the organization inherent in a set of items, for example, may need to remember only the general categories and not every individual item. In speculating about the origins of strategies, Siegler suggests that the various change mechanisms may work together. Once some cognitive activity becomes sufficiently automatized, resources are freed for new encodings, and these new encodings may make new strategies possible.

Encoding
Attending to and forming internal representations of certain features of the environment. A mechanism of change in information-processing theories.

Automatization
An increase in the efficiency with which cognitive operations are executed as a result of practice. A mechanism of change in information-processing theories.

Strategy construction
The creation of strategies for processing and remembering information. A mechanism of change in information-processing theories.

Consider the mnemonic strategy of organization—that is, the tendency to group items into categories as an aid to recall. Children may first need to become skilled at scanning arrays of stimuli (such as lists of words) and encoding important attributes. Once this process has become largely automatic, they can notice and encode higher order attributes (stating, for example, "They're all fruit"). And once they can encode the higher order attributes, they can organize their attention and recall in terms of these general categories—a strategy that will in turn make further cognitive advances possible.

✔ *To Recap...*

Information-processing theorists have set forth several general principles for a theory of cognitive change. One is that theories of change must rest on solid knowledge of the various states of development, so that it is clear exactly what is changing. Another is that the child's current state of knowledge is an important determinant of what kinds of change are possible. A third is that because development has many determinants, a theory of change must encompass a number of specific mechanisms. Among the methods used by information-processing researchers to study cognitive change are self-modifying computer simulations and microgenetic studies.

Three mechanisms that seem to be important are encoding, automatization, and strategy construction. Developmental advances in encoding make developmental advances in reasoning possible. Automatization frees resources for other cognitive activities. Strategy construction can help in overcoming the limitations of the information-processing system. These three mechanisms may often work together; for example, automatization may allow children to make new encodings, which in turn may allow them to formulate new strategies.

CONCLUSION

The emergence of information processing as a dominant approach to the study of cognitive development has been remarkably rapid. Twenty years ago information processing did not really exist as a distinct position within developmental psychology. Today it clearly ranks among the leading approaches to the study of children's intelligence.

The reasons for this rapid emergence should be evident from our discussion of the many successes of information-processing theory and research. Given our focus on these successes, it is reasonable now to ask about limitations. How is the approach, at least as developed to date, limited in what it tells us? Several limitations have been suggested (Kail & Bisanz, 1982; Kuhn, 1992; Miller, 1993).

One limitation concerns scope. Information-processing research, it is true, has addressed many different aspects of child development. Information-processing theories have been more limited. To date, information-processing theorists have been most successful at constructing precise models of specific, but also somewhat limited, aspects of child development (such as Siegler's model [1988] of how children solve arithmetic problems). There is as yet no information-processing theory that rivals Piaget's theory in the scope of phenomena it encompasses.

Another limitation concerns context. Most information-processing studies, in keeping with the underlying computer metaphor, focus on intelligent behavior in tightly controlled and even isolated environments. Information-processing researchers have paid limited attention to the natural context within which thinking and development occur. Some recent work on memory has begun to take context into account (e.g., Ceci et al., 1988). To date, however, such attempts are few.

A third limitation concerns a particular aspect of context, namely the social environment. Humans, unlike computers, interact constantly with other humans, and these interactions are both an important context for exercising cognitive skills and one of the sources of those skills. Although information-processing conceptions have certainly influenced the study of social cognition, the social world has been a relatively neglected topic for most information-processing researchers. Again, recent research on memory provides a promising exception to this statement.

The final limitation has already been mentioned. Despite much recent attention to the issue, information-processing theorists are still far from producing a completely satisfactory explanation of how cognitive change occurs.

These limitations, it should be clear, reflect information processing in its current state of development. They constitute challenges for the future, not inherent deficiencies of the approach.

FOR THOUGHT AND DISCUSSION

1. The term *infantile amnesia* refers to our inability to remember events from the first 2 or 3 years of life. *Think about your own earliest memories. What sorts of events do they include? Why do you think that you remember these events and not numerous others from early childhood? How confident are you that these early memories are accurate?*

2. Mnemonic strategies are techniques that both children and adults use to help themselves remember something. *How often do you employ mnemonic strategies? In what situations are you most likely to use strategies, and what forms do the strategies take? How much of what you remember comes from the deliberate use of strategies?*

3. The accuracy of children's eyewitness testimony is an important and controversial topic. *Imagine that you had the task of designing the program of questioning for a young (say 4- or 5-year-old) suspected victim of abuse. How would you proceed?*

4. We noted the centrality of the computer metaphor to the ways in which information-processing researchers think about and study cognition. *Do you perceive possible limitations to the computer metaphor—that is, aspects of human cognition that cannot be captured in a computer program? If so, what are the differences that you see between human intelligence and computer intelligence?*

5. We discussed how information-processing ideas have been applied to the learning of reading and arithmetic in childhood. *Think about the possible application of the approach to another academic subject, such as writing or science. How would an information-processing researcher study the topic, and what sorts of conclusions might he or she offer?*

6. In Chapter 8 we discussed the Piagetian approach to cognitive change and the constructs of assimilation, accommodation, and equilibration. In the present chapter we considered the information-processing approach and the notions of encoding, automatization, and strategy construction. *How similar or different do you perceive these two approaches as being? Do you prefer one or the other set of change mechanisms? If so, why?*

Chapter 10

COGNITIVE DEVELOPMENT: THE INTELLIGENCE TEST APPROACH

$\mathcal{P}$iaget is hardly a household word, despite the fact that his name probably appears more often in textbooks and professional articles than that of any other child psychologist. The information-processing theorists and programs of research discussed in Chapter 9 are undoubtedly even less familiar. Everyone, however, has heard of IQ. And many people have quite definite opinions, either positive or negative, on the validity and uses of IQ tests.

Debates about IQ are not limited to the popular press. IQ tests have been a source of controversy among psychologists and educators ever since their introduction early in the century. The controversy has waxed and waned, but it has never disappeared (Locurto, 1991; Snyderman & Rothman, 1988; Weinberg, 1989). At present, it appears to be at one of its high points.

Why has the intelligence test, or **psychometric**, approach to cognition been so controversial? At least part of the answer lies in some important differences between this approach and the Piagetian and information-processing perspectives. Some of the differences relate to the distinction between normative and idiographic approaches to development, one of the general issues identified in Chapter 1. Piaget's approach falls clearly under the normative heading, in that his emphasis was always on similarities in children's development—that is, concepts all children develop and stages all children move through. Piaget was never very much interested in individual differences among children. Although information-processing researchers have paid more attention to individual differences than did Piaget, they also have tended to concentrate on basic processes that are common to all children. In contrast, the main point of the intelligence test approach is to identify *differences* in children's cognitive abilities. Furthermore, an IQ test identifies not just differences but *ordered* differences—it says that one child is more or less intelligent than another or that a particular child is above or below average in intelligence. IQ tests thus involve an evaluative component that is impossible to escape from. The fact that such tests force us to make value judgments about children is one reason they have always been controversial.

Another difference between the intelligence test approach and the Piagetian and information-processing approaches concerns purpose and uses. The research discussed in the two preceding chapters is very much theoretically oriented, its goal being to identify basic cognitive processes. We saw that such research has begun to have practical applications (e.g., effects on school curriculum); to date, however, such applications have been limited and secondary to the basic theoretical aims. In contrast, the psychometric approach has been pragmatically oriented from the start. As we will see, IQ tests were designed for practical purposes, and they have always had practical uses—most notably, to determine what kind of schooling a child is to receive. This factor, too, contributes to the controversy. Unlike many of psychologists' measures, IQ tests really can make a difference in a child's life.

In this chapter, we begin by reviewing what IQ tests for children look like, along with some of their strengths and weaknesses. We then move on to some of the theoretical issues that have been the focus of research in the psychometric tradition. Because of the importance of the question, we pay special attention to the role of experience in the development of intelligence, considering both the contribution of the family environment and the effects of schooling. Although our emphasis is on IQ, we occasionally broaden the scope to include other ways to assess differences in intellectual ability. And in the final part of the chapter, we break away from the traditional IQ approach to consider some recent and exciting alternative approaches to studying intelligence.

Psychometric
An approach to the study of intelligence that emphasizes the use of standardized tests to identify individual differences among people.

THE NATURE OF IQ TESTS

Although everyone (at least in our culture) has heard of IQ, not everyone knows how IQ tests are put together or exactly what kinds of abilities such tests measure. We begin, therefore, with an overview of the history and construction of IQ tests. We take a brief look at several specific tests and then turn to the important question of how to evaluate such measures.

The Binet Approach to Measuring Intelligence

The first successful intelligence test was developed in Paris in 1905 by Alfred Binet and Theodore Simon. Binet and Simon had been hired by the Paris school authorities to develop a test that could be given to children who were having difficulty in school. The goal was to distinguish between children who were capable, perhaps with extra help, of succeeding in school and children who were simply not intelligent enough to cope with the regular curriculum. Once the latter group had been identified, they could be placed in special classes from which they might benefit. This sort of "tracking" based on test performance has become controversial in recent years (Linn, 1986). But it originally had a quite humanitarian purpose.

Binet and Simon took a pragmatic approach to their task. They tried out a large number of possible items for their test, looking especially at how two groups of children performed: children who were known to do well in school and children who were known to do poorly in school. Those items that differentiated between these two groups—that is, those on which the academically successful children did better than the academically unsuccessful ones—were the items that they kept for the test. The ability to predict academic success was thus the prime criterion for an item's inclusion as a measure of intelligence. The test items, some of which still appear in

• IQ tests were originally devised for purposes of school placement in Paris school systems in the early 1900s. Such educational applications remain important for contemporary IQ tests.

Figure 10-1   Typical distribution of IQ scores in a sample of children. Tests like the Stanford–Binet are designed to yield a normal distribution of IQs with a mean of 100. These data are from an early form of the Stanford–Binet Intelligence Scale (L—M). From *Stanford–Binet Intelligence Scale* (3rd ed., p. 18) by L. M. Terman and M. A. Merrill, 1973, Chicago: The Riverside Publishing Company. Copyright 1973 by the Riverside Publishing Company. Reproduced with permission of the Riverside Publishing Company, 8420 W. Bryn Mawr Avenue, Chicago, IL 60631.

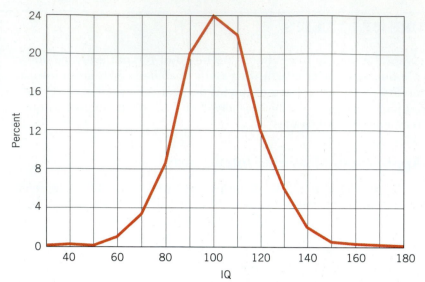

modified form on modern tests, included identification of parts of the body, naming of familiar objects, and distinguishing between abstract words—for example, indicating the difference between *liking* and *respecting*.

The Stanford–Binet Intelligence Scale (Thorndike, Hagen, & Sattler, 1986) is the direct descendant of the original Binet–Simon test. It was developed in 1916 by Lewis Terman at Stanford University and has been revised several times since. The Stanford–Binet shares several features with Binet's original instrument. It is a test of childhood intelligence, applicable to every age group within the span of childhood except infancy. It is a global measure of intelligence, designed to yield a single "intelligence quotient," or IQ, score that summarizes the child's ability. And it stresses the kinds of verbal and academic skills that are important in school. More specifically, the newest version of the Stanford-Binet is intended to assess four general kinds of ability: verbal reasoning, quantitative reasoning, abstract/visual reasoning, and short-term memory.

The Stanford–Binet—and indeed every other standardized test of intelligence—shares one other important feature with Binet's original test. We saw that Binet's approach to measuring intelligence was based on comparing the performances of different groups of children. All contemporary tests of intelligence are comparative, or relative, measures. There is no absolute metric for measuring intelligence, the way that there is for measuring height or weight. Instead, a child's IQ is a function of how that child's performance compares with the performance of other children the same age. Children who perform at the average for their age group have average IQs, which by convention are set at 100. Children who outperform their peers have above-average IQs; children who lag behind their age group have below-average IQs. The greater the discrepancy from average, the higher or lower the IQ will be. Figure 10-1 shows a typical distribution of IQ scores.

Other Tests of Childhood Intelligence

The leading alternative to the Stanford–Binet is a series of tests developed by David Wechsler. There are two Wechsler tests designed for childhood: the Wechsler Intelligence Scale for Children (WISC), which is intended for ages 6 to 16, and the Wechsler Preschool and Primary Scale of Intelligence (WPPSI), which

• Tests such as the Stanford-Binet or Wechsler are individually administered. The tester attempts to elicit the best performance of which the child is capable.

is intended for ages 4 to 6.5 (Wechsler, 1989, 1991). The Wechsler bears many similarities to the Stanford–Binet, including a focus on academically relevant skills. One difference between the two tests is that the Wechsler is divided into a verbal scale (which includes items such as vocabulary and general information) and a performance scale (which includes items such as assembling a puzzle and reproducing a design). The test therefore yields both an overall IQ and separate verbal and performance IQs. Some examples of the kinds of items included on the test are shown in Table 10-1.

Other tests of childhood IQ differ in either the target group for whom they are intended or the way in which they are administered. Some tests are directed to infancy, the one age period not covered by the Stanford–Binet or Wechsler. The best known measure of infant development is the Bayley Scales of Infant Development (Bayley, 1969, 1993). Not surprisingly, measures of infant intelligence tend to stress sensorimotor skills, as opposed to the academic and verbal emphasis found in tests for older children. The Bayley Test, for example, is divided into a motor scale (with items assessing control of the body, muscular coordination, manipulatory skill, and so on) and a mental scale (including items assessing sen-sory-perceptual acuity, vocalization, and memory). Table 10-2 presents some items from the mental scale. The column labeled "Age Placement" refers to the average age at which infants succeed on the item.

In addition to individually administered tests like the Stanford–Binet and Wechsler, there are also group tests of intelligence—that is, tests that can be administered to large numbers of children at the same time. Because of their ease of administration and efficiency, group tests are common in school settings. Undoubtedly the majority of IQ scores that exist in school files come from group tests.

Evaluating the Tests

How can we decide whether a test that claims to measure intelligence really does? A standardized test of intelligence—or indeed of any attribute—must meet two criteria: reliability and validity.

TABLE 10-1 ● Types of Items Included on the Wechsler Intelligence Scale for Children—Third Edition

Subtest	Verbal Scale
Information	How many wings does a bird have?
	How many nickels make a dime?
	What is pepper?
Arithmetic	Sam had three pieces of candy and Joe gave him four more.
	How many pieces of candy did Sam have altogether?
	If two apples cost $.15, what will be the cost of a dozen apples?
Vocabulary	What is a _____ ? or What does _____ mean?
	Hammer
	Protect
	Epidemic

Subtest	Performance Scale
Object assembly	Put the pieces together to make a familiar object.

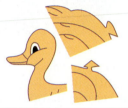

Source: Adapted from *Wechsler Intelligence Scale for Children—Third Edition* by D. Wechsler, 1991, San Antonio: The Psychological Corporation. Copyright 1991 by the Psychological Corporation. Adapted by permission.

Reliability

The consistency or repeatability of measurement is referred to as **reliability**. Does the test give us a consistent picture of what the child can do? Or do scores on the test fluctuate from one testing occasion to the next, perhaps sometimes coming out very high and sometimes very low? Clearly, a test that lacks reliability can hardly give us an accurate measure of the child's ability.

The notion of reliability does not mean that children's IQ scores can never change. Scores often do go up or down as children develop. Reliability refers to short-term consistency—that is, to the constancy of the measuring instrument, not of the child. The major tests of childhood IQ, such as the Stanford–Binet and Wechsler, do possess good reliability.

Validity

The second criterion that a test must meet is **validity**. The issue of validity is easy to summarize: Does the test measure what it claims to measure? Do scores on the Stanford–Binet, for example, really reflect individual differences in children's intelligence? Or do the scores have some other basis—perhaps differences in motivation, or in general test-taking ability, or in familiarity with the specific test content?

The validity of a test can be determined in various ways. The approach most commonly used for IQ tests is labeled *criterion validity*. To determine criterion validity, we first specify some external measure, or criterion, of the attribute that we are attempting to assess. We then see whether scores on our test relate to performance on this external criterion. For tests of childhood IQ, the most common ex-

TABLE 10-2 ● **Examples of Items From the Bayley Scales of Infant Development (2nd ed.)**

Age Placement (in months)	Ability Measured	Procedure	Credit
1	Habituates to rattle	Shake rattle at regular intervals behind child's head	If child shows an initial alerting response that decreases over trials
6	Smiles at mirror image	Place mirror in front of child	If child smiles at image in mirror
12	Pushes car	Push toy car while child watches, then tell child, "Push the car, push the car like I did."	If child intentionally pushes car so that all four wheels stay on table
17–19	Uses two different words appropriately	Record the child's spontaneous word usage throughout the exam	If child uses two (nonimitative) words appropriately
23–25	Points to five pictures	Show pictures of 10 common objects (e.g., dog, book, car), say "Show me the _____ ."	If child either correctly points to or names at least five pictures

Source: From *Bayley Scales of Infant Development* (2nd ed.) (pp. 59, 75, 84, 96, 108) by N. Bayley, 1993, San Antonio: The Psychological Corporation. Copyright 1993 by the Psychological Corporation. Reprinted by permission.

ternal criterion has been the one used by Binet and Simon—performance in school or on standardized tests of academic ability. Tests like the Stanford–Binet do in fact relate to academic performance, with typical correlations falling in the range of .5 to .7 (Minton & Schneider, 1980; Snow & Yalow, 1982). Thus, on the average, the higher the child's IQ, the better the child does in school. It is this ability to predict an important aspect of everyday intelligent behavior that constitutes the argument for IQ tests as valid measures of intelligence.

It is important to note some qualifications to the points just made. A correlation of .5 indicates a moderate relation between IQ and academic performance. But if the correlation is only .5, there must also be a number of exceptions to this on-the-average relation—children with high IQs who do poorly in school, children with average or below-average IQs who do well in school. Knowing a child's IQ does not allow us to predict that child's school performance (or, indeed, anything else) with certainty. Furthermore, as we saw in Chapter 3, a correlation in itself does not allow us to determine the cause and effect. Thus, simply knowing that IQ correlates with school performance does not allow us to conclude that children do well or poorly in school *because* of their IQs. This is one possible explanation for the correlation, but it is not the only one. All we know for certain is that there is some relation between the two variables.

We can note finally that there is obviously a kind of inbred relation between IQ tests and school performance. IQ tests for children were devised to predict school performance, and this is what they do (although not perfectly). Performance in school is important in our culture; so, too, is performance in the occupational contexts that school success often leads to. It is reasonable to argue, therefore, that IQ tests do measure something of what we mean by intelligence in our culture. But the

• IQ tests are most successful at measuring skills necessary for success in school. Such tests may not capture forms of intelligence that are important in other contexts.

qualifications implied by this wording are important. IQ tests may not tap cognitive skills that are important in other cultures, for example (as discussed in Chapter 8), the ability to navigate in a society in which sailing is important, or (as discussed later in this chapter) the ability to succeed as an urban candy vendor at an age when most Western children have barely started school. They may not even tap skills that are important for some subgroups within our culture, such as the ability to do chores on the family farm or to cope with the challenges of life in an inner-city ghetto. And for any individual, they at best measure *something* of intelligence, not everything that we would want this term to mean. The two preceding chapters considered numerous aspects of intelligence that are not well captured by IQ tests. Later in this chapter, we will see that even within the psychometric tradition there are a number of interesting alternatives to IQ.

✔ To Recap...

The intelligence test, or psychometric, approach to intelligence is in several respects different from the Piagetian and information-processing approaches. The purpose of IQ tests is to measure individual differences in intellectual ability. Such tests were originally devised for practical purposes, and they have always had practical applications—school placement, for example. Such real-world applications contribute to the controversy that has always surrounded IQ tests.

Tests of intelligence must be both reliable and valid. IQ tests do possess satisfactory reliability. Whether the tests are valid measures of intelligence has been more difficult to determine. Tests of childhood IQ do relate to measures of academic performance, an important external criterion of childhood intelligence. The relation is not perfect, however. Furthermore, the academic focus of most IQ tests means that they may not be good measures of other kinds of intelligence.

ISSUES IN THE STUDY OF INTELLIGENCE

We have emphasized the pragmatic origins and uses of IQ tests. But the early pioneers of intelligence testing, including Binet, were also interested in theoretical questions about the nature of intelligence. And IQ tests have long served as another context, in addition to Piagetian and information-processing measures, for trying to determine what intelligence is and how it changes with development. In this section, we consider some of the theoretical issues that have most intrigued researchers in the intelligence test tradition.

The Organization of Intelligence

The question of the organization or structure of intelligence is a basic issue that any approach to intelligence must confront. We have seen how Piagetian and information-processing researchers have examined this question. Psychometric researchers also study the organization of intelligence. But the methods they use are different from those that we have encountered thus far.

In the psychometric approach, conclusions about the organization of intelligence are based on the individual differences that IQ tests elicit. The issue is whether these differences show consistent and interpretable patterns, patterns that can tell us something about how intelligence is organized.

Let us consider two opposed possibilities. Suppose that intelligence is a unitary trait—that is, that there is a single "general intelligence" that people possess in varying degrees. If so, then the particular task that we use to measure intelligence should not really matter. Some people—those who are high in general intelligence—will do well whatever the task, and some will do poorly whatever the task. This outcome would be reflected in uniformly high correlations among different measures of intelligence.

Consider now a very different hypothesis. Perhaps there is no such thing as general intelligence. Perhaps instead there are a number of "specific intelligences"—verbal intelligence, mathematical intelligence, spatial intelligence, and so on. People may be high in one form of intelligence but low in some other form. What happens, then, if we administer a test battery that assesses these different forms of intelligence? We no longer expect uniformly high correlations among our measures. Instead, a particular task should correlate most strongly with other tasks that are measuring the same kind of intelligence. Verbal tasks, for example, should correlate strongly with other verbal tasks but weakly or not at all with measures of spatial ability.

The preceding example summarizes the psychometric approach to the organization of intelligence: determine how intelligence is organized by examining the pattern of correlations across different measures of intelligence. In practice, the approach is more complicated than this brief description suggests. Psychometric researchers use a complex statistical procedure called *factor analysis* to make sense of the large number of correlations that their research yields. The goal of factor analysis is to identify the basic components or "factors" that underlie some set of measurements. Items that cluster together in the correlations are assigned to the same underlying factor (such as verbal ability). There are disagreements about exactly how to carry out and interpret factor analyses, and results may vary depending on the method used. Results may also vary across different batteries of tasks or different samples of subjects (Kail & Pellegrino, 1985; Sternberg & Powell, 1983). Thus, psychometric researchers provide no single, agreed-upon answer to the structure question. But they have offered some interesting theories and related findings.

General Versus Specific

We have already previewed the question that has generated the most interest and debate among researchers of the organization of intelligence. Is intelligence a single general ability? Or does intelligence consist instead of a number of specific abilities?

g
General intelligence. *g* is assumed to determine performance on a wide range of intellectual measures.

The earliest proponent of the general intelligence view was the inventor of factor analysis, Charles Spearman. Spearman proposed what has come to be called a two-factor theory of intelligence (Spearman, 1927). One factor is general intelligence, or **g**. In Spearman's view, *g* permeates every form of intellectual functioning and is the most important determinant of individual differences on any test of intelligence. The second factor is *s*, Spearman's label for specific abilities that contribute to performance on particular tasks. Spearman used his newly invented technique of factor analysis to analyze correlations among different measures of intelligence. His conclusion was that the consistently positive correlations across measures were evidence for the existence and importance of *g*.

Other theorists have argued for a more differentiated model. Louis Thurstone, for example, developed an intelligence test designed to assess seven *primary mental abilities*: verbal comprehension, verbal fluency, number, spatial visualization, memory, reasoning, and perceptual speed (Thurstone, 1938; Thurstone & Thurstone, 1962). Thurstone regarded these seven abilities as largely independent and equally important.

Seven is by no means the maximum number of abilities that have been proposed. In J. P. Guilford's *structure of the intellect* model, there are at least 180 somewhat distinct mental abilities (Guilford, 1967, 1988)!

So what is the solution to the general versus specific dispute? As is often the case, the answer probably lies somewhere between extreme positions. The consistent finding of positive correlations among different measures of intelligence is evidence that something like general intelligence does exist. The fact that the correlations are far from perfect is evidence that more specific subskills also exist. This sort of solution is sometimes referred to as a **hierarchical model of intelligence**—a model in which intelligence is seen as being organized in a hierarchical fashion, with broad, general abilities at the top of the hierarchy and more limited, specific skills nested underneath (Sternberg, 1985). It is a model that probably corresponds to the intuitions that most of us hold about intelligence. We have some ability to order people, including ourselves, along some general dimension of intelligence. But we also realize that different people have different strengths and weaknesses and that we may outshine a particular peer in some respects yet lag behind in others.

Hierarchical model of intelligence
A model of the structure of intelligence in which intellectual abilities are seen as being organized hierarchically, with broad, general abilities at the top of the hierarchy and more specific skills nested underneath.

Developmental Changes in Structure

Another question is particularly interesting to child psychologists: Does the structure of intelligence change as the child develops? If so, how?

Two kinds of developmental change have been suggested. One is a differentiation of abilities with increasing age. In this view, the young child's intellectual system is relatively undifferentiated, consisting mainly of general intelligence rather than distinct abilities. As the child develops, however, specific and at least somewhat separate abilities emerge, and the unified intelligence of early childhood gives way to a more differentiated system. This position predicts a change in the pattern of correlations across childhood. In early childhood, different measures of intelligence should correlate strongly, because all tap into the same general cognitive system. In later childhood, the correlations should drop as the child's abilities become more differentiated. Factor-analytic studies provide some support for this prediction (Kail & Pellegrino, 1985; Sternberg, 1988).

The first developmental change, then, is in the number of distinct factors of intelligence that can be identified. The second change concerns the nature of the factors. Various models have been proposed, but most seem to be variants of the same general theme (Sternberg & Powell, 1983). In infancy, intelligence consists mainly of perceptual and motor abilities. As the child develops, symbolic and verbal abilities emerge, and the sensorimotor functioning of infancy is supplanted by more abstract forms of thought. Thus, *intelligence* means somewhat different things at different ages. This claim, too, finds some support in factor-analytic research (Plomin, DeFries, & Fulker, 1988; Sternberg, 1988).

Stability of IQ

Do children's IQs remain stable as they develop, so that we can assume that a child who scores a 100 at age 4 will also score 100 at 8 or 12 or 20? Or can a child's IQ change? This is a question of both theoretical and practical importance.

Answering the question requires a longitudinal approach, in which the same children are tested repeatedly across some span of time. Researchers have conducted many longitudinal studies of IQ, including some essential life-span efforts that began in the 1920s (Bayley, 1970). We therefore have quite a bit of data on this issue. Several conclusions emerge.

Prediction From Infancy

A first conclusion is that traditional tests of infant intelligence do not predict well to tests of later intelligence. The correlation between performance on the Bayley Scales, for example, and performance on later tests is typically close to 0 (Lipsitt, 1992; McCall, 1981). Thus, knowing how fast an infant is developing gives us no basis for predicting whether that infant will turn into an intelligent child or an intelligent adult. There are some exceptions to this statement. Very low scores on infant tests can sometimes be useful to indicate that there is some problem in development (McCall, 1979; Siegel, 1989). Scores on particular subparts of an infant test (such as items dealing with fine motor skills) may relate to measures of similar skills on childhood tests (Siegel, 1992). For the most part, however, individual differences in infant scores do not tell us much about how children will differ later in development. Thus, there is little reason for the parents of a precocious 6-month-old to begin sending away for college catalogues. And there is little reason for parents to become concerned just because their baby cannot stack blocks as early as the neighbors' babies.

Why should there be this gap between infant intelligence and later intelligence? The usual explanation stresses the differences in content between infant tests and childhood tests (Brownell & Strauss, 1984). Tests like the Stanford–Binet and WISC emphasize symbolic abilities (such as language) and abstract, higher order reasoning and problem solving. Infant tests, necessarily, stress quite different things—manual dexterity, visual and auditory alertness, and so on. This explanation is related to the continuity–discontinuity issue introduced in Chapter 1. The argument is that there is a discontinuity in the nature of intelligence between infancy and later childhood. Intelligence in infancy requires different skills than later intelligence, and thus it is not surprising that variations in infant development do not relate to variations in later development. The work on developmental changes in the structure of intelligence, discussed in the preceding section, is compatible with this hypothesis.

There is almost certainly some truth to the discontinuity argument. But to many psychologists, there is something unsatisfactory about any extreme version of the hypothesis. Surely there must be *some* continuity from infancy to childhood, *some* aspect of intelligence that is common across all age periods. But what might this common thread be?

A number of investigators have suggested that the common thread may be response to novelty. It seems reasonable to argue that the ability to make sense of new events is important for intelligence at any age. The form that novelty takes and the way that we respond to it may change greatly from one age period to another. But the ability to cope adaptively with something new should always be a component of intelligence.

Recent longitudinal research provides support for this hypothesis. Investigators have reported positive relations between various sorts of response to novelty in infancy and later measures of intelligence (Bornstein & Sigman, 1986; Colombo, 1993; McCall & Carriger, 1993; McCall & Mash, 1994). For example, babies who show an especially strong preference for new compared with familiar stimuli tend to do well on later IQ tests (Fagan, 1992; Thompson, Fagan, & Fulker, 1991). Similarly, babies who are especially quick to habituate to familiar stimuli tend to perform well on later tests (Slater et al., 1989). The relations that have been demonstrated to date are modest in size (typical correlations are about .35 to .40) and do not extend beyond middle childhood. Nevertheless, these findings do provide a first piece of evidence for some continuity in intelligence from infancy to later childhood.

As might be expected, the studies of response to novelty have led to the creation of a new approach to assessing infant intelligence. In the Fagan Test of Infant Intelligence (Fagan & Detterman, 1992; Fagan & Shepherd, 1986), babies are shown a picture to look at for a brief period, after which the original picture is paired with a slightly different novel picture (see Figure 10-2). The measure of interest is how long the baby looks at the novel compared with the familiar. The greater the interest in novelty, the higher the score on the test. And the higher the Fagan score, the higher, on the average, the later IQ.

Prediction Across Childhood

Beyond infancy, scores from traditional IQ tests do begin to correlate significantly from one age period to another. The correlation is not perfect, however. A typical set of findings is shown in Table 10-3.

Two rules for predicting stability in IQ can be abstracted from the data in Table 10-3 (Bjorklund, 1989). A first rule is that the degree of stability decreases as the time period between tests increases. Thus, we typically find more similarity in IQ between ages 3 and 6 than we do between ages 3 and 12. This pattern fits what we would expect from common sense: The longer we wait between tests, the more chance there is for some change to occur. Indeed, the pattern is not limited to IQ but applies generally whenever we measure stability or change across varying time periods (Nunnally, 1982).

As an illustration of the second rule, consider a comparison between the 3-to-6 correlation and the 9-to-12 correlation. Both reflect a 3-year interval, and hence by our first rule we would expect them to be equivalent. But the correlation is greater between 9 and 12 than it is between 3 and 6. In general, the older the child, the higher the correlation in IQ for any given span of time. This pattern, too, fits common sense: As children get older, major changes in their abilities relative to those of other children become less and less likely.

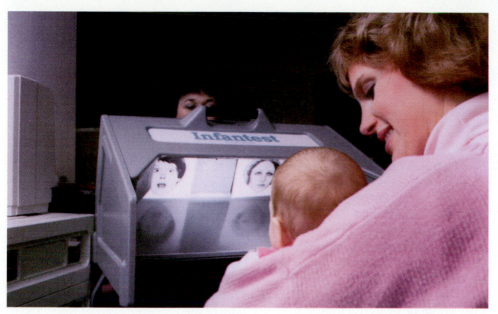

Figure 10-2 The Fagan Test of Infant Intelligence. Infants are first exposed to one of the two members of each stimulus pair, then given a chance to look at either the familiar stimulus or the novel alternative. A relatively strong preference for novelty correlates positively with later IQ. From "Predictive Validity of the Fagan Test of Infant Intelligence" by J. F. Fagan III, P. Shephard, & C. Knevel, 1991, Meeting of the Society for Research in Child Development, Copyright 1993 by J. F. Fagan III. Reprinted by permission.

Another way to examine the stability question is to ask about the magnitude of changes in IQ. If children's IQs do change (and the less-than-perfect correlations tell us that they do), how large can the changes be? One study found that 79% of a sample of children shifted at least 21 points in IQ between the ages of 2.5 and 17. For 14% of the children, the change was 40 points or more (McCall, Applebaum, & Hogarty, 1973).

In summary, probably the most reasonable position on the stability issue is one that avoids extreme statements. It is not correct to suggest that IQ fluctuates all over the place and that childhood IQ therefore has no predictive value. IQ shows moderately good stability, and the stability increases as the child gets older. On the other hand, it is also not correct to suggest that a child's IQ is fixed and unchangeable. IQs do change, and in some cases they change dramatically. We consider some of the reasons for change shortly.

Origins of Individual Differences

Our discussion of IQ has already touched on two of the issues introduced in Chapter 1—normative versus idiographic emphasis and continuity versus discontinuity. We turn next to the third and most general issue—nature versus nurture.

TABLE 10-3 ● Correlations in IQ Across Different Ages

Age	3	6	9	12	18
3		.57	.53	.36	.35
6			.80	.74	.61
9				.90	.76
12					.78

Source: Based on information from "The Stability of Mental Test Performance between Two and Eighteen Years" by M. P. Honzik, J. W. MacFarlan, and L. Allen, 1948, *Journal of Experimental Education, 17,* p. 323.

The question of where differences in intelligence come from has been perhaps the most common—and certainly the most heated—context for debates about the relative contributions of biology and experience to human development.

The question of the origins of individual differences in intelligence was first considered in Chapter 4 in the discussion of hereditary transmission. As noted there, researchers use three main approaches to study this question: family studies, adoption studies, and twin studies.

Family Studies

Family studies capitalize on our knowledge of the degree of genetic relation among different sorts of relatives. Parent and child, for example, have 50% of their genes in common. Two siblings also share an average of 50% of their genes. For grandparent and grandchild, the average genetic overlap is 25%. For first cousins, the overlap is 12.5%. In general, if we know the type of relation between two people, we know their degree of genetic similarity. We can then see whether similarity in IQ relates to similarity in genes.

Similarity in IQ *does* relate to similarity in genes. Typical correlations in IQ across different degrees of relation are shown in Table 10-4. These findings fit nicely with what would be expected from a genetic model of intelligence (Scarr & Kidd, 1983).

Adoption Studies

The problem in interpreting the family studies, of course, is that genetic similarity is not the only possible explanation for similarity in IQ. The pattern shown in Table 10-4 might also be accounted for by environmental factors. Siblings, after all, usually share similar experiences. Parents are typically an important part of their children's environments. We would expect some relation between the parent's IQ and the child's IQ solely for environmental reasons.

You may recall that studies of adopted children offer a way to disentangle the genetic and environmental explanations for parent–child similarity. Two sets of correlations are relevant. One is the correlation between the adopted child's IQ and the biological parents' IQs. In this case, the usual genetic basis for a correlation remains, but the environmental basis is ruled out. The other correlation of interest is that between the adopted child's IQ and the adoptive parents' IQs. In this case, the environmental basis remains, but the genetic contribution is ruled out.

Before discussing findings, we should note that adoption studies are not really as easy to interpret as this description suggests. In some cases, for example, when the separation of mother and infant does not occur at birth, the biological mother

TABLE 10-4 • Correlations in IQ as a Function of Degree of Genetic Relation

Relation	Median Correlation
Siblings	.55
Parent–child	.50
Grandparent–grandchild	.27
First cousins	.26
Second cousins	.16

Source: Adapted from "Genetics and the Development of Intelligence" by S. Scarr-Salapatek, 1975. In F. D. Horowitz (Ed.), *Review of Child Development Research* (Vol. 4, p. 33), Chicago: University of Chicago Press. Copyright 1975 by the University of Chicago Press. Adapted by permission.

provides part of the post-birth environment. In all cases, the biological mother provides the prenatal environment. Some researchers believe that prenatal experiences (e.g., the adequacy of nutrition) make an especially important contribution to later differences in intelligence (Jensen, 1969). There is also the possibility of selective placement, through which adoption agencies attempt to match characteristics of the adoptive parents with characteristics of the biological parents. To the extent that selective placement occurs, parent–child correlations can no longer be clearly interpreted as either genetic or environmental (Horn, 1983; Kamin, 1974).

Two main findings emerge from adoption studies (Turkheimer, 1991). One concerns the pattern of correlations. Typically, the adopted child's IQ correlates more strongly with the IQs of the biological parents than with the IQs of the adoptive parents (Horn, 1983; Loehlin, Horn, & Willerman, 1989; Plomin et al., 1988). This finding provides evidence for the importance of genetic factors. The biological parents make relatively little contribution to an adopted child's environment. But they still provide the child's genes.

The second finding concerns average level of IQ. In most studies the mean IQ for samples of adopted children falls in the range of 105 to 110 (Capron & Duyme, 1989; Scarr & Weinberg, 1983). Adopted children thus tend to have above-average IQs. Why should this be? The most plausible explanation is an environmental one. Parents who adopt children are not a random subset of the population of parents, nor are adoptive homes a random subset of the population of homes. Adoptive parents tend to be highly motivated parents, and adoptive homes tend to be privileged in various ways (such as the number of books in the home and the quality of schools to which the children are sent). These factors apparently boost the IQs of children who grow up in such settings. Thus, the adoption studies provide evidence for both genetic and environmental effects.

• Adoptive homes often offer intellectually stimulating environments, and children who grow up in such homes tend to have above-average IQs.

Twin Studies

The logic of the twin study approach was explained in Chapter 4. There are two types of twins: monozygotic, or identical, twins, who are genetically identical, and dizygotic, or fraternal, twins, who have only a 50% genetic overlap and thus are no more related than ordinary siblings. Researchers have compared correlations in IQ for members of identical twin pairs with correlations in IQ for members of fraternal twin pairs. If genes are important, the first set of correlations should be higher than the second.

The results from many such studies were summarized in Table 4-3 (see page 111). The consistent finding is that identical twins *are* more similar. In the case of general intelligence, the mean correlation is .82 for identical twins, compared with only .59 for fraternal twins (Nichols, 1978). The same pattern emerges for tests of more specific abilities (Plomin, 1988; Segal, 1985).

Like family studies, twin studies are compatible with a genetic model, but they do not prove it correct. Environmental factors again provide an alternative explanation. Perhaps identical twins are treated more similarly than fraternal twins. If so, the greater similarity in IQ may have an environmental rather than a genetic basis.

Researchers have tried in various ways to control for this environmental alternative. Some have attempted to measure aspects of the twins' environments to see whether identical twins are in fact treated more similarly than fraternals. Their conclusion is that such differential treatment is less marked than is often claimed. Furthermore, to the extent that it does occur, it appears to be elicited by preexisting characteristics of the twins, such as the greater physical similarity or more similar temperaments of identical twins. In this view, then, the similarity between identical twins leads to their being treated similarly, not the reverse (Lytton, 1977, 1980; Scarr & Kidd, 1983).

The most widely cited attempt to control for environmental factors comes in the study of twins reared apart. If identical twins are separated early in life and reared in unrelated environments, then there is no environmental basis (other than prenatal experiences) for their developing similarly. The twins still share 100% of their genes, however. Should they still correlate in IQ, powerful evidence for the importance of genes would be gained.

Table 10-5 summarizes the results from a subset of the studies (using U.S. samples) of twins reared apart. The values in the table indicate that separated twins correlate quite substantially in IQ. Indeed, the reported correlations are higher for identical twins reared apart than for fraternal twins reared in the same home!

We noted that some caution is necessary in interpreting the results of adoption studies. The same point applies to studies of twins reared apart. Indeed, most of the data summarized in Table 10-5 come from rather old studies that are subject to a number of methodological criticisms (Farber, 1981; Kamin, 1974, 1981; Taylor, 1980). Separated twins are not easy to find, and they often have not been studied very well once found. On the other hand, two ongoing studies of twins reared apart appear methodologically sound, and these studies confirm the conclusions from the older research: strong similarity in IQ for identical twins, even when the twins have been separated since early in life (Bouchard et al., 1990; Bouchard et al., in press; Pederson et al., 1984).

The Concept of Heritability

The three kinds of evidence that we have considered all point to the same conclusion: Both differences in genes and differences in environments can lead to dif-

TABLE 10-5 • **Correlations in Intelligence of Related and Unrelated Children Under Various Rearing Conditions**

Rearing Condition	Correlation	Number of Pairs
Identical twins raised together	.86	526
Fraternal twins raised together	.53	517
Identical twins raised apart	.74	69
Siblings raised together	.55	1671
Unrelated children raised together	.38	259

Source: Adapted from "The Burt Controversy" by D. C. Rowe and R. Plomin, 1978, *Behavior Genetics, 8,* Table 1, p. 82. Copyright Plenum Publishing Corporation. Adapted by permission.

ferences in IQ. This conclusion is important but very general. Can we go beyond a general statement that both factors are important to say something about their relative importance?

As we discussed in Chapter 4, the question of relative importance makes sense only when we are talking about differences among people. Any individual's intelligence clearly depends on both genes and environments, and there is no way, when we are talking about individual development, ever to disentangle the two factors or to label one factor as more important than the other. We simply would not exist without both genes and environment, let alone have a height or weight or an IQ to explain. Suppose, however, that we are studying a sample of people who differ in IQ and we wish to determine where these differences come from. In this case, the question of relative importance *does* make sense. It is possible that the differences among the members of our sample are totally or predominantly genetic in origin, totally or predominantly environmental in origin, or a reflection of some more even mixture of genetic factors and environmental factors.

Researchers who attempt to determine relative importance make use of exactly the sorts of data that we have been discussing—kinship correlations, adoption studies, and twin studies. What they add to these data is a set of statistical procedures for calculating the heritability of IQ. The term **heritability** refers to the proportion of variance in a trait that can be attributed to genetic variance in the sample being studied. It is, in other words, an estimate of the extent to which differences among people come from differences in their genes as opposed to differences in their environments. The heritability statistic ranges from 0 (all of the differences are environmental in origin) to 1 (all of the differences are genetic in origin). The most widely accepted contemporary estimates of the heritability of IQ place the value at about .5 to .6 (Plomin, 1990; Plomin & McClearn, 1993). By these estimates, then, 50 to 60% of the variation in people's IQs comes from differences in their genes. The conclusion that genes are important should come as no surprise in light of the evidence that we have reviewed. The heritability estimates follow directly from the findings just discussed—the similarity in IQ between identical twins, the correlations in IQ between adopted children and their biological mothers, and so on.

It is important to note some limitations of the heritability statistic. First, heritability can be calculated in different ways, and the value obtained may vary depending on the method used and on the particular data that the researcher decides to emphasize. Published heritability estimates for IQ in fact range from as high as .8 (Burt, 1972; Herrnstein, 1973) to as low as 0 (Kamin, 1974). Second, whatever the heritability may be, the value is specific to the sample studied and can-

Heritability
The proportion of variance in a trait (such as IQ) that can be attributed to genetic variance in the sample being studied.

not be generalized to other samples. The value is specific to the sample studied because it depends on two factors: the range of environmental differences in the sample and the range of genetic differences in the sample. If we increase either range we give that factor more chance to have an effect; conversely, if we decrease either range we give that factor less chance to have an effect. In either case, we change the heritability.

Let us consider an example of this point using not intelligence but height as the outcome that we wish to explain. Imagine an island on which every person receives exactly 100% of his or her nutritional needs (Bjorklund, 1989). In this case, the heritability for height has to be close to 1, since there is no variability in the main environmental contributor to differences in height. If a factor does not vary in some sample of people, it cannot produce differences among those people. Suppose, however, that famine strikes the island. Some people still receive 100% of their nutritional needs; others, however, fall well short of this ideal. Over time, people in the first group grow taller than people in the second group. In this case, the heritability for height becomes less than 1, because environmental as well as genetic differences are now contributing to variations in height. Because the range of environmental differences has grown, the relative importance of genes and environment has changed.

The sample-specific nature of heritability has two further important implications. First, a particular heritability value—based as it is on the current range of genes and environments—tells us nothing for certain about what might happen in the future. In particular, the heritability does not tell us about the possible effects of improvements in the environment. Height, for example, typically shows high heritability, yet average height has increased over the last 100 years, presumably because of improvements in nutrition (Angoff, 1988). Whatever the heritability for IQ may be, improvements in the environment could still lead to gains in children's intelligence. Second, heritability tells us nothing for certain about comparisons between samples that were not included in the heritability estimate. Knowing, for example, what the heritability for height is on Island A does not tell us why its residents are taller or shorter than residents of Island B. Whatever the heritability may be within one group, differences between groups could result solely from differences in their genes, solely from differences in their environments, or from some combination of genes and environment. We will return to this point about between-group comparisons in our discussion of racial differences in IQ.

✔ *To Recap...*

Organization is one major issue in the study of intelligence. Psychometric researchers draw inferences about how intelligence is organized from patterns of correlations across different measures of intelligence. Factor analyses of such correlations provide evidence both for general intelligence, which affects performance on many tasks, and for more specific abilities, which contribute to performance on specific tasks. Such studies have also identified developmental changes in the structure of intelligence across childhood. As children develop, their cognitive abilities become more differentiated, and sensorimotor kinds of functioning give way to more abstract, symbolic skills.

The question of the stability of IQ is another central issue in the psychometric approach to intelligence. Longitudinal studies indicate that infant IQ has little relation to later IQ. This apparent discontinuity in development is usually attributed to the differences in content between infant and childhood intelligence. Recent evidence suggests, however, that response to novelty may provide a link between infancy and later childhood. Beyond infancy, IQ begins to correlate from one age to another, and the stability increases as the child gets older. The correlations are not perfect, however, and substantial changes in IQ do sometimes occur.

The third classic issue in the psychometric approach concerns the origins of individual differences. Three methods of study have been prominent: family studies, adoption studies, and twin studies. All three methods suggest a substantial genetic contribution to individual differences in intelligence, yet all three also indicate the importance of the environment. Estimates of the heritability of IQ suggest that 50 to 60% of the variation among people is genetic in origin.

EXPERIENCE AND INTELLIGENCE

Although we have just discussed some of the limitations of the heritability statistic, we have yet to note what is perhaps the most important limitation. Heritability estimates, at best, answer the question of how much: How much of the variation among people can be attributed to genetic or environmental factors? Such estimates tell us nothing about the processes by which genes or environments exert their effects. *How* is a genotype translated into a particular level of intelligence? And *how* do different environments shape different kinds of cognitive development?

We saw in Chapter 4 that researchers are just beginning to unravel the mysteries of genetic transmission. Some of the basic principles and mechanisms have been discovered, and more seem likely to yield their secrets in the near future. In this section, we focus on the ways in which the environment affects intelligence.

Our starting point is the fact that no two children encounter exactly the same environment as they grow up. The world is, in fact, a natural laboratory for the study of experience and intelligence, offering natural variations in children's experiences on the one hand, and variations in children's intellectual development on the other. The psychologist's task is to discover the relations between the two. Several kinds of evidence have been important in this attempt.

Natural Deprivations

Chapter 5 pointed out that the belief that the placental "barrier" protects the fetus from all harm has only gradually been replaced by an appreciation of the importance of prenatal experience. Much the same historical progression can be traced in the study of early experience and intelligence. Through at least the first third of this century, psychologists showed little concern with the possibility that the early environment might affect later intelligence. Instead, the development of intelligence was believed to be largely under genetic and maturational control, and any effects of early experience were assumed to be minor and transitory.

The first important challenge to this view came from so-called **institutionalization studies** (Hunt, 1961; Thompson & Grusec, 1970). During the 1930s and 1940s, researchers discovered a number of orphanages in which early rearing experiences departed sharply from those typical in a home setting. These orphanages (which, fortunately, were a minority even then) were characterized by very high child-to-caretaker ratios and by frequent changes in caretakers. The children thus had minimal social stimulation and little opportunity to form relationships with others. They also received little perceptual–cognitive input. In some institutions, sheets were hung over the sides of the cribs, thus preventing the children from seeing out. In one orphanage, the children lay so long in one place that they hollowed out a depression in the mattress. When these children reached the age at which they

Institutionalization studies Examinations of the effects of naturally occurring deprivation (such as in certain kinds of orphanage rearing) on children's development.

• Studies of natural deprivations—such as rearing in the Romanian orphanage shown here—provide dramatic evidence for the negative effects of a bad environment on intellectual development.

should have been able to turn over and look around, they could not—because they were trapped in the depression (Spitz, 1945).

In retrospect, it is not surprising that these barren environments had detrimental effects on children's development. The effects were in fact wide-ranging and severe. Children subjected to the deprived orphanage rearing evidenced problems on a number of aspects of later development, including performance on IQ tests and other cognitive measures. In one study, for example, the mean IQ of a group of children reared in a Lebanese orphanage was 50, and no child in the sample reached an IQ of 100 (Dennis, 1973).

One positive finding emerged from the orphanage studies, however. Strong and persistent though the results of early deprivation might have been, the effects were not necessarily permanent. If the children's environments were significantly improved, then at least some of the damage could be undone. The institutionalization studies thus provide evidence about the effects of experience in both directions. Bad early environments can depress children's intelligence, but later improvements in the environment can lead to gains in intellectual performance.

The conclusions that emerged from the orphanage studies are paralleled in occasional case study reports of "attic" or "closet" children (e.g., Davis, 1947). Such reports confirm that an extremely deprived environment (such as being chained in an attic by a disturbed parent) can result in greatly lowered intelligence. Yet these studies also have a more hopeful side, in that therapeutic efforts with such children have succeeded, at least sometimes, in producing remarkable gains (Clarke & Clarke, 1976). So again we see that early experience is important but not all-important. The later environment also plays a role.

Most children, of course, do not encounter such extreme deprivation. What do we know about the less extreme variations in experience that characterize the lives of most children?

Contributions of the Family

For most children, the home environment is one important context within which intellectual skills develop. Several kinds of research provide evidence about the contribution of the family.

Longitudinal Studies

The longitudinal studies mentioned earlier are one source of evidence. Such studies have shown that IQ is far from perfectly stable as children develop and that a particular child's IQ may go up or down by 30 or 40 points across childhood. Researchers have sought to discover whether these changes in IQ can be linked to corresponding changes in the environment. McCall and his colleagues (1973), for example, analyzed patterns of IQ change for 80 children participating in a long-term longitudinal study. They found that two aspects of parental behavior showed the strongest relation to IQ change. Children who declined in IQ tended to have parents who made relatively little effort to stimulate them or to accelerate their development and who also fell at the extremes in their use of punishment, either very high or very low. In contrast, children who increased in IQ tended to have parents who emphasized intellectual acceleration and who were intermediate in the severity of their discipline. Thus, the most adaptive parental pattern appeared to be one that stressed stimulation and intellectual encouragement within a general context of structure and control.

One of the most ambitious attempts to identify the environmental contribution to intelligence comes in the work of Burton White and his associates (White et al., 1978; White & Watts, 1973). These researchers studied 39 mothers and children longitudinally, beginning when the children were either 1 or 2 years old and continuing until they reached the age of 3. Extensive measures were made of both the early environment and the children's intellectual development. The latter included not only standard psychometric tests of intelligence but also a number of other measures of early childhood competence.

Individual differences in children's competence were evident as early as 12 to 15 months. Differences in the mothers' behavior were also evident very early. The mothers whose children were developing relatively well differed on several dimensions from those whose children were developing relatively slowly. Such mothers were characterized by their accessibility to their children and their willingness to give help when the children needed help. The total amount of time a mother spent with her child did not appear to be critical; rather, the important variable was the mother's flexibility and sensitivity to the child's needs. Mothers of the most competent children also ranked high in directing child-appropriate language to their children. And they structured the home environment so that the children were free to explore (as opposed, for example, to being cooped up in a playpen). White and his associates stress the role of the mother as the "designer" of the child's environment. Even when she is not interacting with the child, the mother is an important determinant of what kinds of experiences the child has. Other studies have also demonstrated the importance of the child's freedom to explore within a safe and well-organized physical environment (Wachs, 1992; Wachs & Gruen, 1982).

Research With the HOME

Undoubtedly the most popular contemporary approach to measuring the home environment involves an instrument called the **HOME**. The HOME (for Home Observation for Measurement of the Environment), developed by Caldwell and Bradley (1979), consists of 45 items intended to tap the quality of the child's environment. Each item is scored either yes (this feature is characteristic of the child's environment) or no (this feature is not characteristic). The 45 items are in turn grouped into six general subscales. The items and corresponding subscales for the infant version of the HOME are shown in Table 10-6. (A preschool version is similar, but it consists of 55 items and eight subscales.) Scoring on the HOME is ac-

HOME (Home Observation for Measurement of the Environment) An instrument for assessing the quality of the early home environment. Included are dimensions such as maternal involvement and variety of play materials.

TABLE 10-6 ● Items and Subscales on the HOME (Infant Version)

I. Emotional and Verbal Responsivity of Mother
1. Mother spontaneously vocalizes to child at least twice during visit (excluding scolding).
2. Mother responds to child's vocalizations with a verbal response.
3. Mother tells child the name of some object during visit or says name of person or object in a "teaching" style.
4. Mother's speech is distinct, clear, and audible.
5. Mother initiates verbal interchanges with observer—asks questions, makes spontaneous comments.
6. Mother expresses ideas freely and easily and uses statements of appropriate length for conversation (e.g., gives more than brief answers).
7. Mother permits child occasionally to engage in "messy" types of play.
8. Mother spontaneously praises child's qualities or behavior twice during visit.
9. When speaking of or to child, mother's voice conveys positive feelings.
10. Mother caresses or kisses child at least once during visit.
11. Mother shows some positive emotional responses to praise of child offered by visitor.

II. Avoidance of Restriction and Punishment
12. Mother does not shout at child during visit.
13. Mother does not express overt annoyance with or hostility toward child.
14. Mother neither slaps nor spanks child during visit.
15. Mother reports that no more than one instance of physical punishment occurred during the past week.
16. Mother does not scold or derogate child during visit.
17. Mother does not interfere with child's actions or restrict child's movements more than three times during visit.
18. At least 10 books are present and visible.
19. Family has a pet.

III. Organization of Physical and Temporal Environment
20. When mother is away, care is provided by one of three regular substitutes.
21. Someone takes child into grocery store at least once a week.
22. Child gets out of house at least four times a week.
23. Child is taken regularly to doctor's office or clinic.
24. Child has a special place in which to keep his toys and "treasures."
25. Child's play environment appears safe and free of hazards.

complished during a 1-hour home visit and is based on a combination of interviews with the mother and observation of mother–child interaction. Part of the appeal of the instrument lies in the fact that such a wide range of information can be elicited in such a short time.

Do scores on the HOME relate to children's IQs? Many studies indicate that they do (Bradley et al., 1989; Elardo & Bradley, 1981; Gottfried, 1984a). In general, the higher the score on the HOME (that is, the greater the number of "yes" answers), the better the child's development. Although findings vary across studies, there is some evidence that each of the six subscales relates to IQ. Dimensions that seem to emerge as consistently important are maternal involvement, play materials, and variety of stimulation (Gottfried, 1984b).

Measures on the HOME relate to contemporaneous measures of the child's intelligence. That is, scores on the infant version of the HOME correlate with infant intelligence (Barnard, Bee, & Hammond, 1984b), and scores on the preschool version correlate with preschool intelligence (Siegel, 1984). Measures on the HOME also relate to future intelligence. In one study, for example, the correlation between HOME score at 6 months and IQ at 4.5 years was .50; the correlation between

TABLE 10-6 ● Items and Subscales on the HOME (Infant Version) (*Continued*)

IV. Provision of Appropriate Play Materials
    26. Child has some muscle-activity toys or equipment.
    27. Child has push or pull toy.
    28. Child has stroller or walker, kiddie car, scooter, or tricycle.
    29. Mother provides toys or interesting activities for child during interview.
    30. Provides learning equipment appropriate to age—cuddly toy or role-playing toys.
    31. Provides learning equipment appropriate to age—mobile, table and chairs, high chair, play pen.
    32. Provides eye–hand coordination toys—items to go in and out of receptacle, fit together toys, beads.
    33. Provides eye–hand coordination toys that permit combinations—stacking or nesting toys, blocks or building toys.
    34. Provides toys for literature or music.

V. Maternal Involvement with Child
    35. Mother tends to keep child within visual range and to look at him often.
    36. Mother "talks" to child while doing her work.
    37. Mother consciously encourages developmental advances.
    38. Mother invests "maturing" toys with value via her attention.
    39. Mother structures child's play periods.
    40. Mother provides toys that challenge child to develop new skills.

VI. Opportunities for Variety in Daily Stimulation
    41. Father provides some caretaking every day.
    42. Mother reads stories at least three times weekly.
    43. Child eats at least one meal per day with mother and father.
    44. Family visits or receives visits from relatives.
    45. Child has three or more books of his or her own.

Source: From "174 Children: A Study of the Relationship between Home Environment and Cognitive Development during the First 5 Years" by R. H. Bradley and B. M. Caldwell, 1984. In A. W. Gottfried (Ed.), *Home Environment and Early Cognitive Development* (pp. 7–8), New York: Academic Press. Copyright 1984 by Academic Press. Reprinted by permission.

HOME at 24 months and IQ at 4.5 years was .63 (Bradley & Caldwell, 1984a). Other studies have demonstrated relations between HOME scores in infancy and both IQ and school performance during the grade-school years (Bradley & Caldwell, 1984b; Olson, Bates, & Kaskie, 1992). Thus, the quality of the child's early environment is predictive of various aspects of the child's later intelligence.

    Although the HOME is clearly a valuable source of evidence with respect to experience and intelligence, one caution should be noted. Research suggests that genetic factors may also contribute to findings with the HOME (Braungart, Fulker, & Plomin, 1992; Coon et al., 1990; Plomin & Neiderhiser, 1992). Genetically based characteristics of children may influence the HOME score itself, since such characteristics will affect the treatment that children receive from their parents (recall Bronfenbrenner's notion of developmentally instigative characteristics, discussed in Chapter 2). And genetic characteristics of the parents may affect both the home environment and the child's intelligence, thus contributing to the correlation between HOME measures and children's IQs. Similar points apply to other measures of the early family environment (Plomin et al., 1994). The conclusion that both genes and environment are important for intelligence—and that the two factors are often very difficult to separate—should be familiar by now.

Family Structure

The research that we have considered so far has involved direct measurement of important aspects of the child's environment. In this section, we step back to a more indirect and global level. Doing so will allow us to consider an intriguing theory and a suggestive, but controversial, program of research.

The variable in question is family structure, and the theory is that of Robert Zajonc (1976, 1983; Zajonc & Markus, 1975; Zajonc, Markus, & Markus, 1979). Zajonc has proposed what he calls a **confluence model** of intellectual development. The central notion in the confluence model is that the child's intelligence is affected by the overall intellectual level within the family. The higher the intellectual level, the better the child's development. The intellectual level in turn depends on a number of factors. One important factor is the number of adults in the home. Adults have more intellectual resources than children; hence the intellectual level rises as the number of adults rises. The intelligence of the adults is also important, in the obvious direction: the more intelligent the adults (who typically, of course, are the child's parents), the higher the intellectual level. The number of children is important. Children, in contrast to adults, *decrease* the average intellectual level of the home; the intellectual level drops as the number of children increases. The spacing between children is important, too, with wide spacing more conducive to intellectual development than narrow spacing. When children are widely spaced, the older child has more time within an adult-dominated environment, and the younger child has a more mature older sibling. A final variable is what Zajonc calls the teaching function. Older children act as teachers for their younger siblings and benefit themselves from the chance to be intellectual resources. Lastborn children and only children are thus handicapped, since they have little opportunity to exercise this teaching function.

The confluence model grew out of an attempt to make sense of the voluminous literature on effects of family size and birth order. Family size and birth order do relate to a number of aspects of child development, including performance on IQ tests. On the average, children from large families have lower IQs than children from smaller families, and later-born children have lower IQs than the first children in a family (Terhune, 1976; Zajonc, 1983). Figure 10-3 presents a typical set of findings. Both of these findings (as well as the occasional exceptions to them) fit what would be expected from the confluence model. Other, more specific predictions have also been confirmed. McCall (1984), for example, showed that the birth of a sibling was associated with average declines in IQ in the older children in the family, an outcome compatible with the notion that younger children lower the intellectual level of the home.

On the other hand, not all tests of the confluence model have been positive. Brackbill and Nichols (1982), for example, reported no effects of an extended family structure on children's IQs, even though the extra adults in the home presumably should have boosted the intellectual level. They also found little or no support for several other predictions from the confluence model. Other researchers have also reported negative results and offered severe criticisms of confluence theory and the data offered in support of it (Galbraith, 1982, 1984; Price, Walsh, & Vilberg, 1984; Retherford & Sewell, 1991; Rodgers, 1984). Supporters of the theory have replied that the criticisms are mistaken and the negative tests inappropriate (Berbaum, 1985; Berbaum, Moreland, & Zajonc, 1986; Zajonc et al., 1991). Thus, the validity of the confluence model is at present very much a matter of dispute. And even if the model should prove valid, a cautionary point is worth noting. At best, the effects of family structure on IQ are small and far from inevitable. Growing up with many siblings does not doom anyone to a lower IQ.

Confluence model
A theory of the relation between family structure and the development of intelligence. Intelligence is assumed to relate to the intellectual level of the home, which is determined by factors such as the number and spacing of children.

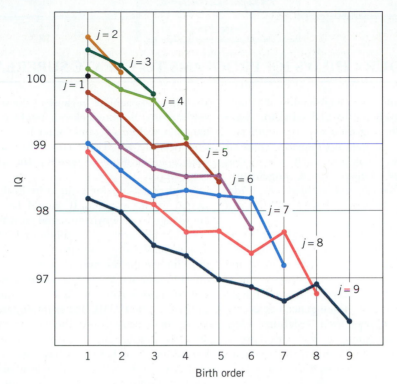

Figure 10-3 Average IQ scores as a function of birth order and number of children (indicated by *j*). These findings are compatible with Zajonc's confluence model of intellectual development. From "Birth Order and Intellectual Development" by R. B. Zajonc and G. B. Markus, 1975, *Psychological Review, 82,* pp. 74-88. Copyright 1975 by the American Psychological Association. Reprinted by permission.

The research that we have considered in this section is of interest not only to psychologists but also to parents who hope to create the best possible environment for their children's intellectual development. In Box 10-1 we discuss one approach to optimizing the early environment: so-called *superbaby programs.*

DEVELOPMENT IN CONTEXT: Families and Achievement: The Message From Cross-Cultural Research

In a study of mathematics achievement in 20 countries, American 8th and 12th graders scored below the international average on virtually every measure taken (Garden, 1987; McKnight et al., 1987). Children from China and Japan, in contrast, were consistently near the top of the range. Other studies across the last 2 decades have provided a similar picture—disappointingly poor performance by American children, coupled with exceptional achievement for children from Asian countries (International Association for the Evaluation of Educational Achievement, 1985; Stevenson et al., 1990).

Why do American children do so poorly in mathematics? It is tempting to indict the school system, and indeed schools can be quite important (Stevenson, 1992). Some differences between Asians and Americans, however, are evident by age 5, before most children have even started school (Stevenson, Lee, & Stigler, 1986). Furthermore, Asian-American students in the United States often outperform Caucasian students, despite the fact that both groups are moving through the same school systems (College Entrance Examination Board, 1982; Sue & Ozaki, 1990). These findings suggest that schools are not the sole explanation; the family environment also contributes.

BOOST YOUR CHILD'S IQ? PROGRAMS TO CREATE SUPERBABIES

As any visitor to the child psychology section of a bookstore knows, some psychologists and educators have not been shy about sharing their expertise with parents. Programs to create high-IQ, superior children abound. Hence, we see book titles such as *Give Your Child a Superior Mind* (Engelmann & Engelmann, 1981), *How to Give Your Baby Encyclopedic Knowledge* (Doman, 1985), and *Awakening Your Child's Natural Genius* (Armstrong, 1991).

Do we in fact know how to manipulate the environment to produce children of superior intelligence? There is no doubt that the environment can be important for intelligence, as the evidence that we have reviewed indicates. There is also no doubt that at least some of the boost-your-child's intelligence books contain many sensible, perhaps even insightful, ideas (Howe, 1990). At least some such books have a grounding in the kinds of research that we have considered. Most are also grounded in their author's extensive experience in working with families and testing out the ideas conveyed in the book. And most include documentation of success in the form of case studies or glowing parental reports.

Despite these positive arguments, many child psychologists are skeptical about the value of such explicit attempts to accelerate development (Elkind, 1988; Rescorla, Hyson, & Hirsh-Pasek, 1991; Sigel, 1987). Various grounds for caution exist. The effects of such acceleration programs have yet to be demonstrated in large-scale and objective studies. Such demonstrations are difficult to achieve because of the self-selection involved. Parents who seek out books or programs to boost their child's IQ may differ in various ways from those who do not. This factor makes it difficult to interpret any differences between the children of the two groups.

Other reasons for caution lie in the evidence reviewed in this chapter. It should be clear that our knowledge of the environmental contributors to intelligence, while growing, is still limited. The clearest evidence concerns the effects of bad environments and the effects of the removal of such bad environments via intervention. We know less about what constitutes a truly superior environment. The relevant data that do exist (from the HOME, for example) are correlational rather than causal, and the effects that have been demonstrated to date are of very modest magnitude. Furthermore, such studies have not verified the importance of the kind of explicit, academically oriented teaching that is stressed in many of the how-to books. Instead, what seems to be important is the parent's flexibility and sensitivity to the child's needs, along with the creation of a generally free and stimulating environment. These variables seem to be important, in fact, not only for IQ but for the development of attachment and overall competence as well. And it could be argued, of course, that creation of a generally competent and secure child, rather than an academic superstar, should be the main goal of child rearing.

The most ambitious attempt to identify family bases for academic achievement is reported in a monograph entitled *Contexts of Achievement* (Stevenson & Lee, 1990). The child participants for the Contexts study were first and fifth graders from the United States, China, and Japan. The children took a variety of achievement tests, and the results confirmed those of previous research—poorer performance in mathematics by American children than by children from China or Japan. The children's mothers also participated in the study, and it was their beliefs and practices that constituted the main focus of the research. The maternal interviews included a variety of questions designed to reveal differences among families and among cultures that might lead to differences in academic performance. Mothers were asked, for example, to judge how well their children were doing in school and to indicate how satisfied they were with this progress. They were asked to give their beliefs about the bases for school success—in particular, to judge the relative contributions of ability and effort to doing well in school. And they were asked about various experiences at home that might contribute to school success, such as parental help with homework or the provision of a quiet place to study.

The results of the Contexts study are in general agreement with those of other studies directed to differences in academic achievement among Chinese, Japanese, and American children (Bacon & Ichikawa, 1988; Hess, Chih-Mei, & McDevitt, 1987). It is clear from such research that mothers in all three cultures are interested in and supportive of their children's academic development. Nevertheless, the maternal interviews revealed cross-cultural differences in beliefs and practices that might well contribute to the superior performance of Asian children. Asian mothers, for example, were more likely than American mothers to regard effort as more important to school success than ability. The emphasis on effort in the Chinese and Japanese families appears to fit with general and long-standing cultural beliefs about the malleability of human nature and the possibility of improving oneself through hard work (Munro, 1977). In line with their beliefs about the importance of effort, Asian mothers were more likely than American mothers to provide help for their children's academic endeavors. In China, for example, 96% of the children received help with homework (the figure in the United States was 67%), and fully 95% of Chinese fifth graders and 98% of Japanese fifth graders had their own desk at home at which to work (the figure for American children was 63%). Similar results emerged from a measure of time spent on academically related activities (e.g., reading, doing workbooks) outside of school: more such time for Asian than American children.

Given the relatively poor performance of their children, American mothers might have been expected to be least satisfied with their children's academic achievement. In fact, just the reverse was true. American mothers were more satisfied with both their children's performance and their children's schools than were Chinese or Japanese mothers. American mothers also gave higher, and therefore less realistic, evaluations of their children's cognitive and academic abilities than mothers in the other two cultures. This pattern suggests a basis for the failure of many American mothers to nurture optimal academic performance in their children. Such mothers may believe that their children are doing better than they in fact are and thus may be satisfied with levels of performance that are in fact not very high. Furthermore, such mothers may believe that academic success is primarily a function of immutable ability rather than changeable effort and thus may see little point in encouraging their children to try harder.

Having presented the main conclusions of the Contexts study, we should also note some qualifications (see also Hatano, 1990). There is no claim in the research that the child-rearing practices of the Asian cultures are producing generally superior children. In fact, American children do just as well as Chinese and Japanese children on measures of general intelligence, and differences in other domains of academic achievement are less marked and less consistent than those found for mathematics. There is also no claim that the differences in mathematics result solely from differences among families. Schools are also important, and schools contribute to the superior performance of Asian children in mathematics. Finally, the Asian superiority in mathematics may be bought at some cost. Although they were more likely to engage in outside-of-school academic activities, the Asian children in the Contexts study were considerably less likely than their American counterparts to be involved in art, music, or sports. As is always the case in child rearing, decisions about practices are intertwined with decisions about values and goals. Children's development is multifaceted, and parents must decide how much emphasis to place on each of the many facets.

Contributions of the School

The average American child spends approximately 15,000 hours in school between the ages of 5 and 18. Clearly, school is a major context within which children in our society exercise—and develop—their intellectual abilities. What do we know about the impact of schooling on cognitive development?

That schooling contributes to the acquisition of specific skills and specific kinds of knowledge is without dispute. Most of us would never come to know state capitals, multiplication tables, or periodic elements without the opportunity (and necessity) of doing so in school. Here, we concentrate on the more general effects that schooling may have on children's intelligence. We consider two kinds of evidence, the first stemming from cross-cultural comparisons and the second from variations within our own culture.

Cross-Cultural Studies

A difficulty in determining the effects of schooling in Western culture is its pervasiveness: Virtually every child goes to school. When we broaden our scope to encompass other cultures, this uniformity no longer holds. Of course, if we simply compare cultures with and without schooling, it will be difficult to interpret our results, because the cultures may differ in a number of ways apart from the presence or absence of school. Most informative, therefore, are cases in which only some children within a culture go to school or in which schooling has been recently introduced, allowing us to make a before-and-after comparison. Psychologists have been able to find and to study a number of such cases (Ceci, 1990; Rogoff, 1981). Several conclusions emerge.

A first conclusion is that some aspects of children's cognitive development seem to be more strongly and consistently affected by schooling than others. Many of the kinds of knowledge studied by Piaget fall in the relatively unaffected category. Schooling does sometimes influence the development of Piagetian concepts—most obviously, effects on the rate at which knowledge is acquired. Most studies, however, report no clear qualitative differences between schooled children and unschooled children in their mastery of concepts like conservation, nor any lasting advantage of the former over the latter. The same conclusion emerges from research on logical reasoning, assuming that the problems are presented in terms that are as familiar to the unschooled children as to the schooled ones.

Other aspects of cognitive development appear to be affected more by schooling. Skill at various kinds of perceptual analysis can be facilitated by schooling—for example, the ability to match stimuli or to construct models of familiar patterns. Schooling can affect memory. Schooled children not only perform better on a variety of memory tasks, but they are also more likely to use mnemonic strategies to help themselves remember. Schooling affects how children classify objects. Children who have been to school are more likely to group objects in terms of general categories (e.g., all of the foods together) rather than functional or thematic relations (e.g., ice cream and spoon together). Similarly, schooling affects how children think about words and use language, with schooled children more likely to think in terms of general categories and abstract relations. And perhaps most generally, schooling improves children's ability to reflect on their own cognitive processes—to think about thinking. As we saw in Chapter 9, such *metacognition* has emerged as an active area of current research interest.

Why does schooling produce these effects? Rogoff (1981) discusses four factors that may play roles. Perhaps the most obvious explanation is that schooling directly teaches many of the specific skills on which schooled children excel.

Classification, for example, is a common activity in school, and committing material to memory is even more common. A more general proposal is that schooling exerts its effects through its emphasis on the search for general rules—for universal systems of knowledge (such as mathematics) within which specific instances can be understood. A third possibility stresses the differences between teaching in school and teaching outside of school. Teaching in school often involves the verbal transmission of information that is far removed from its everyday context, a style of instruction that may promote verbally based, abstract modes of thought. Finally, perhaps the most general explanation concerns a primary goal of most forms of schooling, the development of literacy. It has been argued that literacy, like verbally based teaching, promotes abstract, reflective styles of thinking. And reading, of course, can also be the door to a vast world of experiences and knowledge that could never be acquired firsthand (Stanovich, 1993b).

Schooling in America

What about the effects of schooling within our own culture? Here the comparison shifts from presence versus absence of schooling to either the quantity or the quality of schooling. We begin with the amount of schooling received. It has long been known that there is a positive relation between number of years of education completed and IQ—that is, the more years of schooling people complete, the higher (on the average) are their IQs (Jencks, 1972). The usual explanation has been that more intelligent people stay in school longer. This factor is almost certainly part of the basis for the correlation. Recently, however, Stephen Ceci (1990, 1991, 1992) has argued that the cause and effect may also flow in the opposite direction—that is, that schooling may actually increase IQ.

Ceci cites a variety of evidence in support of his conclusion. Here are three examples. First, children who drop out of school decline in IQ relative to children who stay in school, even when the two groups are initially equal in IQ. Second, children's IQs have been shown to decline slightly across the months of summer vacation and then to rise again during the school year. Third, children whose birthdays make them just barely old enough to qualify for school entry obtain higher IQ scores by age 8 than children whose birthdays make them fall just short. The point

• Not only do IQ tests predict success in school, recent evidence suggests that schooling can increase IQ.

is that the two groups are virtually the same age, but one group has had a year more of schooling. Indeed, Morrison and colleagues (Morrison, Griffith, & Frazier, 1994) have demonstrated, using this "school cut-off" approach, that starting school relatively early can nurture a number of specific cognitive abilities.

In speculating about why schooling boosts IQ, Ceci draws on the cross-cultural evidence just discussed. We saw that schooling affects perceptual analysis, memory, language use, and classification. These skills, Ceci notes, are precisely the kinds of abilities that are stressed on IQ tests. This overlap is, of course, no accident: IQ tests were designed to predict school performance. It is not surprising, therefore, that being good at IQ-type skills is helpful in school. But it is also not surprising that experiences in school can nurture IQ.

As might be expected, quality of schooling is more difficult than quantity to define and to study (Fuller, 1987; Good & Weinstein, 1986). Despite the difficulties, however, few doubt that there can be important differences in the quality of the education that different children receive. Some schools consistently produce more successful outcomes than others—doing so even when the children being served are initially equivalent. And some teachers within a school consistently have happier and more productive classrooms than others.

Michael Rutter (1983) has provided one of the most helpful surveys of the research directed to quality of schooling. One of the interesting messages from his review concerns factors that do *not* make much of a difference. Rutter finds little evidence, for example, that variations in school success (such as performance on standardized tests, attendance rates, and graduation rates) are associated with the financial or physical resources available to the school, with the overall size of the school, or with the size of the class within the school. This conclusion does not mean that such factors are never important—no one would advocate a class size of 50 for kindergartners. But the variations that are normally found along these dimensions do not seem to have much effect on school success.

What factors *do* influence school success? The dimensions that emerge as important in Rutter's review have to do mainly with emphases and organization. Successful schools have a clear emphasis on academic goals, accompanied by clearly defined procedures for achieving those goals. Teachers plan the curriculum together, actively teach important content, assign and grade homework regularly, and in general hold high but realistic expectations for their students. Discipline within successful schools tends to be firm but fair—sufficient to maintain a focus on the task at hand, but not so punitive as to arouse anxiety or resentment. Students in successful schools are helped to feel part of the school through opportunities to participate in school-related activities, as well as by the chance to have a voice in decisions concerning the school. Finally, teachers in successful schools manage their classrooms in an organized and efficient manner, thereby maximizing the time spent on the lesson of the moment rather than on peripheral concerns (e.g., handing out papers, setting up equipment). It is interesting to note that this same variable of classroom management proved important in the Contexts of Achievement study discussed earlier (Stevenson & Lee, 1990). Fifth graders in China and Japan were observed to be engaged in academic activities 92% and 87% of the time, respectively; in American fifth-grade classrooms the figure was 64%.

Cultural compatibility hypothesis
The hypothesis that schooling will be most effective when methods of instruction are compatible with the child's cultural background.

One final point about quality is important. How well school works for a particular child depends not only on general factors like classroom management but also on the fit between the school experience and the child's background and expectations. This principle is expressed in the **cultural compatibility hypothesis**: Classroom instruction is most effective when it matches patterns of learning that are familiar in the child's culture (Slaughter-DeFoe et al., 1990; Tharp, 1989). A nice example of the principle comes in a study of wait-time—that is, the length of time that one participant in a dialogue waits before responding to the other (White & Tharp, 1988). Navajo children tend to pause when giving answers, creating the impression (at least for Anglo teachers) that they have finished responding. The result is that Navajo children are often interrupted before they have completed their answers. In this case, the teacher's wait-time is too short. In contrast, native Hawaiian children prefer a short wait-time, because in their culture prompt response and overlapping speech patterns are signs of interest and involvement. Teachers, however, often interpret the Hawaiian child's quick responses as rude interruptions, and their attempts to curtail such behavior may lead to general uncertainty and inhibition. Thus, in both cases, although in different ways, the teacher's unfamiliarity with the child's cultural background can create problems for the child in school. (Box 10-2 discusses a famous study of the effects of teachers' expectations about their pupils.)

Experimental Interventions

Studies of naturally occurring variations in experience, whether at home or at school, are important but also incomplete. Such studies lack experimental control, and therefore it is difficult to be certain of cause-and-effect relations. We may know, for example, that verbal stimulation from the mother relates to the child's IQ, but why is this? Is it because the mother's verbal input enhances the child's intelligence? Or is it because children who are intelligent elicit a high degree of speech from their mothers? Or does the relation result from some third factor—for example, that mothers who engage in verbal stimulation have genes conducive to intelligence, which they pass on to their children, who therefore have high IQs? If we could experimentally manipulate the child's experiences, we could be much more certain about what the causal relations are.

For obvious ethical reasons, experimental manipulations of children's environments take one direction only. No researcher deliberately makes a child's environment worse. A number of investigators, however, have sought to improve children's environments and thereby enhance their intellectual development. We saw early attempts of this sort when we considered the orphanage and case study reports of severe deprivation. Next we examine more recent and more large-scale intervention projects.

Some Illustrative Intervention Projects

The decade of the 1960s saw the birth of dozens of intervention programs directed to children who were perceived to be at risk for school failure. The Early Training Project (Gray & Ramsey, 1982; Gray, Ramsey, & Klaus, 1982) was one of the first, and it is in many ways a typical example. The participants in the project were ninety 3- and 4-year-old children and mothers of low socioeconomic status. Half of the children were randomly assigned to the intervention condition; the other half constituted an untreated control group. The intervention consisted of two 10-week summer programs in which the children met in small groups with trained teachers. Emphasized in the summer programs were basic skills that the children would need when they started school—perceptual analysis, numerical concepts, and linguistic abilities. Also emphasized was the development of general attitudes necessary for school success, such as achievement motivation. Throughout, the researchers attempted to give the children many one-on-one experiences with a helpful adult in a generally supportive environment. Although the focus was on the summer pro-

PYGMALION IN THE CLASSROOM

Teachers naturally welcome information about their students that might help them to teach more effectively. For many, results from standardized assessment tests—such as IQ and academic achievement measures—are one useful source of information. Normally, of course, such tests are designed to be as accurate as possible. One of the most famous experiments in child psychology, however, was built around the provision of deliberately *inaccurate* test information to teachers.

Robert Rosenthal and Lenore Jacobson (1968) informed a group of elementary-school teachers that a new test of intellectual potential had been developed to measure children's readiness to "bloom." The test, the teachers were told, could identify those children who were most likely to show spurts or leaps forward in their academic performance during the coming year. Each teacher was also given a list of the children from his or her classroom whom the test had identified as likely bloomers. In fact, however, a random-numbers table had been used to select the supposed bloomers. These children were no different from any other children in the class.

What is the point of deliberately misleading teachers in this way? Rosenthal and Jacobson's study grew out of previous research by Rosenthal on a phenomenon known as the *researcher expectancy effect*. Across a series of experiments, Rosenthal (1976) had demonstrated that what researchers expect can affect the results they obtain. For example, testers who are led to believe that their subjects will perform well on some cognitive measure typically elicit better performance than testers who are led to believe that their subjects will perform poorly. The effect extends even to animal research. Testers who are told that they are working with "maze-bright" rats obtain better performance than testers who believe that their rats are "maze-dull."

The work on researcher expectancy effects is of considerable methodological significance, for such research identifies a source of bias that may seriously affect the outcomes of research. The point of the Rosenthal and Jacobson study was to see whether expectancy effects extend beyond the laboratory to the real-life settings within which children develop. Do the expectancies that teachers hold about their students affect the way the students perform? And in particular, can the creation of positive expectancies—as was done with respect to the bloomers—lead to positive outcomes for the children?

The answer to this question turned out to be a qualified yes. Rosenthal and Jacobson did not find any

grams, home visits were made throughout the remainder of the year in an attempt to keep any gains from dissipating.

Effects of the Early Training Project were assessed in various ways. On IQ tests, given when the children entered first grade, the intervention group outperformed the control group by approximately 10 points. By fourth grade, the difference had shrunk to 7 points but was still statistically significant. By age 17, when the last follow-up measures were taken, there were no longer any significant IQ differences; both groups had mean IQs of about 80. On various measures of academic performance, however, effects of the intervention were still evident even a dozen years after its completion. Children in the intervention group were less likely to be placed in special education classes than children in the control group. They were also more likely to graduate from high school than those in the control group. The effects were especially marked for the girls in the sample.

The emphasis in the Early Training Project was on preschool-aged children and on an outside-the-home, school-based intervention program. Other projects have focused on infants and on intervention in the home setting. Slaughter (1983), for example, worked with a sample of mothers and their 1-year-old children.

• Teachers are an important part of any child's life. The Pygmalion study suggests that the expectations teachers form can effect their behavior toward their students.

effects of expectancies for the older children in the study. At first and second grades, however, the effects were dramatic. Children who had been identified as bloomers easily outperformed their classmates on an IQ test given at the end of the year. By the end of the year, the bloomers were also earning better grades in reading and arithmetic. Apparently, the teachers' expectancies acted as self-fulfilling prophecies. Children who were expected to perform well did in fact perform well.

The Rosenthal and Jacobson study is not only one of the most famous but also one of the most controversial experiments in child psychology. The original study has been subjected to a number of criticisms, and its results have not always been replicated in follow-up research (Brophy, 1983; Wineberg, 1987). Clearly, children's intellectual performance has many determinants, and teachers' expectancies are at best one of many contributors. Nevertheless, the weight of the evidence has convinced most critics that expectancies can make a difference—not always, certainly, but in some classrooms and for some children. What teachers expect of their students has been shown to affect how they behave toward those students, and the teachers' behavior has in turn been shown to affect, for better or for worse, how the children perform. Expectancies themselves can have many bases. Among the sources that have been identified are standardized test scores (the basis explored in the Rosenthal and Jacobson study), gender, social class, race, physical attractiveness, and presence of an older sibling in the school system (Dusek & Joseph, 1983). Anyone who has ever followed an older sibling through school should be able to appreciate this last factor.

Rosenthal and Jacobson entitled their book *Pygmalion in the Classroom.* In the Pygmalion legend, a sculptor's skill and devotion transform a mass of stone into a perfect, living woman. Teachers' effects on students are neither this powerful nor (unfortunately) this positive. But teachers can have effects, and the expectancies that they form are one determinant of what these effects may be.

Mothers and infants were randomly assigned to two experimental groups and one control group. The goal of both experimental treatments was to enhance the child's development by working with the mother and improving patterns of mother–child interaction. In one group, mothers met weekly, under the leadership of a trained group leader, to discuss child rearing and early childhood educational experiences. In another, a trained "toy demonstrator" visited the home regularly to show both infants and mothers how to operate various cognitively stimulating toys. Although the group discussions proved somewhat more effective than the toy demonstrations, both had positive effects. At the conclusion of the 2-year treatment, mothers in the experimental groups were superior to those in the control group on a variety of measures. For example, the experimental mothers interacted more with their children during observational sessions, and they were generally more open and flexible in their attitudes toward child rearing. Children in the experimental groups had higher IQs than those in the control group. The latter finding, however, held only on some measures and at some testing times. Furthermore, the group differences in IQ did not arise because the experimental children emerged with above-average or even average IQs. The differences came about be-

381

cause the general decline in IQ across the course of the study was less for the experimental children than for the control children.

General Overview

Intervention projects of the sort just described have been in existence for close to 30 years now. What have they told us about the possibility of modifying intelligence by changing the environment? In answering this question, we draw especially from a report from the Consortium for Longitudinal Studies (1983; Lazar & Darlington, 1982). The authors of this report collated information from 11 independent intervention projects, looking in particular for long-term effects of the interventions. Ages of the participants at the time of final data collection ranged from 9 to 19. Based on this and other recent reviews (Clarke & Clarke, 1989; Darlington, 1991; Ramey & Landesman Ramey, 1990; Seitz, 1990), we can draw several general conclusions.

First, participation in intervention projects has an immediate positive effect on children's IQs. Children who have received intervention typically have higher IQs than children who have not, and the differences typically persist for at least a year or two after the program has ended. The effects, however, do show a definite tendency to diminish with time. In most projects, no differences between experimental and control groups are evident in long-term follow-ups. Furthermore, no project has produced a generally superior level of intellectual functioning in its participants. The main effect of intervention seems to be to minimize the declines in IQ that the children would otherwise experience.

Second, positive effects of intervention are often more marked on other measures than on IQ. The major finding of the Consortium report concerned impact on school performance. Participation in early intervention was associated with higher scores on standardized achievement tests, lower probability of being assigned to special education classes, and lower probability of being retained in a grade. There was also evidence for positive effects on self-concept, achievement motivation, and maternal attitudes toward school. Other studies have also documented beneficial effects of intervention even in the absence of IQ gain. Such findings have reinforced long-standing criticisms of the practice of using IQ scores as the main index of the success of intervention (Schweinhart & Weikart, 1991; Travers & Light, 1982). Not only is IQ an incomplete measure of intellectual ability, but other kinds of effects (such as the effect on school performance) may be more important for the child's development. Furthermore, IQ tests cannot measure the nonintellectual benefits that some programs may have (improved nutritional status, better social competence, and so on).

Third, identifying the specific features of intervention that produce positive effects is difficult. It appears, in fact, that a variety of approaches can be beneficial. The common feature may be the opportunity for close and extended interaction with a supportive adult. Benefits also relate to the intensity of the intervention. Programs that begin in infancy or extend into grade school have greater impact than more short-term efforts, and programs that produce large-scale changes in the child's environment have greater impact than those whose intervention is more limited. Involvement of family members, particularly the mother, is beneficial, especially in ensuring that effects do not disappear once the program ends. In addition to promoting positive forms of mother–child interaction, programs that emphasize parents may produce other changes in the parent's life (such as completion of school or successful employment) that in turn have a positive effect on the child's development (Benasich, Brooks-Gunn, & Clewell, 1992; Larner, Halpern, &

Harkavy, 1992). Finally, with regard to the specific content of the program, an emphasis on language appears to characterize many of the most successful programs. More generally, an explicit focus on academically relevant skills (language, reading, number, and so on) seems, not surprisingly, to increase the chances of later school success.

The points just made are relevant to an evaluation of the most broad-scale and well-known intervention program, Project Head Start. Box 10-3 discusses the history and current status of Head Start.

Race and Intelligence

The intervention programs just discussed have been directed overwhelmingly to poor African-American children. In the consortium projects (Consortium for Longitudinal Studies, 1983), for example, fully 90% of the participants were African American. This emphasis reflects the fact that African-American children are more likely than white children to have problems in school. They also tend to perform more poorly than white children on IQ tests; the average difference is about 15 points (Brody & Brody, 1976; Loehlin, Lindzey, & Spuhler, 1975).

The issue of why race differences in IQ exist is perhaps the most controversial topic in developmental psychology. For years the commonly accepted explanation was an environmentalist one: The environments that African-American children encounter are less likely than those of white children to promote the skills needed to do well on IQ tests. In 1969, however, Arthur Jensen published an article in which he suggested that genetic differences between races might also play a role (Jensen, 1969). Since then, Jensen has often elaborated this position (Jensen, 1972, 1973, 1980, 1981).

Jensen's argument is a complex one that we can only briefly summarize here. He begins by noting that racial differences in IQ have consistently appeared in dozens of studies and on a wide variety of tests. The differences do not seem to relate to the cultural loading of the test; they appear, for example, on nonverbal as well as verbal tests, and on test items that do not seem to require any culture-specific knowledge. Nor are the differences explained by differences in social class, since controlling for social class results in only a small decrease in the discrepancy.

Having established the consistency of racial differences, Jensen goes on to draw inferences from the data concerning heritability. Heritability for white samples, as we saw earlier, is high. Comparable studies with African-American samples have yielded somewhat lower but still substantial heritabilities (Scarr, 1981). It appears, therefore, that genes are an important source of individual differences within a race. Jensen acknowledges the points we made earlier—that heritability is always sample-specific and that heritability within one group cannot be applied directly to a comparison between two groups. He offers, however, a kind of plausibility argument: If genes are so important to differences within races, is it plausible that they make absolutely no contribution to differences between races? In support of this position, he argues that the environmental factors known to be important for intelligence have not been shown to vary appreciably between whites and African Americans. And he maintains that intervention programs designed to increase the intelligence of African-American children have failed to do so. Thus, the environmentalist position has been tested and has failed.

Most developmental psychologists have not been persuaded by Jensen's arguments. Various replies are possible (Angoff, 1988; Eckberg, 1979; Mackenzie, 1984; Scarr, 1981). Many would contend that Jensen's plausibility argument is simply not

PROJECT HEAD START

We noted that the sample size for the Early Training Project (Gray et al., 1982) was 90 mothers and children. The sample for Slaughter's (1983) home-based intervention consisted of 83 families. None of the intervention projects reviewed in the text has been able to include more than a fraction of the families that might benefit from such efforts. The hope has been that such programs can at least help some of the children in need, while perhaps also identifying general principles of intervention that can eventually be applied more broadly.

Project Head Start is enormously larger in scope. Head Start is a nationwide, federally funded intervention program that is directed primarily to low-income preschool children and their families. It was launched in 1965 as part of President Lyndon Johnson's War on Poverty and, unlike many components of the War on Poverty, it continues today: There are more than 2,000 Head Start centers spread across all 50 states.

Because Head Start is many centers rather than one, it can be difficult to say what Head Start "is." Nevertheless, several elements have characterized Head Start classrooms since the beginning of the program (Zigler & Muenchow, 1992). Head Start emphasizes family and community involvement. Parents are encouraged to volunteer in their children's classrooms and parents are also given a voice in decisions about the direction that the program will take. As part of this emphasis on family and community, Head Start attempts to avoid the "deficit" orientation that has characterized some interventions: Rather than seeking only to correct deficiencies in the child's background, Head Start is designed to build upon existing interests and strengths. While academic readiness is always part of a Head Start curriculum, other aspects of the child's development are stressed as well. Social skills are important, as is the development of self-confidence and motivation. So too is the child's physical development; an emphasis on nutrition and dental and medical care has been part of Head Start since its inception.

Does Head Start work? We saw that this question can be difficult to answer for any intervention. It is especially difficult in the case of Head Start, given the many different aspects of development that are stressed in the program, as well as the variations in how the general philosophy is implemented across centers.

• Although preschool intervention projects typically have limited effects on IQ, they can increase children's chances for later success in school.

Initial evaluations of Head Start focused on IQ gain, and many commentators were dismayed when Head Start failed to produce lasting improvements in children's IQs (Westinghouse Learning Center, 1969). In the years since the initial assessment, however, it has become clear that Head Start, like intervention programs in general, can have a number of beneficial effects that are not captured by IQ scores (Lee et al., 1990; Zigler & Finn-Stevenson, 1992; Zigler & Muenchow, 1992; Zigler & Styfco, 1993). These effects include greater success in school, better health status, gains in social competence, and increased involvement of the family in the child's education.

One other benefit of Head Start is worth noting. In addition to directly serving some 11 million children across the last 30 years, Head Start has functioned as a kind of national laboratory for designing and testing intervention programs for children and families (Zigler & Finn-Stevenson, 1992). A number of current social policy initiatives had their origins in programs introduced as part of Head Start, including support programs for needy families and techniques for mainstreaming handicapped children in regular classrooms. Head Start thus qualifies as not only the nation's largest social policy effort but also its largest scientific experiment.

plausible. A high heritability value (and recall that there are disputes about how high the value is) means simply that environmental differences are relatively unimportant *in the sample studied.* Even if differences among white children's environments have little impact, it is still possible that environmental differences between African Americans and whites could produce a 15-point difference in IQ. Recall our example of Island A and Island B. Marked nutritional differences between the two islands might well lead to marked differences in height, no matter how high the heritabilities for each island alone. The same point applies to environmental effects on IQ. To many, this position is more plausible than the claim that African-American children's experiences do not differ in important ways from those of white children.

More direct evidence can also be cited.

1.   Although intervention programs have not been as successful as was hoped, at least some programs have produced genuine and long-term gains in African-American children's intellectual competence. Furthermore, intervention programs to date do not exhaust what might be done. It is quite possible that future programs, building on the knowledge that has been gained, may yield more impressive effects.

2.   "Race" is more a social classification than a biologically determined category. Many African Americans in the United States in fact have white ancestry, in varying degrees. Jensen's position predicts that IQ scores among African Americans should be positively correlated with degree of white ancestry. So-called admixture studies, however, provide no support for this prediction (Scarr et al., 1977).

3.   The finding that adopted children have superior IQs holds also in studies of transracial adoption. On the average, African-American children adopted into white homes have above-average IQs—just as do white children adopted into such homes (Moore, 1986; Scarr & Weinberg, 1983; Weinberg, Scarr, & Waldman, 1992). Thus, rearing in what Scarr and Weinberg call the "culture of the test" diminishes the racial differences in IQ. Clearly, this finding is compatible with an environmentalist position.

✔ *To Recap...*

The issue of experience and intelligence can be studied in two general ways: through examination of the effects of naturally occurring variations in children's experiences and by experimental interventions that change children's environments.

It was the study of naturally occurring deprivations (such as orphanage rearing) that first alerted psychologists to the possible importance of early experience. Such studies demonstrated both the negative effects of a deprived environment and the positive effects of an improvement in environment. Subsequent research has revealed significant, although less dramatic, effects of more normal variations in experience within the home setting. Such studies (often using the HOME instrument) suggest that the child's intellectual development is enhanced by parents who are responsive to the child's needs, who provide a high level of child-appropriate language, and who create a generally stimulating and varied environment in which the child is free to explore. A particular approach to the home environment, Zajonc's confluence model, attempts to relate the child's intelligence to the intellectual level within the home. Tests of the confluence model to date have been mixed.

Schools as well as homes can affect children's intellectual development. Cross-cultural studies indicate that schooling promotes a number of cognitive skills, including memory, classification, and metacognition. Studies within our culture verify that both the quantity and the quality of schooling can be important.

Experimental interventions have been directed mainly to children who are perceived as being at risk for school failure. A variety of intervention programs have had positive effects on children's development. Immediate effects are generally greater than long-term ones, and effects on school performance are generally greater than effects on IQ. Programs that introduce the greatest changes in the child's environment have generally had the greatest impact.

On the average, African-American children score lower than white children on IQ tests. Drawing on the generally high heritability of IQ, Jensen has suggested that genetic factors may contribute to this difference. Most developmental psychologists disagree. Counterarguments include the inappropriateness of applying within-race heritabilities to between-race differences and the positive effect of transracial adoption on African-American children's IQs.

ALTERNATIVES TO IQ

In the discussion of intervention programs, we touched on some ways other than IQ to assess children's competence. In this section, we broaden the scope to consider some recent theories and programs of research that represent significant departures from the traditional IQ perspective.

Vygotsky and the Zone of Proximal Development

As we saw in Chapter 2, Lev Vygotsky was a Soviet psychologist who was a contemporary of Piaget (both were born in 1896) but who died when he was only 37. Vygotsky therefore never had a chance to complete his theorizing or program of research. Nevertheless, he is an important figure, for his ideas have helped to shape the development of modern Soviet child psychology. And in recent years, as translations of his writings have appeared (Vygotsky, 1962, 1978, 1987), Vygotsky has begun to influence Western thinking as well.

Zone of proximal development
Vygotsky's term for the difference between what children can do by themselves and what they can do with help from an adult.

A central construct in Vygotsky's theory is the **zone of proximal development**. The zone is defined as the difference between what the child can do on his or her own and what the child can do with help. Vygotsky refers to what children can do on their own as the *level of actual development*. In his view, it is the level of actual development that standard IQ tests measure. Such a measure is undoubtedly important, but it is also incomplete. Two children might have the same level of actual development, in the sense of being able to solve the same number of problems on some standardized test. Given appropriate help from an adult, however, one child might be able to solve an additional dozen problems while the other child might be able to solve only two or three more. What the child can do with help is referred to as the *level of potential development*. It is the difference between actual and potential that defines a particular child's zone of proximal development.

The emphasis on what the child can do with help is a reflection of a central theme in the theorizing of both Vygotsky and later Soviet psychologists, a theme that we first encountered in Chapter 2 in our discussion of socio-cultural approaches to development. Soviet psychologists believe strongly in the cultural determination of individual development. In their view, much of what children learn is acquired from the culture around them, and much of the child's problem solving is mediated through adult help. Focusing on the child in isolation (as in IQ testing) is therefore misleading. Such a focus at best captures the products of learning; it does not reveal the processes by which children acquire new skills. Furthermore, such a focus may miss important differences among children. In the example given above, the two children appeared equally intelligent when working alone, yet their ability to benefit from help was quite different—they had different zones of proximal development.

In recent years, a number of researchers have attempted to develop methods of assessing intelligence that build on the concept of the zone of proximal development (Belmont, 1989; Brown & Ferrara, 1985; Lidz, 1992). A common research strategy has been a test-train-test procedure. With this approach, the child first attempts to solve a set of problems on his or her own, much as on a standard IQ test. Following this determination of "actual level," the experimenter provides a standardized set of prompts designed to help the child arrive at an answer. The prompts are arranged in a graduated series, starting out fairly subtle and indirect and becoming progressively more explicit until the solution is reached. The child's zone for that kind of problem solving can be determined from the number of hints needed—the fewer the hints, the wider the zone. In the final phase, the child is presented with problems that vary in their similarity to those on which help was given. This final phase provides a measure of the child's ability to transfer the skills learned with adult help.

"Dynamic" assessments of this sort are difficult to carry out, and the approach has yet to result in a generally accepted method of testing intelligence (for critiques, see Paris & Cross, 1988; Sternberg, 1991). Nevertheless, studies using the approach have confirmed Vygotsky's claim that IQ tests provide an incomplete pic-

• In Vygotsky's theory, guidance from a more competent adult is an important source of children's problem-solving skills.

ture of children's intelligence. IQ scores do relate to both speed of initial learning and breadth of transfer. The relation is not perfect, however, and many children's ability to profit from help is not predicted by their IQs. Based on their own studies, Brown and Ferrara (1985) identified six profiles that seemed to capture individual differences in children's learning: (1) low IQ, slow learning, narrow transfer; (2) high IQ, fast learning, wide transfer; (3) low IQ, fast learning, wide transfer; (4) high IQ, slow learning, narrow transfer; (5) fast learning, narrow transfer (labeled "context-bound"); and (6) slow learning, wide transfer (labeled "reflective"). As they note, only the first two profiles fit what would be expected from the IQ perspective and its division of children into "generally intelligent" and "generally not intelligent." The existence of the other profiles is evidence that children are a good deal more variable than IQ tests indicate.

Our emphasis so far has been on the zone of proximal development as a method for assessing intelligence. In Vygotsky's theory, however, social interaction is not only a context within which children demonstrate their intelligence; it is also the primary mechanism through which that intelligence develops. Children acquire knowledge and tools of intellectual adaptation from their interactions with other people, most notably (especially for young children) with their own parents. This aspect of the theory has also been the focus of much recent research, as investigators have sought to determine when and how parents teach things to their children and what children take away from such interactions (Diaz, Neal, & Vachio, 1991; Freund, 1990; Garton, 1992; Rogoff, 1990, 1993). This work has confirmed that children can often perform tasks with appropriate adult help that they are unable to carry out on their own. Of particular interest has been a form of teaching known as **scaffolding**, in which the parent continually adjusts the level of his or her help in response to the child's level of performance, moving to more direct, explicit forms of teaching if the child falters and to less direct, more demanding forms of teaching as the child moves closer to independent mastery. Scaffolding appears to be effective not only in producing immediate success but in instilling the skills necessary for independent problem solving in the future. We consider some specific aspects of this process in the next chapter, when we discuss children's language development.

Although parents have been the focus for much of the research inspired by Vygotsky's theory, other social agents have also received attention. Vygotsky suggested that interactions with more competent peers contribute to children's intellectual development, and recent research supports this idea—benefits from peer teaching have been shown in both experimental studies of problem solving and naturalistic research in classroom settings (Forman, 1992; Phelps & Damon, 1991; Tudge & Rogoff, 1989). More generally, Vygotsky's writings emphasize the importance of not just specific social agents, such as parents or peers, but also the broader culture within which the child develops. Much of the cross-cultural research that we discuss throughout the book has a grounding in Vygotsky's theory, including the studies to which we turn next.

Scaffolding
A method of teaching in which the adult adjusts the level of help provided in relation to the child's level of performance, the goal being to encourage independent performance.

DEVELOPMENT IN CONTEXT: Mathematics in School and on the Streets: Brazilian Candy Vendors

The importance of mathematics in school curricula is reflected in the enshrinement of "'rithmetic" as one of the traditional three Rs. But school is not the only place in which children learn about math. A striking example of out-of-school learning is provided by studies of child candy vendors on the urban streets of Brazil (Nunes, Carraher, & Schliemann, 1993; Saxe, 1988a, 1988b, 1991).

In Brazil, candy selling is one of the occupations available to poor children (usually boys) who need to earn money to help their families survive. Children may enter the selling practice as early as age 5, and they may eventually work as many as 14 hours per day and 60 or 70 hours per week. Many vendors either never go to school or leave school after a few years. In addition to the sheer physical demands of the job, candy selling poses cognitive challenges. Figure 10-4 summarizes the steps that the youthful candy vendor must execute. During the *purchase phase* the seller must buy the candies that he will eventually sell from one of the many available stores. During the *prepare-to-sell phase* the seller must price the candy, translating the wholesale price that he has just paid for a multi-unit box to a retail price for individual units, including a sufficient mark-up to ensure that he makes a profit. During the *sell phase* the seller must negotiate with customers, handling currency and making change as needed and perhaps bargaining on the price as well. Such transactions may take place wherever potential customers are to be found: on the streets, in line at theaters, on buses waiting to depart. Finally, during the *prepare-to-purchase* phase the seller must decide what kind of candies he will buy for his next outing and which store is likely to give him the best price. All of this is complicated by two further factors indicated in the figure: the competition from the many peers who are also engaged in the candy-selling business and the need to cope with Brazil's spiraling inflation rate (250% or higher in recent years).

As this description should make clear, the mathematics involved in candy selling is not of the abstract sort that children often encounter in school. Rather, the mathematical goals that must be met emerge in the context of the candy-selling practice, and children can succeed as candy sellers only if they achieve these goals. That they do succeed is demonstrated both by naturalistic observations of candy vendors at work and by more formal experimental tests of their mathematical ability. On the streets, child candy vendors perform a number of mathematical operations both quickly and accurately: representing the numerical values of different forms of currency, adding and subtracting units of various sizes,

• Child candy vendors in Brazil must develop a number of mathematical skills in order to perform their task successfully.

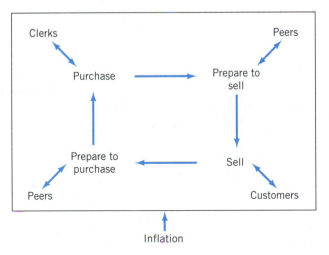

Figure 10-4 Model of the candy-selling practice engaged in by child vendors in Brazil. The children must perform mathematical operations at each phase of the process (purchase, sell, etc.), while interacting with various social agents and adjusting over time to the effects of inflation. From "Candy Selling and Math Learning" by G. B. Saxe, 1988, *Educational Researcher*, August–September, p. 15. Copyright 1988 by the American Educational Research Association. Reprinted by permission.

comparing ratios to determine optimal buying or selling prices (e.g., 3 for 500 versus 7 for 1,000), and adjusting over time for the ever-present inflation. In experimental tests, child candy vendors perform well on problems that are similar to those that they encounter during selling but poorly on traditional school-type problems—just the reverse of the pattern shown by nonvendors who go to school. Neither candy selling nor schooling produces a generally superior level of mathematical functioning; rather, children in both groups do best when operating in the contexts with which they are most familiar (Carraher, Carraher, & Schliemann, 1985; Saxe, 1991).

The studies of child candy vendors are just one of a number of recent examples of the importance of context in both the development and the utilization of cognitive skills (Ceci, 1993; Light & Butterworth, 1993). Other South American research, for example, has demonstrated similar effects in adult samples. Even though Brazilian fisherman receive no formal training in proportional reasoning, they do quite well at calculating ratios as long as the problems are embedded in a context that is similar to their everyday dealings with prices and quantities (Schliemann & Nunes, 1990). Similarly, minimally schooled Brazilian construction foremen are also good at proportional reasoning—but only if the problems are couched in a construction context (Ceci, 1993).

In addition to demonstrating the importance of cultural context, the candy-selling studies illustrate a further Vygotskian theme. This theme concerns the nurturing of children's intellectual development through the teaching and guidance provided by more competent members of the society. Candy vendors, especially the youngest ones, are not expected to master all of the mathematical tasks on their own. Help of various sorts is often provided. Parents may set the day's selling price before the child leaves the house. Storekeepers may help with various calculations. Peers and older siblings may provide both on-the-spot assistance and general models of how to proceed. As the child grows older, these forms of assistance are gradually cut back. Older children are expected to do on their own what they once could do only with help.

One more change that comes with age is worth noting. In general, younger children are less competent vendors than are older ones. They can, for example, often offer just one price ratio rather than several, something that should make their wares less attractive to prospective customers. Despite this seeming disadvantage, 6- to 7-year-old vendors make twice as many sales as do 12- to 15-year-olds. Clearly, being young and cute is one way to elicit help from adults.

Sternberg's Triarchic Theory of Intelligence

Triarchic theory of intelligence
Sternberg's three-part theory of intelligence. The theory includes the components that underlie intelligent behavior, the contexts in which intelligence is exercised, and the experiences or types of tasks that require intelligence.

Robert Sternberg's (1984, 1985) **triarchic theory of intelligence** has roots in both traditional psychometric approaches and information-processing theory and research. As its name implies, the triarchic theory is actually made up of three subtheories: the componential subtheory, the contextual subtheory, and the experiential subtheory.

The goal of the *componential subtheory* is to specify the processes by which intelligent behavior is generated. Although this goal might seem a necessary one for any theory, Sternberg maintains that most psychometric approaches never tell us what the underlying mental processes are. In his view, three kinds of components—performance components, metacomponents, and knowledge-acquisition components—are important. Performance components are the basic operations involved in cognitive activity. Consider, for example, how people solve an analogy problem, such as "trail is to hike as lake is to (a) swim, (b) walk, (c) water, (d) dust." Solving such analogies requires (among other things) encoding the terms of the problem, inferring the relation between the first pair of terms, mapping this relation so that it can be carried over, and applying the relation to the second pair of terms. All of these processes are examples of performance components. Such components are not the whole story, however. Intelligent behavior also requires higher-order control processes that determine which components will be used when. Planning and monitoring cognitive activity are the responsibilities of the metacomponents. Finally, intelligence involves not only execution of existing components but also development of new knowledge. The knowledge-acquisition components are responsible for the acquisition of new information.

The second aspect of Sternberg's theory concerns the contexts within which components are applied. The *contextual subtheory* has to do with the fit between mental activity and the external environment. Intelligence is not simply a matter of internal mental processes (the focus of the componential subtheory); it involves adaptation to the challenges of the external world. Individuals adapt to the environments in which they find themselves. They also select appropriate environments or shape existing environments to make them more appropriate. The processes by which such adaptation, selection, and shaping occur are the concern of the contextual subtheory. Because different environments may present different challenges, the contextual subtheory allows for individual or group differences in the form that intelligence takes. What constitutes intelligent behavior may vary from one setting or one culture to another. As our discussion of Vygotsky should make clear, Sternberg's is not the only theory to stress the importance of context for intelligence.

The final part of Sternberg's theory is the *experiential subtheory*, which addresses the question of what kinds of tasks are appropriate as measures of intelligence. Sternberg argues that two sorts of tasks are most appropriate: those that require response to novelty and those that involve automatization of information processing. We encountered the idea of intelligence as response to novelty in our earlier discussion of the stability of IQ over time. For Sternberg, intelligence is not so much a matter of doing the routine and the familiar as it is a matter of coping adaptively with the new or "nonentrenched." There are a variety of ways in which a task can be novel. Table 10-7 shows one example from Sternberg's research, a sampling of so-called insight problems. The problems in the table are designed to elicit familiar but incorrect methods of solution. The insight lies in the realization that new—and in this case simpler—approaches are necessary.

The notion of automatization is in a sense the converse of response to novelty. Although response to novelty may be the essence of intelligence, much of our intellectual life does involve application of familiar skills to familiar tasks. Common examples are reading and driving a car. Such application is intelligent to the extent that it can be automatized—that is, brought to such a high level of expertise that performance is essentially automatic and little attention need be devoted to the task. Such automatization ensures efficient and intelligent processing and frees cognitive resources for other tasks.

Even from this brief account, the relation of Sternberg's work to the information-processing conceptions discussed in Chapter 9 should be evident. Sternberg's theory represents the major attempt to date to enrich the psychometric perspec-

TABLE 10-7 ● **Tasks Used by Sternberg to Measure Insight**

If you have black socks and brown socks in your drawer, mixed in a ratio of 4 to 5, how many socks will you have to take out to make sure of having a pair of socks the same color?

Water lilies double in area every 24 hours. At the beginning of the summer there is 1 water lily on a lake. It takes 60 days for the lake to become covered with water lilies. On what day is the lake half-covered?

Suppose you and I have the same amount of money. How much must I give you so that you have 10 dollars more than I?

A farmer buys 100 animals for $100. Cows are $10 each, sheep are $3 each, and pigs are 50 cents each. How much did he pay for 5 cows?

Source: From *Beyond IQ: A Triarchic Theory of Human Intelligence* (pp. 81, 285) by R. J. Sternberg, 1985, Cambridge: Cambridge University Press. Copyright 1985 by Cambridge University Press. Reprinted by permission.

tive with insights about cognitive processes gained from the information-processing approach.

Gardner's Multiple Intelligences

Howard Gardner (1983, 1993) has proposed a theory of intelligence that is in some respects similar to those of factor-analytic theorists such as Thurstone and Guilford. Like these theorists, Gardner believes that intelligence is considerably more diversified and multifaceted than the notion of general intelligence admits. Unlike most psychometric researchers, however, Gardner does not rely solely on factor analyses of standardized tests to draw conclusions about different forms of intelligence. And the kinds of intelligence that he proposes go well beyond the ones that psychometric theorists usually consider.

Gardner's general thesis is that humans possess a number of relatively distinct intelligences. We consider what some of these intelligences are shortly. First, however, we must ask about evidence. How can the existence of a distinct intelligence be demonstrated? Gardner suggests a number of kinds of evidence, or signs, that can help point the way. First, there must be experimental evidence in support of the intelligence. The factor-analytic studies discussed earlier in the chapter are one possible experimental approach to distinguishing different sorts of intelligence; information-processing demonstrations of the distinctiveness of different cognitive domains (see Chapter 9) are another. Next, the intelligence should be specifiable in terms of a set of distinct core operations—that is, it should be possible to say what it "is." Third, the intelligence should show a distinct developmental history, progressing predictably from rudimentary to advanced. In addition, it should show a distinct evolutionary history, growing in complexity as the species grows more complex in the course of its evolution.

Two final signs discussed by Gardner concern deviations from the normal developmental path. Gardner argues that isolation by brain damage can be informative. The fact, for example, that linguistic abilities can be either selectively impaired or selectively spared in cases of brain injury is evidence for a separate linguistic intelligence. Similarly, the existence of individuals with exceptional talents in one particular domain is a possible sign. In so-called savants, for example, remarkable mathematical ability may be coupled with subnormal general intelligence, suggesting that a distinct mathematical intelligence exists. And children who compose symphonies at age 10, as did Mozart and Mendelssohn, are evidence for a musical intelligence.

Based on a conjunction of such signs, Gardner proposes the existence of at least six distinct human intelligences. He marshalls evidence in support of a linguistic intelligence, a spatial intelligence, and a logical–mathematical intelligence. Although the evidence that he uses is sometimes unusual (for example, an analysis of the drawings of an autistic child in the discussion of spatial intelligence), these are forms of intelligence that are talked about in some way by every theorist. Other intelligences are less familiar. We have already mentioned the idea of a musical intelligence. In Gardner's view, musical ability meets all of the signs for being considered as a distinct form of intelligence. Musical ability has both an evolutionary and a developmental history, it can appear in isolated form in cases of brain injury or musical prodigy, and it can be analyzed in terms of a set of core elements (pitch, rhythm, timbre, and so on). Similar arguments are offered in support of a bodily-kinesthetic intelligence and a personal intelligence—that is, an intelligence concerned with understanding people, both oneself and others.

Of all the approaches that we consider in this section, Gardner's departs most markedly from traditional approaches to intelligence. This, in fact, is the main point of the theory of multiple intelligences—to broaden the conception of intelligence beyond the verbal, logical, and mathematical abilities that have been almost the sole focus of theories to date.

The Ethological Approach to Intelligence

As we stress throughout this book, the ethological perspective has emerged in recent years as one of the dominant approaches in child psychology. Thus far, ethologists have devoted more attention to aspects of social development (such as attachment and prosocial behavior) than to the development of cognitive abilities. Recently, however, several ethologically oriented writers have begun to address issues of intelligence.

Theorists who discuss intelligence from an ethological perspective emphasize the same themes that characterize ethology in general (Charlesworth, 1983; Jerison, 1982). A basic theme involves the evolutionary basis for behavior. Intelligent behavior is seen as having evolved, and as having done so because it was adaptive in the history of the human species. This emphasis on evolutionary shaping does not mean that ethologists see intelligent behavior as automatic and rigid—humans are above all flexible, learning organisms. But the very capacity for such powerful learning, ethologists maintain, has evolved in response to the varied environmental challenges with which humans have had to cope. One kind of evidence in support of this position is the increase in brain size and brain organization across evolution (Jerison, 1982).

A second theme follows from the first. It is an emphasis on the innate bases for intelligent behavior. This biological emphasis is compatible with the evidence that we have discussed indicating an important genetic contribution to individual differences in intelligence. The ethological approach, however, differs from all the other approaches considered in this chapter in that ethologists' main concern is not with differences but with commonalities. In their view, human intelligence is in basic respects the same the world around, involving the same problem-solving capacities and the same environmental challenges. For ethologists, these similarities stem from the common biological mechanisms and biological heritage of the species.

A third theme is methodological. Ethologists emphasize the naturalistic study of behavior in its natural setting. It is only through naturalistic study that the full

• Ethologists believe that sensorimotor forms of intelligence are similar across babies and across species.

range of the organism's behavioral repertoire, as well as the adaptive significance of that repertoire, can be revealed. This emphasis is directly opposed to the psychometric concern with response to standardized tests. Ethologists are doubtful that performance on a single laboratory test can capture much of the range of human intelligence. It should be clear that this concern is shared by all of the approaches considered in this section.

Let us briefly consider two examples of how ethological thinking has been applied to the study of cognitive development. One concerns the naturalistic methodology. William Charlesworth (1978, 1983) has collected hundreds of hours of observational data of children's problem-solving behavior in the natural environment. In his research, a problem is defined as any block to ongoing behavior (for example, a stuck door that refuses to open) that elicits an attempt at solution (for example, asking a parent for help). Analyses have focused on the frequency and types of problems that children encounter, on the ways in which they respond, and on the success or failure of the response. One finding is that real-life problems often do not look much like those on intelligence tests. Charlesworth reports, for example, that a high proportion of the problems that young children encounter involve social blocks and social interaction, a dimension of intelligence that is seldom tapped on IQ tests. Note that the emphasis on the social context for intelligence is compatible with the Vygotskian position discussed earlier.

The second application is more theoretical. We have seen that variations in sensorimotor forms of intelligence in infancy have little relation to variations in later intelligence. Sandra Scarr (1983) has offered an ethological explanation for this discontinuity. She suggests that the sensorimotor intelligence of infancy evolved earlier in our primate history than did later representational intelligence. Sensorimotor forms of intelligence are in fact quite similar across different primates, in contrast to the marked interspecies differences in adult intelligence. They also are quite similar across human infants, appearing in essentially the same form in every human culture. Scarr suggests that infant intelligence has been shaped through evolution to develop in the same form in any normal environment. Because infant intelligence is so invariable, and because its evolutionary history is so distinct from that of later intelligence, there is little reason to expect infant IQ to predict later IQ. Thus, ethologists offer a theoretical explanation for what to many has been a puzzling empirical finding. More generally, ethology brings a strong theoretical perspective to a field of study that has often been more pragmatic than theoretical.

✔ *To Recap...*

Dissatisfaction with the traditional IQ approach is reflected in four recent alternative approaches to intelligence. Vygotsky and later Soviet psychologists emphasize what children can do with appropriate help from adults. The distinction between what children can do on their own and what they can do with help constitutes the zone of proximal development. Children may differ in their zones of proximal development, even though by standard IQ measures they look equivalent. And appropriate help from an adult or a more competent peer may lead to new forms of intellectual competence.

Sternberg's triarchic theory is composed of three subtheories. The componential subtheory attempts to identify the mental processes, or components, that underlie intelligent behavior. The contextual subtheory concerns adaptation to challenges from the environment. The experiential subtheory concerns the kinds of tasks that are appropriate for assessing intelligence, with an emphasis on tasks that require response to novelty and tasks that involve automatization of cognitive skills.

Gardner's theory of multiple intelligences suggests that certain forms of intelligence fall outside the scope of standard psychometric assessments. Based on a variety of evidence, Gardner posits the existence of six relatively distinct human intelligences: linguistic, spatial, logical-mathematical, musical, bodily-kinesthetic, and personal.

The ethological approach to intelligence stresses themes important to ethological theorizing in general. Among the points emphasized are the evolutionary history of intelligence, the biological bases for intelligent behavior, and the methodological importance of studying intelligence in its natural context.

CONCLUSION

The impact of IQ tests has extended well beyond the academic contexts and professional journals within which most psychological theories and measures are confined. Indeed, a recent survey listed the IQ test as one of the 20 most influential scientific achievements of the 20th century, along with such discoveries as DNA and nuclear fission (Bjorklund, 1989). This evaluation echoed an earlier assessment by a prominent Harvard psychologist, who had labeled the IQ test "psychology's most telling accomplishment to date" (Herrnstein, 1971, p. 45).

For reasons that should be clear by now, most psychologists are not this positive about IQ. Nevertheless, most would agree that the tests do measure something of interest about intelligence and about differences in people's intelligence. And few would deny that the study of differences—in intelligence or in any other important human attribute—is a valid part of the science of psychology. Diversity is a characteristic of any species, and explaining the diversity is one task for those who study the species. Furthermore, the work that we have considered in this chapter has clear practical as well as theoretical significance. If we can discover the factors that lead to variations in intelligence, then we may be able to optimize the intellectual development of children everywhere.

Once these points are made, it must also be acknowledged that work in the psychometric tradition has sometimes been more limiting than illuminating. In particular, the exclusive focus on individual differences may cause us to lose track of the important ways in which all children are similar in their intellectual development. Similarly, the frequent focus on problems in development may cause us to miss the strengths that particular children possess. It is in this respect that the Piagetian and information-processing approaches provide a valuable complement to the intelligence test perspective. These approaches concentrate on basic developments common to all children, and they remind us that all children show impressive intellectual achievements.

The points just made emerge even more clearly in the next chapter, when we turn to the topic of language development. We will see that the focus of most research on language has been on similarities rather than differences among children. And we will see that mastery of language is a remarkable cognitive achievement—perhaps the most impressive achievement that the human species shows.

FOR THOUGHT AND DISCUSSION

1.   We have tried in this chapter to present both the positive and the negative aspects of IQ tests. Some people, however, believe that the negative points so outweigh the positive that the tests should no longer be used. *Do you think that the use of IQ tests should be banned in schools and other applied settings? Why or why not? What would be gained and what would be lost if such tests were no longer used?*

2.   One of the criticisms of the IQ approach to assessing intelligence is that a single score cannot capture the many different aspects of human intelligence. *What are your opinions with respect to the one intelligence versus many intelligences debate? How well does Gardner's theory of multiple intelligences apply to you or to people you know?*

3.   We suggested several ways in which the ethological/evolutionary approach has been applied to the development of intelligence. We also noted, however, that such applications to date have been limited. *Think about the meaning of intelligence within an evolutionary context. What do you see as the most important ways in which an evolutionary perspective might broaden and enrich our understanding of intelligence?*

4.   We noted that the presence or absence of schooling is one important way in which cultures may differ in the opportunities they offer for the development of intellectual skills. *What are other potentially important differences among cultures, and what effects might they have? Are there some aspects of intelligence that you would expect not to vary across cultures? If so, what are they, and why would you expect them not to vary?*

5. Throughout the book, we consider a number of positions that suggest that people in part create their own environments—Bronfenbrenner's notion of developmentally instigative characteristics (Chapter 2), Bandura's model of reciprocal determinism (Chapter 2), and Scarr and McCartney's genotype-environment relationships (Chapter 4). *Consider the application of such models to the interpretation of studies of identical twins reared apart. Is similarity between separated identical twins necessarily a direct result of the genes? Does it make sense to try to identify separate contributions of genes and environment if the two factors are often correlated?*

6. The research discussed in this chapter addresses not only theoretical questions about the nature of intelligence but also practical questions about how best to nurture the intellectual development of all children. Intervention programs for children perceived to be at risk for later problems are a prime example of efforts in this second, applied category. *Imagine that you were to design an intervention program for an at-risk population. What would your program emphasize, and how would you evaluate its effects?*

7. We discuss what research has shown about the contribution of parents to their children's intellectual development. *Do any of the findings affect your ideas of how to interact with your children or of what you will do if you become a parent? Would you consider using any of the stimulation programs discussed in Box 10-1?*

Chapter 11

LANGUAGE DEVELOPMENT

*A*ny student who has spent 4 years in high school or college attempting to learn a second language can appreciate the struggle of trying to memorize how each verb is conjugated or what endings signify past, future, and subjunctive forms. Yet that very same student, during the first 4 years of life, very likely acquired the rudiments of his or her native language rather easily, with no textbooks, classroom instruction, or studying. How is such a remarkable feat accomplished?

The amazing nature of language development would be easiest to understand if it were simply an inherited ability that is passed along in the genes, emerging according to a biological timetable. As we saw in Chapter 2, even animals with very limited cognitive capabilities can display extremely complex behavior if it is the product of millions of years of evolution. But scholars on both sides of the nature–nurture issue agree that certain properties of human language rule out this explanation.

One such property is **productivity**. Whereas communication in other species involves a small set of inborn "messages" that the animal can send and also recognize, humans can produce—and comprehend—an infinite number of sentences. Many of the statements we speak and hear every day are ones we have never used or encountered in exactly the same form, yet they give us little trouble. Such statements are obviously not the sorts of messages that are passed along genetically from generation to generation.

A second property of language that argues against a purely genetic explanation is that it consists not of only one tongue used by all members of the species, but of thousands of languages. More importantly, different languages do not simply substitute one word for another, they use different grammatical structures altogether. The word order used to ask a question in Japanese, for example, is different from the corresponding order in French.

Finally, a third reason why our language cannot simply be transmitted through our genes is that, regardless of their parents' language, children speak and understand only the language or languages to which they are exposed. We are reminded of the story of the little American girl whose parents had just adopted a baby from Korea. "I can't wait until he gets older," she remarked, "so that he can teach me to speak Korean."[1] Whatever language abilities children inherit from their parents, the ability to speak and comprehend their native tongue is not one of them.

We begin, then, by ruling out what would have been the simplest solution to the fascinating puzzle of human language. Children are not born with every possible statement they will ever make or comprehend already stored in their brains. Instead, at least some aspects of language are acquired through interaction with the environment. Nevertheless, the fact that children acquire language so easily and at such an early age suggests that biological processes must play a major role.

It should be clear even from this brief introduction why language development has generated more theoretical debate and research interest than any other topic in child psychology. Our coverage of this active field focuses on the two traditional developmental issues. One is a description of the typical course of language development, beginning with the infant's earliest recognition abilities and continuing through children's first words, sentences, and more complex utterances. The second involves proposed explanations of language acquisition and the research findings that support them.

The chapter is divided into five parts. We begin by considering modern theories of language development. Next, we examine what is known about the period

Productivity
The property of language that permits humans to produce and comprehend an infinite number of statements.

[1]We thank Harriet Rheingold for this story.

before the child begins to speak—a period that many researchers feel is important in laying the groundwork for language development. In the remaining sections, we discuss the development of the three principal areas of language: its meaning (semantics), its structure (grammar), and its functions (pragmatics).

THEORIES OF LANGUAGE DEVELOPMENT

The theoretical debate over language development is not a new one. In ancient Greece, the Stoics and the Skeptics believed that language was natural and instinctual, emerging simply through biological maturation. The Aristotelians, in contrast, believed that language was an invented system that must be learned anew by each succeeding generation. Two thousand years later, these two philosophical positions are still with us (Bates, Bretherton, & Snyder, 1988; Robins, 1968).

Today, the theoretical approaches to language research follow roughly the three traditions we described in Chapter 2, including a biological model, cognitive approaches, and environmental analyses. This section outlines the fundamental ideas of these theories, and later sections examine what the data from research with children have to say about them.

Psycholinguistic Theory

In language research, the evolutionary perspective has found expression in the approach known as **psycholinguistics**. This nativistic model puts heavy emphasis on inborn processes and biological mechanisms.

The modern debate over language development began in about 1960. Before that, most American psychologists viewed language learning in terms of conditioning and learning principles. In his book *Verbal Behavior* (1957), B. F. Skinner had argued that the same operant principles used to explain other forms of human behavior could be used to explain the acquisition of language.

The first important challenge to Skinner's views came from Noam Chomsky, a linguist at the Massachusetts Institute of Technology (MIT). Chomsky and other psycholinguists who have followed him contend that language acquisition must have a strong biological basis because young children acquire it so rapidly, so easily, and during a period of development when their cognitive abilities are still rather unsophisticated (Braine, 1963; Chomsky, 1959, 1965; Lenneberg, 1967; McNeill, 1966). They rule out the possibility that language is acquired by means of rewards, punishments, and imitation for several reasons.

For one, adults do not appear to reinforce or punish children for the accuracy of their speech (a point we will discuss again shortly), as an environmental analysis would seem to suggest. In addition, learning by imitation would require that children be exposed to consistently good models of speech and language. However, much of the everyday adult speech children hear is not well formed and accurate but includes short pieces of sentences, hesitating stops and starts, slang words, and errors of many types. The productivity property of language also argues against learning by imitation because children produce many statements they have never heard spoken precisely in that way. Similarly, they cannot be imitating adult speech when they produce forms like "Mommy goed here" or "me up." Finally, linguistic analyses of human language reveal that the rules we use in speaking or comprehending language are extremely complex. But adults do not specifically teach children these rules. Few of us, in fact, could accurately describe the intricate system of

Psycholinguistics
A theory of language development, originated by Chomsky, that stresses innate mechanisms separate from cognitive processes.

• Noam Chomsky's psycholinguistic theory dominated research on language acquisition throughout the 1960s.

language regulations we use so effortlessly to produce and understand good speech and to recognize when speech is not good. These problems and others have led psycholinguists to conclude that environmental/learning accounts of language development are inadequate. The only alternative, they suggest, is that children are born with special brain mechanisms—separate from other cognitive processes—that allow them to acquire language quickly and easily.

According to Chomsky's original model, language can be described in terms of two types of structures. A language's **surface structure** consists of the rules governing the way that words and phrases can be arranged, which may vary considerably from one language to another. The **deep structure** of language, in contrast, refers to the inborn rules humans possess that underlie *any* language system. Language acquisition, therefore, requires a speech-analyzing mechanism, which Chomsky called the **language acquisition device (LAD)**. Whenever a child hears speech—good, bad, or whatever—this hypothetical brain mechanism begins to develop a **transformational grammar** that translates the surface structure of the language into the deep structure the child can comprehend. The development of these transformational rules is assumed to take place over several years, explaining why the child's initial language skills are rather limited but also why they progress so rapidly.

It should be noted that more recent psycholinguistic models have not adopted Chomsky's notion of a single LAD. They propose, instead, that the brain contains a series of separate *modules*, some of which control cognition and others that are specialized for different aspects of language development (such as grammatical structure, social communication, and conceptual meaning). The language modules are thought to be largely separate from the child's cognitive system and also somewhat independent of one another (Cook, 1988; Jackendoff, 1987; Rosenberg, 1993). Evidence for the modular model has been found, for example, in case studies of intellectually impaired children who can produce long, grammatically correct sentences, but have little understanding of their meaning (Yamada, 1990).

The psycholinguistic model solves several of the problems of an environmental approach. For one, children need only a few critical bits of speech input to develop a transformational grammar and thus to trigger a great deal of language development. Once children grasp the structural rules, or grammar, of the language, they can understand and produce an infinite number of sentences (Caplan & Chomsky, 1980). In addition, the argument goes, the analyzing and processing mechanisms in question have evolved specifically for language acquisition and are concerned only with the abstract structure of speech (e.g., subject–verb–object), not its meaning or content. These two points mean that language acquisition should put few demands on children's cognitive abilities, thus making highly sophisticated language learning possible in a cognitively immature organism. The psycholinguistic model also emphasizes the comprehension side of language—children are assumed to acquire language primarily through hearing it, rather than through speaking it. The rewards and punishments that would be necessary to operantly condition children's speech are thus not important to the psycholinguistic model. Finally, proponents of this view believe that the system of language modules evolved rather suddenly—meaning, in evolutionary terms, during the past 50,000 years or so—which explains why language exists only in our species (Garfield, 1987).

Cognitive-Developmental Language Models

Chomsky's brand of psycholinguistics dominated language research and theory throughout the 1960s. Beginning around 1970, however, alternative views of lan-

---

Surface structure
Chomsky's term for the way words and phrases are arranged in spoken languages.

Deep structure
Chomsky's term for the inborn knowledge humans possess about the properties of language.

Language acquisition device (LAD)
Chomsky's proposed brain mechanism for analyzing speech input—the mechanism that allows young children to quickly acquire the language to which they are exposed.

Transformational grammar
A set of rules developed by the LAD to translate a language's surface structure to a deep structure the child can innately understand.

guage development began to emerge. Some of these grew out of the cognitive-developmental tradition (Rice, 1989).

Whereas psycholinguists believe that language does not depend on children's cognitive abilities and is more or less separate from them, cognitive theorists assume that even very young children have a good deal of knowledge about the world and that they use this knowledge to help them learn language. As these researchers see it, children do not simply acquire a set of abstract linguistic rules. Rather, children acquire language forms that they can "map onto" cognitive concepts they already possess (Bruner, 1979; Johnston, 1986).

Some cognitive language research has been based on Piaget's theory. Most interest has centered on the transition from the later sensorimotor abilities of the toddler to the early preoperational abilities of the preschooler—a time when children are just beginning to combine words into two- and three-word phrases. This research has examined the relations between certain mental operations and corresponding language forms (Gopnik & Meltzoff, 1987a, 1992; Tamis-Lemonda & Bornstein, 1994). For example, it appears that infants need a concept of object permanence before they begin using disappearance words such as *all-gone* (Gopnik & Meltzoff, 1987b).

A second cognitive approach is based on a belief that children actually use their early cognitive concepts as a means of extracting the rules of language from the speech they hear. Recall that the psycholinguistic view is that children analyze speech into its abstract, grammatical structure. This cognitive model, in contrast, holds that children analyze speech into meaning-based, or *semantic*, concepts that involve relations among objects, actions, and events. According to this view, children have a very early, and perhaps innate, understanding of concepts such as *agent* (the person who performs an action), *action* (something that is done to a person or object), and *patient* (the person who is acted upon). When young children hear speech, they presumably analyze it into these cognitive concepts focusing, for example, on who did what to whom. They then develop simple rules regarding these concepts—such as "agents are usually named at the beginning of a statement"—that they use to guide their own speech (Bowerman, 1976; Maratsos, 1988b; Nelson, K. 1985). Even cognitive theorists believe that children eventually become more attuned to the structural aspects of language, as psycholinguists suggest. But the essence of the cognitive approach is that children's early knowledge of how the world operates is what they use to "crack the code" of the speech they hear (Bowerman, 1988; Schlesinger, 1974, 1988).

Information-processing theorists have studied language acquisition using a model called **learnability theory** (Pinker, 1984, 1989; Wexler & Culicover, 1980). These researchers have developed elaborate computer programs that attempt to identify precisely the sorts of grammatical rules required to explain human language. One of the most difficult problems to handle, they contend, is that language acquisition occurs largely without the benefit of *negative evidence*—that is, children are rarely told explicitly when their speech is incorrect (although we will see shortly that this problem may not actually exist). The goals of the learnability approach, then, are to identify language rules that are learnable by young children and to describe mathematically how the learning occurs (Morgan, 1986).

Learnability theory
An information-processing theory of language acquisition that uses computer models to try to identify the structure of language.

Environmental/Learning Approaches

While some psychologists search for the biological or cognitive bases of language, others seek the major sources of influence in the child's environment and social interactions (Bates et al., 1982; Zimmerman, 1983). These models fall into two categories: the learning approach and the functionalist approach.

Learning-Based Analyses

Although Skinner's analysis of language behavior fell out of favor when Chomsky convincingly argued that the environment alone cannot explain the facts of normal language development, learning-based research on the topic did not end. Indeed, in recent years, this tradition has generated some compelling evidence that environmental factors are important in normal language acquisition (Hart & Risley, 1992; Moerk, 1986, 1989). Some learning-based research has remained close to Skinner's original operant model (Michael, 1984; Vargas, 1986). Much of it, however, has followed the social-learning tradition, with its emphasis on observational learning and related cognitive processes (Whitehurst & Vasta, 1975; Zimmerman, 1983).

One of Chomsky's most important criticisms of Skinner's approach was that the environment does not present the child with a good model of language from which to learn. But research has now shown that people do not talk to infants in the same way that they talk to proficient speakers. Instead, mothers (and fathers, and even older children) use a style of speech, termed *motherese,* that is clear, simple, and grammatically accurate when they speak to infants (Hampson & Nelson, 1993; Shatz & Gelman, 1973; Snow & Ferguson, 1977).

Chomsky also argued that children cannot learn language simply by imitating what they hear, because they can produce and understand an unlimited number of new sentences. But social-learning theorists have shown that learning by imitation need not involve exact copying and that modeling may account for the kind of rule-based system that children come to use (Bandura, 1986; Whitehurst & DeBaryshe, 1989).

Finally, psycholinguists have argued that parents do not specifically train children in the rules of language. Recent, detailed analyses of parent–child interactions, however, indicate that parents do respond to the grammatical accuracy of their children's speech, providing them a variety of forms of feedback and instruction (Bohannon & Stanowicz, 1988; Furrow et al., 1993; Moerk, 1989). Taken together, these findings suggest that social and environmental factors may play a significant role in children's language acquisition.

Functionalist Theories

Functionalist model
A theory of language development that stresses the uses of language and the context in which it develops.

A final theoretical view of language development is the **functionalist model**. This approach is not based on learning principles and, in fact, has a distinctly cognitive flavor (Karmiloff-Smith, 1987; Ninio & Snow, 1988). Nevertheless, we have chosen to consider it within the environmental tradition because it emphasizes the social context in which language develops (Hickmann, 1986, 1987; Lempert, 1984).

Psycholinguists, we have seen, believe that the child learns the grammatical structure of language first, whereas most cognitive language theorists believe that the child initially extracts meaning from speech input. Functionalists, in contrast, hold that the child's primary motivation for acquiring language is to communicate ideas and to be understood. The emphasis here is on *pragmatics,* or the functional uses of language. Like the cognitive approach, this model argues that children extract meaning, rather than structure, from speech. But functionalists assign a much larger role to children's social interactions in the language learning process (Bates & MacWhinney, 1982; Bretherton, 1988; MacWhinney & Bates, 1993).

Jerome Bruner has proposed that the typical social environment of infants (in most cases their parents) in fact provides many structured opportunities for lan-

guage learning to take place. These opportunities comprise the **language support system (LASS)**, whose function is to assist children in their efforts to acquire meaning, and eventually grammatical rules, from speech input (Bruner, 1983). The central component of the LASS is the *format*. Formats are similar to the scripts we discussed in Chapter 9 and consist of structured social interactions, or "routines," that commonly take place between infants and their mothers. Familiar formats include looking at books together, playing naming games ("Where's your nose?" "Where's your mouth?") and action games (peekaboo and hide-and-seek), and singing songs with gestures ("The Itsy-Bitsy Spider"). The format allows a child to learn specific language elements within a very restricted context—usually simply by memorizing words and their corresponding actions. Gradually, the parent may change the formats so that they, for example, include more elements or require a greater contribution from the child. In this way, additional language can be learned and previously acquired responses can be applied in new ways. Within these formatted interactions, the parent also provides other sorts of scaffolding for language acquisition, such as simplifying speech, using repetition, and correcting the child's inaccurate or incomplete statements (Snow, Perlmann, & Nathan, 1987). (Recall from Chapter 10 that scaffolding involves providing help appropriate to the child's level of performance.)

Language support system (LASS)
Bruner's proposed process by which parents provide children assistance in learning language.

✔ To Recap...

Until about 1960, the leading theory of language development was Skinner's conditioning and learning account. Since then, the three major traditions have offered additional models.

The evolutionary tradition is represented by Chomsky's psycholinguistic theory. This model holds that learning explanations are inadequate to account for language development. Instead, psycholinguists propose that language is acquired by way of an inborn language acquisition device (LAD), which transforms the surface structure of the language into an internal deep structure that the child innately understands. This hypothetical brain mechanism presumably responds only to the structure, not the meaning, of speech, so language learning is essentially independent of the child's cognitive development.

Cognitive-developmental theorists believe that children's early knowledge and concepts play an important role in language development. Piagetians have attempted to link advances in sensorimotor and early preoperational abilities to corresponding language skills. Others contend that when children hear speech, they analyze it according to its content before extracting its grammatical structure. Information-processing researchers are developing computer programs that attempt to determine the linguistic rules and cognitive processes that would be required for a child to acquire language without the benefit of corrective feedback.

Environmental/learning accounts emphasize the social context in which language learning occurs. Learning-based theories contend that the environment can provide children with the experiences necessary to acquire language and that social-learning principles play a part in this process. Functionalists argue that children's primary motivation to acquire language is to gain a tool for communication. Parents facilitate this process by providing a language support system (LASS), through which children acquire specific language elements as parts of games or songs.

THE PREVERBAL PERIOD

Preverbal period
The period of development preceding the appearance of the child's first word combinations, usually lasting about 18 months.

From the abstract world of theories, we turn to the real world of children learning language. Development in most other areas begins at birth, or even before. But children typically do not produce their first identifiable word until about 1 year of age, and they do not begin to combine words until about 18 months. Just how important is the **preverbal period** in language development?

Some theorists believe that the process of language development is discontinuous, with the events of the preverbal period having little connection to later language development (Bickerton, 1984; Shatz, 1983). Most, however, contend that language acquisition represents a continuous process and that the linguistic abilities developed during infancy form the building blocks of the language skills that appear later on (Golinkoff & Hirsh-Pasek, 1990; Papousek & Papousek, 1991; Vihman et al., 1985). Although scientists have not yet resolved this issue, we will see that infants display some remarkable linguistic skills even before many of the typical signs of language appear.

Speech Perception

Phonology
The study of speech sounds.

Phonetics
The branch of phonology that deals with articulation skills.

Before babies learn to speak, they learn to understand speech. How early is this process apparent? The answer to this question takes us into the area of **phonology**, the study of speech sounds (MacKay, 1987).

Human speech actually consists of a continuous stream of sound. In order to comprehend language, the listener therefore must divide this stream into segments of various sorts, including syllables, words, and statements. The listener must also attend to other characteristics of speech, such as rising and falling intonations, pauses between words and phrases, and stress placed at different points.

Phonologists characterize speech in several ways. Speech therapists, for example, are most concerned with **phonetic** properties, which refer to the different kinds of sounds that can be articulated by our vocal apparatus—the lips, tongue, larynx, and so on. Articulation skills develop in a predictable order, with some sounds, such as *r*, appearing later than others (which explains why a young child might be heard to say "The wabbit is wunning"). A more important characteristic of speech for infants learning language, however, is its **phonemic** properties. These are the contrasts in speech sounds that change the *meaning* of what is heard. Not all sound differences produce different meanings. The *a* in the word *car*, for example, sounds very different when spoken by someone from Mississippi and someone from Brooklyn. But they represent a single **phoneme**, because they fall within a class of sounds that all convey the same meaning. As a result, an English-speaking listener would recognize both words as meaning automobile. If a sound variation crosses the boundary from one phoneme category to another, however, a different meaning is produced, as when *car* becomes *core*. The sound difference between these two words may actually be smaller than between the two regional pronunciations of *car* we just described. But *car* and *core* are perceived as different words—that is, words with different meanings—because in English they represent different phoneme categories. The English language, in fact, uses about 45 phonemes. Other languages use more or fewer.

This topic is important for our understanding of language development because research has shown that babies are surprisingly skilled in this area. From an early age, they show evidence of **categorical perception**—the ability to discriminate when two sounds represent two different phonemes and when, instead, they lie within the same phonemic category. This ability has been investigated extensively in infants and has been demonstrated across a wide range of speech sounds in babies as young as 1 month (Kuhl, 1987; Werker, 1989). Indeed, infants have been shown to display categorical perception of some speech contrasts found only in languages they have never heard (Best, McRoberts, & Sithole, 1988; Trehub, 1976). The age of these subjects suggests that categorical perception is an innate ability and thus universal among children. But biology is only part of the story.

Experience also plays a role in early speech perception. Two-day-old newborns already show a preference for hearing their own language (Moon, Cooper, & Fifer, 1993). Indeed, studies indicate that the more babies are exposed to a language, the sharper their phonemic discriminations become (Burnham, Earnshaw, & Quinn, 1987; Eilers & Oller, 1988). Conversely, lack of exposure may dull these abilities. For example, the distinction between the sounds *r* and *l*, which is not a phonemic contrast in the Japanese language, is a well-known problem for Japanese speakers. Studies show that adult Japanese not only have difficulty pronouncing these sounds but also struggle to discriminate them (Miyawaki et al., 1975). Japanese infants, however, have no difficulty discriminating this contrast, suggesting that they gradually *lose* the ability as a result of having little need to use it (Eimas, 1975). In fact, other research on speech contrasts of various languages indicates that by the end of the 1st year, babies seem to lose a good deal of their ability to discriminate sound contrasts to which they have not been exposed (Werker & Lalonde, 1988; Werker & Tees, 1984).

Experience with language also helps babies conquer the formidable task, mentioned earlier, of segmenting the continuous stream of speech they hear into individual words. One cue that babies use to accomplish this is the location of a word's stress. In English, for example, most words are stressed on the first syllable. One study found that when American babies were exposed to words stressed on either the first or last syllable, 6-month-olds showed no preference, but 9-month-olds preferred listening to the words stressed at the beginning, presumably because it was

Phonemics
The branch of phonology that deals with the relation between speech sounds and meaning.

Phoneme
A sound contrast that changes meaning.

Categorical perception
The ability to detect differences in speech sounds that correspond to differences in meaning—the ability to discriminate phonemic boundaries.

Figure 11-1 When 5-month-olds see side-by-side silent films accompanied by a spoken sound, they look longer at the face that is synchronized with the voice. From "The Bimodal Perception of Speech in Infancy" by P. K. Kuhl and A. N. Meltzoff, 1982, *Science, 218,* p. 1139. Copyright 1982 by the AAAS. Reprinted by permission.

the pattern they were used to hearing (Jusczyk, Cutler, & Redanz, 1993). These results add to the conclusion that infants' speech perception abilities improve as they are exposed to language.

Babies also appear to use visual cues as an aid to language perception. In one study, 5-month-old infants were shown silent films, side by side, of one person saying *ah* and another saying *ee*, as shown in Figure 11-1. At the same time, they heard one of the two sounds presented in synchrony with the films. The babies looked longer at the face that corresponded to the sound they were hearing, indicating that by the age of 5 months, they had developed a kind of lipreading skill to assist them in perceiving speech (Kuhl & Meltzoff, 1982, 1988).

Research on infant speech perception, then, suggests the influence of both nature and nurture. Perhaps from birth, babies possess an ability to discriminate a wide range of speech contrasts. But the environment very quickly begins to fine-tune these discriminations, eliminating those that are not needed and improving the child's ability to use those that remain.

Listening Preferences

Babies not only discriminate various types and properties of speech but they prefer some to others. It may not be surprising to learn that infants prefer listening to their mothers' voices to virtually any other type of sound (DeCasper & Fifer, 1980; Mehler et al., 1978). Also as might be expected, they prefer normal speech to either jumbled words or music (Columbo & Bundy, 1981; Glenn, Cunningham, & Joyce, 1981).

Perhaps even more theoretically important is the type of speech that infants prefer. We said earlier that adults talk to babies differently than they talk to other adults. Several research teams have presented babies with recordings of mothers

speaking to their infants and mothers speaking to other adults. These investigators report that infants consistently prefer the mother-to-baby talk (Cooper & Aslin, 1990; Fernald, 1993; Pegg, Werker & McLeod, 1994). Why should this be the case? The answer appears to lie in the "motherese" intonation patterns, involving a rising and falling in the pitch and the volume of the speaker's voice (Fernald, 1991, 1993; Nelson et al., 1989; Sullivan & Horowitz, 1983). These results are important, because they suggest that the adjustments speakers make when talking to an infant may actually increase the likelihood that the baby will be listening—and perhaps learning.

Early Sounds

Before babies speak words, they produce other sounds. On this topic, the discontinuity view argues that babies' early vocalizations are random and unrelated to their eventual production of words (Jakobson & Waugh, 1979; Studdert-Kennedy, 1986). Continuity theorists, however, feel that early sounds provide the basis for later speech and that the emergence of words represents the continuation of a developmental process that began shortly after birth (Halliday, 1975; Vihman, Ferguson, & Elbert, 1986).

Children's preverbal sounds, in fact, are not random; they follow a reasonably predictable course (Oller, 1986; Roug, Landberg, & Lundberg, 1989; Stark, 1986). The very earliest sounds consist of nonspeech utterances that include whimpers and cries, burps, grunts, and other physiological noises. At about 2 months of age, babies begin to produce one-syllable vowel sounds known as **cooing**—*ah, oo*, and occasionally a consonant–vowel combination like *goo*. Whereas the earlier sounds usually signaled some form of discomfort, these new sounds frequently are accompanied by smiling or laughing and seem to convey more positive emotions (Blount, 1982).

Cooing
A stage in the preverbal period, beginning at about 2 months, when babies primarily produce one-syllable vowel sounds.

• Research indicates that the babbling of infants from different language environments is very similar.

MARVIN   BY TOM ARMSTRONG

Reprinted with permission of North America Syndicate

Reduplicated babbling
A stage in the preverbal period, beginning at about 6 months, when infants produce strings of identical sounds, such as *dadada*.

At about 6 months of age, **reduplicated babbling** appears (Ferguson, 1983). Here, the infant strings together several identical sounds, as in *bababababa*. In the months that follow, the baby adds more and more different sounds, including some that appear only in other languages. Research indicates, in fact, that the babbling of children from different language backgrounds is very similar (Anderson & Smith, 1987; Oller & Eilers, 1982).

As infants approach the end of the 1st year, their babbling loses its duplicated quality, and they begin to combine different sounds, as in *da-doo* or *boo-nee*. This later phase of babbling is characterized by "speechiness"—that is, it begins to include certain fundamental qualities of speech. For example, babies add changing intonation to their sounds, so that their babbling includes the same patterns of rising and falling pitch that we might hear in adult speech (Clumeck, 1980). In addition, many of the sounds that infants produce late in the babbling period are ones that they also display when they first begin to produce words (Ferguson & Macken, 1983; Vihman & Miller, 1988).

Babbling drift
A hypothesis that infants' babbling gradually gravitates toward the language they are hearing and soon will speak.

Babbling is so similar among infants of different language groups that biological mechanisms undoubtedly play a major role. But, as we pointed out earlier, when infants finally begin to speak, they say only words from the language they have been hearing. Does this mean that speech emerges separately from babbling? Or, instead, does the form of babbling steadily gravitate toward the language the child hears—a theoretical notion called **babbling drift** (Brown, 1958b)? Evidence has been reported on both sides of this issue, but it seems to be accumulating in favor of the "drift" hypothesis (Blake & Boysson-Bardies, 1992; Boysson-Bardies et al., 1989; Levit & Utman, 1992; Thevenin et al., 1985). In either case, this issue nicely illustrates the difference between the continuity and discontinuity views of children's preverbal abilities.

The possible role of environmental factors in babbling has also led researchers to examine the vocalizations of deaf infants. If babies do not hear speech, will they still display babbling? This seemingly straightforward research question has not been easy to test, because almost all newborns diagnosed with a hearing problem are provided with some type of hearing device to amplify sound. But the babbling of even these infants is discernibly different from that of normal babies. The differences appear near the end of the babbling stage and include a delay in the onset of reduplicated babbling and a reduced number of well-formed syllables. In the rare situation where no hearing amplification is possible, the indications are that these more complex forms of babbling may not occur at all (Oller & Eilers, 1988). Such findings suggest that, although early babbling is probably guided by innate mechanisms, hearing speech may be a necessary environmental experience for the emergence of the more complex aspects of later babbling.

What about infants who are prevented from babbling? This unusual situation can occur, for example, in children who have severe respiratory problems and must breathe through a surgically implanted tube in the trachea. Clinical studies of such cases show that when the tube is eventually removed and normal breathing is resumed, the child's ability to articulate words lags behind that of age-mates for some time. This finding suggests that the opportunity to babble may provide important practice in the development of articulation. Also, the sounds produced by these children resemble those of deaf children, suggesting further that hearing one's own speech (that is, babbling), along with the speech of others, may be necessary for articulatory skills to develop properly (Locke & Pearson, 1990).

At least one type of babbling, however, does not appear to require vocal skills. Deaf children learning sign language have been shown to display a sort of gestural babbling, producing partial forms of appropriate hand and finger gestures (Petitto & Marentette, 1991). This finding, too, supports the belief that early babbling has a strong biological basis.

Gestures and Nonverbal Responses

Gestures are an important component of human communication (McNeill, 1992). As early as the preverbal period, hearing infants use gestures, combined with other nonverbal responses, to perform many of the functions of vocal language (Acredolo & Goodwyn, 1990; Morford & Goldin-Meadow, 1992). These behaviors have been of particular interest to continuity theorists, who believe that later language is built on early nonverbal skills of this sort (Harding, 1983; Zinober & Martlew, 1985).

Infants first use gestural responses for communicating requests at about 8 to 10 months, usually with their mothers (Bruner, Roy, & Ratner, 1982). Babies who want Mommy to bring a toy, to join in a game, or to open a box learn to signal these desires with various nonverbal behaviors. For example, a baby who wants a toy may reach toward it while looking back and forth between the toy and his mother. Sometimes the reaching includes fussing or crying, which stops when the mother complies with the request (Bates, Camaioni, & Volterra, 1975).

A second function of early gestures is *referential communication*—that is, talking about something in the environment (Bates, O'Connell, & Shore, 1987). This form of responding usually appears at about 11 or 12 months and may initially involve only *showing*, in which the baby holds up objects for adults' acknowledgment. From showing, it may evolve into *giving*, in which the baby offers objects to the adult, again apparently for approval or comment. Eventually, infants develop *pointing* and *labeling*. Here, the baby uses a gesture to draw attention to an object—such as a cat that has just walked into the room—while producing a vocalization and alternating glances between the adult and the object (Leung & Rheingold, 1981).

For these sorts of nonverbal responses to continue, someone must respond to them. A child is not likely to keep requesting toys, for example, unless her mother provides them at least some of the time. In fact, studies have demonstrated that mothers typically react appropriately to their infants' nonverbal behaviors, such as by getting and labeling the object to which the child has just pointed (Murphy, 1978; Ninio & Bruner, 1978). And importantly, this sort of appropriate responding appears to have a positive effect on the child's use of these and related language forms (Masur, 1982, 1983).

Not all infant gestures are used for communicating—some are used for *symbolizing* objects or events. For example, a child may put her fist to her ear and speak

• During language acquisition, children used gestures both to communicate their wants and also to label things.

into it as if it were a telephone or hold her arms out to signify an airplane. Children also use gestures to label events (clapping hands to mean "game show") or to label attributes of objects (raising arms to mean "big"). These gestures frequently are not directed at anyone else—in fact, they often occur when the child is alone—and serve primarily to name things, not to communicate the names to others.

In Chapter 8 we saw that, according to Piagetians, the capacity for symbolic thought emerges late in the sensorimotor period. Cognitive language theorists contend that for children to use language in a symbolic manner, such cognitive abilities must already be in place. This requirement had provoked some controversy, however, in that several studies seemed to indicate that children exposed to early, heavy diets of gestural language—such as deaf children—developed symbolic gesturing earlier than symbolic vocalizing and, importantly, earlier than their levels of cognitive abilities suggested should be possible (Holmes & Holmes, 1980; Prinz & Prinz, 1979). A carefully conducted recent study, however, found that while infants' use of gestures to symbolize events and objects does appear a bit earlier than their vocal symbolizations, the necessary cognitive skills are in fact in place when symbolic gesturing emerges (Goodwyn & Acredolo, 1993).

Several other aspects of gestural naming are worth noting (Acredolo & Goodwyn, 1988). Gesture labeling and word labeling tend to be positively correlated, so that children who do more of one also do more of the other. And once a child acquires a word for an object or event, its gesture label usually disappears. These findings also support the contention of cognitive language theorists that an emerging cognitive skill—the ability to use symbols to represent things in the world—is related to an emerging language ability—the labeling of objects, people, and their characteristics. And they suggest continuity in language development, with gestures serving as a crude form of naming until they are replaced by the more efficient use of spoken labels (Harding, 1983).

Transition to Words

At about 12 months of age, most children utter what their parents consider to be their first word. Students unfamiliar with infants might assume that one morning a baby looks up from her cereal and says "granola." But, in fact, the production of words appears to involve a more gradual and continuous process (Bates et al., 1987; Vihman & Miller, 1988).

Late in their 1st year, infants begin to utter specific sounds (or sound combinations) with increasing frequency—for example, *dee-dee*. Parents often notice that these sounds have become favorites for the child. Soon the baby begins to attach these utterances to particular objects, situations, or people, such as calling the television *dee-dee* (Blake & Fink, 1987; Kent & Bauer, 1985). At this point, such sounds would seem to be functioning as words for the child. But parents may not attribute much significance to this phase, because none of the infant's words correspond to any of their own. Finally, though, the child begins to produce an utterance, even if it is a bit distorted, that the parents recognize, calling the television *dee-vee*. The parents jubilantly record this event as a milestone in the baby's development (Dore, 1985).

The continuity view of language development finds support during this period as well. For example, children more quickly learn words that involve sounds and syllables they are already using, suggesting that early speech builds on babbling skills (Schwartz et al., 1987). Additional evidence is that other preverbal communication forms do not immediately stop when words appear. For some time after the baby's first words, babbling continues, along with communicative and symbolic gesturing (Dobrich & Scarborough, 1984; Vihman & Miller, 1988). Both of these findings suggest that the transition between the preverbal period and the emergence of speech is relatively smooth and continuous rather than abrupt and discontinuous. And they add to the growing belief that the preverbal period serves as an important jumping-off point for later language development.

✔ To Recap...

The importance of the preverbal period in language development has been a subject of interest to both discontinuity theorists, who see preverbal abilities as unrelated to later language, and continuity theorists, who view language development as growing out of earlier nonverbal communication.

Research in early speech perception has shown that babies are born with categorical perception of many speech contrasts, including some that do not occur in their own language. Exposure to specific contrasts of their own language sharpens their ability to discriminate these contrasts, while the ability to discriminate others is often lost. Babies prefer speech (especially that of their mothers) to other sounds, and particularly like the rising and falling intonations many adults use when speaking to young children.

The first sounds of newborns are cries and physiological noises. Cooing sounds appear at about 2 months. Reduplicated babbling begins at 6 months and includes a wide variety of sounds. Near the end of the first year, babbling becomes more speechlike in its sounds and intonations.

Gestures serve many pragmatic functions for infants; preverbal gestures initially take the form of requests and referential communication and later function as symbols to label objects, events, and attributes. Characteristics of early gestures support the cognitive view that gestural and vocal communication are both based on advances in cognitive development.

Babies' first words are often not recognized as such by parents. Early words only gradually replace babbling, gestures, and other nonverbal forms of communication. The combined evidence appears to support a growing consensus that the preverbal period is important for the development of later language.

SEMANTICS

Semantics
The study of how children acquire words and their meanings.

Once children have begun speaking, their use of language expands at a breathtaking rate. We begin our look at this period of language development with the concept of **semantics**, the study of how children acquire words and their meanings.

A well-known investigator of children's language recounts how her 18-month-old daughter began to use the word *hi* to mean that some sort of cloth was covering her hands or feet (for example, her hands were inside a shirt or a blanket was laid across her feet). The child apparently had come to make this unlikely association as a result of her mother's showing her a finger puppet that nodded its head and said "hi." Rather than interpreting the word as a greeting, the child had instead assumed that it meant the mother's fingers were covered by a cloth (Bowerman, 1976).

This anecdote illustrates two points about semantic development. The first is that learning the meaning of words is not as simple a task as it might appear, especially around the age of 2. Not only do children hear adults speaking thousands of different words, but they also must learn that words are of different types, such as those that stand for objects (*hat* and *Mommy*), actions (*eat* and *talk*), and states (*happy* and *red*) (Clark, 1983). Second, the more psychologists study word learning, the more they come to realize how closely this process is tied to children's concept development. Names of things (such as *cat*) usually label an entire class of things (the family's pet kitten, a stuffed toy, Garfield), as do names of actions, states, and so on. Furthermore, the same thing can be called by many different names (for example, animal, horse, stallion, and Champ). How the young child knows what class of things to attach a new word to and how this learning develops are issues of considerable importance to understanding language acquisition (Bloom, 1993).

Early Lexical Development

• Children's first words usually label common objects.

The acquisition of words and their meanings begins in the baby's 2nd year. Infants' first words usually name things that are familiar or important to them, such as food, toys, and family members. These words, we will see, also serve a variety of pragmatic functions, including requesting things, asking questions, and complaining (Griffiths, 1985; Rescorla, 1980). In this section, we examine the emergence of children's first words and the importance of the errors children make when attempting to relate words to objects and events in their world.

First Words and the Naming Explosion

Lexicon
Children's vocabulary, or repertoire of words.

Naming explosion
A period of language development, beginning at about 18 months, when children suddenly begin to acquire words (especially labels) at a high rate.

By the age of 18 months, most children possess a **lexicon**, or vocabulary, of about 50 spoken words and about 100 words that they understand (Benedict, 1979). At around this time, many children display what has been termed the **naming explosion**, in which they begin to label everything in sight. Some psychologists believe that this burst of vocabulary is related to the child's emerging ability to categorize objects (Goldfield & Reznick, 1990; Gopnik & Meltzoff, 1987b, 1992; Reznick & Goldfield, 1992). Word learning continues rapidly for the next few years, and by the age of 6, children have a lexicon of about 10,000 words (Anglin, 1993).

Semantic development proceeds faster for comprehension than for production. Children typically comprehend words before they begin to produce them, and they comprehend many more words than they normally speak (Benedict, 1979; Rescorla, 1981). This pattern is evident from the very beginning and continues even into adulthood.

Throughout language development, nouns (especially object words) are much more common than verbs and action words. In most languages, in fact, nouns are understood earlier, spoken earlier and more frequently, and even pronounced better (Camarata & Leonard, 1986; Gentner, 1982; Nelson, Hampson, & Shaw, 1993).

DEVELOPMENT IN CONTEXT: Social Class, Gender, and Family Influences on Early Word Learning

Children do not all follow the same pattern of lexical development. Early in the word-learning process—before children have acquired 50 spoken words—two types of development are commonly observed (Bates et al., 1988; Bretherton et al., 1983; Nelson, 1973). Some children display a **referential style,** producing a very large proportion of nouns, especially object names, and using language primarily to label things. Others display an **expressive style,** which includes a larger mix of word types and a greater emphasis on language as a pragmatic tool for expressing needs and for social interaction.

What could produce these two different patterns of early language acquisition? A biological explanation is possible, with some children being genetically predisposed to focus more on physical aspects of the environment, such as objects, and others having a greater interest in social interactions and relationships. But an intriguing alternative is that these two styles of vocabulary development result from the context in which language learning takes place (McCabe, 1989).

To explore this possibility, we must first consider some of the other differences between the children exhibiting these two styles. Referential children are more likely to be females. They are usually firstborns and more often have parents who are of high socioeconomic status. These children tend to speak slowly and with good articulation, and they are generally fast language learners. Expressive children are more likely to be males. The majority of them are not firstborns, and they tend to come from lower- or working-class families. These children generally acquire words more slowly and with poorer articulation.

The contextual explanation for these two patterns stresses the *transactional* nature of development discussed in Chapter 2. Certain characteristics that differentiate children with these two styles—such as gender, birth order, and articulation abilities—are thought to affect the type of language environment to which the children are exposed. These different environments, in turn, lead the children to develop either a referential or an expressive pattern of vocabulary acquisition.

Evidence of several types supports this analysis. Parents tend to speak to their infant daughters more than to their infant sons, using more complex speech and better articulation (Cherry & Lewis, 1978; Gurman Bard, & Anderson, 1983). In addition, the types of activities children engage in affect the kinds of speech parents direct toward them. Doll play, for example, evokes a greater use of nouns, whereas toy vehicle play results in less parent speech altogether (O'Brien & Nagle, 1987). Children's gender, then, can affect the sorts of language interactions they have with their parents.

Birth-order differences may involve several factors. One is the amount of time parents spend with their children—firstborns receive more time than those born later. Speech to firstborns also includes more learning devices and greater atten-

Referential style
Vocabulary acquired during the naming explosion that involves a large proportion of nouns and object labels.

Expressive style
Vocabulary acquired during the naming explosion that emphasizes the pragmatic functions of language.

tion to the development of language abilities (Jones & Adamson, 1987). Another factor involves the presence of siblings. Firstborns obviously get most of their language input from their parents, whereas laterborns get a good deal of it from older brothers and sisters. Recall the confluence model of intelligence, described in Chapter 10, in which Zajonc argued that later-born children perform less well because much of their intellectual stimulation comes from other children. A similar argument can be made with regard to language development. Since later-born children spend a good deal of time talking with the other children in the family, they experience less sophisticated language interactions (Dunn, 1983; Jones & Adamson, 1987).

Differences in children's articulation skills also are assumed to produce differences in adult reactions to them. Children who speak slowly and clearly are likely to have more frequent and longer language interactions than children who cannot be understood.

Finally, parents' socioeconomic status has been associated with how much they speak to their children. Middle- and upper-class parents tend to be more concerned with their children's language acquisition, and their speech includes better models and more language-learning devices than are found in the speech of lower-class parents (Hart & Risley, 1992; Hoff-Ginsberg, 1991; Snow et al., 1976).

When these findings are taken together, they provide a compelling argument that the style and quality of speech displayed by youngsters learning language reflects the kinds of language environments to which these children have been exposed. And underscoring the transactional nature of this process, these different environments are to some degree produced by characteristics of the children themselves.

Overextensions

Overextension
An early language error in which children use labels they already know for things whose names they do not yet know.

Psychologists have learned a great deal about children's semantic development by examining the kinds of errors they make. Word learning typically begins with a child attaching a specific label to a specific object, such as learning that the pet poodle is a "doggie." Next, the child begins to extend that label to other examples of the same object, using "doggie" to label the dogs he sees in books or on television. These extensions demonstrate that the child is forming an object category called *doggie* that is defined by certain features.

Most children, however, make errors when attempting to extend these early labels and may also use *doggie* to describe a cat, a fox, a rabbit, and so on. Such **overextensions** are very common in the early stages of semantic development in many languages (Rescorla, 1980). By examining the patterns of children's overextensions, psychologists have been able to learn much about how children construct their object categories (Kay & Anglin, 1982; Kuczaj, 1986).

Why do children overextend labels? One obvious possibility is that their initial categories are simply too broad; they do not yet understand the specific features that define the concept. However, this explanation does not fit very well with the fact that children's overextensions are more common in their productions than in their comprehension. For example, a child who calls an apple a ball might, if shown an apple, a ball, and a pear, be able to *point* to the apple (Fremgen & Fay, 1980; Thomson & Chapman, 1977). If overextensions do not always reflect a lack of understanding, then maybe they reflect a lack of vocabulary. If she does not know the word *apple*, a child may use the name of a similar object, such as *ball*, simply to achieve the communication function of talking about the object. Most likely, both of these reasons are involved in overextension errors (Behrend, 1988; Hoek, Ingram, & Gibson, 1986).

• When young children encounter an object whose name they do not know, they often overextend a label they already have.

Overextended categories eventually give way to more appropriate classification—for example, as children learn that *car* should not be used to label an ambulance, even though the two objects share some characteristics. Mothers appear to play a role in this learning process by correcting their child's mistakes, such as by labeling an overextended object with its correct name or by pointing out the critical features that distinguish the two categories (Mervis & Mervis, 1988).

Underextensions

Another type of semantic error involves applying labels too narrowly, rather than too broadly. A child who has learned to apply the label *bird* to robins and wrens, for example, may not apply it to ostriches. Such **underextensions** are less common in production than are overextensions. Underextensions are frequent, however, in comprehension. For example, when shown a group of different animals, young children often do not point to the ostrich in response to the instruction "show me a bird" but instead select a nonmember of the category, such as a butterfly (Anglin, 1977; Kay & Anglin, 1982).

Underextension
A language error in which children fail to apply labels they know to things for which the labels are appropriate.

Word Coining

Coining occurs when children create new words (Clark, 1982, 1983). We saw earlier that children sometimes name an unfamiliar object by overextending the label of a similar object. Thus, a child who sees a lawn rake for the first time may call it a fork, even though the child understands that the label is not correct. But another device that children use to deal with gaps in their vocabulary is simply to coin a new name for the object. Our first-time viewer of a rake might instead call it a grass-comb (Clark, Gelman, & Lane, 1985). Word coining is common in young children, gradually decreasing as their lexicon grows (Bushnell & Maratsos, 1984; Windsor, 1993).

Coining
Children's creation of new words to label objects or events for which the correct label is not known.

First Word Combinations

Children begin to combine words as they approach age 2. Sometimes they use the same phrase to express different meanings, depending on its function. For example, *Daddy hat* may represent a name for an article of clothing, a demand for the father to take off his hat, or perhaps a simple description of the father's putting on his hat (Bloom, 1973). Some functions of early word combinations are given in Table 11-1. Studies in various language cultures reveal that the same dozen or so functions appear first for all children (Bowerman, 1975; Brown, 1973). This cross-language commonality suggests that the kinds of things children attempt to communicate during this period probably are influenced by their level of cognitive development (Bowerman, 1975, 1981).

Mechanisms of Semantic Development

Since the early 1970s, a number of explanations have been proposed to account for overextensions, underextensions, and other aspects of early word learning. Most of these have focused on children's concept development and on the ways children form object categories and apply labels to them.

Component Models

Some psychologists believe that children construct their object categories one component at a time. An early component approach was the **functional core model** (Nelson, 1974, 1979). This theory held that children's first categories are based on

Functional core model
A component theory of semantic development that holds that children first group object words into categories based on the functions of the objects.

TABLE 11-1 ● **Some Functions of First Word Combinations**

Function	Purpose	Examples
Nomination	Naming, labeling, or identifying	Bunny Ernie
Negation	Rejecting or denying	No nap No wet
Nonexistence	Describing something that is gone or finished	No milk All-gone story
Recurrence	Describing or demanding the repetition of something	More pat-a-cake More drink
Entity–attribute	Describing a characteristic of an object	Ball big
Possessor– possession	Naming two nouns, the first possessing the second	Mommy sock
Agent–action	Describing a person performing an action	Daddy jump
Action–object	Describing an action being performed on an object	Hit ball
Agent–patient	Describing a person doing something to another person	Oscar Bert
Action–patient	Describing an action being performed on a person	Feed baby
Entity–location	Naming a noun and its place	Ball up Baby chair

an object's function. Thus, a child's initial concept of *ball* is more likely to include other things that can be rolled (such as soup cans) than other things that look round (such as the moon). Once the child has formed a category in this way, he then presumably extends (and overextends) its boundaries by also taking into account its perceptual features, such as by realizing that things that roll also are usually round. In support of the functional core model, it has been shown that the more things infants can do with an object, the faster they acquire the object's name (Ross et al., 1986). In addition, this theory is consistent with Piaget's view that children's earliest concepts involve sensorimotor actions and reactions and so also with the view that linguistic concepts are mapped onto the cognitive concepts children already understand. But the functional core model could not account for the fact that many of children's early categories do not involve functions. As a result, it has largely been replaced by other models (Merriman, 1986).

Semantic feature hypothesis
A component theory of semantic development that holds that children first group object words into categories based on the perceptual features (e.g., size, color, shape) of the objects.

According to the **semantic feature hypothesis** (Clark, 1983), children construct categories using the perceptual features of the object. For example, the child may initially define *dog* as "something that has four legs and fur." Later, other features may be added to the definition, such as "barks," "wags tail," and "has no horns." In this way, the child presumably constructs a mental list of components that define the object. When encountering a new example, the child compares its features with those on the list and, if they match, extends the category to include the new object. At first, the small number of components used to define a category will lead the child to overextend frequently. But by systematically refining the category, feature by feature, the child gradually establishes the accurate boundaries of the object category.

It is likely that children's object categories can be based on either perceptual or functional similarities (Mervis, 1987). As early as the preverbal period, children overextend gesture labels both to objects that look like those they already know and to objects with similar functions (Acredolo & Goodwyn, 1988; Anglin, 1983; Bernstein, 1983). And as children grow, both kinds of overextensions continue to occur (Gelman & Markman, 1986, 1987; Nelson & Lucariello, 1985).

Prototypes

A second explanation for the development of lexical categories involves a different type of comparison process. Rather than comparing a new example with a list of features or functions, the child compares the example with a **prototype**, or general model, of the object.

We saw in Chapter 8 that objects often can be categorized at several different levels. The most general level, called the *superordinate level*, includes broad categories, such as *animal*. At the *basic level* are somewhat more specific categories, like *bird*. Research with both adults and children has shown that basic-level categories generally are easiest to learn and use (Rosch & Lloyd, 1978; Rosch & Mervis, 1975). Children's first semantic categories, in fact, usually are at this level (Mervis, 1987). Basic-level categories are composed of even more specific *subordinate-level* examples, such as *robin, owl,* and *ostrich*. Within any basic-level category, such as *bird*, some examples of the object, such as a robin, are considered typical, whereas others, such as an ostrich, are nontypical.

As children begin to form a category of an object (usually at the basic level), they appear to quickly develop a prototype of the object. For most children, the initial prototype of a bird is a small, feathered, two-legged creature with a beak. When children encounter an unfamiliar object, they presumably compare it with the prototype. If it matches closely, they extend the category to the new object. If not, they begin to form a new category. We would predict, therefore, that children should be more likely to extend to typical examples (such as sparrows) and to underextend to nontypical examples (such as storks). Studies have found these predictions to be accurate (Anglin, 1977; White, 1982).

Contrast and Mutual Exclusivity

Regardless of the nature of children's first object categories, it remains to be explained how children so rapidly learn to attach labels they hear to objects they see. Children as young as 3, in fact, can sometimes acquire at least a partial meaning of a word after only one exposure to it, a process called **fast-mapping** (Carey, 1977; Heibeck & Markman, 1987). Preschoolers appear capable of using this process when watching television programs, demonstrating in some studies a very rapid acquisition of new words used by the story characters (Rice & Woodsmall, 1988; Rice et al., 1990).

But note how difficult this task really is. When a child sees a cat and hears Mommy say "There's kitty," how does the child know that *kitty* refers to the cat rather than, say, its fur, its color, or its behavior? Many psychologists who have studied this question agree that children must be predisposed to relate labels to objects in particular ways. That is, when children hear a new word, they automatically make certain assumptions (usually accurate) regarding what it probably refers to. The assumptions permit them to quickly acquire the meaning of the word (Hall & Waxman, 1993; Waxman, 1990).

Consider two examples of semantic-learning mechanisms that assume children have built-in tendencies to treat new words in particular ways. According to **lexical contrast theory** (Clark, 1983, 1987), when children hear an unfamiliar word, they automatically assume the new word has a meaning different from that

Prototype
A general model of an object. The prototype theory of language development holds that children create prototypes as the basis for semantic concepts.

• Children can sometimes acquire the meaning of a new word from only a brief exposure, a process called fast-mapping.

Fast-mapping
A process in which children acquire the meaning of a word after a brief exposure.

Lexical contrast theory
A theory of semantic development holding that (1) children automatically assume a new word has a meaning different from that of any other word they know and (2) children always choose word meanings that are generally accepted over more individualized meanings.

of any word they already know. This assumption motivates them to learn exactly what the new word refers to (Clark, 1988, 1990). A second part of this theory holds that, when a choice must be made, children always replace their current meanings or categories with those that they decide are more conventional or accepted. For example, a child who has been assuming that foxes are called dogs should, upon learning that *fox* has its own separate meaning, replace the incorrect label *dog* with the correct label *fox*. This mechanism helps bring the child's categories in line with those of adults.

Principle of mutual exclusivity
A proposed principle of semantic development stating that children assume an object can have only one name.

The **principle of mutual exclusivity** (Markman, 1989, 1991) states simply that children believe objects can have only one name. So when a youngster hears a new word, she is more likely to attach it to an unknown object than to an object for which she already has a label (Golinkoff et al., 1992; Merriman & Schuster, 1991). This strategy has the advantage of limiting the possibilities a child must choose among when trying to attach meaning to a new word. But the strategy causes problems as children encounter the hierarchical nature of word categories discussed earlier. For example, a dog can also be called an animal, a mammal, a beagle, and so forth. Two-year-olds sometimes balk at referring to their pet pooches by more than one name (Gelman, Wilcox, & Clark, 1989; Mervis, 1987). They may accept two names, however, if the names represent different levels of classification (*dog* and *spaniel*, but not *spaniel* and *retriever*) (Waxman & Senghas, 1992). Similarly, same-level names are acceptable to bilingual children of this age, if the names are in different languages (Au & Glusman, 1990). Mutual exclusivity accounts nicely for some aspects of early word learning, but factors such as an object's shape (Jones, Smith, & Landau, 1991) and familiarity (Hall, 1991) also appear to affect this process in ways we are just beginning to understand.

Modeling

Although babies sometimes make up their own words, much of what they say reflects what they have heard. In fact, babies' early words tend to be those used most frequently by their mothers (Harris et al., 1988; Ninio, 1992); and the more speech parents address to infants the faster their early vocabularies grow (Dunham & Dunham, 1992; Huttenlocher et al., 1991). There is also evidence that infants' first lexicons contain so many object words because objects are what parents usually talk to babies about (Bridges, 1986; Goldfield, 1993). Research has shown, for example, that American mothers tend to label objects more frequently and consistently than Japanese mothers do. And, predictably, the infants of the American mothers have larger noun vocabularies than do the infants of the Japanese mothers (Fernald & Morikawa, 1993). Such findings suggest that modeling at this stage plays an important role in word acquisition. But how important is modeling in attaching words to objects—that is, in the acquisition of meaning?

There is some evidence that infants naturally tend to connect objects and labels. For example, babies are more attentive to toys that have been given names than to those that have not (Baldwin & Markman, 1989). Similarly, babies more easily learn labels for toys they are playing with than for new ones shown to them for the first time (Tomasello & Farrar, 1986). It would seem, then, that frequent object naming by parents would be a good way to help children acquire new semantic categories.

In what has been called the Original Word Game (Brown, 1958a), parents sometimes do, in fact, specifically show a baby an object, tell the baby its name, encourage the baby to say the name, and then provide feedback as to the accuracy of the child's responses. This kind of modeling is given most often to infants and occurs less as children grow older (Goddard, Durkin, & Rutter, 1985). Much of the time, though, parents label objects in a less structured way, simply in their everyday conversations with their children (Howe, 1981). Does either type of modeling actually influence children's acquisition of word meaning?

We do know that parents usually label objects for children at the easiest-to-learn basic level—for example, saying "look at the dog" rather than "look at the animal" or "look at the poodle" (Callanan, 1985; Wales, Colman, & Pattison, 1983). The fact that children first develop semantic categories at this level may be at least partly a result of such modeling. When parents do use subordinate labels for objects, they usually do so for nontypical examples (Shipley, Kuhn, & Madden, 1983; White, 1982)—for example, identifying a robin as a bird but an ostrich as an ostrich. One reason why young children frequently underextend to nontypical examples, failing to extend the bird category to ostriches, for instance, may simply be that they rarely hear anyone refer to ostriches as birds.

Scripts

A final possible mechanism for the development of object categories involves *scripts* and is related to Bruner's notion of formats, described earlier in relation to the LASS. Recall from Chapter 9 that a script is a type of cognitive schema in which a number of familiar actions or events become associated with one another. Taking a bath, going to the supermarket, and having lunch are common examples for most children. Within these routines are certain *slots*, which can be filled by a variety of objects. For example, the dessert slot in the lunch routine can consist of pudding, a cookie, chocolate, and so on. Such slots provide a simple structure by which a child can learn an object category (in this case, *dessert*). If a new object—an eclair— appears in the familiar dessert slot, the child is likely to associate that object with others that have occupied that position and thereby extend the category label *dessert* to it (Camaioni & Laicardi, 1985; Nelson & Gruendel, 1986).

Children are thought to learn many of their object labels within the context of everyday scripts. Indeed, most (though not all) of children's early words have been shown to occur within such structured contexts (Harris et al., 1988; Lucariello, Kyratzis, & Nelson, 1992). Once the object has been categorized, the child can "decontextualize" it—that is, remove it from its scripted context—and use it in situations that may not be so familiar (Barrett, 1986; Nelson, K., 1985).

✔ *To Recap...*

Semantic development is the study of how children acquire words and their meanings. Much semantic research with infants and toddlers has been concerned with how they form and label object categories.

At first, children acquire words slowly. But when their lexicons reach about 50 spoken words, their vocabularies typically increase dramatically and rapidly—the naming explosion. Comprehension of words generally precedes production of those words, and both children and adults understand many more words than they speak. Nouns make up the majority of children's early lexicons, but even very early there are differences among children in the proportion of nouns used, probably because of factors such as social class, gender, and birth order.

Children's language errors help explain their learning processes. Overextension, a common error, appears to occur for two reasons: sometimes children do not understand a concept, and sometimes they lack the vocabulary necessary to express the concept. Underextensions are less common in word production than are overextensions, although

they occur frequently in comprehension. Children sometimes fill gaps in their vocabularies by coining new words.

Several models of semantic development have been proposed. Component models contend that object categories are constructed feature by feature, based on either the functional characteristics of objects (functional core model) or their physical characteristics (semantic feature hypothesis). Prototype theory holds that children create general models, against which they compare new examples. According to this theory, objects can be classified at the superordinate level, the basic level, or the subordinate level. Basic-level concepts are easiest to learn and generally are the first semantic categories formed. Several models have been proposed to explain how children acquire object labels so quickly. Contrast theory is based on two ideas: children assume new words have different meanings from familiar words, and they adopt generally accepted meanings over more individualized meanings. The mutual exclusivity model holds that children believe objects can have only one name.

Children's learning of category labels is aided by parents' modeling, whether direct or in the course of day-to-day interaction. And some labeling occurs in the context of scripts, or everyday routines, where slots serve as structures for learning object categories.

GRAMMAR

Grammar
The study of the structural properties of language, including syntax, inflection, and intonation.

All human languages are structured and follow certain rules called **grammar**. Many of these rules seem arbitrary, such as the English rule that adding *ed* to a verb puts it in the past tense. But, as psycholinguists suggest, some rules may have a biological basis—that is, languages appear to be structured in such a way that humans learn them very easily.

Children must, of course, learn something about the structure of language to comprehend and speak it. Understanding the acquisition of grammar, however, has posed one of the major challenges to language researchers. As noted at the beginning of the chapter, children are not explicitly taught the structure of their language (at least, not before school age), yet they learn it very quickly. And making this feat all the more impressive is the fact that most adults, even those who are well educated, cannot describe our complex linguistic rules in any detail.

Syntax
The aspect of grammar that involves word order.

The grammar of most languages involves three principal devices: word order, inflections, and intonation (Maratsos, 1983). Word order, called **syntax**, is most important for the English language and thus the aspect of grammar on which we focus here. The sentences "John hit the car" versus "The car hit John" or "I did pay" versus "Did I pay?" illustrate how necessary it is to take into account the order of words. Inflections are certain endings added to words. Common examples include plural endings (cat*s*), possessive endings (Mary*'s*), and past-tense endings (work*ed*). Some languages rely much more heavily than English on inflections to communicate meaning. Finally, intonation can alter grammar. A rising tone at the end of a sentence, for example, can transform a statement into a question. Again, some languages make greater use of this device than English.

Development of Grammar

Children's acquisition of knowledge about the structure of their language involves several distinct phases. And as with semantic development, children's errors often reveal a great deal about the rule-learning processes they are using.

One-Word Period

Between the ages of 12 and 24 months, children produce primarily single-word utterances (Barrett, 1985). Over the course of the one-word period, however, the pragmatic functions of these utterances increase, with infants, for example, using single words to both name and request objects (Greenfield & Smith, 1976). Sometimes babies use one word (such as *ball*) to express an entire sentence or idea (such as "That's a ball" or "I want the ball"). We call such words **holophrases**, meaning single-word sentences (Dore, 1975, 1985).

Late in this period, infants begin to produce several single-word utterances in a row. Now the baby may use one word to call the mother's attention to an object, and then a second word to comment on the object (e.g., "Milk—hot"). These multiple one-word utterances can be distinguished from the two-word sentences that will soon appear by the longer pause that occurs between the two single words (Branigan, 1979).

Holophrase
A single word used to express a larger idea; common during the 2nd year of life.

Structure of Word Combinations

By age 2, most children are producing two- and three-word "sentences," such as "Mommy chair" and "all-gone cookie," that can have a variety of meanings. Investigators have discovered that infants' first word combinations are not random but follow certain patterns or orders. As a result, much research has been devoted to trying to understand these earliest indications of syntactic knowledge.

The principal method of investigation here has been to collect samples of a child's speech—usually in the natural environment—and to analyze its structure. Sometimes such samples are gathered over a period of months or years in order to examine how grammar evolves (Bates & Carnevale, 1994).

The first syntactic rules children develop seem to be built around individual words. For example, a child may say "all-gone doggie," "all-gone milk," and "all-gone Mommy," using "all-gone + _____ " as a basic rule (Maratsos, 1983). Children display a degree of individuality in these rules, however. Another child might develop rules around other words, for example " _____ + on" or "I + _____ " (Bloom, Lightbrown, & Hood, 1975; Braine, 1976).

The next phase of grammatical development is the emergence of **telegraphic speech**. As the child's sentences grow from two to three or four words and beyond, they begin to resemble telegram messages. That is, they leave out unnecessary function words, such as *a*, *the*, and *of*, and also certain parts of words, such as endings and unstressed syllables. Thus, a child who hears "Billy, we're going to the parade" may repeat "Billy go 'rade." Within only a few years, however, the telegraphic nature of children's speech greatly diminishes (Bowerman, 1982).

Telegraphic speech
Speech from which unnecessary function words (e.g., *in, the, with*) are omitted; common during early language learning.

Overregularization

As mentioned, the rule learning at the core of children's acquisition of grammar also is evident in certain types of mistakes they make. A good example involves inflections (Kuczaj, 1977). The English language uses inflectional rules to change a verb to the past tense (*ed* is added, as in talk*ed* and play*ed*) and a noun from singular to plural (*s* or *es* is added, as in cup*s* and dish*es*). But unfortunately for English-speaking children, our language also contains a large number of irregular forms that are exceptions to these rules—the verb forms *go-went, eat-ate,* and *see-saw,* for example, and the noun forms *mouse-mice, foot-feet,* and *sheep-sheep.*

At first, children may produce a correct irregular form, if it is part of a "chunk" of adult speech that they are copying. Thus, even 2-year-olds may be heard to say

Overregularization
An early structural language error in which children apply inflectional rules to irregular forms (e.g., adding -*ed* to *say*).

"ate" or "feet." But as they begin to learn the inflectional rules of the language, children **overregularize**, sometimes applying the rules to nouns and verbs that have irregular forms. Now the child will be heard saying "I knowed her" or "Look at the mans." Interestingly, the correct forms do not altogether disappear, so that a child may at one time say "I ate" and at another time say "I eated."

Gradually, the two forms begin to merge, and the inflections are applied to irregular forms. Now the child says "wented" and "mices" (along with "went" and "mice"). The final disappearance of the overregularized forms seems to take place word by word, with some errors persisting longer than others (Kuczaj, 1981).

Children do not overregularize all words at the same rate and seem to be influenced by their exposure to the language forms. Irregular forms that they hear spoken frequently by their parents or others are much less likely to be overregularized (Bybee & Slobin, 1982; Marcus et al., 1992). Likewise, children are more likely to use the correct irregular form if it represents a common class of irregular changes. For example, because *sing-sung* and *swing-swung* are very common (although irregular), children are more likely to say *flung* than they are to say *flinged* (Marcus et al., 1992; Prince & Pinker, 1988). (An early study of grammar acquisition is described in Box 11-1).

Mechanisms of Grammar Acquisition

No area of language development is more complex than that of grammar. As with semantics, many explanations for this complexity have been proposed. Rather than attempting to examine them all, we focus on those that are currently of greatest interest to language researchers.

Form Classes

Form class
A hypothetical innate category for understanding and producing language.

The complexity of language structure and the ease with which children acquire it have led some researchers to conclude that this process requires special inborn mechanisms. The most popular belief has been that infants possess innate categories, called **form classes**, that help them to organize and decode the language input they receive. Debate over the nature of these classes has produced two very different proposals (Braine, 1987; Levy & Schlesinger, 1988).

Some psycholinguists believe that form classes are based on the *structure* of speech. According to this view, when children hear speech, they naturally analyze it into syntactic components, such as subject, verb, and object (Radford, 1990; Valian, 1986). Cognitive theorists, on the other hand, contend that form classes are based on the *meaning* conveyed by speech. When children hear speech, they presumably analyze it into the semantic concepts that were listed in Table 11-1 (Grimshaw, 1981).

Consider, for example, the following sentences:

Jamie walks.

Jamie is hit.

Jamie has freckles.

In English syntax, *Jamie* is the subject of each sentence. Psycholinguists believe that children hearing these sentences can identify the form classes "subject + verb" or "subject + verb + object" and then use them to produce sentences that follow the same syntactic rules. This suggests that children learn the rules of syntax directly, by analyzing speech into its structural components (Valian, Winzemer, & Erreich, 1981).

ADDING ENDINGS TO "WUGS" AND THINGS

Even before the appearance of Chomsky's critique of learning theories of language acquisition, other researchers had questioned the early view that language is learned piecemeal through reinforcement of early babbling or imitation of adult speech. One alternative possibility was that children develop general rules that regulate their early speech productions.

To explore this possibility, Jean Berko, a doctoral student at MIT, conducted a simple but ingenious experiment (Berko, 1958). Children (aged 4 through 7) were shown a series of pictures of nonsense objects and activities that had been given nonsense names—perhaps the most famous being a small birdlike creature that Berko called a wug, shown in Figure 11-2.

The aspect of grammar that Berko examined was inflectional endings, such as adding the *s* or *z* sound to create the plural (e.g., cat*s* or dog*s* and the *d* or *t* sound to create the past tense (e.g., play*ed* or walk*ed*). To investigate a child's use of inflectional endings, Berko might have presented the child with a sequence similar to the following: "This is a cup. Now there is another one. There are two of them. There are two _____."

But what if the child added the correct ending sound to the word? Would that demonstrate that the child knew the rule for plurals? Perhaps. But it could simply mean that the child had previously been reinforced for saying "cups" when more than one was present or that the child was imitating parents' use of this plural form.

To eliminate these alternative explanations, Berko used nonsense terms. For example, on one trial examining possessive endings, the children were told: "This is a bik who owns a hat. Whose hat is it? It is the _____." As predicted, on this and many of the other trials, children supplied the correct inflectional ending. Since these terms were new, the children could not have learned them either through reinforcement or imitation of what they had heard. Rather, this clas-

This is a wug.

Now there is another one.

There are two of them.

There are two _____ .

Figure 11-2 An example of a stimulus used to demonstrate that children's early use of inflectional endings involves rules. From "The Child's Learning of English Morphology" by J. Berko, 1958, *Word, 14*, p. 155. Copyright 1958 by the International Linguistic Association. Reprinted by permission.

sic study showed that the children had acquired a set of inflectional rules that they could systematically apply even to unfamiliar words.

In terms of meaning, by contrast, *Jamie* represents three different functions. In the first sentence, she is an *agent* (someone who produces an action); in the second, she is a *patient* (someone who receives an action); and in the third, she is a *possessor* (someone who has something). Cognitive language theorists believe that young children first analyze speech according to these cognitive, or meaning-based, concepts, which gradually emerge as cognitive development proceeds. Children then use these concepts to learn structural rules. This approach means that children learn the rules of syntax somewhat indirectly, by first extracting semantic form classes and then using them to figure out the structure of the language (Lempert, 1984; Schlesinger, 1974, 1988).

How does the evidence for these two models compare? Studies generally find more support for the semantic analysis regarding children's *initial* word combinations (Braine & Hardy, 1982; Maratsos, 1988b). For example, young children frequently produce sentences of the form "Mommy play" (agent + action) and "Baby washed" (patient + action), because verbs that describe actions appear to involve a concept that infants understand very early. But children of the same age rarely say "Mommy feels" or "Baby liked," because these verbs do not convey action (deVilliers, 1980; Sudhalter & Braine, 1985). The structural form class "subject + verb," therefore, does not characterize these early combinations as accurately as do meaning-based form classes.

Nevertheless, as language development progresses, children's attention to the structure of speech appears to steadily increase (Matthei, 1987). Perhaps semantic form classes serve as early "bootstraps" that help get the process of syntax learning going (Golinkoff & Hirsh-Pasek, 1990; Maratsos, 1988a; Pinker, 1987).

Strategies

Operating principle
A hypothetical innate strategy for analyzing language input.

Another proposed mechanism for learning grammar is that children innately possess cognitive strategies for rapidly acquiring the rules of language. One proposal of this type is based on the notion of **operating principles** (Slobin, 1982, 1985). After studying more than 40 languages, Slobin extracted a number of strategies, which he called operating principles, that described how to learn the rules of almost any language. Among the most important strategies he described are (1) "Pay attention to the order of words," (2) "Avoid exceptions," and (3) "Pay attention to the ends of words."

We have already seen that children do increasingly focus on word order, or syntax, in speech. And children's overregularizations may result, in part, from their avoiding exceptions and applying inflectional rules across the board. Evidence supporting children's use of the third operating principle has been reported in an interesting study.

The method used to address this issue involved teaching English-speaking children several artificial language rules and examining which were acquired most easily. First, the children were taught the names of two new animals—*wugs* and *fips* (Figure 11-3). Next, they learned two new verbs—*pum* (meaning to toss an animal vertically into the air) and *bem* (meaning to toss an animal horizontally across the table surface). Finally, the children were taught two variations of these verbs. If the animal's actions were observed by one other animal, the verbs describing them were *pumabo* or *bemabo*; if the animal's actions were observed by several other animals, the verbs became *akipum* or *akibem*. The researchers hypothesized that if children use a strategy of paying attention to the ends of words, the verbs with a suffix (-*abo*) should be acquired more quickly than the verbs with a prefix (*aki-*). In support of Slobin's model, children learned the suffixed verbs more easily (Daneman & Case, 1981).

Competition model
A proposed strategy children use for learning grammar in which they focus on certain cues in the language.

A more recent proposal that involves strategies for acquiring grammar is the **competition model** (Bates & MacWhinney, 1987; MacWhinney, 1987; MacWhinney & Bates, 1989). According to this account, young children hearing speech examine the various grammatical cues of their language, such as word order, endings, and intonation, and then focus on the one they believe is most useful for learning the structure of the language. The cue they select can vary from one language to another and, very importantly, it is thought to change as the child matures. Initially, children focus on the cue that is most *available*. In English and French, for exam-

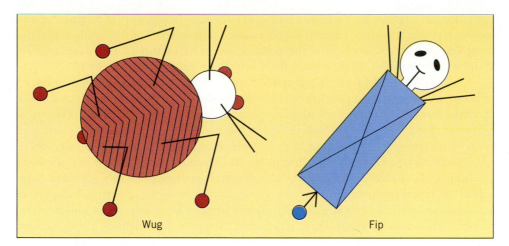

Wug

Fip

Figure 11-3 Artificial language concepts, along with these two imaginary animals, were used to compare children's acquisition of suffixed and prefixed verbs. From "Syntactic Form, Semantic Complexity, and Short-Term Memory: Influences on Children's Acquisition of New Linguistic Structures" by M. Daneman and R. Case, 1981, *Developmental Psychology, 17,* p. 369. Copyright 1981 by the American Psychological Association. Reprinted by permission.

ple, children's first attempts to learn grammar involve word order. Word order is important in these languages and so is a cue that is frequently available to provide information useful for learning language rules. In Turkish, by contrast, where word order is less important, language-learning children typically focus first on the inflections in the speech they hear. In the second stage, children select the cues that are most *reliable*, meaning those that most consistently provide clues to grammatical structure. And in the final stage, children note cues that are in *conflict* with one another and then focus on the one that most often "wins out" and best reveals the language's structure.

Motherese

Recall that Chomsky claimed children should have difficulty extracting structural rules from everyday speech because it typically provides poor models of good language. But research has now demonstrated that both adults and children change aspects of their speech when talking to babies and toddlers in ways that might make language learning easier (Snow & Ferguson, 1977). We have already encountered several characteristics of this **motherese** speaking style, such as the use of greater variations in intonation. These speech adjustments can take a number of other forms as well.

We often think of "baby talk" as containing distortions of pronunciation ("What a pwetty baby!") or word form ("Does the baby want a drink of wah-wah?"). But these sorts of speech changes do not actually occur very frequently, at least in English (Kaye, 1980; Toda, Fogel, & Kawai, 1990). Instead, the speech adjustments that adults make for infants generally are constructive and positive. Mothers tend to speak slowly and use short utterances with babies, often three words or fewer. Usually the words are pronounced very clearly, and the speech rarely contains grammatical errors. When talking about an object or situation, mothers label it frequently and use a good deal of repetition in their descriptions and comments. And the focus of their speech usually is on here-and-now events, rather than on more distant or abstract topics (Messer, 1980; Newport, 1977; Papousek, Papousek, & Haekel, 1987). Motherese is not unique to the English language. Japanese mothers have been found to make similar speech adjustments when talking to their newborns (Fernald & Morikawa, 1993).

Fathers display many of the same speech adjustments, although they generally are less sensitive to the infant's level of linguistic development (McLaughlin et al.,

Motherese
Simplified speech directed at very young children by adults and older children.

• Motherese and other forms of speech adjustment to babies are not exclusive to English-speaking mothers.

1983; Ratner, 1988). In fact, some researchers have suggested that the father's speech serves as a bridge between the fine-tuned adjustments of the mother and the complex and erratic speech of the outside world (Gleason & Weintraub, 1978; Mannle & Tomasello, 1987; Tomasello, Conti-Ramsden, & Ewert, 1990).

Like adults, children vary their speech when interacting with younger children or infants. These adjustments are very similar to those adults make, such as the use of higher pitch, shorter and simpler phrases, and more repetitions (Dunn & Kendrick, 1982; Shatz & Gelman, 1973). In fact, preschoolers sometimes display aspects of motherese when talking to dolls (Warren-Leubeuker & Bohannon, 1983).

But do all these speech adjustments by parents and children have any effect on the infant's language development? The research evidence on this question is incomplete. Attempts to find a convincing connection between the overall degree of maternal speech adjustment and the infant's level of language development have failed to discover a strong relation (Gleitman, Newport, & Gleitman, 1984; Murray, Johnson, & Peters, 1990; Scarborough & Wyckoff, 1986). And attempts to uncover positive effects of more specific speech changes (length of utterance, amount of repetition, and so on) have offered only scattered support (Furrow, Nelson, & Benedict, 1979; Hoff-Ginsberg, 1986, 1990; Hoff-Ginsberg & Shatz, 1982).

Do these results mean that simplifications in the speech directed toward language-learning children are of little value? Probably not. One possibility is that some *minimum* amount of simplification (which almost all babies experience) is important but that the additional degree of motherese provided to some infants is of no extra benefit (Scarborough & Wyckoff, 1986). Of course, it is also possible that the methods and measures used by researchers have simply not been appropriate or sensitive enough to detect all of the relations that exist between the adults' input and the babies' output (Schwartz & Camarata, 1985; Snow, Perlmann, & Nathan, 1987). Whereas motherese is a pervasive phenomenon, then, its role in syntactic development remains unclear (Bohannon & Hirsh-Pasek, 1984; Furrow & Nelson, 1986).

Imitation

The fact that parents present infants with a simplified model of language suggests a possible role for imitation. To what extent do young children acquire grammatical rules by imitating the speech of their parents and other adults?

Certainly, imitation cannot be the whole story. As Chomsky pointed out, our ability to produce entirely novel statements means that language must be based on more than merely copying what we hear. In addition, young children produce word combinations that they have probably not heard ("All-gone Daddy"), along with overregularizations not found in adult speech ("I hurted my foots"). These forms clearly do not arise from imitation in any simple sense.

But perhaps those imitations that occur are *progressive*. That is, perhaps when youngsters do repeat their parents' comments, they tend to imitate language structures more complex than those they use themselves. These structures may then begin to find their way into the children's own spontaneous speech. Whether this is the case seems to depend on how *imitation* is defined (Clark, 1977; Whitehurst & DeBaryshe, 1989).

When imitation is defined as immediate and exact copying of an utterance, several findings emerge. The first is that most children display very little imitation, although a few imitate a great deal (Bloom, Hood, & Lightbrown, 1974). Furthermore, such imitations are rarely progressive. In fact, they often are even shorter and less complex than the syntax the child usually uses (Ervin, 1964; Tager-Flusberg & Calkins, 1990). Finally, the proportion of immediate and exact imitations declines over the first few years of language learning (Kuczaj, 1982).

A different picture emerges when imitation is defined more broadly. For example, we might look for **expanded imitations**, in which the child adds something to the utterance that was just heard; or **deferred imitations**, in which the copying occurs at some later time; or **selective imitations** (which can also be deferred), in which the child imitates the general form of a language structure, such as a prepositional phrase, but uses different words (Snow, 1983; Whitehurst & Novak, 1973). The research evidence suggests that these forms of imitation sometimes *are* progressive. Thus, at least in some cases, a more advanced language structure does first appear in a child's imitation of adult speech and then gradually finds its way into the child's spontaneous, nonimitative speech (Bloom, Hood, & Lightbrown, 1974; Moerk, 1977; Snow & Goldfield, 1983). Moreover, in the speech of young children who imitate frequently, the proportion of expanded imitations generally increases with age, suggesting that these children may have adopted imitation as a mechanism for learning syntax (Kuczaj, 1982; Snow, 1981).

Feedback (Negative Evidence)

Another mechanism for helping children learn language structure is feedback—sometimes called *negative evidence*—when their statements are not grammatically correct. To some extent, this happens automatically. When children say things in ways that cannot be understood, their message often fails to achieve their goal. But research has shown that parents sometimes provide other types of feedback in response to ungrammatical statements.

If we wished to systematically teach linguistic rules to a child, a simple reinforcement procedure might come to mind. Accurate utterances would be rewarded or shown approval, and inaccurate ones would be disapproved of or ignored. This general approach, in fact, has been used successfully in work with language-impaired children (Garcia & DeHaven, 1974; Harris, 1975; Whitehurst et al., 1989) and with children learning vocabulary in a second language (Whitehurst & Valdez-Menchaca, 1988). But does this sort of process operate in the natural environment? Do parents typically reinforce the accuracy of their children's grammar? Once again, the answer to these questions is neither a simple yes nor a simple no (Snow et al., 1987).

Parents rarely respond to their children's ungrammatical statements with simple disapproval, such as "No, you didn't say that right." Instead, feedback regarding the accuracy of a child's remark usually involves its content, or "truth value," such as "No, the block isn't red, it's blue" (Brown & Hanlon, 1970; Demetras, Post, & Snow, 1986). But parents do provide negative evidence in response to ungrammatical statements in more subtle ways (Bohannon & Stanowicz, 1988; Sokolov, 1993).

Research has shown, for example, that mothers frequently respond to their children's ill-formed statements (such as "Mouses runned in hole, Mommy!") in three different ways. **Expansions** involve repeating the child's incorrect statement in a corrected or more complete form ("Yes, the mice ran into the hole!"). **Recasts** involve restating the child's remark using a different structure ("Didn't those mice run into that hole!"). And **clarification questions** signal that the listener did not understand the comment and that the child should attempt the communication again ("What happened? What did those mice do?") (Demetras et al., 1986; Hirsh-Pasek, Treiman, & Schneiderman, 1984; Penner, 1987). Each of these forms of feedback has been found to accelerate children's development of correct grammar (Baker & Nelson, 1984; Farrar, 1990, 1992; Hoff-Ginsberg, 1986; Moerk, 1983; Scherer & Olswang, 1984).

Scaffolding

We saw earlier that formats and scripts are mechanisms that facilitate children's language development. When parents provide children with these structured contexts

Expanded imitation
Imitated speech to which the child has added new elements.

Deferred imitation
Imitated speech that occurs some time after the speech was modeled.

Selective imitation
Imitated speech that repeats only the basic structure of the model, not its precise content.

Expansion
A repetition of speech in which errors are corrected and statements are elaborated.

Recast
A response to speech that restates it using a different structure.

Clarification question
A response that indicates a listener did not understand a statement.

for learning, when they speak to them in motherese, or when they provide them with expansions, recasts, and clarification questions, they are using the general process of *scaffolding* (Bruner, 1975) introduced in Chapter 10. Scaffolding includes behaviors that adults perform to help children learn in many areas, including academics, social skills, motor tasks, and, of course, language acquisition. Usually, this approach begins with what the child is already capable of doing and then provides props, hints, or simply a supportive setting to help the child move up to a more advanced level of skill (Rogoff, 1986, 1990).

With regard to language development, scaffolding can take a variety of forms (Adamson & Bakeman, 1984; Trevarthen & Marwick, 1986). One sort of scaffolding is supplied by the mother who stays closely attuned to what her baby is doing and concentrates her comments on these activities (Akhtar, Dunham, & Dunham, 1991; Baldwin, 1993). If a baby suddenly looks up at the window where a bird has landed, the mother might remark, "See the bird, Timmy, isn't he pretty?" Mothers who engage in "turn-taking" with their babbling infants—first saying something to the baby, then allowing the baby to babble, then saying something else, and so on—are scaffolding as well, providing their children with opportunities both to speak and to listen (Bloom, Russell, & Wassenberg, 1987; Collis, 1985). A third form of scaffolding involves asking questions of the "What?" "Where?" and "Who?" variety. These questions encourage continual language use and interaction (Hoff-Ginsberg, 1986, 1990; Yoder & Kaiser, 1989).

An illustration of scaffolding in language learning can be found in a recent study on children's picture-book reading. Storybook time is a common routine for language-learning youngsters, and correlational studies have repeatedly shown that children who are read to often and from an early age tend to develop language skills earlier (Crain-Thoreson & Dale, 1992; DeBaryshe, 1993; Swinson, 1985; Wells, 1985). Using an experimental approach, researchers hypothesized that a highly scaffolded approach to this activity should have a noticeable impact on children's language development. A group of mothers was trained to use a method called *dialogic reading*, in which the child is encouraged to talk, rather than just listen, during reading time. This technique involved asking the children open-ended questions (such as "What is the bear doing?"), repeating and expanding children's statements, providing praise for speech that was accurate in both content and grammar, and minimizing the proportion of time spent in simply reading. A control group of mothers was lectured on the value of picture-book reading but given no special training or instructions. Both groups were directed to read to their children three or four times a week, and all of these sessions were tape-recorded to ensure that the mothers were following the directions. At the end of 1 month, the children were tested on measures of expressive language ability, and as predicted, the experimental group's scores were significantly higher (Whitehurst et al., 1988). These findings have since been replicated with day-care children from low-income families in Mexico (Valdez-Menchaca & Whitehurst, 1992).

What about children whose speech involves two languages? Box 11-2 describes some research on bilingualism.

• Picture-book reading offers a good opportunity for parents to provide scaffolding to language-learning youngsters.

✔ To Recap...

Grammar is the study of the rules of language structure. These rules include such devices as word order (syntax), inflection, and intonation. The growth of grammar can be seen as children's speech steadily increases in length and complexity. Even during the

one-word period, from 12 to 24 months, the functions of babies' utterances steadily increase, as in the use of holophrases. Children's two-word utterances, which appear around the end of the second year, often display rules built around individual words—for example, combining "all-gone" with various nouns. As sentences grow longer, telegraphic speech emerges. When children first learn inflectional rules, they overregularize them, probably because they do not understand that, for example, each verb generally has only one past tense.

Many explanations of how grammar develops have been proposed. One involves innate form classes. Psycholinguists contend that form classes are based on the structure of speech, whereas cognitive psychologists believe they are based on semantic concepts. Evidence from children's first word combinations supports the semantic interpretation, although structural knowledge becomes increasingly more important as children grow.

An alternative to inborn knowledge are inborn linguistic strategies. Operating principles for acquiring language have been derived from the study of many languages and are supported by observations and experimental investigations of children's language learning.

Environmental influences on grammatical development have also been investigated. Both adults and children use motherese in talking to babies, for example. Attempts to link the use of this simplified speech style to progress in language development have met with mixed success.

Imitation can take several forms. The most important for language learning appear to be the expanded, deferred, and selective forms, which serve to introduce new grammatical constructions to some children. Another environmental factor is feedback. Although parents rarely respond to children's ungrammatical statements with disapproval, they commonly expand, recast, or ask for clarification of ill-formed statements. Such responses have been shown to be of some value for children's language development. Scaffolding of various types has also been shown to substantially affect early language development.

PRAGMATICS

We have seen that language has both structure (grammar) and meaning (semantics). But it also performs functions, in that it gets people to do things we would like them to do. When a toddler points to the refrigerator and says "cup," for example, she is not as likely to be labeling the refrigerator as she is to be asking her mother to fetch her cup of juice. The study of the social uses of language is called **pragmatics**.

Pragmatics is a relatively new area of study and, as a result, we know less about it than semantics or syntactics. But it is the most rapidly growing approach to language study, perhaps because psychologists are focusing more and more on the context in which children learn. As mentioned, functionalist theories have been especially important in this area.

Pragmatics grows out of the functionalists' belief that children continually strive to find better ways of communicating their ideas, requests, and objections to others. From this perspective, children do not learn language simply because of an innate quest to understand linguistic structure. Instead, they are motivated to acquire language because it provides them with a very powerful tool—the ability to communicate with others easily and to achieve their goals effectively (Hickman, 1986; Ninio & Snow, 1988).

To be effective communicators children first must learn to express their needs or desires in ways that can be understood by others. In the beginning, babies can-

Pragmatics
The study of the social uses of language.

BILINGUALISM: TEACHING (AND LEARNING) ONE LANGUAGE OR TWO?

Almost 5 million children in the United States live in households where more than one language is spoken. A similar situation exists in many other countries, such as Canada, where a significant minority of the population speaks both English and French. Most of these children eventually acquire elements of both languages, and many become fluent bilingual speakers (Hyltenstam & Obler, 1989). How should the educational system deal with such children?

Approaches to this problem range from "immersion" programs, in which children are taught in both languages with the goal of making them bilingually fluent, and "transitional" programs, in which minority children are first taught in their own language with the goal of having them later become fluent in the majority language, to "majority-only" policies in which the use of minority languages is explicitly discouraged (Bialystok & Cummins, 1991). Although the types of programs employed often reflect political rather than educational factors, policy makers typically attempt to support their decisions with scientific data regarding bilingual learning. One of the most important questions has been whether children learning two languages have more difficulty learning the majority language. For many scientists, answering this question requires a basic understanding of how the bilingual process works.

One theory has been that bilingual children initially approach the task of learning two languages as if they were learning only one. That is, they do not separate the two forms of speech input but rather develop a single language system that includes elements of each. Only with increasing age do these children presumably learn to differentiate the two tongues, gradually treating them as independent languages (Swain, 1977; Volterra & Taeschner, 1978).

This theory has principally grown out of the observation that younger bilingual children display a good deal of *mixing* (also referred to as *code-switching*), or combining forms from the two languages within the same utterance (Lanza, 1992; Redlinger & Park, 1980). Mixing occurs at all levels of speech, including articulation, vocabulary, inflections, and syntax. The assumption has been that mixing reflects confusion on the part of the bilingual child, who cannot separate the two languages. A related finding is that children in bilingual homes acquire both languages more slowly than peers who are learning only one language, although this lag gradually disappears, and the children's proficiency in both languages eventually reaches that of monolinguals.

Recent research has begun to challenge the single-system hypothesis and to offer alternative interpretations (Genesee, 1989; Pye, 1986). Studies of infant speech perception, for example, indicate clearly that babies can differentiate sounds and phonemes found in different languages (Eilers & Oller, 1988; Moon et al., 1993). Hence, perceptual confusion or immaturity does not appear to be a problem. It has also been suggested that children's substitution of a word in one language for the same word in the second language may simply reflect the overextension principle. Thus, the child may substitute in this way if she does not know the appropriate word in the second language or if it is simply easier to do so (Vihman, 1985). Furthermore, modeling by parents has been implicated in children's language mixing. Detailed studies of bilingual children's home environments indicate that their parents often speak to them using parts of both languages simultaneously (Goodz, 1989). Finally, bilingualism does not result in cognitive deficits, as might be implied by the slower growth of language skills in bilin-

not always accomplish this, and sometimes their attempts to convey their wants are frustrated by their parents' failure to understand exactly what is being requested. This frustration is an important motivator for the child to acquire skills that will make communication easier. But the process operates in the other direction as well. Effective communication also involves understanding what parents and others are saying in order to follow their directions, answer their questions, or comply with their requests. Communication, of course, is a two-way street.

We begin our discussion of pragmatics with a look at how children use speech to control others and to get their own way. Then we examine the development of conversation skills and the ability to communicate effectively with others.

• Research indicates that teaching nonnative children in their own language does not interfere with their learning of the majority language.

guals and the suggestion that hearing two languages confuses children. Bilingual children, in fact, have been shown to be more advanced in some areas of cognition than monolinguals (Diaz, 1983, 1985; Johnson, 1991).

It appears, then, that exposure to two languages does not present an unusually difficult challenge to young children, who can apparently separate and ac-quire both systems (Cummins, 1991; Umbel et al., 1992). This would suggest that attempts by some communities to have schools force nonnative children to learn only English may be misguided and may even de-prive these children of a valuable learning opportunity.

Speech Acts

Before acquiring speech, infants use other tools for communication, such as crying, facial expressions, and gestures. In one study, for example, mothers engaged in a turn-taking game (for example, taking turns squeezing a squeak toy) with their 1-year-old babies. Once the game was going smoothly, they were instructed to not take a turn and to simply sit silently and motionlessly. The babies in this study re-acted by performing a variety of behaviors clearly designed to communicate to the mother that it was her turn. These included vocalizing at her, pointing to the toy, and picking up the toy and giving it to her (Ross & Lollis, 1987).

Speech act
An instance of speech used to perform pragmatic functions, like requesting or complaining.

With the acquisition of language, children add verbal responses to this repertoire of communication devices. Now children achieve various goals by directing words and phrases at other people. Functionalists refer to these pragmatic uses of language as **speech acts** (Astington, 1988; Dore, 1976). Researchers have found that even the earliest words that infants utter usually serve several pragmatic functions (Bretherton, 1988). *Mama,* for example, is generally first used both to call the mother and to request things from her (as when the baby says "mama" while pointing to a toy on a shelf). In time, this word also begins to serve the more common purpose of naming the parent (Ninio & Snow, 1988). Later in the one-word period, babies begin to use *relational words*—those connecting several objects or events—in a number of pragmatic ways. For example, *more* may be used to request that an activity be continued, as well as to describe a block being added to a pile (McCune-Nicolich, 1981).

Mothers also produce speech acts, which must be comprehended by the language-learning infant if the pair is to communicate effectively (Ninio & Wheeler, 1984). The function of speech to babies, however, is not always obvious. When a mother says "May I open it for you?" she is not really asking the child a question as much as she is offering help. And when she says "I didn't mean to break it," she is doing more than describing her intentions; she is actually apologizing to the baby. Researchers are just beginning to study this aspect of pragmatics, as we will see shortly.

DEVELOPMENT IN CONTEXT: Using Speech Style to Convey Cultural Values

When children hear speech, they learn more than just the nature of their parents' language—they also learn a good deal about their culture. Culture, we have seen, is an important macrosystem in which development occurs, and it influences many aspects of children's behavior. One way it affects growing children is through their parents' language. Parents convey information about cultural values to their children not only in the specific content of their speech but also in its style and functions (Schieffelin & Ochs, 1986).

An interesting example can be seen in a comparison of middle-class American and German mothers (Shatz, 1991). These two groups share many similarities. Both represent Western, industrialized societies with affluent middle classes. Their languages are also structurally similar to one another. One important cultural difference between them, however, lies in their philosophies of discipline and socialization. American mothers tend to stress teaching children to express their emotional needs. German mothers, by contrast, display more interest in teaching children obedience and self-reliance.

Of interest to the investigators was whether these differences in cultural values would be reflected in the style of speech the mothers used with their infants. The study focused on verb forms that serve different functions, for example, expressing permission ("you *may* choose..."), obligation ("you *must* put..."), and possibility ("this *can* fit..."). Mothers were tape-recorded as they played with their 2-year-olds, and the speech of both was later analyzed.

As predicted, the German mothers used different kinds of verbs with their children than the American mothers. They tended to focus on obligation verbs and used more negatives (such as "no" and "not there") than did American mothers, who focused more on permission and possibility and also asked more questions.

What about the children? As we have seen, children imitate what they hear and in this study as well a positive correlation was found between the kinds of verbs used by the mothers and those produced by the children. For example, obligation statements were already being produced by many of the German toddlers, whereas not a single American infant used this form. Clearly, the babies seemed already to be acquiring certain cultural expectations from their mothers.

Discourse

Regardless of what theory of language acquisition they favor, all researchers agree that language is most often used in social contexts. Speech during social interaction is called **discourse** or, more commonly, conversation.

Discourse
Language used in social interactions; conversation.

When people have conversations, they must, of course, adhere to the grammatical rules of the language if they are to understand one another. But they also must follow certain social rules of discourse. The most obvious of these is turn-taking, with each participant alternating between being the speaker and being the listener. This basic rule of conversation is one of the first acquired by children. As we have seen, it may actually be learned during the preverbal period (Collis, 1985).

Some other rules of discourse are more difficult, however, and are learned later. One of these is the "answer obviousness" rule. Some statements that are phrased as questions may actually be intended as directives, such as, "Could you hand me that pencil?" How do listeners know in these situations which function the speaker intends? Most often, we solve the problem by considering the context in which the remark is made (Shatz & McCloskey, 1984). For example, we would very likely treat the remark as a directive if the speaker was about to write a note, if a pencil was visible but out of the speaker's reach, and if the pencil was within our reach. Another kind of cue we often use in such situations, however, is the obviousness of the answer. Since we realize that the speaker in our example knows that we *could* pass the pencil, we do not treat the remark as a request for information. Instead, we view it as a directive. Discourse rules of this sort are clearly more difficult to learn than turn-taking, and the answer obviousness rule is not apparent in children until about age 5 (Abbeduto, Davies, & Furman, 1988).

Other discourse rules appear even later. For example, understanding that in a conversation one should (1) say something that relates to what the speaker has just said, (2) say something that is relevant to the topic under discussion, and (3) say something that has not already been said, involves discourse rules that most children do not use consistently until 6 or 7 years of age (Conti & Camras, 1984).

Discourse requires more than rules. It also requires content. Children cannot have a conversation unless they have something to talk about—that is, a topic about which they share some knowledge. Children's early discourse often appears to be built around scripts (Nelson & Gruendel, 1986). As mentioned, these familiar routines, like taking a bath, may help children acquire new vocabulary. It appears that by providing a common topic of conversation, scripts may also facilitate children's learning of discourse rules. One study, for example, found that preschoolers had better conversations and violated fewer rules of discourse when they discussed a scripted topic (such as a trip to the grocery store) than when they discussed a less familiar topic (Furman & Walden, 1990).

Unfortunately, little else is known about how children acquire conversation rules. The rules would seem to require a good foundation of linguistic knowledge, along with considerable experience in conversational situations. But it remains to be discovered whether they are based primarily on trial-and-error learning, modeling and imitation, or some form of scaffolding.

CAN APES LEARN LANGUAGE?

At the beginning of the chapter we said categorically that only humans can acquire true language. At this moment, most developmental psychologists would agree with this assertion. In fact, the proposition that language is unique to humans was first argued scientifically by Descartes (1637) and has never been seriously questioned.

Nevertheless, a small but committed group of scientists has been challenging this claim for many years. Beginning around the turn of the century, one research team after another has attempted to teach language to various species of apes, using a number of different techniques and with varying degrees of success (Wallman, 1992).

The earliest projects were the least successful because they attempted to teach apes to produce the vocal responses used by humans (Furness, 1916; Hayes, 1951; Kellogg & Kellogg, 1933). Although apes are our closest evolutionary relatives—sharing 99% of our genes (King & Wilson, 1975)—and so are also very intelligent, we now know that their vocal apparatus is not adequately developed to allow them to produce the range of sounds necessary to utter many words (Lieberman, Klatt, & Wilson, 1969).

More impressive progress began to be made when investigators moved away from vocal language and attempted to teach other linguistic forms. Some employed the manual sign language used by the deaf community. Most notably, two psychologists at the University of Nevada, Alan and Trixie Gardner, raised a baby chimpanzee named Washoe in a family environment where she was continually signed to and where everyone else communicated using only this system. By the time she was 3 years old, Washoe had developed an impressive vocabulary of gesture (sign) names for common objects and activities, as did a number of other chimps and gorillas who later were trained by the same method (Fouts, 1973; Gardner & Gardner, 1971; Patterson, 1978). This research was criticized, however, because it was never clearly demonstrated that Washoe could produce grammatical statements that were anything more than imitations of what had been signed to her (Seidenberg & Pettito, 1979; Terrace et al., 1979).

A different approach involved training an ape to communicate by pressing symbols on a large keyboard connected to a computer. The symbols were designed to represent words, and the language was based on a very clear system of syntactic rules. This arrangement permitted the ape to ask questions, make statements, or request things of one of her human trainers (or of the computer), who could in turn use the same language to answer the requests or continue the conversation in some other way. Using this approach, Duane Rumbaugh, a psychologist at Georgia State University, reported that he had trained a chimp named Lana to string together symbols to produce new responses with sentence-like qualities (Rumbaugh, Gill, & von Glaserfeld, 1973). Later, he included two chimps in the experiment so that they could use the symbols to communicate with one another (Savage-Rumbaugh & Rumbaugh, 1978; Savage-Rumbaugh, Rumbaugh, & Boysen, 1978). This research was viewed skeptically, however, with many developmentalists remaining unconvinced that it demonstrated true language acquisition (Sebeok & Umiker-Sebeok, 1980; Seidenberg & Pettito, 1987). As a result, interest in this fascinating issue appeared to have waned.

Social Referential Communication

An even more advanced conversational skill involves the ability to effectively communicate information about something that is not known to the other participant in the conversation, as when one child describes his new computer game to a classmate in such a way that the other child understands how it is played. This form of communication is called **social referential communication**. In formal terms, such communication occurs when a *speaker* sends a *message* that is comprehended by a *listener*. The communication is social because it occurs between two people (rather than between a person and a machine, for example); it is referential because the message is in a symbolic form (the child is using language to convey the informa-

Social referential communication
A form of communication in which a speaker sends a message that is comprehended by a listener.

• Attempts to teach language to apes have shown some success, although the evidence remains debatable. Photo made available by Beatrice T. Gardner, PhD, University of Nevada, Reno.

Very recent developments, however, have once again raised the possibility that apes can acquire important aspects of human language. The studies continue to use the symbol keyboard apparatus. But with this latest work, the focus has shifted from the syntactic and semantic elements of language to its pragmatic functions and from language production to language comprehension. The results have been impressive.

One study examined the acquisition of pragmatic forms of communication in four chimps (Greenfield & Savage-Rumbaugh, 1993). In humans, repetition of all or part of a statement just heard can serve a number of important pragmatic functions. For example, upon hearing her mother say "Jenny, let's go inside, it's cold." a young child may use repetition for the purpose of *agreement* ("Go inside!"), *counterclaim* ("No cold, warm"), *denial* ("No inside, stay outside"), *self-reference* ("I cold"), and so forth. In each case, the child is using repetition to accomplish some communication act (Ochs Keenan, 1977). Could chimps use repetition

similarly? When the researchers examined how the four chimps used the symbols on the keyboard apparatus, they found that all four of their subjects did indeed use repetition in these sorts of ways, indicating that language was truly serving a communication function for them.

A second recent study compared language acquisition in a young child and a young chimp who were raised by the same caregiver (Savage-Rumbaugh et al., 1993). For several years, the caregiver spoke English daily to both subjects but also continually exposed them to *lexigrams*, the geometric symbols that served as words in the keyboard apparatus. Any language acquisition occurred only through observational learning, since no rewards or punishments were included in the training. Acquisition was assessed in terms of language comprehension. Throughout the training, the caregiver repeatedly tested each subject's ability to respond appropriately to commands or requests that included a wide variety of object labels and involved various forms of syntax (such as "Put the ball on the table," "Give the cookie to me," and "Go to the refrigerator and get a banana"). By the end of the experiment, the chimp had responded correctly 72% of the time and the child 66% of the time. These results indicated that both subjects had learned to comprehend both semantic and syntactic aspects of the English language.

Taken together, these latest studies suggest that apes may be much more capable of language acquisition than science has assumed. And if future research continues to generate support for this conclusion, Descartes's early pronouncement may finally be disproven.

tion and not simply showing the classmate what to do); and it is communication because it was understood by the listener (Whitehurst & Sonnenschein, 1985).

Research on social referential communication has primarily been conducted in laboratory settings. To study this process, researchers have generally used a task of the following sort. Two children sit across from one another at a table and are separated by a screen or partition. One child is designated as the speaker, the other as the listener. Both children are given sets of cards with pictures on them, such as balls of different sizes and colors. The speaker's task is to send messages that describe a card. The listener's task is to use the messages to select the correct card from the array of cards available. In some experiments, the listener can ask questions or comment on the usefulness of the speaker's descriptions. The success of

• To become effective communicators, young children must acquire both speaker skills and listener skills.

the communication is measured by how often the listener selects the correct card. Using this procedure, psychologists have been able to identify many of the factors that influence children's communication abilities.

In order for children to engage in social referential communication effectively—as speakers or listeners—they must learn a number of important skills. In the role of speaker, children must become aware of *listener cues*, meaning simply that they must adjust messages to meet the needs of the listener. For example, if the listener is far away, the message should be loud; if the listener is running out the door, the message should be brief; and if the listener is someone of high status (for example, a teacher or a preacher), the message should be polite. A good example of a young child's failure to take listener cues into account is the little boy who talks with his grandmother on the telephone and answers her questions by nodding his head. We noted earlier that children do appear to adjust their speech according to one important listener characteristic—age (Sachs & Devin, 1976; Shatz & Gelman, 1973). Children improve in this ability as they get older. Fifth graders, for example, make more effective speech modifications when talking to younger children than do first graders (Sonnenschein, 1988). Another useful listener cue involves *common ground*, the information shared by the speaker and listener. If the listener, for example, knows the speaker's birthday, then the message "Come over on my birthday" will be sufficient; if the listener does not possess the information, the message will be inadequate. Kindergartners have some understanding of the common-ground principle, but this ability too improves with age (Ackerman & Silver, 1990; Ackerman, Szymanski, & Silver, 1990). Perhaps the most important listener cues involve feedback. If the listener does not appear to be comprehending, the speaker should change the message and try again. This skill is not apparent in younger children, who often persist with the same types of messages even though the listener is not understanding (Roberts & Patterson, 1983; Robinson, 1981).

In addition to listener cues, the speaker must also learn to be aware of *context cues*. In other words, the speaker should adjust the message to fit demands of the situation other than those directly related to the listener. One important context cue involves what sort of information has already been given. Attending to this cue helps the speaker to avoid repeating messages and to send the information in a logical order. In addition, the speaker must be sensitive to the array of referents from which the listener must choose. In the experimental situation we described, if only one of the cards has a picture of a large ball, the message "It's the big one" will be effective. But if more than one of the cards has a large ball on it, this message will not help the listener narrow the choice to a single possibility. In tasks of this sort, only after the preschool years do children typically take such context cues into account (Kahan & Richards, 1986; Sodian, 1988; Whitehurst & Sonnenschein, 1985). In real life, too, children often ignore context cues, as when a young child asks her mother to bring her toy without having made any prior reference to a specific toy and without considering that the mother will have dozens to choose from.

As listeners, children need to learn certain rules, as well. Like speakers, listeners must be aware of context cues, including the information that has previously been sent and the nature of the array from which the referent is to be chosen. In addition, when a message is not informative, the child must learn to recognize this fact and to communicate the problem. Children as young as 5 can sometimes detect when a message is poorly constructed or when critical information is missing. At this age, however, they will often proceed with the inadequate information whereas, by age 7, they are more likely to seek clarification or additional information from the speaker (Ackerman, 1993).

How referential communication skills develop is another issue that is just beginning to be studied. They are clearly tied to the emergence of certain cognitive skills. For example, as children's egocentric view of the world decreases, they develop a better appreciation for how another person might view a situation. And as their theory-of-mind understanding improves, they come to realize that listeners with different cognitive capabilities (such as babies versus adults) may interpret the same information differently (Montgomery, 1993; Taylor, Cartwright, & Bowden, 1991). But environmental factors also appear to play a role. One study, for example, found that children whose mothers provided them specific feedback regarding how their messages were inadequate developed their communication skills most rapidly (Robinson, 1981).

✔ To Recap...

Pragmatics is the study of the social uses of language. It is based on the functionalist view that children are motivated to acquire language in order to more effectively communicate their wants and needs. Effective communication abilities involve both speaker skills and listener skills.

Infants at first communicate with crying, gestures, and so on. As they acquire language, they add speech acts to their nonverbal communication skills. They also learn to comprehend speech acts of others.

The ability to communicate effectively involves learning rules of discourse. Turn-taking is one of the earliest discourse rules acquired by infants. Others, such as the answer obviousness rule, are more difficult to learn and are not apparent in children until several years later. The use of scripts as topics of conversation appears to help children learn discourse rules, as well as providing content for their discourse.

Social referential communication occurs when a speaker sends a message that is understood by a listener. Effective communication of this sort involves speaker skills, such as adjusting the messages to the demands of the listener and the context, and listener skills, such as recognizing and communicating when messages are ambiguous.

CONCLUSION

Developmental psychologists, like researchers in the other natural sciences, attempt to identify processes that are general and fundamental. Rather than considering each event or behavior to be unique, scientists search for principles and laws that can explain and interrelate them across the many domains of human development.

During the 1960s, the study of language became somewhat of an exception to this approach. Language was believed to be different, requiring special mechanisms and processes independent of other behaviors. The basic cognitive and learning processes that psychologists used to explain other aspects of development were thought to be inadequate, and even irrelevant, in explaining language acquisition. Perhaps this separation occurred because the psycholinguistic model was developed outside of traditional psychology, by theorists who were trained primarily in linguistic structure rather than human behavior. As we have seen throughout this chapter, however, the situation has changed considerably.

With the development of new theoretical models and better research techniques, language study has come back into the mainstream of child psychology. The view that language is either independent of cognitive abilities or insensitive to social and environmental factors no longer finds much support among developmental researchers. This is not to say that language does not possess its own unique characteristics, which need to be more clearly understood. But there can be little doubt that language development is very much interrelated with other developmental processes, which both affect and are affected by it.

FOR THOUGHT AND DISCUSSION

1. One of the puzzles of human language is this: if it has such a strong biological basis, why are there so many different languages spoken around the world? *How do you think so many languages developed? Do you think the number of languages will change as time goes by? If so, in which direction? Why do you think people in, say, Brooklyn have accents so different from people only several hundred miles away in, say, Boston?*

2. The study of language acquisition has attracted more research than any other single area of developmental psychology. *Why do you think this is true? If you were studying children, what might attract you to investigate their language development?*

3. The growing number of immigrants in many countries is resulting in large numbers of children growing up in households that do not speak the majority language. *Do you think schools should teach in more than one language so that these children will not be at an immediate disadvantage? Or should schools teach the majority language alone?*

4. Most adults simplify their speech (using motherese) when speaking to children although it is not entirely clear why this occurs. *The next time you speak to a child, note whether you make such adjustments. If you do, try to identify exactly what is motivating this behavior. In addition, try speaking to a child without making such adjustments. Does this cause any problems or offer any insights into why motherese occurs?*

5. Whether language is unique to humans is a question that persists in developmental psychology. *Why do you think this issue continues to be pursued? If we can train apes (or other species) to use complex language, what value might this have? What kinds of questions might we want to ask them?*

Part Four

SOCIAL AND PERSONALITY DEVELOPMENT

Chapter 12

EARLY SOCIAL AND EMOTIONAL DEVELOPMENT

Humans are a very social species. We organize into groups ranging in size from families to communities to nations, and we spend a good deal of time interacting with one another. From early on, children form many social relationships. Some of these relationships, such as those with occasional baby-sitters, are very brief and of little consequence. But others, such as those with family members and certain friends, will last for many years and may affect children's later development and personality in important ways (Ainsworth, 1989; Hartup, 1989b).

Understanding social development has not been easy for researchers because the complexity of social interaction poses certain unique obstacles to its scientific study. Consider the following mother–infant interaction, which represents the relatively simple *dyadic*, or two-person, situation.

A mother talks to her baby and he begins to smile; when she moves a toy in front of him, the baby follows it with his eyes; and when she makes a strange face at him, he becomes still and stares attentively. What causes these changes in the baby's behavior? Clearly the changes are being controlled, or caused, by what the mother is doing. But there's more to the interaction than that because the influence here is undoubtedly bidirectional. That is, the baby's responses influence the mother's behavior. For example, if the baby gazes at her with apparent interest, the mother is likely to continue what she is doing. If the baby begins to act bored, she may step up her actions, perhaps tickling him or adding attention-getting vocalizations. And if the baby begins to fret, the mother may tone down her responses or even end the interaction altogether.

This relatively simple example shows why psychologists who attempt to explain social interactions have difficulty drawing simple conclusions as to the causes of human behavior. In the case of the baby's behavior, certainly one determinant is the mother's responses. However, the baby is to some degree controlling her responses. That is, he is a *producer* of his environment, in that his behavior and personal characteristics affect the kinds of things he experiences (Lerner, 1982; Scarr & McCartney, 1983). The example calls to mind Bronfenbrenner's suggestion, mentioned in Chapter 2, that children often display behaviors or traits that are *developmentally instigative*, in that they cause people to respond to them in significant ways. But it also illustrates how the transactional nature of social interactions poses a major challenge to researchers seeking to understand exactly what is affecting whom, and why (Bakeman & Gottman, 1986; Gottman, 1990).

This chapter is the first of five that deal with children's social and personality development. We focus in the present chapter on social interactions during the child's first 2 years of life. To begin, we survey the approaches of the three major theoretical traditions to infant social development. Next, we consider how the infant and caregiver develop an early communication system as they learn to regulate one another's behavior. Then we look at the baby's individual style of responding, an early component of personality called *temperament*. Finally, we examine the topic that traditionally has been of greatest interest to researchers—the nature of the attachment process that produces the unique emotional bond between caregiver and child.

• Children's social interactions are transactional. They not only respond to their environment, they also influence it.

THEORIES OF EARLY SOCIAL DEVELOPMENT

Social development during the first 2 years of life is distinctive in several important ways. First, although children eventually come to have many social contacts—family, friends, teachers, and so on—the infant's social world typically consists of only a few significant individuals, such as the mother, father, and siblings. Second, despite their small number, these initial relationships appear to be more influential and to have longer term effects on the child's social, personality, and even cognitive development than many of the relationships that develop later on. Finally, children appear to develop strong emotional relationships—especially with the mother but also with the father and others—more easily and intensely during the infant years, suggesting that early social development may involve psychological processes that are different from those operating later in life.

Researchers from each of the three major theoretical approaches have taken an interest in early social development. And, as you might expect, their different views have led them to investigate different aspects of this area and to pursue somewhat different questions. Much of the theorizing has been concerned specifically with the attachment process, which we discuss in detail later in the chapter.

Ethology

The ethological explanation of early social interactions is the most extensive and well articulated. Ethological researchers are, of course, most concerned with the evolutionary origins of development, arguing that the social behaviors we observe in today's infants and caregivers represent millions of years of gradual adaptation to the environment (Eibl-Eibesfeldt, 1989; Hess & Petrovich, 1991). Much of this work has involved other species, with theorizing regarding human development based largely on the views of John Bowlby, discussed in Chapter 2 (Ainsworth & Bowlby, 1991; Bretherton, 1992).

Human infants, in contrast to the young of many other species, are relatively helpless at birth and for years remain unable to survive on their own. If babies are not fed, sheltered, and protected, they will certainly die. And because humans produce comparatively few offspring (whereas fish, for example, lay thousands of eggs), our species would quickly become extinct unless a high percentage of babies survive long enough to reproduce.

Ethologists believe that the process of natural selection has provided infants and mothers with innate behaviors designed to ensure the infant's survival (Bowlby, 1969, 1980; Moltz & Rosenblum, 1983). Sociobiologists, you may recall, describe this process a little differently, arguing that evolutionary mechanisms see to it that the species' genes are passed on; the child just happens to be carrying them. By either account, evolution is assumed to have provided a number of built-in responses for the task at hand.

The infant has been evolutionarily programmed to do two sorts of things: keep the **primary caregiver** (usually the mother) nearby and motivate her to provide adequate caregiving. The child keeps the mother in close range by two principal means. For the first 6 or 7 months, the baby can remain close to the mother only by drawing her near. Crying is by far the most effective behavior for doing this. Later, as locomotor abilities develop, the child can stay near the mother by crawling or running after her. The infant promotes caregiving behaviors in several ways. One is by making interactions very pleasant for the mother, such as by smiling, vocalizing, and making eye contact with her. Some ethologists believe that the physical appearance of babies—such as their large heads, round faces, and chubby legs—may also serve to maintain the mother's interactions, because she innately finds it "cute" (Alley, 1983; Fullard & Reiling, 1976; Hildebrandt & Fitzgerald, 1979). Correct caregiving is also encouraged when babies reduce signs of distress in response to the mother's attention, such as when they stop fussing upon being picked up.

Primary caregiver
The person, usually the mother, with whom the infant develops the major attachment relationship.

• According to ethologists, aspects of babies' physical appearance may be innately "cute" and so elicit caregiving.

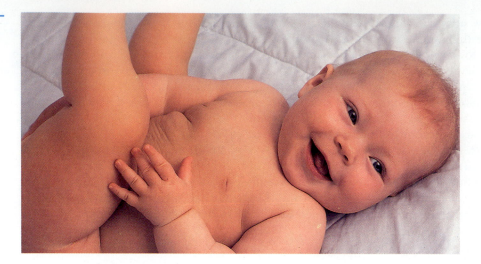

The caregiver, too, presumably has built-in mechanisms for doing what is necessary for the infant's survival. Her job is to "read" the infant's signals and to decide what is wrong, what she should do, and when it is effective. Innate caregiving patterns are obvious in other mammals, where mothers of even first litters appear to know exactly how to care for the young. As we saw in Chapter 2, ethologists characterize these more complex sequences of innate behaviors as modal action patterns and assume they are triggered by stimuli in the environment (such as the sound or smell of the newborn pups). It is not easy to determine what portion of the caregiving provided by human mothers is innate, however, because new mothers in our culture typically acquire much of this information through reading or conversations with others.

In addition to providing mothers and infants with an inborn collection of survival responses during early infancy, evolution also encourages the development of a strong emotional attachment between caregiver and baby across the early months of life and beyond (Ainsworth, 1983, 1989; Hinde & Stevenson-Hinde, 1990). The baby, at first, emits care-seeking behaviors to virtually anyone. But if the mother responds to these bids in a sensitive and consistent way (and sometimes even when she is not so sensitive), the baby gradually focuses them on her, and she becomes the primary caregiver. Bowlby and others of this tradition believe further that the attachment process in humans occurs during a sensitive period in the baby's development, as is the case for the imprinting process that produces attachment in some other species (Scott, 1987).

Environmental/Learning Approaches

Socialization
The process through which society molds the child's beliefs, expectations, and behavior.

Environmentally oriented theorists do not deny that infants and mothers possess many built-in responses that may contribute to early caregiving and the attachment process. But the main concern of these theorists is with the infant's **socialization**—the process by which a child's behavior is molded to fit with the society's roles, beliefs, and expectations (Maccoby, 1992; Maccoby & Martin, 1983). Socialization is assumed to continue throughout childhood, and it later on affects many of the child's more complex social behaviors, such as moral development and interactions with peers. The process, however, begins in infancy and can be observed in the way the baby's first social interactions are influenced by others.

According to the environmental/learning view, caregiver–infant social behaviors result from interaction between the two individuals, with each influencing the behavior of the other. Rather than appealing to special evolutionary mechanisms unique to this area, however, psychologists of this tradition assume that these interactions can be explained by social-learning processes, including reinforcement, punishment, and observational learning (Gewirtz & Pelaez-Nogueras, 1992a; Hay et al., 1985). For example, this approach contends that the reason infants produce behaviors that encourage the mother to approach and remain close (crying, smiling, vocalizing, and so on) is that these behaviors result in either positive reinforcement (milk, a rattle, or being rocked) or negative reinforcement (the removal of a wet diaper). Similarly, the mother learns to respond to these behaviors because they also result in either negative reinforcement (the baby stops crying) or positive reinforcement (the baby smiles, coos, and clings).

Much of the evidence supporting the social-learning model has come from studies showing that infant social behaviors can be influenced by reinforcement processes. Infant vocalizations, for example, will increase if reinforced and decrease if subjected to an extinction procedure (Poulson & Nunes, 1988). The same is true for infant smiling (Etzel & Gewirtz, 1967; Zelazo, 1971). Likewise, certain behaviors common in infants, such as separation protest and social referencing (both of which we will discuss later in the chapter), can be produced through conditioning processes (Gewirtz & Pelaez-Nogueras, 1991a, 1992b). And similar experiments have demonstrated that infant behaviors can serve to increase (reinforce) or decrease (punish) the social behavior of the caregiver (Gewirtz & Boyd, 1976, 1977). Taken together, these studies show that it is theoretically possible to explain changes in caregiver–infant interaction by applying social-learning principles. But exactly how important such principles are in the development of the typical infant–caregiver relationship remains an unresolved question (Hay, 1986; Schaffer, 1986).

Cognitive-Developmental Models

The third major tradition contends that in order to understand children's early social development we should search for the cognitive processes that underlie social behaviors. This approach is based on the concept of social cognition (Brownell, 1986a; Thompson, 1986)—which, as noted in Chapter 2, refers to children's and adults' understanding of human behavior and social interactions.

As applied to attachment, the cognitive tradition overlaps somewhat with the ethological approach in that both are concerned with how infants and mothers cognitively *represent* their relationships with each other (Main, Kaplan, & Cassidy, 1985). Some theorists believe that infants and caregivers develop **internal working models** of each other and use these models to interpret events and to predict what will happen (Bowlby, 1969; Bretherton, 1987, 1990, 1993; Pipp, 1990). For example, an infant may develop expectations regarding the mother's behavior as a result of the type of treatment she provides. If she responds quickly and reliably to the infant's signals of distress or care seeking, the baby may develop the expectation that the mother will be available if needed and so will be less likely to cry when left alone (Lamb, Ketterlinus, & Fracasso, 1992). Likewise, the caregiver may develop an internal working model of the infant that leads her to expect the baby will be eager to interact with her. As a result, she may become more likely to play with the infant (Crowell & Feldman, 1991; George & Solomon, 1989).

Psychologists working within the Vygotskian tradition have been less concerned with the attachment process and more with how infants acquire new social (and cognitive) skills through shared activities with adults and older peers (Rogoff, 1990, 1991). Using an "apprenticeship" model and a process of *guided participation*, the baby and caregiver jointly engage in an activity, with the adult at first directing the

Internal working model
An infant's and a caregiver's cognitive conception of each other, which they use to form expectations and predictions.

learning experience and then gradually transferring control and responsibility to the child. As we said in Chapter 2, Vygotsky believed that infants acquire tools to help them develop. Among these tools are the other people in the child's social world. Beginning at about age 1, infants increasingly attempt to manipulate adults to help them achieve their goals, using techniques such as facial expressions, vocalizations, and various forms of gestures (Rogoff et al., 1992).

An important aspect of the Vygotskian model of early social development is that it puts less emphasis on the mother–infant relationship and recognizes that in many cultures the baby learns a great deal through interactions with others. Across cultures, there is considerable variation in how parents and other adults interact with babies, in who is responsible for child care, and in the kinds of opportunities babies have for interacting with other members of the community (Whiting & Edwards, 1988). In some cultures, for example, children spend a great deal of time with members of their extended family, whereas in others much of the child care is the responsibility of the entire community, including older children. These relationships, too, are assumed to play an important role in the child's early socialization (Rogoff et al., 1991).

Cognitive models of early social development appear to be gaining in popularity (Bretherton, 1991, 1993; Thompson, 1993). This is due largely to the increasing interest in children's social cognition, as psychologists continue to tear down the artificial wall that has traditionally separated research in social and cognitive development.

✔ To Recap...

Early social development differs from later social interactions in that infants have fewer social relationships, these relationships often have long-term significance, and infants form them very easily. The transactional nature of social interactions has made social development a challenge to researchers.

Ethologists contend that evolution has provided many of the responses necessary for the infant's survival. Babies are programmed to produce behaviors that keep the mother close at hand and encourage her to provide appropriate caregiving. The mother, in turn, is biologically prepared to read and respond to the infant's signals. Infant–mother attachment results from these innate behaviors.

Social-learning theorists favor a less biological explanation. They assume that mother-infant attachment responses result from a combination of negative and positive reinforcement processes, with the infant and caregiver each providing consequences for the other's behavior.

Cognitive explanations of early social development consider cognitive development the foundation on which social development is built. Some psychologists contend that children's social behavior reflects their social cognition and that babies and mothers develop expectations, or internal working models, regarding each other's behavior. Vygotskian theorists contend that, through a process of guided participation, parents and others assist infants in acquiring social skills and knowledge.

MUTUAL REGULATION BETWEEN INFANTS AND CAREGIVERS

The attachment process that becomes so evident by the end of the baby's 1st year has roots that extend back to early infancy (Malatesta et al., 1989). Right from birth, mothers and newborns begin to interact in ways that will draw them into a close emotional relationship. A most important feature of these early interactions is that each individual both influences the other's behavior and adjusts to it, producing a smooth-running system of mutual regulation (Bornstein & Tamis-LeMonda, 1990; Tronick, 1989).

The key to the development of this two-way system is effective communication between the infant and the caregiver. Chapter 11 described how babies use gestures and babbling to send messages even before they can speak. But the baby's ability to convey wants and needs, and to mobilize the caregiver into action, begins even earlier.

Crying

By far the most important form of communication in the newborn is crying (Lester, Newman, & Pedersen, in press). Not only is it one of the baby's strongest and clearest responses, but it is one to which caregivers appear to be especially responsive (Demos, 1986; Thompson & Leger, 1994). Crying is part of the infant's larger affective communication system, which we discuss next. But because it has generated so much research on its own, we consider crying here separately.

Darwin believed that crying in newborns evolved as a means of providing the mother with information about the baby's state or condition (Darwin, 1872). Ethologists today continue to assume that crying serves as a stimulus to trigger innate caregiving behaviors by the mother (Eibl-Eibesfeldt, 1989).

Learning theorists, however, point out that crying (like sucking and some other early reflexlike behaviors) soon comes under the baby's voluntary control. When this occurs, crying becomes modifiable by its consequences—that is, it can be conditioned. If a baby's crying results in his caregiver's presence (as it often does), he may learn to use this response purposefully, as a way of summoning her care (Gewirtz, 1991).

For crying to serve as a form of communication, two conditions are necessary. One is that different types of cries should communicate different messages. This is indeed the case, with babies having separate cries for pain, hunger, and fear (Wasz-Hockert, Michelsson, & Lind, 1985). In addition, variations in cries can convey other information. For example, as the pitch of crying increases, adult listeners tend to perceive the baby's problem as becoming more serious and urgent (Thompson & Leger, 1994; Zeskind & Marshall, 1988).

The other condition necessary for crying to be communicative is that listeners must be able to discriminate one type from another. Caregivers must understand whether the baby is saying, for example, "I'm hungry," "I'm wet," or "I'm frightened." Here, too, a number of studies have reported that adult listeners can be quite good at intepreting babies' cries. This ability is based, in part, on experience. In general, parents and other adults who have spent time around newborns are better at decoding infant crying than are adults with little experience (Green, Jones, & Gustafson, 1987; Gustafson & Harris, 1990). And mothers of 4-month-olds are better skilled in this area than mothers of 1-month-olds (Freeburg & Lippman, 1986).

The communication role of crying thus has elements of both nature and nurture. At first, crying is innately elicited by various internal stimuli (such as hunger) and external stimuli (such as a diaper pin). Such crying serves primarily to draw the mother near. With experience, however, the caregiver becomes more accurate at reading the information in these signals, and babies learn to use the crying response as a means of controlling the mother's attention and care.

Emotions and the Affective System

The research on crying indicates that many of the early messages sent by babies involve "dislikes." Newborns also can communicate "likes," using behaviors such as

Emotion
An internal reaction or feeling, which may be either positive (such as joy) or negative (such as anger).

Affect
The outward expression of emotions through facial expressions, gestures, intonation, and the like.

smiling, vocalizing, and gazing at an object they find interesting (Brazelton, 1982). These aversions and preferences are the internal reactions, or feelings, we call **emotions**. On seeing his mother, for example, an infant might experience joy, which might be followed by anger as she prepares to leave, sadness when she is gone, and fear when he hears an unfamiliar sound.

The outward expression of emotions is called **affect**. Many theorists believe that initially there exists a close correspondence between what babies feel and what they express. That is, early on, affect accurately reveals emotion (Malatesta et al., 1989). It is now widely believed that the infant's ability to display and recognize different affective states is the principal basis for mutual regulation between babies and their mothers (Adamson & Bakeman, 1991; Fogel & Thelen, 1987).

Development and Expression of Emotions

Although affective responses can take a number of forms, such as gestures and vocalizations, much of our understanding of babies' early emotional development has come about through the study of facial expressions (Malatesta, Izard, & Camras, 1991). Even newborns possess all of the facial muscle movements necessary to produce virtually any adult emotional expression. However, facial expressions of the basic emotions first appear at different points in development (Camras, Malatesta, & Izard, 1991; Ekman, 1993).

From birth, babies can indicate interest by staring attentively. As we saw in Chapter 7, one stimulus that reliably elicits this expression is the human face, illustrating how evolution encourages infant–mother social interaction right from the beginning. Another inborn facial expression is disgust, which is elicited by unpleasant tastes or odors, usually signaling to the caregiver that feeding is not going the way it should (Rosenstein & Oster, 1988; Steiner, 1979).

By 3 or 4 weeks of age, smiling (reflecting pleasure) appears in response to the human voice or a moving face. Some smiles may be seen before this age, but those occur spontaneously during sleep and are apparently not related to external stimulation (Emde, Gaensbauer, & Harmon, 1976). Sadness and anger—demonstrated experimentally by removal of a teething toy or restraint of the baby's arm—are first evident in facial expressions at 3 or 4 months (Lewis, Alessandri, & Sullivan, 1990; Stenberg, Campos, & Emde, 1983). Facial expressions indicating fear do not appear until about 7 months, and more complex affective responses, like those for shyness and shame, are not apparent until near the end of the baby's 1st year.

The emergence of these emotions is probably guided primarily by biological processes and thus is universal across cultures. Consistent with this possibility, one study has reported that the same progression of facial expressions is found in Japanese and American infants (Camras et al., 1992).

Since infants' expressions are assumed to reflect their emotions, they can be used to infer how a baby is feeling about a situation. For example, researchers taught babies to pull a string tied to one arm to produce a pleasant visual and auditory stimulus. The babies displayed expressions of joy during the learning process but expressions of anger when the pulling no longer produced a reward (Lewis, Alessandri, & Sullivan, 1990; Sullivan, Lewis, & Alessandri, 1992). Thus, the infants appeared to experience the two situations in much the same way adults would. Nevertheless, researchers cannot rule out the possibility that babies' affective responses are not identical to those of adults and that they instead have additional facial expressions for, say, joy or anger that we simply do not recognize as such (Oster, Hegley, & Nagel, 1992). Obviously, we have much more to learn in this area.

Socialization of Emotions

Emotional responses do not emerge simply as a result of a biological timetable. Their development is influenced, in part, by the social environment (Camras et al., 1990; Lewis & Saarni, 1985).

Some of this influence is thought to occur through modeling. Most mothers, for example, display only a few facial expressions to their babies, most of which are positive (Malatesta, 1985). Their babies, in turn, tend to match these expressions (Haviland & Lelwica, 1987). In contrast, infants of depressed mothers display more sad expressions, probably in part because they are imitating the expressions they are seeing (Pickens & Field, 1993).

Whether or not the result of modeling, smiling in 10-month-olds clearly is influenced by social factors and not simply controlled by the emotion the baby is experiencing. One study found that babies this age who were playing with (and smiling at) attractive toys smiled much more when they looked up and found their mothers were looking at them than when they found she was looking away. These findings suggest that the babies' smiles indeed reflect their positive emotions but also serve as a form of communication with the mother (Jones, Collins, & Hong, 1991).

Socialization of emotions also occurs through reinforcement processes. Mothers more often respond positively to infants' expressions of pleasure than to their displays of distress (Keller & Scholmerich, 1987; Malatesta, 1985). This process, perhaps in combination with the modeling just described, may contribute to the fact that, over the course of the first year, infants' positive emotional signals typically increase, while their negative responses decrease (Malatesta et al., 1986; Malatesta et al., 1989).

Older infants generally learn to identify and label their emotions through everyday experiences. For example, parents frequently point out how a child is feeling ("You seem to be angry with Mommy" or "That baby must be feeling upset about dropping her ice cream cone") (Dunn, Bretherton, & Munn, 1987; Smiley & Huttenlocher, 1989).

At first, babies' affective expressions closely mirror their emotions, but with time children learn to control their affective displays, so that what they express may not necessarily reflect what they are feeling (Saarni, 1989, 1990). Such attempts to conceal emotions often result from children's increased understanding of their culture's emotional **display rules**—the expectations or attitudes regarding the expression of affect (Malatesta & Haviland, 1982; Underwood, Coie, & Herbsman, 1992). For example, boys may learn that displaying fear or pain is not seen as appropriate for them, and so they will often try to inhibit such expressions of emotion.

Display rules
The expectations and attitudes a society holds toward the expression of affect.

Recognizing Emotions

Just as the baby influences the mother through the display of affective responses, the mother can influence the baby. But before this form of regulation can occur, the baby must be able to recognize and interpret the mother's responses.

An infant's ability to recognize facial expressions of emotion seems to develop in stages (Nelson, C. A., 1985, 1987; Russell, 1989; Walker-Andrews, 1988). Babies younger than 6 weeks are not very good at scanning faces for detail. As a result, they do not recognize different emotional expressions (Field & Walden, 1982). Next, infants begin to show some evidence of discriminating facial expressions of emotions. For example, babies who have been habituated to a photo of a smiling face show renewed attention when the photo is changed to one depicting a frowning face (Barrera & Maurer, 1981). Babies of this age discriminate even better when they view talking faces displaying various emotions—although under these circumstances the voice may also provide important cues (Caron, Caron, & MacLean, 1988; Haviland & Lelwica, 1987). But do babies in this second stage have any real understanding of the emotions that are being expressed? Probably not. It is more likely that they simply can tell that the faces look different, without appreciating that a sad look represents unhappiness or a smiling face, joy. Once infants reach 6 months of age, however, they appear to develop a clearer understanding of the meanings of emotional expressions. This is shown, for example, by the fact that at this age babies begin to display the same emotion as the face they are viewing (smiling at a happy face) and prefer some emotional expressions to others (Campos et al., 1983; Haviland & Lelwica, 1987; Ludemann, 1991; Nelson & Dolgrin, 1985).

Social referencing
Using information gained from other people to regulate one's own behavior.

Near the end of the 1st year, infants begin to use information about other people's emotional expressions to regulate their own behavior, a process called **social referencing** (Feinman, 1992; Klinnert et al., 1983). Babies are especially likely to look to their mothers or fathers for this type of guidance when they are uncertain what to do next, such as when they encounter an unfamiliar object or person. They then use the parent's expression as a guide to how to react in the situation (Feinman et al., 1992; Rosen, Adamson, & Bakeman, 1992). In a study that illustrates this process very clearly, 1-year-old infants and their mothers were studied as they interacted on the visual-cliff apparatus described in Chapter 7. The baby was placed on the shallow side, while the mother and an attractive toy were positioned at the deep end. This situation appeared to produce uncertainty in the infants, who generally responded cautiously and frequently looked up at their mothers as if attempting to gain information as to how to respond. The mothers were trained to produce a number of affective facial expressions, including fear, happiness, anger, interest, and sadness. The question of interest to the researchers was whether the mother's expression would regulate the infant's behavior on the visual cliff. The results indicated that it did. When the mother expressed joy or interest, most babies crossed over to the deeper side to reach her. If she expressed fear or anger, however, very few of them ventured out onto the deep portion of the apparatus. Thus, babies as young as 1 year old appear to be able to use facial expressions as a cue for understanding the environment and adjusting to it (Sorce et al., 1985; Walden & Ogan, 1988).

Mothers have been shown to use the infant's tendency for social referencing to their advantage. In a study examining the emergence of emotions, mothers were asked how they usually responded when an event—such as abruptly encountering an unfamiliar animal or hearing a loud sound—caused their babies to display surprise. Many mothers reported that immediately after babies exhibit surprise, there is a moment when they appear uncertain how to respond next, and then they continue into a state of either joy or distress. If during that brief moment the mother communicates a positive reaction to the infant, perhaps by smiling or speaking in a pleasant voice, the baby's response is more likely to be a pleasant one, and distress is avoided (Klinnert et al., 1984). This study and others suggest that mothers intuitively understand (or perhaps have learned through experience) that their babies look to them when feeling uncertain and that they have some ability to influence the infant's response to the situation (Hornik & Gunnar, 1988).

Face-to-Face Interactions

During the first 3 or 4 months of life, much of the infant's contact with the caregiver involves face-to-face interactions, such as those that occur during feeding, di-

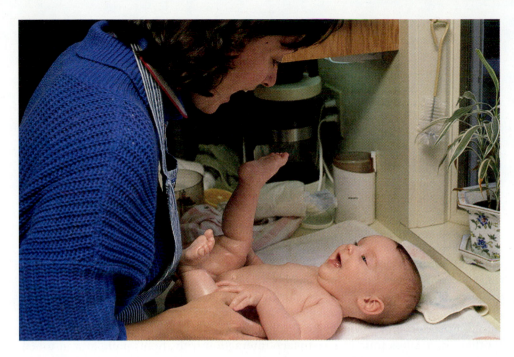

• Face-to-face interactions during the early months appear to play an important role in the development of infant-caregiver attachment.

apering, and many kinds of play. Psychologists have come to attach considerable significance to these early interactions, believing that they are fundamental to the development of an effective communication system between mother and baby and ultimately to the development of a strong attachment relationship (Brazelton & Yogman, 1986; Isabella & Belsky, 1991; Isabella, Belsky, & von Eye, 1989). As a result, a good deal of research has examined these interactions with the aim of understanding exactly what the mother and baby are doing and who is influencing whom (Gable & Isabella, 1992; Symons & Moran, 1987; Tronick & Cohn, 1989).

To understand how these early dyadic interactions develop, researchers have frequently employed a clever laboratory method. The baby and mother sit facing one another, with the mother typically instructed to play with the infant in her normal fashion. As they interact, one camera videotapes the mother's face, and another videotapes the baby's. By replaying the two tapes side by side—sometimes comparing only one frame at a time—investigators can examine the interactions in great detail. This technique, known as **microanalysis**, has helped reveal the subtle ways in which infant and mother influence one another (Kaye, 1982; Lamb, Thompson, & Frodi, 1982).

An important aspect of early interactions involves patterns of behavior in infants. We saw in Chapter 6 that the behavior of newborns is characterized by cycles and rhythms (Cohn & Tronick, 1987; Lester, Hoffman, & Brazelton, 1985). Sleep and feeding are common examples, in that both usually follow quite regular patterns. But newborns also display other behavior cycles that may be important for understanding their social interactions. For example, they appear to cycle from states of attention and interest to states of inattention and avoidance. During the attention phase, they make eye contact with the caregiver and often display positive affect, such as by smiling and vocalizing, whereas during the inattention phase they avoid eye contact and are more likely to show distress. Some psychologists believe that the periods of attention can become too arousing and stressful for the infants and that they keep this stimulation under control by turning away and perhaps by

Microanalysis
A research technique for studying dyadic interactions, in which two individuals are simultaneously videotaped with different cameras, and then the tapes are examined side by side.

self-comforting, such as by putting their thumbs in their mouths (T. M. Field, 1987; Gianino & Tronick, 1988).

These cycles of attention and inattention may be important in establishing a pattern of communication between infant and caregiver. As the mother comes to recognize the baby's cycles, she adjusts her behavior to them. Microanalytic studies of mother–infant interaction during the first 4 months have shown that mothers gradually learn to concentrate their affective displays (talking, tickling, and smiling) during those times when the baby is attending to her. When the baby looks away, the mother's responses decline. Soon the infant and mother develop an **interactional synchrony** in behavior, so that they are both "on" or both "off" at about the same time (Kaye, 1982). In this way, the mother maximizes her opportunities to "teach" the baby, while the baby can regulate the amount of interaction that takes place.

An interesting sidelight involves the problem of child abuse. Although it is not clear why, premature infants have been shown to be at greater risk for being abused than full-term babies. It is possible that this problem results in part from a failure of the infant and caregiver to develop a good communication system. In support of this view, studies have shown that premature babies spend more time asleep, are less alert when awake, are more quickly overaroused by social stimulation, and spend more time averting their gaze from the caregiver. In turn, their mothers spend less time in face-to-face interaction with them, smile at and touch them less, and are less skilled at reading their emotional signals (Kropp & Haynes, 1987; Malatesta et al., 1986). It is important to point out that prematurity does not necessarily prevent the development of a secure attachment relationship (vanIJzendoorn et al., 1992). Nevertheless, the apparent disruption of normal face-to-face affective interaction that results from prematurity may interfere with the establishment of a strong mutual regulation system between mother and baby that, in turn, may increase the likelihood of abuse. We pursue this issue again later in the chapter.

Once a synchronous pattern has developed between mother and baby, a second pattern begins to emerge. The mother waits for the baby to respond, and then she responds back. Sometimes these responses are imitative (the mother produces the same sound that the baby has just made), sometimes they are repetitive (she wiggles the baby's toes after each response), and sometimes they take other forms. But all of them serve to "answer" the infant's responses. As noted in Chapter 11, this *turn-taking* pattern between caregivers and babies may represent the first conversational "dialogues," which later become more obvious as speech and language develop (Beebe et al., 1988; Mayer & Tronick, 1985). Interestingly, this pattern is not exclusive to English-speaking pairs, it has been reported in Japanese mothers and their infants (Masataka, 1993). Babies appear to enjoy turn-taking episodes, often displaying a good deal of smiling and positive vocalizations.

A revealing experimental technique involves having the mother present the baby with no expression at all. The results of this *still-face* procedure have been fairly consistent across a number of studies (Cohn & Tronick, 1983; Ellsworth, Muir, & Hains, 1993; Mayes & Carter, 1990; Toda & Fogel, 1993). Generally, babies at first attempt to engage the mother's attention, sometimes by pointing, vocalizing, or looking at her inquisitively. When the mother fails to respond, the infants usually begin to show signs of distress and protest, and they reduce their overall level of positive affect and often gaze in a different direction. These findings are consistent with the belief that the infant and mother develop an interaction pattern within the first few months that becomes comfortable for both of them. When one member of

Interactional synchrony
The smooth intermeshing of behaviors between mother and baby.

the pair (in this case, the mother) violates that pattern, however, the system is disrupted, and the other member (here, the baby) has difficulty coping with the new interactional style.

More information about interactional patterns comes from studies with mothers who are clinically depressed. These mothers were found to be much less likely to provide positive stimulation to their babies, and they did not synchronize well with the infant's behaviors. The babies, in turn, spent much of their time crying or displaying other forms of distress (Cohn et al., 1990; Field et al., 1990; Pickens & Field, 1993).

Simple face-to-face interaction between the mother and baby peaks at about 3 to 4 months. After that, the baby becomes more interested in objects, and the focus of infant–mother interaction is directed toward other things (Adamson & Bakeman, 1991; Lamb, Morrison, & Malkin, 1987). But the establishment of the reciprocal infant–caregiver relationship appears to lay the groundwork for the attachment bond that will soon emerge.

✔ *To Recap...*

The attachment between mother and infant begins at birth and depends on communication. At first, babies use crying to communicate. But soon other elements of the affective system come into play. The mother and infant regulate each other's behavior through their affective expressions and their recognition of the affective expressions of the other.

Babies begin to express relatively simple emotions facially within the first 2 months, with expression of emotions that require more cognitive sophistication occurring later. Infants also begin to discriminate facial expressions within the first half-year of life. Their understanding of these expressions is not obvious until the second half-year, however, and it is not until the end of the 1st year that they use this understanding to guide their own behavior.

Microanalysis has been used to study face-to-face interactions, the most common interactions of the first 3 or 4 months. These studies reveal that as babies cycle between states of attention and inattention, mothers synchronize their own behavior to match these cycles. Such interactions eventually develop into a turn-taking pattern, which may represent the earliest form of conversation. Experimentally altering the mother's natural behavior toward the child has produced negative reactions in the infant, suggesting that the mother–infant system evolves into a relationship that is comfortable for both of them.

TEMPERAMENT

The child's role in infant–caregiver interactions is greatly influenced by his or her personality. For example, mothers often respond differently to happy, friendly babies who like to cuddle than to fussy, irritable, babies who squirm when held. These different caregiver responses can, in turn, lead to different interaction patterns between mother and baby, once again illustrating the transactional influences that take place during this early period.

For infants, personality does not yet include many components that are evident later on, such as beliefs, attitudes, and values. For this reason, the study of infant personality is generally restricted to emotional expressiveness and responsiveness to environmental stimulation. These components of personality are called **temperament**.

Temperament is meant to describe the baby's behavioral style, reflecting not so much *what* babies do as *how* they do it. For example, two babies may both enjoy rid-

Temperament
The aspect of personality studied in infants; it includes their emotional expressiveness and responsiveness to stimulation.

ing in a mechanical swing. But one may react exuberantly, shrieking with delight, while the other may remain calm and even fall asleep. Most researchers thus view temperament as simply one of the many individual differences, or traits, that make each child unique. Just as babies come in different heights, weights, and body builds, so too do they differ in their overall style of behaving in the world (Bates & Wachs, 1994).

Defining Temperament

Formal definitions of temperament have varied considerably from one investigator to another (Goldsmith et al., 1987). We begin therefore simply by considering three questions that have guided psychologists' attempts to define this concept.

Is Temperament Inherited?

A fundamental question is whether babies inherit their response styles, just as they inherit the shapes of their noses or the color of their hair. Some researchers believe that only those aspects of infants' responsiveness that are clearly genetic in origin should be included in temperament (e.g., Buss & Plomin, 1984, 1986).

As we mentioned in Chapter 4, studies comparing identical, or monozygotic, twins with fraternal, or dizygotic, twins provide strong evidence that at least some portion of temperament is transferred genetically. Identical twins have been found to be more similar to one another than fraternal twins on a variety of behavioral measures and methods, ranging from descriptions by parents of the baby's irritability, to ratings by trained observers of the child's reactions to strangers, to laboratory tests of the infant's fear responses on the visual-cliff apparatus (Emde et al., 1992; Goldsmith & Campos, 1986; Plomin et al., 1993; Saudino & Eaton, 1991; Wilson & Matheny, 1986).

We will see, though, that there is considerable disagreement over which behaviors best represent an infant's temperament, and not all of these behaviors have been shown to have a genetic basis. In addition, even a trait that is inherited can be influenced by the environment (Bates, 1987). We saw in Chapter 6, for example, that a child's height is genetically related to the heights of his or her parents, but also affected by diet, exercise, and illness. Temperamental behaviors may similarly show both genetic and environmental effects.

Is Temperament Stable?

Regardless of the origins of temperament, another theoretical question is whether it remains constant over the years. Does the fearful baby who cries at an unfamiliar face at 6 months also shy away from new people at 20 months and avoid playmates at 42 months? This kind of stability over time and situations has traditionally been viewed by many researchers as an important defining component of responses reflecting temperament.

On this question, research suggests that certain aspects of infants' behavioral style do indeed remain quite stable over time. The most common of these are negative emotionality (such as fear or fussiness), reactions to new situations or people, attention span, and activity level (Campos, Campos, & Barrett, 1989; Fox, 1989; McDevitt, 1986; Pedlow et al., 1993; Robinson et al., 1992; Ruddy, 1993). Not all measures of temperament, however, display this sort of stability.

The question of stability—or the lack of it—has been of interest to both nature and nurture theorists (Hooker et al., 1987). Those who favor a genetic model of temperament argue that when some aspect of a child's response style is found to be stable across years, this stability is most easily explained by the assumption that the trait in question is simply part of the child's genetic structure. Environmentalists, however, contend that such stability could just as easily result from the child's remaining in a fairly constant environment (Bates, 1987; Wachs, 1988). What about traits that are not stable over the years? These would seem to provide evidence for environmental influences. For example, babies who cry a great deal as newborns but then cry very little at 5 months have been shown to have mothers who are more sensitive and responsive than mothers of infants whose crying remains high at both ages, suggesting that the stability or instability of this behavior depends to some extent on the baby's environment (Fish, Stifter, & Belsky, 1991). Nevertheless, theorists who favor the genetic model now argue that even genetically determined, temperamental behaviors need not be stable over time, because some genes turn their influences on and off as the child grows (McCall, 1986; Plomin et al., 1993).

Is Temperament Evident Early in Life?

A third question that has been important in defining temperament is whether the child's response style is apparent from very early on. Here, too, the evidence is inconclusive.

Certain differences among newborns are still observable after several years, according to some reports. Most involve irritability and other forms of negative responding (Plomin et al., 1993; Riese, 1987; Stifter & Fox, 1990; Worobey & Blajda, 1989). Such findings suggest that certain early differences may reflect a stable (and perhaps inborn) behavioral style that is already detectable within only days after birth (Ricciuti & Breitmayer, 1988). Nevertheless, most early differences among newborns disappear. And not all behaviors that are assumed to reflect temperament are evident this early (Bates, 1987).

In short, although many psychologists contend that temperamental behaviors should be genetic, stable, and apparent early, not all agree. And the research evidence, at this point, does not settle the issue. We will see in the sections that follow, however, that the absence of a formal, agreed-upon definition has not prevented researchers from pursuing many investigations of children's temperament.

Types of Temperament

A single definition of temperament would be useful for guiding researchers to the behaviors that best reveal this aspect of personality. But because definitions of temperament have not been consistent from one research team to another, not all investigators have focused on the same behavioral measures (Thompson, 1993). In this section, we examine three current approaches in this area, including both the behavior studied and the methods employed.

NYLS

The oldest and perhaps most widely used classification of temperament was developed in the 1950s by two pediatricians, Alexander Thomas and Stella Chess. Their research project, named the **New York Longitudinal Study (NYLS)**, has continued for over 30 years and represents one of the most important longitudinal efforts in modern child psychology (Thomas & Chess, 1986; Thomas, Chess, & Birch, 1968).

The research began as an effort to predict children's psychological adjustment by identifying potential problems early. The strategy was to develop categories of in-

New York Longitudinal Study (NYLS)
A well-known longitudinal project conducted by Thomas and Chess to study infant temperament and its implications for later psychological adjustment.

fant temperament and then to examine whether these categories relate to the child's social and emotional development at later ages. After extensive interviews with parents of infants, the researchers selected nine behavioral dimensions along which to rate infants' responsiveness. These dimensions are described in Table 12-1. Based on ratings of many infants on these dimensions, Thomas and Chess identified three clusters of characteristics that occurred frequently, leading them to conclude that they had identified three early behavioral styles. They labeled these styles "easy," "difficult," and "slow to warm up."

The easy baby is rhythmic, usually having regular patterns of eating, sleeping, and toileting. He adapts well to changing situations and generally has a positive, happy mood. Easy babies are willing to approach new objects or people, and their reactions (of all types) are typically of low to moderate intensity. About 40% of the babies studied were classified by Thomas and Chess to be of this type.

The difficult baby is just the opposite. She is less predictable in her schedules, is uncomfortable when situations change, and often cries or displays a negative mood. She also withdraws from new experiences and reacts intensely to most environmental stimulation. This pattern was evident in about 10% of the infants.

The slow-to-warm-up baby, too, adapts poorly to changing situations and tends to withdraw from unfamiliar people or objects. He is typically less active, however, and responds at a relatively low intensity. About 15% of the babies were classified as this type.

The remaining 35% of the infants in the project did not fit into any of these three categories. Generally, these babies did not rate high on any of the nine dimensions.

Goodness of fit
A concept describing the relation between a baby's temperament and his or her social and environmental surroundings.

Thomas and Chess (1977) proposed that the infant's temperament influences his or her later development as a result of the **goodness of fit** between the baby's response style and the physical and social surroundings, as we will see in the sections that follow. This notion meshes well with the transactional view of early social development and has become an important concept in temperament research.

Although the NYLS approach remains a widely used method of categorizing infant temperament, it does have its critics. One problem is its heavy reliance on parental report as a means of obtaining information. Although parents' descrip-

TABLE 12-1 ● NYLS Dimensions of Temperament

Activity	The amount of physical and motor activity the infant produces when eating, bathing, and dressing and in other everyday situations
Rhythmicity	The infant's predictability, including feeding schedule, sleep cycle, and elimination habits
Approach/ withdrawal	How positively the infant responds to a new event or stimulus (toy, food, etc.), including mood expression and behavior
Adaptability	The ease with which the infant adjusts to a changed situation
Intensity	The energy level of the infant's responses, both positive and negative
Threshold	The amount of stimulation necessary to provoke a response from the infant
Mood	The number of happy and friendly responses the baby exhibits, in contrast to unhappy and negative behavior
Distractibility	The ease with which the infant's ongoing behavior is disrupted by outside events or stimulation
Attention span and persistence	How long the infant performs an activity and the infant's willingness to continue when faced with obstacles

tions of their babies' behavior have the advantage of reflecting a wide range of situations, this method also is open to biases of several sorts. Some parents are undoubtedly more objective than others, and some are better than others at observing and describing what their children do. Parents also may tend to report the things they assume the researchers would like to hear—presenting, for example, a consistent description of the infant from one interview to the next or portraying the child in a more positive light than is realistic. And parents' descriptions may sometimes reflect their own reactions to the infant's behavior. Some parents, for example, might describe a response style as "stubborn" that other parents would describe as "self-assured" (Bates, 1983; Bates & Bayles, 1984; Matheny, Wilson, & Thoben, 1987).

An alternative to interviews has been the use of questionnaires. Here, parents respond to a series of objective questions about the child's typical behavior and reactions to situations. Several of these instruments have been designed according to the NYLS classification scheme (Carey & McDevitt, 1978; Fullard, McDevitt, & Carey, 1984), although others have been built around different models of temperament (Bates, 1987). Questionnaires offer the advantage of producing quantitative information that can be easily summarized and compared. But they suffer from some of the same potential biases as parent interviews and they involve additional issues, including how well the parents understand the questions, how well they can compare their child with others (as some of the items require), and how they are feeling about the child when they fill out the instrument (Mebert, 1991; Rothbart & Goldsmith, 1985).

EAS Model

Another popular method of classifying infant temperament, which also uses a parent questionnaire, has been developed by a research team headed by Robert Plomin (Buss & Plomin, 1984, 1986). This model is strongly biological in its approach, viewing temperament as inherited personality traits that show an early onset. According to these researchers, a baby's temperament can be measured along three dimensions—emotionality, activity, and sociability. Consequently, this classification is commonly referred to as the **EAS model**.

Emotionality, in this model, refers to how quickly a baby becomes aroused and responds negatively to stimulation from the environment. A baby rating high on this dimension, for example, would be awakened easily by a sudden noise and would cry intensely in reaction. Plomin believes that differences on this dimension represent inherited differences in infants' nervous systems, with some having a quicker "trigger" and automatically experiencing greater arousal than others. During the first few months of life, emotionality reveals itself as general distress reactions (such as crying) in unpleasant situations. Later in the 1st year, emotionality begins to evolve toward either fear or anger responses. Which behavioral style develops, Plomin contends, depends on the infant's experiences.

Activity describes the baby's tempo and energy use. Babies rating high on this dimension are moving all the time, exploring new places, and frequently seeking out vigorous activities. Like most definitions of temperamental traits, this one describes only how the baby behaves and not precisely what the baby likes to do. The researchers use the analogy here of the automobile engine. The activity level presumably determines how fast and how far the infant can go, but the environment determines the direction that the infant will take.

Sociability refers to an infant's preference for being with other people. Babies rating high on this dimension do not like to spend time alone and often initiate

EAS model
Plomin and Buss's theory of temperament, which holds that temperament can be measured along the dimensions of emotionality, activity, and sociability.

contact and interaction with others. This trait is not meant to describe the closeness of a baby's relationship with the caregiver or other significant people, which is assumed to be greatly influenced by the child's experiences. It is simply a measure of how much a given child innately prefers the stimulation derived from people rather than from things, and it is perhaps most clearly assessed in the baby's reactions to unfamiliar people, where the strength of a prior relationship does not come into play.

Although the EAS model views temperament as a biological concept, the researchers are strongly interactionist in their conception of social development. While a baby's levels of emotionality, activity, and sociability may be determined by her genes, the baby's overall social development will depend on how these characteristics interact with characteristics of her social and physical environment.

Rothbart's Model

A third model of temperament has been proposed by Mary Rothbart. This model also has a strong biological flavor, with temperament seen as reflecting inborn differences in infants' physiological functioning. It, too, employs a parent questionnaire to assess an infant's temperament, although this information is supplemented by laboratory measures and by data collected in the home by professional observers (Goldsmith & Rothbart, 1992; Rothbart, 1989). Rothbart views temperament as consisting of individual differences in two areas—reactivity and self-regulation (Rothbart & Derryberry, 1981).

Reactivity is similar to Plomin's dimension of emotionality in that it refers to how easily and intensely a baby responds to stimulation. The major difference is that Rothbart also includes positive arousal, as illustrated by a baby smiling and laughing at a new toy.

The other component of temperament, according to this model, is the baby's ability to increase or reduce this reactivity. This ability, termed *self-regulation*, is assumed to be inborn and to vary from child to child. Control of arousal by infants can take a number of forms, such as how long a baby looks at a stimulating object before turning away or how she approaches and explores it. The specific behaviors used for self-regulation change as the baby gets older, but the underlying temperamental trait presumably continues to govern the infant's success at this task (Rothbart & Posner, 1985).

In a study that illustrates reactivity and self-regulation (LaGasse, Gruber, & Lipsitt, 1989), 2-day-old babies were tested to determine how intensely they sucked on an artificial nipple to obtain sweetened water. Individual babies' reactions to this positive stimulation differed considerably. At 18 months, the intensity of the same babies' reactions to unfamiliar people and situations was examined and found to be positively correlated with their earlier behavior—that is, those who had reacted intensely to the positive stimulation also responded intensely to the aversive stimulation. The researchers interpreted these results as reflecting a stable temperamental trait involving both reactivity and self-regulation. Babies who rated high on this trait were better able both to maximize their exposure to the positive stimulation (by sucking harder) and to minimize their exposure to the aversive stimulation (by withdrawing and hiding). Whether the differences among these babies continue to be stable as they get older, of course, remains to be determined.

Like the other schemes, Rothbart's model holds that inborn traits of temperament interact with the baby's environment to determine the nature and quality of the child's social interactions. Even though the reactivity and self-regulation abilities of babies differ from birth, the child's caregivers and physical surroundings are assumed to play major roles in determining the path that development will take.

Temperament and Social Interactions

It should be clear by now that virtually all researchers who study temperament have an interactional view of its relation to early social development. An infant's social interactions are influenced not only by his or her personality but also by the degree to which these characteristics match the demands or expectations of the environment. For example, if a mother's personality is very methodical, she may have considerable difficulty with a baby whose behavioral style is irregular and unpatterned. As a result, she may frequently attempt to do certain things, such as feeding or putting the baby down for a nap, when the child is not interested, perhaps producing repeated conflict and tension for both of them. That same baby, however, may develop a smoother relationship with a mother whose own behavior is not very structured. A mismatch can similarly occur with the physical environment. A baby who has a high activity level, for example, may have trouble living in a small apartment, and a baby who has a low threshold for distraction may not do well in a noisy neighborhood.

• The match between the baby's temperament and the mother's personality can influence how successfully attachment develops.

The concept of goodness of fit that emerged from the NYLS project has been one way of characterizing the interactional view and has been supported by data from many studies (Lerner, Lerner, & Zabski, 1985; Lerner et al., 1986; Windle & Lerner, 1986). For example, as suggested above, babies who show low rhythmicity would not be expected to fit well in households that are based on structured, predictable schedules. And, in fact, the baby's level of rhythmicity in such households is a good predictor of behavior problems during the first 5 years. In less structured homes, however, this aspect of temperament has little predictive value (Super & Harkness, 1981; Thomas et al., 1974).

The interactional model of temperament and social relationships has implications for the role that infant personality may play in the attachment process. We consider this issue later in the chapter.

Temperament and Behavior Problems

The NYLS project has not been the only research motivated by the search for early predictors of children's psychological adjustment. Other investigators have taken a similar clinical approach to temperament investigations, with most work focusing on two categories of infant personality: the level of difficulty and the level of inhibition.

Difficult Infants

Thomas and Chess reported early in their longitudinal study that babies classifed as "difficult" displayed more behavior problems during early childhood than infants in the other categories (Thomas et al., 1968). This finding has spurred a number of investigations aimed at determining whether this classification scheme might serve as an early screening device for identifying children at risk for later problems.

One question has been whether the difficult response style is stable over time, as many would expect in a true temperamental trait. Although stability has been found for some children identified as difficult, many infants had moved out of this classification when tested several years later (Gibbs, Reeves, & Cunningham, 1987; Korn, 1984; Lee & Bates, 1985). In fact, a follow-up of the longitudinal subjects by Thomas and Chess (1984) indicated that the majority of those displaying temperamental difficulties during early childhood showed no evidence of them by early adulthood.

The most fundamental question regarding this issue, however, is whether assessments of a difficult temperament during infancy correlate with later reports of behavior problems. Some studies have indeed reported such correlations (e.g., Bates, 1987; Bates, Maslin, & Frankel, 1985), but they are open to several interpretations.

The most direct causal explanation is that these temperamental characteristics are symptoms of underlying psychological problems that are present early and remain with the child over the years. There is, at the moment, little scientific evidence to support this interpretation.

A more indirect analysis is that those aspects of the baby's temperament that result in the classification of "difficult," such as frequent crying and irritability, increase the likelihood that parents will respond to the infant in a less-than-optimal manner, leading to problems in the child–caregiver relationship and ultimately to behavior problems in the child. This explanation is related to the goodness-of-fit concept and seems likely to account for some portion of the observed correlation (Bates, 1990; Crockenberg, 1986).

In yet a third explanation, the baby's difficult temperament plays only a minor role in the behavior problems that appear later on, and the correlation lies primarily in the eyes of the beholders (that is, the parents). According to this analysis, the fact that some parents rate their babies as difficult and later report them as having behavior problems results from the parents' attitudes, expectations, or approaches to child-rearing, not from the child's characteristics (Garrison & Earls, 1987; Sanson, Prior & Kyrios, 1990). A number of studies, for example, have found that a baby's temperament during the 1st year—as measured by parent questionnaires—could be accurately predicted by assessment of the mother's personality characteristics and expectations when the child was still in the uterus (e.g., Mebert, 1989, 1991; Vaughn et al., 1987; Zeanah & Anders, 1987)! And a related study found that mothers' perceptions of the temperamental difficulty of their infants were strongly related to their own personal feelings of *self-efficacy*—a concept involving how well someone believes he or she can effectively accomplish a task, which we discuss in the next chapter (Teti & Gelfand, 1991). (A study relating mothers' perceptions to their social class is described in Box 12-1.) In sum, the link between early difficult temperament and later behavior problems remains a subject of some debate.

Finally, having a "difficult" temperament—while perhaps posing certain long-term risks—nevertheless may afford children some ethological advantages. For example, a cross-cultural study of babies during a drought in East Africa found that those classified as difficult were most likely to survive, presumably because they were most demanding of attention and care from their mothers (DeVries & Sameroff, 1984).

Inhibited Infants

Inhibition
Kagan's proposed temperamental response style characterizing infants who react to unfamiliar events and people with timidity and avoidance.

Another personality problem that researchers believe may be linked to temperament involves children who are shy, timid, and fearful, especially when they encounter unfamiliar situations or people. Their typical reaction is to become quiet, to avoid interaction with the strange situation, and to reduce their overall level of activity. This response style corresponds to the NYLS dimension of approach/withdrawal but in more recent work has been referred to as **inhibition** (Asendorpf, 1991, in press; Reznick, 1989). Like the "difficult" temperament, inhibition in infants has been of interest to psychologists in part because it seems to predict later problems in peer interactions (Asendorpf, 1991; Kochanska & Radke-Yarrow, 1992).

The best known research on inhibited children has been conducted by Jerome Kagan and his colleagues. Kagan believes that inhibition may be an inborn temperamental trait that only becomes apparent in certain situations. His research has

WHAT IS "DIFFICULT"? TEMPERAMENT AND SOCIAL CLASS

A fundamental issue for researchers studying "difficult" children is whether this label reflects actual characteristics of the child (as Thomas and Chess believe) and therefore applies in all situations and contexts. Alternatively, this label may simply represent descriptions of the child by parents who hold certain attitudes or expectations regarding what constitutes problem behavior. We have already seen that the NYLS approach—the basis of the "difficult" classification—is not completely objective, because it relies heavily on interviews and subjective ratings by parents. This problem is only partially eliminated by the use of questionnaires, which also can be influenced by parents' prior notions and beliefs.

One factor that researchers have suspected may influence the classification process is social class (Maziade et al., 1984; Sameroff, Seifer, & Elias, 1982). Much of the early research on "difficult" children involved upper-and middle-class families (McDevitt & Carey, 1981). These parents' views on children's behavior and development often differ from those of parents from lower social classes. Such differences in attitude could, in turn, affect parents' ratings of their children on the NYLS measures.

A study in Australia investigated this possibility (Prior et al., 1989). Children from families of both high and low socioeconomic status (SES) were selected for study. Their mothers were asked to describe on rating forms (1) their children's behaviors according to the nine NYLS dimensions, (2) their own child-rearing practices, and (3) how bothered they were by their children's problem behaviors.

Generally, the low-SES mothers described their children in a manner that led them to be classified as "difficult" more often than did the high-SES mothers. Interestingly, the low-SES mothers also reported being less bothered by the "difficult" behaviors. Finally, the two groups reported using different methods of child

rearing. How can these data be interpreted? The researchers offered several possibilities.

One is that the differences in ratings reflect different beliefs regarding children's behavior and how it should be dealt with. Specifically, lower-class mothers were less open to having their children try new experiences, they worried more, and they put more emphasis on early training. This style of child rearing would seem to suggest that the low-SES mothers held lower expectations regarding their children's abilities. Thus, they may have been more likely to view the children as displaying behaviors that would lead to the "difficult" classification. This interpretation is consistent with the finding that the low-SES mothers were less bothered by these behaviors, suggesting again that this is what they would expect of their children.

An alternative explanation is that because the lower-class mothers used different child-rearing practices, they interacted with their children in ways that tended to *produce* "difficult" behaviors. This transactional interpretation would support Thomas and Chess's contention that the "difficult" classification actually reflected characteristics of the child. But it would differ from their view that the "difficult" behaviors were part of the child's inborn constitution, suggesting instead that such behaviors were products of family interactions.

Any way they are interpreted, social-class differences pose problems for the NYLS classification scheme, especially as it relates to the "difficult" category. If this label in fact results either from parents' expectations or from other contextual factors, then the behaviors may not reflect a style of temperament as most researchers have come to view the concept. Current findings regarding "difficult" children should thus be interpreted with caution, perhaps until a more objective method of assessing this category is developed.

involved an impressive longitudinal study designed to determine whether certain behaviors and physiological responses of inhibited children display an early onset and are stable over childhood (Kagan, 1989b; Kagan, Snidman, & Arcus, 1992).

Kagan's approach was to first identify groups of 2-year-olds who were either very inhibited or very uninhibited. He did this by observing how a large group of children reacted in a laboratory setting with unfamiliar people or objects. About 15% of the children responded to the new situations in a very timid manner and were

• Inhibition is a personality style that appears to have a biological basis, but is likely also affected by socialization influences.

thus selected for study. The 15% who responded in the most outgoing and fearless manner were used for comparison. The children were studied again at 5.5 years and at 7.5 years to see whether their early response styles were still apparent, as we would expect if inhibition is a stable trait (Reznick et al., 1986).

Two sorts of measurement were used. The first was a set of behavioral measures, including children's performance on a series of problem-solving tasks with an unfamiliar adult, their interactions with unfamiliar peers, and their social behavior in school. On these measures, about 75% of the children who had been identified as inhibited or uninhibited displayed behaviors consistent with their classification even 6 years later. In addition, most of the inhibited children were found to have developed other fears or anxieties, such as fear of the dark or fear of going away to camp (Kagan et al., 1988).

Suspecting that inhibition might have a biological basis, the researchers also looked at a number of physiological responses in the two groups of children. These included heart rate, pupil dilation, and the release of certain chemicals in the blood during cognitive tests—measures chosen because they are commonly associated with human stress reactions (Fox, 1989; Kagan, Reznick, & Snidman, 1987). The physiological data were reasonably consistent with the behavioral findings. Children identified at age 2 as being inhibited continued to show evidence of greater physiological arousal in new situations as second graders (Kagan, Reznick, & Snidman, 1988). Additional evidence has been reported in recent studies showing that babies who reacted more vigorously to various sorts of arousing stimulation at 4 months of age were more timid and fearful at 14 months than were babies who had displayed smaller reactions to the same stimulation (Kagan & Snidman, 1991; Mullen, Snidman, & Kagan, 1993). Taken together, these studies suggest that some timid children may be displaying a temperamental trait that has been apparent from infancy, that has remained reasonably stable over the years, and that has a biological basis. Recent findings in Sweden by other researchers support these conclusions (Broberg, Lamb, & Hwang, 1990; Kerr et al., 1994).

Even if true, however, these results tell only part of the story. For example, only those children at the extremes of inhibition displayed the sort of stability that is presumed characteristic of a temperamental trait—the rest of the children's levels of inhibition varied considerably over time (Kagan, Reznick, & Gibbons, 1989; Reznick et al., 1989). And even within the extreme groups, some children's inhibition did not remain constant. Finally, shyness and timidity, like a "difficult" temperament, can be caused by a variety of factors, some of which are related to experience and socialization. It has recently been found, for example, that inhibited children are more likely to have depressed mothers than are other children. While this finding could have a genetic basis, the researchers point out other possible causes: depressed mothers may have difficulty getting involved in day-to-day parenting activities or may serve as models of passive, withdrawn, and fearful behavior for their children (Kochanska, 1991).

✔ *To Recap...*

Temperament refers to an infant's overall style of responding. No agreed-upon definition of temperament exists, but many researchers assume it is genetically based, stable, and evident early in life.

Investigators have taken different approaches to temperament research. The NYLS project has been based on a longitudinal study designed to identify the early correlates of later social and emotional problems. Based on parent interviews, this approach has identified three temperament types: the easy baby, the difficult baby, and the slow-to-warm-up baby. It has been criticized, however, for its overreliance on parental reports. Plomin's EAS model has a strong biological orientation. It defines temperament as the baby's emotionality, activity, and sociability. Rothbart contends that temperament reflects the infant's reactivity (emotionality) and self-regulation (ability to control the emotionality).

Temperament is assumed to affect mother–child interactions and attachment through goodness of fit—the degree to which there is a match between the infant's temperamental characteristics and the physical and social environment.

Temperament is also assumed to be involved in children's later behavior problems. Infants classified as difficult have been shown to be at risk for behavior disorders, although the mechanism of this connection remains unclear. Timid children may be displaying an early temperamental trait, inhibition, which is apparent in both their behavioral interactions and their physiological responses to stressful situations.

ATTACHMENT

We come at last to the topic that is most central to this chapter. How do mothers and babies develop the intense emotional relationship that characterizes infancy and early childhood? We have seen that this process appears to be a continuous one, beginning with the earliest mother–infant interactions. In particular, the development of the affective system—which is at the heart of infant–caregiver joint regulation—is important in setting the stage for the social relationship that is about to form. The baby's temperament undoubtedly plays a role in this process as well, although this role tends to be most obvious when it is a source of problems.

Developmental Course of Attachment

The infant's attachment to the caregiver can first be clearly observed at 6 to 8 months of age. However, the actual process begins shortly after birth and continues well beyond this time. Here we describe three general stages of attachment development that roughly correspond to those proposed in several theoretical models of this process (Bowlby, 1969; Schaffer & Emerson, 1964).

Phase 1 (birth–2 months): Indiscriminate Social Responsiveness

At first, babies do not focus their attention exclusively on their mothers and will at times respond positively to anyone. Nevertheless, they do behave in ways that set the stage for the development of an attachment relationship with the caregiver. As we have seen, infants come into the world with a number of built-in responses designed to draw the mother near (such as crying) and to keep her close at hand (quieting and smiling, for example). And while babies in this stage may not reserve their sociability solely for the caregiver, they clearly can recognize her. Experiments have shown that newborns, in fact, prefer to look at their mothers (or at photographs of her) rather than at a stranger within only a few days after birth (Bushnell, Sai, & Mullin, 1989; Field et al., 1985; Walton, Bower, & Bower, 1992).

Caregivers, too, very quickly learn to recognize their babies. Within hours after giving birth, for example, mothers can identify their own children solely on the basis of smell (Kaitz et al., 1987) or by touching a hand or cheek (Kaitz et al., 1992, 1993).

Maternal bonding
The mother's emotional attachment to the child, which appears shortly after birth and which some theorists believe develops through early contact during a sensitive period.

An important difference, however, is that while the baby displays attachment only after some months have passed, the mother's emotional bond to the baby develops very quickly. It was once believed that **maternal bonding** occurs during a sensitive period immediately following birth and requires skin-to-skin contact with the baby (Klaus & Kennell, 1976; Kontos, 1978). Based on this view, many hospitals made it easier for mothers to spend more time with their newborns during the presumably crucial first hours and days of life. Research indicates, however, that although such early contact may be important for some mothers under some circumstances, it certainly does not appear *necessary* for a strong maternal bond (Eyer, 1992; Lamb & Hwang, 1982; Goldberg, 1983; Myers, 1987; Svejda, Pannabecker, & Emde, 1982). Mothers and babies separated during the first days after birth by illness are just as likely to develop strong attachment relationships (Rode et al., 1981). This also holds true for mothers and their adopted babies (Singer et al., 1985).

Phase 2 (2–7 months): Discriminate Social Responsiveness

During the second stage, infants become more interested in the caregiver and other familiar people and direct their social responses to them. While strangers continue to be accepted, they now assume a second-class status.

As we saw earlier, across this period the infant and caregiver develop interactional patterns that permit them to communicate and that establish a unique relationship between them. The child develops a cognitive representation, or *internal working model*, of the caregiver based on how reliable and trustworthy she is perceived to be (Bretherton, 1993). The baby also looks to the mother, when anxious or uncertain, for information regarding how he should feel—the social-referencing process described earlier—and the mother uses this communication system, in turn, to exert some control over the child (Ainsworth, 1992).

Also of importance for the attachment process, babies now begin to develop a sense of "self" and to understand that they are separate from the rest of the world and that they can do things to affect it. We discuss these processes in detail in the chapter that follows.

Phase 3 (8–24 months): Focused Attachment

The attachment bond becomes clearest in the 3rd quarter of the 1st year and remains very strong until about age 2. The appearance of attachment behaviors is very much tied to development in two other areas. One of these is emotional. Somewhere around this time, fear begins to emerge as a dominant emotion. With improvements in memory and other cognitive functions, babies begin to recognize what is strange or unfamiliar, and they generally react to such experiences negatively (Thompson & Limber, 1990). **Wariness of strangers** becomes common, often causing the baby to cry and retreat to the mother (Waters, Matas, & Sroufe, 1975). Being apart from the caregiver produces **separation protest**, which also involves crying and sometimes searching after the mother. One of the clearest indications of attachment is that being close to the caregiver markedly reduces the infant's distress. The trembling, frightened baby is usually soothed simply by achieving contact with the mother. Once this has occurred, the infant may become bold enough to venture out and explore the surrounding area, treating the mother as a secure base to which she can return if new fears arise.

The other related development is physical. At about 6 to 8 months, most babies begin to crawl. This ability, as we saw in Chapter 6, gives infants their first opportunity to have considerable control over where they are. It is crucial in the attachment process, because a baby no longer needs to rely on crying or related behaviors to gain proximity to his mother. The baby need only crawl to her and follow her around.

This pattern of infant behavior—fear of strangers and protest when separated from the caregiver, along with security and boldness when near her—marks the appearance of full-blown infant–caregiver attachment. But exactly how this pattern develops and what significance it has for the child remain issues of continuing research and debate (Sroufe, 1988; Thompson & Limber, 1990).

Assessing Attachment

One method of assessing the strength and quality of the attachment relationship, the **Strange Situation procedure**, has been widely used and is generally accepted as the best available. Although this technique has been criticized, no significant alternative has replaced it. As a result, almost all of the recent work in this area has been based on variations of the same assessment classification, making comparisons among these studies much easier.

The Strange Situation procedure was first described in 1969 by Mary Ainsworth as part of a longitudinal study of the attachment process (Ainsworth & Wittig, 1969). It is conducted in the laboratory, typically when the infant is about 12 months of age, and is based on the belief that attachment can best be observed when the child is studied in an unfamiliar, stress-producing situation (Spangler & Grossmann, 1993).

The method consists of eight episodes, summarized in Table 12-2. Episode 1 simply involves introducing the caregiver and baby to the laboratory room, which contains several chairs and an array of toys and is designed to encourage exploration by the infant. Observers are positioned behind one-way windows, where the behaviors of the infant can be observed and videotaped for later scoring. The next two episodes provide preseparation experiences for the baby. In episode 2, the caregiver and infant are alone, and the observers note the baby's willingness to explore the new toys and situation. In episode 3, a stranger joins them and, after one minute of silence, begins a conversation with the caregiver and also attempts to en-

Wariness of strangers
A general fear of unfamiliar people that appears in many infants at around 8 months of age and indicates the formation of the attachment bond.

Separation protest
Crying and searching by infants separated from their mothers; an indication of the formation of the attachment bond.

• One clear sign that attachment has developed is the infant's reluctance to separate from her caregiver.

Strange Situation procedure
Ainsworth's laboratory procedure for assessing the strength of the attachment relationship by observing the infant's reactions to a series of structured episodes involving the mother and a stranger.

TABLE 12-2 ● Strange Situation Procedure

Episode Number	Persons Present	Duration	Brief Description of Action
1	Mother, baby, and observer	30 sec.	Observer introduces mother and baby to experimental room, then leaves.
2	Mother and baby	3 min.	Mother is nonparticipant while baby explores. If necessary, play is stimulated after 2 min.
3	Stranger, mother, and baby	3 min.	Stranger enters. Min. 1: stranger silent. Min. 2: stranger converses with mother. Min. 3: stranger approaches baby. After 3 min., mother leaves unobtrusively.
4	Stranger and baby	3 min. or less[a]	First separation episode. Stranger's behavior is geared to that of baby.
5	Mother and baby	3 min. or more[b]	First reunion episode. Mother greets and comforts baby, then tries to settle him again in play. Mother then leaves, saying bye-bye.
6	Baby alone	3 min. or less[a]	Second separation episode.
7	Stranger and baby	3 min. or less[a]	Continuation of second separation. Stranger enters and gears her behavior to that of baby.
8	Mother and baby	3 min.	Second reunion episode. Mother enters, greets baby, then picks him up. Meanwhile, stranger leaves unobtrusively.

[a] Episode is curtailed if the baby is unduly distressed.
[b] Episode is prolonged if more time is required for the baby to become reinvolved in play.

gage the baby in play. Episode 4 represents the first separation, in which the caregiver leaves the child alone with the stranger. This episode may last for 3 minutes but is cut short if the baby shows too much distress. Episode 5 involves the return of the caregiver and the departure of the stranger. How the infant reacts to the reunion with the caregiver generally provides some of the most useful information to the researchers. The caregiver remains with the infant for at least 3 minutes, offering comfort and reassurance, and attempts to get the baby reinvolved with the toys. In episode 6, the second separation takes place. Now the caregiver leaves the baby alone in the room, again for a maximum of 3 minutes, depending on the child's level of distress. The stranger returns in episode 7 and attempts to interact with the baby. Episode 8 is the second reunion, during which the caregiver greets and picks up the baby, while the stranger leaves.

Three patterns of responses have generally been found to describe most infants who have undergone this procedure (Ainsworth, 1983). Infants exhibiting pattern B are considered to be *securely attached* to the caregiver. They feel secure enough to explore freely during the preseparation episodes, but they display distress when the caregiver leaves and respond enthusiastically upon her return. About 65% of babies tested react in this manner. Pattern A babies are described as *anxious–avoidant*. They generally show little distress at separation, and when the caregiver returns, they tend to avoid her. This pattern represents about 25% of infants. Pattern C babies are termed *anxious–resistant*. They give evidence of distress throughout the procedure, but particularly during separation. Reunions with the caregiver produce a mixture of relief at seeing her and anger directed toward her. Only about 10% of infants respond in this way.

It is important to understand that, although the Strange Situation focuses on the infant's behavior, it is designed to assess the quality of the *relationship* between caregiver and baby. Pattern B infants are assumed to have developed a secure, healthy attachment to the caregiver, whereas the relationships developed by pattern A and C infants are assumed to be less than optimal.

The Strange Situation procedure and the three categories of attachment derived from it have been used in scores of studies to investigate the attachment process. Two issues have been of primary concern in this research: What factors produce these different attachment patterns? And what significance do they have for the child's development?

Determinants of Attachment

The first issue involves the origin of patterns of attachment. Several factors have been suggested as determining what kind of attachment relationship develops.

Maternal Responsiveness and Attachment

Many theorists believe that the major influence on the quality of attachment is the mother's responsiveness to the baby. Mothers who are more sensitive to their infants' needs and who adjust their behavior to that of their babies are believed more likely to develop a secure attachment relationship (Ainsworth, 1983; Pederson et al., 1990; Sroufe, 1985).

Examples of such interactions can be seen in a number of everyday situations. One of these involves feeding. Pattern B infants have mothers who are more responsive to their signals—feeding them at a comfortable pace, recognizing when they are done or ready for more, and recognizing their taste or texture preferences (Ainsworth et al., 1978; Egeland & Farber, 1984). Another revealing situation in-

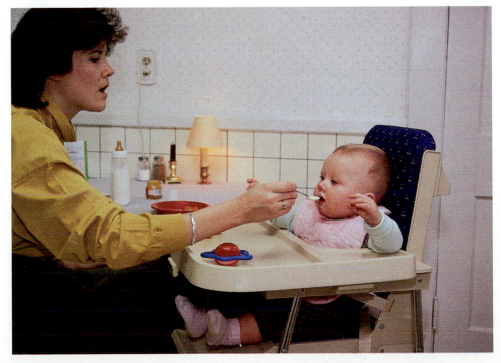

• Secure attachments are most likely to develop when the caregiver is sensitive and responsive to the infant's needs.

volves responsiveness to crying. Mothers of pattern B babies are less likely to ignore their crying, are quicker to respond, and are more effective in comforting the child (Bell & Ainsworth, 1972; Belsky, Rovine, & Taylor, 1984; Del Carmen et al., 1993). A third involves the mother's bodily contact with the infant. When mothers of pattern B babies are holding them, they tend to be more affectionate, playful, and tender toward the children (Ainsworth, 1983; Anisfeld et al., 1990; Tracy & Ainsworth, 1981). Similar results have been found in the face-to-face interactions discussed earlier in the chapter. Here, pattern B infants have caregivers who nicely synchronize their actions to mesh with those of the baby. This practice also serves to lengthen their time together (Isabella & Belsky, 1991; Isabella, Belsky, & von Eye, 1989; Kiser et al., 1986). Finally, overall levels of acceptance, rejection, and sensitivity by mothers across a variety of everyday activities have been shown to predict which of the three attachment classifications their babies will exhibit in the Strange Situation (Isabella, 1993; Rosen & Rothbaum, 1993).

A clever study provides additional support for the importance of the caregiver's sensitivity in the development of a secure attachment relationship. After completing the standard Strange Situation procedure, mothers were asked to stay in the room with their infants to fill out a questionnaire. The toys were removed from the room to make it likely that the child would seek out the mother's attention while she did her work. The researchers unobtrusively observed how the caregivers coped with their babies in this situation and found that mothers of securely attached infants were more sensitive and effective in handling the situation than mothers of pattern A or C infants (Smith & Pederson, 1988).

Still other kinds of evidence link the caregiver's behavior to the quality of the attachment relationship. One is that babies can develop different attachment relationships with different caregivers (e.g., the mother versus the father) (Bridges, Connell, & Belsky, 1988; Goossens & vanIJzendoorn, 1990; Main & Weston, 1981). This should not be surprising if the caregivers are responding differently to the child. Another is that the infant's Strange Situation classification can predict how responsive the mother will be toward an older or younger sibling (Sroufe, 1985). Finally, siblings whose mother responds to them similarly display more similar attachment and social behaviors than siblings whose mother responds to them differently (Ward, Vaughn, & Robb, 1988).

Attachment Across Generations

Given the findings just described, the next question might be why some mothers respond more sensitively to their babies than others. One answer seems to involve the mother's recollections of her own childhood experiences. Using an instrument called the Adult Attachment Interview, researchers have had mothers describe their childhood attachment relationships and have then classified them into three groups (George, Kaplan, & Main, 1985). *Autonomous* mothers present an objective and balanced picture of their childhood, noting both the positive and negative experiences; *dismissing* mothers claim to have difficulty recalling their childhoods and appear to assign little significance to them; and *preoccupied* mothers tend to dwell on their early experiences, often describing them in a confused and highly emotional manner.

Several studies have shown that these classifications are reasonably good predictors of the patterns of attachment these mothers form with their own babies (vanIJzendoorn, 1992). Even more impressively, they can predict both forward and backward. That is, mothers' interviews during pregnancy predict their later attachment to their infants (Fonagy, Steele, & Steele, 1991) and mothers' interviews when their children are age 6 predict their attachments when the children were only 12 months old (Main, Kaplan, & Cassidy, 1985).

It seems clear, then, that the quality of the infant–caregiver relationship results, at least to some degree, from the quality of the infant's care. (A classic study of this issue is described in Box 12-2). But as indicated earlier, attachment in these studies is almost always defined as the infant's reactions in the Strange Situation. Is it possible that other variables may be at work in this testing procedure?

Temperament and Attachment

The alternative suggestion is that the behaviors observed in the Strange Situation result as much from the child's temperament as from the infant–mother relationship (Goldsmith & Alansky, 1987; Kagan, 1984; Lewis & Feiring, 1991; Vaughn et al., 1989). Some findings appear to support this possibility. It seems that babies with more fearful or "difficult" temperaments are likely to show greater distress during separations from their mothers. This greater distress, in turn, affects their reactions during the reunions (Goldsmith & Harman, 1994; Gunnar et al., 1992; Thompson, Connell, & Bridges, 1988; Vaughn et al., 1989). Similar results have been found both with infants who are less sociable, compared with those who prefer to interact with people (Lewis & Feiring, 1989), and with infants who tend to be negative (Del Carmen et al., 1993).

Despite these findings, no study has been able to account for the three patterns of attachment found in the Strange Situation classification solely on the basis of the infant's personality or emotional characteristics (Vaughn et al., 1992). The procedure may well be influenced by *both* the personality characteristics of the child and the quality of the infant–caregiver relationship (Belsky & Isabella, 1988; Calkins & Fox, 1992; Mangelsdorf et al., 1990).

DEVELOPMENT IN CONTEXT: Attachment Across Cultures

Much of the work on attachment has been done in the United States. But increasingly this phenomenon is being studied in other countries and cultures, and it has become obvious that attachment to some degree varies with the cultural context in which it develops (Main, 1990).

Germany represents a Western industrialized culture where we might expect attachment patterns to be similar to those in the United States. This is not exactly the case, however. Researchers have found that fewer infant–caregiver pairs display the secure (Pattern B) attachment relationship than in U.S. samples and that more are classified as pattern A, or anxious–avoidant. This difference does not appear to result from less maternal sensitivity among German mothers. Rather, the investigators speculated that German mothers' emphasis on building independence in their children resulted in the infants appearing less interested in their mothers during reunions (Grossmann & Grossmann, 1990; Grossmann et al., 1985).

The opposite results have been reported in Japanese children, where a higher percentage of pattern C, or anxious–resistant, attachments have been found. But in this culture, mothers rarely leave their babies with others, and so the Strange Situation procedure may prove more stressful for the infants (Miyake, Chen, & Campos, 1985; Takahashi, 1986, 1990).

Yet a different child-rearing situation exists in Israel, where a baby is often cared for with many other infants in a communal kibbutz. Because these infants spend most of their time with a single caregiver, they generally have limited exposure to strangers or unfamiliar settings. Perhaps for this reason, infants in this culture also respond poorly to the Strange Situation procedure, with the majority displaying pattern C attachment (Sagi, 1990; Sagi & Lewkowicz, 1987).

MOTHER LOVE: HARLOW'S STUDIES OF ATTACHMENT

Much of the early work on attachment involved other species. This resulted, in part, from the fact that much of this research was conducted by ethologists—scientists who have traditionally studied behavior in a wide range of animal species. But it also reflects the fact that some questions cannot easily be addressed by studies of human subjects. A classic study that illustrates this point was conducted in the 1950s by Harry Harlow at the University of Wisconsin.

Harlow was interested in determining the role that feeding plays in the attachment process. Many psychologists at that time accepted the learning theory view that a baby's emotional attachment to the mother is based on her role as a powerful reinforcing stimulus. Not only does she provide the infant with stimulation, remove his wet diapers, and comfort him when he is upset, she is, perhaps most importantly, the source of the baby's nourishment. Because food is so fundamental to sustaining life, many researchers assumed that the baby becomes emotionally drawn to the mother as a result of her being associated with it.

In order to test this hypothesis, a researcher would need to experimentally manipulate when, how, and by whom a baby is fed. For ethical reasons, such research cannot be conducted with human babies. Harlow thus approached the issue using what he felt was the best available alternative—baby rhesus monkeys. In addition to feeding, Harlow suspected that the opportunity to cuddle with the mother would also influence the attachment process. So he conducted the following study.

A group of rhesus monkeys were removed from their mothers immediately after birth and raised in a laboratory with two surrogate "mothers" that had been constructed of wood and wire. One of the surrogates was covered with terrycloth, to which the baby monkey could cling; the other surrogate was made only of a wire mesh. For half of the infants, food was made available in a bottle on the cloth mother, while for the other monkeys, the food was attached to the wire mother. To assess the infant's "love" for the mothers, Harlow used two measures. One was the amount of time spent with each surrogate. The other involved the degree to which the mother provided the baby monkey with security in fear-producing situations.

The results were dramatic and surprising. The baby monkeys spent an average of 17 to 18 hours a day on the cloth mother and less than 1 hour a day on the wire mother—regardless of which mother provided

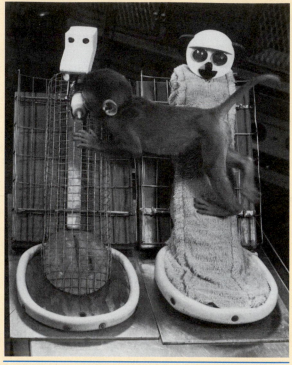

• Harry Harlow found that contact comfort, rather than feeding, was the most important determinant of a rhesus monkey's attachment to its caregiver.

the food. Likewise, when frightened, the monkeys consistently sought out the cloth mother for security; and when only the wire mother was available to them, the infants seemed to find little comfort in its presence (Harlow & Harlow, 1966). Harlow's research thus demonstrated that the most important factor in the development of attachment in rhesus monkeys is not feeding but rather the opportunity to cling and snuggle—a phenomenon he called *contact comfort*.

The relevance of this process to our species remains unclear, partly because we cannot replicate Harlow's procedures by depriving human babies of contact with their caregivers. But this classic research did prompt investigators to begin examining factors other than conditioning and learning principles in their search for the determinants of human attachment. And it also served as a reminder that even widely held ideas regarding the causes of behavior should not be accepted without scientific verification.

Cultural differences need not always mean differences in nationality. Even within the United States, differences in attachment can be found among certain groups. In the African-American culture, for example, child care is commonly shared by multiple family members, rather than left primarily to the mother. As a result, African-American infants often do not seem to find the Strange Situation procedure especially stressful (Jackson, 1993). Similarly, Puerto Rican mothers and Anglo-American mothers tend to differ in how they expect their infants to behave in the Strange Situation. Whereas Anglo mothers stress activity and individualism, Puerto Rican mothers emphasize self-control and respect. As a result, Anglo mothers rated active exploration as the most desirable infant response in the Strange Situation, while Puerto Rican mothers preferred infant behaviors that maintained appropriate public demeanor (such as the absence of crying) and that kept the baby in close contact with her (Harwood, 1992; Harwood & Miller, 1991).

The message from all of these studies is one of caution. Most researchers seem to agree that the Strange Situation remains a valid measure of attachment and that the three classification patterns accurately reflect the quality of the infant–caregiver relationship (Bretherton, 1992). Nevertheless, investigators must be careful not to assume that the values and practices of their own culture are universal and that any deviations from them represent problems or nonoptimal development.

Effects of Attachment on Other Behaviors

The other major issue in attachment research concerns the effects of a secure or insecure attachment on other aspects of the infant's functioning. Many studies have reported that securely attached infants display a variety of other positive characteristics not found in infants whose caregiver relationships are of lower quality.

One of these involves the child's cognitive competence. Several experiments show that securely attached infants later become better problem solvers (Frankel & Bates, 1990; Jacobsen, Edelstein, & Hofmann, 1994; Matas, Arend, & Sroufe, 1978). Pattern B infants also have been reported to be more curious and to do more exploring than other infants (Hazen & Durrett, 1982; Slade, 1987). Finally, one study reported that the cognitive competence of children at 4 years of age can be predicted by their mothers' responsiveness toward them (and presumably the eventual quality of their attachment relationship) at 3 months of age (Lewis, 1993).

Securely attached infants also seem to be more socially competent. For example, they tend to be more cooperative and obedient, and they get along better with their peers (Jacobson & Wille, 1986; Londerville & Main, 1981; Pastor, 1981). In addition, pattern B babies are less likely to develop emotional or behavior problems than are pattern A or C infants (Erickson, Sroufe, & Egeland, 1985; Lewis et al., 1984).

These studies show relatively clearly that the infant's Strange Situation classification can be useful for predicting the child's later cognitive and social competence. Perhaps, as a result of being secure in the caregiver's presence, the infant feels comfortable in exploring the surrounding social and physical environment and thus developing important social and cognitive skills. The details of this process, however, are not yet understood. It remains to be explained, for example, why some infants classified as pattern A or C nevertheless become socially and intellectually competent, while some pattern B babies develop difficulties along these lines. Although these effects may well result from changes in the child's environment, additional research is clearly needed on this issue (Fagot & Kavanagh, 1990; Lamb et al., 1985).

✔ To Recap...

Infant–caregiver attachment develops in three stages. Between birth and 2 months of age, babies respond socially to almost anyone. From ages 2 to 7 months, infants direct social responses principally to familiar people, and they develop a unique affective communication system with the caregiver. Clear-cut attachment becomes evident at 6 to 8 months. At this point the infant is wary of strangers, protests separation, and uses the mother as a source of comfort and a secure base. The appearance of attachment is related to the emergence of two other developmental milestones: the emergence of fear as a major emotion and the ability to crawl.

The most widely used method for assessing attachment is Ainsworth's Strange Situation procedure. This method produces three common patterns of infant response: pattern A, or anxious–avoidant; pattern B, or securely attached; and pattern C, or anxious–resistant. Most babies display pattern B, but the proportion of infants in each classification varies across cultures, apparently reflecting different attitudes toward child rearing.

The quality of the infant–caregiver attachment relationship appears to result primarily from the caregiver's responsiveness. Mothers who are more sensitive to their babies' signals and who adjust their behavior to mesh with that of their children are more likely to develop secure attachment relationships. The mother's recollections of her childhood and the infant's temperament also play a role.

The proportions of attachment classifications have been shown to vary across countries and cultures. These differences probably reflect different attitudes and values regarding child-rearing practices.

Secure attachment to the mother has several positive effects on the child's development. Pattern B babies, for example, display greater cognitive and social competence than babies who are less securely attached.

FAMILY INFLUENCES

Social development, like every other aspect of the child's development, is influenced by the context in which it occurs. During the early years, the most important context is the family. This is where young children spend most of their time, acquire many important social and cognitive skills, and develop—for better or for worse—various attitudes, beliefs, and values.

Recall from Chapter 2 that the family, along with the school, the neighborhood, the church, and so on, is part of Bronfenbrenner's microsystem, the layer of environment that affects the child most directly. But the family itself is a dynamic system, with every member exerting influence on every other member and with the entire system evolving over time (Garbarino & Abramowitz, 1992). The transactional nature of the *family system*, therefore, means that events or changes in any part of it tend to affect everyone—for example, when a new baby comes home, when a child leaves for college, when a disabled grandparent comes to live with the family, when a father loses his job, or when parents get divorced (Minuchin, 1985). Understanding the family's effects on the developing child, therefore, requires that we consider the reciprocal influences, not only between child and parent, but also between siblings, between parents, and so forth (Cowan et al., 1991).

Because the family undoubtedly is the most influential element of the microsystem, it has been studied extensively by developmental researchers (Grotevant, 1989; Parke & Tinsley, 1987). This research has focused on topics ranging from simple parent–child interactions (Maccoby & Martin, 1983), to children's conceptions of the family (Bretherton & Watson, 1990), to the relation of the family to the community and larger society (Goodnow, 1988). In this section, we consider some of the ways in which children's development is influenced in both positive and negative ways by the family context.

The Changing American Family

Adding to the complexity of studying the family system is the fact that the family as an institution has undergone some radical changes in the past several decades. The "traditional" two parent–two child family, idealized in the 1950s, has become increasingly less common as changing values and lifestyles have resulted in a wide range of family types. Today, approximately 50% of children can expect to spend some portion of their childhood living with only one parent, usually the mother. And some of those with two parents may have two mothers or fathers, as gay and lesbian couples are increasingly choosing to have or adopt children (Patterson, 1992). Also, whereas fathers were traditionally the family breadwinners, today about 60% of women with children are employed. In some families, fathers are opting to stay home with the children.

The soaring rate of divorce also means that many remarriages are occurring, often producing blended families that include children from different parents. Today's children can also expect to have older parents, as many mothers are waiting longer to have their first child. And they can expect to have fewer siblings, as many parents are choosing to have fewer children (U.S. Bureau of the Census, 1990).

The impact of these changes on children's development has been of great interest to developmental psychologists, for both theoretical and applied reasons. Much of what psychologists know about child development they have learned by studying children in traditional family contexts. But do these conclusions continue to hold when children are reared in nontraditional contexts? More and more, the answer appears to be no, as researchers repeatedly discover the importance of understanding development in context.

Applied interest in the changing family grows out of the sobering reality that many of today's children are being reared in what are undoubtedly less-than-optimal conditions. Children of single parents, as well as children in two-parent homes whose parents are both employed, frequently become latchkey children, who come

• The transactional nature of the family system means that events like the addition of a new baby can alter the interplay among family members.

home to an empty house and must largely care for themselves (Long & Long, 1983). Hard economic times have resulted in poverty for 14 million children in the United States (Huston, 1991; Houston, McLoyd, & Garcia Coll, 1994). Child abuse is at epidemic levels and appears to be rising (Cicchetti & Carlson, 1989). And drugs, crime, and AIDS have become a part of many children's everyday lives. Clearly, child psychologists must inform policymakers of how such conditions affect children and what interventions will be required to deal with them.

Styles of Parenting

Early social development is very much influenced by parents' child-rearing attitudes and practices. Parents' beliefs regarding the degree to which their behavior determines the child's success in life affects how they approach the task of socializing the child (Goodnow & Collins, 1991; Murphey, 1992). And the child-rearing practices they employ—such as making and enforcing rules, offering support and encouragement, or providing guidance, structure, and predictability in the child's life—can greatly influence the child's development. Approaches to parenting are quite individual and also vary across cultures (Bornstein, 1991; Maccoby, 1992).

Two dimensions of parenting appear to be especially important for the child's development (Maccoby & Martin, 1983). One of these is *parental warmth*—the amount of support, affection, and encouragement the parent provides, as opposed to hostility, shame, or rejection. The other is *parental control*—the degree to which the child is monitored, disciplined, and regulated rather than being left largely unsupervised. The combination of these two dimensions produces four general styles of parenting, which have been found to produce different outcomes in children (Baumrind, 1971, 1989; Dornbusch et al., 1985; MacDonald, 1992).

Parents who are high in both warmth and control are referred to as *authoritative* parents. These parents tend to be caring and sensitive toward their children but set clear limits and maintain a predictable environment. This parenting style clearly has the most positive effects on early social development. Children of these parents generally are the most curious, self-confident, academically successful, and independent. Parents who are low in warmth but high in control are termed *authoritarian* parents. Authoritarian parents are very demanding, exercising strong control over their children's behavior and enforcing their demands with threats and punishment. Most children do not respond well to this approach. Children of authoritarian parents often are easily upset, displaying moodiness, aggression, and conduct problems. Parents who are high in warmth but low in control are called *permissive* parents. These parents are loving and emotionally sensitive but set few limits on behavior. Though they provide acceptance and encouragement to their children, they provide little in the way of structure or predictability. Interestingly, children of these parents in some ways resemble those of authoritarian parents; they are often impulsive, immature, and out of control. Finally, parents who are low on both dimensions are termed *indifferent* parents. These parents set few limits on their children but they also provide little in the way of attention, interest, or emotional support. This detached style of parenting does not foster healthy social development either. Children of indifferent parents tend to be demanding and disobedient and tend not to participate effectively in play and social interactions.

It appears, then, that optimal parenting involves both warmth and control. It is crucial that children feel loved and accepted, but they also must understand the rules of conduct and believe that their parents will require that they be followed.

DEVELOPMENT IN CONTEXT: Maternal Employment, Day Care, and Attachment

One of the most obvious recent societal changes involves the increased number of women working outside the home and leaving some of the job of child rearing to others, such as those who provide care in day-care centers. One topic that has generated a great deal of interest and debate concerns what happens to the mother–infant attachment process under these circumstances. This question is not a minor one, in that over 50% of U.S. mothers place their infants in day care for at least part of the day and the trend toward using day care is increasing (U.S. Bureau of the Census, 1990). As a result, this topic has attracted a great deal of attention from both research psychologists and the general public (Clarke-Stewart, 1989; McCartney, 1990).

A number of studies have found that infants whose mothers are employed are less likely than babies whose mothers stay at home to be classified as securely attached in the Ainsworth Strange Situation procedure (e.g., Barglow, Vaughn, & Molitor, 1987; Belsky, 1988; Belsky & Rovine, 1988; Goossens, 1987; Lamb, Sternberg, & Prodromidis, 1992; Owen & Cox, 1988). And infants whose mothers work full-time are less likely to be securely attached than those working part-time (Clarke-Stewart, 1989). Such evidence appears, at first blush, to suggest that leaving infants with day-care providers may be unadvisable. Not all psychologists, however, agree that a problem exists (Jaeger & Weinraub, 1990; Weinraub & Jaeger, 1990).

One of the main points of contention involves what these findings really mean. As indicated earlier, the Strange Situation has been used almost exclusively to assess the attachment relationship, and there is some disagreement about exactly what it measures. We have also seen that an important requirement of Ainsworth's method is that the infant experience it as somewhat stressful. It is this experience of stress that causes the baby to show anxiety when the mother leaves and to enthusiastically greet her when she returns—reactions that lead to the baby's being classified as securely attached.

The problem with using this method to assess the impact of maternal employment is that infants left frequently in day care may not find the Strange Situation particularly stress-inducing. After all, their mothers routinely leave them with others and then later return to pick them up. Perhaps after babies have gained enough experience with this routine, the Strange Situation does not evoke the level of anxiety necessary for them to display the behaviors that normally indicate secure attachment.

Researchers examining this hypothesis, however, have found that even day-care children often find separations from their mothers in the strange situation to be stressful (Belsky & Braungart, 1991). Nevertheless, the issue may not be fully resolved until an alternative method of measuring the attachment relationship is developed (Lamb & Sternberg, 1990; Weinraub, Jaeger, & Hoffman, 1988).

But suppose that day-care infants are not in fact as strongly attached to their mothers. Not all psychologists believe that this indicates a serious problem. There is evidence, for example, that infants can develop secure attachments to their day-care providers, thus perhaps partially compensating for the typical mother–infant relationship (Goossens & vanIJzendoorn, 1990). Alternatively, or perhaps as a result, day-care infants may be more independent and more confident in dealing with their social environments. Some data, in fact, suggest that among infants who were not classified as securely attached in the Strange Situation, infants whose mothers were employed displayed certain advantages (such as better problem-solving skills and more task persistence) over those whose mothers stayed at home (Clarke-Stewart, 1989; Vaughn, Deane, & Waters, 1985). In addition, among older children, those who have been in day care have been reported in some research to be more sociable, to have better language skills, and to be more skillful in social interactions (McCartney et al., 1982; Ramey, Dorval, & Baker-Ward, 1983; Rubenstein, Howes, & Boyle, 1981). In fact, a longitudinal study in Sweden has found positive social and cognitive effects of entering child care before age 1 on the same children at age 13 (Anderson, 1992).

Another problem with interpreting the effects of day care on attachment involves the mothers themselves. Some mothers are forced to work for economic reasons, whereas others choose to work because their careers are very important to them. Conversely, some mothers who stay home prefer not to work, whereas others would like to work but feel they should remain home to care for the infant. The point here is that whether or not a mother is employed may not be as important as how she feels about her decision (Hock, Morgan, & Hock, 1985). This issue sometimes becomes evident when employment produces **maternal separation anxiety** (Hock, McBride, & Gnezda, 1989; McBride, 1990). For some mothers, being separated from their babies causes a great deal of emotional distress. High levels of anxiety, in turn, often interfere with optimal caregiving. One study found that among employed women, those experiencing the most separation anxiety exhibited an insensitive style of caregiving and had infants who were more likely to be classified as pattern A (Stifter, Coulehan, & Fish, 1993). In these cases, the problem was not the employment itself, but the effect it had on the mother and ultimately on the infant–mother relationship.

Related to all of these findings are issues regarding the day-care setting and staff. The number of children in a classroom, the number of adults supervising them, and the methods of teaching (if any) and discipline all affect the quality of children's day-care experiences (Hennessy et al., 1992; Howes & Hamilton, 1992; Howes, Phillips, & Whitebook, 1992). And these factors may ultimately have as

Maternal separation anxiety Strong negative emotional reactions experienced by some mothers when separated from their children.

• Children who spend time in day care often do not exhibit as strong attachments to their caregivers, but the meaning of this finding is not clear.

much impact on the child's development as whether the child is with or without the mother.

The day-care issue is obviously a complex one that, despite a great deal of study, remains unresolved. What is clear is that unless major governmental or business policy changes can permit mothers to be supported while they stay at home with their newborns, maternal employment will continue to occur in most families (Gamble & Zigler, 1986; Hofferth & Phillips, 1987). The day-care question thus will likely remain a topic of much concern for some time to come.

The Role of Fathers

Most of the research we have discussed has involved mothers. But fathers, too, play a major part in most families and certainly are important figures for young children. This is especially the case today as many fathers are assuming a greater role in child rearing—even in China, as described in Box 12-3 (Bronstein & Cowan, 1988; Hewlett, 1992).

Interestingly, fathers generally spend less time with their children than do mothers, even when both parents are at home (Belsky, Gilstrap, & Rovine, 1984; Lamb, 1981b). This does not mean that fathers do not have the ability to be good caregivers, because the evidence suggests that they do (Belsky et al., 1984; Parke & Tinsley, 1981). But caregiving is not the way fathers typically interact with infants. More often, father–infant interactions involve physical stimulation and play, especially with boys (Lamb, 1981b; Power & Parke, 1983).

Attachment between infants and their fathers has been the subject of much interest. One question has been whether the infant will develop a strong emotional attachment to someone other than the primary caregiver (who is usually the mother). The answer is clearly yes. Infants can become very securely attached to their fathers; fathers, in turn, report similar feelings (Main & Weston, 1981; Palkovitz, 1984).

A second major question has been whether the infant's relationship with the father is necessarily the same as that with the mother. In fact, it appears that an infant's attachment to the father can be quite different (Bridges, Connell, & Belsky, 1988; Fox, Kimmerly, & Schafer, 1991) and that it, too, reflects the father's sensitivity and responsiveness toward the baby (Cox et al., 1992; Easterbrooks & Goldberg, 1984). These findings are important because they offer support for the hypothesis that the security of an infant's attachment to the caregiver depends on the caregiver's responsiveness to the infant. Nevertheless, even when father and baby have a very secure relationship, it is probably not as strong as the baby's relationship with the mother. Studies show that infants, when afraid, are likely to choose contact with the mother over contact with the father (Clarke-Stewart, 1978).

Unfortunately, fathers can also be a source of negative influence on children. Although most of the research examining the effects of parental depression, psychopathology, and maltreatment has involved mothers, the presence of such problems in fathers also can have harmful effects on children's development (Phares, 1992; Phares & Compas, 1992). Finally, fathers appear to play a role in children's development of gender roles. We discuss that issue in Chapter 15.

• Infants also develop attachment relationships with their fathers, although not necessarily of the same type as with their mothers.

The Role of Grandparents

In some families, grandparents play a number of important roles. They can serve as sources of emotional or financial support for the parents and they can, at

THE CHANGING ROLES OF FATHERS IN CHINA

Technology is modernizing the world in dramatic ways. Societies that once were rural are quickly becoming urban. Societies whose economies once were based on farming and fishing are now becoming industrialized. And with these developments have come important changes in the social fabric of these cultures, especially concerning the family (MacFarlane, 1987). Nowhere has this trend been more apparent than in China, where the changing roles of fathers serve to illustrate what is happening in many other cultures around the world (Whyte & Parish, 1984).

The Chinese culture is one of the oldest in the world; for the past 2,000 years or so, its family structure has been rooted in the philosophy of Confucious. This philosophy dictated family roles that were, by Western standards, rigid and traditional. Until recently, the Chinese family was characterized by a strict division of labor between parents. The father was viewed as the major economic provider and absolute head of the household. Children were expected to respect his authority and to obey him without question. His major role was as disciplinarian, and his most important responsibility was to ensure the character development of the child, which included fostering independence, self-sufficiency, and motivation to succeed. In this role, he tended to remain emotionally aloof and to avoid displays of affection. Interestingly, Chinese fathers were also responsible for the child's education. Not only were they expected to instruct the child in many areas, but they also were expected to oversee the child's schooling and eventual entry into the career world. In contrast, the mother's job was to be the nurturant caregiver, who provided children with affection and emotional support and who attended to their daily needs (Ho, 1987).

The rapid industrialization and urbanization of China in the past few decades has produced several trends that are changing this traditional family structure (Jankowiak, 1992). First, many mothers are now entering the work force, leaving some of the child care

to fathers. Thus, fathers' roles have had to extend beyond disciplinarian and educator to include many of the caretaking duties of the mother. In addition, Chinese fathers are becoming involved with their children's education at an earlier age. Also, with many Chinese families now living in small urban apartments, fathers are almost forced into more frequent everyday interactions with their children. Finally, there is a growing attitude in the modern Chinese culture that the father–child relationship should be one of greater warmth and emotionality.

These changes do not mean that Chinese fathers have suddenly become interchangeable with Chinese mothers, who continue to display more patience and affection toward their children. Much of the traditional thinking apparently remains, as illustrated by one anthropologist's recent observations of Chinese mothers and fathers:

> Whenever a child was with both parents, it was assumed and expected that the mother would perform all the necessary caretaking acts, the same acts she performed within the home. This is especially so if the child becomes cranky and starts to cry, a behavior that immediately activates the mother's involvement as it rapidly disengages the father's interest. During the summer [observations] I never saw a father, in a home or in public, holding a crying child in the presence of his wife. (Jankowiak, 1992, p. 353)

Nevertheless, a new breed of fathers in China does appear to be emerging. Unfortunately, with change sometimes come problems. One ironic development is that Chinese school teachers are now complaining that children are too spoiled and indulged by their parents. This trend they attribute largely to modern fathers, who they see as having abandoned their traditional role as strict disciplinarians and who have now become more affectionate and permissive with their children.

times, be mentors, playmates, baby-sitters, or substitute parents for the grandchildren (Cherlin & Furstenberg, 1986; Kornhaber & Woodward, 1985; Tinsley & Parke, 1988). The roles they play and the nature of their relationship with their children and grandchildren appear to depend in part on several factors (Clingempeel et al., 1992).

One of these is the family structure. In families with two parents, grandparents tend to stay more in the background and to have less direct involvement with the grandchildren. When one parent is absent, however, the role of grandparents generally increases and children similarly report an increased closeness to them. This is especially the case for grandfathers. Upon the parent's remarriage, however, grandparents tend to retreat once again to more distant roles.

Grandparents' involvement with their grandchildren also has been found to be related to the children's age and gender. At younger ages, boys and girls generally have equally close relations with their grandparents. But as the children reach puberty, boys tend to become closer to their grandparents, whereas girls become more distant, especially with their grandfathers. One proposed explanation for this difference is that puberty is a time of emotional stress that leads children to distance themselves somewhat from their parents and to seek support elsewhere (Anderson et al., 1989; Steinberg, 1988). Young males will apparently seek out available grandparents to serve this function, whereas young females are more likely to seek support from their girlfriends.

Abusive Parents

Although the family is typically a source of security and protection for the young child, sometimes it can be just the opposite. Child abuse is a tragic reality of some households, and it is a problem that may be growing (Wolfe, 1987).

Abuse and neglect have major developmental consequences for growing children. By 1 year of age, maltreated infants tend to lag in both social and cognitive development (Crittenden, 1988; Lyons-Ruth, Connell, & Zoll, 1989), and these problems typically continue into childhood and adolescence. Many developmental researchers have come to believe that these deficits result from the lack of a secure attachment relationship with the mother. As a result, a great deal of recent research has focused on the attachment process in infants who have been abused or are at risk for abuse (Cicchetti & Carlson, 1989).

Sensitive and responsive caregiving growing out of mutual infant–caregiver regulation, we have seen, is thought to provide the basis for secure attachment. But, as also noted, many abusive mothers fail to develop a smooth and effective communication system with their infants. Although babies will become attached even to mothers whose quality of caregiving is poor, the quality of the attachment relation-

• As boys reach adolescence, they often become closer to their grandfathers.

ship suffers. Perhaps for this reason, the "anxious" attachment patterns occur more frequently among maltreated infants (Aber & Allen, 1987; Carlson et al., 1989b).

Some mothers maltreat their infants in ways that involve physical punishment, active hostility, and intrusiveness into the baby's world. Rather than synchronizing their behavior with that of the child, they often insensitively forge ahead with whatever they are doing (such as feeding a baby before she is hungry), focusing more on their own needs than those of the infant. This caregiving style has been referred to as *overstimulating* and has been linked to physical abuse, such as beating and battering, and to the anxious–avoidant pattern of attachment (pattern A). In contrast, the insensitive care of some mothers takes the form of withdrawal and underinvolvement. This style, termed *understimulation*, has been associated with physical and emotional neglect and appears to be a cause of the anxious–ambivalent pattern of attachment (pattern C) (Belsky et al., 1984; Lyons-Ruth, Connell, & Zoll, 1989).

In addition to Ainsworth's three original patterns, maltreated infants have been found to display several others. For instance, there are babies who, when observed in the Strange Situation, display not only avoidance of their mothers during reunions but also crying, decreased exploration, and resistance to the mothers' overtures for contact. These infants have been characterized as pattern A–C babies (Crittenden, 1985, 1988; Spieker & Booth, 1988). By contrast, some babies cannot be classified into the original three categories because they fail to display any coherent pattern of reactions to the Strange Situation. These infants frequently display elements of each category, sometimes accompanied by bizarre responses like freezing, assuming unusual postures or expressions, and making interrupted or mistimed movements. Such behaviors have led these babies to be classified as "disorganized and disoriented," or pattern D, infants (Main & Solomon, 1986, 1990). Both of these patterns predict problems for the child's development, especially in pattern D infants, who are at risk for developing aggression and antisocial behavior problems (Lyons-Ruth, Alpern, & Repacholi, 1993).

The conclusions that can be drawn from these findings support a transactional model of attachment (Crittenden & Ainsworth, 1989). Evolution has provided that babies will become attached even to caregivers who provide minimal or deviant care. But the interactions between these mothers and their babies clearly affect the quality of the relationship that develops, and this relationship, in turn, affects the child's later social, emotional, and cognitive development (vanIJzendoorn et al., 1992).

✔ To Recap...

The family is the most important context in which early social development occurs. The traditional family has changed dramatically in recent years. Psychologists are interested in these changes as a way of validating previous conclusions regarding human development and also because they involve important societal issues.

One set of findings indicates that children's social behavior is influenced by the parents' style of child rearing. The dimensions of parental warmth and control produce four general styles of parenting. Children of authoritarian, indifferent, or permissive parents often display social and behavioral problems. Authoritative parents produce the most independent and socially competent children.

Infants can develop strong attachment relationships to their fathers, which appear to be based on the father's level of responsiveness. Even secure infant–father attachments, however, are not likely to be as strong as the infant–mother relationship.

Grandparents generally are most involved in children's lives when only a single parent is in the home. At puberty, boys tend to become closer to their grandparents, whereas girls tend to distance themselves.

A fairly new factor in early social development is the current trend for mothers to work outside the home. Some studies have found weaker attachment relationships between mothers and day-care infants, but the meaning and import of these findings are not yet clear.

Child abuse can harm children's cognitive and social development. Infants form attachments to abusive mothers, but the attachment relationships are not secure. Children of mothers who use the overstimulating style of care tend to show the A pattern of attachment, and children of understimulating mothers show the C pattern. Two additional patterns have been noted in abused infants: the A–C pattern and the D, or disoriented and disorganized, pattern.

CONCLUSION

We said at the outset that social development is a complex topic, and by now that message should have emerged quite clearly. It is important to understand the two different sources of this complexity.

The first concerns social interactions themselves. The reciprocal nature of these behaviors makes it difficult to separate the causes of social behaviors from their effects. Even in the infant–mother relationship, as we have seen, social influences can be highly interrelated and subtle. Identifying and disentangling the determinants of further social interactions can be a very challenging task.

The second reason why this topic is so complex is that social development is affected by more than social influences. How the child interacts with other people is the result of biological processes, cognitive abilities, and nonsocial environmental factors—in addition to the influences of the other people. Only recently have psychologists begun to appreciate the extent to which these nonsocial factors are involved in the development of social relationships. This fact will become increasingly evident as we consider the other areas of social development.

In this chapter, we have focused on the attachment phenomenon and its developmental precursors. Other social relationships and processes also occur during infancy, and we consider those in the chapters to follow. In addition, we examine social development beyond the early years as the child grows away from the caregiver and the home to become a member of the larger society.

FOR THOUGHT AND DISCUSSION

1.   The modern study of social development assumes that parent–child interactions are bidirectional and transactional. *Think of some examples of children's behavior (such as exploration) that might previously have been explained one way but now could be interpreted differently.*

2.   Temperamental differences are assumed by many researchers to be stable over time. *How would you characterize your own personality style? Do you think it has been stable since you were a child? Which aspects, if any, have changed?*

3.   A growing number of children spend time in day care. Research has shown that the quality of day care affects children's development. *Should our society ensure that all day-care centers provide high-quality services? If so, who should pay for this? Employers? Federal or state governments?*

4.   The trend to postpone childbearing has resulted in many children having older parents. *What do you see as some advantages and disadvantages for these children? What benefits and problems might result for the parents in being older?*

Chapter 13

DEVELOPMENT OF THE SELF

Existential self
The "I" component of the self, which is concerned with the subjective experience of existing.

Empirical self
The "Me" component of the self, which involves one's objective personal characteristics.

Self-system
The set of interrelated processes—self-knowledge, self-evaluation, and self-regulation—that make up the self.

Self-knowledge (self-awareness)
The part of the self-system concerned with children's knowledge about themselves.

Self-evaluation
The part of the self-system concerned with children's opinions of themselves and their abilities.

Self-regulation
The part of the self-system concerned with self-control.

*W*hat am I really like? How do I feel about myself? Can I exert control over my life? Between infancy and adolescence, as children learn about the world around them, they also seek answers to questions such as these, questions that will help them to understand themselves. The potential importance of this aspect of development has led psychologists to look upon the self as a target for study (Cicchetti & Beeghly, 1990; Yardley & Honess, 1987). And as we will see, it is a topic filled with intriguing and challenging issues.

Psychologists have conceptualized the self using several schemes. In the more traditional view, the self is divided into two domains: the "I," or **existential self**, and the "Me," or **empirical self** (James, 1890). The *I* refers to the subjective experience of existing, which includes, for example, a sense of personal identity, a sense of being able to do things (personal agency), and an awareness of one's continuing existence across time. The *Me* refers to a more objective understanding of one's personal characteristics, such as physical appearance, social status, personality traits, and cognitive abilities. Together, these two components of the self comprise our awareness of who we are (Damon & Hart, 1988, 1992; Lewis, 1991).

A more recent classification scheme for studying the self is the **self-system** (Harter, 1983). This scheme holds that the self is embedded in a system of interrelated processes—some that affect it, others that are affected by it. The self-system has three components. The first is **self-knowledge** (also referred to as **self-awareness**). What do children know about themselves and when do they acquire this knowledge? How is this knowledge related to their understanding of other aspects of their social and physical environment? A second component is **self-evaluation**. What factors influence children's opinions of themselves? How do these opinions affect their behavior? The third component is **self-regulation**. How and when do children acquire self-control? What variables influence this process?

Our coverage of the self in this chapter follows the self-system. Throughout the chapter, we also maintain our interest in the themes that have guided our discussions in other areas: what the three principal theoretical traditions have to say about this topic, how it looks from the nature and the nurture perspectives, and how researchers have investigated it.

THEORIES OF THE SELF

Our discussion of the three components of the self-system crosses areas of research that have historically been quite distinct from one another. Indeed, no theoretical tradition has sought to explain all three of them. Therefore, we do not attempt at this point to present all of the theorizing that has been done on this topic. Instead, we discuss several models here and others in the sections of the chapter where they best apply.

Cognitive-Developmental Approaches

The concept of the self and its relation to other aspects of development have been of considerable interest to cognitive-developmental psychologists. Researchers in the Piagetian tradition have for the most part viewed the development of the self within the context of the four stages of cognitive growth discussed in Chapter 8. We consider their ideas later in the chapter. Other cognitive researchers, however, have constructed separate models of the self. Here, we describe Selman's model and an information-processing model.

Selman's Work on Self-Awareness

The most detailed account of children's self-awareness has been presented by Robert Selman (1980). In the tradition of other cognitive-developmental theorists, Selman has built his model out of extensive clinical interviews with children.

Selman presented children of various ages with brief stories in which the main character faces a conflict or dilemma. The children were then asked a series of questions regarding what the character was thinking and feeling and how the dilemma would be resolved. Selman was interested not so much in the children's solutions as in the type of reasoning they used to arrive at the solutions.

From his interview data, Selman developed a five-stage model of children's awareness of the self. The model is based on assumptions similar to those underlying other theories in this tradition. That is, the stages (1) follow an invariant sequence through which all children pass with no regression to earlier stages, (2) are consistent across different problems and situations, (3) are universal across cultures, and (4) develop as a result of changes in the child's cognitive abilities (Gurucharri & Selman, 1982).

The five stages can be summarized briefly as follows:

Level 0 (infancy): Children understand their physical existence but do not display an awareness of a separate psychological existence. The child does not, for example, distinguish between physical behavior (such as crying) and simultaneous emotional feelings (such as being sad).

Level 1 (early childhood): The child now separates psychological states from behavior and believes that thoughts can control actions. But the child also believes that inner thoughts and feelings are directly represented in outward appearance and behavior, so that someone's self can be known simply by observing the person's actions and statements (for example, that a person who is whistling and smiling *must* be happy).

Level 2 (middle childhood): Here, the child appreciates that feelings and motives can be different from behavior and thus that the self can to some degree be hidden from others. It cannot, however, be hidden from oneself.

Level 3 (preadolescence): Children in later childhood show a growing belief that the self represents a stable component of personality. They believe people can observe and evaluate their inner selves, suggesting that the mind (which does the observing) is somehow separate from the self (which is observed).

Level 4 (adolescence): Ultimately, the adolescent comes to believe that the self cannot ever be completely known, because some aspects of personality remain at an unconscious level.

Here is one of the stories Selman used in developing his model:

THE PUPPY STORY

Tom has just saved some money to buy Mike Hunter a birthday present. He and his friend Greg go downtown to try to decide what Mike will like. Tom tells Greg that Mike is sad these days because Mike's dog Pepper ran away. They see Mike and decide to try to find out what Mike wants without asking him right off. After talking to Mike for a while the kids realize that Mike is really sad because of his lost dog. When Greg suggests that he get a new dog, Mike says *he can't just get a new dog and have things be the same.* Then Mike leaves to run some errands. As Mike's friends shop some more they see a puppy for sale in the pet store. It is the last one left. The owner says that the puppy will probably be sold by tomorrow. Tom and Greg discuss whether to get Mike the puppy. Tom has to decide right away. What do you think Tom will do?

The questions Selman asked of the child listeners were designed to help classify each of them into one of the five stages, as can be seen from the following examples:

If Mike is smiling, could he still be sad? How is that possible? Could someone be happy on the outside, but sad on the inside?
Is it possible that Mike doesn't know how he feels? How is that possible?
What kind of person is Mike if he doesn't care if his dog is lost? Can you tell what kind of person someone is from a situation like this?
How does one get to know someone else's personality? (Selman, 1980, pp. 318–319)

Selman's model is most concerned with children's knowledge and reasoning about the self. Like other cognitive-developmental theories, it has had little to say about children's actual behavior, such as their self-regulation.

Information-Processing Model

Self-schema
An internal cognitive portrait of the self used to organize information about the self.

In the view of psychologists who favor an information-processing model of cognitive development, the self-system is part of the larger memory system (Greenwald & Pratkanis, 1984; Lapsley & Quintana, 1985). According to this model, each of us develops a cognitive schema of who he or she is. The **self-schema** is an internal "self-portrait" that includes the various features and characteristics we ascribe to our personalities. Self-schemas are constructed over time and serve primarily to organize self-related information. Whenever we encounter new events or information, then, we attempt to understand them in terms of these cognitive structures (Markus, 1977).

Support for the existence of such structures comes from studies showing that people are better able to recall self-reference personality descriptors—that is, words they can apply to themselves—than descriptors that do not seem to relate to them (Pullybank et al., 1985; Rogers, 1984). Some such studies investigated whether children's levels of self-esteem and depression would influence their memory for certain types of words. The words were presented one at a time. Half of them were followed by the question "Is this word like you?" and the other half were followed by the question "Is this a long word?" As the self-schema model would predict, all children later were better able to recall the words that they had been asked to relate to themselves. A second independent variable involved the type of words that were presented. Half of the words described positive personal traits (*brave, helpful,* and so on), and the other half described negative personal traits (such as *lonely* and *ugly*). Again as predicted, children who were high in self-esteem and were not depressed showed better recall of the positive traits, whereas depressed children with low self-esteem showed better recall of the negative traits (Hammen & Zupan, 1984; Zupan, Hammen, & Jaenicke, 1987).

This research illustrates how powerfully children's self-schemas can influence the way they relate to the world around them. Children whose self-esteem is high are apparently more attuned to information that is consistent with their positive self-esteem, whereas children with low self-esteem are more aware of information that confirms, and may even perpetuate, their negative views of themselves.

Environmental/Learning Theories

Social-learning theorists have proposed a number of psychological processes that are relevant to the self. Two theoretical models have been developed by

Albert Bandura; one involving self-evaluation, the other concerned with self-regulation.

Bandura's self-evaluation model is built around the concept of **self-efficacy**, a person's ability—as judged by that person—to carry out various behaviors and acts (Bandura, 1977a). Bandura observes that, just as infants and young children do not understand the operations of the physical and social world very well, they do not know much about their own skills and abilities (Bandura, 1981). Studies have shown, for example, that parents (and teachers) can predict how well children will perform on academic tasks much better than children themselves (Miller & Davis, 1992; Stipek & MacIver, 1989). Similarly, in everyday situations parents must frequently warn children, for example, that they are swimming out too far, or that a particular library book will be too difficult for them to understand, or that they can never finish the largest ice-cream sundae on the menu. Such verbal instructions from parents, along with many trial-and-error experiences, help young children to gradually learn the limits of their talents and capabilities—that is, to accurately judge their self-efficacy.

As children grow, two other mechanisms promote the development of self-efficacy judgments. One is modeling, which children come to use as a way of estimating the likelihood of success at a task. For example, a child might reason "If that little girl (who is my size and age) can jump over that fence, I can probably do it, too." Using vicarious experiences in this way obviously involves somewhat sophisticated cognitive abilities, in that the child must determine the appropriate models and situations for making comparisons. Another way in which children learn to estimate their potential for success is through awareness of internal bodily reactions. For example, feelings of emotional arousal (e.g., tension, a nervous stomach, or a fast heart rate) frequently become associated with failures. Bandura believes that, as a result, children begin to interpret these feelings as indications of fear, anxiety, or lack of confidence, and they learn to use them to decide that failure is close at hand. Again, using this type of information requires a fairly high level of cognitive processing and so is more common in older children (Bandura & Schunk, 1981; Schunk, 1983).

Self-efficacy judgments are important because they are believed to significantly affect children's behavior. Bandura contends, for example, that greater feelings of self-efficacy produce increased effort and persistence on a task and thus, ultimately, a higher level of performance. This concept is especially relevant in the area of children's academic achievement and how it relates to their self-evaluations—a topic we discuss later in the chapter.

Bandura also has proposed a theoretical mechanism to explain the development of self-regulation (Bandura, 1991a). Early on, children's behavior is only externally controlled, through such processes as modeling, consequences (reinforcement and punishment), and direct instruction. With experience, however, children learn to anticipate the reactions of others, and they use this knowledge to self-regulate their behavior. For example, as a child learns (through external processes) what the teacher expects of her in the classroom, she comes to regulate her behavior to conform to these rules. Gradually, the child internalizes the rules, and they become personal standards for her. Now the child's behavior comes under the control of her **evaluative self-reactions**—that is, the child notes whether her behavior has met her personal standards and then applies *self-sanctions* in the form of self-approval or self-disapproval. Thus, according to this model, self-regulation occurs as children become motivated to behave in ways that match their internal standards and that result in self-satisfaction rather than self-deprecation.

Self-efficacy
Bandura's term for people's ability to succeed at various tasks, as judged by the people themselves.

Evaluative self-reactions
Bandura's term for consequences people apply to themselves as a result of meeting or failing to meet their personal standards.

• According to Albert Bandura, children learn to self-regulate their behavior by internalizing the rules and standards of adults.

Ethological Theory

Classical ethologists have displayed the least interest in the self-system. Their focus on the entire range of species has tended to discourage their studying the self, which most scientists of this tradition believe is a concept unique to humans (Krebs, Denton, & Higgins, 1987).

Bowlby's writings on attachment, however, discussed his belief that the sense of self begins to develop within the context of infant–caregiver interactions and is promoted by responsive caregiving. These ideas have been echoed and elaborated by more recent developmental theorists (Cicchetti, 1991; Lewis, 1987b; Sander, 1975). For example, we have seen that caregivers who are more responsive to their infants are better at adjusting their behavior to produce reciprocal, turn-taking interactions with the baby. It has been suggested that by participating in such interactions, infants are able to develop their own identities, as well as to understand that they can influence their environments (Sroufe, 1990). Likewise, responsive caregiving leads to a more secure attachment between the baby and mother, which in turn should facilitate the infant's development of internal working models of both the mother and the self (Pipp, 1990). We will see shortly that evidence from both normal and clinical populations of children provides support for these notions.

✔ *To Recap...*

The self-system can be divided into three components: self-knowledge, self-evaluation, and self-regulation. Cognitive–developmental theorists have offered several models concerning self-development. Based on interviews with children, Selman proposed a five-stage model that begins with the infant's being unable to differentiate the physical and psychological selves and ends with the adolescent's believing that aspects of the self remain unconscious and unknowable. Information-processing theorists view the self as part of the larger memory system. Children are believed to construct self-schemas, which they use to organize information related to the self and which influence how they perceive and interact with the world.

Social-learning theory has contributed two models of the self, both proposed by Bandura. Self-efficacy judgments are assumed to be inaccurate in early childhood but to improve gradually with the help of four processes: verbal instruction from parents and other adults, success and failure experiences, observation of relevant models, and monitoring of internal bodily reactions. Self-efficacy judgments appear to have important influences on children's behavior. Self-regulation is assumed to occur when children internalize standards they have acquired through external processes, and then use evaluative self-reactions to keep their behavior consistent with these standards.

Ethologists have had the least to say regarding the self-system, but some have suggested that responsive caregiving and a secure attachment relationship may facilitate aspects of the child's self-development.

SELF-KNOWLEDGE

Our examination of research evidence on the self-system begins with perhaps the most basic questions: What do children know about the self, and when do they know it? It is not uncommon to hear a toddler proudly announce that he is a big boy or that his name is Jeremy. But he may, as yet, have very little understanding of his physical characteristics (heavy or slight), his personality (shy or bold), or his living conditions (middle-class or poor). As we will see, children's self-knowledge develops steadily across the childhood years and is interwoven with the development of other cognitive and socialization processes.

Discovery of the Self in Infancy

When does a baby first understand that he or she exists separately from the surrounding world? This question has long been of interest in developmental psychology. Some researchers believe that babies have an inborn awareness of their existence or at least that awareness develops within the first weeks of life (Samuels, 1986; Stern, 1983, 1985). Others argue that none of what babies do requires us to assume they have self-awareness prior to their first birthday (Kagan, 1991). Unfortunately, like many issues involving nonverbal infants, this one is not easily settled.

The Role of Perception

Perceptual processes are thought to play an important role in infants' first coming to recognize their separateness (Butterworth, 1990; Neisser, 1991). For example, we have seen that, within only weeks after birth, infants can imitate certain adult facial expressions. This finding has been interpreted to mean that almost from the outset babies can connect sensory (visual) input with corresponding motor responses—a capability that lays the groundwork for their realizing that they can interact with and affect the world around them (Meltzoff, 1990).

Studies of perception also have shown that, in the months that follow, the self becomes much more clearly defined. As we saw in Chapter 7, when 6-month-olds are taught to look for an object located in one position relative to themselves—say, to the left—and then are rotated to the opposite orientation, so that the object is to their right, they continue to search for the object by looking left. The addition of visual cues or landmarks to encourage more appropriate searching has little effect on babies of this age (Acredolo, 1985). This phenomenon corresponds nicely to Piaget's belief that between 4 and 10 months, babies view the world egocentrically, understanding everything only in relation to themselves. This perspective, of course, results in unsuccessful searching, and it gradually gives way to more effective, environmentally guided perceptual strategies as the baby approaches 1 year of age. But in using themselves as anchor points when searching, young egocentric infants demonstrate at least a crude awareness of their own separate existence.

Personal Agency

Along with infants' knowledge that they exist apart from the things around them comes an understanding of **personal agency**—that is, an understanding that they can be the agents or causes of events that occur in their worlds. Now babies move toys and put things in their mouths and bang blocks, all suggesting an awareness both that they are separate from these things and that they can do something with them (Case, 1991).

Personal agency also appears to develop through babies' early interactions with caregivers (Emde et al., 1991; Sroufe, 1990). Theorists from all three of the major traditions, in fact, concur that when parents are more sensitive and responsive to their infants' signals, babies more quickly develop an understanding of the impact they can have on their environments (e.g., "I can make Mommy come by crying") (Lamb & Easterbrooks, 1981).

A related question has been whether babies first acquire an understanding of the self or of the mother. In one study, babies aged 6 months and older watched an

Personal agency
The understanding that one can be the cause of events.

adult model eat a Cheerio. They were then given one and instructed either to feed it to themselves or to feed it to their mothers. Significantly more babies at each age level were able to follow the first instruction than the second (Pipp, Fischer, & Jennings, 1987). These findings are consistent with others in showing that infants learn to direct actions or speech toward themselves before they direct those same responses toward their mothers (Bretherton & Beeghly, 1982; Huttenlocher, Smiley, & Charney, 1983), suggesting that, with respect to agency, self-knowledge ("I can do it to me") precedes mother-knowledge ("I can do it to her").

Mastery motivation
An inborn desire to affect or control one's environment.

A sense of personal agency gradually evolves into **mastery motivation** in the child (Jennings, 1991). Now the child begins to do things simply for the pleasure of observing the reactions they produce and for the satisfaction of accomplishing a goal. Recall from Chapter 8 that Piaget discussed the emergence of such behavior during the sensorimotor period. Novel toys or objects appear to be especially effective in eliciting mastery motivation, which may influence the rate and level of the child's cognitive development. For example, one study found that infants who spent more time on a challenging task and were more persistent at trying to solve it also scored higher on measures of cognitive competence several years later (Messer et al., 1986).

Self-Recognition

As babies approach age 2, many display an increasing awareness of the self through their use of pronouns, such as *me* and *mine*, as well as the use of their own names—although, at first, these terms are not always used appropriately (Bates, 1990; Bates, Bretherton, & Snyder, 1989; Stipek, Gralinski, & Kopp, 1990). But the form of self-knowledge during this period that has attracted the most research is infants' ability to recognize what they look like.

Visual Self-Recognition

Visual self-recognition
The ability to recognize oneself; often studied in babies by having them look into mirrors.

A number of researchers have investigated the development of **visual self-recognition** by examining babies' reactions to mirror reflections (Brooks-Gunn & Lewis, 1984). The major issue in this research concerns whether babies actually recognize the reflected images as themselves. But other issues are also of interest (Loveland, 1986).

During their first year, babies smile and vocalize at their mirror reflections (Amsterdam, 1972; Fischer, 1980; Schulman & Kaplowitz, 1977). Some investigators contend that these responses do not indicate self-recognition but are merely the baby's reactions to being able to control the reflected image. The findings from one study of 5-month-olds, however, call this conclusion into question. Each baby was placed before two television screens. On one, the baby saw a live video image of his feet and legs moving about; on the other, he saw another child's feet and legs (whose movements therefore did not correspond to his own). Somewhat surprisingly, the babies spent more time looking at the screen showing the peers' feet than at the one showing their own (Watson, 1985). This suggests that babies' early interest in mirrors does not result simply from their ability to control the image they see (or else they would have preferred to watch their own feet).

As infants move into the second year of life, however, they do appear to develop an interest in outcomes they can control, especially when the outcomes match the behaviors that produced them. This was demonstrated in a clever experiment in which a 14-month-old baby with a toy was seated across the table from two adults with identical toys. Whenever the baby moved or manipulated the toy, the two adults immediately responded—one imitating the baby's actions, the other performing a different action with the toy. The babies in the study smiled and looked longer at the adult who imitated them, indicating not only that they discriminated between the two behaviors, but also that they preferred the imitative to the nonimitative behavior (Meltzoff, 1990). These results suggest that infants' early interest in mirrors may be based on their understanding that what they do in front of the mirror and what they see in it are the same. But does this mean that they also understand that the infants in the mirrors are themselves?

To investigate this issue more effectively, psychologists have used an ingenious procedure. A colored mark is surreptitiously placed on the infant's face in a location where she could not normally see it (such as on her forehead). The baby is then placed before a mirror, and the investigators note whether she attempts to touch the mark. If she does, they conclude that she understands that the marked face in the mirror is her own. Using this measure, researchers have not found self-recognition in infants under 15 months of age; in fact it does not occur reliably until about 24 months (Brooks-Gunn & Lewis, 1984; Bullock & Lutkenhaus, 1990). Babies' interest in mirrors during the first year or so of life, therefore, probably does not mean that they recognize their own reflections.

Visual self-recognition has also been investigated with a number of other techniques. These include comparing infants' reactions to videotapes or photographs of themselves with their reactions to tapes or photos of similar peers (Bigelow, 1981; Johnson, 1983) and having infants point to pictures of themselves in a group after hearing their names (Bertenthal & Fischer, 1978; Damon & Hart, 1982). Evidence from these measures places self-recognition even later, by several months, than the mirror-technique findings (Fischer, 1980).

Regardless of the method used, self-recognition appears at different ages for different infants. Why should this be the case? One possibility is that some babies have more experience with mirrors than others. But it has been demonstrated in chimpanzees, by use of the marked-face method, that self-recognition is not related to how much mirror experience the animal has had (Gallup, 1977). To test this question with humans, researchers compared infants from a nomadic desert culture in Israel, who had had no previous experience with mirrors or other reflective surfaces, with a matched group of Israeli children from a nearby city, again using

• Visual self-recognition has been the most commonly used method of assessing toddlers' self-awareness.

the marked-face measure. Consistent with the chimpanzee results, the researchers found no self-recognition differences between the two groups (Priel & de Schonen, 1986). Thus, experience with mirrors does not appear to be important in visual self-recognition.

Self-Recognition in Maltreated Infants

Another proposed influence is the infant–caregiver relationship. As we indicated earlier, some psychologists believe that it is through caregiver–infant interaction that the infant first develops a concept of a separate self. And as mentioned in Chapter 12, a secure attachment to the caregiver promotes exploration and cognitive development in the baby. Thus, we might predict that more securely attached infants would show greater self-recognition than less securely attached infants of the same age. Using the Strange Situation procedure (described in Chapter 12) as the measure of attachment and the marked-face technique as the measure of self-recognition, one research team compared the responses of infants who had been abused and neglected with those who had experienced more normal interactions with their caregivers. The maltreated infants were found to be less securely attached, and they also displayed less evidence of self-recognition (Schneider-Rosen & Cicchetti, 1984, 1991). Moreover, the maltreated infants responded more negatively to their mirror reflections, which the researchers speculate may reflect the beginnings of a low sense of self-worth (Cicchetti et al., 1990). Other research with abused children has found that their language is less likely to involve descriptions of themselves or of their internal states and feelings (Cicchetti, 1991; Coster et al., 1989). Recent studies with nonabused infants have confirmed that securely attached babies have a better understanding of both personal agency and physical characteristics than do infants in other classifications (Pipp, Easterbrooks, & Harmon, 1992). Thus a secure attachment relationship appears to promote the development of the self.

Self-Recognition and the Awareness of Others

One proposed outcome of infants' increasing awareness of their individual identities is a greater awareness of the separateness and distinctiveness of others. That is, as we become more self-aware, we should simultaneously become more other-aware. Evidence for children's developing appreciation of the existence and individuality of others comes from several sources.

One of these involves *synchronic imitation,* in which two preverbal children play with similar toys in a similar fashion that involves coordinated action (Eckerman & Stein, 1990; Nadel & Fontaine, 1989). In order to synchronize his play with that of a peer, a child must have some understanding of the other child's intentions and behavior. This type of play would thus seem to require some degree of self-and other-awareness. And consistent with this view, 18-month-olds who give evidence of mirror self-recognition display more synchronic imitation with same-age peers than do infants who do not recognize themselves in the mirror (Asendorpf & Baudonniere, 1993).

Other-awareness has also been demonstrated by young children's reactions to another person's distress. If the emergence of the self leads to an increased understanding of the separate feelings of others, we might expect this to be reflected in greater concern for someone in pain or discomfort. This prediction, too, has been supported. Research has shown that 2-year-olds who display mirror self-recognition are more likely to help someone in distress (Zahn-Waxler et al., 1992).

Developmental Changes in Self-Descriptions

Psychologists have typically assessed older children's self-knowledge by examining their descriptions of themselves. This method has taken a number of forms, ranging from very unstructured interviews—which might include such general questions as "Who are you?"—to very structured questionnaires, which might require answers to written items like "How old are you?" and "What is your favorite outdoor game?" Regardless of the method used, researchers have found a relatively predictable pattern of development (Damon & Hart, 1988, 1992).

By the age of 2, many children display knowledge of some of their most basic characteristics. For example, they know whether they are girls or boys and they know that they are children rather than adults (Harter, 1988; M. Lewis, 1981). These category labels are undoubtedly learned through modeling and reinforcement, as children repeatedly hear themselves referred to with phrases such as "my little boy" and as they receive approval when they correctly state their age or other personal characteristic. But as we will see, cognitive development also plays a role in the self-discovery process.

In the preschool years, as shown in Table 13-1, self-descriptions usually involve physical features, possessions, and preferences (Hart & Damon, 1985; Keller, Ford, & Meacham, 1978). Thus, a 4-year-old might say that she lives in a big house, has a dog, and likes ice cream. The accuracy of this information, however, is not always what it might be. Descriptions during this period typically focus on objective, here-and-now attributes—a finding that corresponds well with Piaget's description of preoperational children's view of the world. But it is incorrect to assume, as some psychologists have, that children of this age can only comprehend specific characteristics of themselves and do not understand more general traits, such as being messy or having a big appetite. The self-description a young child offers seems to depend heavily on how the information is sought. Children give more general responses when questions are structured to encourage generality ("Tell me how you are at school with your friends") than when the questions focus on more specific information ("Tell me what you did at school with friends today") (Eder, 1989, 1990).

TABLE 13-1 ● Children's Self-Descriptions at Three Stages of Development

Piagetian Stage	Nature of Comments	Focus of Self-Descriptions	Examples
Early childhood			
Preoperational	Objective focus on here-and-now	Physical characteristics, possessions, preferences	"I have freckles." "I have a big-wheel bike." "I like pizza."
Middle childhood			
Concrete operational	Emphasize category membership, nontangibles	Behavioral traits, abilities, emotions	"I'm a good singer." "I'm a cheerleader."
Adolescence			
Formal operational	Abstract, hypothetical	Attitudes, personality attributes, beliefs	"I'm patriotic." "I could be a convincing lawyer." "I don't need drugs to be happy."

In middle childhood, self-descriptions change in several ways, reflecting the shift to concrete operational abilities (Harter, 1994; Markus & Nurius, 1984). Rather than limiting their statements to the here-and-now and the physical, 6-to 10-year-olds begin to talk about less tangible characteristics such as emotions ("Sometimes I feel sad"), and to fit themselves into categories ("I'm a Yankees fan" or "I'm a Boy Scout"). They also base their descriptions more often on social comparisons with other children and may describe their skills or talents relative to those of friends or classmates ("I'm the best skater on the street") (Aboud, 1985; Ruble, 1983; Ruble & Frey, 1987). The accuracy of children's information also improves during this period (Glick & Zigler, 1985).

As children enter adolescence, their self-descriptions continue to change (Harter, 1990c; Harter & Monsour, 1992). The formal operational child thinks and self-describes in more abstract and hypothetical terms. Rather than focusing on physical characteristics and possessions (as in early childhood) or on behavioral traits and abilities (as in middle childhood), the adolescent is concerned with attitudes ("I hate chemistry"), personality attributes ("I'm a curious person"), and beliefs involving hypothetical situations ("If I meet someone who has a different idea about something, I try to be tolerant of it") (Hart & Damon, 1985; Rosenberg, 1986b). The adolescent self also differentiates into more roles. For example, adolescents give different responses when asked to describe themselves in the classroom, at home, and with friends. Moreover, for the first time these differences involve opposing or conflicting attributes, such as being shy in the classroom but outgoing with friends (Harter & Monsour, 1992). The limits of self development are not yet known, but the self apparently continues to differentiate throughout adolescence and adulthood (Block & Robins, 1993; Harter, 1990; Marsh, 1989).

✔ To Recap...

Children's knowledge about the self increases steadily through childhood. It is not yet known whether babies are born with any understanding of the self. Perceptual processes, such as those involved in neonatal imitation and early space perception, likely play an important role in early self development. During the second half of the first year, babies begin to display a sense of personal agency by acting on toys and other objects in their environments. A sense of agency evolves into mastery motivation, as infants begin to engage in activities simply for the sake of mastering them.

As infants approach the end of their second year, they begin to show recognition of themselves. Research with mirrors, videotapes, and photographs indicates reliable self-recognition by about 2 years of age. The development of self-recognition does not appear to be related to experience with mirrors. Research with maltreated infants suggests that it does seem to be influenced by the security of infant–caregiver attachment.

Increases in self-awareness are accompanied by increases in other-awareness. Infants who display self-recognition are more likely to also engage in synchronic imitation and to help someone in distress.

Self-knowledge in children beyond the infant years has been assessed principally through examination of their self-descriptions. Self-descriptions by preschoolers reflect preoperational thinking and typically include references only to objective, here-and-now characteristics. In middle childhood, the concrete operational child focuses to a greater degree on nontangible characteristics, such as emotions, and on membership in various categories. Adolescents' formal operational abilities lead to more abstract and hypothetical self-descriptions, concerned often with attitudes, personality characteristics, and personal beliefs, sometimes involving conflicting attributes.

SELF-EVALUATION

As children grow, they not only come to understand more about themselves but they also begin to evaluate this information. Social involvements, as in school or on athletic teams, encourage children to compare themselves with other children and also with their images of whom they would like to be. Such self-evaluations usually bring both good news and bad, as children come to recognize their strengths and weaknesses and their positive and negative attributes. Self-evaluation, like self-knowledge, develops as children grow, and is influenced by both cognitive and socialization variables (Ruble et al., 1990).

Measuring Self-Worth

The opinions children develop about themselves have been referred to as their **self-esteem**, or **self-worth** (Harter, 1985, 1987). Self-esteem is assumed to include not only children's cognitive judgments of their abilities but also their affective reactions to these self-evaluations. However, in practice, the measurement of self-worth has typically emphasized the cognitive component.

Self-esteem (self-worth)
A person's evaluation of himself or herself, and his or her affective reactions to that evaluation.

The most common method of assessing children's self-esteem has used questionnaires. Typically, such instruments present children with a list of questions designed to tap their evaluations of themselves in a variety of situations or contexts (such as "How good are you at sports?" and "Do you think you are creative?"). The responses to these questions can be combined and analyzed to produce an overall score representing the child's level of self-esteem (Coopersmith, 1967; Piers & Harris, 1969).

Attempts to capture self-esteem in a single score, however, have met with the same problems as attempts to describe children's intelligence with a single IQ score. Intuitively, it seems unlikely that children would evaluate themselves similarly in all areas—academics, appearance, athletics, and so on. And research has demonstrated that evaluations across different areas are usually not consistent (Harter, 1985; Rosenberg, 1986a).

An alternative to the single-score method is to divide children's lives conceptually into a number of domains (social skills, physical skills, and so on) and then to assess their self-evaluations separately in each. The results are then reported as a "profile" across the various domains rather than being combined into a single composite score. The best example of this approach is the *Self-Perception Profile for Children*, described in more detail in Box 13-1 (Harter, 1985, 1988). The notion of an overall measure of self-esteem is retained to some extent by this instrument. Additional questions are included to assess children's global impressions and feelings about themselves, and these are combined into a separate single index of the child's self-worth.

The Stability of Self-Worth

The results of many studies give a relatively clear picture of the development of self-esteem across the childhood years. Children under about 8 years of age do not have a well-developed sense of overall self-worth (Harter, 1988). We do know, however, that kindergartners' self-esteem scores tend to be reasonably high and related to a secure attachment to the caregiver (Cassidy, 1988) and a general optimism about the future (Fischer & Leitenberg, 1986). During the middle and later childhood years, self-esteem scores are generally stable, with perhaps a small trend toward im-

SELF-PERCEPTION PROFILE FOR CHILDREN

Susan Harter has developed the most useful instrument available for measuring children's self-esteem, a questionnaire designed to assess children's opinions of their overall worth as well as their self-evaluations in five separate domains: scholastic competence, athletic competence, social acceptance, behavioral conduct, and physical appearance. It can be used with children aged 8 and older.

Each item on the questionnaire presents two related statements, one describing a competent child and the other describing a less competent child. A child completing the instrument selects the statement that best describes him and then marks the box indicating whether the statement is "really true for me" or just "sort of true for me." Below are sample items from the scholastic competence area and the domain of behavioral conduct.

Children respond to six items in each of the six areas, and their scores are used to construct a profile of their self-esteem. The sample profiles below depict

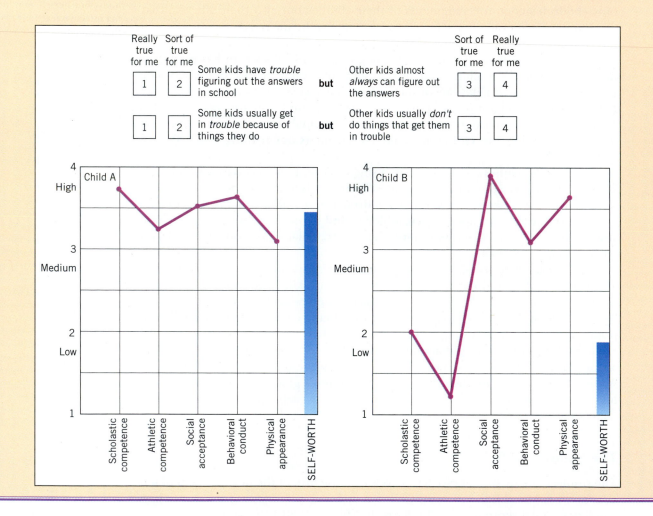

one child (A) who has a relatively consistent view of her competence across the five domains and whose self-worth is very high. The other child (B) has self-evaluations that vary considerably among the five areas and a low level of global self-worth.

For children between the ages of 4 and 7, items consist of pictures—for example, a girl who is good at puzzles (left) and a girl who is not good at puzzles (right). The child points to the circle indicating whether a picture is a little like her (small circle) or a lot like her (large circle). Because children below age 8 cannot form an overall judgment of their self-worth, only the five individual areas are assessed (Harter & Pike, 1984).

The scores for self-worth in the older children, in fact, do not simply reflect a composite of the child's other five scores. Harter has explained this by examining the degree to which children's global self-worth is influenced by the two traditional models described in the text: the looking-glass self (Cooley, 1902) and the child's feelings of competence in areas where success is important (James, 1892).

To assess the first of these, she constructed additional items that asked children to rate how they believed other people felt about them. Consistent with the looking-glass model, youngsters who felt others had high regard for them also rated themselves high on the self-worth items. To examine the competence model, she asked children to rate how important each of the five areas was to them. In support of this model, children who rated themselves as very competent in areas they felt were important also had high self-worth scores (Harter, 1986). Harter has concluded from these studies and others that have followed that older children's feelings of self-esteem are based on *both* how they perceive others evaluate them and how they evaluate themselves (Harter, 1988, 1990a).

provement (Cairns & Cairns, 1988; Dunn, 1994). But the transition to adolescence at times poses problems. Many investigators have found that at about age 11 or 12, self-esteem scores dip, only to increase again during the high-school years (Harter, 1990a; Nottleman, 1987; Wigfield et al., 1991).

Self-consciousness
A concern about the opinions others hold about oneself.

Looking-glass self
The conception of the self based on how one thinks others see him or her.

One factor that may play a role in this temporary deterioration of self-esteem is the child's level of **self-consciousness**, or concern about the opinions of others. It has long been believed that we tend to view other people's reactions to us as reflections of who we are. For this reason, the psychological portraits we paint of ourselves are based in part on what has been called the **looking-glass self** (Cooley, 1902). In other words, at least to some extent, we see ourselves as we think others see us. Cognitive-developmentalists suggest that this tendency increases with the emergence of formal operational abilities. At this stage, children become so much better at taking the perspective of others that they develop a preoccupation with how other people regard their appearance, behavior, and so forth (Elkind, 1980; Hart, 1988a). The increased self-consciousness leads to more critical self-evaluations, which in turn lower self-esteem (Adams, Abraham, & Markstrom, 1987; Rosenberg, 1985). This process appears to be especially true of females, who display both greater self-consciousness (Gray & Hudson, 1984) and lower self-esteem (Abramowitz, Petersen, & Schulenberg, 1981; Simmons et al., 1979) during this period than males.

Another factor that may cause the dip in self-worth among early adolescents are the biological changes associated with puberty. Some researchers have suggested that pubertal changes produce physical and psychological stress in children that lead to depression and other negative emotional states (Simmons & Blyth, 1987).

An environmental variable that has been found to contribute to the drop in self-esteem involves whether children remain in their own school during this period or move to a new one following sixth grade. Several studies report that moving to a new school usually produces a noticeable decline in self-esteem scores, especially if it is large and ethnically diverse (Blyth, Simmons, & Carlton-Ford, 1983; Simmons, Carlton-Ford, & Blyth, 1987). Children who remain in the same school, by contrast, show no such change (Demo & Savin-Williams, 1983; Rosenberg, 1986b). We consider the role that changing schools may play in academic problems in a later section.

• Conformity to peer pressures during adolescence may result from an increase in self-consciousness and a dip in self-esteem.

Academic Self-Concept

Whereas one traditional view holds that self-esteem is constructed largely from the opinions of others (Cooley, 1902), another contends that it primarily reflects our feelings of **competence** (James, 1892). Competence involves a combination of what we would like to achieve and how confident we feel about achieving it, making the competence component of a child's self-esteem essentially the same as the child's perceived self-efficacy (Harter, 1988). The factors affecting self-esteem have also been investigated in the classroom, especially with regard to children's perceptions of their academic competence, or **academic self-concept** (Stipek, 1992).

Age and Gender Differences

Prior to entering school, children have no basis for an academic self-concept. Some research has examined the reactions of infants and preschoolers to other sorts of achievement tasks, however, and has found that a developmental progression does exist (Stipek, Recchia, & McClintic, 1992). Infants, for example, have little understanding of success and failure and so do not behave in ways that give any evidence of self-evaluation. However, even before they reach age 2, children begin to show that they anticipate how adults will react to their (often small) achievements, such as when they look up for approval after making a stack of blocks. They also express delight at their successes and display negative reactions to their failures. By age 3, most children prefer to engage in activities at which they win rather than lose.

Interestingly, children's academic self-concept generally is highest in kindergarten and steadily declines through at least fourth grade. This trend has been noted in children's spontaneous classroom comments to other students (Ruble & Frey, 1987), in their statements during interviews (Benenson & Dweck, 1986), and in their responses to questionnaires (Butler, 1990; Eccles et al., 1993b). One cause of this decline may be as simple as the fact that older children realize "bragging" is not socially appropriate and so increasingly avoid giving glowing descriptions of their abilities (Ruble & Frey, 1987).

During this period, boys express more self-competence in sports and mathematics, whereas girls are more positive regarding their abilities in reading and music (Eccles et al., 1993b; Frey & Ruble, 1987). Girls, however, tend to base their academic self-image largely on classroom conduct and much less on academic achievement. The reverse is true for boys (Entwisle et al., 1987). This gender difference is not completely understood, but it may be related to the different ways teachers respond to males and females, as we will see shortly.

Competence
Self-evaluation that includes both what one would like to achieve and one's confidence in being able to achieve it.

Academic self-concept
The part of self-esteem involving children's perceptions of their academic abilities.

DEVELOPMENT IN CONTEXT: Children's Self-Evaluations in Single-Parent Families

Millions of children, especially those living in poverty, grow up in families where the mother is the only parent. Clearly, this social context would appear to put children at risk for problems in development and adjustment (L. W. Hoffman, 1984, 1989). For this reason, psychologists have been interested in determining whether being raised in a mother-headed household affects children's evaluations of their personal and academic competence. As it turns out, a crucial factor is whether the mother is employed.

In one study, inner-city children in Philadelphia were given Harter's Self-Perception Profile (Alessandri, 1992). All of the children lived in single-parent households and had been raised from birth by their mothers alone. For one third of the subjects, the mother was employed full-time; for another third, she worked part-time; and for the final third, she stayed at home and received public assistance. The three groups of mothers did not differ in age, ethnic background, or education.

Children whose mothers worked either full- or part-time had more favorable self-perceptions of global self-worth than did children whose mothers stayed at home. Mothers who worked appeared to be especially good role models for their daughters, because the researchers also found that these girls evaluated themselves significantly higher in scholastic competence than did the girls whose mothers were unemployed. Moreover, these evaluations proved to be accurate in that school records showed the academic achievement of daughters of working mothers to be higher than that of any other children in the study. Finally, the researchers examined how mothers described their children's characteristics, as well as how children described their own characteristics. Families with working mothers were found to show a better correspondence between the mothers' descriptions and the children's self-descriptions, and this was especially true for mothers and daughters. This finding suggests that these families were more in tune with one another and shared more similar beliefs and expectations.

It seems, then, that when mothers are forced to play the dual roles of wage earner and parent, their children's development does not necessarily suffer. Any problems or inconveniences caused by mothers working (such as eating schedules, and transportation problems) appear to be compensated for by children's greater self-esteem and, in the case of females, higher academic self-concept and achievement.

• When mothers play the roles of both wage-earner and parent, their children's development does not necessarily suffer.

Learned Helplessness

Learned helplessness Acquired feelings of incompetence, often brought about as a result of repeated failure experiences.

A major determinant of children's academic self-concept is, of course, their academic performance. Children who do well in school are likely to develop high opinions of their competence, as poor performers are likely to develop low opinions. But the feedback children receive for their work, and the way they interpret it, also can have surprisingly powerful effects on their self-images.

The most striking example of this is a phenomenon called **learned helplessness** (Dweck & Reppucci, 1973). When children are unsuccessful at a task, they may attribute their failure to a lack of effort, a lack of ability, or both. Which attribution they make can be very significant. When children attribute failure to lack of effort, the failure usually has little impact on their feelings of academic competence. A child who has failed a math test, for example, might reason, "I could have done well on that test if only I had studied harder." This child is likely to approach the next test with at least the same motivation as before. However, a child who concludes that failure on a task resulted from lack of ability is likely to make a broader self-evaluation, such as "I'm lousy at math." This sort of conclusion may lead the child to approach future math tests in a less motivated, more pessimistic manner. Indeed, the child's expectations may be lowered so much that she can no longer pass even a relatively easy math test. These acquired feelings of incompetence are called *learned helplessness,* and they may continue to affect the child's future work unless steps are taken to reverse them (Fincham, Hokoda, & Sanders, 1989).

Learned helplessness is generally not seen until middle and later childhood (Boggiano, Barrett, & Kellam, 1993; Rholes et al., 1980). When it does appear, it is much more common in girls. The cause of this gender difference seems to lie in the way teachers typically provide feedback to the two genders. When boys fail, they are more often told that they did not try hard enough (indicating a lack of effort); when girls fail, they are usually told simply that they have the wrong answers (implying a lack of ability) (Dweck & Goetz, 1980). Because all children sometimes fail, all receive such feedback, and all can thus be influenced by it. In general, then, girls may eventually come to believe that their abilities are inadequate and therefore approach new tasks in a pessimistic manner, whereas boys may continue to assume that their failures derive from too little effort and so remain motivated in the face of new challenges.

Children as young as 6 may be vulnerable to a form of helplessness that results from repeated criticism. One investigator had kindergartners imagine they had constructed something that had one small element missing (such as a picture of a family in which one person's feet were missing). The child next imagined presenting the construction to a teacher. Some children were then told that the teacher reacted by criticizing the work. This procedure was repeated several times with different constructions, after which the children were asked a number of questions. These children responded in ways typical of learned helplessness. For example, they rated their constructions lower, they said they would switch to a different type of activity, they reported feeling bad (for example, sad or angry), and they made more negative self-evaluations (Heyman, Dweck, & Cain, 1992).

Fortunately, a number of studies have shown that learned helplessness can be at least partially remediated. One method involves changing the nature of the teachers' feedback so that girls are not led to believe their failures necessarily reflect a lack of ability (Dweck et al., 1978). Another involves a program to "retrain" helpless children to attribute their failures to effort rather than ability (Dweck, 1975). And a third involves rearranging the learning materials to reduce the likelihood that discouraging failures will occur at the beginning of the lessons (Licht & Dweck, 1984). Learned helplessness is thus a problem that can be successfully treated. It is also one that can be prevented, if adults understand its source.

• Whether children attribute failure to effort or ability can strongly affect their academic self-concept.

The Role of Social Comparisons

We have seen that academic self-image is affected by children's academic performance and by the types of attributions they make regarding failure. But the general decline over the elementary grades in children's self-evaluations of competence may involve yet another factor.

Children, like adults, evaluate their abilities at least in part by comparing them with those of others—a process called **social comparison** (Festinger, 1954; Suls & Wills, 1991). This process begins as early as kindergarten, but its function changes with age (Stipek, 1992).

Kindergartners use what their classmates are doing or saying primarily as a way of making friends or learning how things are done. For example, a child may comment to a classmate that they are coloring on the same page of their books. Social comparisons, at this point, do not appear to have much impact on the child's self-image (Aboud, 1985; Stipek & Tannatt, 1984). As children proceed through the early grades, however, their social comparisons increasingly involve academic performance, and they begin to use the comparisons to evaluate their own competence relative to others (Butler, 1992; Ruble & Frey, 1991).

By second grade, children's spontaneous self-evaluative remarks become positively correlated with the number of social comparisons they make; that is, children with lower opinions of their competence make fewer social comparisons (Frey & Ruble, 1987). One interpretation of this finding is that in continually comparing their performance with that of peers, many children unhappily discover that their work is not as good as they had believed. A child who once found great pleasure in drawing may discover that his artwork is not as attractive as that of his classmates. As a result, he may both lower his opinion of his drawings and begin to avoid com-

Social comparison
Comparing one's abilities to those of others.

• Children's willingness to make social comparisons is related to their academic competence.

paring his work with that of other children. If this interpretation is correct, we would expect academically successful children to seek out more information about their performance than children who are lower achievers. And research has found just that: High-achieving students show more interest in comparing their performance with classmates' and also in discovering the correct answers to problems (Ruble & Flett, 1988). (The role of social comparison and other contextual factors in junior high school is discussed in Box 13-2).

This developmental progression in the function of social comparisons is not inevitable, however, and can be influenced by the atmosphere of the educational environment. For example, in Israel the communal kibbutz environment places greater emphasis on cooperative, rather than competitive, learning and fosters more concern with mastering skills rather than surpassing others. As a result, even older children in the kibbutz environment have been found to use social comparison primarily as a means of acquiring new abilities and much less for self-evaluation (Butler & Ruzany, 1993).

The relation between social comparison and academic self-concept, then, is bidirectional. Social comparisons can affect children's self-image by giving them information about how they are performing relative to other children. But children's self-image may affect their willingness to engage in social comparisons, depending on how pleasant or aversive they expect the resulting information to be.

Parenting Styles

Children's academic self-concept is also affected by the attitudes, expectations, and behaviors of parents. Studies have shown that parents' perceptions of their children's academic abilities are, in fact, one of the best predictors of the children's self-perceptions of ability (Phillips & Zimmerman, 1990; Stevenson & Newman, 1986). And, as we will see in Chapter 15, parents generally hold higher opinions and expect greater achievements of their sons than their daughters (Phillips, 1987; Phillips & Zimmerman, 1990).

How do such expectations produce their effects on children's self-perceptions? One likely possibility involves the way parents interact with children on academic tasks. For example, we know that parents who display an authoritative style of discipline and child rearing tend to use more scaffolding techniques when working with their children (Pratt et al., 1988), and that these children, in turn, tend to be more cognitively competent (Baumrind, 1989, 1991).

To determine whether differences in parents' interaction styles also influence academic self-concept, researchers in one study observed academically successful students working on several tasks with either their mothers or their fathers (Wagner & Phillips, 1992). The children were divided into those whose academic self-concepts were high and those whose academic self-concepts were low. Interestingly, no differences in interaction style were found among the mothers of these two groups. However, the fathers behaved quite differently. Fathers of children with high academic self-concept were warmer and more supportive in their interactions than were the fathers of the other children. This finding is consistent with other research in which college students recalled that continuing support from their fathers was instrumental in their success in school (Schaffer & Blatt, 1990).

Effects of Academic Self-Concept

Children's perception of their academic competence has perhaps been of such interest to psychologists because of its applied significance—academic self-concept strongly influences academic achievement, as we saw in the discussion of learned helplessness (Nolen-Hoeksema, Girgus, & Seligman, 1986). Studies examining feelings of competence and perceived self-efficacy report that children who view themselves as academically skilled are more motivated to succeed, more persistent in their work, and more willing to seek out challenging tasks or problems (Boggiano, Main, & Katz, 1988; Harter, 1988; Harter & Connell, 1984; Schunk, 1984). A high academic self-concept, even when it is an overestimate of the child's abilities, also correlates positively with (and probably contributes to) a high level of self-esteem (Connell & Ilardi, 1987; Harter, 1985).

As importantly, children with low opinions of their academic abilities are less motivated to work. One study, in fact, found that even among children whose academic skills were high, students who held an incorrectly low opinion of their competence approached new tasks with less effort and optimism than their classmates (Phillips, 1984, 1987). Thus, for some children, academic success may hinge as much on academic self-concept as it does on academic ability.

✔ *To Recap...*

The opinions children form about themselves comprise their self-esteem. Self-esteem is assumed to have both cognitive and affective components. Researchers have focused on the former and have typically measured self-esteem by use of questionnaires.

Kindergartners tend to have a relatively high level of self-esteem, which remains stable until early adolescence. At about age 12, children report a dip in self-esteem, which has been attributed to several changes that typify adolescence, including an increase in self-consciousness.

An important component of self-esteem is a feeling of competence. Academic self-concept, representing the child's perceived competence in the classroom, has been of particular interest to researchers. The academic self-image of the kindergartner is high, but it steadily decreases over the elementary school years. Girls display lower academic self-images during these years than boys.

Academic self-concept is affected by feedback regarding failure. Feedback that leads children to attribute failure to insufficient effort has little effect on their subsequent motivation. But feedback leading children to attribute failure to insufficient ability can lower their expectations of success to such an extent that they may eventually fail even in easy tasks—a phenomenon called learned helplessness. Females in middle childhood display more learned helplessness than males, partly because males and females receive different types of feedback from teachers. A form of learned helplessness resulting from repeated criticism has been found in children as young as 6.

As children move through the early grades, they increasingly use social comparisons in developing academic self-concepts. This process may explain the general decline in acade-

DO AMERICAN SCHOOLS DEPRESS
ADOLESCENTS' ACADEMIC SELF-CONCEPT?

The dip in self-esteem that is common during early adolescence usually includes a decline in feelings of academic competence and motivation (Eccles, Midgley, & Adler, 1984; Harter, 1981). Some have attributed this decline also to the physical and emotional changes associated with puberty or to other developmental processes (Simmons & Blyth, 1987).

An alternative explanation, however, views the problem more as a mismatch between predictable developmental changes of adolescence and the educational context to which students are exposed (Seidman et al., 1994). Specifically, Jacquelynne Eccles contends that most junior high schools are not well suited to the developmental needs of adolescents, resulting in what she describes as a poor *stage/environment fit* (Eccles et al., 1993a; Eccles & Midgley, 1989).

Eccles argues that the typical junior high school environment produces mismatches in several areas. First, junior high teachers tend to put more emphasis on teacher control and discipline at a time when the adolescent is attempting to become more independent and self-reliant. A related problem is that teachers at this level frequently report feeling discouraged and ineffective, especially in their attempts to teach lower ability students, whereas students during this period

are in special need of support and encouragement. Third, having students move from class to class and grouping them according to their abilities tend to encourage social comparisons among adolescents at a time when their feelings of self-consciousness are just beginning to emerge. Finally, junior high teachers tend to use higher standards of grading, which results in some students' suddenly encountering more failures than before (Eccles & Midgley, 1990).

Eccles supports these contentions with data from a longitudinal study across a number of sixth-and seventh-grade classrooms. The study investigated the beliefs and behaviors of teachers and students regarding mathematics. One finding was that seventh-grade math teachers reported having less trust and confidence in their students and feeling less effective in working with them than the sixth-grade teachers (Midgley, Feldlaufer, & Eccles, 1988b). The students, in turn, viewed teachers in seventh grade as being less supportive, less friendly, and less fair (Feldlaufer, Midgley, & Eccles, 1988). The researchers also compared the self-efficacy levels of the teachers with those of their students. Students who had moved from a sixth-grade teacher whose self-efficacy level was high to a seventh-grade teacher whose level was low ended the

mic self-image, because many children must lower their assessments of their abilities as they compare them with those of other children. Parents' (especially fathers') interaction styles also influence children's academic self-concept.

Academic self-concept influences children's academic achievement. High self-image improves motivation and success, and low self-image reduces them, even among children whose low self-image inaccurately reflects their high academic ability.

SELF-REGULATION

We have examined how growing children gain knowledge of the self and how their continual evaluation of this knowledge produces a concept of the self. In this section, we consider a third process—how the self comes to regulate, or control, children's behavior.

Self-regulation is a crucial aspect of human development. If children did not learn to control their own behavior—to avoid the things they must avoid, to wait for the things they cannot have right away, to alter strategies that are not working—

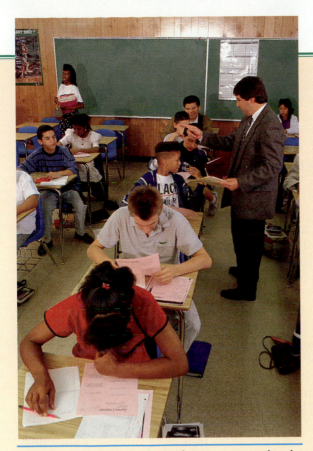

• The increased emphasis on classroom control and discipline in many junior high schools may serve to depress self-esteem in adolescent students, who are in the process of developing independence and self-reliance.

year with lower expectations regarding their abilities in math than students whose seventh-grade teacher reported high self-efficacy. This pattern was most pronounced among students at lower ability levels (Midgley, Feldlaufer, & Eccles, 1988b). Finally, the students' perceptions of how much support they received from their teachers were compared with the value the students attached to mathematics. When students moved to a seventh-grade teacher they viewed as higher in support, their view of math was enhanced; when they moved to a teacher they viewed as nonsupportive, the value they attached to math declined (Midgley, Feldlaufer, & Eccles, 1988a).

These results suggest that at least some declines in academic self-concept and motivation that occur during adolescence may not be inevitable. What seems to be necessary is for educational policymakers to adjust school environments to better fit the developmental needs of young adolescents. Such changes might include keeping students together in the same classrooms, fostering better student–teacher relationships, and adjusting grading standards to more closely match those to which students have been accustomed (Eccles et al., 1993a). These changes may not eliminate all of the problems associated with adolescence, but they can help provide a more appropriate educational context for learning to take place.

they would be constantly at the mercy of the moment-to-moment pushes and pulls of their environments. They would simply be "weathervanes," as Bandura puts it (1986, p. 335). The development of self-control is one of the child's most impressive accomplishments. Self-control indicates at the very least that the child knows what demands are made by the surrounding world, realizes what behaviors relate to those demands, and understands how to adjust the behaviors to meet the demands (Vaughn, Kopp, & Krakow, 1984).

The hallmark of self-regulation is internal control. Throughout childhood, a great deal of children's behavior is regulated by commands or consequences that flow from parents and others. But some portion of behavior gradually comes to be performed under the children's own private commands and instructions, sometimes even followed by self-administered rewards or punishments. How does such self-control develop, and what are its effects?

The Emergence of Self-Control

Many theoretical models have been proposed to explain the emergence of self-regulation (e.g., Bandura, 1991a; Harter, 1982; Kopp, 1991; Mischel, Shoda, &

Rodriguez, 1989; Vygotsky, 1934/1962), and all of them share a common belief. Children's behavior is assumed to be completely controlled at first by external sources. Then, gradually, some of this control is internalized. Although the theories disagree on the contributions of biological, cognitive, and social influences to this process, they all propose this fundamental shift from external to internal regulation.

Self-regulation is primitive during early infancy and mostly involves involuntary biological processes (Rothbart & Posner, 1985). As we have seen, babies reflexively squint in response to a bright light and turn away when the caregiver is providing too much verbal stimulation. Such responses serve important regulatory functions, but they offer no evidence that the infants who engage in them are cognitively aware of what is happening.

By the beginning of the second year, babies have developed many voluntary behaviors and can act on their environments in purposeful ways. Children now act in order to accomplish things or to reach goals, as when a baby grabs for a toy he would like to play with or pushes over a tower of blocks to watch it crash to the floor. But at this point, the child's ability to monitor his behaviors and to adjust them as necessary is still not very impressive (Bullock & Lutkenhaus, 1988).

Compliance
Willingness to obey the requests of others.

The goals of 2-year-olds may involve other people. Children now show the first evidence of **compliance** by following the commands or requests of others (Howes & Olenick, 1986; Schneider-Rosen & Wenz-Gross, 1990). Social consequences undoubtedly play a role in this process, because compliance often results in attention or social approval and noncompliance in disapproval (Kuczynski & Kochanska, 1990; Schaffer & Crook, 1980). There is also evidence suggesting that babies at this age sometimes follow directions (such as "Put the blanket on the teddy bear") simply because they find doing so pleasurable in its own right (Kaler & Kopp, 1990; Rheingold, Cook, & Kolowitz, 1987). But even here, the child's behavior remains largely under external, rather than internal, control.

Self-control makes its first appearance during the 3rd year, as children begin to resist having everything done for them and to assert their desire to do things themselves (Bullock & Lutkenhaus, 1990; Geppert & Kuster, 1983). Much of the external control these children have experienced involves verbal instruction from the parent. In asserting their independence, the children now sometimes attempt to take on this role themselves, and they adopt some of the same regulating commands. A 2-year-old might be overheard, for example, to say "no, no" as she reaches for a forbidden object. Or she may direct her own behavior in much the same way her mother has directed it previously ("Put the spoon in the bowl"). At this point, then, some verbal control over the child's behavior has begun to move from external sources to the child herself. But the progression is not yet complete. The final step comes when the child internalizes the control, directing her behavior silently with thought rather than speech. This form of self-regulation generally is not apparent before 3 years of age.

Beyond age 3, self-control quickly becomes much more elaborate and sophisticated. Children develop strategies to resist the many temptations they encounter every day. They also learn to delay gratification by passing up smaller immediate rewards in exchange for larger delayed ones. And they acquire a host of additional techniques for guiding other aspects of their behavior. We consider some of these more complex forms of self-regulation a little later in the chapter.

The Role of Private Speech

Many psychologists believe that the transition from external control to self-control is guided primarily by the child's language. This proposition has been most clearly articulated in the writings of two Soviet psychologists, Lev Vygotsky and Alexander Luria.

Vygotsky's Model

Earlier, we noted that Vygotsky was a contemporary of Piaget. Like Piaget, he believed that a good way to learn about young children's development is by observing them in problem-solving situations (Vygotsky, 1934/1962). Vygotsky was intrigued by the common observation that preschoolers sometimes talk to themselves while working on a task—a behavior now generally referred to as **private speech** (Diaz & Berk, 1992; Zivin, 1979). Piaget had labeled this self-directed behavior *egocentric speech* and believed that it was only minimally relevant to children's cognitive development and self-regulation (Hodapp & Goldfield, 1985).

Vygotsky did not agree. He argued that young children's private speech grows out of their interactions with parents and other adults as they work together on various tasks (Behrend, Rosengren, & Perlmutter, 1992; Rizzo & Corsaro, 1988). Much of a parent's speech in such situations involves guiding and regulating the child. Over the course of many such interactions, children begin to use their parents' instructional comments (although not always in versions as complete or well formed) to direct their own behavior. Gradually, the controlling speech becomes internalized as thought, and children eventually produce silent statements similar to the verbal ones. Vygotsky thus viewed self-regulation as developing out of the child's social interactions—a process he called **sociogenesis** (Van der Veer & Valsiner, 1988).

Research is offering more and more support for Vygotsky's model. If the model is correct, we would expect children's production of private speech to increase over the early years, as they increasingly adopt the language of adults, and then to diminish gradually as the speech "goes underground." Developmental studies have shown that this pattern is indeed apparent across the ages 4 to 10 (Bivens & Berk, 1990; Frauenglass & Diaz, 1985; Kohlberg, Yaeger, & Hjertholm, 1968). Researchers have also found that in middle and later childhood, an increasing proportion of private speech takes the form of whispering, presumably also reflecting its gradual internalization (Frauenglass & Diaz, 1985). Furthermore, private speech is most evident at the beginning of a new task and at other points where children are having the greatest difficulty. But it decreases (becomes internalized) as they master the task (Behrend et al., 1992; Meichenbaum & Goodman, 1979). Finally, a number of studies have closely examined parent–child interaction during problem-solving activities, with a special focus on the changes that occur over time. Parents have been found to adjust their behaviors to the demands of the situation—for example, being more directive with children who are younger or who are just learning a task—and children have shown evidence of taking on the regulating role and guiding their own behavior to solve the problems (Freund, 1990; Pratt et al., 1988; Saxe, Guberman, & Gearhart, 1987).

Luria's Model

Vygotsky's interest in verbal regulation was carried on by his colleague Alexander Luria (1961, 1982). Whereas Vygotsky focused on the transfer of parental speech to children, Luria was more interested in the role speech plays in controlling young children's behavior. And whereas Vygotsky's work was based largely on naturalistic observations of children at play, Luria used a simple but ingenious laboratory method (Vocate, 1987).

The behavior of interest was the way in which children pressed a rubber bulb with their hands. The bulb allowed Luria to investigate, among other things, what factors were effective in getting the child either to start pressing the bulb or to in-

Private speech
Speech children produce and direct toward themselves during a problem-solving activity.

Sociogenesis
The process of acquiring knowledge or skills through social interactions.

hibit (either stop or not start) pressing it. Here, we consider only two of the factors Luria studied. The first involved whether the child responded to the *semantic content* (the meaning) of a spoken command or instead responded only to its sound or rhythm, which Luria called its *pulse*. The second factor was whether the command was given by someone else or was spoken by the child. The results of Luria's many studies indicate that verbal regulation of this sort changes as the child grows (Waters & Tinsley, 1982; Zivin, 1979).

Between 18 months and 3 years of age, only adult, external speech can influence the child's responding; self-verbalizations are ineffective. Furthermore, speech can only start the behavior; it cannot inhibit it. If a 2-year-old is pressing the bulb, for example, the instruction "Stop!" usually leads to even harder pressing. This is because the aspect of speech that controls behavior during this period is its pulse rather than its meaning. For the same reason, these youngsters are just as likely to begin pressing when they hear the command "Don't press!" as when they hear the command "Press!"

From ages 3 to 4.5, external speech can control both starting and inhibiting, indicating that the semantic content of commands presented by others has become relevant. Children's own self-directed speech (under the experimenter's instructions) now can cause them to start pressing the bulb. But because children during this period respond only to the pulse of their own speech, they cannot yet produce self-controlled inhibiting.

By 5 years of age, children's self-directed speech can control their behavior almost as well as speech from the experimenter. Luria contended that at this point children's vocal speech becomes internalized as they begin to guide their responses with silent instructions. His own research, however, did not go on to examine this final part of the process.

Luria's model has inspired a great deal of research, although not all of it has supported his views (Miller, Shelton, & Flavell, 1970). We consider one study here and discuss some others in the following section. This experiment nicely illustrates Luria's distinction between the semantic content and the pulse of speech. Children in the study participated in a game similar to Simon Says. On each turn, the experimenter modeled a response—for example, touched her toes—and simultaneously gave either a command to start ("Touch your toes!") or to inhibit ("Don't touch your toes!"). For one third of the children, the experimenter used a soft voice; for one third, a medium voice; and for one third, a loud voice. The dependent measures of interest were the number of starting errors (not responding when they should) and the number of inhibiting errors (responding when they should not). Luria's model would predict more inhibiting errors, because verbal control over inhibition develops later. And indeed, the children made about seven times as many inhibiting errors. The researchers also predicted that for younger children, louder commands, which are more effective in grabbing the children's attention, should produce more inhibiting errors, because these children should be responding only to the pulse aspect of the speech and not to its content. For older children, to whom the content is relevant, louder commands should be better for controlling behavior. The results of this study, depicted in Figure 13-1, confirmed these predictions (Saltz, Campbell, & Skotko, 1983).

Luria's research adds further support to Vygotsky's belief that self-regulation begins as external control and is gradually internalized. But perhaps more importantly, it illustrates the limited information-processing capabilities of younger children, who tend to respond more to the presence or absence of a command than to its content. As the data from the study just described suggest, shouting at a toddler

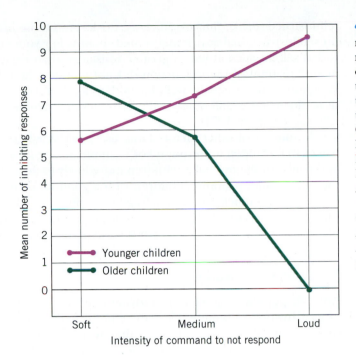

Figure 13-1 Mean number of inhibiting errors for younger and older children as a function of the intensity of the verbal command not to respond. From "Verbal Control of Behavior: The Effects of Shouting" by E. Saltz, S. Cambell, and D. Skotko, 1983, *Developmental Psychology, 19,* pp. 461–464. Copyright 1983 by The American Psychological Association. Reprinted by permission.

to inhibit a response ("Don't touch the stove!") may actually make the child more likely to carry out a dangerous act.

Resistance to Temptation

Luria's laboratory studies of self-regulation were somewhat abstract and were not designed to deal directly with everyday events or problems. United States researchers, by contrast, have used experimental procedures that bear a closer resemblance to situations children commonly encounter in their daily lives.

One such situation arises when children must resist the temptation to do something that they are prohibited from doing. Babies have no self-control in this regard and immediately go after whatever appeals to them. The only deterrent is control by the parent, who either prevents or punishes the response. However, children eventually learn to inhibit forbidden behaviors, even when no one is watching them. How does this kind of self-control come about?

A common method for studying resistance to temptation uses the **forbidden toy technique**. Typically, an experimenter puts a child in a room where there is an attractive toy but tells the child not to touch or play with the toy. Outside the room, observers surreptitiously monitor the child's behavior through a two-way mirror. The investigators usually are interested in how long the child waits before breaking the rule or how much time the child spends playing with the forbidden toy.

One example of this type of research has some relevance for Luria's analysis. The researchers wanted to find out whether having children produce self-instructional statements during their waiting time would affect their ability to resist temptation. The children were placed in a room with several attractive toys on a table behind them and were instructed not to turn around and look at the toys while the experimenter was out of the room. Some of the children were also told that, to help them keep from looking, they should repeat out loud a relevant statement, like "I must not turn around." Children in a second group were told to use an irrelevant

Forbidden toy technique
An experimental procedure for studying children's resistance to temptation in which the child is left alone with an attractive toy and instructed not to play with it.

self-instruction, like "hickory, dickory, dock." And those in a third group were given no self-instructional advice and waited silently. For younger children, producing a verbal self-instruction led to greater resistance than remaining silent. But the semantic content of the instruction did not matter—the relevant and irrelevant instructions worked equally well. For older children, the content of the self-instruction did make a difference, with the relevant statement proving most effective (Hartig & Kanfer, 1973).

A number of other factors have also been shown to influence children's behavior in forbidden toy settings. For example, seeing an adult model break the rule and play with the toy makes children more likely to do so (Grusec et al., 1979). On the other hand, providing children with a good rationale for following the prohibition ("Don't touch the toy; it's fragile and might break") increases the likelihood that they will resist (Parke, 1977), as does teaching children to develop their own plans or strategies for dealing with the temptation (C. J. Patterson, 1982).

Delay of Gratification

Delay of gratification technique
An experimental procedure for studying children's ability to postpone a smaller, immediate reward in order to obtain a larger, delayed one.

Another popular approach to studying children's self-control has been the **delay of gratification technique**. Here the child usually is presented with two choices: a small reward that is available immediately or a larger reward that can only be obtained later. This situation, of course, is analogous to many choices children (and adults) encounter every day. Should I use this week's allowance to buy a small toy or combine it with next week's and buy a larger toy? Should I eat this snack now or save my appetite for a better meal later? Perhaps because this experimental task is a bit more complex than that involving resistance to temptation, more factors have been shown to influence children's ability to delay gratification (Mischel et al., 1989).

Here, too, Luria's model has found support. In one study, while waiting for the preferred reward, children were directed to produce either a relevant statement ("I am waiting for the marshmallow"), an irrelevant statement ("one, two, three"), or nothing. Once again, either of the self-statements increased waiting time for younger children, but only the relevant verbalizations were of assistance to the older children (Karniol & Miller, 1981).

• The ability to delay gratification appears to be a personality trait that remains quite stable over the years.

Another method for helping children to delay gratification is to reduce or alter the attention they pay to the tempting object (the smaller but immediately available reward) (Mischel et al., 1991). When the object is out of sight, for example, children will wait much longer. The same is true when they spend the waiting time playing with a toy or engaging in some other distracting activity. Even when they are thinking about the tempting object, children will wait longer if they are instructed to think only about certain of its objective properties (say, the shape or color of a candy bar) rather than about its appealing properties (the candy bar's smell or taste).

As children grow older, their understanding of these delay strategies increases. For example, when presented with various waiting techniques and asked to select the ones that would work best, preschoolers display little knowledge of what strategies would be more effective. Third graders, however, show an impressive understanding. And by sixth grade, the large majority of children clearly seem to know that redirecting one's attention from the reward and various other forms of distraction are the methods most useful in delaying gratification (Mischel et al., 1989; Yates, Yates, & Beasley, 1987).

Finally, children's ability to cope with temptation in this type of experimental situation appears to reflect a surprisingly stable personality characteristic. In a recent study, adolescents who had participated as preschoolers in delay of gratification research of the type just described were studied again 10 years later. Parents were asked to complete several questionnaires concerned with aspects of their children's present cognitive skills, social competence, and ability to cope with stress. The results indicated that children who had been better at delaying gratification in their early years were much more likely to be rated by parents as stronger in each of these three areas. For example, the children who had waited the longest during the experimental procedures (especially those who had spontaneously developed good coping strategies) were now reported to be the most academically successful, the best at getting along with peers, the best at coping with problems, and the most confident and self-reliant (Mischel et al., 1991; Mischel, Shoda, & Peake, 1988). These rather remarkable findings indicate that a child's early ability to delay gratification may be one long-term predictor of that child's eventual success and happiness.

A practical application of research into self-regulation in general is described in Box 13-3.

✔ *To Recap...*

The development of self-regulation is a major achievement that represents a shift from external environmental control to internal regulation. Little meaningful self-regulation is evident during the 1st year of life. During the 2nd year, children's voluntary behaviors are principally under environmental control, but some of this control gradually moves to the child during the 3rd year in the form of self-directing speech and, eventually, self-directing thought. Self-control strategies after age 3 become more numerous and increasingly complex.

Verbal self-regulation has been investigated extensively by Soviet psychologists. Lev Vygotsky studied children's private speech, concluding that, through social interactions and shared problem-solving activities, children gradually adopt the regulating speech of parents and internalize it as thought. Alexander Luria studied the effects of speech on children's starting and inhibiting behaviors. He contends that children at about 5 years of age can control their behavior using internalized, self-directed speech.

Resistance to temptation studies examine the common situation in which children must withhold a prohibited behavior. Using the forbidden toy technique, investigators have found that the ability to resist temptation is influenced by a number of factors, including

TEACHING CHILDREN TO TALK TO THEMSELVES

An exciting outgrowth of research on children's self-control has been the application of self-regulation procedures to problems in the classroom. Much of this work has been concerned with behavior problems and has trained children to monitor the appropriateness of their own behavior and to dispense self-rewards accordingly (Kendall & Braswell, 1985; Rosenbaum & Drabman, 1979). An interesting study illustrates how these methods can be applied to children's academic performance (Roberts, Nelson, & Olson, 1987).

The subjects were first and second graders who were having difficulty with math skills. The researchers believed that the children's performance could be improved if they were taught to approach each problem in a systematic, step-by-step manner, which would be guided by self-instructional statements.

Following a baseline period, in which the researchers simply observed the children's unaided performance, the training was begun with the modeling of self-instructions. For a simple addition problem, the approach modeled to the child might be as follows:

$$8 + \square = 15$$

"First, I have to read the problem. Eight plus some number equals 15. This is an addition problem, so I have to circle the sign. I circle the plus. Now I put eight sticks over the 8 and put sticks over the box until I get 15. 1, 2, 3, 4, 5, 6, 7, 8 and 9, 10, 11, 12, 13, 14, 15. Now I count the sticks over the box. 1, 2, 3, 4, 5, 6, 7. There are seven sticks over the box. Seven is my answer, so I write it in the box. Eight plus 7 equals 15."

Children then practiced and were given feedback on more problems until they could reliably produce the correct self-instructions on their own. At this point, a reinforcement system was introduced. The experiment involved several conditions, but of particular interest is the condition in which children earned rewards simply for continuing to use the self-instructions as they performed their daily math problems.

The data from three of these students over several weeks are presented in Figure 13-2. The dependent variable (on the vertical axis) indicates the number of math problems solved correctly during the baseline condition and then during the reward procedures. Recall that these children did not receive reinforcement for the accuracy of their math answers; they were rewarded only for producing the self-instructional statements. Their improvement in math performance thus can be attributed directly to the production of

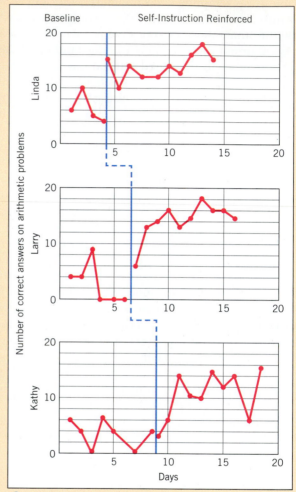

Figure 13-2 Number of math problems solved by 3 first and second graders participating in the self-instructional training project. During the baseline period, when no training was involved, performance was low. When children were taught to self-instruct and were reinforced for doing so correctly, the number of problems they solved increased markedly. From "Self-instruction: An analysis of the differential effects of instruction and reinforcement" by R. N. Roberts, R. O. Nelson, and T. W. Olson, 1987, *Journal of Applied Behavior Analysis, 20,* pp. 235–242. Copyright 1987 by the Society for the Experimental Analysis of Behavior.

self-guiding verbalizations. These results illustrate clearly how training in self-regulation can be used as a tool in the classroom.

appropriate self-statements, modeling, and a good rationale or plan for resisting the prohibited act.

Delay of gratification studies examine children's ability to forego smaller immediate rewards in order to receive larger delayed ones. Factors that affect waiting time include self-statements and various methods of reducing attention to the tempting, immediately available reward. Children's understanding of effective delay strategies increases as they get older. The ability to delay gratification during the preschool years has been linked with parents' ratings of their adolescents' cognitive, social, and coping abilities.

CONCLUSION

This chapter has covered a number of topics that may seem only loosely connected to one another. Why a baby watches her feet in a mirror may seem unrelated to why she does or does not give up a smaller reward to wait for a larger one in kindergarten or why she lowers her opinion of herself in junior high school. The lack of an immediately obvious connection between these aspects of child development reflects the fact that the self has only recently become a topic of major research interest. As noted, no single theory, as yet, has even attempted to explain all three components of the self-system.

But whatever its theoretical underpinnings, our examination of the self has nicely illustrated an important theme of this book and of modern child psychology. The theme is that social and cognitive development are so interdependent that it is difficult to study either one alone. Although for clarity we have often discussed these two domains separately, it should be apparent that one cannot be completely understood without the other. We have seen, for example, that children's growing knowledge about themselves and their increasingly accurate evaluations of their abilities have major influences on their interactions with other people. On the other hand, Vygotsky and others have demonstrated that social interactions play an important role in the development of children's thinking and problem-solving skills. This theme has emerged in earlier chapters and will continue to find its way into our discussions as we look further at children's social development.

FOR THOUGHT AND DISCUSSION

1. Our awareness of who we are involves both the subjective I-self and the objective Me-self. *Think about who you are. Which of these two selves do you tend to focus on? Why do you think this is the case? Would you guess this is true for everyone?*

2. Our self-efficacy judgments are believed to influence our behavior. *Can you think of several things you recently decided to __not__ do as a direct result of your own self-efficacy judgments? Do you think that following these judgments is always wise?*

3. Presumably, the self continues to differentiate beyond the adolescent years. *Have you begun to think about yourself in any new ways since entering college? What additional "selves" might you expect to emerge as you grow older (such as the "parent-self")?*

4. Junior high schools do not seem well suited to the needs of young adolescents. *Beyond the suggestions mentioned in the text, what are some other changes that would be useful, and why would they be useful? What about in high school?*

5. Bandura noted that in the absence of self-control we would all be "weathervanes." *What exactly did he mean by this? Give some everyday examples. Do other species demonstrate self-control? Give examples of some behavior that supports your answer.*

6. Children who are better at delaying gratification grow up to be more competent in a variety of ways. *Why do you think this ability is so important?*

Chapter 14

MORAL DEVELOPMENT

Moral rules
Rules used by a society to protect individuals and to guarantee their rights.

Social conventions
Rules used by a society to govern everyday behavior and to maintain order.

Moral conduct
The aspect of children's moral development concerned with behavior.

Moral reasoning
The aspect of children's moral development concerned with knowledge and understanding of moral issues and principles.

A major challenge of childhood is to develop an understanding of exactly how the world operates—that is, to learn "the rules of the game." For example, physical rules, such as gravity and object permanence, govern the environment, and complex linguistic rules govern communication. As if these were not enough, however, children must also come to understand another major set of rules—the laws, sanctions, and everyday practices that govern the social world in which they live.

Social rules are of two main types (Turiel, Killen, & Helwig, 1987). **Moral rules** protect the welfare of individuals, guarantee people's rights, and determine what is fair and what is unjust. In most societies, for example, people are not permitted to kill one another or to steal one another's property. Added to such formal laws are the many **social conventions** that govern everyday behavior and maintain order in the society. These might include giving up a seat to an older person, saying "please" and "thank you," and waiting in line for one's turn. Furthermore, children must learn that both moral and social rules can vary from one setting to another and that there may be important differences between, for example, the rules of their family and those of their classroom or between the behavior expected by parents and the behavior encouraged by peers. Needless to say, acquiring social rules of this type comprises a very important part of children's development (Gralinski & Kopp, 1993; Maccoby & Martin, 1983).

Social rules are designed primarily to guide children in discerning what is "right" behavior and what is "wrong" behavior. For this reason, the study of how children come to understand and follow these rules has traditionally come under the heading of "morality" or "moral development." Until early in this century, moral development was an area of academic concern only to philosophers and religious scholars. Today, developmental psychology also has a great deal of interest in this topic.

Contemporary research in moral development falls into two major categories. Researchers who focus on **moral conduct** are interested in explaining children's behavior—for example, why children steal, which children are more likely to start fights, and what factors promote sharing and cooperation among youngsters. Researchers concerned with **moral reasoning** investigate how children think about what they and others do. Studies of this type focus on children's ability to examine a moral situation and to decide such questions as, Was the behavior appropriate or not? Should the person be punished for the behavior? If so, how much?

We begin this chapter by considering the approaches to moral development that have been taken by the three major theoretical traditions. Then we examine what psychologists have learned about the development of moral reasoning abilities. Next we focus on issues of moral conduct—first the factors affecting children's *prosocial*, or desirable, behaviors and then the causes of aggression and other *antisocial* behaviors.

THEORIES OF MORAL DEVELOPMENT

Two theoretical issues have dominated the study of moral development (Gibbs & Schnell, 1985; Wainryb, 1993). One is whether children's moral beliefs and behaviors reside in the child and simply emerge over time or, instead, reside in the culture and are transmitted to the child. You will, of course, recognize this issue as a form of the nature–nurture debate. The second issue involves the generality of moral rules. If they emerge from the child, they must have a large biological component, making them universal for all members of our species. On the other hand, if they develop within the social group, they are more arbitrary and thus can vary from one culture to the next. These two questions lie at the heart of much of the research on this topic.

Cognitive-Developmental Models

As might be expected, the cognitive tradition has been most concerned with the development of children's moral reasoning. Theorists in this tradition contend that cognitive development forms the basis for moral development and that to understand children's moral conduct, we must first understand their reasoning abilities and their knowledge of moral issues (DeVries, 1991; Rest, 1983). The cognitive approach further holds that a child's moral conduct should display considerable consistency from one situation to another and should reflect a unitary process in which moral reasoning and moral conduct are clearly related. Finally, because these models are closely associated with theories of cognitive development, they typically view moral development as involving a distinct series of stages (Krebs & Van Hesteren, 1994).

Cognitive-developmentalists begin with the observation that moral questions are often complex. Issues such as abortion rights, gun control, and the death penalty involve compelling arguments on both sides. Older children and adults, they point out, typically examine the various arguments and weigh the evidence on all sides. Young children, in contrast, have difficulty appreciating that an issue may look very different from another person's perspective, and so they tend to base their opinions on only certain aspects of the information and arrive at simplistic conclusions (Turiel, Hildebrandt, & Wainryb, 1991). These observations have led cognitive-developmentalists to conclude that advances in moral reasoning abilities are dependent on increasing cognitive abilities as the child grows. These advances, in turn, are thought to produce more mature moral behaviors.

Two models have guided most of the cognitive research on moral development. Here we simply describe the models; in the next section, we will examine some of the research findings that relate to them.

Piaget's Theory

Piaget's model of moral development grew out of his early work with children in Geneva, Switzerland, during the 1920s and 1930s. To investigate how children's conceptions of morality develop, Piaget used two very different methods.

One was a naturalistic approach in which he observed children playing common street games, such as marbles. Piaget closely examined how youngsters created and enforced the rules of their games, and he questioned them about circumstances under which the rules could be modified or even ignored. The second approach was more experimental and involved presenting individual children with **moral dilemmas** to solve. These took the form of short stories in which the child had to determine which of two characters was "naughtier." For example, in one story a little boy named Augustine accidentally makes a large ink stain on the tablecloth while trying to be helpful and fill his father's inkpot, whereas a little boy named Julian makes a small ink spot on the tablecloth while engaging in the forbidden act of playing with his father's pen.

From this research, Piaget developed a model of moral development, which focused on the way children follow rules and which consisted of four stages (Damon,

Moral dilemmas
Stories used by Piaget and others to assess children's levels of moral reasoning.

• Piaget studied common street games as a way of examining children's conceptions of rules.

Moral realism
Piaget's second stage of moral development, in which children's reasoning is based on objective and physical aspects of a situation and is often inflexible.

Objective responsibility
Responsibility assigned solely in terms of an action's objective and physical consequences. Children in Piaget's stage of moral realism evaluate situations using this concept.

Immanent justice
Literally, inherent justice; refers to the expectation of children in Piaget's stage of moral realism that punishment must follow any rule violation, including those that appear to go undetected.

1983; Piaget, 1932). In the first stage (2 to 4 years), children have no real conception of morality. Much of their behavior involves play and imaginative games that have no formal rules, although at times they may invent certain restrictions as part of the play (e.g., all green blocks must be put in the same pail). The idea of following someone else's rules does not appear consistently until the second stage (5 to 7 years). But when rule following does emerge, children approach the concept in a very absolute manner. Social rules are viewed as *heteronomous*, or externally dictated, commands presented by people in authority (usually parents), and they cannot be changed. Children in this second stage, called the stage of **moral realism**, do not think to question the purpose or correctness of a rule, even though they may not like to follow it. Thus, Piaget observed that younger children playing marble games were usually very inflexible about changing any rules, even if it would have made the game more convenient or more fun.

Piaget noted two interesting characteristics that grow out of this absolutist orientation. Most children in the second stage display **objective responsibility**, meaning that they evaluate moral situations only in terms of their physical and objective consequences. In the moral dilemmas, for example, these children saw acts causing more damage as more morally wrong than acts causing less damage—regardless of the character's motives or intentions. Hence, the helpful Augustine was usually seen as naughtier than the disobedient Julian because he made the larger ink stain. Another characteristic of this stage is **immanent justice**. Because these children believe so firmly in the authority of a rule, they feel that punishment must always occur when the rule is broken. Thus, if a child steals a cookie when no one is looking and then loses his baseball the following day, he is likely to assume that he has been punished for the theft.

Piaget's third stage (8 to 11 years) finds the child gradually realizing that rules are agreements created by people to help or protect one another. Obeying these rules is no longer viewed as simply following someone else's orders, but as a per-

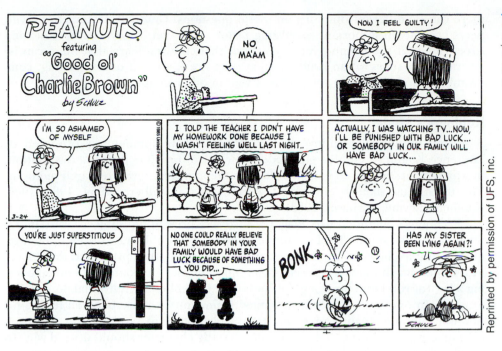

• A belief in immanent justice characterizes children's reasoning in Piaget's stage of moral realism.

sonal, *autonomous* decision to cooperate with others. Piaget observed, for example, that third-stage children could adapt marble-game rules, if necessary, to fit the circumstances of the moment (too many players, too few marbles, and so on). Furthermore, at this stage, children's more advanced cognitive abilities allow new factors to enter into their moral evaluations. What a person was trying to do—that is, the person's motives or intentions—may become as important as the outcome of the behavior. Accordingly, with increasing age, children were more likely to judge Julian's forbidden behavior naughtier, even though it caused less damage. Because the morality of following a rule is now evaluated in relation to other factors in the situation, Piaget referred to this third level as the stage of **moral relativism**.

In the final stage, which Piaget discussed only briefly, children become capable of developing new rules. Their formal operational abilities now enable them to imagine hypothetical situations that could arise in a game and to create rules that would handle them, for example. They also begin to extend their moral reasoning beyond the personal level to larger societal and political concerns. At this point, the adolescent may develop an interest in wider moral issues, such as protecting the environment or helping the homeless.

Piaget believed that moral reasoning, like cognitive development, is guided by both innate and environmental factors. On the nature side, children's advancing cognitive abilities, including their movement away from egocentric thinking, enable them to consider more information and several different perspectives when evaluating the morality of a situation. Thus, the narrow focusing on unchangeable rules and objective consequences gives way to a broader and more flexible view of the world. From the nurture perspective, Piaget believed that social experiences play an important role in the child's movement from stage to stage. During their early years, children learn that parents usually dictate and enforce the rules of behavior. In their desire to please their parents, children adopt the belief that they live in a world where rules must be followed. But the one-way nature of this rule system keeps children from expressing their own points of view or appreciating that

Moral relativism
Piaget's third stage of moral development, in which children view rules as agreements that can be altered and consider people's motives or intentions when evaluating their moral conduct.

there can be different opinions on moral questions. Gradually, interactions with peers become an important socializing factor. As Piaget discovered by observing street games, it is through peer interactions that children learn that there can be several perspectives on an issue and that rules are the result of negotiating, compromising, and respecting the points of view of other people.

Kohlberg's Model

A second influential cognitive theory of moral development was proposed by Lawrence Kohlberg. Kohlberg's model grew out of his 1958 doctoral dissertation, in which he attempted to examine Piaget's theory using newer research methods. The theory has since been revised several times (Kohlberg, 1969, 1984, 1986; Kohlberg, Levine, & Hewer, 1983).

Kohlberg's method, like Piaget's, involved presenting subjects with moral dilemmas to assess their level of moral reasoning. But Kohlberg's stories did not require a simple choice as to who was naughtier. Instead, they presented the subject with a dilemma in which a story character must choose, for example, between obeying a law (or rule) and breaking the law for the benefit of an individual person. For example, in one story a poor man named Heinz must choose between letting his sick wife die and stealing medicine from a drugstore to save her life. For each dilemma, the subject is asked to indicate what the character should do and why. In Kohlberg's model, the second question is the more important, because it presumably reveals the subject's level of reasoning.

From his research, Kohlberg concluded that moral reasoning develops in three predictable levels, termed **preconventional, conventional**, and **postconventional.** Within each level are two stages, and each stage can be divided into a social perspective component and a moral content component. The model is described in Table 14-1. In his later writings, Kohlberg suggested that the sixth stage is actually more theoretical than real. Few individuals attain this level, and none of the subjects that Kohlberg studied ever displayed it. Nevertheless, Kohlberg speculated that a seventh stage of moral development might also exist that goes beyond conventional moral reasoning and enters the realm of religious faith (Kohlberg et al., 1983).

An important aspect of Kohlberg's model is how the two components of each stage interact. The social perspective component indicates the point of view from which the moral decision is made. For example, the child in the first stage is egocentric and sees all situations from a personal point of view. With development, the child becomes better able to appreciate the dilemma from the perspective of others or in terms of what is best for society as a whole. Advances in this area are thought to be related to the individual's cognitive development and to have a strong biological basis. But advances in perspective taking are not sufficient for moral reasoning to advance. They must be accompanied by development of the moral content component, which is assumed to be more strongly influenced by the child's experiences with moral situations. Kohlberg's theory thus resembles Piaget's in assuming that moral development results from a combination of improving cognitive skills and repeated encounters with moral issues.

Movement from stage to stage in Kohlberg's model closely follows the Piagetian process of accommodation. Movement occurs when the child can no longer handle new information within her current view of the world—or in Piagetian terms, when she can no longer assimilate new information within her existing structure of schemes. Kohlberg's model places particular importance on *role-*

Preconventional level
Kohlberg's first two stages of moral development. Moral reasoning is based on the assumption that individuals must serve their own needs.

Conventional level
Kohlberg's third and fourth stages of moral development. Moral reasoning is based on the view that a social system must be based on laws and regulations.

Postconventional level
Kohlberg's final stages of moral development. Moral reasoning is based on the assumption that the value, dignity, and rights of each individual person must be maintained.

TABLE 14-1 ● Kohlberg's Stage Model of Moral Reasoning

	Social Perspective	*Moral Content*
Level I Preconventional		
Stage 1: Heteronomous morality ("Morality derives from power and authority.")	Children cannot consider more than one person's perspective. They tend to be egocentric, assuming that their feelings are shared by everyone.	This stage is equivalent to Piaget's moral realism. Evaluations of morality are absolute and focus on physical and objective characteristics of a situation. Morality is defined only by authority figures, whose rules must be obeyed.
Stage 2: Individualism and instrumental purpose ("Morality means looking out for yourself.")	Children understand that people have different needs and points of view, although they cannot yet put themselves in the other's place. Other people are assumed to serve their own self-interests.	Moral behavior is seen as valuable if it serves one's own interests. Children obey rules or cooperate with peers with an eye toward what they will get in return. Social interactions are viewed as deals and arrangements that involve concrete gains.
Level II Conventional		
Stage 3: Interpersonal conformity ("Morality means doing what makes you liked.")	People can view situations from another's perspective. They understand that an agreement between two people can be more important than each individual's self-interest.	The focus is on conformity to what most people believe is right behavior. Rules should be obeyed so that people you care about will approve of you. Interpersonal relations are based on the Golden Rule ("Do unto others. . .").
Stage 4: Law and order ("What's right is what's legal.")	People view morality from the perspective of the social system and what is necessary to keep it working. Individual needs are not considered more important than maintaining the social order.	Morality is based on strict adherence to laws and on performing one's duty. Rules are seen as applying to everyone equally and as being the correct means of resolving interpersonal conflicts.
Level III Postconventional		
Stage 5: Social contract ("Human rights take precedence over laws.")	People take the perspective of all individuals living in a social system. They understand that not everyone shares their own values and ideas but that all have an equal right to exist.	Morality is based on protecting each individual's human rights. The emphasis is on maintaining a social system that will do so. Laws are created to protect, rather than restrict, individual freedoms, and they should be changed as necessary. Behavior that harms society is wrong, even if it is not illegal.
Stage 6: Universal ethical principles ("Morality is a matter of personal conscience.")	People view moral decisions from the perspective of personal principles of fairness and justice. They believe each person has personal worth and should be respected, regardless of ideas or characteristics. The progression from stage 5 to stage 6 can be thought of as a move from a socially directed to an inner-directed perspective.	It is assumed that there are universal principles of morality that are above the law, such as justice and respect for human dignity. Human life is valued above all else.

Source: Based on information from L. Kohlberg, "Moral Stages and Moralization: The Cognitive-Developmental Approach," 1976. In T. Likona (Ed.), *Moral Development and Behavior: Theory, Research, and Social Issues,* New York: Holt, Rinehart and Winston.

taking opportunities, which occur when children participate in decision-making situations with others and exchange differing points of view on moral questions. The contrasting viewpoints produce cognitive conflict, which the child eventually resolves by reorganizing her thinking into a more advanced stage of reasoning. This process occurs gradually, so although any individual's reasoning can be generally classified into one of the stages, he may approach certain moral issues at a higher or lower stage.

Several other characteristics of Kohlberg's stage model are similar to Piaget's theory. One is that each stage forms an integrated whole, with children in that stage generally responding consistently to different dilemmas and situations. Another is that the stages follow an invariant sequence, so all children experience them in the same order and with no regression to earlier stages. Finally, the progression of stages is universal for all people and all cultures.

Kohlberg did not attempt to construct a model that deals with all aspects of moral reasoning. He developed his dilemmas specifically to assess children's *justice reasoning*—how children decide which of the story characters has the most valid rights and claims (for example, Heinz's sick wife or the druggist who owns the store). Kohlberg assumed that this aspect of moral development would be most likely to display the Piagetian stage characteristics just described, because justice reasoning emphasizes children's abstract cognitive approach to the moral issue rather than their emotional feelings about it. Moral decisions in which the child has a more personal stake were not of interest to Kohlberg, although they have been to other researchers (Gilligan & Wiggins, 1987; Noddings, 1984).

The cognitive models of Piaget and Kohlberg have inspired most of the research on children's moral reasoning. We examine how well the two theories have held up to experimental scrutiny when we review the research findings later in the chapter.

Environmental/Learning Theories

The social-learning tradition also has had a great deal to say about moral development, and most of it contrasts sharply with the cognitive-developmental perspective. The essence of the social-learning view is that the social behaviors we traditionally label in terms of moral development are acquired and maintained through the same principles that govern most other behaviors. Although social-learning theorists do agree that these processes are affected by developmental advances in cognitive abilities (Perry & Perry, 1983), they emphasize environmental mechanisms like reinforcement, punishment, and observational learning (modeling and imitation). This emphasis argues against a stage model of development in which moral behaviors emerge according to an internal timetable that is universal for all children. Instead, it predicts that behaviors should develop more individually, depending primarily on each child's social environment and personal experiences.

Most of the research within the social-learning tradition has involved moral conduct—both prosocial and antisocial behaviors—rather than moral reasoning. This difference has resulted principally from the fact that social-learning theorists, unlike cognitive-developmentalists, believe that moral reasoning and moral conduct are somewhat independent processes that can be influenced by different factors. As a result, social-learning theorists are less inclined to expect a child's moral behavior to show consistency across situations or between knowledge and conduct (Gewirtz & Pelaez-Nogueras, 1991b).

The principal spokesman for the social-learning account of moral development has been Albert Bandura; most of the research conducted within this tradition is based on his views (Bandura, 1986, 1989, 1991b). Bandura's theory, described in Chapter 2, holds that reinforcement and punishment are major processes by which children acquire moral behaviors. In simplest terms, children tend to increase the likelihood of behaviors (prosocial or antisocial) that are approved or result in reward and decrease the likelihood of behaviors that are ignored or punished. In addition, children come to discriminate the reinforcement possibilities that exist in different settings, such as the praise parents provide for good grades versus the pressure peers may exert for skipping school.

Another process that Bandura considers crucial for understanding moral development is observational learning. Children learn many of the rules and practices of their social world by watching others, such as parents and peers (Brody & Shaffer, 1982; Mills & Grusec, 1988). Also of interest is the role of the media and how children's behavior is affected by what they observe on television or read in books and magazines (Eron & Huesmann, 1986; Williams, 1986).

With development, reinforcement and observational processes become internalized, and children learn to use them to regulate their own behavior. As we saw in Chapter 13, Bandura proposes that, through the use of evaluative self-reactions and self-sanctions, children come to regulate their behavior to match the moral standards they set for themselves.

The Ethological Perspective

Human ethologists and sociobiologists have both investigated aspects of moral conduct. Much of their work has involved relating the behavior observed in other species to the moral conduct of humans. Two areas of particular interest have been altruism and aggression (Hinde, 1986; MacDonald, 1988b, 1988c; Zahn-Waxler, Cummings, & Iannotti, 1986).

Altruism

Altruistic behaviors are those that benefit someone else but offer no obvious benefit—and perhaps even some cost—to the individual performing them. Giving money to a charity, sharing a candy bar, and risking one's life to save someone else's are examples. As mentioned in Chapter 2, this prosocial behavior has been a particular challenge to classical evolutionary models, because self-sacrifice would not seem to fit with Darwin's proposed mechanisms. How can a behavior that does not increase a person's own chances of survival and reproduction be passed on in the species? It would seem, instead, that people who act selfishly and think first about themselves would be more likely to survive to pass along their genes. This dilemma, called the **paradox of altruism**, was discussed by Darwin and has been studied and debated ever since (Krebs, 1987; MacDonald, 1988a).

Sociobiologists have attempted to resolve this problem by adding two concepts to Darwin's "survival of the fittest" notion (Dawkins, 1976; Maynard Smith, 1976). **Kin selection** proposes that humans, and some other animals, behave in ways that increase the chances for the survival and reproduction of their genes rather than themselves. A person can pass on his genes either by reproducing himself *or* by increasing the reproductive chances of someone who has the same or similar genes. The more genes the second individual shares with the first, the more reasonable it becomes to try to save that individual's life (and reproductive capability). Therefore, we would predict that a mother should be more likely to risk her life for her child than for her husband, because her child shares many of her genes. Similarly, any family member, or *kin*, should be favored over any unrelated individual.

Paradox of altruism
The logical dilemma faced by ethological theorists who try to reconcile self-sacrificial behavior with the concepts of natural selection and survival of the fittest.

Kin selection
A proposed mechanism by which an individual's altruistic behavior toward a kin member increases the likelihood of the survival of genes similar to those of the individual.

Reciprocal altruism
A proposed mechanism by which an individual's altruistic behavior toward members of the social group may promote the survival of the individual's genes through reciprocation by others or may ensure the survival of similar genes.

But people perform acts of altruism directed toward nonfamily members every day. How does evolutionary theory explain such behavior? Here a process called **reciprocal altruism** comes into play. According to this idea, people are genetically programmed to be helpful because (1) it increases the likelihood that they will someday in turn receive aid from the person they helped or from some other altruistic member of their group or (2) by helping someone else in their social group, they help to ensure that genes similar to their own will be passed on in the species (Trivers, 1971, 1983). We have more to say about altruistic behavior later in the chapter.

Aggression

Aggression and dominance relationships have been another favorite area of research for human ethologists (Cairns, 1986; Omark, Strayer, & Freedman, 1980). One function of aggression is, again, to increase the likelihood of survival of an individual's genes—believed by some to be the most important evolutionary function of any behavior. Aggression serves this purpose in many ways, such as by helping the individual to obtain food, protect the young, or preserve valuable hunting territory. In such cases, evolutionary processes clearly favor the stronger, smarter, or more skillful members of the species.

Dominance hierarchy
A structured social group in which members higher on the dominance ladder control those who are lower, initially through aggression and conflict but eventually simply through threats.

Aggression in many species can lead to physical combat. Some conflicts, however, do not progress to this point but are resolved when one animal displays threatening gestures (such as certain facial expressions and body postures) and the other animal backs down, perhaps making submissive gestures. Such behaviors also have adaptive value for both individuals—the attacker gains possession of the desired property while the retreating animal avoids injury or death. In some species that form social groups, such as monkeys, a **dominance hierarchy** develops, in which each member of the group fits somewhere on a dominance ladder. Each monkey controls those lower in the hierarchy (often simply by threats) but submits to those higher on the ladder. Even though it is initially created through aggression, such a structure ultimately reduces the overall physical conflict that might otherwise occur in the group. The structure and function of dominance hierarchies in children's social interactions has been a favorite focus of ethologists (Lore & Schultz, 1993), as we will see in Chapter 16.

DEVELOPMENT IN CONTEXT: An Evolutionary Account of the Development of Antisocial Behavior

A newer evolutionary model, proposed by Jay Belsky and his colleagues (Belsky, Steinberg, & Draper, 1991), is concerned with the development of "reproductive strategies," the behaviors and attitudes children display regarding interpersonal relationships, mating, and parenting. According to this model, evolution has primed humans to be sensitive to their early rearing experiences and to develop, in response, behavior patterns or strategies that maximize their chances of successful reproduction. Such strategies thus result from a combination of the child's evolutionary heritage and early experiences, and they are assumed to emerge during the first 5 to 7 years of life.

Two behavior patterns, in particular, predominate. Children who are raised in secure and supportive environments, where they have ample food, clothing, and other resources, are likely to develop more positive attitudes toward family life and toward personal relationships in general. As a result, they focus on finding a single mate for a long-term relationship, and they invest heavily in raising their children. In contrast, children who have stressful, unstable early home experiences, and who fail to develop close emotional bonds with caregivers and others, develop reproductive patterns that are more individualistic and oriented toward personal survival. These children have less interest in forming long-term interpersonal relationships. They tend to seek many sexual partners but have minimal interest in their offspring.

The relevance of this evolutionary theory to moral development lies in its prediction that children (especially males) displaying the second pattern of development will be more likely to engage in antisocial behaviors, such as aggression, delinquency, and generally self-oriented conduct. Children reared in more nurturant environments, on the other hand, should display more interpersonal cooperation, altruism, and other-oriented behaviors.

Belsky's model is very contextualist in that he argues that the two behavior patterns should not be viewed as better or worse, but simply as two strategies for coping with very different environmental contexts. For children who experience nurturant caregiving and secure attachments, developing trust and concern for others may be a sensible approach to life. But for children raised in unpredictable environments, where resources are scarce and others cannot necessarily be trusted, developing an opportunistic lifestyle may have evolutionary survival value by offering a realistic and effective response to the situation. This model, then, suggests that understanding children's moral behavior requires an appreciation of how evolutionary mechanisms promote development in context.

✔ *To Recap...*

Research in moral development falls into two major categories: investigations of moral conduct and of moral reasoning. Two questions have guided much of this research: Are moral beliefs and behaviors innate and emergent, or are they socially created and acquired through experience? And do moral rules follow a universal pattern, or are they arbitrary, differing from one culture to the next?

Cognitive-developmentalists are most concerned with moral reasoning, and they argue that moral development depends on cognitive development. It is marked by consistency across situations and between moral thought and moral conduct, and it proceeds through stages.

Piaget proposed a four-stage model. Children in the first stage show very little understanding of rule following. In the second stage, the stage of moral realism, children view rules as absolute and base their moral evaluations largely on physical and objective aspects of a situation. Increased interaction with peers combines with a movement away from egocentric thinking in the third stage, the stage of moral relativism. Children in this stage approach rules more flexibly and are able to take subjective factors, such as intentions, into account. In the final stage, children's moral reasoning can extend to hypothetical situations and to issues in the larger society.

Kohlberg's model consists of three levels of moral reasoning—preconventional, conventional, and postconventional—each composed of two stages. The two components of each stage, social perspective and moral content, represent inborn and environmental influences, respectively. Movement from stage to stage occurs when the child experiences cognitive conflict. In Kohlberg's view, each stage represents an integrated whole, movement from stage to stage follows an invariant sequence, and the model is universal across cultures. Kohlberg's theory focuses on justice reasoning, which he believed was most likely to display structured stage characteristics.

Social-learning theory emphasizes environmental influences on moral development and is most concerned with moral conduct. Bandura has been the most influential proponent of this view. Reinforcement and punishment principles, along with observational learning processes and self-regulation, are assumed to be the major determinants of children's moral behavior according to the social-learning model.

The ethological tradition has attempted to explain patterns of moral development in terms of evolutionary principles. The so-called paradox of altruism has been one area of interest. Sociobiologists have argued that self-sacrificial behavior can be explained by a focus on the survival of the genes, rather than of the individual, through the processes of kin selection and reciprocal altruism. In the area of aggression, ethologists have been especially interested in how aggression reduces the overall level of conflict in a social group through the formation of dominance hierarchies. Belsky's model predicts that children will develop different reproductive strategies depending on their early rearing environments. Children raised in secure environments tend to have greater interest in interpersonal relations, marriage, and children and to be more prosocial. Those raised in unstable settings are likely to become more opportunistic, self-oriented, and antisocial.

MORAL REASONING

How well has research evidence supported the theoretical positions of the theories we have just examined? We investigate this question, along with other issues, with reference to three important topic areas: moral reasoning, prosocial behavior, and aggression. We begin with a discussion of research on children's moral reasoning.

Evaluating Piaget's Model

Some studies of moral reasoning have specifically addressed Piaget's model. For example, researchers have investigated—and supported—Piaget's concept of immanent justice reasoning (Jose, 1990; Karniol, 1980). Overall, research indicates that Piaget's model was basically correct. Many studies of Piaget's work, however, have examined the possibility that his research methods distorted his conclusions to some extent. Consider an example.

In Piaget's stories, the character's intentions were always stated before the amount of damage was described. Thus, children were first told that Julian was disobeying his father and then that he caused little damage. Because very young children may have difficulty processing much information at one time, the part of the story they hear last might be the one they remember best. So if the damage done is always mentioned at the end, younger children may focus on this factor. Studies have in fact shown that if the character's motives or intentions are presented at the end of Piaget's stories, children as young as 5 may decide that the naughtier character was not the one who did less damage but the one who had bad motives (Austin, Ruble, & Trabasso, 1977; Moran & McCullers, 1984; Nummedal & Bass, 1976).

These results, combined with results from related experiments, suggest that Piaget somewhat underestimated younger children's moral reasoning abilities (Grueneich, 1982; Karniol, 1978). Even very young children seem capable of taking into account a number of factors when making a moral judgment. But for a younger child to use a piece of information (such as a character's motives), that information must be made very *salient*—that is, clear and noticeable. Some techniques that have been successfully used to increase the salience of a character's intentions include (1) placing the information at the end of the story, as we have already seen, (2) adding pictures, slides, or videotapes to the stories, as in Figure 14-1 (Chandler, Greenspan, & Barenboim, 1973; Nelson, 1980), (3) training the child to examine the story carefully before making a moral judgment (Rotenberg, 1980), and (4) asking the child to describe the character's intentions (Brandt & Strattner-Gregory, 1980).

Research designed to improve on Piaget's methods has provided a more complete picture of how moral reasoning typically develops. Although they are capable of using motives and intentions earlier, children up to 5 or 6 years of age nevertheless base their moral evaluations primarily on the amount of damage produced by the story character. From that point until they are 8 to 10 years of age, children consider damage and motives about equally. And beginning at about age 10, the character's motives become the most important factor (Surber, 1982).

In addition to motives and damage, children also use other factors in assessing a story character's morality. For example, they judge the breaking of moral rules more harshly than the violation of social conventions (Smetana & Braeges, 1990; Smetana, Schlagman, & Adams, 1993; Tisak, 1993). They evaluate a harmful act less severely if it involves retaliation (getting back at someone for an earlier wrongdoing) (Ferguson & Rule, 1988). They are more tolerant of acts that were unforeseeable (such as accidentally hitting someone who has just come around the corner) (Sanvitale, Saltzstein, & Fish, 1989; Yuill & Perner, 1988) and acts that were followed by an apology or an admission of guilt (Leon, 1982; Nunner-Winkler & Sodian, 1988). Younger children also evaluate personal injury (breaking a person's leg) more harshly than property damage (breaking a person's bicycle) (Moran & McCullers, 1984).

Evaluating Kohlberg's Model

A great deal more research has been directed toward studying Kohlberg's model. And it, too, has been the target of some criticism.

Figure 14-1 An example of drawings used to convey motive, action, and outcome in stories. When pictures such as these accompany stories involving moral dilemmas, even 4- to 6-year-olds sometimes use story characters' motives as a basis for evaluating their behavior. From "Factors Influencing Young Children's Use of Motives and Outcomes as Moral Criteria" by S. A. Nelson, 1980, *Child Development, 51,* pp. 823–829. Copyright 1980 by The Society for Research in Child Development. Reprinted by permission.

Some problems Kohlberg addressed himself, in his revisions of the model. For example, the original scoring method by which he determined the stage of each subject's reasoning was faulted for requiring a great deal of subjective interpretation (Kurtines & Grief, 1974; Liebert, 1984). In response, Kohlberg and his associates developed a new scoring procedure, the *Moral Judgment Interview (MJI)*, that is considerably more objective and precise (Colby & Kohlberg, 1987). Another criticism was that Kohlberg's highest stage of reasoning, the sixth stage, has not been demonstrated to exist. As we saw earlier, Kohlberg conceded that this stage is more theoretical than actual.

Other questions regarding specific elements of Kohlberg's model can only be answered with data from well-conducted experiments. The most important of these questions involve five characteristics of the model, several of which we discussed earlier: prerequisite abilities, consistency, invariant sequence, universal stages, and movement through stages as the result of cognitive conflict.

Prerequisite Abilities

A fundamental tenet of any cognitive-developmental model, including Kohlberg's, is that advances in cognitive and perspective-taking abilities form the basis for advances in moral reasoning. Researchers have tested this belief in two ways. One has been to determine whether children at more advanced levels of moral reasoning also display greater cognitive and perspective-taking abilities. Several studies have found that they do (Krebs & Gillmore, 1982; Rowe & Marcia, 1980). But, as discussed in Chapter 3, such correlational findings cannot confirm that improved cognitive and perspective-taking abilities *caused* improvements in moral reasoning abilities. All these abilities could simply advance at about the same time (or, for that matter, cognitive advances might be brought on by advances in moral reasoning). A better way to approach this question would be to induce advances in cognitive and perspective-taking abilities experimentally—for example, through educational programs—and then examine whether increases in moral reasoning follow. Several studies of this sort have been conducted and appear to support Kohlberg's claims (Arbuthnot et al., 1983; Walker, 1980; Walker & Richards, 1979).

Consistency

A second issue is whether Kohlberg was correct in his belief that each stage of moral reasoning forms an integrated whole, with the child using the same level of reasoning to approach most problems and situations. Research using Kohlberg's original scoring system failed to find this sort of consistency (Rest, 1983). However, recent studies employing the newer scoring method suggest that children's reasoning does follow this pattern (Walker, 1988; Walker & Taylor, 1991b). A typical study, for example, found that over 60% of the time, subjects used reasoning appropriate to a single stage across a series of moral dilemmas. Over 90% of the time, subjects used reasoning from two adjacent stages (Walker, deVries, & Trevarthen, 1987).

Invariant Sequence

Another source of controversy has involved the assertion that stages follow an invariant sequence through which all children proceed in the same order without regressing. Again, longitudinal investigations using Kohlberg's earlier scoring system reported that stage-skipping and regression to lower stages were frequent (Holstein, 1976; Kuhn, 1976; Kuhn et al., 1977). But more recent research seems to indicate that such violations of sequence are actually uncommon (Page, 1981; Walker, 1986, 1989).

Universal Stages

The two issues just discussed can also be examined with regard to a larger question raised by Kohlberg's theory: Is the model universal, applying equally well to people of all cultures? Cross-cultural studies have examined the issues of consistency across situations (Bersoff & Miller, 1993; Lei & Cheng, 1989; Snarey, Reimer, & Kohlberg, 1985) and invariant sequence (Edwards, 1986; Lei & Cheng, 1989; Snarey et al., 1985; Tietjen & Walker, 1985) and have found these characteristics in cultures as diverse as those in Israel, Indonesia, and the Bahamas.

But some cultural differences have been found. In many nonindustrial societies, for example, individuals rarely progress to the fifth stage, although many people in more technologically advanced cultures do (Snarey, 1985). This finding is not a major problem to Kohlberg's theory, which incorporates the idea that culture and experiences help determine what stage a person ultimately reaches (Kohlberg, 1984). A more serious concern is that Kohlberg's moral dilemmas do not adequately address certain moral issues and concepts found in other cultures (Snarey & Keljo, 1991). For example, in some Chinese cultures, the conflict between what is right for the individual and what is right for society is not ideally resolved by choosing one over the other (as is required in Kohlberg's hypothetical dilemmas). Instead, the solution seen as most appropriate is to reconcile the two interests by arriving at a compromise solution (Dien, 1982). And according to Hindu beliefs in India, the very fact that Heinz finds himself in a dilemma is an indication of his prior sins or negligence, which he will not escape by committing further sinful actions such as stealing (Shweder & Much, 1987). Kohlberg's model, then, is not applicable to everyone in these cultures.

What about generalizing principles of morality from one culture to another? Kohlberg's theory would predict that moral reasoning is universal in that an individual should view a particular behavior in the same way regardless of the customs or standards of the culture in which the behavior takes place. Research with children and adolescents in the United States, however, indicates that most subjects do not feel they must impose their own moral beliefs on the behavior of individuals in cultures very different from their own (Wainryb, 1993).

Applicability should be universal not only across cultures but between sexes as well. Recall that Kohlberg's theory focuses on justice reasoning as the best indicator of moral development. In some early research, Kohlberg reported that the moral reasoning of females generally was not as advanced as that of males (Kohlberg, 1969; Kohlberg & Kramer, 1969). One of Kohlberg's students, however, subsequently conducted a study that challenged this suggestion. In a book entitled *In a Different Voice*, Carol Gilligan (1982) argued that Kohlberg's model underestimates the moral reasoning of females because their moral orientation is less concerned with justice—whether someone has the *right* to do something, based on laws or rules—and more concerned with issues of responsibility and care—whether someone has an *obligation* to do something, based on the value of a personal relationship. For example, arguing that Heinz should steal the drug because saving a life is more important than obeying laws reflects a justice orientation, whereas arguing that Heinz should steal the drug because he has an obligation to help someone he loves represents a care orientation. This book sparked a heated debate that continues today (Haste & Baddeley, 1991; Larrabee, 1993; Puka, 1991).

• Moral reasoning appears to advance fastest when issues are discussed one stage above the child's own level. It is wise for parents to take this into account when reasoning with children, and adjust their arguments to the appropriate level.

+1 stage technique
A method of investigating the hierarchical organization of moral stages; children are exposed to reasoning one stage above their own in order to maximize cognitive conflict and thus induce movement to the higher stage.

Research has examined the charge that Kohlberg's system produces lower scores for females and has found that few gender differences have, in fact, been reported in studies using Kohlberg's moral dilemmas (Donenberg & Hoffman, 1988; Greeno & Maccoby, 1986; Thoma, 1986; Walker, 1989, 1991). Studies do suggest that adult females may be more likely to use a care orientation in resolving moral issues, but both sexes typically use both orientations to some degree (Garrod, Beal, & Shin, 1990; Gilligan & Attanucci, 1988; Smetana, Killen, & Turiel, 1991; Walker, 1989; Walker, deVries, & Trevarthen, 1987).

Movement Through Stages

Finally, another aspect of Kohlberg's model that has been studied extensively involves two related assertions—that each stage represents a reorganization of the child's previous moral reasoning and that this reorganization occurs when the child experiences cognitive conflict over a moral dilemma and cannot resolve it by reasoning at the current stage. If Kohlberg's model is correct, we would expect children to be most likely to experience such cognitive conflict when they are exposed to arguments at the level of reasoning just above their own.

Research on reorganization generally has supported Kohlberg's claims. Although children are better able to understand arguments at stages lower than their own, they tend to agree more with arguments at higher stages, *if they can understand them* (Boom & Molenaar, 1989; Carroll & Rest, 1981; Walker, deVries, & Bichard, 1984).

Much of the research on cognitive conflict has involved a method known as the **+1 stage technique** (Turiel, 1966; Walker, 1988). Subjects in these studies typically are asked to solve a moral dilemma and then are exposed to arguments that either agree or disagree with their own and that are either lower, higher, or at the same stage level as theirs. Kohlberg's theory predicts that subjects who display the greatest change in moral reasoning will be those exposed to the most conflict and presented with reasoning just slightly more advanced than their own (that is, at +1 stage above). Although the findings of studies using the +1 stage technique have not been entirely consistent, for the most part they have supported this prediction (Matefy & Acksen, 1976; Norcini & Snyder, 1986; Walker, 1983; Walker & Richards, 1979).

Kohlberg's model has thus stood up fairly well under experimental testing. Children's moral reasoning does appear to progress through stages and to display the characteristics suggested by Kohlberg and other cognitive-developmental theorists. The role of moral reasoning in children's actual moral behavior, however, is not quite so clear, as we will see.

Other Forms of Justice

We have been focusing on the ideas of Piaget and Kohlberg, but the moral concepts assessed by their methods are not the only areas of moral reasoning that have been of interest to psychologists. Here we briefly consider research on two other aspects of children's moral reasoning: distributive justice and retributive justice (Berndt, 1982; Siegal, 1982).

Distributive Justice

One issue involves how to distribute a limited amount of resources among a group of deserving people—a concept called *distributive justice* (Damon, 1983).

Researchers usually assess this form of moral reasoning using a reward allocation task. In the typical study, a group of children perform a task together for which they are to receive some sort of payment. One child is then asked to divide the pay among the participants. Usually the situation is designed so that the children have performed different amounts of work.

Children's reasoning regarding distributive justice appears to develop in several stages. Up until about 4 years of age, children's reward distribution is characterized by self-interest; they tend to take a large portion of the earnings for themselves, regardless of the amount of work they contributed (Lane & Coon, 1972; Nelson & Dweck, 1977). As they reach 5 or 6 years of age, children begin to divide rewards according to an equality principle, with all children receiving the same share, whatever their input (Berndt, 1981; Damon & Colby, 1987; Damon & Killen, 1982). By about 7 years of age, children start to use equity as the basis for reward allocation. Children who did more work are given more of the reward, although not always in correct proportions (Hook, 1982, 1983; Kourilsky & Kehret-Ward, 1984).

Children's allocation of rewards appears to be influenced not only by their cognitive development—for example, their understanding of proportions—but also by situational variables (Sigelman & Waitzman, 1991). For example, children distribute more reward to those whom they consider to be in greater need or whom they see as kind and helpful (Enright et al., 1984; Nisan, 1984). Also, if children believe that they will interact with another child again, a child who has done relatively little work, they tend to reward the child using the equality rule rather than the more advanced equity rule (Graziano, 1987).

Retributive Justice

Children's concepts of justice have also been examined with a view toward determining what factors children use in assigning blame or responsibility—that is, their concept of *retributive justice*. Even young children appear to approach such problems in essentially the same way as adults. When presented with a story about a character who broke a rule, both children and adults first examine whether any harm or damage was done. If none occurred, the subjects typically do not pursue the issue of responsibility and justice. When damage is perceived to have occurred, people in both age groups then attempt to try to determine whether the story character was responsible. If no blame can be assigned to the character, punishment typically is not considered necessary. But if the character is deemed responsible for the harm, both children and adults proceed to the questions of whether punishment is warranted and, if so, how much. At both ages, then, subjects appear to follow a three-step line of reasoning: Harm? Responsibility? Punishment? (Shultz & Darley, 1991; Shultz & Wright, 1985; Shultz, Wright, & Schleifer, 1986).

Interestingly, although their approach to punishment situations may be similar to that of adults, children *predict* that adults' approach will be different from their own. For example, when children were presented with several stories in which a character had bad intentions and produced a bad outcome, they rated the character's behavior negatively. When asked to predict how adults would evaluate the behavior, the children predicted that the adults would also view the behavior negatively but would focus more on the outcome of the bad behaviors than on the character's motives and would evaluate the character's behavior more harshly than they had—predictions that proved to be false when the children's parents were then also asked to rate the story characters (Saltzstein et al., 1987). These findings indicate that children's moral reasoning in situations involving responsibility for damage does not represent a simple imitation of what they expect from adults.

Furthermore, children's predictions about the harshness of adults' judgments may reflect their view of adults as the creators and enforcers of social rules.

Social Influences on Moral Reasoning

We have already seen that cognitive-developmental and social-learning theorists agree that social factors play a role in moral development, although they disagree as to the nature and importance of that role. In this section, we consider several of the most important forms of social influence on the development of moral reasoning.

Peer Interaction

Both Piaget and Kohlberg believed that peer interactions play a major role in producing more sophisticated forms of moral thought. In their view, as children are forced to wrestle with the many moral conflicts encountered in everyday interactions with friends and playmates, they gradually ascend to new cognitive stages where they can confront such dilemmas with a more complex and effective style of reasoning.

• Both Piaget and Kohlberg believed that children's moral reasoning is strongly influenced by their interactions with peers.

Research supports this hypothesis, but not very strongly. Correlational studies generally have demonstrated a positive relation between children's peer interactions and their moral maturity (Brody & Shaffer, 1982; Higgins, Power, & Kohlberg, 1984). For example, children who are popular and who engage in many social activities tend to score higher on measures of moral reasoning (Enright & Satterfield, 1980; Keasey, 1971). However, the correlational nature of such research makes it impossible to be sure that peer interaction was, in fact, the cause of the advances in moral reasoning.

Few experimental investigations of this issue have been conducted. In one study, male and female adolescents were tested on several of Kohlberg's dilemmas and then assigned to same-sex pairs. To generate conflict and discussion, researchers made sure each pair was made up of subjects who had offered very different views on the moral dilemmas. In some of the pairs, both subjects were at the same stage of reasoning; in others, they were less than one stage apart; and in others, they were one full stage apart. The pairs were then given additional dilemmas to resolve over a 2-month period. Finally, all subjects were again tested on a different set of Kohlberg's dilemmas. In the groups where the subjects were at different levels, the lower level subject generally advanced more than the higher level subject. Greatest advancement occurred in the pairs whose members were only slightly different from one another. These data not only demonstrate the potential influence of peer interactions on moral reasoning but also support the belief that arguments just above a subject's own stage are most effective in inducing movement to the next stage (Berkowitz, Gibbs, & Broughton, 1980).

Modeling

Children learn a good deal by observing others, and researchers have investigated whether this process extends to moral reasoning. It has been shown, for example, that parents tend to use higher stage levels of reasoning as their children grow older (Denney & Duffy, 1974), which might contribute to changes in the style of the children's reasoning. Parents also lower their level of moral reasoning when discussing a moral issue with a child, much as they lower their language level using motherese with language-learning children (Walker & Taylor, 1991a).

Social-learning theorists contend that if modeling and imitation play a role in children's moral reasoning, there is no reason why moral development should follow an invariant sequence of stages. Rather, if a child who reasons at one level can be persuaded that a less sophisticated approach is somehow better, the child should regress to the more primitive form of reasoning (Perry & Bussey, 1984).

To examine this possibility, social-learning researchers have employed methods such as the following. A child is exposed to a peer or adult model who attempts to solve a moral dilemma using reasoning that is lower by one stage than that of the child. The model then is praised and rewarded for the answer, and this procedure continues over a number of dilemmas. Next, the child is asked to respond to a series of moral dilemmas and is rewarded for answers at lower stages and not rewarded for those that tend toward higher levels of reasoning. By using modeling, in combination with direct and vicarious reinforcement procedures, social-learning theorists have reported a number of demonstrations of children regressing to earlier stages of moral reasoning (Brody & Henderson, 1977; Dorr & Fey, 1974; Harvey & Liebert, 1979; Saltzstein, Sanvitale, & Supraner, 1978).

This research is not without its critics. One question that remains unanswered is whether the children's reasoning was affected for more than a very brief time. Another is whether the children would have been as easily influenced in the natural environment, where children are rarely praised for less mature modes of thinking and where they are unlikely to witness such praise being offered to others. Although the techniques used in this research may, in principle, influence children's level of reasoning, they may have no role in everyday life.

Parents' Disciplinary Practices

One way in which children learn about moral issues is through discipline for misconduct. When parents punish children they generally hope that children will not only avoid performing the inappropriate behaviors again but also will gradually assume responsibility for enforcing the rules. As we saw in the previous chapter, the development of self-regulation often involves learning to control the desire to engage in forbidden behavior. And just as Vygotskians and others have argued, children seem to accomplish this by *internalizing* the rules and prohibitions presented by their parents, usually during disciplinary situations (Gralinski & Kopp, 1993; Hoffman, 1994).

The effectiveness of discipline in promoting internalization of the parents' values and morals depends on a number of factors (Grusec & Goodnow, 1994). One involves the style of punishment parents employ. Three general classes of parental discipline have been identified (Hoffman, 1970, 1984b). *Power assertion* involves the use of commands, threats, and physical force. *Love withdrawal* refers to the use of verbal disapproval, ridicule, or the withholding of affection from the child. *Induction* involves reasoning with the child to explain why certain behaviors are prohibited, and it often encourages feelings of guilt in the child by pointing out how the misbehavior may have caused harm or distress to someone else. Evidence from a number of studies indicates that children whose discipline involves more induction display the most advanced levels of moral reasoning. Love withdrawal techniques result in somewhat lower levels, while power assertion produces the least mature forms of reasoning (Boyes & Allen, 1993; Brody & Shaffer, 1982; Hart, 1988b; Weiss et al., 1992). It should be noted, however, that most parents use some combination of these methods, so simple conclusions may be misleading.

In fact, parents' styles of discipline seem to interact with other aspects of the situation in determining the likelihood of internalization by the child. For example, children will not internalize a rule unless they understand its meaning and agree, at least to some extent, that it is appropriate and reasonable (Grusec & Goodnow, 1994). Whether internalization occurs also seems to depend on the affective response of the child. For example, if the discipline produces mainly fear, the child is not likely to internalize the parents' message; however, if it produces empathy with someone who has been hurt by the child's actions, then internalization becomes more likely (Hoffman, 1994). Finally, internalization is thought to depend in part on the child's temperament. Two behavioral characteristics in particular—the level of children's emotional reaction to having done something wrong and their ability to inhibit prohibited behaviors in tempting situations—appear to have inborn, temperamental qualities and are believed to determine how easily parents can socialize moral standards in their children (Kochanska, 1991, 1993).

Moral Reasoning and Moral Conduct

A fundamental question that arises in the area of moral development is whether children's moral reasoning is related to their moral conduct. That is, does a child who displays a more sophisticated understanding of moral issues behave more appropriately than a child who reasons at a lower level (Burton, 1984; Kutnick, 1986)?

Cognitive-developmentalists, you will recall, contend that these elements should be consistent with each other, as well as across situations. Kohlberg, for example, believed that moral thought and moral action should be consistent (although not perfectly so), and he claimed that the evidence shows that they are (Kohlberg, 1987; Kohlberg & Candee, 1984). Social-learning theorists make a different prediction. They argue that moral reasoning and conduct may show some correspondence but that it need not be very strong, because what children say and what they do involve somewhat independent processes (Bandura, 1991; Liebert, 1984).

The evidence on this question has not, in fact, supported Kohlberg's position. Studies based on Kohlberg's method have found only a modest relation between a child's level of moral reasoning and the child's moral behavior (Blasi, 1980, 1983; Rholes & Lane, 1985; Straughan, 1986). In most children, this relation simply does not hold. (Box 14-1 describes a classic study on cross-situational consistency.)

Children's moral behavior is undoubtedly influenced by many factors; moral reasoning is just one of these (Hoffman, 1991; Widaman & Little, 1985). Rather than attempting to make global statements about children's moral reasoning and moral actions, therefore, many researchers have found that a more fruitful approach is to examine relations between specific cognitive processes and specific behaviors. We consider some of these studies in the sections that follow.

✔ *To Recap...*

Research aimed at evaluating Piaget's model generally supports his ideas but suggests that he somewhat underestimated younger children's moral reasoning. When, in the classic moral dilemmas, the story characters' motives are made salient, even preschoolers can use this information as a basis for moral evaluations.

Experimental studies of Kohlberg's model generally support his contention that certain cognitive and perspective-taking abilities are prerequisite to the development of moral reasoning abilities. The data also are in line with Kohlberg's view that moral reasoning displays consistency across situations and that children proceed through the stages in an invariant order. The universality of the model is less well documented. Although cross-cultural research indicates a similar pattern of moral development in a number of diverse societies, there are cultures where Kohlberg's theory clearly does not apply. Some researchers have also questioned the universality of the model across genders. Finally,

A STUDY IN MORAL CHARACTER: ARE THERE "GOOD KIDS" AND "BAD KIDS"?

Are there "good kids" and "bad kids," or does children's morality depend on the situation and circumstances in which they find themselves? This question formed the basis for a classic early study of children's character, conducted by Hugh Hartshorne and Mark May (1928–1930).

The question they raised is really one of *cross-situational consistency*. We might state it this way: Does morality represent a consistent personality trait that each of us carries with us?

Cognitive-developmental theorists, we have seen, expect cross-situational consistency to be high, because they assume children's moral behavior is guided by their current levels of moral reasoning. Environmental/learning theorists expect much less consistency, arguing that children's behavior is more likely to be influenced by the risks and rewards that exist in a given situation.

Hartshorne and May explored this problem by exposing over 10,000 children, aged 8 to 16, to situations that provided opportunities for dishonesty. The settings ranged from homes to schools to churches, and the behaviors of interest were various forms of lying, cheating, and stealing. Each situation was designed so that dishonest behavior would "pay off" for the child, but the apparent risk of being detected varied. In reality, the researchers were always aware of whether the child was being honest. The children were also interviewed as to their attitudes regarding dishonesty.

The results seemed very straightforward at the time. The investigators reported almost no consistency across situations for the children they studied. The fact that a child stole in one context was not useful in predicting whether the child would cheat in another. And there was very little correspondence between children's verbal pronouncements of moral values and their actual behavior. Hartshorne and May thus concluded that children's moral behavior does not reflect a personality trait but is *situation-specific*, depending primarily on the circumstances at hand.

This conclusion has since been modified to some degree. A reanalysis of the project's data indicated that some degree of consistency did exist (Burton, 1963, 1984). This was particularly true for situations that were similar to one another. It nevertheless remained clear that the children observed in this classic study were, for the most part, willing to adjust their moral conduct to fit the demands of the moment.

Kohlberg's belief that each stage represents a reorganization that results from cognitive conflict also has been supported by experimental data.

Children's allocation of rewards appears to follow a predictable sequence, moving from self-interest (up to age 4), to equality (ages 5 and 6), and then to equity (age 7 and older). But reward allocation also is influenced by situational variables. Children's reasoning about distribution of punishment uses much the same pattern found in adults: Was harm done? If so, was the person in question responsible? If so, is punishment warranted?

Studies of social influences on moral reasoning have confirmed that interactions with peers, especially in situations of moral conflict, stimulate development. Researchers also have caused children's level of reasoning to regress by use of modeling techniques in combination with direct and vicarious rewards. But the durability of these influences is uncertain. Parental disciplinary techniques are another influence on moral reasoning and affect the degree to which children internalize parents' standards. Induction is most effective in stimulating moral development and internalization. But children's ability to process the information contained in the discipline, along with their affective reaction to it, also affect internalization.

The relation between moral reasoning and moral behavior is a fundamental issue in moral development research. Kohlberg asserted that the two should be closely related, but this assertion has not been strongly supported.

PROSOCIAL BEHAVIOR

Prosocial behavior
The aspect of moral conduct that includes socially desirable behaviors such as sharing, helping, and cooperating; often used interchangeably with *altruism* by modern researchers.

We turn now to moral conduct—the way children act as opposed to how they think. Specifically, we examine **prosocial behavior**, those acts that society considers desirable and attempts to encourage in children. Three forms of prosocial behavior have been studied most extensively: sharing, cooperation, and helping (which includes comforting and caregiving) (Eisenberg & Mussen, 1989).

We said at the beginning of the chapter that altruism presented classical ethology with a paradox, because altruism is presumably performed solely for the benefit of someone else. Ethologists solved this dilemma by proposing several evolutionary mechanisms that make altruistic behaviors of value not only to the person being helped but also to the helper (that is, the helper's genes). Other psychologists have come to the similar conclusion that most, if not all, prosocial behaviors produce some form of positive consequence for the helper, even if it is only at the emotional level. Because of the similarities between altruism and prosocial behavior, the terms have come to be used interchangeably by modern researchers. We follow that practice here.

Prosocial Behavior in Infancy

Until recently, many theorists believed that before children can display altruism, they must develop two abilities: perspective taking, or the ability to perceive a situation from someone else's point of view, and empathy, the ability to experience the emotions of someone else. If perspective taking and empathy are indeed prerequisites to prosocial behavior, then we should see little or no altruism in infants, whose abilities along these lines are, as yet, poorly developed. Yet there is considerable evidence that altruism begins early. For example, babies cry when they hear the crying of other babies but not when they hear their own tape-recorded crying—suggesting at least a primitive level of empathy (Martin & Clark, 1982). And researchers have repeatedly reported examples of sharing and comforting by children younger than age 2 (Hay et al., 1991; Lamb, 1991; Rheingold, 1988; Zahn-Waxler et al., 1992).

Defining altruism in infants is not a simple matter, however. Because the infant's language is so limited, researchers must rely on other behaviors that can be clearly observed and agreed upon. For example, one series of laboratory studies in which infants played with their parents defined sharing as any of the following behaviors: (1) pointing at or holding up a toy to draw the parent's attention, (2) giving a toy to the parent, or (3) giving a toy to the parent and then playing with it together. Using these behavioral definitions, the researchers found evidence of sharing in almost all of their subjects, with most of the older infants displaying all three types of behavior (Rheingold, Hay, & West, 1976). Later experiments found that toddlers are eager to help their parents perform everyday tasks, such as folding laundry and dusting furniture (Rheingold, 1982b), and that they display nurturing and caregiving toward both toys and their parents (Rheingold & Emery, 1986).

The prosocial behavior of infants has also been studied in naturalistic settings. One major project had mothers observe and record their infants' behavior at home every day over many months. The focus of this research concerned children's reactions to seeing someone in distress. To guarantee that enough of these situations occurred, the mothers provided some staged events, such as by faking an injury (such as hurting an ankle) or displaying strong emotions (for example, getting angry on the telephone). Hundreds of these episodes were recorded over the course of the project, and in a large proportion of them, the children responded in a prosocial manner. Two general categories of reaction were observed. Younger infants primarily showed only empathic distress, such as crying. But many of the older toddlers actually attempted to help the victim, although the help was not always appropriate, as when one youngster tried to feed his cereal to his ailing father (Radke-Yarrow & King, 1979; Radke-Yarrow & Zahn-Waxler, 1984; Zahn-Waxler et al., 1992).

Sharing also can serve a variety of interpersonal functions for toddlers. It appears to be one way they initiate or maintain social interactions with adults or peers (Eckerman, Davis, & Didow, 1989; Hay et al., 1991). And it also is a means by which infants resolve conflicts among themselves, such as when the number of available toys is small (Caplan et al., 1991).

Sharing and helping behaviors are certainly not always observed in infants, however. Several studies suggest that, at this age, such behaviors are likely to occur only when the infant has previously been involved in a give-and-take relationship with the other person and has experienced some "receiving" as well as "giving" (Hay & Murray, 1982; Levitt et al., 1985).

Age and Gender Differences in Prosocial Behavior

If children's prosocial behavior is influenced by advances in their cognitive and affective processes, we would expect altruism to increase with age. And many laboratory studies have found this to be the case—older children are more likely to share and help than are younger ones (e.g., Eisenberg, 1990; Froming, Allen, & Jensen, 1985; Froming, Allen, & Underwood, 1983; Midlarsky & Hannah, 1985). Nevertheless, the issue is a bit more complex than this.

Under some circumstances, no age differences are observed. In one study, for example, older children shared money they had just earned more readily than younger children—but only when it was first made clear to them that (1) sharing is a good thing to do, (2) they were participating in an experiment on sharing, or (3) the experimenter was watching. In the absence of such information, the older children were no more generous than the younger ones (Zarbatany, Hartmann, & Gelfand, 1985). Similarly, another study found that younger children could be just as helpful as older children, if it was first made clear to them that they had the knowledge and skills needed to provide assistance (Peterson, 1983). Finally, age differences often are not found when children's sharing and helping is observed in naturalistic, rather than laboratory, settings (Farver & Branstetter, 1994; Radke-Yarrow, Zahn-Waxler, & Chapman, 1983).

Older children have generally been found to cooperate more than younger ones, and here the difference appears to be more clearly based on differences in cognitive abilities. When participating in a task or game, older children can better determine the strategies that will benefit the majority of the other participants, whereas younger children typically can identify only the strategies that are good for themselves (Knight et al., 1987). Furthermore, older children are more flexible in adjusting their behavior to match their goals. For example, older children are able to shift between a competitive strategy that permits them to obtain the most points and a cooperative strategy that maximizes the points obtained by the children and their partners. Younger children cannot easily adjust their behavior in this way and tend to remain with their initial strategy (Schmidt, Ollendick, & Stanowicz, 1988).

• Although girls have the reputation of being more generous, research indicates that girls are only slightly more altruistic than boys.

The question of sex differences has produced mixed findings as well. When teachers and peers are asked to rate which children are most helpful, generous, and comforting, they consistently rate girls higher (Shigetomi, Hartmann, & Gelfand, 1981; Zarbatany et al., 1985). Yet most studies indicate only a slight tendency for females to be more altruistic (Eagly & Crowley, 1987; Moore & Eisenberg, 1984) or to display more empathy (Farver & Branstetter, 1994; Lennon & Eisenberg, 1987).

Cognitive and Affective Determinants of Prosocial Behavior

We have so far seen that prosocial behaviors can take various forms and begin to appear at an early age. What factors determine when prosocial behaviors emerge and how much altruism a child will exhibit? And why are some children much more altruistic than others? In this section, we consider cognitive and emotional factors that may affect prosocial development.

Moral Reasoning

We have seen that cognitive-developmental psychologists, like Piaget and Kohlberg, believe that moral reasoning processes lie at the heart of moral development. Their models would predict, then, that a positive relation should exist between a child's moral reasoning and altruistic behavior (Krebs & Van Hesteren, 1994).

Investigations of this issue have typically evaluated the child's level of moral reasoning through the use of *prosocial dilemmas*. These stories differ from those of Piaget and Kohlberg in that they place less emphasis on breaking rules or laws. Instead, the story character usually must decide whether to help someone, often at some personal expense. For example, one story requires a little girl to choose between helping a hurt child and being on time for a birthday party (Eisenberg, 1982).

Investigations comparing children's prosocial reasoning with their prosocial behavior have generally found a small positive relation (Eisenberg, 1986, 1987; Eisenberg et al., 1991). This finding is similar to research on Kohlberg's justice-reasoning dilemmas. There, too, only a modest relation exists between how children think about moral issues and how they act.

Perspective Taking

The ability to understand a situation from someone else's point of view is also basic to cognitive-developmental explanations of prosocial behavior. Perspective taking can be physical, social, or affective.

Physical perspective taking involves simply taking another's physical point of view. The best known task for measuring this ability in children is Piaget's three-mountains task (Piaget & Inhelder, 1956), discussed in Chapter 8. Studies using this method have found only a small relation between physical perspective-taking abilities and altruistic behavior (Moore & Eisenberg, 1984; Underwood & Moore, 1982).

Research on social perspective taking—the ability to identify the thoughts and attitudes of someone else—has produced stronger results. For example, in several studies, children who were better at telling a story from another person's point of view were more often altruistic with peers (Chalmers & Townsend, 1990; Froming, Allen, & Jensen, 1985).

There has been less research on children's affective perspective taking, which involves understanding (but not necessarily experiencing) the feelings and emotions of another person. It, too, displays a positive correlation with altruism (Bryant, 1987; Moore & Eisenberg, 1984). A study related to affective perspective taking is described in Box 14-2.

Empathy

Empathy differs from affective perspective taking in that the empathic child not only identifies with but also *feels* the emotions of the other person, although perhaps not as strongly (Barnett, 1987). The concept of empathy has been central to some theories of prosocial development, in particular that of Martin Hoffman (1982, 1984a, 1991).

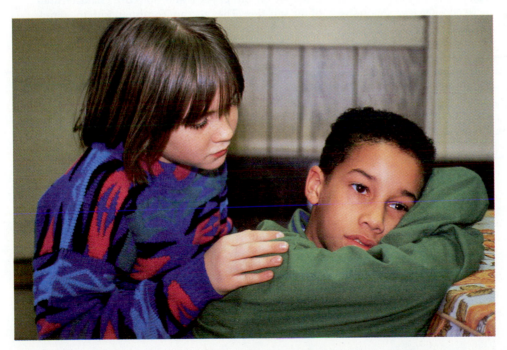

• Empathy involves the ability not only to understand someone else's feelings, but also to share them.

HOW DOES THE BULLY FEEL?

When one child bullies another—such as by threats, stealing money or a toy, or physical assault—we would expect the victim to feel bad (that is, sad, angry, or frustrated) and we would probably predict that young children will have the same expectation. But how will children expect the bully, or victimizer, to feel?

Research has shown that most adults indeed predict that children expect the victim to feel very bad, and they also predict that children will expect the victimizer to experience some negative emotions as well (Zelko et al., 1986). Interestingly, only the first prediction is accurate.

An important early study reported that young children, after hearing a story in which a child is victimized by another child, expect the bully to experience mainly, or even exclusively, positive emotions (Barden et al., 1980). These "happy victimizer" results have generated considerable interest among developmental psychologists studying moral development because they are both surprising and potentially important.

They are surprising, in part, because they are inconsistent with what adults expect children to say. In addition, they do not fit well with most theories of moral development, which suggest that either (a) viewing the victim in distress should evoke empathy in the bully or (b) that having concern about being caught and punished should produce anxiety. In either case, the victimizer should experience negative emotions, such as remorse, guilt, or fear.

The findings may be important to our understanding of moral development because they shed light on why some children continue to victimize others and how we might deal with this problem (Guerra & Slaby, 1990; Slaby & Guerra, 1988). They also add to our more general understanding of children's social cognition (Harris, 1989; Masters & Carlson, 1984).

More detailed investigations have found that the "happy victimizer" expectation is most prevalent among the youngest children studied (4 to 6 years old). By ages 8 to 10 many children have come to believe that the bully will have negative, as well as positive, emotions (Arsenio, 1988; Nunner-Winkler & Sodian, 1988). What changes in moral reasoning are responsible for this shift in expectations?

It appears that children of different ages focus on different aspects of the situation. Younger children appear to concentrate on the bully's material gain, such as the money that was stolen or the opportunity to play with the other child's toy, and to expect that these gains make the victimizer feel happy. As children mature, their focus shifts to the plight of the victim and the harm the antisocial behavior has caused.

This hypothesis received support in a recent study that manipulated the salience of the victim's experience. When children heard stories in which the victim's pain or loss was emphasized, subjects as young as age 6 attributed both negative and positive emotions to the bully. Even under these conditions, however, 4- and 5-year-olds continued to express the "happy victimizer" expectations (Arsenio & Kramer, 1992).

These findings fit well with Piaget's belief that the moral reasoning of younger children tends to be based primarily on the physical and objective characteristics of the situation. They also are consistent with the developmental advances in affective perspective-taking and empathy that occur during middle childhood. In fact, a related study found that "happy victimizer" expectations could serve as a measure of moral reasoning development. Holding these expectations predicted the likelihood that children would cheat on a task if given the opportunity (Asendorpf & Nunner-Winkler, 1992).

Hoffman believes that empathy is involved in altruistic behavior in two ways. First, the empathic child experiences emotional distress when observing another person in need. The child can often relieve this distress by helping or sharing with that person. Second, when a prosocial act produces joy or happiness in the other person, the empathic child can also experience these positive emotions.

Hoffman and others assume that the development of empathy is guided in part by biological processes (Eisenberg, 1986, 1989; Zahn-Waxler, Robinson, & Emde, 1992). As a species, humans are believed to be innately capable of emotionally responding to another person's distress. This ability is present in a primitive form during infancy (Ungerer et al., 1990)—although we have seen that, at this point, babies cannot clearly separate other people's feelings from their own. With increasing cognitive development, children come to better understand what others feel and why, and by 2 to 3 years of age, their first genuinely empathic responses occur. In later childhood, empathy develops fully, enabling children to generalize empathic responding to entire groups, such as the poor or oppressed.

Although biology may play an important role in the emergence of empathy, Hoffman and others feel that children's experiences influence how rapidly and completely it develops (Barnett, 1987; Hoffman, 1984b, 1987). For example, parents who teach children to identify their own emotions and those of others may be facilitating empathic development. Similarly, inductive discipline, which involves pointing out how a child's misbehavior makes someone else feel, may promote the development of empathy. And when parents frequently verbalize their own empathic responses, children are likely to pay more attention to these processes and thus achieve a greater understanding of how they operate (Eisenberg et al., 1992, 1993; Fabes, Eisenberg, & Miller, 1990).

The role of empathy in prosocial behavior has been studied more extensively than any other cognitive or affective variable (Batson & Oleson, 1991). But as with perspective taking, although the two variables might seem to be logically and theoretically related, the relation between them is inconsistent. The strength of the relation seems to depend on how empathy is measured. In many studies, children have listened to stories about characters in emotional situations and then reported their own feelings (which were taken as indicators of the children's empathy with the character). When empathy is assessed in this manner, researchers have found only small associations between empathic responding and prosocial behaviors. However, researchers who have assessed empathy by having teachers rate children on this characteristic or by observing children's emotional arousal in their facial expressions have found clearer positive correlations with altruism (Chapman et al., 1987; Eisenberg & Fabes, 1991; Eisenberg & Miller, 1987; Marcus, 1986).

Attributions

Adults often base their decisions to help someone on the causes to which they attribute the person's problems. So do children. When children attribute problems to factors beyond the person's control (such as bad luck), they are more likely to be sympathetic and altruistic toward the person. However, when they view the person's dilemma as resulting from laziness, greed, or some other controllable factor, they are less likely to offer help (Barnett & McMinimy, 1988; Eisenberg, 1990).

Social and Family Determinants of Prosocial Behavior

Children's willingness to share, help, and cooperate are, of course, affected by social and situational factors. Social-learning theorists contend that these behaviors are influenced by the same learning processes that affect other social behaviors—namely, reinforcement and observational learning.

Reinforcement

Will children be more altruistic if they are reinforced for altruism? This straightforward question has been answered positively many times in laboratory studies, demonstrating clear effects of reward and praise on children's prosocial behaviors (Gelfand & Hartmann, 1982; Grusec, 1981). Praise is especially effective in promoting altruism if it emphasizes that the child is a generous or helpful person ("You were a very nice girl for sharing your candy") rather than focusing on the specific behavior ("I like the way you shared your candy") (Mills & Grusec, 1989). Applied psychologists have used reward programs as a way of increasing prosocial behaviors in the classroom and other naturalistic settings (Barton, 1981; Kohler & Fowler, 1985; Serbin, Tonick, & Sternglanz, 1977).

But do reinforcement processes play a role in maintaining altruism under everyday circumstances, when no psychologist is involved? Here, too, the answer appears to be yes. One study investigating preschool children's naturally occurring altruistic behavior found that peers often responded positively to this type of behavior, such as by smiling, thanking the child, or doing something nice in return (Eisenberg et al., 1981). Similar research conducted in home settings has indicated that mothers, like peers, usually respond to altruistic behavior with some form of praise or verbal approval (Grusec & Dix, 1986; Mills & Grusec, 1988). And older siblings who are cooperative and helpful also tend to promote prosocial interactions among younger family members (Dunn & Munn, 1986).

Finally, even in the absence of external rewards or approval, reinforcement processes can still be in operation. Witnessing the joy experienced by someone we have just helped, for example, or sharing that person's relief from distress can serve to reinforce our helping behavior. Whether "pure" altruism ever occurs remains a matter of debate. But there can be no doubt that much of children's prosocial behavior occurs because it rewards the giver, as well as the receiver.

Modeling and the Media

Children's prosocial behavior is very much influenced by what they see others do. Laboratory studies have shown that children share more or are more helpful after observing a model performing similar behaviors (e.g., Eron & Huesmann, 1986; Lipscomb, McAllister, & Bregman, 1985; Radke-Yarrow & Zahn-Waxler, 1986). Not all models are imitated equally, however. Models who are seen as more powerful, competent, or important tend to be imitated more often (Eisenberg-Berg & Geisheker, 1979).

Some psychologists have attempted to use modeling in applied settings to increase prosocial behavior. Children's educational television, for example, often includes moral themes and prosocial messages. Programs like "Sesame Street," "Barney," and "Care Bears" are designed explicitly to encourage young children to help and cooperate. And research in field settings has shown that regular exposure to prosocial television can increase altruistic and socially desirable behaviors at all age levels (Friedrich & Stein, 1973, 1975; Friedrich-Cofer et al., 1979).

What about other television viewing? Children's viewing habits are, in part, influenced by parents. Much of this influence occurs through the rules parents impose, but there is also evidence that children to some degree imitate the viewing preferences of their parents—both good and bad (St. Peters et al., 1991).

✔ *To Recap...*

Prosocial, or altruistic, behaviors include sharing, cooperating, and helping. Even infants display some types of prosocial behavior. With age, prosocial behavior increases, although the relation is not a simple one. Typical experimental procedures may exaggerate differences in sharing and helping between younger and older children. However, older children do seem better able to cooperate than younger ones. Although girls are generally rated as more altruistic by teachers and peers, the observed differences in actual behaviors of boys and girls are small.

Cognitive and affective factors influence prosocial behavior. Children's levels of moral reasoning, as measured by responses to prosocial dilemmas, display a small positive correlation with altruistic behavior. Physical, social, and affective perspective taking also correlate positively, although only modestly, with prosocial actions.

Empathy develops gradually through childhood and is believed to be the product of both innate processes and socialization. Parental child-rearing practices appear especially important. Depending on how it is measured, empathy may correlate weakly or strongly with altruistic behavior.

Two environmental determinants clearly affect prosocial behavior. In both laboratory and classroom, systematically applied reinforcement increases altruism. Reinforcement also appears to operate in the natural environment, with peers and parents often providing social approval for altruistic acts. Modeling can increase prosocial responding in the laboratory. Television programs with prosocial content have also been demonstrated to increase children's altruism.

AGGRESSION

At the opposite end of the spectrum from prosocial behavior is the antisocial behavior of **aggression**. Whether it takes the form of destroying a preschool playmate's block tower, teasing and taunting by a fourth grader, or fighting between teenage gangs, aggression is a common and important aspect of child development. It too has been studied extensively (Baron & Richardson, 1994).

Aggression
Behavior that is intended to cause harm to persons or property and that is not socially justifiable.

Defining Aggression

Aggression can take many forms, and its scientific definition must include the elements common to all of them. But it has not been easy to settle on a definition that is both objective enough for research purposes (that is, easy to observe and measure) and at the same time consistent with a commonsense understanding of what is and is not aggressive behavior.

Aggression might appear to be any behavior that hurts someone or damages property. But accidentally spilling hot coffee on a friend or his new carpet is not aggression. And throwing a brick at someone or her car, but missing, *is* aggression. So aggression would appear to be based less on its *consequences* and more on the *intention* to cause harm. But dentists sometimes cause pain that is not altogether accidental, and house wreckers intentionally damage property. Moreover, intention is much more difficult for a researcher to observe and measure than is the behavior it produces.

These sorts of problems have led researchers to adopt a definition of aggression similar to the following: *behavior that is intended to cause harm to persons or property and that is not socially justifiable.* Notice that by this definition, aggression is always based on a social judgment that takes into account both the individual's motives and the circumstances or context in which the behavior occurs (Parke & Slaby, 1983).

Aggression can be divided into types based on its form and function. For example, verbal aggression, involving name calling, teasing, threats, and so forth, can be distinguished from physical aggression, such as hitting, kicking, and biting. In addition, aggressive behavior whose purpose is to obtain something (e.g., shoving another child away from a desired toy) is termed **instrumental aggression**, whereas aggression aimed specifically at inflicting pain or harm is termed **hostile aggression** (or **retaliatory aggression**, if it is carried out in response to the aggression of someone else).

Instrumental aggression
Aggression whose purpose is to obtain something desired.

Hostile (retaliatory) aggression
Aggression whose purpose is to cause pain or injury.

Age and Gender Differences in Aggression

The various types of aggression are worth distinguishing, because they occur in different proportions among children of different ages and sexes. Most of our knowledge regarding aggression during the preschool years has been based on direct observation of peer interactions. Between the ages of 18 months and 5 years, there is no simple relation between children's ages and their overall aggression (Hay, 1984). There is some evidence, however, that physical and instrumental aggression are more prevalent at the younger ages, with verbal and hostile aggression becoming more common as children reach school age (Hartup, 1974; McCabe & Lipscomb, 1988). Aggression in older children often is measured by use of the *peer nomination* method (discussed again in Chapter 16), in which each child rates classmates. Ratings of children in first through fifth grades have indicated that overall aggression does appear to increase with age (Eron et al., 1983).

Gender differences in aggression are well documented (Crowell, 1987; Eagly & Steffen, 1986). Males begin to display more aggression during the preschool years (Cummings, Iannotti, & Zahn-Waxler, 1989; Hyde, 1986) and continue to do so throughout the elementary school years (Eron et al., 1983; Parke & Slaby, 1983). In the later elementary grades, another gender difference begins to become apparent that extends into junior high school. Male aggression toward other boys becomes increasingly physical in nature, but male aggression toward girls drops markedly. Aggression by females grows more social in nature (such as name calling and gossiping) and is directed predominantly, but not entirely, toward other girls (Cairns et al., 1989). Overall sex differences in aggression, however, tend to decrease as children reach adolescence (Hyde, 1986).

Gender can also play a role in the measurement of aggression; expectations based on gender influence how observers evaluate children's aggression. In one study, adults viewed a film of two snowsuited preschoolers playing roughly in the snow. Some of the adults were told that the children were two boys, some that they were two girls, and some that they were a boy and a girl. Despite having viewed the same film, both male and female adults rated the "girls" as displaying more aggression than the "boys" (Condry & Ross, 1985). These results can be interpreted in a number of ways. For example, rough play may be seen as so inherent in little boys that it is viewed as a normal part of their behavior. In little girls, however, rough-

• In young males, aggression is often physical, whereas in young females it is often verbal.

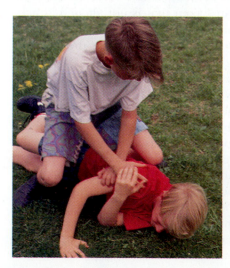

housing is not expected and so may warrant a different label. Regardless of the explanation, the findings illustrate the "social judgment" aspect of defining aggression.

Biological Determinants of Aggression

Much of the research on children's aggression has been concerned with identifying its causes. Here, we consider the determinants that have primarily a biological basis and then move on to social and cognitive influences.

An individual's level of aggression has proved to be remarkably stable over many years (Cairns et al., 1989; Cummings et al., 1989). Longitudinal research indicates that peer nominations of aggression at age 8 are excellent predictors of aggression and various other antisocial behaviors at age 30 (Eron, 1987; Eron et al., 1987). This degree of stability lends itself well to a genetic or biological explanation of the behavior. Hormones, inborn temperament styles, and dominance mechanisms are among the mechanisms that have been suggested.

Hormones

The hormones produced by our bodies are responsible for some of the physical and behavioral differences between males and females (a topic we discuss in more detail in Chapter 15). Indeed, injecting hormones from male laboratory animals into female animals causes the females to display more fighting and other forms of aggressive behavior (Svare, 1983). Studies with adolescent males suggest that the hormone testosterone plays a role in human aggression.

In a well-known Swedish study, 15- to 17-year-old boys were rated by peers for aggressive behavior and then tested for their levels of testosterone. The blood level of the hormone correlated significantly with peer ratings of both verbal and physical aggression—particularly for retaliatory aggression. The researchers explained this relation by noting that boys with higher levels of the hormone described themselves as being more irritable and impatient, perhaps making them especially susceptible to threats and provocations (Olweus, 1983, 1986).

Temperament

We saw in Chapter 12 that some babies are born with "difficult" response styles. They fuss, cry, and are more demanding than other infants of the same age. This personality dimension is quite stable across childhood (Thomas & Chess, 1986), prompting researchers to investigate whether it bears some relation to the development of aggressive behavior.

One group of researchers tested this hypothesis by asking a group of mothers to rate their 6-month-old infants on a temperament questionnaire that allowed the researchers to identify "difficult" babies. Over the course of the next five years, the same mothers periodically evaluated their children's aggressive behavior. As predicted, the early temperament ratings were quite good predictors of which children would display greater amounts of aggression (Bates, 1987; Bates, Maslin, & Frankel, 1985). Another study examined the question by asking identical and fraternal adult twins to describe how aggressive they had been as children. Identical twins reported a much higher correspondence than fraternal twins (Rushton et al., 1986). Both of these findings, of course, could have resulted from environmental influences interacting with certain inborn traits. But they suggest that at least some portion of aggressive behavior may be attributed to genetic factors (Cummings et al., 1986).

Dominance

Another way in which nature factors may affect the development of aggression involves the evolutionary mechanisms described earlier. Unlike most other explanations of aggression—which treat it solely as undesirable behavior that is best eliminated or controlled—ethologists argue that aggression has been passed along through generations because it has value to the individual and to the species (Cairns, 1986).

The dominance relationships that characterize some other species—monkeys, for example—also appear to exist among young children. Observational studies of children in naturalistic settings suggest that intact social groups, such as classrooms or children in a neighborhood, often develop a dominance hierarchy (Ginsburg, 1980; Strayer & Noel, 1986). The more dominant children establish their position through overt fighting and physical force. But eventually they maintain control over less dominant children using only nonviolent threats and gestures. The strong resemblance of these groups to those found in other species supports the idea that aggression may have evolutionary origins (Fishbein, 1984; Sluckin, 1980).

Social and Environmental Determinants of Aggression

Social and situational factors are also very important determinants of aggressive behavior. One common argument against the ethologists' claim that aggression is innate in humans, for example, is that there are some primitive cultures in which interpersonal conflict is very rare (Montague, 1968).

As might be expected, social-learning theorists believe aggression is controlled largely by learning principles (Bandura, 1973, 1986, 1989). Their research has shown, for example, that gender differences in physical aggression may be explained by the fact that little boys report that they expect less disapproval for this sort of behavior and are less bothered by the disapproval when it occurs (Boldizar, Perry, & Perry, 1989; Perry, Perry, & Weiss, 1989). Environmental influences can also be illustrated by a consideration of two familiar contexts in which aggressive behavior develops: family interactions and the viewing of violence on television (Pearl, 1987).

Family Processes

Children's aggression often stems from their interactions with parents and siblings. Parents of aggressive children have been found to deal with misbehavior more through power-assertion methods of discipline, using physical punishment, than through verbal explanation or reasoning (Dodge, Pettit, & Bates, 1994; Morton, 1986; Patterson, Reid, & Dishion, 1992). To social-learning theorists, this finding suggests that two processes may be at work in these situations. First, the parents may be modeling aggressive behavior to their children, who go on to imitate what they see. And second, these parents may be interacting with their children in ways that actually promote aggression.

An example of the first of these processes can be found in a cross-cultural study of two neighboring communities in Mexico. In one village, the level of adult conflict and violence was quite high, whereas the other village was unusually peaceful and nonviolent. As predicted, the behavior of the children in these communities paralleled that of the adults. In the violent village, children engaged in more frequent play-fighting and real aggression, suggesting that they were imitating the behaviors they frequently observed in their parents and other adults (Fry, 1988).

The other process is illustrated by a series of observational studies conducted by Gerald Patterson and his colleagues (Baldwin & Skinner, 1989; Patterson, 1982, 1986; Patterson et al., 1992). Patterson found that families of aggressive children commonly display a troublesome pattern of interactions he terms **coercive family process.** These households are characterized by very few friendly, cooperative comments or behaviors and by a high rate of hostile and negative responses. Commonly, the parents spend a good deal of time scolding, berating, or threatening the children, while the children nag or disobey the parents and tease or frustrate one another.

In such environments, aggression is used as a means of stopping or escaping from these sorts of aversive experiences. For example, a little girl may tease and taunt her brother, who punches her to make her stop, which leads his mother to spank him for punching his sister. These aggressive behaviors serve to end an aversive situation, if only temporarily. Thus, the behaviors are negatively reinforced and so become likely to occur again. In this way, both the children and parents end up using aggression to control one another and to get what they want. Patterson refers to this pattern as coercion because the family members achieve their goals through threats, commands, and other coercive behaviors rather than cooperative, prosocial means. Children who learn this style of interaction at home—and who fail to learn more positive interpersonal skills—also display aggression in other settings and often go on to delinquency and other serious forms of antisocial behavior (Conger et al., 1994; DeBaryshe, Patterson, & Capaldi, 1993; Patterson, DeBaryshe, & Ramsey, 1989; Vuchinich, Bank, & Patterson, 1992).

Coercive family process
Gerald Patterson's term for the method by which some families control one another through aggression and other coercive means.

Violence on Television

No topic concerning childhood aggression has provoked as much interest as the possible effects of violence on television (Eron & Huesmann, 1984, 1986; Freedman, 1984; Friedrich-Cofer & Huston, 1986; Gadow & Sprafkin, 1993; Sawin, 1990). And with good reason. The average child spends more time viewing television than in any other activity except sleep—about 2.5 to 4 hours each day—and by the time he reaches age 21 has witnessed about 8,000 television murders (Liebert & Sprafkin, 1988).

Beginning with Bandura in the 1960s, researchers have repeatedly demonstrated that children can learn new forms of aggression, and can be stimulated to perform them, by viewing a violent film model (Bandura, 1973, 1983). But does the average child really become more aggressive simply as a result of watching a typical diet of current network programming? The answer, based on dozens of studies and reports, appears to be yes (Eron & Huesmann, 1984, 1986; Huesmann & Miller, 1994). Moreover, the effects of violence can take several forms.

The most obvious effect is that children imitate the violent acts they see (For a discussion of this, see Box 14-3). They are especially likely to do so when the violence is performed by the "good guys" and also when the aggression successfully achieves its purpose. A somewhat less obvious effect is that television violence increases the likelihood of all other forms of aggression in children, even those that do not resemble the behavior of the television models. Violence on television can also make children more tolerant of aggression and less bothered by it (Parke & Slaby, 1983). To make matters worse, the relation between violence and aggression appears to be circular. While television violence stimulates aggression, more aggressive children also tend to watch more violent television (Huesmann, Lagerspetz, & Eron, 1984). And in keeping with the sex differences noted earlier, boys watch more violent cartoons and action stories than girls (Huston et al., 1990).

SHOULD THE GOVERNMENT REGULATE MEDIA VIOLENCE?

In the summer of 1993, the MTV network aired a program in which the cartoon characters Beavis and Butthead (Figure 14-2) demonstrated to their young viewers how to start fires in unusual ways. Shortly thereafter, a 5-year-old boy in Moraine, Ohio, imitated what he had seen and set his house afire, killing his younger sister. During the same summer, a movie was released entitled *The Program.* It included a scene in which characters lay down on the white line of a highway while cars sped by. Teenagers in two different states attempted the same stunt and were run over and killed.

Incensed by these senseless deaths, U.S. Attorney General Janet Reno announced to the television and movie industries that if they did not voluntarily control the kinds of material to which they exposed children and adolescents, Congress would pass legislation to do so. Unfortunately, neither enacting such laws nor convincing all involved that this is the appropriate remedy are simple matters (Morganthau, 1993).

An obvious obstacle to decreasing such programming is resistance from the entertainment industry. Television and movie violence are very popular and so generate enormous profits.

More important is the issue of First Amendment rights. The First Amendment to the U.S. Constitution guarantees the right to freedom of expression. The courts and many legislatures have taken this to mean that government should be severely limited in its ability to censor what is broadcast over the airwaves or portrayed in film. In a free and open society, some argue, individuals, not the government, should choose what to watch and what to avoid. As New York governor Mario Cuomo put it "Do we really want a thought-police crackdown? Government censorship—and that's what it would be—would mean seizing an important part of our freedom and delivering it to a government we already distrust; substituting the opinions of faceless and unaccountable bureaucrats for our own judgments about what is valuable or interesting or entertaining" (*Los Angeles Times,* 1994). Others contend, however, that our society clearly has allowed government to impose restrictions of various sorts on our choices. Our children are required to ride in car seats, attend school, and be inoculated against certain diseases. And governmental restrictions have been imposed on manufacturers of children's toys, food, and clothing.

An alternative to direct government intervention has been action by interest groups, such as the *National*

Figure 14-2   A scene from "Beavis and Butt-head," in which a cartoon character demonstrates lighting a fire.

Coalition on Television Violence, which apply pressure through letter-writing campaigns, consumer boycotts, and other lobbying techniques. In some areas, the movie industry has responded—for example, by adopting the familiar rating system that warns parents whether movies have too much sex or violence. Similar rating systems are being developed by the cable industry and the major television networks. In response to the outcry generated by the cases described earlier, MTV decided to move "Beavis and Butt-head" to a later time slot, in the hope that it would be seen by fewer young children. And Disney Studios recalled *The Program* and edited out the highway scene. Of course, these changes came too late to save the lives of the children whose deaths were prompted by them. More importantly, they do not guarantee that similar problems will not appear in future movies or television programs.

A second alternative is to focus on changing children's attitudes toward media violence. One study found that the negative impact of such material could be reduced by reminding children that the programs are not real or by emphasizing the unacceptability of violent behavior (Huesmann et al., 1983).

This issue, thus, remains unsettled. For the present, the best solution probably is for parents to sit down and watch television with their children so they can help the children comprehend and interpret what is being presented on the screen.

Reprinted by permission of NEA, Inc.

• Violence on television has been shown to be a common cause of children's aggression.

Cognitive Influences on Aggression

Any complete understanding of children's aggression must include the cognitive processes that control it. Much research in this area has involved the development of social cognition, or how children come to understand the social world in which they live (Dodge, 1986b; Turiel, 1987).

Aggression is a subject with which most youngsters are familiar. From an early age, children can identify aggressive behavior and realize that it is considered undesirable. Even first graders show strong agreement on peer nominations of aggression, and they use this information to decide whom they would prefer as friends (Younger & Piccinin, 1989; Younger, Schwartzman, & Ledingham, 1985). By the age of 5, children can comprehend more complex forms of aggressive behavior—such as **displaced aggression**, in which a child who has been the object of aggression reacts by striking out at something else (Miller & DeMarie-Dreblow, 1990; Weiss & Miller, 1983).

Aggressive children (especially boys) show certain cognitive differences from their classmates. For example, their level of moral reasoning tends to be lower (Bear, 1989), and they are less likely to take into account a character's motives when making a moral judgment (Sanvitale et al., 1989). In addition, these children show less empathy (Bryant, 1982; Ellis, 1982).

Aggressive children also differ in another aspect of social cognition—attributions. Kenneth Dodge and his associates have conducted research that demonstrates that aggressive children have difficulty reading social cues in the environment (Dodge, 1985; Dodge & Crick, 1990; Quiggle et al., 1992). Their studies typically involve videotaped episodes in which one child is harmed or provoked by a peer whose intentions are unclear. In these situations, aggressive children are much more likely to attribute hostile or malicious motives to the provoker. And when cues are provided to suggest that the provoker's intentions were not hostile, aggressive children have more difficulty understanding and using these cues (Dodge & Crick, 1990; Dodge & Somberg, 1987). These findings suggest that some children may be aggressive because they do not view the world in the same way most children do (Waas, 1988). (A related attributional model of aggression that focuses on inner-city youth will be describe later, in Box 14-4.)

The studies described in this section, together with the research already discussed, indicate that aggression is a complex social behavior with biological, social, and cognitive elements. This complexity has made the task of preventing or reducing the frequency of aggression a major challenge.

Displaced aggression Retaliatory aggression directed at a person or object other than the one against whom retaliation is desired.

Applications
Box 14-4

UNDERSTANDING AND REDUCING AGGRESSION IN INNER-CITY YOUTH

In the United States, problems involving aggression have been prevalent among inner-city youths during the past decade. It is generally accepted that these problems stem principally from sociocultural factors, including poverty, failure to complete high school, and family instability (Boone, 1991; Leadbeater & Bishop, 1994; Gibbs, 1988; Patterson, Kupersmidt, & Vaden, 1990).

A recent analysis has added faulty attributional processes as a contributor to the aggressive behavior of these youths (Graham & Hudley, 1994; Graham, Hudley, & Williams, 1992). Like the attributional model of Dodge, described earlier, this analysis also begins by suggesting that aggressive children are more likely to interpret ambiguous, provocative actions by their peers (such as bumping into them in the school hallway) as intentional and hostile. However, as shown in Figure 14-3, this model adds a third step—emotional arousal, or anger—which is thought to energize the aggressive, retaliatory behavior.

Using this model as a basis, the researchers went on to develop a cognitive intervention program designed to interrupt the sequence leading up to the aggression (Hudley & Graham, 1993). Some earlier intervention programs had also assumed that anger plays a role in causing aggression and so focused on methods of reducing the anger (Bash & Camp, 1985; Goldstein & Glick, 1987). The present program, by contrast, attacks the problem a step earlier, focusing on the attributions that are believed to generate the anger.

The study involved urban African-American children in grades 4 to 6, who had been selected on the basis of teacher and peer ratings of their aggression. Most of the subjects had been rated high on aggression, but some had been rated low (so that not all children selected to participate in the study were stigmatized as problem students). Each subject was assigned to one of three groups: an experimental group that received attribution training, an attention control group that received training only in academic skills, and a second control group that received no training.

The attribution training involved teaching the children to recognize cues to another person's intentions (such as facial expressions), to encourage nonhostile attributions when the peer's actions were ambiguous (for example, "he probably did it by accident"), and to generate nonaggressive responses to the peer's behavior. The training continued for 6 weeks and included a variety of methods, such as storytelling, role-playing, videos, and group brainstorming.

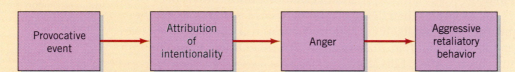

Figure 14-3 A model illustrating the roles of faulty attributions and anger in causing retaliatory aggression. Adapted from "Attributional and Emotional Determinants of Aggression Among African-American and Latino Young Adolescents" by S. Graham et al., 1992, *Developmental Psychology, 28,* 731–740. Copyright 1992 by the American Psychological Association. Reprinted by permission.

DEVELOPMENT IN CONTEXT: Does Being Aggressive Mean Being Rejected?

Aggression is considered a social problem primarily because it causes harm to others. But psychologists have also warned that the aggressive child, by failing to acquire appropriate social skills, runs the risk of being rejected by the peer group and becoming an outcast (Asher & Coie, 1990).

Before and after the training, all subjects were given a series of assessments designed to determine how likely they were to (a) attribute hostile intentions in an ambiguous situation, (b) become angry in reponse to such attributions, and (c) respond with aggressive behavior. The data for those subjects initially rated high on aggression are shown in Figure 14-4. Obviously, the attributional training worked very well. On each of the three measures, the subjects in the experimental group scored the lowest on the posttest that followed the training and showed by far the greatest change. These data suggest not only that attributions play a role in producing aggression toward peers in everyday classroom situations but also that cognitive interventions designed to change these attributions can reduce such aggression.

The researchers caution, however, that other factors in the situation should not be overlooked. One is that not all aggression is directed toward peers and that this approach may not reduce problems involving vandalism, defiance of authority, theft, and so forth. Perhaps a more important point is that given the extremely difficult conditions under which many of these urban children live, attributing hostile intentions to peer provocations may often be accurate and retaliating with aggression may be a useful survival response in this setting.

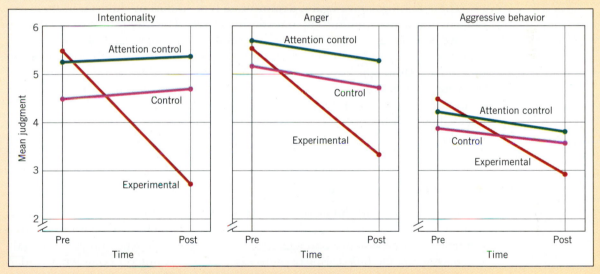

Figure 14-4 Results of an intervention study with African-American children. The Experimental Group received attributional training and decreased the most on the three measures of interest. Adapted from "An Attributional Intervention to Reduce Peer-directed Aggression Among African-American Boys" by C. Hudley & S. Graham, 1993, *Child Development, 64*, 124–138. Copyright 1993 by the Society for Research in Child Development. Reprinted by permission.

We will see in Chapter 16 that these concerns have some foundation. Aggressive children often have poor interpersonal skills, and aggression runs high among unpopular, rejected children (although the cause-and-effect relation probably operates in both directions). But does this mean that highly aggressive children never have friends? Or that they are never members of stable social groups?

These questions were addressed in a large-scale study of the social patterns of aggressive children (Cairns et al., 1988). To begin, the researchers identified a group of males and females in the fourth and seventh grades as being very aggressive, based on reports from their teachers, principals, and counselors. Next, for comparison, the researchers selected a group of nonaggressive children who were similar in age, gender, race, and other related characteristics. The social patterns of the two groups were measured by a number of means, including interviews with classmates, ratings by teachers, and self-ratings.

The data from these measures were analyzed to answer several questions. First, did the children group themselves into social clusters, in which certain children spent a great deal of time together? If so, which children were members of these groups? Were any of the clusters made up predominantly of aggressive children? Finally, how often were aggressive children nominated as "best friends" by their classmates?

The results proved somewhat surprising. In the social clusters that were identified, aggressive subjects were just as likely to be members as nonaggressive subjects. Children high in aggression often tended to hang around together, forming their own clusters. And aggressive children had just as many peer nominations as "best friend" as did nonaggressive children. The best-friend relationships, however, involved aggressive children nominating one another and nonaggressive children nominating one another.

These findings, once again, demonstrate how studies of children in their natural environments often turn up unexpected results. The widely held belief that aggressive behavior automatically sentences a child to a life of social isolation is clearly overstated. Many aggressive children have a network of friends who are similar to themselves. Although these clusters may encourage and thus perpetuate antisocial behavior, they also appear to provide friendships and social support. Thus, while many aggressive children may fail to develop good interpersonal skills and may be rejected by their peers, some are socially competent enough to make and maintain friends.

Controlling Aggression

Parents, teachers, and public officials often look to developmental psychology for help in solving real-life problems. This has been very much the case with regard to reducing juvenile violence and aggression, a task in which legal and judicial methods have generally failed. But because researchers do not yet completely understand the mechanisms of antisocial behavior, attempts to control it through psychological or educational methods have been only partially successful (Kazdin, 1987). We examine some of these methods next.

Catharsis

Catharsis
The psychoanalytic belief that the likelihood of aggression can be reduced by viewing aggression or by engaging in high-energy behaviors.

It was once believed that aggression is a means of "venting steam" and that it can thus be prevented by having the aggressive child channel energy into other behaviors or experience aggression vicariously. Hitting a punching bag or watching a wrestling match, then, could take the place of engaging in aggressive behaviors. Psychoanalytic theory refers to these substitute behaviors as forms of **catharsis**. The catharsis process has been used to defend the existence of violent television programs and aggression-related toys (Feshbach & Singer, 1971).

Research evidence, however, does not support this theory. As we have seen, viewing violence on television increases rather than decreases the likelihood of aggression. And studies with both children and adults indicate that engaging in high-activity behaviors does not make aggression any less likely (Geen, 1983). Not surprisingly, methods aimed at curbing aggression through the catharsis process have generally proved ineffective (Parke & Slaby, 1983).

Parent Training

It is well established that parents' child-rearing methods are related to their children's aggression. One of the most straightforward and successful approaches to handling this source of aggression has been the use of parent training techniques (Kazdin, 1987). Drawing on principles of behavior modification, psychologists have trained parents in more effective ways of interacting with their children. Parents learn to reduce the use of negative remarks, such as threats and commands, and replace them with positive statements and verbal approval of children's prosocial behaviors. They are also trained in applying nonphysical punishment in a consistent and reasonable manner when discipline is required. The results of this form of intervention have often been dramatic in changing both the parents' and children's behavior (Horne & Sayger, 1990). Similar techniques have been used to train teachers and other child-care workers (Kazdin, 1987).

Cognitive Methods

Another way to reduce aggression is to focus on cognitive processes, which tend to be different for aggressive children. This approach has been used with children ranging in age from preschoolers to adolescents (Gibbs, 1991).

One cognitive method focuses on the emotions that accompany behaviors. Aggression is often accompanied by anger. Laboratory studies with adults have shown that if this emotional response can be replaced with an incompatible response, such as empathy, aggression can be prevented or decreased (Baron, 1983). Similarly, programs for increasing children's empathy—by teaching them to take the perspective of the other child and to experience that child's emotional reactions—have found some success in reducing conflict and aggression (Feshbach & Feshbach, 1982; Gibbs, 1987).

A second cognitive approach involves preventing aggression through training in problem-solving techniques. This method teaches children to deal with problem situations more effectively by first generating and examining various strategies for confronting the problem and then following a systematic plan for dealing with it. With younger children, problem-solving training often is begun in a laboratory setting. The children first hear stories in which a character faces potential conflict, then are trained to analyze the problem and develop constructive solutions. Gradually, the children are encouraged to apply these new skills in real-life situations (Lochman et al., 1984; Shure, 1989). Similar programs have been used with aggressive adolescents (Goldstein & Glick, 1987; Guerra & Slaby, 1990). One approach is described in Box 14-4.

✔ *To Recap...*

Aggression is often defined as behavior that is intended to cause harm and that is not socially justifiable. This definition always involves a social judgment as to the person's motives and the situational appropriateness of the behavior. Aggression can be classified as verbal versus physical or as instrumental versus hostile or retaliatory. To measure aggression, researchers may use direct observation or the peer nomination method.

In preschoolers, physical and instrumental aggression gradually give way to verbal and hostile aggression. In school-age children, the overall level of aggression tends to increase

with age. Males are more aggressive than females—especially, beginning in the later elementary school years, toward one another. Females at this age begin to display more social aggression, primarily toward other girls.

The fact that aggression is a very stable characteristic over the lifespan lends itself to a biological explanation of aggressive behavior. Biological explanations of aggression have linked it to blood levels of the hormone testosterone, to "difficult" temperament during infancy, and to the evolutionary processes that operate in dominance relationships.

Situational factors are assumed to influence aggression by way of the social-learning principles of reinforcement, punishment, and observational learning. The families of aggressive children engage in an ongoing pattern of coercive interactions in which members control one another through forms of aggressive behavior. Violence on television also increases the likelihood of aggression in child viewers. The effects may include direct imitation of the violent behavior, an increase in overall aggression, and an increase in children's tolerance of aggression in others.

Aggressive children appear to be deficient in a number of cognitive areas, including moral reasoning and empathy. These children have difficulty interpreting social cues and are more likely to attribute hostile motives to other children.

Various methods have been used in attempts to control children's aggression. Techniques based on the catharsis model have been of little value. Methods designed to teach parents more effective ways to discipline and interact with their children have proved very successful, however, as have cognitive approaches aimed at directly changing children's beliefs and attitudes regarding interpersonal violence.

CONCLUSION

In many respects, children's moral development is the same as any other aspect of their behavior. Hence, it is treated by developmental psychologists as simply one more topic of study. Yet issues of morality have an added element that makes them different.

It should be clear from this chapter that moral development can be studied scientifically. By viewing moral reasoning in terms of the development of rule following, psychologists can examine how this process changes with age and what factors influence it. Similarly, prosocial and antisocial behaviors can be conceptualized as forms of social behavior influenced by biological, cognitive, and environmental variables.

But although science will eventually answer many of the questions regarding moral development, it cannot answer all of them. Most moral issues—like those involving capital punishment, racial discrimination, and animal rights—are based on *values*. Values are both personal and societal, and they reflect the priorities that we attach to certain things in our lives. Each of us encounters moral decisions every day. And each of us participates in a society that is continually wrestling with moral struggles. The choices we make will sometimes be influenced by information that science has provided us. But science alone cannot dictate what we choose.

Can we develop a science of values? Those who have considered the question think it unlikely (Kurtines, Alvarez, Azmitia, 1990; Schwartz, 1990). The solutions to many of the moral issues we face may ultimately reside in the principles we develop as we grow from children to adults. Perhaps we will someday more clearly understand this process. But even if we do, the solutions still may not be obvious.

FOR THOUGHT AND DISCUSSION

1. Some psychologists believe that pure altruism does not exist and that all of our acts of kindness are really based on getting something in return. *Do you believe that pure altruism ever occurs? If so, try to generate an example of an altruistic act in which no reward of any sort is possible.*

2. The world seems to be perpetually at war. Whenever one dispute is settled, another erupts. *Do you believe that humans are innately aggressive and therefore that wars are inevitable? If not, how do you explain the constant presence of international conflict?*

3. According to Kohlberg, moral reasoning develops through stages. *Read the descriptions of stages given in Table 14-1. Which stage do you think best describes you? Can you think of people you know who could be characterized by each of the other stages?*

4. Females have the reputation of being more altruistic than males, yet research shows that the sexes differ little in this regard. *Why do you think females have acquired this reputation (given that it apparently cannot be based on personal experience)? What do you think are some of the ramifications of this incorrect belief? How might things be different if everyone held a more accurate view?*

5. The study by Condry and Ross (1985) found that adults' judgments as to whether children's behavior was aggressive depended on whether they believed the snowsuited youngsters were males or females. *How do you feel about the interpretation of this finding that was suggested in the text? Can you think of any other possible interpretations? What implications do you think these results have for how researchers should go about studying aggression?*

6. For children living in some inner-city neighborhoods, responding to aggression with retaliation may be a useful survival response. *Under such circumstances, would there be any justification for intervention programs to encourage such behavior (or at least not discourage it)? Can you think of other potential responses that might be encouraged in an intervention program for this type of situation?*

Chapter 15

GENDER-ROLE DEVELOPMENT AND SEX DIFFERENCES

*M*en and women typically differ in a number of ways—such as physical appearance and dress, personality styles, occupational preferences, parenting roles, and some specific talents and abilities—not only in Western society but in most cultures around the world. Many such differences can be traced to childhood and even infancy. What is the source of these sex-related characteristics, and how do they emerge?

Until the 1960s, most psychologists believed that after an infant had come into the world as either a boy or a girl, the child's gender-role development simply followed, more or less routinely, from there. Most sex differences in behavior were thought to have their roots in inborn factors, with the environment playing only a minor role.

The rise of the Women's Movement in the United States during the late 1960s had an important effect on scientific thinking on this issue. As many of society's legal and cultural barriers to women were being challenged, so too were many scientific ideas regarding gender-role acquisition and behavior. Some researchers began to question whether many of the traditional gender differences found in our culture are really inevitable products of biology. Perhaps, instead, they are partially or totally created by the social environment. This newer point of view resulted in an explosion of scientific research during the 1970s. This research, which continues today, has reexamined many previous beliefs and assumptions about sex differences (Carter, 1987a; Huston, 1985; Jacklin, 1989; Lutz & Ruble, 1994).

In this chapter, we present a view of children's gender-role development that has resulted both from changes in societal attitudes and from important advances in research methodology (Fagot, 1982; Jacklin, 1981). Biological differences remain a major factor. But a growing understanding of cognitive and social influences, and of their interactions at different points in development, gives us a much clearer picture of how this aspect of development unfolds.

THEORIES OF GENDER-ROLE DEVELOPMENT

Sex, or gender
An individual's biological maleness or femaleness.

Sex differentiation
The process through which biological sex differences emerge.

Sex difference
A behavior or characteristic in which males and females usually differ as a result of either biological or environmental factors.

Gender role, or sex-role stereotype
A pattern of behaviors that is considered appropriate for males or females by the culture in which they live.

Sex typing
The process by which children develop the sex role considered appropriate by their culture.

Before we go on to examine the major developmental theories, we should clarify the terminology we will be using throughout the chapter. The labels **sex** and **gender** are used interchangeably to refer to an individual's biological maleness or femaleness. The biological process through which these physical differences emerge is called **sex differentiation**. When we refer to a **sex difference**, however, we are saying simply that males and females differ on the particular characteristic under discussion; we are not assuming anything about the biological or environmental origins of that difference. The term **gender role** (or **sex-role stereotype**) refers to a pattern or set of behaviors considered appropriate for males or females within a particular culture (Deaux, 1987, 1993; Gentile, 1993). In most cultures, for example, the male gender role is characterized by such traits as leadership, independence, and aggressiveness, whereas females are expected to be nurturant, dependent, and sensitive (Block, 1973; Williams & Best, 1990). **Sex typing** is the process by which children develop the behaviors and attitudes considered appropriate for their gender. This process is assumed to involve a combination of biological, cognitive, and social mechanisms (Huston, 1983, 1985; Serbin, Powlishta, & Gulko, 1993).

The study of gender roles has covered many different questions and issues. And as usual, theorists from the three major traditions have had different things to say about the nature and causes of this aspect of development.

Ethological and Biological Explanations

The most traditional approach holds that evolutionary and biological processes are principally responsible for sex differences and gender-role development (MacDonald, 1988b). There is no doubt, of course, that biological sex differences exist. Certainly, males and females have anatomical differences, and they also play very different roles in sexual reproduction—a fact that is true for almost all other species, as well. Among species most closely related to our own (such as primates and other mammals), males and females display clear differences in social behavior that undoubtedly have a genetic basis (Hinde, 1983). Certain aspects of hormonal and brain functioning, which we consider later in the chapter, also appear to differ for males and females (Goy & McEwen, 1980; Hines & Green, 1991).

The existence of such marked biological differences has led some theorists to suspect that most other aspects of gender-role behavior also are guided primarily by inborn processes. For example, some ethologists and sociobiologists argue that sex differences in social behavior—such as females' being more nurturant toward the young and males' being more exploratory and aggressive—may have evolved because they are valuable to the survival of the species. Similar arguments have been made for certain sex differences in cognitive abilities (MacDonald, 1988a, 1988c; Silverman & Eals, 1992).

Some proposals within this tradition, however, may be described as *biosocial* models (Ehrhardt, 1985; Hood et al., 1987; Moore, 1985). The biosocial approach suggests that biological elements—namely, genes and hormones—set the process of sex differentiation into motion but that environmental conditions complete and maintain this process. One model, for example, refers to the "nature–critical period–nurture" principle. According to this principle, biological and social factors work together to produce normal development (in this case, sex differentiation), but only if they occur during specific developmental periods (Money, 1987; Money & Annecillo, 1987).

The idea that nature and nurture interact in gender-role development is not unique to biosocial models. In fact, it characterizes both the cognitive-developmental and social-learning theories. The differences among these approaches lie mainly in what mechanisms are believed to be involved and how much emphasis is placed on biological versus socialization influences.

Cognitive-Developmental Models

The cognitive approach to gender-role development focuses on the child's ability to understand the concepts of male and female and to identify with one of them. The emphasis is on the child's increasing knowledge regarding gender and gender roles and how this knowledge translates into the sex-typed behaviors that we commonly observe (Huston, 1983; Liben & Signorella, 1987; Martin, 1993).

A Stage Model

The early cognitive-developmental account of this process was based on a three-stage model of development. First, children develop **gender identity**—the ability to categorize themselves as male or female. This self-classification is followed by the emergence of **gender stability**—an awareness that all boys grow up to be men and all girls become women. Finally, children develop **gender consistency**—the recognition that an individual's gender is permanent and cannot change simply with changes in dress or behavior. Taken together, these three cognitive stages repre-

Gender identity
Knowing one's gender.

Gender stability
Understanding that one's gender will remain the same throughout life.

Gender consistency
Understanding that one's gender cannot be changed by superficial changes in clothing, occupation, etc.

• Gender stability refers to the understanding that boys grow up to be men and girls grow up to be women.

Gender constancy
Understanding that one's gender is a fixed part of the self; it includes gender identity, gender stability, and gender consistency.

Gender schema
A cognitive structure used to organize information regarding one's gender.

Gender script
A familiar routine or sequence of events that is typically associated with only one gender.

sent the child's understanding of **gender constancy**—the knowledge that our gender is an integral and fixed part of ourselves (Kohlberg & Ullian, 1974; Slaby & Frey, 1975).

As is typical of stage theories, the stages are assumed to be universal for all cultures, and all children are assumed to pass through them in an invariant order. More importantly, these changes in cognitive sophistication and awareness are thought to be the underlying causes of the changes in the child's gender-role behavior. That is, this model predicts that children will not show sex-typed behaviors until they have attained a clear understanding of gender constancy. As we will see in later sections, however, stereotyped sex differences in behavior appear much earlier than this.

Information-Processing Models

Newer cognitive-developmental accounts of sex-role development have been based on the information-processing concepts of the **gender schema** and the **gender script**. As we saw in Chapter 9, a schema is a cognitive representation of the general structure of something familiar, and a script is a type of schema that involves a familiar sequence of events.

The gender-schema model proposes that, early in life, children develop schemas for "boy" and "girl" (Bem, 1981, 1987; Liben & Signorella, 1987; Martin, 1991; Martin & Halverson, 1987). These schemas result principally from two factors. One is the child's inborn tendency to organize and classify information from the environment. The other is our culture's heavy emphasis on providing gender-distinguishing cues (such as clothing, names, and occupations), which make these concepts easily identifiable. The child then adopts one of the schemas—boy or girl—and the schema, in turn, affects the child in three ways. First, it prompts the child to pay greater attention to information relevant to his or her own gender. A girl may notice television advertisements for new Barbie dolls, for example, whereas a boy may be more attuned to sportscasts giving last night's baseball scores. Second, it influences the child's self-regulated behavior. For instance, a girl may decide to play with Barbie dolls and a boy to play baseball. Third, the gender schema may lead the child to make certain inferences, as when the child assumes that the new "quarterback" on the street is a boy (Berndt & Heller, 1986; Martin, 1991). This model predicts that gender-stereotyped behavior will appear when the child has developed a gender schema, which seems to occur at about the same point as gender stability or perhaps even gender identity (Martin, 1993; Martin, Wood, & Little, 1990).

Research support for this cognitive model is growing. In Chapter 13 we saw that children can recall information better when they see it as relevant to their self-schemas. Similar findings have been reported regarding gender-related materials—children show better recall for material relevant to their own gender (Bauer, 1993; Boston & Levy, 1991; Liben & Signorella, 1993; Martin et al., 1990; Welch-Ross & Schmidt, 1994). A related finding is that children recall information better when it is consistent with the gender schemas they have formed. For example, in several studies, children were shown a series of pictures or photographs, each depicting either a male or female performing a gender-stereotyped activity. The children later were shown two pictures and asked which one they had seen earlier. Children had more accurate memory for gender-consistent pictures (such as a woman ironing clothes) than for gender-inconsistent pictures (such as a man ironing clothes) (Bigler & Liben, 1990; Boston & Levy, 1991; Liben & Signorella, 1993). A similar study recently extended this finding to personality traits. Children recalled more things about a female character if they were told she was shy (gender-consistent) than if she was outgoing (gender-inconsistent); the reverse was found if the character was a male (McAninch et al., 1993). Adding further support to this model, other researchers report that these patterns of schema-related findings are clearest among children who display the greatest knowledge of traditional sex stereotypes (Carter & Levy, 1988; Levy, 1989) and who hold the strongest sex-stereotyped attitudes (List, Collins, & Westby, 1983; Signorella & Liben, 1984).

We saw in Chapters 9 and 11 that scripts are familiar routines, like going to McDonald's or taking a bath. A child acquires such a script as a whole and then gradually learns to use it in more flexible ways, such as by replacing elements of it with new objects or behaviors. The script model of gender role development is, in a sense, the opposite of the gender schema approach (Levy & Fivush, 1993). It holds that children first learn to behave in ways that follow predictable scripts for their gender, such as having a tea party (female) or building a fort (male). Once these scripts have become familiar, the children use their experiences as one basis for constructing cognitive schemas around the categories of male and female. In this way, the sex-typed behavior is seen as inducing the creation of the cognitive structures rather than vice versa.

Environmental/Learning Approaches

Social-learning theorists view gender roles as primarily learned patterns of behavior that are acquired through experience. According to this approach, many sex-typed behaviors are products of the same learning principles that govern other social behaviors, including reinforcement processes, observational learning, and self-regulation (Bandura, 1989, 1991; Bussey & Bandura, 1992). Little boys, for example, are more likely to behave in traditionally masculine ways because they receive social approval for this type of behavior and disapproval when they exhibit traditionally feminine behavior or preferences. They also observe and imitate models in their environments—ranging from parents to classmates to television characters—who display gender-related behaviors. And, by learning to anticipate how others will respond to their behavior, they gradually internalize standards regarding what are appropriate and inappropriate gender behaviors and then self-regulate their behavior to conform to these standards.

Support for this model can be found, for example, in a recent study which determined that (a) there was no clear relation between young children's gender constancy and their sex-typed behavior, but that (b) the same children's sex-typed behaviors could be predicted by their anticipation of the consequences they would receive for playing with traditionally same-sex or opposite-sex toys (Bussey & Bandura, 1992). We will consider other research supporting the environmental/learning approach in later sections.

Social-learning theorists do not deny that biological distinctions separate males and females, but they argue that many of the sex differences in children's social behavior and cognitive abilities are not inevitable results of their genetic makeup. Nor do they deny that children develop a cognitive understanding of different gender roles. But this understanding, they believe, is not necessarily the cause of the sex differences we observe in behavior, especially during early childhood (Bandura, 1991).

One implication of the social-learning approach has to do with the possibility for change. If sex-typed behaviors are learned, they can be unlearned or modified by changes in the child's environment or experiences. Psychologists who prefer a biological model, in contrast, do not generally believe that most sex differences can, or should, be changed. (Box 15-1 describes some classic research that sheds light on whether gender roles are inevitable.)

✔ *To Recap...*

The biological analysis of gender-role development has looked to genetic and structural differences as the most likely causes of sex differences in behavior. Current theories, referred to as biosocial models, incorporate both biological and socialization processes.

The cognitive-developmental tradition has generated two theoretical approaches to gender-role development. The older is a stage model, in which children's understanding of gender-role issues proceeds through three stages: gender identity, gender stability, and gender consistency. As usual for stage models, the stages are assumed to follow an invariant order and to be universal across cultures. Newer approaches involve information-processing models based on the concepts of the gender schema and the gender script. The gender schema is a cognitive representation of gender believed to help children organize gender-related information, regulate their gender-role behavior and make inferences regarding gender-role issues. Both the gender schema model and the stage model predict that children will not display sex-typed behavior until they have attained the appropriate cognitive level of development. In contrast, the gender script model proposes that gender scripts are used as models for behavior, which in turn help induce the construction of gender schemas.

Social-learning theory views gender-role behaviors as simply another class of social responses acquired and maintained by learning principles, including reinforcement, modeling, and self-regulation. Sex differences in this view are not inevitable and may change with environmental conditions.

STUDYING GENDER ROLES IN CROSS-CULTURAL CONTEXT

Are the traditional gender roles we find in Western societies the inevitable products of our evolutionary past, as some sociobiologists would have us believe? Have females been genetically programmed to assume the stereotyped "feminine" roles and responsibilities in any culture, whereas males are biologically destined to display stereotypical "masculine" attitudes and behaviors? This issue, which forms the basis of much modern research on gender, was in fact investigated many years ago in a classic cross-cultural study.

The research was conducted in the 1930s by Margaret Mead, a renowned anthropologist and writer. In the course of studying primitive cultures in the South Pacific, Mead became interested in three tribes on the island of New Guinea. Although the tribes lived within 100 miles of each other, their cultures and social structures were remarkably different.

The Arapesh were peaceful mountain dwellers. In their culture, few role distinctions existed between females and males. Instead, all tribal members displayed a traditionally "feminine" personality. Both mothers and fathers were gentle, nurturant, and highly involved in rearing their children. The atmosphere of the society was cooperative, with an emphasis on communal, rather than individual, goals and welfare.

The Mundugumor were fierce, cannibalistic warriors. Here, too, few distinctions could be found in the roles of males and females. However, Mead described the personality style of this tribe as stereotypically "masculine." Men and women fought and hunted side by side. Child-rearing was given only minimal attention. The tribe had considerable wealth and resources, so little cooperation among families was required or observed. Although the society had many rules, tribal members frequently broke them and disputes were common, leading to a general atmosphere of hostility and suspicion.

Perhaps most interesting were the Tchambuli. In their culture, the traditional gender roles were reversed. Men focused their energies on artistic activities, including music, dance, and frequent ceremonies of all sorts. They paid great attention to their physical appearance, wearing makeup, elaborate costumes, and exotic hairstyles. In contrast, the women held most of the social and economic power. They took responsibility for obtaining food—mainly by fishing and trapping—as well as the other goods necessary for the family's survival. They also controlled the family's resources, which men could spend only with their permission. At the community level, the women served as the managers and administrators, seeing to it that the day-to-day affairs of the tribe were attended to.

Mead summarized the three tribes in this way: "The Arapesh ideal is the mild, responsive man married to the mild, responsive woman; the Mundugumor ideal is the violent, aggressive man married to the violent, aggressive woman. . . . In the Tschambuli we found a genuine reversal of the sex attitudes of our own culture, with the woman the dominant, impersonal, managing partner, the man the less responsible and the emotionally dependent person" (1935, p. 279).

Mead concluded from her observations that there is no inevitable relation between one's biological sex and the role one plays in a society. Our traditional gender roles, she contended, are culturally determined and socialized into our children. As we have seen, this conclusion proved to be years ahead of its time and foreshadowed much of what would be asserted by social activists and investigated by behavioral scientists 30 years later.

Mead's overall view of human development, in fact, puts a major emphasis on culture as a socializing agent:

"We are forced to conclude that human nature is almost unbelievably malleable. . . . the differences between individuals who are members of different cultures, like the differences between individuals within a culture, are almost entirely to be laid to differences in conditioning, especially during early childhood, and the form of this conditioning is culturally determined" (p. 280).

This research has not escaped criticism, however. Some critics have suggested that Mead's data collection methods were faulty and that her conclusions were inaccurate (Caton, 1990; Daly & Wilson, 1983). Nevertheless, her work drew attention to the important role that culture plays in human development, and it challenged the view that many of the social behaviors witnessed in Western society are the inevitable products of our genetic heritage.

SEX TYPING AND THE SOCIALIZATION OF GENDER DIFFERENCES

Of all the questions concerning gender-role development, the most intriguing and perhaps the most fundamental involves sex typing. Why do little girls and boys typically adopt the stereotyped behaviors and preferences of their gender? Most developmentalists would agree that sex typing involves biological, cognitive, and socialization processes, all operating together in the growing child (Huston, 1983, 1985; Serbin et al., 1993). The real question, then, involves how we can identify these processes in more detail and understand precisely how they interact. In this section, we examine the role of socialization processes, which social-learning theorists contend are most influential in producing sex typing. We begin very early in development.

Early Sex Differences

We turn first to sex differences among infants and preschoolers. Differences here are especially relevant to the nature–nurture issue, because genetic influences can occur even before birth, whereas cognitive and socialization factors would seem to require some time to produce their effects.

Infancy

At birth, the most obvious sex differences, of course, involve the sexual anatomy. But several other biological differences are apparent in newborns as well. The female newborn generally is healthier and more developmentally advanced than the male, despite being somewhat smaller and lighter. Although she is less muscular and somewhat more sensitive to pain, she is better coordinated neurologically and physically (Garai & Sheinfeld, 1968; Tanner, 1974).

Few clear differences in behavior have been demonstrated between male and female newborns (Phillips, King, & Dubois, 1978). During the first weeks of life, females maintain greater eye contact (Hittleman & Dickes, 1979). Males display more motor activity and also spend more time awake (Eaton & Enns, 1986; Feldman, Brody, & Miller, 1980). They may also be more irritable, although this finding remains uncertain (Feldman et al., 1980; Moss, 1974). Sex differences also are apparent in some early lower-body reflexes (such as foot grasp and Babinski). Females produce stronger reflexes on the right side whereas males produce stronger reflexes on the left side (Grattan et al., 1992). Similarly, at 5 months of age, females are more likely to reach for objects with their right hands, while males show no preference (Humphrey & Humphrey, 1987). These differences may be related to brain laterality, which we discuss later in the chapter.

During the first 2 years, additional sex differences begin to emerge. Females generally are more vocal and begin to use language earlier (Harris, 1977). During this period, males are more likely to show illness, disease, and abnormalities of various kinds (Lahey et al., 1980; Singer, Westphal, & Miswander, 1968). A few researchers have reported sex differences in auditory and visual sensory abilities, but the results in this area are contradictory and difficult to interpret (Birns, 1976).

It appears, then, that a number of anatomical and physiological differences, along with a few behavioral distinctions, separate the sexes during infancy. But for the most part, the major gender distinctions that are so clear later in childhood do not yet exist in the newborn and young infant.

Preschool Period

Beginning at about 2 years of age, clear and pervasive sex differences in behaviors and activity preferences emerge. These differences very closely follow traditional gender stereotypes (Lewis, 1987a).

Males show more interest in blocks, transportation toys (such as trucks and airplanes), and objects that can be manipulated. They also engage in more large-motor activities, including rough-and-tumble play, which tend to include more physical aggression (O'Brien & Huston, 1985; Roopnarine, 1984). Different socialization patterns also become evident in early childhood, with males spending more time with peers and nonfamily members than females do (Feiring & Lewis, 1987).

Girls prefer doll play, dress-up, artwork, and domestic activities like sewing and cooking. They also prefer more sedentary activities, such as reading and drawing, over more vigorous ones. However, whereas males tend to stick to a rather narrowly defined group of toys and games, females display a wider range of interests and are more likely than males to engage in activities preferred by the opposite sex (Bussey & Bandura, 1992; Eisenberg, Tryon, & Cameron, 1984; Fagot & Leinbach, 1983). This asymmetrical pattern of sex-typing is important and will appear again at other points in our discussion.

It is also during this period that **gender segregation** (also called **sex cleavage**) first emerges (Maccoby, 1990; Maccoby & Jacklin, 1987). This is the commonly observed pattern of male and female children playing in same-sex groups alone and sometimes strenuously avoiding contact with members of the other sex (Hayden-Thomson, Rubin, & Hymel, 1987; Sroufe et al., 1993). Girls generally exhibit this form of social grouping earlier than boys, but once it appears in both sexes, it remains very strong throughout most of childhood (LaFreniere, Strayer, & Gauthier, 1984; Powlishta, Serbin, & Moller, 1993; Thorne, 1986). Furthermore, girls' groups and boys' groups differ in several ways. Boys play in larger groups, whereas girls

Gender segregation, or sex cleavage
The tendency for male and female children to play in same-sex groups.

• During the preschool period, boys and girls develop clear differences in their toy and activity preferences.

generally limit their group size to two or three. Boys tend to play in public places away from adult observation, whereas girls tend to stay closer to adults. And social interaction among boys often involves issues of dominance and who will be the leader, whereas girls' interactions stress turn taking and more equal participation by group members (Benenson, 1993; Carter, 1987b; Charlesworth & Dzur, 1987; Maccoby, 1988).

If these early sex differences are primarily the products of socialization, rather than biology, then there should be evidence that male and female children are raised and treated differently by the people in their world. We turn next to the research that has examined this possibility.

Differential Treatment of Males and Females

Typically, parents anxiously await the news as to whether their newborn baby is a boy or a girl. The very high interest in this characteristic—as opposed to the baby's length or blood type, for example—provides an important hint of what is to come. From the moment the child receives a gender label, he or she is in many ways treated according to that label (Block, 1983; Stern & Karraker, 1989). Let us consider some of what researchers have learned about the differential treatment of the sexes during the early childhood years.

Infancy

Even before newborns leave the hospital, parents use very different terms to describe their little boys (e.g., "firmer," "better coordinated," "stronger") (Rubin, Provenzano, & Luria, 1974). Once newborns arrive at home, many features of their environments are often based entirely on their gender, such as whether their nurseries are pink or blue, whether their toys are dolls or trucks, and whether their clothes have ruffles or not (Pomerleau et al., 1990; Shakin, Shakin, & Sternglanz,

• Society makes distinctions between males and females right from infancy.

1985). Children's names and hairstyles, of course, also typically correspond to their gender.

More important differences in treatment involve how the parents interact with their babies. Boys receive more encouragement to crawl and walk, as well as more overall physical stimulation (Frisch, 1977; MacDonald & Parke, 1986). Girls, on the other hand, usually experience a richer language environment. Mothers vocalize more to them, imitate their vocalizations more, and generally maintain a higher level of mother–infant vocal exchange (Cherry & Lewis, 1976; Moss, 1974; Wasserman & Lewis, 1985). Finally, when interacting with their infants, parents are more likely to encourage play with a toy that is neutral or that is considered to match the child's sex than to select one that is traditionally viewed as appropriate for the other sex (Caldera, Huston, & O'Brien, 1989; Eisenberg et al., 1985).

Although children display few sex differences in behavior before 2 years of age, differential treatment by parents and other adults during this early period may begin to promote the differences that soon will appear. An example can be seen in a study of children's communication styles. One-year-old infants were observed in a child-care center as they interacted with their teachers. One measure of interest was the frequency of assertive behaviors, defined as grabbing for objects, kicking, pushing, and the like. At this age, boys and girls exhibited an equal number of assertive behaviors. Teachers, however, were likely to respond in some way when a boy was involved but to ignore the behavior if it was performed by a girl. One year later, the children were observed again in the same setting. Boys now displayed more assertive behaviors than girls (Fagot et al., 1985). These findings suggest, although they do not prove, that the later difference in assertiveness resulted from the greater attention given to the little boys for these behaviors. (Another method of investigating differential treatment is described in Box 15-2.)

Preschool Period

After 2 years of age, differential reactions to males and females become more pronounced. Parents are likely to respond favorably to their children for gender-appropriate play and activities and to respond negatively to behaviors considered characteristic of the other sex (Fagot & Leinbach, 1983, 1987). This difference is also apparent in the toys parents provide for their children. A simple examination of children's rooms and toy collections usually reveals that they have been furnished mainly with sex-stereotyped games and activities (Lewis, 1987a; Rheingold & Cook, 1975). A similar situation exists for the Christmas presents parents give to their children. Here, however, we find that girls often receive at least some toys appropriate for males, whereas boys are unlikely to be given any presents considered appropriate for females (Robinson & Morris, 1986).

For some children, nursery school or day care is the next step into the social world. Studies here have shown that teachers, too, react differently to the two sexes. Boys receive criticism and disapproval for engaging in cross-sex activities more often than girls (Etaugh, Collins, & Gerson, 1975; Fagot, 1977). In addition, other children begin to respond similarly, typically showing disapproval to males who perform female activities but not to girls whose interests are "boyish" (Carter & McCloskey, 1984; Lamb & Roopnarine, 1979). What effects on gender-role development might we expect from these reactions by parents, teachers, and peers? Because girls meet with little disapproval when they engage in masculine activities, their range of acceptable behaviors should be reasonably large. Males, however, cannot stray from the traditional masculine behaviors without negative consequences. Their range of gender-appropriate behaviors should thus be more re-

THE "BABY X" TECHNIQUE

When adults see or play with a baby girl, they act differently than they do toward a baby boy. Why? One possible reason is the different expectations and stereotypes that adults hold for boys and girls. However, we cannot rule out the possibility that male and female babies are treated differently because they behave differently. The greater physical stimulation of little boys, for example, may result from the way they react to such treatment or perhaps from things they do to initiate it.

To separate these two explanations, investigators have used a research method that has come to be known as the Baby X technique. In this approach, adult subjects observe or interact with a baby labeled male for some subjects and female for others. Because the same infant is used for both groups, any differences in the adults' behavior toward the baby can only be caused by the different labels.

Researchers have used a number of variations on this method. In an early study, parents listened to a tape recording of a child's voice, which some were told was male and others were told was female (Rothbart & Maccoby, 1966). Subsequent research has used both live and filmed infants and has investigated both children's and adults' descriptions of the babies, along with their actual interactions with them (Bell & Carver, 1980; Condry & Condry, 1976; Delk et al., 1986; Seavy, Katz, & Zalk, 1975; Sidorowicz & Lunney, 1980; Smith & Lloyd, 1978).

The results across the studies have been reasonably consistent. Responses to babies labeled male are

• Adults' reactions to infants often depend on what they believe a baby's sex to be. (For example, do you think the baby on the cover of this book is a boy or girl?)

generally different from responses to the same babies labeled female. For example, negative emotionality (such as crying) was interpreted as anger when the baby was labeled male and fear when labeled female. Interestingly, children show even greater distinctions between gender-labeled babies than adults do (Stern & Karraker, 1989).

Overall, the findings from the Baby X method indicate that it is indeed the gender labels that produce differences in the observers' reactions. These findings thus offer strong support for the hypothesis that children are treated differently solely as a result of their gender.

stricted. These patterns, of course, are precisely what we described earlier for even younger children—being a "tomboy" is at least tolerated, but being a "sissy" is not (Feinman, 1981; Martin, 1990).

The evidence regarding differential treatment of males and females thus offers support for the important role of reinforcement and punishment processes in children's sex typing. Socialization influences, as we have seen, also can occur through the process of observational learning.

Modeling: Gender-Role Information From the Environment

Other chapters have shown that various aspects of children's social behavior can be acquired and maintained through modeling and imitation. Psychologists have therefore investigated whether sex typing might not also result from the observation of models displaying gender-stereotyped behaviors, preferences, and attitudes.

Laboratory studies have revealed that this is indeed possible. And some interesting relation have been found. Child observers focus more attention on models of the same sex, and they also recall and imitate these models' behavior to a greater degree (Bussey & Bandura, 1984; Perry & Bussey, 1979). In addition, children are sensitive to the gender-appropriateness of the model's activity. If a male child, for example, believes that a behavior is "female," he is unlikely to imitate it even if it is modeled by a male (Masters et al., 1979; Raskin & Israel, 1981). An important sex difference emerges with respect to modeling, however. Boys imitate adult males, and they tend to avoid imitating behaviors modeled by adult females. In contrast, although girls prefer to imitate adult women, they will also imitate adult men (Bussey & Perry, 1982). This cross-sex imitation by girls may reflect their perception that our culture invests males with higher status and greater rewards (Williams, 1987). And it probably contributes to the fact that, as we have seen, the female gender role appears to be less restricted than that of the male.

Children, then, do imitate sex-typed behaviors in the laboratory. But what about the modeling children are exposed to in real life? Does it support traditional sex stereotypes?

Modeling (like so many things) begins at home. In many U.S. households, children see their mothers and fathers engaged daily in traditional gender-role behaviors and activities (such as mothers cooking and fathers repairing). Children in homes where parents perform nontraditional jobs and chores have been found to be less sex-stereotyped than most (Serbin et al., 1993). But even these children will likely be exposed to neighbors, relatives, classmates, and friends whose behaviors are consistent with gender stereotypes. So real-life models of traditional gender roles are abundant.

The mass media is another important source of information for children. Television, in particular, communicates to youngsters a great deal about social practices and behavior (Liebert & Sprafkin, 1988). Analyses of the contents of both network programs and commercials indicate that television has generally portrayed characters in very traditional gender roles, although this appears to have changed

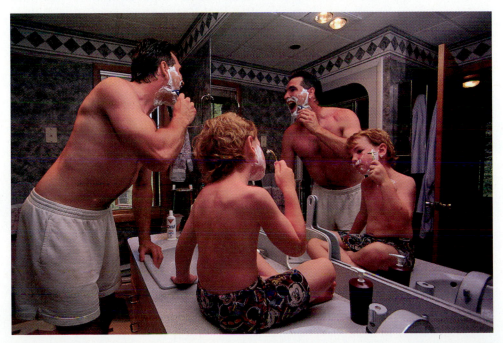

• Modeling is an important process through which children become sex-typed.

somewhat in recent years (Bretl & Cantor, 1988; Calvert & Huston, 1987; Lovdal, 1989; Signorielli, 1989). Perhaps it should not be surprising that children who are the heaviest television viewers also hold the most stereotyped perceptions of male and female sex roles (McGhee & Frueh, 1980; Signorella, Bigler, & Liben, 1993). Newspaper comics have also been analyzed for their gender-stereotyped messages, and here, too, males are more often portrayed in career situations outside the home, whereas females are shown performing domestic chores or caring for children inside the home (Brabant & Mooney, 1986; Chavez, 1985).

Finally, children's storybooks and schoolbooks represent another possible source of sex typing through modeling. Examination of recent children's books suggests that some efforts have been made to minimize sex stereotyping and to portray both males and females in a wide array of social roles (Purcell & Stewart, 1990). But what writers try to do, mothers sometimes undo. One study, for example, reported on how mothers read picture books to their preschool children. Even when they read books that presented some of the characters (usually animals) as gender-neutral, mothers referred to these characters as "he" about 95% of the time (DeLoache, Cassidy, & Carpenter, 1987).

Fathers and Sex Typing

Most young children spend a good deal more time with their mothers than with their fathers. We might expect, then, that the mother is the parent primarily responsible for the child's gender-role development. Research indicates, however, that fathers may also play an important part in this process (Lamb, 1981c, 1986).

Fathers differ somewhat from mothers in the area of gender-role socialization of their children; the differences are strongest during infancy, however, and by the end of the preschool period fathers and mothers differ much less (Fagot & Hagan, 1991; Lytton & Romney, 1991; Stern & Karraker, 1989). Fathers appear to be more concerned both that their male child be "masculine" and that their female child be "feminine," whereas mothers tend to treat their sons and daughters alike (Fisher-Thompson, 1990; Jacklin, DiPietro, & Maccoby, 1984; Langlois & Downs, 1980). These more rigid attitudes are expressed in fathers' descriptions of what constitutes appropriate gender-role behaviors, as well as in their actual interactions with their sons and daughters (MacDonald & Parke, 1986; McGillicuddy-DeLisi, 1988; Siegal, 1987; Snow, Jacklin, & Maccoby, 1983).

The fact that fathers may have greater concern for children's gender-related activities does not necessarily mean that they exert an influence on these activities. How can we determine the father's effects on the child's gender-role development? One approach, using a correlational method, suggests that fathers who hold more sex-stereotyped views have children who learn gender distinctions at an earlier age (Fagot, Leinbach, & O'Boyle, 1992; McHale et al., 1990; Weinraub et al., 1984). Another research approach, discussed later in the chapter, has examined the effects on children of being raised without a father.

There is much evidence, then, for the role of socialization processes in sex typing. But we will see next that the processes proposed by cognitive-developmental theorists are also involved in children's sex typing.

✔ *To Recap...*

Sex typing is a fundamental aspect of gender-role development. Sex typing is minimal in newborns and infants younger than about 2 years of age. Preschoolers older than about 2 years, however, display traditional sex-stereotyped toy and activity preferences. Boys show

a narrower range of interests than girls, who more often engage in cross-sex activities. Gender segregation begins during this period and remains strong throughout childhood.

From birth, children's treatment is influenced by their gender. Newborns are immediately exposed to traditional cultural distinctions, and parents and other adults interact with male and female babies in stereotyped ways. In the preschool period, differential treatment of the sexes becomes even more pronounced. Parents provide children with gender-appropriate toys and encourage sex-stereotyped behaviors and interests. Nursery school and day-care teachers, as well as peers, dispense social approval and disapproval for gender-stereotyped behavior. Girls are permitted greater latitude, however, whereas boys receive criticism for straying from the more narrowly defined male role.

Modeling may also be a mechanism of sex typing. Laboratory studies report that children focus more attention on same-sex models and more often imitate their behavior. Here again, though, females display more cross-sex imitation. Real-life models of traditional gender roles are common in the everyday lives of most children. Television programs and commercials also portray characters in sex-stereotyped roles, as do newspaper comic strips.

Fathers appear to be more concerned than mothers with maintaining traditional gender-role behavior in their children. Fathers who make more sex-stereotyped distinctions have children who learn these distinctions earlier.

UNDERSTANDING GENDER ROLES AND STEREOTYPES

We have reviewed considerable evidence that socialization processes are involved in sex typing. In this section, we turn to the cognitive processes that influence gender-role development. Of particular interest is the developing child's increasing understanding of gender roles and stereotypes.

Awareness of Gender Roles

A fundamental question regarding cognitive influences concerns when children first become aware of gender-related issues. This awareness involves a developing understanding of one's gender as well as an understanding of the gender-role characteristics and expectations of others (Martin & Halverson, 1983b; Serbin et al., 1993; Signorella et al., 1993; Stangor & Ruble, 1987).

The ability to discriminate the categories of male and female develops remarkably early. By 2 months of age, infants can discriminate male and female voices (Jusczyk, Pisoni, & Mullenix, 1992), by 5 months of age, some can learn to respond differently to pictures of men and women (Leinbach & Fagot, 1993), and by 9 months, babies can match female voices to female faces (Poulin-Dubois, Serbin, Kenyon, & Derbyshire, 1994).

We have already introduced the stage model of gender constancy, which includes gender identity ("I am a boy/girl"), gender stability ("I will grow up to be a man/woman"), and gender consistency ("I cannot change my sex") (Kohlberg & Ullian, 1974; Slaby & Frey, 1975). Data from a number of studies have confirmed this theoretical progression. By 3 years of age, almost all children display gender identity. Gender stability follows at about 4 years, and gender consistency at about 5. Males and females progress through these stages at approximately the same rate (Bem, 1989; Fagot, 1985; Martin & Little, 1990). This progression has been demonstrated in a variety of cultures, although children in many non-Western cultures appear to proceed through the stages more slowly (Munroe, Shimmin, & Munroe, 1984).

Conceptually, gender constancy is similar to Piagetian conservation. In both cases, children must come to understand that a thing may remain the same even when a perceptual aspect of it changes. Thus, children learn that just as the number of coins remains the same whether they are piled up or spread out, a person's gender does not change when he or she wears different clothes or has a different occupation. Predictably, then, a significant correlation has been found between children's level of gender constancy and their conservation abilites (Marcus & Overton, 1978).

Gender-role knowledge
Understanding that a certain toy, activity, or personal characteristic is considered more appropriate for one sex than the other.

Other cognitive aspects of gender roles have also been investigated. The awareness that "male" and "female" are separate categories and that certain characteristics, objects, and activities are typically associated with each is termed **gender-role knowledge** (Fagot & Leinbach, 1993; Martin, 1993). By about 2 years, children can reliably sort pictures of males and females and their accessories (clothes, tools, and appliances) into separate piles and can accurately point to pictures of things for males and things for females—two tasks commonly used to assess children's gender-role knowledge (Fagot, Leinbach, & Hagan, 1986; O'Brien & Huston, 1985; Thompson, 1975). Interestingly, children do not accurately label sex-stereotyped toys until about a year later (Weinraub & Brown, 1983; Weinraub et al., 1984). Four-year-olds associate certain colors with males (blue, brown, and maroon) and females (pink and lavender) in the same way that adults do (Picariello, Greenberg, & Pillemer, 1990). But knowledge about sex-stereotyped social behavior does not emerge consistently until age 5. Before that age, few children categorize behavior traits like aggression, dominance, kindness, or emotionality as more masculine or feminine; this sort of classifying increases only gradually over childhood (Flerx, Fidler, & Rogers, 1976; Weinraub & Brown, 1983; Williams, Bennett, & Best, 1975). Finally, as we saw earlier, children tend to both learn and remember the characteristics of their own gender stereotype before those of the opposite-sex stereotype (Bauer, 1993; Boston & Levy, 1991; Stangor & Ruble, 1987).

Another kind of gender awareness involves an understanding of the rigidity of gender-role stereotypes. During the preschool years, most children view gender roles in inflexible, absolutist terms (consistent with preoperational thinking) and consider cross-sex behaviors to be violations of social standards. This attitude is stronger in males, however, perhaps relating to their narrower view of gender-appropriate activities (Lobel & Menashri, 1993; Smetana, 1986). By middle childhood, children generally have begun to view gender roles as socially determined rules and conventions that can be approached somewhat flexibly and broken without major consequences (Carter & Patterson, 1982; Stoddart & Turiel, 1985)—a finding supported by a longitudinal study of German children (Trautner et al, 1989). Nevertheless, males continue to hold less flexible attitudes than females regarding gender roles (Katz & Ksansnak, 1994; Serbin et al., 1993).

Gender Awareness and the Emergence of Sex-Typed Behavior

We have seen that some forms of gender knowledge are present relatively early in childhood. But how does this knowledge relate to sex-typed behavior?

Recall that cognitive-developmentalists view the understanding of gender roles as the fundamental process in sex typing. Once a child develops an awareness of being male, for example, he presumably becomes motivated to behave like a male, and he seeks information from his social environment to learn how this is done (Kohlberg & Ullian, 1974; Martin & Halverson, 1987).

This analysis leads to three predictions (Huston, 1985). First, the emergence of gender constancy or accurate gender-role knowledge should *precede* the corresponding sex-typed behavior. For example, children should believe that trucks are for boys and dolls are for girls *before* they display a gender-related preference for these toys. Second, gender-role knowledge should correlate with gender-role behavior. That is, at least during early childhood, the more developed the child's understanding of gender roles, the more sex-typed that child's behavior should be. And third, if we can alter a child's gender-related cognitions—for example, by providing information that reduces sex-stereotyping of occupations or abilities—we should see changes in corresponding sex-typed behaviors and preferences. Consider the evidence available on each of the three predictions.

Many studies have shown that preference for sex-typed activities does not clearly depend on the emergence of gender-role knowledge, gender identity, or gender constancy (Blakemore, LaRue, & Olejnik, 1979; Bussey & Bandura, 1992; Carter & Levy, 1988; Fagot et al., 1986; Lobel & Menashri, 1993; Perry, White, & Perry, 1984; Weinraub et al., 1984). Many 2-year-olds exhibit preferences for sex-typed toys, for example, but cannot yet identify those toys as being more appropriate or typical for girls or boys. It has also been found that gender constancy is not a prerequisite for imitation of same-sex models (Bussey & Bandura, 1984, 1992). And gender knowledge does not appear to be clearly related to the degree of sex-stereotyping in children's attitudes (Serbin & Sprafkin, 1986).

The second prediction—that gender-role knowledge should correlate with gender-role behavior—has not been studied extensively. The available evidence, however, does not show a strong relation between levels of cognitive awareness and sex-typed preferences or behavior in young children (Hort, Leinbach, & Fagot, 1991; Levy & Carter, 1989; Martin & Little, 1990; Signorella et al., 1992)—although level of gender knowledge does influence how well children can recall gender-related information (Carter & Levy, 1988; Levy, 1989).

Finally, attempts to change sex-typed behaviors by changing gender-role cognitions have produced both positive and negative results (Box 15-3 describes two successful interventions). But the long-term success of the interventions remains to be determined.

It should be noted that children who display gender knowledge early eventually show more sex-typed behavior than those who display it later (Fagot & Leinbach, 1989). And without doubt, children's understanding and acceptance of gender-role stereotypes exerts considerable influence on their behavior from middle childhood onward (Galambos, Almeida, & Petersen, 1990; Serbin et al., 1993; Signorella, 1987). It seems fair to conclude, though, that a sophisticated understanding of gender and gender roles is not critical to the *appearance* of sex-typed activities and preferences, which may mean that socialization processes play the major role here (Bussey & Bandura, 1992; Fagot & Leinbach, 1993; Martin, 1993; Serbin et al., 1993).

Effects of Sex-Typed Labeling

There is one very important way in which gender-related cognitions affect behavior. This is through the influence of the gender labels that are attached to objects and activities. Once children begin to view items as "for boys" or "for girls," they will prefer the same-sex ones and tend to avoid the cross-sex ones (Eaton, VonBargen, & Keats, 1981; Masters et al., 1979; Ruble, Balaban, & Cooper, 1981). Younger children—meaning those who do not yet display gender constancy—may play with a

CHANGING CHILDREN'S GENDER STEREOTYPES

Many scholars contend that if women are to gain a more equal status in society, it is crucial that inaccurate stereotypes regarding gender be eliminated. For example, if women are to have equal access to occupations traditionally viewed as appropriate only for males, it will be necessary that our thinking regarding the stereotyped nature of these jobs be replaced with a more flexible view.

Most educators and psychologists believe that the place to begin such change is with children. Unless little boys and little girls grow up understanding that occupations are not restricted to one sex, the opportunities available to both males and females will remain limited.

Researchers within the social-learning tradition, in response to these concerns, have attempted to change children's sex-typed attitudes and behaviors using learning principles—especially modeling and reinforcement (Katz, 1986). One study, for example, investigated the effectiveness of vicarious reinforcement for cross-sex behavior. Eight- and 11-year-old subjects watched a film of a child who modeled various activities that were stereotyped for the opposite sex and then received praise and approval for those activities from either another child or an adult. Subjects who observed a film model became more likely to then engage in cross-sex activities and games themselves. Interestingly, the younger subjects were more influenced by seeing a peer show approval, whereas the older subjects' behavior changed more when they saw an adult dispense the reinforcement (Katz & Walsh, 1991).

Other interventions have been designed by cognitive-developmentalists. One study taught children the qualifications needed for various jobs. For example, they were taught that being a construction worker did not require being a man but did require being able to drive machinery. This intervention was effective in changing children's stereotyped attitudes toward these jobs, but it did not affect their own career aspirations (Bigler & Liben, 1990). A follow-up study focused on the cognitive abilities children need in order to display flexible attitudes regarding gender and occupations. Specifically, the investigators specu-

• Achieving equal access to occupations will require changing gender stereotypes and attitudes. Intervention programs with children suggest that this may be possible.

lated that in order to understand, for example, that the same person can be both a woman and an engineer, the child needs to have a good understanding of the classification skills discussed in Chapter 8. Supporting this hypothesis, the researchers found that children with better classification skills held fewer sex-stereotyped attitudes. More importantly, after the children had received a week of training on classification skills—such as learning to sort pictures of people into different piles—their attitudes toward the gender-appropriateness of occupations became more flexible (Bigler & Liben, 1992).

These studies indicate that changing children's sex-stereotyped attitudes and behavior is possible. But given the strong stereotypes that exist in society, it remains to be determined whether the changes produced by such interventions will extend to all areas of the child's life and hold up over time (Lutz & Ruble, 1994). Moreover, for gender stereotypes to be reduced significantly at a societal level, it will be necessary eventually to move beyond the small-scale intervention projects described here to more fundamental institutional changes, such as in classrooms, the workplace, and the media.

cross-sex toy if it is especially attractive. But older children, and especially boys, will tend to choose an own-sex toy, even if it is less attractive than an available opposite-sex toy (Frey & Ruble, 1992).

A second effect of sex-typed labels is their influence on children's performance of the labeled activity. For example, in one study children were presented with unfamiliar objects and told that they were things boys liked or things girls liked. Not only did children later have better recall of the objects labeled as appropriate to their sex, but they spent more time handling and exploring them (Bradbard et al., 1986). Moreover, other research has shown that in skill tasks, such as dropping marbles into a container or solving shape puzzles, children's level of performance was better when the task was labeled as an activity appropriate to their gender (Gold & Berger, 1978; Montemayor, 1974).

These findings illustrate the powerful role that gender labels may play in perpetuating sex differences in preferences and abilities. Once children decide that an activity is more appropriate for the other sex (for example, that "math is for boys"), their performance on the activity may suffer. In this way, the gender label serves to maintain both the stereotype and the sex difference (Carter & Levy, 1988; Levy & Carter, 1989).

✔ To Recap...

Cognitive issues in gender-role development include children's awareness of gender and gender roles, the relation between gender-role knowledge and emerging sex-typed behaviors, and the effects of sex-typed labeling.

Awareness of gender roles involves both knowledge of one's own gender and knowledge of the gender-role characteristics and expectations of others. Even young infants can learn to discriminate the categories of male and female. More sophisticated gender awareness develops in three stages: gender identity (at about 3 years of age), gender stability (at about 4 years), and gender consistency (at 5 years). Gender constancy has been correlated with Piagetian conservation abilities.

Gender-role knowledge involves awareness of the concepts of male and female and their culturally defined stereotypes. Children generally understand the basic male–female concept by age 2. Gender labeling of toys appears at age 3, and an awareness of sex-typed personality traits at about age 5. As children get older, they increasingly view gender roles as socially determined, and their attitudes toward violations become more tolerant and flexible.

Cognitive-developmental theory holds that the various forms of gender knowledge precede the corresponding sex-typed behaviors. Research generally fails to support this view, though a few studies have found relations between gender-role cognitions and aspects of sex-typed behavior.

Sex-typed labels do affect childrens' behavior. When activities or objects are seen as being for one gender or the other, children prefer the same-sex activities and avoid the cross-sex ones. Children also tend to perform better on same-sex-labeled activities than on those with cross-sex labels.

FAMILY INFLUENCES ON GENDER-ROLE DEVELOPMENT

Gender-role development, like all aspects of children's development, takes place in a social context that influences it in important ways. The most influential of these contexts is the family. Many studies have been devoted to identifying those characteristics of families that affect children's gender-role development and sex-typed behavior. These characteristics range from general attributes, like the family's social class, to very specific ones, like the types of child-rearing practices a parent uses. In this section we examine several of the most important family influences on the sex-typing process.

Socioeconomic Status

It is commonly believed that parents in higher social classes, perhaps because they tend to be more worldly and better educated, rear their children in less gender-stereotyped ways and thus have children who display less rigid sex typing. The research evidence only partly supports this belief (Katz, 1987). Although older children and adolescents tend to display less traditional attitudes and preferences if their families are of higher socioeconomic status (Canter & Ageton, 1984; Emmerich & Shepard, 1982; Romer & Cherry, 1980; Serbin et al., 1993), this relation is not as clear among younger children (Cummings & Taebel, 1980). In fact, some researchers have found the opposite to be true, with middle- and upper-class families having preschoolers who are more sex-stereotyped in their behaviors and attitudes than lower-class children (Nadelman, 1974). The absence of a simple and strong relation here is probably not surprising, however, since social class is such a broad dimension on which to classify families.

DEVELOPMENT IN CONTEXT: Growing Up in a Single-Parent Household

Gender-role development has traditionally been studied in the context of two-parent families. But many children are not raised in such families. In fact, it is estimated that about half of the children born today will spend some portion of their lives in a single-parent environment, primarily as a result of divorce (Hernandez, 1988). Is gender-role development different for these children? And does divorce have different effects on boys and girls?

The answer to both questions is yes. Divorce can have a number of deleterious effects on children's development, including gender-role development (Hetherington, Stanley-Hagan, & Anderson, 1989; Wallerstein, Corbin, & Lewis, 1988). The nature and severity of these problems depend on a number of factors, including the gender of the children.

In about 90% of divorces, mothers end up with custody of the children. Eventually, approximately 75% of these mothers remarry. But during the period immediately following divorce, children frequently experience problems of various sorts (Hetherington & Clingempeel, 1992). These problems often differ from one sibling to another (Monahan et al., 1993), so it may not be surprising that they also differ for males and females.

Boys generally react more negatively to divorce than girls. Most often their problems involve conduct disorders at home and at school. Aggression and non-compliance, in fact, sometimes persist for several years after the breakup (Hetherington et al., 1989). Gender-role development can also be affected in boys living in households without fathers, especially if the breakup occurs during the boys' infancy or early childhood (Adams, Milner, & Schrepf, 1984). These boys typically exhibit fewer male sex-typed behaviors and attitudes than boys living in intact families (Brenes, Eisenberg, & Helmstadter, 1985; Serbin et al., 1993; Stevenson & Black, 1988). If separation occurs later, and particularly if an alternative male—

such as an older brother—is available, the effects typically are less obvious (Biller, 1981; Santrock, 1970). And when boys remain in the custody of their fathers, they generally show still fewer effects (Camara & Resnick, 1988; Hanson, 1988).

The effects of divorce on girls are less clear (Allison & Furstenberg, 1989; Emery, 1988). Although most researchers agree that girls react less negatively than boys, some problems may nevertheless occur. The immediate emotional upheaval that follows the parents' breakup usually seems to disappear more quickly for girls, often within the first 2 years. But longer-term problems, especially in gender-role development, have been observed. Among girls whose fathers are absent, very little gender-role disruption occurs before adolescence (Stevenson & Black, 1988). During the teenage years, however, several patterns of problem behavior may emerge. These girls tend to have more difficulty interacting with males of their own age. Some become shy and withdrawn, whereas others display overly outgoing and attention-seeking behavior (Newcomer & Udry, 1987; Wallerstein et al., 1988).

A more recent departure from the traditional American family involves children being raised by parents who are lesbian or gay (Patterson, 1992, 1994). Because this phenomenon is relatively recent (Blumenfeld & Raymond, 1988), not a great deal of research has been conducted in this area. Those studies that have compared gender-role development in children of single, lesbian mothers, however, have found no apparent differences from children in traditional households (Golombok, Spencer, & Rutter, 1983; Green, 1978; Green et al., 1986; Hoeffer, 1981; Kirkpatrick, Smith, & Roy, 1981).

Interestingly, remarriage often intensifies children's problems, particularly in females (Bray, 1988; Wallerstein et al., 1988). Adolescent girls who are close to their mothers may have difficulty adjusting to the introduction of a stepfather. Their relationships with their mothers frequently become hostile and antagonistic, and they tend to remain distant from their stepfathers. Boys, however, sometimes benefit from the addition of a stepfather, although usually only after a period of time (Hetherington, 1988).

The long-term effects of divorce need not be negative. Many children eventually adapt to the new family situation, whether it involves living with a single parent or with a new stepparent. Not all of the factors that ease these transitions are known. But a predictable, structured environment, routines, both at home and at school, and emotional support appear to be major contributors to successful coping (Hetherington, 1989).

Maternal Employment

We discussed the effects of maternal employment on infant–caregiver attachment in Chapter 12. Other research indicates that when mothers work, their children's gender-role development tends to be affected; children of working mothers are less sex-stereotyped in their attitudes, preferences, and behaviors than are the children of mothers who stay at home (Huston, 1983; Katz & Boswell, 1986; Levy, 1989; MacKinnon, Stoneman, & Brody, 1984; Signorella, Bigler, & Liben, 1993; Weinraub et al., 1984). This effect appears to be especially true for males and for younger children (Katz, 1987). Once again, the processes at work here are a matter of speculation. Children of working mothers often spend time in day-care centers. Perhaps the staff in these centers tend to treat children in less sex-stereotyped ways or to encourage more cross-sex activities. It is also possible that mothers who work maintain less traditional attitudes regarding gender roles than do mothers who stay at home, and so they tend to rear their children in less stereotyped ways. In either case, as children get older, the effects of maternal employment on sex typing become increasingly less evident.

Parental Attitudes and Child-Rearing Methods

Parents' gender-related beliefs and behaviors have long been assumed to exert a good deal of influence on their children's sex typing (Block, 1983; Huston, 1983). As we have seen, the nature of this influence may take several forms (Katz, 1987). One is based on modeling. The attitudes parents express, the kinds of household chores each engages in, whether the mother works and what she does—all may affect children's understanding and adoption of gender roles. A more direct source of influence involves the gender-role activities and behaviors that parents encourage and approve of in their children. The toys they buy, the teams or organizations they have their children join, the rules they establish for dress and social conduct, and many other specific child-rearing practices can directly shape the sorts of sex-typed behaviors in which their children will engage (Katz, 1986).

One fruitful approach to studying this question has been to look at the sex typing and gender knowledge of children raised by counterculture parents (Eiduson et al., 1982; Weisner & Eiduson, 1986). During the 1960s and early 1970s, the peace movement spawned a subculture of parents who challenged many of society's traditional social and political views. One aspect of this challenge was a belief in egalitarian gender roles, with males and females assumed to have equal abilities and to deserve equal opportunities and responsibilities. Many counterculture parents not only expressed these attitudes but put them into practice in their family interactions and lifestyles. If socialization by parents can influence children's gender-role knowledge and sex-typed behavior, we might expect to see relatively clear effects within counterculture families.

An interesting pattern of results has emerged from this research (Weisner & Wilson-Mitchell, 1990). Children of counterculture parents have indeed shown less sex stereotyping, for example, in their beliefs regarding occupations, in their own occupational preferences, and in the degree to which they associate specific objects with a given sex. That is, at the cognitive level, they espouse beliefs and attitudes similar to those of their parents. But when toy and activity preferences have been assessed, these children tend to display the same gender stereotyping as children from more conventional families. One explanation for these findings is that counterculture parents differ principally from conventional parents primarily in terms of the attitudes they model—what they say and how they live. Their actual interactions with their children involving gender-related behaviors and activities, however, turn out to be not very different from those of conventional parents (Eiduson, 1980; Weitzman, Birns, & Friend, 1985). Hence, the relation between parents' socialization practices and their children's sex typing is not as clearly testable among counterculture families as we might have expected.

The role of parents as gender-role socializers, of course, must be viewed within the larger social context. Parents are simply one of the many socializing agents to which growing children are exposed. And though they may be the strongest influence, a great deal of pressure to conform to societal gender stereotypes is continually being exerted on children by peers, siblings, teachers, and the media.

✔ To Recap...

The family is the most influential social context in which sex typing occurs. Various characteristics of the family affect children's gender-role knowledge and behavior. Families from higher socioeconomic levels tend to have children who are less sex-typed in their behaviors and beliefs. This effect is strongest among older children and adolescents.

Children from single-parent families, usually headed by the mother, tend to be less gender-stereotyped than children from traditional two-parent households, perhaps because of the absence of the father or because of the dual-gender behaviors modeled by the single parent. Mothers who work have children who display less sex-typed attitudes and behavior than do the children of mothers who stay at home. This effect is particularly strong among males and younger children, and it decreases with age.

Finally, gender-related attitudes and behaviors displayed by parents influence children's sex-typed beliefs and behaviors. The clearest evidence involves a similarity in parent–child attitudes.

SOME COMMON SEX DIFFERENCES

The toy and activity differences that distinguish boys and girls during early childhood are not the only ones commonly observed in growing children. Although some of the sex differences we will consider in this section are small, and all of them represent only the *average* difference across all males and females, they nevertheless remain to be explained.

Cognitive Differences

We begin with differences in cognition and related processes. Some appear early; others do not emerge until later. In all cases, the nature–nurture debate remains very much alive as researchers seek the sources of these differences in both biological and environmental variables.

Language and Verbal Abilities

There is little doubt that young females have greater abilities in some kinds of verbal skills (Feingold, 1992, 1993; Wentzel, 1988). Female infants produce more sounds at an earlier age than males (Harris, 1977). They use words sooner, and the size of their early vocabularies is much larger (Nelson, 1973). Grammatical development also progresses more rapidly in females. On a variety of measures of language complexity (such as sentence length, use of pronouns, use of conjunctions, and so on), girls begin to show a marked superiority at about 2 years of age, with the differences continuing through adolescence (Koenigsknecht & Friedman, 1976; Schacter et al., 1978). But comprehension abilities (such as understanding the meanings of words) do not favor females quite as strongly (Harris, 1977).

Recall that research indicates that mothers provide a richer language environment for their infant daughters than for their sons. These and related findings suggest that socialization factors may play a role in this sex difference. But most psychologists agree that a biological basis for early female verbal superiority probably also exists.

The sex differences in this area diminish with age. By late adolescence, females no longer display an obvious superiority in verbal abilities (Hyde & Linn, 1988).

Quantitative Abilities

The ability to deal with numbers and mathematical concepts reveals an interesting pattern of sex differences. Girls usually begin counting and using numbers before boys. Throughout the elementary years and junior high school, girls tend to be better at computational problems whereas boys do better with math reasoning problems (Fennema & Tartre, 1985; Marshall, 1984). During this period, girls also tend to get higher grades (Kimball, 1989). By high school, however, males begin to perform better, especially at the higher levels of ability, as evidenced by their consistently better performance on the math portion of the SAT exams (Benbow & Stanley, 1981, 1985; Hyde, Fennema, & Lamon, 1990; Kimball, 1989; Stanley et al., 1991). This advantage seems to derive, in part, from males' use of more effective strategies when approaching mathematics problems (Byrnes & Takahira, 1993).

It has been suggested that the sex differences come about to some degree because girls view math as a male activity and therefore have less interest in it and because parents and teachers offer greater encouragement to males in this area. Some studies support this analysis (Eccles & Midgely, 1990; Jacobs, 1991; Kimball, 1989; Lummis & Stevenson, 1990), but others do not (Raymond & Benbow, 1986). Here, too, biological and socialization factors probably combine to produce the observed differences (Chipman, Brush, & Wilson, 1985).

In a related area, researchers have found that boys are more likely than girls to use computers in their schoolwork and play. They also express a more positive attitude toward computers and are more likely to enroll in computer courses or attend computer camp (Chen, 1985; Hess & Miura, 1985). These findings do not mean that males are better at using computers than females. They do suggest, however, the beginning of a stereotype that says computers are for males. Females who accept this stereotype may shy away from computers, and so their performance may lag behind. In this way, a new, and perhaps avoidable, gender difference may be created (Lockheed, 1985).

Spatial Abilities

One area in which males repeatedly have been found to outperform females is spatial abilities (Feingold, 1993; Halpern, 1992). Researchers have studied spatial skills using a number of tasks and techniques; some have produced larger and clearer differences than others (Horan & Rosser, 1984; Linn & Petersen, 1985; Merriman, Keating, & List, 1985).

One type of task on which males and females differ markedly involves mental rotation (Halpern, 1992; Linn & Petersen, 1985). An example of a mental rotation task appears in Figure 15-1. Another task where females generally have more difficulty than males is the water-level task, shown in Figure 15-2 (Liben, 1991; Vasta, Belongia, & Ribble, in press; Vasta, Lightfoot, & Cox, 1993). Some sex differences in spatial abilities are present during early and middle childhood (Herman & Siegel, 1978; Vasta & Green, 1982), but the differences tend to increase in adolescence and adulthood (Johnson & Meade, 1987; Linn & Petersen, 1985).

Figure 15-1 A mental rotation task in which the subject must decide whether the two objects are the same (as in *a*) or different (as in *b*).

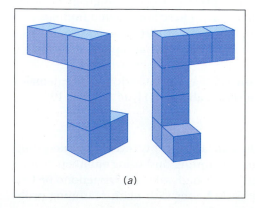

(a)

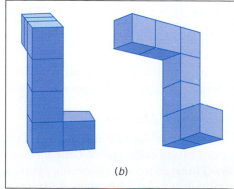

(b)

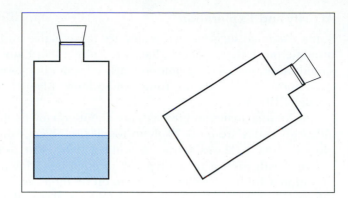

Figure 15-2 A water-level task in which the subject is asked to predict how the water will look when the bottle is tilted.

Biological explanations of these sex differences have involved several processes. The pattern of differences corresponds reasonably well with what would be predicted by a genetic model if spatial ability were controlled by a recessive gene carried on the X chromosome (McGee, 1982; Thomas, 1983). Some research also points to differences in the way the left and right hemispheres of the brain are organized in males and females (Waber, 1977, 1979a). A later section discusses these biological processes and the roles they may play in sex differentiation. For now, we simply note that neither of these explanations has escaped major criticism (Caplan, MacPherson, & Tobin, 1985), nor can either account for all of the findings in this area (Newcombe & Dubas, 1992).

Socialization analyses have been proposed, as well. Some theorists believe that little girls are discouraged from engaging in activities that promote the development of spatial skills (such as playing with blocks and mechanical toys), because they are male-stereotyped activities. Thus, boys improve in these skills, as girls fall behind—which, as we have seen, is consistent with the data (Baenninger & Newcombe, 1989; Newcombe & Dubas, 1992; Signorella, Jamison, & Krupa, 1989; Tracy, 1987).

In all likelihood, this sex difference, like many others, has both nature and nurture components. Males probably do have a biological advantage in some spatial skills, owing perhaps to one or both of the proposed biological mechanisms mentioned. But the influences of experience cannot be dismissed, and such influences may maintain or even magnify inherent differences in spatial abilities.

Complex Processes

Boys and girls do not appear to display major differences in traditional aspects of cognition, such as memory, reasoning, and problem solving. Those differences that have been found may actually reflect differences in the areas we have already discussed.

Some research, for example, indicates that females are better at using organizational strategies to help them in memory tasks (Cox & Waters, 1986; Waters, 1981; Waters & Schreiber, 1991). They also exhibit better recall in tasks that involve verbal material rather than spatial location (Kail & Siegel, 1977). These findings, however, may reflect females' superior verbal abilities rather than superiority in the memory processes themselves.

Social and Personality Differences

Sex differences also exist in some areas of social and personality functioning (Eagly, 1987). These differences, for the most part, have been discussed in earlier chapters and so will be described here only briefly.

Activity and Exploration

Some evidence suggests that males are more active and like to explore and manipulate more than females (Eaton & Enns, 1986; Eaton & Yu, 1989). Males also spend more time playing outdoors, use considerably more physical space, and engage more frequently in rough-and-tumble play (DiPietro, 1981; Harper & Sanders, 1975).

As infants, males and females are about equally likely to explore a new object, although males are more likely to touch the object, whereas females tend to explore it visually (Mayes, Carter, & Stubbe, 1993). But an interesting sex difference emerges with respect to the type of parental behavior that encourages infant exploration. Children's willingness to go off on their own can be predicted from how the caregiver reacts when the child is playing alone. Boys become more independent when their mothers do not interfere with their play and permit them to remain by themselves. Daughters treated in this manner, however, respond in the opposite way: They become less likely to explore and more likely to stay close to their mothers. Only when caregivers frequently join in the solitary play of their daughters do these children increase their independent exploration—although, even then, female infants are more likely to "check in" with the mother or seek her contact while exploring (Martin, 1981; Martin, Maccoby, & Jacklin, 1981; Mayes et al., 1993). Perhaps related to the last finding, a recent study of social referencing found that changes in caregivers' facial expressions influenced how closely their infant daughters would approach an unfamiliar object, but they had no effect on their infant sons (Rosen, Adamson, & Bakeman, 1992).

The reasons for the sex differences in exploratory behavior remain unclear. Some research suggests that mothers interact with their male babies in ways that encourage autonomy and independence, whereas they tend to encourage more interpersonal closeness in their female babies (Robinson, Little, & Biringen, 1993). But it also is possible that males may simply be biologically more predisposed to explore than females, who need more encouragement to venture out.

Social Influence

The two sexes react differently in situations involving social influence (Maccoby, 1990; Pettit et al., 1990). When attempting to resolve a conflict or influence others to do something, boys take a more heavy-handed approach, often using threats or physical force. Girls are more likely to use verbal persuasion or to abandon the conflict altogether (Miller, Danaher, & Forbes, 1986; Pettit et al., 1990; Sheldon, 1990). Similarly, in stories written by male children, conflict is more often resolved through the use of violence, whereas conflict resolution in girls' stories usually involves reasoning and compromise (Pierce & Edwards, 1988).

Prosocial Behavior

We saw in the previous chapter that females are generally rated as more generous, helpful, and cooperative by their teachers and peers (Shigetomi, Hartmann, & Gelfand, 1981; Zarbatany et al., 1985). Some evidence does suggest that they have better affective perspective-taking abilities and experience more empathy (Dodge & Feldman, 1990; Zahn-Waxler et al., 1992; Zahn-Waxler, Robinson, & Emde, 1992). But when researchers have examined children's actual behavior, they have found few sex differences in this area (Eagly & Crowley, 1987; Moore & Eisenberg, 1984). So if a difference exists here, it is very small.

• Infants' willingness to explore their environments is related to their gender and to how their mothers interact with them.

Aggression

Males generally display more aggression than females. But once again, there exists a good deal of controversy as to exactly what forms it takes and when it occurs (Crowell, 1987; Hyde, 1984; Tieger, 1980). Preschool and elementary-school males display more physical aggression, such as kicking, pinching, and hitting, than do females of the same age; they are also rated as more aggressive by their peers (Eron et al., 1983; McCabe & Lipscomb, 1988). These behaviors decrease with age, but other forms of aggression may take their place (Eagly & Steffen, 1986; Hyde, 1986). As indicated in Chapter 14, all of these findings need to be considered with caution, since observers' ratings of aggression tend to be influenced by the gender of the child (Condry & Ross, 1985; Lyons & Serbin, 1986).

In addition, one source of the sex differences in aggression may lie in cognitive differences between boys and girls. As we also saw in the previous chapter, aggressive children are more likely to make hostile attributions in response to ambiguous events than are nonaggressive children. One study found that when girls experience such events they are more likely than boys to either interpret them in a positive way or to walk away from them. Males, in contrast, tend to respond to ambiguous provocations in ways that are more likely to lead to retaliatory aggression (Dodge & Feldman, 1990).

✔ *To Recap...*

Sex differences in some cognitive and social areas persist well beyond early childhood. In the cognitive area, females outperform males in rate of language acquisition and in overall verbal abilities, although these differences disappear by late adolescence. The fact that mothers more often interact verbally with their infant daughters may combine with biological factors to produce this difference. Although females begin counting earlier and solve computational problems better during middle childhood, male superiority in math, especially in math reasoning, becomes apparent during adolescence. Both socialization and biological variables are assumed to be involved. Males also display superior performance on many spatial tasks, a sex difference that increases into adulthood. Neither biological nor socialization explanations of this difference have proved conclusive. Sex differences in complex processes, such as memory, also have been reported but may simply reflect differences in verbal and math abilities.

In the area of social and personality differences, males are more physically active, use more space, and display more rough-and-tumble play than females. Male infants are more likely to explore by touch and if left alone; female infants are more likely to explore visually and if given support and encouragement. Social influence by boys often involves threats and physical force; girls use verbal persuasion and reasoning. Girls also have a reputation for being more altruistic, helpful, and cooperative, but few sex differences in these behaviors have actually been observed. Males do display more physical aggression than females during childhood, a sex difference that decreases with age. However, other forms of aggression may appear.

BIOLOGICAL INFLUENCES ON GENDER-ROLE DEVELOPMENT

We turn again now to the biological component of gender-role development, which includes the genetic, structural, and physiological processes that distinguish males and females. As these mechanisms have become better understood in recent years,

DO SCHOOLS CHEAT GIRLS?

We have seen in earlier chapters that adolescence is a time when children undergo marked physical, cognitive, and social changes. Gender-role development is no exception. With the onset of puberty and an increase in self-consciousness, both males and females become more aware of gender-role expectations and strive harder to adhere to them (Hill & Lynch, 1983). As a result, some sex differences tend to increase during adolescence.

Many researchers are coming to believe that schools inadvertently contribute to this process (Huston & Alvarez, 1990). For example, a recent report entitled *How Schools Shortchange Girls* (American Association of University Women, 1992) and a new book called *Failing at Fairness: How America's Schools Cheat Girls* (Sadker & Sadker, 1994) both arrive at the conclusion that, in school, girls are at a disadvantage in how they are viewed, how they are treated, and what is expected of them. These problems are especially evident in the typical junior high school, where aspects of the educational environment clearly seem to favor males.

One of these aspects is the nature of the courses students take. As children move beyond the elementary grades, schools place more emphasis on math and science. Children in the elementary grades generally view these courses as equally appropriate for either gender. But older students increasingly rate math and science as more appropriate for males (Wilder, Mackie, & Cooper, 1985), and girls' attitudes toward these subjects become less positive as they progress toward high school (Tittle, 1986). As noted earlier, attitudes toward computer work follow a similar course, a trend that may be especially troublesome given the increasing emphasis schools are placing on computer skills (Chen, 1985; Lockheed, 1985).

A second issue involves the relation between school structure and students' learning styles. Studies have shown that males and females approach school-

• Studies suggest that beginning in junior high, the typical school environment is better suited to males than to females.

work in different ways. Girls generally favor familiar activities in which teachers or other adults are involved. Boys, on the other hand, tend to prefer tasks that are new and challenging and that they can work on independently (Dweck, 1986; Huston et al., 1986).

Some researchers believe that, beginning at the junior high level, schools provide a more "masculine" learning environment (Chipman et al., 1985; LaTorre et al., 1983). Independent learning appears to be particularly suited to math and science courses. In addition, work in these areas often jumps quickly from familiar concepts to new ones. Thus, males are likely to make the transition to such courses more easily than females.

When we consider alongside these findings the fact that adolescent females tend to experience greater self-consciousness and lower self-esteem than adolescent males, we might well conclude that junior high school is a more hospitable environment for young males and a more intimidating one for young females.

---

it has become increasingly clear that they interact in important ways with cognitive and socialization influences (Ehrhardt, 1985; Hood et al., 1987).

Sexual dimorphism
The existence in some species of biological differences between males and females for the purpose of reproduction.

Like most other species, humans exhibit **sexual dimorphism**—that is, the male and female are biologically different for the purpose of reproduction. The process through which these biological differences emerge is called *sex differentiation*. Many of the biological influences on gender-role development appear to result from Nature's preparing the individual in this way to participate in the reproduction process (Parsons, 1982).

Genetic Influences

As noted in Chapter 4, human body cells contain 46 chromosomes, which carry the genetic material that makes us who we are. These chromosomes consist of 22 matched pairs plus an additional pair of sex chromosomes. In the female, both sex chromosomes are called Xs; in the male, one chromosome is called X and the other Y. The chromosomes of the human female thus are designated 46,XX; those of the male, 46,XY. Human germ cells, however, contain only half as many chromosomes as the body cells. In females, the ovum contains 22 chromosomes plus an X chromosome; in males, each sperm contains 22 chromosomes plus either an X or a Y. During fertilization, then, the mother contributes 22 chromosomes and an X, and the father contributes 22 chromosomes and either an X or a Y. Thus, at the moment of conception, the child becomes genetically male or female, and it is the father who determines the sex of the baby. But the process of sex differentiation has only just begun.

The X chromosome is relatively large and contains many genes that direct growth and functioning. The Y chromosome is about one quarter the size, with much less genetic material. The sex chromosomes have no influence at all on the fertilized zygote for about 6 weeks. At that point, if the embryo is genetically male (XY), the Y chromosome causes a portion of the embryo to become the male gonadal structure—the **testes**. Once this is accomplished, the Y chromosome does not appear to play any further role in the process of sex differentiation. If the embryo is genetically female (XX), the sex chromosomes produce no change at 6 weeks. At 10 to 12 weeks, however, one X chromosome causes a portion of the embryo to become female gonads—the **ovaries**. From this point on, sex differentiation is guided primarily by the hormones produced by the testes and the ovaries.

Testes
The male gonadal structure that produces the sperm.

Ovaries
The female gonadal structure that produces the ovum.

Chromosomal Abnormalities

The process just described occasionally does not work as it should. When this happens, the embryo may have an unusual arrangement of sex chromosomes (Grumback, 1979).

One such abnormality occurs when an ovum is fertilized by a sperm that carries no sex chromosome at all or when the sperm provides an X and the ovum has no sex chromosome. In either case, the resulting embryo has only an X and is designated 45,XO. Most of these embryos fail to develop in the uterus and are aborted by the mother's body without her even being aware that conception had occurred. But in the few cases in which the fetus develops completely, the child displays a variety of abnormalities referred to as **Turner's syndrome**. At birth, the baby is female in appearance, but the ovaries have already disappeared and do not produce the hormones necessary for the sex differentiation process to continue. As a result, women with Turner's syndrome do not develop breasts or menstruate unless they are given hormone therapy. Physically, they typically are short and have an unusual neck and chest structure. They have been described as having "ultrafeminine" personalities, and their cognitive abilities are consistent with this orientation—very high in verbal abilities and well below average in spatial skills (McCauley et al., 1987; Rovet, 1991).

Another chromosomal problem occurs when an egg carrying two X chromosomes is fertilized by a sperm carrying a Y. In this case, a 47,XXY child is produced, with characteristics referred to as **Klinefelter's syndrome**. The presence of the Y chromosome causes the child to have a male appearance, but he is somewhat feminized, because his male hormone levels are low. Men with Klinefelter's syndrome have long arms, very little body hair, an underdeveloped penis, and sometimes

Turner's syndrome
A chromosomal disorder of females in which one X chromosome is absent. Women with the syndrome have no ovaries, do not menstruate, are short in stature, and display "ultrafeminine" personality characteristics.

Klinefelter's syndrome (XXY)
A chromosomal disorder of males in which an extra X chromosome is present. Men with the syndrome have long arms, little body hair, an underdeveloped penis, and somewhat feminine personality characteristics.

overdeveloped breasts. They often are somewhat timid and unassertive in their interpersonal interactions (Bancroft, Axworthy, & Ratcliffe, 1982; Raboch, Mellan, & Starka, 1979).

A third chromosomal abnormality occurs when the sperm provides two, rather than one, Y chromosomes. The **47,XYY** males produced when this occurs are perhaps the opposite of the 45,XO females in that they have large body builds and very masculine personality characteristics (Owen, 1972, 1979). There has been some controversy over whether these men are more likely than others to become criminals or to display antisocial behavior. Data indicate that they are found in unexpectedly large proportions in prisons and psychiatric institutions and that they are more impulsive and less tolerant of frustration than other men (Gardner & Neu, 1972; Hook, 1973; Ratcliffe & Field, 1982). But it is not clear that the genetic abnormality leads directly to the antisocial behavior; more likely, social factors are responsible for the observed problems (Delozier & Engel, 1982; Witkin et al., 1976).

Sex-Linked Traits

We have seen that the sex chromosomes normally influence sex differentiation by causing the embryo to develop either testes or ovaries, which then produce different sex hormones. But another way in which sex chromosomes occasionally affect males and females differently involves certain genes.

Some genes are found only on the sex chromosomes and thus are called **sex-linked genes**, or more commonly, **X-linked genes,** because they almost always occur on the X chromosome. If a child inherits an X-linked trait carried by a recessive gene from one parent, the trait only becomes apparent if the corresponding gene from the other parent is also recessive or if there is no corresponding gene on the other parent's sex chromosome. Thus, when a girl inherits a recessive X-linked trait from one parent, it usually is blocked by a dominant gene on the X chromosome donated by the other parent. For this reason, most recessive X-linked traits are not expressed in women. But typically when a boy inherits a recessive X-linked trait from his mother, no matching gene is present on the Y chromosome, because the Y chromosome carries so few genes. In such cases, the trait is expressed. Thus, recessive X-linked traits are much more common in males.

An example of a disorder caused by an X-linked gene is **fragile X syndrome** (Hagerman & Silverman, 1991). This genetic abnormality only became clearly understood in the 1980s, but it is believed to be the most common form of inherited mental retardation. The large majority of males who carry the gene display symptoms that include physical characteristics (such as a long face, and large ears), difficulties with language and cognitive abilities, and hyperactivity or related problems of impulsivity and self-control. By contrast, only about 30% of females who carry the gene on one X chromosome show clear evidence of the syndrome (Hagerman, 1991).

About 70 traits are sex-linked (Hutt, 1972). Most of them are either dangerous (e.g., muscular dystrophy, hemophilia, and some forms of diabetes) or troublesome (e.g., poor night vision, and color blindness). As indicated earlier, some researchers have speculated that spatial abilities may be a recessive X-linked trait, but the evidence for this is mixed (Boles, 1980; Thomas, 1983).

Sex-Limited Traits

Some genes that are not carried on the sex chromosomes may also affect males and females differently. Usually, this occurs when the expression of a trait requires the

47,XYY syndrome
A chromosomal disorder of males in which an extra Y chromosome is present. Men with the syndrome have large body builds and very masculine personality characteristics.

Sex-linked, or X-linked, genes
Genes found only on the sex chromosomes, most often the X chromosome.

Fragile X syndrome
An X-linked genetic disorder, more often expressed in males, producing retarded intellectual development, language and behavior problems, and identifiable physical characteristics.

presence of certain levels of sex hormones. Such traits are called **sex-limited**. The gene for baldness, for example, may be carried by either men or women, but the characteristic appears only in men because high levels of male hormones are needed for it to be expressed.

Hormonal Influences

A major step in sex differentiation begins when the newly formed embryonic gonads begin to secrete hormones of different types. These chemical substances travel in the bloodstream, affecting the development and functioning of various parts of the body (Moore, 1985).

Up until about the 3rd month of gestation, the internal sex organs of the fetus can become either male or female. When a Y chromosome causes testes to develop in the embryo, these glands secrete hormones called **androgens** that cause the male internal reproductive organs to grow (and they also secrete a chemical that causes the female organs to shrink). At 5 months, if androgens are present, the external sex organs also develop as male, producing a penis and scrotal sac. If androgens are not present at 3 months, the internal sex organs, and later the external sex organs, develop as female. No special hormone is needed for this to occur. The hormones produced mainly by the ovaries are **estrogen** and **progesterone**, but they do not play their principal role in sex differentiation until puberty.

Somewhere between 3 and 8 months after conception, sex hormones are believed to affect the development and organization of the fetal brain (Hines & Gorski, 1985; McEwen, 1987). The two major types of organizing effects involve hormonal regulation (how often the body releases various hormones) and **brain lateralization** (how the two hemispheres of the brain function differently). We discuss possible sex differences in brain lateralization in a later section.

Hormonal Regulation and Abnormalities

The different proportions of sex hormones in male and female fetuses primarily affect the development of the **hypothalamus**, a structure in the brain that regulates the *pituitary gland*. In adults, this gland controls the production of hormones by the gonads. These hormones, in turn, maintain certain body functions (such as menstruation in the female), but they also appear to activate aspects of certain social behaviors, including aggression, maternal behaviors, and sexual activity. Some theorists believe that sex differences in these and other social behaviors may therefore have their roots in the structural differences of the hypothalamus that are produced before birth (Ehrhardt, 1985; Hines & Green, 1991).

Much of the nonhuman research on this question has involved manipulating the amount of sex hormones to which a fetus is exposed and then observing the animal's behavior in early life and maturity. For example, if pregnant hamsters or monkeys are given extra doses of testosterone (a type of androgen), the female offspring tend to be more aggressive, dominant, and exploratory—characteristics found more frequently in males of the species (Hines, 1982; Money & Annecillo, 1987). These sorts of studies, of course, cannot be conducted with humans, so we must look to other methods of research when examining hormonal effects in our species.

As with chromosomes, hormonal processes sometimes go awry. Two such hormonal abnormalities are **congenital adrenal hyperplasia (CAH)**, in which too much androgen is produced during pregnancy, and **androgen insensitivity**, in which the fetus cannot respond to the presence of the masculinizing hormone.

Sex-limited traits
Genes that affect males and females differently but that are not carried on the sex chromosomes.

Androgens
Hormones that have masculinizing effects and are more abundant in males.

Estrogens and progesterone
Hormones that have feminizing effects and are more abundant in females.

Brain lateralization
The organization of the human brain into left and right hemispheres that perform different functions.

Hypothalamus
The structure in the brain that regulates the pituitary gland.

Congenital adrenal hyperplasia (CAH)
A hormonal disorder caused by an overproduction of androgens during pregnancy. Afflicted females have large genitals and display male personality characteristics; afflicted males tend to be slightly more masculine in their interests and interactions.

Androgen insensitivity
A genetic disorder in which the fetus does not respond to masculinizing hormones. Affected individuals (XX or XY) usually are feminine in appearance and interests.

CAH usually results from an inherited enzyme deficiency that causes the adrenal glands to produce androgens, regardless of whether testes are present (Berenbaum, 1990; White, New, & Dupont, 1987). This problem typically begins after the internal sex organs have been formed but before the external sex organs appear. If the fetus is genetically female (XX), she will have ovaries and normal internal sex organs, but the excessive androgen will cause the external organs to develop in a masculine direction. Often the clitoris will be very large, resembling a penis, and sometimes a scrotal sac will develop (but it will be empty, because there are no testes). In a number of reported cases, such females have been mistaken at birth for males and raised as boys (Money & Annecillo, 1987). In most cases, however, the problem is discovered at birth and corrected by surgically changing the external sex organs and by administering drugs to reduce the high levels of androgens. While these procedures return the girls to biological normality, the early androgen exposure appears to have some long-term effects. Many of these girls become "tomboys," preferring rough outdoor play and traditional male-stereotyped toys, while having little interest in dolls, jewelry, makeup, or activities typical of young females. They also show less interest in marriage and motherhood. At adolescence, the spatial abilities of CAH females are typically markedly better than those of normal females. The males who have received the extra dose of androgens react less dramatically. These boys are somewhat more inclined toward intense physical activity than normal boys, but they do not appear to be more aggressive or antisocial (Berenbaum & Hines, 1992; Resnick et al., 1986).

Androgen insensitivity is a genetic defect in males that causes the body cells not to respond to androgens. The testes of an XY fetus will produce hormones, but neither internal nor external male sex organs will develop. The substance that usually shrinks the potential female internal sex organs will be effective, however, leaving the fetus with neither a uterus nor an internal male system. But the external organs will develop as female. Studies have shown that androgen-insensitive individuals are generally feminine in appearance, preferences, and abilities (Ehrhardt & Meyer-Bahlburg, 1981; Money & Ehrhardt, 1972).

Taken together, evidence from animals and humans suggests that fetal sex hormones play an important part in producing differences between males and females. But we must be very careful about drawing broad conclusions. Hormonal processes are quite complex, and scientists still do not understand exactly how they affect the brain or how they interact with socialization processes (Harway & Moss, 1983; Hines & Green, 1991; Moore, 1985).

Brain Lateralization

The human brain is *lateralized*—that is, it is divided into left and right hemispheres that perform different functions (Molfese & Segalowitz, 1989). The left half both controls and receives information from the right side of the body, including the right ear, hand, and foot and the right visual field of each eye. The right hemisphere controls and receives information from the left side. The left hemisphere is primarily responsible for language and speech processes, whereas the right side appears to be more involved with quantitative and spatial abilities (Springer & Deutsch, 1989). Because the division of these functions corresponds to the cognitive sex differences we discussed earlier, some psychologists believe that differences in brain laterality may be important for understanding certain differences in male and female behavior (Levy, 1981; Witelson & Kigar, 1989). Of particular interest are data suggesting that males are *more* lateralized—that is, their left and right hemispheres function more independently—than females (Bryden, 1982; McGlone, 1980). As noted, this difference may result from the actions of fetal androgens that operate selectively on males (Finegan, Niccols, & Sitarenios, 1992; Jacklin, Wilcox, & Maccoby, 1988).

Studies of language and verbal abilities provide some support for the idea that brain lateralization plays a role in gender differences. For example, in both 3- and 6-month-old infants, sex differences in hemisphere specialization have been found. When they responded to recordings of a voice speaking, female infants showed stronger brain-wave reactions to right-ear (left-hemisphere) presentations, whereas male infants showed stronger reactions to left-ear (right-hemisphere) presentations (Shucard et al., 1981; Shucard & Shucard, 1990). At 2 and 3 years of age, both sexes begin to process verbal stimuli (such as spoken words) through the right ear and nonverbal stimuli (such as music) through the left ear (Harper & Kraft, 1986; Kamptner, Kraft, & Harper, 1984). But at this point, males begin to show evidence of greater lateralization than females—for example, performing much better in response to verbal stimuli presented in the right ear than the left ear but showing the opposite tendency for nonverbal stimuli (Kraft, 1984).

Other research has reported that verbal abilities in males whose left hemispheres have been damaged (such as through strokes or tumors) are much more impaired than in females with a similar degree of damage in that area (McGlone, 1980; Sasanuma, 1980). These results suggest that language functioning in females is more equally spread between the two hemispheres, whereas in males it is more concentrated in the left hemisphere.

The role of brain lateralization in spatial abilities has also been examined (Newcombe, Dubas, & Baenninger, 1989; Springer & Deutsch, 1989; Waber, 1979a). Evidence for greater lateralization in males has been reported—for example, in a study of children's haptic performance. Children in the study first felt a pair of hidden shapes, one with each hand, for 10 seconds. They were then asked to pick out the two shapes from a visual display. For boys, left-hand (right-hemisphere) performance was better than right-hand performance. For girls, left-and right-hand performance were equal (Witelson, 1976).

The evidence that males seem to be more lateralized than females does not provide a simple explanation of verbal and spatial sex differences. It has, however, led researchers to pursue this line of inquiry in the hope of determining whether structural brain differences may form the bases of certain sex differences in behavior.

✔ *To Recap...*

In humans, the male and female are different for the purpose of reproduction, a characteristic called sexual dimorphism. The process through which these differences emerge is called sex differentiation.

Human body cells possess 46 chromosomes, including two sex chromosomes. In females, both sex chromosomes are Xs (46,XX); and in males, one is X and the other, Y (46,XY). The sex chromosomes of the embryo cause the development of either testes or ovaries. Chromosomal abnormalities can produce individuals with unusual sex chromosome arrangements. Turner's syndrome (XO), Klinefelter's syndrome (XXY), and 47,XYY syndrome are examples.

Traits carried by genes found only on the sex chromosomes (usually on an X) are called sex-linked or X-linked traits. They are usually recessive and often dangerous. X-linked traits almost always are found in men, where the Y chromosome fails to block the expression of the recessive problem gene.

Sex-limited traits are carried by genes that are not on the sex chromosomes but that require male or female sex hormones for their expression.

The principal fetal hormones are androgens in males and progesterone and estrogens in females. The production of androgens by the testes is necessary for the embryo to develop as male. Androgens also affect the organization of the fetal brain. Hormonal abnormalities in humans illustrate the role of hormones in gender-related behaviors. Congenital Adrenal Hyperplasia (CAH) results from the overproduction of androgens during gestation. Even with treatment, the personalities of CAH females remain masculinized. CAH males are only somewhat more masculinized than normal males. Androgen insensitivity involves a failure of the body cells to respond to androgens. The personalities of androgen-insensitive males are feminized.

Brain lateralization refers to the specialization in function of the brain hemispheres. Each controls and receives input from the opposite side of the body. The right hemisphere is principally involved with quantitative and spatial abilities, and the left hemisphere is more involved with verbal abilities. Males appear to be more lateralized than females. This sex difference may be related to behavioral sex differences on verbal and spatial tasks.

ANDROGYNY

Two assumptions have guided much of the research on gender-role development conducted during the past 2 decades. The first is that many observed sex differences are not inevitable. We have seen that a substantial amount of evidence is consistent with this contention. The second assumption is that many of the sex differences that exist should be reduced or eliminated. Here the evidence and arguments are a bit more complicated (Katz, 1986).

When we examine the personality traits or characteristics traditionally considered desirable for males or females, we find two distinct clusters (Cook, 1985). The masculine gender role includes principally what have been called *instrumental* characteristics, such as independence, ambition, and self-confidence. The feminine gender role is predominantly characterized by *expressive* traits, including compassion, sensitivity, and warmth. The early view in psychology was that these masculine and feminine clusters represented opposite ends of a continuum. This view further held that our psychological well-being is maximized when we adopt the cluster of personality traits that matches our gender.

Androgyny
A personality type composed of desirable characteristics of the masculine and feminine personality types.

The modern challenge to these views is based on the concept of **androgyny**. According to this concept, masculine and feminine traits are not opposite ends of one dimension but two separate dimensions. An individual thus may possess attributes from each. More importantly, the most psychologically healthy individuals are believed to be androgynous—that is, to possess a blend of desirable traits from both the masculine and the feminine cluster. These androgynous personality types can be, for example, bold yet kind, self-assured yet humble, assertive yet nurturing, and so forth. The presumed benefit of this blending is flexibility. The androgynous person should possess a wider range of available responses that can be brought to bear in a variety of situations (Bem, 1985; Spence, 1985).

A number of instruments have been developed to assess androgyny. The two most popular are the Bem Sex-Role Inventory (Bem, 1974, 1979) and the Personal Attributes Questionnaire (Spence & Helmreich, 1978). These instru-

• Children with androgynous personalities presumably possess a wider range of abilities and interests.

ments list socially desirable traits or attributes, some instrumental and some expressive. Respondents are asked to rate themselves on each one. An overall gender-role rating can then be calculated and the individual classified as masculine, feminine, or androgynous.

As suggested earlier, proponents of the androgyny concept contend that androgynous individuals should exhibit more flexibility and better psychological adjustment than people with either strongly masculine or strongly feminine personalities. Although the results of some studies have been consistent with this view (Baucom & Danker-Brown, 1979; Bem, 1975; Boldizar, 1991; Spence, Helmreich, & Holahan, 1979), the evidence has not been overwhelming (Taylor & Hall, 1982).

Recent studies suggest that it is the masculine component of androgyny—that is, the desirable traits from the instrumental cluster—that is primarily responsible for the individual's level of psychological well-being. Thus, both men and women who rate themselves higher on these items are likely to be better adjusted than those who rate themselves lower (Markstrom-Adams, 1989; Whitely, 1985).

This last finding, however, need not force us to abandon androgyny as a useful concept or a desirable condition. It is always possible that the concept is sound but that our instruments are not accurately measuring the process. Nor should we assume that feminine characteristics are not valuable for success or happiness in our culture. Traits from the female cluster may operate in subtle ways that researchers have not thoroughly studied, and they may thus exert more influence over psychological health than we realize (Cook, 1985).

CONCLUSION

Far from being the simple and straightforward matter that psychologists once thought, gender-role development appears to be a complex and delicate process. As in other areas of development, biological, cognitive, and environmental factors all play important parts in guiding the child's progress toward a sexual identity.

An important aspect of research in this area is that it reveals the intimate relations between scientific investigation and the social environment in which research is conducted. As indicated at the beginning of the chapter, the explosion of research on gender roles that occurred in the 1970s grew primarily out of a political and sociological movement rather than a scientific one. It is, of course, likely that the earlier theoretical notions would eventually have been challenged anyway. But it is doubtful that as much attention would have been focused on this topic had it not been for the formation of women's studies departments in colleges, the debate over the Equal Rights Amendment, the creation of affirmative action programs, and so on. In some sense, then, society often dictates to scientists what needs to be studied.

Such pressure can pose problems for the research community. Even now, though some of the myths of gender-role development have been discarded and new views are replacing the old, many of the most important questions remain unanswered. Yet parents are clamoring to know what are the best methods for raising their children in nonsexist ways, educators want to know whether males and females require different types of instruction, employers want to know whether both sexes really can do any job equally well, and so forth.

Most psychologists are reluctant to provide firm answers to these questions at this point. For now, what we can say with some certainty is that the child's gender-role development does not occur automatically and that it is sensitive to how parents, teachers, peers, and the culture respond to the child. But the next step—prescribing the best rearing and teaching practices—remains a controversial and difficult business.

FOR THOUGHT AND DISCUSSION

1.   Studies have shown that one result of developing gender schemas and associating ourselves with either the male or female schema is that we then become selectively attuned to information relevant to our gender. *Can you think of several examples of things in your everyday life that you pay attention to probably because they are related to your gender schema? Are there things that you probably ignore because they are part of the other gender schema? Repeat this exercise with another schema, besides gender, to which you relate.*

2.   Research indicates that by the preschool years, girls and boys (especially boys) tend to play with different kinds of toys and engage in different sorts of play activities. *Should preschool or day-care teachers actively attempt to engage children in activities more typical of the other gender, even if the children resist doing so? For example, should boys be encouraged (or required) to spend time in the cooking area, even if they find this activity unappealing? If not, do you think there is another way for teachers to break down children's strong gender stereotypes?*

3.   When a gender label is attached to an object or activity, members of the opposite sex are more likely to avoid it. *Think of an object or activity that you tend to avoid because it is sex-typed. Can you think of a way the label could be altered that would cause you to stop doing so?*

4.   One reason males are better than females on some spatial tasks may be that they have had more experience with activities that promote the development of spatial skills. *What are some specific activities that you believe might do this? Can you think*

of any activities more common in females that could promote spatial skills and that would offer evidence counter to this hypothesis?

5. The concept of androgyny suggests that the optimal personality style is one that borrows the best traits from the traditional male and female stereotypes. *What is your reaction to this idea? Do you believe males and females should develop more similar personality styles? If androgyny is more effective than masculinity or femininity, why do you think evolution hasn't made this personality type much more common?*

Chapter 16

PEER RELATIONS

$\mathcal{A}$ny visitor to a day-care center, playground, or park can readily see that children interact with other children from early in life. And the importance of peers is not limited to our culture. Societies the world around promote contact among children, in some cases more strongly than does our society (Draper & Harpending, 1988). As one psychologist writes, "None of the world's cultures rears its children solely through interaction with adults" (Hartup, 1983, p. 104).

Nevertheless, until fairly recently the study of children's social development concentrated largely on relations within the family. This focus is understandable: The family is clearly important and is stressed in every theory of socialization. However, in recent years the interest in families has begun to be supplemented by research directed to the role of peers. After years of relative neglect, peer relations has emerged as one of the "hot" topics in child psychology.

We touched on the role of peers in development at several points in the preceding chapters. The topic of peer relations is important enough, however, to merit a focus of its own, and that is the purpose of the present chapter. Two very general questions will be of interest. One is how children relate to other children—that is, peers as objects or targets of the child's social behaviors. The other is how interaction with peers affects the child's development—that is, peers as sources of developmental change.

THEORIES OF PEER RELATIONS

The three major theoretical traditions have addressed somewhat different aspects of children's peer relations. To a great extent, therefore, the pictures they provide complement rather than contradict each other.

Cognitive-Developmental Theory

Cognitive-developmental theorists discuss peers in both of the senses just identified—as objects of behavior and as sources of change. An example of the latter is Piaget's (1932) theory of how peers contribute to changes in moral reasoning, a theory discussed in Chapter 14. In Piaget's view, the child, lacking the power and authority of the adult, conforms to what he or she perceives to be the adult's views. The result is moral realism, characterized by a rigid conception of right and wrong. When the child interacts with peers, however, the relation is much more one of equals, and there is a continual need for cooperating, negotiating, and taking the point of view of the other. It is interaction with peers, therefore, that leads to the ability to consider different perspectives, an ability central to the more advanced form of reasoning known as moral relativism. More generally, interaction with peers is important in breaking down the child's egocentrism and encouraging more mature forms of thought (Musatti, 1986).

Peers are also important in Kohlberg's (1987) theory of moral development. As in Piaget's theory, movement through Kohlberg's stages results partly from biological maturation. Achieving a new stage, however, requires not only a sufficient level of maturation but also experience with moral issues. Kohlberg especially stresses experiences in which the child encounters different points of view and thus is forced to consider and to integrate different perspectives. Such experiences of cognitive conflict may be especially likely in the give-and-take of the peer group.

As we saw in Chapter 10, peers also play a role in Vygotsky's theory (Tudge & Rogoff, 1989). Just as children benefit from interactions with a parent or teacher, so they may be helped to new levels of understanding when they interact with a more competent peer.

In addition to their role in promoting cognitive change, peers are also important as objects of the child's thought. Thinking about other children falls under the heading of *social cognition*—the child's understanding of the social and interpersonal world. Of course, peers are not the only targets for social cognition; children think about adults, about social institutions, and about themselves. But peers are undoubtedly frequent objects of social cognition for most children from early in life.

Piaget's discussions of social cognition (Piaget, 1950, 1967) stress its similarities to the child's reasoning about the physical world. Young children's egocentrism, for example, colors both their logical reasoning and their thinking about other people. More generally, the limitations of preoperational thought find their way into the child's attempts to make sense of other people (Flavell et al., 1993). And as these limitations are overcome, the child is seen as entering new stages of social reasoning. The idea that social cognition, like physical cognition, develops in stages is found in a number of models of social-cognitive development. Robert Selman (1980), for example, has proposed a five-stage model of social understanding, ranging from Piagetian egocentrism in very young children to mastery of social systems and social institutions by adolescence (Chapter 13 discusses how Selman's theory applies to understanding of the self). Similarly, William Damon (1977, 1980) has developed stage models to account for developmental changes in children's understanding of such concepts as fairness, justice, and friendship.

Despite these perceived similarities between physical and social cognition, modern cognitive-developmentalists tend to stress differences between understanding of the physical world and understanding of the social world (Damon, 1981; Hoffman, 1981). A primary difference is that other people, unlike inanimate objects, are themselves conscious, thinking organisms capable of spontaneous and intentional behavior. Furthermore, our relations with other people involve not just action but interaction, and such interaction requires mutual coordination of intention and action. Because of these complexities, understanding other people, including peers, can present challenges that go beyond those posed by the physical world.

Children's understanding of other children is an interesting topic in itself. But it is also important because of its possible effects on the child's social behavior. A basic principle of the cognitive-developmental approach is that the child's cognitive level is an important determinant of how the child behaves, including behavior toward other people. Thus, the cognitive theorist would expect older children to show more complex and mature forms of social behavior because of their greater cognitive maturity. And within an age group, the theorist would expect children who are advanced in their level of social reasoning also to be advanced in their social behavior. We will consider shortly how well these expectations are borne out by research.

The Environmental/Learning Approach

We have seen that social-learning theory attempts to identify basic learning principles that apply across a range of situations, age groups, and types of behavior. It should come as no surprise, then, to learn that the social-learning concepts already stressed are also important for the topic of peer relations.

Peers can affect a child's behavior and development in several ways. One way is through peer reinforcement and punishment. Peers provide many reinforcing or punishing consequences as a child develops—attention, praise, acquiescence to the child's wishes, sharing or refusing to share, criticism, disapproval. Many of these consequences are, to be sure, unintended, but they may function as reinforcers or punishers nonetheless. Peers are also important as models of behavior. As discussed in Chapter 2, Bandura (1977b, 1986, 1989) places a heavy emphasis on the various ways in which exposure to models can affect a child's behavior. Finally, peers contribute to the development of self-efficacy, or children's conceptions of which behaviors they are capable of performing. One source of self-efficacy judgments is the child's observation of the behavior of others, and peers are clearly a natural comparison group.

Of course, none of the roles just cited is unique to peers. But peers may be especially important sources of such effects, especially as children grow older. The sheer amount of time spent with peers guarantees that any child will be exposed frequently to the behavior of other children and will experience frequent consequences from other children as the result of his or her behavior. Furthermore, the importance, at least for most children, of being accepted by other children guarantees that peers will be effective agents of reinforcement and punishment, as well as potent models for a wide range of behaviors. And, of course, the behaviors that peers model and reinforce may differ from the behaviors that adults try to promote.

Interaction with peers also provides a good example of Bandura's (1978) principle of reciprocal determinism. Recall that the model of reciprocal determinism attempts to capture the interplay among three factors: the person, the person's behavior, and the environment (see Figure 2-2). Each of these factors influences the others when children interact. Characteristics of the child (such as cognitive level) affect the behaviors directed toward other children. Characteristics of the environment also affect behavior. We will see, for example, that children may behave differently in small groups than in large groups, and with friends than with nonfriends. The environment is in turn affected by the child and the child's behaviors. Particular behaviors may change group size by attracting or repelling other children, and general characteristics of the child certainly affect the probability that friends will be available to play with. Finally, the child's behavior affects characteristics of the child. The success or failure of various efforts with peers, for example, may affect feelings of self-efficacy, which in turn will affect future behavior toward peers.

Ethological Theory

The ethological approach brings several emphases to the study of peer relations (Attili, 1990; Hinde, 1983; Miller, 1993). Theoretically, there is the familiar emphasis on the innate basis for behavior, a basis established during the evolutionary history of the species. Many of the social behaviors that children show, including behaviors toward other children, are assumed to have been selected for during evolution because of their adaptive value. We have already seen this argument applied to two important classes of social behavior: altruism and aggression. Ethologists do not claim that such behaviors are totally under genetic control, because experience is clearly necessary for their emergence. But they do claim that there is an important genetic component (Zahn-Waxler, Cummings, & Iannotti, 1986).

A second emphasis concerns the value of comparative study. Ethology began as the study of animal behavior, and ethologists always look for informative comparisons across different species. Relations with peers are important in the development of a number of species, including all nonhuman primates (Suomi & Harlow, 1975). Furthermore, the ways in which peers relate show interesting similarities across species. The study of other species can therefore provide clues as to the nature and importance of peer relations in human development.

Let us consider an example that will illustrate both of the points just made. We have seen that ethologists believe the tendency to be aggressive was selected for during evolution. But unchecked aggression is not adaptive for a species; evolution must also produce controls on aggression. One form of control, which is found in a number of species, is known as a *dominance hierarchy*. Recall from Chapter 14 that a dominance hierarchy is a kind of pecking order that determines who wins out over whom in social disputes. Over time, the members of a group come to realize, and to acknowledge in their behavior, that A dominates B, B dominates C, and so on. Some degree of aggression, or at least of rough-and-tumble-play, may be necessary as the hierarchy is developing; once it is established, however, disputes can be resolved simply through members' knowledge of their relative status and thus without use of force. It is the reduction in actual aggression that represents the adaptive value of dominance hierarchies. Other evidence for an evolutionary basis to dominance hierarchies includes their universality within a species as well as their similar form across species.

As we saw in Chapter 14, children also form dominance hierarchies. Such hierarchies are evident in the preschool, once children have had sufficient experience to sort out the relative ordering (LaFreniere & Charlesworth, 1983; Strayer & Strayer, 1976). And although their exact form may be different, dominance hierarchies are also apparent among groups of well-acquainted adolescents (Savin-Williams, 1987). That such hierarchies are effective in minimizing actual aggression is shown by one study of adolescents at a summer camp. Of 7000 dominance encounters, only 1% resulted in fights (Savin-Williams, 1979).

Note again that the biological emphasis in ethological theorizing does not rule out the contribution of other factors. Experience and environmental circumstances are important in the formation of a hierarchy. Children cannot learn the standing of particular peers until they have experience with those peers. Cognitive abilities also enter in as the child weighs various cues and makes decisions about dominance. What ethological theory adds is the belief that there is a biologically based tendency, set by evolution, to utilize experience in this way.

The work on dominance can also serve to introduce a final ethological theme— the importance of naturalistic observation. Ethologists learn about dominance by observing how children interact in their natural settings—nursery schools for 3- and 4-year-olds, summer camps or boarding schools for adolescents. More generally, the ethological approach has always emphasized the need to study the natural behaviors of organisms in their natural settings (Eibl-Eibesfeldt, 1989; Strayer, 1980). Although the value of the naturalistic approach is now generally accepted, ethologists deserve credit for being among its first and most forceful advocates.

✔ To Recap...

The three major theoretical perspectives in child psychology offer their own distinct views on peer relations. In the cognitive-developmental approach, peers are important as an impetus for cognitive change. Both Piaget and Kohlberg stress cognitive conflict with peers as one source of the ability to consider different points of view, whereas Vygotsky's theory emphasizes the instructional role played by more competent peers. Peers are also important as objects of thought, a topic that falls under the heading of social cognition.

Cognitive-developmental theorists maintain that how children think about their peers is one determinant of how they behave toward peers.

According to the social-learning approach, peers contribute to the socialization of the child in three main ways. Peers reinforce or punish certain behaviors and thereby increase or decrease their likelihood of occurring. Peers also serve as models who may influence the child's subsequent behavior. Finally, peers are one source for self-efficacy judgments. Interactions among peers provide a good example of reciprocal determinism, or the mutual influences among person, behavior, and situation.

Ethological approaches reflect the assumption that behaviors toward peers (such as altruism and aggression) have an innate basis that reflects the evolutionary history of the species. Peer relations are important for a number of species, and comparative study is therefore a valuable guide in assessing their role in human development. Finally, ethologists stress the value of naturalistic observation of behavior, including behavior with peers.

TYPICAL PEER RELATIONS

How do children interact with each other? To answer this question, we first consider how peer relations change as children grow older—that is, the developmental aspect of peer relations. We then explore situational and cognitive factors that can affect the nature of children's interactions.

Developmental Changes

The most obvious developmental change in peer relations is an increase in amount. As children grow older, they spend more and more time with peers and relatively less time with adults, including their parents (Hartup, 1992c). In one study, for example, the proportion of time children spent with other children increased from approximately 30% at ages 1 and 2 to almost 60% by age 11. Conversely, time spent with adults dropped from 55% at 1 and 2 to less than 10% at 11 (Ellis, Rogoff, & Cromer, 1981).

The change in amount of time spent with peers is a backdrop to the issue on which we now concentrate—changes in the nature or quality of children's relations with their peers. Here, too, the changes with age are dramatic.

Infancy

Unlike older children, infants cannot spontaneously seek out their peers for companionship or pleasure. If infants find themselves together, it is because adults have placed them together. Adults often do place babies together, however, and the likelihood of such contact is increasing as more and more mothers enter the labor force. Three or four infants may be cared for in the home of one mother, or half a dozen or so may occupy the "baby room" of a day-care center. One survey indicates that more than 50% of American babies between the ages of 6 and 12 months see other babies at least once a week (Vandell & Mueller, 1980). And even infants who do not have such experiences may be brought together by researchers for the purposes of study, a procedure that has been labeled the "baby party" technique (Perry & Bussey, 1984).

Interest in other children emerges quite early. Infants as young as 6 months look at, vocalize to, smile at, and touch other infants (Hay, 1985; Hay, Nash, & Pedersen, 1983). Such behaviors are, to be sure, limited in both frequency and complexity. They also have been characterized as *object-centered*, because infants' early in-

• For many children, interaction with peers begins very early in life.

teractions often center around some toy of mutual interest (Perry & Bussey, 1984). Indeed, toys remain an important context for interaction throughout infancy.

Relations with peers change in various ways as babies develop (Brownell, 1990; Brownell & Brown, 1992; Howes, 1987a, 1987b). Initially simple and discrete behaviors, such as a touch, begin to be coordinated into more complex combinations, such as a touch in conjunction with a smile, perhaps followed by a vocalization. Reciprocity becomes more and more likely as one-way social acts evolve into more truly social interchanges. Thus, a social overture from Baby 1, such as the offer of a toy, elicits an appropriate response from Baby 2, which in turn elicits a further response from Baby 1. Positive emotional responses become more marked as infants begin to take obvious pleasure in the company and the behavior of their peers. Unfortunately, negative responses also become more evident, especially in disputes over toys. Nevertheless, most social interchanges among infants are positive. And the cognitive level of a child's play is generally higher when peers are present than when they are not (Rubenstein & Howes, 1976).

Experience with peers has a definite effect on how infants interact. Specific experience is important; like any of us, infants are more likely to be sociable with acquaintances than with a peer whom they have never seen before (Field & Roopnarine, 1982). General experience also contributes; infants with a relatively extended history of peer interaction are more likely to initiate contact with new peers (Becker, 1977). The conclusion that experience affects peer relations is, in fact, a general one that should be kept in mind as we review developmental changes beyond infancy. In addition to differences based on age, there always are individual differences in how children of the same age relate, and past experience is one source of these differences.

The Preschool Period

The years between 2 and 5 are a time of expanding peer relations. Developmental trends first evident during infancy continue, and new forms of social interaction and social competence emerge. Although relations within the family remain critical, for most preschoolers peers begin to constitute a second important social system.

We have already seen numerous differences between what infants can do and what preschoolers can do. It should be no surprise to learn that peer relations also differ between the two periods. The preschooler occupies a larger social world than the infant, with a greater number and variety of playmates (Howes, 1983, 1987b). The preschooler's social world is also more differentiated; that is, the child can direct different behaviors to different social objects and form somewhat different relations with different peers (Howes, 1987b; Ross & Lollis, 1989). The complexity of social interactions increases as symbolic forms of behavior begin to predominate over physical ones. The same goal that was once accomplished with a pull or a shove can now be achieved (at least sometimes) with a verbal request. Children also become more skilled at adjusting such communications to the different needs of different listeners (Garvey, 1986; Shatz & Gelman, 1973), and the first truly collaborative problem solving emerges (Brownell & Carriger, 1990; Cooper, 1980). Of course, none of these developments is instantaneous—skill in interacting with peers increases gradually in the years between 2 and 5, and indeed for some time afterward. The preschooler's social competence is impressive compared with that of the infant, but there is still a long way to go.

Much of the research concerned with peer relations during the preschool years has focused on children's play. One common approach to categorizing play is shown in Table 16-1. As can be seen, the categories vary in the cognitive complex-

TABLE 16-1 • Types of Play Classified According to Cognitive Level

Type	Description	Examples
Functional	Simple, repetitive muscular movements performed with or without objects	Shaking a rattle; jumping up and down
Constructive	Manipulation of objects with intention of creating somethng	Building a tower of blocks; cutting and pasting pictures
Pretend (or dramatic)	Use of an object or person to symbolize something that it is not	Pretending that a log is a boat; playing Batman and Robin with a friend
Games with rules	Playing games in accordance with prearranged rules and limits	Playing hopscotch; playing checkers

Source: Based on information from *The Effects of Sociodramatic Play on Disadvantaged Preschool Children* by S. Smilansky, 1968, New York: John Wiley & Sons.

ity of the play, ranging from the simple motor exercise of functional play to the give-and-take intricacies of games with rules. As would be expected, children of different ages are likely to engage in different types of play. Functional play emerges early and predominates during the infant and toddler years; games with rules, in contrast, are infrequent among children younger than grade-school age (Rubin, Fein, & Vanderberg, 1983). The category of **pretend play** has been of special interest to students of preschool development. Research demonstrates that both the frequency and the complexity of pretend play increase across the preschool years. Such research also suggests that pretend play can have beneficial effects on both the child's cognitive development and the child's relations with peers (Fisher, 1992; Stambak & Sinclair, 1993).

Another popular approach to categorizing play is shown in Table 16-2. Here, the focus is on the social organization rather than the cognitive level of the child's play. The usual assumption has been that the various types of play develop in the order shown in the table. Thus, 2-year-olds are most likely to be found in solitary or onlooker behavior; in 5- and 6-year-olds, cooperative and associative play are com-

Pretend play
A form of play in which children use an object or person as a symbol to stand for something else.

TABLE 16-2 • Types of Play Classified According to Social Level

Type	Description
Onlooker	Watching others play without participating oneself
Solitary	Playing alone and independently, with no attempt to get close to other children
Parallel	Playing alongside other children and with similar materials but with no real interaction or cooperation
Associative	Playing with other children in some common activity but without division of labor or subordination to some overall group goal
Cooperative	Playing in a group that is organized for the purpose of carrying out some activity or attaining some goal, with coordination of individual members' behavior in pursuit of the common goal

Source: Based on information from "Social Participation Among Preschool Children" by M.B. Parten, 1932, *Journal of Abnormal and Social Psychology, 27*, pp. 243–269.

• Children's play undergoes characteristic changes across the preschool and gradeschool years (see Table 16-2). For very young children, the onlooker role is a common one.

• Solitary play is common prior to the onset of social play.

mon. A particularly interesting category is that of **parallel play,** in which two or more children play next to each other, using the same sorts of materials and perhaps even talking, yet without any genuine interaction. Anyone who has watched groups of 3- and 4-year-olds can verify that such "semisocial" play is common.

The categories listed in Table 16-2 were developed more than 60 years ago (Parten, 1932). Although recent research verifies that children today show the same general patterns of play, such research also suggests some qualifications and complexities in the developmental picture (Howes & Matheson, 1992; Rubin & Coplan, 1992). Not all children progress in the order shown in the table; a child might move directly from solitary behavior to cooperative play, for example, without an intervening phase of parallel play (Smith, 1978). Nor do the early categories of play necessarily disappear as children grow older; solitary and parallel play are still common among 4- and 5-year-olds (Tieszen, 1979). What does change with age is the cognitive maturity of the play. The nonsocial play of 2- and 3-year-olds consists mainly of various kinds of functional play (see Table 16-1). Older children are more likely to embed even their nonsocial play in a constructive or dramatic context (Rubin, Watson, & Jambor, 1978). Because of this interplay of cognitive and social factors, modern scales to assess play typically include both cognitive and social dimensions (Howes, Unger, & Seidner, 1989; Rubin, 1989).

As noted, the preschool years are a time of expanding peer interaction, especially for children who attend a nursery school or day-care center. This period is a good one, therefore, for a first look at the processes stressed in social-learning accounts of peer relations. One important process is modeling. Children clearly imitate other children in preschool settings; one study reports an average of 13 imitative acts per child per hour (Abramovitch & Grusec, 1978). A variety of behaviors have been shown to be susceptible to the effects of preschool peer models, including compliance with adult instructions (Ross, 1971), sharing (Elliott & Vasta, 1970), social participation (O'Connor, 1969), and problem solving (Morrison & Kuhn, 1983). Indeed, some capacity for imitative learning emerges even before the usual age for preschool attendance. Several recent studies have shown simple forms of peer imitation in children as young as 15 to 20 months (Asendorpf & Baudonniere, 1993; Eckerman, Davis, & Didow, 1989; Hanna & Meltzoff, 1993).

Parallel play
A form of play in which children play next to each other and with similar materials but with no real interaction or cooperation.

• Parallel play is a familiar sight among preschoolers.

• The appearance of associative play marks an advance in the social organization of the child's play.

• The most advanced form of social play is found in the cooperation and coordination of cooperative play.

Reinforcement, too, occurs frequently in the preschool (Charlesworth & Hartup, 1967; Furman & Gavin, 1989). Among the reinforcers children deliver are help giving, praise, smiling or laughing, affection, and compliance. Preschool children also deliver punishment to each other; examples include noncompliance, blaming, disapproval, physical attack, and ignoring. That such behaviors do function as reinforcements or punishments is suggested by children's reactions to them; reinforcers tend to elicit positive responses in their recipients, whereas punishments tend to elicit negative ones (Furman & Masters, 1980). The reinforcing or punishing nature of such events is also verified by their effects on subsequent behavior. Children are most likely to repeat a response that results in reinforcement and least likely to repeat one that results in punishment (Hartup, 1983). Among the aspects of social development that have been shown to be responsive to peer consequences in the preschool are gender-typed behaviors (Lamb, Easterbrooks, & Holden, 1980), modes of initiating interaction (Leiter, 1977), and aggression (Patterson, Littman, & Bricker, 1967).

We noted earlier that children's reinforcement of their peers is often unintentional. The same is true, of course, for many instances of modeling. These processes are not necessarily inadvertent, however, even in children as young as preschoolers. Research indicates that preschool children often use imitation of peers as a technique to win friends or to enter ongoing groups (Grusec & Abramovitch, 1982)—a successful technique, in that imitation is generally responded to positively. And anyone who has spent much time around young children is familiar with their deliberate manipulation of reinforcement through such promises as "I'll be your friend if . . ." and the corresponding threat "I won't be your friend unless. . . ."

Later Childhood and Adolescence

We have already touched on some of the ways in which peer relations change during the grade-school years. Children's play continues to evolve through the hierarchies shown in Tables 16-1 and 16-2. By age 8 or 9, children have become enthusiastic participants in games with rules, as any visit to a school playground or toy store will readily verify (Eifermann, 1971). By middle childhood, children's play is also more likely to fall within the most advanced of the categories in Table 16-2, that of cooperative play. These changes in both the cognitive level and the social organization of play in turn relate to more general factors in the child's development. Increased experience with peers clearly plays a role as children spend more and more time with a wider and wider variety of children. Advances in cognitive level also contribute. In particular, gains in perspective-taking skills during middle childhood may underlie both the newfound facility at games with rules and the general ability to interact cooperatively.

One of the most striking developmental changes in peer relations is the increased importance of groups as a context for peer interaction. For psychologists, the term **group** means something more than just a collection of individuals. Hartup (1983) suggests the following criteria for determining that a group exists: "social interaction occurs regularly, values are shared over and above those maintained in society at large, individual members have a sense of belonging, and a structure exists to support the attitudes that members should have toward one another" (p. 144).

Preschool children occasionally interact in ways that seem to fit this definition. The same four boys, for example, may play together in similar ways every day, demonstrating clear leader-and-follower roles in their play as well as a clear sense

Group
A collection of individuals who interact regularly in a consistent, structured fashion and who share values and a sense of belonging to the group.

of "we" versus "they" in their relations with those outside their group. Indeed, children as young as 2 may show some of the criteria of group formation (Lakin, Lakin, & Constanzo, 1979). Nevertheless, it is during the grade-school years that membership in groups assumes a clear significance in the lives of most children. Some such groups are formal ones with a substantial degree of adult input, such as Brownies, Cub Scouts, 4-H, and Little League. Other groups are more informal, child-created, and child-directed, reflecting mutual interests of the group members. The cliques and gangs that are such a familiar part of adolescent life are the culmination of this developmental progression.

How does membership in a group affect peer relations? A classic study of this question is the Robbers Cave Experiment (Sherif et al., 1961). For this study, 22 fifth-grade boys, initially unacquainted, were recruited to attend one of two summer camps. In each camp, the boys engaged in typical activities—hiking, sports, crafts, and the like. They also, thanks to the manipulation of the experimenters, coped with various unexpected challenges—for example, preparing a meal when the staff had failed to do so. In both camps, divisions of labor and cooperative problem solving ensued, both in response to immediate crises and with respect to longer-term group organization and group goals. Leaders and followers emerged. And both camps adopted names—Rattlers in one case, Eagles in the other.

Initially, neither group was aware of the other. After 5 days, however, the experimenters arranged for the two groups to meet "accidentally." A series of competitions (baseball, tug of war, and so on) followed, engineered so that neither group enjoyed more success than the other. The immediate effects of the competitions on group cohesiveness were detrimental; bickering followed any defeat, and the leader of one group was actually overthrown. Over time, however, the between-group competitions led to a heightened sense of within-group—"us" as opposed to "them"—solidarity. At the same time, the rivalry between groups escalated, eventually reaching the point of physical violence. Only through cooperative efforts to solve further experimentally engineered "crises" (for example, a nonfunctioning water supply on a hot day) did the two groups begin to resolve their conflict and develop between-group friendships.

The Robbers Cave experiment suggests several conclusions about children's groups that are verified by more recent research (Fine, 1987; Hartup, 1992c). Most

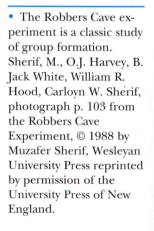

• The Robbers Cave experiment is a classic study of group formation. Sherif, M., O.J. Harvey, B. Jack White, William R. Hood, Carloyn W. Sherif, photograph p. 103 from the Robbers Cave Experiment, © 1988 by Muzafer Sherif, Wesleyan University Press reprinted by permission of the University Press of New England.

generally, it is clear that children tend to form groups based on common interests and goals and that groups serve as a source of self-identity and gratification. Groups are organized, with rules and norms that must be adhered to and divisions of the members into leaders and followers. Work in support of common goals is one source of group cohesiveness; competition with other groups is another source. Between-group rivalry is clearly the most worrisome aspect of group functioning, since attitudes and behaviors toward outsiders may become quite negative. More positively, the same factors that promote within-group cohesion—in particular, working toward a common goal—can also serve to reduce between-group hostility. These conclusions are not limited to children but apply to adults' groups as well. At the most far-reaching level, they have implications for relations between ethnic groups and between nations (Hartup, 1983). (In Box 16-1 we consider a classic study of a group-oriented method of socialization.)

The work on groups raises the general question of peers' influence on a child's development. To many adults, the importance of peer-group membership for the grade-schooler or adolescent raises the disturbing possibility that peers may come to outweigh parents as a source of behaviors and values. What do we know about the influence of peers in general and about the relative influence of peers and parents in particular? (Table 16-3 summarizes the results from one survey of the relative influence of parents and peers.)

TABLE 16-3 ● Percentage of Teenagers Seeking Peer Advice on Different Issues[a]

Issue	Boys	Girls
1. On what to spend money	19%	2%
2. Whom to date	41	47
3. Which clubs to join	54	60
4. Advice on personal problems	27	53
5. How to dress	43	53
6. Which courses to take at school	8	16
7. Which hobbies to take up	46	36
8. In choosing the future occupation	0	2
9. Which social events to attend	66	60
10. Whether to go or not go to college	0	0
11. What books to read	38	40
12. What magazines to buy	46	51
13. How often to date	35	24
14. Participating in drinking parties	46	40
15. In choosing future spouse	8	9
16. Whether to go steady or not	30	29
17. How intimate to be on a date	35	24
18. Information about sex	30	44

[a]Subjects chose among three alternatives: peers, parents, and undecided.

Source: Adapted from "Adolescents' Peer Orientation: Changes in the Support System during the Past Three Decades" by H. Sebald, 1989, *Adolescence, 24*, pp. 940, 941. Copyright 1989 by Libra Publishers. Adapted by permission.

TWO WORLDS OF CHILDHOOD: A SOVIET–AMERICAN COMPARISON

In every culture, peers play certain roles—reinforcing and punishing particular actions, serving as models for a wide range of behaviors, providing standards for social comparisons and for judgments of self-efficacy, and establishing group norms and practices to which other children must adhere. Furthermore, adults in every culture make deliberate use of the power of peers—citing particular peers as models of good behavior, pointing out the consequences of the child's behavior for the peer group as a whole, and so forth. In most instances, this sort of peer-based socialization is casual and unsystematic—just one of many ways in which perceptive parents and teachers attempt to instill desired behavior. But what would happen if a society as a whole decided to make the peer group a major vehicle of socialization?

A classic study by Urie Bronfenbrenner (1962, 1970) sought to answer this question. Bronfenbrenner's test case was the Soviet Union of the 1950s and 1960s. Child-rearing methods in the Soviet Union during this time—in keeping with the overall Communist philosophy that guided the country—placed a heavy emphasis on various collectives, or organized peer groups, to which children belonged as they grew up. For many children, collective upbringing began with enrollment in infant nurseries and public preschools. For all children, collectives of various levels and sizes were important throughout the school years—the classroom as a whole; the individual rows, or "links," within the classroom; and the broader Communist youth groups to which virtually all children belonged and of which each classroom was a unit. Between the ages of 10 and 15, the youth group was the Pioneers. Figure 16-1 shows examples of posters that were used to illustrate some of the Laws of the Pioneers.

The kind of social structure just described guarantees an important role for peers, simply because children spend so much time with other children from early in life. The Soviet emphasis on peers, however, went well beyond simple proximity. Rather, for Soviet children, the collective, rather than the individual child, was the primary unit for achievement and for evaluation. The frequent school competitions, for example, were structured always in terms of the collective: the best row within a class, the best class within a school, the best school within a district. The rewards for success in such competitions—for example, large "Who Is Best?" charts displayed throughout the school—listed not the winning children but the winning groups. Because any one child's success was tied to that of the group, children had a clear incentive for monitoring and regulating their peers' behavior, as well as a clear reason for being responsive themselves to suggestions or criticisms from the group. That such criticisms would be forthcoming was ensured by the designation of some children as "monitors," whose job was to help the teacher maintain order and elicit optimal performance. As the following examples from a third-grade monitor illustrate, the monitors were quite willing to be critical: "Today Valodya did the wrong problem. Masha didn't write neatly and forgot to underline the right words in her lesson; Alyosha had a dirty shirt collar" (Bronfenbrenner, 1970, p. 60). Far from being resentful of the negative evaluations, the targets for such criticisms were expected to enter into the group evaluation process themselves, generating both further self-criticisms and their own peer commentaries.

The issue of peer influence turns out to be one of those "it depends" issues (Berndt, 1989a; Newman, 1982). Peers can clearly be an important source of values. But how important they are depends on a number of factors. Peer influence varies with age, reaching a peak, at least by some measures, in early adolescence and declining thereafter (Berndt, 1979; Constanzo, 1970). Peer influence varies from child to child (Perry & Bussey, 1984). And peer influence, as well as the relative importance of peers and parents, varies from one area of life to another. In areas such as clothing, music, and choice of friends, peers are often more important than parents, especially by adolescence. In areas such as academic planning and occupational aspirations, however, it is parents who usually have the dominant voice (Berndt, Miller, & Park, 1989; Sebald, 1989).

Figure 16-1 Posters illustrating the laws of the Pioneers, a Communist youth group to which many children in the Soviet Union belonged during the 1950s and 1960s. From *Two Worlds of Childhood* (pp. 45, 48) by U. Bronfenbrenner, 1970, New York: Russell Sage Foundation.

How does such socialization affect children's development? In attempting to answer this question, Bronfenbrenner drew on two sources of evidence: informal observations of the behavior of Soviet children in a variety of settings and controlled experiments comparing the responses of Soviet children to the responses of children from the United States and other Western countries. Both kinds of evidence led to the same conclusion. Soviet children appeared in general to be well-mannered, hardworking, obedient, and respectful of others, both peers and adults. Naturally occurring instances of antisocial behavior were rare among the Soviet youths, and Soviet children were also less likely than their Western counterparts to act antisocially or immorally when given a chance to do so in experimental settings (for example, to cheat on a test). One Soviet-American experimental comparison proved especially instructive with respect to the role of the peer group. When told that classmates would be informed of any misconduct, Soviet children became even less likely to behave antisocially. American children, in contrast, became more likely.

Bronfenbrenner's general conclusion was that the Soviet system of socialization appeared to accomplish its goal: namely, production of well-behaved and responsible citizens who would conform to the dictates of Soviet society. He also noted, however, that by the late 1960s cracks were becoming evident in the socialization edifice and various forms of dissatisfaction were creeping in. And as the recent events in the former Soviet Union make clear, even a group-oriented and conformity-based method of socialization does not remove the possibility of individual initiative and social change.

This discussion is not meant to imply that peers are never a negative influence. In particular cases, they clearly can be—in problem areas as serious as smoking (Stanton & Silva, 1992), drug use (Brock, Nomura, & Cohen, 1989; Dinges & Oetting, 1993), and delinquency (Jessor & Jessor, 1977). Box 16-2 discusses perhaps the most worrisome manifestation of peer group membership in adolescence—teenage gang violence. Despite these cautionary points, it is important to remember that membership in groups, in addition simply to being enjoyable for children, promotes a number of social skills that will remain valuable throughout life. Furthermore, surveys reveal that the common perception of a clash in values between peers and parents is overstated; on most questions, peers and parents are more similar than different in their views (Brown, 1990; Newman, 1982). Finally, decisions about many issues, especially by adolescence, are not a matter simply of acquiescence to either peers or parents; rather, individuals may arrive at positions of their own that do not mirror those of any outside group (Berndt, 1979; Savin-Williams & Berndt, 1990). Thus, one legacy of effective socialization, including membership in peer groups, may be a healthy capacity for independent thought.

Situational Factors

Children's age is one determinant of how they interact. The situation in which they find themselves is another. Situational factors are of particular importance in social-learning theory. Social-learning theorists believe that behaviors are always learned within particular situations and that the immediate situation is therefore always an important determinant of how children behave. It follows that children's behavior may vary from one situation to another. The same child who is a model of decorum at home, for example, may be the terror of the playground at nursery school. Understanding behavior, then—including behavior with peers—requires knowledge of the setting in which the behavior occurs.

Space and Resources

Research has identified a variety of situational factors that can affect behavior in both animals and humans. One such factor is crowding. When many organisms are packed into a small space, negative consequences often ensue, including increased aggression, heightened emotional arousal, and decreased problem solving. Such effects have been demonstrated in species ranging from rats (Calhoun, 1962) to adult humans (Epstein, 1981).

Crowding can also affect children. In one study, 4th-, 8th-, and 11th-grade children spent 30 minutes together under one of two conditions: four children in a 20- by 24-foot space or four children in a 5- by 8-foot space. Children in the latter condition showed greater physiological arousal and reported more discomfort and annoyance. Later, when they were asked to choose a game to play together, they were more likely to choose competitive rather than cooperative options (Aiello, Nicosia, & Thompson, 1979). Other studies have demonstrated effects of more extended periods of crowding under naturalistic circumstances, such as in the preschool (Liddell & Kruger, 1987, 1989). Children have been found, for example, to engage in less cooperative play in crowded classrooms than in less crowded ones. More fights occur on small playgrounds than on large ones (Ginsburg, 1975).

The resources available can also affect how children interact. As we saw, toys often facilitate peer interaction, especially for young children. On the other hand, a scarcity of toys sometimes leads to an increase in play with peers, presumably because the environment presents the child with fewer interesting alternatives (Vandell, Wilson, & Buchanan, 1980). The nature of the toys or other resources also plays a role. Not surprisingly, solitary and parallel play are most common in the art and book corners and other "quiet" areas within a school. Conversely, the doll area is a likely setting for cooperative and dramatic play (Rubin, 1977). Outdoor settings and areas encouraging large-muscle activity (running, throwing, etc.) are also associated with more cooperative play, along, of course, with a general increase in the energy level and physical nature of the play (Hartup, 1983).

Familiarity

It has long been known that the familiarity of the setting can affect how young children interact with adults, both their own parents and strangers. Familiarity also in-

CONTROLLING GANG VIOLENCE

In 1990 the number of gang homicides in Los Angeles reached an all-time high of 329. This figure represented 34% of the homicides in the city that year. Homicide is now the leading cause of death among African-American youths in the United States and the second leading cause of death (after automobile accidents) for Caucasian youths.

Attempts to control the violent activities of teenage gangs have a long and mostly unsuccessful history (Covey, Menard, & Franzese, 1992). In 1987 the Office of Juvenile Justice and Delinquency Prevention established the National Youth Gang Suppression and Intervention Program (Spergel, Chance, & Curry, 1990; Spergel & Curry, 1990). The mandate of the National Program was to coordinate information about gang activities and intervention efforts from 45 communities around the United States. The ultimate goal was to use such information to develop and to disseminate effective intervention programs. Because many of us tend to think of gangs as a problem only in big cities, it is worth noting that the survey was not limited to large urban areas—among the communities sampled were Benton Harbor, Michigan, Chino, California, and Cicero, Illinois.

How have communities attempted to combat teenage violence? The National Program identified five strategies. Most common (44% of the cases) was *suppression*—that is, an emphasis on tactics such as surveillance, arrest, and imprisonment. The next most common policy (31.5%) was *social intervention*—an emphasis on crisis intervention, treatment for the youths and their families, and referral to social services. *Organizational development* accounted for 10.9% of the cases; here the primary strategy was the creation of special units for handling the problem, such as new police units and special youth agency crisis programs. In *community mobilization* (8.9%) the focus was on improved communication and joint policy and program development among various community agencies. Finally,

the least common strategy (4.8%) was *social opportunities*—the provision of basic or remedial education, training, work incentives, and jobs.

How well do such strategies work? Answering this question is not an easy task. Intervention projects seldom take the form of neat, well-controlled experiments, and obtaining clear indications of their success or failure can be difficult. The evaluative component of the National Program relied on two main sources of data: evaluations from various members of the juvenile justice system (such as police officers, judges, and church leaders) and objective data concerning changes in gang activity over time (number of gangs, number of gang members, number of gang homicides, and so on). In part, the conclusions from both sorts of data confirmed the caution and pessimism of previous reviews: In only 8 of the 45 cities was there evidence of improvement in the gang situation over time. More positively, the survey did provide information about variations in effectiveness among the five intervention strategies. The authors summarize their conclusions as follows: "Community mobilization was the factor that most powerfully predicted a decline in the gang problem. The provision of basic social opportunities to gang youth, that is, education and employment, was also very important in cities with chronic gang problems" (Spergel et al., 1990, p. 3).

Because of the complexities noted, the results from the National Program must be regarded as tentative. Indeed, not all reviews have reached the same conclusions (Lundman, 1984). Nevertheless, the National Program does represent an ambitious and promising attempt to provide a scientific grounding for efforts to address one of the nation's most pressing social problems. And it does send a disquieting message in the conjunction of two of its findings: The most effective intervention strategies were also the ones that were least often employed.

---

fluences interactions with peers. Infants are more likely to direct social behaviors toward fellow infants when they are in their own homes than when they are in the other babies' homes (Becker, 1977). Comparable effects have been found for nursery-school children. In one study, 32 sets of two initially unacquainted preschoolers were observed playing together twice, first in the experimenter's home and then in the home of one of the children. Based on the sessions in the experimenter's home, one member of each pair was identified as relatively sociable and the other as relatively shy. During the second session all 16 of the initially sociable children who were observed at home remained socially dominant. But 15 of the 16 "shy" children became socially dominant when observed in *their* homes. The greater social activity included both a higher frequency of positive behaviors, such as initiating play, and a higher frequency of negative behaviors, such as aggression (Jeffers & Lore, 1979). As the researchers note, parents are often surprised when told that the outgoing child they know is timid or withdrawn at school. Studies such as this suggest that the child's behavior may in fact be different at home than it is in other settings. And they carry a message for parents of a shy child: Arranging opportunities to play with peers in the familiar home setting may help to break down the shyness and increase social confidence.

Another way to examine familiarity is in terms not of the physical environment but of the people in it. We have already seen that babies behave differently with familiar playmates than with strangers. Acquaintanceship also affects interaction in older children. Social interaction is both more frequent and more positive with familiar peers than with unfamiliar ones. The cognitive level of play increases with familiar peers; cooperative and associative play become more common, and solitary and onlooker behavior less common (Doyle, Connolly, & Rivest, 1980). Collaborative problem solving proceeds more smoothly and efficiently among familiar peers than among unfamiliar ones (Brody, Graziano, & Musser, 1983). And finally, as they become acquainted, children become more likely to show behaviors that may be the precursors of friendship, such as sharing information about the self (Furman, 1987). Friendship is obviously a significant step beyond mere acquaintanceship, and it has a major impact on how children interact. We return to the topic of friendship shortly.

Group Size

Group size is both a dependent variable and an independent variable in the study of peer relations. It is dependent in the sense that it is one of the outcomes we can study: What size play groups do children prefer? The answer varies some with age. Toddlers and preschoolers play most often in groups of two. Even when more children are present, social behaviors in this age group often involve only two children at a time (Bronson, 1981). Older children are more likely to interact with several peers simultaneously, although one-on-one interaction remains important (Hartup, 1992c). Recall that there is also a gender difference in this aspect of development: Boys, on the average, play in larger groups than girls (Waldrop & Halverson, 1975).

Group size can also be examined as an independent variable that may affect the quality of children's interactions. It is a variable that is hard to study in isolation, because the number of children in a group often varies with other factors, such as the amount of space per child and the number of available adults. At least sometimes, however, smaller numbers seem to be better than larger numbers. For example, children have been observed to engage in more conversational interchanges (Howes & Rubenstein, 1979), to ask more questions of adults (Torrance, 1970), and to show more imaginative play (Smith & Connolly, 1981) in small groups than in large groups. In one researcher's words, "the smaller, more focused situation promotes greater intensity, vigor, and cohesiveness in child–child interactions" (Hartup, 1983, p. 124). This is a conclusion of practical as well as theoretical importance. It has implications, for example, for policies concerning classroom size and the number of children in day-care groups (Belsky, 1984; Howes, Phillips, & Whitebook, 1992).

Cognitive Contributions

We turn finally to the role that cognitive development plays in peer relations. As the name suggests, cognitive factors are stressed most heavily in the cognitive-developmental approach. But any theoretical perspective must allow some role for cognitive factors. It seems obvious that the way children think about peers must affect their behavior toward peers. The question is exactly how do these factors contribute.

A reasonable first step is to ask which cognitive factors might be important. The most popular candidate has been perspective taking. The ability to adopt the perspective of another—to figure out what someone else feels, thinks, wishes, or the like—seems clearly relevant to the ability to interact with others. More broadly, researchers have stressed various aspects of social cognition—the child's thoughts and level of reasoning with respect to other people. How, for example, do children reason about the causes of other people's behavior, or about the morality of various behaviors, or about the nature of friendship (Shantz, 1983)? Finally, some investigators have moved closer to actual social interaction by focusing on **social problem-solving skills**, the skills needed to resolve social dilemmas (Rubin & Krasnor, 1986; Rubin & Rose-Krasnor, 1992). An example of an approach to assessing social problem-solving skills is shown in Table 16-4. As can be seen, the dilemmas in this case involve sharing resources and initiating friendship. Models of the skills needed to solve such problems have often been grounded in information-processing conceptions of the components—such as attention, representation, and memory—of problem solving in general (Dodge, 1986a).

Whatever cognitive abilities are stressed, three kinds of evidence can be examined for links between cognitive development and social behavior. We can look for parallel changes with age, examine correlations within an age grouping, or determine the effects of training.

Social problem-solving skills Skills needed to resolve social dilemmas.

Changes With Age

Chapters 8, 9, and 10 described the gradual emergence of the wide range of knowledge and skills that constitute childhood cognitive development. Similarly, more recent chapters have discussed the gradual development of a broad and powerful repertoire of social behaviors. The general progression in both the cognitive and social realms is the same: from initially simple, limited, often less-than-optimal responding to increasingly complex, sophisticated, and adaptive behavior. This parallel course of development is compatible with the hypothesis that cognitive advances lead to social advances. As children can do more cognitively, they also can do more socially.

The kind of similarities just discussed are obviously very general. Clearer support for the contribution of cognitive factors comes from a demonstration of more specific parallels between cognitive changes and social changes. Celia Brownell (1986a, 1988), for example, has attempted to identify cognitive prerequisites for the emergence of particular social relations in infancy. She focuses on two general cognitive abilities that develop across infancy: the capacity to integrate behaviors into larger combinations and the capacity to separate oneself from the environment, or Piagetian decentration. These general advances are implicated in a number of more specific cognitive changes, including language learning and object permanence. They also, according to Brownell, contribute to changes in peer relations. We saw, for example, that peer interactions become increasingly complex and reciprocal as infants develop. These changes, Brownell argues, are made possible by increases in the general capacity for sustained and integrated behavior

TABLE 16-4 ● Examples of Items Used to Assess Children's Social Problem-Solving Skills

Stimulus	Narration	Questions
Picture of one girl swinging and another girl standing nearby	This girl's name is Laurie, and this is Kathy. Laurie is five years old. Kathy is seven years old. Kathy is older than Laurie. Kathy has been on the swing for a long, long time. Laurie would really like to play on the swing.	What do you think Laurie could say or do so that she could play on the swing? If that didn't work, what else could Laurie do or say so that she could play on the swing? What do you think you would do or say if you wanted to play on the swing?
Picture of a boy riding a tricycle and a girl standing nearby	This boy's name is Bert and this girl's name is Erika. They are both five years old. Bert, the boy, has been on the tricycle for a long, long time. Erika, the girl, would like to ride the tricycle.	What do you think Erika could say or do so that she could ride the tricycle? If that didn't work, what else could Erika do or say so that she could have the tricycle? What do you think you would do or say if you wanted to ride on the tricycle?
Picture of a school setting with two girls sitting near each other	This girl's name is Kim and this is Jenny. Kim and Jenny are both five years old. They are both the same age. Kim and Jenny are in the same class at school, but this is Jenny's first day at the school. Jenny is a new girl in the class. Kim would like to get to know Jenny better.	What do you think Kim could say or do to get to know Jenny? If that didn't work, what else could Kim do or say to get to know Jenny? What do you think you would do or say to get to know Jenny?

Source: Excerpted from *The Social Problem-Solving Test—Revised* (pp. 3,4) by K.H. Rubin, 1988, Waterloo, Ontario: University of Waterloo. Copyright 1988 by K.H. Rubin. Reprinted by permission.

across infancy. Similarly, babies' play becomes less object-centered and more symbolic and more truly peer-oriented as they grow older. Changes of this sort are assumed to reflect general changes in babies' ability to decenter from the immediate environment.

We have already noted a similar argument with respect to changes in peer relations in later childhood. The cognitive ability that has been stressed most in this case is perspective taking. Children's ability to take the role of others increases steadily throughout childhood. At the same time, the ways in which children relate to others also change, and many of the changes seem to involve perspective taking. We have seen numerous examples of changes in peer relations that can be plausibly linked to advances in perspective taking—cooperative play, collaborative problem solving, games with rules, group organization, and so on.

Parallel changes of the sort just discussed are a useful source of evidence, but they are hardly definitive proof for the importance of cognitive factors. After all, *many* aspects of children's development change more or less in synchrony as children get older, and it is difficult to know what the cause-and-effect relations are. If cognitive abilities are really important for peer relations, then it should be possible to demonstrate cognitive-social links *within* an age grouping. Children who are advanced in the relevant cognitive ability should also be advanced in their peer relations.

Correlations Within Age Groupings

In a correlational study, a researcher measures two aspects of development simultaneously to see whether they are related. A researcher investigating the relationship of peer interaction and cognitive skills would direct one measure to some aspect of peer relations (such as the frequency of cooperative play) and the other to the presumed cognitive prerequisite (such as perspective taking). Support for the importance of cognitive factors would come from a significant positive correlation between cognitive ability and social development.

Many studies have looked for such correlations. The general conclusion has been that there *is* a positive relation between level of cognitive development and level of peer relations. Perspective taking has been the most frequently examined cognitive variable, and a variety of forms of perspective taking have been shown to relate to how children interact (Kurdek, 1978). Not surprisingly, measures of communication skill, both in speaking and listening, also relate positively to peer interaction (Gottman, Gonso, & Rasmussen, 1975). So do various measures of social cognition—for example, level of moral judgment (Blasi, 1980) and attributions concerning the intentions underlying behavior (Dodge, Murphy, & Buchsbaum, 1984). And so do measures of the kind of social problem-solving skills described in Table 16-4 (Rubin & Krasnor, 1986; Yeates, Schultz, & Selman, 1991). Among the aspects of peer relations that have been found to relate to cognitive development are play (Rubin & Maioni, 1975), prosocial behavior (Wentzel & Erdley, 1993), and aggression (Rubin, Bream, & Rose-Krasnor, 1991).

Although the evidence for cognitive–social links is generally positive, several cautions should be noted. First, not all of the evidence is positive; a number of studies have reported no relation between cognitive ability and behavior with peers (Kurdek, 1978; Shantz, 1983). Furthermore, when significant relations do emerge, they usually are not very large. Thus, cognitive measures account for only a modest amount of the variation in the way children behave with peers. This conclusion is perhaps not surprising. No study, after all, assesses every aspect of cognitive development that might be relevant. And no one would claim that cognitive level is the *sole* determinant of peer relations. At best it is one contributor.

One final caution concerns the conclusions that can be drawn from a significant correlation. As we discussed in Chapter 3, correlational data do not permit clear cause-and-effect conclusions. Simply knowing, for example, that perspective taking is correlated with cooperation does not allow us to conclude that perspective taking *causes* cooperation. To determine causality with certainty, we need an experimental design in which one of the variables can be experimentally manipulated. And this brings us to the final source of evidence.

Training

If cognitive advances underlie social advances, then we should expect that teaching children relevant cognitive skills will lead to changes in their social behavior as well.

Consider the hypothesized link between perspective taking and cooperation. If a causal relation exists, then training children in perspective taking should also produce gains in cooperation.

In general, the results from training studies are compatible with those from correlational research. Not all training studies produce positive results, and the effects that do occur are generally modest in magnitude. Nevertheless, most of the evidence suggests that training in relevant cognitive skills does have some effect on the way children behave with peers. Training in perspective taking, for example, has been shown to lead to decreased aggression (Chandler, 1973) and increased helpfulness and cooperation (Iannotti, 1978). Teaching children social problem-solving skills has been shown to result in improvements in prosocial behavior and general social adjustment (Weissberg, 1985).

Training studies of this sort are not only of scientific interest. Such interventions are also one way to attempt to help children who are having difficulties in social adjustment. We consequently return to training studies later, in our discussion of problems in peer relations.

Our discussion in this section has concentrated on one of the two emphases in the cognitive-developmental approach: the effects of cognitive level on social behavior. Cognitive-developmental theorists, as you may recall, also stress the reverse causal direction: the effects of social experience on children's cognitive development. In Box 16-3 we consider one form of research that reflects this second emphasis—studies of **peer tutoring** in school settings.

Peer tutoring
An educational procedure in which children act as teachers for other children.

✔ *To Recap...*

Children's peer relations undergo dramatic changes with development. Infants as young as 6 months show interest in and positive behaviors toward other infants, and as infants develop, their interactions with peers become more frequent, more complex, and more reciprocal. Such interactions are affected not only by age but by experience, a point that remains true throughout childhood.

During the preschool years, peer interactions continue to grow in frequency and complexity. Relations with peers become more differentiated, and symbolic forms of interaction begin to predominate over physical ones. Play increases in both cognitive level and social organization as cooperative play becomes increasingly likely. As they interact more and more, children become important socializing agents for each other, especially by delivering reinforcements and punishments for particular behaviors and by serving as models.

Development during the grade-school years is in part a continuation of trends present earlier. Play, for example, continues to evolve in both complexity and social organization. In addition, groups, both formal and informal, begin to assume a prominent role. Studies of children's groups reveal the importance of common interests and goals for group formation, as well as the importance of organization and agreed-upon norms for effective group functioning. Although the peer group can be an influential source of values and behavior, parents remain influential as well, and on most issues the views of peers and of parents are more similar than different.

Situational factors affect how peers interact. Aspects of the physical environment—such as the familiarity of the setting, the amount of space per child, and the nature of the available resources—can be important. The social environment also plays a role; for example, the number and familiarity of the other children present can affect how children interact.

A factor stressed especially in the cognitive-developmental approach to peer relations is the cognitive level of the child. Cognitive level is by no means a perfect predictor of peer interaction; cognitive-social relations are only sometimes found, and when they do

PEERS AS TEACHERS

A visitor to any elementary school will soon see many of the phenomena discussed in this chapter—imitation, reinforcement, group formation, play of various sorts. But the visitor will see something else as well, and that is children teaching other children. Some of the peer teaching that occurs in school is child-initiated, as children spontaneously—and perhaps furtively—help other children. Some peer teaching is hardly furtive, however, for it occurs as a deliberate part of the school curriculum. Such *peer-tutoring* efforts date back to at least the late 1700s (Gerber & Kauffman, 1981). It has been estimated that by the early 1970s, over 10,000 elementary schools had instituted some sort of peer-tutoring program (Melaragno, 1974).

Various rationales underlie the use of children as teachers of other children. Some of the arguments are derived from theory or research. Cognitive-developmental theory has offered various ideas about the role that peers might play as tutors. Especially influential has been Vygotsky's conception of the zone of proximal development, which stresses the child's ability to profit from interaction with more competent others, including peers (Damon & Phelps, 1989; Rogoff, 1990; Vygotsky, 1978). Social-learning theory and research have also contributed. Work in this tradition has shown that children can influence the behavior of other children through the models they provide and the reinforcements they dispense. Why not apply this power to the development of academic skills?

Other arguments for peer tutoring are more pragmatic. Every school system faces the perennial problem of not having the resources to do what it would like to do, perhaps especially with respect to individualizing instruction to fit the needs of particular children. The use of children as teachers is one way to try to overcome such person-power shortages.

Given the diversity of peer-tutoring programs, it is difficult to draw general conclusions about how well such programs work, especially in comparison with more traditional forms of instruction. Nevertheless, it is clear that many peer-tutoring programs have bene-

• Peer tutoring programs are a part of the curriculum in many schools. Such programs can benefit both the children being tutored and the tutors themselves.

fited those tutored, producing gains both in school performance and on standardized tests (Gerber & Kauffman, 1981; Hartup, 1983). A variety of factors can influence the success of peer tutoring. Tutoring is generally most effective when it is extended rather than brief and when the tutors have received some training in how they are supposed to teach. Children prefer tutors who are older than themselves, and tutoring is in fact usually more effective when the tutor is somewhat older. Although children also prefer tutors who are the same gender as themselves, there is no evidence that this variable affects the success of tutoring.

That tutoring has a positive effect on the children who are tutored is not surprising; they, after all, are the targets of the tutoring effort. More intriguing is the fact that tutoring can also benefit the tutors. Serving as a tutor has been shown to lead to gains in self-esteem, prosocial behavior, attitudes toward school, and academic performance (Hartup, 1983). Such gains are not always found, just as gains for those tutored are not always found. Nevertheless, the evidence suggests that one way to promote children's development may be to have them serve as teachers for other children.

occur, they are modest in magnitude. Nevertheless, three kinds of evidence suggest that cognitive factors do contribute to peer relations: parallel changes with age in the level of children's cognitive development and the complexity of their social interactions; within-age correlations between cognitive abilities and social behavior; and effects of training in relevant cognitive abilities on subsequent social behavior.

FRIENDSHIP

According to the dictionary, the word *peer* means "equal." Clearly, however, some peers (to borrow from George Orwell's *Animal Farm*) are more equal than others. Relations among peers, like peers themselves, differ. In this section, we focus on the most important peer relationship—friendship. We begin by considering what children themselves mean by the word *friend*. We then examine how friendships are formed and how friendship influences children's behavior.

Conceptions of Friendship

Consider the following answers in response to the question "What is a friend?"

"A friend is a person you like. You play around with them."

"Friends don't snatch or act snobby, and they don't argue or disagree. If you're nice to them, they'll be nice to you."

"A person who helps you do things. When you need something, they get it. You do the same for them."

"Someone you can share things with and who shares things with you. Not material things; feelings. When you feel sad, she feels sad. They understand you."

"A stable, affective, dyadic relationship marked by preference, reciprocity, and shared positive affect."

It does not take much psychological insight to guess that these answers were given by subjects of different ages—or to figure out which is the definition offered by professional researchers. In fact, the first four answers (which are drawn from studies by Rubin, 1980, and Youniss and Volpe, 1978) came from children ranging in age from 6 to 13. The last (which is from Howes, 1987b, p. 253) is typical of the way psychologists define **friendship**.

Friendship
An enduring relationship between two individuals, characterized by loyalty, intimacy, and mutual affection.

Despite their diversity, the different definitions do share some common elements. All agree that there is something special about a friend that does not apply to peers in general. All state or imply that friendship is not just any sort of relationship but a relationship of affection: friends like each other. And all acknowledge that friendship is a two-way, reciprocal process. One child may like another child, but liking alone does not make one a friend. For friendship to exist, the affection must be returned.

As the examples indicate, the presence of these common elements does not rule out the possibility that children's reasoning about friendship might change with age. At a general level, a description of the changes that occur should sound familiar, for such changes parallel more general advances in the way children think about the world (Berndt, 1988; Rawlins, 1992). Young children's thinking about friendship tends to focus on concrete, external attributes; a friend is someone who is fun to play with and who shares things. Older children are more capable of penetrating beneath the surface to take into account more abstract aspects of friendship, such as caring for another person. For young children, friendship is often a momentary state dependent on specific acts just performed or about to be performed. Older children are more likely to see friendship as an enduring relationship that persists across time and even in the face of occasional conflicts. Finally, although even young children realize the importance of mutual liking between friends, it is only in late childhood or adolescence that qualities such as loyalty and intimacy become central in children's thinking about friendship.

TABLE 16-5 ● A Stage Model of Conceptions of Friendship

Stage Level	Description	Typical Statements
Level 1 (approximately 5 to 7)	Friends are associates who are nice to me and who are fun to play with. Friendship is a temporary relationship, easily established and easily terminated.	"He's my friend because he plays with me and gives me lots of toys." "She likes me because I let her come to my house and play with me."
Level 2 (approximately 8 to 10)	Friends are people who help each other in a relationship of reciprocal trust. The friend is liked because of certain dispositions or traits and not merely because of frequent play contacts.	"A friend is someone who helps you, like if you fall down on your bike." "You do a lot for them and they do a lot for you and you can trust them."
Level 3 (approximately 11)	Friends are people who understand each other and share their innermost thoughts and feelings. Friendship is a long-term relationship based on compatibility of interest and personality.	"Someone you can talk to and tell your problems to and they understand you." "You like the same kinds of things and you can say what you want around each other."

Source: Based on information from *The Social World of the Child* by W. Damon, 1977, San Francisco: Jossey-Bass.

The kinds of findings just sketched have led to the formation of several stage models of conceptions of friendship (Damon, 1977; Keller & Wood, 1989; Selman, 1980; Youniss & Volpe, 1978). Whether changes in how children think about friendship are best conceptualized in terms of stages is still a subject of dispute (Hartup, 1992b). Nevertheless, such models provide interesting attempts to capture the major transformations in children's thinking. Table 16-5 provides an example of how one stage model conceptualizes understanding of friendship.

Determinants of Friendship

How do children become friends? The studies just considered are one relevant source of evidence, for they tell us what children themselves say is important to look for in a friend. Other common ways to study the determinants of friendship are to interview parents about their children's friends (e.g., Hayes, Gershman, & Bolin, 1980) and to observe children as they become acquainted over time (e.g., Gottman, 1983). Here, we consider two general questions about determinants: which children become friends and how friendships are formed.

Friendship Selection

Friends are not selected randomly. As they develop, children are exposed to many different people, but only a few of these potential friends ever become actual friends. On what basis are these selections made?

Studies of friendship formation show a rare unanimity in agreeing that one general factor is central to most friendship choices (Berndt, 1988; Epstein, 1986,

1989). This factor is similarity. Children tend to pick friends who are similar to themselves. Similarity is not the only basis that is used; children may sometimes seek out friends who are more popular than they (Hirsch & Renders, 1986) or who have a higher socioeconomic status (Epstein, 1983). Nevertheless, similarity seems to be a major contributor to most friendship selections.

Various kinds of similarity are important. One is similarity in age. Friendships are most common among children who are close in age. Mixed-age friendships are found, of course, especially when children move outside the same-age groupings imposed by school (Epstein, 1989). Even when not constrained by adults, however, most children tend to pick friends who are about the same age (Berndt, 1988).

Similarity in gender is also important. As we saw in Chapter 15, a preference for same-sex friends emerges in the preschool years and becomes quite strong by middle childhood. Indeed, throughout much of childhood, gender is a better predictor of friendship choices than age (Epstein, 1986). Even in adolescence, when cross-sex romantic relationships have begun to emerge, same-sex friendships continue to predominate (Hartup, 1993). Finally, still another contributor is similarity in race. As with gender, a preference for same-race friends is evident as early as preschool and generally increases with age (Fishbein & Imai, 1993). It should be noted, however, that the strength of this tendency depends on a number of factors, including the degree of integration in the school system and in the neighborhood (DuBois & Hirsch, 1990; Epstein, 1986).

Although the variables of age, gender, and race are important, they do not completely explain friendship selection. Most children encounter a number of peers who are similar to themselves in age, gender, and race; yet only some of these peers are selected as friends. What further sorts of similarity might influence this selection? Thomas Berndt (1988) suggests two. Friends tend to be similar in their orientation toward school; they show correlations, for example, in educational aspirations and achievement test scores (Ide et al., 1981). Friends also tend to be similar

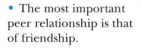

• The most important peer relationship is that of friendship.

in what Berndt labels their "orientation toward children's culture," or what they like to do outside of school (music, sports, games, and so on). In short, one reason that friends are friends is that they like to do the same sorts of things.

This last conclusion raises a question about causality. Do children become friends because they have similar interests and preferences? Or do children develop similar interests and preferences because they are friends? Answering this question requires longitudinal study, in which patterns of similarity can be traced over time, and few such studies have been carried out. There is some evidence, however, that the cause and effect flow in both directions (Epstein, 1989; Hartup, 1992c). Children who later become friends are more similar initially than children who do not become friends, indicating that similarity is indeed a determinant of friendship selection. But children who are friends become more similar over time, indicating that friendship also promotes further similarity.

A final issue with respect to friendship choices concerns their stability. Do children tend to keep the same friends over time, or is childhood friendship a more transient phenomenon? As is often the case regarding questions about stability, the answer depends on a number of factors (Berndt, 1988; Epstein, 1986). One is age. Young children's friendship choices are often only moderately stable, at best, over time—a finding in keeping with how young children reason about friendship. The stability of friendship increases as children get older. Another important factor is the stability of the environment. Fluctuations in friendship are most likely when children experience changes in their environment, as when they move to a new school. Conversely, friendships may remain quite stable when children remain together in the same setting. In one study, for example, two thirds of a sample of fourth graders retained the same best friend across the course of the school year (Berndt & Hoyle, 1985).

Friendship Formation.

Consider the following exchange:

> Interviewer: Is it easy or hard to make friends?
> Child [4 years old]: Hard, because sometimes if you wave to the other person, they might not see you wave, so it's hard to get that friend.
> Interviewer: What if they see you?
> Child: Then it's easy. (Selman & Jaquette, 1977, p. 18)

For some children, making friends may indeed be (or at least seem) this easy. Generally, however, the process is more complicated. A study by John Gottman (1983) provides an exceptionally detailed account of how children become friends.

The subjects in Gottman's research were children between the ages of 3 and 9, none of whom knew each other at the start of the study. Pairs of same-aged children were randomly formed, and each pair then met in the home of one of the children for three play sessions across a period of 4 weeks. The questions were whether the children would become friends and, if so, what the processes would be that led to friendship formation. The answer to the first question was provided by the mothers' responses to a questionnaire concerned with whether, and how strongly, their children had become friends with their new playmates. The answer to the second question came from observations of the children's behavior during the play sessions. These sessions were tape-recorded, and the children's conversations were later coded for a variety of aspects of social interaction.

Gottman found that some of the children did indeed become friends, whereas others did not. What aspects of the interaction differentiated the two groups? A variety of processes proved important. Children who became friends were more successful at establishing a *common-ground activity*—that is, agreeing on what to do—than children who did not become friends. Eventual friends showed greater *communication clarity* and were more successful at *exchanging information* than nonfriends. Eventual friends were more skillful at *resolving conflict*—an important skill, for conflict is frequent in young children's interactions. And eventual friends were more likely to engage in *self-disclosure*, or sharing of personal information about the self.

Considering its importance, the topic of friendship formation has received surprisingly little study (perhaps because of the difficulty of such study—it took several years to analyze the tapes in Gottman's research!). Nevertheless, the available evidence supports Gottman's conclusion that processes such as exchange of information and resolution of conflict are central to friendship formation (Grusec & Lytton, 1988). As we will see, processes of this sort do not disappear once a friendship has been formed. The same kinds of skills that help to build a friendship are also central to how friends interact with each other.

Behavior With Friends

That behavior is different with friends than with nonfriends seems almost part of the definition of friendship. But exactly how does behavior differ as a function of friendship? Some differences are obvious. Children spend more time with friends than with nonfriends, and they typically derive more pleasure from interacting with friends (Hartup, 1989a). Friends, clearly, are fun to be with. In this section we focus on three further areas of possible differences between friends and nonfriends.

Prosocial Behavior

As we saw in Chapter 14, the term *prosocial behavior* refers to forms of conduct that society considers desirable and whose development is thus encouraged in children. Examples of prosocial behavior include helping someone in need, comforting someone in distress, and sharing with others. It seems reasonable to expect that such clearly positive behaviors will be more likely with friends than with peers in general.

For the most part, this commonsense prediction is borne out by research. Children share more with friends than with classmates who are merely acquaintances (Jones, 1985). Cooperation in carrying out some common task is generally greater among friends than nonfriends, as is equity in dividing any rewards that are obtained (Berndt, 1981). Even as early as the preschool years, children may cooperate and share more with friends than with nonfriends (Birch & Billman, 1986; Matsumoto et al., 1986), and they are more likely to offer help to a friend in distress than to a mere acquaintance (Costin & Jones, 1992). Preschoolers also deliver reinforcements more often to friends than to peers in general (Masters & Furman, 1981).

Despite this positive evidence, not all studies find that prosocial behaviors are more likely with friends. Berndt (1986c) summarizes a series of studies in which elementary-school children actually shared less with friends than with acquaintances. According to Berndt, the critical element may be the presence of perceived competition with the friend. Research indicates that children believe friends should be equal (Tesser, 1984). Sharing too freely threatens this principle, because it may result in the friend "winning the contest" by ending up with the greater amount. Allowing a nonfriend to "win" is less threatening, and hence children are more willing to share with nonfriends. Anyone who has watched best friends compete in some contest (or can think back to his or her own such experiences) will probably agree that there is an especially strong resistance to being bested by a friend. By adolescence, this "can't let him beat me" attitude has diminished, and sharing is more likely with friends even under competitive conditions.

Conflict

We turn next to a less positive side of peer interaction. The definition psychologists give to *conflict* is a broad one: Conflict occurs "when one person does something to which a second person objects" (D.F. Hay, 1984, p. 2). The core notion is thus one of opposition between individuals, a notion conveyed by words such as *refusing, denying, objecting,* and *disagreeing* (Hartup, 1992a).

Defined this broadly, conflict is clearly a frequent component of peer interaction. Conflict is also a frequent component of interaction between friends. Indeed, in terms of sheer frequency, conflicts probably occur most often among friends (Hartup, 1992a; Shantz, 1987). In part this finding results simply from the fact that friends spend so much time together. But it also reflects the freedom and security that friends feel with each other, and thus their ability to criticize and to disagree without threatening the relationship (Hartup et al., 1993).

The important difference between friends and nonfriends, therefore, is not the probability of conflict but the ways in which the conflict is handled (Hartup et al., 1988; Laursen, 1993; Vespo & Caplan, 1993). Although exceptions certainly occur, conflicts are generally less heated among friends than among nonfriends. Friends use what Hartup (1992a) refers to as "softer" modes of managing conflict than nonfriends: They are more likely to attempt to reason with the other person and less likely to get into extended chains of disagreement. They are also more likely to resolve the conflict in an equitable, mutually satisfactory way. And they are more likely to let bygones be bygones and to continue playing together following the conflict. We saw that the ability to resolve conflicts satisfactorily plays a role in forming a

• Occasional conflicts are an inevitable part of friendship. But friends are skilled at defusing conflict and restoring positive relations.

friendship. The findings just mentioned indicate that such skills are also important for maintaining a friendship. Indeed, the ability to overcome conflict and remain close could be seen as one definition of the term *friendship*.

Intimacy

The idea that intimacy is central to friendship is expressed clearly in the fourth of the quotations we gave earlier: A friend is someone with whom to share one's innermost thoughts and feelings. The quotation that expressed this view came from a 13-year-old, and it is usually not until late childhood or adolescence that the emphasis on intimacy emerges. This emphasis is found not only in what adolescents themselves say about friendship but also in theoretical writings about adolescence. As one researcher notes, "intimacy is often treated as the prototypical feature of adolescent friendships" (Berndt, 1988, p. 167).

Do friends in fact interact in more intimate ways than nonfriends? Children's own statements about friendship provide one source of evidence. If a girl says she shares things with her best friend that she can share with no one else, there seems little reason to doubt the accuracy of her statement. In one series of studies, statements of this sort were absent among kindergarteners but were offered by approximately 40% of the sixth-grade subjects (Berndt, 1986a). Table 16-6 presents examples of items from one such self-report approach to assessing the intimacy of friendships.

Researchers have also attempted to probe the intimacy of friendships by direct observation of how friends interact. Here, however, we run into an obvious methodological problem: The presence of the observer may change the behavior being observed. It seems unrealistic to think that friends will share intimate secrets when they know that their conversation is being tape-recorded! In fact, some studies of this sort have reported few, if any, differences in the intimacy of conversations between friends and between nonfriends (Berndt, 1986b; Mettetal, 1983). Some differences do emerge, however, when observations are made in more natural set-

TABLE 16-6 ● Examples of Items From the Sharabany Intimacy Scale

Dimension of Intimacy	Sample Item[a]
1. Frankness and Spontaneity	I feel free to talk with her about almost everything.
2. Sensitivity and Knowing	I know how she feels about things without her telling me.
3. Attachment	I feel close to her.
4. Exclusiveness	I do things with her that are quite different from what other kids do.
5. Giving and Sharing	If she wants something I let her have it even if I want it, too.
6. Imposing and Taking	I can count on her help whenever I ask for it.
7. Common Activities	Whenever you see me you can be sure that she is also around.
8. Trust and Loyalty	I speak up to defend her when other kids say bad things about her.

[a]Subjects rate their extent of agreement or disagreement with each statement on a 7-point scale.

Source: Adapted from "Girlfriend, Boyfriend: Age and Sex Differences in Intimate Friendship" by R. Sharabany, R. Gershoni, and J. E. Hofman, 1981, *Developmental Psychology, 17*, p. 802. Copyright 1981 by the American Psychological Association. Adapted by permission.

tings. Children who are friends or are in the process of becoming friends are more likely than nonfriends to talk about feelings and to engage in various forms of self-disclosure (Gottman, 1983). Because this difference emerges as early as the preschool years, these data suggest that intimacy may be a characteristic of friendship long before children begin to talk about intimacy as being important. On the other hand, the frequency of such intimate disclosures does increase as children grow older (Berndt & Perry, 1990; Rotenberg & Sliz, 1988). And the importance of intimacy as a determinant of the quality of friendship is greater for adolescents than for younger children (Buhrmester, 1990; Hartup, 1993). It is worth noting that in addition to age differences there are gender differences in this aspect of friendship: Girls' friendships are characterized by a higher degree of intimacy than are those of boys (Jones & Dembo, 1989; Youniss & Smollar, 1986).

Another approach to the study of intimacy is to examine children's knowledge of their friends. If friendship is characterized by the exchange of intimate information about the self, then friends should know quite a bit about each other. In fact, children do show fairly good knowledge of their friends' characteristics, including both nonintimate information (such as their friend's phone number) and more intimate information (their friend's likes and dislikes, for example) (Diaz & Berndt, 1982; Ladd & Emerson, 1984). Table 16-7 presents examples of the kinds of questions that have been used in this research.

Does knowledge of friends change with age? Two main sorts of developmental change have been identified. The first concerns the distinction between the intimate and the nonintimate. With development comes an increase, in particular, in knowl-

TABLE 16-7 ● Questions to Test Children's Knowledge About Their Friends

External Characteristics

1. What is your friend's telephone number?
2. What is your friend's birthdate?
3. Can you tell me the first name of your friend's parents?
4. Can you tell me the name of the street where your friend lives?
5. What clubs or teams does your friend belong to?
6. Can you tell me the first name of your friend's siblings?

Preferences

7. What is your friend's favorite sport?
8. What are the foods that your friend really hates?
9. Who are the classmates your friend prefers to play with?
10. What is your friend's favorite TV show?
11. What would your friend like to be when he or she grows up?
12. What is your friend's favorite subject at school?

Personality Characteristics

13. How does your friend react when he or she is teased?
14. What does your friend worry about most?
15. What things make your friend really mad?
16. What things make your friend really proud of him/herself?
17. How does your friend usually spend his or her allowance?
18. When your friend is upset, what can you do to make him or her feel better?

Source: From "Knowledge of a Best Friend: Fact or Fancy?" by R. M. Diaz and T. J. Berndt, 1982, *Developmental Psychology, 18,* p. 790. Copyright 1982 by the American Psychological Association. Reprinted by permission.

edge of intimate information, a finding in keeping with the idea that friendships become increasingly intimate as children get older (Diaz & Berndt, 1982). The second change concerns knowledge of similarities and differences between oneself and one's friend. Even young children have a fairly good awareness of ways in which they and their friends are similar. With development, children become increasingly aware of how they and their friends are different, a potentially important kind of knowledge with respect to maintaining a friendship (Ladd & Emerson, 1984).

DEVELOPMENT IN CONTEXT: Children's Social Networks and Social Supports

Social network
The people with whom an individual regularly interacts.

Social support
Resources (both tangible and intangible) provided by other people in times of uncertainty or stress.

Consider the range of people that a typical grade-schooler encounters in the course of a week. Peers of various sorts are certain to be represented, both at school and in the neighborhood. These peers include friends of varying degrees, acquaintances (both liked and disliked), and strangers. For many children, siblings are also important, perhaps both older and younger versions. Parents, of course, are a prominent part of most children's social worlds. And other adults have roles to play—teachers, neighbors, grandparents, and other relatives.

In recent years, many psychologists have begun to move beyond the study of single relationships (such as with a parent or a friend) to attempt to encompass the entire range of interpersonal experiences just sketched. Such psychologists work with the construct of a **social network** (Belle, 1989a). A social network has been defined as "the cast of characters in an individual's social world" (Belle, 1989b, p. 1). Studies of social networks attempt to identify all of the people with whom the child regularly interacts, as well as to provide information about the frequency, the nature, and perhaps the quality of the interactions.

What is the significance of a child's social network? Most generally, the interest in social networks reflects a growing awareness of the multiple contexts, both situational and interpersonal, within which children develop (recall our discussion of Bronfenbrenner's work in Chapter 2). Studies of children's social networks, both in our society and in other cultures, confirm that most children do in fact have extensive and varied social contacts from early in life (Belle, 1989a). Furthermore, one aspect of a child's social network may influence other aspects. As we discuss shortly, for example, the quality of attachment to the parents can affect how a child relates to peers. In some cases, one part of the social network may at least partly compensate for problems with other parts. Having an intimate friend may be especially important when family relations are not going smoothly. Similarly, general difficulties within the peer group—for example, lack of popularity—may be less damaging if the child has at least one good friend to whom to turn.

The examples just given illustrate another reason to study social networks. Social networks are closely related to a topic of great current interest—**social support**. Social support refers to the resources provided by other people in times of uncertainty or stress. The support can take many forms, depending on the situation and the recipient's needs—comforting, reassuring, advising, helping, or perhaps simply "being there." An individual's social network identifies his or her potential sources of support, but the network does not guarantee that support will be forthcoming. Research with adults has shown that success in obtaining support is an important determinant of people's ability to cope in times of stress (Cohen & Wills, 1985).

What sorts of support do children receive from their social networks? Researchers have devised various methods to probe children's perception of social

• Children may receive social support from a number of sources. For many children, grandparents are an important part of the social network.

support. One ingenious technique is labeled "The Neighborhood Walk" (Bryant, 1985). With this procedure, experimenter and child take a walk around the child's neighborhood while the experimenter asks the child about the people and places he or she regularly visits and about the kinds of support the different sources provide (e.g., "Are there adults at church that you have special talks with?"). The Neighborhood Walk thus focuses on contexts that are important to the particular child, and it does so in a relaxed, natural manner that helps children to remember and to talk about their experiences. Another instrument is labeled "My Family and Friends" (Reid et al., 1989). Figure 16-2 shows the props used in the Family and Friends measure. The experimenter begins by identifying the members of the child's social network and placing their names (or perhaps photographs) on cards. Questions then are asked to determine which people provide particular kinds of support—for example, "When you want to share your feelings, which person do you go to most often?" The child responds by placing the cards in order in the tray, thus providing a rank ordering of the various support sources. A final question explores the child's satisfaction with the support: "When you talk to [specific person] about your feelings, how much better do you feel?" It is here that the barometer enters in, for children respond by moving the indicator to the marker that expresses their degree of satisfaction.

Several findings emerge from studies of children's social supports (Berndt, 1989b; Bryant, 1985; Furman & Buhrmester, 1992; Reid et al., 1989). The most gen-

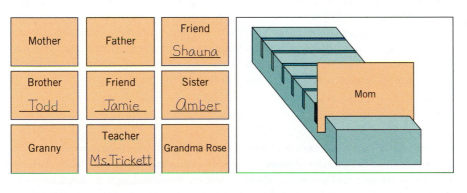
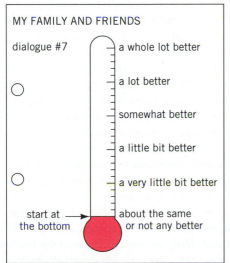
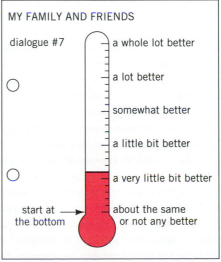

Figure 16-2 Materials used in the "My Family and Friends" measure of social support. Children indicate the relative importance of different support sources by placing the cards in order in the tray. They indicate their satisfaction with a particular source by moving the indicator on the barometer. From "My Family and Friends: Six- to Twelve-Year-Old Children's Perceptions of Social Support" by M. Reid, S. Landesman, R. Treder, and J. Jaccard, 1989, *Child Development, 60,* p. 900. Copyright 1989 by The Society for Research in Child Development, Inc. Reprinted by permission.

eral conclusion is that children, like adults, do have social supports and do benefit from them. Supports take a variety of forms. One important category is emotional support—behaviors of others that offer needed comfort or reassurance and enhance the self-esteem of the recipient. Other forms include instrumental support (provision of tangible resources to help solve practical tasks), informational support (provision of information or advice about how to cope with problems), and companionship support (sharing of activities and experiences). Just as they can take many forms, supports can come from many sources. Not surprisingly, parents tend to be the most important sources of support for most children. A variety of other sources can also be important, however, including peers, siblings, grandparents, teachers, and even pets. Children's supports change some with age: Older children's social networks and sources of support are generally more extensive and more differentiated than those of younger children. Finally, children whose support system is relatively strong tend to score better on measures of social adjustment than children to whom support is less available (Dubow et al. 1991; Ladd, 1994; Levitt, Guacci-Franco, & Levitt, 1993). As Thomas Berndt (1989b) points out, the cause and effect underlying such relations may go in both directions: Support may contribute to children's social adjustment, and children who are well adjusted may be most successful at obtaining support.

We noted that peers are one source of support for children. As would be expected, it is friends who are the most important peers in times of need. In one study, friends were ranked second only to parents as sources of emotional support, and friends headed the list when children were in need of companionship (Reid et al., 1989). As would also be expected, the value of friends as sources of support increases as children grow older (Berndt, 1989b). Older children, as we have seen, emphasize such qualities as intimacy and trust in their thinking about friendship and in their behavior with friends. It is not surprising, then, that development brings an increased tendency to turn to friends in times of need.

✔ *To Recap...*

A particularly important peer relation is friendship. Children themselves agree with this assessment; from the preschool years on, children talk about friends as being different from peers in general. Children reason about friendship in increasingly sophisticated ways as they develop. Young children tend to think of friends in concrete terms as sources of immediate pleasure; older children are more likely to see friendship as an enduring relationship characterized by attributes such as intimacy and loyalty. These changes in conceptions of friendship parallel more general changes in children's cognitive abilities.

Children tend to pick friends who are similar to themselves. Similarities in age, gender, and race have all been shown to influence selection. Similarities of a more behavioral sort also play a role; friends tend to be similar in academic orientation, and they often share the same outside-of-school interests. Studies of friendship formation suggest that a variety of processes contribute, including exchange of information, self-disclosure, and successful resolution of conflict.

Behavior with friends differs from that with nonfriends in a number of ways. Prosocial behaviors, such as sharing and helping, are generally more common with friends (although not always, because perceived competition sometimes leads to reduced sharing with a friend). Although conflict does not disappear once a friendship has been formed, resolution of conflict is generally more successful among friends than among nonfriends. Finally, sharing of intimate information is more likely among friends, and the importance of intimacy for friendship increases as children get older. Friends eventually become an integral part of most children's social networks, and friends can be an important source of social support in times of need.

POPULARITY AND PROBLEMS

Our emphasis thus far has been on general processes in peer relations and general changes that accompany development. But peer relations do not follow a single general pattern. For some children, life in the peer group is a good deal more enjoyable and fulfilling than for others. In this section, our focus shifts to individual differences in the quality of peer relations. We begin with the more positive side and the question of popularity. We then move on to the various kinds of problems in peer relations that some children develop.

Popularity

Before we can explore where differences in peer relations come from, we must know what the differences are. A first question, therefore, concerns measurement. How can we determine which children are doing well in the peer group and which children are not?

Measuring Popularity

The most common approach to assessing popularity has been to ask children themselves, the assumption being that a child's peers should be the best judges of that child's standing among peers. Such peer-based evaluations of social standing are referred to as **sociometric techniques** (Asher & Hymel, 1981; Terry & Coie, 1991). Researchers have used a variety of specific sociometric approaches (and conclusions vary to some extent depending on the approach used). In the *nomination technique*, the child is asked to name some specific number of well-liked peers—for example, "Tell me the names of three kids in the class you especially like." The technique can also be directed to negative relations: "Tell me the names of three kids in the class you don't like very much." In the *rating-scale technique*, the child is asked to rate each of his or her classmates along the dimension of interest. The child might be asked, for example, to rate each classmate on a 5-point scale ranging from "really like to play with" to "really don't like to play with." Finally, in the *paired-comparison technique*, the child is presented with the names of two classmates at a time and asked to pick the one that he or she likes better. Because all pairs are eventually presented, the technique yields an overall measure of liking for each target child.

What is the evidence that sociometric measures yield a valid picture of a child's social standing? In a sense, this question might seem a silly one to ask: If a child is rated as "liked" by everyone in the class, what better measure of popularity might we hope to find? Sociometric techniques, after all, focus directly on what we are trying to determine—what the peer group thinks of the child. Nevertheless, the uncertainty of verbal-report measures with children, especially young children, makes it necessary to ask whether such techniques correlate with other ways of assessing a child's social standing. The answer is that they do. Sociometric scores correlate with teacher ratings of popularity or social competence—that is, the children who are identified by their peers as well liked also tend to be the ones whom teachers identify as popular (Green et al., 1980). Sociometric scores also correlate with direct observations of children's social interactions (Bukowski & Hoza, 1989). Even socio-

Sociometric techniques Procedures for assessing children's social status based on evaluations by the peer group. Sociometric techniques may involve ratings of degree of liking, nominations of liked or disliked peers, or forced-choice judgments between pairs of peers.

metric assessments by children as young as preschool age show correlations with such external measures and thus some evidence of validity (Denham & McKinley, 1993; Hymel, 1983).

Determinants of Popularity

However it is measured, *popularity* is easy to define. A popular child is one who is well liked by his or her peers. In terms of sociometric techniques, such children receive high ratings and are the objects of many positive and few, if any, negative choices. These children are sometimes referred to as the "stars" in sociometric classification systems (Gronlund, 1959). But what underlies such star status?

Some examinations of this question have focused on relatively indirect predictors of popularity. Birth order, for example, has been found to relate to popularity. Last-born children tend to be more popular than middle-borns or first-borns (Miller & Maruyama, 1976). (It should be recognized, of course, that there are plenty of exceptions to this and to all of the other on-the-average findings that we present.) Hartup (1983) suggests an explanation for this finding. Last-born children may have the greatest need to develop interpersonal skills within the family (such as tolerance, and persuasiveness), and these skills continue to serve them when they interact with peers. Intellectual ability also relates to popularity. Both IQ scores (Roff, Sells, & Golden, 1972) and measures of academic performance (Green et al., 1980) have been found to correlate with sociometric ratings.

That intellectual ability relates to popularity is perhaps not surprising, given the importance of the school as a context for observations of peers. Other correlates of popularity are perhaps less easily explained. Physical attractiveness shows a relation. On the average, relatively attractive children (as rated either by adults or by children themselves) are more popular than relatively unattractive children (Dion & Berscheid, 1974). Even children's names relate to how popular they are. In one study, one sample of grade-school children rated the attractiveness of the names possessed by a second sample of children. Even though the first group did not know the second, these attractiveness ratings showed a moderately strong correlation with measures of popularity within the second sample (McDavid & Harari, 1966). Thus, children with more attractive (and, in general, less offbeat) names tended to be more popular.

Why should one's physical attractiveness or one's name relate to popularity? No one knows. In the case of names, there are at least two possible explanations. One is that children with offbeat names are subject to ridicule, resulting in lowered self-esteem and loss of popularity. The other is that parents who give their children offbeat names treat them unusually in other ways as well, resulting in lowered social competence (Hartup, 1983). Research to date has not distinguished between these two possibilities. An intriguing suggestion with respect to the variable of attractiveness is that attractive and unattractive children may actually behave differently. In one study, 5-year-olds rated as unattractive showed more aggression and were more boisterous in their play than their more attractive counterparts (Langlois & Downs, 1979). Thus, part of the reason for the unattractive child's social problems may lie in the child's behavior. On the other hand, there is also ample evidence that both adults and children in U.S. society tend to hold a "beauty is good" stereotype, evaluating attractive individuals positively even in the absence of objective evidence (Ritts, Patterson, & Tubbs, 1992). Part of the reason may thus lie in stereotyped expectations about what attractive and unattractive people are like.

As noted, the research we have considered thus far has concerned relatively indirect predictors of popularity. We turn next to direct measures of behavior.

Presumably, popular children become popular because they behave in ways that other children find attractive. What do we know about behavioral contributors to popularity?

In general, the behavioral correlates of popularity are not at all surprising. Popular children tend to be friendly, socially visible, outgoing in their behavior, and reinforcing in their interactions with others (Newcomb, Bukowski, & Pattee, 1993). At a more specific level, three sets of skills seem to be especially important for popularity (Asher, Renshaw, & Hymel, 1982). Popular children are skilled at *initiating interaction* with other children. They enter ongoing groups smoothly and they set about making friends in a carefully paced but confident manner, not forcing themselves on other children but also not giving up at the slightest rebuff. Popular children are also skilled at *maintaining interaction.* They reinforce other children, show sensitivity to the needs and wishes of others, and communicate effectively in the role of both speaker and listener. Finally, popular children are skilled at *resolving conflict.* The popular child knows how to defuse touchy situations in ways agreeable to all parties, using reasoning rather than force and drawing on general principles of fairness and general rules for how people should interact.

This list of contributors to popularity should sound familiar. The kinds of social skills that help make a child popular are the same sorts of skills that we saw are important for forming and maintaining friendships. The concurrence is what we would expect: Popular children are children who have the qualities desirable in a friend.

Problems in Peer Relations

Popularity is the bright side of the sociometric picture. But not everyone is popular, and not everyone develops satisfactory friendships. Problems in peer relations are a topic not only of scientific interest but also of great practical importance in the lives of many children.

Measuring Problems

The techniques used to assess problems in children's relations with their peers are the same ones used to measure popularity. Indeed, the two constructs are often measured at the same time in the same sample; after all, not everyone can be a "star," and some children will come out at the negative end in any assessment of social standing. Sociometric techniques are therefore again prominent. Teacher assessments and direct observations of behavior are also sometimes used (Schneider, Rubin, & Ledingham, 1985).

Much debate in the study of social problems has concerned not the initial assessments but how to classify children based on these assessments. Popularity, as we saw, is easy to define. Problems, however, can take many forms, and different investigators have proposed different classification systems (Asher & Coie, 1990; Newcomb et al., 1993). One often used system distinguishes rejected children, neglected children, and controversial children. A **rejected child** is one who receives few positive but many negative nominations from his or her peers. The rejected child seems to be actively disliked. A **neglected child**, in contrast, is one who receives few nominations of any sort, positive or negative, from peers. The neglected child seems to be less disliked than ignored. Finally, the **controversial child**, as the name suggests, receives a mixed evaluation from the peer group, earning both many positive and many negative nominations. The rejected–neglected–controversial distinction has been the focus of much research, and so we begin by reviewing

Rejected child
A child who receives few positive and many negative nominations in sociometric assessments by his or her peers. Such children seem to be disliked by the peer group.

Neglected child
A child who receives few nominations of any sort, positive or negative, in sociometric assessments by his or her peers. Such children seem to be ignored by the peer group.

Controversial child
A child who receives both many positive and many negative nominations in sociometric assessments by his or her peers.

findings concerning these three groups. As we go, however, we also note some qualifications to the general conclusions, as not all children with problems fall clearly into one of these categories.

Determinants of Problems

We have already discussed the kinds of social skills that seem to underlie popularity. This work gives us a start toward understanding the source of problems in peer relations. Children who develop problems fall well short of the level of social skills that popular children show. But rejected children and neglected children fall short in somewhat different ways.

Studies of the behavior of rejected children suggest several ways in which the rejected child's behavior may contribute to his or her social difficulties (Cillessen et al., 1992; Coie, Dodge, & Kupersmidt, 1990; Dodge et al., 1990). Probably the most consistent correlate of peer rejection is aggression. Peers report, and behavioral observations confirm, that many rejected children are well above average in levels of aggression. More generally, rejected children often show behavior that is antisocial, inappropriate to the situation at hand, and disruptive of ongoing group activities. Their attempts to enter new groups or to make new friends tend to be especially maladroit, consisting of overly intrusive and even bizarre overtures whose outcome, predictably, is exactly the opposite of their intent (Putallaz & Wasserman, 1990).

The picture for neglected children is different (Coie & Kupersmidt, 1983). Neglected children are often perceived by their peers as being shy. This perception is not surprising, in that neglected children are less talkative and less socially active than children in general. Compared with most children, neglected children make fewer and more hesitant attempts to enter groups and to make new friends. And neglected children give up quickly when their tentative and not very skilled efforts do not meet with success.

As befits their in-between sociometric status, controversial children typically show a mixture of positive and negative social behaviors (Newcomb et al., 1993). Like rejected children, controversial children tend to rank high on measures of aggression. But they also, like popular children, tend to score high on measures of sociability.

The patterns just described reflect typical, on-the-average differences among groups of children. As such, they do not apply to all rejected or neglected children. Only some neglected children, for example, show the shy behavioral style just described; others are indistinguishable in their behaviors from sociometrically average children (Rubin et al., 1989). Similarly, only some rejected children seem to earn their status through high aggression and lack of control; for others, social withdrawal appears to be a more important contributor (French, 1988, 1990). Some researchers have argued, in fact, that **social withdrawal**—that is, self-imposed isolation from the peer group—can be an important problem in itself, even in the absence of rejection or neglect (Asendorpf, 1990; Rubin, 1993; Rubin, LeMare, & Lollis, 1990). Finally, not all unpopular children are totally lacking in friends. As we saw in Chapter 14, aggressive, rejected children, in particular, may have a small set of close, long-term friends. These children are not generally liked by the peer group, however, and the friends they do have are often other aggressive children who are more likely to maintain than to moderate their antisocial behavior (Cairns et al., 1988).

The response of peers can be important more generally to the problems of the unpopular child. Children develop reputations within the peer group (fools around in class, hits other kids, never wants to play). Research reveals that these

Social withdrawal
Self-imposed isolation from the peer group.

reputations are to some extent self-perpetuating—that is, the unpopular child's behavior may be interpreted in negative ways by peers, even when the behavior does not fit the expectation (Hymel, Wagner, & Butler, 1990). Clearly, such effects make the task of winning peer acceptance even more difficult.

The message from this discussion is that problems in peer relations can take many forms and can have many sources. Despite their diversity, however, the various problems may have a common underlying core. The common element that has been proposed is a cognitive one. Earlier we reviewed evidence indicating that social-cognitive skills are important for successful peer relations. Children with social problems may acquire their status because they lack such skills. Simply put, such children do not know how to make or maintain friends.

Research to investigate the hypothesis that cognitive deficits underlie social problems is similar to the research discussed earlier in the chapter under the heading "Cognitive Contributions." Again, the literature is mixed. Not all studies find relations between cognitive and social skills, and when relations do emerge, they are seldom large (Crick & Dodge, 1994; Dodge & Feldman, 1990). It is clear that cognitive deficits are at best only one contributor to problems in peer relations. A variety of studies suggest, however, that cognitive problems do indeed contribute. Unpopular children are often lower in perspective-taking skills than their more popular peers (Jennings, 1975). Rejected children have difficulty in judging the intentions behind the behavior of others, a deficiency that may contribute to their high levels of aggression (Dodge, 1986; Quiggle et al., 1992). And both rejected and neglected children show deficits in the kind of social problem-solving skills illustrated in Table 16-4 (Rubin & Krasnor, 1986; Rubin & Rose-Krasnor, 1992). This finding makes sense, because the kinds of solutions such dilemmas call for are precisely the behaviors that rejected and neglected children fail to show.

Interventions

Can children with problems in peer relations be helped by intervention programs? Before we attempt intervention, it is important to ask about the stability of such problems. Perhaps children who have difficulties in relating to peers early in childhood will simply outgrow their problem as they get older—become less shy or less aggressive, for example. If so, there may be little point in intervening.

Longitudinal studies indicate that children with problems do *not* automatically outgrow them (Coie et al., 1992; Dodge, 1993; Kupersmidt, Coie, & Dodge, 1990; Rubin, 1993). Some, of course, do; early peer status is no more perfectly predictive of later development than is any other early childhood measure. For many children, however, early rejection or neglect or withdrawal does predict continuing rejection or neglect or withdrawal. The category of rejection is especially stable over time. And rejected children are the ones who are at greatest risk for a number of problems later in life, including juvenile delinquency, dropping out of school, and mental illness (Coie & Cillessen, 1993; Parker & Asher, 1987). Although less is known about the long-term consequences of early social withdrawal, recent evidence suggests that withdrawn children are also at risk for later problems (Rubin & Asendorpf, 1993).

A variety of intervention approaches have been tried (LaGreca, 1993; Ramsey, 1991; Schneider et al., 1985). Some are grounded in social-learning theory. Modeling, for example, has been used in an attempt to increase social skills and social acceptance (Schunk, 1987). Shaping of desirable social behaviors through reinforcement has also been explored (O'Connor, 1972). Other approaches have their origins in cognitive-developmental theory. Included in this category are attempts to improve peer relations through teaching perspective-taking skills (Chandler, 1973) and through training in social problem-solving abilities (Pepler, King, & Byrd, 1991; Selman & Schultz, 1990; Urbain & Kendell, 1980). Still other approaches are more eclectic, encompassing a number of different training techniques in an attempt to promote the needed social skills (Mize & Ladd, 1990).

Intervention efforts do have beneficial effects (Asher, 1985; Erwin, 1993; Schneider & Byrne, 1985). Indeed, all of the approaches sketched in the preceding paragraph have yielded positive results, including effects on both the social skills being taught and the subsequent sociometric status. These effects are, to be sure, limited in various ways in research to date. Not all children benefit from intervention, and at present we know little about the long-term impact of such programs. Nevertheless, the picture is an encouraging one. Especially heartening is the fact that rejected children, the group that may be most at risk for later problems, can be helped through intervention to improve their social status (Asher, 1985). It is interesting to note that one technique that has proved especially effective with such children is training in academic skills (Coie & Krehbiel, 1984). Apparently, the improvement in the rejected child's academic performance has a beneficial impact on the child's self-concept and general classroom behavior, changes that in turn affect how the peer group evaluates the child. (See Box 16-4 for a discussion of peer-based intervention programs.)

✔ To Recap...

Children show important individual differences in the quality of their peer relations. Typically, such differences have been assessed through sociometric techniques—judgments offered by the child's peers. Children are defined as popular if they are the objects of many positive and few negative judgments.

Studies of the determinants of popularity have explored both relatively indirect predictors and more direct behavioral correlates. Variables in the first category that correlate (although far from perfectly) with popularity include birth order, intellectual ability, physical attractiveness, and name. The behavioral skills that seem to distinguish popular from less popular children are of three sorts: skill in initiating interaction, skill in maintaining interaction, and skill in resolving conflict.

Sociometric assessments also identify children with problems in peer relations. The rejected child receives few positive but many negative nominations from the peer group, whereas the controversial child receives many choices in both categories and the neglected child receives few nominations of any sort. Both rejected and neglected children show deficits in social skills, although their behavioral problems take different forms. Many (although not all) rejected children are characterized by aggressive, antisocial, and inappropriate behavior, whereas many (although again not all) neglected children are characterized by shy and withdrawn behavior. Although problems in peer relations are often predictive of continuing difficulties, intervention programs have produced improvements in both social skills and sociometric status.

THE FAMILY

For most children, the family and the peer group are the two most important microsystems within which development occurs. In this final section of the chapter we consider how these two major social worlds relate. We begin by examining how children's relations with their siblings compare with their peer relations. We then explore the contribution of parents to children's peer relations.

PEERS AS THERAPISTS

Whatever specific social skills are stressed, most intervention programs are similar in the general teaching model they adopt—a model in which an adult teaches a child. By definition, however, the unpopular child's problems concern behavior with peers, and whatever skills are acquired through intervention will eventually need to be applied in the peer group. Perhaps peers can be made part of the change process from the start.

A number of peer-based intervention programs have been developed in recent years (Kohler & Strain, 1990). According to Odom and Strain (1984), such programs can be divided into three types. In a *proximity intervention*, socially competent children are placed with the target children and instructed to play with them and try to elicit play in return. The peer "therapists" are not given any special training; rather, the hope is that a natural transmission of social skills will occur when more competent children interact with less competent ones. In a *prompt-and-reinforce intervention*, in contrast, children are trained to behave in specific ways that will help unpopular children learn social skills. The behaviors include prompts to engage in some social activity (e.g., "Come play") and reinforcements for desired response (e.g., "I like to play with you"). Finally, a *peer-mediated intervention* also involves training of the intervention agents—the socially competent children—but in this case the emphasis is on the production of more general social overtures, which may elicit a variety of social responses from the target children. Such social overtures might include sharing a toy, initiating a game, or suggesting a new play idea.

Each of these three general approaches has been shown to have some success in promoting social skills. Perhaps not surprisingly, the more focused techniques have generally worked better than the simple exposure of the proximity approach (Odom & Strain, 1984). Beneficial effects have been demonstrated not only for children of low sociometric status but for a variety of other groups (such as children with mental retardation or autism) as well. Interestingly, there is evidence that benefits may occur not just for the targets of the interventions but for the peer therapists themselves (Kohler et al., 1989)—something that we saw is also true with peer tutoring. Finally, there is evidence that at least some of the gains from intervention hold up across settings and over short periods of time. To date, however, the evidence for long-term benefits from peer-based interventions remains limited—as, indeed, is the case for intervention efforts in general. The question of whether intervention programs in childhood can prevent social problems later in life remains an important challenge for future research.

Siblings and Peers

Much like the topic of peer relations, the topic of siblings has enjoyed a resurgence of research interest in recent years (Boer & Dunn, 1992; Brody & Stoneman, 1994; Hetherington, Reiss, & Plomin, 1994; Mendelson, 1990). We have already mentioned some of the ways in which siblings can affect development—the effects on intellectual development stressed in the confluence model, for example (Chapter 10), or the contribution of older siblings to children's language development (Chapter 11). We focus here on questions relevant to the present chapter: How do sibling relations compare with peer relations, and how does experience with siblings contribute to behavior with peers?

There are both obvious similarities and obvious differences in children's relations with their siblings and their relations with their peers, especially friends. On the one hand, both sibships and friendships are intimate, long-lasting relationships that are the context for frequent and varied interactions—interactions that are usually positive in tone but can include moments of conflict and rivalry as well. Both relationships involve partners who are close in age, and hence interactions are likely to be more egalitarian and symmetrical than interactions with adults, such as parents or teachers. On the other hand, siblings (unless they are twins) are not identical in age, and the younger–older contrast introduces a basic asymmetry not necessarily found with friends. Furthermore, siblings, unlike friends, are not together by choice and they do not have the option of terminating the relationship if negative aspects begin to outweigh positive. As one researcher puts it, "siblings do not choose each other, very often do not trust or even like each other, and may be competing strongly for parental affection and interest; the sources of conflict and hostility in this relationship are likely to be very different from those leading to tension in a friendship" (Dunn, 1992, p. 7).

This analysis suggests that we should expect some similarity—but hardly perfect similarity—between sibling relations and peer relations. And this, in fact, is what research shows. Let us first consider some similarities. Siblings clearly can perform the same roles and fulfill the same needs as we have seen are important among friends—as objects of pleasure or companionship, for instance, or as sources of affection, or as confidants for intimate interchanges (Buhrmester, 1992). Less positively, siblings, like friends, may also sometimes be targets for hostility and conflict; especially among younger children, conflicts among siblings are a depressingly familiar experience for many parents (Dunn, 1993). Some conflict is inevitable in any long-term, intimate relationship, and sibships, like friendships, are no exception to this rule.

Along with these general similarities in sibling and peer relations come differences. Some differences follow from the differences in age between siblings and the contrasting roles played by the younger and older child. Older siblings usually take the lead in dealings with their younger siblings, initiating both more positive and more negative actions and generally directing the course of the interaction; younger siblings, in turn, are more likely to give in to and to imitate their older partner (Teti, 1992). Such asymmetry does lessen with age, however, and by adolescence the relations between siblings are typically more egalitarian; now the younger sibling is sometimes the dominant member, and now the younger sibling

• Both conflict and cooperation are frequent components of sibling interaction.

is the one who provides nurturance or help (Buhrmester & Furman, 1990). Another change that is evident by adolescence—and another contrast between siblings and friends—is a decline in the relative importance of siblings as sources of intimacy or help; as friends come to play these roles more often, children have less need to turn to their siblings for emotional or instrumental support (Buhrmester & Furman, 1990). Finally, the domain of conflict reveals differences as well as similarities between sibling relations and peer relations. Although conflicts occur in both relationships, they tend to be more frequent between siblings than between friends (Buhrmester, 1992) and they also take somewhat different forms in the two contexts. Children are less likely to reason with siblings than with friends, less likely to attempt to take the sibling's point of view, and more likely to judge perceived transgressions negatively when the perpetrator is a sibling (Dunn, 1993; Rafaelli, 1991; Slomkowski & Dunn, 1993). This more negative quality of sibling conflicts may reflect the forced, "not chosen" nature of the sibling relationship.

Our discussion thus far has concerned general similarities or differences between sibling relations and peer relations. But it is also important to ask about *within-child* links between the two social worlds. Does a particular child tend to show the same sorts of behaviors with peers as he or she shows with siblings? And does the overall quality of a child's peer relations mirror the quality of relations with siblings?

The answer, once again, turns out to be of the "sometimes but not always" sort (Dunn & McGuire, 1992). Research makes clear that there is no simple, direct carryover of relations forged with siblings to relations with peers. Indeed, some examinations of the issue report little if any association between how children behave with siblings and how they behave with peers (Abramovitch et al., 1986; Berndt & Bulleit, 1985). Such findings demonstrate, once again, the importance of context for children's behavior—what we see in one social context does not necessarily hold true when we move to a different context. In other studies sibling–peer connections do emerge, but they are seldom strong. As we might expect, links tend to be greater with friendship (another intense, dyadic relationship) than with peer relations in general (Stocker & Dunn, 1990). In some cases the direction of the relation is positive. For example, studies have shown positive correlations between cooperation with siblings and cooperation with friends (Stocker & Mantz-Simmons, 1993), as well as between aggression with siblings and aggression toward peers (Vandell et al., 1990). In other cases the direction is negative. For example, children with relatively hostile sibling relations sometimes form especially close friendships (Stocker & Dunn, 1990); similarly, children who are unpopular with peers may rank high on affection and companionship with their siblings (East & Rook, 1992). What seems to be happening in these cases is a kind of compensation: When one component of children's social networks is unsatisfactory, they may try especially hard to obtain pleasure and support from other components.

A general conclusion to take away from these studies is that growing up with siblings can affect a number of aspects of children's development, including their behavior with peers. The links between siblings and peers are neither simple nor inevitable, however, and in any case experience with siblings is just one contributor to how children fare with peers. We turn next to another potentially important contributor: parents' child-rearing practices.

Parents and Peers

The question to be examined now is one of interest to any parent: What do parents do that helps or hinders their children's success with peers? The answer, we will see, is that parents do a variety of things that can be important (Dunn, 1993; Parke & Ladd, 1992; Putallaz & Heflin, 1990).

Parents' contribution to peer relations can begin very early in life, before most children have even begun to interact with peers. As we saw in Chapter 12, infants differ in the security of the attachments they form with the caregiver, and these differences in turn relate to the sensitivity and responsiveness of caregiving practices. As we also saw in Chapter 12, secure attachment in infancy is associated with a number of positive outcomes in later childhood, including various aspects of peer relations. Children who were securely attached as infants tend to do well on measures of social competence and popularity later in childhood (Elicker, Englund, & Sroufe, 1992; LaFreniere & Sroufe, 1985). Security of attachment is also related to quality of friendships; children with a history of secure attachment tend to form more harmonious and well-balanced friendships than do children with less satisfactory attachments (Park & Waters, 1989; Youngblade & Belsky, 1992). Although most studies to date have examined outcomes in preschool or grade-school children, recent research indicates that some links between infant attachment and social competence are evident even in adolescence (Englund, Reed, & Sroufe, 1993).

Parents may also contribute to the development of the forms of play that occupy such a central position in children's early interactions with their peers. Before they embark on pretend or dramatic play with peers, many children have spent dozens of hours engaged in such play with their mothers and fathers at home. Observational studies verify that joint pretend play is a frequent activity in many households and that parents (mothers in particular in these studies) often assume an active and directive role in such play (Haight & Miller, 1992, 1993; O'Reilly & Bornstein, 1993). Especially among toddlers or young preschoolers, it is often the mother who initiates and provides the content for play episodes, and play with the mother tends to be more complex and more sustained than does play alone. With development, the initiative and direction gradually shift to the child, and peers come to supplant parents as play partners.

It is interesting to note that there may be cultural differences in the extent to which parents structure children's early play. Active participation by mothers has been found mostly with middle-class Western samples. Researchers who have ex-

• Parents are important contributors to the emergence of play and to the development of peer relations. But the kinds of experiences that parents provide may vary across different cultural settings.

amined other cultural contexts report less maternal interest in and involvement with children's early play (Farver, 1993; Farver & Howes, 1993; Rogoff et al., 1993). This finding does not reflect a general lack of involvement on the mothers' part, but rather a difference in focus that reflects a difference in cultural circumstances and cultural goals. In non-Western settings, children are often involved in the activities of the adult community from early in life, and parents are more likely to teach and to model culturally desired behaviors than to serve as play partners. As one research team summarizes the difference, in the United States mothers and children play together with baby dolls; in Mexico, children help their mothers take care of real babies (Farver & Howes, 1993).

Parents' involvement in early play represents a relatively indirect contribution to eventual peer relations. Parents may also take a more direct role in promoting and managing their children's encounters with peers. Ladd (1992) identifies four ways in which parents may influence the frequency and nature of peer interactions: (a) as "designers" of the child's environment, parents make choices that affect the availability of peers and the settings (such as a safe versus a hazardous neighborhood) within which peer interactions take place; (b) as "mediators," parents arrange peer contacts for their children and regulate their choice of play partners; (c) as "supervisors," parents monitor their children's peer interactions and offer guidance and support; and finally, (d) as consultants, parents provide more general advice and emotional support with respect to peer relations, especially in response to questions and concerns from the child. Research indicates that parents vary in the frequency and the skill with which they perform these various roles and that these variations in parental behavior in turn relate to variations in children's peer relations (Ladd & Coleman, 1993; Ladd, Profilet, & Hart, 1992; Lollis, Ross, & Tate, 1992). It has been found, for example, that peer acceptance in the preschool is related to the extent to which parents initiate play opportunities for their children (Ladd & Hart, 1992). Play among children, especially toddlers or preschoolers, proceeds more smoothly and happily when a parent is present to facilitate and direct (Bhavnagri & Parke, 1991). And play opportunities are more frequent and friendship networks larger when children grow up in safe neighborhoods with closely spaced houses than when conditions are less conducive to peer interaction (Medrich et al., 1982).

Although the kinds of direct management just discussed can undoubtedly be important, most attempts to identify the parental contribution to peer relations have focused on general child-rearing strategies that either nurture or fail to nurture the social skills necessary for success with peers. Several dimensions emerge as important (Cassidy et al., 1992; Parke et al., 1992; Putallaz & Heflin, 1990). One consistent correlate of sociometric status and social skills is parental warmth (MacDonald, 1992). Children who come from homes that are characterized by high levels of warmth, nurturance, and emotional expressiveness tend to do well in the peer group; conversely, children whose home lives are less harmonious are at risk for peer problems as well. The extreme of the latter situation comes in cases of physical abuse or neglect. Children who have been abused show special difficulty in responding appropriately when peers exhibit signs of distress (Klimes-Dougan & Kistner, 1990). Children who have been maltreated also show heightened levels of aggressiveness and social withdrawal (Mueller & Silverman, 1989). Not surprisingly, abused children tend to fare poorly on sociometric measures, and their unskilled behavior with peers often perpetuates their difficulties (Cicchetti et al., 1992; Salzinger et al., 1993).

The parent's methods of controlling and disciplining the child can also be important (Dekovic & Janssens, 1992; Dishion, 1990; Hart et al., 1992). Parents of popular children tend to be intermediate in the degree of control that they exert, neither rigidly directing the child's every action nor allowing too much leeway because of lack of time or interest. Such parents are involved in the lives of their children, but the goal of their socialization seems to be to promote autonomy and not merely immediate compliance. When discipline becomes necessary, parents of popular children tend to prefer verbal rather than physical methods, reasoning with the child and negotiating rather than imposing solutions. In contrast, techniques of power assertion (threats, and physical punishment) are likely to characterize the home lives of children with peer problems.

As Putallaz and Heflin (1990) note, these conclusions about the contribution of parents to peer relations should not sound new or surprising. They fit, rather, with general conclusions about the effects of parental practices on children's social development. They are reminiscent, therefore, of evidence that we discussed in the preceding chapters with regard to parents' contributions to their children's prosocial behavior, or level of aggressiveness, or self-concept. The main way in which parents affect their children's success with peers is by promoting (or failing to promote) attributes that are important to peer interaction. The conclusions also fit with what we would expect from theory. Support for cognitive-developmental positions is evident in the value of rational, cognitively oriented techniques of control and discipline. Support for social-learning theory can be seen in the clear role of parental reinforcements and parental models in fostering social skills. Indeed, the importance of parents as models is perhaps the clearest conclusion to be drawn from studies of the family's contribution to peer relations. Parents who are warm and friendly and effective with others have children who are warm and friendly and effective with others.

✔ To Recap...

Experiences within the family are one contributor to children's behavior with friends. Siblings are in many respects similar to peers as social objects, and sibling relations show many of the characteristics important in relations with peers, especially friends. Sibships and friendships are different in some respects, however, and specific qualities of sibling relations are only sometimes reflected in relations with peers.

Parents can contribute to their children's behavior with peers in a number of ways. Secure attachment to the parent during infancy is associated with positive peer relations in later childhood. Parents' participation in early pretend play may facilitate the emergence of play with peers. Both the frequency and the nature of peer interactions may be affected by various parental actions, ranging from choice of neighborhood to direct initiation and management of peer encounters. Finally, parents' child-rearing practices can help instill the social skills necessary for success in the peer group. Among the parental practices that can be beneficial are creation of a warm and supportive family atmosphere, use of cognitively oriented techniques of discipline, and provision of models of socially appropriate actions in the parents' own behavior.

CONCLUSION

The topic of peer relations is a good one with which to conclude our survey of the modern science of child psychology, because in considering how peers relate to and affect each other we can see again many of the themes and issues that we have encountered throughout this book. The influence of the three major theoretical perspectives is again evident; indeed, much of the contemporary interest in peer relations can be traced to the emergence of the cognitive-developmental, social-learning, and ethological positions. Issues that are fundamental to child psychology in general, such as the nature versus nurture debate and the continuity of early and later development, are also central to the study of peer relations. And the methodological approaches that characterize child psychology are all represented in the study of peer relations: laboratory studies, naturalistic observations, questionnaires and interviews, experimental and correlational designs.

The topic is representative in another respect as well. The advances in our understanding of peer relations in just the last dozen or so years have been truly remarkable. We know much more than we used to, for example, about the ways in which peers influence each other, and about the importance of friendship in children's development, and about links between cognitive abilities and social abilities. We have also made great progress with respect to the pragmatically important question of how to identify and help children who are having problems with peers. At the same time, there is still much to be learned about almost every topic we have considered. The power of the scientific approach is verified daily in the study of child psychology. But the mysteries of human development yield their secrets slowly.

FOR THOUGHT AND DISCUSSION

1. Each of the major theoretical positions emphasizes the role of peers in children's development. *But is experience with peers necessary for development? Imagine a scenario in which a child is reared solely in the company of loving and sensitive adults. Could such a child develop normally? Why or why not?*

2. Consider the discussion of age changes in the social organization of children's play (onlooker, solitary, parallel, associative, cooperative). *Do you think that the popularity of video games promotes or hinders the development of more mature levels of social organization during play? Why? How would you study this question?*

3. Consider the topic of friendship selection. *Suppose you wished to determine how a group of kindergartners select playmates. How would you go about finding out? If you asked the children directly, what would you ask?*

4. Research indicates that initial similarity between children is one basis for friendship selection but that friends also become more similar over time. *Think about your own friendships, either past or present. To what extent have you sought out friends who were similar to yourself, and to what extent have you and your friends grown more similar across the course of the relationship?*

5. We noted that social withdrawal—that is, self-imposed isolation from the peer group—can pose serious problems for children's social development. *Consider the problem of social withdrawal from the perspective of social learning theory. How might a social learning theorist explain the development of social withdrawal? What steps might such a theorist advocate to help a withdrawn child become more socially accepted?*

6. We have seen that family members influence children's peer relations. *But does the reverse occur? In what ways could experience with peers affect a child's relations with parents and siblings?*

GLOSSARY

AB̄ error Infants' tendency to search in the original location where an object was found rather than in the most recent hiding place. A characteristic of stage 4 of object permanence.

academic self-concept The part of self-esteem involving children's perceptions of their aca-demic abilities.

accommodation Changing existing cognitive structures to fit with new experiences. One of the two components of adaptation in Piaget's theory.

adaptation The tendency to fit with the environment in ways that promote survival. One of the two biologically based functions stressed in Piaget's theory.

affect The outward expression of emotions through facial expressions, gestures, intonation, and the like.

aggression Behavior that is intended to cause harm to persons or property and that is not socially justifiable.

amniocentesis A procedure for collecting cells that lie in the amniotic fluid surrounding the fetus. A needle is passed through the mother's abdominal wall into the amniotic sac to gather discarded fetal cells. These cells can be examined for chromosomal and genetic defects.

amniotic sac A fluid-containing enclosure, secured by a watertight membrane, that surrounds and protects the embryo and fetus.

androgen insensitivity A genetic disorder in which the fetus does not respond to masculinizing hormones. Affected individuals (XX or XY) usually are feminine in appearance and interests.

androgens Hormones that have masculinizing effects and are more abundant in males.

androgyny A personality type composed of desirable characteristics of the masculine and feminine personality types.

anorexia nervosa A severe eating disorder, usually involving excessive weight loss through self-starvation, typically found in teenage girls.

anoxia A deficit of oxygen supply to the cells, that can produce brain or other tissue damage.

appearance–reality distinction Distinction between how objects appear and what they really are. Understanding the distinction implies an ability to judge both appearance and reality correctly when the two diverge.

assimilation Interpreting new experiences in terms of existing cognitive structures. One of the two components of adaptation in Piaget's theory.

at risk A term describing babies who have a higher likelihood of experiencing developmental problems than other babies.

attention The selection of particular sensory input for perceptual and cognitive processing and the exclusion of competing input.

autobiographical memory Specific, personal, and long-lasting memory regarding the self.

automatization An increase in the efficiency with which cognitive operations are executed as a result of practice. A mechanism of change in information-processing theories.

autosome One of the 22 pairs of chromosomes other than the sex chromosomes.

axon A long fiber extending from the cell body in a neuron; conducts activity from the cell body to another cell.

babbling drift A hypothesis that infants' babbling gradually gravitates toward the language they are hearing and soon will speak.

behavior analysis B. F. Skinner's environmental/learning theory, which emphasizes the role of operant learning in changing observable behaviors.

behavior genetics A field of study that explores the role of genes in producing individual differences in behavior.

behaviorism A theory of psychology, first advanced by John B. Watson, that human development results primarily from conditioning and learning processes.

binocular vision The ability of the two eyes to see the same aspects of an object simultaneously.

bone age The degree of maturation of an individual as indicated by the extent of hardening of the bones.

brain lateralization The organization of the human brain into left and right hemispheres that perform different functions.

brainstem The lower part of the brain, closest to the spinal cord; includes the cerebellum, which is important for maintaining balance and coordination.

brightness constancy The experience that the physical brightness of an object remains the same even though the amount of light it reflects back to the eye changes (because of shadows or changes in the illuminating light).

bulimia A disorder of food binging and sometimes purging by self-induced vomiting or excessive use of laxatives, typically observed in teenage girls.

Cartesian dualism René Descartes's idea that the mind and body are separate, which helped clear the way for the scientific study of human development.

categorical perception The ability to detect differences in speech sounds that correspond to differences in meaning—the ability to discriminate phonemic boundaries.

catharsis The psychoanalytic belief that the likelihood of aggression can be reduced by viewing aggression or by engaging in high-energy behaviors.

centration Piaget's term for the young child's tendency to focus on only one aspect of a problem at a time, a perceptually biased form of responding that often results in incorrect judgments.

cephalocaudal Literally, head-to-tail. This principle of development refers to the tendency of body parts to mature in a head-to-foot progression.

cerebral cortex The thin sheet of gray matter, consisting of six layers of neurons, that covers the brain.

cerebrum The highest brain center; includes both hemispheres of the brain and the interconnections between them.

chorionic villus sampling (CVS) A procedure for gathering fetal cells earlier in pregnancy than is possible through amniocentesis. A tube is passed through the vagina and cervix so that fetal cells can be gathered at the site of the developing placenta.

chromosome One of the bodies in the cell nucleus along which the genes are located. The nucleus of each human cell has 46 chromosomes, with the exception of the germ cells, which have 23.

clarification question A response that indicates a listener did not understand a statement.

class inclusion The knowledge that a subclass cannot be larger than the superordinate class that includes it. In Piaget's theory, a concrete operational achievement.

clinical method Piaget's principal research method, which involved a semi-structured interview with questions designed to probe children's understanding of various concepts.

coercive family process Gerald Patterson's term for the method by which some families control one another through aggression and other coercive means.

cognition Higher order mental processes, such as reasoning and problem solving, through which humans attempt to understand the world.

cognitive structures Piaget's term for the interrelated systems of knowledge that underlie and guide intelligent behavior.

cohort effect A problem sometimes found in cross-sectional research, in which subjects of a given age are affected by factors unique to their generation.

coining Children's creation of new words to label objects or events for which the correct label is not known.

color constancy The experience that the color of an object remains the same even though the wavelengths it reflects back to the eye change (because of changes in the color of the illuminating light).

comparative research Research conducted with nonhuman species in order to provide information relevant to human development.

competence Self-evaluation that includes both what one would like to achieve and one's confidence in being able to achieve it.

competition model A proposed strategy children use for learning grammar in which they focus on certain cues in the language.

compliance Willingness to obey the requests of others.

computer simulation Programming a computer to perform a cognitive task in the same way that humans are thought to perform it. An information-processing method for testing theories of underlying process.

conception The entry of the genetic material from a male germ cell (sperm) into a female germ cell (ovum); fertilization.

concrete operations Form of intelligence in which mental operations make logical problem solving with concrete objects possible. The third of Piaget's periods, extending from about 6 to 11 years.

conditioned reflex method John B. Watson's name for the Pavlovian conditioning process in which reflexive responses can be conditioned to stimuli in the environment.

conditioned stimulus (CS) A neutral stimulus that comes to elicit a response (UCR) through a conditioning process in which it is consistently paired with another stimulus (UCS) that naturally evokes the response.

confluence model A theory of the relation between family structure and the development of intelligence. Intelligence is assumed to relate to the intellectual level of the home, which is determined by factors such as the number and spacing of children.

congenital adrenal hyperplasia (CAH) A hormonal disorder caused by an overproduction of androgens during pregnancy.

Afflicted females have large genitals and display male personality characteristics; afflicted males tend to be slightly more masculine in their interests and interactions.

conservation The knowledge that the quantitative properties of an object or collection of objects are not changed by a change in appearance. In Piaget's theory, a concrete operational achievement.

constructive memory The effects of the general knowledge system on how information is interpreted and thus remembered.

constructivism Piaget's belief that children actively create knowledge rather than passively receive it from the environment.

continuity versus discontinuity debate The scientific controversy regarding whether development is constant and connected (continuous) or uneven and disconnected (discontinuous).

controversial child A child who receives both many positive and many negative nominations in sociometric assessments by his or her peers.

conventional level Kohlberg's third and fourth stages of moral development. Moral reasoning is based on the view that a social system must be based on laws and regulations.

cooing A stage in the preverbal period, beginning at about 2 months, when babies primarily produce one-syllable vowel sounds.

correlation The relation between two variables, described in terms of its direction and strength.

correlation coefficient (r) A number between +1.00 and -1.00 that indicates the direction and strength of a correlation between two variables.

cross-cultural studies Research designed to determine the influence of culture on some aspect of development and in which culture typically serves as an independent variable.

crossing over The exchange of genetic material between chromosomes during meiosis.

cross-sectional design A research method in which subjects of different ages are studied simultaneously to examine the effects of age on some aspect of behavior.

cross-sequential design A research method combining longitudinal and cross-sectional designs.

cultural compatibility hypothesis The hypothesis that schooling will be most effective when methods of instruction are compatible with the child's cultural background.

cultural relativism The idea that certain behaviors or patterns of development vary from one culture to another.

deep structure Chomsky's term for the inborn knowledge humans possess about the properties of language.

defensive reflex A natural reaction to novel stimuli that tends to protect the organism from further stimulation and that may include orientation of the stimulus receptors away from the stimulus source and a variety of physiological changes.

deferred imitation Imitation of a model observed some time in the past.

delay of gratification technique An experimental procedure for studying children's ability to postpone a smaller, immediate reward in order to obtain a larger, delayed one.

dendrite One of a net of short fibers extending out from the cell body in a neuron; receives activity from nearby cells and conducts that activity to the cell body.

deoxyribonucleic acid (DNA) The chemical material that carries genetic information on chromosomes. Capable of self-replication, the DNA molecule is made up of complementary nucleotides wound in a stairlike, double-helix structure.

dependent variable The variable that is predicted to be affected by an experimental manipulation. In psychology, usually some aspect of behavior.

deprivation experiment Rearing a group of organisms without access to a particular kind of experience. An ethological method for studying the effects of experience on development.

descriptive research Research based solely on observations, with no attempt to determine systematic relations among the variables.

developmental pacing The rate at which spurts and plateaus occur in an individual's physical and mental development.

developmental psychology The branch of psychology devoted to the study of changes in behavior and abilities over the course of development.

dialectical process The process in Vygotsky's theory whereby children learn through problem-solving experiences shared with others.

discourse Language used in social interactions; conversation.

discrimination learning A type of learning in which children come to adjust their behavior according to stimuli that signal the opportunity for reinforcement or the possibility of punishment.

discriminative stimuli Stimuli that provide information as to the possibility for reinforcement or punishment.

dishabituation The recovery of a habituated response that results from a change in the eliciting stimulus.

displaced aggression Retaliatory aggression directed at a person or object other than the one against whom retaliation is desired.

display rules The expectations and attitudes a society holds toward the expression of affect.

distal properties The actual properties of an object—color, size, and so on—as opposed to proximal stimulation.

dominance hierarchy A structured social group in which members higher on the dominance ladder control those who are lower, initially through aggression and conflict but eventually simply through threats.

Down syndrome A chromosomal disorder typically associated with an extra chromosome 21. Its effects include mental retardation and a characteristic physical appearance.

EAS model Plomin and Buss's theory of temperament, which holds that temperament can be measured along the dimensions of emotionality, activity, and sociability.

ecological approach An approach to studying development that focuses on individuals within their environmental contexts.

ecological systems theory Bronfenbrenner's theory that emphasizes the interrelations of the individual with layers of environmental context.

effectance motivation The desire of the infant or child to become effective in acting on the environment and in coping with the objects and people in it.

egocentrism In infancy, an inability to distinguish the self (e.g., one's actions or perceptions) from the outer world. In later childhood, an inability to distinguish one's own perspective (e.g., visual experience, thoughts, feelings) from that of others.

electroencephalograph (EEG) An instrument that measures brain activity by sensing minute electrical changes at the top of the skull.

embryo The developing organism from the 3rd week, when implantation is complete, through the 8th week after conception.

emotion An internal reaction or feeling, which may be either positive (such as joy) or negative (such as anger).

empirical self The "Me" component of the self, which involves one's objective personal characteristics.

encoding Attending to and forming internal representations of certain features of the environment. A mechanism of change in information-processing theories.

environmentalism The theory that human development is best explained by an examination of the individual's experiences and environmental influences.

equilibration Piaget's term for the biological process of self-regulation that propels the cognitive system to higher and higher forms of equilibrium.

equilibrium A characteristic of a cognitive system in which assimilation and accommodation are in balance, thus permitting adaptive, nondistorted response to the world.

erogenous zones According to Freud's theory of psychosexual development, the areas of the body where the libido resides during successive stages of development. The child seeks physical pleasure at the erogenous zone at which the libido is located.

estrogen and progesterone Hormones that have feminizing effects and are more abundant in females.

ethology The study of development from an evolutionary perspective.

evaluative self-reactions Bandura's term for consequences people apply to themselves as a result of meeting or failing to meet their personal standards

existential self The "I" component of the self, which is concerned with the subjective experience of existing.

exosystem Social systems that can affect children but in which they do not participate directly. Bronfenbrenner's third layer of context.

expanded imitation Imitated speech to which the child has added new elements.

expansion A repetition of speech in which errors are corrected and statements are elaborated.

expertise Organized factual knowledge with respect to some content domain.

expressive style Vocabulary acquired during the naming explosion that emphasizes the pragmatic functions of language.

false belief The realization that people

can hold beliefs that are not true. Such understanding, which is typically acquired during the preoperational period, provides evidence of the ability to distinguish the mental from the nonmental.

fast-mapping A process in which children acquire the meaning of a word after a brief exposure.

fetal alcohol syndrome A set of features in the infant caused by the mother's ingestion of alcohol during pregnancy; typically includes facial malformations and other physical and mental disabilities.

fetal distress A condition of abnormal stress in the fetus; may be reflected during the birth process in an abnormal fetal heart rate.

fetus The developing organism from the 9th week to the 38th week after conception.

fixation The condition in which some of the libido inappropriately remains in one of the erogenous zones, causing the adult to continually seek physical pleasure in that area.

forbidden toy technique An experimental procedure for studying children's resistance to temptation in which the child is left alone with an attractive toy and instructed not to play with it.

formal operations Form of intelligence in which higher-level mental operations make possible logical reasoning with respect to abstract and hypothetical events and not merely concrete objects. The fourth of Piaget's periods, beginning at about 11 years.

form class A hypothetical innate category for understanding and producing language.

fragile X syndrome An X-linked genetic disorder, more often expressed in males, producing retarded intellectual development, language and behavior problems, and identifiable physical characteristics.

fraternal (dizygotic) twins Twins who develop from separately fertilized ova and who thus are no more genetically similar than other siblings.

friendship An enduring relationship between two people, characterized by loyalty, intimacy, and mutual affection.

functional core model A component theory of semantic development that holds that children first group object words into categories based on the functions of the objects.

functionalist model A theory of language development that stresses the uses of language and the context in which it develops.

functions Piaget's term for the biologically based tendencies to organize knowledge into cognitive structures and to adapt to challenges from the environment.

g General intelligence. *g* is assumed to determine performance on a wide range of intellectual measures.

gender consistency Understanding that one's gender cannot be changed by superficial changes in clothing, occupation, and so on.

gender constancy Understanding that one's gender is a fixed part of the self; it includes gender identity, gender stability, and gender consistency.

gender identity Knowing one's gender.

gender role (sex-role stereotype) A pattern of behaviors that is considered appropriate for males or females by the culture in which they live.

gender-role knowledge Understanding that a certain object, activity, or personal characteristic is considered more appropriate for one sex than the other.

gender schema A cognitive structure used to organize information regarding one's gender.

gender script A familiar routine or sequence of events that is typically associated with only one gender.

gender segregation (sex cleavage) The tendency for male and female children to play in same-sex groups.

gender stability Understanding that one's gender will remain the same throughout life.

gene The unit of inheritance; a segment of DNA on the chromosome that can guide the production of a protein or an RNA molecule.

genetic counseling The advising of prospective parents about genetic diseases and the likelihood that they might pass on defective genetic traits to their offspring.

genetic epistemology Jean Piaget's term for the study of children's knowledge and how it changes with development.

genetic psychology G. Stanley Hall's original term for developmental psychology that stressed the evolutionary basis of development.

genotype The genetic constitution that an individual inherits; may refer to the inherited basis of a single trait, a set of traits, or all a person's traits.

goodness of fit A concept describing the relation between a baby's temperament and his or her social and environmental surroundings.

grammar The study of the structural properties of language, including syntax, inflection, and intonation.

group A collection of individuals who interact regularly in a consistent, structured fashion and who share values and a sense of belonging to the group.

habituation The decline or disappearance of a reflex response as a result of repeated elicitation. The simplest type of learning.

haptic perception The perceptual experience that results from active exploration of objects by touch.

heritability The proportion of variance in a trait (such as IQ) that can be attributed to genetic variance in the sample being studied.

hierarchical model of intelligence A model of the structure of intelligence in which intellectual abilities are seen as being organized hierarchically, with broad, general abilities at the top of the hierarchy and more specific skills nested underneath

holophrase A single word used to express a larger idea; common during the 2nd year of life.

HOME (Home Observation for Measurement of the Environment) An instrument for assessing the quality of the early home environment. Included are dimensions such as maternal involvement and variety of play materials.

hostile (retaliatory) aggression Aggression whose purpose is to cause pain or injury.

Huntington's chorea An inherited disease in which the nervous system suddenly deteriorates, resulting in uncontrollable muscular movements and disordered brain function. The disease typically strikes people between about 30 and 40 years of age and ultimately causes death.

hypothalamus The structure in the brain that regulates the pituitary gland.

hypothesis A predicted relation between a phenomenon and a factor assumed to affect it that is not yet supported by a great deal of evidence. Hypotheses are tested in experimental investigations.

hypothetical–deductive reasoning A form of problem solving characterized by the ability to generate and test hypotheses and to draw logical conclusions from the results of the tests. In Piaget's theory, a formal operational achievement.

identical (monozygotic) twins Twins who develop from a single fertilized ovum and thus inherit identical genetic material.

identification The Freudian process through which the child adopts the characteristics of the same-sex parent during the phallic stage.

imitation Behavior of an observer that results from and is similar to the behavior of a model.

immanent justice Literally, inherent justice; refers to the expectation of children in Piaget's stage of moral realism that punishment must follow any rule violation, including those that appear to go undetected.

imprinting A biological process in which the young of some species acquire an emotional attachment to the mother.

incomplete dominance The case in which a dominant gene does not completely suppress the effect of a recessive gene on the phenotype.

independent variable The variable in an experiment that is systematically manipulated.

infantile amnesia The inability to remember experiences from the first 2 or 3 years of life.

inhibition Kagan's proposed temperamental response style characterizing infants who react with timidity and avoidance to unfamiliar events and people.

innate releasing mechanism A stimulus that triggers an innate sequence or pattern of behaviors. Also called a sign stimulus.

institutionalization studies Examinations of the effects of naturally occurring deprivation (such as in certain kinds of orphanage rearing) on children's development.

instrumental aggression Aggression whose purpose is to obtain something desired.

intentional behavior In Piaget's theory, behavior in which the goal exists prior to the action selected to achieve it; made possible by the ability to separate means and end.

interactional synchrony The smooth intermeshing of behaviors between mother and baby.

interactionist perspective The theory that human development results from the combination of nature and nurture factors.

internalization Vygotsky's term for the child's incorporation, primarily through language, of bodies of knowledge and tools of thought from the culture.

internal working model An infant's and a caregiver's cognitive conception of each other, which they use to form expectations and predictions.

introspection A research method for investigating the workings of the mind by asking subjects to describe their mental processes.

invariance The stability in the relations among some properties of an object as other properties change.

invariants Aspects of the world that remain the same even though other aspects have changed. In Piaget's theory, different forms of invariants are understood at different stages of development.

kin selection A proposed mechanism by which an individual's altruistic behavior toward a kin member increases the likelihood of the survival of genes similar to those of the individual.

kinetic cue A visual cue that informs the observer about the relative distance of an object either through movement of the object or movement of the observer.

Klinefelter's syndrome (XXY) A chromosomal disorder of males in which an extra X chromosome is present. Men with the syndrome have long arms, little body hair, an underdeveloped penis, and somewhat feminine personality characteristics.

language acquisition device (LAD) Chomsky's proposed brain mechanism for analyzing speech input—the mechanism that allows young children to quickly acquire the language to which they are exposed.

language support system (LASS) Bruner's proposed process by which parents provide children assistance in learning language.

law (principle) A predicted relation between a phenomenon and a factor assumed to affect it that is supported by a good deal of scientific evidence.

learnability theory An information-processing theory of language acquisition that uses computer models to try to identify the structure of language.

learned helplessness Acquired feelings of incompetence, often brought about as a result of repeated failure experiences.

learning A relatively permanent change in behavior that results from practice or experience.

lexical contrast theory A theory of semantic development holding that (1) children automatically assume a new word has a meaning different from that of any other word they know and (2) children always choose word meanings that are generally accepted over more individualized meanings.

lexicon Children's vocabulary, or repertoire of words.

libido Sigmund Freud's term for the sexual energy that he believed is possessed by all children from birth and then moves to different locations on the body over the course of development.

life-span developmental psychology The study of developmental issues across the life cycle.

locomotion The movement of an individual through space. Psychologists have been most interested in movements that individuals control themselves, such as walking and crawling.

longitudinal design A research method in which the same subjects are studied repeatedly over time.

looking-glass self The conception of the self based on how one thinks others see him or her.

macrosystem The culture or subculture in which the child lives. Bronfenbrenner's fourth layer of context.

magical causality The belief that a generally effective causal action can produce any outcome of interest, even in the absence of physical contact between cause and effect. A characteristic of stage 3 of the sensorimotor period.

mastery motivation An inborn desire to affect or control one's environment.

maternal bonding The mother's emotional attachment to the child, which appears shortly after birth and which some theorists believe develops through early contact during a sensitive period.

maternal separation anxiety Strong negative emotional reactions experienced by some mothers when separated from their children.

maturation The biological processes assumed by some theorists to be primarily responsible for human development.

meiosis Replication in sex cells, which consists of two cell divisions, resulting in four cell nuclei that are all genetically different.

mesosystem The interrelations among the child's microsystems. The second of Bronfen-brenner's layers of context.

metamemory Knowledge about memory.

microanalysis A research technique for studying dyadic interactions, in which two individuals are simultaneously videotaped with different cameras, and then the tapes are examined side by side.

microgenetic method A research method in which a small number of subjects are observed repeatedly in order to study an expected change in a developmental process.

microsystem The environmental system closest to the child, such as the family or school. The first of Bronfenbrenner's layers of context.

midbrain A part of the brain that lies above the brainstem; serves as a relay station and as a control area for breathing and swallowing and houses part of the auditory and visual systems.

mitosis Replication of the chromosomal mate-rial of the cell nucleus followed by cell division, resulting in two identical nuclei.

mnemonic strategies Techniques (such as rehearsal or organization) that people use in an attempt to remember something.

modal action pattern A sequence of behaviors elicited by a specific stimulus.

monocular cue A visual cue that is available to one eye only or that does not depend on the combined information available to the two eyes.

moral conduct The aspect of children's moral development concerned with behavior.

moral dilemmas Stories used by Piaget and others to assess children's levels of moral reasoning.

moral realism Piaget's second stage of moral development, in which children's reasoning is based on objective and physical aspects of a situation and is often inflexible.

moral reasoning The aspect of children's moral development concerned with knowledge and understanding of moral issues and principles.

moral relativism Piaget's third stage of moral development, in which children view rules as agreements that can be altered and consider people's motives or intentions when evaluating their moral conduct.

moral rules Rules used by a society to protect individuals and guarantee their rights.

moro reflex The infant's response to loss of head support or to a loud sound, consisting of thrusting of the arms and fingers outward, followed by clenching of the fists and a grasping motion of the arms across the chest.

motherese Simplified speech directed at very young children by adults and older children.

motion parallax An observer's experience that a closer object moves across the field of view faster than a more distant object when both objects are moving at the same speed or when the objects are stationary and the observer moves.

myelin A sheath of fatty material that surrounds and insulates the axon, resulting in speedier transmission of neural activity.

naming explosion A period of language development, beginning at about 18 months, when children suddenly begin to acquire words (especially labels) at a high rate.

nativism The theory that human development results principally from inborn processes that guide the emergence of behaviors in a predictable manner.

natural selection An evolutionary process proposed by Charles Darwin in which characteristics of an individual that increase its chances of survival are more likely to be passed along to future generations.

nature versus nurture debate The scientific controversy regarding whether the primary source of developmental change rests in biological (nature) factors or environmental and experiential (nurture) factors.

negative correlation A correlation in which two variables change in opposite directions.

negative punisher A punishing consequence that involves the removal of something pleasant following a behavior.

negative reinforcer A reinforcing consequence that involves the removal of something unpleasant following a behavior.

neglected child A child who receives few nominations of any sort, positive or negative, in sociometric assessments by his or her peers. Such children seem to be ignored by the peer group.

neuron A nerve cell consisting of a cell body, axons, and dendrites. Neurons transmit activity from one part of the nervous system to another.

neurotransmitter A chemical that transmits electrical activity from one neuron across the synaptic junction to another neuron.

New York Longitudinal Study (NYLS) A well-known longitudinal project conducted by Thomas and Chess to study infant temperament and its implications for later psychological adjustment.

normative versus idiographic development debate The question of whether research should focus on identifying commonalities in human development (normative development) or on the causes of individual differences (idiographic development).

norms A timetable of age ranges indicating when normal growth and developmental milestones are reached.

obesity A condition of excess fat storage; often defined as weight more than 20 percent over a standardized 'ideal' weight.

object permanence The knowledge that objects have a permanent existence that is independent of our perceptual contact with them. In Piaget's theory, a major achievement of the sensorimotor period.

objective responsibility Responsibility assigned solely in terms of an action's objective and physical consequences. Children in Piaget's stage of moral realism evaluate situations using this concept.

objectivity A characteristic of scientific research; it requires that the procedures and subject matter of investigations should be formulated so that they could, in principle, be agreed on by everyone.

observational learning A form of learning in which an observer's behavior changes as a result of observing a model.

operant behavior Voluntary behavior controlled by its consequences. The larger category of human behaviors.

operant conditioning A form of learning in which the probability of occurrence of an operant behavior changes as a result of its reinforcing or punishing consequences.

operating principle A hypothetical innate strategy for analyzing language input.

operating space In Case's theory, the resources necessary to carry out cognitive operations.

operations Piaget's term for the various forms of mental action through which older children solve problems and reason logically.

organization The tendency to integrate knowledge into interrelated cognitive structures. One of the two biologically based functions stressed in Piaget's theory.

orienting reflex A natural reaction to novel stimuli that enhances stimulus processing and includes orientation of the eyes and ears to optimize stimulus reception, inhibition of ongoing activity, and a variety of physiological changes.

ovaries The female gonadal structure that produces the ovum.

overextension An early language error in which children use labels they already know for things whose names they do not yet know.

overregularization An early structural language error in which children apply inflectional rules to irregular forms (e.g., adding *-ed* to *say*).

palmar reflex The infant's finger grasp of an object that stimulates the palm of the hand.

paradox of altruism The logical dilemma faced by ethological theorists who try to reconcile self-sacrificial behavior with the concepts of natural selection and survival of the fittest.

parallel play A form of play in which children play next to each other and with similar materials but with no real interaction or cooperation.

peer tutoring Educational procedure in which children act as teachers for other children.

perception The interpretation of sensory stimulation based on experience.

periods Piaget's term for the four general stages into which his theory divides development. Each period is a qualitatively distinct form of functioning that characterizes a wide range of cognitive activities.

peripheral vision The perception of visual input outside the area on which the individual is fixating.

personal agency The understanding that one can be the cause of events.

phenotype The observable expression of a genotype.

phenylketonuria (PKU) An inherited metabolic disease caused by a recessive gene. It can produce severe mental retardation if dietary intake of phenylalanine is not controlled for the first several years of life.

phobia A fear that has become serious and may have been generalized to an entire class of objects or situations.

phoneme A sound contrast that changes meaning.

phonemics The branch of phonology that deals with the relations between speech sounds and meaning.

phonetics The branch of phonology that deals with articulation skills.

phonics An approach to reading instruction that stresses letter-sound correspondences and the build-up of words from individual units.

phonological awareness The realization that letters correspond to sounds and the ability to perform specific letter-to-sound translations.

phonology The study of speech sounds.

placenta An organ formed by both embryonic and uterine tissue where the embryo attaches to the uterus. This organ exchanges nutrients, oxygen, and wastes between the embryo or fetus and the mother through a very thin membrane that does not allow the passage of blood.

positive correlation A correlation in which two variables change in the same direction.

positive punisher A punishing consequence that involves the presentation of something unpleasant following a behavior.

positive reinforcer A reinforcing consequence that involves the presentation of something pleasant following a behavior.

postconventional level Kohlberg's final stages of moral development. Moral reasoning is based on the assumption that the value, dignity, and rights of each individual person must be maintained.

postural development The increasing ability of babies to control parts of their body, especially the head and the trunk.

pragmatics The study of the social uses of language.

preconventional level Kohlberg's first two stages of moral development. Moral reasoning is based on the assumption that individuals must serve their own needs.

prehension The ability to grasp and manipulate objects with the hands.

preoperational Form of intelligence in which symbols and mental actions begin to replace objects and overt behaviors. The second of Piaget's periods, extending from about 2 to 6 years.

pretend play A form of play in which children use an object or person as a symbol to stand for something else.

preterm A term describing babies born before the end of the normal gestation period.

preverbal period The period of development preceding the appearance of the child's first word combinations, usually lasting about 18 months.

primary caregiver The person, usually the mother, with whom the infant develops the major attachment relationship.

principle of mutual exclusivity A proposed principle of semantic development stating that children assume an object can have only one name.

private speech Speech children produce and direct toward themselves during a problem-solving activity.

production deficiency The failure to generate a mnemonic strategy spontaneously.

productivity The property of language that permits humans to produce and comprehend an infinite number of statements.

progressive decentering Piaget's term for the gradual decline in egocentrism that occurs across development.

prosocial behavior The aspect of moral conduct that includes socially desirable behaviors such as sharing, helping, and cooperating; often used interchangeably with *altruism* by modern researchers.

prospective memory Memory directed to the performance of future activities.

prototype A general model of an object. The prototype theory of language development holds that children create prototypes as the basis for semantic concepts.

proximal stimulation Physical energies that reach sensory receptors.

proximodistal Literally, near-to-far. This principle of development refers to the tendency of body parts to develop in a trunk-to-extremities direction.

psycholinguistics A theory of language development, originated by Chomsky, that stresses innate mechanisms separate from cognitive processes.

psychometric An approach to the study of intelligence that emphasizes the use of standardized tests to identify individual differences among people.

psychoteratology The discovery and study of the harmful effects of teratogens through the use of behavioral measures, such as learning ability.

puberty The period in which chemical and physical changes in the body occur to enable sexual reproduction.

punisher A consequence that decreases the likelihood of a behavior that it follows.

qualitative identity The knowledge that the qualitative nature of something is not changed by a change in its appearance. In Piaget's theory, a preoperational achievement.

rapid eye movement (REM) sleep A stage of irregular sleep in which the individual's eyes move rapidly while the eyelids are closed.

reaction range The amount by which a trait can vary as a result of experience within the limits set by genetic inheritance.

reactivation The preservation of the memory for an event through reencounter with at least some portion of the event in the interval between initial experience and memory test.

recall memory   The retrieval of some past stimulus or event that is not perceptually present.

recapitulation theory   An early biological notion, adopted by G. Stanley Hall, that the development of the individual repeats the development of the species.

recast   A response to speech that restates it using a different structure.

reciprocal altruism   A proposed mechanism by which an individual's altruistic behavior toward members of the social group may promote the survival of the individual's genes through reciprocation by others or may ensure the survival of similar genes.

reciprocal determinism   Bandura's proposed process describing the interaction of a person's characteristics and abilities (P), behavior (B), and environment (E).

recognition memory   The realization that some perceptually present stimulus or event has been encountered before.

reduplicated babbling   A stage in the preverbal period, occurring at about 6 months, when infants produce strings of identical sounds, such as dadada.

referential style   Vocabulary acquired during the naming explosion that involves a large proportion of nouns and object labels.

reflex   An automatic and stereotyped response to a specific stimulus.

reinforcer   A consequence that increases the likelihood of a behavior that it follows.

rejected child   A child who receives few positive and many negative nominations in sociometric assessments by his or her peers. Such children seem to be disliked by the peer group.

reliability   The consistency or repeatability of a measuring instrument. A necessary property of a standardized test.

representation   The use of symbols to picture and act on the world internally.

repression   Freud's term for the process through which desires or motivations are driven into the unconscious, as typically occurs during the phallic stage.

respondent behavior   Responses based on reflexes, which are controlled by specific eliciting stimuli. The smaller category of human behaviors.

respondent (classical) conditioning   A form of learning, involving reflexes, in which a neutral stimulus acquires the power to elicit a reflexive response (UCR) as a result of being associated (paired) with the naturally eliciting stim-

ulus (UCS). The neutral stimulus then becomes a conditioned stimulus (CS).

respondent extinction   A process related to respondent conditioning in which the conditioned stimulus (CS) gradually loses its power to elicit the response as a result of no longer being paired with the unconditioned stimulus (UCS).

response inhibition (counterimitation)   Behavior of an observer that is directly opposite that of a model; often the result of vicarious punishment.

reversal-replication (ABAB) design   An experimental design in which the independent variable is systematically presented and removed several times. It can be used in studies involving very few subjects.

reversibility   Piaget's term for the power of operations to correct for potential disturbances and thus arrive at correct solutions to problems.

rooting reflex   The turning of the infant's head toward the cheek at which touch stimulation is applied, followed by opening of the mouth.

rules   Procedures for acting on the environment and solving problems.

scaffolding   A method of teaching in which the adult adjusts the level of help provided in relation to the child's level of performance, the goal being to encourage independent performance.

scatter diagram   A graphic illustration of a correlation between two variables.

schema   A general representation of the typical structure of familiar experiences.

schemes   Piaget's term for the cognitive structures of infancy. A scheme consists of a set of skilled, flexible action patterns through which the child understands the world.

scientific method   The system of rules used by scientists to conduct and evaluate their research.

script   A representation of the typical sequence of actions and events in some familiar context.

selective attention   A concentration on a stimulus or event with attendant disregard for other stimuli or events.

selective imitation   Behavior of an observer that follows the general form or style of the behavior of a model but is not a precise copy.

self-consciousness   A concern about the opinions others hold about oneself.

self-efficacy   Bandura's term for people's ability to succeed at various tasks, as judged by the people themselves.

self-esteem (self-worth)   A person's evalu-

ation of himself or herself, and his or her affective reactions to that evaluation.

self-evaluation   The part of the self-system concerned with children's opinions of themselves and their abilities.

self-knowledge (self-awareness)   The part of the self-system concerned with children's knowledge about themselves.

self-regulation   The part of the self-system concerned with self-control.

self-schema   An internal cognitive portrait of the self used to organize information about the self.

self-system   The set of interrelated processes—self-knowledge, self-evaluation, and self-regulation—that make up the self.

semantic feature hypothesis   A component theory of semantic development that holds that children first group object words into categories based on the perceptual features (e.g., size, color, shape) of the objects.

semantics   The study of how children acquire words and their meanings.

sensation   The experience resulting from the stimulation of a sense organ.

sensitive (critical) period   A period of development during which certain behaviors are more easily learned.

sensorimotor   Form of intelligence in which knowledge is based on physical interactions with people and objects. The first of Piaget's periods, extending from birth to about 2 years.

sensorimotor schemes   Skilled and generalizable action patterns by which infants act on and understand the world. In Piaget's theory, the cognitive structures of infancy.

separation protest   Crying and searching by infants separated from their mothers; an indication of the formation of the attachment bond.

seriation   The ability to order stimuli along some quantitative dimension, such as length. In Piaget's theory, a concrete operational achievement.

sex (gender)   An individual's biological maleness or femaleness.

sex difference   A behavior or characteristic in which males and females usually differ as a result of either biological or environmental factors.

sex differentiation   The process through which biological sex differences emerge.

sex-limited traits   Genes that affect males and females differently but that are not carried on the sex chromosomes.

sex-linked (X-linked) genes   Genes found only on the sex chromosomes, most often the X chromosome.

sex typing The process by which children develop the gender role considered appropriate by their culture.

sexual dimorphism The existence in most species of biological differences between males and females for the purpose of reproduction.

shape constancy The experience that the physical shape of an object remains the same even though the shape of its projected image on the eye varies.

short-term storage space In Case's theory, the resources necessary to store results from previous cognitive operations while carrying out new ones.

sickle-cell anemia (SCA) An inherited blood disease caused by a recessive gene. The red blood cells assume a sickled shape and do not distribute oxygen efficiently to the cells of the body.

size constancy The experience that the physical size of an object remains the same even though the size of its projected image on the eye varies.

small for gestational age (SGA) A term describing babies born at a weight in the bottom 10% of babies of a particular gestational age.

social cognition Understanding of the social and interpersonal world. Social cognition includes both thoughts about other people, such as parents and peers, and thoughts about the self.

social comparison Comparing one's abilities to those of others.

social conventions Rules used by a society to govern everyday behavior and to maintain order.

socialization The process through which society molds the child's beliefs, expectations, and behavior.

social-learning theory A form of environmental/learning theory that adds observational learning to respondent and operant learning as a process through which children's behavior changes.

social network The people with whom an individual regularly interacts.

social policy The principles used by a society to decide which social problems to address and how to deal with them.

social problem-solving skills Skills needed to resolve social dilemmas.

social referencing Using information gained from other people to regulate one's own behavior.

social referential communication A form of communication in which a speaker sends a message that is comprehended by a listener.

social support Resources (both tangible and intangible) provided by other people in times of uncertainty or stress.

social withdrawal Self-imposed isolation from the peer group.

sociobiology A branch of biology that attempts to discover the evolutionary origins of social behavior.

sociogenesis The process of acquiring knowledge or skills through social interactions.

sociometric techniques Procedures for assessing children's social status based on evaluations by the peer group. Sociometric techniques may involve ratings of degree of liking, nominations of liked or disliked peers, or forced-choice judgments between pairs of peers.

speech act An instance of speech used to perform pragmatic functions, like requesting or complaining.

+1 stage technique A method of investigating the hierarchical organization of moral stages; children are exposed to reasoning one stage above their own in order to maximize cognitive conflict and thus induce movement to the higher stage.

stepping reflex The infant's response to being held in a slightly forward, upright position with feet touching a horizontal surface, consisting of stepping movements.

stimulus generalization A process related to respondent conditioning in which stimuli that are similar to the conditioned stimulus (CS) also acquire the power to elicit the response.

Strange Situation procedure Ainsworth's laboratory procedure for assessing the strength of the attachment relationship by observing the infant's reactions to a series of structured episodes involving the mother and a stranger.

strategy construction The creation of strategies for processing and remembering information. A mechanism of change in information-processing theories.

surface structure Chomsky's term for the way words and phrases are arranged in spoken languages.

symbolic function The ability to use one thing (such as a mental image or word) as a symbol to represent something else.

symbolic play Form of play in which the child uses one thing in deliberate pretense to stand for something else.

synapse The small space between neurons where neural activity is communicated from one cell to another.

syntax The aspect of grammar that involves word order.

tabula rasa Latin phrase, meaning "blank slate," used to describe the newborn's mind as entirely empty of inborn abilities, interests, or ideas.

Tay-Sachs disease An inherited disease in which the lack of an enzyme that breaks down fats in brain cells causes progressive brain deterioration. Affected children usually die by the age of 6.

telegraphic speech Speech from which unnecessary function words (e.g., *in, the, with*) are omitted; common during early language learning.

temperament The aspect of personality studied in infants; it includes their emotional expressiveness and responsiveness to stimulation.

teratogen An agent that can cause abnormal development in the fetus.

testes The male gonadal structure that produces the sperm.

theory A broad set of statements describing the relation between a phenomenon and the factors assumed to affect it.

theory of mind Thoughts and beliefs concerning the mental world.

tonic neck reflex The infant's postural change when the head is turned to the side, consisting of extension of the arm on that side and clenching of the other arm in what looks like a fencer's position.

tools of intellectual adaptation Vygotsky's term for the techniques of thinking and problem solving that children internalize from their culture.

transactional influence A bidirectional, or re-ciprocal, relationship in which individuals influence one another's behaviors.

transformational grammar A set of rules developed by the LAD to translate a language's surface structure to a deep structure the child can innately understand.

transitivity The ability to combine relations logically to deduce necessary conclusions—for example, if A > B and B > C then A > C. In Piaget's theory, a concrete operational achievement.

triarchic theory of intelligence Sternberg's three-part theory of intelligence. The theory includes the components that underlie intelligent behavior, the contexts in which intelligence is exercised, and the experiences or types of tasks that require intelligence.

Turner's syndrome A chromosomal disorder of females in which one X chromosome is absent. Women with the syndrome have no ovaries, do not menstruate, are short in stature, and display "ultrafeminine" personality characteristics.

ultrasound imaging A noninvasive procedure for detecting physical defects in the fetus. A device that produces soundlike waves of energy is moved over the pregnant woman's abdomen, and reflections of these waves form an image of the fetus.

umbilical cord A soft cable of tissue and blood vessels that connects the fetus to the placenta.

unconditioned response (UCR) The response portion of a reflex, which is reliably elicited by a stimulus (UCS).

unconditioned stimulus (UCS) The stimulus portion of a reflex, which reliably elicits a respondent behavior (UCR).

underextensions A language error in which children fail to apply labels they know to things for which the labels are appropriate.

universals of development Aspects of development or behavior that are common to children everywhere.

utilization deficiency The failure of a recently developed mnemonic strategy to facilitate recall.

validity The accuracy with which a measuring instrument assesses the attribute that it is designed to measure. A necessary property of a standardized test.

variable Any factor that can take on different values along a dimension.

vestibular sensitivity The perceptual experience that results from motion of the body and from the pull of gravity.

vicarious consequences Consequences of a model's behavior that affect an observer, through observation, in the same way they affect the model.

vicarious punishment Punishing consequences experienced by a model that affect an observer similarly through observation.

vicarious reinforcement Reinforcing consequences experienced by a model that affect an observer similarly through observation.

visual accommodation The automatic adjustment of the lens of the eye to produce a focused image of an object on the light-sensitive tissue at the back of the eye.

visual self-recognition The ability to recognize oneself; often studied in babies by having them look into mirrors.

wariness of strangers A general fear of unfamiliar people that appears in many infants at around 8 months of age and indicates the formation of the attachment bond.

whole-word An approach to reading instruction that stresses learning and visual retrieval of entire words.

47,XYY syndrome A chromosomal disorder of males in which an extra Y chromosome is present. Men with the syndrome have large body builds and very masculine personality characteristics.

Zeitgeist "The spirit of the times," or the ideas shared by most scientists during a given period.

zone of proximal development Vygotsky's term for the difference between what children can do by themselves and what they can do with help from an adult.

zygote A fertilized ovum.

REFERENCES

An asterisk (*) indicates a reference new to this edition.

ABBEDUTO, L., DAVIES, B., & FURMAN, L. (1988). The development of speech act comprehension in mentally retarded individuals and nonretarded children. *Child Development, 59,* 1460–1472.

ABEL, E. L. (1980). Fetal alcohol syndrome: Behavioral teratology. *Psychological Bulletin, 87,* 29–50.

ABEL, E. L. (1981). Behavioral teratology of alcohol. *Psychological Bulletin, 90,* 564–581.

ABER, J. L., & ALLEN, J. P. (1987). Effects of maltreatment on young children's socioemotional development: An attachment theory perspective. *Developmental Psychology, 23,* 406–414.

ABOUD, F. E. (1985). Children's application of attribution principles to social comparisons. *Child Development, 56,* 682–688.

*ABRAMOVITCH, R., CORTER, C., PEPLER, D. J., & STANHOPE, L. (1986). Sibling and peer interaction: A final follow-up and a comparison. *Child Development, 57,* 217–229.

ABRAMOVITCH, R., & GRUSEC, J. E. (1978). Peer imitation in a natural setting. *Child Development, 49,* 60–65.

ABRAMOWITZ, R. H., PETERSEN, A. C., & SCHULENBERG, J. E. (1981). Changes in self-image during early adolescence. In D. Offer, E. Ostrov, & K. I. Howard (Eds.), *Patterns of adolescent self-image.* San Francisco: Jossey-Bass.

ABRAVANEL, E., & SIGAFOOS, A. D. (1984). Exploring the presence of imitation during early infancy. *Child Development, 55,* 381–392.

*ACKERMAN, B. P. (1993). Children's understanding of the speaker's meaning in referential communication. *Journal of Experimental Child Psychology, 55,* 56–86.

ACKERMAN, B. P., & SILVER, S. (1990). Children's understanding of private keys in referential communication. *Journal of Experimental Child Psychology, 50,* 217–242.

ACKERMAN, B. P., SZYMANSKI, J., & SILVER, D. (1990). Children's use of common ground in interpreting ambiguous referential utterances. *Developmental Psychology, 26,* 234–245.

*ACKERMAN, S. J. (1992). Research on the genetics of alcoholism is still in ferment. The *Journal of NIH Research, 4,* 61–65.

ACREDOLO, L. P. (1978). Development of spatial orientation in infancy. *Developmental Psychology, 14,* 224–234.

ACREDOLO, L. P. (1985). Coordinating perspectives on infant spatial orientation. In R. Cohen (Ed.), *The development of spatial cognition.* Hillsdale, NJ: Erlbaum.

ACREDOLO, L. P., & EVANS, D. (1980). Developmental changes in the effects of landmarks on infant spatial behavior. *Developmental Psychology, 16,* 312–318.

ACREDOLO, L. P., & GOODWYN, S. W. (1988). Symbolic gesturing in normal infants. *Child Development, 59,* 450–466.

ACREDOLO, L. P., & GOODWYN, S. W. (1990). Development of communicative gesturing. In R. Vasta (Ed.), *Annals of child development* (Vol. 7). Greenwich, CT: JAI Press.

ADAMS, G. R., ABRAHAM, K. G., & MARKSTROM, C. A. (1987). The relations among identity development, self-consciousness, and self-focusing during middle and late adolescence. *Developmental Psychology, 23,* 292–297.

*ADAMS, M. J. (1990). *Beginning to read: Thinking and learning about print.* Cambridge, MA: MIT Press.

ADAMS, P. L., MILNER, J. R., & SCHREPF, N. A. (1984). *Fatherless chidren.* New York: Wiley.

ADAMS, R. J. (1987). An evaluation of color preference in early infancy. *Infant Behavior and Development, 10,* 143–150.

ADAMS, R. J. (1989). Newborns' discrimination among mid- and long-wavelength stimuli. *Journal of Experimental Child Psychology, 47,* 130–141.

ADAMSON, L. B., & BAKEMAN, R. (1984). Mothers' communicative acts: Changes during infancy. *Infant Behavior and Development, 7,* 467–478.

ADAMSON, L. B., & BAKEMAN, R. (1991). The development of shared attention during infancy. In R. Vasta (Ed.), *Annals of child development* (Vol. 8). London: Kingsley.

*ADOLPH, K. E., EPPLER, M. A., & GIBSON, E. J. (1993). Development of perception of affordances. In C. Rovee-Collier & L. P. Lipsitt (Eds.), *Advances in infancy research* (Vol. 8). Norwood, NJ: Ablex.

AIELLO, J. R., NICOSIA, G., & THOMPSON, D. E. (1979). Physiological, social, and behavioral consequences of crowding on children and adolescents. *Child Development, 50,* 195–202.

AINSWORTH, M. D. S. (1973). The development of infant–mother attachment. In B. M. Caldwell & H. N. Ricciuti (Eds.), *Review of child development research* (Vol. 3). Chicago: University of Chicago Press.

AINSWORTH, M. D. S. (1983). Patterns of infant–mother attachment as related to maternal care: Their early history and their contribution to continuity. In D. Magnusson & V. Allen (Eds.), *Human development: An interactional perspective.* New York: Academic Press.

AINSWORTH, M. D. S. (1989). Attachments beyond infancy. *American Psychologist, 44,* 709–716.

*AINSWORTH, M. D. S. (1992). A consideration of social referencing in the context of attachment theory and research. In S. Feinman (Ed.), *Social referencing and the social construction of reality in infancy.* New York: Plenum.

AINSWORTH, M. D. S., BLEHAR, M. C., WATERS, E., & WALL, S. (1978). *Patterns of attachment: A psychological study of the strange situation.* Hillsdale, NJ: Erlbaum.

*AINSWORTH, M. D. S., & BOWLBY, J. (1991). An ethological approach to personality development. *American Psychologist, 46,* 331–341.

AINSWORTH, M. D. S., & WITTIG, B. A. (1969). Attachment and exploratory behavior of one-year-olds in a strange situation. In B. M. Foss (Ed.), *Determinants of infant behavior* (Vol. 4). London: Methuen.

AKHTAR, N., DUNHAM, F., & DUNHAM, P. J. (1991). Directive interactions and early vocabulary development: The role of joint attentional focus. *Journal of Child Language, 18,* 41–49.

*ALDHOUS, P. (1993). Disease gene search goes big science. *Science, 259,* 591–592.

*ALESSANDRI, S. M. (1992). Effects of maternal work status in single-parent families on children's perception of self and family and school achievement. *Journal of Experimental Child Psychology, 54,* 417–433.

ALLEN, M. C. (1984). Developmental outcome

and follow-up of the small for gestational age infant. *Seminars in Perinatology, 8,* 123–156.

ALLEY, T. R. (1983). Infantile head shape as an elicitor of adult protection. *Merrill-Palmer Quarterly, 29,* 411–427.

ALLISON, A. C. (1954). Protection afforded by sickle-cell trait against subtertian malarial infections. *British Medical Journal, 1,* 290–294.

ALLISON, P. D., & FURSTENBERG, F. F. (1989). How marital dissolution affects children: Variations by age and sex. *Developmental Psychology, 25,* 540–549.

ALS, H., DUFFY, F. H., & McANULTY, G. B. (1988). Behavioral differences between preterm and full-term newborns as measured with the APIB System Scores: I. *Infant Behavior and Development, 11,* 305–318.

ALS, H., TRONICK, E., ADAMSON, L., & BRAZELTON, T. B. (1976). The behavior of the full-term yet underweight newborn. *Develop-mental Medicine and Child Neurology, 18,* 590.

*ALTMAN, L. (1993, July 7). World Bank reports health gains for poor. *New York Times,* p. A6.

*AMERICAN ASSOCIATION OF UNIVERSITY WOMEN. (1992). *How schools shortchange women.* Wellesley, MA: AAUW and NEA.

*AMES, B. N. (1979). Identifying environmental chemicals causing mutations and cancer. *Science, 204,* 587–593.

AMSTERDAM, B. K. (1972). Mirror self-image reactions before age two. *Developmental Psychology, 5,* 297–305.

ANDERSON, D. R., LORCH, E. P., FIELD, D. E., COLLINS, P. A., & NATHAN, J. G. (1986). Television viewing at home: Age trends in visual attention and time with T.V. *Child Development, 57,* 1024–1033.

*ANDERSON, E., HETHERINGTON, E. M., & CLINGEMPEEL, W. G. (1989). Transformations in family relations at puberty: Effects of family context. *Journal of Early Adolescence, 9,* 310–334.

*ANDERSON, G. C. (1993, March). *Effects of environment on perinatal behavior.* Paper presented at the meeting of the Society for Research in Child Development. New Orleans.

ANDERSON, G. M., & ALLISON, D. J. (1990). Intrauterine growth retardation and the routine use of ultrasound. In R. B. Goldbloom & R. S. Lawrence (Eds.), *Preventing disease: Beyond the rhetoric.* New York: Springer-Verlag.

ANDERSON, R., & SMITH, B. L. (1987). Phonological development of two-year-old monolingual Puerto Rican Spanish-speaking children. *Journal of Child Language, 14,* 57–78.

*ANDERSSON, B.-E. (1992). Effects of day-care on cognitive and socioemotional competence of thirteen-year-old Swedish schoolchildren. *Child Development, 63,* 20–36.

ANGLIN, J. M. (1977). *Word, object, and conceptual development.* New York: Norton.

ANGLIN, J. M. (1983). Extensional aspects of the preschool child's word concepts. In T. Seiler & W. Wannamacher (Eds.), *Concept development and the development of word meaning.* Berlin: Springer-Verlag.

*ANGLIN, J. M. (1993). Vocabulary development: A morphological analysis. *Monographs of the Society for Research in Child Development, 58*(10, Serial No. 238).

ANGOFF, W. H. (1988). The nature–nurture debate, aptitudes, and group differences. *American Psychologist, 43,* 713–720.

*ANISFELD, E., BROWN, J., CUNNINGHAM, N., MILENTIJEVIC, I., REUSCH, N., & SOTO, L. (1993, March). *The role of vestibular-proprioceptive stimulation in preterm infant development: New evidence.* Paper presented at the meeting of the Society for Research in Child Development, New Orleans.

ANISFELD, E., CASPER, V., NOZYCE, M., & CUNNINGHAM, N. (1990). Does infant carrying promote attachment? An experimental study of the effects of increased physical contact on the development of attachment. *Child Development, 61,* 1617–1627.

ANISFELD, M. (1991). Neonatal imitation. *Developmental Review, 11,* 60–97.

*ANTONINI, A., & STRYKER, M. P. (1993). Rapid remodeling of axonal arbors in the visual cortex. *Science, 260,* 1819–1821.

APGAR, V. (1953). A proposal for a new method of evaluation of the newborn infant. *Current Researches in Anesthesia and Analgesia, 32,* 260–267.

APGAR, V., & BECK, J. (1974). *Is my baby all right?* New York: Pocket Books.

APPEL, L. F., COOPER, R. G., McCARRELL, N., SIMS-KNIGHT, J., YUSSEN, S. R., & FLAVELL, J. H. (1972). The development of the distinction between perceiving and memorizing. *Child Development, 43,* 1365–1381.

APPELBAUM, M. I., & McCALL, R. B. (1983). Design and analysis in developmental psychology. In W. Kessen (Ed.), *Handbook of child psychology: Vol. I. History, theory, and methods.* New York: Wiley

APPLEY, M. (1986). G. Stanley Hall: Vow on Mount Owen. In S. H. Hulse & B. F. Green (Eds.), *One hundred years of psychological research in America.* Baltimore: Johns Hopkins University Press.

ARBUTHNOT, J., SPARLING, Y., FAUST, D., & KEE, W. (1983). Logical and moral development in preadolescent children. *Psychological Reports, 52,* 209–210.

*ARCHER, J. (1992). *Ethology and human development.* London: Harvester Wheatsheaf and Barnes & Noble.

ARDREY, R. (1966). *The territorial imperative.* London: Anthony Blond.

ARIES, P. (1962). *Centuries of childhood: A social history of family life.* New York: Knopf.

*ARMSTRONG, T. (1991). *Awakening your child's natural genius.* Los Angeles: Jeremy P. Tarcher, Inc.

*ARSENIO, W. F. (1988). Children's conceptions of the situational affective consequences of sociomoral events. *Child Development, 59,* 1611–1622.

*ARSENIO, W. F., & KRAMER, R. (1992). Victimizers and their victims: Children's conceptions of the mixed emotional consequences of moral transgressions. *Child Development, 63,* 915–927.

*ARTERBERRY, M. E., BENSEN, A. S., & YONAS, A. (1991). Infants' responsiveness to static-monocular depth information: A recovery from habituation approach. *Infant Behavior and Development, 14,* 241–251.

*ASENDORPF, J. B. (1990). Beyond social withdrawal: Shyness, unsociability, and peer avoidance. *Human Development, 33,* 250–259.

*ASENDORPF, J. B. (1991). Development of inhibited children's coping with unfamiliarity. *Child Development, 62,* 1460–1474.

*ASENDORPF, J. B. (in press). Social inhibition: A general-developmental perspective. In J. Pennebaker & H. C. Traue (Eds.), *Emotional expression and inhibition in health and illness.* Toronto: Hogrefe & Huber.

*ASENDORPF, J. B., & BAUDONNIERE, P. (1993). Self-awareness and other-awareness: Mirror self-recognition and synchronic imitation among unfamiliar peers. *Developmental Psychology, 29,* 88–95.

*ASENDORPF, J. B., & NUNNER-WINKLER, G. (1992). Children's moral motive strength and temperamental inhibition reduce their immoral behavior in real moral conflicts. *Child Development, 63,* 1223–1235.

ASERINSKY, E., & KLEITMAN, N. (1955). A motility cycle in sleeping infants as manifested by ocular and gross bodily activity. *Journal of Applied Physiology, 8,* 11–18.

*ASHCRAFT, M. H. (1990). Strategic processing in children's mental arithmetic: A review and proposal. In D. F. Bjorklund (Ed.), *Children's strategies: Contemporary views of cognitive development.* Hillsdale, NJ: Erlbaum.

ASHER, S. R. (1985). An evolving paradigm in social skill training research with children. In B. H. Schneider, K. H. Rubin, & J. E. Ledingham (Eds.), *Children's peer relations: Issues in assessment and intervention.* New York: Springer-Verlag.

ASHER, S. R., & COIE, J. D. (Eds.). (1990). *Peer rejection in childhood.* New York: Cambridge University Press.

ASHER, S. R., & HYMEL, S. (1981). Children's social competence in peer relations: Sociometric and behavioral assessment. In J. D. Wine & M. D. Smye (Eds.), *Social competence.* New York: Guilford.

ASHER, S. R., RENSHAW, P. D., & HYMEL, S. (1982). Peer relations and the development of social skills. In S. G. Moore (Ed.), *The young child: Reviews of research* (Vol. 3). Washington, DC: National Association for the Education of Young Children.

*ASHMEAD, D. H., DAVIS, D. L., WHALEN, T., & ODOM, R. D. (1991). Sound localization and sensitivity to interaural time differences in human infants. *Child Development, 62,* 1211–1226.

ASHMEAD, D. H., & PERLMUTTER, M. (1980). Infant memory in everyday life. In M. Perlmutter (Ed.), *New directions for child development: No. 10. Children's memory.* San Francisco: Jossey-Bass.

ASLIN, R. N. (1987a). Motor aspects of visual development in infancy. In P. Salapatek & L. Cohen (Eds.), *Handbook of infant perception: Vol. 1. From sensation to perception.* New York: Academic Press.

ASLIN, R. N. (1987b). Visual and auditory development in infancy. In J. D. Osofsky (Ed.),

Handbook of infant development (2nd ed.). New York: Wiley.

ASLIN, R. N., & SHEA, S. L. (1990). Velocity thresholds in human infants: Implications for the perception of motion. *Developmental Psychology, 26,* 589–598.

ASLIN, R. N., & SMITH, L. B. (1988). Perceptual development. *Annual Review of Psychology, 39,* 435–473.

ASLIN, R. N., PISONI, D. B., JUSCZYK, P. W. (1983). Auditory development and speech perception in infancy. In M. M. Haith & J. J. Campos (Eds.), *Handbook of child psychology: Vol. 2. Infancy and developmental psychobiology.* New York: Wiley.

ASTINGTON, J. W. (1988). Children's production of commissive speech acts. *Journal of Child Language 15,* 411–423.

*ASTINGTON, J. W. (1993). *The child's discovery of the mind.* Cambridge, MA: Harvard University Press.

ATKINSON, J., & BRADDICK, O. (1988). Infant precursors of later visual disorders: Correlation or causality? In A. Yonas (Ed.), *Minnesota symposia on child psychology: Vol. 20. Perceptual development in infancy.* Hillsdale, NJ: Erlbaum.

ATKINSON, R. C., & SHIFFRIN, R. M. (1971). The control of short-term memory. *Scientific American, 225,* 82–90.

ATTILI, G. (1990). Successful and disconfirmed children in the peer group: Indices of social competence within an evolutionary perspective. *Human Development, 33,* 238–249.

AU, T. K., & GLUSMAN, M. (1990). The principle of mutual exclusivity in word learning: To honor or not to honor. *Child Development, 61,* 1474–1490.

AUSTIN, V. D., RUBLE, D. N., & TRABASSO, T. (1977). Recall and order effects as factors in children's moral judgments. *Child Development, 48,* 470–474.

BACON, W. F., & ICHIKAWA, V. (1988). Maternal expectations, classroom experiences, and achievement among kindergarteners in the United States and Japan. *Human Development, 31,* 378–383.

*BAENNINGER, M., & NEWCOMBE, N. (1989). The role of experience in spatial test performance: A meta-analysis. *Sex Roles, 20,* 327–344.

BAHRICK, L. E. (1983). Infants' perception of substance and temporal synchrony in multimodal events. *Infant Behavior and Development, 6,* 429–451.

BAHRICK, L. E. (1988). Intermodal learning in infancy: Learning on the basis of two kinds of invariant relations in audible and visual events. *Child Development, 59,* 197–209.

*BAHRICK, L. E. (1992). Infants' perceptual differentiation of amodal and modality-specific audio-visual relations. *Journal of Experimental Child Psychology, 53,* 180–199.

BAHRICK, L. E., WALKER, A. S., & NEISSER, U. (1981). Selective looking by infants. *Cognitive Psychology, 13,* 377–390.

*BAILEY, M. (1992). Children and AIDS. In J. M. Mann, D. J. M. Tarantola, & T. W. Netter (Eds.), *AIDS in the world.* Cambridge, MA: Harvard University Press.

BAILEY, S. M., & GARN, S. M. (1986). The genetics of maturation. In F. Falkner & J. M. Tanner (Eds.), *Human growth: A comprehensive treatise.* New York: Plenum.

*BAILLARGEON, R. (1986). Representing the existence and the location of hidden objects: Object permanence in 6- and 8-month-old infants. *Cognition, 23,* 21–41.

BAILLARGEON, R. (1987a). Object permanence in 3½- and 4½-month-old infants. *Developmental Psychology, 23,* 655–664.

*BAILLARGEON, R. (1987b). Young infants' reasoning about the physical and spatial properties of a hidden object. *Cognitive Development, 2* 179–200.

*BAILLARGEON, R. (1993). The object concept revisited: New directions in the investigation of infants' physical knowledge. In H. W. Reese (Ed.), *Advances in child development and behavior* (Vol. 23). New York: Academic Press.

BAILLARGEON, R., DeVOS, J., & GRABER, R. (1989). Location memory in 8-month-old infants in a non-search AB task: Further evidence. *Cognitive Development, 4,* 345–367.

BAKEMAN, R., & GOTTMAN, J. M. (1986). *Observing interactions: An introduction to sequential analysis.* Cambridge: Cambridge University Press.

BAKER, N. D., & NELSON, K. E. (1984). Recasting and related conversational techniques for triggering syntactic advances in young children. *First Language, 5,* 3–22.

BAKER-WARD, L., ORNSTEIN, P. A., & HOLDEN, D. J. (1984). The expression of memorization in early childhood. *Journal of Experimental Child Psychology, 37,* 555–575.

BALAZS, R., JORDAN, T., LEWIS, P. D., & PATEL, A. J. (1986). Undernutrition and brain development. In F. Falkner & J. M. Tanner (Eds.), *Human growth: A comprehensive treatise* New York: Plenum.

*BALDWIN, D. A. (1993). Infants' ability to consult the speaker for clues to word reference. *Journal of Child Language, 20,* 395–418.

BALDWIN, D. A., & MARKMAN, E. M. (1989). Establishing word-object relations: A first step. *Child Development, 60,* 381–398.

BALDWIN, D. V., & SKINNER, M. L. (1989). Structural model for antisocial behavior: Generalization to single-mother families. *Developmental Psychology, 25,* 45–50.

BANCROFT, J., AXWORTHY, D., & RATCLIFFE, S. (1982). The personality and psycho-sexual development of boys with XXY chromosome constitution. *Journal of Child Psychology and Psychiatry, 23,* 169–180.

BANDURA, A. (1965). Influence of models' reinforcement contingencies on the acquisition of imitative responses. *Journal of Personality and Social Psychology, 1,* 589–595.

BANDURA, A. (1973). *Aggression: A social learning analysis.* Englewood Cliffs, NJ: Prentice Hall.

BANDURA, A. (1977a). Self-efficacy: Toward a unifying theory of behavioral change. *Psychological Review, 84,* 191–215.

BANDURA, A. (1977b). *Social learning theory.* Englewood Cliffs, NJ: Prentice Hall.

BANDURA, A. (1978). The self system in reciprocal determinism. *American Psychologist, 33,* 344–358.

BANDURA, A. (1981). Self-referent thought: A developmental analysis of self-efficacy. In J. H. Flavell & L. Ross (Eds.), *Social cognitive development: Frontiers and possible futures.* New York: Cambridge University Press.

BANDURA, A. (1983). Psychological mechanisms of aggression. In R. G. Geen & E. I. Donnerstein (Eds.), *Aggression: Theoretical and empirical reviews* (Vol. 1). New York: Academic Press.

BANDURA, A. (1986). *Social foundations of thought and action: A social cognitive theory.* Englewood Cliffs, NJ: Prentice Hall.

BANDURA, A. (1989). Social cognitive theory. In R. Vasta (Ed.), *Annals of child development* (Vol. 6). Greenwich, CT: JAI Press.

*BANDURA, A. (1991a). Self-regulation of motivation through anticipatory and self-regulatory mechanisms. In R. A. Dienstbier (Ed.), *Perspectives on motivation: Nebraska symposium on motivation* (Vol. 38). Lincoln: University of Nebraska Press.

*BANDURA, A. (1991b). Social cognitive theory of moral thought and action. In W. M. Kurtines & J. L. Gewirtz (Eds.), *Handbook of moral behavior and development: Vol. 1. Theory.* Hillsdale, NJ: Erlbaum.

BANDURA, A., & SCHUNK, D. H. (1981). Cultivating competence, self-efficacy, and intrinsic interest through proximal self-motivation. *Journal of Personality and Social Psychology, 41,* 586–598.

BANDURA, A., & WALTERS, R. H. (1959). *Adolescent aggression.* New York: Ronald Press.

BANKS, M. S., & SALAPATEK, P. (1983). Infant visual perception. In M. M. Haith & J. J. Campos (Eds.), *Handbook of child psychology: Vol. 2. Infancy and developmental psychobiology.* New York: Wiley.

BARD, C., HAY, L., & FLEURY, M. (1990). Timing and accuracy of visually directed movements in children: Control of direction and amplitude components. *Journal of Experimental Child Psychology, 50,* 102–118.

*BARDEN, R. C., ZELKO, F. A., DUNCAN, S. W., & MASTERS, J. C. (1980). Children's consensual knowledge about the experiential determinants of emotion. *Journal of Personality and Social Psychology, 39,* 968–976.

BARGLOW, P., VAUGHN, B. E., & MOLITOR, N. (1987). Effects of maternal absence due to employment on the quality of infant–mother attachment. *Child Development, 58,* 945–954.

*BARINAGA, M. (1993). Death gives birth to the nervous system. But how? *Science, 259,* 762–763.

*BARINAGA, M. (1994). From fruit flies, rats, mice: Evidence of genetic influence. *Science, 264,* 1690–1693.

BARKER, R. G., & WRIGHT, H. F. (1951). *One boy's day: A specimen record of behavior.* New York: Harper & Row.

BARKER, R. G., & WRIGHT, H. F. (1955). *Midwest and its children.* New York: Harper & Row.

BARNARD, K. E., BEE, H. L., & HAMMOND, M. A. (1984a). Developmental changes in maternal interactions with term and preterm infants. *International Journal of Behavior and Development, 7,* 101–113.

BARNARD, K. E., BEE, H. L., & HAMMOND, M. A. (1984b). Home environment and cognitive development in a healthy, low-risk sample: The Seattle study. In A. W. Gottfried (Ed.), *Home environment and early cognitive development*. New York: Academic Press.

*BARNARD, K. E., MORISSET, C. E., & SPIEKER, S. (1993). Preventive interventions: Enhancing parent–infant relationships. In C. H. Zeanah, Jr. (Ed.), *Handbook of infant development*. New York: Guilford.

BARNES, D. M. (1986). Brain architecture. *Science, 233,* 155–156.

BARNES, D. M. (1988). Schizophrenia genetics: A mixed bag. *Science, 242,* 1009.

BARNES, D. M. (1990). Silver Spring monkeys yield unexpected data on brain reorganization. *Journal of NIH Research, 2,* 19–20.

BARNETT, C. R., LEIDERMAN, P. H., GROB-STEIN, R., & KLAUS, M. H. (1970). Neonatal separation: The maternal side of interactional deprivation. *Pediatrics, 45,* 197–205.

BARNETT, M. A. (1987). Empathy and related responses in children. In N. Eisenberg & J. Strayer (Eds.), *Empathy and its development*. New York: Cambridge University Press.

BARNETT, M. A., & McMINIMY, V. (1988). Influence of the reason for the other's affect on preschoolers' empathy response. *Journal of Genetic Psychology, 149,* 153–162.

BARON, R. A. (1983). The control of human aggression: A strategy based on incompatible responses. In R. G. Geen & E. I. Donnerstein (Eds.), *Aggression: Theoretical and empirical reviews* (Vol. 2). New York: Academic Press.

BARON, R. A., & RICHARDSON, D. R. (Eds.). (1994). *Human aggression* (2nd ed.). New York: Plenum.

*BARONE, D. (1993). Wednesday's child: Literacy development of children prenatally exposed to crack or cocaine. *Research in the Teaching of English, 27,* 7–45.

*BAROODY, A. J. (1992). The development of kindergartners' mental-addition strategies. *Learning and Individual Differences, 4,* 215–235.

BARRERA, M., & MAURER, D. (1981). The perception of facial expressions by the three-month-old. *Child Development, 52,* 203–206.

BARRETT, D. E., RADKE-YARROW, M., & KLEIN, R. E. (1982). Chronic malnutrition and child behavior: Effects of early caloric supplementation on social and emotional functioning at school age. *Developmental Psychology, 18,* 541–556.

BARRETT, M. D. (Ed.). (1985). *Children's single-word speech*. New York: Wiley.

BARRETT, M. D. (1986). Early semantic representations and early word usage. In S. A. Kuczaj & M. D. Barrett (Eds.), *The development of word meaning*. New York: Springer-Verlag.

BARTON, E. J. (1981). Developing sharing: An analysis of modeling and other behavioral techniques. *Behavior Modification, 5,* 386–398.

BASH, M. A. S., & CAMP, B. W. (1985). *Think Aloud: Classroom program*. Champaign, IL: Research Press.

*BATES, E. (1990). Language about me and you: Pronominal reference and the emerging concept of self. In D. Cicchetti & M. Beeghly (Eds.), *The self in transition: Infancy to childhood*. Chicago: University of Chicago Press.

BATES, E., BRETHERTON, I., BEEGHLY-SMITH, M., & McNEW, S. (1982). Social bases of language development: A reassessment. In D. S. Palermo (Ed.), *Advances in child development and behavior* (Vol. 17). New York: Academic Press.

BATES, E., BRETHERTON, I., SHORE, C., & McNEW, S. (1983). Names, gestures, and objects: Symbolization in infancy and aphasia. In K. E. Nelson (Ed.), *Children's language* (Vol. 4). Hillsdale, NJ: Erlbaum.

BATES, E., BRETHERTON, I., & SNYDER, L. (1988). *From first words to grammar: Individual differences and dissociable mechanisms*. New York: Cambridge University Press.

BATES, E., CAMAIONI, L., & VOLTERRA, V. (1975). The acquisition of performatives prior to speech. *Merrill-Palmer Quarterly, 21,* 205–226.

*BATES, E., & CARNEVALE, G. F. (1993). New directions in research on language development. *Developmental Review, 13,* 436–470.

BATES, E., & MacWHINNEY, B. (1982). Functionalist approaches to grammar. In E. Wanner & L. Gleitman (Eds.), *Language acquisition: The state of the art*. New York: Cambridge University Press.

*BATES, E., & MacWHINNEY, B. (1987). Competition, variation, language learning. In B. MacWhinney (Ed.), *Mechanisms of language acquisition*. Hillsdale, NJ: Erlbaum.

BATES, E., O'CONNELL, B., & SHORE, C. (1987). Language and communication in infancy. In J. D. Osofsky (Ed.), *Handbook of infant development* (2nd ed.). New York: Wiley.

BATES, J. E. (1983). Issues in the assessment of difficult temperament. *Merrill-Palmer Quarterly, 29,* 89–97.

BATES, J. E. (1987). Temperament in infancy. In J. D. Osofsky (Ed.), *Handbook of infant development* (2nd ed.). New York: Wiley.

BATES, J. E. (1990). Conceptual and empirical linkages between temperament and behavior problems: A commentary on the Sanson, Prior, and Kyrios study. *Merrill-Palmer Quarterly, 36,* 193–199.

BATES, J. E., & BAYLES, K. (1984). Objective and subjective components in mothers' perceptions of their children from age 6 months to 3 years. *Merrill-Palmer Quarterly, 30,* 111–130.

BATES, J. E., MASLIN, C. A., & FRANKEL, K. A. (1985). Attachment security, mother–child interaction, and temperament as predictors of behavior-problem ratings at age three years. In I. Bretherton & E. Waters (Eds.), *Growing points of attachment theory and research*. *Monographs of the Society for Research in Child Development, 50* (Nos. 1–2).

*BATES, J. E., & WACHS, T. D. (1994). *Temperament: Individual differences at the interface of biology and behavior*. Washington, DC: APA.

BATESON, P. P. G. (1979). How do sensitive periods arise and what are they for? *Animal Behaviour, 27,* 470–486.

*BATSON, C. D., & OLESON, K. C. (1991). Current status of the empathy-altruism hypothesis. In M. S. Clark (Ed.), *Review of personality and social psychology: Prosocial behavior*. Newbury Park, CA: Sage.

BAUCOM, D. H., & DANKER-BROWN, P. (1979). Influence of sex roles on the development of learned helplessness. *Journal of Consulting and Clinical Psychology, 47,* 928–936.

*BAUER, P. J. (1992). Holding it all together: How enabling relations facilitate young children's event recall. *Cognitive Development, 7,* 1–28.

*BAUER, P. J. (1993a). Identifying subsystems of autobiographical memory: Commentary on Nelson. In C. A. Nelson (Ed.), *Minnesota symposia on child psychology: Vol. 26. Memory and affect in development*. Hillsdale, NJ: Erlbaum.

*BAUER, P. J. (1993b). Memory for gender-consistent and gender-inconsistent event sequences by twenty-five-month-old children. *Child Development, 64,* 285–297.

*BAUER, P. J., & MANDLER, J. M. (1992). Putting the horse before the cart: The use of temporal order in recall of events by one-year-old children. *Developmental Psychology, 28,* 441–452.

*BAUERFELD S. L., & LACHENMEYER, J. R. (1992). Prenatal nutritional status and intellectual development: Critical review and evaluation. In B. B. Lahey & A. E. Kazdin (Eds.), *Advances in clinical child psychology* (Vol. 14). New York: Plenum.

BAUMRIND, D. (1971). Current patterns of parental authority. *Developmental Psychology Monograph, 4,* 1–103.

BAUMRIND, D. (1989). Rearing competent children. In W. Damon (Ed.), *Child development today and tomorrow*. San Francisco: Jossey-Bass.

*BAUMRIND, D. (1991). The influence of parenting style on adolescent competence and substance abuse. *Journal of Early Adolescence, 11,* 56–95.

BAYLEY, N. (1969). *Bayley Scales of Infant Development: Birth to Two Years*. New York: The Psychological Corporation.

BAYLEY, N. (1970). Development of mental abilities. In P. H. Mussen (Ed.), *Carmichael's manual of child psychology* (3rd ed., Vol. 1). New York: Wiley.

*BAYLEY, N. (1993). *Bayley Scales of Infant Development: Birth to Two Years* (2nd ed.). New York: The Psychological Corporation.

BEACONSFIELD, P., BIRDWOOD, G., & BEACONSFIELD, R. (1980). The placenta. *Scientific American, 243,* 94–103.

BEAR, G. G. (1989). Sociomoral reasoning and antisocial behaviors among normal sixth graders. *Merrill-Palmer Quarterly, 35,* 181–196.

*BEARDSLEY, T. (1991). Smart genes. *Scientific American, 265,* 87–95.

*BEBKO, J. M., BURKE, L., CRAVEN, J., & SARLO, N. (1992). The importance of motor activity in sensorimotor development: A perspective from children with physical handicaps. *Human Development, 35,* 226–240.

BECHTOLD, A. G., BUSHNELL, E. W., & SALAPATEK, P. (1979, April). *Infants' visual localization of visual and auditory targets*. Paper presented at the meeting of the Society for Research in Child Development, San Francisco.

*BECKER, J. (1993). Young children's numerical use of number words: Counting in many-to-one situations. *Developmental Psychology, 29,* 458–465.

BECKER, J. M. F. (1977). A learning analysis of the development of peer-oriented behavior in nine-month-old infants. *Developmental Psychology, 13,* 481–491.

BECKWITH, L., & PARMELEE, A. (1986). EEG patterns of preterm infants, home environment, and later IQ. *Child Development, 57,* 777–789.

BEEBE, B., ALSON, D., JAFFE, J., FELDSTEIN, S., & CROWN, C. (1988). Vocal congruence in mother–infant play. *Journal of Psycholinguistic Research, 17,* 245–259.

BEEBE, T. P., Jr., WILSON, T. E., OGLETREE, D. F., KATZ, J. E., BALHORN, R., SALMERON, M. D., & SIEKHAUS, W. J. (1989). Direct observation of native DNA structures with the scanning tunneling microscope. *Science, 243,* 370–372.

BEHREND, D. A. (1988). Overextensions in early language comprehension: Evidence from a signal detection approach. *Journal of Child Language, 15,* 63–75.

*BEHREND, D. A., ROSENGREN, K. S., & PERLMUTTER, M. (1992). The relation between private speech and parental interactive style. In R. M. Diaz & L. E. Berk (Eds.), *Private speech: From social interaction to self-regulation.* Hillsdale, NJ: Erlbaum.

BEHRMAN, R. E., & VAUGHAN, V. C., III. (1987). *Nelson textbook of pediatrics* (3rd ed.). Philadelphia: Saunders.

*BEIER, E. G. (1991). Freud: Three contributions. In G. A. Kimble, M. Wertheimer, & C. L. White (Eds.), *Portraits of pioneers in psychology.* Hillsdale, NJ: Erlbaum.

BEILIN, H. (1971). Developmental stages and developmental processes. In D. Green, M. Ford, & G. Flamer (Eds.), *Measurement and Piaget.* New York: McGraw-Hill.

BEILIN, H. (1978). Inducing conservation through training. In G. Steiner (Ed.), *Psychology of the 20th century: Vol. 7. Piaget and beyond.* Zurich: Kindler.

BEILIN, H. (1989). Piagetian theory. In R. Vasta (Ed.), *Annals of child development* (Vol. 6). Greenwich, CT: JAI Press.

*BEILIN, H. (1992a). Piaget's enduring contribution to developmental psychology. *Developmental Psychology, 28,* 191–204.

*BEILIN, H. (1992b). Piaget's new theory. In H. Beilin & P. B. Pufall (Eds.), *Piaget's theory: Prospects and possibilities.* Hillsdale, NJ: Erlbaum.

*BELL, M. A., & FOX, N. A. (1992). The relations between frontal brain electrical activity and cognitive development during infancy. *Child Development, 63,* 1142–1163.

BELL, N. J., & CARVER, W. (1980). A reevaluation of gender label effects: Expectant mothers' responses to infants. *Child Development, 51,* 925–927.

BELL, R. Q. (1979). Parent, child, and reciprocal influences. *American Psychologist, 34,* 821–826.

BELL, S., & AINSWORTH, M. D. S. (1972). Infant crying and maternal responsiveness. *Child Development, 43,* 1171–1190.

BELLE, D. (Ed.). (1989a). *Children's social networks and social supports.* New York: Wiley.

BELLE, D. (1989b). Introduction: Studying children's social networks and social supports. In D. Belle (Ed.), *Children's social networks and social supports.* New York: Wiley.

BELLINGER, D., LEVITON, A., NEEDLEMAN, H. L., WATERNAUX, C., & RABINOWITZ, M. (1986). Low-level lead exposure and infant development in the first year. *Neurobehavioral Toxicology and Teratology, 8,* 151–161.

BELMONT, J. M. (1989). Cognitive strategies and strategic learning: The socio-instructional approach. *American Psychologist, 44,* 142–148.

BELSEY, E. M., ROSENBLATT, D. B., LIEBERMAN, B. A., REDSHAW, M., CALDWELL, J., NOTARIANNI, L., SMITH, R. L., & BEARD, R. W. (1981). The influence of maternal analgesia on neonatal behavior: I. Pethidine. *British Journal of Obstetrics & Gynecology, 887,* 398–406.

BELSKY, J. (1980). Child maltreatment: An ecological integration. *American Psychologist, 35,* 320–335.

BELSKY, J. (1984). Two waves of day care research: Developmental effects and conditions of quality. In R. C. Ainslie (Ed.), *The child and the day care setting.* New York: Praeger.

BELSKY, J. (1988). The "effects" of infant day care reconsidered. *Early Childhood Research Quarterly, 3,* 235–272.

*BELSKY, J., & BRAUNGART, J. M. (1991). Are insecure-avoidant infants with extensive daycare experience less stressed by and more independent in the Strange Situation? *Child Development, 62,* 567–571.

BELSKY, J., GILSTRAP, B., & ROVINE, M. (1984). The Pennsylvania Infant and Family Development Project: I. Stability and change in mother–infant and father–infant interaction in a family setting at one, three, and nine months. *Child Development, 55,* 692–705.

BELSKY, J., & ISABELLA, R. A. (1988). Maternal, infant, and social-contextual determinants of attachment security. In J. Belsky & T. Nezworski (Eds.), *Clinical implications of attachment.* Hillsdale, NJ: Erlbaum.

BELSKY, J., & ROVINE, M. (1988). Nonmaternal care in the first year of life and infant–parent attachment security. *Child Development, 59,* 157–167.

BELSKY, J., ROVINE, M., & TAYLOR, D. G. (1984). The Pennsylvania Infant and Family Development Project, III. The origins of individual differences in infant–mother attachment: Maternal and infant contributions. *Child Development, 55,* 718–728.

*BELSKY, J., STEINBERG, L., & DRAPER, P. (1991). Childhood experience, interpersonal development, and reproductive strategy: An evolutionary theory of socialization. *Child Development, 62,* 647–670.

BEM, S. L. (1974). The measurement of psychological androgyny. *Journal of Consulting and Clinical Psychology, 42,* 155–162.

BEM, S. L. (1975). Sex role adaptability: One consequence of psychological androgyny. *Journal of Personality and Social Psychology, 31,* 634–643.

BEM, S. L. (1979). Theory and measurement of androgyny: A reply to the Pedhazur-Tetenbaum and Locksley-Colten critiques. *Journal of Personality and Social Psychology, 37,* 1047–1054.

BEM, S. L. (1981). Gender schema theory: A cognitive account of sex-typing. *Psychological Review, 88,* 354–364.

*BEM, S. L. (1985). Androgyny and gender schema theory. In T. B. Sonderegger (Ed.), *Nebraska symposium on motivation: Psychology and gender* (Vol. 32). Lincoln: University of Nebraska Press.

BEM, S. L. (1987). Masculinity and femininity exist only in the mind of the perceiver. In J. M. Reinisch, L. A. Rosenblum, & S. A. Sanders (Eds.), *Masculinity/femininity: Basic perspectives.* New York: Oxford.

*BEM, S. L. (1989). Genital knowledge and gender constancy in preschool children. *Child Development, 60,* 649–662.

*BENASICH, A. A., BROOKS-GUNN, J., & CLEWELL, B. C. (1992). How do mothers benefit from early intervention programs? *Journal of Applied Developmental Psychology, 13,* 311–362.

BENBOW, C. P., & STANLEY, J. C. (1981). Mathematical ability: Is sex a factor? *Science, 212,* 118–119.

BENBOW, C. P., & STANLEY, J. C. (1985). Sex differences in mathematical reasoning ability: More facts. *Science, 222,* 1029–1031.

BENEDICT, H. (1979). Early lexical development: Comprehension and production. *Journal of Child Language, 6,* 183–200.

*BENENSON, J. F. (1993). Greater preference among females than males for dyadic interaction in early childhood. *Child Development, 64,* 544–555.

*BENENSON, J. F., & DWECK, C. S. (1986). The development of trait explanations and self-evaluations in the academic and social domains. *Child Development, 57,* 1179–1187.

*BENOIT, D. (1993). Failure to thrive and feeding disorders. In C. H. Zeanah, Jr. (Ed.), *Handbook of infant mental development.* New York: Guilford.

BENSON, J. B. (1990). The significance and development of crawling in human infancy. In J. E. Clark & J. H. Humphrey (Eds.), *Advances in motor development research* (Vol. 3). New York: AMS Press.

BENSON, J. B., & UZGIRIS, I. C. (1985). Effects of self-initiated locomotion on infant search activity. *Developmental Psychology, 21,* 923–931.

BERBAUM, M. L. (1985). Explanation and prediction: Criteria for assessing the confluence model. *Child Development, 56,* 781–784.

BERBAUM, M. L., MORELAND, R. L., & ZAJONC, R. B. (1986). Contentions over the confluence model: A reply to Price, Walsh, and Vilburg. *Psychological Bulletin, 100,* 270–274.

*BERENBAUM, S. A. (1990). Congenital adrenal hyperplasia: Intellectual and psychosexual functioning. In C. Holmes (Ed.), *Psychoneuroendocrinology: Brain, behavior, and hormonal interactions.* New York: Springer-Verlag.

*BERENBAUM, S. A., & HINES, M. (1992). Early androgens are related to childhood sex-typed toy preferences. *Psychological Science, 3,* 203–206.

BERG, W. K., & BERG, K. M. (1987). Psychophysiological development in infancy: State, startle, and attention. In J. Osofsky (Ed.), *Handbook of infant development* (2nd ed.). New York: Wiley.

BERGSMA, D. (1979). *Birth defects compendium.* New York: Alan R. Liss.

BERKO, J. (1958). The child's learning of English morphology. *Word, 14,* 150–177.

KOWITZ, M. W., GIBBS, J. C., & BROUGHTON, J. M. (1980). The relation of moral judgment stage disparity to developmental effects of peer dialogues. *Merrill-Palmer Quarterly, 26,* 341–357.

BERNDT, T. J. (1979). Developmental changes in conformity to peers and parents. *Developmental Psychology, 15,* 608–616.

BERNDT, T. J. (1981). Age changes and changes over time in prosocial intentions and behavior between friends. *Developmental Psychology, 17,* 408–416.

BERNDT, T. J. (1982). Fairness and friendship. In K. H. Rubin & H. S. Ross (Eds.), *Peer relationships and social skills in childhood.* New York: Springer-Verlag.

BERNDT, T. J. (1986a). Children's comments about their friendships. In M. Perlmutter (Ed.), *Minnesota symposia on child psychology: Vol. 18. Cognitive perspectives on children's social and behavioral development.* Hillsdale, NJ: Erlbaum.

BERNDT, T. J. (1986b, August). *The distinctive features of conversations between friends.* Paper presented at the meeting of the American Psychological Association, Washington, DC.

BERNDT, T. J. (1986c). Sharing between friends: Contexts and consequences. In E. C. Mueller & C. R. Cooper (Eds.), *Process and outcome in peer relationships.* New York: Academic Press.

BERNDT, T. J. (1988). The nature and significance of children's friendships. In R. Vasta (Ed.), *Annals of child development* (Vol. 5). London: JAI Press.

BERNDT, T. J. (1989). Friendships in childhood and adolescence. In W. Damon (Ed.), *Child development today and tomorrow.* San Francisco: Jossey-Bass.

BERNDT, T. J. (1989b). Obtaining support from friends during childhood and adolescence. In D. Belle (Ed.), *Children's social networks and social supports.* New York: Wiley.

*BERNDT, T. J., & BULLEIT, T. N. (1985). Effects of sibling relationships on preschoolers' behavior at home and at school. *Developmental Psychology, 21,* 761–767.

BERNDT, T. J., & HELLER, K. A. (1986). Gender stereotypes and social inferences: A developmental study. *Journal of Personality and Social Psychology, 50,* 889–898.

BERNDT, T. J., & HOYLE, S. G. (1985). Stability and change in childhood and adolescent friendships. *Developmental Psychology, 21,* 1007–1015.

*BERNDT, T. J., MILLER, K. E., & PARK, K. (1989). Adolescents' perceptions of friends' and parents' influence on aspects of their school adjustment. *Journal of Early Adolescence, 9,* 419–435.

BERNDT, T. J., & PERRY, T. B. (1990). Distinctive features and effects of adolescent friendships. In R. Montemayor, G. R. Adams, & T. P. Gullotta (Eds.), *From childhood to adolescence: A transitional period?* London: Sage.

BERNSTEIN, M. E. (1983). Formation of internal structure in a lexical category. *Journal of Child Language, 10,* 381–399.

*BERSOFF, D. M., & MILLER, J. G. (1993). Culture, context, and the development of moral accountability judgments. *Developmental Psychology, 29,* 664–676.

*BERTENTHAL, B. I. (1993, March). *Emerging trends in perceptual development.* Paper presented at the meeting of the Society for Research in Child Development, New Orleans.

*BERTENTHAL, B. I., & CAMPOS, J. J. (1990). A systems approach to the organizing effects of self-produced locomotion during infancy. In C. Rovee-Collier & L. P. Lipsitt (Eds.), *Advances in infancy research* (Vol. 6). Norwood, NJ: Ablex.

BERTENTHAL, B. I., CAMPOS, J. J., & HAITH, M. M. (1980). Development of visual organization: The perception of subjective contours. *Child Development, 51,* 1072–1080.

BERTENTHAL, B. I., & FISCHER, K. W. (1978). Development of self-recognition in the infant. *Developmental Psychology, 11,* 44–50.

*BERTENTHAL, B. I., & PINTO, J. (in press). Complementary processes in the perception and production of human movements. In E. Thelen & L. Smith (Eds.), *Dynamical systems in development: Vol. 2. Applications.* Cambridge, MA: Bradford Books.

BEST, C. T., McROBERTS, G. W., & SITHOLE, N. M. (1988). Examination of perceptual reorganization for nonnative speech contrasts: Zula click discrimination by English-speaking adults and infants. *Journal of Experimental Psychology: Human Perception and Performance, 14,* 345–360.

*BHAVNAGRI, N., & PARKE, R. D. (1991). Parents as direct facilitators of children's peer relationships: Effects of age of child and sex of parent. *Journal of Social and Personal Relationships, 8,* 423–440.

*BIALYSTOK, E., & CUMMINS, J. (1991). Language, cognition, and education of bilingual children. In E. Bialystok (Ed.), *Language processing in bilingual children.* Cambridge: Cambridge University Press.

*BIBACE, R., & WALSH, M. E. (1981). Children's conceptions of illness. In R. Bibace & M. E. Walsh (Eds.), *New directions for child development: No. 14. Children's conceptions of health, illness, and bodily functions.* San Francisco: Jossey-Bass.

BICKERTON, D. (1984). The language bioprogram hypothesis. *Behavioral and Brain Sciences, 7,* 173–187.

BIGELOW, A. E. (1981). The correspondence between self- and image movement as a cue to self-recognition for young children. *Journal of Genetic Psychology, 139,* 11–26.

BIGLER, R. S., & LIBEN, L. S. (1990). The role of attitudes and interventions in gender-schematic processing. *Child Development, 61,* 1440–1452.

*BIGLER, R. S., & LIBEN, L. S. (1992). Cognitive mechanisms in children's gender stereotyping: Theoretical and educational implications of a cognitive-based intervention. *Child Development, 63,* 1351–1363.

*BIGLER, R. S., & LIBEN, L. S. (1993). A cognitive-developmental approach to social stereotyping and reconstructive memory in Euro-American children. *Child Development, 64,* 1507–1518.

BIJOU, S. W. (1989). Behavior analysis. In R. Vasta (Ed.), *Annals of child development* (Vol. 6). Greenwich, CT: JAI Press.

BIJOU, S. W., & BAER, D. M. (1961). *Child development: Vol. 1. A systematic and empirical theory.* Englewood Cliffs, NJ: Prentice Hall.

BIJOU, S. W., & BAER, D. M. (1965). *Child development: Vol. 2. Universal stage of infancy.* Englewood Cliffs, NJ: Prentice Hall.

BIJOU, S. W., & BAER, D. M. (1978). *Behavior analysis of child development.* Englewood Cliffs, NJ: Prentice Hall.

BILLER, H. B. (1981). The father and sex role development. In M. E. Lamb (Ed.), *The role of the father in child development* (2nd ed.). New York: Wiley.

BINSACCA, D. B., ELLIS, J., MARTIN, D. G., & PETITTI, D. B. (1987). Factors associated with low birthweight in an inner-city population: The role of financial problems. *American Journal of Public Health, 77,* 505–506.

BIRCH, L. L., & BILLMAN, J. (1986). Preschool children's food sharing with friends and acquaintances. *Child Development, 57,* 387–395.

BIRNHOLZ, J. C., & BENACERRAF, B. R. (1983). The development of human fetal hearing. *Science, 222,* 516–518.

BIRNS, B. (1976). The emergence and socialization of sex differences in the earliest years. *Merrill-Palmer Quarterly, 22,* 229–254.

*BISANZ, J., & LEFEVRE, J. (1990). Strategic and nonstrategic processing in the development of mathematical cognition. In D. F. Bjorklund (Ed.), *Children's strategies: Contemporary views of cognitive development.* Hillsdale, NJ: Erlbaum.

BIVENS, J. A., & BERK, L. E. (1990). A longitudinal study of the development of elementary school children's private speech. *Merrill-Palmer Quarterly, 36,* 443–463.

BJORK, E. L., & CUMMINGS, E. M. (1984). Infant search errors: Stage of concept development or stage of memory development. *Memory and Cognition, 12,* 1–19.

BJORKLUND, D. F. (1987a). How age changes in knowledge base contribute to the development of children's memory: An interpretive review. *Developmental Review, 7,* 93–130.

BJORKLUND, D. F. (1987b). A note on neonatal imitation. *Developmental Review, 7,* 86–92.

BJORKLUND, D. F. (1989). *Children's thinking.* Pacific Grove, CA: Brooks/Cole.

BJORKLUND, D. F. (Ed.). (1990). *Children's strategies: Contemporary views of cognitive development.* Hillsdale, NJ: Erlbaum.

*BJORKLUND, D. F., GAULTNEY, J. F., & GREEN, B. L. (1993). "I watch, therefore I can do": The development of meta-imitation during the preschool years and the advantage of optimism about one's imitative skills. In R. Pasnak & M. L. Howe (Eds.), *Emerging themes in cognitive development: Vol. 2. Competencies.* New York: Springer-Verlag.

*BJORKLUND, D. F., & GREEN, B. L. (1992). The adaptive nature of cognitive immaturity. *American Psychologist, 47,* 46–54.

*BJORKLUND, D. F., MUIR-BROADDUS, J. E., & SCHNEIDER, W. (1990). The role of knowledge in the development of strategies. In D. F. Bjorklund (Ed.), *Children's strategies: Contemporary views of cognitive development.* Hillsdale, NJ: Erlbaum.

BJORKLUND, D. F., & ZEMAN, B. R. (1982). Children's organization and metamemory awareness in their recall of familiar information. *Child Development, 53,* 799–810.

*BLAKE, J., & BOYSSON-BARDIES, B. (1992). Patterns in babbling: A cross-linguistic study. *Journal of Child Language, 19,* 51–74.

BLAKE, J., & FINK, R. (1987). Sound-meaning correspondences in babbling. *Journal of Child Language, 14,* 229–253.

BLAKEMORE, J. E. O., LaRUE, A. A., & OLEJNIK, A. B. (1979). Sex-appropriate toy preferences and the ability to conceptualize toys as sex-role related. *Developmental Psychology, 15,* 339–340.

BLASI, A. (1980). Bridging moral cognition and moral action: A critical review of the literature. *Psychological Bulletin, 88,* 1–45.

BLASI, A. (1983). Moral cognition and moral action: A theoretical perspective. *Developmental Review, 3,* 178–210.

BLASS, E. M., GANCHROW, J. R., & STEINER, J. E. (1984). Classical conditioning in newborn humans 2–48 hours of age. *Infant Behavior and Development, 7,* 223–235.

*BLASS, E. M., & SMITH, B. A. (1992). Differential effects of sucrose, fructose, glucose, and lactose. *Developmental Psychology, 28,* 804–810.

*BLOCK, J., & ROBINS, R. W. (1993). A longitudinal study of consistency and change in self-esteem from early adolescence to early adulthood. *Child Development, 64,* 909–923.

BLOCK, J. H. (1973). Conceptions of sex role: Some cross-cultural and longitudinal perspectives. *American Psychologist, 28,* 512–526.

BLOCK, J. H. (1983). Differential premises arising from differential socialization of the sexes: Some conjectures. *Child Development, 54,* 1335–1354.

BLOOM, K., RUSSELL, A., & WASSENBERG, K. (1987). Turn taking affects the quality of infant vocalizations. *Journal of Child Language, 14,* 211–227.

BLOOM, L. (1973). *One word at a time.* The Hague: Mouton.

*BLOOM, L. (1993, Winter). Word learning. *SRCD Newsletter,* pp. 1–13.

BLOOM, L., HOOD, L., & LIGHTBROWN, P. (1974). Imitation in language development: If, when, and why. *Cognitive Psychology, 6,* 380–420.

BLOOM, L., LIFTER, K., & BROUGHTON, J. (1985). The convergence on early cognition and language in the second year of life: Problems in conceptualization and measurement. In M. Barrett (Ed.), *Single-word speech.* New York: Wiley.

BLOOM, L., LIGHTBROWN, P., & HOOD, L. (1975). Structure and variation in child language. *Monographs of the Society for Research in Child Development, 40* (2, No. 160).

BLOUNT, B. G. (1982). The ontogeny of emotions and their vocal expression in infants. In S. A. Kuczaj (Ed.), *Language development* (Vol. 2). Hillsdale, NJ: Erlbaum.

*BLUMENFELD, W. J., & RAYMOND, D. (1988). *Looking at gay and lesbian life.* Boston: Beacon.

BLURTON-JONES, N. (1972). *Ethological studies of child behavior.* Cambridge: Cambridge University Press.

BLYTH, D. A., SIMMONS, R. G., & CARLTON-FORD, S. (1983). The adjustment of early adolescents to school transitions. *Journal of Early Adolescence, 3,* 105–120.

*BOER, F., & DUNN, J. (Eds.). (1992). *Children's sibling relationships: Developmental and clinical issues.* Hillsdale, NJ: Erlbaum.

*BOGGIANO, A. K., BARRETT, M., & KELLAM, T. (1993). Competing theoretical analyses of helplessness: A social-developmental analysis. *Journal of Experimental Child Psychology, 55,* 194–207.

BOGGIANO, A. K., MAIN, D. S., & KATZ, P. A. (1988). Children's preference for challenge: The role of perceived competence and control. *Journal of Personality and Social Psychology, 54,* 134–141.

BOHANNON, J. N., & HIRSH-PASEK, K. (1984). Do children say as they're told? A new perspective on motherese. In L. Feagans, C. Garvey, & R. Golinkoff (Eds.), *The origins and growth of communication.* Norwood, NJ: Ablex.

BOHANNON, J. N., & STANOWICZ, L. (1988). The issue of negative evidence: Adult responses to children's language errors. *Developmental Psychology, 24,* 684–689.

BOISMER, J. D. (1977). Visual stimulation and wake-sleep behavior in human neonates. *Developmental Psychology, 10,* 219–227.

*BOLDIZAR, J. P. (1991). Assessing sex typing and androgyny in children: The children's sex-role inventory. *Developmental Psychology, 27,* 505–515.

BOLDIZAR, J. P., PERRY, D. G., & PERRY, L. C. (1989). Outcome values and aggression. *Child Development, 60,* 571–579.

BOLES, D. B. (1980). X-linkage of spatial ability: A critical review. *Child Development, 51,* 625–635.

BOLLES, R. C., & BEECHER, M. D. (Eds.). (1988). *Evolution and learning.* Hillsdale, NJ: Erlbaum.

BOOM, J., & MOLENAAR, P. C. M. (1989). A developmental model of hierarchical stage structure in objective moral judgments. *Developmental Review, 9,* 133–145.

*BOONE, S. L. (1991). Aggression in African-American boys: A discriminant analysis. *Genetic, Social, and General Psychology Monographs, 117,* 205–228.

BORKE, H. (1975). Piaget's mountains revisited: Changes in the egocentric landscape. *Developmental Psychology, 11,* 240–243.

BORKOWSKI, J. G., MILSTEAD, M., & HALE, C. (1988). Components of children's metamemory: Implications for strategy generalization. In F. E. Weinert & M. Perlmutter (Eds.), *Memory development: Universal changes and individual differences.* Hillsdale, NJ: Erlbaum.

BORNSTEIN, M. H. (Ed.). (1987). *Sensitive periods in development: Interdisciplinary perspectives.* Hillsdale, NJ: Erlbaum.

*BORNSTEIN, M. H. (Ed.). (1991). *Cultural approaches to parenting.* Hillsdale, NJ: Erlbaum.

*BORNSTEIN, M. H., & LAMB, M. E. (1992). *Development in infancy* (3rd ed.). New York: McGraw-Hill.

BORNSTEIN, M. H., & SIGMAN, M. D. (1986). Continuity in mental development from infancy. *Child Development, 57,* 251–274.

BORNSTEIN, M. H., & TAMIS-LeMONDA, C. S. (1990). Activities and interactions of mothers and their firstborn infants in the first six months of life: Covariation, stability, continu-

ity, correspondence, and prediction. *Child Development, 61,* 1206–1217.

BORSTELMANN, L. J. (1983). Children before psychology: Ideas about children from antiquity to the later 1800s. In W. Kessen (Ed.), *Handbook of child psychology: Vol. 1. History, theory, and methods.* New York: Wiley.

*BOSTON, M. B., & LEVY, G. D. (1991). Changes and differences in preschoolers' understanding of gender scripts. *Cognitive Psychology, 6,* 417–432.

*BOTTOMS, B. L., GOODMAN, G. S., SCHWARTZ-KENNEY, B. M., SACHSEN-MAIER, T., & THOMAS, S. (1990, March). *Keeping secrets: Implications for children's testimony.* Paper presented at the American Psychology and Law Society Meeting, Williamsburg, VA.

*BOUCHARD, T. J., Jr. (1994). Genes, environment, and personality. *Science, 264,* 1700–1701.

*BOUCHARD, T. J., Jr., LYKKEN, D. T., McGUE, M., SEGAL, N. L., & TELLEGEN, A. (1990). Sources of human psychological differences: The Minnesota Study of Twins Reared Apart. *Science, 250,* 223–228.

*BOUCHARD, T. J., Jr., LYKKEN, D. T., TELLEGEN, A., & McGUE, M. (in press). Genes, drives, environment and experience: EPD theory–revised. In C. Benbow & D. Lubinski (Eds.), *From psychometrics to giftedness: Essays in honor of Julian Stanley.* Baltimore: John Hopkins University Press.

BOWER, T. G. R. (1966). Slant perception and shape constancy in infants. *Science, 151,* 832–834.

BOWER, T. G. R. (1974). The evolution of sensory systems. In R. B. MacLeod & H. L. Pick Jr. (Eds.), *Perception: Essays in honor of James J. Gibson.* Ithaca, NY: Cornell University Press.

BOWER, T. G. R., BROUGHTON, J. M., & MOORE, M. K. (1970). Demonstration of intention in the reaching behavior of neonate humans. *Nature, 228,* 679–680.

BOWERMAN, M. (1975). Cross-linguistic similarities at two stages of syntactic development. In E. H. Lenneberg & E. E. Lenneberg (Eds.), *Foundations of language: A multidisciplinary approach.* New York: Academic Press.

BOWERMAN, M. (1976). Semantic factors in the acquisition of rules for word use and sentence construction. In D. M. Morehead & A. E. Morehead (Eds.), *Normal and deficient child language.* Baltimore: University Park Press.

BOWERMAN, M. (1981). Language development. In H. C. Triandis & A. Heron (Eds.), *Handbook of cross-cultural psychology: Vol. 4. Developmental psychology.* Boston: Allyn & Bacon.

BOWERMAN, M. (1982). Reorganizational processes in lexical and syntactic development. In E. Wanner & L. R. Gleitman (Eds.), *Language acquisition: The state of the art.* New York: Cambridge University Press.

BOWERMAN, M. (1988). Inducing the latent structure of language. In F. S. Kessel (Ed.), *The development of language and language researchers: Essays in honor of Roger Brown.* Hillsdale, NJ: Erlbaum.

BOWLBY, J. (1969). *Attachment and loss: Vol. I. Attachment.* New York: Basic Books.

BOWLBY, J. (1973). *Attachment and loss: Vol. 2. Separation.* New York: Basic Books.

_____, J. (1980). _Attachment and loss: Vol. 3._ New York: Basic Books.

____WLBY, J. (1988). _A secure base: Parent–child attachment and healthy human development._ New York: Basic Books.

*BOYER, M., BARRON, K. S., & FARRAR, M. J. (in press). Three-year-olds remember a novel event from 20 months: Evidence for long-term memory in children? _Memory._

*BOYES, M. C., & ALLEN, S. G. (1993). Styles of parent–child interaction and moral reasoning in adolescence. _Merrill-Palmer Quarterly, 39,_ 551–570.

BOYSSON-BARDIES, B., HALLE, P., SAGART, L., & DURAND, C. (1989). A crosslinguistic investigation of vowel formants in babbling. _Journal of Child Language, 16,_ 1–17.

BRABANT, S., & MOONEY, L. (1986). Sex role stereotyping in the Sunday comics: Ten years later. _Sex Roles, 14,_ 141–148.

BRACKBILL, Y. (1975). Continuous stimulation and arousal level in infancy: Effects of stimulus intensity and stress. _Child Development, 46,_ 364–369.

BRACKBILL, Y., ADAMS, G., CROWELL, D. H., & GRAY, M. L. (1966). Arousal level in neonates and preschool children under continuous auditory stimulation. _Journal of Experimental Child Psychology, 4,_ 178–188.

BRACKBILL, Y., & NICHOLS, P. L. (1982). A test of the confluence model of intellectual development. _Developmental Psychology, 18,_ 192–198.

BRADBARD, M. R., MARTIN, C. L., ENDSLEY, R. C., & HALVERSON, C. F. (1986). Influence of sex stereotypes on children's exploration and memory: A competence versus performance distinction. _Developmental Psychology, 22,_ 481–486.

BRADDICK, O., & ATKINSON, J. (1988). Sensory selectivity, attentional control, and cross-channel integration in early visual development. In A. Yonas (Ed.), _Minnesota symposia on child psychology: Vol. 20. Perceptual development in infancy._ Hillsdale, NJ: Erlbaum.

BRADLEY, R. H., & CALDWELL, B. M. (1984a). 174 children: A study of the relationship between home environment and cognitive development during the first 5 years. In A. W. Gottfried (Ed.), _Home environment and early cognitive development._ New York: Academic Press.

BRADLEY, R. H., & CALDWELL, B. M. (1984b). The relation of infants' home environments to achievement test performance in first grade: A follow-up study. _Child Development, 55,_ 803–809.

BRADLEY, R. H., CALDWELL, B. M., ROCK, S. L., BARNARD, K. E., GRAY, C., HAMMOND, M. A., MITCHELL, S., SIEGEL, L., RAMEY, C. T., GOTTFRIED, A. W., & JOHNSON, D. L. (1989). Home environment and cognitive development in the first 3 years of life: A collaborative study involving six sites and three ethnic groups in North America. _Developmental Psychology, 25,_ 217–235.

BRAINE, M. D. S. (1963). The ontogeny of English phrase structure: The first phase. _Language, 39,_ 1–13.

BRAINE, M. D. S. (1976). Children's first word combinations. _Monographs of the Society for Research in Child Development, 41_ (1, Serial No. 164).

BRAINE, M. D. S. (1987). What is learned in acquiring word classes–a step toward an acquisition theory. In B. MacWhinney (Ed.), _Mechanisms of language acquisition._ Hillsdale, NJ: Erlbaum.

BRAINE, M. D. S., & HARDY, J. A. (1982). On what case categories there are, why they are, and how they develop: An amalgam of _a priori_ considerations, speculations, and evidence from children. In E. Wanner & L. R. Gleitman (Eds.), _Language acquisition: The state of the art._ Cambridge: Cambridge University Press.

BRAINE, M. D. S., & RUMAINE, B. (1983). Logical reasoning. In J. H. Flavell & E. M. Markman (Eds.), _Handbook of child psychology: Vol. 3. Cognitive development._ New York: Wiley.

BRANDT, M. M., & STRATTNER-GREGORY, M. J. (1980). Effect of highlighting intention on intentionality and restitutive justice. _Developmental Psychology, 16,_ 147–148.

BRANIGAN, G. (1979). Some reasons why successive single word utterances are not. _Journal of Child Language, 6,_ 411–421.

*BRAUNGART, J. M., FULKER, D. W., & PLOMIN, R. (1992). Genetic mediation of the home environment during infancy: A sibling adoption study of the HOME. _Developmental Psychology, 28,_ 1048–1055.

*BRAUNGART, J. M., PLOMIN, R., DeFRIES, J. C., & FULKER, D. W. (1992). Genetic influence on tester-rated infant temperament as assessed by Bayley's Infant Behavior Record: Non-adoptive and adoptive siblings and twins. _Developmental Psychology, 28,_ 40–47.

BRAY, J. H. (1988). Children's development during early remarriage. In E. M. Hetherington & J. D. Arasteh (Eds.), _Impact of divorce, single parenting, and stepparenting on children._ Hillsdale, NJ: Erlbaum.

BRAZELTON, T. B. (1973). _Neonatal Behavioral Assessment Scale._ Clinics in developmental medicine (No. 50). Philadelphia: Lippincott.

BRAZELTON, T. B. (1982). Joint regulation of neonate-parent behavior. In E. Z. Tronick (Ed.), _Social interchange in infancy: Affect, cognition, and communication._ Baltimore: University Park Press.

BRAZELTON, T. B. (1984). _Brazelton Behavior Assessment Scale_ (rev. ed.). Philadelphia: Lippincott.

BRAZELTON, T. B., NUGENT, J. K, & LESTER, B. M. (1987). Neonatal behavioral assessment scale. In J. D. Osofsky (Ed.), _Handbook of infant development_ (2nd ed.). New York: Wiley.

BRAZELTON, T. B., & YOGMAN, M. W. (Eds.). (1986). _Affective development in infancy._ Norwood, NJ: Ablex.

BREINER, S. J. (1990). _Slaughter of the innocents: Child abuse through the ages._ New York: Plenum.

*BREMNER, J. G. (1993). Motor abilities as causal agents in infant cognitive development. In G. J. P. Savelsbergh (Ed.), _The development of coordination in infancy._ Amsterdam: Elsevier.

BRENES, M. E., EISENBERG, N., & HELM-STADTER, G. C. (1985). Sex role development of preschoolers from two-parent and one-parent families. _Merrill-Palmer Quarterly, 31,_ 33–41.

BRETHERTON, I. (1987). New perspectives on attachment relations: Security, communication, and internal working models. In J. D. Osofsky (Ed.), _Handbook of infant development_ (2nd ed.). New York: Wiley.

BRETHERTON, I. (1988). How to do things with one word: The ontogenesis of intentional message making in infancy. In M. D. Smith & J. L. Locke (Eds.), _The emergent lexicon._ San Diego: Academic Press.

BRETHERTON, I. (1990). Open communication and internal working models: Their role in the development of attachment relationships. In R. A. Thompson (Ed.), _Nebraska symposium on motivation: Vol. 36. Socioemotional development._ Lincoln: University of Nebraska Press.

*BRETHERTON, I. (1992). The origins of attachment theory: John Bowlby and Mary Ainsworth. _Developmental Psychology, 28,_ 759–775.

*BRETHERTON, I. (1993). From dialogue to internal working models: The co-construction of self in relationships. In C. A. Nelson (Ed.), _Minnesota symposium on child development: Vol. 26. Memory and affect in development._ Hillsdale, NJ: Erlbaum.

BRETHERTON, I., & BEEGHLY, M. (1982). Talking about internal states: The acquisition of an explicit theory of mind. _Developmental Psychology, 18,_ 906–921.

BRETHERTON, I., McNEW, S., SNYDER, L., & BATES, E. (1983). Individual differences at 20 months: Analytic and wholistic strategies in language acquisition. _Journal of Child Language, 10,_ 293–320.

BRETHERTON, I., & WATSON, M. W. (Eds.). (1990). _New directions for child development: No. 48. Children's perspectives on the family._ San Francisco: Jossey-Bass.

BRETL, D. J., & CANTOR, J. (1988). The portrayal of men and women in U.S. television commercials: A recent content analysis and trends over 15 years. _Sex Roles, 18,_ 595–609.

*BREWER, C. L. (1991). Perspectives on John B. Watson. In G. A. Kimble, M. Wertheimer, & C. L. White (Eds.), _Portraits of pioneers in psychology._ Hillsdale, NJ: Erlbaum.

BRIDGES, A. (1986). Actions and things: What adults talk about to 1-year-olds. In S. A. Kuczaj & M. D. Barrett (Eds.), _The development of word meaning._ New York: Springer-Verlag.

BRIDGES, L. J., CONNELL, J. P., & BELSKY, J. (1988). Similarities and differences in infant–mother and infant–father interaction in the Strange Situation: A component process analysis. _Developmental Psychology, 24,_ 92–100.

BROBERG, A., LAMB, M. E., & HWANG, P. (1990). Inhibition: Its stability and correlates in sixteen- to forty-month-old children. _Child Development, 61,_ 1153–1163.

BROCK, J. S., NOMURA, C., & COHEN, P. (1989). A network of influences on adolescent drug involvement: Neighborhood, school, peer, and family. _Genetic, Social, and General Psychology Monographs, 115,_ 123–145.

BRODY, E. B., & BRODY, N. (1976). _Intelligence: Nature, determinants, and consequences._ New York: Academic Press.

BRODY, G. H., GRAZIANO, W. G., & MUSSER, L. M. (1983). Familiarity and children's behavior in same-age and mixed-age peer groups. _Developmental Psychology, 19,_ 568–576.

BRODY, G. H., & HENDERSON, R. W. (1977). Effects of multiple model variations and rationale provision on the moral judgments and explanations of young children. *Child Development, 48,* 1117–1120.

BRODY, G. H., & SHAFFER, D. R. (1982). Contributions of parents and peers to children's moral socialization. *Developmental Review, 2,* 31–75.

*BRODY, G. H., & STONEMAN, Z. (1994). Understanding sibling relationships in middle childhood: A review of a decade of research. In R. Vasta (Ed.), *Annals of child development* (Vol. 10). Greenwich, CT: JAI Press.

*BRONFENBRENNER, U. (1962). Soviet methods of character education: Some implications for research. *Religious Education, 57,* 545–561.

*BRONFENBRENNER, U. (1970). *Two worlds of childhood: U.S. and U.S.S.R.* New York: Russell Sage Foundation.

BRONFENBRENNER, U. (1979). *The ecology of human development: Experiments by nature and design.* Cambridge, MA: Harvard University Press.

BRONFENBRENNER, U. (1986). Ecology of the family as a context for human development: Research perspectives. *Developmental Psychology, 22,* 723–742.

BRONFENBRENNER, U. (1989). Ecological systems theory. In R. Vasta (Ed.), *Annals of child development* (Vol. 6). Greenwich, CT: JAI Press.

*BRONFENBRENNER, U. (1993). The ecology of cognitive development: Research models and fugitive findings. In R. H. Wozniak & K. W. Fischer (Eds.), *Development in context: Acting and thinking in specific environments.* Hillsdale, NJ: Erlbaum.

BRONSHTEIN, A. I., ANTONOVA, T. G., KAMENETSKAYA, A. G., LUPPOVA, M. N., & SYTOVA, V. A. (1958). On the development of the functions of analyzers in infants and some animals at the early stage of ontogenesis. In *Problems of evolution of physiological functions* (Report No. 60–61006, pp. 106–116). Washington, DC: Office of Technical Services.

BRONSON, W. C. (1981). *Toddlers' behaviors with agemates: Issues of interaction, cognition, and affect.* Norwood, NJ: Ablex.

*BRONSTEIN, P., & COWAN, C. P. (Eds.). (1988). *Fatherhood today: Men's changing roles in the family.* New York: Wiley.

*BROOKE, J. (1991, June 15). Signs of life in Brazil's industrial valley of death. *New York Times International,* p. 2.

BROOKS-GUNN, J. (1987). Pubertal processes and girls' psychological adaptation. In R. M. Lerner & T. L. Foch (Eds.), *Biological psychosocial interactions in early adolescence.* Hillsdale, NJ: Erlbaum.

*BROOKS-GUNN, J. (1991). Maturational timing variations in adolescent girls, consequences of. In R. M. Lerner, A. C. Peterson, & J. Brooks-Gunn (Eds.), *Encyclopedia of adolescence* (Vol. 2). New York: Garland.

*BROOKS-GUNN, J., KLEBANOV, P. K., LIAW, F., & SPIKER, D. (1993). Enhancing the development of low-birthweight premature infants: Changes in cognition and behavior over the first three years. *Child Development, 64,* 736–753.

BROOKS-GUNN, J., & LEWIS, M. (1984). The development of early visual self-recognition. *Developmental Review, 4,* 215–239.

*BROOKS-GUNN, J., & REITER, E. O. (1990). The role of pubertal processes. In S. S. Feldman & G. R. Elliott (Eds.), *At the threshold: The developing adolescent.* Cambridge, MA: Harvard University Press.

BROPHY, J. E. (1983). Research on the self-fulfilling prophecy and teacher expectations. *Journal of Educational Psychology, 75,* 631–661.

BROWN, A. L., BRANSFORD, J. D., FERRARA, R. A., & CAMPIONE, J. C. (1983). Learning, remembering, and understanding. In J. H. Flavell & E. M. Markman (Eds.), *Handbook of child psychology: Vol. 3. Cognitive development.* New York: Wiley.

BROWN, A. L., & CAMPIONE, J. C. (1990). Communities of learning and thinking, or a context by any other name. In D. Kuhn (Ed.), *Developmental perspectives on teaching and learning thinking skills.* Basel, Switzerland: Karger.

BROWN, A. L., & FERRARA, R. A. (1985). Diagnosing zones of proximal development. In J. V. Wertsch (Ed.), *Culture, communication, and cognition: Vygotskian perspectives.* Cambridge: Cambridge University Press.

BROWN, A. L., PALINCSAR, A. S., & ARMBRUSTER, B. B. (1984). Instructing comprehension-fostering activities in interactive learning situations. In H. Mandl, N. L. Stein, & T. Trabasso (Eds.), *Learning and comprehension of text.* Hillsdale, NJ: Erlbaum.

*BROWN, B. B. (1990). Peer groups and peer cultures. In S. S. Feldman & G. R. Elliott (Eds.), *At the threshold: The developing adolescent.* Cambridge, MA: Harvard University Press.

BROWN, J. S., & BURTON, R. D. (1978). Diagnostic models for procedural bugs in basic mathematical skills. *Cognitive Science, 2,* 155–192.

BROWN, J. S., & VANLEHN, K. (1982). Towards a generative theory of "bugs." In T. P. Carpenter, J. M. Moser, & T. A. Romberg (Eds.), *Addition and subtraction: A cognitive perspective.* Hillsdale, NJ: Erlbaum.

BROWN, K. W., & GOTTFRIED, A. W. (1986). Development of cross-modal transfer in early infancy. In L. P. Lipsitt & C. K. Rovee-Collier (Eds.), *Advances in infancy research* (Vol. 4). Norwood, NJ: Ablex.

BROWN, R. (1958). How shall a thing be called? *Psychological Review, 65,* 14–21.

BROWN, R. (1973). *A first language: The early stages.* Cambridge, MA: Harvard University Press.

BROWN, R., & HANLON, C. (1970). Derivational complexity and order of acquisition in child speech. In J. R. Hayes (Ed.), *Cognition and the development of language.* New York: Wiley.

BROWNELL, C. A. (1986). Convergent developments: Cognitive-developmental correlates of growth in infant/toddler peer skills. *Child Development, 57,* 275–286.

BROWNELL, C. A. (1988). Combinatorial skills: Converging developments over the second year. *Child Development, 59,* 675–685.

BROWNELL, C. A. (1990). Peer social skills in toddlers: Competencies and constraints illustrated by same-age and mixed-age interaction. *Child Development, 61,* 838–848.

*BROWNELL, C. A., & BROWN, E. (1992). Peer and play in infants and toddlers. In V. B. Van Hasselt & M. Hersen (Eds.), *Handbook of social development.* New York: Plenum.

*BROWNELL, C. A., & CARRIGER, M. S. (1990). Changes in cooperation and self–other differentiation during the second year. *Child Development, 61,* 1164–1174.

BROWNELL, C. A., & STRAUSS, M. A. (1984). Infant stimulation and development: Conceptual and empirical considerations. *Journal of Children in Contemporary Society, 6,* 109–130.

BRUNER, J. (1975). From communication to language: A psychological perspective. *Cognition, 3,* 255–287.

BRUNER, J. (1979). Learning how to do things with words. In D. Aaronson & R. W. Rieber (Eds.), *Psycholinguistic research: Implications and applications.* Hillsdale, NJ: Erlbaum.

BRUNER, J. (1983). *Child's talk: Learning to use language.* New York: Norton.

BRUNER, J., & GOODMAN, C. C. (1947). Value and need as organizing factors in perception. *Journal of Abnormal and Social Psychology, 42,* 33–44.

BRUNER, J., GOODNOW, J. J., & AUSTIN, G. A. (1956). *A study of thinking.* New York: Wiley.

BRUNER, J., ROY, C., & RATNER, N. (1982). The beginnings of request. In K. E. Nelson (Ed.), *Children's language* (Vol. 3). Hillsdale, NJ: Erlbaum.

*BRUNNER, H. G., NELEN, M. R., ZANDVOORT, P. VAN, ABELING, N. G. G. M., GENNIP, A. H. VAN, WOLTERS, E. C., KUIPER, M. A., ROPERS, H. H., & OOST, B. A. VAN. (1993). X-linked borderline mental retardation with prominent behavioral disturbance: Phenotype genetic localization, and evidence for disturbed monoamine metabolism. *American Journal of Human Genetics, 52,* 1032–1039.

BRYANT, B. K. (1982). An index of empathy for children and adolescents. *Child Development, 53,* 413–425.

BRYANT, B. K. (1985). The Neighborhood Walk: Sources of support in middle childhood. *Monographs of the Society for Research in Child Development, 50* (3, Serial No. 210).

BRYANT, B. K. (1987). Mental health, temperament, family, and friends: Perspectives on children's empathy and social perspective taking. In N. Eisenberg & J. Strayer (Eds.), *Empathy and its development.* Cambridge: Cambridge University Press.

BRYDEN, M. P. (1982). *Laterality: Functional asymmetry in the intact brain.* New York: Academic Press.

BUCHER, B., & SCHNEIDER, R. E. (1973). Acquisition and generalization of conservation by pre-schoolers, using operant training. *Journal of Experimental Child Psychology, 16,* 187–204.

BUHRMESTER, D. (1990). Intimacy of friendship, interpersonal competence, and adjustment during preadolescence and adolescence. *Child Development, 61,* 1101–1111.

*BUHRMESTER, D. (1992). The developmental courses of sibling and peer relationships. In F. Boer & J. Dunn (Eds.), *Children's sibling relationships: Developmental and clinical issues.* Hillsdale, NJ: Erlbaum.

...TER, D., & FURMAN, W. (1990). ...ions of sibling relationships during mid-...childhood and adolescence. *Child Development, 61,* 1387–1398.

BUKOWSKI, W. M., & HOZA, B. (1989). Popularity and friendship: Issues in theory, measurement, and outcome. In T. J. Berndt & G. W. Ladd (Eds.), *Peer relationships in child development.* New York: Wiley.

BULLOCK, M., & LUTKENHAUS, P. (1988). The development of volitional behavior in the toddler years. *Child Development, 59,* 664–674.

BULLOCK, M., & LUTKENHAUS, P. (1990). Who am I? Self-understanding in toddlers. *Merrill-Palmer Quarterly, 36,* 217–238.

*BURKHALTER, A. (1991). Developmental status of intrinsic connections in visual cortex of newborn humans. In P. Bagnoli & W. Hodos (Eds.), *The changing visual system.* New York: Plenum.

BURNHAM, D. K. (1987). The role of movement in object perception by infants. In B. E. McKenzie & R. H. Day (Eds.), *Perceptual development in early infancy: Problems and issues.* Hillsdale, NJ: Erlbaum.

BURNHAM, D. K., EARNSHAW, L. J., & QUINN, M. C. (1987). The development of the categorical identification of speech. In B. E. McKenzie & R. H. Day (Eds.), *Perceptual development in early infancy: Problems and issues.* Hillsdale, NJ: Erlbaum.

BURT, C. (1972). Inheritance of general intelligence. *American Psychologist, 27,* 175–190.

BURTON, R. V. (1963). The generality of honesty reconsidered. *Psychological Review, 70,* 481–499.

BURTON, R. V. (1984). A paradox in theories and research in moral development. In W. M. Kurtines & J. L. Gewirtz (Eds.), *Morality, moral behavior, and moral development.* New York: Wiley.

BUSHNELL, E. W. (1982). Visual-tactual knowledge in 8-, 9-, and 11-month-old infants. *Infant Behavior & Development, 5,* 63–75.

*BUSHNELL, E. W. (in press). A dual-processing approach to cross-modal matching: Implications for development. In D. J. Lewkowicz & R. Lickliter (Eds.), *The development of intersensory perception: Comparative perspectives.* Hillsdale, NJ: Erlbaum.

*BUSHNELL, E. W., & BOUDREAU, J. P. (1993). Motor development and the mind: The potential role of motor abilities as a determinant of aspects of perceptual development. *Child Development, 64,* 1005–1021.

BUSHNELL, E. W., & MARATSOS, M. P. (1984). *Spooning* and *basketing:* Children's dealing with accidental gaps in the lexicon. *Child Development, 55,* 893–902.

*BUSHNELL, I. W. R., SAI, F., & MULLIN, J. T. (1989). Neonatal recognition of the mother's face. *British Journal of Developmental Psychology, 7,* 3–15.

BUSS, A. H., & PLOMIN, R. (1984). *Temperament: Early developing personality traits.* Hillsdale, NJ: Erlbaum.

BUSS, A. H., & PLOMIN, R. (1986). The EAS approach to temperament. In R. Plomin & J. Dunn (Eds.), *The study of temperament: Changes, continuities and challenges.* Hillsdale, NJ: Erlbaum.

BUSSEY, K., & BANDURA, A. (1984). Gender constancy, social power, and sex-linked modeling. *Journal of Personality and Social Psychology, 47,* 1292–1302.

*BUSSEY, K., & BANDURA, A. (1992). Self-regulatory mechanisms governing gender development. *Child Development, 63,* 1236–1250.

BUSSEY, K., & PERRY, D. G. (1982). Same-sex imitation: The avoidance of cross-sex models or the acceptance of same-sex models? *Sex Roles, 8,* 773–784.

BUTLER, R. (1990). The effects of mastery and competitive conditions on self-assessment at different ages. *Child Development, 61,* 201–210.

*BUTLER, R. (1992). What young people want to know when: The effects of mastery and ability on social information seeking. *Journal of Social and Personality Psychology, 62,* 934–943.

*BUTLER, R., & RUZANY, N. (1993). Age and socialization effects on the development of social comparison motives and normative ability assessment in kibbutz and urban children. *Child Development, 64,* 532–543.

*BUTTERWORTH, G. (1990). Self-perception in infancy. In D. Cicchetti & M. Beeghly (Eds.), *The self in transition: Infancy to childhood.* Chicago: University of Chicago Press.

*BYBEE, J. L., & SLOBIN, D. I. (1982). Rules and schemes in the development and use of the English past tense. *Language, 58,* 265–289.

BYRNES, J. P. (1988a). Formal operations: A systematic reformulation. *Developmental Review, 8,* 66–87

BYRNES, J. P. (1988b). What's left is closer to right. A response to Keating. *Developmental Review, 8,* 385–392

*BYRNES, J. B., & TAKAHIRA, S. (1993). Explaining gender differences on SAT-math items. *Developmental Psychology, 29,* 805–810.

CAIRNS, R. B. (1983). The emergence of developmental psychology. In W. Kessen (Ed.), *Handbook of child psychology: Vol. 1. History, theory, and methods.* New York: Wiley.

CAIRNS, R. B. (1986). An evolutionary and developmental perspective on aggressive patterns. In C. Zahn-Waxler, E. M. Cummings, & R. Iannotti (Eds.), *Altruism and aggression: Biological and social origins.* Cambridge: Cambridge University Press.

CAIRNS, R. B., & CAIRNS, B. D. (1988). The sociogenesis of self concepts. In N. Bolger, A. Caspi, G. Downey, & M. Moorehouse (Eds.), *Persons in context: Developmental processes.* New York: Cambridge University Press.

CAIRNS, R. B., CAIRNS, B. D., NECKERMAN, H. J., FERGUSON, L. L., & GARIEPY, J. (1989). Growth and aggression: I. Childhood to early adolescence. *Developmental Psychology, 25,* 320–330.

CAIRNS, R. B., CAIRNS, B. D., NECKERMAN, H. J., GEST, S. D., & GARIEPY, J. (1988). Social networks and aggressive behavior: Peer support or peer rejection? *Developmental Psychology, 24,* 815–823.

CALDERA, Y. M., HUSTON, A. C., & O'BRIEN, M. (1989). Social interactions and play patterns of parents and toddlers with feminine, masculine, and neutral toys. *Child Development, 60,* 70–76.

CALDWELL, B. M. (1964). The effects of infant care. In M. L. Hoffman & L. W. Hoffman (Eds.), *Review of child development research* (Vol. 1). New York: Russell Sage Foundation.

CALDWELL, B. M., & BRADLEY, R. (1979). *Home Observation for Measurement of the Environment.* Unpublished manuscript, University of Arkansas Press.

CALHOUN, J. B. (1962). Population density and social pathology. *Scientific American, 206,* 139–148.

*CALKINS, S. D., & FOX, N. A. (1992). The relations among infant temperament, security of attachment, and behavioral inhibition at twenty-four months. *Child Development, 63,* 1456–1472.

CALLANAN, M. A. (1985). How parents label objects for young children: The role of input in the acquisition of category hierarchies. *Child Development, 56,* 508–523.

CALVERT, S. L., & HUSTON, A. C. (1987). Television and children's gender schemata. In L. S. Liben & M. L. Signorella (Eds.), *New directions for child development: No. 38. Children's gender schemata.* San Francisco: Jossey-Bass.

CAMAIONI, L., & LAICARDI, C. (1985). Early social games and the acquisition of language. *British Journal of Developmental Psychology, 3,* 31–39.

CAMARA, K. A., & RESNICK, G. (1988). Interpersonal conflict and cooperation: Factors moderating children's post-divorce adjustment. In E. M. Hetherington & J. D. Arasteh (Eds.), *Impact of divorce, single parenting, and stepparenting on children.* Hillsdale, NJ: Erlbaum.

CAMARATA, S., & LEONARD, L. B. (1986). Young children pronounce object words more accurately than action words. *Journal of Child Language, 13,* 51–65.

CAMPOS, J. J., BARRETT, K. C., LAMB, M. E., GOLDSMITH, H. H., & STENBERG, C. (1983). Socioemotional development. In M. M. Haith & J. J. Campos (Ed.), *Handbook of child psychology: Vol. 2. Infancy and developmental psychobiology.* New York: Wiley.

CAMPOS, J. J., & BERTENTHAL, B. I. (1989). Locomotion and psychological development in infancy. In F. J. Morrison, C. Lord, & D. P. Keating (Eds.), *Applied developmental psychology* (Vol. 3). New York: Academic Press.

*CAMPOS, J. J., BERTENTHAL, B. I., & KERMOIAN, R. (1992). Early experience and emotional development. *Psychological Science, 3,* 61–64.

CAMPOS, J. J., CAMPOS, R. G., & BARRETT, K. C. (1989). Emergent themes in the study of emotional development and emotion regulation. *Developmental Psychology, 25,* 394–402.

CAMPOS, J. J., HIATT, S., RAMSAY, D., HENDERSON, C., & SVEJDA, M. (1978). The emergence of fear on the visual cliff. In M. Lewis & L. Rosenblum (Eds.), *The origins of affect.* New York: Plenum

CAMPOS, R. G. (1989). Soothing pain-elicited distress in infants with swaddling and pacifiers. *Child Development, 60,* 781–792.

*CAMRAS, L. A., MALATESTA, C. Z., & IZARD, C. E. (1991). The development of facial expressions in infancy. In R. Felman & B. Rime (Eds.),

Fundamentals of nonverbal behavior. Cambridge: Cambridge University Press.

*CAMRAS, L., OSTER, L. A., CAMPOS, J. J., MIYAKE, K., & BRADSHAW, D. (1992). Japanese and American infants' responses to arm restraint. *Developmental Psychology, 28,* 578–583.

CAMRAS, L. A., RIBORDY, S., HILL, J., MARTINO, S., SACHS, V., SPACCARELLI, S., & STEFANI, R. (1990). Maternal facial behavior and the recognition and production of emotional expression by maltreated and nonmaltreated children. *Developmental Psychology, 20,* 304–312.

CANTER, R. J., & AGETON, S. S. (1984). The epidemiology of adolescent sex-role attitudes. *Sex Roles, 11,* 657–676.

CANTOR, C. R. (1990). Orchestrating the Human Genome Project. *Science, 248,* 49–51.

*CAPECCHI, M. R. (1994, March). Targeted gene replacement. *Scientific American,* pp. 52–59.

CAPLAN, D., & CHOMSKY, N. (1980). Linguistic perspectives on language development. In D. Caplan (Ed.), *Biological studies of mental processes.* Cambridge, MA: MIT Press.

*CAPLAN, M., VESPO, J. E., PEDERSEN, J., & HAY, D. F. (1991). Conflict and its resolution in small groups of one- and two-year-olds. *Child Development, 62,* 1513–1524.

CAPLAN, P. J., MacPHERSON, G. M., & TOBIN, P. (1985). Do sex-related differences in spatial abilities exist? A multilevel critique with new data. *American Psychologist, 40,* 786–799.

*CAPRON, C., & DUYME, M. (1989). Assessment of effects of socio-economic status on IQ in a full cross-fostering study. *Nature, 340,* 552–554.

CAPUTE, A. J., ACCARDO, P. J., VINING, E. P. G., RUBENSTEIN, J. F., & HARRYMAN, S. (1978). *Primitive reflex profile.* Baltimore: University Park Press.

*CARDON, L. R., & FULKER, D. W. (1991). Sources of continuity in infant predictors of later IQ. *Intelligence, 15,* 279–293.

*CARDON, L. R., & FULKER, D. W. (1994). A model of developmental change in hierarchical phenotypes with application to specific cognitive abilities. *Behavior Genetics, 24,* 1–16.

*CARDON, L. R., FULKER, D. W., & DeFRIES, J. C. (1992). Continuity and change in general cognitive ability from 1 to 7 years of age. *Developmental Psychology, 28,* 64–73.

CAREY, S. (1977). The child as word learner. In M. Halle, J. Bresnan, & G. A. Miller (Eds.), *Linguistic theory and psychological reality.* Cambridge, MA: MIT Press.

CAREY, W. B., & McDEVITT, S. C. (1978). Revision of the Infant Temperament Questionnaire. *Pediatrics, 61,* 735–739.

CARLSON, V., CICCHETTI, D., BARNETT, D., & BRAUNWALD, C. (1989a). Disorganized/disoriented attachment relationships in maltreated infants. *Developmental Psychology, 25,* 525–531.

CARLSON, V., CICCHETTI, D., BARNETT, D., & BRAUNWALD, K. G. (1989b). Finding order in disorganization: Lessons from research on maltreated infants' attachments to their caregivers. In D. Cicchetti & V. Carlson (Eds.), *Child mal-*

treatment: Theory and research on the causes and consequences of child abuse and neglect. New York: Cambridge University Press.

CARON, A. J., CARON, R. F., & CARLSON, V. R. (1979). Infant perception of the invariant shape of objects varying in slant. *Child Development, 50,* 716–721.

CARON, A. J., CARON, R. F., & MacLEAN, D. J. (1988). Infant discrimination of naturalistic emotional expressions: The role of face and voice. *Child Development, 59,* 604–616.

*CARRAHER, T. N., CARRAHER, D. W., & SCHLIEMANN, A. D. (1985). Mathematics in the streets and schools. *British Journal of Developmental Psychology, 3,* 21–29.

CARROLL, J. L., & REST, J. R. (1981). Development in moral judgment as indicated by rejection of lower-style statements. *Journal of Research in Personality, 15,* 538–544.

CARTER, D. B. (Ed.). (1987a). *Current conceptions of sex roles and sex-typing: Theory and research.* New York: Praeger.

CARTER, D. B. (1987b). The role of peers in sex role socialization. In D. B. Carter (Ed.), *Current conceptions of sex roles and sex-typing: Theory and research.* New York: Praeger.

CARTER, D. B., & LEVY, G. D. (1988). Cognitive aspects of early sex-role development: The influence of gender schemas on preschoolers' memories and preferences for sex-typed toys and activities. *Child Development, 59,* 782–792.

CARTER, D. B., & McCLOSKEY, L. A. (1984). Peers and maintenance of sex-typed behavior: The development of children's conceptions of cross-gender behavior in their peers. *Social Cognition, 2,* 294–314.

CARTER, D. B., & PATTERSON, C. J. (1982). Sex roles as social conventions: The development of children's conceptions of sex-role stereotypes. *Developmental Psychology, 18,* 812–824.

CASE, R. (1985). *Intellectual development.* New York. Academic Press.

CASE, R. (1986). The new stage theories in cognitive development: Why we need them; what they assert. In M. Perlmutter (Ed.), *Minnesota symposia on child psychology: Vol. 19. The development of intelligence.* Hillsdale, NJ: Erlbaum.

*CASE, R. (1991). Stages in the development of the young child's first sense of self. *Developmental Review, 11,* 210–230.

*CASE, R. (1992a). *The mind's staircase: Exploring the conceptual underpinnings of children's thought and knowledge.* Hillsdale, NJ: Erlbaum.

*CASE, R. (1992b). Neo-Piagetian theories of intellectual development. In H. Beilin & P. B. Pufall (Eds.), *Piaget's theory: Prospects and possibilities.* Hillsdale, NJ: Erlbaum.

CASPI, A., & ELDER, G. H. (1988). Childhood precursors of the life course: Early personality and life disadvantage. In E. M. Hetherington, R. M. Lerner, & M. Perlmutter (Eds.), *Child development in a life-span perspective.* Hillsdale, NJ: Erlbaum.

CASPI, A., ELDER, G. H., & BEM, D. J. (1987). Moving against the world: Life-course patterns of explosive children. *Developmental Psychology, 23,* 308–313.

CASPI, A., ELDER, G. H., & BEM, D. J. (1988). Moving away from the world: Life-course pat-

terns of shy children. *Developmental Psy[chology], 24,* 824–831.

CASSIDY, J. (1988). Child–mother attach[ment] and the self in six-year-olds. *Child Developmen[t], 59,* 121–134.

*CASSIDY, J., PARKE, R. D., BUTKOVSKY, L., & BRAUNGART, J. M. (1992). Family–peer connections: The roles of emotional expressiveness within the family and children's understanding of emotions. *Child Development, 63,* 603–618.

*CATON, H. (1990). *The Samoa reader.* Lanham, MD: University Press of America.

CAVANAUGH, J. C., & PERLMUTTER, M. (1982). Metamemory: A critical examination. *Child Development, 53,* 11–28.

CAVDAR, A. D., ARACASOY, A., BAYCU, T., & HIMMETOGLU, D. (1980). Zinc deficiency and anencephaly in Turkey. *Teratology, 22,* 141.

CECI, S. J. (1990). *On intelligence. . . . more or less: A bioecological theory.* Englewood Cliffs, NJ: Prentice Hall.

*CECI, S. J. (1991). How much does schooling influence general intelligence and its cognitive components? A reassessment of the evidence. *Developmental Psychology, 27,* 703–722.

*CECI, S. J. (1992, September/October). Schooling and intelligence. *Psychological Science Agenda,* pp. 7–9.

*CECI, S. J. (1993). Contextual trends in intellectual development. *Developmental Review, 13,* 403–435.

CECI, S. J., & BRONFENBRENNER, U. (1985). Don't forget to take the cupcakes out of the oven: Prospective memory, strategic time-monitoring, and context. *Child Development, 56,* 150–165.

CECI, S. J., BRONFENBRENNER, U., & BAKER, J. G. (1988). Memory in context: The case of prospective remembering. In F. E. Weinert & M. Perlmutter (Eds.), *Memory development: Universal changes and individual differences.* Hillsdale, NJ: Erlbaum.

*CECI, S. J., & BRUCK, M. (1993a). Child witnesses: Translating research into policy. *Society for Research in Child Development Social Policy Report, 7,* 1–30.

*CECI, S. J., & BRUCK, M. (1993b). Suggestibility of the child witness: A historical review and synthesis. *Psychological Bulletin, 113,* 403–439.

*CHALL, J. S. (1983). *Learning to read: The great debate.* (updated ed.). New York: McGraw-Hill.

CHALMERS, J. B., & TOWNSEND, M. A. R. (1990). The effects of training in social perspective taking on socially maladjusted girls. *Child Development, 61,* 178–190.

CHANDLER, M. J. (1973). Egocentrism and antisocial behavior: The assessment and training of social perspective-taking skills. *Developmental Psychology, 9,* 326–332.

CHANDLER, M. J., GREENSPAN, S., & BARENBOIM, C. (1973). Judgments of intentionality in response to videotaped and verbally presented moral dilemmas: The medium is the message. *Child Development, 44,* 315–320.

*CHAPMAN, M. (1988). *Constructive evolution: Origins and development of Piaget's thought.* Cambridge: Cambridge University Press.

*CHAPMAN, M. (1992). Equilibration and the dialectics of organization. In H. Beilin & P. B.

R..........

..), *Piaget's theory: Prospects and possi-
...llsdale, NJ: Erlbaum.

.....N, M., ZAHN-WAXLER, C., COOPER-
.....G., & IANNOTTI, R. (1987). Empathy
....d responsibility in the motivation of chil-
.....ren's helping. *Developmental Psychology, 23,*
140–145.

CHARLESWORTH, R., & HARTUP, W. W.
(1967). Positive social reinforcement in the
nursery school peer group. *Child Development,
38,* 993–1002.

CHARLESWORTH, W. R. (1978). Ethology: Its relevance for observational studies of human adaptation. In G. P. Sackett (Ed.), *Observing behavior*
(Vol. 1). Baltimore: University Park Press.

CHARLESWORTH, W. R. (1983). An ethological
approach to cognitive development. In C. J.
Brainerd (Ed.), *Recent advances in cognitive-developmental theory: Progress in cognitive development
research.* New York: Springer-Verlag.

*CHARLESWORTH, W. R. (1992). Darwin and
developmental psychology: Past and present.
Developmental Psychology, 28, 5–16.

CHARLESWORTH, W. R., & DZUR, C. (1987).
Gender comparisons of preschoolers' behavior
and resource utilization in group problem-solving. *Child Development, 58,* 191–200.

CHASNOFF, I. J., SCHNOLL, S. H., BURNS, W.
J., & BURNS, K. (1984). Maternal narcotic substance abuse during pregnancy: Effects on
infant development. *Neurobehavioral Toxicology
and Teratology, 6,* 277–280.

CHAVEZ, D. (1985). Perpetuation of gender
inequality: A content analysis of comic strips.
Sex Roles, 13, 93–102.

CHEN, M. (1985). Gender differences in adolescents' use of and attitudes toward computers.
In M. McLaughlin (Ed.), *Communication yearbook* (Vol. 10). Beverly Hills, CA: Sage.

*CHERLIN, A. J., & FURSTENBERG, F. F.
(1986). *The new American grandparent.* New York:
Basic Books.

CHERRY, L., & LEWIS, M. (1976). Mothers and
two-year-olds: A study of sex differentiated
aspects of verbal interaction. *Developmental
Psychology, 12,* 278–282.

CHERRY, L., & LEWIS, M. (1978). Differential
socialization of girls and boys: Implications for
sex differences in language development. In N.
Waterhouse & C. Snow (Eds.), *The development of
communication.* New York: Wiley.

CHI, M. T. H. (1978). Knowledge structures and
memory development. In R. S. Siegler (Ed.),
Children's thinking: What develops? Hillsdale, NJ:
Erlbaum.

CHI, M. T. H., & CECI, S. J. (1987). Content
knowledge: Its role, representation, and
restructuring in memory development. In
H. W. Reese (Ed.), *Advances in child development
and behavior* (Vol. 20). New York: Academic
Press.

*CHI, M. T. H., GLASER, R., & FARR, M. J.
(Eds.). (1988). *The nature of expertise.* Hillsdale,
NJ: Erlbaum.

*CHI, M. T. H., & KOESKE, R. D. (1983).
Network representation of a child's dinosaur
knowledge. *Developmental Psychology, 19,* 29–39.

Children in poverty: Excerpts from testimony
given by Nicholas Lill, Subcommittee on
Human Resources, U.S. House of Representatives September 1992 (1993, Winter). *SRCD
Newsletter,* 14.

CHIPMAN, S. F., BRUSH, L., & WILSON, D.
(Eds.). (1985). *Women and mathematics:
Balancing the equation.* Hillsdale, NJ: Erlbaum.

CHISZAR, D. (1981). Learning theory, ethological theory, and developmental plasticity. In E. S.
Gollin (Ed.), *Developmental plasticity: Behavioral
and biological aspects of variations in development.*
New York: Academic Press.

CHOMSKY, N. (1959). A review of B. F. Skinner's
Verbal Behavior. Language, 35, 26–58.

CHOMSKY, N. (1965). *Aspects of the theory of syntax.* Cambridge, MA: MIT Press.

CHOMSKY, N. (1980). *Rules and representations.*
New York: Columbia University Press.

*CICCHETTI, D. (1991). Fractures in the crys-
tal: Developmental psychopathology and the
emergence of self. *Developmental Review, 11,*
271–287.

CICCHETTI, D., & BEEGHLY, M. (Eds.). (1990).
The self in transition: Infancy to childhood.
Chicago: University of Chicago Press.

*CICCHETTI, D., BEEGHLY, M., CARLSON, V.,
& TOTH, S. (1990). The emergence of self in
atypical populations. In D. Cicchetti & M.
Beegly (Eds.), *The self in transition: Infancy to
childhood.* Chicago: University of Chicago
Press.

CICCHETTI, D., & CARLSON, V. (Eds.). (1989).
*Child maltreatment: Theory and research on the
causes and consequences of child abuse and neglect.*
New York: Cambridge University Press.

*CICCHETTI, D., LYNCH, M., SHONK, S., &
MANLY, J. T. (1992). An organizational per-
spective on peer relations in maltreated chil-
dren. In R. D. Parke & G. W. Ladd (Eds.),
Family-peer relationships: Modes of linkage.
Hillsdale, NJ: Erlbaum.

*CILLESSEN, A. H. N., VANIJZENDOORN,
H. W., VAN LIESHOUT, C. F. M., & HARTUP,
W. W. (1992). Heterogeneity among peer-
rejected boys: Subtypes and stabilities. *Child
Development, 63,* 893–905.

CLARK, E. V. (1982). The young word-maker: A
case study of innovation in the child's lexicon.
In E. Wanner & L. R. Gleitman (Eds.), *Language
acquisition: The state of the art.* Cambridge:
Cambridge University Press.

CLARK, E. V. (1983). Meanings and concepts. In
J. H. Flavell & E. M. Markman (Eds.), *Handbook
of child psychology: Vol. 3. Cognitive development.*
New York: Wiley.

CLARK, E. V. (1987). The principle of contrast: A
constraint on language acquisition. In B.
MacWhinney (Ed.), *Mechanisms of language
acquisition.* Hillsdale, NJ: Erlbaum.

CLARK, E. V. (1988). On the logic of contrast.
Journal of Child Language, 15, 317–335.

CLARK, E. V. (1990). On the pragmatics of contrast. *Journal of Child Language, 17,* 417–431.

CLARK, E. V., GELMAN, S. A., & LANE, N. M.
(1985). Compound nouns and category structure in young children. *Child Development, 56,*
84–94.

CLARK, R. (1977). What's the use of imitation?
Journal of Child Language, 4, 341–358.

CLARKE, A. M., & CLARKE, A. D. B. (1976).
Early experience: Myth and evidence. New York:
Free Press.

CLARKE, A. M., & CLARKE, A. D. B. (1989). The
later cognitive effects of early intervention.
Intelligence, 13, 289–297.

CLARKE-STEWART, K. A. (1978). And daddy
makes three: The father's impact on the
mother and the young child. *Child Development,
49,* 466–478.

CLARKE-STEWART, K. A. (1989). Infant day
care: Maligned or malignant? *American
Psychologist, 44,* 266–273.

CLEWELL, W. H., JOHNSON, M. L., MEIER,
P. R., NEWKIRK, J. B., ZIDE, S. L., HENDEE,
R. W., BOWES, W. A., Jr., HECHT, F., O'KEEFE,
D., HENRY, G. P., & SHIKES, R. H. (1982). A
surgical approach to the treatment of fetal
hydrocephalus. *New England Journal of Medicine,
306,* 1320–1325.

CLIFTON, R. K., GRAHAM, F. K., & HATTON,
H. M. (1968). Newborn heart-rate response
and response habituation as a function of stimulus duration. *Journal of Experimental Child
Psychology, 6,* 265–278.

CLIFTON, R. K., GWIAZDA, J., BAUER, J. A.,
CLARKSON, M. G., & HELD, R. M. (1988).
Growth in head size during infancy: Implications
for sound localization. *Developmental Psychology,
24,* 477–483.

CLIFTON, R. K., MORRONGIELLO, B. A.,
KULIG, J. W., & DOWD, J. M. (1981).
Developmental changes in auditory localiza-
tion in infancy. In R. N. Aslin, J. R. Alberts, &
M. R. Petersen (Eds.), *Development of perception:
Psychobiological perspectives: Vol. 1. Audition,
somatic perception, and the chemical senses.* New
York: Academic Press.

*CLINGEMPEEL, W. G., COLYAR, J. J., BRAND,
E., & HETHERINGTON, E. M. (1992).
Children's relations with maternal grandparents: A longitudinal study of family structure
and pubertal status effects. *Child Development,
63,* 1404–1422.

CLUMECK, H. V. (1980). The acquisition of
tone. In G. H. Yeni-Komshian, J. Kavanagh, &
C. A. Ferguson (Eds.), *Child phonology: Vol. 1.
Production.* New York: Academic Press.

COHEN, D. (1979). *J. B. Watson: The founder of
behaviorism.* London: Routledge & Kegan Paul.

*COHEN, J. (1992). Pediatric AIDS vaccine trials
set. *Science, 258,* 1568–1570.

*COHEN, J. (1993). AIDS. The mood is unfamil-
iar. *Science, 260,* 1254–1255.

COHEN, L. B., & STRAUSS, M. S. (1979).
Concept acquisition in the human infant. *Child
Development, 50,* 419–424.

COHEN, S., & WILLS, T. A. (1985). Stress, social
support, and the buffering hypothesis.
Psychological Bulletin, 98, 310–357.

COHEN, S. E. (1974). Developmental differences
in infants' attentional responses to face–voice
incongruity of mother and stranger. *Child
Development, 45,* 1155–1158.

COHN, J. F., CAMPBELL, S. B., MATIAS, R., &
HOPKINS, J. (1990). Face-to-face interactions
of postpartum depressed and nondepressed
mother–infant pairs at 2 months. *Developmental
Psychology, 26,* 15–23.

COHN, J. F., & TRONICK, E. Z. (1983). Three-month-old infants' reaction to simulated maternal depression. *Child Development, 54,* 185–193.

COHN, J. F., & TRONICK, E. Z. (1987). mother–infant face-to-face interaction: The sequence of dyadic states at 3, 6, and 9 months. *Developmental Psychology, 23,* 68–77.

*COIE, J. D., & CILLESSEN, A. H. N. (1993). Peer rejection: Origins and effects on children's development. *Current Directions in Psychological Science, 2,* 89–92.

COIE, J. D., DODGE, K. A., & KUPERSMIDT, J. B. (1990). Peer group behavior and social status. In S. R. Asher & J. D. Coie (Eds.), *Peer rejection in childhood.* New York: Cambridge University Press.

COIE, J. D., & KREHBIEL, G. (1984). Effects of academic tutoring on the social status of low-achieving, socially rejected children. *Child Development, 55,* 1465–1478.

COIE, J. D., & KUPERSMIDT, J. (1983). A behavioral analysis of emerging social status in boys' groups. *Child Development, 54,* 1400–1416.

*COIE, J. D., LOCHMAN, J. E., TERRY, R., & HYMAN, C. (1992). Predicting early adolescent disorder from childhood aggression and peer rejection. *Journal of Consulting and Clinical Psychology, 60,* 783–792.

COLBY, A., & KOHLBERG, L. (1987). *The measurement of moral judgment* (Vols. 1–2). New York: Cambridge University Press.

COLE, C. B., & LOFTUS, E. F. (1987). The memory of children. In S. J. Ceci, M. P. Toglia, & D. F. Ross (Eds.), *Children's eyewitness memory.* New York: Springer-Verlag.

*COLE, M. (1992). Culture in development. In M. H. Bornstein & M. E. Lamb (Eds.), *Developmental psychology: An advanced textbook* (3rd ed.). Hillsdale, NJ: Erlbaum.

COLEMAN, W. (1971). *Biology in the nineteenth century: Problems of form, function, and transformation.* New York: Wiley.

COLLEGE ENTRANCE EXAMINATION BOARD. (1982). *Profiles, college-bound seniors.* New York: Author.

*COLLINS, F., & GALAS, D. (1993). A new five-year plan for the Human Genome Project. *Science, 262,* 43–46.

COLLINS, W. A. (1988). Research on the transition to adolescence: Continuity in the study of developmental processes. In M. R. Gunnar & W. A. Collins (Eds.), *Minnesota symposia on child psychology: Vol. 21. Development during the transition to adolescence.* Hillsdale, NJ: Erlbaum.

COLLIS, G. M. (1985). On the origins of turn-taking: Alternation and meaning. In M. D. Barrett (Ed.), *Children's single-word speech.* New York: Wiley.

*COLOMBO, J. (1993). *Infant cognition: Predicting later intellectual functioning.* Thousand Oaks, CA: Sage.

COLOMBO, J., & BUNDY, R. S. (1981). A method for the measurement of infant auditory selectivity. *Infant Behavior and Development, 4,* 219–223.

*COMMITTEE ON SUBSTANCE ABUSE. (1990). Drug-exposed infants. *Pediatrics, 86,* 639–642.

COMMONS, M. L., MILLER, P. M., & KUHN, D.

(1982). The relation between formal operational reasoning and academic course selection and performance among college freshmen and sophomores. *Journal of Applied Developmental Psychology, 3,* 1–10.

CONDRY, J. C., & CONDRY, S. (1976). Sex differences: A study in the eye of the beholder. *Child Development, 47,* 812–819.

CONDRY, J. C., & ROSS, D. F. (1985). Sex and aggression: The influence of gender label on the perception of aggression in children. *Child Development, 56,* 225–233.

*CONGER, R. D., GE, X., ELDER, G. H., LORENZ, F. O., & SIMONS, R. L. (1994). Economic stress, coercive family process, and developmental problems of adolescents. *Child Development, 65,* 541–561.

CONNELL, J. P., & ILARDI, B. C. (1987). Self-system concomitants of discrepancies between children's and teachers' evaluations of academic competence. *Child Development, 58,* 1297–1307.

CONSORTIUM FOR LONGITUDINAL STUDIES. (1983). *As the twig is bent. . . Lasting effects of preschool programs.* Hillsdale, NJ: Erlbaum.

CONSTANZO, P. R. (1970). Conformity development as a function of self-blame. *Journal of Personality and Social Psychology, 14,* 366–374.

CONTI, D. J., & CAMRAS, L. A. (1984). Children's understanding of conversational principles. *Journal of Experimental Child Psychology, 38,* 456–463.

COOK, E. P. (1985). *Psychological androgyny.* New York: Pergamon.

COOK, M., & BIRCH, R. (1984). Infant perception of the shapes of tilted plane forms. *Infant Behavior and Development, 7,* 389–402.

*COOK, V. J. (1988). *Chomsky's universal grammar.* Oxford: Blackwell.

COOLEY, C. H. (1902). *Human nature and the social order.* New York: Charles Scribner's Sons.

COON, H., FULKER, D. W., DeFRIES, J. C., & PLOMIN, R. (1990). Home environment and cognitive ability of 7-year-old children in the Colorado Adoption Project: Genetic and environmental etiologies. *Developmental Psychology, 26,* 459–468.

COOPER, C. R. (1980). Development of collaborative problem solving among preschool children. *Developmental Psychology, 16,* 433–440.

COOPER, R. G. (1984). Early number development: Discovering number space with addition and subtraction. In C. Sophian (Ed.), *Origins of cognitive skills.* Hillsdale, NJ: Erlbaum.

COOPER, R. P., & ASLIN, R. N. (1989). The language environment of the young infant: Implications for early perceptual development. *Canadian Journal of Psychology, 43,* 247–265.

COOPER, R. P., & ASLIN, R. N. (1990). Preference for infant-directed speech in the first month after birth. *Child Development, 61,* 1584–1595.

COOPERSMITH, S. (1967). *The antecedents of self-esteem.* San Francisco: W. H. Freeman.

COPANS, S. A. (1974). Human prenatal effects: Methodological problems and some suggested solutions. *Merrill-Palmer Quarterly, 20,* 43–52.

*CORINA, D. P., VAID, J., & BELLUGI, U. (1992). The linguistic basis of left hemisphere specialization. *Science, 255,* 1258–1260.

*COSTER, W. J., GERSTEN, M. S., BEEGHLY, M., & CICCHETTI, D. (1989). Communicative functioning in maltreated toddlers. *Developmental Psychology, 25,* 1020–1029.

*COSTIN, S. E., & JONES, D. C. (1992). Friendship as a facilitator of emotional responsiveness and prosocial interventions among young children. *Developmental Psychology, 28,* 941–947.

*COVEY, H. C., MENARD, S., & FRANZESE, R. J. (1992). *Juvenile gangs.* Springfield, IL: Charles C Thomas.

*COWAN, C. P., COWAN, P. A., HEMING, G., & MILLER, N. B. (1991). Becoming a family: Marriage, parenting and child development. In P. A. Cowan & E. M. Hetherington (Eds.), *Family transitions.* Hillsdale, NJ: Erlbaum.

*COWAN, P. A. (1978). *Piaget: With feeling.* New York: Holt, Rinehart and Winston.

COWAN, W. M. (1979). *The brain.* San Francisco: W. H. Freeman.

COX, D., & WATERS, H. S. (1986). Sex differences in the use of organization strategies: A developmental analysis. *Journal of Experimental Child Psychology, 41,* 18–37.

*COX, M. J., OWEN, M. T., HENDERSON, V. K., & MARGAND, N. A. (1992). Prediction of infant–father and infant–mother attachment. *Developmental Psychology, 28,* 474–483.

*CRAIN-THORESON, C., & DALE, P. S. (1992). Do early talkers become early readers? Linguistic precocity, preschool language, and emergent literacy. *Developmental Psychology, 28,* 421–429.

CRATTY, B. J. (1986). *Perceptual and motor development in infants and children.* Englewood Cliffs, NJ: Prentice Hall.

*CRAVENS, H. (1992). A scientific project locked in time: The Terman genetic studies of genius, 1920s–1950s. *American Psychologist, 47,* 183–189.

CRAVIOTO, J., & ARRIETA, R. (1986). Nutrition, mental development, and learning. In F. Falkner & J. M. Tanner (Eds.), *Human growth: A comprehensive treatise.* New York: Plenum.

*CRICK, N. R., & DODGE, K. A. (1994). A review and reformulation of social information-processing mechanisms in children's social adjustment. *Psychological Bulletin, 115,* 74–101.

CRITTENDEN, P. M. (1985). Maltreated infants: Vulnerability and resilience. *Journal of Child Psychology and Psychiatry, 26,* 85–96.

CRITTENDEN, P. M. (1988). Relationships at risk. In J. Belsky & T. Nezworski (Eds.), *Clinical implications of attachment.* Hillsdale, NJ: Erlbaum.

CRITTENDEN, P. M., & AINSWORTH, M. D. S. (1989). Child maltreatment and attachment theory. In D. Cicchetti & V. Carlson (Eds.), *Child maltreatment: Theory and research on the causes and consequences of child abuse and neglect.* New York: Cambridge University Press.

CROCKENBERG, S. B. (1986). Are temperamental differences in babies associated with predictable differences in care-giving? In J. V. Lerner & R. M. Lerner (Eds.), *Temperament and social interaction in infants and children.* San Francisco: Jossey-Bass.

CROCKETT, L. J., & PETERSEN, A. C. (1987). Pubertal status and psychosocial development:

Findings from the early adolescence study. In R. M. Lerner & T. L. Foch (Eds.), *Biological psychosocial interactions in early adolescence.* Hillsdale, NJ: Erlbaum.

CROOK, C. K. (1979). The organization and control of infant sucking. In H. W. Reese & L. P. Lipsitt (Eds.), *Advances in child development and behavior. (Vol. 14).* New York: Academic Press.

CROOK, C. K. (1987). Taste and olfaction. In P. Salapatek & L. Cohen (Eds.), *Handbook of infant perception: Vol. 1. From sensation to perception.* New York: Academic Press.

CROUCHMAN, M. (1985). What mothers know about their newborns' visual skills. *Developmental Medicine and Child Neurology, 27,* 455–460.

CROWELL, D. H. (1987). Childhood aggression and violence: Contemporary issues. In D. H. Crowell, I. M. Evans, & C. R. O'Donnell (Eds.), *Childhood aggression and violence: Sources of influence, prevention, and control.* New York: Plenum.

CROWELL, J. A., & FELDMAN, S. S. (1991). Mothers' working models of attachment relationships and mother and child behavior during separation and reunion. *Developmental Psychology, 27,* 597–605.

CUMMINGS, E. M., HOLLENBECK, B., IANNOTTI, R., RADKE-YARROW, M., & ZAHN-WAXLER, C. (1986). Early organization of altruism and aggression: Developmental patterns and individual differences. In C. Zahn-Waxler, E. M. Cummings, & R. Iannotti (Eds.), *Altruism and aggression: Biological and social origins.* New York: Cambridge University Press.

CUMMINGS, E. M., IANNOTTI, R. J., & ZAHN-WAXLER, C. (1989). Aggression between peers in early childhood: Individual continuity and developmental change. *Child Development, 60,* 887–895.

CUMMINGS, S., & TAEBEL, D. (1980). Sex inequality and the reproduction consciousness: An analysis of sex-role stereotyping among children. *Sex Roles, 6,* 631–644.

*CUMMINS, J. (1991). Interdependence of first- and second-language proficiency in bilingual children. In E. Bialystok (Ed.), *Language processing in bilingual children.* Cambridge: Cambridge University Press.

CUNNINGHAM, F. G., MacDONALD, P. C., & GANT, N. F. (1989). *Williams obstetrics* (18th ed.). London: Appleton & Lange.

*CUOMO, M. (1994, January 17). Clintons should lead fight on media violence. *Los Angeles Times,* p. 12.

CURTIS, H. (1983). *Biology.* New York: Worth.

CUTTS, K., & CECI, S. J. (1988, August). *Hidden memories from infancy: Memory for cheerios, or cheerio, memory?* Paper presented at the meeting of the American Psychological Association, Atlanta, GA.

*DALY, M., & WILSON, M. (1983). *Sex, evolution, and behavior* (2nd ed.). Boston: PWS.

DAMON, W. (1977). *The social world of the child.* San Francisco: Jossey-Bass.

DAMON, W. (1980). Patterns of change in children's social reasoning: A two-year longitudinal study. *Child Development, 51,* 1010–1017.

DAMON, W. (1981). Exploring children's social cognition on two fronts. In J. H. Flavell & L.

Ross (Eds.), *Social cognitive development.* Cambridge: Cambridge University Press.

DAMON, W. (1983). *Social and personality development.* New York: Norton.

DAMON, W., & COLBY, A. (1987). Social influence and moral change. In W. M. Kurtines & J. L. Gewirtz (Eds.), *Moral development through social interaction.* New York: Wiley.

DAMON, W., & HART, D. (1982). The development of self-understanding from infancy through adolescence. *Child Development, 53,* 841–864.

DAMON, W., & HART, D. (1988). *Self-understanding in childhood and adolescence.* New York: Cambridge University Press.

*DAMON, W., & HART, D. (1992). Self-understanding and its role in social and moral development. In M. H. Bornstein & M. E. Lamb (Eds.), *Developmental psychology: An advanced textbook* (3rd ed.). Hillsdale, NJ: Erlbaum.

DAMON, W., & KILLEN, M. (1982). Peer interaction and the process of change in children's moral reasoning. *Merrill-Palmer Quarterly, 28,* 347–367.

DAMON, W., & PHELPS, E. (1989). Strategic uses of peer learning in children's education. In T. J. Berndt & G. W. Ladd (Eds.), *Peer relationships in child development.* New York: Wiley.

DANEMAN, M., & CASE, R. (1981). Syntactic form, semantic complexity, and short-term memory: Influences on children's acquisition of new linguistic structures. *Developmental Psychology, 17,* 367–378.

DANNEMILLER, J. L. (1985). The early phase of dark adaptation in human infants. *Vision Research, 25,* 207–212.

DANNEMILLER, J. L., & HANKO, S. A. (1987). A test of color constancy in 4-month-old infants. *Journal of Experimental Child Psychology, 44,* 255–267.

DANNER, F. W., & DAY, M. C. (1977). Eliciting formal operations. *Child Development, 48,* 1600–1606.

*DARLINGTON, R. B. (1991). The long-term effects of model preschool programs. In L. Okagaki & R. J. Sternberg (Eds.), *Directors of development: Influences on the development of children's thinking.* Hillsdale, NJ: Erlbaum.

DARWIN, C. (1872). *The expression of emotions in man and animals.* London: Murray.

DARWIN, C. (1877). A biographical sketch of an infant. *Mind, 2,* 285–294.

DASEN, P. R. (1975). Concrete operational development in three cultures. *Journal of Cross-Cultural Psychology, 6,* 156–172.

DASEN, P. R., & HERON, A. (1981). Cross-cultural tests of Piaget's theory. In H. C. Triandis & A. Heron (Eds.), *Handbook of cross-cultural psychology: Vol. 4. Developmental psychology.* Boston: Allyn & Bacon.

DAVIDS, A., DeVAULT, S., & TALMADGE, M. (1961). Anxiety, pregnancy, and childbirth abnormalities. *Journal of Consulting Psychology, 25,* 74–77.

*DAVIDSON, D., & HOE, S. (1993). Children's recall and recognition memory for typical and atypical actions in script-based stories. *Journal of Experimental Child Psychology, 55,* 104–126.

*DAVIES, G. M. (1993). Children's memory for

other people: An integrative review. In C. A. Nelson (Ed.), *Minnesota symposia on child psychology: Vol. 26. Memory and affect in development.* Hillsdale, NJ: Erlbaum.

DAVIS, K. (1947). Final note on a case of extreme isolation. *American Journal of Sociology, 45,* 554–565.

DAWKINS, R. (1976). *The selfish gene.* New York: Oxford University Press.

DAY, M. C. (1975). Developmental trends in visual scanning. In H. W. Reese (Ed.), *Advances in child development and behavior* (Vol. 10). New York: Academic Press.

DAY, R. H. (1987). Visual size constancy in infancy. In B. E. McKenzie & R. H. Day (Eds.), *Perceptual development in early infancy: Problems and issues.* Hillsdale, NJ: Erlbaum.

DAY, R. H., & McKENZIE, B. E. (1973). Perceptual shape constancy in early infancy. *Perception, 2,* 315–320.

De LISI, R., & STAUDT, J. (1980). Individual differences in college students' performance on formal operations tasks. *Journal of Applied Developmental Psychology, 1,* 201–208.

De VRIES, R. (1969). Constancy of generic identity in the years three to six. *Monographs of the Society for Research in Child Development, 34,* (3, Serial No. 127).

*de RIBAUPIERRE, A., RIEBEN, L., & LAUTREY, J. (1991). Developmental change and individual differences: A longitudinal study using Piagetian tasks. *Genetic, Social, and General Psychology Monographs, 117,* 285–311.

DEAUX, K. (1987). Psychological constructions of masculinity and femininity. In J. M. Reinisch, L. A. Rosenblum, & S. A. Sanders (Eds.), *Masculinity/femininity: Basic perspectives.* New York: Oxford University Press.

*DEAUX, K. (1993). Sorry, wrong number—A reply to Gentile's call. *Psychological Science, 4,* 125–126.

*DeBARYSHE, B. D. (1993). Joint picture-book reading correlates of early oral language skill. *Journal of Child Language, 20,* 455–461.

*DeBARYSHE, B. D., PATTERSON, G. R., & CAPALDI, D. M. (1993). Performance model for academic achievement in early adolescent boys. *Developmental Psychology, 29,* 795–804.

DeCASPER, A. J., & FIFER, W. P. (1980). Of human bonding: Newborns prefer their mothers' voices. *Science, 208,* 1174–1176.

DeCASPER, A. J., & PRESCOTT, P. A. (1984). Human newborns' perception of male voices: Preference, discrimination, and reinforcing value. *Developmental Psychobiology, 17,* 481–491.

DeCASPER, A. J., & SPENCE, M. J. (1986). Newborns prefer a familiar story over an unfamiliar one. *Infant Behavior and Development, 9,* 133–150.

DeCASPER, A. J., & SPENCE, M. J. (1991). Auditory mediated behavior during the perinatal period: A cognitive view. In M. J. S. Weiss & P. R. Zelazo (Eds.), *Newborn attention: Biological constraints and the influence of experience.* Norwood, NJ: Ablex.

*DeFRIES, J. C., & GILLIS, J. J. (1993). Genetics of reading disability. In R. Plomin & G. E. McClearn (Eds.), *Nature, nurture, and psychology.* Washington, DC: APA.

*DeKAY, W. T., & BUSS, D. M. (1992). Human nature, individual differences, and the importance of context: Perspectives from an evolutionary psychology. *Current Directions, 1,* 184–189.

*DEKOVIC, M., & JANSSENS, J. M. A. M. (1992). Parents' child-rearing style and child's sociometric status. *Developmental Psychology, 28,* 925–932.

*DEL CARMEN, R., PEDERSEN, F. A., HUFFMAN, L. C., & BRYAN, Y. E. (1993). Dyadic distress management predicts subsequent security of attachment. *Infant Behavior and Development, 16,* 131–147.

DELK, J. L., MADDEN, R. B., LIVINGSTON, M., & RYAN, T. T. (1986). Adult perceptions of the infant as a function of gender labeling and observer gender. *Sex Roles, 15,* 527–534.

DeLOACHE, J. S., CASSIDY, D. J., & BROWN, A. L. (1985). Precursors of mnemonic strategies in very young children's memory. *Child Development, 46,* 125–137.

DeLOACHE, J. S., CASSIDY, D. J., & CARPENTER, C. J. (1987). The three bears are all boys: Mothers' gender labeling of neutral picture book characters. *Sex Roles, 17,* 163–178.

DELOZIER, C. D., & ENGEL, E. (1982). Sexual differentiation as a model for genetic and environmental interaction affecting physical and psychological development. In W. R. Gove & G. R. Carpenter (Eds.), *The fundamental connection between nature and nurture: A review of the evidence.* Lexington, MA: Lexington.

DEMAITRE, L. (1977). The idea of childhood and child care in medieval writing of the Middle Ages. *Journal of Psychohistory, 4,* 461–490.

DEMETRAS, M. J., POST, K. N., & SNOW, C. E. (1986). Feedback to first language learners: The role of repetitions and clarification questions. *Journal of Child Language, 13,* 275–292.

*DEMETRIOU, A., SHAYER, M., & EFKLIDES, A. (Eds.). (1993). *Neo-Piagetian theories of cognitive development.* New York: Routledge.

DEMO, D. H., & SAVIN-WILLIAMS, R. C. (1983). Early adolescent self-esteem as a function of social class: Rosenberg and Pearlin revisited. *American Journal of Sociology, 88,* 763–774.

DEMOS, V. (1986). Crying in early infancy: An illustration of the motivational function of affect. In T. B. Brazelton & M. Yogman (Eds.), *Affect and early infancy.* Norwood, NJ: Ablex.

*DENENBERG, V., & THOMAN, E. (1981). Evidence for a functional role for active (REM) sleep in infancy. *Sleep, 4,* 185–191.

*DENHAM, S. A., & MCKINLEY, M. (1993). Sociometric nominations of preschoolers: A psychometric analysis. *Early Education and Development, 4,* 109–122.

DENNEY, N. W., & DUFFY, D. M. (1974). Possible environmental causes of stages in moral reasoning. *Journal of Genetic Psychology, 125,* 277–284.

DENNIS, W. (1960). Causes of retardation among institutional children: Iran. *Journal of Genetic Psychology, 96,* 47–59.

DENNIS, W. (1973). *Children of the Creche.* New York: Appleton-Century-Crofts.

DENNIS, W., & NAJARIAN, P. (1957). Infant development under environmental handicap. *Psychological Monographs, 71* (No. 436).

*DESCARTES, R. (1960). *Discourse on method and meditations.* Indianapolis: Bobbs-Merrill. (Original work published 1637)

deVILLIERS, J. G. (1980). The process of rule learning in child speech: A new look. In K. E. Nelson (Ed.), *Children's language* (Vol. 2). New York: Gardner.

DeVRIES, M. W., & SAMEROFF, A. J. (1984). Culture and temperament: Influences on infant temperament in three East African societies. *American Journal of Orthopsychiatry, 54,* 83–96.

*DeVRIES, R. (1991). The cognitive-developmental paradigm. In W. M. Kurtines & J. L. Gewirtz (Eds.), *Handbook of moral behavior and development: Vol. 1. Theory.* Hillsdale, NJ: Erlbaum.

DEWSBURY, D. A. (1978). *Comparative animal behavior.* New York: McGraw-Hill.

*DIAMOND, A. (1985). Development of the ability to use recall to guide actions, as indicated by infants' performance on A$\overline{\text{B}}$. *Child Development, 56,* 868–883.

DIAMOND, A. (1991a). Frontal lobe involvement in cognitive changes during the first year of life. In K. Gibson, M. Konner, & A. Petersen (Eds.), *Brain and behavioral development.* New York: Aldine.

*DIAMOND, A. (1991b). Neuropsychological insights into the meaning of object concept development. In S. Carey & R. Gelman (Eds.), *The epigenesis of mind: Essays on biology and cognition.* Hillsdale, NJ: Erlbaum.

*DIAMOND, A. (1993). *Nature and causes of cognitive deficits in phenylketonuria (PKU) even with dietary treatment: Longitudinal study and animal model.* Paper presented at the meeting of the Society for Research in Child Development, New Orleans.

*DIAMOND, A., CRUTTENDEN, L., & NEIDERMAN, D. (1994). A$\overline{\text{B}}$ with multiple wells: 1. Why are multiple wells sometimes easier than two wells? 2. Memory or memory + inhibition? *Developmental Psychology, 30,* 192–205.

*DIAMOND, M. C. (1991). Environmental influences on the young brain. In K. R. Gibson & A. C. Petersen (Eds.), *Brain maturation and cognitive development.* New York: Aldine De Gruyter.

DIAZ, R. M. (1983). Thought and two languages: The impact of bilingualism on cognitive development. *Review of Research in Education, 10,* 23–54.

DIAZ, R. M. (1985). Bilingual cognitive development: Addressing three gaps in current research. *Child Development, 56,* 1376–1388.

*DIAZ, R. M., & BERK, L. E. (Eds.). (1992). *Private speech: From social interaction to self-regulation.* Hillsdale, NJ: Erlbaum.

DIAZ, R. M., & BERNDT, T. J. (1982). Children's knowledge of a best friend: Fact or fancy? *Developmental Psychology, 18,* 787–794.

DIAZ, R. M., NEAL, C. J., & VACHIO, A. (1991). Maternal teaching in the zone of proximal development: A comparison of low- and high-risk dyads. *Merrill-Palmer Quarterly, 37,* 83–108.

DICK-READ, G. (1933). *Natural childbirth.* New York: Dell.

DICK-READ, G. (1944). *Childbirth without fear.* New York: Dell.

DIEN, D. S. F. (1982). A Chinese perspective on Kohlberg's theory of moral development. *Developmental Review, 2,* 331–341.

*DINGES, M. M., & OETTING, E. R. (1993). Similarity in drug use patterns between adolescents and their friends. *Adolescence, 28,* 253–266.

DION, K. K., & BERSCHEID, E. (1974). Physical attractiveness and peer perception among children. *Sociometry, 37,* 1–12.

DiPIETRO, J. A. (1981). Rough and tumble play: A function of gender. *Developmental Psychology, 17,* 50–58.

DISHION, T. J. (1990). The family ecology of boys' peer relations in middle childhood. *Child Development, 61,* 874–892.

*DIXON, R. A., & LERNER, R. M. (1992). A history of systems in developmental psychology. In M. H. Bornstein & M. E. Lamb (Eds.), *Developmental psychology: An advanced textbook* (3rd ed.). Hillsdale, NJ: Erlbaum.

*DNA tests free 9-year inmate. (1993, June 29). *Denver Post,* p. 4A.

DOBRICH, W., & SCARBOROUGH, H. S. (1984). Form and function in early communication: Language and pointing gestures. *Journal of Experimental Child Psychology, 38,* 475–490.

DOBSON, V., & TELLER, D. Y. (1978). Visual acuity in human infants: A review and comparison of behavioral and electrophysiological studies. *Vision Research, 18,* 1469–1483.

DODGE, K. A. (1985). Attributional bias in aggressive children. In P. Kendall (Ed.), *Advances in cognitive-behavioral research and therapy* (Vol. 4). New York: Academic Press.

DODGE, K. A. (1986a). A social information processing model of social competence in children. In M. Perlmutter (Ed.), *Minnesota symposia on child psychology: Vol. 18. Cognitive perspectives on children's social and behavioral development.* Hillsdale, NJ: Erlbaum.

DODGE, K. A. (1986b). Social information-processing variables in the development of aggression and altruism in children. In C. Zahn-Waxler, E. M. Cummings, & R. Iannotti (Eds.), *Altruism and aggression: Biological and social origins.* New York: Cambridge University Press.

*DODGE, K. A. (1993, March). *Social information processing and peer rejection factors in the development of behavior problems in children.* Paper presented at the meeting of the Society for Research in Child Development, New Orleans.

DODGE, K. A., COIE, J. D., PETTIT, G. S., & PRICE, J. M. (1990). Peer status and aggression in boys' groups: Developmental and contextual analyses. *Child Development, 61,* 1289–1309.

*DODGE, K. A., & CRICK, N. R. (1990). Social-information processing bases of aggressive behavior in children. *Personality and Social Psychology Bulletin, 16,* 8–22.

DODGE, K. A., & FELDMAN, E. (1990). Issues in social cognition and sociometric status. In S. R. Asher & J. D. Coie (Eds.), *Peer rejection in childhood.* Cambridge: Cambridge University Press.

DODGE, K. A., MURPHY, R. R., & BUCHSBAUM, K. (1984). The assessment of intention-cue detection skills in children: Implications for developmental psychopathology. *Child Development, 55,* 163–173.

*DODGE, K. A., PETTIT, G. S., & BATES, J. E. (1994). Socialization mediators of the relation between socioeconomic status and child conduct problems. *Child Development, 65,* 649–665.

DODGE, K. A., & SOMBERG, D. R. (1987). Hostile attributional biases among aggressive boys are exacerbated under conditions of threats to the self. *Child Development, 58,* 213–224.

DODWELL, P. C., HUMPHREY, G. K., & MUIR, D. W. (1987). Shape and pattern perception. In P. Salapatek & L. Cohen (Eds.), *Handbook of infant perception: Vol. 2. From perception to cognition.* New York: Academic Press.

DOMAN, G. (1985). *How to give your baby encyclopedic knowledge.* New York: Doubleday.

DONALDSON, M. (1982). Conservation: What is the question? *British Journal of Psychology, 73,* 199–207.

DONENBERG, G. R., & HOFFMAN, L. W. (1988). Gender differences in moral development. *Sex Roles, 18,* 701–717.

DORE, J. (1975). Holophrases, speech acts and language universals. *Journal of Child Language, 2,* 21–40.

DORE, J. (1976). Children's illocutionary acts. In R. Freedle (Ed.), *Comprehension and production.* Hillsdale, NJ: Erlbaum.

DORE, J. (1985). Holophrases revisited: Their "logical" development during dialog. In M. D. Barrett (Ed.), *Children's single-word speech.* New York: Wiley.

*DORIS, J. (Ed.). (1991). *The suggestibility of children's recollections: Implications for eyewitness testimony.* Washington, DC: APA.

DORNBUSCH, S. M., GROSS, R. T., DUNCAN, P. D., & RITTER, P. L. (1987). Stanford studies of adolescence using the national health examination survey. In R. M. Lerner & T. L. Foch (Eds.), *Biological-psychosocial interactions in early adolescence.* Hillsdale, NJ: Erlbaum.

*DORNBUSCH, S. M., RITTER, P. L., LEIDERMAN, P. H., ROBERTS, D. F., & FRALEIGH, M. J. (1985). The relation of parenting style to adolescent school performance. *Child Development, 58,* 1244–1257.

DORR, D., & FEY, S. (1974). Relative power of symbolic and peer models in the modification of children's moral choice behavior. *Journal of Personality and Social Psychology, 29,* 335–341.

*DOUGHERTY, T., & HAITH, M. M. (1993, March). *Processing speed in infants and children: A component of IQ?* Paper presented at the meeting of the Society for Research in Child Development, New Orleans.

DOWLING, M., & BENDELL, D. (1988). Characteristics of small-for-gestational-age infants. *Infant Behavior and Development, 11,* 77.

DOYLE, A., CONNOLLY, J., & RIVEST, L. (1980). The effect of playmate familiarity on the social interactions of young children. *Child Development, 51,* 217–223.

DRAPER, P., & HARPENDING, H. (1988). A sociobiological perspective on the development of human reproductive strategies. In K. B. MacDonald (Ed.), *Sociobiological perspectives on human development.* New York: Springer-Verlag.

*DREHER, M. C. (1989). Poor and pregnant: Perinatal ganja use in rural Jamaica. *Advances in Alcohol & Substance Abuse, 8,* 45–53.

*DREHER, M. C., & HAYES, J. S. (1993). Triangulation in cross-cultural research of child development in Jamaica. *Western Journal of Nursing Research, 15,* 216–229.

*DREHER, M. C., NUGENT, K. & HUDGINS, R. (1994). Prenatal marijuana exposure and neonatal outcomes in Jamaica: An ethnographic study. *Pediatrics, 93,* 254–260.

DROTAR, D. K. (1988). Failure to thrive. In D. K. Routh (Ed.), *Handbook of pediatric psychology.* New York: Guilford.

*DROTAR, D. K., ECKERLE, D., SATOLA, J., PALLOTTA, J., & WYATT, B. (1990). Maternal interactional behavior with nonorganic failure-to-thrive infants: A case comparison study. *Child Abuse and Neglect, 14,* 41–51.

DUBIGNON, J., & CAMPBELL, D. (1968). Intra-oral stimulation and sucking in the newborn. *Journal of Experimental Child Psychology, 6,* 154–166.

DuBOIS, D. L., & HIRSCH, B. J. (1990). School and neighborhood friendship patterns of blacks and whites in early adolescence. *Child Development, 61,* 524–536.

*DUBOW, E. F., TISAK, J., CAUSEY, D., HRYSHKO, A., & REID, G. (1991). A two-year longitudinal study of stressful life events, social support, and social problem-solving skills: Contributions to children's behavioral and academic adjustment. *Child Development, 62,* 583–599.

DUCKWORTH, E. (1987). *The having of wonderful ideas and other essays on teaching and learning.* New York: Teachers College Press.

DUFFY, F. H., ALS, H., & McANULTY, G. B. (1990). Behavioral and electrophysiological evidence for gestational age effects in healthy preterm and full-term infants studied two weeks after expected due date. *Child Development, 61,* 1271–1286.

*DUFRESNE, A., & KOBASIGAWA, A. (1989). Children's spontaneous allocation of study time: Differential and sufficient aspects. *Journal of Experimental Child Psychology, 47,* 274–296.

*DUNCAN, G. J., BROOKS-GUNN, J., & KLEBANOV, P. K. (1994). Economic deprivation and early childhood development. *Child Development, 65,* 296–318

*DUNHAM, P., & DUNHAM, F. (1992). Lexical development during middle infancy: A mutually driven infant-caregiver process. *Developmental Psychology, 28,* 414–420.

DUNN, J. (1983). Sibling relationships in early childhood. *Child Development, 54,* 787–811.

*DUNN, J. (1992). Sisters and brothers: Current issues in developmental research. In F. Boer & J. Dunn (Eds.), *Children's sibling relatioinships: Developmental and clinical issues.* Hillsdale, NJ: Erlbaum.

*DUNN, J. (1993). *Young children's close relationships.* Newbury Park, CA: Sage.

*DUNN, J. (1994). Sibling relationships and perceived self-competence: Patterns of stability between childhood and early adolescence. In A. Sameroff & M. M. Haith (Eds.), *Reason and responsibility: The passage through childhood.* Chicago: University of Chicago Press.

DUNN, J., BRETHERTON, I., & MUNN, P. (1987). Conversations about feeling states between mothers and their young children. *Developmental Psychology, 23,* 132–139.

DUNN, J., & KENDRICK, C. (1982). The speech of two- and three-year-olds to infant siblings: "Baby talk" and the context of communication. *Journal of Child Language, 9,* 579–595.

*DUNN, J., & McGUIRE, S. (1992). Sibling and peer relationships in childhood. *Journal of Child Psychology & Psychiatry & Allied Disciplines, 33,* 67–105.

DUNN, J., & MUNN, P. (1986). Siblings and the development of prosocial behaviors. *International Journal of Behavioral Development, 9,* 265–284.

*DURKIN, K. (1993). The representation of number in infancy and early childhood. In C. Pratt & A. F. Garton (Eds.), *Systems of representation in children.* New York: Wiley.

DUSEK, J. B., & JOSEPH, G. (1983). The bases of teacher expectancies: A meta-analysis. *Journal of Educational Psychology, 75,* 327–346.

DWECK, C. S. (1975). The role of expectations and attributions in the alleviation of learned helplessness. *Journal of Personality and Social Psychology, 31,* 674–685.

DWECK, C. S. (1986). Motivational processes affecting learning. *American Psychologist, 41,* 1040–1048.

DWECK, C. S., DAVIDSON, W., NELSON, S., & ENNA, B. (1978). Sex differences in learned helplessness: II. The contingencies of evaluative feedback in the classroom, and III. An experimental analysis. *Developmental Psychology, 14,* 268–276.

DWECK, C. S., & GOETZ, T. E. (1980). Attributions and learned helplessness. In J. H. Harvey, W. Ickles, & R. F. Kidd (Eds.), *New directions in attribution research* (Vol. 2). Hillsdale, NJ: Erlbaum.

DWECK, C. S., & REPPUCCI, N. D. (1973). Learned helplessness and reinforcement responsibility in children. *Journal of Personality and Social Psychology, 25,* 109–116.

EAGLY, A. H. (1987). *Sex differences: A social-role interpretation.* Hillsdale, NJ: Erlbaum.

EAGLY, A. H., & CROWLEY, M. (1987). Gender and helping behavior: A meta-analytic review of the social psychological literature. *Psychological Bulletin, 100,* 283–308.

EAGLY, A. H., & STEFFEN, V. J. (1986). Gender and aggressive behavior: A meta-analytic review of the social psychological literature. *Psychological Bulletin, 100,* 309–330.

*EAST, P. L., & ROOK, K. S. (1992). Compensatory patterns of support among children's peer relationships: A test using school friends, nonschool friends, and siblings. *Developmental Psychology, 28,* 163–172.

EASTERBROOKS, M. A., & GOLDBERG, W. A. (1984). Toddler development in the family: Impact of father involvement and parenting characteristics. *Child Development, 55,* 740–752.

EATON, W. O., & ENNS, L. R. (1986). Sex differences in human motor activity level. *Psychological Bulletin, 100,* 19–28.

EATON, W. O., & YU, A. P. (1989). Are sex differences in child motor activity level a function of sex differences in maturational status? *Child Development, 60,* 1005–1011.

ECCLES, J. S., & MIDGLEY, C. (1989). Stage/environment fit: Developmentally appropriate classrooms for early adolescents. In R. E. Ames & C. Ames (Eds.), *Research on motivation in education* (Vol. 3). New York: Academic Press.

ECCLES, J. S., & MIDGLEY, C. (1990). Changes in academic motivation and self-perception during early adolescence. In R. Montemayor, G. R. Adams, & T. P. Gullotta (Eds.), *From childhood to adolescence: A transitional period?* Newbury Park, CA: Sage.

ECCLES, J. S., MIDGLEY, C., & ADLER, T. (1984). Grade-related changes in the school environment: Effects on achievement motivation. In J. G. Nicholls (Ed.), *The development of achievement motivation.* Greenwich, CT: JAI Press.

*ECCLES, J. S., MIDGLEY, C., WIGFIELD, A., BUCHANAN, C. M., REUMAN, D., FLANA-GAN, C., & MacIVER, D. (1993). Development during adolescence: The impact of stage-environment fit on young adolescents' experiences in schools and in families. *American Psychologist, 48,* 90–101.

*ECCLES, J., WIGFIELD, A., HAROLD, R. D., & BLUMENFELD, P. (1993). Age and gender differences in children's self- and task perceptions during elementary school. *Child Development, 64,* 830–847.

ECKBERG, D. L. (1979). *Intelligence and race: The origins and dimensions of the IQ controversy.* New York: Praeger.

*ECKERMAN, C. O., DAVIS, C. C., & DIDOW, S. (1989). Toddlers' emerging ways of achieving social coordinations with a peer. *Child Development, 60,* 440–453.

*ECKERMAN, C. O., & STEIN, M. R. (1990). How imitation begets imitation and toddlers' generation of games. *Developmental Psychology, 26,* 370–378.

*ECKSTEIN, S., & SHEMESH, M. (1992). The rate of acquisition of formal operational schemata in adolescence: A secondary analysis. *Journal of Research in Science Teaching, 29,* 441–451.

EDELMAN, G. M. (1987). *Neural Darwinism: The theory of neuronal group selection.* New York: Basic Books.

*EDELMAN, G. M. (1993). Neural Darwinism: Selection and reentrant signaling in higher brain function. *Neuron, 10,* 115–125.

EDER, R. A. (1989). The emergent personologist: The structure and content of 3½-, 5½-, and 7½-year-olds' concepts of themselves and others. *Child Development, 60,* 1218–1228.

EDER, R. A. (1990). Uncovering young children's psychological selves: Individual and developmental differences. *Child Development, 61,* 849–863.

EDWARDS, C. P. (1986). Cross-cultural research on Kohlberg's stages: The basis for consensus. In S. Modgil & C. Modgil (Eds.), *Lawrence Kohlberg: Consensus and controversy.* Philadelphia: Falmer.

EGELAND, B., & FARBER, E. (1984). Infant-mother attachment: Factors related to its development and changes over time. *Child Development, 55,* 753–771.

EHRHARDT, A. A. (1985). The psychobiology of gender. In A. S. Rossi (Ed.), *Gender and the life course.* New York: Aldine.

EHRHARDT, A. A., & MEYER-BAHLBURG, H. F. L. (1981). Effects of prenatal sex hormones on gender-related behavior. *Science, 211,* 1312–1318.

EIBL-EIBESFELDT, I. (1975). *Ethology: The biology of behavior* (2nd ed.). New York: Holt, Rinehart and Winston.

EIBL-EIBESFELDT, I. (1989). *Human ethology.* Hawthorne, NY: Aldine de Gruyter.

EICHORN, D. (1979). Physical development: Current foci of research. In J. D. Osofsky (Ed.), *Handbook of infant development.* New York: Wiley.

EICHORN, D. (1970). Physiological development: In P. H. Mussen (Ed.), *Carmichael's Manual of Child Psychology* (3rd ed.). New York: Wiley.

EIDUSON, B. T. (1980). Changing sex roles in alternative family styles: Implications for young children. In E. J. Anthony & C. Chiland (Eds.), *The child in his family: Preventive child psychiatry in an age of transition* (Vol. 6). New York: Wiley.

EIDUSON, B. T., KORNFEIN, M., ZIMMERMAN, I. L., & WEISNER, T. S. (1982). Comparative socialization practices in alternative family settings. In M. E. Lamb (Ed.), *Nontraditional families.* New York: Plenum.

EIFERMANN, R. R. (1971). Social play in childhood. In R. E. Herron & B. Sutton-Smith (Eds.), *Child's play.* New York: Wiley.

EILERS, R. E., & OLLER, D. K. (1988). Precursors to speech: What is innate and what is acquired? In R. Vasta (Ed.), *Annals of child development* (Vol. 5). Greenwich, CT: JAI Press.

EIMAS, P. D. (1975). Auditory and phonetic coding of the cues for speech: Discrimination of the [r-l] distinction by young infants. *Perception and Psychophysics, 18,* 341–347.

EISENBERG, N. (1982). The development of reasoning regarding prosocial behavior. In N. Eisenberg (Ed.), *The development of prosocial behavior.* New York: Academic Press.

EISENBERG, N. (1986). *Altruistic emotion, cognition, and behavior.* Hillsdale, NJ: Erlbaum.

EISENBERG, N. (1987). The relation of altruism and other moral behaviors to moral cognition: Methodological and conceptual issues. In N. Eisenberg & J. Strayer (Eds.), *Empathy and its development.* New York: Cambridge University Press.

EISENBERG, N. (1989). Empathy and sympathy. In W. Damon (Ed.), *Child development today and tomorrow.* San Francisco: Jossey-Bass.

EISENBERG, N. (1990). Prosocial development in early and mid-adolescence. In R. Montemayor, G. R. Adams, & T. P. Gullotta (Eds.), *From childhood to adolescence: A transitional period?* Newbury Park, CA: Sage.

EISENBERG, N., CAMERON, E., TRYON, K., & DODEZ, R. (1981). Socialization of prosocial behavior in the preschool classroom. *Developmental Psychology, 17,* 773–782.

*EISENBERG, N., & FABES, R. A. (1991). Prosocial behavior and empathy: A multimethod, developmental perspective. In P. Clark (Ed.), *Review of personality and social psychology.* Newbury Park, CA: Sage.

*EISENBERG, N., FABES, R. A., CARLO, G., SPEER, A. L., SWITZER, G., KARBON, M., & TROYER, D. (1993). The relations of empathy-related and maternal practices to children's comforting behavior. *Journal of Experimental Child Psychology, 55,* 131–150.

*EISENBERG, N., FABES, R. A., CARLO, G., TROYER, D., SPEER, A. L., KARBON, M., & SWITZER, G. (1992). The relations of maternal practices and characteristics of children's vicarious emotional responsiveness. *Child Development, 63,* 583–602.

EISENBERG, N., & MILLER, P. A. (1987). The relation of empathy to prosocial and related behaviors. *Psychological Bulletin, 101,* 91–119.

*EISENBERG, N., MILLER, P. A., SHELL, R., McNALLEY, S., & SHEA, C. (1991). Prosocial development in adolescence: A longitudinal study. *Developmental Psychology, 27,* 849–857.

EISENBERG, N., & MUSSEN, P. H. (1989). *The roots of prosocial behavior in children.* New York: Cambridge University Press.

EISENBERG, N., TRYON, K., & CAMERON, E. (1984). The relation of preschoolers' peer interaction to their sex-typed toy choices. *Child Development, 55,* 1044–1050.

EISENBERG, N., WOLCHIK, S. A., HERNANDEZ, R., & PASTERNACK, J. F. (1985). Parental socialization of young children's play: A short-term longitudinal study. *Child Development, 56,* 1506–1513.

EISENBERG, R. B. (1970). The organization of auditory behavior. *Journal of Speech and Hearing Research, 13,* 454–471.

EISENBERG, R. B. (1976). *Auditory competence in early life.* Baltimore: University Park Press.

EISENBERG-BERG, N., & GEISHEKER, E. (1979). Content of preachings and power of the model/preacher: The effect on children's generosity. *Developmental Psychology, 15,* 168–175.

*EKMAN, P. (1993). Facial expression and emotion. *American Psychologist, 48,* 384–392.

ELARDO, R., & BRADLEY, R. H. (1981). The Home Observation for Measurement of the Environment (HOME) scale: A review of research. *Developmental Review, 1,* 113–145.

ELDER, G. H. (1974). *Children of the Great Depression.* Chicago: University of Chicago Press.

ELDER, G. H. (1985). *Life course dynamics: Trajectories and transitions, 1968–1980.* Ithaca, NY: Cornell University Press.

ELDER, G. H., & CASPI, A. (1988). Human development and social change: An emerging perspective on the life course. In N. Bolger, A. Caspi, G. Downey, & M. Moorehouse (Eds.), *Persons in context: Developmental processes.* New York: Cambridge University Press.

ELDER, G. II., CASPI, A., & DOWNEY, G. (1986). Problem behavior and family relationships: Life course and intergenerational themes. In A. B. Sorensen, F. E. Weinert, & L. R. Sherrod (Eds.), *Human development and the life course: Multidisciplinary perspectives.* Hillsdale, NJ: Erlbaum.

*ELICKER, J., ENGLUND, M., & SROUFE, L. A. (1992). Predicting peer competence and peer relationships in childhood from early parent–child relationships. In R. D. Parke & G. W. Ladd (Eds.), *Family-peer relationships: Modes of linkage.* Hillsdale, NJ: Erlbaum.

ELKIND, D. (1980). Strategic interactions in early adolescence. In J. Adelson (Ed.),

Handbook of adolescent psychology. New York: Wiley.

ELKIND, D. (1988). *Miseducation.* New York: Knopf.

ELLIOTT, R., & VASTA, R. (1970). The modeling of sharing: Effects associated with vicarious reinforcement, symbolization, age, and generalization. *Journal of Experimental Child Psychology, 10,* 8–15.

ELLIS, P. L. (1982). Empathy: A factor in antisocial behavior. *Journal of Abnormal Child Psychology, 10,* 123–134.

ELLIS, S., ROGOFF, B., & CROMER, C. C. (1981). Age segregation in children's social interactions. *Developmental Psychology, 17,* 399–407.

*ELLSWORTH, C. P., MUIR, D. W., & HAINS, S. M. J. (1993). Social competence and person-object differentiation: An analysis of the still-face effect. *Developmental Psychology, 29,* 63–73.

*ELMER-DeWITT, P. (1994, January 17). The genetic revolution. *Time,* pp. 46–53.

*EMDE, R. N. (1992). Individual meaning and increasing complexity: Contributions of Sigmund Freud and Rene Spitz to developmental psychology. *American Psychologist, 28,* 347–359.

*EMDE, R. N. (1994). Individuality, context, and the search for meaning. *Child Development, 65,* 719–737.

EMDE, R. N., & HARMON, R. J. (Eds.). (1984). *Continuities and discontinuities in development.* New York: Plenum.

*EMDE, R. N., BIRINGEN, Z., CLYMAN, R. B., & OPPENHEIM, D. (1991). The moral sense of infancy: Affective core and procedural knowledge. *Developmental Review, 11,* 251–270.

EMDE, R. N., GAENSBAUER, T. J., & HARMON, R. J. (1976). Emotional expression in infancy: A biobehavioral study. *Psychological Issues Monograph Series, 10.* (No. 37). New York: International Universities Press.

*EMDE, R. N., PLOMIN, R., ROBINSON, J., CORLEY, R., DeFRIES, J., FULKER, D. W., REZNICK, J. S., CAMPOS, J., KAGAN, J., & ZAHN-WAXLER, C. (1992). Temperament, emotion, and cognition at fourteen months: The MacArthur Longitudinal Twin Study. *Child Development, 63,* 1437–1455.

EMDE, R. N., SWEDBERG, J., & SUZUKI, B. (1975). Human wakefulness and biological rhythms after birth. *Archives of General Psychiatry, 32,* 780–783.

EMERY, R. E. (1988). *Marriage, divorce, and children's adjustment.* Beverly Hills, CA: Sage.

EMMERICH, W., & SHEPARD, K. (1982). Development of sex-differentiated preferences during late childhood and adolescence. *Developmental Psychology, 18,* 406–417.

ENGELMANN, S., & ENGELMANN, T. (1981). *Give your child a superior mind.* New York: Simon & Schuster.

*ENGLUND, M. M., REED, T., & SROUFE, L. A. (March, 1993). *Continuity of social competence from infancy to adolescence.* Paper presented at the meeting of the Society for Research in Child Development, New Orleans.

ENNIS, R. H. (1976). An alternative to Piaget's conceptualization of logical competence. *Child Development, 47,* 903–919.

ENRIGHT, R. D., BJERSTEDT, A., ENRIGHT, W. F., LEVY, V. M., LAPSLEY, D. K., BUSS, R. R., HARWELL, M., & ZINDLER, M. (1984). Distributive justice development: Cross-cultural, contextual, and longitudinal evaluations. *Child Development, 55,* 1737–1751.

ENRIGHT, R. D., & SATTERFIELD, S. J. (1980). An ecological validation of social cognitive development. *Child Development, 51,* 156–161.

ENTWISTLE, D. R., ALEXANDER, K. L., PALLAS, A. M., & CADIGAN, D. (1987). The emergent academic self-image of first-graders: Its response to social structure. *Child Development, 58,* 1190–1206.

EPSTEIN, J. L. (1983). Selections of friends in differently organized schools and classrooms. In J. L. Epstein & M. Karweit (Eds.), *Friends in school.* New York: Academic Press.

EPSTEIN, J. L. (1986). Friendship selection: Developmental and environmental influences. In E. C. Mueller & C. R. Cooper (Eds.), *Process and outcome in peer relationships.* New York: Academic Press.

EPSTEIN, J. L. (1989). The selection of friends: Changes across the grades and in different school environments. In T. J. Berndt & G. W. Ladd (Eds.), *Peer relationships in child development.* New York: Wiley.

EPSTEIN, Y. M. (1981). Crowding stress and human behavior. *Journal of Social Issues, 37,* 126–144.

ERICKSON, J. D., & BJERKEDAL, T. (1982). Fetal and infant mortality in Norway and the United States. *Journal of the American Medical Association, 247,* 987–991.

ERICKSON, M. F., SROUFE, L. A., & EGELAND, B. (1985). The relationship between quality of attachment and behavior problems in pre-school in a high-risk sample. In I. Bretherton & E. Waters (Eds.), *Growing points of attachment theory and research. Monographs of the Society for Research in Child Development, 50* (1–2, Serial No. 209).

ERON, L. D. (1982). Parent–child interaction, television violence, and aggression of children. *American Psychologist, 37,* 197–211.

ERON, L. D. (1987). The development of aggressive behavior from the perspective of a developing behaviorism. *American Psychologist, 42,* 435–442.

ERON, L. D., & HUESMANN, L. R. (1984). Television violence and aggressive behavior. In B. B. Lahey & A. E. Kazdin (Eds.), *Advances in clinical child psychology* (Vol. 7). New York: Plenum.

ERON, L. D., & HUESMANN, L. R. (1986). The role of television in the development of prosocial and antisocial behavior. In D. Olweus, J. Block, & M. Radke-Yarrow (Eds.), *Development of antisocial and prosocial behavior.* Orlando, FL: Academic Press.

ERON, L. D., HUESMANN, L. R., BRICE, P., FISCHER, P., & MERMELSTEIN, R. (1983). Age trends in the development of aggression, sex typing, and related television habits. *Developmental Psychology, 19,* 71–77.

ERON, L. D., HUESMANN, L. R., DUBOW, E., ROMANOFF, R., & YARMEL, R. W. (1987). Aggression and its correlates over 22 years. In D. H. Crowell, I. M. Evans, & C. R. O'Donnell

(Eds.), *Childhood aggression and violence: Sources of influence, prevention, and control.* New York: Plenum.

ERVIN, S. M. (1964). Imitation and structural change in children's language. In E. H. Lenneberg (Ed.), *New directions in the study of language.* Cambridge, MA: MIT Press.

*ERWIN, P. (1993). *Friendship and peer relations in children.* Chichester, England: Wiley.

ETAUGH, C., COLLINS, G., & GERSON, A. (1975). Reinforcement of sex-typed behaviors of two-year-old children in a nursery school setting. *Developmental Psychology, 11,* 255.

ETZEL, B. C., & GEWIRTZ, J. L. (1967). Experimental modification of caretaker-maintained high rate operant crying in a 6- and a 20-week old infant *(Infans tyrannotearus):* Extinction of crying with reinforcement of eye contact and smiling. *Journal of Experimental Child Psychology, 5,* 303–317.

EUROPEAN COLLABORATIVE STUDY. (1991). Children born to women with HIV-1 infection: Natural history and risk of transmission. *Lancet, 337,* 253–260.

EVANS, W. F. (1973). *The stage IV error in Piaget's theory of object concept development: An investigation of the role of activity.* Unpublished doctoral dissertation, University of Houston.

EVELYTH, P. B. (1986). Population differences in growth. In F. Falkner & J. M. Tanner (Eds.), *Human growth: A comprehensive treatise.* New York: Plenum.

*EYER, D. E. (1992). *Mother–infant bonding: A scientific fiction.* New Haven: Yale University Press.

FABES, R. A., EISENBERG, N., & MILLER, P. A. (1990). Maternal correlates of children's vicarious emotional responsiveness. *Developmental Psychology, 26,* 639–648.

FABRICIUS, W. V., & CAVALIER, L. (1989). The role of causal theories about memory in young children's memory strategy choice. *Child Development, 60,* 298–308.

*FABRICIUS, W. V., HODGE, M. H., & QUINAN, J. R. (1993). Processes of scene recognition memory in young children and adults. *Cognitive Development, 8,* 343–360.

FABRICIUS, W. V., & STEFFE, L. (1989, April). *Considering all possible combinations: The early beginnings of a formal operational skill.* Paper presented at the meeting of the Society for Research in Child Development, Kansas City, MO.

FADIMAN, A. (1983, April). The unborn patient. *Life,* pp. 38–44.

FAGAN, J. F., III. (1973). Infants' delayed recognition memory and forgetting. *Journal of Experimental Child Psychology, 16,* 424–450.

FAGAN, J. F., III. (1976). Infants' recognition of invariant features of faces. *Child Development, 47,* 627–638.

*FAGAN, J. F., III. (1992). Intelligence: A theoretical viewpoint. *Current Directions in Psychological Science, 1,* 82–86.

*FAGAN, J. F., III, & DETTERMAN, D. H. (1992). The Fagan Test of Infant Intelligence: A technical summary. *Journal of Applied Developmental Psychology, 13,* 173–193.

FAGAN, J. F., III, & SHEPHERD, P. A. (1986). *The

Fagan Test of Infant Intelligence: Training manual. Cleveland: Infantest Corporation.

FAGAN, J. F., III, SHEPHERD, P. A., & KNEVEL, C. R. (1991, April). *Predictive validity of the Fagan Test of Infant Intelligence.* Paper presented at the meeting of the Society for Research in Child Development, Seattle.

FAGEN, J. W., MORRONGIELLO, B. A., ROVEE-COLLIER, C. K., & GEKOSKI, M. J. (1984). Expectancies and memory retrieval in three-month-old infants. *Child Development, 55,* 936–943.

FAGOT, B. I. (1977). Consequences of moderate cross-gender behavior in preschool children. *Child Development, 48,* 902–907.

FAGOT, B. I. (1982). Sex role development. In R. Vasta (Ed.), *Strategies and techniques of child study.* New York: Academic Press.

FAGOT, B. I. (1985). Stages in thinking about early sex role development. *Developmental Review, 5,* 83–98.

*FAGOT, B. I., & HAGAN, R. (1991). Observations of parent reactions to sex-stereotyped behaviors: Age and sex effects. *Child Development, 62,* 617–628.

FAGOT, B. I., HAGAN, R., LEINBACH, M. D., & KRONSBERG, S. (1985). Differential reactions to assertive and communicative acts of toddler boys and girls. *Child Development, 56,* 1499–1505.

FAGOT, B. I., & KAVANAGH, K. (1990). The prediction of antisocial behavior from avoidant attachment classifications. *Child Development, 61,* 864–873.

FAGOT, B. I., & LEINBACH, M. D. (1983). Play styles in early childhood: Social consequences for boys and girls. In M. B. Liss (Ed.), *Social and cognitive skills: Sex roles and children's play.* New York: Academic Press.

FAGOT, B. I., & LEINBACH, M. D. (1987). Socialization of sex roles within the family. In D. B. Carter (Ed.), *Current conceptions of sex roles and sex typing: Theory and research.* New York: Praeger.

FAGOT, B. I., & LEINBACH, M. D. (1989). The young child's gender schema: Environmental input, internal organization. *Child Development, 60,* 663–672.

*FAGOT, B. I., & LEINBACH, M. D. (1993). Gender-role development in young children: From discrimination to labeling. *Developmental Review, 13,* 205–224.

FAGOT, B. I., LEINBACH, M. D., & HAGAN, R. (1986). Gender labeling and the adoption of sex-typed behaviors. *Developmental Psychology, 22,* 440–443.

*FAGOT, B. I., LEINBACH, M. D., & O'BOYLE, C. (1992). Gender labeling, gender stereotyping, and parenting behaviors. *Developmental Psychology, 28,* 225–230.

FANTZ, R. L. (1961). The origin of form perception. *Scientific American, 204,* 66–72.

FANTZ, R. L. (1963). Pattern vision in newborn infants. *Science, 140,* 296–297.

FARBER, S. L. (1981). *Identical twins reared apart: A reanalysis.* New York: Basic Books.

FARRAR, M. J. (1990). Discourse and the acquisition of grammatical morphemes. *Journal of Child Language, 17,* 607–624.

*FARRAR, M. J. (1992). Negative evidence and grammatical morpheme acquisition. *Developmental Psychology, 28,* 90–98.

FARRAR, M. J., & GOODMAN, G. S. (1990). Developmental differences in the relation between scripts and episodic memory: Do they exist? In R. Fivush & J. Hudson (Eds.), *Knowing and remembering in young children.* New York: Cambridge University Press.

*FARRAR, M. J., & GOODMAN, G. S. (1992). Developmental changes in event memory. *Child Development, 63,* 173–187.

FARROW, J. A., REES, J. M., & WORTHINGTON-ROBERTS, B. S. (1987). Health developmental and nutritional states of adolescent alcohol and marijuana abusers. *Pediatrics, 79,* 218–223.

*FARVER, J. M. (1993). Cultural influences in scaffolding play: A comparison of American and Mexican mother–child and sibling–child pairs. In K. MacDonald (Ed.), *Parents and children playing.* Albany: SUNY Press.

*FARVER, J. M., & BRANSTETTER, W. H. (1994). Preschoolers' prosocial responses to their peers' distress. *Developmental Psychology, 30,* 334–341.

*FARVER, J. M., & HOWES, C. (1993). Cultural differences in American and Mexican mother–child pretend play. *Merrill-Palmer Quarterly, 39.* 334–358

FEIN, G. G., SCHWARTZ, P. M., JACOBSON, S. W., & JACOBSON, J. L. (1983). Environmental toxin and behavioral development: A new role for psychological research. *American Psychologist, 38,* 1198–1205.

*FEINGOLD, A. (1992). Sex differences in variability in intellectual abilities: A new look at an old controversy. *Review of Educational Research, 62,* 61–84.

*FEINGOLD, A. (1993). Cognitive gender differences: A developmental perspective. *Sex Roles, 29,* 91–112.

*FEINMAN, S. (1981). Why is cross-sex role behavior more approved for girls than for boys? *Sex Roles, 7,* 289–300.

*FEINMAN, S. (1992). (Ed.). *Social referencing and the social construction of reality in infancy.* New York: Plenum.

*FEINMAN, S., ROBERTS, D., HSIEH, K., SAWYER, D., & SWANSON, D. (1992). A critical review of social referencing in infancy. In S. Feinman (Ed.), *Social referencing and the social construction of reality in infancy.* New York: Plenum.

FEIRING, C., & LEWIS, M. (1987). The child's social network: Sex differences from three to six years. *Sex Roles, 17,* 621–636.

FELDLAUFER, H., MIDGLEY, C., & ECCLES, J. S. (1988). Student, teacher, and observer perceptions of the classroom environment before and after the transition to junior high school. *Journal of Early Adolescence, 8,* 133–156.

FELDMAN, J. F., BRODY, N., & MILLER, S. A. (1980). Sex differences in non-elicited neonatal behaviors. *Merrill-Palmer Quarterly, 26,* 63–73.

*FENNEMA, E., & TARTRE, L. A. (1985). The use of spatial visualization in mathematics by girls and boys. *Journal for Research in Mathematics Education, 16,* 184–206.

FENWICK, K., HILLIER, L., & MORRONGIELLO, B. (1991, April). *Newborn's head orientation toward sounds within hemifields.* Poster presented at the meeting of the Society for Research in Child Development, Seattle.

FERGUSON, C. A. (1983). Reduplication in child phonology. *Journal of Child Language, 10,* 239–243.

FERGUSON, C. A., & MACKEN, M. A. (1983). The role of play in phonological development. In K. E. Nelson (Ed.), *Children's language* (Vol. 4). Hillsdale, NJ: Erlbaum

FERGUSON, L. R. (1970). Dependency motivation in socialization. In R. A. Hoppe, G. A. Milton, & E. C. Simmel (Eds.), *Early experience and the process of socialization.* New York: Academic Press.

FERGUSON, T. J., & RULE, B. G. (1988). Children's evaluations of retaliatory aggression. *Child Development, 59,* 961–968.

FERNALD, A. (1991). Prosodic speech to children: Prelinguistic and linguistic functions. In R. Vasta (Ed.), *Annals of child development* (Vol. 8). London: Kingsley.

*FERNALD, A. (1993). Approval and disapproval: Infant responsiveness to vocal affect in familiar and unfamiliar languages. *Child Development, 64,* 657–674.

*FERNALD, A., & MORIKAWA, H. (1993). Common themes and cultural variations in Japanese and American mothers' speech to infants. *Child Development, 64,* 637–656.

FERRIERA, A. J. (1969). *Prenatal environment.* Springfield, IL: Charles C Thomas.

FESHBACH, N. D., & FESHBACH, S. (1982). Empathy training and the regulation of aggression: Potentialities and limitations. *Academic Psychology Bulletin, 4,* 399–413.

FESHBACH, S., & SINGER, R. D. (1971). *Television and aggression: An experimental field study.* San Francisco: Jossey-Bass.

FESTINGER, L. (1954). A theory of social comparison processes. *Human Relations, 1,* 117–140.

FIELD, D. (1987). A review of preschool conservation training: An analysis of analyses. *Developmental Review, 7,* 210–251.

FIELD, J. (1987). The development of auditory-visual localization in infancy. In B. E. McKenzie & R. H. Day (Eds.), *Perceptual development in early infancy: Problems and issues.* Hillsdale, NJ: Erlbaum.

FIELD, T. M. (1987). Affective and interactive disturbances in infants. In J. D. Osofsky (Ed.), *Handbook of infant development* (2nd ed.). New York: Wiley.

*FIELD, T. M., COHEN, D., GARCIA, R., & GREENBERG, R. (1985). Mother–stranger face discrimination by the newborn. *Infant Behavior and Development, 7,* 19–25.

FIELD, T. M., HEALY, B., GOLDSTEIN, S., & GUTHERTZ, M. (1990). Behavior-state matching and synchrony in mother–infant interactions of nondepressed versus depressed dyads. *Developmental Psychology, 26,* 7–14.

FIELD, T. M., & ROOPNARINE, J. L. (1982). Infant–peer interactions. In T. M. Field, A. Huston, H. C. Quay, L. Troll, & G. E. Finley (Eds.), *Review of human development.* New York: Wiley.

*FIELD, T., SANDBERG, D., GARCIA, R., VEGA-LAHR, N., GOLDSTEIN, S., & GUY, L. (1985).

Pregnancy problems, postpartum depression, and early mother–infant interactions. *Developmental Psychology, 21,* 1152–1156.

FIELD, T. M., & WALDEN, T. A. (1982). Production and perception of facial expressions in infancy and early childhood. In H. W. Reese & L.P. Lipsitt (Eds.), *Advances in child development and behavior* (Vol. 16). New York: Academic Press.

FINCHAM, F. D., HOKODA, A., & SANDERS, R. (1989). Learned helplessness, test anxiety, and academic achievement: A longitudinal analysis. *Child Development, 60,* 138–145.

*FINE, G. A. (1987). *With the boys: Little league baseball and preadolescent culture.* Chicago: University of Chicago Press.

*FINEGAN, J. K., NICCOLS, G. A., & SITARENIOS, G. (1992). Relations between prenatal testosterone levels and cognitive abilities at 4 years. *Developmental Psychology, 28,* 1075–1089.

*FINLAY, D., & IVINSKIS, A. (1987). Cardiac change responses and attentional mechanisms in infants. In B. E. McKenzie & R. H. Day (Eds.), *Perceptual development in early infancy: Problems and issues.* Hillsdale, NJ: Erlbaum.

FINNEGAN, L. P., & FEHR, K. O. (1980). The effects of opiates, sedative-hypnotics, amphetamines, cannabis, and other psychoactive drugs on the fetus and newborn. In O. J. Kalant (Ed.), *Research advances in alcohol and drug problems: Vol. 5. Alcohol and drug problems in women.* New York: Plenum.

FIREMAN, G., & BEILIN, H. (1990, May). *Preformationism and Piaget's stage concept.* Paper presented at the meeting of the Jean Piaget Society, Philadelphia.

FIRSCH, R. E. (1984). Fatness, puberty, and fertility. In J. Brooks-Gunn & A. C. Petersen (Eds.), *Girls at puberty: Biological, psychological, and social perspectives.* New York: Plenum.

FISCHER, K. W. (1980). A theory of cognitive development: The control and construction of hierarchies of skills. *Psychological Review, 87,* 477–531.

*FISCHER, K. W., & BIDELL, T. (1991). Constraining nativist inferences about cognitive capacities. In S. Carey & R. Gelman (Eds.), *The epigenesis of mind.* Hillsdale, NJ: Erlbaum.

FISCHER, M., & LEITENBERG, H. (1986). Optimism and pessimism in elementary school-aged children. *Child Development, 57,* 241–248.

*FISH, M., STIFTER, C. A., & BELSKY, J. (1991). Conditions of continuity and discontinuity in infant negative emotionality: Newborn to five months. *Child Development, 62,* 1525–1537.

FISHBEIN, H. D. (1984). *The psychology of infancy and childhood: Evolutionary and cross-cultural perspectives.* Hillsdale, NJ: Erlbaum.

*FISHBEIN, H. D., & IMAI, S. (1993). Preschoolers select playmates on the basis of gender and race. *Journal of Applied Developmental Psychology, 14,* 303–316.

FISHER, C. B., & TRYON, W. W. (1988). Ethical issues in the research and practice of applied developmental psychology. *Journal of Applied Developmental Psychology, 9,* 27–39.

FISHER, C. B., & TRYON, W. W. (1990). *Ethics in applied developmental psychology: Emerging issues in an emerging field.* Norwood, NJ: Ablex.

*FISHER, E. P. (1992). The impact of play on development: A meta-analysis. *Play & Culture, 5,* 159–181.

*FISHER-THOMPSON, D. (1990). Adult gender typing of children's toys. *Sex Roles, 23,* 291–303.

*FIVUSH, R. (1991). The social construction of personal narratives. *Merrill-Palmer Quarterly, 37,* 59–82.

*FIVUSH, R. (1993). Emotional content of parent–child conversations about the past. In C. A. Nelson (Ed.), *Minnesota symposia on child psychology: Vol. 26. Memory and affect in development.* Hillsdale, NJ: Erlbaum.

*FIVUSH, R., KUEBLI, J., & CLUBB, P. A. (1992). The structure of events and event representations: A developmental analysis. *Child Development, 63,* 188–201.

*FIVUSH, R., & REESE, E. (1992). The social construction of autobiographical memory. In M. A. Conway, S. Rubin, H. Spinnler, & W. Wagenaar (Eds.), *Theoretical perspectives on autobiographical memory.* Norwell, MA: Kluwer Academic.

FLAVELL, J. H. (1963). *The developmental psychology of Jean Piaget.* Princeton, NJ: Van Nostrand.

*FLAVELL, J. H. (1970). Developmental studies of mediated memory. In H. W. Reese & L. P. Lipsitt (Eds.), *Advances in child development and behavior* (Vol. 5). New York: Academic Press.

FLAVELL, J. H. (1971). First discussant's comments: What is memory development the development of? *Human Development, 14,* 272–278.

FLAVELL, J. H. (1982a). On cognitive development. *Child Development, 53,* 1–10.

FLAVELL, J. H. (1982b). Structures, stages, and sequences in cognitive development. In W. A. Collins (Ed.), *Minnesota symposia on child psychology Vol. 15. The concept of development.* Hillsdale, NJ: Erlbaum.

FLAVELL, J. H. (1984). Discussion. In R. J. Sternberg (Ed.), *Mechanisms of cognitive development.* New York: W. H. Freeman.

FLAVELL, J. H. (1985). *Cognitive development* (2nd ed.). Englewood Cliffs, NJ: Prentical Hall.

FLAVELL, J. H. (1986). The development of children's knowledge about the appearance–reality distinction. *American Psychologist, 41,* 418–425.

*FLAVELL, J. H. (1992a). Cognitive development: Past, present, and future. *Developmental Psychology, 28,* 998–1005.

*FLAVELL, J. H. (1992b). Perspectives on perspective taking. In H. Beilin & P. B. Pufall (Eds.), *Piaget's theory: Prospects and possibilities.* Hillsdale, NJ: Erlbaum.

FLAVELL, J. H., BEACH, D. H., & CHINSKY, J. M. (1966). Spontaneous verbal rehearsal in a memory task as a function of age. *Child Development, 37,* 283–299.

FLAVELL, J. H., FLAVELL, E. R., & GREEN, F. L. (1983). Development of the appearance–reality distinction. *Cognitive Psychology, 15,* 95–120.

FLAVELL, J. H., FRIEDRICHS, A., & HOYT, J. (1970). Developmental changes in memorization processes. *Cognitive Psychology, 1,* 324–340.

FLAVELL, J. H., GREEN, F. L., & FLAVELL, E. R. (1989). Young children's ability to differentiate appearance–reality and Level 2 perspectives in the tactile modality. *Child Development, 60,* 201–213.

*FLAVELL, J. H., LINDBERG, N. A., GREEN, F. L., & FLAVELL, E. R. (1992). The development of children's understanding of the appearance–reality distinction between how people look and what they are really like. *Merrill-Palmer Quarterly, 38,* 513–524.

*FLAVELL, J. H., MILLER, P. H., & MILLER, S. A. (1993). *Cognitive development* (3rd ed.). Englewood Cliffs, NJ: Prentice Hall.

FLAVELL, J. H., SHIPSTEAD, S. G., & CROFT, K. (1980). What young children think you see when their eyes are closed. *Cognition, 8,* 369–387.

*FLAVELL, J. H., ZHANG, H.-D., ZOU, H., DONG, Q., & QI, S. (1983). A comparison between the development of the appearance–reality distinction in the People's Republic of China and the United States. *Cognitive Psychology, 15,* 459–466.

FLETCHER, J. C. (1983). Ethics and trends in applied human genetics. *Birth defects: Original article series, 11,* 143–158.

FLERX, W. C., FIDLER, D. S., & ROGERS, R. W. (1976). Sex role stereotypes: Developmental aspects and early intervention. *Child Development, 47,* 998–1007.

FLODERUS-MYRHED, B., PEDERSON, N., & RASMUSON, I. (1980). Assessment of heritability for personality based on a short-form of the Eyesenck Personality Inventory: A study of 12,898 twin pairs. *Behavior Genetics, 10,* 158–162.

FODOR, J. (1980). Fixation of belief and concept acquisition. In M. Piattell-Palmarini (Ed.), *Language and learning: The debate between Jean Piaget and Noam Chomsky.* Cambridge, MA: Harvard University Press.

FOGEL, A., & THELEN, E. (1987). Development of early expressive and communicative action: Reinterpreting the evidence from a dynamic systems perspective. *Developmental Psychology, 23,* 747–761.

FOGELMAN, K. (1980). Smoking in pregnancy and subsequent development of the child. *Child Care, Health and Development, 6,* 233–249.

*FOGLE, S. (1992). Pretty BABI: Blastomere screen detects CF gene. *Journal of NIH Research, 4,* 46.

*FONAGY, P., STEELE, H., & STEELE, M. (1991). Maternal representations of attachment during pregnancy predict the organization of infant–mother attachment at one year of age. *Child Development, 62,* 891–905.

*FORMAN, E. A. (1992). Discourse, intersubjectivity, and the development of peer collaboration: A Vygotskian approach. In L. T. Winegar & J. Valsiner (Eds.), *Children's development within social context: Vol. 1. Metatheory and theory.* Hillsdale, NJ: Erlbaum.

*FORRESTER, M. A. (1992). *The development of young children's social-cognitive skills.* Hillsdale, NJ: Erlbaum.

FORSLUND, M., & BJERRE, I. (1983). Neurological assessment of preterm infants at term conceptional age in comparison with normal full-term infants. *Early Human Development, 8,* 195–208.

*FOUTS, R. S. (1973). Acquisition and testing of gestural signs in four young chimpanzees. *Science, 180,* 978–980.

FOX, N. A. (1989). Psychophysiological correlates of emotional reactivity during the first year of life. *Developmental Psychology, 25,* 364–372.

FOX, N. A., KAGAN, J., & WEISKOPF, S. (1979). The growth of memory during infancy. *Genetic Psychology Monographs, 99,* 91–130.

FOX, N. A., KIMMERLY, N. L., & SCHAFER, W. D. (1991). Attachment to mother/attachment to father: A meta-analysis. *Child Development, 62,* 210–225.

FOX, R., ASLIN, R. N., SHEA, S. L., & DUMAIS, S. T. (1980). Stereopsis in human infants. *Science, 207,* 323–324.

FRANCIS, P. L., SELF, P. A., & HOROWITZ, F. D. (1987). The behavioral assessment of the neonate: An overview. In J. D. Osofsky (Ed.), *Handbook of infant development* (2nd ed.). New York: Wiley.

FRANKEL, K. A., & BATES, J. E. (1990). Mother–toddler problem solving: Antecedents of attachment, home behavior, and temperament. *Child Development, 61,* 810–819.

FRAUENGLASS, M. H., & DIAZ, R. M. (1985). Self-regulatory functions of children's speech: A critical analysis of recent challenges to Vygotsky's theory. *Developmental Psychology, 21,* 357–364.

*FREDA, M. C., ANDERSON, F. H., DAMUS, K., PROUST, D., BRUSTMAN, L., & MERKATZ, I. R. (1990). Lifestyle for inner city women at high risk for preterm birth. *Journal of Advanced Nursing, 15,* 364–372.

FREEBURG, T. J., & LIPPMAN, M. Z. (1986). Factors influencing discrimination of infant cries. *Journal of Child Language, 13,* 3–13.

*FREEDLAND, R. L. (1993). *Interlimb patterning during the onset of creeping in human infants.* Paper presented at the meeting of the Society for Research in Child Development. New Orleans.

*FREEDMAN, D. G., & FREEDMAN, M. (1969). Behavioral differences between Chinese-American and American newborns. *Nature, 224,* 1227.

FREEDMAN, J. L. (1984). Effect of television violence on aggressiveness. *Psychological Bulletin, 96,* 227–246.

FREMGEN, A., & FAY, D. (1980). Overextensions in production and comprehension: A methodological clarification. *Journal of Child Language, 7,* 205–211.

FRENCH, D. C. (1988). Heterogeneity of peer-rejected boys: Aggressive and nonaggressive subtypes. *Child Development, 59,* 976–985.

*FRENCH, D. C. (1990). Heterogeneity of peer rejected girls. *Child Development, 61,* 2028–2031.

FREUND, L. S. (1990). Maternal regulation of children's problem-solving behavior and its impact on children's performance. *Child Development, 61,* 113–126.

FREY, K. S., & RUBLE, D. N. (1987). What children say about classroom performance: Sex and grade differences in perceived competence. *Child Development, 58,* 1066–1078.

*FREY, K. S., & RUBLE, D. N. (1992). Gender constancy and the "cost" of sex-typed behavior: A test of the conflict hypothesis. *Developmental Psychology, 28,* 714–721.

*FRIED, P. A., O'CONNELL, C. M., & WATKINSON, M. A. (1992). 60- and 72-month follow-up of children prenatally exposed to marijuana, cigarettes, and alcohol: Cognitive and language assessment. *Developmental and Behavioral Pediatrics, 13,* 383–391.

*FRIED, P. A., WATKINSON, B., & GRAY, R. (1992). A follow-up study of attentional behavior in 6-year-old children exposed prenatally to marijuana, cigarettes, and alcohol. *Neurotoxicology and Teratology, 14,* 299–311.

FRIEDMAN, J. M. (1981). Genetic disease in the offspring of older fathers. *Obstetrics and Gynecology, 57,* 745–749.

FRIEDRICH, L. K., & STEIN, A. H. (1973). Aggressive and prosocial television programs and the natural behavior of preschool children. *Monographs of the Society for Research in Child Development, 38* (4, Serial No. 151).

FRIEDRICH, L. K., & STEIN, A. H. (1975). Prosocial television and young children: The effects of verbal labeling and role playing on learning and behavior. *Child Development, 46,* 27–38.

FRIEDRICH-COFER, L. K., & HUSTON, A. C. (1986). Television violence and aggression: The debate continues. *Psychological Bulletin, 100,* 364–371.

FRIEDRICH-COFER, L. K., HUSTON-STEIN, A., KIPNIS, D. M., SUSMAN, E. J., & CLEWETT, A. S. (1979). Environmental enhancement of prosocial television content: Effects on interpersonal behavior, imaginative play, and self-regulation in a natural setting. *Developmental Psychology, 15,* 637–646.

FRISCH, H. L. (1977). Sex stereotypes in adult–infant play. *Child Development, 48,* 1671–1675.

*FRITH, U. (1989). *Autism: Explaining the enigma.* Oxford: Basil Blackwell.

FRODI, A. M., LAMB, M. E., LEAVITT, L. A., & DONOVAN, W. L. (1978). Fathers' and mothers' responses to infant smiles and cries. *Infant Behavior and Development, 1,* 187–198.

FRODI, A. M., SENCHAK, M., GARFIELD, A., & SCOVILLE, J. (1988). Verbal and behavioral responsiveness to the cries of atypical infants. *Infant Behavior and Development, 11,* 100.

FROMING, W. J., ALLEN, L., & JENSEN, R. (1985). Altruism, role-taking, and self-awareness: The acquisition of norms governing altruistic behavior. *Child Development, 56,* 1223–1228.

FROMING, W. J., ALLEN, L., & UNDERWOOD, B. (1983). Age and generosity reconsidered: Cross-sectional and longitudinal evidence. *Child Development, 54,* 585–593.

FRY, D. P. (1988). Intercommunity differences in aggression among Zapotec children. *Child Development, 59,* 1008–1019.

FUKAHARA, H., SHIMURA, Y., & YAMANOUCHI, I. (1988, November). *The transmission of ambient noise and self-produced sound into the human body.* Poster presented at the second joint meeting of the Acoustical Society of America and the Acoustical Society of Japan, Honolulu.

*FULKER, D. W., & CARDON, L. R. (1993). What can twin studies tell us about the structure and correlates of cognitive abilities? In T. J. Bouchard, Jr. & P. Propping (Eds.), *Twins as a tool of behavioral genetics.* New York: Wiley.

FULLARD, W., McDEVITT, S. C., & CAREY, W. B. (1984). Assessing temperament in one to three year old children. *Journal of Pediatric Psychology, 9,* 205–217.

FULLARD, W., & REILING, A. M. (1976). An investigation of Lorenz's "babyness." *Child Development, 47,* 1191–1193.

*FULLER, B. (1987). Defining school quality. In J. Hannway & M. Lockhead (Eds.), *The contribution of social sciences to educational policy and practice: 1965–1985.* Berkeley, CA: McCuthan.

FURMAN, L. N., & WALDEN, T. A. (1990). Effect of script knowledge on preschool children's communicative interactions. *Developmental Psychology, 26,* 227–233.

FURMAN, W. (1987). Acquaintanceship in middle childhood. *Developmental Psychology, 23,* 563–570.

*FURMAN, W., & BUHRMESTER, D. (1992). Age and sex differences in perceptions of networks of personal relationships. *Child Development, 63,* 103–115.

FURMAN, W., & GAVIN, L. A. (1989). Peers' influence on adjustment and development. In T. J. Berndt & G. W Ladd (Eds.), *Peer relationships in child development.* New York: Wiley.

FURMAN, W., & MASTERS, J. C. (1980). Affective consequences of social reinforcement, punishment, and neutral behavior. *Developmental Psychology, 16,* 100–104.

*FURNESS, W. (1916). Observations on the mentality of chimpanzees and orangutans. *Proceedings of the American Philosophical Society, 45,* 281–290.

*FURROW, D., BAILLIE, C., McLAREN, J., & MOORE, C. (1993). Differential responding to two- and three-year-olds' utterances: The roles of grammaticality ambiguity. *Journal of Child Language, 20,* 363–375.

FURROW, D., & NELSON, K. (1986). A further look at the motherese hypothesis: A reply to Gleitman, Newport, and Gleitman. *Journal of Child Language, 13,* 163–176.

FURROW, D., NELSON, K., & BENEDICT, H. (1979). Mothers' speech to children and syntactic development: Some simple relationships. *Journal of Child Language, 6,* 423–442.

*GABLE, S., & ISABELLA, R. A. (1992). Maternal contributions to infant regulation of arousal. *Infant Behavior and Development, 15,* 95–107.

*GADOW, K. D., & SPRAFKIN, J. (1993). Television "violence" and children with emotional and behavioral disorders. *Journal of Emotional and Behavioral Disorders, 1,* 54–63.

GALAMBOS, N. L., ALMEIDA, D. M., & PETERSEN, A. C. (1990). Masculinity, femininity, and sex role attitudes in early adolescence: Exploring gender intensification. *Child Development, 61,* 1905–1914.

GALBRAITH, R. C. (1982). Sibling spacing and intellectual development: A closer look at the confluence model. *Developmental Psychology, 18,* 151–173.

GALBRAITH, R. C. (1984). Individual differences in intelligence: A reappraisal of the confluence model. *Intelligence, 17,* 185–194.

GALLAHUE, D. L. (1989). *Understanding motor development* (2nd ed.). Carmel, IN: Benchmark Press.

GALLUP, G. G. (1977). Self-recognition in primates: A comparative approach to the bidirectional properties of consciousness. *American Psychologist, 32,* 329–338.

GAMBLE, T. J., & ZIGLER, E. F. (1986). Effects of infant day care: Another look at the evidence. *American Journal of Orthopsychiatry, 56,* 26–42.

GARAI, J. E., & SCHEINFELD, A. (1968). Sex differences in mental and behavioral traits. *Genetic Psychology Monographs, 77,* 169–299.

*GARBARINO, J., & ABRAMOWITZ, R. H. (1992a). The ecology of human development. In J. Garbarino (Ed.), *Children and families in the social environment* (2nd ed.). New York: Aldine de Gruyter.

*GARBARINO, J., & ABRAMOWITZ, R. H. (1992b). The family as a social system. In J. Garbarino (Ed.), *Children and families in the social environment* (2nd ed.). New York: Aldine de Gruyter.

*GARBARINO, J., GABOURY, M. T., & PLANTZ, M. C. (1992). Social policy, children, and their families. In J. Garbarino (Ed.), *Children and families in the social environment* (2nd ed.). New York: Aldine de Gruyter.

GARCIA, E. E., & DeHAVEN, E. D. (1974). The use of operant techniques in the establishment and generalization of language: A review and analysis. *American Journal of Mental Deficiency, 79,* 169–172.

GARCIA-COLL, C. T., EMMONS, L., VOHR, B. R., WARD, A. M., BRANN, B. S., SHAUL, P. W., MAYFIELD, S. R., & OH, W. (1988). Behavioral responsiveness in preterm infants with intraventricular hemorrhage. *Pediatrics, 81,* 412–418.

GARDEN, R. A. (1987). The second IEA mathematics study. *Comparative Education Review, 31,* 47–68.

*GARDNER, B. T., & GARDNER, R. A. (1971). Two-way communication with an infant chimpanzee. In A. M. Schrier & F. Stollnitz (Eds.), *Behavior of nonhuman primates* (Vol. 4). New York: Academic Press.

GARDNER, H. (1983). *Frames of mind: The theory of multiple intelligences.* New York: Basic Books.

*GARDNER, H. (1993). *Multiple intelligences.* New York: Basic Books.

*GARDNER, J. M., KARMEL, B. Z., & MAGNANO, C. L. (1992). Arousal/visual preference interactions in high-risk neonates. *Developmental Psychology, 28,* 821–830.

GARDNER, L., & NEU, R. (1972). Evidence linking an extra Y chromosome to sociopathic behavior. *Archives of General Psychiatry, 26,* 220–222.

GARFIELD, J. L. (1987). Introduction: Carving the mind at its joints. In J. L. Garfield (Ed.), *Modularity in knowledge representation and natural-language understanding.* Cambridge, MA: MIT Press.

*GARNER, R. (1990). Children's use of strategies in reading. In D. F. Bjorklund (Ed.), *Children's strategies: Contemporary views of cognitive development.* Hillsdale, NJ: Erlbaum.

*GARNER, R. (1993). Skilled and less skilled readers' ability to distinguish important and unimportant information in expository text. In S. R. Yussen & M. C. Smith (Eds.), *Reading across the life span.* New York: Springer-Verlag.

GARRISON, W. T., & EARLS, F. J. (1987). *Temperament and child psychopathology.* Newbury Park, CA: Sage.

GARROD, A., BEAL, C., & SHIN, P. (1990). The development of moral orientation in elementary school children. *Sex Roles, 22,* 13–26.

*GARTON, A. F. (1992). *Social interaction and the development of language and cognition.* Hove and London: Erlbaum.

GARVEY, C. (1986). Peer relations and the growth of communication. In E. C. Mueller & C. R. Cooper (Eds.), *Process and outcome in peer relationships.* New York: Academic Press.

*GAULTNEY, J. F., BJORKLUND, D. F., & SCHNEIDER, W. (1992). The role of children's expertise in a strategic memory task. *Contemporary Educational Psychology, 17,* 244–257.

GEBER, M., & DEAN, R. F. A. (1957). Gesell tests on African children. *Pediatrics, 202,* 1055–1065.

GEEN, R. G. (1983). Aggression and television violence. In R. G. Geen & E. I. Donnerstein (Eds.), *Aggression: Theoretical and empirical reviews* (Vol. 2). New York: Academic Press.

GELFAND, D. M., & HARTMANN, D. P. (1982). Response consequences and attributions: Two contributors to prosocial behavior. In N. Eisenberg (Ed.), *The development of prosocial behavior.* New York: Academic Press.

GELMAN, R. (1972). Logical capacity of very young children: Number invariance rules. *Child Development, 43,* 75–90.

GELMAN, R. (1982). Basic numerical abilities. In R. J. Sternberg (Ed.), *Advances in the psychology of human intelligence* (Vol. 1). Hillsdale, NJ: Erlbaum.

*GELMAN, R. (1991). Epigenetic foundations of knowledge structures: Initial and transcendent constructions. In S. Carey & R. Gelman (Eds.), *The epigenesis of mind.* Hillsdale, NJ: Erlbaum.

GELMAN, R., & BAILLARGEON, R. (1983). A review of some Piagetian concepts. In J. H. Flavell & E. M. Markman (Eds.), *Handbook of child psychology: Vol. 3. Cognitive development.* New York: Wiley.

GELMAN, R., & GALLISTEL, C. R. (1978). *The child's understanding of number.* Cambridge, MA: Harvard University Press.

GELMAN, S. A., & MARKMAN, E. M. (1986). Categories and induction in young children. *Cognition, 23,* 183–209.

GELMAN, S. A., & MARKMAN, E. M. (1987). Young children's inductions from natural kinds: The role of categories and appearances. *Child Development, 58,* 1532–1541.

*GELMAN, S. A., & WELLMAN, H. M. (1991). Insides and essences: Early understanding of the non-obvious. *Cognition, 38,* 213–244.

GELMAN, S. A., WILCOX, S. A., & CLARK, E. V. (1989). Conceptual and lexical hierarchies in young children. *Cognitive Development, 4,* 309–326.

GENESEE, F. (1989). Early bilingual development: One language or two? *Journal of Child Language, 16,* 161–179.

*GENTILE, D. A. (1993). Just what are sex and gender anyway? *Psychological Science, 4,* 120–124.

GENTNER, D. (1982). Why nouns are learned before verbs: Linguistic relativity versus natural partitioning. In S. A. Kuczaj (Ed.), *Language development* (Vol. 2). Hillsdale, NJ: Erlbaum.

*GEORGE, C., KAPLAN, N., & MAIN, M. (1985). *The Adult Attachment Interview.* Unpublished manuscript, University of California, Department of Psychology, Berkeley.

*GEORGE, C., & SOLOMON, J. (1989). Internal working models of parenting and security of attachment at age six. *Infant Mental Health Journal, 10,* 222–237.

GEPPERT, U., & KUSTER, U. (1983). The emergence of "wanting to do it onself": A precursor of achievement motivation. *International Journal of Behavioral Development, 6,* 355–369.

GERBER, M., & KAUFFMAN, J. M. (1981). Peer tutoring in academic settings. In P. S. Strain (Ed.), *The utilization of classroom peers as behavior change agents.* New York: Plenum.

GESELL, A. (1954). The ontogeneses of infant behavior. In L. Carmichael (Ed.), *Manual of child psychology* (2nd ed.). New York: Wiley.

GESELL, A., & ILG, F. L. (1943). *Infant and child in the culture of today.* New York: Harper.

GESELL, A., & THOMPSON, H. (1929). Learning and growth in identical infant twins: An experimental study by the method of co-twin control. *Genetic Psychological Monographs, 6,* 1–24.

GESELL, A., & THOMPSON, H. (1938). *The psychology of early growth.* New York: Macmillan.

*GEWIRTZ, J. L. (1991). Social influence on child and parent via stimulation and operant learning mechanisms. In M. Lewis & S. Feinman (Eds.), *Social influences and socialization in infancy.* New York: Plenum.

GEWIRTZ, J. L., & BOYD, E. F. (1976). Mother–infant interaction and its study. In H. W. Reese (Ed.), *Advances in child development and behavior* (Vol. 11). New York: Academic Press.

GEWIRTZ, J. L., & BOYD, E. F. (1977). Experiments on mother–infant interaction underlying mutual attachment acquisition: The infant conditions the mother. In T. Alloway, P. Pliner, & L. Kramer (Eds.), *Advances in the study of communication and affect: Vol. 3. Attachment behavior.* New York: Plenum.

*GEWIRTZ, J. L., & PELAEZ-NOGUERAS, M. (1991a). The attachment metaphor and the conditioning of infant separation protests. In J. L. Gewirtz & W. M. Kurtines (Eds.), *Intersections with attachment.* Hillsdale, NJ: Erlbaum.

*GEWIRTZ, J. L., & PELAEZ-NOGUERAS, M. (1991b). Proximal mechanisms underlying the acquisition of moral behavior patterns. In W. M. Kurtines & J. L. Gewirtz (Eds.), *Handbook of moral behavior and development: Vol. 1. Theory.* Hillsdale, NJ: Erlbaum.

*GEWIRTZ, J. L., & PELAEZ-NOGUERAS, M. (1992a). B. F. Skinner's legacy to human infant behavior and development. *American Psychologist, 47,* 1411–1422.

*GEWIRTZ, J. L., & PELAEZ-NOGUERAS, M. (1992b). Social referencing as a learned process. In S. Feinman (Ed.), *Social referencing and the social construction of reality in infancy.* New York: Plenum.

GHATALA, E. S., LEVIN, J. R., PRESSLEY, M., & LODICO, M. G. (1985). Training cognitive strategy monitoring in children. *American Educational Research Journal, 22,* 199–216.

GIANINO, A., & TRONICK, E. Z. (1988). The mutual regulation model: The infant's self and interactive regulation coping and defense. In T. Field, P. McCabe, & N. Schneiderman (Eds.), *Stress and coping.* Hillsdale, NJ: Erlbaum.

GIBBS, J. C. (1987). Social processes in delinquency: The need to facilitate empathy as well as sociomoral reasoning. In W. M. Kurtines & J. L. Gewirtz (Eds.), *Moral development through social interaction.* New York: Wiley.

*GIBBS, J. C. (1991). Sociomoral developmental delay and cognitive distortion: Implications for the treatment of antisocial youth. In W. M. Kurtines & J. L. Gewirtz (Eds.), *Handbook of moral behavior and development: Vol. 3. Application.* Hillsdale, NJ: Erlbaum.

GIBBS, J. C., & SCHNELL, S. V. (1985). Moral judgment "versus" socialization: A critique. *American Psychologist, 40,* 1071–1080.

*GIBBS, J. T. (Ed.). (1988). *Young, black, and male in America: An endangered species.* Dover, MA: Auburn House.

GIBBS, M. V., REEVES, D., & CUNNINGHAM, C. C. (1987). The application of temperament questionnaires to a British sample: Issues of reliability and validity. *Journal of Child Psychology and Psychiatry, 28,* 61–77.

GIBSON, E. J. (1988). Exploratory behavior in the development of perceiving, acting, and the acquiring of knowledge. *Annual Review of Psychology, 39,* 1–41.

GIBSON, E. J., OWSLEY, C. J., & JOHNSTON, J. (1978). Perception of invariants by five-month-old infants: Differentiation of two types of motion. *Developmental Psychology, 14,* 407–415.

GIBSON, E. J., & WALK, R. D. (1960). The "visual cliff." *Scientific American, 202,* 64–71.

GIBSON, E. J., & WALKER, A. (1984). Development of knowledge of visual-tactual affordances of substance. *Child Development, 55,* 453–460.

GIBSON, J. J. (1966). *The senses considered as perceptual systems.* Boston: Houghton Mifflin.

GILLIGAN, C. (1982). *In a different voice: Psychological theory and women's development.* Cambridge, MA: Harvard University Press.

GILLIGAN, C., & ATTANUCCI, J. (1988). Two moral orientations: Gender differences and similarities. *Merrill-Palmer Quarterly, 34,* 223–237.

GILLIGAN, C., & WIGGINS, G. (1987). The origins of morality in early childhood relationships. In J. Kagan & S. Lamb (Eds.), *The emergence of morality in young children.* Chicago: University of Chicago Press.

*GINGRAS, J. L., WEESE-MAYER, D. E., HUME, R. F., Jr., & O'DONNELL, K. J. (1992). Cocaine and development: Mechanisms of fetal toxicity and neonatal consequences of prenatal cocaine exposure. *Early Human Development, 31,* 1–24.

GINSBURG, H., & OPPER, S. (1988). *Piaget's theory of intellectual development* (3rd ed.). Englewood Cliffs, NJ: Prentice Hall.

*GINSBURG, H. J. (1975, April). *Variations of aggressive interaction among male elementary school children as a function of spatial density.* Paper presented at the meeting of the Society for Research in Child Development, Denver.

GINSBURG, H. J. (1980). Playground as laboratory: Naturalistic studies of appeasement, altruism, and the Omega child. In D. R. Omark, F. F. Strayer, & D. G. Freedman (Eds.), *Dominance relations: An ethological view of human conflict and social interaction.* New York: Garland.

*GLASSMAN, M. (1994). All things being equal: The two roads of Piaget and Vygotsky. *Developmental Review, 114,* 186–214.

GLEASON, J. B., & WEINTRAUB, S. (1978). Input and the acquisition of communicative competence. In K. E. Nelson (Ed.), *Children's language* (Vol. 1). New York: Gardner.

GLEITMAN, L. R., NEWPORT, E. L., & GLEITMAN, H. (1984). The current status of the motherese hypothesis. *Journal of Child Language, 11,* 43–79.

GLENN, S. M., CUNNINGHAM, C. C., & JOYCE, P. F. (1981). A study of auditory preferences in nonhandicapped infants and infants with Down's syndrome. *Child Development, 52,* 1303–1307.

GLICK, M., & ZIGLER, E. (1985). Self-image: A cognitive-developmental approach. In R. L. Leahy (Ed.), *The development of the self.* Orlando, FL: Academic Press.

*GOCHMAN, D. S. (1988). Assessing children's health concepts. In P. Karoly (Ed.), *Handbook of child health assessment: Biopsychosocial perspectives.* New York: Wiley.

GODDARD, M., DURKIN, K., & RUTTER, D. R. (1985). The semantic focus of maternal speech: A comment on Ninio and Bruner (1978). *Journal of Child Language, 12,* 209–213.

GOLBUS, M. S. (1983). Prenatal diagnosis. *Birth Defects: Original Article Series, 11,* 121–125.

GOLD, D., & BERGER, C. (1978). Problem-solving performance of young boys and girls as a function of task appropriateness and sex identity. *Sex Roles, 4,* 183–193.

GOLD, R. (1987). *The description of cognitive development: Three Piagetian themes.* Oxford: Clarendon Press.

GOLDBERG, S. (1983). Parent–infant bonding: Another look. *Child Development, 54,* 1355–1382.

*GOLDFIELD, B. A. (1993). Noun bias in maternal speech to one-year-olds. *Journal of Child Language, 20,* 85–99.

GOLDFIELD, B. A., & REZNICK, J. S. (1990). Early lexical acquisition: Rate, content, and the vocabulary spurt. *Journal of Child Language, 17,* 171–183.

GOLDMAN, A. S. (1980). Critical periods of prenatal toxic insults. In R. H. Schwartz & S. J. Yaffe (Eds.), *Drug and chemical risks to the fetus and newborn.* New York: Alan R. Liss.

*GOLDSMITH, H. H. (1993). Nature–nurture issues in behavior-genetic context: Overcoming barriers to communication. In R. Plomin & G. E. McClearn (Eds.), *Nature, nurture, and psychology.* Washington, DC: APA.

GOLDSMITH, H. H., & ALANSKY, J. A. (1987). Maternal and infant temperamental predictors of attachment: A meta-analytic review. *Journal of Consulting and Clinical Psychology, 55,* 805–816.

GOLDSMITH, H. H., BUSS, A. H., PLOMIN, R., ROTHBART, M. K., THOMAS, A., CHESS, S., HINDE, R. A., & McCALL, R. B. (1987). Roundtable: What is temperament: Four approaches. *Child Development, 58,* 505–529.

GOLDSMITH, H. H., & CAMPOS, J. (1986). Fundamental issues in the study of early temperament: The Denver Twin Temperament Study. In M. E. Lamb, A. L. Brown, & B. Rogoff (Eds.), *Advances in developmental psychology* (Vol. 4). Hillsdale, NJ: Erlbaum.

*GOLDSMITH, H. H., & HARMAN, C. (1994). Temperament and attachment: Individuals and relationships. *Current Directions in Psychological Science, 3,* 53–57.

*GOLDSMITH, H. H., & ROTHBART, M. K. (1992). *The Laboratory Temperament Assessment Battery.* Eugene, OR: Personality Development Laboratory.

GOLDSTEIN, A. P., & GLICK, B. (1987). *Aggression replacement training: A comprehensive intervention for aggressive youth.* Champaign, IL: Research Press.

GOLINKOFF, R. M., & HIRSH-PASEK, K. (1990). Let the mute speak: What infants can tell us about language acquisition. *Merrill-Palmer Quarterly, 36,* 67–92.

*GOLINKOFF, R. M., HIRSH-PASEK, K., BAILEY, L. M., & WENGER, N. R. (1992). Young children and adults use lexical principles to learn new nouns. *Developmental Psychology, 28,* 99–108.

*GOLOMBOK, S., COOK, R., BISH, A. & MURRAY, C. (1993). Families created by the new reproductive technologies: Quality of parenting and social and emotional development of the children. Unpublished manuscript.

*GOLOMBOK, S., SPENCER, A., & RUTTER, M. (1983). Children in lesbian and single-parent households: Psychosexual and psychiatric appraisal. *Journal of Child Psychology and Psychiatry, 24,* 551–572.

GOOD, T. L., & WEINSTEIN, R. S. (1986). Schools make a difference: Evidence, criticisms, and new directions. *American Psychologist, 41,* 1090–1097.

GOODMAN, G. S., AMAN, C., & HIRSCHMAN, J. (1987). Child sexual and physical abuse: Children's testimony. In S. J. Ceci, M. P. Toglia, & D. F. Ross (Eds.), *Children's eyewitness memory.* New York: Springer-Verlag.

*GOODMAN, G. S., & BOTTOMS, B. L. (Eds.). (1993). *Child victims, child witnesses.* New York: Guilford.

GOODMAN, G. S., HIRSCHMANN, J. E., HEPPS, D., & RUDY, L. (1991). Children's memory for stressful events. *Merrill-Palmer Quarterly, 37,* 109–158.

*GOODMAN, G. S., PYLE TAUB, E., JONES, D. P. H., ENGLAND, P., PORT, L. K., RUDY, L., & PRADO, L. (1992). Testifying in criminal court. *Monographs of the Society for Research in Child Development, 57* (5, Serial No. 229).

*GOODMAN, G. S., & SCHWARTZ-KENNEY, B. M. (1992). Why knowing a child's age is not enough: Influences of cognitive, social, and emotional factors on children's testimony. In H. Dent & R. Flin (Eds.), *Children as witnesses.* New York: Wiley.

GOODNOW, J. J. (1988). Children, families, and communities: Ways of viewing their relationships to each other. In N. Bolger, A. Caspi, G. Downey, & M. Moorehouse (Eds.), *Persons in context.* New York: Cambridge University Press.

*GOODNOW, J. J., & COLLINS, W. A. (1990).

Development according to parents: The nature, sources, and consequences of parents' ideas. Hillsdale, NJ: Erlbaum.

*GOODWYN, S. W., & ACREDOLO, L. P. (1993). Symbolic gesture versus word: Is there a modality advantage for onset of symbolic use? *Child Development, 64,* 688–701.

GOODZ, N. S. (1989). Parental language mixing in bilingual families. *Journal of Infant Mental Health, 10,* 25–34.

GOOSSENS, F. A. (1987). Maternal employment and day care: Effects on attachment. In L. W. C. Tavecchio & M. H. vanIJzendoorn (Eds.), *Attachment in social networks.* Amsterdam: North-Holland.

GOOSSENS, F. A., & vanIJZENDOORN, M. H. (1990). Quality of infants' attachments to professional caregivers: Relation to infant–parent attachment and day-care characteristics. *Child Development, 61,* 832–837.

GOPNIK, A., & MELTZOFF, A. N. (1987a). The development of categorization in the second year and its relation to other cognitive and linguistic developments. *Child Development, 58,* 1523–1531.

GOPNIK, A., & MELTZOFF, A. N. (1987b). Early semantic developments and their relationship to object permanence, means–ends understanding and categorization. In K. Nelson & A. VanKleek (Eds.), *Children's language* (Vol. 6). Hillsdale, NJ: Erlbaum.

*GOPNIK, A., & MELTZOFF, A. N. (1992). Categorization and mapping: Basic-level sorting in eighteen-month-olds and its relation to language. *Child Development, 63,* 1091–1103.

*GORMAN, K. S., & POLLITT, E. (1992). Relationship between weight and body proportionality at birth, growth during the first year of life, and cognitive development at 36, 48, and 60 months. *Infant Behavior and Development, 15,* 279–296.

*GOSWAMI, U., & BRYANT, P. (1990). *Phonological skills and learning to read.* Hove, England: Erlbaum.

GOTLIEB, S. J., BAISINI, F. J., & BRAY, N. W. (1988). Visual recognition memory in IVGR and normal birthweight infants. *Infant Behavior and Development, 11,* 223–228.

GOTTESMAN, I. I. (1974). Developmental genetics and ontogenetic psychology: Overdue detente and propositions from a matchmaker. In A. Pick (Ed.), *Minnesota symposium on child psychology.* Minneapolis: University of Minnesota Press.

*GOTTESMAN, I. I. (1993). Origins of schizophrenia: Past as prologue. In R. Plomin & G. E. McClearn (Eds.), *Nature, nurture, and psychology.* Washington, DC: APA.

GOTTESMAN, I. I., & SHIELDS, J. (1982). *Schizophrenia.* Cambridge: Cambridge University Press.

GOTTFRIED, A. W. (Ed.). (1984a). *Home environment and early cognitive development.* New York: Academic Press.

GOTTFRIED, A. W. (1984b). Home environment and early cognitive development: Integration, meta-analyses, and conclusions. In A. W. Gottfried (Ed.), *Home environment and early cognitive development.* New York: Academic Press.

*GOTTLIEB, G. (1991). Behavioral pathway to evolutionary change. *Rivista Di Biologia—Biology Forum, 84*(3), 385–409.

*GOTTLIEB, G. (1992). *Individual development and evolution: The genesis of novel behavior.* New York: Oxford University Press.

GOTTMAN, J. M. (1983). How children become friends. *Monographs of the Society for Research in Child Development, 48* (3, Serial No. 201).

GOTTMAN, J. M. (1990). *Sequential analysis: A guide for behavioral researchers.* New York: Cambridge University Press.

GOTTMAN, J. M., GONSO, J., & RASMUSSEN, B. (1975). Social interaction, social competence, and friendship in children. *Child Development, 46,* 709–718.

GOULD, J. L. (1982). *Ethology: The Mechanisms and evolution of behavior.* New York: Norton.

GOY, R. W., & McEWEN, B. S. (1980). *Sexual differentiation of the brain.* Cambridge, MA: MIT Press.

*GRAHAM, F. K., & CLIFTON, R. K. (1966). Heart-rate change as a component of the orienting response. *Psychological Bulletin, 65,* 305–320.

GRAHAM, S., & HUDLEY, C. (1994). Attributions of aggressive and nonaggressive African-American male early adolescents: A study of construct accessibility. *Developmental Psychology, 30,* 365–373.

*GRAHAM, S., HUDLEY, C., & WILLIAMS, E. (1992). Attributional and emotional determinants of aggression among African-American and Latino young adolescents. *Developmental Psychology, 28,* 731–740.

*GRALINSKI, J. H., & KOPP, C. B. (1993). Everyday rules for behavior: Mothers' requests to young children. *Developmental Psychology, 29,* 573–584.

GRANRUD, C. E., & YONAS, A. (1984). Infants' perception of pictorially specified interposition. *Journal of Experimental Child Psychology, 37,* 500–511.

GRATCH, G. (1972). A study of the relative dominance of vision and touch in six-month-old infants. *Child Development, 43,* 615–623.

GRATCH, G., & LANDERS, W. F. (1971). Stage IV of Piaget's theory of infants' object concepts: A longitudinal study. *Child Development, 42,* 359–372.

*GRATTAN, M. P., De VOS, E., LEVY, J., & McCLINTOCK, M. K. (1992). Asymmetric action in the human newborn: Sex differences in patterns of organization. *Child Development, 62,* 273–289.

GRAY, S. W., & RAMSEY, B. K. (1982). The Early Training Project: A life-span view. *Human Development, 25,* 48–57.

GRAY, S. W., RAMSEY, B. K., & KLAUS, R. A. (1982). *From 3 to 20: The early training project.* Baltimore: University Park Press.

*GRAY, W. M. (1990). Formal operational thought. In W. F. Overton (Ed.), *Reasoning, necessity, and logic: Developmental perspectives.* Hillsdale, NJ: Erlbaum.

GRAY, W. M., & HUDSON, L. M. (1984). Formal operations and the imaginary audience. *Developmental Psychology, 20,* 619–627.

GRAZIANO, W. G. (1987). Lost in thought at the choice point: Cognition, context, and equity. In J. C. Masters & W. P. Smith (Eds.), *Social comparison, social justice, and relative deprivation.* Hillsdale, NJ: Erlbaum.

GREEN, J. A., JONES, L. E., & GUSTAFSON, G. E. (1987). Perception of cries by parents and nonparents: Relation to cry acoustics. *Developmental Psychology, 23,* 370–382.

GREEN, K. D., FOREHAND, R., BECK, S. J., & VOSK, B. (1980). An assessment of the relationship among measures of children's social competence and children's academic achievement. *Child Development, 51,* 1149–1156.

GREEN, M. (1989). *Theories of human development: A comparative approach.* Englewood Cliffs, NJ: Prentice Hall.

*GREEN, R. (1978). Sexual identity of 37 children raised by homosexual or transsexual parents. *American Journal of Psychiatry, 135,* 692–697.

*GREEN, R., MANDEL, J. B., HOTVEDT, M. E., GRAY, J., & SMITH, L. (1986). Lesbian mothers and their children: A comparison with solo parent heterosexual mothers and their children. *Archives of Sexual Behavior, 15,* 167–184.

*GREENFIELD, P. M., & CHILDS, C. P. (1991). Developmental continuity in biocultural context. In R. Cohen & A. W. Siegel (Eds.), *Context and development.* Hillsdale, NJ: Erlbaum.

*GREENFIELD, P. M., & SAVAGE-RUMBAUGH, E. S. (1993). Comparing communicative competence in child and chimp: The pragmatics of repetition. *Journal of Child Language, 20,* 1–26.

GREENFIELD, P. M., & SMITH, J. H. (1976). *The structure of communication in early language development.* New York: Academic Press.

GREENLEAF, B. K. (1978). *Children through the ages: A history of childhood.* New York: McGraw-Hill.

*GREENO, C. G., & MACCOBY, E. E. (1986). How different is the "different voice"? *Signs: Journal of Women in Culture and Society, 11,* 310–316.

GREENO, J. G., RILEY, M. S., & GELMAN, R. (1984). Conceptual competence and children's counting. *Cognitive Psychology, 16,* 94–143.

GREENOUGH, W. T., & BLACK, J. E. (1992). Induction of brain structure by experience: Substrates for cognitive development. In M. R. Gunnar & C. A. Nelson (Eds.), *Minnesota symposia on child psychology:* Vol. 24. *Developmental behavioral neuroscience.* Hillsdale, NJ: Erlbaum.*

GREENOUGH, W. T., BLACK, J. E., & WALLACE, C. S. (1987). Experience and brain development. *Child Development, 58,* 539–559.

GREENWALD, A., & PRATKANIS, A. (1984). The self. In R. Wyer & T. Srull (Eds.), *Handbook of social cognition* (Vol. 3). Hillsdale, NJ: Erlbaum.

GRIFFITHS, P. (1985). The communicative functions of children's single-word speech. In M. D. Barrett (Ed.), *Children's single-word speech.* New York: Wiley.

GRIMSHAW, J. (1981). Form, function, and the language acquisition device. In C. L. Baker & J. J. McCarthy (Eds.), *The logical problem of language acquisition.* Cambridge, MA: MIT Press.

GRINDER, R. E. (1967). *A history of genetic psychology: The first science of human development.* New York: Wiley.

GRONLUND, N. (1959). *Sociometry in the classroom.* New York: Harper.

*GROSSMANN, K., GROSSMANN, K. E., SPANGLER, G., SUESS, G., & UNZNER, L. (1985). Maternal sensitivity and newborns' orientation responses as related to quality of attachment in northern Germany. In I. Bretherton & E. Waters (Eds.), Growing points of attachment theory and research. *Monographs of the Society for Research in Child Development, 50*(1–2, Serial No. 209).

*GROSSMANN, K. E., & GROSSMANN, K. (1990). The wider concept of attachment in cross-cultural research. *Human Development, 33,* 31–47.

GROTEVANT, H. D. (1989). Child development within the family context. In W. Damon (Ed.), *Child development today and tomorrow.* San Francisco: Jossey-Bass.

GRUENEICH, R. (1982). Issues in the developmental study of how children use intention and consequence information to make moral evaluations. *Child Development, 53,* 29–43.

GRUMBACK, M. (1979). Genetic mechanisms of sexual development. In H. L. Vallet & I. H. Porter (Eds.), *Genetic mechanisms of sexual development.* New York: Academic Press.

GRUSEC, J. E. (1981). Socialization processes and the development of altruism. In J. P. Rushton & R. M. Sorrentino (Eds.), *Altruism and helping behavior: Social, personality, and developmental perspectives.* Hillsdale, NJ: Erlbaum.

*GRUSEC, J. E. (1992). Social learning theory and developmental psychology: The legacies of Robert Sears and Albert Bandura. *Developmental Psychology, 28,* 776–786.

GRUSEC, J. E., & ABRAMOVITCH, R. (1982). Imitation of peers and adults in a natural setting: A functional analysis. *Child Development, 53,* 636–642.

GRUSEC, J. E., & DIX, T. (1986). The socialization of prosocial behavior: Theory and reality. In C. Zahn-Waxler, E. M. Cummings, & R. Iannotti (Eds.), *Altruism and aggression: Biological and social origins.* New York: Cambridge University Press.

*GRUSEC, J. E., & GOODNOW, J. J. (1994). Impact of parental discipline methods on the child's internalization of values: A reconceptualization of current points of view. *Developmental Psychology, 30,* 4–19.

GRUSEC, J. E., KUCZYNSKI, L., RUSHTON, J. P., & SIMUTIS, Z. M. (1979). Learning resistance to temptation through observation. *Developmental Psychology, 15,* 233–240.

GRUSEC, J. E., & LYTTON, H. (1988). *Social development: History, theory, and research.* New York: Springer-Verlag.

GUERRA, N. G., & SLABY, R. G. (1990). Cognitive mediators of aggression in adolescent offenders: 2. Intervention. *Developmental Psychology, 26,* 269–277.

GUILFORD, J. P. (1967). *The nature of human intelligence.* New York: McGraw-Hill.

GUILFORD, J. P. (1988). Some changes in the structure-of-the-intellect model. *Educational and Psychological Measurement, 48,* 1–4.

*GUILLEMIN, J. (1993). Cesarean birth: Social and political aspects. In B. K. Rothman (Ed.), *Encyclopedia of childbearing.* Phoenix, AZ: Oryx Press.

GUNNAR, M. R., FISCH, R. O., & MALONE, S. (1984). The effects of a pacifying stimulus on behavioral and adrenocortical responses to circumcision in the newborn. *Journal of the American Academy of Child Psychiatry, 23,* 34–38.

*GUNNAR, M. R., LARSON, M. C., HERTSGAARD, L., HARRIS, M. L., & BRODERSEN, L. (1992). The stressfulness of separation among nine-month-old infants: Effects of social context variables and infant temperament. *Child Development, 63,* 290–303.

GURMAN BARD, E., & ANDERSON, A. (1983). The unintelligibility of speech to children. *Journal of Child Language, 10,* 265–292.

GURUCHARRI, C., & SELMAN, R. L. (1982). The development of interpersonal understanding during childhood, preadolescence, and adolescence: A longitudinal follow-up study. *Child Development, 53,* 924–927.

GUSTAFSON, G. E., & HARRIS, K. L. (1990). Women's responses to young infants' cries. *Developmental Psychology, 26,* 144–152.

GUTTMACHER, A. F. (1973). *Pregnancy, birth and family planning.* New York: Viking.

HAECKEL, E. (1977). Last words on evolution. In D. N. Robinson (Ed.), *Significant contributions to the history of psychology: 1750–1920.* Washington, DC: University Publications of America. (Original work published 1906)

HAGEN, J. W., & HALE, G. A. (1973). The development of attention in children. In A. D. Pick (Ed.), *Minnesota symposia on child psychology.* (Vol. 7). Minneapolis: University of Minnesota Press.

*HAGERMAN, R. J. (1991). Fragile X syndrome. *Encyclopedia of human biology* (Vol. 3). San Diego: Academic Press.

*HAGERMAN, R. J., & SILVERMAN, A. C. (Eds.). (1991). *Fragile X syndrome: Diagnosis, treatment, and research.* Baltimore: Johns Hopkins University Press.

*HAIGHT, W., & MILLER, P. J. (1992). The development of everyday pretend play: A longitudinal study of mothers' participation. *Merrill-Palmer Quarterly, 38,* 331–349.

*HAIGHT, W., & MILLER, P. J. (1993). *Pretending at home.* Albany: SUNY Press.

HAINLINE, L., & ABRAMOV, I. (1992). Assessing visual development: Is infant vision good enough? In C. Rovee-Collier & L. P. Lipsitt (Eds.), *Advances in infancy research* (Vol. 7). Norwood, NJ: Ablex.

HAITH, M. M. (1966). The response of the human newborn to visual movement. *Journal of Experimental Child Psychology, 3,* 235–243.

HAITH, M. M. (1980). *Rules that babies look by.* Hillsdale, NJ: Erlbaum.

HAITH, M. M. (1986). Sensory and perceptual processes in early infancy. *Journal of Pediatrics, 109,* 158–171.

HAITH, M. M. (1991). Gratuity, perception-action integration and future orientation in infant vision. In F. Kessel, A. Sameroff, & M. Bornstein (Eds.), *The past as prologue in developmental psychology: Essays in honor of William Kessen.* Hillsdale, NJ: Erlbaum.

*HAITH, M. M. (1993). Preparing for the 21st century: Some goals and challenges for studies of infant sensory and perceptual development. *Developmental Review, 13,* 354–371.

*HAITH, M. M. (in press). Visual expectations as the first step toward the development of future-oriented processes. In M. M. Haith, J. B. Benson, R. J. Roberts Jr., & B. F. Pennington (Eds.), *The development of future-oriented processes.* Chicago: University of Chicago Press.

HAITH, M. M., BERGMAN, T., & MOORE, M. J. (1977). Eye contact and face scanning in early infancy. *Science, 198,* 853–855.

HAITH, M. M., HAZAN, C., & GOODMAN, G. S. (1988). Expectation and anticipation of dynamic visual events by 3.5-month old babies. *Child Development, 59,* 467–479.

*HAITH, M. M., WENTWORTH, N., & CANFIELD, R. L. (1993). The formation of expectations in early infancy. In C. Rovee-Collier & L. P. Lipsitt (Eds.), *Advances in infancy research* (Vol. 8). Norwood, NJ: Ablex.

HALE, G. A. (1979). Development of children's attention to stimulus components. In G. A. Hale & M. Lewis (Eds.), *Attention and cognitive development.* New York: Plenum.

*HALE, S. (1990). A global development trend in cognitive processing speed. *Child Development, 61,* 653–663.

HALFORD, G. S. (1989). Reflections on 25 years of Piagetian cognitive developmental psychology, 1963–1988. *Human Development, 32,* 325–357.

*HALFORD, G. S. (1993). *Children's understanding: The development of mental models.* Hillsdale, NJ: Erlbaum.

*HALL, D. G. (1991). Acquiring proper nouns for familiar and unfamiliar animate objects: Two-year-olds' word-learning biases. *Child Development, 62,* 1142–1154.

*HALL, D. G., & WAXMAN, S. R. (1993). Assumptions about word meaning: Individuation and basic-level kinds. *Child Development, 64,* 1550–1570.

HALL, G. S. (1904). *Adolescence: Its psychology and its relations to physiology, anthropology, sociology, sex, crime, religion, and education* (2 vols.). New York: Appleton.

HALLIDAY, M. A. K. (1975). *Learning to mean: Explorations in the development of language.* New York: Edward Arnold.

*HALPERN, D. F. (1992). *Sex differences in cognitive abilities* (2nd ed.). Hillsdale, NJ: Erlbaum.

*HALPERN, R. (1993). Poverty and infant development. In C. H. Zeanah, Jr. (Ed.), *Handbook of infant mental development.* New York: Guilford.

HALVERSON, H. M. (1946). A study of feeding mechanisms in premature infants. *Journal of Genetic Psychology, 68,* 205–217.

*HAMER, D. H., HU, S., MAGNUSON, V. L., HU, N., & PATTATUCCI, A. M. L. (1993). A linkage between DNA markers on the X chromosome and male sexual orientations. *Science, 261,* 321–327.

HAMMEN, C., & ZUPAN, B. A. (1984). Self-schemas, depression, and the processing of personal information in children. *Journal of Experimental Child Psychology, 37,* 598–608.

*HAMPSON, I., & NELSON, K. (1993). The relation of maternal language to variation in rate and style of language acquisition. *Journal of Child Language, 20,* 313–342.

*HANDYSIDE, A. H., LESKO, J. G., TARÍN, J. J., WINSTON, R. M. L., & HUGHES, M. R. (1992). Birth of a normal girl after in vitro fertilization and preimplantation diagnostic testing for cystic fibrosis. *New England Journal of Medicine, 327,* 905–909.

*HANNA, E., & MELTZOFF, A. N. (1993). Peer imitation by toddlers in laboratory, home, and day-care contexts: Implications for social learning and memory. *Developmental Psychology, 29,* 701–710.

*HANSON, D. R., GOTTESMAN, I. I., & MEEHL, P. E. (1977). Genetic theories and the validation of psychiatric diagnoses: Implica-tions for the study of children of schizophrenics. *Journal of Abnormal Psychology, 86,* 575–588.

HANSON, S. M. H. (1988). Divorced fathers with custody. In P. Bronstein & C. P. Cowan (Eds.), *Fatherhood today: Men's changing role in the family.* New York: Wiley.

*HARBECK, C., & PETERSON, L. (1992). Elephants dancing in my head: A developmental approach to children's concepts of specific pains. *Child Development, 63,* 138–149.

*HARBECK-WEBER, C., & PETERSON, L. Children's conceptions of illness and pain. In R. Vasta (Ed.), *Annals of child development* (Vol. 9). London: Kingsley.

HARDING, C. G. (1983). Setting the stage for language acquisition: Communication development in the first year. In R. M. Golinkoff (Ed.), *The transition from prelinguistic to linguistic communication.* Hillsdale, NJ: Erlbaum.

HARKNESS, S., & SUPER, C. M. (1987). The use of cross-cultural research in child development. In R. Vasta (Ed.), *Annals of child development* (Vol. 4). Greenwich, CT: JAI Press.

HARLOW, H. F., & HARLOW, M. K. (1966). Learning to love. *American Scientist, 54,* 244–272.

HARPER, L., & KRAFT, R. H. (1986). Lateralization of receptive language in preschoolers: Test–retest reliability in a dichotic listening task. *Developmental Psychology, 22,* 553–556.

HARPER, L., & SANDERS, K. M. (1975). Preschool children's use of space: Sex differences in outdoor play. *Developmental Psychology, 11,* 119.

HARPER, P. S. (1981). *Practical genetic counseling.* Baltimore: University Park Press.

HARRIS, G., THOMAS, A., & BOOTH, D. A. (1990). Development of salt preference in infancy. *Developmental Psychology, 26,* 534–538.

HARRIS, L. J. (1977). Sex differences in the growth and use of language. In E. Donelson & J. E. Gullahorn (Eds.), *Women: A psychological perspective.* New York: Wiley.

HARRIS, M., BARRETT, M., JONES, D., & BROOKES, S. (1988). Linguistic input and early word meaning. *Journal of Child Language, 15,* 77–94.

HARRIS, P. L. (1983). Infant cognition. In M. M. Haith & J. J. Campos (Eds.), *Handbook of child psychology: Vol. 2. Infancy and developmental psychobiology.* New York: Wiley.

*HARRIS, P. L. (1989a). *Children and emotion: The development of psychological understanding.* Oxford: Basil Blackwell.

*HARRIS, P. L. (1989b). Object permanence in infancy. In A. Slater & G. Bremner (Eds.), *Infant development.* Hillsdale, NJ: Erlbaum.

HARRIS, S. L. (1975). Teaching language to nonverbal children—with emphasis on problems of generalization. *Psychological Bulletin, 82,* 565–580.

*HART, B., & RISLEY, T. R. (1992). American parenting of language-learning children: Persisting differences in family–child interactions observed in natural home environments. *Developmental Psychology, 28,* 1096–1105.

*HART, C. H., DeWOLF, D. M., WOZNIAK, P., & BURTS, D. C. (1992). Maternal and paternal disciplinary styles: Relations with preschoolers' playground behavioral orientations and peer status. *Child Development, 63,* 879–892.

HART, D. (1988a). The development of personal identity in adolescence: A philosophical dilemma approach. *Merrill-Palmer Quarterly, 34,* 105–114.

HART, D. (1988b). A longitudinal study of adolescents' socialization and identification as predictors of adult moral judgment development. *Merrill-Palmer Quarterly, 34,* 245–260.

HART, D., & DAMON, W. (1985). Contrasts between understanding self and understanding others. In R. L. Leahy (Ed.), *The development of the self.* Orlando, FL: Academic Press.

*HART, S. N. (1991). From property to person status: Historical perspective on children's rights. *American Psychologist, 46,* 53–59.

HARTER, S. (1981). A new self-report scale of intrinsic versus extrinsic orientation in the classroom: Motivational and informational components. *Developmental Psychology, 17,* 300–312.

HARTER, S. (1982). A developmental perspective on some parameters of self-regulation in children. In P. Karoly & F. H. Kanfer (Eds.), *Self-management and behavior change: From theory to practice.* New York: Pergamon.

HARTER, S. (1983). Developmental perspectives on the self-system. In E. M. Hetherington (Ed.), *Handbook of child psychology: Vol. 4. Socialization, personality, and social development.* New York: Wiley.

HARTER, S. (1985). Competence as a dimension of self-evaluation: Toward a comprehensive model of self-worth. In R. L. Leahy (Ed.), *The development of the self.* Orlando, FL: Academic Press.

HARTER, S. (1986). Processes underlying the construction, maintenance and enhancement of the self-concept in children. In J. Suls & A. Greenwald (Eds.), *Psychological perspectives on the self* (Vol. 3). Hillsdale, NJ: Erlbaum.

HARTER, S. (1987). The determinants and mediational role of global self-worth in children. In N. Eisenberg (Ed.), *Contemporary topics in developmental psychology.* New York: Wiley.

HARTER, S. (1988). Developmental processes in the construction of the self. In T. D. Yawkey & J. E. Johnson (Eds.), *Integrative processes and socialization: Early to middle childhood.* Hillsdale, NJ: Erlbaum.

*HARTER, S. (1990a). Causes, correlates and the functional role of self-worth: A life-span perspective. In R. J. Sternberg & J. Kolligian (Eds.), *Competence considered.* New Haven, CT: Yale University Press.

HARTER, S. (1990b). Processes underlying adolescent self-concept formation. In R. Montemayor, G. R. Adams, & T. P. Gullotta (Eds.), *From childhood to adolescence: A transitional period?* Newbury Park, CA: Sage.

*HARTER, S. (1994). Developmental changes in self-understanding across the 5 to 7 shift. In A. Sameroff & M. M. Haith (Eds.), *Reason and responsibility: The passage through childhood.* Chicago: University of Chicago Press.

HARTER, S., & CONNELL, J. P. (1984). A model of the relationship among children's academic achievement and their self-perceptions of competence, control, and motivational orientation. In J. Nicholls (Ed.), *The development of achievement motivation.* Greenwich, CT: JAI Press.

*HARTER, S., & MONSOUR, A. (1992). Developmental analysis of conflict caused by opposing attributes in the adolescent self-portrait. *Developmental Psychology, 28,* 251–260.

HARTER, S., & PIKE, R. (1984). The Pictorial Scale of Perceived Competence and Social Acceptance for Young Children. *Child Development, 55,* 1969–1982.

HARTIG, M., & KANFER, F. H. (1973). The role of verbal self-instructions in children's resistance to temptation. *Journal of Personality and Social Psychology, 25,* 259–267.

HARTSHORNE, H., & MAY, M. S. (1928–1930). *Studies in the nature of character* (3 vols.). New York: Macmillan.

HARTUP, W. W. (1974). Aggression in childhood: Developmental perspectives. *American Psychologist, 29,* 336–341.

HARTUP, W. W. (1983). Peer relations. In E. M. Hetherington (Ed.), *Handbook of child psychology: Vol. 4. Socialization, personality, and social development.* New York: Wiley.

HARTUP, W. W. (1989a). Behavioral manifestations of children's friendships. In T. J. Berndt & G. W. Ladd (Eds.), *Peer relationships in child development.* New York: Wiley.

HARTUP, W. W. (1989b). Social relationships and their developmental significance. *American Psychologist, 44,* 120–126.

*HARTUP, W. W. (1992a). Conflict and friendship relations. In C. U. Shantz & W. W. Hartup (Eds.), *Conflict in child and adolescent development.* Cambridge: Cambridge University Press.

*HARTUP, W. W. (1992b). Friendships and their developmental significance. In H. McGurk (Ed.), *Childhood social development: Contemporary perspectives.* Hillsdale, NJ: Erlbaum.

*HARTUP, W. W. (1992c). Peer relations in early and middle childhood. In V. B. Van Hasselt & M. Hersen (Eds.), *Handbook of social development.* New York: Plenum.

*HARTUP, W. W. (1993). Adolescents and their friends. In B. Laursen (Ed.), *New directions for child development: No. 60. Close friendships in adolescence.* San Francisco: Jossey-Bass.

*HARTUP, W. W., FRENCH, D. C., LAURSEN, B., JOHNSON, M. K., & OGAWA, J. R. (1993). Conflict and friendship relations in middle childhood: Behavior in a closed-field situation. *Child Development, 64,* 445–454.

HARTUP, W. W., LAURSEN, B., STEWART, M. I., & EASTERSON, A. (1988). Conflict and the friendship relations of young children. *Child Development, 59,* 1590–1600.

HARVEY, S. E., & LIEBERT, R. M. (1979). Abstraction, inference, and acceptance in children's processing of an adult model's moral judgments. *Developmental Psychology, 15,* 552–558.

HARWAY, M., & MOSS, L. T. (1983). Sex differences: The evidence from biology. In M. B. Liss (Ed.), *Social and cognitive skills: Sex roles and children's play.* New York: Academic Press.

*HARWOOD, R. L. (1992). The influence of culturally derived values on Anglo and Puerto Rican mothers' perceptions of attachment behavior. *Child Development, 63,* 822–839.

*HARWOOD, R. L., & MILLER, J. G. (1991). Perceptions of attachment behavior: A comparison of Anglo and Puerto Rican mothers. *Merrill-Palmer Quarterly, 37,* 583–599.

HASSELHORN, M. (1990). The emergence of strategic knowledge activation in categorical clustering during retrieval. *Journal of Experimental Child Psychology, 50,* 59–80.

*HASSELHORN, M. (1992). Task dependency and the role of category typicality and metamemory in the development of an organizational strategy. *Child Development, 63,* 202–214.

*HASTE, H., & BADDELEY, J. (1991). Moral theory and culture: The case of gender. In W. M. Kurtines & J. L. Gewirtz (Eds.), *Handbook of moral behavior and development: Vol. 1. Theory.* Hillsdale, NJ: Erlbaum.

HATANO, G. (1990). Commentary: Toward the cultural psychology of mathematical cognition. *Monographs of the Society for Research in Child Development, 55* (1–2, Serial No. 221).

*HATANO, G., SIEGLER, R. S., RICHARDS, D. D., INAGAKI, K., STAVY, R., & WAX, N. (1993). The development of biological knowledge: A multi-national study. *Cognitive Development, 8,* 47–62.

*HAUSER, P., ZAMETKIN, A. J., MARTINEZ, P., VITIELLO, B., MATOCHIK, J. A., MIXSON, A. J., & WEINTRAUB, B. D. (1993). Attention-deficit-hyperactivity disorder in people with generalized resistance to thyroid hormone. *New England Journal of Medicine, 328,* 997–1039.

HAVILAND, J. M., & LELWICA, M. (1987). The induced affect response: 10-week-old infants' response to three emotion expressions. *Developmental Psychology, 23,* 97–104.

*HAWLEY, T. L., & DISNEY, E. R. (1992). Crack's children: The consequences of maternal cocaine abuse. Social Policy Report. *Society for Research in Child Development, 6,* 1–23.

*HAWLEY, T. L., HALLE, T., DRASIN, R., & THOMAS, N. (1993). *Children of the crack epidemic: The cognitive, language, and emotional development of preschool children of addicted mothers.* Presented at the biennial meeting of the Society for Research in Child Development, New Orleans.

HAY, D. F. (1984). Social conflict in early childhood. In G. J. Whitehurst (Ed.), *Annals of child development* (Vol. 1). Greenwich, CT: JAI Press.

HAY, D. F. (1985). Learning to form relationships in infancy: Parallel attainments with parents and peers. *Developmental Review, 5,* 122–161.

HAY, D. F. (1986). Learning to be social: Some comments on Schaffer's *The child's entry into a social world. Developmental Review, 6,* 107–114.

*HAY, D. F., CAPLAN, M., CASTLE, J., & STIMSON, C. A. (1991). Does sharing become increasingly "rational" in the second year of life? *Developmental Psychology, 27,* 987–993.

HAY, D. F., & MURRAY, P. (1982). Giving and requesting: Social facilitation of infants' offers to adults. *Infant Behavior and Development, 5,* 301–310.

HAY, D. F., MURRAY, P., CECIRE, S., & NASH, A. (1985). Social learning of social behavior in early life. *Child Development, 56,* 43–57.

HAY, D. F., NASH, A., & PEDERSEN, J. (1983). Interaction between six-month-old peers. *Child Development, 54,* 557–562.

HAY, L. (1984). Discontinuity in the development of motor control in children. In W. Prinz & A. F. Sanders (Eds.), *Cognition and motor processes.* Berlin: Springer-Verlag.

HAYDEN-THOMSON, L., RUBIN, K. H., & HYMEL, S. (1987). Sex preferences in sociometric choices. *Developmental Psychology, 23,* 558–562.

*HAYES, C. (1951). *The ape in our house.* New York: Harper.

HAYES, D. S., GERSHMAN, E., & BOLIN, L. J. (1980). Friends and enemies: Cognitive bases for preschool children's unilateral and reciprocal relationships. *Child Development, 51,* 1276–1279.

*HAYES, J. S., LAMPART, R., DREHER, M. C., & MORGAN, L. (1991). Five-year follow-up of rural Jamaican children whose mothers used marijuana during pregnancy. *W.I. Medical Journal, 40,* 120–123.

*HAYNE, H., GRECO-VIGORITO, C., & ROVEE-COLLIER, C. (1993). Forming contextual categories in infancy. *Cognitive Development, 8,* 63–82.

HAYNE, H., ROVEE-COLLIER, C. K., & PERRIS, E. E. (1987). Categorization and memory retrieval by three-month-olds. *Child Development, 58,* 750–767.

HAYNES, H., WHITE, B. L., & HELD, R. (1965). Visual accommodation in human infants. *Science, 148,* 528–530.

HAZEN, N. L., & DURRETT, M. E. (1982). Relationship of security of attachment to exploration and cognitive mapping abilities in 2-year-olds. *Developmental Psychology, 18,* 751–759.

HEBB, D. O. (1949). *The organization of behavior.* New York: Wiley.

HEIBECK, T., & MARKMAN, E. M. (1987). Word learning in children: An examination of fast mapping. *Child Development, 58,* 1021–1034.

HELLER, J. (1987). What do we know about the risk of caffeine consumption in pregnancy? *British Journal of Addiction, 82,* 885–889.

*HENNESSY, E., MARTIN, S., MOSS, P., & MELHUISH, E. (1992). *Children and day care: Lessons from research.* London: Paul Chapman.

HERMAN, J. F., & SIEGEL, A. W. (1978). The development of cognitive mapping of the large-scale environment. *Journal of Experimental Child Psychology, 26,* 389–406.

*HERNANDEZ, D. J. (1988). Demographic trends and the living arrangements of children. In E. M. Hetherington & J. D. Arasteh (Eds.), *Impact of divorce, single parenting and stepparenting on children.* Hillsdale, NJ: Erlbaum.

HERRNSTEIN, R. J. (1971, September). I.Q. *Atlantic Monthly,* pp. 43–64.

HERRNSTEIN, R. J. (1973). *IQ in the meritocracy.* Boston: Little, Brown.

HERSHENSON, M. (1964). Visual discrimination in the human newborn. *Journal of Comparative and Physiological Psychology, 58,* 270–276.

HESS, E. H. (1973). *Imprinting: Early experience and the developmental psychobiology of attachment.* New York: Van Nostrand.

*HESS, E. K., & PETROVICH. S. (1991). Ethology and attachment: A historical perspective. In J. L. Gewirtz & W. M. Kurtines (Eds.), *Intersections with attachment.* Hillsdale, NJ: Erlbaum.

HESS, R. D., CHIH-MEI, C., & McDEVITT, T. M. (1987). Cultural variations in family beliefs about children's performance in mathematics: Comparisons among People's Republic of China, Chinese-American, and Caucasian-American families. *Journal of Educational Psychology, 79,* 179–188.

HESS, R. D., & MIURA, I. T. (1985). Gender differences in enrollment in computer-camps and classes. *Sex Roles, 13,* 193–203.

HETHERINGTON, E. M. (1988). Parents, children, and siblings: Six years after divorce. In R. A. Hinde & J. Stevenson-Hinde (Eds.), *Relationships within families: Mutual influences.* Oxford: Clarendon.

HETHERINGTON, E. M. (1989). Coping with family transitions: Winners, losers, and survivors. *Child Development, 60,* 1–14.

*HETHERINGTON, E. M., & CLINGEMPEEL, W. G. (Eds.). (1992). Coping with marital transitions. *Monographs of the Society for Research in Child Development, 57* (2–3, Serial No. 227).

*HETHERINGTON, E. M., REISS, D., & PLOMIN, R. (Eds.). (1994). *Separate social worlds of siblings: The impact of nonshared environment on development.* Hillsdale, NJ: Erlbaum.

HETHERINGTON, E. M., STANLEY-HAGAN, M., & ANDERSON, E. R. (1989). Marital transitions: A child's perspective. *American Psychologist, 44,* 303–312.

*HEWLETT, B. S. (Ed.). (1992). *Father–child relations: Cultural and biosocial contexts.* New York: Aldine de Gruyter.

*HEYMAN, G. D., DWECK, C. S., & CAIN, K. M. (1992). Young children's vulnerability to self-blame and helplessness: Relationship to beliefs about goodness. *Child Development, 63,* 401–415.

*HEYMAN, J. (1992). Is breast feeding at risk? The challenge of AIDS. In J. M. Mann, D. J. M. Tarantola, & T. W. Netter (Eds.), *AIDS in the world.* Cambridge, MA: Harvard University Press.

HICKMANN, M. (1986). Psychosocial aspects of language acquisition. In P. Fletcher & M. Garman (Eds.), *Language acquisition: Studies in first language acquisition* (2nd ed.). New York: Cambridge University Press.

HICKMANN, M. (1987). The pragmatics of reference in child language: Some issues in developmental theory. In M. Hickmann (Ed.), *Social* and functional approaches to language and thought. Orlando, FL: Academic Press.

HIGGINS, A., POWER, C., & KOHLBERG, L. (1984). The relationship of moral atmosphere to judgments of responsibility. In W. M. Kurtines & J. L. Gewirtz (Eds.), *Morality, moral behavior, and moral development*. New York: Wiley.

HILDEBRANDT, K. A., & FITZGERALD, H. E. (1979). Facial feature determinants and perceived infant attentiveness. *Infant Behavior and Development, 2,* 329–340.

HILGARD, E. R. (1987). *Psychology in America: A historical survey.* San Diego: Harcourt Brace Jovanovich.

HILL, J. P., & LYNCH, M. E. (1983). The intensification of gender-related role expectations during early adolescence. In J. Brooks-Gunn & A. C. Petersen (Eds.), *Girls at puberty: Biological and psychological perspectives.* New York: Plenum.

HINDE, R. A. (1983). Ethology and child development. In M. M. Haith & J. J. Campos (Eds.), *Handbook of child psychology: Vol. 2. Infancy and developmental psychobiology.* New York: Wiley.

HINDE, R. A. (1986). Some implications of evolutionary theory and comparative data for the study of human prosocial and aggressive behavior. In D. Olweus, J. Block, & M. Radke-Yarrow (Eds.), *Development of antisocial and prosocial behavior.* New York: Academic Press.

HINDE, R. A. (1989). Ethological and relationships approaches. In R. Vasta (Ed.), *Annals of child development* (Vol. 6). Greenwich, CT: JAI Press.

*HINDE, R. A., & STEVENSON-HINDE, J. (1990). Attachment: Biological, cultural and individual desiderata. *Human Development, 33,* 62–72.

HINES, M. (1982). Prenatal gonad hormones and sex differences in human behavior. *Psychological Bulletin, 92,* 56–80.

HINES, M., & GORSKI, R. A. (1985). Hormonal influences on the development of neural asymmetries. In D. F. Benson & E. Zaidel (Eds.), *The dual brain: Hemispheric specialization in humans.* New York: Guilford.

*HINES, M., & GREEN, R. (1991). Human hormonal and neural correlates of sex-typed behaviors. *Review of Psychiatry, 10,* 536–555.

HIRSCH, B. J., & RENDERS, R. J. (1986). The challenge of adolescent friendships: A study of Lisa and her friends. In S. E. Hobfolk (Ed.), *Stress, social support, and women.* Washington, DC: Hemisphere.

HIRSH-PASEK, K., TREIMAN, R., & SCHNEI-DERMAN, M. (1984). Brown & Hanlon revisited: Mothers' sensitivity to ungrammatical forms. *Journal of Child Language, 11,* 81–88.

HITTLEMAN, J. H., & DICKES, R. (1979). Sex differences in neonatal eye contact time. *Merrill-Palmer Quarterly, 25,* 171–184.

*HO, D. Y. F. (1987). Fatherhood in Chinese culture. In M. E. Lamb (Ed.), *The father's role: Cross-cultural perspectives.* Hillsdale, NJ: Erlbaum.

*HOCK, E., McBRIDE, S., & GNEZDA, M. T. (1989). Maternal separation anxiety: Mother-infant separation from the maternal perspective. *Child Development, 60,* 793–802.

HOCK, E., MORGAN, K. C., & HOCK, M. D. (1985). Employment decisions made by mothers of infants. *Psychology of Women Quarterly, 9,* 383–402.

HODAPP, R. M., & GOLDFIELD, E. C. (1985). Self- and other regulation during the infancy period. *Developmental Review, 5,* 274–288.

*HOEFFER, B. (1981). Children's acquisition of sex-role behavior in lesbian-mother families. *American Journal of Orthopsychiatry, 5,* 536–544.

HOEK, D., INGRAM, D., & GIBSON, D. (1986). Some possible causes of children's early word overextensions. *Journal of Child Language, 13,* 477–494.

HOFF-GINSBERG, E. (1986). Function and structure in maternal speech: The relation to the child's development of syntax. *Developmental Psychology, 22,* 155–163.

HOFF-GINSBERG, E. (1990). Maternal speech and the child's development of syntax: A further look. *Journal of Child Language, 17,* 85–99.

*HOFF-GINSBERG, E. (1991). Mother–child conversation in different social classes and communicative settings. *Child Development, 62,* 782–796.

HOFF-GINSBERG, E., & SHATZ, M. (1982). Linguistic input and the child's acquisition of language. *Psychological Bulletin, 92,* 3–26.

HOFFERTH, S., & PHILLIPS, D. (1987). Children in the United States, 1970–1995. *Journal of Marriage and the Family, 59,* 559–571.

HOFFMAN, H. S. (1987). Imprinting and the critical period for social attachments: Some laboratory investigations. In M. H. Bornstein (Ed.), *Sensitive periods in development: Interdisciplinary perspectives.* Hillsdale, NJ: Erlbaum.

*HOFFMAN, L. W. (1984). Work, family, and the socialization of the child. In R. D. Parke (Ed.), *The family: Review of child development research* (Vol. 7). Chicago: University of Chicago Press.

*HOFFMAN, L. W. (1989). Effects of maternal employment in the two-parent family. *American Psychologist, 44,* 283–292.

*HOFFMAN, L. W. (1991). The influence of the family environment on personality: Accounting for sibling differences. *Psychological Bulletin, 110,* 187–203.

HOFFMAN, M. L. (1970). Moral development. In P. H. Mussen (Ed.), *Carmichael's manual of child psychology* (3rd ed., Vol. 2). New York: Wiley.

HOFFMAN, M. L. (1981). Perspectives on the difference between understanding people and understanding things: The role of affect. In J. H. Flavell & L. Ross (Eds.), *Social cognitive development.* New York: Cambridge University Press.

HOFFMAN, M. L. (1982). Development of prosocial motivation: Empathy and guilt. In N. Eisenberg-Berg (Ed.), *Development of prosocial behavior.* New York: Academic Press.

HOFFMAN, M. L. (1984a). Empathy, its limitations, and its role in a comprehensive moral theory. In W. M. Kurtines & J. L. Gewirtz (Eds.), *Morality, moral behavior, and moral development.* New York: Wiley.

HOFFMAN, M. L. (1984b). Parent discipline, moral internalization, and development of prosocial motivation. In E. Staub, D. Bar-Tal, J. Karylowski, & J. Reykowski (Eds.), *Development and maintenance of prosocial behavior.* New York: Plenum.

HOFFMAN, M. L. (1987). The contribution of empathy to justice and moral judgment. In N. Eisenberg & J. Strayer (Eds.), *Empathy and its development.* New York: Cambridge University Press.

*HOFFMAN, M. L. (1991). Empathy, social cognition, and moral action. In W. M. Kurtines & J. L. Gewirtz (Eds.), *Handbook of moral behavior and development: Vol. 1. Theory.* Hillsdale, NJ: Erlbaum.

*HOFFMAN, M. L. (1994). Discipline and internalization. *Developmental Psychology, 30,* 26–28.

*HOGGE, W. A. (1990). Teratology. In I. R. Merkatz & J. E. Thompson (Eds.), *New perspectives on prenatal care.* New York: Elsevier.

HOLDEN, C. (1986). High court says no to administration's Baby Doe rules. *Science, 232,* 1595–1596.

HOLDEN, C. (1987). The genetics of personality. *Science, 237,* 598–601.

*HOLMES, K. M., & HOLMES, D. W. (1980). Signed and spoken language development in a hearing child of hearing parents. *Sign Language Studies, 28,* 239–254.

HOLSTEIN, C. (1976). Irreversible, stepwise sequence in the development of moral judgment: A longitudinal study of males and females. *Child Development, 47,* 51–61.

HOLZMAN, P. S., & MATTHYSSE, S. (1990). The genetics of schizophrenia: A review. *Psychological Science, 1,* 279–286.

HONZIK, M. P., McFARLANE, J. W., & ALLEN, L. (1948). The stability of mental test performance between two and eighteen years. *Journal of Experimental Education, 17,* 309–323.

HOOD, K. E., DRAPER, P., CROCKETT, L. J., & PETERSEN, A. C. (1987). The ontogeny and phylogeny of sex differences in development: A biosocial synthesis. In D. B. Carter (Ed.), *Current conceptions of sex roles and sex-typing: Theory and research.* New York: Praeger.

HOOK, E. B. (1973). Behavioral implication of the human XXY genotype. *Science, 179,* 139–150.

HOOK, E. G., & LINDSJO, A. (1978). Down syndrome in live births by single year maternal age interval in a Swedish study: Comparison with results from a New York State study. *American Journal of Human Genetics, 30,* 19–27.

HOOK, J. (1982). Development of equity and altruism in judgments of reward and damage allocation. *Developmental Psychology, 18,* 825–834.

HOOK, J. (1983). The development of children's equity judgments. In R. L. Leahy (Ed.), *The child's construction of social equality.* New York: Academic Press.

HOOKER, D. (1958). *Evidence of prenatal function of the central nervous system in man.* New York: American Museum of Natural History.

HOOKER, K., NESSELROADE, D. W., NESSELROADE, J. R., & LERNER, R. M. (1987). The structure of intraindividual temperament in the context of mother–child dyads: P-technique factor analyses of short-term change. *Developmental Psychology, 23,* 332–346.

*HOOPER, C. (1992). Encircling a mechanism in Alzheimer's disease. *Journal of NIH Research, 4,* 48–54.

HOPKINS, A. (1987). Prescribing in pregnancy: Epilepsy and anticonvulsant drugs. *British Medical Journal, 294,* 497–501.

HORAN, R. F., & ROSSER, R. A. (1984). Multivariable analysis of spatial abilities by sex. *Developmental Review, 4,* 381–411.

*HORGAN, J. (1993, June). Trends in behavioral genetics: Eugenics revisited. *Scientific American,* pp. 123–131.

HORN, J. M. (1983). The Texas Adoption Project: Adopted children and their intellectual resemblance to biological and adoptive parents. *Child Development, 54,* 268–275.

HORNE, A. M., & SAYGER, T. V. (1990). *Treating conduct and oppositional defiant disorders in children.* New York: Pergamon.

HORNIK, R., & GUNNAR, M. R. (1988). A descriptive analysis of infant social referencing. *Child Development, 59,* 626–634.

HOROWITZ, F. D. (1992). John B. Watson's legacy: Learning and environment. *Developmental Psychology, 28,* 360–367.

HORT, B. E., LEINBACH, M. D., & FAGOT, B. I. (1991). Is there coherence among the cognitive components of gender acquisition? *Sex Roles, 24,* 195–207.

HOUSEHOLDER, J., HATCHER, R., BURNS, W., & CHASNOFF, I. (1982). Infants born to narcotic-addicted mothers. *Psychological Bulletin, 92,* 453–468.

HOWE, C. (1981). *Acquiring language in a conversational context.* Orlando, FL: Academic Press.

*HOWE, M. J. A. (1990). *Sense and nonsense about hothouse children: A practical guide for parents and teachers.* Leicester, England: British Psychological Society.

*HOWE, M. L., & COURAGE, M. L. (1993). On resolving the enigma of infantile amnesia. *Psychological Bulletin, 113,* 305–326.

HOWE, M. L., & RABINOWITZ, F. M. (1990). Resource panacea? Or just another day in the developmental forest? *Developmental Review, 10,* 125–154.

HOWES, C. (1983). Patterns of friendship. *Child Development, 54,* 1041–1053.

HOWES, C. (1987a). Peer interaction of young children. *Monographs of the Society for Research in Child Development, 53* (1, Serial No. 217).

HOWES, C. (1987b). Social competence with peers in young children: Developmental sequences. *Developmental Review, 7,* 252–272.

*HOWES, C., & HAMILTON, C. E. (1992). Children's relationships with caregivers: Mothers and child care teachers. *Child Development, 63,* 859–866.

*HOWES, C., & MATHESON, C. C. (1992). Sequences in the development of competent play with peers: Social and social pretend play. *Developmental Psychology, 28,* 961–974.

HOWES, C., & OLENICK, M. (1986). Family and child care influences on toddlers' compliance. *Child Development, 57,* 202–216.

*HOWES, C., PHILLIPS, D. A., & WHITEBOOK, M. (1992). Thresholds of quality: Implications for the social development of children in center-based child care. *Child Development, 63,* 449–460.

HOWES, C., & RUBENSTEIN, J. L. (1979). *Influences on toddler peer behavior in two types of daycare.* Unpublished manuscript, Harvard University, Cambridge, MA.

*HOWES, C., UNGER, O., & SEIDNER, L. B. (1989). Social pretend play in toddlers.

Parallels with social play and with solitary pretend. *Child Development, 60,* 77–84.

HOY, E. A., BILL, J. M., & SYKES, D. H. (1988). Very low birthweight: A long-term developmental impairment? *International Journal of Behavioral Development, 11,* 37–67.

HOYLES, M. (1979). Childhood in historical perspective. In M. Hoyles (Ed.), *Changing childhood.* London: Writers and Readers Publishing Cooperative.

HRONSKY, S. L., & EMORY, E. K. (1987). Neurobehavioral effects of caffeine on the neonate. *Infant Behavior and Development, 10,* 61–80.

*HSU, L. K. G. (1990). *Eating disorders.* New York: Guilford.

*HUDLEY, C., & GRAHAM, S. (1993). An attributional intervention to reduce peer-directed aggression among African-American boys. *Child Development, 64,* 124–138.

HUDSON, J. A. (1990a). Constructive processing in children's event memory. *Developmental Psychology, 26,* 180–187.

*HUDSON, J. A. (1990b). The emergence of autobiographical memory in mother–child conversation. In R. Fivush & J. A. Hudson (Eds.), *Knowing and remembering in young children.* Hillsdale, NJ: Erlbaum.

HUDSON, J. A., & NELSON, K. (1983). Effects of script structure on children's story recall. *Developmental Psychology, 19,* 625–635.

*HUDSON, J. A., & SIDOTI, F. (1988, April). *Two-year-olds' autobiographic memory in mother–child conversation.* Paper presented at the International Conference on Infant Studies, Washington, DC.

HUESMANN, L. R., ERON, L. D., KLEIN, R., BRICE, P., & FISCHER, P. (1983). Mitigating the imitation of aggressive behaviors by changing children's attitudes about media violence. *Journal of Personality and Social Psychology, 44,* 899–910.

HUESMANN, L. R., LAGERSPETZ, K., & ERON, L. D. (1984). Intervening variables in the television violence–aggression relation: Evidence from two countries. *Developmental Psychology, 20,* 746–775.

*HUESMANN, L. R., & MILLER, L. S. Long-term effects of repeated exposure to media violence in childhood. In L. R. Huesmann (Ed.), *Aggressive behavior: Current perspectives.* New York: Plenum.

*HUMPHREY, D. E., & HUMPHREY, G. K. (1987). Sex differences in infant reaching. *Neuropsychologia, 25,* 971–975.

HUNT, J. McV. (1961). *Intelligence and experience.* New York: Ronald Press.

*HUNTINGTON'S DISEASE COLLABORATIVE RESEARCH GROUP. (1993). A novel gene containing a trinucleotide repeat that is expanded and unstable on Huntington's disease chromosomes. *Cell, 72,* 971–983.

HUSTON, A. C. (1983). Sex-typing. In E. M. Hetherington (Ed.), *Handbook of child psychology: Vol. 4. Socialization, personality, and social development.* New York: Wiley.

HUSTON, A. C. (1985). The development of sex typing: Themes from recent research. *Developmental Review, 5,* 1–17.

*HUSTON, A. C. (Ed.). (1992). *Children in poverty: Child development and public policy.* New York: Cambridge University Press.

HUSTON, A. C., & ALVAREZ, M. M. (1990). The socialization context of gender role development in early adolescence. In R. Montemayor, G. R. Adams, & T. P. Gullotta (Eds.), *From childhood to adolescence: A transitional period?* Newbury Park, CA: Sage.

HUSTON, A. C., CARPENTER, J. C., ATWATER, J. B., & JOHNSON, L. M. (1986). Gender, adult structuring of activities, and social behavior in middle childhood. *Child Development, 57,* 1200–1209.

HUSTON, A. C., McLOYD, V. C., GARCIA-COLL, C. (1994). Children and poverty: Issues in contemporary research. *Child Development, 65,* 275–282.

HUSTON, A. C., WRIGHT, J. C., RICE, M. L., KERKMAN, D., & ST. PETERS, H. (1990). Development of television viewing patterns in early childhood: A longitudinal analysis. *Developmental Psychology, 26,* 409–420.

*HUTCHINS, E. (1983). Understanding Micronesian navigation. In D. Gentner & A. Stevens (Eds.), *Mental models.* Hillsdale, NJ: Erlbaum.

HUTT, C. (1972). *Males and females.* Baltimore: Penguin.

HUTTENLOCHER, J., HAIGHT, W., BRYK, A., SELTZER, M., & LYONS, T. (1991). Early vocabulary growth: Relation to language input and gender. *Developmental Psychology, 27,* 236–248.

HUTTENLOCHER, J., SMILEY, P., & CHARNEY, R. (1983). Emergence of action categories in the child: Evidence from verb meanings. *Psychological Review, 90,* 72–93.

*HUTTENLOCHER, P. R. (1990). Morphometric study of human cerebral cortex development. *Neuropsychologia, 28,* 517–527.

HUXLEY, A. (1932). *Brave new world.* New York: Harper and Brothers.

HYDE, J. S. (1984). How large are gender differences in aggression? A developmental meta-analysis. *Developmental Psychology, 20,* 722–736.

HYDE, J. S. (1986). Gender differences in aggression. In J. S. Hyde & M. C. Linn (Eds.), *The psychology of gender differences: Advances through meta-analysis.* Baltimore: Johns Hopkins University Press.

*HYDE, J. S., FENNEMA, E., & LAMON, S. J. (1990). Gender differences in mathematics performance: A meta-analysis. *Psychological Bulletin, 107,* 139–153.

*HYDE, J. S., & LINN, M. C. (1988). Gender differences in verbal ability: A meta-analysis. *Psychological Bulletin, 104,* 53–69.

HYLTENSTAM, K., & OBLER, L. (Eds.). (1989). *Bilingualism across the lifespan: Aspects of acquisition, maturity and loss.* Cambridge: Cambridge University Press.

HYMEL, S. (1983). Preschool children's peer relations: Issues in sociometric assessment. *Merrill-Palmer Quarterly, 29,* 237–260.

HYMEL, S., WAGNER, E., & BUTLER, L. J. (1990). Reputational bias: View from the peer group. In S. R. Asher & J. D. Coie (Eds.), *Peer rejection in childhood.* New York: Cambridge University Press.

IANNOTTI, R. (1978). Effect of role-taking experiences on role taking, empathy, altruism, and aggression. *Developmental Psychology, 14,* 119–124.

IDE, J. K., PARKERSON, J., HAERTEL, G. D., & WALBERG, H. J. (1981). Peer group influence on educational outcomes: A quantitative synthesis. *Journal of Educational Psychology, 73,* 472–484.

IMMELMANN, K., & SUOMI, S. J. (1981). Sensitive phases in development. In K. Immelmann, G. W. Barlow, L. Petrinovich, & M. Main (Eds.), *Behavioral development: The Bielefeld interdisciplinary project.* Cambridge: Cambridge University Press.

INHELDER, B., & PIAGET, J. (1958). *The growth of logical thinking from childhood to adolescence.* New York: Basic Books.

INHELDER, B., & PIAGET, J. (1964). *The early growth of logic in the child.* New York: Norton.

INTERNATIONAL ASSOCIATION FOR THE EVALUATION OF EDUCATIONAL ACHIEVEMENT. (1985). *Second study of mathematics: Summary report, United States.* Urbana-Champaign, IL: U.S. National Coordinating Center.

*ISABELLA, R. A. (1993). Origins of attachment: Maternal interactive behavior across the first year. *Child Development, 64,* 605–621.

ISABELLA, R. A., & BELSKY, J. (1991). Interactional synchrony and the origins of infant–mother attachment: A replication study. *Child Development, 62,* 373–384.

ISABELLA, R. A., BELSKY, J., & vonEYE, A. (1989). Origins of infant–mother attachment. An examination of interactional synchrony during the infant's first year. *Developmental Psychology, 25,* 12–21.

ISTVAN, J. (1986). Stress, anxiety, and birth outcomes: A critical review of the evidence. *Psychological Bulletin, 100,* 331–348.

*JACKENDOFF, R. (1987). *Consciousness and the computational mind.* New York: Academic Press.

JACKLIN, C. N. (1981). Methodological issues in the study of sex-related differences. *Developmental Review, 1,* 266–273.

JACKLIN, C. N. (1989). Female and male: Issues of gender. *American Psychologist, 44,* 127–133.

JACKLIN, C. N., DiPIETRO, J. A., & MACCOBY, E. E. (1984). Sex-typing behavior and sex-typing pressure in child/parent interactions. *Archives of Sexual Behavior, 13,* 413–425.

*JACKLIN, C. N., WILCOX, K. T., & MACCOBY, E. E. (1988). Neonatal sex steroid hormones and intellectual abilities of six year old boys and girls. *Developmental Psychobiology, 21,* 567–574.

*JACKSON, J. F. (1993). Multiple caregiving among African Americans and infant attachment: The need for an emic approach. *Human Development, 36,* 87–102.

*JACOBS, J. E. (1991). Influence of gender stereotypes on parent and child mathematics attitudes. *Journal of Educational Psychology, 83,* 518–527.

*JACOBSEN, T., EDELSTEIN, W., & HOFMANN, V. (1994). A longitudinal study of the relation between representations of attachment in childhood and cognitive functioning in childhood and adolescence. *Developmental Psychology, 30,* 112–124.

JACOBSON, A. G. (1966). Inductive processes in embryonic development. *Science, 152,* 25–34.

JACOBSON, J. L., & JACOBSON, S. W. (1988). New methodologies for assessing the effects of prenatal toxic exposure on cognitive functioning in humans. In M. Evans (Ed.), *Toxic contaminants and ecosystem health: A Great Lakes focus.* New York: Wiley.

*JACOBSON, J. L., JACOBSON, S. W., PADGETT, R. J., BRUMITT, G. A., & BILLINGS, R. L. (1992). Effects of prenatal PCB exposure on cognitive processing efficiency and sustained attention. *Developmental Psychology, 28,* 297–306.

JACOBSON, J. L., & WILLE, D. E. (1986). The influence of attachment pattern on developmental changes in peer interaction from the toddler to the preschool period. *Child Development, 57,* 338–347.

JACOBSON, S., FEIN, G. G., JACOBSON, J. L., SCHWARTZ, P. M., & DOWLER, J. K. (1984). Neonatal correlates of prenatal exposure to smoking, caffeine, and alcohol. *Infant Behavior and Development, 7,* 253–265.

JACOBSON, S., FEIN, G. G., JACOBSON, J. L., SCHWARTZ, P. M., & DOWLER, J. K. (1985). The effect of intrauterine PCB exposure on visual recognition memory. *Child Development, 56,* 853–860.

JAEGER, E., & WEINRAUB, M. (1990). Early nonmaternal care and infant attachment: In search of process. In K. McCartney (Ed.), *New directions for child development: No. 49. Child care and maternal employment: A social ecology approach.* San Francisco: Jossey-Bass.

JAKOBSON, R., & WAUGH, L. (1979). *The sound shape of language.* Bloomington: Indiana University Press.

*JAMES, W. (1890). *Principles of psychology.* New York: Holt.

JAMES, W. (1892). *Psychology: The briefer course.* New York: Holt.

JAMISON, W. (1977). Developmental inter-relationships among concrete operational tasks: An investigation of Piaget's stage concept. *Journal of Experimental Child Psychology, 24,* 235–253.

*JANKOWIAK, W. (1992). Father–child relations in urban China. In B. S. Hewlett (Ed.), *Father–child relations: Cultural and biosocial contexts.* New York: Aldine de Gruyter.

JAROFF, L. (1989, March 20). The gene hunt. *Time,* pp. 62–67.

JEFFERS, V. W., & LORE, R. K. (1979). Let's play at my house: Effects of the home environment on the social behavior of children. *Child Development, 50,* 837–841.

*JEFFREYS, A. J., BROOKFIELD, J. F. Y., & SEMEONOFF, R. (1992). Positive identification of an immigration test-case using human DNA fingerprints. *Journal of NIH Research, 4,* 81–87.

JENCKS, C. (1972). *Inequality.* New York: Basic Books.

JENNINGS, K. D. (1975). People vs. object orientation, social behavior, and intellectual abilities in preschool children. *Developmental Psychology, 11,* 511–519.

*JENNINGS, K. D. (1991). Early development of mastery motivation and its relation to the self-concept. In M. Bullock (Ed.), *The development of*

intentional action: Cognitive, motivational, and interactive process.* Basel: Karger.

JENSEN, A. R. (1969). How much can we boost IQ and scholastic achievement? *Harvard Educational Review, 39,* 1–123.

JENSEN, A. R. (1972). *Genetics and education.* New York: Harper & Row.

JENSEN, A. R. (1973). *Educability and group differences.* New York: Harper & Row.

JENSEN, A. R. (1980). *Bias in mental testing.* New York: Free Press.

JENSEN, A. R. (1981). *Straight talk about mental tests.* New York: Free Press.

JERISON, H. J. (1982). The evolution of biological intelligence. In R. J. Sternberg (Ed.), *Handbook of human intelligence.* New York: Cambridge University Press.

JESSOR, R., & JESSOR, S. L. (1977). *Problem behavior and psychosocial development.* New York: Academic Press.

JOFFE, J. M. (1969). *Prenatal determinants of behavior.* Oxford: Pergamon.

JOHANSSEN, G. (1973). Visual perception of biological motion and a model of its analysis. *Perception and Psychophysics, 14,* 201–211.

JOHNSON, D. B. (1983). Self-recognition in infants. *Infant Behavior and Development, 6,* 211–222.

JOHNSON, E. S., & MEADE, A. C. (1987). Developmental patterns of spatial ability: An early sex difference. *Child Development, 58,* 725–740.

*JOHNSON, J. (1991). Constructive processes in bilingualism and their cognitive growth effects. In E. Bialystok (Ed.), *Language processing in bilingual children.* Cambridge: Cambridge University Press.

*JOHNSON, M. H., DZIURAWIEC, S., BARTRIP, J., & MORTON, J. (1992). The effects of movement of internal features on infants' preferences for face-like stimuli. *Infant Behavior and Development, 15,* 129–136.

JOHNSTON, J. R. (1986). Cognitive prerequisites: The evidence from children learning English. In D. I. Slobin (Ed.), *The crosslinguistic study of language acquisition: Vol. 2. Theoretical issues.* Hillsdale, NJ: Erlbaum.

JONES, C., & ADAMSON, L. (1987). Language use in mother–child and mother–child–sibling interactions. *Child Development, 58,* 356–366.

*JONES, C., & LOPEZ, R. (1990). Drug abuse and pregnancy. In I. R. Merkatz & J. E. Thompson (Eds.), *New perspectives on prenatal care.* New York: Elsevier.

JONES, D. C. (1985). Persuasive appeals and responses to appeals among friends and acquaintances. *Child Development, 56,* 757–763.

JONES, G. E., & DEMBO, M. H. (1989). Age and sex role differences in intimate friendships during childhood and adolescence. *Merrill-Palmer Quarterly, 35,* 445–462.

*JONES, K. L., JOHNSON, K. A., & CHAMBERS, C. C. (1992). Pregnancy outcome in women treated with phenobarbital monotherapy. *Teratology, 45,* 452–453.

JONES, K. L., LACRO, R. V., JOHNSON, K. A., & ADAMS, J. (1988). Pregnancy outcome in women treated with Tegretol. *Teratology, 37,* 468–469.

JONES, K. L., SMITH, D. W., ULLELAND, C. N., & STREISSGUTH, A. P. (1973). Pattern of malformation in offspring of chronic alcoholic mothers. *Lancet, 1,* 1267–1271.

JONES, M. C. (1924). A laboratory study of fear: The case of Peter. *Pedagogical Seminary, 31,* 308–315.

JONES, M. C. (1957). The later careers of boys who were early- or late-maturing. *Child Development, 28,* 113–128.

*JONES, S. S., COLLINS, K., & HONG, H. (1991). An audience effect on smile production in 10-month-old infants. *Psychological Science, 2,* 45–49.

*JONES, S. S., & RIDGE, B. (1991, April). *Mouth opening and tongue protrusion are exploratory behaviors in very young infants.* Paper presented at the meeting of the Society for Research in Child Development, Seattle.

*JONES, S. S., SMITH, L. B., & LANDAU, B. (1991). Object properties and knowledge in early lexical learning. *Child Development, 62,* 499–516.

JOOS, S. K., POLLITT, E., MUELLER, W. H., & ALBRIGHT, D. L. (1983). The Bacon Chow study: Maternal nutritional supplementation and infant behavioral development. *Child Development, 54,* 669–676.

JOSE, P. E. (1990). Just world reasoning in children's immanent justice judgments. *Child Development, 61,* 1024–1033.

*JUSCZYK, P. W., PISONI, D. B., & MULLENIX, J. (1992). Some consequences of stimulus variability on speech processing by two-month-old infants. *Cognition, 43,* 253–291.

*JUSCZYK, P. W., CUTLER, A., & REDANZ, N. J. (1993). Infants' preference for the predominant stress patterns of English words. *Child Development, 64,* 675–687.

KABACK, M. M. (1982). Screening for reproductive counseling: Social, ethical, and medicolegal issues in the Tay-Sachs disease experience. In *Human genetics: Part B. Medical aspects.* New York: Alan R. Liss.

KAGAN, J. (1970). Attention and psychological change in the young child. *Science, 170,* 826–832.

KAGAN, J. (1984). *The nature of the child.* New York: Basic Books.

KAGAN, J. (1989). Temperamental contributions to social behavior. *American Psychologist, 44,* 668–674.

*KAGAN, J. (1991). The theoretical utility of constructs for self. *Developmental Review, 11,* 244–250.

*KAGAN, J., ARCUS, D., & SNIDMAN, N. (1993). The idea of temperament: Where do we go from here? In R. Plomin & G. E. McClearn (Eds.), Nature, nurture, and psychology. Washington, DC: APA.

KAGAN, J., REZNICK, J. S., & GIBBONS, J. (1989). Inhibited and uninhibited types of children. *Child Development, 60,* 838–845.

KAGAN, J., REZNICK, J. S., & SNIDMAN, N. (1987). The physiology and psychology of behavioral inhibition. *Child Development, 58,* 1459–1473.

KAGAN, J., REZNICK, J. S., & SNIDMAN, N.

(1988). Biological bases of childhood shyness. *Science, 240,* 167–171.

KAGAN, J., REZNICK, J. S., SNIDMAN, N., GIBBONS, J., & JOHNSON, M. O. (1988). Childhood derivatives of inhibition and lack of inhibition to the unfamiliar. *Child Development, 59,* 1580–1589.

*KAGAN, J., & SNIDMAN, N. (1991). Infant predictors of inhibited and uninhibited profiles. *Psychological Science, 2,* 40–44.

*KAGAN, J., SNIDMAN, N., & ARCUS, D. M. (1992). Initial reactions to unfamiliarity. *Current Directions in Psychological Science, 1,* 171–174.

KAHAN, L. D., & RICHARDS, D. D. (1986). The effects of context on referential communication strategies. *Child Development, 57,* 1130–1141.

*KAIL, R. (1991). Developmental change in speed of processing during childhood and adolescence. *Psychological Bulletin, 109,* 490–501.

*KAIL, R. (1992). Evidence for global developmental change is intact. *Journal of Experimental Child Psychology, 54,* 308–314.

KAIL, R., & BISANZ, J. (1982). Cognitive development: An information-processing perspective. In R. Vasta (Ed.), *Strategies and techniques of child study.* New York: Academic Press.

*KAIL, R., & BISANZ, J. (1992). The information-processing perspective on cognitive development in childhood and adolescence. In R. J. Sternberg & C. A. Berg (Eds.), *Intellectual development.* New York: Cambridge University Press.

*KAIL, R., & PARK, Y. (1992). Global developmental change in processing time. *Merrill-Palmer Quarterly, 38,* 525–541.

*KAIL, R., & PARK, Y. (1994). Processing time, articulation time, and memory span. *Journal of Experimental Child Psychology, 57,* 281–291.

KAIL, R., & PELLEGRINO, J. W. (1985). *Human intelligence: Perspectives and prospects.* New York: W. H. Freeman.

KAIL, R., & SIEGEL, A. W. (1977). Sex differences in retention of verbal and spatial characteristics of stimuli. *Journal of Experimental Child Psychology, 23,* 341–347.

*KAITZ, M., GOOD, A., ROKEM, A. M., & EIDELMAN, A. I. (1987). Mothers' recognition of their newborns by olfactory cues. *Developmental Psychology, 20,* 587–591.

*KAITZ, M., LAPIDOT, P., BRONNER, R., & EIDELMAN, A. I. (1992). Parturient women can recognize their infants by touch. *Developmental Psychology, 28,* 35–39.

*KAITZ, M., MEIROV, H., LANDMAN, I., & EIDELMAN, A. I. (1993). Infant recognition by tactile cues. *Infant Behavior and Development, 16,* 333–341.

KAITZ, M., MESCHULACH-SARFATY, O., AUERBACH, J., & EIDELMAN, A. (1988). A reexamination of newborns' ability to imitate facial expressions. *Developmental Psychology, 24,* 3–7.

KALER, S. R., & KOPP, C. B. (1990). Compliance and comprehension in very young toddlers. *Child Development, 61,* 1997–2003.

KALLMAN, F. J. (1953). *Heredity in health and mental disorder.* New York: Norton.

KAMII, C. (1985). *Young children reinvent arith-*

metic: Implications of Piaget's theory. New York: Teachers College Press.

KAMII, C. (1989). *Young children continue to reinvent arithmetic.* New York: Teachers College Press.

*KAMII, C., & DeVRIES, R. (1993). *Physical knowledge in preschool education: Implications of Piaget's theory* (rev. ed.). New York: Teachers College Press.

KAMIN, L. (1974). *The science and politics of IQ.* Hillsdale, NJ: Erlbaum.

KAMIN, L. (1981). Commentary. In S. Scarr (Ed.), *Race, social class, and individual differences in IQ.* Hillsdale, NJ: Erlbaum.

KAMPTNER, L., KRAFT, R. H., & HARPER, L. V. (1984). Lateral specialization and social-verbal development in preschool children. *Brain and Cognition, 3,* 42–50.

*KANDEL, E. R., & O'DELL, T. J. (1992). Are adult mechanisms also used for development? *Science, 258,* 243–245.

KARMEL, B. Z., & MAISEL, E. B. (1975). A neuronal activity model for infant visual attention. In L. B. Cohen & P. Salapatek (Eds.), *Infant perception: From sensation to cognition: Vol. 1. Basic visual processes.* New York: Academic Press.

KARMILOFF-SMITH, A. (1987). Function and process in comparing language and cognition. In M. Hickmann (Ed.), *Social and functional approaches to language and thought.* Orlando, FL: Academic Press.

*KARMILOFF-SMITH, A. (1992). *Beyond modularity: A developmental perspective on cognitive science.* Cambridge, MA: MIT Press.

KARNIOL, R. (1978). Children's use of intention cues in evaluating behavior. *Psychological Bulletin, 85,* 76–85.

KARNIOL, R. (1980). A conceptual analysis of immanent justice responses in children. *Child Development, 51,* 118–130.

KARNIOL, R., & MILLER, D. T. (1981). The development of self-control in children. In S. S. Brehm, S. M. Kassin, & F. X. Gibbons (Eds.), *Developmental social psychology: Theory and research.* New York: Oxford University Press.

*KARSON, E. M., POLVINO, W., & ANDERSON, W. F. (1992). Prospects for human gene therapy. *Journal of Reproductive Medicine, 37,* 508–514.

KATCHADOURIAN, H. (1977). *The biology of adolescence.* San Francisco: Freeman.

KATZ, P. A. (1986). Modification of children's gender stereotyped behavior: General issues and research considerations. *Sex Roles, 14,* 591–602.

KATZ, P. A. (1987). Variations in family constellation: Effects of gender schemata. In L. S. Liben & M. L. Signorella (Eds.), *New directions for child development: Vol. 38. Children's gender schemata.* San Francisco: Jossey-Bass.

KATZ, P. A., & BOSWELL, S. L. (1986). Flexibility and traditionality in children's gender roles. *Genetic, Social, and General Psychology Monographs, 112,* 105–147.

*KATZ, P. A., & KSANSNAK, K. R. (1994). Developmental aspects of gender role flexibility and traditionality in middle childhood and adolescence. *Developmental Psychology, 30,* 272–282.

*KATZ, P. A., & WALSH, P. V. (1991). Modification of children's gender-stereotyped behavior. *Child Development, 62,* 338–351.

KAY, D. A., & ANGLIN, J. M. (1982). Overextension and underextension in the child's expressive and receptive speech. *Journal of Child Language, 9,* 83–98.

KAYE, H. (1967). Infant sucking behavior and its modification. In L. P. Lipsitt & C. C. Spiker (Eds.), *Advances in child development and behavior* (Vol. 3). New York: Academic Press.

KAYE, K. (1980). Why we don't talk "baby talk" to babies. *Journal of Child Language, 7,* 489–507.

KAYE, K. (1982). *The mental and social life of babies.* Chicago: University of Chicago Press.

KAZDIN, A. E. (1987). *Conduct disorders in childhood and adolescence.* Newbury Park, CA: Sage.

KEARSLEY, R. B. (1973). The newborn's response to auditory stimulation: A demonstration of orienting and defensive behavior. *Child Development, 44,* 582–590.

KEASEY, C. B. (1971). Social participation as a factor in the moral development of preadolescents. *Developmental Psychology, 5,* 216–220.

KEATING, D. P. (1988). Byrnes' reformulation of Piaget's formal operations: Is what's left what's right? Commentary. *Developmental Review, 8,* 376–384.

*KEE, D. W., & GUTTENTAG, R. (1994). Resource requirements of knowledge access and recall benefits of associative strategies. *Journal of Experimental Child Psychology, 57,* 211–223.

*KEEFE, M. R. (1987). Comparison of neonatal nighttime sleep–wake patterns in nursery versus rooming-in environments. *Nursing Research, 36,* 140–144.

*KEIL, F. C. (1992). The origins of an autonomous biology. In M. R. Gunnar & M. Maratsos (Eds.), *Minnesota symposia on child psychology: Vol. 25. Modularity and constraints in language and cognition.* Hillsdale, NJ: Erlbaum.

KELLER, A., FORD, L. H., & MEACHAM, J. A. (1978). Dimensions of self-concept in preschool children. *Developmental Psychology, 14,* 483–489.

KELLER, M., & WOOD, P. (1989). Development of friendship reasoning: A study of interindividual differences in intraindividual change. *Developmental Psychology, 25,* 820–826.

KELLMAN, P. J., & SPELKE, E. S. (1983). Perception of partly occluded objects in infancy. *Cognitive Psychology, 15,* 483–524.

KELLMAN, P. J., SPELKE, E. S., & SHORT, K. R. (1986). Infant perception of object unity from translatory motion in depth and vertical translation. *Child Development, 57,* 72–86.

*KELLMAN, P. J., & VON HOFSTEN, C. (1992). The world of the moving infant: Perception of motion, stability, and space. In C. Rovee-Collier & L. P. Lipsitt (Eds.), *Advances in infancy research* (Vol. 7). Norwood, NJ: Ablex.

*KELLOGG, W. N., & KELLOGG, L. A. (1933). *The ape and the child.* New York: McGraw-Hill.

KENDALL, P. C., & BRASWELL, L. (1985). *Cognitive-behavioral therapy for impulsive children.* New York: Guilford.

KENDLER, K. S., & ROBINETTE, C. D. (1983). Schizophrenia in the National Academy of Sciences–National Research Council twin registry: A 16-year update. *American Journal of Psychiatry, 140,* 1551–1563.

KENT, R. D., & BAUER, H. R. (1985).

Vocalizations of one-year-olds. *Journal of Child Language, 12,* 491–526.

*KERKMAN, D. D., & SIEGLER, R. S. (1991). Individual differences and adaptive flexibility in lower-income children's strategy choices. *Learning and Individual Differences, 5,* 113–136.

*KERR, M., LAMBERT, W. W., STATTIN, H., & KLACKENBERG-LARSSON, I. (1994). Stability of inhibition in a Swedish longitudinal sample. *Child Development, 65,* 138–146.

KESSEN, W., HAITH, M. M., & SALAPATEK, P. H. (1970). Human infancy: A bibliography and guide. In P. H. Mussen (Ed.), *Carmichael's manual of child psychology* (3rd ed., Vol. 1). New York: Wiley.

KESSEN, N., & LEUTZENDORFF, A. M. (1963). The effect of non-nutritive sucking on movement in the human newborn. *Journal of Comparative and Physiological Psychology, 56,* 69–72.

*KIMBALL, M. M. (1989). A new perspective on women's math achievement. *Psychological Bulletin, 105,* 198–214.

*KING, M. C., & WILSON, A. C. (1975). Evolution at two levels in humans and chimpanzees. *Science, 188,* 107–116.

*KIRKPATRICK, M., SMITH, C., & ROY, R. (1981). Lesbian mothers and their children: A comparative survey. *American Journal of Orthopsychiatry, 51,* 545–551.

KISER, L. J., BATES, J. E., MASLIN, C. A., & BAYLES, K. (1986). Mother–infant play at six months as a predictor of attachment security at thirteen months. *Journal of the American Academy of Child Psychiatry, 25,* 68–75.

KISILEVSKY, B. S., & MUIR, D. W. (1984). Neonatal habituation and dishabituation to tactile stimulation during sleep. *Developmental Psychology, 20,* 367–373.

*KISTER, M. C., & PATTERSON, C. J. (1980). Children's conceptions of the causes of illness: Understanding of contagion and use of immanent justice. *Child Development, 51,* 839–846.

KLAHR, D. (1989). Information processing approaches to cognitive development. In R. Vasta (Ed.), *Annals of child development* (Vol. 6). Greenwich, CT: JAI Press.

*KLAHR, D. (1992). Information-processing approaches to cognitive development. In M. H. Bornstein & M. E. Lamb (Eds.), *Developmental psychology: An advanced textbook* (3rd ed.). Hillsdale, NJ: Erlbaum.

KLAHR, D., & ROBINSON, M. (1981). Formal assessment of problem solving and planning processes in preschool children. *Cognitive Psychology, 13,* 113–148.

KLAHR, D., & WALLACE, J. G. (1976). *Cognitive development: An information processing view.* Hillsdale, NJ: Erlbaum.

KLAUS, M. H., & KENNELL, J. H. (1976). *Maternal–infant bonding.* St. Louis: Mosby.

KLEINER, K. A., & BANKS, M. S. (1987). Stimulus energy does not account for 2-month olds' face preferences. *Journal of Experimental Psychology: Human Perception and Performance, 13,* 594–600.

KLEMCHUK, H. P., BOND, L. A., & HOWELL, D. C. (1990). Coherence and correlates of level 1 perspective taking in young children. *Merrill-Palmer Quarterly, 36,* 369–387.

KLIMES-DOUGAN, B., & KISTNER, J. (1990). Physically abused preschoolers' responses to peers' distress. *Developmental Psychology, 26,* 599–602.

KLINNERT, M. D., CAMPOS, J. J., SORCE, J. F., EMDE, R. N., & SVEJDA, M. (1983). Emotions as behavior regulators: Social referencing in infancy. In R. Plutchik & H. Kellerman (Eds.), *Emotions in early development: Vol. 2. The emotions.* New York: Academic Press.

KLINNERT, M. D., SORCE, J. F., EMDE, R. N., STENBERG, C., & GAENSBAUER, T. (1984). Continuities and change in early emotional life: Maternal perceptions of surprise, fear, and anger. In R. N. Emde & R. J. Harmon (Eds.), *Continuities and discontinuities in development.* New York: Plenum.

KNIGHT, G. P., BERNING, A. L., WILSON, S. L., & CHAO, C. (1987). The effects of information-processing demands and social-situational factors on the social decision making of children. *Journal of Experimental Child Psychology, 43,* 244–259.

*KOCH, R., & De La CRUZ, F. (1991). The danger of birth defects in the children of women with phenylketonuria. *Journal of NIH Research, 3,* 61–63.

*KOCHANSKA, G. (1991a). Patterns of inhibition to the unfamiliar in children of normal and affectively ill mothers. *Child Development, 62,* 250–263.

*KOCHANSKA, G. (1991b). Socialization and temperament in the development of guilt and conscience. *Child Development, 62,* 1379–1392.

*KOCHANSKA, G. (1993). Toward a synthesis of parental socialization and child temperament in early development of conscience. *Child Development, 64,* 325–347.

*KOCHANSKA, G., & RADKE-YARROW, M. (1992). Inhibition in toddlerhood and the dynamics of the child's interaction with an unfamiliar peer at age five. *Child Development, 63,* 325–335.

KOENIGSKNECT, R. A., & FRIEDMAN, P. (1976). Syntax development in boys and girls. *Child Development, 47,* 1109–1115.

*KOHLBERG, K. (1993). Human embryo cloning reported. *Science, 262,* 652–653.

KOHLBERG, L. (1969). Stage and sequence: The cognitive-developmental approach to socialization. In D. A. Goslin (Ed.), *Handbook of socialization theory and research.* Chicago: Rand McNally.

KOHLBERG, L. (1984). *The psychology of moral development: The nature and validity of moral stages.* San Francisco: Harper & Row.

KOHLBERG, L. (1986). A current statement on some theoretical issues. In S. Modgil & C. Modgil (Eds.), *Lawrence Kohlberg: Consensus and controversy.* Philadelphia: Falmer.

KOHLBERG, L. (1987). The development of moral judgment and moral action. In L. Kohlberg (Ed.), *Child psychology and childhood education: A cognitive-developmental view.* New York: Longman.

KOHLBERG, L., & CANDEE, D. (1984). The relationship of moral judgment to moral action. In W. M. Kurtines & J. L. Gewirtz (Eds.), *Morality, moral behavior, and moral development.* New York: Wiley.

KOHLBERG, L., & KRAMER, R. (1969). Continuities and discontinuities in childhood and adult moral development. *Human Development, 12,* 93–120.

KOHLBERG, L., LEVINE, C., & HEWER, A. (1983). *Moral stages: A current formulation and a response to critics.* Basel, Switzerland: Karger.

KOHLBERG, L., & ULLIAN, D. Z. (1974). Stages in the development of psychosexual concepts and attitudes. In R. C. Friedman, R. M. Richart, & R. L. VandeWiele (Eds.), *Sex differences in behavior.* New York: Wiley.

KOHLBERG, L., YAEGER, J., & HJERTHOLM, E. (1968). Private speech: Four studies and a review of theories: *Child Development, 39,* 817–826.

KOHLER, F. W., & FOWLER, S. A. (1985). Training prosocial behaviors to young children: An analysis of reciprocity with untrained peers. *Journal of Applied Behavior Analysis, 18,* 187–200.

*KOHLER, F. W., & STRAIN, P. S. (1990). Peer assisted interventions: Early promises, notable achievements, and future aspirations. *Clinical Psychology Review, 10,* 441–452.

*KOHLER, F. W., SCHWARTZ, I., CROSS, J., & FOWLER, S. A. (1989). The effects of two alternating intervention roles on independent work skills. *Education and Treatment of Children, 12,* 205–218.

KOLATA, G. (1983). Fetal surgery for neural defects. *Science, 221,* 441.

KOLATA, G. (1986). Genetic screening raises questions for employers and insurers. *Science, 232,* 317–319.

KOLATA, G. (1989, April 18). Survival of the fetus: A barrier is reached. *New York Times,* 25.

KOLB, B. (1989). Brain development, plasticity, and behavior. *American Psychologist, 44,* 1203–1212.

KONNER, M. J. (1976). Maternal care, infant behavior and development among the Kung. In R. B. Lee & I. DeVore (Eds.), *Kalahari hunter-gatherers.* Cambridge, MA: Harvard University Press.

KONTOS, D. (1978). A study of the effects of extended mother–infant contact on maternal behavior at one and three months. *Birth and the Family Journal, 5,* 133–140.

KOPP, C. B. (1979). Perspectives on infant motor system development. In M. Bornstein & W. Kessen (Eds.), *Psychological development from infancy: Image to intention.* Hillsdale, NJ: Erlbaum.

KOPP, C. B. (1983). Risk factors in development. In M. M. Haith & J. J. Campos (Eds.), *Handbook of child psychology: Vol. 2. Infancy and developmental psychobiology.* New York: Wiley.

*KOPP, C. B. (1991). Young children's progression to self-regulation. In M. Bullock (Ed.), *The development of intentional action: Cognitive, motivational, and interactive process.* Basel, Switzerland: Karger.

KOPP, C. B., & KALER, S. R. (1989). Risk in infancy: Origins and implications. *American Psychologist, 44,* 224–230.

KOPP, C. B., & PARMELEE, A. H. (1979). Prenatal and perinatal influences on infant behavior. In J. D. Osofsky (Ed.), *Handbook of infant development.* New York: Wiley.

KORN, S. J. (1984). Continuities and discontinuities in difficult/easy temperament: Infancy to young adulthood. *Merrill-Palmer Quarterly, 30,* 189–199.

*KORNER, A. F. (1985). Preventive intervention with high-risk newborns: Theoretical, conceptual and methodological perspectives. In J. D. Osofsky (Ed.), *Handbook for infant development* (2nd ed.). New York: Wiley.

KORNER, A. F., BROWN, B. W., READE, E. P., STEVENSON, D. K., FERNBACH, S., & THOM, V. (1988). State behavior of preterm infants as a function of development, individual, and sex differences. *Infant Behavior and Development, 11,* 111–124.

KORNER, A. F., & THOMAN, E. (1970). Visual alertness in neonates as evoked by maternal care. *Journal of Experimental Child Psychology, 10,* 67–78.

KORNER, A. F., ZEANAH, C. H., LINDEN, J., BERKOWITZ, R. I., KRAEMER, H. C., & AGRAS, S. W. (1985). The relation between neonatal and later activity and temperament. *Child Development, 56,* 38–42.

*KORNHABER, A., & WOODWARD, K. L. (1985). *Grandparents, grandchildren: The vital connection.* New Brunswick, NJ: Transaction.

KOURILSKY, M., & KEHRET-WARD, T. (1984). Kindergartners' attitudes toward distributive justice: Experiential mediators. *Merrill-Palmer Quarterly, 30,* 49–64.

*KOZULIN, A. (1990). *Vygotsky's psychology.* Cambridge, MA: Harvard University Press.

KRAFT, R. H. (1984). Lateral specialization and verbal/spatial ability in preschool children: Age, sex, and familial handedness differences. *Neuropsychologia, 22,* 319–335.

KREBS, D. (1987). The challenge of altruism in biology and psychology. In C. Crawford, M. Smith, & D. Krebs (Eds.), *Sociobiology and psychology: Ideas, issues, and applications.* Hillsdale, NJ: Erlbaum.

KREBS, D., DENTON, K., & HIGGINS, N. C. (1987). On the evolution of self-knowledge and self-deception. In K. B. MacDonald (Ed.), *Sociobiological perspectives on human development.* New York: Springer-Verlag.

KREBS, D., & GILLMORE, J. (1982). The relationship and the first stages of cognitive development, role-taking abilities, and moral development. *Child Development, 53,* 877–886.

KREBS, D. L., & VAN HESTEREN, F. (1994). The development of altruism: Toward an integrative model. *Developmental Review, 14,* 103–158.

KREIPE, R. E., & STRAUSS, J. (1989). Adolescent medical disorders, behavior and development. In G. R. Adams, R. Montemayor, & T. P. Gullotta (Eds.), *Biology of adolescent behavior and development.* Newbury Park, CA: Sage.

KREITLER, S., & KREITLER, H. (1989). Horizontal decalage: A problem and its solution. *Cognitive Development, 4,* 89–119.

KREUTZER, M. A., LEONARD, C., & FLAVELL, J. H. (1975). An interview study of children's knowledge about memory. *Monographs of the Society for Research in Child Development, 40* (1, Serial No. 159).

*KRISTOF, N. D. (1993, July 21). Ultrasound undertaker: China's peasants find new way to avoid unwanted daughters. *The Denver Post,* p. 2A.

KROLL, J. (1977). The concept of childhood in the middle ages. *Journal of the History of Behavioural Sciences, 13,* 384–393.

KROPP, J. P., & HAYNES, O. M. (1987). Abusive and nonabusive mothers' ability to identify general and specific emotion signals of infants. *Child Development, 58,* 187–190.

KUCHUK, A., VIBBERT, M., & BORNSTEIN, M. H. (1986). The perception of smiling and its experiential correlates in three-month-old infants. *Child Development, 57,* 1054–1061.

*KUCZAJ, S. A. (1977). The acquisition of regular and irregular past tense forms. *Journal of Verbal Learning and Verbal Behavior, 16,* 589–600.

KUCZAJ, S. A. (1978). Children's judgments of grammatical and ungrammatical irregular past tense verbs. *Child Development, 49,* 319–326.

KUCZAJ, S. A. (1981). More on children's initial failures to relate specific acquisitions. *Journal of Child Language, 8,* 485–487.

KUCZAJ, S. A. (1982). Language play and language acquisition. In H. W. Reese (Ed.), *Advances in child development and behavior* (Vol. 17). New York: Academic Press.

KUCZAJ, S. A. (1986). Thoughts on the intentional basis of early object word extension: Evidence from comprehension and production. In S. A. Kuczaj & M. D. Barrett (Eds.), *The development of word meaning.* New York: Springer-Verlag.

KUCZYNSKI, L., & KOCHANSKA, G. (1990). Development of children's noncompliance strategies from toddlerhood to age 5. *Developmental Psychology, 26,* 398–408.

KUHL, P. K. (1987). Perception of speech and sound in early infancy. In P. Salapatek & L. Cohen (Eds.), *Handbook of infant perception: Vol. 2. From perception to cognition.* Orlando, FL: Academic Press.

*KUHL, P. K. (1993). Early linguistic experience and phonetic perception: Implications for theories of developmental speech perception. *Journal of Phonetics, 21,* 125–139.

KUHL, P. K., & MELTZOFF, A. N. (1982). The bimodal perception of speech in infancy. *Science, 218,* 1138–1140.

KUHL, P. K., & MELTZOFF, A. N. (1988). Speech as an intermodal object of perception. In A. Yonas (Ed.), *Minnesota symposia on child psychology: Vol. 20. Perceptual development in infancy.* Hillsdale, NJ: Erlbaum.

KUHN, D. (1974). Inducing development experimentally: Comments on a research paradigm. *Developmental Psychology, 10,* 590–600.

KUHN, D. (1976). Short-term longitudinal evidence for the sequentiality of Kohlberg's early stages of moral development. *Developmental Psychology, 12,* 162–166.

*KUHN, D. (1991). *The skills of argument.* New York: Cambridge University Press.

*KUHN, D. (1992a). Cognitive development. In M. H. Bornstein & M. E. Lamb (Eds.), *Developmental psychology: An advanced textbook* (3rd ed.). Hillsdale, NJ: Erlbaum.

*KUHN, D. (1992b). Piaget's child as scientist. In H. Beilin & P. B. Pufall (Eds.), *Piaget's theory: Prospects and possibilities.* Hillsdale, NJ: Erlbaum.

KUHN, D., HO, V., & ADAMS, C. (1979). Formal reasoning among pre- and late-adolescents. *Child Development, 50,* 1128–1135.

KUHN, D., LANGER, J., KOHLBERG, L., & HAAN, N. S. (1977). The development of formal operations in logical and moral judgment. *Genetic Psychology Monographs, 95,* 97–188.

*KULIN, H. E. (1991). Puberty, hypothalamic-pituitary changes of. In R. M. Lerner, A. C. Peterson, & J. Brooks-Gunn (Eds.), *Encyclopedia of adolescence* (Vol 2.). New York: Garland.

KUPERSMIDT, J. B., COIE, J. D., & DODGE, K. A. (1990). The role of poor peer relationships in the development of disorder. In S. R. Asher & J. D. Coie (Eds.), *Peer rejection in childhood.* New York: Cambridge University Press.

KURDEK, L. A. (1978). Perspective taking as the cognitive basis of children's moral development: A review of the literature. *Merrill-Palmer Quarterly, 34,* 3–28.

KURENT, J. E., & SEVER, J. L. (1977). Infectious diseases. In J. G. Wilson & F. C. Fraser (Eds.), *Handbook of teratology: Vol. 1. General principles and etiology.* New York: Plenum.

KURTINES, W. M., ALVAREZ, M., & AZMITIA, M. (1990). Science and morality: The role of values in science and the study of moral phenomena. *Psychological Bulletin, 107,* 283–295.

KURTINES, W. M., & GRIEF, E. B. (1974). The development of moral thought: Review and evaluation of Kohlberg's approach. *Psychological Bulletin, 81,* 453–470.

KURTZ, B. E., & BORKOWSKI, J. G. (1987). Development of strategic skills in impulsive and reflective children: A longitudinal study of metacognition. *Journal of Experimental Child Psychology, 43,* 129–148.

KUTNICK, P. (1986). The relationship of moral judgment and moral action: Kohlberg's theory, criticism and revision. In S. Modgil & C. Modgil (Eds.), *Lawrence Kohlberg: Consensus and controversy.* Philadelphia: Falmer.

LABORATORY OF COMPARATIVE HUMAN COGNITION. (1983). Culture and cognitive development. In W. Kessen (Ed.), *Handbook of child psychology: Vol. 1. History, theory, and methods.* New York: Wiley.

*LADD, G. W. (1992). Themes and theories: Perspectives on processes in family–peer relationships. In R. D. Parke & G. W. Ladd (Eds.), *Family–peer relationships: Modes of linkage.* Hillsdale, NJ: Erlbaum.

*LADD, G. W. (1994). Shifting ecologies during the 5–7 period: Predicting children's adjustment during the transition to grade school. In A. Sameroff & M. Haith (Eds.), *Reason and responsibility: The passage through childhood.* Chicago: University of Chicago Press.

*LADD, G. W., & COLEMAN, C. (1993). Young children's peer relationships: Forms, features, and functions. In B. Spodek (Ed.), *Handbook of research on the education of young children* (2nd ed.). New York: Macmillan.

LADD, G. W., & EMERSON, E. S. (1984). Shared knowledge in children's friendships. *Developmental Psychology, 20,* 932–940.

*LADD, G. W., & HART, C. H. (1992). Creating informal play opportunities: Are parents' and preschoolers' initiations related to children's competence with peers? *Developmental Psychology, 28,* 1179–1187.

*LADD, G. W., PROFILET, S. M., & HART, C. H. (1992). Parents' management of children's peer relations: Facilitating and supervising children's activities in the peer culture. In R. D. Parke & G. W. Ladd (Eds.), *Family–peer relationships: Modes of linkage.* Hillsdale, NJ: Erlbaum.

LaFRENIERE, P., & CHARLESWORTH, W. R. (1983). Dominance, attention, and affiliation in a preschool group: A nine-month longitudinal study. *Ethology and Sociobiology, 4,* 55–67.

LaFRENIERE, P., & SROUFE, L. A. (1985). Profiles of peer competence in the preschool: Interrelations between measures, influence of social ecology, and relation to attachment history. *Developmental Psychology, 21,* 56–69.

LaFRENIERE, P., STRAYER, F. F., & GAUTHIER, R. (1984). The emergence of same-sex affiliative preferences among preschool peers: A developmental/ethological perspective. *Child Development, 55,* 1958–1965.

LaGASSE, L. L., GRUBER, C. P., & LIPSITT, L. P. (1989). The infantile expression of avidity in relation to later assessments of inhibition and attachment. In J. S. Reznick (Ed.), *Perspectives on behavioral inhibition.* Chicago: University of Chicago Press.

*LaGRECA, A. M. (1993). Social skills training with children: Where do we go from here? *Journal of Clinical Child Psychology, 22,* 288–298.

LAHEY, B. B., HAMMER, D., CRUMRINE, P. L., & FOREHAND, R. L. (1980). Birth order × sex interactions in child behavior problems. *Developmental Psychology, 16,* 608–615.

LAKIN, M., LAKIN, M. G., & CONSTANZO, P. R. (1979). Group processes in early childhood: A dimension of human development. *International Journal of Behavioral Development, 2,* 171–183.

*LALLEMONT, M., LaPOINTE, N., M'PELÉ, P., & COEUR, S. L.-L. (1992). Perinatal HIV transmission. In J. M. Mann, D. J. M. Tarantola, & T. W. Netter (Eds.), *AIDS in the world.* Cambridge, MA: Harvard University Press.

LAMAZE, F. (1970). *Painless childbirth: Psychoprophylactic method.* Chicago: Henry Regneny.

LAMB, M. E. (1981a). The development of father–infant relationships. In M. E. Lamb (Ed.), *The role of the father in child development* (2nd ed.). New York: Wiley.

LAMB, M. E. (1981b). *The role of the father in child development.* New York: Wiley.

LAMB, M. E. (1986). The changing roles of fathers. In M. E. Lamb (Ed.), *The father's role: Applied perspectives.* New York: Wiley.

LAMB, M. E., & EASTERBROOKS, M. A. (1981). Individual differences in parental sensitivity: Origins, components, and consequences. In M. E. Lamb & L. R. Sherrod (Eds.), *Infant social cognition: Empirical and theoretical considerations.* Hillsdale, NJ: Erlbaum.

LAMB, M. E., EASTERBROOKS, M. A., & HOLDEN, G. W. (1980). Reinforcement and punishment among preschoolers: Characteristics, effects, and correlates. *Child Development, 51,* 1230–1236.

LAMB, M. E., & HWANG, C. (1982). Maternal attachment and mother–neonate bonding: A critical review. In M. E. Lamb & A. L. Brown (Eds.), *Advances in developmental psychology* (Vol. 2). Hillsdale, NJ: Erlbaum.

*LAMB, M. E., KETTERLINUS, R. D., & FRACASSO, M. P. (1992). Parent–child relationships. In M. H. Bornstein & M. E. Lamb (Eds.), *Developmental psychology: An advanced textbook* (3rd ed.). Hillsdale, NJ: Erlbaum.

LAMB, M. E., MORRISON, D. C., & MALKIN, C. M. (1987). The development of infant social expectations in face-to-face interaction: A longitudinal study. *Merrill-Palmer Quarterly, 33,* 241–254.

LAMB, M. E., & ROOPNARINE, J. L. (1979). Peer influences on sex-role development in preschoolers. *Child Development, 50,* 1219–1222.

*LAMB, M. E., & STERNBERG, K. (1990). Do we really know how day care affects children? *Journal of Applied Developmental Psychology, 11,* 351–379.

*LAMB, M. E., STERNBERG, K., & PRODROMIDIS, M. (1992). Nonmaternal care and the security of infant–mother attachment: A reanalysis of the data. *Infant Behavior and Development, 15,* 71–83.

LAMB, M. E., THOMPSON, R. A., & FRODI, A. M. (1982). Early social development. In R. Vasta (Ed.), *Strategies and techniques of child study.* New York: Academic Press.

LAMB, M. E., THOMPSON, R. A., GARDNER, W., & CHARNOV, E. L. (1985). *Infant–mother attachment: The origins and developmental significance of individual differences in Strange Situation behavior.* Hillsdale, NJ: Erlbaum.

*LAMB, S. (1991). First moral sense: Aspects of and contributors to a beginning morality in the second year of life. In W. M. Kurtines & J. L. Gewirtz (Eds.), *Handbook of moral behavior and development: Vol. 2. Research.* Hillsdale, NJ: Erlbaum.

*LANDAU, B. (1991). Spatial representation of objects in the young blind child. *Cognition, 38,* 145–178.

LANDEGREN, V., KAISER, R., CASKEY, C. T., & HOOD, L. (1988). DNA diagnostics: Molecular techniques and automation. *Science, 242,* 229–237.

LANE, I. M., & COON, R. C. (1972). Reward allocation in preschool children. *Child Development, 43,* 1382–1389.

*LANGER, O. (1990). Critical issues in diabetes and pregnancy. In I. R. Merkatz & J. E. Thompson (Eds.), *New perspectives on prenatal care.* New York: Elsevier.

LANGER, W. L. (1974). Infanticide: A historical survey. *History of Childhood Quarterly, 1,* 353–365.

LANGLOIS, J. H., & DOWNS, A. C. (1979). Peer relations as a function of physical attractiveness: The eye of the beholder or behavioral reality? *Child Development, 50,* 409–418.

LANGLOIS, J. H., & DOWNS, A. C. (1980). Mothers, fathers, and peers as socialization agents of sex-typed play behaviors in young children. *Child Development, 51,* 1237–1247.

*LANZA, E. (1992). Can bilingual two-year-olds code-switch? *Journal of Child Language, 19,* 633–658.

LAPSLEY, D. K., & QUINTANA, S. M. (1985). Integrative themes in social and developmental theories of self. In J. B. Pryor & J. D. Day (Eds.), *The development of social cognition.* New York: Springer-Verlag.

LARGO, R. H., MOLINARI, L., WEBER, M., PINTO, L. C., & DUC, G. (1985). Early development of locomotion: Significance of prematurity, cerebral palsy and sex. *Developmental Medicine and Child Neurology, 27,* 183–191.

*LARNER, M., HALPERN, R., & HARKAVY, O. (Eds.). (1992). *Fair start for children: Lessons learned from seven demonstration projects.* New Haven, CT: Yale University Press.

*LARRABEE, M. J. (Ed.). (1993). *An ethic of care: Feminist and interdisciplinary perspectives.* New York: Routledge.

LARSSON, G., BOHLIN, A. B., & TUNELL, R. (1985). Prospective study of children exposed to variable amounts of alcohol in utero. *Archives of Disease in Childhood, 60,* 316–321.

LaTORRE, R. A., YU, L., FORTIN, L., & MARRACHE, M. (1983). Gender-role adoption and sex as academic and psychological risk factors. *Sex Roles, 9,* 1127–1136.

*LAURSEN, B. (1993). Conflict management among close peers. In B. Laursen (Ed.), *New directions for child development: No. 60. Close friendships in adolescence.* San Francisco: Jossey-Bass.

LAZAR, I., & DARLINGTON, R. (1982). Lasting effects of early education: A report from the consortium for longitudinal studies. *Monographs of the Society for Research in Child Development, 47* (2–3, Serial No. 195).

*LEADBEATER, B. J., & BISHOP, S. J. (1994). Predictors of behavior problems in preschool children of inner-city Afro-American and Puerto Rican adolescent mothers. *Child Development, 65,* 638–648.

LEBOYER, F. (1975). *Birth without violence.* New York: Knopf.

LEE, C., & BATES, J. E. (1985). Mother–child interaction at the age of two years and perceived difficult temperament. *Child Development, 56,* 1314–1325.

LEE, D. N., & ARONSON, E. (1974). Visual proprioceptive control of standing in human infants. *Perception and Psychophysics, 15,* 529–532.

LEE, V. E., BROOKS-GUNN, J., SCHNUR, E., & LIAW, F.-R. (1990). Are Head Start effects sustained? A longitudinal follow-up comparison of disadvantaged children attending Head Start, no preschool, and other preschool programs. *Child Development, 61,* 495–507.

LEI, T., & CHENG, S. (1989). A little but special light on the universality of moral judgment development. In L. Kohlberg, D. Candee, & A. Colby (Eds.), *Rethinking moral development.* Cambridge, MA: Harvard University Press.

LEIDERMAN, P. H., & SEASHORE, M. J. (1975). mother–infant separation: Some delayed consequences. In *Parent-infant interaction* (CIBA Foundation Symposium No. 33). New York: Elsevier.

LEIJON, I. (1980). Neurology and behavior of newborn infants delivered by vacuum extraction of maternal indication. *Acta Paediatrica Scandinavica, 69,* 626–631.

*LEINBACH, M. D., & FAGOT, B. I. (1993). Categorical habituation to male and female faces: Gender schematic processing in infancy. *Infant Behavior and Development, 16,* 317–332.

LEITER, M. P. (1977). A study of reciprocity in preschool play groups. *Child Development, 48,* 1288–1295.

LEMPERS, J. D., FLAVELL, E. R., & FLAVELL, J. H. (1977). The development in very young children of tacit knowledge concerning visual perception. *Genetic Psychology Monographs, 95,* 3–53.

LEMPERT, H. (1984). Topic as starting point for syntax. *Monographs of the Society for Research in Child Development, 49* (5, Serial No. 208).

LENNEBERG, E. H. (1967). *Biological foundations of language.* New York: Wiley.

LENNON, R., & EISENBERG, N. (1987). Gender and age differences in empathy and sympathy. In N. Eisenberg & J. Strayer (Eds.), *Empathy and its determinants.* New York: Cambridge University Press.

*LEON, G. R. (1991). Bulimia nervosa in adolescence. In R. M. Lerner, A. C. Peterson, & J. Brooks-Gunn (Eds.), *Encyclopedia of Adolescence.* New York: Garland.

LEON, M. (1982). Rules in children's moral judgments: Integration of intent, damage, and rationale information. *Developmental Psychology, 18,* 835–842.

LEPPERT, P. C., NAMEROW, P. B., & BARKER, D. (1986). Pregnancy outcomes among adolescent and older women receiving comprehensive prenatal care. *Journal of Adolescent Health Care, 7,* 112–117.

LERNER, J. V., LERNER, R. M., & ZABSKI, S. (1985). Temperament and elementary school children's actual and rated academic performance: A test of a "goodness-of-fit" model. *Journal of Child Psychology and Psychiatry, 26,* 125–136.

LERNER, R. M. (1982). Children and adolescents as producers of their own development. *Developmental Review, 2,* 342–370.

LERNER, R. M. (1987). A life-span perspective for early adolescence. In R. M. Lerner & T. L. Foch (Eds.), *Biological-psychosocial interactions in early adolescence.* Hillsdale, NJ: Erlbaum.

LERNER, R. M., & LERNER, J. V. (1987). Children in their contexts: A goodness of fit model. In J. B. Lancaster, J. Altmann, A. S. Rossi, & L. B. Sherrod (Eds.), *Parenting across the life span: Biosocial dimensions.* Hawthorne, NY: Aldine.

LERNER, R. M., & LERNER, J. V. (1989). Organismic and social-contextual bases of development: The sample case of early adolescence. In W. Damon (Ed.), *Child development today and tomorrow.* San Francisco: Jossey-Bass.

LERNER, R. M., LERNER, J. V., & TUBMAN, J. (1989). Organismic and contextual bases of development in adolescence: A developmental contextual view. In G. R. Adams, R. Montemayor, & T. P. Gullotta (Eds.), *Biology of adolescent behavior and development.* Newbury Park, CA: Sage.

LERNER, R. M., LERNER, J. V., WINDLE, M., HOOKER, K., LENERZ, K., & EAST, P. L. (1986). Children and adolescents in their contexts: Tests of a goodness of fit model. In R.

Plomin & J. Dunn (Eds.), *The study of temperament: Changes, continuities, and challenges.* Hillsdale, NJ: Erlbaum.

*LERNER, R. M., & VON EYE, A. (1992). Sociobiology and human development: Arguments and evidence. *Human Development, 35,* 12–33.

LESLIE, A. M. (1988). The necessity of illusion: Perception and thought in infancy. In L. Weiskrantz (Ed.), *Thought without language.* Oxford: Oxford University Press.

LESLIE, A. M., & KEEBLE, S. (1987). Do six-month-old infants perceive causality? *Cognition, 25,* 265–288.

LESTER, B. M. (1976). Spectrum analysis of the cry sounds of well-nourished and malnourished infants. *Child Development, 47,* 237–241.

LESTER, B. M. (1984). A biosocial model of infant crying. In H. W. Reese (Ed.), *Advances in infancy research. (Vol. 3).* Norwood, NJ: Ablex.

LESTER, B. M., HOFFMAN, J., & BRAZELTON, T. B. (1985). The rhythmic structure of mother–infant interaction in term and preterm infants. *Child Development, 56,* 15–27.

*LESTER, B. M., NEWMAN, J., & PEDERSEN, F. (Eds.). (in press). *Biological and social aspects of infant crying.* New York: Plenum.

LEUNG, E. H. L., & RHEINGOLD, H. L. (1981). Development of pointing as a social gesture. *Developmental Psychology, 17,* 215–220.

*LEVIT, A. G., & UTMAN, J. G. A. (1992). From babbling towards the sound systems of English and French: A longitudinal two-case study. *Journal of Child Language, 19,* 19–49.

*LEVITT, M. J., GUACCI-FRANCO, N., & LEVITT, J. L. (1993). Convoys of social support in childhood and early adolescence: Structure and function. *Developmental Psychology, 29,* 811–818.

LEVITT, M. J., WEBER, R. A., CLARK, M. C., & McDONNELL, P. (1985). Reciprocity of exchange in toddler sharing behavior. *Developmental Psychology, 21,* 122–123.

*LEVY, G. D. (1989). Developmental and individual differences in preschoolers' recognition memories: The influences of gender schematization and verbal labeling of information. *Sex Roles, 21,* 305–324.

LEVY, G. D., & CARTER, D. B. (1989). Gender schema, gender constancy, and gender-role knowledge: The roles of cognitive factors in preschoolers' gender-role stereotype attributions. *Developmental Psychology, 25,* 444–449.

*LEVY, G. D., & FIVUSH, R. (1993). Scripts and gender: A new approach for examining gender-role development. *Developmental Psychology, 13,* 126–146.

LEVY, J. (1981). Lateralization and its implications for variation in development. In E. S. Gollin (Ed.), *Developmental plasticity.* New York: Academic Press.

LEVY, Y., & SCHLESINGER, I. M. (1988). The child's early categories: Approaches to language acquisition theory. In Y. Levy, I. M. Schlesinger, & M. D. S. Braine (Eds.), *Categories and processes in language acquisition.* Hillsdale, NJ: Erlbaum.

LEWIS, M. (1981). Self-knowledge: A social cognitive perspective on gender identity and sex-role development. In M. E. Lamb & L. R. Sherrod

(Eds.), *Infant social cognition: Empirical and theoretical considerations*. Hillsdale, NJ: Erlbaum.

LEWIS, M. (1987a). Early sex role behavior and school age adjustment. In J. M. Reinisch, L. A. Rosenblum, & S. A. Sanders (Eds.), *Masculinity/femininity: Basic perspectives*. New York: Oxford, University Press.

LEWIS, M. (1987b). Social development in infancy and early childhood. In J. D. Osofsky (Ed.), *Handbook of infant development* (2nd ed.). New York: Wiley.

*LEWIS, M. (1991). Ways of knowing: Objective self-awareness or consciousness. *Developmental Review, 11*, 231–243.

*LEWIS, M. (1993). Early socioemotional predictors of cognitive competency at 4 years. *Developmental Psychology, 29*, 1036–1045.

*LEWIS, M., ALESSANDRI, S. M., & SULLIVAN, M. W. (1990). Violation of expectancy, loss of control, and anger expression in young infants. *Developmental Psychology, 26*, 745–751.

LEWIS, M., & FEIRING, C. (1989). Infant, mother, and mother–infant interaction behavior and subsequent attachment. *Child Development, 60*, 831–837.

*LEWIS, M., & FEIRING, C. (1991). Attachment as personal characteristic or a measure of the environment. In J. L. Gewirtz & W. M. Kurtines (Eds.), *Intersections with attachment*. Hillsdale, NJ: Erlbaum.

LEWIS, M., FEIRING, C., McGUFFOG, C., & JASKIR, J. (1984). Predicting psychopathology in six-year-olds from early social relations. *Child Development, 55*, 123–136.

LEWIS, M., & SAARNI, C. (Eds.). (1985). *The socialization of emotions*. New York: Plenum.

*LEWKOWICZ, D. J. (1992a). Infants' response to temporally based intersensory equivalence: The effect of synchronous sounds on visual preferences for moving stimuli. *Infant Behavior and Development, 15*, 297–324.

*LEWKOWICZ, D. J. (1992b). The development of temporally based intersensory perception in human infants. In F. Macar, V. Pouthas, & W. J. Friedman (Eds.), *Time, action and cognition: Towards bridging the gap*. Dordrecht, The Netherlands: Kluwer Academic.

*LEYENDECKER, B., & SCHOLMERICH, A. (1991). An ecological perspective on infant development. In M. E. Lamb & H. Keller (Eds.), *Infant development: Perspectives from German-speaking countries*. Hillsdale, NJ: Erlbaum.

*LIBEN, L. S. (1991). The Piagetian water-level task: Looking beneath the surface. In R. Vasta (Ed.), *Annals of child development* (Vol. 8). London: Kingsley.

LIBEN, L. S., & SIGNORELLA, M. L. (Eds.). (1987). *New directions for child development: No. 38. Children's gender schemata*. San Francisco: Jossey-Bass.

*LIBEN, L. S., & SIGNORELLA, M. L. (1993). Gender-schematic processing in children: The role of initial interpretations of stimuli. *Developmental Psychology, 29*, 141–149.

LICHT, B. G., & DWECK, C. S. (1984). Determinants of academic achievement: The interaction of children's achievement orientations with skill area. *Developmental Psychology, 20*, 628–636.

LIDDELL, C., & KRUGER, P. (1987). Activity and social behavior in a South African township nursery: Some effects of crowding. *Merrill-Palmer Quarterly, 33*, 195–211.

LIDDELL, C., & KRUGER, P. (1989). Activity and social behavior in a crowded South African nursery: A follow-up study on the effects of crowding at home. *Merrill-Palmer Quarterly, 35*, 209–226.

*LIDZ, C. S. (1992). Dynamic assessment: Some thoughts on the model, the medium, and the message. *Learning and Individual Differences, 4*, 125–136.

*LIEBERMAN, P. D., KLATT, H., & WILSON, W. (1969). Vocal tract limitations of the vocal repertoires of rhesus monkeys and other nonhuman primates. *Science, 164*, 1185–1187.

LIEBERT, R. M. (1984). What develops in moral development? In W. M. Kurtines & J. L. Gewirtz (Eds.), *Morality, moral behavior, and moral development*. New York: Wiley.

LIEBERT, R. M., & SPRAFKIN, J. (1988). *The early window: Effects of television on children and youth* (3rd ed.). New York: Pergamon.

*LIGHT, P., & BUTTERWORTH, G. (Eds.). (1993). *Context and cognition*. Hillsdale, NJ: Erlbaum.

LINDBERG, M. A. (1980). Is knowledge base development a necessary and sufficient condition for memory development? *Journal of Experimental Child Psychology, 30*, 401–410.

LINN, M. C., & PETERSEN, A. C. (1985). Emergence and characterization of sex differences in spatial ability: A meta-analysis. *Child Development, 56*, 1479–1498.

LINN, R. L. (1986). Educational testing and assessment: Research needs and policy issues. *American Psychologist, 41*, 1153–1160.

LIPSCOMB, T. J., McALLISTER, H. A., & BREGMAN, N. J. (1985). A developmental inquiry into the effects of multiple models on children's generosity. *Merrill-Palmer Quarterly, 31*, 335–344.

LIPSITT, L. P. (1977). Taste in human neonates: Its effect on sucking and heart rate. In J. M. Weiffenbach (Ed.), *Taste and development: The genesis of sweet preference*. Washington, DC: Government Printing Office.

LIPSITT, L. P. (1990). Learning and memory in infants. *Merrill-Palmer Quarterly, 36*, 53–66.

*LIPSITT, L. P. (1992). Discussion: The Bayley Scales of Infant Development: Issues of prediction and outcome revisited. In C. Rovee-Collier & L. P. Lipsitt (Eds.), *Advances in infancy research* (Vol. 7). Norwood, NJ: Ablex.

LIPSITT, L. P., ENGEN, T., & KAYE, H. (1963). Developmental changes in the olfactory threshold of the neonate. *Child Development, 34*, 371–376.

LIPSITT, L. P., & KAYE, H. (1965). Change in neonatal response to optimizing and non-optimizing sucking stimulation. *Psychonomic Science, 2*, 221–222.

LIPSITT, L. P., & LEVY, N. (1959). Electrotactual threshold in the neonate. *Child Development 30*, 547–554.

LIST, J. A., COLLINS, W. A., & WESTBY, S. D. (1983). Comprehension and inferences from traditional and nontraditional sex-role portrayals on television. *Child Development, 54*, 1579–1587.

*LOBEL, M., DUNKEL-SCHETTER, C., & SCRIMSHAW, S. C. M. (1992). Prenatal maternal stress and prematurity: A prospective study of socioeconomically disadvantaged women. *Health Psychology, 11*(1), 32–40.

*LOBEL, T. E., & MENASHRI, J. (1993). Relations of conceptions of gender-role transgressions and gender constancy to gender-typed toy preferences. *Developmental Psychology, 29*, 150–155.

LOCHMAN, J. E., BURCH, P. P., CURRY, J. F., & LAMPRON, L. B. (1984). Treatment and generalization effects of cognitive-behavioral and goal-setting interventions with aggressive boys. *Journal of Consulting and Clinical Psychology, 52*, 915–916.

LOCKE, J. (1824). *An essay concerning human understanding*. New York: Seaman. (Original work published 1694).

LOCKE, J. L., & FEHR, F. S. (1970). Young children's use of the speech code in a recall task. *Journal of Experimental Child Psychology, 10*, 367–373.

LOCKE, J. L., & PEARSON, D. M. (1990). Linguistic significance of babbling: Evidence from a tracheostomized infant. *Journal of Child Language, 17*, 1–16.

LOCKHEED, M. (1985). Women, girls, and computers: A first look at the evidence. *Sex Roles, 13*, 115–122.

LOCKMAN, J. J. (1984). The development of detour ability during infancy. *Child Development, 55*, 482–491.

*LOCURTO, C. (1991). *Sense and nonsense about IQ: The case for uniqueness*. New York: Praeger.

LOEHLIN, J. C., HORN, J. M., & WILLERMAN, L. (1989). Modeling IQ change: Evidence from the Texas Adoption Project. *Child Development, 60*, 993–1004.

LOEHLIN, J. C., LINDZEY, G., & SPUHLER, J. N. (1975). *Race differences in intelligence*. San Francisco: W. H. Freeman.

*LOEHLIN, J. C., & ROWE, D. C. (1992). Genes, environment, and personality. In G. Caprara & G. L. VanHeck (Eds.), *Modern personality psychology: Critical reviews and new directions*. Hertfordshire, UK: Harvester-Wheatsheaf.

*LOEHLIN, J. C., WILLERMAN, L., & HORN, J. M. (1988). Human behavior genetics. *Annual Review of Psychology, 39*, 101–133.

*LOLLIS, S. P., ROSS, H. S., & TATE, E. (1992). Parents' regulation of children's peer interactions: Direct influences. In R. D. Parke & G. W. Ladd (Eds.), *Family-peer relationships: Modes of linkage*. Hillsdale, NJ: Erlbaum.

LONDERVILLE, S., & MAIN, M. (1981). Security of attachment, compliance, and maternal training methods in the second year of life. *Developmental Psychology, 17*, 289–299.

*LONG, L., & LONG, T. (1983). *The handbook for latchkey children and their parents*. New York: Arbor House.

*LORE, R. K., & SCHULTZ, L. A. (1993). Control of human aggression: A comparative perspective. *American Psychologist, 48*, 16–25.

LORENZ, K. Z. (1937). The companion in the bird's world. *Auk, 54*, 245–273.

LORENZ, K. Z. (1950). Innate behaviour patterns. *Symposia for the Society of Experimental Biology, 4*, 211–268.

LORENZ, K. Z. (1981). *The foundations of ethology.* New York: Springer-Verlag.

LOUNSBURY, M. L., & BATES, J. E. (1982). The cries of infants of differing levels of perceived temperamental difficultness: Acoustic properties and effects on listeners. *Child Development, 53*, 677–686.

LOVDAL, L. T. (1989). Sex role messages in television commercials: An update. *Sex Roles, 21*, 715–724.

LOVELAND, K. A. (1986). Discovering the affordances of a reflecting surface. *Developmental Review, 6*, 1–24.

LOWREY, G. H. (1978). *Growth and development of children* (7th ed.). Chicago: Year Book Medical Publishers.

*LOZOFF, B. (1989). Nutrition and behavior. *American Psychologist, 44*, 231–236.

LUBCHENKO, L. O. (1981). Gestational age, birthweight, and the high-risk infant. In C. C. Brown (Ed.), *Infants at risk.* Palm Beach, FL: Johnson & Johnson.

*LUCARIELLO, J., KYRATZIS, A., & NELSON, K. (1992). Taxonomic knowledge: What kind and when? *Child Development, 63*, 978–998.

LUDEMANN, P. M. (1991). Generalized discrimination of positive facial expressions by seven- and ten-month-old infants. *Child Development, 62*, 55–67.

*LUDEMANN, P. M., & NELSON, C. A. (1988). Categorical representation of facial expression by 7-month-old infants. *Developmental Psychology, 24*, 492–501.

LUMMIS, M., & STEVENSON, H. W. (1990). Gender differences in beliefs and achievement: A cross-cultural study. *Developmental Psychology, 26*, 254–263.

*LUNDMAN, R. J. (1984). *Prevention and control of juvenile delinquency.* New York: Oxford University Press.

LURIA, A. R. (1961). *The role of speech in the regulation of normal and abnormal behavior.* New York: Liveright.

LURIA, A. R. (1982). *Language and cognition.* New York: Wiley.

*LUTZ, S. E., & RUBLE, D. N. (1994). Children and gender prejudice: Context, motivation, and the development of gender conceptions. In R. Vasta (Ed.), *Annals of child development* (Vol. 10). London: Kingsley.

*LYKKEN, D. T., McGUE, M., TELLEGEN, A., & BOUCHARD, T. J., Jr. (1992). Emergenesis: Genetic traits that may not run in families. *American Psychologist, 47*, 1565–1577.

LYNCH, M. P., EILERS, R. E., OLLER, K. D., & URBANO, R. C. (1990). Innateness, experience, and music perception. *Psychological Science, 1*, 272–276.

*LYON, T. D., & FLAVELL, J. H. (1993). Young children's understanding of forgetting over time. *Child Development, 64*, 789–800.

LYONS, J. A., & SERBIN, L. A. (1986). Observer bias in scoring boys' and girls' aggression. *Sex Roles, 14*, 301–313.

*LYONS-RUTH, K., ALPERN, L., & REPACHOLI, B. (1993). Disorganized infant attachment classification and maternal psychosocial problems as predictors of hostile-aggressive behavior in the preschool classroom. *Child Development, 64*, 572–585.

LYONS-RUTH, K., CONNELL, D. B., & ZOLL, D. (1989). Patterns of maternal behavior among infants at risk for abuse: Relations with infant attachment behavior and infant development at 12 months of age. In D. Cicchetti & V. Carlson (Eds.), *Child maltreatment: Theory and research on the causes and consequences of child abuse and neglect.* New York: Cambridge University Press.

LYTTON, H. (1977). Do parents create, or respond to, differences in twins? *Developmental Psychology, 13*, 456–459.

LYTTON, H. (1980). *Parent–child interaction: The socialization process observed in twin and singleton families.* New York: Plenum.

*LYTTON, H., & ROMNEY, D. M. (1991). Parents' sex-related differential socialization of boys and girls: A meta-analysis. *Psychological Bulletin, 109*, 267–296.

MACCOBY, E. E. (1967). Selective and auditory attention in children. In L. P. Lipsitt & C. C. Spiker (Eds.), *Advances in child development and behavior* (Vol. 3). New York: Academic Press.

MACCOBY, E. E. (1969). The development of stimulus selection. In J. P. Hill (Ed.), *Minnesota symposia on child psychology.* (Vol. 3). Minneapolis: University of Minnesota Press.

MACCOBY, E. E. (1988). Gender as a social category. *Developmental Psychology, 24*, 755–765.

*MACCOBY, E. E. (1990). Gender and relationships: A developmental account. *American Psychologist, 45*, 513–521.

*MACCOBY, E. E. (1992). The role of parents in the socialization of children: An historical overview. *Developmental Psychology, 28*, 1006–1017.

MACCOBY, E. E., & JACKLIN, C. N. (1987). Gender segregation. In H. W. Reese (Ed.), *Advances in child development and behavior* (Vol. 20). Orlando, FL: Academic Press.

MACCOBY, E. E., & MARTIN, J. A. (1983). Socialization in the context of the family: Parent–child interaction. In E. M. Hetherington (Ed.), *Handbook of child psychology: Vol. 4. Socialization, personality, and social development.* New York: Wiley.

MacDONALD, K., & PARKE, R. D. (1986). Parent–child physical play: The effects of sex and age of children and parents. *Sex Roles, 15*, 367–378.

MacDONALD, K. B. (1988a). The interfaces between sociobiology and developmental psychology. In K. B. MacDonald (Ed.), *Sociobiological perspectives on human development.* New York: Springer-Verlag.

MacDONALD, K. B. (1988b). *Social and personality development: An evolutionary synthesis.* New York: Plenum.

MacDONALD, K. B. (1988c). Sociobiology and the cognitive-developmental tradition in moral development research. In K. B. MacDonald (Ed.), *Sociobiological perspectives on human development.* New York: Springer-Verlag.

*MacDONALD, K. B. (1992). Warmth as a developmental construct: An evolutionary analysis. *Child Development, 63*, 753–773.

MacFARLANE, A. (1975). Olfaction in the development of social preferences in the human neonate. In *Parent–infant interaction* (CIBA Foundation Symposium No. 33). Amsterdam: Elsevier.

MacFARLANE, A. (1977). *The psychology of childbirth.* Cambridge, MA: Harvard University Press.

*MacFARLANE, A. (1987). *The culture of capitalism.* Oxford: Basil Blackwell.

MacKAY, I. R. A. (1987). *Phonetics: The science of speech production.* Boston: Little, Brown.

MacKENZIE, B. (1984). Explaining race differences in IQ: The logic, the methodology, and the evidence. *American Psychologist, 39*, 1214–1233.

MacKINNON, C. E., STONEMAN, Z., & BRODY, G. H. (1984). The impact of maternal employment and family form on children's sex-role stereotypes and mothers' traditional attitudes. *Journal of Divorce, 8*, 51–60.

*MacWHINNEY, B. (1987). The competition model. In B. MacWhinney (Ed.), *Mechanisms of language acquisition.* Hillsdale, NJ: Erlbaum.

*MacWHINNEY, B., & BATES, E. (1989). *The crosslinguistic study of sentence processing.* Cambridge: Cambridge University Press.

*MacWHINNEY, B., & BATES, E. (1993). *The crosslinguistic study of sentence processing.* Cambridge: Cambridge University Press.

*MAGNUSSON, D., BERGMAN, L. R., RUDIGER, G., & TORESTAD, B. (Eds.). (1991). *Problems and methods in longitudinal research: Stability and change.* Cambridge: Cambridge University Press.

*MAIN, M. (1990). Cross-cultural studies of attachment organization: Recent studies, changing methodologies, and the concept of conditional strategies. *Human Development, 33*, 48–61.

*MAIN, M., KAPLAN, N., & CASSIDY, J. (1985). Security in infancy, childhood and adulthood: A move to the level of representation. In I. Bretherton & E. Waters (Eds.), Growing points of attachment theory and research. *Monographs of the Society for Research in Child Development, 50*(1–2, Serial No. 209).

MAIN, M., & SOLOMON, J. (1986). Discovery of a disorganized/disoriented attachment pattern. In T. B. Brazelton & M. W. Yogman (Eds.), *Affective development in infancy.* Norwood, NJ: Ablex.

MAIN, M., & SOLOMON, J. (1990). Procedures for identifying infants as disorganized/disoriented during the Ainsworth Strange Situation. In M. Greenberg, D. Cicchetti, & M. Cummings (Eds.), *Attachment during the preschool years.* Chicago: University of Chicago Press.

MAIN, M., & WESTON, D. (1981). The quality of the toddler's relationship to mother and father. *Child Development, 52*, 932–940.

MAJEWSKI, F., & STEGER, M. (1984). Fetal head growth retardation associated with maternal phenobarbitone/primidone and/or phenytoin therapy. *European Journal of Pediatrics, 141*, 188–189.

*Making pregnancy and childbearing safer for women in West Africa. (1993). *Carnegie Quarterly, 38*, 1–17.

MALATESTA, C. Z. (1985). Developmental course of emotion expression in the human infant. In G. Zivin (Ed.), *The development of expressive behavior: Biology–environment interactions*. Orlando, FL: Academic Press.

MALATESTA, C. Z., CULVER, C., TESMAN, J. R., & SHEPARD, B. (1989). The development of emotion expression during the first two years of life. *Monographs of the Society for Research in Child Development, 54* (1–2, Serial No. 219).

MALATESTA, C. Z., GRIGORYEV, P., LAMB, C., ALBIN, M., & CULVER, C. (1986). Emotion socialization and expressive development in preterm and full term infants. *Child Development, 57,* 316–330.

MALATESTA, C. Z., & HAVILAND, J. M. (1982). Learning display rules: The socialization of emotion expression in infancy. *Child Development, 53,* 991–1003.

*MALATESTA, C. Z., IZARD, C. E., & CAMRAS, L. (in press). Conceptualizing early infant affect: Emotions as fact, fiction, or artifact? In K. Strongman (Ed.), *International review of studies on emotion*. New York: Wiley.

MALINA, R. M. (1990). Physical growth and performance during the transitional years (9–16). In R. Montemayor, G. R. Adams, & T. Gullotta (Eds.), *From childhood to adolescence: Vol. 2. Advances in adolescent development*. London: Sage.

MANDLER, J. M. (1983). Representation. In J. H. Flavell & E. M. Markman (Eds.), *Handbook of child psychology: Vol. 3. Cognitive development*. New York: Wiley.

MANDLER, J. M. (1984). *Stories, scripts, and scenes: Aspects of schema theory*. Hillsdale, NJ: Erlbaum.

MANDLER, J. M. (1988). How to build a baby: On the development of an accessible representational system. *Cognitive Development, 3,* 113–136.

*MANDLER, J. M. (1990). Recall of events by preverbal children. In A. Diamond (Ed.), *The development and neural bases of higher cognitive functions*. New York: New York Academy of Sciences.

*MANDLER, J. M. (1992). How to build a baby: II. Conceptual primitives. *Psychological Review, 99,* 587–605.

MANDLER, J. M., & GOODMAN, M. S. (1982). On the psychological validity of story structure. *Journal of Verbal Learning and Verbal Behavior, 21,* 507–523.

MANGELSDORF, S., GUNNAR, M., KESTENBAUM, R., LANG, S., & ANDREAS, D. (1990). Infant proneness-to-distress temperament, maternal personality, and mother–infant attachment: Associations and goodness of fit. *Child Development, 61,* 820–831.

MANN, C. C. (1994). Behavioral genetics in transition. *Science, 264,* 1686–1689.

*MANN, J. M., TARANTOLA, D. J. M., & NETTER, T. W. (1992a). A global epidemic out of control? In J. M. Mann, D. J. M. Tarantola, & T. W. Netter (Eds.), *AIDS in the world*. Cambridge, MA: Harvard University Press.

*MANN, J. M., TARANTOLA, D. J. M., & NETTER, T. W. (1992b). The HIV pandemic: status and trends. In J. M. Mann, D .J. M. Tarantola, & T. W. Netter (Eds.), *AIDS in the world*. Cambridge, MA: Harvard University Press.

MANNLE, S., & TOMASELLO, M. (1987). Fathers, siblings, and the Bridge Hypothesis. In K. E. Nelson & A. VanKleeck (Eds.), *Children's language* (Vol. 6). Hillsdale, NJ: Erlbaum.

MARATSOS, M. (1983). Some current issues in the study of the acquisition of grammar. In J. H. Flavell & E. M. Markman (Eds.), *Handbook of child psychology: Vol. 3. Cognitive development*. New York: Wiley.

MARATSOS, M. (1988a). Crosslinguistic analysis, universals, and language acquisition. In F. S. Kessel (Ed.), *The development of language and language researchers: Essays in honor of Roger Brown*. Hillsdale, NJ: Erlbaum.

MARATSOS, M. (1988b). The acquisition of formal word classes. In Y. Levy, I. M. Schlesinger, & M. D. S. Braine (Eds.), *Categories and processes in language acquisition*. Hillsdale, NJ: Erlbaum.

MARCH OF DIMES BIRTH DEFECTS FOUNDATION. (1989). *Annual Report*.

MARCUS, D. E., & OVERTON, W. E. (1978). The development of gender constancy and sex role preferences. *Child Development, 49,* 434–444.

*MARCUS, G. F., PINKER, S., ULLMAN, M., HOLLANDER, M., ROSEN, T. J., & XU, F. (1992). Overregularization in language acquisition. *Monographs of the Society for Research in Child Development, 57*(4, No. 228).

MARCUS, R. (1986). Naturalistic observation of cooperation, helping, and sharing and their associations with empathy and affect. In C. Zahn-Waxler, E. M. Cummings, & R. Iannotti (Eds.), *Altruism and aggression*. New York: Cambridge University Press.

MARINI, Z., & CASE, R. (1989). Parallels in the development of preschoolers' knowledge about their physical and social worlds. *Merrill-Palmer Quarterly, 35,* 63–87.

*MARINI, Z., & CASE, R. (1994). The development of abstract reasoning about the physical and social world. *Child Development, 65,* 147–159.

MARKMAN, E. M. (1981). Two different principles of conceptual organization. In M. E. Lamb & A. L. Brown (Eds.), *Advances in developmental psychology* (Vol. 1). Hillsdale, NJ: Erlbaum.

*MARKMAN, E. M. (1989). *Categorization and naming in children: Problems of induction*. Cambridge, MA: MIT Press.

*MARKMAN, E. M. (1991). The whole object, taxonomic, and mutual exclusivity assumptions as initial constraints on word meanings. In S. A. Gelman & J. P. Byrnes (Eds.), *Perspectives on language and thought: Interrelations in development*. Cambridge: Cambridge University Press.

MARKSTROM-ADAMS, C. (1989). Androgyny and its relation to adolescent psychosocial well-being: A review of the literature. *Sex Roles, 21,* 325–340.

MARKUS, H. J. (1977). Self-schemata and processing information about the self. *Journal of Personality and Social Psychology, 35,* 63–78.

MARKUS, H. J., & NURIUS, P. S. (1984). Self-understanding and self-regulation in middle childhood. In W. A. Collins (Ed.), *Development during middle childhood: The years from six to twelve*. Washington, DC: National Academy Press.

*MARSH, H. W. (1989). Age and sex effects in multiple dimensions of self-concept: Preadolescence to early adulthood. *Journal of Educational Psychology, 81,* 417–430.

MARSHALL, S. P. (1984). Sex differences in children's mathematics achievement: Solving computations and story problems. *Journal of Educational Psychology, 76,* 194–204.

MARTIN, C. L. (1990). Attitudes and expectations about children with nontraditional and traditional gender roles. *Sex Roles, 22,* 151–165.

*MARTIN, C. L. (1991). The role of cognition in understanding gender effects. In H. W. Reese (Ed.), *Advances in child development and behavior* (Vol. 23). San Diego, CA: Academic Press.

*MARTIN, C. L. (1993). New directions for investigating children's gender knowledge. *Developmental Review, 13,* 184–204.

MARTIN, C. L., & HALVERSON, C. F. (1983a). The effects of sex-typing schemas on young children's memory. *Child Development, 54,* 563–574.

MARTIN, C. L., & HALVERSON, C. F. (1983b). Gender constancy: A methodological and theoretical analysis. *Sex Roles, 9,* 775–790.

MARTIN, C. L., & HALVERSON, C. F. (1987). The roles of cognition in sex role acquisition. In D. B. Carter (Ed.), *Current conceptions of sex roles and sex typing*. New York: Praeger.

MARTIN, C. L., & LITTLE, J. K. (1990). The relation of gender understanding to children's sex-typed preferences and gender stereotypes. *Child Development, 61,* 1427–1439.

*MARTIN, C. L., WOOD, C. H., & LITTLE, J. K. (1990). The development of gender stereotype components. *Child Development, 61,* 1891–1904.

MARTIN, G. B., & CLARK, R. D. (1982). Distress crying in neonates: Species and peer specificity. *Developmental Psychology, 18,* 3–9.

MARTIN, J. A. (1981). A longitudinal study of the consequences of early mother–infant interaction: A microanalytic approach. *Monographs of the Society for Research in Child Development, 46* (3, Serial No. 190).

MARTIN, J. A., MACCOBY, E. E., & JACKLIN, C. N. (1981). Mothers' responsiveness to interactive bidding and nonbidding in boys and girls. *Child Development, 52,* 1064–1067.

*MARTIN, T. R., & BRACKEN, M. B. (1986). Association of low birth weight with passive smoke exposure in pregnancy. *American Journal of Epidemiology, 124,* 633–642.

MARTORANO, S. C. (1977). A developmental analysis of performance on Piaget's formal operational tasks. *Developmental Psychology, 13,* 666–672.

*MARX, J. (1992). Homeobox genes go evolutionary. *Science, 255,* 399–401.

*MARX, J. (1993). ALS (Gene linked to Lou Gehrig's disease). *Science, 259,* 1393.

*MASATAKA, N. (1993). Effects of contingent and noncontingent maternal stimulation on the vocal behaviour of three- to four-month-old Japanese infants. *Journal of Child Language, 20,* 303–312.

*MASTERS, J. C., & CARLSON, C. R. (1984). Children's and adults' understanding of the causes and consequences of emotional states. In C. Izard, J. Kagan, & R. Zajonc (Eds.), *Emotions, cognition, and behavior*. Cambridge: Cambridge University Press.

MASTERS, J. C., FORD, M. E., AREND, R., GROTEVANT, H. D., & CLARK, L. V. (1979). Modeling and labeling as integrated determinants of children's sex-typed imitative behaviors. *Child Development, 50,* 364–371.

MASTERS, J. C., & FURMAN, W. (1981). Popularity, individual friendship selection, and specific peer interaction among children. *Developmental Psychology, 17,* 344–350.

MASUR, E. F. (1982). Mothers' responses to infants' object-related gestures: Influences on lexical development. *Journal of Child Language, 9,* 23–30.

MASUR, E. F. (1983). Gestural development, dual-directional signaling, and the transition to words. *Journal of Psycholinguistic Research, 12,* 93–109.

MATAS, L., AREND, R., & SROUFE, L. A. (1978). Continuity of adaptation in the second year: The relationship between quality of attachment and later competence. *Child Development, 49,* 547–556.

MATEFY, R. E., & ACKSEN, B. A. (1976). The effect of role-playing discrepant positions on change in moral judgments and attitudes. *Journal of Genetic Psychology, 128,* 189–200.

MATHENY, A. P. (1980). Bayley's Infant Behavior Record: Behavioral components and twin analysis. *Child Development, 51,* 1157–1167.

MATHENY, A. P. (1983). A longitudinal twin study of stability of components from Bayley's Infant Behavior Record. *Child Development, 54,* 356–360.

MATHENY, A. P., WILSON, R. S., & THOBEN, A. S. (1987). Home and mother: Relations with infant temperament. *Developmental Psychology, 23,* 323–331.

MATSUMOTO, D., HAAN, N., YABROVE, G., THEODOROU, P., & CARNEY, C. C. (1986). Preschoolers' moral actions and emotions in Prisoner's Dilemma. *Developmental Psychology, 22,* 663–670.

MATTHEI, E. H. (1987). Subject and agent in emerging grammars: Evidence for a change in children's biases. *Journal of Child Language, 14,* 295–308.

MAURER, D. (1985). *Infants' perception of facedness.* In T. M. Field & N. A. Fox (Eds.), *Social perception in infants.* Norwood, NJ: Ablex.

MAURER, D., & SALAPATEK, P. (1976). Developmental changes in the scanning of faces by young infants. *Child Development, 47,* 523–527.

MAYER, N. K., & TRONICK, E. Z. (1985). Mothers' turn-giving signals and infant turn-taking in mother–infant interaction. In T. M. Field & N. A. Fox (Eds.), *Social perception in infants.* Norwood, NJ: Ablex.

*MAYES, L. C. (1992). Prenatal cocaine exposure and young children's development. *Annals, AAPSS, 521,* 11–27.

MAYES, L. C., & CARTER, A. S. (1990). Emerging social regulatory capacities as seen in the still-face situation. *Child Development, 61,* 754–763.

*MAYES, L. C., CARTER, A. S., & STUBBE, D. (1993). Individual differences in exploratory behavior in the second year of life. *Infant Behavior and Development, 16,* 269–284.

MAYNARD SMITH, J. (1976). Group selection. *Quarterly Review of Biology, 51,* 277–283.

MAZIADE, M., BOUDREAULT, M., THIVIERGE, J., CAPERAA, P., & COTE, R. (1984). Infant temperament: SES and gender differences and reliability of measurement in a large Quebec sample. *Merrill-Palmer Quarterly, 30,* 213–226.

*McANINCH, C. B., MANOLIS, M. B., MILICH, R., & HARRIS, M. J. (1993). Impression formation in children: Influence of gender and expectancy. *Child Development, 64,* 1492–1506.

McBRIDE, S. (1990). Maternal modulators of child care: The role of maternal separation anxiety. In K. McCartney (Ed.), *New directions for child development: No. 49. Child care and maternal employment: A social ecology approach.* San Francisco: Jossey-Bass.

McCABE, A., & LIPSCOMB, T. J. (1988). Sex differences in children's verbal aggression. *Merrill-Palmer Quarterly, 34,* 389–401.

*McCABE, A., & PETERSON, C. (1991). Getting the story: A longitudinal study of parental styles in eliciting narratives and developing narrative skill. In A. McCabe & C. Peterson (Eds.), *Developing narrative structure.* Hillsdale, NJ: Erlbaum.

McCABE, A. E. (1989). Differential language learning styles in young children: The importance of context. *Developmental Review, 9,* 1–20.

McCALL, R. B. (1977). Challenges to a science of developmental psychology. *Child Development, 48,* 333–344.

McCALL, R. B. (1979). The development of intellectual functioning in infancy and the prediction of later IQ. In J. D. Osofsky (Ed.), *Handbook of infant development.* New York: Wiley.

McCALL, R. B. (1981). Early predictors of later IQ: The search continues. *Intelligence, 5,* 141–148.

McCALL, R. B. (1984). Developmental changes in mental performance: The effect of the birth of a sibling. *Child Development, 55,* 1317–1321.

McCALL, R. B. (1986). Issues of stability and continuity in temperamental research. In R. Plomin & J. Dunn (Eds.), *The study of temperament: Changes, continuities and challenges.* Hillsdale, NJ: Erlbaum.

McCALL, R. B., APPLEBAUM, M. I., & HOGARTY, P. S. (1973). Developmental changes in mental performance. *Monographs of the Society for Research in Child Development, 38* (3, Serial No. 150).

*McCALL, R. B., & CARRIGER, M. S. (1993). A meta-analysis of infant habituation and recognition memory as predictors of later IQ. *Child Development, 64,* 57–79.

*McCALL, R. B., & MASH, C. W. (1994). Infant cognition and its relation to mature intelligence. In R. Vasta (Ed.), *Annals of child development* (Vol. 10). London: Kingsley.

McCARTNEY, K. (Ed.). (1990). *New directions for child development: No. 49. Child care and maternal employment: A social ecology approach.* San Francisco: Jossey-Bass.

McCARTNEY, K., & NELSON, K. (1981). Children's use of scripts in story recall. *Discourse Processes, 4,* 59–70.

McCARTNEY, K., SCARR, S., PHILLIPS, D., GRAJEK, S., & SCHWARZ, J. C. (1982). Environmental differences among day care centers and their effects on children's development. In E. F. Zigler & E. W. Gordon (Eds.), *Day care: Scientific and social policy studies.* Boston: Auburn House.

McCAULEY, E., KAY, T., ITO, J., & TREDER, R. (1987). The Turner syndrome: Cognitive deficits, affective discrimination, and behavior problems. *Child Development, 58,* 464–473.

*McCLEARN, G. E., PLOMIN, R., GORA-MASLAK, G., & CRABBE, J. C. (1991). The gene chase in behavioral science. *Psychological Science, 2,* 222–229.

*McCLELLAND, J. L., MUNAKATA, Y., JOHNSON, M. H., & SIEGLER, R. S. (1993). *The development and neural basis of object permanence.* Unpublished manuscript.

*McCOY, E. (1988). Childhood through the ages. In K. Finsterbusch (Ed.), *Sociology 88/89.* Guildford, CT: Dushkin.

McCUNE-NICOLICH, L. (1981). The cognitive bases of relational words in the single word period. *Journal of Child Language, 8,* 15–34.

McDAVID, J. W., & HARARI, H. (1966). Stereotyping of names and popularity in grade-school children. *Child Development, 35,* 453–459.

McDEVITT, S. C. (1986). Continuity and discontinuity of temperament in infancy and early childhood: A psychometric perspective. In R. Plomin & J. Dunn (Eds.), *The study of temperament: Changes, continuities and challenges.* Hillsdale, NJ: Erlbaum.

McDEVITT, S. C., & CAREY, W. B. (1981). Stability of ratings vs. perceptions of temperament from early infancy to 1–3 years. *Journal of Orthopsychiatry, 51,* 342–345.

McDONNELL, P. M. (1979). Patterns of eye-hand coordination in the first year of life. *Canadian Journal of Psychology, 33,* 253–267.

*McDONOUGH, L., & MANDLER, J. M. (1989, April). *Immediate and deferred imitation with 11-month-olds: A comparison between familiar and novel actions.* Paper presented at the meeting of the Society for Research in Child Development, Kansas City, MO.

McEWEN, B. S. (1987). Observations on brain sexual differentiation: A biochemist's view. In J. M. Reinisch, L. A. Rosenblum, & S. A. Sanders (Eds.), *Masculinity/femininity: Basic properties.* New York: Oxford University Press.

McGEE, M. G. (1982). Spatial abilities: The influence of genetic factors. In M. Potegal (Ed.), *Spatial abilities: Development and physiological foundations.* New York: Academic Press.

McGHEE, P. E., & FRUEH, T. (1980). Television viewing and the learning of sex-role stereotypes. *Sex Roles, 6,* 179–188.

McGILLICUDDY-DeLISI, A. V. (1988). Sex differences in parental teaching behaviors. *Merrill-Palmer Quarterly, 34,* 147–162.

McGLONE, J. (1980). Sex differences in human brain asymmetry: Critical survey. *Behavioral and Brain Sciences, 3,* 215–227.

McGRAW, M. B. (1935). *Growth: A study of Johnny and Jimmy.* New York: Appleton-Century-Crofts.

McGRAW, M. B. (1940). Suspension grasp behavior of the human infant. *American Journal of the Disabled Child, 60,* 799–811.

*McGUE, M., BOUCHARD, T. J., IACANO, W. G., & LYKKEN, D. T. (1993). Behavioral genetics of cognitive ability: A life-span perspective. In R. Plomin & G. B. McClearn (Eds.), *Nature, nurture, and psychology.* Washington, DC: APA.

*McGUE, M., & LYKKEN, D. T. (1992). Genetic influence on risk of divorce. *Psychological Science, 3,* 368–373.

*McGUFFIN, P., & KATZ, R. (1993). Genes, adversity, and depression. In R. Plomin & G. E. McClearn (Eds.), *Nature, nurture, and psychology.* Washington, DC: APA.

McGURK, H. (1970). The role of object orientation in infant perception. *Journal of Experimental Child Psychology, 9,* 363–373.

McHALE, S. M., BARTKO, W. T., CROUTER, A. C., & PERRY-JENKINS, M. (1990). Children's housework and psychosocial functioning: The mediating effects of parents' sex-role behaviors and attitudes. *Child Development, 61,* 1413–1426.

McKNIGHT, C. C., CROSSWHITE, F. J., DOSSEY, J. A., KIFER, E., SWAFFORD, J. O., TRAVERS, K. J., & COONEY, T. J. (1987). *The underachieving curriculum: Assessing U.S. school mathematics from an international perspective.* Champaign, IL: Stipes.

*McKUSICK, V. A. (1992). *Mendelian inheritance in man.* Baltimore: Johns Hopkins University Press.

McLAUGHLIN, B., WHITE, D., McDEVITT, T., & RASKIN, R. (1983). Mothers' and fathers' speech to their young children: Similar or different? *Journal of Child Language, 10,* 245–252.

McNEILL, D. (1966). Developmental psycholinguistics. In F. Smith & G. A. Miller (Eds.), *The genesis of language: A psycholinguistic approach.* Cambridge, MA: MIT Press.

*McNEILL, D. (1992). *Hand and mind: What gestures reveal about thought.* Chicago: University of Chicago Press.

*MEAD, M. (1935). *Sex and temperament in three primitive societies.* New York: William Morrow.

MEAD, M., & NEWTON, N. (1967). Cultural patterning of perinatal behavior. In S. A. Richardson & A. F. Guttmacher (Eds.), *Childbearing: Its social and psychological factors.* Baltimore: Williams & Wilkins.

MEBERT, C. J. (1989). Stability and change in parents' perceptions of infant temperament: Early pregnancy to 13.5 months postpartum. *Infant Behavior and Development, 2,* 237–244.

MEBERT, C. J. (1991). Dimensions of subjectivity in parents' ratings of infant temperament. *Child Development, 62,* 352–361.

*MEDRICH, E. A., ROIZEN, J. A., RUBIN, V., & BUCKLEY, S. (1982). *The serious business of growing up: A study of children's lives outside school.* Berkeley: University of California Press.

MEHLER, J., BERTONCINI, J., BARRIERE, M., & JASSIK-GERSHENFELD, D. (1978). Infant recognition of mother's voice. *Perception, 7,* 491–497.

MEHLER, J., JUSCZYK, P. W., LAMBERTZ, G., HALSTED, N., BERTONCINI, J., & AMIEL-TISON, C. (1988). A precursor of language acquisition in young infants. *Cognition, 29,* 143–178.

MEICHENBAUM, D., & GOODMAN, S. (1979). Clinical use of private speech and critical ques-

tions about its study in natural settings. In G. Zivin (Ed.), *The development of self-regulation through private speech.* New York: Wiley.

MELARAGNO, R. J. (1974). Beyond decoding: Systematic schoolwide tutoring in reading. *The Reading Teacher, 27,* 157–160.

*MELOT, A.-M., & CORROYER, D. (1992). Organization of metacognitive knowledge: A condition for strategy use in memorization. *European Journal of Psychology of Education, 7,* 23–38.

*MELTON, D. A. (1991). Pattern formation during animal development. *Science, 252,* 234–241.

*MELTZOFF, A. N. (1988a). Infant imitation after a 1-week delay: Long-term memory for novel and multiple stimuli. *Developmental Psychology, 24,* 470–476.

MELTZOFF, A. N. (1988b). Infant imitation and memory: Nine-month-olds in immediate and deferred tests. *Child Development, 59,* 217–225.

MELTZOFF, A. N. (1990a). Foundations for developing a concept of self: The role of imitation in relating self to other and the value of social mirroring, social modeling, and self practice in infancy. In D. Cicchetti & M. Beeghly (Eds.), *The self in transition: Infancy to childhood.* Chicago: University of Chicago Press.

*MELTZOFF, A. N. (1990b). Towards a developmental cognitive science: The implications of cross-modal matching and imitation for the development of representation and memory in infancy. In A. Diamond (Ed.), *The development and neural bases of higher cognitive functions.* New York: New York Academy of Sciences.

MELTZOFF, A. N., & BORTON, R. W. (1979). Intermodal matching by human neonates. *Nature, 282,* 403–404.

MELTZOFF, A. N., & MOORE, M. K. (1977). Imitation of facial and manual gestures by human neonates. *Science, 198,* 75–78.

MELTZOFF, A. N., & MOORE, M. K. (1983a). Newborn infants imitate adult facial gestures. *Child Development, 54,* 702–709.

MELTZOFF, A. N., & MOORE, M. K. (1983b). The origins of imitation in infancy: Paradigm, phenomena, and theory. In L. P. Lipsitt & C. Rovee-Collier (Eds.), *Advances in infancy research* (Vol. 2). Norwood, NJ: Ablex.

MELTZOFF, A. N., & MOORE, M. K. (1985). Cognitive foundations and social functions of imitation and intermodal representation in infancy. In J. Mehler & R. Fox (Eds.), *Neonate cognition: Beyond the blooming buzzing confusion.* Hillsdale, NJ: Erlbaum.

MELTZOFF, A. N., & MOORE, M. K. (1989). Imitation in newborn infants: Exploring the range of gestures imitated and the underlying mechanisms. *Developmental Psychology, 25,* 954–962.

*MELTZOFF, A. N., & MOORE, M. K. (1992). Early imitation within a functional framework: The importance of person identity, movement, and development. *Infant Behavior and Development, 15,* 479–505.

*MENARD, S. (1991). *Longitudinal research.* Newbury Park, CA: Sage.

MENDELSON, M. J. (1990). *Becoming a brother.* Cambridge, MA: MIT Press.

MENDELSON, M. J., & FERLAND, M. B. (1982).

Auditory–visual transfer in four-month-old infants. *Child Development, 53,* 1022–1027.

MENDELSON, M. J., & HAITH, M. M. (1976). The relation between audition and vision in the human newborn. *Monographs of the Society for Research in Child Development, 41* (4, Serial No. 167).

MENIG-PETERSON, C. L. (1975). The modification of communicative behaviors in preschool-aged children as a function of the listener's perspective. *Child Development, 46,* 1015–1018.

MEREDITH, H. V. (1963). Change in the stature and body weight of North American boys during the last 80 years. In L. P. Lipsitt & C. C. Spiker (Eds.), *Advances in child development and behavior* (Vol. 1). New York: Academic Press.

MERRIMAN, W. E. (1986). How children learn the reference of concrete nouns: A critique of current hypotheses. In S. A. Kuczaj & M. D. Barrett (Eds.), *The development of word meaning.* New York: Springer-Verlag.

MERRIMAN, W. E., KEATING, D. P., & LIST, J. A. (1985). Mental rotation of facial profiles: Age-, sex-, and ability-related differences. *Developmental Psychology, 21,* 888–900.

*MERRIMAN, W. E., & SCHUSTER, J. M. (1991). Young children's disambiguation of object name reference. *Child Development, 62,* 1288–1301.

*MERSON, M. H. (1993). Slowing the spread of HIV: Agenda for the 1990s. *Science, 260,* 1266–1268.

MERVIS, C. B. (1987). Child-basic object categories and early lexical development. In U. Neisser (Ed.), *Concepts and conceptual development: Ecological and intellectual factors in categorization.* New York: Cambridge University Press.

MERVIS, C. B., & CRISAFI, M. A. (1982). Order of acquisition of subordinate-, basic-, and superordinate-level categories. *Child Development, 53,* 250–266.

MERVIS, C. B., & MERVIS, C. A. (1988). Role of adult input in young children's category evolution: I. An observational study. *Journal of Child Language, 15,* 257–272.

MESSER, D. J. (1980). The episodic structure of maternal speech to young children. *Journal of Child Language, 7,* 29–40.

*MESSER, D. J., McCARTHY, M. E., McQUISTON, S., MacTURK, R. H., YARROW, L. J., & VIETZE, P. M. (1986). Relation between mastery motivation in infancy and competence in early childhood. *Developmental Psychology, 22,* 366–372.

METTETAL, G. (1983). Fantasy, gossip, and self-disclosure: Children's conversations with friends. In R. N. Bostrom (Ed.), *Communication yearbook* (Vol. 7). Beverly Hills, CA: Sage.

MICHAEL, J. (1984). Verbal behavior. *Journal of the Experimental Analysis of Behavior, 42,* 363–376.

MIDGLEY, C., FELDLAUFER, H., & ECCLES, J. (1988a). Student/teacher relations and attitudes towards mathematics before and after the transition to junior high school. *Child Development, 60,* 375–395.

MIDGLEY, C., FELDLAUFER, H., & ECCLES, J. (1988b). The transition to junior high school: Beliefs of pre- and post-transition teachers. *Journal of Youth and Adolescence, 17,* 543–562.

MIDLARSKY, E., & HANNAH, M. E. (1985). Competence, reticence, and helping by children and adolescents. *Developmental Psychology, 21*, 534–541.

MILLER, N., & MARUYAMA, G. (1976). Ordinal position and peer popularity. *Journal of Personality and Social Psychology, 33*, 123–131.

*MILLER, P. H. (1990). The development of strategies of selective attention. In D. F. Bjorklund (Ed.), *Children's strategies: Contemporary views of cognitive development.* Hillsdale, NJ: Erlbaum.

*MILLER, P. H. (1993). *Theories of developmental psychology* (3rd ed.). New York: W. H. Freeman.

MILLER, P. H., & ALOISE, P. A. (1989). Young children's understanding of the psychological causes of behavior: A review. *Child Development, 60*, 257–285.

MILLER, P. H., & DeMARIE-DREBLOW, D. (1990). Social-cognitive correlates of children's understanding of displaced aggression. *Journal of Experimental Child Psychology, 49*, 488–504.

*MILLER, P. H., & SEIER, W. L. (in press). Strategy utilization deficiencies in children: When, where, and why? In H. W. Reese (Ed.), *Advances in child development and behavior* (Vol. 25). New York: Academic Press.

MILLER, P. M., DANAHER, D. L., & FORBES, D. (1986). Sex-related strategies for coping with interpersonal conflict in children aged five to seven. *Developmental Psychology, 22*, 543–548.

MILLER, S. A. (1976). Nonverbal assessment of Piagetian concepts. *Psychological Bulletin, 83*, 405–430.

MILLER, S. A. (1982). Cognitive development: A Piagetian perspective. In R. Vasta (Ed.), *Strategies and techniques of child study.* New York: Academic Press.

MILLER, S. A. (1986). Certainty and necessity in the understanding of Piagetian concepts. *Developmental Psychology, 22*, 3–18.

MILLER, S. A. (1987). *Developmental research methods.* Englewood Cliffs, NJ: Prentice Hall.

*MILLER, S. A., & DAVIS, T. L. (1992). Beliefs about children: A comparative study of mothers, teachers, peers, and self. *Child Development, 63*, 1251–1265.

MILLER, S. A., SHELTON, J., & FLAVELL, J. H. (1970). A test of Luria's hypothesis concerning the development of verbal self-regulation. *Child Development, 41*, 651–665.

MILLS, R. S. L., & GRUSEC, J. E. (1988). Socialization from the perspective of the parent–child relationship. In S. Duck (Ed.), *Handbook of personal relationships.* Chichester, England: Wiley.

MILLS, R. S. L., & GRUSEC, J. E. (1989). Cognitive, affective, and behavioral consequences of praising altruism. *Merrill-Palmer Quarterly, 35*, 299–326.

*MINDE, K. (1993). Prematurity and illness in infancy: Implications for development and intervention. In C. H. Zeanah Jr. (Ed.), *Handbook of infant development.* New York: Guilford.

MINKOWSKI, M. (1928). In *Abderhalden's Handbook of Biological Methods* (Issue 253, Section V, Pt. 5B). Cited in A. Peiper (1963), *Cerebral function in infancy and adulthood.* New York: Consultants Bureau.

MINTON, H. L., & SCHNEIDER, F. W. (1980). *Differential psychology.* Monterey, CA: Brooks/Cole.

*MINUCHIN, P. (1985). Families and individual development: Provocations from the field of family therapy. *Child Development, 56*, 289–302.

MISCHEL, W., SHODA, Y., & PEAKE, P. K. (1988). The nature of adolescent competencies predicted by preschool delay of gratification. *Journal of Personality and Social Psychology, 54*, 687–696.

*MISCHEL, W., SHODA, Y., & RODRIGUEZ, M. L. (1989). Delay of gratification in children. *Science, 244*, 933–938.

MITZENHEIM, P. (1985). The importance of Rousseau's developmental thinking for child psychology. In G. Eckardt, W. G. Bringmann, & L. Sprung (Eds.), *Contributions to a history of developmental psychology.* Berlin: Mouton.

*MIYAKE, K., CHEN, S. J., & CAMPOS, J. J. (1985). Infant temperament, mother's mode of interaction, and attachment in Japan: An interim report. In I. Bretheron & E. Waters (Eds.), Growing points of attachment theory and research. *Monographs of the Society for Research in Child Development, 50*(1–2, Serial No. 209).

MIYAWAKI, K., STRANGE, W., VERBRUGGE, R., LIBERMAN, A. M., JENKINS, J. J., & FUJIMURA, O. (1975). An effect of linguistic experience: The discrimination of the [r] and [l] by native speakers of Japanese and English. *Perception and Psychophysics, 18*, 331–340.

MIZE, J., & LADD, G. W. (1990). A cognitive-social learning approach to social skill training with low-status preschool children. *Developmental Psychology, 26*, 388–397.

MODGIL, S., & MODGIL, C. (1976). *Piagetian research: Compilation and commentary* (Vols. 1–8). Windsor, England: NFER.

MOELY, B. E. (1977). Organizational factors in the development of memory. In R. V. Kail & J. W. Hagen (Eds.), *Perspectives on the development of memory and cognition.* Hillsdale, NJ: Erlbaum.

*MOELY, B. E., HART, S. S., LEAL, L., SANTULLI, K. A., RAO, N., JOHNSON, T., & HAMILTON, L. B. (1992). The teacher's role in facilitating memory and study strategy development in the elementary school classroom. *Child Development, 63*, 653–672.

MOERK, E. L. (1977). Processes and products of imitation: Additional evidence that imitation is progressive. *Journal of Psycholinguistic Research, 6*, 187–202.

MOERK, E. L. (1983). *The mother of Eve: As a first language teacher.* Norwood, NJ: Ablex.

MOERK, E. L. (1986). Environmental factors in early language acquisition. In G. J. Whitehurst (Ed.), *Annals of child development* (Vol. 3). Greenwich, CT: JAI Press.

MOERK, E. L. (1989). The LAD was a lady and the tasks were ill-defined. *Developmental Review, 9*, 21–57.

MOFFITT, A. R. (1973). Intensity discrimination and cardiac reaction in young infants. *Developmental Psychology, 8*, 357–359.

*MOFFITT, T. E., CASPI, A., BELSKY, J., & SILVA, P. A. (1992). Childhood experience and the onset of menarche: A test of a sociobiological model. *Child Development, 63*, 47–58.

MOLFESE, D. L., & MOLFESE, V. J. (1979). Hemispheric and stimulus differences as reflected in the cortical responses of newborn infants to speech stimuli. *Developmental Psychology, 15*, 505–511.

*MOLFESE, D. L., & SEGALOWITZ, S. J. (1989). *Brain lateralization in children: Developmental implications.* New York: Guilford.

MOLTZ, H., & ROSENBLUM, L. A. (1983). A conceptual framework for the study of parent–young symbiosis. In L. A. Rosenblum & H. Moltz (Eds.), *Symbiosis in parent–offspring interactions.* New York: Plenum.

*MONAHAN, S. C. BUCHANAN, C., M., MACCOBY, E. E., & DORNBUSCH, S. M. (1993). Sibling differences in divorced families. *Child Development, 64*, 152–168.

MONEY, J. C. (1987). Propaedeutics of diecious G-I/R: Theoretical foundations for understanding dimorphic gender-identity/role. In J. M. Reinisch, L. A. Rosenblum, & S. A. Sanders (Eds.), *Masculinity/femininity: Basic perspectives.* New York: Oxford University Press.

MONEY, J. C., & ANNECILLO, C. (1987). Crucial period effect in psychendocrinology: Two syndromes, abuse dwarfism and female (CVAH) hermaphroditism. In M. H. Bornstein (Ed.), *Sensitive periods in development: Interdisciplinary perspectives.* Hillsdale, NJ: Erlbaum.

MONEY, J. C., & EHRHARDT, A. A. (1972). *Man & woman, boy & girl.* Baltimore: Johns Hopkins University Press.

MONTAGUE, M. F. A. (1968). *Man and aggression.* New York: Oxford University Press.

MONTEMAYOR, R. (1974). Children's performance in a game and their attraction to it as a function of sex-typed labels. *Child Development, 45*, 152–156.

*MONTGOMERY, D. E. (1992). Young children's theory of knowing: The development of a folk epistemology. *Developmental Review, 12*, 410–430.

*MONTGOMERY, D. E. (1993). Young children's understanding of interpretive diversity between different-age listeners. *Developmental Psychology, 29*, 337–345.

*MOON, C., COOPER, R. P., & FIFER, W. P. (1993). Two-day-olds prefer their native language. *Infant Behavior and Development, 16*, 495–500.

MOORE, B. S., & EISENBERG, N. (1984). The development of altruism. In G. J. Whitehurst (Ed.), *Annals of child development* (Vol. 1). Greenwich, CT: JAI Press.

MOORE, C. L. (1985). Another psychobiological view of sexual differentiation. *Developmental Review, 5*, 18–55.

*MOORE, D. (1993, March). *Simultaneous auditory and visual depth perception in 4- and 7-month-olds.* Paper presented at the meeting of the Society for Research in Child Development, New Orleans.

MOORE, E. G. J. (1986). Family socialization and the IQ test performance of traditionally and transracially adopted black children. *Developmental Psychology, 22*, 317–326.

MOORE, K. L. (1983). *Before we are born.* Philadelphia: Saunders.

MORAN, G. F., & VINOVSKIS, M. A. (1985). The

great care of godly parents: Early childhood in Puritan New England. In A. B. Smuts & J. W. Hagen (Eds.), History and research in child development. *Monographs of the Society for Research in Child Development, 50* (4–5, Serial No. 211).

MORAN, J. D., III, & McCULLERS, J. C. (1984). The effects of recency and story content on children's moral judgments. *Journal of Experimental Child Psychology, 38,* 447–455.

*MORELL, V. (1993). The puzzle of the triple repeats. *Science, 260,* 1422–1423.

*MORFORD, M., & GOLDIN-MEADOW, S. (1992). Comprehension and production of gesture in combination with speech in one-word speakers. *Journal of Child Language, 19,* 559–580.

*MORGAN, B., & GIBSON, K. R. (1991). Nutritional and environmental interactions in brain development. In K. R. Gibson and A. C. Petersen (Eds.), *Brain maturation and cognitive development.* New York: Aldine de Gruyter.

MORGAN, J. L. (1986). *From simple input to complex grammar.* Cambridge, MA: MIT Press.

*MORGANE, P. J., AUSTIN-LaFRANCE, R., BRONZINO, J., TONKISS, J., DÍAZ-CINTRA, S., CINTRA, L., KEMPER, T., & GALLER, J. R. (1993). Prenatal malnutrition and development of the brain. *Neuroscience and Biobehavioral Reviews, 17,* 91–128.

*MORGANTHAU, T. (1993, November 1). Can TV violence be curbed? *Newsweek,* p. 16.

MORIN, N. C., WIRTH, F. H., JOHNSON, D. H., FRANK, L. M., PRESBURG, H. J., VAN DE WATER, V. L., CHEE, E. M., & MILLS, J. L. (1989). Congenital malformations and psychosocial development in children conceived by in vitro fertilization. *Journal of Pediatrics, 115,* 222–227.

MORO, E. (1918). Das erste Trimenon. *Munch. med. Wschr., 65,* 1147–1150.

MORRIS, D. (1967). *The naked ape.* New York: McGraw-Hill.

*MORRISON, F. J., GRIFFITH, E. M., & FRAZIER, J. A. (1994). Schooling and the 5–7 shift: A natural experiment. In A. Sameroff & M. M. Haith (Eds.), *Reason and responsibility: The passage through childhood.* Chicago: University of Chicago Press.

MORRISON, H., & KUHN, D. (1983). Cognitive aspects of preschoolers' peer imitation in a play situation. *Child Development, 54,* 1054–1063.

MORRONGIELLO, B. A. (1988a). Discrimination of sound localization by very young infants. *Infant Behavior and Development, 11,* 225.

MORRONGIELLO, B. A. (1988b). Infants' localization of sounds along two spatial dimensions: Horizontal and vertical axes. *Infant Behavior and Development, 11,* 127–143.

MORRONGIELLO, B. A. (1988c). Infants' localization of sounds in the horizontal plane: Estimates of minimal audible angle. *Developmental Psychology, 24,* 8–13.

*MORRONGIELLO, B. A., & FENWICK, K. D. (1991). Infants' coordination of auditory and visual depth information. *Journal of Experimental Child Psychology, 52,* 277–296.

*MORRONGIELLO, B. A., HEWITT, K. L., & GOTOWIEC, A. (1991). Infants' discrimination of relative distance in the auditory modality: Approaching versus receding sound sources. *Infant Behavior and Development, 14,* 187–208.

MORTON, T. (1986). Childhood aggression in the context of family interaction. In D. H. Crowell, I. M. Evans, & C. R. O'Donnell (Eds.), *Childhood aggression and violence: Sources of influence, prevention, and control.* New York: Plenum.

MOSS, H. A. (1974). Early sex differences and mother–infant interaction. In R. C. Friedman, R. N. Richart, & R. L. VandeWiele (Eds.), *Sex differences in behavior.* New York: Wiley.

MOSSLER, D. G., MARVIN, R. S., & GREENBERG, M. D. (1976). Conceptual perspective taking in 2- to 6-year-old children. *Developmental Psychology, 12,* 85–86.

MOUNTEER, C. A. (1987). Roman childhood, 200 B.C. to A.D. 600. *Journal of Psychohistory, 14,* 233–254.

*MRAZEK, P. J. (1993). Maltreatment and infant development. In C. H. Zeanah Jr. (Ed.), *Handbook of infant mental development.* New York: Guilford.

*MRC VITAMIN STUDY/RESEARCH GROUP. (1991). Prevention of neural tube defects: Results of the Medical Research Council vitamin study. *Lancet, 338,* 131–137.

MUELLER, E., & SILVERMAN, N. (1989). Peer relations in maltreated children. In D. Cicchetti & V. Carlson (Eds.), *Child maltreatment: Theory and research on the causes and consequences of child abuse and neglect.* New York: Cambridge University Press.

MUELLER, W. H. (1986). The genetics of size and shape in children and adults. In F. Falkner & J. M. Tanner (Eds.), *Human growth: A comprehensive treatise* (2nd ed., Vol. 3). New York: Plenum.

MUIR, D., & CLIFTON, R. K. (1985). Infants' orientation to the location of sound sources. In G. Gottlieb & N. A. Krasnegor (Eds.), *Measurement of audition and vision in the first year of postnatal life: A methodological overview.* Norwood, NJ: Ablex.

*MULLEN, M., SNIDMAN, N., & KAGAN, J. (1993). Free-play behavior in inhibited and uninhibited children. *Infant Behavior and Development, 16,* 383–389.

MUNRO, D. J. (1977). *The concept of man in contemporary China.* Ann Arbor: University of Michigan Press.

MUNROE, R. H., SHIMMIN, H. S., & MUNROE, R. L. (1984). Gender understanding and sex role preference in four cultures. *Developmental Psychology, 20,* 673–682.

*MURATA, P. J., McGLYNN, E. A., SIU, A. L., & BROOK, R. H. (1992). *Prenatal care.* Santa Monica, CA: Rand.

*MURPHEY, D. A. (1992). Constructing the child: Relations between parents' beliefs and child outcomes. *Developmental Review, 12,* 199–232.

MURPHY, C. M. (1978). Pointing in the context of a shared activity. *Child Development, 49,* 371–380.

MURRAY, A. D., JOHNSON, J., & PETERS, J. (1990). Fine-tuning of utterance length to preverbal infants: Effects on later language development. *Journal of Child Language, 17,* 511–525.

MURRAY, F. B. (1982). Learning and development through social interaction and conflict: A challenge to social learning theory. In L. Liben

(Ed.), *Piaget and the foundation of knowledge.* Hillsdale, NJ: Erlbaum.

MUSATTI, T. (1986). Early peer relations: The perspectives of Piaget and Vygotsky. In E. C. Mueller & C. R. Cooper (Eds.), *Process and outcome in peer relationships.* New York: Academic Press.

MUSSEN, P. H. (1987). Longitudinal study of the life span. In N. Eisenberg (Ed.), *Contemporary topics in developmental psychology.* New York: Wiley.

MUSSEN, P., & JONES, M. C. (1957). Self-conceptions, motivations, and interpersonal attitudes of late- and early-maturing boys. *Child Development, 28,* 243–256.

*MWAMWENDA, T. S. (1992). Cognitive development in African children. *Genetic, Social, and General Psychology Monographs, 118,* 5–72.

MYERS, B. J. (1987). Mother–infant bonding as a critical period. In M. H. Bornstein (Ed.), *Sensitive periods in development: Interdisciplinary perspectives.* Hillsdale, NJ: Erlbaum.

MYERS, M., & PARIS, S. G. (1978). Children's metacognitive knowledge about reading. *Journal of Educational Psychology, 70,* 680–690.

*NADEL, J., & FONTAINE, A. (1989). Communicating by imitation: A developmental and comparative approach to transitory social competence. In B. H. Schneider, G. Attili, J. Nadel, & R. P. Weissberg (Eds.), *Social competence in developmental perspective.* Dordrecht, The Netherlands: Kluwer.

NADELMAN, L. (1974). Sex identity in American children: Memory, knowledge, and preference tests. *Developmental Psychology, 10,* 413–417.

NAEYE, R. L., DIENER, M. M., & DELLINGER, W. S. (1969). Urban poverty: Effects on prenatal nutrition. *Science, 166,* 1026.

*NAKAHARA, T., UOZUMI, T., MONDEN, S., MUTTAGIN, Z., KURISU, K., ARITA, K., KUWABARA, S., OHAMA, K., KUMAGAI, M., & NAKAHARA, K. (1993). Prenatal diagnosis of open spina bifida by MRI and ultrasonography. *Brain & Development, 15,* 75–78.

*NATIONAL INSTITUTES OF HEALTH. (1993). The human genome: A race to the 3 billionth base. *Journal of NIH Research, 5,* 44.

NEEDHAM, J. (1959). *A history of embryology.* Cambridge: Cambridge University Press.

NEEDLEMAN, H. L., SCHELL, A. S., BELLINGER, D., LEVITON, A., & ALLDRED, E. N. (1990). The long-term effects of exposure to low doses of lead in childhood: An 11-year follow-up report. *New England Journal of Medicine, 322,* 83.

*NEISSER, U. (1991). Two perceptually given aspects of the self and their development. *Developmental Review, 11,* 197–209.

NELSON, C. A. (1985). The perception and recognition of facial expressions in infancy. In T. M. Field & N. A. Fox (Eds.), *Social perception in infants.* Norwood, NJ: Ablex.

NELSON, C. A. (1987). The recognition of facial expressions in the first two years of life: Mechanisms of development. *Child Development, 58,* 889–909.

NELSON, C. A., & DOLGRIN, K. G. (1985). The generalized discrimination of facial expressions by seven-month-old infants. *Child Development, 56,* 58–61.

NELSON, C. A., & HOROWITZ, F. D. (1987). Visual motion perception in infancy: A review and synthesis. In P. Salapatek & L. Cohen (Eds.), *Handbook of infant perception: Vol. 2. From perception to cognition.* New York: Academic Press.

NELSON, D. G. K., HIRSH-PASEK, K., JUSCZYK, P. W., & CASSIDY, K. W. (1989). How the prosodic cues in motherese might assist language learning. *Journal of Child Language, 16,* 55–68.

NELSON, K. (1973). Structure and strategy in learning to talk. *Monographs of the Society for Research in Child Development, 38* (1–2, Serial No. 149).

NELSON, K. (1974). Concept, word, and sentence: Interrelationships in acquisition and development. *Psychological Review, 81,* 267–285.

NELSON, K. (1979). Explorations in the development of a functional semantic system. In W. Collins (Ed.), *Minnesota symposia on child psychology: Vol. 12. Children's language and communication.* Hillsdale, NJ: Erlbaum.

NELSON, K. (1985). *Making sense: The acquisition of shared meaning.* Orlando, FL: Academic Press.

*NELSON, K. (1986). *Event knowledge: Structure and function in development.* Hillsdale, NJ: Erlbaum.

*NELSON, K. (1993a). Events, narratives, memory: What develops? In C. A. Nelson (Ed.), *Minnesota symposia on child psychology: Vol. 26. Memory and affect in development.* Hillsdale, NJ: Erlbaum.

*NELSON, K. (1993b). The psychological and social origins of autobiographical memory. *Psychological Science, 4,* 7–14.

NELSON, K., & GRUENDEL, J. (1981). Generalized event representations: Basic building blocks of cognitive development. In M. E. Lamb & A. L. Brown (Eds.), *Advances in developmental psychology* (Vol. 1). Hillsdale, NJ: Erlbaum.

NELSON, K., & GRUENDEL, J. (1986). Children's scripts. In K. Nelson (Ed.), *Event knowledge: Structure and function in development.* Hillsdale, NJ: Erlbaum.

NELSON, K., & HUDSON, J. (1988). Scripts and memory: Functional relationships in development. In F. E. Weinert & M. Perlmutter (Eds.), *Memory development: Universal changes and individual differences.* Hillsdale, NJ: Erlbaum.

*NELSON, K., HAMPSON, J., & SHAW, L. K. (1993). Nouns in early lexicons: Evidence, explanations, and implications. *Journal of Child Language, 20,* 61–84.

NELSON, K., & LUCARIELLO, J. (1985). The development of meaning in first words. In M. D. Barrett (Ed.), *Children's single-word speech.* New York: Wiley.

NELSON, S. A. (1980). Factors influencing young children's use of motives and outcomes as moral criteria. *Child Development, 51,* 823–829.

NELSON, S. A., & DWECK, C. S. (1977). Motivation and competence as determinants of young children's reward allocation. *Developmental Psychology, 13,* 192–197.

NEWBERGER, C. M., MELNICOE, L., & NEW-

BERGER, E. H. (1986). The American family in crisis: Implications for children. *Current Problems in Pediatrics, 16,* 674–721.

*NEWCOMB, A. F., BUKOWSKI, W. M., & PATTEE, L. (1993). Children's peer relations: A meta-analytic review of popular, rejected, neglected, controversial, and average sociometric status. *Psychological Bulletin, 113,* 99–128.

NEWCOMBE, N. (1989). The development of spatial perspective taking. In H. W. Reese (Ed.), *Advances in child development and behavior* (Vol. 22). San Diego, CA: Academic Press.

*NEWCOMBE, N., & DUBAS, J. S. (1992). A longitudinal study of predictors of spatial ability in adolescent females. *Child Development, 63,* 37–46.

NEWCOMBE, N., DUBAS, J. S., & BAENNINGER, M. (1989). Associations of timing of puberty, spatial ability, and lateralization in adult women. *Child Development, 60,* 246–254.

*NEWCOMBE, N., & HUTTENLOCHER, J. (1992). Children's early ability to solve perspective-taking problems. *Developmental Psychology, 28,* 635–643.

NEWCOMER, S., & UDRY, J. R. (1987). Parental marital status effects on adolescent sexual behavior. *Journal of Marriage and the Family, 48,* 235–240.

NEWMAN, P. R. (1982). The peer group. In B. B. Wolman (Ed.), *Handbook of developmental psychology.* Engelwood Cliffs, NJ: Prentice-Hall.

NEWPORT, E. L. (1977). Motherese: The speech of mothers to young children. In N. J. Castellan, D. B. Pisoni, & G. Potts (Eds.), *Cognitive theory* (Vol. 2). Hillsdale, NJ: Erlbaum.

*NEWPORT, E. L. (1991). Contrasting concepts of the critical period for language. In S. Carey & R. Gelman (Eds.), *The epigenesis of mind: Essays on biology and cognition.* Hillsdale, NJ: Erlbaum.

NICHOLS, R. C. (1978). Heredity and environment: Major findings from twin studies of ability, personality, and interests. *Homo, 29,* 158–173.

*NINIO, A. (1992). The relation of children's single-word utterances to single-word utterances in the input. *Journal of Child Language, 19,* 87–110.

NINIO, A., & BRUNER, J. (1978). The achievement and antecedents of labeling. *Journal of Child Language, 5,* 1–15.

NINIO, A., & SNOW, C. E. (1988). Language acquisition through language use: The functional sources of children's early utterances. In Y. Levy, I. M. Schlesinger, & M. D. S. Braine (Eds.), *Categories and processes in language acquisition.* Hillsdale, NJ: Erlbaum.

NINIO, A., & WHEELER, P. (1984). Functions of speech in mother–infant interaction. In L. Feagans, C. Garvey, & R. Golinkoff (Eds.), *The origins and growth of communication.* Norwood, NJ: Ablex.

NISAN, M. (1984). Distributive justice and social norms. *Child Development, 55,* 1020–1029.

NODDINGS, N. (1984). *Caring: A feminist approach to ethics and moral education.* Berkeley: University of California Press.

NOLEN-HOEKSEMA, S., GIRGUS, J. S., & SELIGMAN, M. E. P. (1986). Learned helpless-

ness in children: A longitudinal study of depression, achievement, and explanatory style. *Journal of Personality and Social Psychology, 51,* 435–442.

NORCINI, J. J., & SNYDER, S. S. (1986). Effects of modeling and cognitive induction on moral reasoning. In G. L. Sapp (Ed.), *Handbook of moral development: Models, processes, techniques, and research.* Birmingham: Religious Education Press.

NOTTLEMAN, E. D. (1987). Competence and self-esteem during transition from childhood to adolescence. *Developmental Psychology, 23,* 441–450.

*NOWAK, R. (1994). Mining treasures from "Junk DNA." *Science, 263,* 608–610.

NOWLIS, G. H., & KESSEN, W. (1976). Human newborns differentiate differing concentrations of sucrose and glucose. *Science, 191,* 865–866.

NUMMEDAL, S. G., & BASS, S. C. (1976). Effects of the salience of intention and consequences on children's moral judgments. *Developmental Psychology, 12,* 475–476.

*NUNES, T., CARRAHER, D. W., & SCHLIEMANN, A. D. (1993). *Street mathematics and school mathematics.* New York: Cambridge University Press.

NUNNALLY, J. C. (1982). The study of human change: Measurement, research strategies, and methods of analysis. In B. B. Wolman (Ed.), *Handbook of developmental psychology.* Englewood Cliffs, NJ: Prentice Hall.

NUNNER-WINKLER, G., & SODIAN, B. (1988). Children's understanding of moral emotions. *Child Development, 59,* 1323–1338.

O'BRIEN, M., & HUSTON, A. C. (1985). Development of sex-typed play behavior in toddlers. *Developmental Psychology, 21,* 866–871.

O'BRIEN, M., & NAGLE, K. (1987). Parents' speech to toddlers: The effect of play context. *Journal of Child Language, 14,* 269–279.

O'CONNOR, R. D. (1969). Modification of social withdrawal through symbolic modeling. *Journal of Applied Behavior Analysis, 2,* 15–22.

*OCHS KEENAN, E. (1977). Making it last: Repetition in children's discourse. In S. Ervin-Tripp & C. Mitchell-Kernan (Eds.), *Child discourse.* New York: Academic Press.

O'CONNOR, R. D. (1972). Relative efficacy of modeling, shaping, and the combined procedures for modification of social withdrawal. *Journal of Abnormal Psychology, 79,* 327–334.

ODOM, S. L., & STRAIN, P. S. (1984). Peer-mediated approaches to promoting children's social interaction: A review. *American Journal of Orthopsychiatry, 54,* 544–557.

OEHLER, J. M., & ECKERMAN, C. D. (1988). Regulatory effects of human speech and touch in premature infants prior to term age. *Infant Behavior and Development, 11,* 249.

*OHLENDORF-MOFFAT, P. (1991, February). Surgery before birth. *Discover,* pp. 59–65.

OLLER, D. K. (1986). Metaphonology and infant vocalizations. In B. Lindblom & R. Zetterstrom (Eds.), *Precursors of early speech.* New York: Stockton.

OLLER, D. K., & EILERS, R. E. (1982). Similarity

of babbling in Spanish- and English-learning babies. *Journal of Child Language, 9,* 565–577.

OLLER, D. K., & EILERS, R. E. (1988). The role of audition in infant babbling. *Child Development, 59,* 441–449.

OLSON, G. M., & SHERMAN, T. (1983). Attention, learning, and memory in infants. In M. M. Haith & J. J. Campos (Eds.), *Handbook of child psychology: Vol. 2. Infancy and developmental psychobiology.* New York: Wiley.

*OLSON, S. L., BATES, J. E., & KASKIE, B. (1992). Caregiver–infant interaction antecedents of children's school-age cognitive ability. *Merrill-Palmer Quarterly, 38,* 309–330.

*OLVERA-EZZELL, N., POWER, T. G., & COUSINS, J. H. (1990). Maternal socialization of children's eating habits: Strategies used by obese Mexican-American mothers. *Child Development, 61,* 395–400.

OLWEUS, D. (1983). The role of testosterone in the development of aggressive, antisocial behavior in human adolescents. In K. T. VanDusen & S. A. Mednick (Eds.), *Prospective studies in crime and delinquency.* Boston: Kluwer-Nijhoff.

OLWEUS, D. (1986). Aggression and hormones: Behavioral relationship with testosterone and adrenaline. In D. Olweus, J. Block, & M. Radke-Yarrow (Eds.), *Development of antisocial and prosocial behavior.* Orlando, FL: Academic Press.

OMARK, D. R., STRAYER, F. F., & FREEDMAN, D. G. (1980). *Dominance relations: An ethological view of human conflict and social interaction.* New York: Garland.

*O'REILLY, A. W., & BORNSTEIN, M. (1993). Caregiver–child interaction in play. In M. H. Bornstein & A. W. O'Reilly (Eds.), *New directions for child development: No. 59. The role of play in the development of thought.* San Francisco, CA: Jossey-Bass.

ORNSTEIN, P. A., BAKER-WARD, L., & NAUS, M. J. (1988). The development of mnemonic skill. In F. E. Weinert & M. Perlmutter (Eds.), *Memory development: Universal changes and individual differences.* Hillsdale, NJ: Erlbaum.

*ORNSTEIN, P. A., LARUS, D. M., & CLUBB, P. A. (1991). Understanding children's testimony: Implications of research on the development of memory. In R. Vasta (Ed.), *Annals of child development* (Vol. 8). London: Kingsley.

ORNSTEIN, P. A., NAUS, M. J., & LIBERTY, C. (1975). Rehearsal and organizational processes in children's memory. *Child Development, 46,* 818–830.

*OSHERSON, D. N. (1990). *An invitation to cognitive science.* Cambridge, MA: MIT Press.

*OSTER, H., HEGLEY, D., & NAGEL, L. (1992). Adult judgments and fine-grained analysis of infant facial expressions: Testing the validity of a priori coding formulas. *Developmental Psychology, 28,* 1115–1131.

OTTINGER, D. R., & SIMMONS, J. E. (1964). Behavior of human neonates and prenatal maternal anxiety. *Psychological Reports, 14,* 391–394.

*OVERTON, W. F. (Ed.). (1990). *Reasoning, necessity, and logic: Developmental perspectives.* Hillsdale, NJ: Erlbaum.

OWEN, D. R. (1972). The 47,XYY male: A review. *Psychological Bulletin, 78,* 209–233.

OWEN, D. R. (1979). Psychological studies in XYY men. In H. L. Vallet & I. H. Porter (Eds.), *Genetic mechanisms of sexual development.* New York: Academic Press.

OWEN, M., & COX, M. (1988). Maternal employment and the transition to parenthood. In A. E. Gottfried & A. W. Gottfried (Eds.), *Maternal employment and children's development: Longitudinal research.* New York: Plenum.

PAGE, R. A. (1981). Longitudinal evidence for the sequentiality of Kohlberg's stages of moral judgment in adolescent males. *Journal of Genetic Psychology, 139,* 3–9.

PAIKOFF, R. L., & BROOKS-GUNN, J. (1990). Physiological processes: What role do they play during the transition to adolescence? In R. Montemayor, G. R. Adams, & T. Gullotta (Eds.), *From childhood to adolescence: Vol. 2. Advances in adolescent development.* London: Sage.

*PAINE, P., DOREA, J. G., PASQUALI, L., & MONTEIRO, A. M. (1992). Growth and cognition in Brazilian school children: A spontaneously occurring intervention. *International Journal of Child Development, 15,* 169–183.

PALCA, J. (1990). AIDS and the future. *Science, 248,* 1484.

*PALCA, J. (1991). Fetal brain signals time for birth. *Science, 253,* 1360.

PALKOVITZ, R. (1984). Parental attitudes and fathers' interactions with their 5-month-old infants. *Developmental Psychology, 20,* 1054–1060.

*PAPOUSEK, M., & PAPOUSEK, H. (1991). Early verbalizations as precursors of language development. In M. E. Lamb & H. Keller (Eds.), *Infant development: Perspectives from German-speaking countries.* Hillsdale, NJ: Erlbaum.

PAPOUSEK, M., PAPOUSEK, H., & HAEKEL, M. (1987). Didactic adjustments in fathers' and mothers' speech to their 3-month-old infants. *Journal of Psycholinguistic Research, 16,* 491–516.

PAREKH, V. C., PHERWANI, A., UDANI, P. M., & MUKKERJIE, S. (1970). Brain weight and head circumference in fetus, infant, and children of different nutritional and socioeconomic groups. *Indian Pediatrics, 7,* 347–358.

PARIS, S. G. (1975). Integration and inference in children's comprehension and memory. In F. Restle, R. Shiffrin. J. Castellan, H. Lindman, & D. Pisoni (Eds). *Cognitive theory* (Vol. 1). Hillsdale, NJ: Erlbaum.

*PARIS, S. G., & CROSS, D. R. (1988). The zone of proximal development: Virtues and pitfalls of a metaphorical representation of children's learning. *Genetic Epistemologist, 16*(1), 27–37.

PARIS, S. G., & LINDAUER, B. K. (1976). The role of inference in children's comprehension and memory for sentences. *Cognitive Psychology, 8,* 217–227.

PARIS, S. G., & OKA, E. R. (1986). Children's reading strategies, metacognition, and motivation. *Developmental Review, 6,* 25–56.

PARK, K. A., & WATERS, E. (1989). Security of attachment and preschool friendships. *Child Development, 60,* 1076–1081.

PARKE, R. D. (1977). Some effects of punishment on children's behavior—revisited. In E. M. Hetherington & R. D. Parke (Eds.), *Contem-*

porary readings in child psychology. New York: McGraw-Hill.

PARKE, R. D., & BEITEL, A. (1986). Hospital-based intervention for fathers. In M. E. Lamb (Ed.), *The father's role: Applied perspectives.* New York: Wiley.

*PARKE, R. D., CASSIDY, J., BURKS, V. M., CARSON, J. L., & BOYUM, L. (1992). Familial contribution to peer competence among young children: The role of interactive and affective processes. In R. D. Parke & G. W. Ladd (Eds.), *Family–peer relationships: Modes of linkage.* Hillsdale, NJ: Erlbaum.

PARKE, R. D., & COLLMER, C. (1975). Child abuse: An interdisciplinary analysis. In E. M. Hetherington (Ed.), *Review of child development research* (Vol. 5). Chicago: University of Chicago Press.

*PARKE, R. D., & LADD, G. W. (Eds.). (1992). *Family–peer relationships: Modes of linkage.* Hillsdale, NJ: Erlbaum.

PARKE, R. D., & SLABY, R. G. (1983). The development of aggression. In E. M. Hetherington (Ed.), *Handbook of child psychology: Vol. 4. Socialization, personality, and social development.* New York: Wiley.

*PARKE, R. D., & TINSLEY, B. J. (1987). Family interaction in infancy. In J. Osofsky (Ed.), *Handbook of infant development* (2nd ed.). New York: Wiley.

PARKER, J. G., & ASHER, S. R. (1987). Peer relations and later personal adjustment: Are low-accepted children at risk? *Psychological Bulletin, 102,* 357–389.

PARMELEE, A. H., & GARBANATI, J. (1987). Clinical neurobehavioral aspects of state organization in newborn infants. In A. Kobayashi (Ed.), *Neonatal brain and behavior.* Nagoya, Japan: University of Nagoya Press.

PARMELEE, A. H., & SIGMAN, M. D. (1983). Perinatal brain development and behavior. In M. M. Haith & J. J. Campos (Eds.), *Handbook of child psychology: Vol. 2. Infancy and developmental psychobiology.* New York: Wiley.

PARSONS, C. (1960). Inhelder and Piaget's "The growth of logical thinking": II. A logician's viewpoint. *British Journal of Psychology, 51,* 75–84.

PARSONS, J. E. (1982). Biology, experience, and sex-dimorphic behaviors. In W. R. Gove & G. R. Carpenter (Eds.), *The fundamental connection between nature and nurture: A review of the evidence.* Lexington, MA: Lexington.

PARTEN, M. B. (1932). Social participation among preschool children. *Journal of Abnormal and Social Psychology, 27,* 243–269.

PASTOR, D. L. (1981). The quality of mother–infant attachment and its relationship to toddlers' initial sociability with peers. *Developmental Psychology, 17,* 326–335.

*PATTERSON, C. J. (1982). Self-control and self-regulation in childhood. In T. M. Field, A. Huston, H. C. Quay, L. Troll, & G. E. Finley (Eds.), *Review of human development.* New York: Wiley.

*PATTERSON, C. J. (1992). Children of lesbian and gay parents. *Child Development, 63,* 1025–1042.

*PATTERSON, C. J. (1994). Lesbian and gay families. *Current Directions in Psychological Science, 3,* 62–64.

*PATTERSON, C. J., KUPERSMIDT, J. B., & VADEN, N. A. (1990). Income level, gender, ethnicity, and household composition as predictors of children's school-based competence. *Child Development, 61,* 485–494.

*PATTERSON, F. G. (1978). The gestures of a gorilla: Language acquisition in another pongid. *Brain and Language, 5,* 72–97.

PATTERSON, G. R. (1982). *Coercive family process.* Eugene, OR: Castalia.

PATTERSON, G. R. (1986). The contribution of siblings to training for fighting: A microsocial analysis. In D. Olweus, J. Block, & M. Radke-Yarrow (Eds.), *Development of antisocial and prosocial behavior.* Orlando, FL: Academic Press.

PATTERSON, G. R., DeBARYSHE, B. D., & RAMSEY, E. (1989). A developmental perspective on antisocial behavior. *American Psychologist, 44,* 329–335.

PATTERSON, G. R., LITTMAN, R. A., & BRICKER, W. (1967). Assertive behavior in children: A step toward a theory of aggression. *Monographs of the Society for Research in Child Development, 32* (5, Serial No. 113).

*PATTERSON, G. R., REID, J. B., & DISHION, T. J. (1992). *Antisocial boys.* Eugene, OR: Castalia.

PEARL, D. (1987). Familial, peer, and television influences on aggressive and violent behavior. In D. H. Crowell, I. M. Evans, & C. R. O'Donnell (Eds.), *Childhood aggression and violence: Sources of influence, prevention, and control.* New York: Plenum.

*PEARSON, D. A. (1991). Auditory attention switching: A developmental study. *Journal of Experimental Child Psychology, 51,* 320–334.

PEDERSEN, D. R., MORAN, G., SITKO, C., CAMPBELL, K., GHESQUIRE, K., & ACTON, H. (1990). Maternal sensitivity and the security of infant–mother attachment: A Q-sort study. *Child Development, 61,* 1974–1983.

PEDERSON, D. R., & TER VRUGT, D. (1973). The influence of amplitude and frequency of vestibular stimulation on the activity of two-month-old infants. *Child Development, 44,* 122–128.

PEDERSON, N. L., FRIBERG, L., FLODERUS-MYRHED, B., McCLEARN, G. E., & PLOMIN, R. (1984). Swedish early-separated twins: Identification and characterization. *Acta Geneticae Medicae et Gemelogiae, 33,* 243–250.

*PEDLOW, R., SANSON, A., PRIOR, M., & OBERKLAID, F. (1993). Stability of maternally reported temperament from infancy to 8 years. *Developmental Psychology, 29,* 998–1007.

*PEGG, J. E., WERKER, J. F., & MCLEOD, P. J. (1992). Preferences for infant-directed over adult-directed speech: Evidence from 7-week-old infants. *Infant Behavior and Development, 15,* 325–345.

PEIPER, A. (1963). *Cerebral function in infancy and adulthood.* New York: Consultants Bureau.

PENNER, S. G. (1987). Parental responses to grammatical and ungrammatical child utterances. *Child Development, 58,* 376–384.

PENNINGTON, B. F., & SMITH, S. D. (1983). Genetic influences on learning disabilities and speech and language disorders. *Child Development, 54,* 369–387.

*PEPLER, D. J., KING, G., & BYRD, W. (1991). A social-cognitively based social skills training program for aggressive children. In D. J. Pepler & K. H. Rubin (Eds.), *The development and treatment of childhood aggression.* Hillsdale, NJ: Erlbaum.

*PERFETTI, C. A. (1991). The psychology, pedagogy, and politics of reading. *Psychological Science, 2,* 70–76.

*PERNER, J., & ASTINGTON, J. W. (1992). The child's understanding of mental representation. In H. Beilin & P. B. Pufall (Eds.), *Piaget's theory: Prospects and possibilities.* Hillsdale, NJ: Erlbaum.

PERRY, D. G., & BUSSEY, K. (1979). The social learning theory of sex differences: Imitation is alive and well. *Journal of Personality and Social Psychology, 37,* 1699–1712.

PERRY, D. G., & BUSSEY, K. (1984). *Social development.* Englewood Cliffs, NJ: Prentice Hall.

PERRY, D. G., & PERRY, L. C. (1983). Social learning, causal attribution, and moral internalization. In J. Bizanz, G. L. Bizanz, & R. Kail (Eds.), *Learning in children: Progress in cognitive development research.* New York: Springer-Verlag.

PERRY, D. G., PERRY, L. C., & WEISS, R. J. (1989). Sex differences in the consequences that children anticipate for aggression. *Developmental Psychology, 25,* 312–319.

PERRY, D. G., WHITE, A. J., & PERRY, L. C. (1984). Does early sex typing result from children's attempts to match their behavior to sex role stereotypes? *Child Development, 55,* 2114–2121.

*PETERS, D. P. (1991). The influence of stress and arousal on the child witness. In J. Doris (Ed.), *The suggestibility of children's recollections.* Washington, DC: APA.

PETERSEN, A. C. (1987). The nature of biological-psychosocial interactions: The sample case of early adolescence. In R. M. Lerner & T. L. Foch (Eds.), *Biological-psychosocial interactions in early adolescence.* Hillsdale, NJ: Erlbaum.

PETERSON, L. (1983). Role of donor competence, donor age, and peer presence on helping in an emergency. *Developmental Psychology, 19,* 873–880.

PETTIT, G. S., BAKSHI, A., DODGE, K. A., & COIE, J. D. (1990). The emergence of social dominance in young boys' play groups: Developmental differences and behavioral correlates. *Developmental Psychology, 26,* 1017–1025.

*PETITTO, L. A., & MARENTETTE, P. F. (1991). Babbling in the manual mode: Evidence for the ontogeny of language. *Science, 251,* 1493–1496.

PETTERSON, L., YONAS, A., & FISCH, R. O. (1980). The development of blinking in response to impending collision in preterm, full-term, and postterm infants. *Infant Behavior and Development, 3,* 155–165.

*PHARES, V. (1992). Where's Poppa?: The relative lack of attention to the role of fathers in child and adolescent psychopathology. *American Psychology, 47,* 656–664.

*PHARES, V., & COMPAS, E. (1992). The role of fathers in child and adolescent psychopathology: Make room for daddy. *Psychological Bulletin, 111,* 387–412.

PHAROAH, P., CONNOLLY, K., HETZEL, B., & ELKINS, R. (1981). Maternal thyroid function and motor competence in the child. *Developmental Medicine and Child Neurology, 23,* 76–82.

*PHELPS, E., & DAMON, W. (1991). Peer collaboration as a context for cognitive growth. In L. T. Landsmann (Ed.), *Culture, schooling, and psychological development.* Norwood, NJ: Ablex.

PHILLIPS, D. A. (1984). The illusion of incompetence among academically competent children. *Child Development, 55,* 2000–2016.

PHILLIPS, D. A. (1987). Socialization of perceived academic competence among highly competent children. *Child Development, 58,* 1308–1320.

*PHILLIPS, D. A., & ZIMMERMAN, M. (1990). The developmental course of perceived competence and incompetence among competent children. In R. J. Sternberg & J. Kolligian (Eds.), *Competence considered.* New Haven, CT: Yale University Press.

PHILLIPS, S., KING, S., & DuBOIS, L. (1978). Spontaneous activities of female versus male newborns. *Child Development, 49,* 590–597.

PIAGET, J. (1926). *The language and thought of the child.* New York: Harcourt Brace.

PIAGET, J. (1929). *The child's conception of the world.* London: Routledge & Kegan Paul.

PIAGET, J. (1932). *The moral judgment of the child.* London: Routledge & Kegan Paul.

PIAGET, J. (1950). *The psychology of intelligence.* New York: Harcourt Brace.

PIAGET, J. (1951). *Plays, dreams, and imitation in childhood.* New York: Norton.

PIAGET, J. (1952). *The origins of intelligence in children.* New York: International Universities Press.

PIAGET, J. (1954). *The construction of reality in the child.* New York: Basic Books.

PIAGET, J. (1957). Logique et equilibre dans les comportements du sujet. In L. Apostel, B. Mandelbrot, & J. Piaget (Eds.), *Etudes d' epistemologie genetique* (Vol. 2). Paris: Presses Universitaires de France.

PIAGET, J. (1964). Development and learning. In R. E. Ripple & V. N. Rockcastle (Eds.), *Piaget rediscovered.* Ithaca, NY: Cornell University Press.

PIAGET, J. (1965). *The moral judgment of the child.* New York: Free Press. (Original work published 1932).

PIAGET, J. (1967). *Six psychological studies.* New York: Random House.

PIAGET, J. (1968). *On the development of memory and identity.* Barre, MA: Clark University Press and Barre Publishers.

PIAGET, J. (1969). *The child's conception of time.* London: Routledge & Kegan Paul.

PIAGET, J. (1970). *The child's conception of movement and speed.* London: Routledge & Kegan Paul.

PIAGET, J. (1971). *Science of education and the psychology of the child.* New York: Viking.

PIAGET, J. (1972). Intellectual evolution from adolescence to adulthood. *Human Development, 15,* 1–12.

PIAGET, J. (1976). *To understand is to invent: The future of education.* New York: Penguin.

PIAGET, J. (1977). *The development of thought:*

Equilibration of cognitive structures. New York: Viking.

PIAGET, J. (1979). Correspondence and transformation. In F. B. Murray (Ed.), *The impact of Piagetian theory.* Baltimore: University Park Press.

PIAGET, J. (1980). Recent studies in genetic epistemology. *Cashiers Foundation Archives, Jean Piaget, No. 1.*

PIAGET, J. (1983). Piaget's theory. In W. Kessen (Ed.), *Handbook of child psychology: Vol. 1. History, theory, and methods.* New York: Wiley.

PIAGET, J., & INHELDER, B. (1956). *The child's conception of space.* London: Routledge & Kegan Paul.

PIAGET, J., & INHELDER, B. (1969). *The psychology of the child.* New York: Basic Books.

PIAGET, J., & INHELDER, B. (1973). *Memory and intelligence.* New York: Basic Books.

PIAGET, J., & INHELDER, B. (1974). *The child's construction of quantities.* London: Routledge & Kegan Paul.

PIAGET, J., INHELDER, B., & SZEMINSKA, A. (1960). *The child's conception of geometry.* New York: Basic Books.

PIAGET, J., & SZEMINSKA, A. (1952). *The child's conception of number.* New York: Basic Books.

PICARIELLO, M. L., GREENBERG, D. N., & PILLEMER, D. B. (1990). Children's sex-related stereotyping of colors. *Child Development, 61,* 1453–1460.

*PICK, H. L., Jr., (1992). Eleanor J. Gibson: Learning to perceive and perceiving to learn. *Developmental Psychology, 28,* 787–794.

PICK, H. L., Jr., & PICK, A. D. (1970). Sensory and perceptual development. In P. H. Mussen (Ed.), *Carmichael's manual of child psychology* (3rd ed., Vol. 1). New York: Wiley.

*PICKENS, J., & FIELD, T. (1993). Facial expressivity in infants of depressed mothers. *Developmental Psychology, 29,* 986–988.

PIERCE, K., & EDWARDS, E. D. (1988). Children's construction of fantasy stories: Gender differences in conflict resolution strategies. *Sex Roles, 18,* 393–404.

PIERS, E., & HARRIS, D. (1969). *The Piers-Harris Children's Self-Concept Scale.* Nashville, TN: Counselor Recordings and Tests.

PINKER, S. (1984). *Language learnability and language development.* Cambridge, MA: Harvard University Press.

PINKER, S. (1987). The bootstrapping problem in language acquisition. In B. MacWhinney (Ed.), *Mechanisms of language acquisition.* Hillsdale, NJ: Erlbaum.

*PINKER, S. (1989). *Learnability and cognition: The acquisition of argument structure.* Cambridge, MA: MIT Press.

*PIPP, S. (1990). Sensorimotor and representational internal working models of self, other, and relationship: Mechanisms of connection and separation. In D. Cicchetti & M. Beeghly (Eds.), *The self in transition: Infancy to childhood.* Chicago: University of Chicago Press.

*PIPP, S., EASTERBROOKS, M. A., & HARMON, R. J. (1992). The relation between attachment and knowledge of self and mother in one- to three-year-old infants. *Child Development, 63,* 738–750.

PIPP, S., FISCHER, K. W., & JENNINGS, S. (1987). Acquisition of self- and mother knowledge in infancy. *Developmental Psychology, 23,* 86–96.

PLOMIN, R. (1986). *Development, genetics, and psychology.* Hillsdale, NJ: Erlbaum.

PLOMIN, R. (1988). The nature and nurture of cognitive abilities. In R. J. Sternberg (Ed.), *Advances in the psychology of human intelligence* (Vol. 4). Hillsdale, NJ: Erlbaum.

*PLOMIN, R. (1990). *Nature and nurture.* Belmont, CA: Wadsworth.

*PLOMIN, R. (1993). Nature and nurture: Perspective and prospective. In R. Plomin & G. E. McClearn (Eds.), *Nature, nurture, and psychology.* Washington, DC: APA.

PLOMIN, R., & DANIELS, D. (1987). Why are children in the same family so different from one another? *Behavioral and Brain Sciences, 10,* 1–16.

PLOMIN, R., & DeFRIES, J. C. (1985). *Origins of individual differences in infancy: The Colorado Adoption Project.* Orlando, FL: Academic Press.

PLOMIN, R., DeFRIES, J. C., & FULKER, D. W. (1988). *Nature and nurture during infancy and early childhood.* Cambridge: Cambridge University Press.

*PLOMIN, R., EMDE, R. N., BRAUNGART, J. M., CAMPOS, J., CORLEY, R., FULKER, D. W., KAGAN, J., REZNICK, J. S., ROBINSON, J., ZAHN-WAXLER, C., & DeFRIES, J. C. (1993). Genetic change and continuity from fourteen to twenty months: The MacArthur Longitudinal Twin Study. *Child Development, 64,* 1354–1376.

*PLOMIN, R., LOEHLIN, J. C., & DeFRIES, J. C. (1985). Genetic and environmental components of "environmental" influences. *Developmental Psychology, 21,* 391–402.

*PLOMIN, R., & McCLEARN, G. E. (Eds.). (1993). *Nature, nurture, and psychology.* Washington, DC: APA.

*PLOMIN, R., & NEIDERHISER, J. M. (1992). Genetics and experience. *Current Directions in Psychological Science, 1,* 160–164.

PLOMIN, R., OWEN, M. J., McGUFFIN, P. (1994). The genetic basis of complex human behaviors. *Science, 246,* 1733–1739.

PLOMIN, R., REISS, D., HETHERINGTON, E. M., & HOWE, G. W. (1994). Nature and nurture: Genetic contributions to measures of the family environment. *Developmental Psychology, 30,* 32–43.

POLLOCK, L. (1983). *Forgotten children: Parent–child relations from 1500 to 1900.* Cambridge: Cambridge University Press.

POLLOCK, L. (1987). *A lasting relationship: Parents and children over three centuries.* London: Fourth Estate.

POMERLEAU, A., BOLDUC, D., MALCUIT, G., & COSSETTE, L. (1990). Pink or blue: Environmental gender stereotypes in the first two years of life. *Sex Roles, 22,* 359–367.

PORTER, R. H., & LANEY, M. D. (1980). Attachment theory and the concept of inclusive fitness. *Merrill-Palmer Quarterly, 26,* 35–51.

*PORTER, R. H., MAKIN, J. W., DAVIS, L. B., & CHRISTENSON, K. M. (1992). Breast-fed infants respond to olfactory cues from their own mother and unfamiliar lactating females. *Infant Behavior and Development, 15,* 85–93.

POSNER, M. C., PETERSEN, S. E., FOX, P. T., & RAICHLEY, M. E. (1988). Localization of cognitive operations in the human brain. *Science, 240,* 1627–1631.

*POSNER, M. I. (1989). *The foundations of cognitive science.* Cambridge, MA: MIT Press.

POULIN-DUBOIS, D., SERBIN, L. A., KENYON, B., & DERBYSHIRE, A. (1994). Infants' intermodal knowledge about gender. *Developmental Psychology, 30,* 436–442.

*POULSON, C. L., & NUNES, L. R. P. (1988). The infant vocal-conditioning literature: A theoretical and methodological review. *Journal of Experimental Child Psychology, 46,* 438–450.

POULSON, C. L., NUNES, L. R. P., & WARREN, S. F. (1989). Imitation in infancy: A critical review. In H. W. Reese (Ed.), *Advances in child development and behavior* (Vol. 22). San Diego, CA: Academic Press.

POWELL, G. F., BRASEL, J. A., & BLIZZARD, R. M. (1967). Emotional deprivation and growth retardation simulating ideopathic hypopituitarism: I. Clinical evaluation of the syndrome. *New England Journal of Medicine, 276,* 1271–1278.

POWELL, L. F. (1974). The effect of extra stimulation and maternal involvement on the development of low-birth-weight infants and on maternal behavior. *Child Development, 45,* 106–113.

POWER, T. G., & PARKE, R. D. (1983). Patterns of mother and father play with their 8-month-old infant: A multiple analyses approach. *Infant Behavior and Development, 6,* 453–459.

*POWLEDGE, T. M. (1993). The genetic fabric of human behavior. *BioScience, 43,* 362–367.

*POWLISHTA, K. K., SERBIN, L. A., & MOLLER, L. C. (1993). The stability of individual differences in gender typing: Implications for understanding gender segregation. *Sex Roles, 29,* 723–737.

PRADER, A., TANNER, J. M., & VON HARNACK, G. A. (1963). Catch up growth following illness or starvation. *Journal of Paediatrics, 62,* 646–659.

PRATT, M. W., KERIG, P., COWAN, P. A., & COWAN, C. P. (1988). Mothers and fathers teaching 3-year-olds: Authoritative parenting and adult scaffolding of young children's learning. *Developmental Psychology, 24,* 832–839.

PRECHTL, H. F. R. (1968). Neurological findings in newborn infants after pre- and paranatal complications. In J. H. P. Jonxis, H. K. A. Visser, & J. A. Troelstra (Eds.), *Aspects of prematurity and dysmaturity.* Springfield, IL: Charles C Thomas.

PRECHTL, H. F. R. (1977). *The neurological examination of the full-term newborn infant* (2nd ed.). London: Heinemann.

PRECHTL, H. F. R., & BEINTEMA, D. (1964). *The neurological examination of the full-term newborn infant.* London: Heinemann.

PRESSLEY, M. (1982). Elaboration and memory development. *Child Development, 53,* 296–309.

*PRESSLEY, M. (1992). How not to study strategy discovery. *American Psychologist, 47,* 1240–1241.

PRESSLEY, M., BORKOWSKI, J. G., & O'SULLIVAN, J. (1985). Children's metamemory and the teaching of memory strategies. In D. L.

Forrest-Pressley, G. E. MacKinnon, & T. G. Waller (Eds.), *Metacognition, cognition, and human performance: Vol. 1. Theoretical perspectives.* New York: Academic Press.

PRESSLEY, M., FORREST-PRESSLEY, D., & ELLIOT-FAUST, D. J. (1988). What is strategy instructional enrichment and how to study it: Illustrations from research on children's prose memory and comprehension. In F. E. Weinert & M. Perlmutter (Eds.), *Memory development: Universal changes and individual differences.* Hillsdale, NJ: Erlbaum.

PRESSLEY, M., LEVIN, J. R., & BRYANT, S. L. (1983). Memory and strategy instruction during adolescence: When is explicit instruction needed? In M. Pressley & J. R. Levin (Eds.), *Cognitive strategy research: Psychological foundations.* New York: Springer-Verlag.

PRICE, G. G., WALSH, D. J., & VILBERG, W. R. (1984). The confluence model's good predictions of mental age beg the question. *Psychological Bulletin, 96,* 195–200.

PRIEL, B., & deSCHONEN, S. (1986). Self-recognition: A study of a population without mirrors. *Journal of Experimental Child Psychology, 41,* 237–250.

*PRINCE, A., & PINKER, S. (1988). Rules and connections in human language. *Trends in Neuroscience, 11,* 195–202.

*PRINZ, P. M., & PRINZ, E. A. (1979). Simultaneous acquisition of ASL and spoken English. *Sign Language Studies, 25,* 283–296.

PRIOR, M., SANSON, A., CARROLL, R., & OBERKLAID, F. (1989). Social class differences in temperament ratings by mothers of preschool children. *Merrill-Palmer Quarterly, 35,* 239–248.

PRYOR, J. B., & DAY, J. D. (Eds.). (1985). *The development of social cognition.* New York: Springer-Verlag.

*PUKA, B. (1991). Interpretive experiments: Probing the care-justice debate in moral development. *Human Development, 34,* 61–80.

PULLYBANK, J., BISANZ, J., SCOTT, C., & CHAMPION, M. A. (1985). Developmental invariance in the effects of functional self-knowledge on memory. *Child Development, 56,* 1447–1454.

PURCELL, P., & STEWART, L. (1990). Dick and Jane in 1989. *Sex Roles, 22,* 177–185.

PUTALLAZ, M., & HEFLIN, A. H. (1990). Parent–child interaction. In S. R. Asher & J. D. Coie (Eds.), *Peer rejection in childhood.* New York: Cambridge University Press.

PUTALLAZ, M., & WASSERMAN, A. (1990). Children's entry behavior. In S. R. Asher & J. D. Coie (Eds.), *Peer rejection in childhood.* New York: Cambridge University Press.

PYE, C. (1986). One lexicon or two? An alternative interpretation of early bilingual speech. *Journal of Child Language, 13,* 591–593.

*QUIGGLE, N. L., GARBER, J., PANAK, W. F., & DODGE, K. A. (1992). Social information processing in aggressive and depressed children. *Child Development, 63,* 1305–1320.

RABOCH, J., MELLAN, I., & STARKA, L. (1979). Klinefelter's syndrome: Sexual development and activity. *Archives of Sexual Behavior, 8,* 333–339.

*RACHELL, P. L., & GOTTLIEB, G. (1992). Developmental intersensory interference: Augmented prenatal sensory experience interferes with auditory learning in duck embryos. *Developmental Psychology, 28,* 795–803.

*RACK, J. P., HULME, C., & SNOWLING, M. J. (1993). Learning to read: A theoretical synthesis. In H. W. Reese (Ed.), *Advances in child development and behavior* (Vol. 24). San Diego, CA: Academic Press.

*RADFORD, A. (1990). *Syntactic theory and the acquisition of English syntax: The nature of early child grammars of English.* Oxford: Blackwell.

RADKE-YARROW, M., & ZAHN-WAXLER, C. (1984). Roots, motives, and patterns in children's prosocial behavior. In E. Staub, D. Bar-Tal, J. Karylowski, & J. Reykowski (Eds.), *Development and maintenance of prosocial behavior.* New York: Plenum.

RADKE-YARROW, M., & ZAHN-WAXLER, C. (1986). The role of familial factors in the development of prosocial behavior: Research findings and questions. In D. Olweus, J. Block, & M. Radke-Yarrow (Eds.), *Development of antisocial and prosocial behavior.* Orlando, FL: Academic Press.

RADKE-YARROW, M., ZAHN-WAXLER, C., & CHAPMAN, M. (1983). Children's prosocial dispositions and behavior. In E. M. Hetherington (Ed.), *Handbook of child psychology: Vol. 4. Socialization, personality, and social development.* New York: Wiley.

*RAFF, M. C., BARRES, B. A., BURNE, J. F., COLES, H. S., ISHIZAKI, Y., & JACOBSON, M. D. (1993). Programmed cell death and the control of cell survival: Lessons from the nervous system. *Science, 262,* 695–700.

*RAFFAELLI, M. (1991, April). *Conflict with siblings and friends in late childhood and adolescence.* Paper presented at the meeting of the Society for Research in Child Development, Seattle.

RAKIC, P. (1988). Specification of cerebral cortical areas. *Science, 241,* 170–176.

*RAKIC, P. (1991). Development of the primate visual system throughout life. In P. Bagnoli & W. Hodos (Eds.), *The changing visual system.* New York: Plenum.

RAKIC, P., BOURGEOIS, J. P., ECKENHOFF, M. F., ZECEVIC, N., & GOLDMAN-RAKIC, P. S. (1986). Concurrent overproduction of synapses in diverse regions of the primate cerebral cortex. *Science, 232,* 232–234.

RAMEY, C. T., DORVAL, B., & BAKER-WARD, L. (1983). Group day care and socially disadvantaged families: Effects on the child and the family. In S. Kilmer (Ed.), *Advances in early education and day care* (Vol. 3). Greenwich, CT: JAI Press.

RAMEY, C. T., & LANDESMAN RAMEY, S. (1990). Intensive educational intervention for children of poverty. *Intelligence, 14,* 1–9.

*RAMSEY, P. G. (1991). *Making friends in school: Promoting peer relationships in early childhood.* New York: Teachers College Press.

RASKIN, P. A., & ISRAEL, A. C. (1981). Sex-role imitation in children: Effects of sex of child, sex of model, and sex-role appropriateness of modeled behavior. *Sex Roles, 7,* 1067–1077.

RATCLIFFE, S. G., & FIELD, M. A. S. (1982). Emotional disorder in XYY children: Four case reports. *Journal of Child Psychology and Psychiatry, 23,* 401–406.

RATNER, H. H., & MYERS, N. A. (1981). Long-term memory and retrieval at ages 2, 3, 4. *Journal of Experimental Child Psychology, 31,* 365–386.

RATNER, N. B. (1988). Patterns of parental vocabulary selection in speech to very young children. *Journal of Child Language, 15,* 481–492.

RAUH, V. A., ACHENBACH, T. M., NURCOMBE, B., HOWELL, C. T., & TETI, D. M. (1988). Minimizing adverse effects of low birthweight: Four-year results of an early intervention program. *Child Development, 59,* 544–553.

RAVN, K. E., & GELMAN, S. A. (1984). Rule usage in children's understanding of "big" and "little". *Child Development, 55,* 2141–2150.

*RAWLINS, W. K. (1992). *Friendship matters: Communication, dialectics, and the life course.* New York: Aldine de Gruyter.

RAYMOND, C. L., & BENBOW, C. P. (1986). Gender differences in mathematics: A function of parental support and student sex typing? *Developmental Psychology, 22,* 808–819.

*RAYNER, K. (1993). Eye movements in reading: Recent developments. *Current Directions in Psychological Science, 2,* 81–85.

REDLINGER, W. E., & PARK, T. (1980). Language mixing in young bilinguals. *Journal of Child Language, 7,* 337–352.

REES, J. M., & TRAHMS, C. M. (1989). Nutritional influences on physical growth and behavior in adolescence. In G. R. Adams, R. Montemayor, & T. P. Gullotta (Eds.), *Biology of adolescent behavior and development.* Newbury Park, CA: Sage.

*REESE, E., & FIVUSH, R. (1993). Parental styles of talking about the past. *Developmental Psychology, 29,* 596–606.

REID, M., LANDESMAN, S., TREDER, R., & JACCARD, J. (1989). "My Family and Friends": Six-to twelve-year-old children's perceptions of social support. *Child Development, 60,* 896–910.

REISMAN, J. E. (1987). Touch, motion and perception. In P. Salapatek & L. Cohen (Eds.), *Handbook of infant perception: Vol. 1. From sensation to perception.* New York: Academic Press.

RESCORLA, L. A. (1980). Overextension in early language development. *Journal of Child Language, 7,* 321–335.

RESCORLA, L. A. (1981). Category development in early language. *Journal of Child Language, 8,* 225–238.

*RESCORLA, L. A., HYSON, M. C., & HIRSH-PASEK, K. (Eds.). (1991). *New directions for child development: No. 53. Academic instruction in early childhood: Challenge or pressure?* San Francisco: Jossey-Bass.

RESNICK, S. M., BERENBAUM, S. A., GOTTESMAN, I. I., & BOUCHARD, T. J. (1986). Early hormonal influences on cognitive functioning in congenital adrenal hyperplasia. *Developmental Psychology, 22,* 191–198.

REST, J. R. (1983). Morality. In J. H. Flavell & E. M. Markman (Eds.), *Handbook of child psychology: Vol. 3. Cognitive development.* New York: Wiley.

*RETHERFORD, R. D., & SEWELL, W. H. (1991). Birth order and intelligence: Further tests of the confluence model. *American Sociological Review, 56,* 141–158.

REZNICK, J. S. (Ed.). (1989). *Perspectives on behavioral inhibition.* Chicago: University of Chicago Press.

REZNICK, J. S., GIBBONS, J. L., JOHNSON, M. O., & McDONOUGH, P. M. (1989). Behavioral inhibition in a normative sample. In J. S. Reznick (Ed.), *Perspectives on behavioral inhibition.* Chicago: University of Chicago Press.

*REZNICK, J. S., & GOLDFIELD, B. A. (1992). Rapid change in lexical development in comprehension and production. *Developmental Psychology, 28,* 406–413.

REZNICK, J. S., KAGAN, J., SNIDMAN, N., GERSTEN, M., BAAK, K., & ROSENBERG, A. (1986). Inhibited and uninhibited behavior: A follow-up study. *Child Development, 51,* 660–680.

RHEINGOLD, H. L. (1982a). Ethics as an integral part of research in child development. In R. Vasta (Ed.), *Strategies and techniques of child study.* New York: Academic Press.

RHEINGOLD, H. L. (1982b). Little children's participation in the work of adults: A nascent prosocial behavior. *Child Development, 53,* 114–125.

RHEINGOLD, H. L. (1988). The infant as a member of society. *Acta Paediatrica Scandinavica, 77,* 9–20.

RHEINGOLD, H. L., & COOK, K. (1975). The contents of boys' and girls' rooms as an index of parents' behavior. *Child Development, 46,* 459–463.

RHEINGOLD, H. L., COOK, K. V., & KOLOWITZ, V. (1987). Commands activate the behavior and pleasure of 2–year-old children. *Developmental Psychology, 23,* 146–151.

RHEINGOLD, H. L., & EMERY, G. N. (1986). The nurturant acts of very young children. In D. Olweus, J. Block, & M. Radke-Yarrow (Eds.), *Development of antisocial and prosocial behavior.* Orlando, FL: Academic Press.

RHEINGOLD, H. L., HAY, D. F., & WEST, M. J. (1976). Sharing in the second year of life. *Child Development, 47,* 1148–1158.

RHOLES, W. S., & LANE, J. W. (1985). Consistency between cognitions and behavior: Cause and consequence of cognitive moral development. In J. B. Pryor & J. D. Day (Eds.), *The development of social cognition.* New York: Springer-Verlag.

RHOLES, W. S., BLACKWELL, J., JORDAN, C., & WALTERS, C. (1980). A developmental study of learned helplessness. *Developmental Psychology, 16,* 616–624.

RICCIUTI, H. N., & BREITMAYER, B. J. (1988). Observational assessments of infant temperament in the natural setting of the newborn nursery: Stability and relationship to perinatal status. *Merrill-Palmer Quarterly, 34,* 281–299.

RICE, M. L. (1989). Children's language acquisition. *American Psychologist, 44,* 149–156.

RICE, M. L., HUSTON, A. C., TRUGLIO, R., & WRIGHT, J. (1990). Words from "Sesame Street": Learning vocabulary while viewing. *Developmental Psychology, 26,* 421–428.

RICE, M. L., & WOODSMALL, L. (1988). Lessons from television: Children's word learning when viewing. *Child Development, 59,* 420–429.

RIESE, M. L. (1987). Temperament stability between the neonatal period and 24 months. *Developmental Psychology, 23,* 216–222.

RIESER, J. (1979). Spatial orientation of six-month-old infants. *Child Development, 50,* 1078–1087.

RIESER, J., YONAS, A., & WIKNER, K. (1976). Radial localization of odors by human newborns. *Child Development, 47,* 856–859.

*RITTS, V., PATTERSON, M. L., & TUBBS, M. E. (1992). Expectations, impressions, and judgments of physically attractive students: A review. *Review of Educational Research, 62,* 413–426.

RIZZO, T. A., & CORSARO, W. A. (1988). Toward a better understanding of Vygotsky's process of internalization: Its role in the development of the concept of friendship. *Developmental Review, 8,* 219–237.

ROBERTS, K. (1988). Retrieval of a basic-level category in prelinguistic infants. *Developmental Psychology, 24,* 21–27.

ROBERTS, L. (1988). Carving up the human genome. *Science, 242,* 1244–1246.

ROBERTS, L. (1990). To test or not to test? *Science, 247,* 17–19.

*ROBERTS, L. (1991). Does egg beckon sperm when the time is right? *Science, 252,* 214.

ROBERTS, R. (1989, October). *The acquisition of complex action skills.* Paper presented at the meeting of the MacArthur Interest Group on Future-Oriented Processes, New Haven, CT.

*ROBERTS, R. J., BROWN, D., WIEBKE, S., & HAITH, M. M. (1991). A computer-automated laboratory for studying complex perception-action skills. *Behavior Research Methods and Instrumentation, 23,* 493–504.

ROBERTS, R. J., & PATTERSON, C. J. (1983). Perspective taking and referential communication: The question of correspondence reconsidered. *Child Development, 54,* 1005–1014.

ROBERTS, R. N., NELSON, R. O., & OLSON, T. W. (1987). Self-instruction: An analysis of the differential effects of instruction and reinforcement. *Journal of Applied Behavior Analysis, 20,* 235–242.

ROBINS, R. H. (1968). *A short history of linguistics.* Bloomington: Indiana University Press.

ROBINSON, C. C., & MORRIS, J. T. (1986). The gender-stereotyped nature of Christmas toys received by 36-, 48-, and 60-month old children: A comparison between nonrequested vs. requested toys. *Sex Roles, 15,* 21–32.

ROBINSON, E. J. (1981). The child's understanding of inadequate messages and communication failure: A problem of ignorance or egocentrism? In W. P. Dickson (Ed.), *Children's oral communication skills.* New York: Academic Press.

*ROBINSON, J., LITTLE, C., & BIRINGEN, Z. (1993). Emotional communication in mother–toddler relationships: Evidence for early gender differentiation. *Merrill-Palmer Quarterly, 39,* 496–517.

*ROBINSON, J. L., REZNICK, J. S., KAGAN, J., & CORLEY, R. (1992). The heritability of inhibited and uninhibited behavior: A twin study. *Developmental Psychology, 28,* 1030–1037.

ROCHAT, P. (1989). Object manipulation and exploration in 2- to 5-month-old infants. *Developmental Psychology, 25,* 871–884.

*ROCHAT, P. (1993). Hand–mouth coordination in the newborn: Morphology, determinants, and early development of a basic act. In G. J. P. Savelsbergh (Ed.), *The development of coordination in infancy.* London: Elsevier.

RODE, S., CHANG, P., FISCH, R., & SROUFE, L. A. (1981). Attachment patterns of infants separated at birth. *Developmental Psychology, 17,* 188–191.

RODGERS, J. L. (1984). Confluence effects: Not here, not now! *Developmental Psychology, 20,* 321–331.

ROFF, M., SELLS, S. B., & GOLDEN, M. M. (1972). *Social adjustment and personality development in children.* Minneapolis: University of Minnesota Press.

ROFFWARG, H. P., MUZIO, J. N., & DEMENT, W. C. (1966). Ontogenetic development of the human sleep–dream cycle. *Science, 152,* 604–619.

ROGAN, W. J. (1982). PCB's and cola-colored babies: Japan, 1968, and Taiwan, 1979. *Teratology, 26,* 259–261.

ROGERS, T. B. (1984). An analysis of two central stages underlying responding to personality items: The self-referent decision and response selection. *Journal of Research in Personality, 8,* 128–138.

ROGOFF, B. (1981). Schooling and the development of cognitive skills. In H. C. Triandis & A. Heron (Eds.), *Handbook of cross-cultural psychology: Vol. 4. Developmental psychology.* Boston: Allyn & Bacon.

ROGOFF, B. (1986). Adult assistance of children's learning. In T. E. Raphael (Ed.), *Contexts of school-based literacy.* New York: Random House.

ROGOFF, B. (1990). *Apprenticeship in thinking: Cognitive development in social context.* New York: Oxford University Press.

*ROGOFF, B. (1991). The joint socialization of development by young children and adults. In M. Lewis & S. Feinman (Eds.), *Social influences and socialization in infancy.* New York: Plenum.

*ROGOFF, B. (1993). Children's guided participation and participatory appropriation in sociocultural activity. In R. H. Wozniak & K. W. Fischer (Eds.), *Development in context.* Hillsdale, NJ: Erlbaum.

*ROGOFF, B., MISTRY, J., GONCU, A., & MOSIER, C. (1991). Cultural variation in the role relations of toddlers and their families. In M. H. Bornstein (Ed.), *Cultural approaches to parenting.* Hillsdale, NJ: Erlbaum.

*ROGOFF, B., MISTRY, J., GONCU, A., & MOSIER, C. (1993). Guided participation in cultural activity by toddlers and caregivers. *Monographs of the Society for Research in Child Development 58,* (Serial No. 236).

*ROGOFF, B., MISTRY, J., RADZISZEWSKA, B., & GERMOND, J. (1992). Infants' instrumental social interaction with adults. In S. Feinman (Ed.), *Social referencing and the social construction of reality in infancy.* New York: Plenum.

ROMER, N., & CHERRY, D. (1980). Ethnic and social class differences in children's sex-role concepts. *Sex Roles, 6,* 245–263.

ROOPNARINE, J. L. (1984). Sex-typed socialization in mixed-age preschool classrooms. *Child Development, 55,* 1078–1084.

ROSCH, E. (1973). On the internal structure of perceptual and semantic categories. In T. E. Moore (Ed.), *Cognitive development and the acquisition of language*. New York: Academic Press.

ROSCH, E., & LLOYD, B. (Eds.). (1978). *Cognition and categorization*. Hillsdale, NJ: Erlbaum.

ROSCH, E., & MERVIS, C. B. (1975). Family resemblances: Studies in the internal structure of categories. *Cognitive Psychology, 7*, 573–605.

ROSCH, E., MERVIS, C. B., GRAY, W. D., JOHNSON, D. M., & BOYES-BRAEM, P. (1976). Basic objects in natural categories. *Cognitive Psychology, 8*, 382–439.

ROSE, R. J., & DITTO, W. B. (1983). A developmental-genetic analysis of common fears from early adolescence to early childhood. *Child Development, 54*, 361–368.

ROSE, S. A. (1981). Developmental changes in infants' retention of visual stimuli. *Child Development, 52*, 227–233.

ROSE, S. A., GOTTFRIED, A. W., & BRIDGER, W. H. (1981a). Cross-modal transfer and information processing by the sense of touch in infancy. *Developmental Psychology, 17*, 90–98.

*ROSE, S. A., GOTTFRIED, A. W., & BRIDGER, W. H. (1981b). Cross-modal transfer in 6-month-old infants. *Developmental Psychology, 17*, 661–669.

*ROSE, S. A., & ORLIAN, E. K. (1991). Asymmetries in cross-modal transfer. *Child Development, 62*, 706–718.

ROSE, S. A., & RUFF, H. A. (1987). Cross-modal abilities in human infants. In J. D. Osofsky (Ed.), *Handbook of infant development* (2nd ed.). New York: Wiley.

*ROSEN, K. S., & ROTHBAUM, F. (1993). Quality of parental caregiving and security of attachment. *Developmental Psychology, 29*, 358–367.

*ROSEN, W. D., ADAMSON, L. B., & BAKEMAN, R. (1992). An experimental investigation of infant social referencing: Mothers' messages and gender differences. *Developmental Psychology, 28*, 1172–1178.

ROSENBAUM, M. S., & DRABMAN, R. S. (1979). Self-control training in the classroom: Review and critique. *Journal of Applied Behavior Analysis, 12*, 467–485.

ROSENBERG, M. (1985). Self-concept and psychological well-being in adolescence. In R. L. Leahy (Ed.), *The development of the self*. Orlando, FL: Academic Press.

ROSENBERG, M. (1986a). *Conceiving the self*. Melbourne, FL: Krieger.

ROSENBERG, M. (1986b). Self-concept from middle childhood through adolescence. In J. Suls (Ed.), *Psychological perspectives on the self* (Vol. 3). Hillsdale, NJ: Erlbaum.

*ROSENBERG, S. (1993). Chomsky's theory of language: Some recent observations. *Psychological Science, 4*, 15–19.

ROSENBLITH, J. F. (1961). The modified Graham Behavior Test for neonates: Test-retest reliability, normative data and hypotheses for future work. *Biology of the Neonate, 3*, 174–192.

*ROSENGREN, K. S., GELMAN, S. A., KALISH, C. W., & McCORMICK, M. (1991). As time goes by: Children's early understanding of growth in animals. *Child Development, 62*, 1302–1320.

ROSENSTEIN, D., & OSTER, H. (1988). Differential facial responses to four basic tastes in newborns. *Child Development, 59*, 1555–1568.

ROSENTHAL, R. (1976). *Experimenter effects in behavioral research* (enl. ed.). New York: Halsted Press.

ROSENTHAL, R., & JACOBSON, L. (1968). *Pygmalion in the classroom*. New York: Holt, Rinehart & Winston.

ROSETT, H. L. (1980). The effects of alcohol on the fetus and offspring. In O. J. Kalant (Ed.), *Research advances in alcohol and drug problems: Vol. 5. Alcohol and drug problems in women*. New York: Plenum.

ROSS, D. S. (1972). *G. Stanley Hall: The psychologist as prophet*. Chicago: University of Chicago Press.

ROSS, G. (1980). Categorization in 1- to 2-year-olds. *Developmental Psychology, 16*, 391–396.

ROSS, G., NELSON, K., WETSTONE, H., & TANOUYE, E. (1986). Acquisition and generalization of novel object concepts by young language learners. *Journal of Child Language, 13*, 67–83.

ROSS, H. S., & LOLLIS, S. P. (1987). Communication within infant social games. *Developmental Psychology, 23*, 241–248.

ROSS, H. S., & LOLLIS, S. P. (1989). A social relations analysis of toddler peer relationships. *Child Development, 60*, 1082–1091.

ROSS, S. A. (1971). A test of the generality of the effects of deviant preschool models. *Developmental Psychology, 4*, 262–267.

*ROSSO, P. (1990). *Nutrition and metabolism in pregnancy*. New York: Oxford University Press.

ROTENBERG, K. J. (1980). Children's use of intentionality in judgments of character and disposition. *Child Development, 51*, 282–284.

ROTENBERG, K. J., & SLIZ, D. (1988). Children's restrictive disclosure to friends. *Merrill-Palmer Quarterly, 34*, 203–215.

ROTHBART, M. K. (1989). Temperament in childhood: A framework. In G. A. Kohnstamm, J. E. Bates, & M. K. Rothbart (Eds.), *Temperament in childhood*. New York: Wiley.

ROTHBART, M. K., & DERRYBERRY, D. (1981). Development of individual differences in temperament. In M. E. Lamb & A. Brown (Eds.), *Advances in developmental psychology* (Vol. 1). Hillsdale, NJ: Erlbaum.

ROTHBART, M. K., & GOLDSMITH, H. H. (1985). Three approaches to the study of infant temperament. *Developmental Review, 5*, 237–260.

ROTHBART, M. K., & MACCOBY, E. E. (1966). Parents' differential reactions to sons and daughters. *Journal of Personality and Social Psychology, 4*, 237–243.

ROTHBART, M. K., & POSNER, M. I. (1985). Temperament and the development of self-regulation. In L. C. Hartledge & C. F. Telzrow (Eds.), *The neuropsychology of individual differences: A developmental perspective*. New York: Plenum.

ROTMAN, B. (1977). *Jean Piaget: Psychologist of the real*. Hassocks, England: Harvester Press.

ROUG, L., LANDBERG, I., & LUNDBERG, L. J. (1989). Phonetic development in early infancy: A study of four Swedish children during the first eighteen months of life. *Journal of Child Language, 16*, 19–40.

ROVEE-COLLIER, C. K. (1987). Learning and memory in infancy. In J. D. Osofsky (Ed.), *Handbook of infant development* (2nd ed.). New York: Wiley.

*ROVEE-COLLIER, C. K., & BHATT, R. S. (1993). Evidence of long-term memory in infancy. In R. Vasta (Ed.), *Annals of child development* (Vol. 9). London: Kingsley.

ROVEE-COLLIER, C. K., & HAYNE, H. (1987). Reactivation of infant memory: Implications for cognitive development. In H. W. Reese (Ed.), *Advances in child development and behavior* (Vol. 20). New York: Academic Press.

ROVEE-COLLIER, C. K., & SHYI, G. (1992). A functional and cognitive analysis of infant long-term retention. In M. L. Howe, C. J. Brainerd, & V. F. Reyna (Eds.), *Development of long-term retention*. New York: Springer-Verlag.

*ROVET, J. F. (1991). The cognitive and neuropsychological characteristics of females with Turner syndrome. In B. Bender & D. Berch (Eds.), *Sex chromosome abnormalities and behavior: Psychological studies*. Boulder, CO: Westview.

*ROWE, D. C. (1993). Genetic perspectives on personality. In R. Plomin & G. E. McClearn (Eds.), *Nature, nurture, and psychology*. Washington, DC: APA.

ROWE, D. C., & PLOMIN, R. (1978). "The Burt Controversy." *Behavior Genetics, 8*, 81–83.

ROWE, I., & MARCIA, J. E. (1980). Ego identity status, formal operations, and moral development. *Journal of Youth and Adolescence, 9*, 87–99.

ROWLEY, P. T. (1984). Genetic screening: Marvel or menace? *Science, 225*, 138–144.

RUBENSTEIN, J., & HOWES, C. (1976). The effect of peers on toddler interaction with mother and toys. *Child Development, 47*, 597–605.

RUBENSTEIN, J. L., HOWES, C., & BOYLE, P. (1981). A two year follow-up of infants in community based infant day care. *Journal of Child Psychology and Psychiatry, 22*, 209–218.

RUBIN, J. Z., PROVENZANO, F. J., & LURIA, Z. (1974). The eye of the beholder: Parents' views on sex of newborns. *American Journal of Orthopsychiatry, 44*, 512–519.

RUBIN, K. H. (1977). The social and cognitive value of preschool toys and activities. *Canadian Journal of Behavioral Science/Review of Canadian Science, 9*, 382–385.

*RUBIN, K. H. (1988). *The Social Problem-Solving Test—Revised*. Unpublished manuscript. University of Waterloo, Waterloo, Ontario.

*RUBIN, K. H. (1989). *The Play Observation Scale (POS)*. Unpublished manuscript. University of Waterloo, Waterloo, Ontario.

*RUBIN, K. H. (1993). The Waterloo Longitudinal Project: Correlates and consequences of social withdrawal from childhood to adolescence. In K. H. Rubin & J. B. Asendorpf (Eds.), *Social withdrawal, inhibition, and shyness in childhood*. Hillsdale, NJ: Erlbaum.

*RUBIN, K. H., & ASENDORPF, J. B. (Eds.). (1993). *Social withdrawal, inhibition, and shyness in childhood*. Hillsdale, NJ: Erlbaum.

*RUBIN, K. H., BREAM, L., & ROSE-KRASNOR, L. (1991). Social problem solving and aggression in childhood. In D. J. Pepler & K. H. Rubin (Eds.), *The development and treatment of childhood aggression*. Hillsdale, NJ: Erlbaum.

*RUBIN, K. H., & COPLAN, R. J. (1992). Peer relationships in childhood. In M. H. Bornstein & M. E. Lamb (Eds.), *Developmental psychology: An advanced textbook* (3rd ed.). Hillsdale, NJ: Erlbaum.

RUBIN, K. H., FEIN, G. G., & VANDENBERG, B. (1983). Play. In E. M. Hetherington (Ed.), *Handbook of child psychology: Vol. 4. Socialization, personality, and social development.* New York: Wiley.

RUBIN, K. H., & KRASNOR, L. R. (1986). Social-cognitive and social behavioral perspectives on problem solving. In M. Perlmutter (Ed.), *Minnesota symposia on child psychology: Vol. 19. Cognitive perspectives on children's social and behavioral development.* Hillsdale, NJ: Erlbaum.

RUBIN, K. H., LeMARE, L. J., & LOLLIS, S. (1990). Social withdrawal in childhood: Developmental pathways to peer rejection. In S. R. Asher & J. D. Coie (Eds.), *Peer rejection in childhood.* New York: Cambridge University Press.

RUBIN, K. H., & MAIONI, T. L. (1975). Play preference and its relationship to egocentrism, popularity and classification skills in preschoolers. *Merrill-Palmer Quarterly, 21,* 171–179.

RUBIN, K. H., & ROSE-KRASNOR, L. (1992). Interpersonal problem solving and social competence in children. In W. B. Van Hasselt & M. Hersen (Eds.), *Handbook of social development.* New York: Plenum.*

RUBIN, K. H., WATSON, K. S., & JAMBOR, T. W. (1978). Free-play behaviors in preschool and kindergarten children. *Child Development, 49,* 534–536.

RUBIN, Z. (1980). *Children's friendships.* Cambridge, MA: Harvard University Press.

RUBLE, D. N. (1983). The development of social-comparison processes and their role in achievement-related self-socialization. In E. T. Higgins, D. N. Ruble, & W. W. Hartup (Eds.), *Social cognition and social development: A sociocultural perspective.* Cambridge: Cambridge University Press.

RUBLE, D. N., BALABAN, T., & COOPER, J. (1981). Gender constancy and the effects of sex-typed televised toy commercials. *Child Development, 52,* 667–675.

RUBLE, D. N., & FLETT, G. L. (1988). Conflicting goals in self-evaluative information seeking: Developmental and ability level analyses. *Child Development, 59,* 97–106.

RUBLE, D. N., & FREY, K. S. (1987). Social comparison and outcome evaluation in group contexts. In J. C. Masters & W. P. Smith (Eds.), *Social comparison, social justice, and relative deprivation.* Hillsdale, NJ: Erlbaum.

*RUBLE, D. N., & FREY, K. S. (1991). Changing patterns of behavior as skills are acquired: A functional model of self-evaluation. In J. Suls & T. A. Wills (Eds.), *Social comparison: Contemporary theory and research.* Hillsdale, NJ: Erlbaum.

RUBLE, D. N., GROSOVSKY, E. H., FREY, K. S., & COHEN, R. (1990). Developmental changes and competence assessment. In A. K. Boggiano & T. S. Pittman (Eds.), *Achievement motivation.* New York: Cambridge University Press.

*RUDDY, M. G. (1993a). Attention shifting and temperament at 5 months. *Infant Behavior and Development, 16,* 255–259.

*RUDDY, M. G. (1993b). *Attention shifting in the laboratory at 5 months as a predictor of sustained attention at 3.5 years.* Paper presented at the meeting of the Society for Research in Child Development, New Orleans.

RUFF, H. A., & KOHLER, C. J. (1978). Tactual-visual transfer in six-month-old infants. *Infant Behavior and Development, 1,* 259–264.

RUGH, R., & SHETTLES, L. (1971). *From conception to birth: The drama of life's beginning.* New York: Harper & Row.

*RUMBAUGH, D. M., GILL, T. V., & VON GLASERFELD, E. C. (1973). Reading and sentence completion by a chimpanzee *(Pan.).* *Science, 182,* 731–733.

RUSHTON, J. P., FULKER, D. W., NEALE, M. C., NIAS, D. K. B., & EYSENCK, H. J. (1986). Altruism and aggression: The heritability of individual differences. *Journal of Personality and Social Psychology, 50,* 1192–1198.

*RUSSELL, J. (1992). The theory theory: So good they named it twice? *Cognitive Development, 7,* 485–519.

RUSSELL, J. A. (1989). Culture, scripts, and children's understanding of emotion. In C. Saarni & P. L. Harris (Eds.), *Children's understanding of emotion.* Cambridge: Cambridge University Press.

*RUTKOWSKA, J. C. (1991). Looking for "constraints" in infants' perceptual-cognitive development. *Mind and Language, 6,* 215–238.

RUTTER, M. (1983). School effects on pupil progress: Research findings and policy implications. *Child Development, 54,* 1–29.

RUTTER, M. (1987). Continuities and discontinuities from infancy. In J. D. Osofsky (Ed.), *Handbook of infant development* (2nd ed.). New York: Wiley.

SAARNI, C. (1989). Children's understanding of strategic control of emotional expression in social transactions. In C. Saarni & P. L. Harris (Eds.), *Children's understanding of emotion.* Cambridge: Cambridge University Press.

SAARNI, C. (1990). Emotional competence: How emotions and relationships become integrated. In R. A. Thompson (Ed.), *Nebraska symposium on motivation: Vol. 36. Socioemotional development.* Lincoln: University of Nebraska Press.

*SAARNIO, D. A. (1993a). Scene memory in young children. *Merrill-Palmer Quarterly, 39,* 196–212.

*SAARNIO, D. A. (1993b). Understanding aspects of pictures: The development of scene schemata in young children. *Journal of Genetic Psychology, 154,* 41–51.

SACHS, J., & DEVIN, J. (1976). Young children's use of age-appropriate speech styles in social interaction and role-playing. *Journal of Child Language, 3,* 81–98.

*SADEH, A., & ANDERS, T. F. (1993). Sleep disorders. In C. H. Zeanah Jr. (Ed.), *Handbook of infant development.* New York: Guilford.

*SADKER, M., & SADKER, D. (1994). *Failing at fairness: How America's schools cheat girls.* New York: Scribner.

*SAGI, A. (1990). Attachment theory and research from a cross-cultural perspective. *Human Development, 33,* 10–22.

*SAGI, A., & LEWKOWICZ, K. S. (1987). A cross-cultural evaluation of attachment research. In L. W. C. Tavecchio & M. H. vanIJzendoorn (Eds.), *Attachment in social networks. Contributions to the Bowlby–Ainsworth attachment theory.* Amsterdam: Elsevier.

SALTZ, E., CAMPBELL, S., & SKOTKO, D. (1983). Verbal control of behavior: The effects of shouting. *Developmental Psychology, 19,* 461–464.

SALTZSTEIN, H. D., SANVITALE, D., & SUPRANER, A. (1978). Social influence on children's standards for judging criminal culpability. *Developmental Psychology, 14,* 125–131.

*SALZINGER, S., FELDMAN, R. S., HAMMER, M., & ROSARIO, M. (1993). The effects of physical abuse on children's social relationships. *Child Development, 64,* 169–187.

SALZSTEIN, H. D., WEINER, A. S., MUNK, J. J., SUPRANER, A., BLANK, R., & SCHWARZ, R. P. (1987). Comparison between children's own moral judgments and those they attribute to adults. *Merrill-Palmer Quarterly, 33,* 33–51.

SAMEROFF, A. J. (1975). Transactional models in early social relations. *Human Development, 18,* 65–79.

SAMEROFF, A. J., & CHANDLER, M. J. (1975). Reproductive risk and the continuum of caretaking casualty. In F. Horowitz (Ed.), *Review of child development research* (Vol. 4). Chicago: University of Chicago Press.

*SAMEROFF, A. J., SEIFER, R., BALDWIN, A., & BALDWIN, C. (1993). Stability of intelligence from preschool to adolescence: The influence of social and family risk factors. *Child Development, 64,* 80–97.

SAMEROFF, A. J., SEIFER, R., & ELIAS, P. K. (1982). Sociocultural variability in infant temperament ratings. *Child Development, 53,* 164–173.

SAMUELS, C. A. (1986). Bases for the infant's developing self-awareness. *Human Development, 29,* 36–48.

SANDER, L. (1975). Infant and caretaking environment. In E. J. Anthony (Ed.), *Explorations in child psychiatry.* New York: Plenum.

SANDER, L. W., SNYDER, P. A., ROSETT, H. L., LEE, A., GOULD, J. B., & OUELLETTE, E. (1977). Effects of alcohol intake during pregnancy on newborn state regulation: A progress report. *Alcoholism: Clinical and Experimental Research, 1,* 233–241.

SANDER, L. W., STECHLER, G., BURNS, P., & JULIA, H. L. (1970). Early mother–infant interaction and 24-hour patterns of activity and sleep. *Journal of the American Academy of Child Psychiatry, 9,* 103–123.

SANSON, A., PRIOR, M., & KYRIOS, M. (1990). Contamination of measures in temperament research. *Merrill-Palmer Quarterly, 36,* 179–192.

SANTROCK, J. W. (1970). Paternal absence, sex typing, and identification. *Developmental Psychology, 2,* 264–272.

SANVITALE, D., SALTZSTEIN, H. D., & FISH, M. C. (1989). Moral judgments by normal and conduct-disordered preadolescent and adolescent boys. *Merrill-Palmer Quarterly, 35,* 463–481.

SASANUMA, S. (1980). Do Japanese show sex differences in brain asymmetry? Supplementary findings. *Behavioral and Brain Sciences, 3,* 247–248.

*SAUDINO, K. J., & EATON, W. O. (1991). Infant temperament and genetics: An objective twin study of motor activity level. *Child Development, 62,* 1167–1174.

*SAVAGE-RUMBAUGH, E. S., MURPHY, J., SEVCIK, R. A., BRAKKE, K. E., WILIAMS, S. L., & RUMBAUGH, D. M. (1993). Language comprehension in ape and child. *Monographs of the Society for Research in Child Development, 58*(3–4, Serial No. 233).

*SAVAGE-RUMBAUGH, E. S., & RUMBAUGH, D. M. (1978). Symbolization, language and chimpanzees: A theoretical reevaluation based on initial language acquisition processes in four young *Pan troglodytes. Brain and Language, 6,* 265–300.

*SAVAGE-RUMBAUGH, E. S., RUMBAUGH, D. M., & BOYSEN, S. (1978). Symbolic communication between two chimpanzees *(Pan troglodytes). Science, 201,* 641–644.

SAVIN-WILLIAMS, R. C. (1979). Dominance hierarchies in groups of early adolescents. *Child Development, 50,* 923–935.

SAVIN-WILLIAMS, R. C. (1987). *Adolescence: An ethological perspective.* New York: Springer-Verlag.

*SAVIN-WILLIAMS, R. C., & BERNDT, T. J. (1990). Friendship and peer relations. In S. S. Feldman & G. R. Elliott (Eds.), *At the threshold: The developing adolescent.* Cambridge, MA: Harvard University Press.

*SAWIN, D. G. (1990). Aggressive behavior among children in small playgroup settings with violent television. In K. D. Gadow (Ed.), *Advances in learning and behavioral disabilities.* (Vol. 6). Greenwich, CT: JAI Press.

*SAXE, G. B. (1988a). Candy selling and math learning. *Educational Researcher, 17,* 14–21.

*SAXE, G. B. (1988b). The mathematics of child street vendors. *Child Development, 59,* 1415–1425.

*SAXE, G. B. (1991). *Culture and cognitive development: Studies in mathematical understanding.* Hillsdale, NJ: Erlbaum.

SAXE, G. B., GUBERMAN, S., & GEARHART, M. (1987). Social processes in early number development. *Monographs of the Society for Research in Child Development, 52* (2, Serial No. 216).

SAYEGH, Y., & DENNIS, W. (1965). The effect of supplementary experiences upon the behavioral development of infants in institutions. *Child Development, 36,* 81–90.

*SAYWITZ, K. J., GOODMAN, G. S., NICHOLAS, E., & MOAN, S. F. (1991). Children's memories of a physical examination involving genital touch: Implications for reports of child sexual abuse. *Journal of Consulting and Clinical Psychology, 59,* 682–691.

SCAFADI, F. A., FIELD, T. M., SCHANBERG, S. M., BAUER, C. R., VEGA-LAHR, N., GARCIA, R., POIRIER, J., NYSTROM, G., & COHN, C. M. (1986). Effects of tactile/kinesthetic stimulation on the clinical course and sleep/wake behavior of preterm neonates. *Infant Behavior and Development, 9,* 91–105.

SCARBOROUGH, H., & WYCKOFF, J. (1986). Mother, I'd still rather do it myself: Some further non-effects of "motherese." *Journal of Child Language, 13,* 431–437.

SCARR, S. (1981). *Race, social class, and individual differences in IQ: New studies of old problems.* Hillsdale, NJ: Erlbaum.

SCARR, S. (1983). An evolutionary perspective on infant intelligence: Species patterns and individual variations. In M. Lewis (Ed.), *Origins of intelligence: Infancy and early childhood* (2nd ed.). New York: Plenum.

SCARR, S. (1988). How genotypes and environments combine: Development and individual differences. In N. Bolger, A. Caspi, G. Downey, & M. Moorehouse (Eds.), *Persons in context: Developmental processes.* Cambridge: Cambridge University Press.

*SCARR, S. (1992). Developmental theories for the 1990s: Development and individual differences. *Child Development, 63,* 1–19.

*SCARR, S. (1993). Biological and cultural diversity: The legacy of Darwin for development. *Child Development, 64,* 1333–1353.

SCARR, S., & KIDD, K. K. (1983). Developmental behavior genetics. In M. M. Haith & J. J. Campos (Eds.), *Handbook of child psychology: Vol. 2. Infancy and developmental psychobiology.* New York: Wiley.

SCARR, S., & McCARTNEY, K. (1983). How people make their own environments: A theory of genotype–environment effects. *Child Development, 54,* 424–435.

SCARR, S., & SALAPATEK, P. (1970). Patterns of fear development during infancy. *Merrill-Palmer Quarterly, 16,* 53–90.

SCARR, S., PAKSTIS, A. J., KATZ, S. H., & BARKER, W. B. (1977). Absence of a relationship between degree of white ancestry and intellectual skills within a black population. *Human Genetics, 39,* 69–86.

SCARR, S., WEBBER, P. L., WEINBERG, R. A., & WITTIG, M. A. (1981). Personality resemblance among adolescents and their parents in biologically related and adoptive families. *Journal of Personality and Social Psychology, 40,* 885–898.

SCARR, S., & WEINBERG, R. A. (1983). The Minnesota Adoption Studies: Genetic differences and malleability. *Child Development, 54,* 260–267.

*SCARR-SALAPATEK, S. (1975). Genetics and the development of intelligence. In F. D. Horowitz (Ed.), *Review of child development research* (Vol. 4). Chicago: University of Chicago Press.

SCARR-SALAPATEK, S., & WILLIAMS, M. (1973). The effects of early stimulation on low-birthweight infants. *Child Development, 44,* 94–101.

*SCHACTER, D. L., MOSCOVITCH, M., TULVING, E., McLACHLAN, D. R., & FREEDMAN, M. (1986). Mnemonic precedence in amnesic patients: An analogue of the AB error in infants? *Child Development, 57,* 816–823.

SCHACTER, F. F., SHORE, E., HODAPP, R., CHALFIN, S., & BUNDY, C. (1978). Do girls talk earlier? Mean length of utterance in toddlers. *Developmental Psychology, 14,* 388–392.

*SCHAFFER, C. E., & BLATT, S. J. (1990). Interpersonal relationships and the experience of perceived efficacy. In R. J. Sternberg & J. Kolligian (Eds.), *Competence considered.* New Haven, CT: Yale University Press.

SCHAFFER, H. R. (1986). Some thoughts of an ordinologist. *Developmental Review, 6,* 115–121.

SCHAFFER, H. R., & CROOK, C. K. (1980). Child compliance and maternal control techniques. *Developmental Psychology, 16,* 54–61.

*SCHAFFER, H. R., & EMERSON, P. E. (1964). The development of social attachments in infancy. *Monographs of the Society for Research in Child Development, 29*(3, Serial No. 94).

*SCHEINFELD, A. (1972). *Heredity in humans.* Philadelphia: Lippincott.

SCHERER, N. J., & OLSWANG, L. B. (1984). Role of mother's expansions in stimulating children's language production. *Journal of Speech and Hearing Research, 27,* 387–396.

*SCHIEFFELIN, B. B., & OCHS, E. (Eds.), (1986). *Language socialization across cultures.* Cambridge: Cambridge University Press.

*SCHLEIDT, M. (1991). An ethological perspective on infant development. In M. E. Lamb & H. Keller (Eds.), *Infant development: Perspectives from German-speaking countries.* Hillsdale, NJ: Erlbaum.

SCHLESINGER, I. M. (1974). Relational concepts underlying language. In R. L. Schiefelbusch & L. L. Lloyd (Eds.), *Language perspectives: Acquisition, retardation, and intervention.* Baltimore: University Park Press.

SCHLESINGER, I. M. (1988). The origin of relational categories. In Y. Levy, I. M. Schlesinger, & M. D. S. Braine (Eds.), *Categories and processes in language acquisition.* Hillsdale, NJ: Erlbaum.

*SCHLIEMANN, A. D., & NUNES, T. (1990). A situated schema of proportionality. *British Journal of Developmental Psychology, 8,* 259–268.

SCHMIDT, C. R., OLLENDICK, T. H., & STANOWICZ, L. B. (1988). Developmental changes in the influence of assigned goals on cooperation and competition. *Developmental Psychology, 24,* 574–579.

SCHMIDT, H., & SPELKE, E. S. (1984, April). *Gestalt relations and object perception in infancy.* Paper presented at the meeting of the International Conference on Infant Studies, New York.

*SCHMUCKLER, M. A. (1993). Perception-action coupling in infancy. In G. J. P. Savelsbergh (Ed.), *The development of coordination in infancy.* London: Elsevier.

SCHNEIDER, B. A., & TREHUB, S. E. (1985a). Behavioral assessment of basic capabilities. In S. E. Trehub & B. A. Schneider (Eds.), *Auditory development in infancy.* New York: Plenum.

*SCHNEIDER, B. A., & TREHUB, S. E. (1985b). Infant auditory psychophysics: An overview. In G. Gottlieb & N. A. Krasnegor (Eds.), *Measurement of audition and vision in the first year of postnatal life: A methodological overview.* Norwood, NJ: Ablex.

SCHNEIDER, B. A., TREHUB, S. E., & BULL, D. (1980). High-frequency sensitivity in infants. *Science, 207,* 1003–1004.

SCHNEIDER, B. H., & BYRNE, B. M. (1985). Children's social skills training: A meta-analysis. In B. H. Schneider, K. H. Rubin, & J. E. Ledingham (Eds.), *Children's peer relations: Issues in assessment and intervention.* New York: Springer-Verlag.

SCHNEIDER, B. H., RUBIN, K. H., & LEDINGHAM, J. E. (Eds.). (1985). *Children's peer relations: Issues in assessment and intervention.* New York: Springer-Verlag.

SCHNEIDER, W., KORKEL, J., & WEINERT, F. E. (1987). *The knowledge base and memory performance: A comparison of academically successful and unsuccessful learners.* Paper presented at the meeting of the American Educational Research Association, Washington, DC.

*SCHNEIDER, W., KORKEL, J., & WEINERT, F. E. (1989). Domain-specific knowledge and memory performance: A comparison of high- and low-aptitude children. *Journal of Educational Psychology, 81,* 306–312.

SCHNEIDER, W., & PRESSLEY, M. (1989). *Memory development between 2 and 20.* New York: Springer-Verlag.

SCHNEIDER-ROSEN, K., & CICCHETTI, D. (1984). The relationship between affect and cognition in maltreated infants: Quality of attachment and the development of visual self-recognition. *Child Development, 55,* 648–658.

*SCHNEIDER-ROSEN, K., & CICCHETTI, D. (1991). Early self-knowledge and emotional development: Visual self-recognition and affective reactions to mirror self-image in maltreated and nonmaltreated toddlers. *Developmental Psychology, 27,* 471–478.

SCHNEIDER-ROSEN, K., & WENZ-GROSS, M. (1990). Patterns of compliance from eighteen to thirty months of age. *Child Development, 61,* 104–112.

SCHULMAN, A. H., & KAPLOWITZ, C. (1977). Mirror-image response during the first two years of life. *Developmental Psychobiology, 10,* 133–142.

SCHUNK, D. H. (1983). Reward contingencies and the development of children's skills and self-efficacy. *Journal of Educational Psychology, 75,* 511–518.

SCHUNK, D. H. (1984). Self-efficacy perspective on achievement behavior. *Educational Psychologist, 19,* 48–58.

*SCHUNK, D. H. (1987). Peer models and children's behavioral change. *Review of Educational Research, 57,* 159–174.

SCHWARTZ, B. (1990). The creation and destruction of value. *American Psychologist, 45,* 7–15.

SCHWARTZ, R. G., & CAMARATA, S. (1985). Examining relationships between input and language development: Some statistical issues. *Journal of Child Language, 12,* 199–207.

SCHWARTZ, R. G., LEONARD, L. B., FROME-LOEB, D. M., & SWANSON, L. A. (1987). Attempted sounds are sometimes not: An expanded view of phonological selection and avoidance. *Journal of Child Language, 14,* 411–418.

*SCHWEINHART, L. J., & WEIKART, D. P. (1991). Response to "Beyond IQ in Preschool Programs?" *Intelligence, 15,* 313–315.

SCHWEITZER, L. B., & DESNICK, R. J. (1983). Inherited metabolic diseases: Advances in delineation, diagnosis and treatment. *Birth Defects: Original Article Series, 19,* 11–37.

SCIENCE. (1988, June 10). Biological systems, p. 1383.

SCOTT, J. P. (1987). Critical periods in the processes of social organization. In M. H. Bornstein (Ed.), *Sensitive periods in development: Interdisciplinary perspectives.* Hillsdale, NJ: Erlbaum.

*SEARS, R. R. (1977). Sources of life satisfactions of the Terman gifted men. *American Psychologist, 32,* 119–128.

SEASHORE, M. J., LEIFER, A. D., BARNETT, C. R., & LEIDERMAN, P. H. (1973). The effects of denial of early mother–infant interaction on maternal self-confidence. *Journal of Personality and Social Psychology, 26,* 369–378.

SEAVY, C., KATZ, P., & ZALK, S. (1975). Baby X: The effect of gender labels on adult responses to infants. *Sex Roles, 1,* 103–109.

*SEBALD, H. (1989). Adolescent peer orientation: Changes in the support system during the last three decades. *Adolescence, 24,* 937–945.

*SEBEOK, T. A., & UMIKER-SEBEOK, J. (1980). *Speaking of apes: A critical anthology of two-way communication with man.* New York: Plenum.

SEGAL, N. L. (1985). Monozygotic and dizygotic twins: A comparative analysis of mental ability profiles. *Child Development, 56,* 1051–1058.

*SEIDENBERG, M. S., & PETTITO, L. A. (1979). Signing behavior in apes: A critical review. *Cognition, 7,* 177–215.

*SEIDENBERG, M. S., & PETTITO, L. A. (1987). Communication, symbolic communication, and language: Comment on Savage-Rumbaugh, McDonald, Sevcik, Hopkins and Rubert (1986). *Journal of Experimental Psychology: General, 116,* 279–287.

SEIDMAN, E., ALLEN, L., ABER, J. L., MITCHELL, C., A FEINMAN, J. (1994). The impact of school transition in early adolescence on the self-system and perceived social context of poor urban youth. *Child Development, 65,* 507–522.

SEITZ, V. (1990). Intervention programs for impoverished children: A comparison of educational and family support models. In R. Vasta (Ed.), *Annals of child development* (Vol. 7). London: Kingsley.

SELF, P. A., & HOROWITZ, F. D. (1979). The behavioral assessment of the neonate: An overview. In J. D. Osofsky (Ed.), *Handbook of infant development.* New York: Wiley.

*SELIK, R. M., CHU, S. Y. & BUEHLER, J. W. (1993). HIV infection as leading cause of death among young adults in US cities and states. *Journal of the American Medical Association, 269,* 2991–2994.

SELMAN, R. L. (1980). *The growth of interpersonal understanding: Development and clinical analyses.* New York: Academic Press.

SELMAN, R. L., & JAQUETTE, D. (1977). *The development of interpersonal awareness.* Unpublished manuscript.

SELMAN, R. L., & SCHULTZ, L. H. (1990). *Making a friend in youth: Developmental theory and pair therapy.* Chicago: University of Chicago Press.

*SERBIN, L. A., POWLISHTA, K. K., & GULKO, J. (1993). The development of sex typing in middle childhood. *Monographs of the Society for Research in Child Development, 58*(Serial No. 232).

SERBIN, L. A., & SPRAFKIN, C. (1986). The salience of gender and the process of sex typing in three- to seven-year-old children. *Child Development, 57,* 1188–1199.

SERBIN, L. A., TONICK, I. J., & STERNGLANZ, S. H. (1977). Shaping cooperative cross-sex play. *Child Development, 48,* 924–929.

SHAKIN, M., SHAKIN, D., & STERNGLANZ, S. H. (1985). Infant clothing: Sex labeling for strangers. *Sex Roles, 12,* 955–963.

SHANTZ, C. U. (1983). Social cognition. In J. H. Flavell & E. M. Markman (Eds.), *Handbook of child psychology: Vol. 3. Cognitive development.* New York: Wiley.

SHANTZ, C. U. (1987). Conflicts between children. *Child Development, 58,* 283–305.

SHAPIRO, B., HAITH, M. M., CAMPOS, J., BERTENTHAL, B., & HAZAN, C. (1983, November). *Motion enhances object perception for infants.* Paper presented at the meeting of the Psychonomic Society, San Diego, CA.

*SHARABANY, R., GERSHONI, R., & HOFMAN, J. E. (1981). Girlfriend, boyfriend: Age and sex differences in intimate friendship. *Developmental Psychology, 17,* 800–808.

*SHARPE, R. M., & SKAKKEBAEK, N. E. (1993). Are oestrogens involved in falling sperm counts and disorders of the male reproductive tract? *Lancet, 341,* 1392–1395.

*SHATZ, C. J. (1992). Dividing up the cortex. *Science, 258,* 237–240.

SHATZ, M. (1983). On transition, continuity, and coupling: An alternative approach to communicative development. In R. M. Golinkoff (Ed.), *The transition from prelinguistic to linguistic communication.* Hillsdale, NJ: Erlbaum.

*SHATZ, M. (1991). Using cross-cultural research to inform us about the role of language development: Comparisons of Japanese, Korean, and English, and of German, American English, and British English. In M. H. Bornstein (Ed.), *Cultural approaches to parenting.* Hillsdale, NJ: Erlbaum.

SHATZ, M., & GELMAN, R. (1973). The development of communication skills: Modifications in the speech of young children as a function of the listener. *Monographs of the Society for Research in Child Development, 38* (5, Serial No. 152).

SHATZ, M., & McCLOSKEY, L. (1984). Answering appropriately: A developmental perspective on conversational knowledge. In S. A. Kuczaj (Ed.), *Discourse development: Progress in cognitive developmental research.* New York: Springer-Verlag.

SHAVELSON, R. J., HUBNER, J. J., & STANTON, G. C. (1976). Self-concept: Validation of construct interpretations. *Educational Research, 46,* 407–441.

SHAYER, M., KUCHEMAN, D. E., & WYLAM, H. (1976). The distribution of Piagetian stages of thinking in British middle and secondary school children. *British Journal of Educational Psychology, 46,* 164–173.

SHAYER, M., & WYLAM, H. (1978). The distribution of Piagetian stages of thinking in British middle and secondary school children: II. 14 to 16 year old and sex differentials. *British Journal of Educational Psychology, 48,* 62–70.

*SHELDON, A. (1990). Pickle fights: Gendered talk in preschool disputes. *Discourse Processes, 13,* 5–31.

SHEPARD, T. H. (1977). Maternal metabolic and endocrine imbalances. In J. G. Wilson & F. C. Fraser (Eds.), *Handbook of teratology: Vol. 1. General principles of etiology.* New York: Plenum.

SHEPARD, T. H. (1986). Human teratogenicity. *Advances in Pediatrics, 33,* 225–268.

SHERIF, M., HARVEY, O. .J., WHITE, B. J., HOOD, W. R., & SHERIF, C. W. (1961). *Intergroup conflict and cooperation: The Robbers Cave experiment.* Norman: University of Oklahoma Press.

SHIGETOMI, C. C., HARTMANN, D. P., & GELFAND, D. M. (1981). Sex differences in children's altruistic behavior and reputations for helpfulness. *Developmental Psychology, 17,* 434–437.

SHIPLEY, E. F., KUHN, I. F., & MADDEN, E. C. (1983). Mothers' use of superordinate category terms. *Journal of Child Language, 10,* 571–588.

SHUCARD, J. L., & SHUCARD, D. W. (1990). Auditory evoked potentials and hand preference in 6-month-old infants: Possible gender-related differences in cerebral organization. *Developmental Psychology, 26,* 923–930.

SHUCARD, J. L., SHUCARD, D. W., CUMMINS, K. R., & CAMPOS, J. J. (1981). Auditory evoked potentials and sex-related differences in brain development. *Brain and Language, 13,* 91–102.

*SHULTZ, T. R., & DARLEY, J. M. (1991). An information-processing model of retributive moral judgments based on "legal reasoning." In W. M. Kurtines & J. L. Gewirtz (Eds.), *Handbook of moral behavior and development: Vol. 2. Research.* Hillsdale, NJ: Erlbaum.

SHULTZ, T. R., & WRIGHT, K. (1985). Concepts of negligence and intention in the assignment of moral responsibility. *Canadian Journal of Behavioural Science, 17,* 97–108.

SHULTZ, T. R., WRIGHT, K., & SCHLEIFER, M. (1986). Assignment of moral responsibility and punishment. *Child Development, 57,* 177–184.

SHURE, M. B. (1989). Interpersonal competence training. In W. Damon (Ed.), *Child development today and tomorrow.* San Francisco: Jossey-Bass.

*SHURKIN, J. N. (1992). *Terman's kids: The groundbreaking study of how the gifted grow up.* Boston: Little, Brown.

SHWEDER, R. A., & MUCH, M. C. (1987). Determinations of meaning: Discourse and moral socialization. In W. M. Kurtines & J. L. Gewirtz (Eds.), *Moral development through social interaction.* New York: Wiley.

SIDOROWICZ, L. S., & LUNNEY, G. S. (1980). Baby X revisited. *Sex Roles, 6,* 67–73.

*SIEBER, J. E. (1992). *Planning ethically responsible research: A guide for students and internal review boards.* Newbury Park, CA: Sage.

SIEGAL, M. (1982). *Fairness in children.* New York: Academic Press.

SIEGAL, M. (1987). Are sons and daughters treated more differently by fathers than by mothers? *Developmental Review, 7,* 183–209.

*SIEGAL, M. (1988). Children's knowledge of contagion and contamination as causes of illness. *Child Development, 59,* 1353–1359.

*SIEGAL, M. (1991). *Knowing children: Experiments in conversation and cognition.* Hillsdale, NJ: Erlbaum.

*SIEGAL, M., & SHARE, D. L. (1990). Contam-ination sensitivity in young children. *Developmental Psychology, 26,* 455–458.

SIEGEL, L. S. (1984). Home environment influences on cognitive development in preterm and full-term children during the first 5 years. In A. W. Gottfried (Ed.), *Home environment and early cognitive development.* New York: Academic Press.

*SIEGEL, L. S. (1989). A reconceptualization of prediction from infant test scores. In M. H. Bornstein & N. Krasnegor (Eds.), *Stability and continuity in mental development.* Hillsdale, NJ: Erlbaum.

*SIEGEL, L. S. (1992). Infant, motor, and language behaviors as predictors of achievement at school age. In C. Rovee-Collier & L. P. Lipsitt (Eds.), *Advances in infancy research* (Vol. 7). Norwood, NJ: Ablex.

*SIEGEL, L. S. (1993a). The development of reading. In H. W. Reese (Ed.), *Advances in child development and behavior* (Vol. 24). San Diego: Academic Press.

*SIEGEL, L. S. (1993b). Phonological processing deficits as the basis of a reading disability. *Developmental Review, 13,* 246–257.

SIEGLER, R. S. (1976). Three aspects of cognitive development. *Cognitive Psychology, 8,* 481–520.

SIEGLER, R. S. (1978). The origins of scientific reasoning. In R. S. Siegler (Ed.), *Children's thinking: What develops?* Hillsdale, NJ: Erlbaum.

SIEGLER, R. S. (1981). Developmental sequences within and between concepts. *Monographs of the Society for Research in Child Development, 46* (2, Serial No. 189).

SIEGLER, R. S. (1983). Information processing approaches to development. In W. Kessen (Ed.), *Handbook of child psychology: Vol. 1. History, theory, and methods.* New York: Wiley.

SIEGLER, R. S. (1986). A panoramic view of development [Review of intellectual development: Birth to adulthood]. *Contemporary Psychology, 31,* 329–331.

SIEGLER, R. S. (1988). Individual differences in strategy choices: Good students, not-so-good students, and perfectionists. *Child Development, 59,* 833–851.

SIEGLER, R. S. (1989). Mechanisms of cognitive development. *Annual Review of Psychology, 40,* 353–379.

SIEGLER, R. S. (1991). *Children's thinking* (2nd ed.). Englewood Cliffs, NJ: Prentice Hall.

*SIEGLER, R. S., & CROWLEY, K. (1991). The microgenetic method: A direct means for studying cognitive development. *American Psychologist, 46,* 606–620.

*SIEGLER, R. S., & CROWLEY, K. (1992). Microgenetic methods revisited. *American Psychologist, 47,* 1241–1243.

SIEGLER, R. S., & JENKINS, E. (1989). *How children discover new strategies.* Hillsdale, NJ: Erlbaum.

SIEGLER, R. S., & LIEBERT, R. M. (1975). Acquisition of formal scientific reasoning by 10 to 13 year olds: Designing a factorial experiment. *Developmental Psychology, 11,* 401–402.

*SIEGLER, R. S., & MUNAKATA, Y. (1993, Winter). Beyond the immaculate transition: Advances in the understanding of change. *SRCD Newsletter,* pp. 3, 10–11, 13.

*SIEGLER, R. S., & SHIPLEY, C. (in press). A new model of strategy choice. In G. Halford & P. Simon (Eds.), *Developing cognitive competence: New approaches to process modeling.* Hillsdale, NJ: Erlbaum.

*SIEGLER, R. S., & SHRAGER, J. (1984). Strategy choices in addition and subtraction: How do children know what to do? In C. Sophian (Ed.), *Origins of cognitive skills.* Hillsdale, NJ: Erlbaum.

SIGEL, I. E. (1987). Does hothousing rob children of their childhood? *Early Childhood Research Quarterly, 2,* 211–225.

*SIGELMAN, C., MADDOCK, A., EPSTEIN, J., & CARPENTER, W. (1993). Age differences in understandings of disease causality: AIDS, colds, and cancer. *Child Development, 64,* 272–284.

*SIGELMAN, C. K., & WAITZMAN, K. A. (1991). The development of distributive justice orientations: Contextual influences of children's resource allocations. *Child Development, 62,* 1367–1378.

SIGNORELLA, M. L. (1987). Gender schemata: Individual differences and context effects. In L. S. Liben & M. L. Signorella (Eds.), *New directions for child development: No. 38. Children's gender schemata.* San Francisco: Jossey-Bass.

*SIGNORELLA, M. L., BIGLER, R. S., & LIBEN, L. S. (1993). Developmental differences in children's gender schemata about others: A meta-analytic review. *Developmental Review, 13,* 147–183.

SIGNORELLA, M. L., JAMISON, W., & KRUPA, M. H. (1989). Predicting spatial performance from gender stereotyping in activity preferences and self-concept. *Developmental Psychology, 25,* 89–95.

SIGNORELLA, M. L., & LIBEN, L. S. (1984). Recall and reconstruction of gender-related pictures: Effects of attitude, task difficulty, and age. *Child Development, 55,* 393–405.

SIGNORIELLI, N. (1989). Television and conceptions about sex roles: Maintaining conventionality and the status quo. *Sex Roles, 21,* 341–360.

*SILVERMAN, I., & EALS, M. (1992). Sex differences in spatial abilities: Evolutionary theory and data. In J. H. Barkow, L. Cosmides, & J. Tooby (Eds.), *The adapted mind: Evolutionary psychology and the generation of culture.* New York: Oxford University Press.

*SIMEONSSON, R. J., BUCKLEY, L., & MONSON, L. (1979). Conceptions of illness causality in hospitalized children. *Journal of Pediatric Psychology, 4,* 77–84.

SIMMONS, R. G., & BLYTH, D. A. (1987). *Moving into adolescence: The impact of pubertal change and social context.* Hawthorne, NY: Aldine de Gruyter.

SIMMONS, R. G., BLYTH, D. A., VanCLEAVE, E. F., & BUSH, D. M. (1979). Entry into early adolescence. *American Sociological Review, 44,* 948–967.

SIMMONS, R. G., CARLTON-FORD, S. L., & BLYTH, D. A. (1987). Predicting how a child will age with the transition to junior high school. In R. M. Lerner & T. M. Foch (Eds.), *Biological-psychosocial interactions in early adolescence.* Hillsdale, NJ: Erlbaum.

SINGER, J. E., WESTPHAL, M., & MISWANDER,

K. R. (1968). Sex differences in the incidence of neonatal abnormalities and abnormal performance in early childhood. *Child Development, 39,* 103–112.

SINGER, L. M., BRODZINSKY, D. M., RAMSAY, D., STEIR, M., & WATERS, E. (1985). Mother-infant attachment in adoptive families. *Child Development, 56,* 1543–1551.

SKINNER, B. F. (1953). *Science and human behavior.* New York: Macmillan.

SKINNER, B. F. (1957). *Verbal behavior.* New York: Appleton-Century-Crofts.

SLABY, R. G., & FREY, K. S. (1975). Development of gender constancy and selective attention to same-sex models. *Child Development, 46,* 849–856.

SLABY, R. G., & GUERRA, N. G. (1988). Cognitive mediators of aggression in adolescent offenders: 1. Assessment. *Developmental Psychology, 24,* 580–588.

SLADE, A. (1987). Quality of attachment and early symbolic play. *Developmental Psychology, 23,* 78–85.

*SLATER, A., COOPER, R., ROSE, D., & MORISON, V. (1989). Prediction of cognitive performance from infancy to early childhood. *Human Development, 32,* 137–147.

*SLATER, A., MATTOCK, A., BROWN, E., & BREMNER, J. G. (1991). Form perception at birth: Cohen and Younger (1984) revisited. *Journal of Experimental Child Psychology, 51,* 395–406.

*SLATER, A., & MORISON, V. (1991). Visual attention and memory at birth. In M. J. S. Weiss & P. R. Zelazo (Eds.), *Newborn attention: Biological constraints and the influence of experience.* Norwood, NJ: Ablex.

SLATER, A., MORISON, V., & ROSE, D. (1984). Habituation in the newborn. *Infant Behavior and Development, 7,* 183–200.

SLATER, A., MORISON, V., SOMERS, M., MATTOCK, A., BROWN, E., & TAYLOR, D. (1990). Newborn and older infants' perception of partly occluded objects. *Infant Behavior and Development, 13,* 33–49.

SLAUGHTER, D. T. (1983). Early intervention and its effects on maternal and child development. *Monographs of the Society for Research in Child Development, 48* (4, Serial No. 202).

SLAUGHTER-DEFOE, D. T., NAKAGAWA, K., TAKANISHI, R., & JOHNSON, D. J. (1990). Toward cultural/ecological perspectives on schooling and achievement in African- and Asian-American children. *Child Development, 61,* 363–383.

SLOBIN, D. I. (1982). Universal and particular in the acquisition of language. In E. Wanner & L. R. Gleitman (Eds.), *Language acquisition: The state of the art.* Cambridge: Cambridge University Press.

SLOBIN, D. I. (1985). *The cross-linguistic study of language* (Vols. 1 and 2). Hillsdale, NJ: Erlbaum.

*SLOMKOWSKI, C., & DUNN, J. (1993, March). *Conflict in close relationships.* Paper presented at the meeting of the Society for Research in Child Development, New Orleans.

SLUCKIN, A. (1980). Dominance relationships in preschool children. In D. R. Omark, F. F. Strayer, & D. G. Freedman (Eds.), *Dominance*

relations: An ethological view of human conflict and social interaction.* New York: Garland.

*SLUTSKER, L., BRUNET, J.-B., KARON, J. M., & CURRAN, J. W. (1992). The shape of the pandemic. In J. M. Mann, D. J. M. Tarantola, & T. W. Netter (Eds.), *AIDS in the world.* Cambridge, MA: Harvard University Press.

*SMETANA, J. G. (1986). Preschool children's conceptions of sex-role transgressions. *Child Development, 57,* 862–871.

*SMETANA, J. G., & BRAEGES, J. L. (1990). The development of toddlers' moral and conventional judgments. *Merrill-Palmer Quarterly, 36,* 329–346.

*SMETANA, J. G., KILLEN, M., & TURIEL, E. (1991). Children's reasoning about interpersonal and moral conflicts. *Child Development, 62,* 629–644.

*SMETANA, J. G., SCHLAGMAN, N., & ADAMS, P. W. (1993). Preschool children's judgments about hypothetical and actual transgressions. *Child Development, 64,* 202–214.

SMILANSKY, S. (1968). *The effects of sociodramatic play on disadvantaged preschool children.* New York: Wiley.

SMILEY, P., & HUTTENLOCHER, J. (1989). Young children's acquisition of emotion concepts. In C. Saarni & P. L. Harris (Eds.), *Children's understanding of emotion.* Cambridge: Cambridge University Press.

*SMITH, B. A., STEVENS, K., TORGERSON, W. S., & KIM, J. H. (1992). Diminished reactivity of postmature human infants to sucrose compared with term infants. *Developmental Psychology, 28,* 811–820.

SMITH, C., & LLOYD, B. (1978). Maternal behavior and perceived sex of infant: Revisited. *Child Development, 49,* 1263–1265.

*SMITH, C. L. (1979). Children's understanding of natural language hierarchies. *Journal of Experimental Child Psychology, 27,* 437–458.

SMITH, E. A. (1989). A biosocial model of adolescent sexual behavior. In G. R. Adams, R. Montemayor, & T. P. Gullota (Eds.), *Biology of adolescent behavior and development.* London: Sage.

SMITH, P. B., & PEDERSON, D. R. (1988). Maternal sensitivity and patterns of infant-mother attachment. *Child Development, 59,* 1097–1101.

SMITH, P. K. (1978). A longitudinal study of social participation in preschool children: Solitary and parallel play reexamined. *Developmental Psychology, 14,* 517–523.

SMITH, P. K., & CONNOLLY, K. J. (1981). *The ecology of preschool behavior.* Cambridge: Cambridge University Press.

*SMITH, S. D., KIMBERLING, W. J., & PENNINGTON, B. F. (1991). Screening for multiple genes influencing dyslexia. *Reading and Writing, 3,* 285–298.

SNAREY, J. R. (1985). Cross-cultural universality of social-moral development: A critical review of Kohlbergian research. *Psychological Bulletin, 97,* 202–232.

*SNAREY, J. R., & KELJO, K. (1991). In a *Gemeinschaft* voice: The cross-cultural expansion of moral development theory. In W. M. Kurtines & J. L. Gewirtz (Eds.), *Handbook of*

moral behavior and development: Vol. 1. Theory.* Hillsdale, NJ: Erlbaum.

SNAREY, J. R., REIMER, J., & KOHLBERG, L. (1985). Development of social-moral reasoning among kibbutz adolescents: A longitudinal cross-cultural study. *Developmental Psychology, 21,* 3–17.

SNOW, C. E. (1981). The uses of imitation. *Journal of Child Language, 8,* 205–212.

SNOW, C. E. (1983). Saying it again: The role of expanded and deferred imitations in language acquisition. In K. E. Nelson (Ed.), *Children's language* (Vol. 4). Hillsdale, NJ: Erlbaum.

SNOW, C. E., ARLMAN-RUPP, A., HASSING, Y., JOBSE, J., JOOSTER, J., & VORSTER, J. (1976). Mothers' speech in three social classes. *Journal of Psycholinguistic Research, 5,* 1–20.

SNOW, C. E., & FERGUSON, C. (1977). *Talking to children: Language input and acquisition.* Cambridge: Cambridge University Press.

SNOW, C. E., & GOLDFIELD, B. A. (1983). Turn the page please: Situation-specific language acquisition. *Journal of Child Language, 10,* 551–569.

SNOW, C. E., PERLMAN, R., & NATHAN, D. (1987). Why routines are different: Toward a multiple-factors model of the relation between input and language acquisition. In K. E. Nelson & A. VanKleeck (Eds.), *Children's language* (Vol. 6). Hillsdale, NJ: Erlbaum.

SNOW, M. E., JACKLIN, C. N., & MACCOBY, E. E. (1983). Sex-of-child differences in father–child interaction at one year of age. *Child Development, 54,* 227–232.

SNOW, R. E., & YALOW, E. (1982). Education and intelligence. In R. J. Sternberg (Ed.), *Handbook of human intelligence.* Cambridge: Cambridge University Press.

SNYDERMAN, M., & ROTHMAN, S. (1988). *The IQ controversy, the media, and public policy.* New Brunswick, NJ: Transaction Books.

SODIAN, B. (1988). Children's attributions of knowledge to the listener in a referential communication task. *Child Development, 59,* 378–385.

SOKOLOV, E. N. (1960). *Perception and the conditioned reflex.* New York: Macmillan.

*SOKOLOV, J. L. (1993). A local contingency analysis of the fine-tuning hypothesis. *Developmental Psychology, 29,* 1008–1023.

SOMMERVILLE, J. (1978). English Puritans and children: A social-cultural explanation. *Journal of Psychohistory, 6,* 113–137.

SOMMERVILLE, J. (1982). *The rise and fall of childhood.* Beverly Hills, CA: Sage.

SONNENSCHEIN, S. (1988). The development of referential communication: Speaking to different listeners. *Child Development, 59,* 694–702.

SONTAG, L. W. (1944). War and fetal maternal relationship. *Marriage and Family Living, 6,* 1–5.

SONTAG, L. W. (1966). Implications of fetal behavior and environment for adult personalities. *Annals of the New York Academy of Sciences, 134,* 782–786.

SOPHIAN, C., & SAGE, S. (1983). Development in infants' search for displaced objects. *Journal of Experimental Child Psychology, 35,* 143–160.

SOPHIAN, C., & WELLMAN, H. M. (1983). Selective information use and perseveration in the search behavior of infants and young children. *Journal of Experimental Child Psychology, 35,* 369–390.

SORCE, J. F., EMDE, R. N., CAMPOS, J. J., & KLINNERT, M. D. (1985). Maternal emotional signaling: Its effect on the visual cliff behavior of 1-year-olds. *Developmental Psychology, 21,* 195–200.

SORENSON, J. R., SWAZEY, J. P., & SCOTCH, N. A. (1981). Reproductive pasts, reproductive futures. Genetic counseling and its effectiveness. *Birth Defects: Original Article Series, 17* (No. 4).

SOSTEK, A. M., SMITH, Y. F., KATZ, K. S., & GRANT, E. G. (1987). Developmental outcome of preterm infants with intraventricular hemorrhage at one and two years of age. *Child Development, 58,* 779–786.

*SPANGLER, G., & GROSSMANN, K. E. (1993). Biobehavioral organization in securely and insecurely attached infants. *Child Development, 64,* 1439–1450.

SPEARMAN, C. (1927). *The abilities of man.* New York: Macmillan.

SPEER, J. R., & FLAVELL, J. H. (1979). Young children's knowledge of the relative difficulty of recognition and recall memory tasks. *Developmental Psychology, 15,* 214–217.

SPELKE, E. S. (1976). Infants' intermodal perception of events. *Cognitive Psychology, 8,* 533–560.

SPELKE, E. S. (1979). Perceiving bimodally specified events in infancy. *Developmental Psychology, 15,* 626–636.

SPELKE, E. S. (1985). Perception of unity, persistence, and identity: Thoughts on infants' conceptions of objects. In J. Mehler & R. Fox (Eds.), *Neonate cognition: Beyond the blooming buzzing confusion.* Hillsdale, NJ: Erlbaum.

SPELKE, E. S. (1987). The development of intermodal space perception. In P. Salapatek & L. Cohen (Eds.), *Handbook of infant perception: Vol. 2. From perception to cognition.* Orlando, FL: Academic Press.

SPELKE, E. S. (1988). Where perceiving ends and thinking begins: The apprehension of objects in infancy. In A. Yonas (Ed.), *Minnesota symposia on child psychology: Vol. 20. Perceptual development in infancy.* Hillsdale, NJ: Erlbaum.

*SPELKE, E. S. (1991). Physical knowledge in infancy: Reflections on Piaget's theory. In S. Carey & R. Gelman (Eds.), *The epigenesis of mind.* Hillsdale, NJ: Erlbaum.

*SPELKE, E. S., BREINLINGER, K., MACOMBER, J., & JACOBSON, K. (1992). Origins of knowledge. *Psychological Review, 99,* 605–632.

SPELKE, E. S., & OWSLEY, C. J. (1979). Intermodal exploration and knowledge in infancy. *Infant Behavior and Development, 2,* 13–28.

*SPENCE, J. T. (1985). Gender identity and its implications for concepts of masculinity and femininity. In T. B. Sonderegger (Ed.), *Nebraska symposium on motivation: Psychology and gender* (Vol. 32). Lincoln: University of Nebraska Press.

SPENCE, J. T., & HELMREICH, R. L. (1978). *Masculinity and femininity: Their psychological dimensions, correlates, and antecedents.* Austin: University of Texas Press.

SPENCE, J. T., HELMREICH, R. L., & HOLA-

HAN, C. K. (1979). Negative and positive components of psychological masculinity and femininity and their relationships to self-reports of neurotic and acting out behaviors. *Journal of Personality and Social Psychology, 37,* 1673–1682.

*SPERGEL, I. A., CHANCE, R. L., & CURRY, G. D. (1990, June). National Youth Gang Suppression and Intervention Program. *National Institute of Justice Reports, #222,* 1–4.

*SPERGEL, I. A., & CURRY, G. D. (1990). Strategies and perceived effectiveness in dealing with the youth gang problem. In C. R. Huff (Ed.), *Gangs in America.* Newbury Park, CA: Sage.

SPIEKER, S. J., & BOOTH, C. L. (1988). Maternal antecedents of attachment quality. In J. Belsky & T. Nezworski (Eds.), *Clinical implications of attachment.* Hillsdale, NJ: Erlbaum.

SPITZ, R. (1945). Hospitalism: An inquiry into the genesis of psychiatric conditions in early childhood. *Psychoanalytic Study of the Child, 1,* 53–74.

*SPRINGER, K., & BELK, A. (1993, March). *Children's understanding of physical mediation between cause and effect: The example of contamination.* Paper presented at the meeting of the Society for Research in Child Development, New Orleans.

*SPRINGER, K., & KEIL, F. C. (1991). Early differentiation of causal mechanisms appropriate to biological and nonbiological kinds. *Child Development, 62,* 767–781.

*SPRINGER, K., & RUCKEL, J. (1992). Early beliefs about the cause of illness: Evidence against immanent justice. *Child Development, 7,* 429–443.

SPRINGER, S. P., & DEUTSCH, G. (1989). *Left brain, right brain* (3rd ed.). New York: W. H. Freeman.

SROUFE, L. A. (1985). Attachment classification from the perspective of infant–caregiver relationships and infant temperament. *Child Development, 56,* 1–14.

SROUFE, L. A. (1986). Bowlby's contribution to psychoanalytic theory and developmental psychology: Attachment: Separation: Loss. *Journal of Child Psychology and Psychiatry, 27,* 841–849.

SROUFE, L. A. (1988). The role of infant-caregiver attachment in development. In J. Belsky & T. Nezworski (Eds.), *Clinical implications of attachment.* Hillsdale, NJ: Erlbaum.

SROUFE, L. A. (1990). An organizational perspective on the self. In D. Cicchetti & M. Beeghly (Eds.), *The self in transition: Infancy to childhood.* Chicago: University of Chicago Press.

*SROUFE, L. A., BENNETT, C., ENGLUND, M., URBAN, J., & SHULMAN, S. (1993). The significance of gender boundaries in preadolescence: Contemporary correlates and antecedents of boundary violation and maintenance. *Child Development, 64,* 455–466.

*ST. PETERS, M., FITCH, M., HUSTON, A. C., WRIGHT, J. C., & EAKINS, D. J. (1991). Television and families: What do young children watch with their parents? *Child Development 62,* 1409–1423.

*STACK, D. M., & MUIR, D. W. (1992). Adult tactile stimulation during face-to-face interactions modulates five-month-olds' affect and attention. *Child Development, 63,* 1509–1525.

*STAMBAK, M., & SINCLAIR, H. (1993). *Pretend play among 3–year-olds.* Hillsdale, NJ: Erlbaum.

STANGOR, C., & RUBLE, D. N. (1987). Development of gender role knowledge and gender constancy. In L. S. Liben & M. L. Signorella (Eds.), *New directions for child development: No. 38. Children's gender schemata.* San Francisco: Jossey-Bass.

STANHOPE, R. (1989). The endocrine control of puberty. In J. M. Tanner & M. A. Preece (Eds.), *The physiology of human growth.* London: Cambridge University Press.

*STANLEY, J. C., BENBOW, C. P., BRODY, L. E., DAUBER, S., & LUPKOWSKI, A. E. (1991). Gender differences in eighty-six nationally standardized aptitude and achievement tests. In N. Colangelo, S. G. Assouline, & D. Ambroson (Eds.), *National research symposium on talent development.* Iowa City: University of Iowa Press.

*STANOVICH, K. E. (Ed.). (1988). *Children's reading and the development of phonological awareness.* Detroit: Wayne State University Press.

*STANOVICH, K. E. (Ed.). (1993a). The development of rationality and critical thinking [Special issue]. *Merrill-Palmer Quarterly, 39*(1).

*STANOVICH, K. E. (1993b). Does reading make you smarter? Literacy and the development of verbal intelligence. In H. W. Reese (Ed.), *Advances in child development and behavior* (Vol. 24). San Diego: Academic Press.

*STANTON, W. R., & SILVA, P. A. (1992). A longitudinal study of the influence of parents and friends on children's imitation of smoking. *Journal of Applied Developmental Psychology, 13,* 423–434.

STARK, R. E. (1986). Prespeech segmental feature development. In P. Fletcher & M. Garman (Eds.), *Language acquisition: Studies in first language development* (2nd ed.). New York: Cambridge University Press.

STARKEY, P., & COOPER, R. (1980). Perception of numbers by human infants. *Science, 210,* 1033–1034.

STEIN, N. L., & GLENN, C. G. (1982). Children's concept of time: The development of a story schema. In W. J. Friedman (Ed.), *The developmental psychology of time.* New York: Academic Press.

STEIN, Z. A., & SUSSER, M. W. (1976). Prenatal nutrition and mental competence. In J. D. Lloyd-Still (Ed.), *Malnutrition and intellectual development.* Littleton, MA: Publishing Sciences Group.

*STEINBERG, L. D. (1988). Pubertal maturation and family relations: Evidence for the distancing hypothesis. In G. Adams, R. Montemayor, & T. Gullotta (Eds.), *Advances in adolescent development.* Beverly Hills, CA: Sage.

STEINER, J. E. (1977). Facial expressions of the neonate infant indicating the hedonics of food-related chemical stimuli. In J. M. Weiffenbach (Ed.), *Taste and development: The genesis of sweet preference.* Washington, DC: Government Printing Office.

STEINER, J. E. (1979). Human facial expressions in response to taste and smell stimulation. In H. W. Reese & L. P. Lipsitt (Eds.), *Advances in child behavior and development* (Vol. 13). New York: Academic Press.

STENBERG, C. R.; CAMPOS, J. J., & EMDE, R. N. (1983). The facial expression of anger in seven-month-old infants. *Child Development, 54,* 178–184.

STEPHENS, T. (1990). Blocking fetal AIDS: Immune intervention paces science. *Journal of NIH Research, 2,* 21–24.

*STEPHENS, T. (1991). A close look at pot use in pregnancy. *Journal of NIH Research, 3,* 53–54.

*STERN, C. D. (1992). Pioneers of embryology. In S. F. Gilbert (Ed.), *A conceptual history of modern embryology.* New York: Plenum.

STERN, D. N. (1983). The early development of schemas of self, other, and "self with other." In J. D. Lichtenberg & S. Kaplan (Eds.), *Reflections on self psychology.* Hillsdale, NJ: Erlbaum.

STERN, D. N. (1985). *The interpersonal world of the infant.* New York: Basic Books.

STERN, M., & KARRAKER, K. (1989). Sex stereotyping of infants: A review of gender labeling studies. *Sex Roles, 20,* 501–522.

*STERN, M., & KARRAKER, K. (1992). Modifying the prematurity stereotype in matters of premature and ill full-term infants. *Journal of Clinical Child Psychology, 21,* 76–82.

STERNBERG, R. J. (1984). Toward a triarchic theory of human intelligence. *Behavioral and Brain Sciences, 7,* 269–287.

STERNBERG, R. J. (1985). *Beyond IQ: A triarchic theory of human intelligence.* New York: Cambridge University Press.

STERNBERG, R. J. (1988). Intellectual development: Psychometric and information-processing approaches. In M. H. Bornstein & M. E. Lamb (Eds.), *Developmental psychology: An advanced textbook* (2nd ed.). Hillsdale, NJ: Erlbaum.

*STERNBERG, R. J. (1991). Death, taxes, and bad intelligence tests. *Intelligence, 15,* 257–269.

STERNBERG, R. J., & POWELL, J. S. (1983). The development of intelligence. In J. H. Flavell & E. M. Markman (Eds.), *Handbook of child psychology: Vol. 3. Cognitive development.* New York: Wiley.

*STEVENSON, H. W. (1992). *The learning gap: Why our schools are failing and what we can learn from Japanese and Chinese education.* New York: Summit Books.

STEVENSON, H. W., & LEE, S. (1990). Contexts of achievement: A study of American, Chinese, and Japanese children. *Monographs of the Society for Research in Child Development, 55* (1–2, Serial No. 221).

STEVENSON, H. W., LEE, S., CHEN, C., STIGLER, J., FAN, L., & GE, F. (1990). Mathematics achievement of children in China and the United States. *Child Development, 61,* 1053–1066.

STEVENSON, H. W., LEE, S. Y., & STIGLER, J. W. (1986). Mathematics achievement of Chinese, Japanese, and American children. *Science, 231,* 693–699.

*STEVENSON, H. W., & NEWMAN, R. S. (1986). Long-term prediction of achievement and attitudes in mathematics and reading. *Child Development, 57,* 646–659.

STEVENSON, M. R., & BLACK, K. N. (1988). Paternal absence and sex-role development: A meta-analysis. *Child Development, 59,* 793–814.

*STIFTER, C. A., COULEHAN, C. M., & FISH, M. (1993). Linking employment to attachment: The mediating effects of maternal separation anxiety and interactive behavior. *Child Development, 64,* 1451–1460.

STIFTER, C. A., & FOX, N. A. (1990). Infant reactivity: Physiological correlates of newborn and 5-month temperament. *Developmental Psychology, 26,* 582–588.

*STIPEK, D. (1984). Young children's performance expectations: Logical analysis or wishful thinking? In J. G. Nicholls (Ed.), *Advances in motivation and achievement: Vol. 3. The development of achievement motivation.* Greenwich, CT: JAI Press.

*STIPEK, D. (1992). The child at school. In M. E. Lamb & M. H. Bornstein (Eds.), *Developmental psychology: An advanced textbook* (3rd ed.). Hillsdale, NJ: Erlbaum.

STIPEK, D., GRALINSKI, J. H., & KOPP, C. B. (1990). Self-concept development in the toddler years. *Developmental Psychology, 26,* 972–977.

*STIPEK, D., & MacIVER, D. (1989). Developmental change in children's assessment of intellectual competence. *Child Development, 60,* 521–538.

*STIPEK, D., RECCHIA, S., & McCLINTIC, S. (1992). Self-evaluation in young children. *Monographs of the Society for Research in Child Development, 57*(1, Serial No. 226).

STIPEK, D., & TANNATT, L. (1984). Children's judgments of their own and their peers' academic competence. *Journal of Educational Psychology, 76,* 75–84.

*STJERNFELDT, M., BERGLUND, K., LINDSTEN, J., & LUDVIGSSON, J. (1986). Maternal smoking during pregnancy and risk of childhood cancer. *Lancet, 1,* 1350–1352.

*STOCKER, C., & DUNN, J. (1990). Sibling relationships in childhood: Links with friendships and peer relationships. *British Journal of Developmental Psychology, 8,* 227–244.

*STOCKER, C. M., & MANTZ-SIMMONS, L. M. (1993). *Children's friendship and peer status: Links with family relationships, temperament, and social skills.* Unpublished manuscript.

STODDART, T., & TURIEL, E. (1985). Children's concepts of cross-gender activities. *Child Development, 56,* 1241–1252.

*STOLL, C., DOTT, B., ALEMBIK, Y., & ROTH, M. (1993). Evaluation of routine prenatal ultrasound examination in detecting fetal chromosomal abnormalities in a low risk population. *Human Genetics, 91,* 37–41.

STONE, C. A., & DAY, M. C. (1978). Levels of availability of a formal operational strategy. *Child Development, 49,* 1054–1065.

STOTT, D. H. (1969). The child's hazards *in utero.* In J. G. Howells (Ed.), *Modern perspectives in international child psychiatry.* Edinburgh: Oliver & Boyd.

STRAUGHAN, R. (1986). Why act on Kohlberg's moral judgments? (Or how to reach Stage 6 and remain a bastard). In S. Modgil & C. Modgil (Eds.), *Lawrence Kohlberg: Consensus and controversy.* Philadelphia: Falmer.

STRAUSS, M. S., & CURTIS, L. E. (1984). Development of numerical concepts in infancy. In C. Sophian (Ed.), *Origins of cognitive skills.*

The 18th annual Carnegie symposium on cognition. Hillsdale, NJ: Erlbaum.

STRAWN, J. (1992a). Children in poverty: Excerpts from testimony given by Nicholas Zill, Subcommittee on Human Resources, U.S. House of Representatives September 1992.

STRAWN, J. (1992b, Fall). The states and the poor: Child poverty rises as the safety net shrinks. *Social Policy Report, Society for Research in Child Development, 6* (3), 1–19.

STRAYER, F. F. (1980). Social ecology of the preschool peer group. In W. A. Collins (Ed.), *Minnesota symposia on child psychology: Vol. 13. Development of cognition, affect, and social relations.* Hillsdale, NJ: Erlbaum.

STRAYER, F. F., & NOEL, J. M. (1986). The prosocial and antisocial functions of preschool aggression: An ethological study of triadic conflict among young children. In C. Zahn-Waxler, E. M. Cummings, & R. Iannotti (Eds.), *Altruism and aggression: Biological and social origins.* Cambridge: Cambridge University Press.

STRAYER, F. F., & STRAYER, J. (1976). An ethological analysis of social agonism and dominance relations among preschool children. *Child Development, 47,* 980–989.

STREISSGUTH, A. P., BARR, H. M., JOHNSON, J. C., MARTIN, D. C., & KIRCHNER, G. L. (1985). Attention and distraction at age 7 years related to maternal drinking during pregnancy. *Alcoholism: Clinical and Experimental Research, 9,* 195.

STREISSGUTH, A. P., SAMPSON, P. D., & BARR, H. M. (1989). Neurobehavioral dose-response effects of prenatal alcohol exposure in humans from infancy to adulthood. *Annals of the New York Academy of Sciences, 562,* 145–158.

STRERI, A., & PECHEUX, M. G. (1986). Vision to touch and touch to vision transfer of form in 5-month-old infants. *British Journal of Developmental Psychology, 4,* 161–167.

STUDDERT-KENNEDY, M. (1986). Sources of variability in early speech in infancy. In G. Yeni-Konshian, C. Kavanaugh, & C. Ferguson (Eds.), *Child phonology: Perception and production.* New York: Academic Press.

SUDHALTER, V., & BRAINE, M. D. S. (1985). How does comprehension of passive develop? A comparison of actional and experiential verbs. *Journal of Child Language, 12,* 455–470.

SUE, S., & OZAKI, S. (1990). Asian-American educational achievements: A phenomenon in search of an explanation. *American Psychologist, 45,* 913–920.

SUGARMAN, S. (1983). *Children's early thought: Developments in classification.* Cambridge: Cambridge University Press.

SUGARMAN, S. (1987). *Piaget's construction of the child's reality.* Cambridge: Cambridge University Press.

SULLIVAN, J. W., & HOROWITZ, F. D. (1983). The effects of intonation on infant attention: The role of the rising intonation contour. *Journal of Child Language, 10,* 521–534.

SULLIVAN, M. W. (1982). Reactivation: Priming forgotten memories in human infants. *Child Development, 53,* 516–523.

*SULLIVAN, M. W., LEWIS, M., & ALESSANDRI, S. M. (1992). Cross-age stability in emotional expressions: During learning and extinction. *Developmental Psychology, 28,* 58–63.

*SULS, J., & WILLS, T. A. (Eds.). (1991). *Social comparison: Contemporary theory and research.* Hillsdale, NJ: Erlbaum.

SUN, M. (1988). Anti-acne drug poses dilemma for FDA. *Science, 240,* 714–715.

SUOMI, S. J., & HARLOW, H. F. (1975). The role and reason of peer relationships in rhesus monkeys. In M. Lewis & L. A. Rosenblum (Eds.), *Friendship and peer relations.* New York: Wiley.

SUPER, C. M. (1981). Cross-cultural research on infancy. In H. C. Triandis & A. Heron (Eds.), *Handbook of cross-cultural psychology: Vol. 4. Developmental psychology.* Boston: Allyn & Bacon.

SUPER, C. M., & HARKNESS, S. (1981). Figure, ground and gestalt: The cultural context of the active individual. In R. M. Lerner & N. A. Busch-Rossnagel (Eds.), *Individuals as producers of their development: A life-span perspective.* New York: Academic Press.

*SUPER, C. M., HERRERA, M. G., & MORA, J. O. (1990). Long-term effects of food supplementation and psychosocial intervention on the physical growth of Colombian infants at risk of malnutrition. *Child Development, 61,* 29–49.

SURBER, C. F. (1982). Separable effects of motives, consequences, and presentation order on children's moral judgments. *Developmental Psychology, 18,* 257–266.

SVARE, B. (1983). Psychobiological determinants of maternal aggressive behavior. In E. C. Simmel, M. E. Hahn, & J. K. Walters (Eds.), *Aggressive behavior: Genetic and neural approaches.* Hillsdale, NJ: Erlbaum.

SVEJDA, M. J., PANNABECKER, B. J., & EMDE, R. N. (1982). Parent-to-infant attachment: A critique of the early "bonding" model. In R. N. Emde & R. J. Harmon (Eds.), *The development of attachment and affiliative systems.* New York: Plenum.

*SWAIN, I. U., ZELAZO, P. R., & CLIFTON, R. K. (1993). Newborn infants' memory for speech sounds retained over 24 hours. *Developmental Psychology, 29,* 313–323.

SWAIN, M. (1977). Bilingualism, monolingualism, and code acquisition. In W. Mackey & T. Andersson (Eds.), *Bilingualism in early childhood.* Rowley, MA: Newbury House.

SWINSON, J. (1985). A parental involvement project in a nursery school. *Educational Psychology in Practice, 1,* 19–22.

SYMONS, D. K., & MORAN, G. (1987). The behavioral dynamics of mutual responsiveness in early face-to-face mother–infant interactions. *Child Development, 58,* 1488–1495.

TAGER-FLUSBERG, H., & CALKINS, S. (1990). Does imitation facilitate the acquisition of grammar? Evidence from a study of autistic, Down's syndrome and normal children. *Journal of Child Language, 17,* 591–606.

*TAKAHASHI, K. (1986). Examining the Strange Situation procedure with Japanese mothers and 12-month-old infants. *Developmental Psychology, 22,* 265–270.

*TAKAHASHI, K. (1990). Are the key assumptions of the "Strange Situation" procedure universal? A view from Japanese research. *Human Development, 33,* 23–30.

*TAMIS-LEMONDA, C. S., & BORNSTEIN, M. H. (1994). Specificity in mother–toddler language-play relations across the second year. *Developmental Psychology, 30,* 283–292.

TANNER, J. M. (1963). The regulation of human growth. *Child Development, 34,* 817–847.

TANNER, J. M. (1974). Variability of growth and maturity in newborn infants. In M. Lewis & L. A. Rosenblum (Eds.), *The effect of the infant on its caregiver.* New York: Wiley.

TANNER, J. M. (1987). Issues and advances in adolescent growth and development. *Journal of Adolescent Health Care, 8,* 470–478.

*TANNER, J. M. (1990). *Fetus into man: Physical growth from conception to maturity.* (2nd ed.). Cambridge, MA: Harvard University Press.

TAYLOR, H. J. (1980). *The IQ game: A methodological inquiry into the heredity–environment controversy.* New Brunswick, NJ: Rutgers University Press.

*TAYLOR, M., CARTWRIGHT, B. S., & BOWDEN, T. (1991). Perspective taking and theory of mind: Do children predict interpretive diversity as a function of differences in observers' knowledge? *Child Development, 62,* 1334–1351.

TAYLOR, M. C., & HALL, J. A. (1982). Psychological androgyny: Theories, methods, and conclusions. *Psychological Bulletin, 92,* 347–366.

TELLER, D. Y., & BORNSTEIN, M. H. (1987). Infant color vision and color perception. In P. Salapatek & L. Cohen (Eds.), *Handbook of infant perception: Vol. 1. From sensation to perception.* New York: Academic Press.

TELZROW, R., CAMPOS, J., ATWATER, S., BERTENTHAL, B., BENSON, J., & CAMPOS, R. (1988). Delays and spurts in spatial cognitive development in locomotor-handicapped infants. *Infant Behavior and Development, 11,* 312.

TERHUNE, K. W. (1976). *A review of the actual and expected consequences of family size* (Publication No. NIH 76-779). Washington, DC: U.S. Department of Health, Education and Welfare.

*TERMAN, L. M. (1925). *Genetic studies of genius: Vol. 1. Mental and physical traits of a thousand gifted children.* Stanford: Stanford University Press.

TERMAN, L. M., & MERRILL, M. A. (1973). Stanford-Binet Intelligence Scale (3rd ed.). Chicago: Riverside Publishing Company.

*TERRACE, H. S., PETTITO, L. A., SANDERS, R. J., & BEVER, T. G. (1979). Can an ape create a sentence? *Science, 206,* 891–900.

*TERRY, R., & COIE, J. D. (1991). A comparison of methods for defining sociometric status among children. *Developmental Psychology, 27,* 867–880.

TESSER, A. (1984). Self-evaluation maintenance processes: Implications for relationships and for development. In J. C. Masters & K. Yarkin-Levin (Eds.), *Boundary areas in social and developmental psychology.* New York: Academic Press.

*TESSLER, M. (1991). *Making memories together: The influence of mother–child joint encoding on the development of autobiographical memory style.* Unpublished doctoral dissertation, City University of New York Graduate Center, New York.

*TETI, D. M. (1992). Sibling interaction. In V. B. Van Hasselt & M. Hersen (Eds.), *Handbook of social development.* New York: Plenum.

*TETI, D. M., & GELFAND, D. M. (1991). Behavioral competence among mothers of infants in the first year: The mediational role of maternal self-efficacy. *Child Development, 62,* 918– 929.

THARP, R. G. (1989). Psychocultural variables and constants: Effects on teaching and learning in schools. *American Psychologist, 44,* 349–359.

THELEN, E. (1981). Rhythmical behavior in infancy: An ethological perspective. *Developmental Psychology, 17,* 237–257.

*THELEN, E., & ADOLPH, K. E. (1992). Arnold L. Gesell: The paradox of nature and nurture. *Developmental Psychology, 28,* 368–380.

THEVENIN, D. H., EILERS, R. E., OLLER, D. K., & LAVOIE, L. (1985). Where's the drift in babbling drift? A cross-linguistic study. *Applied Psycholinguistics, 6,* 3–15.

THOMA, S. J. (1986). Estimating gender differences in the comprehension and preference of moral issues. *Developmental Review, 6,* 165–180.

THOMAN, E. B. (1990). Sleeping and waking states in infants. A functional perspective. *Neuroscience and Behavioral Reviews, 14,* 93–107.

*THOMAN, E. B. (1993). Obligation and option in the premature nursery. *Developmental Review, 13,* 1–30.

THOMAN, E. B., DENENBERG, V. H., SIEVEL, J., ZEIDNER, L. P., & BECKER, P. (1981). State organization in neonates: Developmental inconsistency indicates risk for developmental dysfunction. *Neuropediatrics, 12,* 45–54.

*THOMAN, E. B., & INGERSOLL, E. W. (1993). Learning in premature infants. *Developmental Psychology, 29,* 692–700.

*THOMAN, E. B., INGERSOLL, E. W., & ACEBO, C. (1991). Premature infants seek rhythmic stimulation, and the experience facilitates neurobehavioral development. *Journal of Developmental and Behavioral Pediatrics, 12,* 11–18.

THOMAS, A., & CHESS, S. (1977). *Temperament and development.* New York: Bruner/Mazel.

THOMAS, A., & CHESS, S. (1984). Genesis and evaluation of behavioral disorder: From infancy to early adult life. *American Journal of Psychiatry, 141,* 1–9.

THOMAS, A., & CHESS, S. (1986). The New York Longitudinal Study: From infancy to early adult life. In R. Plomin & J. Dunn (Eds.), *The study of temperament: Changes, continuities and challenges.* Hillsdale, NJ: Erlbaum.

THOMAS, A., CHESS, S., & BIRCH, H. G. (1968). *Temperament and behavior disorders in children.* New York: New York University Press.

THOMAS, A., CHESS, S., SILLEN, J., & MENDEZ, O. (1974). Cross-cultural study of behavior in children with special vulnerabilities to stress. In D. F. Ricks, A. Thomas, & M. Roff (Eds.), *Life history research in psychopathology.* Minneapolis: University of Minnesota Press.

THOMAS, H. (1983). Familial correlational analyses, sex differences, and the X-linked gene hypothesis. *Psychological Bulletin, 93,* 427–440.

THOMAS, R. M. (1979). *Comparing theories of child development.* Belmont, CA: Wadsworth.

*THOMPSON, J. E. (1990). Maternal stress, anxiety, and social support during pregnancy as possible directions for prenatal intervention. In I. R. Merkatz & J. E. Thompson (Eds.), *New perspectives on prenatal care.* New York: Elsevier.

*THOMPSON, L. A., FAGAN, J. F., III, & FULKER, D. W. (1991). Longitudinal prediction of specific cognitive abilities from infant novelty preference. *Child Development, 62,* 530–538.

THOMPSON, R. A. (1986). Temperament, emotionality, and infant social cognition. In J. V. Lerner & R. M. Lerner (Eds.), *New directions for child development: No. 31. Temperament and social interaction in infants and children.* San Francisco: Jossey-Bass.

*THOMPSON, R. A. (1993a). Developmental research and legal policy: Toward a two-way street. In D. Cicchetti & S. Toth (Eds.), *Child abuse, child development, and social policy.* Norwood, NJ: Ablex.

THOMPSON, R. A. (1993b). Social development: Enduring issues and new challenges. *Developmental Review, 13,* 372–402.

THOMPSON, R. A., CONNELL, J. P., & BRIDGES, L. J. (1988). Temperament, emotion, and social interactive behavior in the Strange Situation: A component process analysis of attachment system functioning. *Child Development, 59,* 1102–1110.

*THOMPSON, R. A., & LEGER, D. W. (1994). From squalls to calls: The cry as a developing socioemotional signal. In B. Lester, J. Newman, & F. Pedersen (Eds.), *Biological and social aspects of infant crying.* New York: Plenum.

*THOMPSON, R. A., & LIMBER, S. (1990). "Social anxiety" in infancy: Stranger wariness and separation distress. In H. Leitenberg (Ed.), *Handbook of social and evaluation anxiety.* New York: Plenum.

THOMPSON, S. K. (1975). Gender labels and early sex role development. *Child Development, 46,* 339–347.

THOMPSON, W. R., & GRUSEC, J. E. (1970). Studies of early experience. In P. H. Mussen (Ed.), *Carmichael's manual of child psychology* (3rd ed., Vol. 1). New York: Wiley.

THOMSON, J. R., & CHAPMAN, R. S. (1977). Who is "Daddy" revisited: The status of two-year-olds' over-extended words in use and comprehension. *Journal of Child Language, 4,* 359–375.

THORNDIKE, R. L., HAGEN, E. P., & SATTLER, J. M. (1986). *Stanford-Binet Intelligence Scale* (4th ed.). Chicago: Riverside Publishing Company.

*THORNE, B. (1986). Girls and boys together . . . but mostly apart: Gender arrangements in elementary schools. In W. W. Hartup & Z. Rubin (Eds.), *Relationships and development.* Hillsdale, NJ: Erlbaum.

THURSTONE, L. L. (1938). *Primary mental abilities.* Chicago: University of Chicago Press.

THURSTONE, L. L., & THURSTONE, T. G. (1962). *SRA Primary Mental Abilities.* Chicago: Science Research Associates.

TIEGER, T. (1980). On the biological basis of sex differences in aggression. *Child Development, 51,* 943–963.

TIESZEN, H. R. (1979). Children's social behavior in a Korean preschool. *Journal of Korean Home Economics Association, 17,* 71–84.

TIETJEN, A. M., & WALKER, L. J. (1985). Moral reasoning and leadership among men in Papua

New Guinea society. *Developmental Psychology, 21,* 982–992.

TINBERGEN, N. (1951). *The study of instinct.* London: Oxford University Press.

TINBERGEN, N. (1973). *The animal in its world: Explorations of an ethologist, 1932–1972* (Vols. 1 and 2). Cambridge, MA: Harvard University Press.

*TINSLEY, B. J. (1992). Multiple influences on the acquisition and socialization of children's health attitudes and behavior: An integrative review. *Child Development, 63,* 1043–1069.

*TINSLEY, B. J., & PARKE, R. D. (1988). The role of grandfathers in the context of the family. In P. Bronstein & C. P. Cowan (Eds.), *Fatherhood today: Men's changing roles in the family.* New York: Wiley.

*TISAK, M. S. (1993). Preschool children's judgments of moral and personal events following physical harm and property damage. *Merrill-Palmer Quarterly, 39,* 375–390.

TITTLE, C. K. (1986). Gender research in education. *American Psychologist, 41,* 1161–1168.

*TOBEY, A. E., & GOODMAN, G. S. (1992). Children's eyewitness memory: Effects of participation and forensic context. *Child Abuse and Neglect, 16,* 779–796.

*TODA, S., & FOGEL, A. (1993). Infant response to the still-face situation at 3 and 6 months. *Developmental Psychology, 29,* 532–538.

TODA, S., FOGEL, A., & KAWAI, M. (1990). Maternal speech to three-month-old infants in the United States and Japan. *Journal of Child Language, 17,* 279–294.

TOMASELLO, M., CONTI-RAMSDEN, G., & EWERT, B. (1990). Young children's conversations with their mothers and fathers: Differences in breakdown and repair. *Journal of Child Language, 17,* 115–130.

TOMASELLO, M., & FARRAR, M. J. (1986). Joint attention and early language. *Child Development, 57,* 1454–1463.

TORRANCE, E. P. (1970). Influence of dyadic interaction on creative functioning. *Psychological Reports, 26,* 391–394.

TOUCHETTE, N. (1990). Evolutions: Fertilization. *Journal of NIH Research, 2,* 94–97.

TOUSSAINT, N. A. (1974). An analysis of synchrony between concrete-operational tasks in terms of structural and performance demands. *Child Development, 45,* 992–1001.

TOUWEN, B. C. L. (1976). *Neurological development in infancy* (Clinics in Developmental Medicine, No. 58). London: Spastics International.

TRABASSO, T., ISEN, A. M., DOLECKI, P., McLANAHAN, A. G., RILEY, C. A., & TUCKER, T. (1978). How do children solve class-inclusion problems? In R. S. Siegler (Ed.), *Children's thinking: What develops?* Hillsdale, NJ: Erlbaum.

TRABASSO, T., STEIN, N. L., & JOHNSON, L. R. (1981). Children's knowledge of events: A causal analysis of story structure. In G. H. Bower & A. R. Lang (Eds.), *The psychology of learning and motivation* (Vol. 15). New York: Academic Press.

TRACY, D. M. (1987). Toys, spatial ability, and science and mathematics achievement: Are they related? *Sex Roles, 17,* 115–138.

TRACY, R. L., & AINSWORTH, M. D. S. (1981). Maternal affectionate behavior and infant–

mother attachment patterns. *Child Development, 52,* 1341–1343.

*TRAUTNER, H. M., HELBING, N., SAHM, W. B., & LOHAUS, A. (1989, April). *Beginning awareness–rigidity–flexibility: A longitudinal analysis of sex-role stereotyping in 4- to 10-year-old children.* Paper presented at the meeting of the Society for Research in Child Development, Kansas City.

TRAVERS, J. R., & LIGHT, R. J. (Eds.). (1982). *Learning from experience: Evaluating early childhood demonstration programs.* Washington, DC: National Academy Press.

TREHUB, S. E. (1976). The discrimination of foreign speech contrasts by infants and adults. *Child Development, 47,* 466–472.

TREHUB, S. E., & SCHNEIDER, B. A. (1983). Recent advances in the behavioral study of infant audition. In S. E. Gerber & G. T. Mencher (Eds.), *Development of auditory behavior.* New York: Grune & Stratton.

TREHUB, S. E., SCHNEIDER, B. A., MORRONGIELLO, B. A., & THORPE, L. A. (1988). Auditory sensitivity in school-age children. *Journal of Experimental Child Psychology, 46,* 273–285.

*TREHUB, S. E., THORPE, L. A., & COHEN, A. J. (1991, April). *Infants' auditory processing of numerical information.* Paper presented at the meeting of the Society for Research in Child Development, Seattle.

TREHUB, S. E., THORPE, L. A., & MORRONGIELLO, B. A. (1987). Organizational processes in infants' perception of auditory patterns. *Child Development, 58,* 741–749.

TREVARTHEN, C., & MARWICK, H. (1986). Signs of motivation for speech in infants, and the nature of mother's support for development of language. In B. Lindblom & R. Zetterstrom (Eds.), *Precursors of early speech.* New York: Stockton.

TREXLER, R. C. (1973). The foundlings of Florence, 1395–1455. *History of Childhood Quarterly, 1,* 259–284.

TRIEBER, F., & WILCOX, S. (1984). Discrimination of number by infants. *Infant Behavior and Development, 7,* 93–100.

TRIVERS, R. L. (1971). The evolution of reciprocal altruism. *Quarterly Review of Biology, 46,* 35–57.

TRIVERS, R. L. (1983). The evolution of cooperation. In D. L. Bridgeman (Ed.), *The nature of prosocial development.* New York: Academic Press.

TRONICK, E. Z. (1989). Emotions and emotional communication in infants. *American Psychologist, 44,* 112–119.

TRONICK, E. Z., & COHN, J. F. (1989). Infant–mother face-to-face interaction: Age and gender differences in coordination and the occurrence of miscoordination. *Child Development, 60,* 85–92.

*TUCHMANN-DUPLESSIS, H. (1975). *Drug effects on the fetus.* Sydney, Australia: ADIS Press.

*TUDGE, J., & ROGOFF, B. (1989). Peer influences on cognitive development: Piagetian and Vygotskian perspectives. In M. H. Bornstein & J. S. Bruner (Eds.), *Interaction in human development.* Hillsdale, NJ: Erlbaum.

TURIEL, E. (1966). An experimental test of the

sequentiality of developmental stages in the child's moral judgments. *Journal of Personality and Social Psychology, 3,* 611–618.

TURIEL, E. (1987). Potential relations between the development of social reasoning and childhood aggression. In D. H. Crowell, I. M. Evans, & C. R. O'Donnell (Eds.), *Childhood aggression and violence: Sources of influence, prevention, and control.* New York: Plenum.

*TURIEL, E., HILDEBRANDT, C., & WAINRYB, C. (1991). Judging social issues. *Monograph of the Society for Research in Child Development, 56*(Serial No. 224).

*TURIEL, E., KILLEN, M., & HELWIG, C. C. (1987). Morality: Its structure, functions, and vagaries. In J. Kagan & S. Lamb (Eds.), *The emergence of moral concepts in young children.* Chicago: University of Chicago Press.

*TURKHEIMER, E. (1991). Individual and group differences in adoption studies of IQ. *Psychological Bulletin, 110,* 392–405.

TYNAN, W. D. (1986). Behavioral stability predicts morbidity and mortality in infants from a neonatal intensive care unit. *Infant Behavior and Development, 9,* 71–79.

*U.S. BUREAU OF THE CENSUS. (1990). *Current population reports.* Washington, DC: Government Printing Office.

*UMBEL, V. M., PEARSON, B. Z., FERNANDEZ, M. C., & OLLER, D. K. (1992). Measuring bilingual children's receptive vocabularies. *Child Development, 63,* 1012–1020.

*UNDERWOOD, B., & MOORE, B. (1982). Perspective-taking and altruism. *Psychological Bulletin, 91,* 143–173.

*UNDERWOOD, M. K., COIE, J. D., & HERBSMAN, C. R. (1992). Display rules for anger and aggression in school-age children. *Child Development, 63,* 366–380.

*UNGERER, J. A., DOLBY, R., WATERS, B., BARNETT, B., KEIK, N., & LEWIN, V. (1990). The early development of empathy: Self-regulation and individual differences in the first year. *Motivation and Emotion, 14,* 93–106.

UNYK, A., & SCHELLENBERG, E. G. (1991, April). *Lullabies: Form and function.* Paper presented at the meeting of the Society for Research in Child Development, Seattle.

URBAIN, E. S., & KENDELL, P. C. (1980). Review of social-cognitive problem-solving interventions with children. *Psychological Bulletin, 88,* 109–143.

UZGIRIS, I. C., & HUNT, J. McV. (1975). *Assessment in infancy: Ordinal scales of psychological development.* Urbana: University of Illinois Press.

*VALDEZ-MENCHACA, M. C., & WHITEHURST, G. J. (1992). Accelerating language development through picture book reading: A systematic extension to Mexican day care. *Developmental Psychology, 28,* 1106–1114.

VALIAN, V. (1986). Syntactic categories in the speech of young children. *Developmental Psychology, 22,* 562–579.

VALIAN, V., WINZEMER, J., & ERREICH, A. (1981). A little-linguist model of syntax learning. In S. Tavakolian (Ed.), *Language acquisition and linguistic theory.* Cambridge, MA: MIT Press.

*VAN DE WALLE, G. A., & SPELKE, E. S. (1993, March). *Integrating information over time: Infant perception of partly occluded objects.* Paper presented at the meeting of the Society for Research in Child Development, New Orleans.

VAN DER VEER, R., & VALSINER, J. (1988). Lev Vygotsky and Pierre Janet: On the origin of the concept of sociogenesis. *Developmental Review, 8,* 52–65.

VAN GIFFEN, K., & HAITH, M. M. (1984). Infant visual response to gestalt geometric forms. *Infant Behavior and Development, 7,* 335–346.

VAN LOOSBROEK, E., & SMITSMAN, A. W. (1990). Visual perception of numerosity in infancy. *Developmental Psychology, 26,* 916–922.

*VANDELL, D. L., MINNET, A. M., JOHNSON, B. S., & SANTROCK, J. W. (1990). *Siblings and friends: Experiences of school-aged children.* Unpublished manuscript, University of Texas at Dallas.

VANDELL, D. L., & MUELLER, E. C. (1980). Peer play and friendships during the first two years. In H. C. Foot, A. J. Chapman, & J. R. Smith (Eds.), *Friendship and social relations in children.* New York: Wiley.

VANDELL, D. L., WILSON, K. S., & BUCHANAN, N. R. (1980). Peer interaction in the first year of life: An examination of its structure, content, and sensitivity to toys. *Child Development, 51,* 481–488.

*VANIJZENDOORN, M. H. (1992). Intergenerational transmission of parenting: A review of studies in nonclinical populations. *Developmental Review, 2,* 76–99.

*VANIJZENDOORN, M. H., GOLDBERG, S., KROONENBERG, P. M., & FRENKEL, O. J. (1992). The relative effects of maternal and child problems on the quality of attachment: A meta-analysis of attachment in clinical samples. *Child Development, 63,* 840–858.

VARGAS, E. A. (1986). Intraverbal behavior. In P. N. Chase & L. J. Parrott (Eds.), *Psychological aspects of language: The West Virginia Lectures.* Springfield, IL: Thomas.

VASTA, R. (1979). *Studying children: An introduction to research methods.* San Francisco: W. H. Freeman.

VASTA, R. (1982a). Child study: Looking toward the eighties. In R. Vasta (Ed.), *Strategies and techniques of child study.* New York: Academic Press.

VASTA, R. (Ed.). (1982b). *Strategies and techniques of child study.* New York: Academic Press.

*VASTA, R., BELONGIA, C., & RIBBLE, C. (in press). Investigating the orientation effect on the water-level task: Who? When? and Why? *Developmental Psychology.*

VASTA, R., & GREEN, P. J. (1982). Differential cue utilization by males and females in pattern copying. *Child Development, 53,* 1102–1105.

*VASTA, R., LIGHTFOOT, C., & COX, B. D. (1993). Understanding gender differences on the water-level problem: The role of spatial perception. *Merrill-Palmer Quarterly, 39,* 391–414.

VAUGHN, B. E., BRADLEY, C. F., JOFFE, L. S., SEIFER, R., & BARGLOW, P. (1987). Maternal characteristics measured prenatally are predictive of ratings of temperamental "difficulty" on the Carey Infant Temperament Questionnaire. *Developmental Psychology, 23,* 152–161.

VAUGHN, B. E., DEANE, K. E., & WATERS, E. (1985). The impact of out-of-home care and the quality of infant–mother attachment in an economically disadvantaged population. *Child Development, 51,* 1203–1214.

VAUGHN, B. E., KOPP, C. B., & KRAKOW, J. B. (1984). The emergence and consolidation of self-control from eighteen to thirty months of age: Normative trends and individual differences. *Child Development, 55,* 990–1004.

VAUGHN, B. E., LEFEVER, G. B., SEIFER, R., & BARGLOW, P. (1989). Attachment behavior, attachment security, and temperament during infancy. *Child Development, 60,* 728–737.

*VAUGHN, B. E., STEVENSON-HINDE, J., WATERS, E., KOTSAFTIS, A., LEFEVER, G. B., SHOULDICE, A., TRUDEL, M., & BELSKY, J. (1992). Attachment security and temperament in infancy and early childhood: Some conceptual clarifications. *Developmental Psychology, 28,* 463–473.

*VELLUTINO, F. R. (1991). Commentary: Has basic research in reading increased our understanding of developmental reading and how to teach reading? *Psychological Science, 2,* 70, 81–83.

VENTURA, S. J. (1989). Trends and variations in first births to older women, United States, 1970–1986 (Vital and Health Statistics Series 21, No. 47). Bethesda, MD: National Center for Health Statistics.

*VESPO, J. E., & CAPLAN, M. (1993). Preschoolers' differential conflict behavior with friends and acquaintances. *Early Education and Development, 4,* 45–58.

VIETZE, P. M., & VAUGHAN, H. G. (1988). *Early identification of infants with developmental disabilities.* Philadelphia: Grune & Stratton.

VIHMAN, M. M. (1985). Language differentiation by the bilingual infant. *Journal of Child Language, 12,* 297–324.

VIHMAN, M. M., FERGUSON, C. A., & ELBERT, M. (1986). Phonological development from babbling to speech: Common tendencies and individual differences. *Applied Psycholinguistics, 7,* 3–40.

VIHMAN, M. M., MACKEN, M. A., MILLER, R., SIMMONS, H., & MILLER, J. (1985). From babbling to speech: A re-assessment of the continuity issue. *Language, 61,* 397–444.

VIHMAN, M. M., & MILLER, R. (1988). Words and babble at the threshold of language acquisition. In M. D. Smith & J. L. Locke (Eds.), *The emergent lexicon.* Orlando, FL: Academic Press.

VOCATE, D. R. (1987). *The theory of A. R. Luria.* Hillsdale, NJ: Erlbaum.

VOLTERRA, V., & TAESCHNER, T. (1978). The acquisition and development of language by bilingual children. *Journal of Child Language, 5,* 311–326.

VON HOFSTEN, C. (1982). Eye-hand coordination in the newborn. *Developmental Psychology, 18,* 450–461.

VON HOFSTEN, C. (1988, June). *A perception-action perspective on the development of manual movements.* Paper presented at Attention and Performance meetings, Saline Royale, France.

VON HOFSTEN, C. (1989). Motor development as the development of systems: Comments on the special section. *Developmental Psychology, 25,* 950–953.

VON WRIGHT, M. R. (1989). Body image satisfaction in adolescent girls and boys: A longitudinal study. *Journal of Youth and Adolescence, 18,* 71–83.

VOORHEES, C. V., & BUTCHER, R. E. (1982). Behavioral teratogenicity. In K. Snell (Ed.), *Developmental toxicology.* New York: Praeger.

VOORHEES, C. V., & MOLLNOW, E. (1987). Behavioral teratogenesis: Long-term influences on behavior from early exposure to environmental agents. In J. D. Osofsky (Ed.), *Handbook of infant development* (2nd ed.). New York: Wiley.

VOYAT, G. E. (1982). *Piaget systematized.* Hillsdale, NJ: Erlbaum.

*VUCHINICH, S., BANK, L., & PATTERSON, G. R. (1992). Parenting, peers, and the stability of antisocial behavior in preadolescent boys. *Developmental Psychology, 28,* 510–521.

VURPILLOT, E. (1968). The development of scanning strategies and their relation to visual differentiation. *Journal of Experimental Child Psychology, 6,* 632–650.

VURPILLOT, E., & BALL, W. A. (1979). The concept of identity and children's selective attention. In G. A. Hale & M. Lewis (Eds.), *Attention and cognitive development.* New York: Plenum.

VUYK, R. (1981). *Overview and critique of Piaget's genetic epistemology 1965–1980.* New York: Academic Press.

VYGOTSKY, L. S. (1962). *Thought and language.* Cambridge, MA: MIT Press. (Original work published 1934)

VYGOTSKY, L. S. (1978). *Mind in society: The development of higher psychological processes.* Cambridge, MA: Harvard University Press.

*VYGOTSKY, L. S. (1987). *The collected works of L. S. Vygotsky: Vol. 1. Problems of general psychology.* New York: Plenum.

WAAS, G. A. (1988). Social attributional biases of peer-rejected and aggressive children. *Child Development, 59,* 969–975.

WABER, D. P. (1977). Sex differences in mental activities, hemispheric lateralization, and rate of physical growth at adolescence. *Developmental Psychology, 13,* 29–38.

WABER, D. P. (1979). Cognitive abilities and sex-related variations in the maturation of cerebral cortical functions. In M. A. Wittig & A. C. Petersen (Eds.), *Sex-related differences in cognitive functioning.* New York: Academic Press.

WACHS, T. D. (1988). Relevance of physical environment influences for toddler temperament. *Infant Behavior and Development, 11,* 431–445.

*WACHS, T. D. (1992). *The nature of nurture.* Newbury Park, CA: Sage.

WACHS, T. D., & GRUEN, G. E. (1982). *Early experience and human development.* New York: Plenum.

WADSWORTH, B. J. (1978). *Piaget for the classroom teacher.* New York: Longman.

WAGHORN, L., & SULLIVAN, E. V. (1970). The exploration of transition rules in conservation of quantity (substance) using film mediated modeling. *Acta Psychologica, 32,* 65–80.

*WAGNER, B. M., & PHILLIPS, D. A. (1992). Beyond beliefs: Parent and child behaviors and

children's perceived academic competence. *Child Development, 63,* 1380–1391.

WAGNER, D. A., & STEVENSON, H. W. (Eds.). (1982). *Cultural perspectives on child development.* San Francisco: W. H. Freeman.

*WAINRYB, C. (1993). The application of moral judgments to other cultures: Relativism and universality. *Child Development, 64,* 924–933.

WALDEN, T. A., & OGAN, T. A. (1988). The development of social referencing. *Child Development, 59,* 1230–1240.

WALDROP, M. F., & HALVERSON, C. F., Jr. (1975). Intensive and extensive peer behavior: Longitudinal and cross-sectional analyses. *Child Development, 46,* 19–26.

WALES, R., COLMAN, M., & PATTISON, P. (1983). How a thing is called—a study of mothers' and children's naming. *Journal of Experimental Child Psychology, 36,* 1–17.

WALK, R. D., & DODGE, S. H. (1962). Visual depth perception of a 10-month-old monocular human infant. *Science, 137,* 529–530.

WALKER, A. S. (1982). Intermodal perception of expressive behaviors by human infants. *Journal of Experimental Child Psychology, 33,* 514–535.

WALKER, L. J. (1980). Cognitive and perspective-taking prerequisites for moral development. *Child Development, 51,* 131–139.

WALKER, L. J. (1983). Sources of cognitive conflict for stage transition in moral development. *Developmental Psychology, 19,* 103–110.

WALKER, L. J. (1986). Cognitive processes in moral development. In G. L. Sapp (Ed.), *Handbook of moral development: Models, processes, techniques, and research.* Birmingham, AL: Religious Education Press.

WALKER, L. J. (1988). The development of moral reasoning. In R. Vasta (Ed.), *Annals of child development* (Vol. 5). Greenwich, CT: JAI Press.

WALKER, L. J. (1989). A longitudinal study of moral reasoning. *Child Development, 60,* 157–166.

*WALKER, L. J. (1991). Sex differences in moral reasoning. In W. M. Kurtines & J. L. Gewirtz (Eds.), *Handbook of moral behavior and development: Vol. 2. Research.* Hillsdale, NJ: Erlbaum.

WALKER, L. J., & RICHARDS, B. S. (1979). Stimulating transitions in moral reasoning as a function of stage of cognitive development. *Developmental Psychology, 15,* 95–103.

WALKER, L. J., & TAYLOR, J. H. (1991a). Family interactions and the development of moral reasoning. *Child Development, 62,* 264–283.

WALKER, L. J., & TAYLOR, J. H. (1991b). Stage transitions in moral reasoning: A longitudinal study of developmental processes. *Developmental Psychology, 27,* 330–337.

WALKER, L. J., deVRIES, B., & BICHARD, S. L. (1984). The hierarchical nature of stages of moral development. *Developmental Psychology, 20,* 960–966.

WALKER, L. J., deVRIES, B., & TREVARTHEN, S. D. (1987). Moral stages and moral orientations in real-life and hypothetical dilemmas. *Child Development, 58,* 842–858.

WALKER-ANDREWS, A. S. (1988). Infants' perception of the affordances of expressive behaviors. In C. K. Rovee-Collier & L. P. Lipsitt

(Eds.), *Advances in infancy research* (Vol. 5). Norwood, NJ: Ablex.

*WALKER-ANDREWS, A. S., & DICKSON, L. (1993, March). *A taxonomy for intermodal relations: Developmental evidence.* Paper presented at the meeting of the Society for Research in Child Development, New Orleans.

WALKER-ANDREWS, A. S., & RAGLIONI, S. S. (1988). Infants' intermodal matching of male and female faces and voices. *Infant Behavior and Development, 11,* 336.

WALLACH, L., WALL, A. J., & ANDERSON, L. (1967). Number conservation: The role of reversibility, addition-subtraction, and misleading perceptual cues. *Child Development, 38,* 425–442.

*WALLER, N. G., KOJETIN, B. A., BOUCHARD, T. J., Jr., LYKKEN, D. T., & TELLEGEN, A. (1990). Genetic and environmental influences on religious interests, attitudes, and values: A study of twins reared apart and together. *Psychological Science, 1,* 138–142.

WALLERSTEIN, J. S., CORBIN, S. B., & LEWIS, J. M. (1988). Children of divorce: A 10-year study. In E. M. Hetherington & J. D. Arasteh (Eds.), *Impact of divorce, single parenting, and step-parenting on children.* Hillsdale, NJ: Erlbaum.

*WALLMAN, J. (1992). *Aping language.* Cambridge: Cambridge University Press.

*WALTON, G. E., BOWER, N. J. A., & BOWER, T. G. R. (1992). Recognition of familiar faces by newborns. *Infant Behavior and Development, 15,* 265–269.

WAPNER, S. (1969). Organismic-developmental theory: Some applications to cognition. In P. H. Mussen, J. Langer, & M. Covington (Eds.), *Trends and issues in developmental psychology.* New York: Holt, Rinehart and Winston.

WAPNER, S., & WERNER, H. (1965). An experimental approach to body perception from the organismic-developmental point of view. In S. Wapner & H. Werner (Eds.), *The body percept.* New York: Random House.

WARD, M. J., VAUGHN, B. E., & ROBB, M. D. (1988). Social-emotional adaptation and infant–mother attachment in siblings: Role of the mother in cross-sibling consistency. *Child Development, 59,* 643–651.

WARKANY, J. (1977). History of teratology. In J. G. Wilson & F. C. Fraser (Eds.), *Handbook of teratology: Vol. 1. General principles and etiology.* New York: Plenum.

WARKANY, J. (1981). Prevention of congenital malformations. *Teratology, 23,* 175–189.

WARREN, K. R., & BAST, R. J. (1988). Alcohol-related birth defects: An update. *Public Health Reports, 103,* 638–642.

WARREN-LEUBECKER, A., & BOHANNON, J. N. (1983). The effects of verbal feedback and listener type on the speech of preschool children. *Journal of Experimental Child Psychology, 35,* 540–548.

WASSERMAN, G. A., & LEWIS, M. (1985). Infant sex differences: Ecological effects. *Sex Roles, 12,* 665–675.

WASSERMAN, P. M. (1988). Fertilization in mammals. *Scientific American, 259,* 78–84.

WASZ-HOCKERT, O., MICHELSSON, K., & LIND, J. (1985). Twenty-five years of Scandinavian cry research. In B. M. Lester & C. Z. Boukydis (Eds.), *Infant crying: Theoretical and research perspectives.* New York: Plenum.

WATERS, E., MATAS, L., & SROUFE, L. A. (1975). Infants' reactions to an approaching stranger: Description, validation, and functional significance of wariness. *Child Development, 46,* 348–356.

WATERS, H. S. (1981). Organization strategies in memory for prose: A developmental analysis. *Journal of Experimental Child Psychology, 32,* 223–246.

*WATERS, H. S., & SCHREIBER, L. L. (1991). Sex differences in elaborative strategies: A developmental analysis. *Journal of Experimental Child Psychology, 52,* 319–335.

WATERS, H. S., & TINSLEY, V. S. (1982). The development of verbal self-regulation: Relationships between language, cognition, and behavior. In S. Kuczaj (Ed.), *Language development: Language, cognition, and culture.* Hillsdale, NJ: Erlbaum.

WATSON, J. B., & RAYNER, R. (1920). Conditioned emotional reactions. *Journal of Experimental Psychology, 3,* 1–14.

WATSON, J. D. (1968). *The double helix: A personal account of the discovery of the structure of DNA.* New York: Atheneum.

WATSON, J. D. (1990). The Human Genome Project: Past, present, and future. *Science, 248,* 44–49.

WATSON, J. D., & CRICK, F. H. C. (1953). Molecular structure of nucleic acid: A structure for deoxyribose nucleic acid. *Nature, 171,* 737–738.

WATSON, J. S. (1985). Contingency perception in early social development. In T. M. Field & N. A. Fox (Eds.), *Social perception in infants.* Norwood, NJ: Ablex.

WAXMAN, S. R. (1990). Linguistic biases and the establishment of conceptual hierarchies. *Cognitive Development, 5,* 123–150.

*WAXMAN, S. R., & SENGHAS, A. (1992). Relations among word meanings in early lexical development. *Developmental Psychology, 28,* 862–873.

WECHSLER, D. (1989). *Wechsler Preschool and Primary Scale of Intelligence—Revised.* New York: The Psychological Corporation.

WECHSLER, D. (1991). *Wechsler Intelligence Scale for Children—Third Edition.* New York: The Psychological Corporation.

*WEGLAGE, J., FUNDERS, B., WILKEN, B., SCHUBERT, D., & ULLRICK, K. (1993). School performance and intellectual outcome in adolescents with phenylketonuria. *Acta Paediatrica, 81,* 582–586.

WEINBERG, R. A. (1989). Intelligence and IQ: Landmark issues and great debates. *American Psychologist, 44,* 98–104.

*WEINBERG, R. A., SCARR, S., & WALDMAN, I. D. (1992). The Minnesota Transracial Adoption Study: A follow-up of IQ test performance at adolescence. *Intelligence, 16,* 117–135.

WEINRAUB, M., & BROWN, L. M. (1983). The development of sex-role stereotypes in children: Crushing realities. In V. Franks & E. D. Rothblum (Eds.), *The stereotyping of women: Its effects on mental health.* New York: Springer.

WEINRAUB, M., CLEMENS, L. P., SOCKLOFF, A., ETHRIDGE, T., GRACELY, E., & MYERS, B. (1984). The development of sex role stereotypes in the third year: Relationships to gender labeling, gender identity, sex-typed toy preference, and family characteristics. *Child Development, 55,* 1493–1503.

WEINRAUB, M., & JAEGER, E. (1990). The timing of mothers' return to the workplace: Effects on the developing mother–infant relationship. In J. S. Hyde & M. J. Essex (Eds.), *Parental leave and child care: Setting a research and policy agenda.* Philadelphia: Temple University Press.

WEINRAUB, M., JAEGER, E., & HOFFMAN, L. W. (1988). Predicting infant outcomes in families of employed and non-employed mothers. *Early Childhood Research Quarterly, 3,* 361–378.

WEISNER, T. S., & EIDUSON, B. T. (1986). Children of the '60's as parents. *Psychology Today, 20,* 60–66.

WEISNER, T. S., & WILSON-MITCHELL, J. E. (1990). Nonconventional family life styles and sex typing in six-year-olds. *Child Development, 61,* 1915–1933.

WEISS, B. (1983). Behavioral toxicology and environmental health science: Opportunity and challenge for psychology. *American Psychologist, 38,* 1188–1197.

*WEISS, B., DODGE, K. A., BATES, J. E., & PETTIT, G. S. (1992). Some consequences of early harsh discipline: Child aggression and a maladaptive social information processing style. *Child Development, 63,* 1321–1335.

WEISS, M. G., & MILLER, P. H. (1983). Young children's understanding of displaced aggression. *Journal of Experimental Child Psychology, 35,* 529–539.

*WEISS, R.A. (1993). How does HIV cause AIDS? *Science, 260,* 1273–1279.

WEISSBERG, R. P. (1985). Designing effective social problem-solving programs for the classroom. In B. H. Schneider, K. H. Rubin, & J. E. Ledingham (Eds.), *Children's peer relations: Issues in assessment and intervention.* New York: Springer-Verlag.

WEITZMAN, N., BIRNS, B., & FRIEND, R. (1985). Traditional and nontraditional mothers' communication with their sons and daughters. *Child Development, 56,* 894–898.

WELCH-ROSS, M. K., & SCHMIDT, C. R. (1994). *Children's reconstructive memory for gender-related story content.* Presented at the Conference on Human Development, Pittsburgh.

WELD, N. (1968). Some possible genetic implications of Carthaginian child sacrifice. *Perspectives in Biology and Medicine, 12,* 69–78.

WELLMAN, H. M. (1977). Preschoolers' understanding of memory-relevant variables. *Child Development, 48,* 1720–1723.

WELLMAN, H. M. (1988). The early development of memory strategies. In F. E. Weinert & M. Perlmutter (Eds.), *Memory development: Universal changes and individual differences.* Hillsdale, NJ: Erlbaum.

*WELLMAN, H. M. (1990). *The child's theory of mind.* Cambridge, MA: Bradford Books/MIT Press.

WELLMAN, H. M., CROSS, D., & BARTSCH, K.

(1986). Infant search and object permanence: A meta-analysis of the A-not-B error. *Monographs of the Society for Research in Child Development, 51* (3, Serial No. 214).

*WELLMAN, H. M., & GELMAN, S. A. (1992). Cognitive development: Foundational theories of core domains. *Annual Review of Psychology, 43,* 337–375.

WELLMAN, H. M., RITTER, K., & FLAVELL, J. H. (1975). Deliberate memory behavior in the delayed reactions of very young children. *Developmental Psychology, 11,* 780–787.

*WELLS, G. (1985). Preschool literacy-related activities and success in school. In D. R. Olson, N. Torrance, & A. Hilyard (Eds.), *Literacy, language, and learning.* New York: Cambridge University Press.

*WELSH, M. C., PENNINGTON, B. F., OZONOFF, S., ROUSE, B., & McCABE, E. R. B. (1990). Neuropsychology of early-treated phenylketonuria: Specific executive function deficits. *Child Development, 61,* 1697–1713.

WENTZEL, K. R. (1988). Gender differences in math and English achievement: A longitudinal study. *Sex Roles, 18,* 691–699.

*WENTZEL, K. R., & ERDLEY, C. A. (1993). Strategies for making friends: Relations to social behavior and peer acceptance in early adolescence. *Developmental Psychology, 29,* 819–826.

WERKER, J. F. (1989). Becoming a native listener. *American Scientist, 77,* 54–59.

*WERKER, J. F. (1991). The ontogeny of speech perception. In I. G. Mattingly & M. Studdert-Kennedy (Eds.), *Modularity and the motor theory of speech perception.* Hillsdale, NJ: Erlbaum.

WERKER, J. F., & LALONDE, C. E. (1988). Cross-language speech perception: Initial capabilities and developmental change. *Developmental Psychology, 24,* 672–683.

WERKER, J. F., & TEES, R. C. (1984). Cross-language speech perception: Evidence for perceptual reorganization during the first year of life. *Infant Behavior and Development, 7,* 49–63.

WERNER, J. S., & LIPSITT, L. P. (1981). The infancy of human sensory systems: Developmental plasticity. In E. F. Gollin (Ed.), *Developmental plasticity: Behavioral and biological aspects of variation in development.* New York: Academic Press.

WERNER, J. S., & SIQUELAND, E. R. (1978). Visual recognition memory in the preterm infant. *Infant Behavior and Development, 1,* 79–94.

*WERNER, L. A., & BARGONES, J. Y. (1992). Psychoacoustic development of human infants. In C. Rovee-Collier & L. P. Lipsitt (Eds.), *Advances in infancy research* (Vol. 7). Norwood, NJ: Ablex.

WERTHEIMER, M. (1985). The evolution of the concept of development in the history of psychology. In G. Eckardt, W. G. Bringmann, & L. Sprung (Eds.), *Contributions to a history of developmental psychology.* Berlin: Mouton.

*WERTSCH, J. V., & TULVISTE, P. (1992). L. S. Vygotsky and contemporary developmental psychology. *Developmental Psychology, 28,* 548–557.

WESTINGHOUSE LEARNING CENTER. (1969). *The impact of Head Start: An evaluation of the effects of Head Start on children's cognitive and* affective development. Washington, DC: Clearinghouse for Federal Scientific and Technical Information.

WEXLER, K., & CULICOVER, P. W. (1980). Formal principles of language acquisition. Cambridge, MA: MIT Press.

WHITE, B. L., & HELD, R. (1966). Plasticity of sensorimotor development in the human infant. In J. F. Rosenblith & W. Allinsmith (Eds.), The causes of behavior (2nd ed.). Boston: Allyn & Bacon.

WHITE, B. L., CASTLE, P., & HELD, R. (1964). Observations on the development of visually directed reaching. Child Development, 35, 349–364.

WHITE, B. L., KABAN, B. T., ATTANUCCI, J., & SHAPIRO, B. B. (1978). Experience and environment: Major influences on the development of the young child (Vol. 2). Englewood Cliffs, NJ: Prentice Hall.

WHITE, B. L., & WATTS, J. C. (1973). Experience and environment: Major influences on the development of the young child (Vol. 1). Englewood Cliffs, NJ: Prentice Hall.

*WHITE, P. C., NEW, M. I., & DUPONT, B. (1987). Congenital adrenal hyperplasia. New England Journal of Medicine, 316, 1519–1524.

WHITE, R. W. (1959). Motivation reconsidered: The concept of competence. Psychological Review, 66, 297–333.

WHITE, S., & THARP, R. G. (1988, April). Questioning and wait-time: A cross-cultural analysis. Paper presented at the meeting of the American Educational Research Association, New Orleans.

*WHITE, S. H. (1992). G. Stanley Hall: From philosophy to developmental psychology. Developmental Psychology, 28, 25–34.

WHITE, T. G. (1982). Naming practices, typicality, and underextension in child language. Journal of Experimental Child Psychology, 33, 324–346.

WHITEHURST, G. J., & DeBARYSHE, B. D. (1989). Observational learning and language acquisition: Principles of learning, systems, and tasks. In G. E. Speidel & K. E. Nelson (Eds.), The many faces of imitation in language learning. New York: Springer-Verlag.

WHITEHURST, G. J., FALCO, F. L., LONIGAN, C. J., FISCHEL, J. E., DeBARYSHE, B. D., VALDEZ-MENCHACA, M. C., & CAULFIELD, M. (1988). Accelerating language development through picture book reading. Developmental Psychology, 24, 552–559.

WHITEHURST, G. J., FISCHEL, J. E., CAULFIELD, M., DeBARYSHE, B., & VALDEZ-MENCHACA, M. C. (1989). Assessment and treatment of early expressive language delay. In P. Zelazo & R. Barr (Eds.), Challenges to developmental paradigms: Implications for theory, assessment, and treatment. Hillsdale, NJ: Erlbaum.

WHITEHURST, G. J., & NOVAK, G. (1973). Modeling, imitation training, and the acquisition of sentence phrases. Journal of Experimental Child Psychology, 16, 332–345.

WHITEHURST, G. J., & SONNENSCHEIN, S. (1985). The development of communication: A functional analysis. In G. J. Whitehurst (Ed.), Annals of child development (Vol. 2). Greenwich, CT: JAI Press.

WHITEHURST, G. J., & VALDEZ-MENCHACA, M. C. (1988). What is the role of reinforcement in language acquisition? Child Development, 59, 430–440.

WHITEHURST, G. J., & VASTA, R. (1975). Is language acquired through imitation? Journal of Psycholinguistic Research, 4, 37–59.

WHITELY, B. E. (1985). Sex-role orientation and psychological well-being: Two meta-analyses. Sex Roles, 12, 207–225.

*WHITING, B. B., & EDWARDS, C. P. (1988). Children of different worlds: The formation of social behavior. Cambridge, MA: Harvard University Press.

*WHITLEY, R., & GOLDENBERG, R. (1990). Infectious disease in the prenatal period and the recommendations for screening. In I. R. Merkatz & J. E. Thompson (Eds.), New perspectives on prenatal care. New York: Elsevier.

*WHYTE, M., & PARISH, W. (1984). Urban life in contemporary China. Chicago: University of Chicago Press.

WIDAMAN, K. F., & LITTLE, D. (1985). Contextual influences on sociomoral judgment and action. In J. B. Pryor & J. D. Day (Eds.), The development of social cognition. New York: Springer-Verlag.

*WIDAMAN, K. F., LITTLE, T. D., GEARY, D. C., & CORMIER, P. (1992). Individual differences in the development of skill in mental addition: Internal and external validation of chronometric models. Learning and Individual Differences, 4, 167–213.

WIGFIELD, A., ECCLES, J. S., MacIVER, D., REUMAN, D. A., & MIDGLEY, C. (1991). Transitions during early adolescence: Changes in children's domain-specific self-perceptions and general self-esteem across the transition to junior high school. Developmental Psychology, 27, 552–565.

WILDER, G., MACKIE, D., & COOPER, J. (1985). Gender and computers: Two surveys of computer-related attitudes. Sex Roles, 13, 215–228.

WILLATTS, P. (1990). Development of problem-solving strategies in infancy. In D. F. Bjorklund (Ed.), Children's strategies: Contemporary views of cognitive development. Hillsdale, NJ: Erlbaum.

*WILLIAMS, C. B., & MILLER, C. A. (1991). Preventive health care for young children: A ten country study with analysis of relevance to U.S. policy. Washington, DC: National Center for Clinical Infant Programs.

WILLIAMS, J. (1987). Psychology of women: Behavior in a biosocial context. New York: Norton.

WILLIAMS, J., BENNETT, S., & BEST, D. (1975). Awareness and expression of sex stereotypes in young children. Developmental Psychology, 11, 635–642.

*WILLIAMS, J. E., & BEST, D. L. (1990). Measuring sex stereotypes: A multinational study. Newbury Park, CA: Sage.

WILLIAMS, T. M. (1986). The impact of television. New York: Academic Press.

WILSON, E. O. (1975). Sociobiology: The new synthesis. Cambridge, MA: Harvard University Press.

WILSON, J. G. (1977a). Embryotoxicity of drugs in man. In J. G. Wilson & F. C. Fraser (Eds.), Handbook of teratology: Vol. 1. General principles and etiology. New York: Plenum.

WILSON, J. G. (1977b). Current status of teratology: General principles and mechanisms derived from animal studies. In J. G. Wilson & F. C. Fraser (Eds.), Handbook of teratology: Vol. 1. General principles and etiology. New York: Plenum.

WILSON, J. G. (1977c). Environmental chemicals. In J. G. Wilson & F. C. Fraser (Eds.), Handbook of teratology: Vol. 1. General principles and etiology. New York: Plenum.

WILSON, R. S. (1983). The Louisville Twin Study: Developmental synchronies in behavior. Child Development, 54, 298–316.

WILSON, R. S. (1986a). Continuity and change in cognitive ability profile. Behavior Genetics, 16, 45–60.

WILSON, R. S. (1986b). Growth and development of human twins. In F. Falkner & J. M. Tanner (Eds.), Human growth: A comprehensive treatise. New York: Plenum.

WILSON, R. S., & MATHENY, A. P. (1986). Behavior-genetics research in infant temperament: The Louisville Twin Study. In R. Plomin & J. Dunn (Eds.), The study of temperament: Changes, continuities and challenges. Hillsdale, NJ: Erlbaum.

WINDLE, M., & LERNER, R. M. (1986). The "goodness-of-fit" model of temperament-context relations: Interaction or correlation? In J. V. Lerner & R. M. Lerner (Eds.), New directions for child development: No. 31. Temperament and social interaction in infants and children. San Francisco: Jossey-Bass.

*WINDSOR, J. (1993). The functions of novel word compounds. Journal of Child Language, 20, 119–138.

WINEBERG, S. S. (1987). The fulfillment of the self-fulfilling prophecy. Educational Researcher, 16, 28–36.

WINER, G. A. (1978). Enhancement of class-inclusion reasoning through verbal context. Journal of Genetic Psychology, 132, 299–306.

WINER, G. A. (1980). Class-inclusion reasoning in children: A review of the empirical literature. Child Development, 51, 309–328.

WINICK, M. (1971). Cellular growth during early malnutrition. Pediatrics, 47, 969–978.

WINICK, M., KNARIG, K. M., & HARRIS, R. C. (1975). Malnutrition and environmental enrichment by early adoption. Science, 190, 1173–1175.

*WINSTON, R. M. L., & HANDYSIDE, A. H. (1993). New challenges in human in vitro fertilization. Science, 260, 932–936.

WITELSON, S. F. (1976). Sex and the single hemisphere: Specialization of the right hemisphere for spatial processing. Science, 193, 425–427.

*WITELSON, S. F., & KIGAR, S. (1989). Anatomical development of the corpus callosum in humans: A review with reference to sex and cognition. In D. L. Molfese & S. J. Segalowitz (Eds.), Brain lateralization in children: Developmental implications. New York: Guilford.

WITKIN, H. A., MEDNICK, S. A., SCHULSINGER, R., BAKKESTROM, E., CHRISTIANSEN, K. O., GOODENOUGH, D. R., HIRSCHORN, K., LUNDSTEEN, C., OWEN, D. R., PHILLIP, J., RUBIN, D. B., & STOCKING, M. (1976). Criminality in XYY and XXY men. Science, 193, 547–555.

WOLFE, D. A. (1987). *Child abuse: Implications for child development and psychopathology.* Newbury Park, CA: Sage.

WOLFF, P. H. (1959). Observations on newborn infants. *Psychosomatic Medicine, 21,* 110–118.

WOLFF, P. H. (1966). The causes, controls and organization of behavior in the neonate. *Psychological Issues, 5* (No. 17).

WOLFF, P. H. (1969). The natural history of crying and other vocalizations in early infancy. In B. Foss (Ed.), *Determinants of infant behavior* (Vol. 4). London: Methuen.

WOROBEY, J., & BLAJDA, V. M. (1989). Temperament ratings at 2 weeks, 2 months, and 1 year: Differential stability of activity and emotionality. *Developmental Psychology, 25,* 257–263.

*WYNN, K. (1992a). Addition and subtraction by human infants. *Nature, 358,* 749–750.

*WYNN, K. (1992b). Children's acquisition of the number words and the counting system. *Cognitive Psychology, 24,* 220–251.

*WYNN, K. (1993, April). *Evidence for innate knowledge of number.* Invited address to the Western Psychological Association, Phoenix, AZ.

*YAMADA, J. E. (1990). *Laura: A case for the modularity of language.* Cambridge, MA: MIT Press.

YARDLEY, K., & HONESS, T. (1987). *Self and identity: Psychosocial perspectives.* New York: Wiley.

YATES, G. C. R., YATES, S. M., & BEASLEY, C. J. (1987). Young children's knowledge of strategies in delay of gratification. *Merrill-Palmer Quarterly, 33,* 159–169.

YEATES, K. O., SCHULTZ, L. H., & SELMAN, R. L. (1991). The development of interpersonal negotiation strategies in thought and action: A social-cognitive link to behavioral adjustment and social status. *Merrill-Palmer Quarterly, 37,* 369–406.

YODER, P. J., & KAISER, A. P. (1989). Alternative explanations for the relationship between maternal interaction style and child language development. *Journal of Child Language, 16,* 141–160.

YONAS, A., ARTERBERRY, M. E., & GRANRUD, C. E. (1987). Space perception in infancy. In R. Vasta (Ed.), *Annals of child development* (Vol. 4). Greenwich, CT: JAI Press.

YONAS, A., & GRANRUD, C. E. (1985). Development of visual space perception in young infants. In J. Mehler & R. Fox (Eds.), *Neonate cognition: Beyond the blooming buzzing confusion.* Hillsdale, NJ: Erlbaum.

YONAS, A., & OWSLEY, C. (1987). Development of visual space perception. In P. Salapatek & L. Cohen (Eds.), *Handbook of infant perception: Vol. 2. From perception to cognition.* New York: Academic Press.

*YOUNGBLADE, L. M., & BELSKY, J. (1992). Parent–child antecedents of 5-year-olds' close friendships: A longitudinal analysis. *Developmental Psychology, 28,* 700–713.

YOUNGER, A. J., & PICCININ, A. M. (1989). Children's recall of aggressive and withdrawn behaviors: Recognition memory and likability judgments. *Child Development, 60,* 580–590.

YOUNGER, A. J., SCHWARTZMAN, A. E., & LEDINGHAM, J. E. (1985). Age-related changes in children's perceptions of aggression and withdrawal in their peers. *Developmental Psychology, 21,* 70–75.

*YOUNGER, B. (1993). Understanding category members as "the same sort of thing": Explicit categorization in ten-month infants. *Child Development, 64,* 309–320.

*YOUNISS, J., & SMOLLAR, J. (1986). *Adolescent relations with mothers, fathers and friends.* Chicago: University of Chicago Press.

YOUNISS, J., & VOLPE, J. (1978). A relational analysis of children's friendship. In W. Damon (Ed.), *New directions for child development: No. 1. Social cognition.* San Francisco: Jossey-Bass.

YUILL, N., & PERNER, J. (1988). Intentionality and knowledge in children's judgments of actor's responsibility and recipient's emotional reaction. *Developmental Psychology, 24,* 358–365.

YUNIS, J. J. (1983). The chromosomal basis of human neoplasia. *Science, 221,* 227–236.

*YUSSEN, S. R., & LEVY, V. M. (1975). Developmental changes in predicting one's own span of short-term memory. *Journal of Experimental Child Psychology, 19,* 502–508.

ZAHN-WAXLER, C., CUMMINGS, E. M., & IANNOTTI, R. (Eds.). (1986). *Altruism and aggression: Biological and social origins.* Cambridge: Cambridge University Press.

*ZAHN-WAXLER, C., RADKE-YARROW, M., WAGNER, E., & CHAPMAN, M. (1992). Development of concern for others. *Developmental Psychology, 28,* 126–136.

*ZAHN-WAXLER, C., ROBINSON, J. L., & EMDE, R. N. (1992). The development of empathy in twins. *Developmental Psychology, 28,* 1038–1047.

ZAJONC, R. B. (1976). Family configuration and intelligence. *Science, 192,* 227–236.

ZAJONC, R. B. (1983). Validating the confluence model. *Psychological Bulletin, 93,* 457–480.

ZAJONC, R. B., & MARKUS, G. B. (1975). Birth order and intellectual development. *Psychological Review, 82,* 74–88.

*ZAJONC, R. B., MARKUS G. B., BERBAUM, M. L., BARGH, J. A., & MORELAND, R. L. (1991). One justified criticism plus three flawed analyses equal two unwarranted conclusions: A reply to Retherford and Sewell. *American Sociological Review, 56,* 159–165.

ZAJONC, R. B., MARKUS, H., & MARKUS, G. B. (1979). The birth order puzzle. *Journal of Personality and Social Psychology, 37,* 1325–1341.

ZARBATANY, L., HARTMANN, D. P., & GELFAND, D. M. (1985). Why does children's generosity increase with age: Susceptibility to experimenter influence or altruism? *Child Development, 56,* 746–756.

ZARBATANY, L., HARTMANN, D. P., GELFAND, D. M., & VINCIGUERRA, P. (1985). Gender differences in altruistic reputation: Are they artifactual? *Developmental Psychology, 21,* 97–101.

ZEANAH, C., & ANDERS, T. (1987). Subjectivity in parent-infant relationships: A discussion of internal working models. *Infant Mental Health Journal, 8,* 237–250.

*ZELAZO, N. A., ZELAZO, P. R., COHEN, K. M., & ZELAZO, P. D. (1993). Specificity of practice effects on elementary neuromotor patterns. *Developmental Psychology, 29,* 686–691.

ZELAZO, P. R. (1971). Smiling to social stimuli: Eliciting and conditioning effects. *Developmental Psychology, 4,* 32–42.

ZELAZO, P. R. (1976). From reflexive to instrumental behavior. In L. Lipsitt (Ed.), *Developmental psychobiology: The significance of infancy.* Hillsdale, NJ: Erlbaum.

*ZELAZO, P. R., WEISS, M. J. S., & TARQUINO, N. (1991). Habituation and recovery of neonatal orienting to auditory stimuli. In M. J. S. Weiss & P. R. Zelazo (Eds.), *Newborn attention: Biological constraints and the influence of experience.* Norwood, NJ: Ablex.

ZELAZO, P. R., ZELAZO, N., & KOLB, S. (1972). "Walking" in the newborn. *Science, 177,* 314–315.

*ZELKO, F. A., DUNCAN, S. W., BARDEN, R. C., GARBER, J., & MASTERS, J. C. (1986). Adults' expectancies about children's emotional responsiveness: Implications for the development of implicit theories of affect. *Developmental Psychology, 22,* 109–114.

ZESKIND, P. S. (1983). Production and spectral analysis of neonatal crying and its relation to other biobehavioral systems in the infant at risk. In T. Field & A. Sostek (Eds.), *Infants born at risk: Psychological and perceptual processes.* New York: Grune & Stratton.

*ZESKIND, P. S., KLEIN, L., & MARSHALL, T. R. (1992). Adult's perceptions of experimental modifications of durations of pauses and expiratory sounds in infant crying. *Developmental Psychology, 28,* 1153–1162.

ZESKIND, P. S., & LESTER, B. M. (1978). Acoustic features and auditory perceptions of the cries of newborns with prenatal and perinatal complications. *Child Development, 49,* 580–589.

ZESKIND, P. S., & MARSHALL, T. R. (1988). The relation between variations in pitch and maternal perceptions of infant crying. *Child Development, 59,* 193–196.

ZESKIND, P. S., & RAMEY, C. T. (1981). Preventing intellectual and interactional sequelae of fetal malnutrition: A longitudinal, transactional and synergistic approach to development. *Child Development, 52,* 213–218.

*ZIGLER, E. F., & FINN-STEVENSON, M. (1992). Applied developmental psychology. In M. H. Bornstein & M. E. Lamb (Eds.), *Developmental psychology: An advanced textbook* (3rd ed.). Hillsdale, NJ: Erlbaum.

*ZIGLER, E. F., HOPPER, P., & HALL, N. W. (1993). Infant mental health and social policy. In C. H. Zeanah, Jr. (Ed.), *Handbook of infant mental health.* New York: Guilford.

ZIGLER, E. F., & MUENCHOW, S. (1992). *Head Start: The inside story of America's most successful educational experiment.* New York: Basic Books.

*ZIGLER, E. F., & STYFCO, S. J. (Eds.). (1993). *Head Start and beyond: A national plan for extended childhood intervention.* New Haven, CT: Yale University Press.

ZIMMERMAN, B. J. (1983). Social learning theory: A contextualist account of cognitive functioning. In C. J. Brainerd (Ed.), *Recent advances in cognitive-developmental theory: Progress in cognitive development research.* New York: Springer-Verlag.

ZIMMERMAN, B. J., & BLOM, D. E. (1983). Toward an empirical test of the role of cognitive conflict in learning. *Developmental Review, 3,* 18–38.

ZINOBER, B., & MARTLEW, M. (1985). The development of communicative gestures. In M. D. Barrett (Ed.), *Children's single-word speech.* New York: Wiley.

ZIVIN, G. (1979). Removing common confusions about egocentric speech, private speech, and self-regulation. In G. Zivin (Ed.), *The development of self-regulation through private speech.* New York: Wiley.

ZUPAN, B. A., HAMMEN, C., & JAENICKE, C. (1987). The effects of current mood and prior depressive history on self-schematic processing in children. *Journal of Experimental Child Psychology, 43,* 149–158.

AUTHOR INDEX

Abbeduto, L., 435
Abel, E. L., 149
Aber, J. L., 482
Aboud, F. E., 496, 503
Abraham, K. G., 500
Abramov, I., 223
Abramovitch, R., 605, 607, 639
Abramowitz, R. H., 59, 474, 500
Abravanel, E., 266
Acebo, C., 172
Ackerman, B. P., 104, 438, 439
Ackerman, Ss. J., 439
Acksen, B. A., 532
Acredolo, L. P., 236, 411, 412, 419, 491
Acredolo, L., 236
Adams, G. R., 223, 500
Adams, C., 289
Adams, M. J., 343
Adams, P. L., 578
Adams, P. W., 529
Adamson, L. B., 416, 430, 450, 452, 455, 584
Adler, T., 506
Adolph, K. E., 20, 212
Ageton, S. S., 578
Aiello, J. R., 612
Ainsworth, M., 466–469
Ainsworth, M. D. S., 58, 187, 444, 445, 446, 470, 482
Akhtar, N., 30
Alansky, J. A., 471
Aldhous, P., 104
Alessandri, S. M., 450, 502
Allen, L., 539, 541
Allen, J. P., 482
Allen, M. C., 167
Allen, S. G., 535
Alley, T. R., 445
Allison, A. C., 104
Allison, D. J., 152
Allison, D. M., 579

Allison, P. D., 164
Almeida, D. M., 575
Aloise, P. H., 37
Alpern, L., 482
Als, H., 167–168
Altman, L., 202
Altz, L., 511
Alvarez, M. M., 556
Aman, C., 322
American Association of University Women, 586
Ames, B. N., 150
Amsterdam, B. K., 492
Anders, T., 173, 462
Anderson, A., 415
Anderson, B. E., 478
Anderson, E., 481, 578
Anderson, G. C., 163
Anderson, G. M., 152, 164
Anderson, D. R., 242
Anderson, L., 294
Anderson, R., 410
Anderson, W. F., 157
Anglin, J. M., 414, 416, 417, 419
Angoff, W. H., 366, 383
Anisfeld, E., 171, 267, 478
Annecillo, C., 56, 589–590
Antonini, A., 211
Apgar, V., 167, 169
Appel, L. F., 315
Appelbaum, M. I., 66
Applebaum, M. I., 371
Appley, M., 13
Arbuthnot, J., 530
Archer, M., 57
Arcus, D., 114
Arcus, D. M., 463
Ardrey, Ro., R., 57
Arend, R., 473
Aries, P., 8
Armbruster, B. B., 313

Armstrong, T., 374
Aronson, E., 216
Arrieta, R., 201
Arsenio, W. F., 542
Arterberry, M. E., 235, 236
Asendorpf, J. B., 462, 494, 542, 605, 634, 635
Aserinsky, E., 175, 176
Ashcraft, M. H., 338
Asher, S. R., 552, 631, 633, 635, 636
Ashmead, D. H., 220, 309
Aslin, R. N., 217, 218, 219, 221, 223, 224, 229, 230,2 35, 242, 409
Astington, J. W., 271, 434
Atkinson, J., 220, 223, 224
Attanucci, J., 532
Attili, G., 600
Au, T. K., 420
Austin, G. A., 212
Austin, V. D., 528
Axworthy, D., 588
Azmitia, M., 556

Bacon, W. F., 375
Baddeley, J., 531
Baenninger, M., 583, 591
Baer, D., 41
Bahrick, L. E., 240
Bailey, S. M., 139, 200
Baillargeon, R., 263, 264, 265, 284
Baisini, F. J., 167
Bakeman, R., 430, 444, 450, 452, 455, 584
Baker, N. D., 313
Baker, S. W., 429
Baker-Ward, L., 311, 315, 478
Balaban, T., 575
Balazs, R., 201
Baldwin, D. A., 420, 430
Baldwin, D. V., 549
Ball,W. A., 246
Bancroft, J., 588

Patterson, M. L., 632
Pattison, P., 421
Peake, P. K., 515
Pearl, D., 548
Pearson, D. M., 243, 411
Pecheux, M. G., 240
Pedersen, 449
Pedersen, J., 602
Pederson, 112
Pederson, D. R., 176, 216, 469, 470
Pederson, N. L., 364
Pedlow, R., 456
Pegg, J. E., 409
Peiper, A., 177, 178, 179. 191
Pelaez-Nogueras, M., 40, 447, 524
Pellegrino, J. W., 357, 359
Penner, S. G., 429
Pennington, B. F., 108, 109
Pepler, D. J., 636
Perfetti, C. A., 343
Periss, E. E., 308
Perlmann, R., 405, 428
Perlmutter, M., 309, 315, 509
Perner, J., 271, 529
Perry, D. G., 524, 535, 548, 571, 575, 602, 603
Perry, L. C., 548, 571. 575
Perry, T. B., 609, 627
Peters, D. P., 322, 428
Petersen, A. C., 199, 500, 575, 582
Peterson, L., 235, 286, 326, 539
Petitto, L. A., 411, 436
Petrovich, S., 445
Pettit, G. S., 548, 584
Phares, V., 481
Pharoah, P., 140, 141
Phelps, E., 388, 619
Philips, D., 479
Phillips, D., 479
Phillips, D. A., 505, 614
Phillips, S., 566
Piaget, J., 33, 37, 181, 213, 238, 254, 258, 262, 266, 268, 269, 271, 272, 273, 275, 277, 278, 286, 288, 289, 290, 291, 292, 294, 319, 332, 333, 520, 541, 598, 599
Picariello, M. L., 574
Piccinin, A. M., 551
Pick, A. D., 214
Pick, H. L., 214, 243
Pickens, J., 451, 455
Pierce, K., 584
Piers, E., 497
Pike, R., 499
Pillemer, D. B., 574
Pinker, S., 403, 424, 426
Pinto, J., 232
Pipp, S., 447, 490, 492, 494
Pisoni, D. B., 217, 218, 219, 573
Plantz, M. C., 6
Plomin, R., 24, 110, 111, 113, 114, 116, 119, 359, 363, 364, 365, 371, 456, 457, 459, 637

Pollitt, E., 167
Pollock, L., 8, 9
Polvino, W., 157
Pomerleau, A., 568
Porter, R. H., 56, 215
Posner, M., 36, 193, 460, 508
Post, K. N., 429
Poulin-Dubois, 573
Poulson, C. L., 266, 447
Powell, G. F., 204
Powell, J. S., 357, 359
Powell, L. F., 171
Power, T. G., 201, 479, 534
Powledge, T. M., 104
Powlishta, K. K., 560, 567
Prader, A., 195
Pratkanis, A., 488
Pratt, M. W., 505, 510
Prechtl, H. F. R., 169
Prescott, P. A., 218
Pressley, M., 80, 311, 312, 313, 315, 316
Price, G. G., 372
Priel, B., 494
Prince, A., 424
Prinz, E. A., 412
Prinz, P. M., 412
Prior, M., 462, 463
Prodromidis, M., 477
Profilet, S. M., 641
Provenzano, F. J., 568
Pryor, J. B., 37
Puka, B., 531
Pullybank, J., 488
Purcell, P., 572
Putallaz, M., 634, 640, 641, 642
Pye, C., 432

Qi, S., 271
Quiggle, N. L., 551, 635
Quinan, J. R., 332
Quinn, M. C., 219, 407
Quintana, S. M., 488

Rabinowitz, F. M., 337
Raboch, J., 588
Rachell, P. L., 214
Rack, J. P., 343
Radford, A., 424
Radke-Yarrow, M., 141, 462, 539, 543
Rafaelli, M., 639
Raff, M. C., 191
Raglioni, S. S., 240
Rakic, P., 130, 191, 211
Ramey, C. T., 141, 382, 478
Ramsey, B. K., 379, 549, 635
Raskin, P. A., 571
Rasmuson, 112
Rasmussen, B., 617
Ratcliffe, S., 588
Ratner, H. H., 332
Ratner, N., 411

Ratner, N. B., 428
Rauh, V. A., 172
Raven, K. E., 333
Rawlins, W. K., 620
Raymond, D., 579
Rayner, R., 44, 343
Recchia, S., 501
Redanz, N. J., 408
Redlinger, W. E., 432
Reed, T., 640
Rees, J. M., 201
Reese, E., 326, 328
Reeves, D., 461
Reid, M., 548, 629, 630
Reiling, A. M., 445
Reimer, J., 531
Reisman, J. E., 214, 216
Reiss, D., 637
Reiter, E. O., 199
Renders, R. J., 622
Renshaw, P. D., 633
Repacholi, B., 482
Reppucci, N. D., 502
Rescorla, L. A., 374, 414, 415, 416
Resnick, G., 579, 590
Rest, J. R., 519, 530, 532
Retherford, R. D., 372
Reznick, J. S., 414, 462, 464, 465
Rheingold, H. L., 82, 281, 411, 508, 538, 569
Rholes, W. S., 503, 536
Ribble, C., 582
Ricciuti, H. N., 457
Rice, M. L., 403, 419
Richards, D. D., 439
Richards, B. S., 530, 532
Richardson, 545
Ridge, B., 266
Rieben, L., 280
Riese, M. L., 457
Rieser, J., 214, 236
Riley, M. S., 282
Risley, T. R., 404, 416
Ritter, P. L., 312
Ritts, V., 632
Rivest, L., 614
Rizzo, T. A., 509
Robb, M. D., 470
Roberts, K., 231
Roberts, L., 105, 125, 153
Roberts, R., 248
Roberts, R. J., 247, 438
Roberts, R. N., 514
Robinette, C. D., 110
Robins, R. H., 401
Robins, R. W., 496
Robinson, C. C., 569
Robinson, E. J., 438, 439
Robinson, J., 584
Robinson, J. L., 456, 542, 584
Robinson, M., 333

SUBJECT INDEX

ABAB design, 73
AB error, object permanence, 262, 265
Abortion, 154
Abuse, *see* Child abuse
Academic achievement, cross-cultural research, 373–375
Academic self-concept:
  age and gender differences, 501, 506
  defined, 501
  effects of, 505–507
  learned helplessness, 502–503, 506
  parenting styles and, 504–505
  schools and, 506–507
  social comparison role, 503–504, 506–507
Accommodation, Piaget's theory, 34–35, 39
Accutane, birth defects and, 148
Achondroplasia, 102, 143
Acquired immunodeficiency disease (AIDS), *see* AIDS
Acquired (conditioned) reinforcers, 45
Action skills, 246–248
Action systems:
  in infancy, 243–245
  in older children, 245–248
Activity:
  sex differences in, 584
  temperament and, 459
Activity reinforcers, 45
ADA deficiency, fetal treatment, 156–157
Adaptation, Piaget's theory, 34, 39
Adolescents, *see also* Puberty
  formal operational stage, 487–488
  peer relations, 607–609
  physical growth in, 196
  puberty and, 197–198
Adoption studies:
  function of, 109–110
  intelligence performance, 113, 362–363, 367

personality, 113
psychiatric disorders, 110
Adulthood, formal operational stage, 287–288
Adult processes, childhood influence on, 5
Affect, emotional development and, 450
Age level:
  academic self-concept, 501
  action systems, 243–248
  aggression and, 546
  attention, 241–243
  hearing and, 218–219
  maturation, 195
  memory and, 304–329
  peer relations and, 615–619
  prosocial behavior, 539
Aggression:
  age and gender differences, 546–547, 585
  biological determinants, 547–548
  cognitive influences, 551
  controlling, 554–556
  defined, 545
  displaced, 551
  genetics and, 104
  inner-city youth study, 552–553
  media violence:
    government regulation of, 550
    television violence, 549
  moral development and, 526
  punishment and, 46
  rejection and, 552–554
  social and environmental determinants, 548–549
AIDS:
  prenatal development and, 134, 137
  statistics, 138–139
  transmission of, 155
Alcohol abuse:
  as genetic disorder, 104
  prenatal development and, 148–151

Alertness, in newborns, 173–176, 182
Alpha-feto protein (FEP), 153
Altruism:
  defined, 525–526, 528
  empathy and, 542
  family and, 543–544
Alzheimer's Disease, 104
American Psychological Association:
  Ethical Principles in the Conduct of Research with Human Participants, 83
  history of, 15–16
Amniocentesis, 153–154, 158
Amniotic sac, 128
Anal stage, Freudian theory, 18
Androgen insensitivity, 589
Androgens, 589
Androgyny, 592
Anencephaly, 140
Anorexia nervosa, 201
Anoxia, 167, 172
Antisocial behavior, evolutionary account of, 526–527
Anxiety, prenatal development and, 142
Apgar examination, 168–169, 172
Appearance-reality distinction, 270
Arithmetic, ability for, 337–339, 341. *See also* Mathematics
Artificialism, 276
Assessment, birth and perinatal period, 168–170
Assimilation, Piaget's theory, 34–35, 39
At-risk babies, environmental influences, 170–172. *See also* Birth and perinatal period, risk concept
Attachment:
  assessment of, 467–469
  behavior, effect on, 473–474
  cross-cultural study, 471, 473
  determinants of:
    caregiving and, 472
    generational attachment, 470–471

Moro reflex, 177–178
Mortality rates:
　childhood, 202
　infants, 165
Mother(s):
　age level, *see* Maternal age
　bonding with, *see* Maternal bonding
　responsiveness of, 469–470
　stress, influence of, 141–142
Mother-child relationship, social development and, 445, 447, 452–455, 465, 469–470
Mother-infant bond, study of, 58
Motherese, language development, 427–428, 431
Motion, objects and, 232
Motion parallax, 234–235
Motivational processes, observational learning, 50
Motor development:
　infancy:
　　maturation and experience, 186
　　principles and sequence, 183–184
　　psychological implications, 186–187
　　toddlers, 188
　preschool age, 188
Multiple intelligence, 392–393, 395
Mumps, prenatal development and, 137
Muscular dystrophy, 102
Mutual exclusivity principle, language development, 420, 422
Myelin, 191
Myelination, 192

Naming explosion, 414
National Center on Child Abuse and Neglect, 204–205
Nativism, 12, 24
Natural selection, 12–13, 445
Nature vs. nurture debate, 24–26, 55, 107
Negative correlation, 69
Negative reinforcement, 44–45
Neglect:
　impact of, 204–205
　peer relations and, 633
Neonates, *see* Birth and perinatal period; Infancy; Newborns
Neurons, 190–191, 193
Neurotransmitter, 191
Newborns:
　hearing in, 218–219
　imitation inn, 266
　intermodal relations, 238
　memory in, 305–307
　physical compromise of, 167–168
　reflexes in, 177–179, 182
　smell and, 215
　vestibular sensitivity in, 216
　vision in, 221–228, 237
　touch and, 217
Niche-picking, 118–119

Nicotine, prenatal development and, 148–149, 151
Nonverbal communication, language development and, 411–412
Normative development, idiographic development vs., 26–27
Norms, establishment of, 20
Numerical understanding, concrete operations, 282–283
Nutrition:
　growth and, 195, 200–201, 205
　prenatal development and, 132, 134, 137–130, 166, 200

Obesity, 201
Object permanence:
　Piagetian theory, 260–263
　recent studies of, 263–267
Objective responsibility, 520
Observational learning theory:
　moral development and, 528
　overview, 47–50, 52
Ontogeny, 133
Operant behavior, 41
Operant conditioning, 43–45, 52
Operating principle, language development, 426
Operating space, 334–335, 337
Operations, Piagetian theory, 279–280
Oral stage, Freudian theory, 18–19
Organization, Piaget's theory, 34, 39
Orienting reflex, 241, 243
Ovaries, 587
Overextension, 416–417, 421
Overregularization, language development, 424

Pain, sensory and perceptual development, 214
Palmar reflex, 177–178
Palmarmental reflex, 179
Paradox of altruism, 525, 528
Parallel play, 605
Parental age, prenatal development and, 132
Parental attitudes, sex role development and, 580
Parent-child interactions:
　abusive parents, 481–482
　peer relations, 639–642
Parent-infant relationship, environmental factors, 170–171
Parent training, aggression control and, 555
Patellar tendon reflex, 178
Peer relations:
　cross-cultural study, 610–611
　family and, 637–642
　friendship:
　　behavior and, 624–628
　　concepts of, 620–621

　determinants of, 621–624
　social networks and, 628–631
　gang violence, 613
　moral development and, 534
　peers:
　　parents and, 639–642
　　as teachers, 619
　　as therapists, 637
　　siblings and, 637–639
　　popularity, 631–633
　　problems in, 633–636
　　socialization and, 446
　theories of:
　　cognitive-developmental theory, 598–599
　　environmental/learning approach, 599–600
　　ethological theory, 600–601
　typical interactions:
　　cognitive contributions, 615–619
　　developmental changes, 602–609
　　situational factors, 610–614
Peer review, ethical research and, 83
Peer tutoring, 618
Perception, defined, 210. *See also* Sensory and perceptual development
Peripheral vision, 223
Permissive parenting, 476–477
Permissiveness:
　Freudian theory and, 18
　historical perspective, 12
Personal agency, 491–492
Personal Attributes Questionnaire, 593
Personality, genetics and, 112–114
Perspective taking:
　concrete operations, 281–282
　prosocial behavior, 541
Phallic stage, Freudian theory, 18
Phenotypes:
　defined, 96
　examples of, 97
　genetic disorders and, 99
　influences on, 98
Phenylalanine, 101, 103, 141
Phenylketonuria (PKU):
　as genetic disorder, 101–102
　maternal nutrition and, 141
　prenatal development and, 1334
　screening for, 152
Phobia, 43
Phocomelia, 145
Phonemics, 407
Phoneme, 407
Phonetics, 406–407
Phonics, 343
Phonological awareness, 343
Phonology, 406
Photography, in research, 20
Phylogeny, 13
Physical abnormalities, 203–204
Physical abuse, effects of, 46

PHOTO CREDITS